Encyclopedia of
American Indian History

Encyclopedia of
American Indian History

VOLUME IV

Bruce E. Johansen
Barry M. Pritzker
EDITORS

A B C ● C L I O

Santa Barbara, California • Denver, Colorado • Oxford, England

Copyright 2008 by ABC-CLIO, Inc.

Cataloging-in-Publication Data is on file with the Library of Congress

ISBN: 978-1-85109-817-0   ebook: 978-1-85109-818-7

12   11   10   09   08   1   2   3   4   5   6   7   8

Production Editor: Vicki Moran
Editorial Assistant: Sara Springer
Production Manager: Don Schmidt
Media Editor: John Whithers
Media Resources Coordinator: Ellen Brenna Dougherty
Media Resources Manager: Caroline Price
File Manager: Paula Gerard

ABC-CLIO, Inc.
130 Cremona Drive, P.O. Box 1911
Santa Barbara, California 93116-1911

This book is also available on the World Wide Web as an ebook. Visit http://www.abc-clio.com for details.

This book is printed on acid-free paper. ∞

Manufactured in the United States of America

For our families,
and for future generations

Bruce E. Johansen
Barry M. Pritzker

Contents

VOLUME I

Chronological Essays
Issues in American Indian History
Events in American Indian History

VOLUME II

Culture and American Indian History
Governments and American Indian History

VOLUME III

People and Groups in American Indian History
Primary Source Documents

VOLUME IV

Indian Nation Histories
Resources

Volume IV

Introduction, xiii

Indian Nation Histories

Native Americans of the Southwest

Acoma Pueblo	998
Apache, Chiricahua	1001
Apache, Jicarilla	1003
Apache, Lipan	1004
Apache, Mescalero	1005
Apache, Western	1006
Chemehuevi	1007
Cochiti Pueblo	1008
Cocopah	1009
Havasupai	1010
Hopi	1012
Hopi-Tewa	1014
Hualapai	1014
Isleta Pueblo	1015
Jemez Pueblo	1016
Laguna Pueblo	1017
Mojave or Mohave	1018
Nambé Pueblo	1020
Navajo (Dine'é)	1021
Pee-Posh	1024
Picuris Pueblo	1025
Pima	1026
Pojoaque Pueblo	1028
Quechan	1029
Sandia Pueblo	1030
San Felipe Pueblo	1031
San Ildefonso Pueblo	1032
San Juan Pueblo	1033
Santa Ana Pueblo	1034
Santa Clara Pueblo	1034

Santo Domingo Pueblo	1035
Taos Pueblo	1035
Tesuque Pueblo	1037
Tigua	1038
Tohono O'odham	1039
Yaqui	1040
Yavapai	1042
Zia Pueblo	1044
Zuni	1044

Native Americans of California

Achumawi	1047
Cahto	1048
Cahuilla	1049
Chumash	1051
Costanoan	1053
Cupeño	1054
Hupa	1055
Karuk	1057
Luiseño	1059
Maidu	1060
Miwok	1062
Mono	1063
Pomo	1065
Salinan	1067
Serrano	1068
Shasta	1069
Tipai-Ipai	1071
Tolowa	1072
Tubatulabal	1073
Wailaki	1073

Wintun   1074
Wiyot   1076
Yana   1077
Yokuts   1078
Yurok   1079

Native Americans of the Northwest Coast
Bella Bella   1082
Bella Coola   1083
Chinook   1085
Coosans   1087
Haida   1089
Kwakiutl   1092
Makah   1094
Nootkans   1096
Quileute   1098
Salish, Central Coast   1099
Salish, Northern Coast   1102
Salish, Southern Coast   1103
Salish, Southwestern Coast   1106
Tillamook   1109
Tlingit   1110
Tsimshian   1114
Upper Umpqua   1116

Native Americans of the Great Basin
Paiute, Northern   1119
Paiute, Owens Valley   1121
Paiute, Southern   1123
Shoshone, Eastern or Wind River   1125
Shoshone, Northern   1127
Shoshone, Western   1129
Ute   1131
Washoe   1133

Native Americans of the Plateau
Cayuse   1136
Coeur d'Alene   1137
Colville   1137
Kalispel   1138
Klamath   1139
Klikitat   1140
Kootenai   1141

Lillooet   1141
Modoc   1142
Nez Percé   1144
Okanagon   1146
Salish   1147
Sanpoil   1147
Shuswap   1149
Sinkiuse   1149
Spokan   1151
Thompson   1152
Umatilla   1153
Wishram   1154
Yakima (Yakama)   1155

Native Americans of the Great Plains
Apache, Plains   1157
Arapaho   1158
Arikara   1160
Assiniboine   1161
Blackfeet   1162
Cheyenne   1165
Comanche   1167
Cree, Plains   1170
Crow   1171
Dakota   1174
Gros Ventres   1176
Hidatsa   1177
Ioway   1179
Kaw   1180
Kiowa   1181
Lakota   1183
Mandan   1189
Missouria   1191
Nakota   1192
Ojibwa, Plains   1193
Omaha   1196
Osage   1197
Otoe   1198
Pawnee   1200
Ponca   1202
Quapaw   1204
Tonkawa   1205
Wichita   1206

Native Americans of the Southeast

Alabama	1208
Caddo	1209
Catawba	1210
Cherokee	1212
Chickasaw	1215
Chitimacha	1217
Choctaw	1217
Creek	1220
Houma	1222
Lumbee	1223
Natchez	1224
Powhatan	1226
Seminole	1228
Tunica	1230
Tuscarora	1231
Yuchi	1233

Native Americans of the Northeast Woodlands

Abenaki	1235
Algonquin	1236
Anishinabe	1238
Cayuga	1240
Fox	1242
Illinois	1244
Kickapoo	1245
Lenápe	1247
Mahican	1249
Maliseet	1251
Menominee	1252
Miami	1254
Micmac	1256
Mohawk	1258
Nanticoke	1261
Narragansett	1262
Oneida	1264
Onondaga	1267
Ottawa	1270
Passamaquoddy	1271

Penobscot	1272
Pequot	1274
Potawatomi	1276
Sauk	1278
Seneca	1280
Shawnee	1284
Wampanoag	1287
Winnebago	1288
Wyandotte	1290

Native American of the Subarctic

Beaver	1294
Carrier	1295
Chilcotin	1297
Chipewyan	1299
Cree	1300
Dogrib	1304
Gwich'in	1305
Hare	1307
Ingalik	1308
Kaska	1309
Naskapi/Montagnais	1311
Sekani	1313
Slavey	1314
Tahltan	1316
Tanaina	1318

Native Americans of the Arctic

Alutiiq	1321
Iglulik	1323
Inuit, Baffinland	1325
Inuit, Caribou	1328
Inuit, Copper	1330
Inuit, Labrador or Ungava	1332
Inupiat	1335
Inuvialuit	1338
Netsilik	1340
Unangan	1343
Yup'ik	1346

Resources

Discontinued Indian Mascots, 1969–2002   1352

Indian Mascots   1353

Tribal Governments in the United States, 2006   1354

Largest Tribes in the United States, 1980–2000   1379

National Indian Organizations   1380

American Indian Population 1860–1990   1382

Poverty on American Indian Reservations and Trust Lands   1382

Native American Terminated Tribes, 1955–1969   1392

Canadian First Nations   1393

Heads of Indian Affairs, 1824–2007   1417

Native American Treaties with the United States, 1778–1883   1419

Index, I-1
About the Editors

Introduction

A BOOK CAN BE A TIME MACHINE, opening a window on the unquestioned judgments and assumptions of authors in other times. Many of these have been delivered with a sense of European-American self-congratulation. Consider John D. Hicks, who, in *The Federal Union: A History of the United States to 1865* (1937) opens a 700-page tome with the words "The civilization that grew up in the United States . . ." implying that nothing worth the name occurred before Columbus planted European seeds here (Hicks, 1937, 1). Paragraph two begins: "America before the time of Columbus had developed no great civilizations of its own" (Hicks, 1937, 1). This text states authoritatively that the Mayas, Aztecs, and Incas could not match "the best that Europe had to offer" (Hicks, 1937, 1), despite the fact that accounts of the Cortez invasion expressed a sense of awe at the Aztecs' capital city Tenochtitlan when they first saw it. In the same paragraph, Hicks develops reasons why he believes that Europeans surpassed America's "primitive civilization": "racial traits may account in part for this failure, but the importance of the environment cannot be overlooked" (Hicks, 1937, 1).

No time and no people speak with a single voice, however. So while Hicks' assumptions of racial superiority remind us of Richard Henry Pratt's advertising slogan for the boarding schools he built ("Kill the Indian, Save the Man") even Pratt's and Hicks' time were informed by other voices that asserted enduring value to Native American peoples and cultures. While Pratt's slogan is sometimes interpreted as an endorsement of genocide in our time, to him it was friendly advice to peoples whom he assumed would die culturally as well as genetically if they held fast to cultures that he considered out of date in a modern world. Multicultural ideas that inform public discourse (as well as census reports) in our time had precedents in Pratt's and Hicks' time. The majority society was just not listening. Consider Walt Whitman, for example, during 1883, as Pratt was fashioning his campaign to save Indians by killing their cultures:

As to our aboriginal or Indian population . . . I know it seems to be agreed that they must gradually dwindle as time rolls on, and in a few generations more leave only a reminiscence, a blank. But I am not at all clear about that. As America . . . develops, adapts, entwines, faithfully identifies its own—are we to see it cheerfully accepting using all the contributions of foreign lands from the whole outside globe—and then rejecting the only ones distinctly its own? (Moquin, 1973, 5–6).

One newspaper, the *Omaha World-Herald*, sent a native woman, Susette LaFlesche (an Omaha), to describe the aftermath of the Wounded Knee massacre. She was married to Thomas Tibbles. Together, a decade earlier, they had roused their city of Omaha in anger over the torturous treatment suffered by the Ponca Standing Bear and his band. Exiled in Indian Territory from their homeland along the Niobrara River (in northernmost Nebraska), the Poncas had escaped and walked home, stopping in the city, their feet bleeding in the snow, so hungry that they had chewed on their moccasins. General George Crook volunteered to be the defendant in a legal case that established the Poncas' right to return home.

History is full of surprises. The same year that Hicks' book was published, Matthew W. Stirling, chief and later director of the American Bureau of Ethnology for thirty years (1928–1958), stated in *National Geographic* that the Albany Plan of Union (1754) was fundamentally shaped by the Iroquois Confederacy through Benjamin Franklin (Stirling, 1937). Such an idea is hardly universally accepted, even in our time. For one, Steven Pinker, in *The Blank Slate*, asserted that the same idea was flimsy enough to dismiss without explanation in two words: "1960s granola" (Pinker, 2002, 298).

Historically, we stand with Whitman and Stirling. *The Encyclopedia of American Indian History* attempts to redress assumptions that any single culture is superior to any other. American Indian voices were available to historians in the 1930s; it was, after

all, a time of major Native rights assertion under the Indian Reorganization Act, but many non-Native historians seemed not to be listening. The writings of Dr. Charles A. Eastman (or, to use his Dakota name, Ohiyesa) and Luther Standing Bear were widely published, among many others. Major nineteenth-century feminists (Elizabeth Cady Stanton and Matilda Joslyn Gage, to name two) had acknowledged their debt to Native matriarchal societies. Still, one can hardly imagine Hicks having any use for an encyclopedia entry titled "American Indian Contributions to the World."

We start with six essays, written by our co-editors and members of our editorial board, which focus on the themes that dominate particular eras in American Indian history. So, for example, if a reader wants to find out why the Trail of Tears migration happened when it did, s/he would find that context covered in the essay dealing with the period from 1800 to 1850. The late Vine Deloria, Jr. once advised non-Indian scholars to study the history of topics of contemporary importance to Native peoples, and a section of the encyclopedia addresses those issues that are prominent both in the history of Native peoples and in Native societies today. These entries range from archaeology and pre-contact Native history to topics like gaming and water rights, which are still so relevant. Subsequent sections deal with the most important events of American Indian history, aspects of Native cultures that have had ramifications in history, Native interactions with non-Indian governments, and the roles of both individuals and groups in American Indian history. One of the most important sections of the encyclopedia, the histories of particular Native nations, is absolutely vital to the stories we're seeking to have told and deserves to be highlighted. Also, primary sources from throughout American Indian history are presented so that readers can get a flavor of how different people viewed these events as they happened.

The occupancy of most of North America by Europeans on a sustained basis is less than 200 years

old—four consecutive human lives then, less than three now. Thus, the importance of American Indian history to the recent history of all peoples on this continent is clear. The history is written in what we call our homeland—many of our cities, half the constituent states in the federal union that calls itself the United States, bear names that have Native roots.

If there is one thing we've learned from trying to organize and do justice to such a vast and important subject, it is that there is no way to present this material that is perfect for everyone. Different people learn best in different ways. However, we've endeavored to be as clear as possible, making the large number of materials and resources as easy to locate and use as possible. An encyclopedia is not a cast-iron product, but a collection of many contributors' work. In our case, this is a mixture of Native and non-Native voices. Selection of subject matter is subject to judgment, and interpretation, and will be reviewed—something or someone is included, someone or something else is ignored, or given short shrift. We can say only that we have done our best.

Bruce E. Johansen and Barry M. Pritzker, Editors
Steven L. Danver, Project Editor

References and Further Reading

Hicks, John D. *The Federal Union: A History of the United States to 1865.* 1937. Boston: Houghton-Mifflin.

Moquin, Wayne. *Great Documents in American Indian History.* 1973. New York: Praeger.

Pinker, Steven. *The Blank Slate: The Modern Denial of Human Nature.* 2002. New York: Viking (Penguin Putnam).

Pritzker, Barry M. *Native America Today: A Guide to Community Politics and Culture.* 1999. Santa Barbara, CA: ABC-CLIO.

Stirling, Matthew W. "America's First Settlers, the Indians." *National Geographic* 72:5 (1937), cited in Bruce E. Johansen, comp. *Native America and the Evolution of Democracy: A Supplementary Bibliography.* 1999, 140. Westport, CT: Greenwood.

Encyclopedia of
American Indian History

Indian Nation Histories

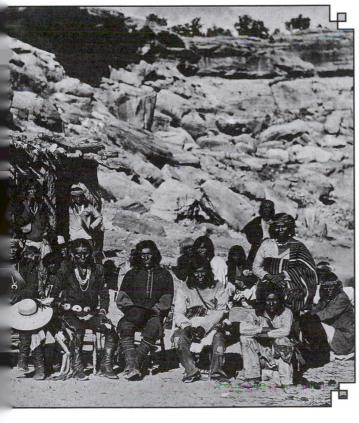

Native Americans
of the Southwest — 998

Native Americans
of California — 1047

Native Americans
of the Northwest Coast — 1082

Native Americans
of the Great Basin — 1119

Native Americans
of the Plateau — 1136

Native Americans
of the Great Plains — 1157

Native Americans
of the Southeast — 1208

Native Americans of the
Northeast Woodlands — 1235

Native Americans
of the Subarctic — 1294

Native Americans
of the Arctic — 1321

Native Americans of the Southwest

Acoma Pueblo

"Acoma" is from the Acoma and Spanish *acoma*, or *acú*, meaning "the place that always was" or "People of the White Rock." "Pueblo" is from the Spanish for "village." It refers both to a certain style of Southwest Indian architecture, characterized by multistory buildings made of stone and adobe (pueblo), and to the people themselves (Pueblo). The Rio Grande Pueblos are known as eastern Pueblos; Zuni, Hopi, and sometimes the Acomas and Lagunas are known as western Pueblos.

Acoma is located roughly 60 miles west of Albuquerque, New Mexico. The reservation consists of three main communities: Sky City (Old Acoma), Acomita, and McCartys. The traditional lands of Acoma Pueblo encompassed roughly 5 million acres. Of this, roughly 10 percent is included in the reservation. The pueblo's population was perhaps 5,000 in 1550. Acoma is a western Keresan dialect.

All Pueblo people are thought to be descended from Ancestral Puebloan, perhaps Mogollon, and several other ancient peoples. From them they learned architecture, farming, pottery, and basketry. Larger population groups became possible with effective agriculture and the development of ways to store food surpluses. In the context of a relatively stable existence, the people devoted increasing amounts of time and attention to religion, arts, and crafts.

In the 1200s, the Ancestral Puebloans abandoned their traditional canyon homelands in response to climatic and social upheavals. A century or two of migrations ensued, followed by the slow reemergence of their culture in the historic pueblos. Acoma

Pueblo was established at least 800 years ago.

Pueblo governments are derived from two traditions. Elements that are probably indigenous include the cacique, or head of the Pueblos, and the war captain, both chosen for life. These officials were intimately related to the religious structures of the pueblo and reflected the essentially theocratic nature of Pueblo government. A parallel but in most cases distinctly less powerful group of officials was imposed by the Spanish authorities. They generally dealt with external matters and included a governor, two lieutenant governors, and a council. In addition, the All Indian Pueblo Council, dating from 1598, began meeting again in the twentieth century.

One mechanism that works to keep Pueblo societies coherent is a pervasive aversion to individualistic behavior. Children were traditionally raised with gentle guidance and a minimum of discipline. Pueblo Indians were generally monogamous, and divorce was relatively rare. The dead were prepared ceremonially and quickly buried. A vigil of four days and nights was generally observed. Acoma Pueblo recognized roughly twenty matrilineal clans. The economy was basically a socialistic one, whereby labor was shared and produce was distributed equally. In modern times photography by outsiders is discouraged. At Acoma, a formal, traditional education system under the direction of the kiva headmen includes courses on human behavior, the human spirit, the human body, ethics, astrology, child psychology, oratory, history, music, and dance.

The Acoma pueblo featured three rows of three-story, apartment-style dwellings, facing south

Pottery in the interior of an Acoma dwelling, photographed in 1900. (National Archives and Records Administration)

on top of a 350-foot-high mesa. The lower levels were reserved mainly for storage. The buildings were constructed of adobe (earth-and-straw) bricks, with beams across the roof that were covered with poles, brush, and plaster. The roof of one level served as the floor of another. The levels were interconnected by ladders. As an aid to defense, the traditional design included no doors or windows; entry was through the roof. Baking ovens stood outside the buildings. Water was primarily obtained from two natural cisterns. Acoma also features seven rectangular pithouses, or kivas, that served as ceremonial chambers and clubhouses. The village plaza is the spiritual center of the village, where all the balanced forces of the world come together.

Before the Spanish arrived, people living at the Acoma pueblo ate primarily corn, beans, and squash. *Mut-tze-nee* was a favorite thin corn bread. They also grew sunflowers and tobacco and kept turkeys. They hunted deer, antelope, and rabbits and gathered a variety of wild seeds, nuts, berries, and other foods. Favorite foods as of circa 1700 included a blue corn drink, corn mush, pudding, wheat cake, corn balls, paper bread, peach-bark drink, flour bread, wild berries, and prickly pear fruit. The Acomas also raised herds of sheep, goats, horses, and donkeys after the Spanish introduced these animals into the region.

Irrigation techniques included dams and terraces. Pottery was an important technological adaptation, as were weaving baskets and weaving cotton and tanning leather. Farming implements were made of stone and wood. Corn was ground using manos and metates.

All Pueblos were part of extensive Native American trading networks that reached for 1,000 miles in every direction. With the arrival of other cultures, Pueblo Indians also traded with the Hispanic American villages and then U.S. traders. At fixed times during summer or fall, enemies declared truces so that trading fairs might be held. The largest and best-known was at Taos with the Comanches. Nomads exchanged slaves, buffalo hides, buckskins, jerked meat, and horses for agricultural and manufactured pueblo products. Pueblo Indians traded for shell and copper ornaments, turquoise, and macaw feathers. Trade along the Santa Fe Trail began in 1821. By the 1880s and the arrival of railroads, the Pueblos were dependent on many American-made goods, and the Native American manufacture of weaving and pottery declined and nearly died out.

Acoma Pueblo was first visited by non-Indians in 1539, probably by Estevan, an advance scout of the Coronado expedition. The following year the people welcomed Hernando de Alvarado, also a member of Coronado's group. In 1598, Juan de Oñate arrived in the area with settlers, founding the colony of New Mexico. However, that year Acomas killed some of his representatives, for which they faced a Spanish reprisal in 1599: The Spanish killed 800 people, tortured and enslaved others, and destroyed the pueblo. The survivors rebuilt shortly thereafter and began a process of consolidating several farming sites near Acoma, which were later recognized by the Spanish as two villages.

Oñate carried on the process, already underway, of subjugating the local Indians, forcing them to pay taxes in crops, cotton, and work and opening the door for Catholic missionaries to attack the Indians' religion. The Spanish renamed the pueblos with saints' names and began a program of church construction. At the same time, they introduced such new crops as peaches, wheat, and peppers into the region. In 1620, a royal decree created civil offices at each pueblo; silver-headed canes, many of which remain in use today, symbolized the governor's authority. In 1629, the Franciscan Juan Ramirez founded a mission at Acoma and built a huge church there.

The Pueblo Indians organized and instituted a general revolt against the Spanish in 1680. For years, the Spaniards had routinely tortured Indians for practicing traditional religion. They also forced the Indians to labor for them, sold them into slavery, and let Spaniard-owned cattle overgraze Indian land, a situation that eventually led to drought, erosion, and famine. Popé of San Juan Pueblo and other Pueblo religious leaders planned the revolt, sending runners carrying cords of maguey fibers to mark the day of rebellion. On August 10, 1680, a virtually united stand on the part of the Pueblos drove the Spanish from the region. The Indians killed many Spaniards but refrained from mass slaughter, allowing them to leave Santa Fe for El Paso.

The Pueblos experienced many changes during the following decades: Refugees established communities at Hopi, guerrilla fighting continued against the Spanish, and certain areas were abandoned. By the 1700s, excluding Hopi and Zuni, only Taos, Picuris, Isleta, and Acoma Pueblos had not changed locations since the arrival of the Spanish. Although Pueblo unity did not last, and Santa Fe was officially reconquered in 1692, Spanish rule was notably less severe from then on. Harsh forced labor all but ceased, and the Indians reached an understanding with the Church that enabled them to continue practicing their traditional religion. The Acomas resisted further Spanish contact for several years thereafter, then bowed to Spanish power and accepted a mission.

In general, the Pueblo eighteenth century was marked by smallpox epidemics and increased raiding by the Apache, Comanche, and Ute. Occasionally Pueblo Indians fought with the Spanish against the nomadic tribes. The people practiced their religion, more or less in secret. During this time, intermarriage and regular exchange between Hispanic villages and Pueblo Indians created a new New Mexican culture, neither Spanish nor strictly Indian, but rather a blend of the two.

Mexican "rule" in 1821 brought little immediate change to the Pueblos. The Mexicans stepped up what had been a gradual process of appropriating Indian land and water, and they allowed the nomadic tribes even greater latitude to raid. As the presence of the United States in the area grew, it attempted to enable the Pueblo Indians to continue their generally peaceful and self-sufficient ways and recognized Spanish land grants to the Pueblos. Land disputes with neighboring Laguna Pueblos were not settled so easily, however.

During the nineteenth century, the process of acculturation among Pueblo Indians quickened markedly. In an attempt to retain their identity, Pueblo Indians clung even more tenaciously to their heritage, which by now included elements of the once-hated Spanish culture and religion. By the 1880s, railroads had largely put an end to the traditional geographical isolation of the pueblos. Paradoxically, the U.S. decision to recognize Spanish land grants to the Pueblos denied the Indians certain rights granted under official treaties and left them particularly open to exploitation by squatters and thieves.

After a gap of more than 300 years, the All Indian Pueblo Council began to meet again in the 1920s, specifically in response to a congressional threat to appropriate Pueblo lands. Partly as a result of the Council's activities, Congress confirmed Pueblo title to their lands in 1924 by passing the Pueblo Lands Act. The United States also acknowledged its trust responsibilities in a series of legal decisions and other acts of Congress. Still, especially after 1900, Pueblo culture was increasingly threatened by highly intolerant Protestant evangelical missions and schools. The Bureau of Indian Affairs also weighed in on the subject of acculturation, forcing Indian children to leave their homes and attend culture-killing boarding schools. In 1922, most Acoma children had been sent away to such schools.

Following World War II, the issue of water rights took center stage at most pueblos. Also, the All Indian Pueblo Council succeeded in slowing the threat against Pueblo lands as well as religious persecution. Making crafts for the tourist trade became an important economic activity during this period. Since the late nineteenth century, but especially after the 1960s, Pueblos have had to cope with onslaughts by (mostly white) anthropologists and seekers of Indian spirituality. The region is also known for its major art colonies at Taos and Santa Fe.

See also All Indian Pueblo Council; Land, Identity and Ownership of, Land Rights; Pueblo Revolt; Water Rights.

Apache, Chiricahua

"Chiricahua" is a name taken from their stronghold in the Chiricahua Mountains, in southeast Arizona, and "Apache" is from the Zuni word *apachu*, mean-ing "enemy." The Apaches call themselves Ndee, or Dine'é, "the People."

The Apaches arrived in the Southwest from present-day Canada around 1400. By the early 1600s, the Chiricahua were living in southwestern New Mexico, southeastern Arizona, and northern Mexico. Late twentieth-century Chiricahua communities include the Mescalero Apache Reservation in southeastern New Mexico and a presence at Fort Sill, Oklahoma.

Ancestors of today's Apaches began the trek from Asia to North America relatively late, in roughly 1000 BCE. Most members of this group, which included the Athapaskans, were known as the Nadene. By 1300, the group that was to become the southern Athapaskans (Apaches and Navajos) broke away from other Athapaskan tribes and began migrating southward, reaching the American Southwest around 1400 and crystallizing into separate cultural groups.

The Apaches generally filtered into the mountains surrounding the Pueblo-held valleys. This process ended in the 1600s and 1700s, with a final push southward and westward by the Comanches. Before contact with the Spanish, the Apaches were relatively peaceful and may have engaged in some agricultural activities.

Traditionally, the Chiricahuas knew little tribal cohesion and no central political authority. They were a tribe based on common territory, language, and culture. As much central authority as existed was found in the local group (thirty-five to 200 people), composed of extended families. Its leader, or chief, enjoyed authority because of personal qualities, such as persuasiveness and bravery, often in addition to ceremonial knowledge. (All the famous Apache "chiefs" were local group leaders.) Decisions were made by consensus. One of the chief's most important functions was to minimize friction among his people.

Local groups joined to form three Chiricahua bands. One was the eastern, or Cihene (Red Paint People), also known as Mimbreños, Coppermine, Warm Spring, or Mogollon Apaches; the second was the central (Chokonen). The third band was the southern (Nednai, Enemy People, also called Pinery or Bronco Apaches), who lived mainly in Mexico. Some intermarriage occurred between bands.

Women were the anchors of the Apache family. Residence was matrilocal. Besides the political organization, society was divided into a number of

matrilineal clans. Apaches in general respected the elderly and valued honesty above all other qualities.

Gender roles were clearly defined but not rigidly enforced. Women gathered, prepared, and stored food; built the home; carried water; gathered fuel; cared for the children; tanned, dyed, and decorated hides; and wove baskets. Men hunted, raided, and waged war. They also made weapons and were responsible for their horses and equipment. They also made musical instruments.

Girls as well as boys practiced with the bow and arrow, sling, and spear, and both learned to ride expertly. Although actual marriage ceremonies were brief or nonexistent, the people practiced a number of formal preliminary rituals, designed to strengthen the idea that a man owed deep allegiance to his future wife's family. Out of deference, married men were not permitted to speak directly with their mothers-in-law. Divorce was relatively easy to obtain.

All Apaches had a great fear of ghosts. Chiricahuas who died had their faces painted red and were buried the same day. Their personal possessions were burned or destroyed, including their house and favorite horse.

Chiricahua Apaches lived in dome-shaped brush wikiups, which they covered with hides in bad weather. The doors always faced east. Eastern Chiricahuas sometimes used teepees.

Chiricahua Apaches were primarily hunters and gatherers. They hunted buffalo prior to the sixteenth century, and afterward they continued to hunt deer, elk, antelope, rabbits, and other game. They did not eat bear, turkey, or fish.

Wild foods included agave; cactus shoots, flowers, and fruit; berries; seeds; nuts; honey; and wild onions, potatoes, and grasses. Nuts and seeds were often ground into flour. The agave or century plant was particularly important. Baking its base in rock-lined pits for several days yielded mescal, a sweet, nutritious food that was dried and stored.

Traditional farm crops were obtained from the Pueblos by trade or raid. The Chiricahuas, particularly the eastern band, also practiced some agriculture: Corn, for instance, was used to make *tiswin*, a weak beer.

The Chiricahuas traditionally wore buckskin clothing and moccasins. As they acquired cotton and later wool through trading and raiding, women tended to wear two-piece calico dresses, with long, full skirts and long blouses outside the skirt belts. They occasionally carried knives and later ammunition belts. Girls wore their hair over their ears, shaped around two willow hoops. Some older women wore their hair Plains-style, parted in the middle with two braids. Men's postcontact styles included calico shirts, muslin breechclouts with belts, cartridge belts, moccasins, and headbands.

Historically, the Apache made formidable enemies. Raiding was one of their most important activities. The main purpose of raiding, in which one sought to avoid contact with the enemy, was to gain wealth and honor. It differed fundamentally from warfare, which was undertaken primarily for revenge. Chiricahua Apaches did not generally take scalps, nor did they maintain formal warrior societies.

Thrust into contact with the Spanish, the Apaches, having acquired horses, began raiding Spanish and Pueblo settlements. This dynamic included trading as well as raiding and warfare, but the Spanish habit of selling captured Apaches into slavery led to Apache revenge and increasingly hostile conditions along the Spanish frontier. After 1821, the Mexicans put a bounty on Apache scalps, increasing Apache enmity and adding to the cycle of violence in the region.

Following the war between Mexico and the United States (1848), the Apaches, who did their part to bring misery to Mexico, assumed that the Americans would continue to be their allies. They were shocked and disgusted to learn that their lands were now considered part of the United States and that the Americans planned to "pacify" them. Having been squeezed by the Spanish, the Comanches, the Mexicans, and now miners, farmers, and other landgrabbers from the United States, the Apaches were more than ever determined to protect their way of life.

Some Chiricahua bands tried to stay out of trouble in the 1850s by planting fields under the supervision of federal agents, but when raiding resumed as a result of broken promises of food and protection, all sides were caught in a spiral of violence. Mangas Coloradas, a peaceful Mimbreño chief, turned to war after he was bullwhipped by U.S. miners in 1860. Cochise, son-in-law of Mangas Coloradas and leader of the central band of Chiricahua, began a guerrilla war along the Butterfield Trail after whites killed some of his men. Cochise began as central band war chief, but by force of personality and integrity he eventually claimed authority over other Chiricahua bands as well. Resistance continued until 1874, when Cochise, hungry and exhausted, surrendered. He

could no longer control other Chiricahua bands, though, and their raiding continued.

Meanwhile, the U.S. policy of concentration via forced marches resulted in thousands of Chiricahua and western Apaches living on the crowded and disease-ridden San Carlos Reservation. There, a handful of dissident chiefs, confined in chains, held out for the old life of freedom and self-respect. Victorio fled in 1877, taking 350 Indians with him. He battled the army and Apache scouts until he was killed in Mexico in 1880. Nana, his successor, continued the raids until joining the Mescalero Reservation.

When soldiers killed a White Mountain Apache medicine man in 1881, Geronimo, a southern band shaman, led a group of Chiricahua away from San Carlos. In 1883 he agreed to return peacefully, but two years later, when soldiers banned the Indians' ceremonial drink *tiswin*, the Chiricahua fled again. In 1886 Geronimo surrendered in Mexico but on the way back to the United States escaped with thirty-six other Apaches. Their final surrender and the effective end of Apache military resistance came several months later: General Nelson Miles and one-quarter of the U.S. Army, plus Apache scouts, were needed to find and capture them. Geronimo regretted his surrender until his death as a prisoner of war in 1909.

As punishment for the freedom fighting activities of some of their group, the U.S. government sent all the Chiricahuas, including those who had been living peacefully at San Carlos, to prison in Alabama and Florida, where roughly one-quarter of them died over the following few years. Since the citizens of New Mexico opposed the return of the Apaches to San Carlos, the Chiricahuas who remained alive were sent in 1894 to the Kiowa Reservation at Fort Sill, Oklahoma, where they took up cattle raising and farming. In 1913, the Chiricahua were granted full freedom, although no reservation. Although some remained at Fort Sill, most moved back to New Mexico and life on the Mescalero Reservation.

Cattle raising and timber sales proved lucrative in the early twentieth century. Eventually, day schools replaced the hated, culture-killing boarding schools. By the late 1940s, every family had a house, and the economy at Mescalero was relatively strong. The reservation is managed cooperatively with the Mescalero and the Lipan Apaches.

See also Apache Wars; Geronimo: His Own Story; Mangas Coloradas; Relocation; Victorio.

Apache, Cibecue

See Apache, Western.

Apache, Fort Sill

See Apache, Chiricahua.

Apache, Jicarilla

"Jicarilla" is from the Spanish for "little basket" or "chocolate basket," and "Apache" is from the Zuni word *apachu*, meaning "enemy." The Apaches call themselves Ndee, or Dine'é, "the People." Jicarillas spoke a dialect of southern Athapaskan, or Apachean.

Beginning around the nineteenth century, the Jicarillas recognized two distinct bands. The Llaneros lived in the eastern Sangre de Cristo Mountains in adobe houses with nearby farms. From the pueblos, especially Taos, they learned pottery and social and religious customs. The Olleros gave up plains life somewhat later. In addition to hunting buffalo, they had picked up some Plains technology, such as teepees, parfleches, and travois.

Jicarilla Apaches were primarily hunters and gatherers. They hunted buffalo into the seventeenth century, and afterward they continued to hunt deer, mountain sheep, elk, antelope, rabbits, and other game. They did not eat bear, turkey, or fish.

Wild foods included agave shoots, flowers, and fruit; berries; seeds; nuts; honey; and wild onions, potatoes, and grasses. Nuts and seeds were often ground into flour. The agave or century plant was particularly important. Baking its base in rock-lined pits for several days yielded mescal, a sweet, nutritious food that was dried and stored.

In the late 1600s they learned farming from the Pueblos, and by the early nineteenth century they farmed river bottomlands and built irrigation ditches, growing some corn, beans, squash, pumpkins, peas, wheat, and melons. When supplies ran low, crops were obtained from the Pueblos by trade or raid.

Following the war between Mexico and the United States (1848), the Apaches, who did their part to bring misery to Mexico, assumed that the Americans would continue as allies. They were shocked and disgusted to learn that their lands were now considered part of the United States and that the

Americans planned to "pacify" them. Having been squeezed by the Spanish, the Comanches, the Mexicans, and now miners, farmers, and other land-grabbers from the United States, the Apaches were more than ever determined to protect their way of life.

Increased military activity led to a treaty in 1851 that called for the cessation of hostilities on all sides and, in exchange for aid, bound the Jicarillas to remain at least fifty miles from all settlements. When U.S. promises of food and protection went unkept, however, the Jicarillas returned to raiding, and the region was plunged into a spiral of violence. Another treaty in 1855 created agencies: Options for the Jicarillas now included either begging for food at the agency or raiding.

In the 1860s, the tribe escaped confinement at the deadly Bosque Redondo (Fort Sumner) only because the camp failed before they could be rounded up. By 1873 they were the only Southwestern tribe without an official reservation. At about this time, leaders of the two Jicarilla bands, the Olleros and the Llaneros, began consulting with each other, creating a new tribal consciousness. They sent a joint delegation to Washington, D.C., where they lobbied for a reservation, but in 1883 the tribe was moved to the Mescalero Reservation. Finding all the good land already taken, the Jicarillas began shortly to drift back north to their old lands. In 1887, the government granted them an official home.

Unfortunately, the climate on the new reservation was unfavorable for farming, and in any case non-Indians owned whatever good arable land existed. This, plus the existence of individual allotments and centralized government control, slowed economic progress. The tribe sold some timber around the turn of the century. In 1903, the government established a boarding school in Dulce, the reservation capital, but turned it into a sanatorium in 1918 following a tuberculosis epidemic (90 percent of the Jicarillas had tuberculosis by 1914). The Dutch Reformed Church of America opened a school in 1921.

A major addition to the reservation in 1907 provided the Jicarillas with land suitable for herding sheep. They began this activity in the 1920s, and the tribe soon realized a profit. Livestock owners and the "progressive" proacculturation group tended to be Olleros, whereas the Llaneros were the farmers, the conservatives, and guardians of tradition. In the early 1930s bad weather wiped out most of the sheep

herd, although by 1940 it had largely been rebuilt. Also by this time the people were generally healthy again, and acculturation quickened.

The postwar years saw a huge increase in tribal income from oil and gas development. With part of this money, the tribe bought out most non-Indian holdings on the reservation. Education levels, health, and morale all rose. In the 1950s, a decline in the sheep industry brought much of the population to live in Dulce. The tribe began per-capita payments at that time, partly to offset a lack of economic opportunities in Dulce. This action kept families going until more help arrived with the federal programs of the 1960s as well as an increasingly diversified economy. In the 1970s the tribe won $9 million in land claims.

See also Agriculture; Assimilation; Land, Identity and Ownership of, Land Rights; Relocation.

Apache, Lipan

"Lipan" may mean "warriors of the mountains." "Apache" comes from the Zuni word *apachu,* meaning "enemy." The Apaches call themselves Ndee, or Dine'é, "the People." The Apaches arrived in the Southwest from present-day Canada around 1400. By about 1700, the Lipans were living on the south central Texas plains, as far south as Texas's Colorado River. Today they live on the Mescalero Reservation in southeast New Mexico.

Lipan Apaches generally lived in hide teepees. Occasionally, and especially when they were moved off the Plains, they used dome-shaped brush wiki-ups, which they covered with grass thatch or with hides in bad weather.

Lipan Apaches were primarily hunters and gatherers. They hunted buffalo into the eighteenth century, and afterward they continued to hunt deer, elk, antelope, rabbits, and other game. They ate few birds and did not eat fish, coyote, snake, or owl.

Wild foods included agave; cactus shoots, flowers, and fruit; berries; seeds; nuts; honey; and wild onions, potatoes, and grasses. Nuts and seeds were often ground into flour. The agave or century plant was particularly important. Baking its base in rock-lined pits for several days yielded mescal, a sweet, nutritious food that was dried and stored. The Lipans moved often to follow animal migrations as well as the ripening of their wild foods. Traditional farm crops were obtained by trade or raid and by practicing some agriculture.

By about 1700 the Lipans had become separated from the Jicarillas and had migrated into the central and south Texas plains. They had also acquired horses and had become expert buffalo hunters and raiders of the western Plains from Kansas to Mexico. Caddoan villages felt the wrath of Lipan raiders and slavers until they acquired guns from French traders and were able to drive the Lipan back into Texas.

A Lipan request for Spanish protection against the Comanches, who were pressing them from the north and east, resulted in the establishment of a mission in 1757, which the Comanches promptly destroyed the following year. By the late eighteenth century, the Comanches had forced most Lipans from Texas into New Mexico to join other Apache bands there.

By the early nineteenth century, the remaining Lipans had established good terms with the Texans, serving as their scouts, guides, and trading partners. Following the war between Mexico and the United States (1848), the Apaches, who did their part to bring misery to Mexico, assumed that the Americans would continue as allies. Instead, the Texans adopted an extermination policy, and the Lipans who escaped went to live in Mexico. In the late 1870s, some Lipans fought with the Chiricahua leader Victorio in his last stand against the United States and captivity. He and they were killed in Mexico.

In 1873, the U.S. government had granted the Mescalero Apaches a small reservation surrounding the Sierra Blanca Mountains. The Mescaleros absorbed Apache refugees and immigrants in hopes that the increased numbers would help them gain the elusive title to their land. In 1903, thirty-seven Mexican Lipan Apaches arrived, followed in 1913 by 187 Chiricahuas from Fort Sill, Oklahoma. Eventually, largely through intermarriage, these peoples evolved into the modern Mescalero community.

The United States engaged in extreme repression and all-out assault on traditional culture at the end of the nineteenth century. Cattle raising and timber sales proved lucrative in the early twentieth century. Eventually, day schools replaced the hated, culture-killing boarding schools. By the late 1940s, every family had a house, and the Mescalero economy was relatively stable. The reservation is managed cooperatively with the Mescalero and the Chiricahua Apaches.

See also Apache Wars; Land, Identity and Ownership of, Land Rights; Victorio.

Apache, Mescalero

"Mescalero," from mescal, a food derived from the agave, or century, plant and an important part of their diet. "Apache" comes from the Zuni *apachu,* or "enemy." The Apaches call themselves Ndee, or Dine'é, "the People." Mescalero is a southern Athapaskan, or Apachean dialect.

The Mescaleros traditionally lived from east of the Rio Grande to the Pecos and beyond to the west Texas plains. The Mescalero Reservation is located in southeast New Mexico, northeast of Alamogordo.

The Mescaleros had moved into southern New Mexico by the early sixteenth century and had acquired horses at about the same time. They and the Jicarillas raided (and traded with) Spanish settlements and pueblos on the Rio Grande, and after 1680 they controlled the Camino Real, the main route from El Paso to Santa Fe. They hunted buffalo on the southern Plains and were the de facto masters of the Plains.

Some Mescalero bands tried to stay out of trouble in the 1850s by planting fields under the supervision of federal agents, but, when raiding resumed owing to broken promises of food and protection, all sides became caught up in a spiral of violence. By 1863, General James Carleton forced them off their informal reservation in the Sierra Blanca Mountains to Fort Sumner, at Bosque Redondo, on the Pecos. It was a concentration camp: Living with 9,000 Navajos, the Mescalero endured overcrowding, disease, bad water, and starvation. Two years later they escaped into the mountains, where they lived for seven years.

In 1873, the U.S. government granted the Mescaleros a small reservation surrounding the Sierra Blanca, which included their traditional summer territory. This land made for a harsh home in winter, however, and in any case it was too small for hunting and gathering. That decade was marked by disease, white incursions, and violence directed against them. In 1880, in retaliation after some Mescaleros joined the Chiricahuas in their wars against the United States, the army placed the Mescaleros under martial law, disarmed them, and penned them in a corral filled deep with manure.

By the mid-1880s, gambling had replaced traditional raiding. Missionaries arrived, as did a day school, which the Indians hated for separating the children from their elders. Meanwhile, their population plummeted from 3,000 in 1850 to 431 in 1888. These were years marked by dependency, agent

thievery, tyranny, disease, starvation and malnourishment, and uncertainty about the status of their reservation. Still, they survived the epidemics and efforts to steal their reservation by turning it into a national park (a move that proved unsuccessful in the long run).

The Mescaleros had absorbed Apache refugees and immigrants in hopes that increased numbers would help them gain the elusive title to their land. In 1883, the Jicarillas arrived, although they left by 1887. In 1903, thirty-seven Lipan Apaches arrived, followed in 1913 by 187 Chiricahuas from Fort Sill, Oklahoma. Eventually, largely through intermarriage, all evolved into the modern Mescalero community.

The United States engaged in extreme repression and all-out assault on traditional culture at the end of the nineteenth century. Cattle raising and timber sales proved lucrative in the early twentieth century. Eventually, day schools replaced the hated, culture-killing boarding schools. By the late 1940s, every family had a house, and the reservation economy was relatively strong. The reservation is managed cooperatively with the Chiricahua and the Lipan Apaches.

See also Apache Wars; Assimilation; Gambling;
Land, Identity and Ownership of, Land Rights.

Apache, Mimbreño

See Apache, Chiricahua.

Apache, Northern Tonto

See Apache, Western.

Apache, San Carlos

See Apache, Western.

Apache, Southern Tonto

See Apache, Western.

Apache, Western

The word "Apache" comes from the Zuni *apachu*, meaning "enemy." These people are properly known as Ndee, or Dine'é, "the People." "Western Apache" is a somewhat artificial designation given to an Apache tribe composed, with some exceptions, of bands living in Arizona. After 1850 these bands were primarily the San Carlos, White Mountain, Tonto (divided into northern and southern Tonto by anthropologists), and Cibecue. Apaches spoke southern Athapaskan, or Apachean.

Traditionally, western Apache bands covered nearly all but the northwesternmost quarter of Arizona. Their territory encompassed an extreme ecological diversity. Today's reservations include Fort Apache (Cibecue and White Mountain); San Carlos

An Apache bride. (National Archives and Records Administration)

(San Carlos); Camp Verde, including Clarkdale and Middle Verde (mostly Tonto, shared with the Yavapai); and Payson. Tontos also live in the Middle Verde, Clarkdale, and Payson communities.

Each of the western Apache tribes was considered autonomous and distinct, although intermarriage did occur. Tribal cohesion was minimal; there was no central political authority. A tribe was based on a common territory, language, and culture. Each was made up of between two and five bands of greatly varying size. Bands formed the most important Apache unit, which were in turn composed of local groups (thirty-five to 200 people in extended families, themselves led by a headman) headed by a chief. The chief lectured his followers before sunrise every morning on proper behavior. His authority was based on his personal qualities and perhaps his ceremonial knowledge. Decisions were made by consensus. One of the chief's most important functions was to mitigate friction among his people.

Having acquired the horse, the western Apache groups established a trading and raiding network with at least a dozen other groups, from the Hopi to Spanish settlements in Sonora. Although the Spanish policy of promoting docility by providing liquor to Native Americans worked moderately well from the late eighteenth century through the early nineteenth, Apache raids remained ongoing into the nineteenth century. By 1830, the Apaches had drifted away from the presidios and resumed a full schedule of raiding.

Following the war between Mexico and the United States (1848), the Apaches, who did their part to bring misery to Mexico, assumed that the Americans would continue to be their allies. The Apaches were shocked and disgusted to learn that their lands were now considered part of the United States and that the Americans planned to "pacify" them. Having been squeezed by the Spanish, the Comanches, the Mexicans, and now miners, farmers, and other land-grabbers from the United States, some Apaches were more than ever determined to protect their way of life.

Throughout the 1850s most of the anti-Apache attention was centered on the Chiricahuas. The White Mountain and Cibecue people never fought to the finish with the Americans; out of range of the mines and settlements, they continued their lives of farming and hunting. When Fort Apache was created (1863), these people adapted peacefully to reservation life and went on to serve as scouts against the Tontos and Chiricahuas.

The Prescott gold strike (1863) heralded a cycle of raid, murder, and massacre for the Tonto. By 1865 a string of forts ringed their territory; they were defeated militarily eight years later. A massacre of San Carlos (Aravaipa) women in 1871 led to Grant's Peace Policy, a policy of concentration via forced marches. The result was that thousands of Chiricahuas and western Apaches lived on the crowded and disease-ridden San Carlos Reservation. There, a handful of dissident chiefs, confined in chains, held out for the old life of freedom and self-respect. The Chiricahua Victorio bolted with 350 followers and remained at large and raiding for years. More fled in 1881. By 1884 all had been killed or had returned, at least temporarily. In general, the western Apaches remained peaceful on the reservations while corrupt agents and settlers stole their best land.

The White Mountain people joined Fort Apache in 1879. As the various bands were spuriously lumped together, group distinctions as well as traditional identity began to break down. A man named Silas John Edwards established a significant and enduring religious cult at Fort Apache in the 1920s. Though not exactly Christian, it did substitute a new set of ceremonies in place of the old ones, contributing further to the general decline of traditional life. In 1918 the government issued cattle to the Apaches, and lumbering began in the 1920s. In 1930, the government informed the Apaches that a new dam (the Coolidge) would flood old San Carlos. All residents were forced out, and subsistence agriculture ended for them. The Bureau of Indian Affairs (BIA) provided them with cattle and let all Anglo leases expire; by the late 1930s these Indians were stockherders.

See also Apache Wars; Horse, Economic Impact; Victorio; Warfare, Intertribal.

Apache, White Mountain

See Apache, Western.

Chemehuevi

"Chemehuevi" is Yuman for "nose in the air like a roadrunner," referring to a running style of the original settlers of the Chemehuevi Valley. These Indians traditionally called themselves *Nuwu*, "the People,"

or *Tantáwats*, "Southern Men." Chemehuevis spoke Paiute, a group of the Shoshonean branch of the Uto-Aztecan language family.

Since the late nineteenth and early twentieth centuries, these people have lived in the Chemehuevi Valley, California (part of the Colorado River Valley east of Joshua Tree National Monument), and southwestern California. Their traditional territory was located in southwestern Utah, the Mojave Desert, and finally the Chemehuevi Valley, near the present Lake Havasu.

Toward the end of the eighteenth century, the Chemehuevis and the Las Vegas band of southern Paiutes may have exterminated the Desert Mojaves. In the midnineteenth century, the Chemehuevis took over their territory as well as that of the Pee-Posh (Maricopa) Indians, who had been driven away by the Mojave Indians and who had gone to live on the Gila River. The Mojaves either actively or passively accepted the Chemehuevis. On the Colorado River, the Chemehuevis developed a crop-based economy and at the same time began to think of themselves as a distinct political entity. They also became strongly influenced in many ways by the Mojaves, notably in their interest in warfare and their religious beliefs. Some Chemehuevis raided miners in northern Arizona from the 1850s through the 1870s.

In 1865 the Chemehuevis and Mojaves fought each other. The Chemehuevis lost and retreated to the desert. Two years later, however, many returned to the California side of the Colorado River, where they resumed their lives on the Colorado River Reservation, established two years earlier. Many Chemehuevis also remained in and around the Chemehuevi Valley, combining wage labor and traditional subsistence. By the turn of the century, most Chemehuevis were settled on the Colorado River Reservation and among the Serranos and Cahuillas in southern California. In 1885, after a particularly severe drought, a group moved north to farm the Chemehuevi Valley. When a reservation was established there, in 1907, the tribal split became official.

The creation of Hoover Dam in 1935 and Parker Dam in 1939 spelled disaster for the Chemehuevis. The Hoover stopped the seasonal Colorado River floods, which the Chemehuevi people had depended on to nourish their crops. The Parker Dam created Lake Havasu, placing most of the Chemehuevi Valley under water. At that point, most Indians in the Chemehuevi Valley moved south again to join their

people at the Colorado River Reservation. A government relocation camp operated on the reservation from 1942 to 1945.

By the end of World War II, 148 Navajo and Hopi families had also colonized the reservation; they, with the Chemehuevis and Mojaves, became known as the Colorado River Indian Tribes (CRIT). As a result of a 1951 lawsuit, the Chemehuevis were awarded $900,000 by the United States for land taken to create Lake Havasu. The tribe was not formally constituted until they adopted a constitution in 1971. At about that time, some Chemehuevis began a slow return to the Chemehuevi Valley, where they remain today, operating a resort on their tribal lands.

Before their move to the Colorado River, the Chemehuevis had little tribal consciousness or government per se. They roamed their territory in many bands, each with a relatively powerless chief. They assumed a tribal identity toward the midnineteenth century. At the same time, the chief, often a generous, smart, wealthy man succeeded by his eldest son, assumed a stronger leadership role.

Following their move to the river, a diet based on foods obtained by hunting and by gathering desert resources was partially replaced by crops such as corn, beans, pumpkins, melons, grasses (semicultivated), and wheat. The Chemehuevis also ate fish from the river; game, including turtles, snakes, and lizards; and a variety of wild plants, such as mesquite beans (a staple) and piñon nuts.

See also Environment and Pollution; Reservation Economic and Social Conditions; Warfare, Intertribal.

Cochiti Pueblo

"Cochiti" comes from the original Keresan via a Spanish transliteration. The word "pueblo" comes from the Spanish for "village." It refers both to a certain style of Southwest Indian architecture, characterized by multistory, apartment-like buildings made of adobe (pueblo), and to the people themselves (Pueblo). Rio Grande Pueblos are known as eastern Pueblos; Zunis, Hopis, and sometimes Acomas and Lagunas are known as western Pueblos. Cochiti is a Keresan dialect.

In the sixteenth century, Cochiti Pueblo featured two- to three-story, apartment-style dwellings as well as individual houses, facing south. The buildings were constructed of adobe (earth-and-straw) bricks, with beams across the roof that were covered with poles, brush, and plaster. Floors were of wood plank or packed earth. The roof of one level served as the floor of another. The levels were interconnected by ladders. As an aid to defense, the traditional design included no doors or windows; entry was through the roof. Pithouses, or kivas, served as ceremonial chambers and clubhouses. The village plaza, around which all dwellings were clustered, is the spiritual center of the village where all the balanced forces of the world come together.

Cochitis were farmers. Before the Spanish arrived, they ate primarily corn, beans, and pumpkins. They also grew sunflowers and tobacco. They hunted deer, mountain lion, bear, antelope, and rabbits. Occasionally, men from Cochiti and Santo Domingo pueblos would travel east to hunt buffalo. Cochitis also gathered a variety of wild seeds, nuts, berries, and other foods. The Spanish introduced wheat, alfalfa, sheep, cattle, and garden vegetables, which soon became part of the regular diet.

All Pueblos were part of extensive Native American trading networks. With the arrival of other cultures, Pueblo Indians also traded with the Hispanic American villages and then U.S. traders. At fixed times during summer or fall, enemies declared truces so that trading fairs might be held. The largest and best-known was at Taos with the Comanches. Nomads exchanged slaves, buffalo hides, buckskins, jerked meat, and horses for agricultural and manufactured pueblo products. Pueblo Indians traded for shell and copper ornaments, turquoise, and macaw feathers. Trade along the Santa Fe Trail began in 1821. By the 1880s and the arrival of railroads, the Pueblos were dependent on many American-made goods, and the Native American manufacture of weaving and pottery declined and nearly died out.

Though often depicted as passive and docile, most Pueblo groups regularly engaged in warfare. The great revolt of 1680 stands out as the major military action, but they also skirmished at other times with the Spanish and defended themselves against attackers such as Apaches, Comanches, and Utes. They also contributed auxiliary soldiers to provincial forces under Spain and Mexico, which were used mainly against raiding Indians and to protect merchant caravans on the Santa Fe Trail. After the raid-

ing tribes began to pose less of a threat in the late nineteenth century, Pueblo military societies began to wither away, with the office of war captain changing to civil and religious functions.

See also Agriculture; All Indian Pueblo Council; Pueblo Revolt.

Cocopah

"Cocopah" is from the Mojave *kwi-ka-pah*. The Cocopahs called themselves *Xawil Kunyavaei*, "Those Who Live on the River." The traditional home of the Cocopahs is near the Colorado River delta. Presently, many tribal members live in northwestern Mexico and on a reservation near Somerton, Arizona. Cocopahs spoke River Yuman, a member of the Hokan-Siouan language family.

The Cocopahs traditionally maintained little political leadership. They lived in small settlements, or rancherias, of ten to twelve families. Society was organized into clans, with each clan having a leader. Other quasi officials included dance and war leaders and funeral orators. Leadership was generally determined by experience, ability, and, as with everything else, dreams.

Originally concentrated in nine rancherias, the Cocopahs built two different types of homes. In winter they built conical, partially excavated (later four-post rectangular) structures, covering the walls of sticks with earth. In summer they built oval-domed, brush-covered huts. They also used a circular, unroofed ramada for dwelling and/or cooking and small granaries with elevated floors for storing food.

Corn, beans, black-eyed peas, pumpkins, and later melons were planted, usually in July. Gathered food, such as the seeds of wild saltgrass, roots, fruits, eggs, and especially mesquite, were also important, as was fish (such as mullet and bass) from the river and the Gulf of California. Wild game included deer, boar, and smaller animals. Much of the food was dried and stored for the winter. In general, the women gathered and cooked food, and the men hunted.

The Cocopahs planted seeds in holes rather than plowed rows in order to preserve topsoil. They used pottery (jars, seed-toasting trays), crude baskets, fire drills, vegetable-fiber fishing nets, clubs and bow and arrow for warfare, stone and wooden mortars, and stone and clamshell tools. Their musical instruments included a scraped and

drummed basket, gourd rattles, and cane flutes and whistles. They also used small earthen dikes for irrigation.

Warfare united the Cocopahs. They observed formalized war patterns and respected special war leaders. They prepared for war by dreaming, fasting, and painting their bodies and underwent purification rituals upon their return. Traditional enemies included the Mojave and the Quechan; allied peoples included the O'odham, Pee-Posh, and Pai. Their weapons were the war club, bow and arrow, lance, and deerskin shield.

By 1540 the Mojave and Quechan Indians had forced them down the Colorado River, to a place where they farmed 50,000 acres of delta land, made rich by the annual spring floods. The Cocopahs encountered Spanish soldiers and travelers during the mid-sixteenth century but remained in place and relatively unaffected by contact with the Europeans until U.S. dams stopped the Colorado from flooding in the late nineteenth century.

In 1853, the Gadsden Treaty separated the four bands of Cocopahs: Two remained in Mexico, and two moved north near Somerton, Arizona. By the mid-1800s, with the cessation of warfare with their ancient enemies, the Quechans, the Cocopahs lost a certain sense of purpose. A generation of men obtained employment as river pilots and navigators along the Colorado River, whetting their appetite for American goods and foods. Riverboat traffic ended when the railroad reached Yuma in 1877. In 1905, an accidental diversion of the Colorado River (the Salton Sea debacle) led to the Cocopahs' final displacement. Lacking strong political, religious, or social leadership, they quickly fell further into disintegration and impoverishment.

Thanks mainly to the work of Frank Tehanna, the U.S. government established a reservation in 1917 for the Cocopahs and some Quechans and Pee-Posh. The government then almost completely abandoned them for the next sixty years. By the end of World War II, fewer than sixty Cocopahs remained on the desolate reservation; the rest lived elsewhere, generally in even worse poverty. In the 1960s, the tribe organized and won from the government electricity and improved housing, building their first tribal building and rewriting their constitution.

In 1986, the tribe received an additional 615 acres, now known as the North Reservation. In the 1970s and 1980s, the tribe made improvements in education as well as other social and cultural pro-

grams. That period also witnessed a revival of crafts such as beadwork and the development of fine arts.

See also Agriculture; Reservation Economic and Social Conditions; Warfare, Intertribal.

Havasupai

"Havasupai" is a name meaning "People of the Blue-Green Water." With the Hualapais, from whom they may be descended, they are also called the Pais (Pa'as) Indians ("the People"; Hualapais are western Pais, and Havasupais are eastern Pais). With the Hualapais and the Yavapais, the Havasupais are also Upland Yumans, in contrast to River Yumans such as the Mojaves and Quechans. The Havasupais spoke Upland Yuman, a member of the Hokan-Siouan language family.

Since approximately 1100, the Havasupais have lived at Cataract Canyon in the Grand Canyon as well as on the nearby upland plateaus.

The Havasupais probably descended from the prehistoric Cohoninas, a branch of the Hakataya culture. Thirteen bands of Pais originally hunted, farmed, and gathered in northwest Arizona along the Colorado River. By historic times, the Pais were divided into three subtribes: the Middle Mountain People; the Plateau People (including the Blue Water People, also called Cataract Canyon Band, who were ancestors of the Havasupais); and the Yavapai Fighters.

The Blue Water People were comfortable in an extreme range of elevations. They gathered desert plants from along the Colorado River at 1,800 feet and hunted on the upper slopes of the San Francisco peaks, their center of the world, at 12,000 feet.

Formal authority among the Havasupais was located in chiefs, hereditary in theory only, of ten local groups. Their only real power was to advise and persuade. The Havasupais held few councils; most issues were dealt with by men informally in the sweat lodge.

The Havasupais were individualists rather than band or tribe oriented. The family was the main unit of social organization. In place of a formal marriage ceremony, a man simply took up residence with a woman's family. The couple moved into their own home after they had a child. Women owned no

property. Babies stayed mainly on basket cradle boards until they were old enough to walk. With some exceptions, work was roughly divided by gender.

In winter and summer, dwellings consisted of domed or conical wickiups of thatch and dirt over a pole frame. People also lived in rock shelters. Small domed lodges were used as sweat houses and clubhouses.

In Cataract Canyon the people grew corn, beans, squash, sunflowers, and tobacco. During the winter they lived on the surrounding plateau and ate game such as mountain lion and other cats, deer, antelope, mountain sheep, fowl, and rabbit, which were killed in communal hunting drives. Wild foods included piñon nuts, cactus and yucca fruits, agave hearts, mesquite beans, and wild honey.

Traditional implements included stone knives, bone tools, bows and arrows, clay pipes for smoking, and nets of yucca fiber. The Havasupais tilled their soil with sticks. Baskets and pottery were used for a number of purposes. Grinding was accomplished by means of a flat rock and rotary mortars.

The Havasupais often traded with the Hopis and other allied tribes, exchanging deerskins, baskets, salt, lima beans, and red hematite paint for food, pottery, and cloth. They also traded with tribes as far away as the Pacific Ocean.

Buckskin, worked by men, was the main clothing material. Women wore a two-part dress, with a yucca-fiber or textile belt around the waist, and trimmed with hoof tinklers. In the nineteenth century they began wearing ornamental shawls. Moccasins, when worn, were made with a high upper part wrapped around the calf. Men wore shirts, loincloths, leggings, headbands, and high-ankle moccasins. Personal decoration consisted of necklaces, earrings of Pueblo and Navajo shell and silver, and occasionally painted faces.

With the possible exception of Francisco Garces, in 1776, few if any Spanish or other outsiders disturbed them into the 1800s. Spanish influences did reach them, however, primarily in the form of horses, cloth, and fruit trees through trading partners such as the Hopis.

In the early 1800s, a trail was forged from the Rio Grande to California that led directly through Pai country. By around 1850, with invasions and treaty violations increasing, the Pais occasionally reacted with violence. When mines opened in their territory in 1863, they perceived the threat and readied for war. Unfortunately for them, the Hualapai War (1865–1869) came just as the Civil War ended. After their military defeat by the United States, some Pais served as army scouts against their old enemies, the Yavapais and the Tonto Apaches.

Although the Hualapais were to suffer deportation, the United States paid little attention to those who returned to their isolated homes. At this point the two tribes became increasingly distinct. Despite their remote location, Anglo encroachment eventually affected even the Havasupais, and an 1880 executive order established their reservation along Havasu Creek. The final designation in 1882 included just 518 acres in the canyon; the Havasupais also lost their traditional upland hunting and gathering grounds (some people continued to use the plateau in winter but were forced off in 1934, when the National Park Service destroyed their homes).

The Havasupais intensified farming on their little remaining land and began a wide-scale cultivation of peaches. In 1912 they purchased cattle. Severe epidemics in the early twentieth century reduced their population to just over 100. At the same time the Bureau of Indian Affairs, initially slow to move into the canyon, proceeded with a program of rapid acculturation. By the 1930s, Havasupai economic independence had given way to a reliance on limited wage labor. Traditional political power declined as well, despite the creation in 1939 of a tribal council.

Feeling confined in the canyon, the Havasupai stepped up their fight for permanent grazing rights on the plateau. The 1950s were a grim time for the people, with no employment and little tourism. Conflict over land led to deep familial divisions, which in turn resulted in serious cultural loss. Food prices at the local store were half again as high as those in neighboring towns. In the 1960s, however, an infusion of federal funds provided employment in tribal programs as well as modern utilities. Still, croplands continued to shrink, as more and more land was devoted to the upkeep of pack animals for the tourists, the tribe's limited but main source of income. In 1975, after an intensive lobbying effort, the government restored 185,000 acres of land to the Havasupai.

See also Agriculture; Environment and Pollution; Reservation Economic and Social Conditions.

Hopi

"Hopi" comes from *Hopituh Shi-nu-mu*, "Peaceful People." They were formerly called the Moki (or Moqui) Indians, a name probably taken from a Zuni epithet. The Hopis are the westernmost of the Pueblo peoples. First, Second, and Third Mesas are all part of Black Mesa, located on the Colorado Plateau between the Colorado River and the Rio Grande, in northeast Arizona. Of the several Hopi villages, all but Old Oraibi are of relatively recent construction. Hopi, a Shoshonean language, is a member of the Uto-Aztecan language family.

According to legend, the Hopis agreed to act as caretakers of this Fourth World in exchange for permission to live here. Over centuries of a stable existence based on farming, they evolved an extremely rich ceremonial life. The Hopi Way, whose purpose is to maintain a balance between nature and people in every aspect of life, is ensured by the celebration of their ceremonies.

The Hopis recognize two major ceremonial cycles, masked (January or February until July) and unmasked, which are determined by the position of the sun and the lunar calendar. The purpose of most ceremonies is to bring rain. As the symbol of life and well-being, corn, a staple crop, is the focus of many ceremonies. All great ceremonies last nine days, including a preliminary day. Each ceremony is controlled by a clan or several clans. Central to Hopi ceremonialism is the kiva, or underground chamber, which is seen as a doorway to the cave world from whence their ancestors originally came.

Katsinas are guardian spirits, or intermediaries between the creator and the people. They are said to dwell at the San Francisco peaks and at other holy places. Every year at the winter solstice, they travel to inhabit people's bodies and remain until after the summer solstice. Recreated in dolls and masks, they deliver the blessings of life and teach people the proper way to live. Katsina societies are associated with clan ancestors and with rain gods. All Hopis are initiated into katsina societies, although only men play an active part in them.

Perhaps the most important ceremony of the year is Soyal, or the winter solstice, which celebrates the Hopi worldview and recounts their legends. Another important ceremony is Niman, the harvest festival. The August Snake Dance has become a well-known Hopi ceremony.

Like other Pueblo peoples, the Hopis recognize a dual division of time and space between the upper world of the living and the lower world of the dead. Prayer may be seen as a mediation between the upper and lower, or human and supernatural, worlds. These worlds coexist at the same time and may be seen in oppositions such as summer and winter, day and night, life and death. In all aspects of Hopi ritual, ideas of space, time, color, and number are all interrelated in such a way as to provide order to the Hopi world.

Traditionally, the Hopis favored a weak government coupled with a strong matrilineal, matrilocal clan system. They were not a tribe in the usual sense of the word but were characterized by an elaborate social structure, each village having its own organization and each individual his or her own place in the community. The "tribe" was "invented" in 1936, when the non-Native Oliver La Farge wrote their constitution. Although a tribal council exists, many people's allegiance remains with the village kikmongwi (cacique). A kikmongwi is appointed for life and rules in matters of traditional religion. Major villages include Walpi (First Mesa), Shungopavi (Second Mesa), and Oraibi (Third Mesa).

Hopi children learn their traditions through katsina dolls, including scare-katsinas, as well as social pressure, along with an abundance of love and attention. This approach tends to encourage friendliness and sharing in Hopi children. In general, women owned (and built) the houses and other material resources, whereas men farmed and hunted away from the village. Special societies included katsina and other men's and women's organizations concerned with curing, clowning, weather control, and war.

Distinctive one- or two-floor pueblo housing featured sandstone and adobe walls and roof beams of pine and juniper, gathered from afar. The dwellings were entered via ladders through openings in the roofs and were arranged around a central plaza. This architectural arrangement reflects and reinforces cosmological ideas concerning emergence from an underworld through successive world levels.

Hopis have been expert dry farmers for centuries, growing corn, beans, squash, cotton, and tobacco on floodplains and sand dunes or, with the use of irrigation, near springs. The Spanish brought crops such as wheat, chilies, peaches, melons, and other fruit. Men were the farmers and hunters of game such as deer, antelope, elk, and rabbits. The Hopi also kept domesticated turkeys. Women gathered wild food and herbs, such as pine nuts, prickly

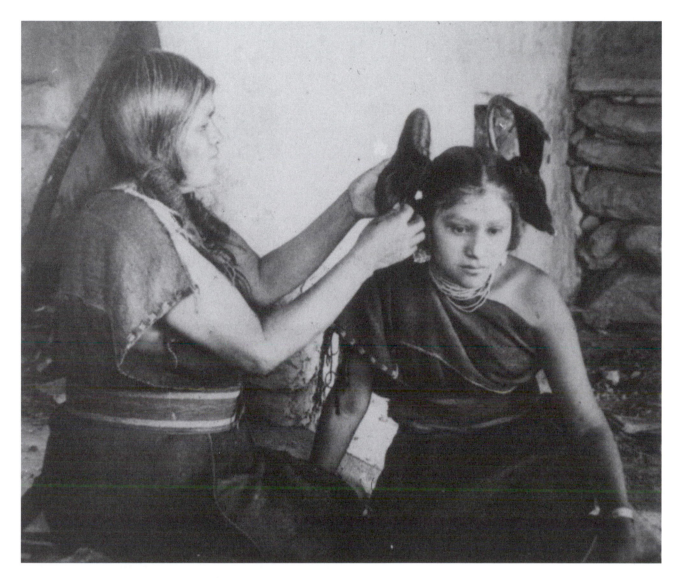

Hopi woman dressing hair of unmarried girl, ca. 1900. (National Archives and Records Administration)

pear, yucca, berries, currants, nuts, and seeds. Crops were dried and stored against drought and famine.

Farming technology included digging sticks (later the horse and plow), small rock or brush-and-dirt dams and sage windbreaks, and an accurate calendar on which each year's planting time was based. Grinding tools were made of stone. Men wove clothing and women made pottery, which was used for many purposes. Men also hunted with the bow and arrow and used snares and nets to trap animals.

The Hopis are probably descended from the prehistoric Ancestral Puebloan culture. Ancestors of the Hopis have been in roughly the same location for at least 10,000 years. During the fourteenth century, the Hopis became one of three centers of

Pueblo culture, along with the Zuni/Acoma and Rio Grande Pueblos. Between the fourteenth and sixteenth centuries, three traits in particular distinguished the Hopi culture: a highly specialized agriculture, including selective breeding and various forms of irrigation; a pronounced artistic impulse, as seen in mural and pottery painting; and the mining and use of coal (after which the Hopi returned to using wood for fuel and sheep dung for firing pottery).

The Hopis first met non-Native Americans when members of Coronado's party came into their country in 1540. The first missionary arrived in 1629, at Awatovi. Although the Spanish did not colonize Hopis, they did make the Indians swear allegiance to

the Spanish crown and attempted to undermine their religious beliefs. For this reason, the Hopis joined the Pueblo Revolt of 1680. They destroyed all local missions and established new pueblos at the top of Black Mesa that were easier to defend. The Spanish reconquest of 1692 did not reach Hopi land, and the Hopis welcomed refugees from other pueblos who sought to live free of Spanish influence. In 1700, the Hopis destroyed Awatovi, the only village with an active mission, and remained free of Christianity for almost 200 years thereafter.

During the nineteenth century the Hopis endured an increase in Navajo raiding. Later in the century they again encountered non-Natives, this time permanently. The U.S. government established a Hopi reservation in 1882, and the railroad began bringing in trading posts, tourists, missionaries, and scholars. The new visitors in turn brought disease epidemics that reduced the Hopi population dramatically.

Like many tribes, the Hopis struggled to deal with the upheaval brought about by these new circumstances. Following the Dawes Act (1887), surveyors came in preparation for parceling the land into individual allotments; the Hopis met them with armed resistance. Although there was no fighting, Hopi leaders were imprisoned. They were imprisoned as well for their general refusal to send their children to the new schools, which were known for brutal discipline and policies geared toward cultural genocide. Hopi children were kidnapped and sent to the schools anyway.

Factionalism also took a toll on Hopi life. Ceremonial societies split between "friendly" and "hostile" factions. This development led in 1906 to the division of Oraibi, which had been continuously occupied since at least 1100, into five villages. Contact with the outside world increased significantly after the two world wars. By the 1930s, the Hopi economy and traditional ceremonial life were in shambles (yet perhaps the latter remained more intact than that of any other U.S. tribe). Most people who could find work worked for wages or the tourist trade. For the first time, alcoholism became a problem.

In 1943, a U.S. decision to divide the Hopi and Navajo Reservations into grazing districts resulted in the loss of most Hopi land. This sparked a major disagreement between the tribes and the government that continues to this day. Following World War II, the "hostile" traditionalists emerged as the caretakers of land, resisting Cold War–related policies such as mineral development and nuclear testing and mining. The official ("friendly") tribal council, however, instituted policies that favored the exploitation of the land, notably permitting Peabody Coal to strip-mine Black Mesa, beginning in 1970.

> *See also* Agriculture; Ancestral Puebloan Culture; Katsinas; Navajo-Hopi Land Dispute; Uranium Mining.

Hopi-Tewa

The Hopi-Tewas are a small group (roughly 700) of Native Americans living mostly on the Hopi Reservation. These Indians are descended from immigrants who settled at First Mesa (Tewa Village [Hano] and Polacca) following the Pueblo Revolt, around 1700. They speak a variety of Tewa, a Tanoan language, and have some distinct cultural attributes.

> *See also* Ancestral Puebloan Culture; Pueblo Revolt.

Hualapai

The Hualapai, or Walapai (Xawálapáiya), "Pine Tree People," were named after the piñon pine nut. With the Havasupais, they are called the Pais (Pa'as) Indians ("the People"; the Hualapais are the western Pais, and the Havasupais are the eastern Pais). They are also described, with the Havasupais and the Yavapais, as Upland Yumans, in contrast to the River Yumans, such as the Mojaves and Quechans. Hualapais spoke Upland Yuman, a member of the Hokan-Siouan language family.

The Pai Indians, who traditionally considered themselves one people, probably descended from the prehistoric Patayans of the ancient Hakataya culture. Thirteen bands of Pais originally ranged in northwest Arizona along the Colorado River, hunting, farming, and gathering. By historic times, three subtribes had been organized: the Middle Mountain People, the Plateau People, and the Yavapai Fighters. Each subtribe was further divided into several bands, which in turn were divided into camps and families.

Traditional political authority was decentralized. The headmen of both a camp (roughly twenty people) and a band (roughly eighty-five to 200 people) led by fostering consensus. They served as

war chiefs and spokespeople when necessary. The position of headman was occasionally hereditary but more often based on personality and ability. There was little or no tribal identity until the early twentieth century, when the Hualapais created a fledgling tribal council. In the 1930s they adopted a constitution and elected their first tribal president.

Occasionally the Hualapais grew the standard American crops (corn, beans, and squash) near springs and ditches. Corn was made into mush, soup, and bread; pumpkins were dried in long strips. In the main, however, they obtained their food by hunting and gathering, leaving their summer camps to follow the seasonal ripening of wild foods. The women gathered piñon nuts, cactus and yucca fruits, agave (mescal) hearts, mesquite beans, and other plants. The men hunted deer, antelope, mountain sheep, rabbits (in drives), and small game. Meat was dried and stored in skin bags. The Hualapais also ate fish.

The Hualapais were part of an extensive system of exchange that stretched from the Pacific Ocean to the Pueblos. Shell decorations and horses came from the Mojaves and the Quechans. Rich red ocher pigment was a key trade item, as were baskets and dried mescal and dressed skins. Meat and skins went for crops; lima beans for Hopi peaches.

Although the Pais encountered non-Natives in 1540, or perhaps as late as 1598, neither the Spanish nor the Mexicans developed Hualapai country, which remained fairly isolated until the 1820s. Around that time, a trail was blazed from the Rio Grande to California that led directly through Pai country. After the Mexican cession (1848), Hualapais began working in white-owned mines. With Anglo invasions and treaty violations increasing and the mines ever exploitative, the Hualapais, in 1865, met violence with violence. A warrior named Cherum forced a key U.S. retreat but later scouted for his old enemy. Later, the United States selected Hualapai Charley and Leve Leve as principal chiefs because they were amenable to making peace. The Hualapai War ended in 1869.

Because the eastern Pais played a minor role in the war, they were allowed to return home afterward; it was at this juncture that the two "tribes," Hualapais and Havasupais, became increasingly separate. The army forced the Hualapais who failed to escape to march in 1874 to the Colorado River Reservation. There, the low altitude combined with disease and poor rations brought the Hualapais much suffering and death. When they filtered back home several years later, they found their land in non-Native hands. Still, they applied for and received official permission to remain, and a reservation was established for them in 1883.

The reservation consisted of 1 million acres on the South Rim of the Grand Canyon, a fraction of their original land. Before long, overgrazing by non-Indians had ruined the Native food supply, and ranchers and cattlemen were directly threatening the Indians with physical violence. A series of epidemics struck the Hualapais. Most Hualapais lived off the reservation, scrambling for wage work and sending their children to Anglo schools. As the Hualapais formed an underclass of cheap, unskilled labor, their way of life began to vanish. The railroad depot at Peach Springs became the primary Hualapai village, but the railroad brought only dislocation, disease, and some jobs. Their new condition strengthened their differences with the still isolated Havasupais.

The Hualapais began herding cattle in 1914, although their herds were greatly outnumbered by those of non-Natives. Extensive prejudice against the Indians diminished somewhat after World War I, out of respect for Indian war heroes. Through the midtwentieth century the Hualapais retained a strong sense of their culture, although economic progress was extremely slow up to then.

See also Disease, Historic and Contemporary; Reservation Economic and Social Conditions; Trade.

Isleta Pueblo

"Isleta" is a name taken from the Spanish missions San Antonio de la Isleta and San Augustin de la Isleta (*isleta* means "little island"). The word "pueblo" comes from the Spanish for "village." It refers both to a certain style of Southwest Indian architecture, characterized by multistory, apartment-like buildings made of adobe (pueblo), and to the people themselves (Pueblo). The Pueblos along the Rio Grande are known as eastern Pueblos; Zunis, Hopis, and sometimes Acomas and Lagunas are known as western Pueblos. The Tiwa name for Isleta Pueblo is Shiewhibak, meaning "flint kick-stick place." The Isletas spoke southern Tiwa, a Kiowa-Tanoan language.

Since at least the eighteenth century, the Isleta Pueblo has been located on the Rio Grande several

miles south of Albuquerque. The pueblo consists of a main village (San Agustín) and two farm villages (Chikal and "town chief") three miles to the south.

Like many Pueblos, Isleta was governed by a dual leadership system: a cacique (head of the Pueblo), intimately related to traditional religion, and a governor and his staff, which derived from Spanish colonial rule. The last correctly installed cacique at Isleta died in 1896. After that date, disruptions of installation rituals caused the war chiefs to serve for decades as acting caciques. This situation came to a head in the 1940s, when a political revolution split the pueblo into several factions and postponed elections. With the help of the Bureau of Indian Affairs, a constitution was drawn up; elections were held and the proper officers installed in 1950.

Isleta Pueblo was organized into seven corn groups. Men led the groups, although there were women's auxiliaries. The groups were ritual units, similar to kiva groups, functioning for personal crises and societal ceremonies. The tribe was also divided into Red Eyes (summer) and Black Eyes (winter) groups. Each had a war captain and two or three assistants. Four men from each group served for life as grandfathers or disciplinarians. Each group had ceremonial, irrigation, clowning, hunting, ballplaying, and other group responsibilities.

Two medicine societies (for illness due to misbehavior or witchcraft) were the Town Fathers and the Laguna Fathers. A warrior's society consisted of people who had taken a scalp and had been ritually purified. Closely associated with the kiva, this group also had a women's component, with special duties. The economy was basically a socialistic one, whereby labor was shared and produce was distributed equally. In modern times photography by outsiders is discouraged.

The Isleta Pueblo featured apartment-style dwellings as high as five stories, as well as individual houses, facing south. The buildings were constructed of adobe (earth-and-straw) bricks, with beams across the roof that were covered with poles, brush, and plaster. Floors were of wood plank or packed earth. The roof of one level served as the floor of another.

The levels were interconnected by ladders. As an aid to defense, the traditional design included no doors or windows; entry was through the roof. Pithouses, or kivas, served as ceremonial chambers and clubhouses. The village plaza, around which all dwellings were clustered, is the spiritual center of the village where all the balanced forces of the world come together. A track for ceremonial foot races was also part of the village.

Isletas were farmers. Before the Spanish arrived, they ate primarily corn, beans, and squash. They also grew cotton and tobacco. They hunted deer, mountain lion, bear, antelope, and rabbits. Occasionally, men from Isleta would travel east to hunt buffalo. Isletas also gathered a variety of wild seeds, nuts, berries, and other foods and fished in rivers and mountain streams. The Spanish introduced wheat, alfalfa, chilies, fruit trees, grapes (often made into wine for sale to the Laguna Pueblo or nearby Spanish-American villages), sheep, cattle, and garden vegetables, which soon became part of the regular diet.

See also Agriculture; All Indian Pueblo Council; Pueblo Revolt.

Jemez Pueblo

Jemez is from the Spanish *Jémez*, taken from the Jemez self-designation. The Jemez name for their pueblo is *Walatowa*, "at the pueblo in the cañada" or "this is the place." The word "pueblo" comes from the Spanish for "village." It refers both to a certain style of Southwest Indian architecture, characterized by multistory, apartment-like buildings made of adobe (pueblo), and to the people themselves (Pueblo). Rio Grande Pueblos are known as eastern Pueblos; Zunis, Hopis, and sometimes Acomas and Lagunas are known as western Pueblos. The people spoke Towa, a Kiowa-Tanoan language. The Jemez Pueblo is located along the east bank of the Jemez River, twenty-five miles north of Bernalillo, New Mexico.

The Jemez people lived near Stone Canyon, south of Dulce, New Mexico, around 2,000 years ago. They moved to near their present location after the arrival of the Athapaskans, around the fourteenth century. However, some of them moved to the San Diego Canyon–Guadalupe Canyon area, south of Santa Fe, where they established numerous large fortresses and hundreds of small houses.

The Jemez recognized two divisions, or kiva groups: Squash and Turquoise. The people were further arranged into matrilineal clans with specific ceremonial functions. In modern times photography by outsiders has been discouraged.

More than any other pueblo, Jemez was built on the heights of mesas. It featured apartment-style dwellings of up to four stories, containing as many as 2,000 rooms, as well as one- and two-room houses. The buildings were constructed of adobe (earth-and-straw) bricks, with pine beams across the roof that were covered with poles, brush, and plaster. Floors were of wood plank or packed earth. The roof of one level served as the floor of another. The levels were interconnected by ladders. As an aid to defense, the traditional design included no doors or windows; entry was through the roof. Two rectangular pithouses, or kivas, served as ceremonial chambers and clubhouses. The village plaza, around which all dwellings were clustered, is the spiritual center of the village where all the balanced forces of the world come together. Jemez people also built cliff dwellings to guard access to important places and monitor trails.

Before the Spanish arrived, Jemez people ate primarily corn, beans, and squash. They also grew cotton and tobacco. They hunted deer, mountain lion, bear, antelope, and rabbits. Twice a year, after planting and again after the harvest, men would travel east to hunt buffalo. The women also gathered a variety of wild foods including piñon seeds, yucca fruit, berries, and wild potatoes. The Spanish introduced wheat, alfalfa, chilies, fruit trees, grapes, sheep, cattle, and garden vegetables, which soon became part of the regular diet.

The Spaniards found them in 1540 and built a mission at Giusewa Pueblo in the late sixteenth century. In 1621, they began another mission at the Pueblo de la Congregación, the present Jemez Pueblo. In 1628, Fray Martin de Arvide arrived at the Mission of San Diego de la Congregación with orders to unite the scattered Jemez communities, after which the Jemez Pueblo became an important center for missionary activity.

Despite the pueblo's position as a missionary center, the Jemez people actively resisted Spanish efforts to undermine their religion. They joined in rebellion with the Navajo about 1645, a crime for which twenty-nine Jemez leaders were hanged. They also took a leading part in the Pueblo Revolt of 1680. For years, the Spaniards had routinely tortured Indians for practicing traditional religion. They also forced the Indians to labor for them, sold them into slavery, and let Spaniard-owned cattle overgraze Indian land, a situation that eventually led to drought, erosion, and famine. Popé of the San Juan Pueblo and other Pueblo religious leaders planned the great revolt, sending runners carrying cords of maguey fibers to mark the day of rebellion. On August 10, 1680, a virtually united stand on the part of the Pueblos drove the Spanish from the region. The Indians killed many Spaniards but refrained from mass slaughter, allowing most of them to leave Santa Fe for El Paso.

The Jemez people withdrew to sites on the top of the San Diego Mesa in 1681. When the Spanish left they descended, only to reascend in 1689 when they sighted a new Spanish force. Some returned again to the pueblo in 1692, when they, along with Keresans from the Zia Pueblo, arrived at an understanding with the Spanish. Most Jemez, however, still resisted the Spanish, a situation that resulted in fighting between the Jemez and the Keresan pueblos of Zia and Santa Ana. This in turn resulted in a punitive Spanish–Keresan expedition in 1694, ending in the death or capture of over 400 Jemez people. All prisoners were pardoned after they helped the Spanish defeat the Tewas at Black Mesa.

By 1696, the Jemez Pueblo had been rebuilt and reoccupied at or near the original site. The following year, however, after joining again with the Navajo in an anti-Spanish revolt, the Jemez returned to their ancestral homeland near Stone Canyon. Others went west to Navajo country; of these, some eventually returned to Jemez but many remained with the Navajo. Some Jemez also fled to the Hopi Pueblo but were returned several years later by missionaries. The Jemez exile did not end until the early eighteenth century, when members of the tribe returned and settled at Walatowa, twelve miles south of their former mesa homes. At that time they built a new church, San Diego de los Jémez.

See also Agriculture; All Indian Pueblo Council; Pueblo Revolt.

Laguna Pueblo

"Laguna," Spanish for "lake," refers to a large pond near the pueblo. The word "pueblo" comes from the Spanish for "village." It refers both to a certain style of Southwest Indian architecture, characterized by multistory, apartment-like buildings made of adobe (pueblo), and to the people themselves (Pueblo). The Pueblos along the Rio Grande are known as eastern Pueblos; Zunis, Hopis, and sometimes Acomas and Lagunas are known as western Pueblos.

The Lagunas call their pueblo *Kawaika*, "Lake." The people spoke a Keresan dialect similar to that of the Acoma Pueblo. The Laguna Pueblo is made up of six major villages in central New Mexico, forty-two miles west of Albuquerque.

All Pueblo people are thought to be descended from Ancestral Puebloan, perhaps Mogollon, and several other ancient peoples, although the precise origin of the Keresan peoples is unknown. From them they learned architecture, farming, pottery, and basketry. Larger population groups became possible with effective agriculture and ways to store food surpluses. In the context of a relatively stable existence, the people devoted increasing amounts of time and attention to religion, arts, and crafts.

The Laguna Pueblo featured multistory, apartment-style dwellings. The lower levels were reserved mainly for storage. The buildings were constructed of adobe (earth-and-straw) bricks, with beams across the roof that were covered with poles, brush, and plaster. The roof of one level served as the floor of another. The levels were interconnected by ladders. As an aid to defense, the traditional design included no doors or windows; entry was through the roof. Baking ovens stood outside the buildings. Water was primarily obtained from two natural cisterns. Laguna also features two rectangular pithouses, or kivas, for ceremonial chambers and clubhouses. Herders stayed in caves, small rectangular houses, logs in a horseshoe shape covered with brush, or dugouts. The village plaza is the spiritual center of the village where all the balanced forces of the world come together.

Before the Spanish arrived, people living at the Laguna Pueblo ate primarily corn, beans, and squash. They also grew sunflowers and tobacco and kept turkeys. They hunted deer, antelope, and rabbits and gathered a variety of wild seeds, nuts, berries, and other foods. Favorite foods as of about 1700 included a blue corn drink, corn mush, pudding, wheat cake, corn balls, paper bread, peach-bark drink, flour bread, wild berries, and prickly pear fruit. The Lagunas also raised herds of sheep, goats, horses, and donkeys after the Spanish introduced these animals into the region.

Lagunas practiced dry farming and ditch irrigation technology. They used mica for window lights. Fine white clay yielded excellent pottery, and wicker baskets were fashioned of red willow shoots.

See also Agriculture; All Indian Pueblo Council; Pueblo Revolt.

Maricopa

See Pee-Posh.

Mojave or Mohave

The original name is *Tzi-na-ma-a*. "Mojave" is a Hispanicization of the Yuman *aha-makave*, meaning "beside the water." The Mojaves traditionally lived in the Mojave Valley and along the northern lower Colorado River. Today, Mojave Indians live primarily on the Fort Mojave Reservation (Arizona) and on the Colorado River Indian Reservation (Arizona and California). Mojaves spoke River Yuman, a member of the Hokan-Siouan language family. Roughly 20,000 Mojaves lived along the river in the early sixteenth century. Their number was reduced to 3,000 by 1770.

The modern Mojave Indians settled the Mojave Valley around 1150. These people farmed soil enriched from sediment left by the annual spring floods. The Mojave may have encountered non-Natives as early as 1540. Although they served as scouts for Father Francisco Garces's Grand Canyon expedition in 1776, among others, they generally resisted Spanish interference and maintained their independence.

The Mojaves believed, as did all Yumans, that they originally emerged into this world from a place near Spirit Mountain, Nevada. Dreaming was the key to the Mojave religious experience. Dreams were seen as visits with ancestors. There were omen dreams and, more rarely, great dreams, which brought the power to cure, to lead in battle, to orate at a funeral, or to do almost anything. However, dreams were considered of questionable authenticity unless they conferred success. Dreams permeated every aspect of Mojave culture. They were the source of constant discussion and meditation. Shamans had the most elaborate great dreams, which were considered to have begun in the womb. Shamans could cause disease as well as cure it, a situation that made for a precarious existence for them.

The Mojaves performed few public ceremonies or rituals. Instead, they sang song cycles for curing, funerals, and entertainment. The cycles consisted of dreams and tribal mythology and were accompanied by people shaking rattles and beating sticks on baskets. A complete cycle could take a night or more to sing, and the Mojaves knew about thirty cycles, each with 100 to 200 songs.

Four Mojave chiefs with a Yuma, second from left, acting as interpreter, ca. 1887. (Library of Congress)

Positions of authority, such as subchiefs or local leaders, derived from dreaming or oratory. Hereditary chiefs in the male line did exist, although with obscure functions. Despite their loose division into bands and local groups, the Mojaves thought of themselves as a true tribe; that is, they possessed a national consciousness, and they came together for important occasions such as warfare. Men planted the crops and women harvested them. Leaders addressed the people from rooftops in the morning about proper ways of living. Hunters generally gave away what they killed. Both men and women tattooed and painted their bodies. The dead were cremated, and their possessions and homes were also burned after a special ceremony during which mourners sang song cycles. No formal marriage ceremony existed: Marriages were arranged by the couple, and divorce was easy and common. Women carried babies on the hip, never on the back. Mojaves often traveled widely for trade and fun, covering up to 100 miles by foot in a day.

Bands and families lived in scattered rancherias, or farms. In warm weather they lived in flat-roofed, open-sided structures. Cold weather dwellings were low and rectangular, with roofs of thatch-covered poles; sand and earth or river mud were piled over the exterior. Doors faced south against the cold north winds. The people also used cylindrical granaries with flat roofs.

Crops such as corn, beans, and pumpkins (and wheat and melons after the Spanish arrived) constituted 50 percent of the Mojave diet. They also caught fish; hunted game such as rabbits and beaver with bows and arrows, traps, or deadfalls; and gathered wild foods. Mesquite beans in particular were a staple, used for food, drink, flour (pith from pods), shoes and clothing (bark), hair dye, instruments (roots), glue (sap), fuel for firing pottery, and funeral pyres.

Men and women wore loincloths; women also wore willow-bark aprons. Both went barefoot except when traveling, when they wore badger-hide sandals. Rabbit-skin blankets and robes kept them warm in winter. Both sexes wore their hair long; women's hung loose, and men rolled theirs into strands. Both tattooed their chins and painted their faces.

The Mojaves were fierce fighters. A warrior society (*kwanamis*) led three different fighting groups: archers, clubbers, and stick (or lance) men. In addition to those three types of weapons, they also used deer-hide shields, mesquite or willow bows, and arrows in coyote or wildcat quivers. War leaders

experienced dreams conferring power in battle. Traditional enemies included the Pimas, O'odhams, Pee-Posh, and Cocopahs; allies included the Quechans, Chemehuevis, Yavapais, and western Apaches. The Mojaves often took girls or young women as prisoners, giving them to old men as an insult to the enemy.

Contact with non-Natives remained sporadic until the nineteenth century. At about that time they began raiding Anglo-American fur trappers. They also allowed a band of Paiute Indians called the Chemehuevis to settle in the southern portion of their territory. The Mexican cession and discovery of gold in California brought more trespassers and led to more raids. In 1857, the Mojaves suffered a decisive military loss to their ancient enemies, the Pima and Pee-Posh (Maricopa) Indians. Two years later, the United States built Forts Mojave and Yuma to stem Mojave raiding. By this time, however, the Mojaves, defeated in battle and weakened by disease, settled for peace.

In 1865, the Mojave leader Irrateba (or Yara Tav) convinced a group of his followers to relocate to the Colorado River Valley area. The same year, Congress created the Colorado River Reservation for "all the tribes of the Colorado River drainage," primarily the Mojaves and Chemehuevis. Roughly 70 percent of the Mojaves had remained in the Mojave Valley, however, and they received a reservation in 1880. This split occasioned intratribal animosities for decades.

The early twentieth century was marked by influenza epidemics and non-Indian encroachment. The first assimilationist government boarding school had opened at the Colorado River Reservation in 1879. Legal allotments began in 1904. Traditional floodplain agriculture disappeared in the 1930s when the great dams tamed the Colorado River. During World War II, many U.S. citizens of Japanese heritage were interned on the Colorado River Reservation: For this operation the United States summarily appropriated 25,000 acres of Indian land.

For nineteen years after the war, until 1964, the Bureau of Indian Affairs (BIA) opened the reservation to Hopi and Navajo settlement (tribal rejection of this rule in 1952 was ignored by the BIA). Now all members of four tribes call the reservation home, having evolved into the CRIT (Colorado River Indian Tribes) Indians, a difficult development for the few remaining Mojave elders. In 1963 a federal court case guaranteed the tribes title to federal water rights. They received a deed to the reservation the following year.

See also Agriculture; Reservation Economic and
    Social Conditions.

Nambé Pueblo

"Nambé" is a Spanish rendition of a similar sounding Tewa name, loosely interpreted as "rounded earth." The word "pueblo" comes from the Spanish for "village." It refers both to a certain style of Southwest Indian architecture, characterized by multistory, apartment-like buildings made of adobe (pueblo), and to the people themselves (Pueblo). The Pueblos along the Rio Grande are known as eastern pueblos; Zunis, Hopis, and sometimes Acomas and Lagunas are known as western Pueblos. The Nambé Pueblo is located about fifteen miles north of Santa Fe, New Mexico. The Nambé people spoke a dialect of Tewa, a Kiowa-Tanoan language.

The Nambé people built small, irregular dwellings clustered around a central plaza. The buildings were constructed of adobe (earth-and-straw) bricks, with beams across the roof that were covered with poles, brush, and plaster. Floors were of wood plank or packed earth. Pithouses, or kivas, served as ceremonial chambers and clubhouses. The village plaza, around which all dwellings were clustered, is the spiritual center of the village where all the balanced forces of the world come together.

Before the Spanish arrived, people from the Nambé Pueblo ate primarily corn, beans, and squash. They also grew cotton and tobacco. They hunted deer, mountain lion, antelope, and rabbit, and gathered a variety of wild seeds, nuts, berries, and other foods. The Spanish introduced wheat, alfalfa, chilies, fruit trees, grapes, sheep, cattle, and garden vegetables, which soon became part of the regular diet.

In the Pueblo Way, art and life are inseparable. Nambé artists specialized in making embroidered dresses. Songs, dances, and dramas also qualify as traditional arts. Many Pueblos experienced a renaissance of traditional arts in the twentieth century, beginning in 1919 with San Ildefonso pottery.

See also Agriculture; All Indian Pueblo Council;
    Pueblo Revolt.

Navajo (Dine'é)

"Navajo" is a Tewa word meaning "planted fields." The Navajos call themselves Dine'é, "the People." Like the Apaches, they are of Athapaskan descent. Dinetah, the traditional Navajo homeland, is located on the lower Colorado Plateau, between the San Juan and Little Colorado Rivers, about seventy-five miles northwest of Santa Fe. Today's Navajo Nation occupies a 28,800-square-mile reservation in northern Arizona and New Mexico and southern Utah. This land is mostly plateau (above 5,000 feet) and is marked by deep, sheer-walled canyons. The winters are cold, the summers are hot, and there is little water.

The Dine'é are the most numerous Indian tribe in the United States. In 1990, 144,000 Indians lived on the Navajo Reservation, plus 1,177 at Cañoncito and 191 at Ramah. Many thousands also live off-reservation. More than 200,000 Indians now qualify for membership in the Navajo Nation (officially 219,198 in 1990). Perhaps 6,000 Navajos lived in the Dinetah in 1800. Navajo is an Athapaskan language.

Roughly 3,000 years ago, the Athapaskans, along with others (all called the Na-Dene), began a new wave of Asian migration into North America. Nomadic hunter-gatherers, the southern Athapaskans arrived in the Southwest in roughly 1400 and filled in the mountains around the Pueblo-held valleys. The northern Athapaskans remained in the subarctic.

Sa'ah Naaghei Bik'en Hozho, which may be characterized as being grounded to the earth, whole, and in harmony with life, is the Navajo Way. Everything is sacred and interrelated. For instance, religion equals identity equals clan equals place. The chief role of ceremonialism is to maintain or restore this harmony. Therefore, most ceremonies are for curing illness, broadly defined as being off balance for any number of reasons, such as contact with non-Natives, ghosts, witches, or the dead.

Navajo hogan and cornfield near Holbrook, Arizona, ca. 1889. (National Archives and Records Administration)

According to legend, Navajos (and all other beings) came to this world 600 to 800 years ago through a progression of underworlds. They were assisted by powerful and mysterious spiritual beings such as coyote, changing woman, spider woman, spider man, and the hero twins. These beings exist in the natural and supernatural worlds and may be called upon for help with curing. Most ceremonies are held when needed, not according to the calendar.

Many important aspects of Navajo ceremonialism, such as the use of masked dancers, feathered prayer sticks, altars, dry (sand) painting, cornmeal, and pollen, were borrowed from the Hopi and other Pueblo people. Traditional Navajo religion excludes organized priesthoods or religious societies. Instead, ceremonies are conducted by "singers" who have mastered one or more of twenty-four chantway systems. The systems are divided into six main groups: blessingway, warway, gameway (hunting), and the three curing ceremonials—holyway, evilway (ghostway), and lifeway. Each group might be composed of fifty or more chants, which in turn might have hundreds of songs or prayers. Specific sandpaintings and social functions often accompany each chant.

As part of the ceremony, the singers use bundles containing items such as rattles, feathered wands and brushes, various stones, and herbal medicines. The most important is the mountain earth bundle, which contains pinches of soil from the tops of the four sacred (bordering) mountains. Around 1940, the Native American Church took its place in Navajo religious practice.

Traditionally, the Navajos were organized in a number of bands, each led by a headman (appointed for life) and a clan leader, who were assisted by one or more war leaders. The leaders met formally only every few years. Decisions were made by consensus.

In general, the individual takes precedence over the group in Navajo culture. Property ownership is individual. The residence group, which was organized around a head mother, a sheep herd, and a customary land-use area, was the largest traditional Navajo organization. Clans were both matrilineal and matrilocal. Men were not allowed to see or talk with their mothers-in-law, so families lived near the wife's mother but in their own homes. The Navajos had a great fear of death. After the dead were buried, their belongings were destroyed.

The extended family was an important economic and social unit, as was the "outfit" in later times, a grouping that consisted of two or more extended families. Home, crops, pottery, and livestock belonged to women and were considered women's work; men made jewelry and represented the family in public and at ceremonies. A four-day girls' puberty ceremony ranked among the most important occasions.

Navajos lived in hogans. At first they were cone-shaped structures, framed with logs and poles and covered with earth and bark. Later the hogans had six or eight sides and were covered with stone and adobe. Doorways always faced east. The hogans were grouped in rancherias, or small settlements. Other structures included sweat lodges, brush corrals, and ramadas.

To the Athapaskans, Spanish influence (beginning in the early seventeenth century) meant primarily horses, guns, and places to raid. Consequently their interest in raiding grew, and they effectively established the northern Spanish frontier. Spanish missionaries had little success with the Navajos. Navajos also raided Pueblo Indians for food, women, slaves, and property. Between raids, Navajo and Pueblo people traded with each other. From this contact, the Navajos adopted some Pueblo habits, arts, and customs, especially farming, and settled down. They became farmers, then herders of sheep, goats, and horses.

Navajos helped the Pueblo people in their great revolt against the Spanish (1680), mainly by accepting, occasionally on a permanent basis, fugitives and refugees. Throughout much of the eighteenth century, the Navajos came in greater contact with Pueblo people and adopted more and more of their ways. Dine'é-Pueblo "pueblitas" became almost a distinct culture in parts of the Dinetah. What is now considered the traditional Navajo culture arose out of this cultural mix.

Animal husbandry, agriculture, hunting, gathering, and weaving wool made up the economic base of the Navajos as they began slowly to spread west and south. The early nineteenth century saw much reciprocal raiding with Mexicans, Spaniards, and early U.S. travelers on the Santa Fe Trail. Faced with the Mexicans' better firepower, Navajos, especially children, became targets of slave traders during the first half of the nineteenth century. At this time the Navajos possessed no tribal consciousness. They traveled with their livestock in clans (there were over sixty) to summer and winter hogans.

In the 1840s, the Navajos held out against U.S. troops in their sacred stronghold, Canyon de Chelly. However, treaties signed then did not stop

the conflict over grazing lands; white abuses of Indians, including the slave trade; and U.S. Army depredations. Following the Mexican Cession (1848), the Navajos were shocked to learn that the United States considered itself the "owner" of all traditional Navajo territory. In the face of Navajo resistance, the United States determined to take the land by force.

The great warrior and war chief Manuelito attacked and almost took Fort Defiance in 1860. Kit Carson defeated the Navajos in 1864 through a scorched-earth policy: He destroyed their fields, orchards, and livestock, and then he invaded Canyon de Chelly. Band by band the Navajos surrendered. Manuelito surrendered in 1866. The United States then forcibly relocated 8,000 Navajos to Bosque Redondo (Fort Sumner) in eastern New Mexico, with plans to transform them into farmers. Hundreds of Navajos died on the 400-mile walk, and 2,000 more died in a smallpox epidemic the following year. The Navajos who had not been captured hid in and around Navajo country.

In 1868 the Navajos were allowed to return and were granted 3.5 million acres of land for a reservation. Although the treaty called for a U.S. government–appointed tribal chief, local headmen retained their power. Manuelito returned home to serve as a Bureau of Indian Affairs (BIA)–appointed subchief and then head chief of the Navajos. He also served as the head of the Navajo Cavalry, the local police dedicated to ending Navajo raiding. After their return, the Navajos turned successfully to horse and sheep herding. Navajo culture changed quickly at that time: Trading posts opened, rug weaving for tourists began to take the place of traditional blanket weaving, children were sent to U.S. boarding schools (although this was fiercely resisted at first), Navajos began working for the railroads, missionaries arrived in force, and non-Native health care made inroads into traditional cultural practices.

By 1886 the reservation had grown from 3.5 to 11.5 million acres, although much of the best land was taken for railroad rights of way. Tremendous sheep and goat herds made the Navajos relatively prosperous and independent until the mid-1890s, when economic and natural disasters combined to reduce the herds by 75 percent. Following this period the Navajos switched from subsistence herding to raising stock for market.

The Navajos remained organized primarily by band into the twentieth century and thus knew little

or no true tribal consciousness until a business council began to meet in 1922. Local business councils, the first and most important community-level political entities, had been created in 1904 (well over a hundred chapters of the councils now exist). In 1915, the BIA divided the Navajo Reservation into six districts (which were in turn reorganized in 1955), each with a non-Indian superintendent. These communities retain their character as government towns. In 1923 the Secretary of the Interior appointed a tribal commissioner and a tribal council. In 1923 Henry Chee Dodge, who had assumed the position of head chief after Manuelito, became the first tribal chair. He provided the tribe with valuable leadership until his death in 1947.

Overgrazing was the key issue in the 1930s; a BIA-mandated stock reduction at that time led to dramatically lower standards of living. It also led to rejection by the tribe of the Indian Reorganization Act (IRA), of which the stock reduction plan was a part. World War II was a watershed for the tribe: Navajos traveled off the reservation in numbers for the first time, and those who returned came home not only with some money but also with a sense of honor gained from fighting as well as from using their language as a code the enemy was unable ever to break. Still, a crisis of unemployment and even starvation marked the immediate postwar years for the Navajos.

The 1950s brought large-scale energy development and with it jobs, money, and new social problems. Coal, oil, and uranium were the most important resources. The number of tribal programs increased dramatically, as did the power of the tribal council. The tribe adopted its own court system and legal code in 1959. The new programs culminated in 1965 with the Office of Navajo Economic Opportunity (ONEO), led by Peter MacDonald. The ONEO funneled tens of millions of dollars into social programs. MacDonald dominated Navajo politics for twenty years, both as head of the ONEO and as tribal chairman in 1970, 1974, 1978, and 1986.

However, the coal leases of the 1960s included provisions for massive strip mining. Soon the once pristine region was seriously polluted, and by the late 1970s there was strong sentiment against further development. MacDonald himself was convicted in 1990 and 1992 of several felony corruption-related crimes and later jailed. Peterson Zah served as tribal chairman in 1982, as president of the Navajo Nation in 1990, and as chair of the Nation in 1992. The controversy over the degree and type of economic

development continues today, the Navajos having achieved a large degree of self-determination.

> *See also* Dodge, Henry Chee; Long Walk; MacDonald, Peter; Manuelito; Navajo-Hopi Land Dispute.

Papago

See Tohono O'odham.

Pecos Pueblo

See Jemez Pueblo.

Pee-Posh

"Pee-Posh" or "Pipatsje" means "the People." These people are also known as the Maricopas. (*See also* Pima.) The Pee-Posh lived for centuries along the lower Colorado River and then began migrating to the Gila River region in the 1600s. Today the majority of Pee-Posh live outside Arizona and California, although the greatest concentrations live with the Pima on the Gila River and Salt River Reservations in Arizona (none live on the Maricopa Reservation). The Pee-Posh spoke a dialect of River Yuman, a Hokan-Siouan language.

The people whom the Spanish called the Opas or the Cocomaricopas were one of several small Yuman tribes (including the related groups—the Halchidomas, Kahwans, Kavelchadoms, and the Halyikwamais) who lived along the lower Colorado River. Contact with the Spanish was minimal and sporadic. By the early eighteenth century, these peoples had relocated up the Gila River, owing to an escalation of attacks by the Quechans and Mojaves. The Pimas offered them land and protection, and the two groups soon formed a confederation. By the early nineteenth century, the Pee-Posh had all but absorbed the smaller tribes.

The Pima–Maricopa confederacy went a long way toward making non-Indian settlement of that part of the desert possible, protecting Anglos from Apaches, starvation, and thirst. For example, the Indians used much of their surplus wheat to pro-

vide food for the so-called forty-niners on their way to California. (By 1870, their wheat production had reached 3 million pounds, an achievement that aroused the wrath of Anglo wheat farmers.) The Indians also sold wheat to the U.S. Army. Beginning in the 1840s, and continuing throughout the century, epidemics took a heavy toll on the Indian population. In 1857, the confederacy decisively defeated the Quechans and Mojaves at Maricopa Wells, marking the last major formal battle between Indian nations in the Southwest.

In recognition of its alliance with the confederation, the U.S. government established a reservation on the Gila River in 1863 for the Pimas and the Pee-Posh. However, river water levels soon began to fall to such low levels as a result of upstream diversions by non-Natives that a group of Indians moved to the confluence of the Gila and Salt Rivers. Now known as Laveen, this community was first called Maricopa Colony. Halchidoma descendents soon relocated to the Salt River, around the present site of Lehi. In 1879, the original reservation was enlarged, and the Salt River Reservation was established.

During that decade several factors conspired to ruin the Indians' thriving economy: a decline in rainfall, a doubling of the population, and, in particular, huge diversions of Gila River water by non-Indians. By the 1880s, Indian crops routinely failed and famine threatened. Many Pimas and Pee-Posh were forced into the wage economy at the lowest levels. With the loss of the river, the heart of their culture also disappeared. The U.S. government continued to ignore the key problem of water rights, and Pima and Pee-Posh impoverishment continued well into the twentieth century.

In the late nineteenth century, the Bureau of Indian Affairs (BIA) began a campaign to assimilate local Indians. With its blessing, the Presbyterian Church became very active at Gila River, beginning a day school and in general imposing a religious structure on the tribes. The issue of Christianity proved to be a very divisive one on the reservation. In 1914, allotment hit both reservations (against active Indian opposition), scattering the people and further disrupting community life. In 1926, the BIA formed a Pima Advisory Council in an effort to create a formal body that spoke for the tribe. In 1934, the Pimas created a constitution, which was revised by the Pima and Pee-Posh community two years later.

By 1930, non-Native water diversions had effectively ended Gila River surface water flowing to the

Pee-Posh. Rather than redress the situation, the BIA forced the Indians to use brackish well water. This water was suitable only for growing cotton and some grains, however, and the people could no longer grow edible crops. Several other factors worked to cancel any benefits that might have come with the well water, including a dependency of Indians on wage work, continued ongoing water shortages, and the hated allotments (heirships), which had destroyed their effective land base.

In 1934, the Pimas and the Pee-Posh accepted the Indian Reorganization Act (IRA) and formed the Gila River Indian Community. Following World War II, many Pee-Posh (encouraged by the BIA's relocation program) moved away from the reservation. For years outsiders thought that the Pee-Posh had died out and become a subgroup of the Pima Indians.

Nominal village chiefs exerted little influence. Recognized specialists had the true authority, as curers, calendar stick keepers, singers, potters, and dancers. All obtained their power from dreams.

Entire villages moved when someone died, after the body, residence, and possessions had been burned. Special singers sang elaborate song cycles for funerals and transmitted legends, such as ancestral wanderings or conflicts with other groups. Girls celebrated a special puberty ceremony, after which they were tattooed. Both sexes cultivated a high tolerance of pain. As was true for other River Yumans, farming, including ownership of the farm site, was essentially an individual activity. Boundary disputes were solved by mediation or by controlled fighting. The Pee-Posh recognized patrilineal clan as well as village divisions.

Flattened-dome houses were built with a frame of mesquite or cottonwood uprights and covered with willow ribs and arrowweed thatch. Walls were packed with earth. Rectangular ramadas often adjoined the houses. All dwelling entrances faced east. Other structures included storage sheds, woven basket granaries, and sweat lodges.

The Pee-Posh used floodwater agriculture in their farming. Their staples were mesquite beans and corn. Men planted and cultivated, and women harvested. Much food was also gathered, including seeds, berries, nuts, cactus fruit, honey, caterpillars, and beans. The people also ate jackrabbits and fish (caught with nets or bare hands).

See also Agriculture; Confederacies; Indian Reorganization Act.

Picuris Pueblo

"Picuris" comes from the Spanish *picurís*, "at the mountain gap." The word "pueblo" comes from the Spanish for "village." It refers both to a certain style of Southwest Indian architecture, characterized by multistory, apartment-like buildings made of adobe (pueblo), and to the people themselves (Pueblo). Rio Grande Pueblos are known as eastern Pueblos; Zunis, Hopis, and sometimes Acomas and Lagunas are known as western Pueblos. The people call their pueblo *pingultha*, which means either "mountain warrior place" or "mountain pass place." People from Picuris spoke a dialect of northern Tiwa, a Tanoan language.

The Picuris Pueblo is located on the western slopes of the Sangre de Cristo Mountains, eighteen miles south of Taos Pueblo. The average elevation is about 7,000 feet, which makes for a relatively short and somewhat precarious growing season.

The relative isolation of the Picuris delayed the assimilationist pressures faced by other pueblos. However, a government day school, in which children learned Anglo ways and values, opened in 1899. Adults were encouraged to engage in wage work off the pueblo. Timber operations also began, damaging the fragile irrigation system. In an attempt to retain their identity, the Pueblo Indians clung even more tenaciously to their heritage, which by now included elements of the once hated Spanish culture and religion. By the 1880s, railroads had largely put an end to the traditional geographical isolation of the pueblos. Paradoxically, the U.S. decision to recognize Spanish land grants to the Pueblos denied them certain rights granted under official treaties and left them particularly open to exploitation by squatters and thieves.

In 1947, the adult men of the Picuris voted to change the name of the pueblo to San Lorenzo; however, the name "Picuris" was again adopted in 1955.

The Picuris Pueblo featured apartment-style dwellings as high as nine stories. The buildings were constructed of adobe (earth-and-straw) bricks, with beams across the roof that were covered with poles, brush, and plaster. Floors were of wood plank or packed earth. The roof of one level served as the floor of another. The levels were interconnected by ladders. As an aid to defense, the traditional design included no doors or windows; entry was through the roof. Pithouses, or kivas, served as ceremonial chambers and clubhouses. The village plaza, around

which all dwellings were clustered, is the spiritual center of the village where all the balanced forces of world come together.

See also Agriculture; All Indian Pueblo Council; Pueblo Revolt.

Pima

"Pima" is derived from *pi-nyi-match*, "I don't know" (a reply to early questioners). The Pimas were originally called Akimel O'odhams, or River People, and they are also known as One Villagers because of their relatively settled lives. The O'odham Indians include the Pimas, Tohono O'odhams (Papagos, or Desert People, also known as Two Villagers because of their traditional migration patterns), Sand Papagos (Hia C-ed O'odham, or No Villagers because of their more or less constant migrations in search of food), and the Ak-chin O'odhams. Piman is a language of the Uto-Aztecan family.

Traditionally, the Pimas lived in rancherias in present-day southern Arizona and northern Sonora, Mexico (the Sonoran Desert). The Spanish categorized them as the Pima Alto (upper Pimas, who lived near the Gila and Salt Rivers) and the Pima Bajo (or Nevones, lower Pimas, who lived along the Yaqui and Sonora Rivers). Today's (upper) Pima reservations are located in southern Arizona. There were roughly 50,000 Pimas in 1500 and perhaps 3,000 in 1700.

The Pimas are probably descended from ancient Hohokam Indians. They lived and farmed in permanent settlements (rancherias) near rivers on the northern edge of the Spanish frontier, which at the time was at present-day Tucson. The first non-Indian to visit the Pimas was Marcos de Niza (1589). In 1684, Father Eusebio Francisco Kino organized several missions and introduced livestock, wheat, and metal tools into the region.

An accommodation between the Pimas and Spanish masked resentments over religious, political, and cultural imperialism, not to mention forced labor. In 1695 the lower Pimas, under Luis Oacpicagigua and others, revolted against the Spanish, and in 1751 the upper Pima rebelled. The latter had little support from other tribes or even a majority of Pimas, however, and peace was soon established.

Around 1800 the Pee-Posh (Maricopa) Indians came to live near the upper Pimas. At the same time the area came under more frequent attacks by

Apache raiders. The twin factors of winter wheat production plus increased conflict with the Apaches led to a thorough transformation of Pima society. Pima bands engaged in closer cooperation and began to produce agricultural surpluses. This led in turn to an increased integration of their society. By the midnineteenth century the position of governor had become hereditary, and the Pimas had become a true tribe. They were also the only effective force in the area against the Apaches as well as an important economic power.

Despite Pima food assistance to the forty-niners and the U.S. Army, Anglo settlers along the Gila River took the best farmland and diverted water for their own use. After the Gadsden Purchase (1853) split O'odham country in two, Anglos began using the term "Pima" for residents on the Gila River and "Papago" for Piman speakers south of the Gila. The United States established a Pima–Maricopa reservation on the Gila River in 1859. However, as a result of failing water supplies, many Indians moved north, where another reservation was established in 1879 on the Salt River. From the 1850s on, three generations of the Azul family led the Pima–Maricopa confederation.

By 1870, Pima annual wheat production had reached 3 million pounds. Non-Natives reacted to this achievement with fear, envy, and retaliation. Major Anglo water diversions soon left the Pimas with little water for their crops. Combined with a drought and population increases, this led to Pima impoverishment in the late nineteenth and early twentieth centuries. Many Pimas were forced into the wage economy at the lowest levels. The U.S. government ignored the key problem of Pima water rights.

The loss of the river and the growing influence of Presbyterians brought about a severe decline in Pima culture and traditional religion. The Presbyterians replaced the Pima religious structure with one of their own creation. The Presbyterian Church and the Bureau of Indian Affairs (BIA) opened day and boarding schools, respectively. Allotment hit the reservation in 1914, breaking up tribal land patterns and further disrupting community life.

In 1926, the BIA created a Pima Advisory Council to meet the bureau's need for a body that spoke for the tribe. Eight years later the Pimas adopted a constitution and tribal council, which remained quite powerless, because the Pima "tribe" had virtually disappeared. The Pima and Maricopa community revised the constitution and bylaws in 1936. In the 1930s the San Carlos Project began returning irri-

A Pima home with a woman seated by the doorway, ca. 1907. (Library of Congress)

gation water to the Pimas, but several factors worked to cancel its benefits, including the dependency of Indians on wage work (at that point they were reluctant to return to subsistence farming), a complex water management bureaucracy that mandated required crops, chronic ongoing water shortages, and the fact that allotments (heirship) had destroyed their effective land base. The post–World War II period has been a time for Pimas once again to assume a degree of control over their own resources and lives.

A civil leader and one or more shamans presided over economically and politically independent Pima villages. Village ceremonial leaders were known as "keepers of the smoke." Village chiefs elected a tribal chief, who ran council meetings. His other responsibilities included overseeing farm projects and defending against Apache raiders. In the midnineteenth century, the chieftainship went from

a position of power and no wealth to one of wealth and no power. In 1936 the adoption of a new constitution under the Indian Reorganization Act marked the beginning of the Pima battle for legal rights.

Each village was divided into two groups, Red Ant and White Ant, who opposed each other in games and other ceremonial functions. The groups were further divided into patrilineal clans. In general, men farmed, fished, hunted, built the houses, and wove cotton; women gathered food and made baskets, pottery, and clothing. They also carried firewood and food on their backs in burden baskets. The Pimas used a lunar calendar. Their year began with the rainy season and the appearance of flowers on certain plants, such as the saguaro cactus. Viikita was a celebration held every fourth harvest to celebrate and ensure the favor of the gods.

Pimas lived in small, round, flat-topped, poleframed structures, covered with grass and mud. In

warm weather they moved into simple open-sided brush arbors. They also built cylindrical bins in which they stored mesquite beans. Ramadas, used for clubhouses, also dotted each village.

Farm products such as corn, squash (cut into strips and dried), and tepary beans accounted for up to 60 percent of the Pima diet. The people also grew tobacco and cotton and, after the Spanish arrived, wheat (winter wheat ensured protection against starvation and made farms very productive) and alfalfa. Wild foods included cactus fruit, mesquite beans, greens, chilies, and seeds, which, with corn, were ground into meal on a cottonwood mortar and used in gruel and cakes. Pimas also ate fish and hunted deer, rabbit, mountain sheep, antelope, and reptiles. They drank saguaro wine for ceremonial purposes.

To irrigate their crops, Pimas diverted water from rivers with dams of logs and brush. They also built canals and feeder ditches. Farm tools consisted of digging sticks and a flat board used for hoeing and harvesting. Hunting bows were made of Osage orange or willow. After a great meteor shower in 1833, the people used calendar sticks—saguaro ribs with cuts—to mark certain events. The Spanish brought horse- and oxen-drawn wagons, plows, and metal picks and shovels into the region.

See also Agriculture; Hohokam Culture; Reservation Economic and Social Conditions.

Pojoaque Pueblo

"Pojoaque" is an adaptation of the Tewa *posuwaegeh*, meaning "drink-water place." The word "pueblo" comes from the Spanish for "village." It refers both to a certain style of Southwest Indian architecture, characterized by multistory, apartment-like buildings made of adobe (pueblo), and to the people themselves (Pueblo). Rio Grande Pueblos are known as eastern Pueblos; Zunis, Hopis, and sometimes Acomas and Lagunas are known as western Pueblos. The Pojoaque Pueblo is located sixteen miles north of Santa Fe; it is the smallest of the six Tewa villages. Tewa is a Kiowa-Tanoan language.

Pojoaque took an active part in the 1680 Pueblo Revolt against the Spanish. For years, the Spaniards had routinely tortured Indians for practicing traditional religion. They also forced the Indians to labor for them, sold them into slavery, and let Spaniard-owned cattle overgraze Indian land, a situation that

eventually led to drought, erosion, and famine. Popé of San Juan Pueblo and other Pueblo religious leaders planned the revolt, sending runners carrying cords of maguey fibers to mark the day of rebellion. On August 10, 1680, a virtually united stand on the part of the Pueblos drove the Spanish from the region. The Indians killed many Spaniards but refrained from mass slaughter, allowing them to leave Santa Fe for El Paso.

Pojoaque suffered greatly in the aftermath of the revolt. Spanish recolonizers took much of their best land. The tribe was decimated and scattered but was able to reestablish itself in 1706. However, by then most of their population had been absorbed by other pueblos. Although Pueblo unity did not last, and Santa Fe was officially reconquered in 1692, Spanish rule was notably less severe from then on. Harsh forced labor all but ceased, and the Indians reached an understanding with the Church that enabled them to continue practicing their traditional religion.

During the nineteenth century the population at Pojoaque became so small (it was recorded as thirty-two in 1870) that the people could no longer hold their ceremonies. A steady loss of their land base contributed to the tribe's degeneration. Many people left to live at other pueblos or to make their way in the outside world. At the same time, documents attesting to Spanish land grants and water rights were lost, although the United States did confirm their holding in 1858; shortly afterward, leaders traveled to Washington to receive the patent as well as a silver-headed Lincoln cane. Paradoxically, the U.S. decision to recognize Spanish land grants to the Pueblos denied them certain rights granted under official treaties and left them particularly open to exploitation by squatters and thieves.

By the early twentieth century, the Pojoaque Pueblo was all but abandoned, although it had become a small Spanish-American settlement by the 1930s. At that time a handful of Pojoaque families returned, evicted non-Indians, and fenced the land. Antonio José Tapia was instrumental in reestablishing the pueblo during this period. Government payment for losses suffered over the years acted as an incentive for other Pojoaques to return. Partly because of lobbying from the All Indian Pueblo Council, Congress confirmed Pueblo title to their lands in 1924 by passing the Pueblo Lands Act. The United States also acknowledged its trust responsibilities in a series of legal decisions and other acts of Congress. Still, the Bureau of Indian Affairs (BIA) forced Indian children to leave their homes and

attend culture-killing boarding schools and in general did its best to undermine Indian identity and survival.

At Pojoaque, in contrast with most other pueblos, seasons were traditionally delineated not so much by the solstice as by the actual change in seasons. Formerly a summer and a winter cacique, appointed for life, oversaw the pueblo. Society was divided into two groups: summer (associated with the Squash kiva) and winter (associated with the Turquoise kiva). Membership in a group was patrilineal. These groups were further divided into clans. A number of secret societies also existed. For instance, the warrior society was concerned with hunting, war, crops, fertility, and curing. Each society had its own dances and ritual paraphernalia.

See also Agriculture; All Indian Pueblo Council; Pueblo Revolt.

Quechan

"Quechan" comes from *xam kwatcan*, "another going down" (a reference to their ancestral migration). Quechans are also known as Yuma Indians; *Yuma* is an O'odham word for "People of the River." Quechan farmers began using the floodwaters of the Colorado River for irrigation around 2,500 years ago. The Quechans lived in several small settlements, or rancherias, along the bottomlands of the Colorado River, near the mouth of the Gila. Many Quechans now live on the Fort Yuma Reservation as well as on the Cocopah Reservation with Pee-Posh and Cocopas, having once been allied with these tribes. Quechan is a dialect of River Yuman.

The Quechans were organized into patrilineal clans. Little or no status differences existed among family groups. Rancheria leaders addressed the people from rooftops on correct behavior. All possessions of the deceased, even the house, were given away or destroyed. Dung was burned to keep away mosquitoes.

Like those of all Yumans, Quechan religion and knowledge were based on dreaming. Dreams were seen as visits with ancestors. The most powerful dreamer was their religious leader. Dreams also brought power to lead in battle, to orate at a funeral, or to do almost anything. However, dreams were considered of questionable authenticity unless they conferred success. Shamans were specialists who were able to cure using supernatural powers acquired through very powerful dreams, perhaps begun in the womb. They also controlled the weather.

Quechans sang extended song cycles for curing, funerals, and entertainment. The cycles consisted of dreams and tribal mythology and were accompanied by people shaking rattles and beating sticks on baskets. Important Quechan ceremonies included a four-day-long girls' puberty rite and a boy's nose-piercing ceremony (at age seven, which also included racing and fasting). A mesquite harvest festival in the summer and a crop harvest festival in the fall both featured games, contests, gambling, and songs. Quechans also observed a four-day-long mourning ceremony.

All political authority among the Quechans was based on dreams, as was the authority of singers, speakers, and curers. Each rancheria had one or more headmen: Although they might meet in council to discuss tribal matters, decision making was by consensus. Other offices included the war leader and funeral orator.

Quechans considered war essential to the acquisition and maintenance of their spiritual power. They distinguished between raiding, an activity whose main purpose was to acquire horses or captives, and warfare, the purpose of which was revenge. The Mojaves were traditional allies; their enemies included the Cocopahs, Pee-Posh, and Pimas. The Quechan warrior hierarchy included the leader, then spearmen and clubmen, archers, horsepeople (after contact) with spears, and finally women with clubs. For weapons they used mesquite bows, clubs, stone knives, hide shields, and spears.

The Quechans first encountered a non-Native person in 1540, in the person of Hernando de Alarcón. Father Eusebio Francisco Kino arrived in 1698 and Father Francisco Garces in 1775. The Quechans generally resisted Spanish missions and settlements. A rebellion in 1781 ended Spanish control of a key river crossing, and the Quechans were able to continue their traditional way of life.

In the midnineteenth century, Quechans occasionally raided overland travelers (on the Southern Overland Trail, or Butterfield Route), partly in retaliation for crop thievery. The number of non-Indians passing through their territory increased greatly in and after 1849, due to the California gold rush. At that time, the Quechans provided a ferry service across the Colorado. When Anglos attempted to

open a competing service, the Quechans blocked the passage. When the U.S. Army intervened to keep the passage open, the Quechans fought back, driving the U.S. forces away for a year. In 1852, the soldiers returned and built Fort Yuma, effectively ending Quechan resistance in the area. Five years later, the Quechans and their Mojave allies were defeated by the Pimas and Maricopas in the last big intra-Indian fight near the Colorado River.

In 1853 the United States established the Fort Yuma Reservation with 45,000 acres, on the California side of the Colorado. Steamship and railroad travel, as well as the town of Yuma, boomed in the following decades. Quechans worked as steamship pilots and woodcutters until railroads ended the industry and then as laborers and domestics.

By the end of the century the tribe, devastated by disease, was in a state of cultural eclipse. Factionalism also weakened the tribe, and Anglos took the opportunity to appoint Quechan leaders unilaterally. Clan and village affiliations broke down when youths were taken away forcibly to boarding school. The Quechans relinquished most of their land in 1893 and lost the best of what was left to Anglos by 1910. Upstream dams prevented natural flooding, and Quechan farmers, people of the river for centuries, found themselves in the position of having to pay for irrigation water.

Quechans lived in poverty well into the twentieth century. The mandated allotment of their land in 1912 led to endless subdivision and rendered it useless for agriculture; most was leased to non-Indians. The federal War on Poverty arrived in the 1960s, and with it new opportunities for decent housing and economic development. In 1978 the government returned 25,000 acres (minus the vital water rights) and paid for even more in the 1980s.

See also Boarding Schools, United States and Canada; Reservation Economic and Social Conditions; Warfare, Intertribal.

Sandia Pueblo

"Sandia" comes from the Spanish for "watermelon," referring to the size, shape, and color of the nearby Sandia Mountains. The word "pueblo" comes from the Spanish for "village." It refers both to a certain style of Southwest Indian architecture, characterized by multistory, apartment-like buildings made of adobe (pueblo), and to the people themselves (Pueblo). Rio Grande Pueblos are known as eastern Pueblos; Zunis, Hopis, and sometimes Acomas and Lagunas are known as western Pueblos. The Tiwa name for Sandia Pueblo is *Napeya* or *Nafiat*, "at the dusty place." Southern Tiwa is a Kiowa-Tanoan language.

Sandia Pueblo is located fifteen miles north of Albuquerque, on the east bank of the Rio Grande. The altitude ranges from 5,000 to 10,670 feet, and the land contains good farmland, game, and wild foods.

Francisco Vasquez de Coronado probably visited Sandia Pueblo in 1540. In 1598, Juan de Oñate arrived in the area with settlers, founding the colony of New Mexico. Oñate carried on the process, already underway in nearby areas, of subjugating the local Indians; forcing them to pay taxes in crops, cotton, and work and opening the door for Catholic missionaries to attack their religion. The Spanish renamed the pueblos with saints' names and began a program of church construction, constructing the Mission of San Francisco Sandia in 1617. At the same time, the Spanish introduced such new crops as peaches, wheat, and peppers into the region. In 1620, a royal decree created civil offices at each pueblo; silver-headed canes, many of which remain in use today, symbolized the governor's authority.

Sandia joined the Pueblo Revolt of 1680. For years, the Spaniards had routinely tortured Indians for practicing traditional religion. They also forced the Indians to labor for them, sold them into slavery, and let Spaniard-owned cattle overgraze Indian land, a situation that eventually led to drought, erosion, and famine. Popé of San Juan Pueblo and other Pueblo religious leaders planned the great revolt, sending runners carrying cords of maguey fibers to mark the day of rebellion. On August 10, 1680, a virtually united stand on the part of the Pueblos drove the Spanish from the region. The Indians killed many Spaniards but refrained from mass slaughter, allowing most of them to leave Santa Fe for El Paso.

The Spanish burned the Sandia Pueblo after the revolt. It was then reoccupied but later burned or abandoned several times in the 1680s and 1690s; the pueblo was in ruins in 1692. The Sandias first fled to the nearby mountains and then lived for a time at the Hopi Pueblo. The Sandia Pueblo was permanently reoccupied in 1748 by a mixed group of refugees from various pueblos. Meanwhile, Santa Fe was officially reconquered in 1692, although Spanish rule was notably less severe from then on. Harsh

forced labor all but ceased, and the Indians reached an understanding with the Church that enabled them to continue practicing their traditional religion.

Sandia Pueblo featured multistoried apartment-style dwellings constructed of adobe (earth-and-straw) bricks, with beams across the roof that were covered with poles, brush, and plaster. Floors were of wood plank or packed earth. The roof of one level served as the floor of another. The levels were interconnected by ladders. As an aid to defense, the traditional design included no doors or windows; entry was through the roof. Pithouses, or kivas, served as ceremonial chambers and clubhouses. The village plaza, around which all dwellings were clustered, is the spiritual center of the village where all the balanced forces of the world come together.

> See also Agriculture; All Indian Pueblo Council; Pueblo Revolt.

Sand Papago, or Hia C-ed O'odham

See Tohono O'odham.

San Felipe Pueblo

The Spanish assigned the patron saint San Felipe Apóstol to this pueblo in 1598. The word "pueblo" comes from the Spanish for "village." It refers both to a certain style of Southwest Indian architecture, characterized by multistory, apartment-like buildings made of adobe (pueblo), and to the people themselves (Pueblo). Rio Grande Pueblos are known as eastern Pueblos; Zunis, Hopis, and sometimes Acomas and Lagunas are known as western Pueblos. The Native name for this pueblo is Katishtya. The San Felipe people spoke a dialect of Keresan.

The San Felipe Pueblo is located at the foot of Santa Ana Mesa on the west bank of the Rio Grande, six miles north of its junction with the Jemez River (twenty-five miles north of Albuquerque). One or more other San Felipe pueblos may have existed in the area prior to the sixteenth century.

Keresans have been traced to an area around Chaco Canyon north to Mesa Verde. In the 1200s, the Keresans abandoned their traditional canyon homelands in response to climatic and social

Ancient Puebloan ruins known as the Long House, the second-largest cliff dwelling at Mesa Verde in present-day Colorado. The area was later populated by the San Felipe Pueblo. (Corel)

upheavals. A century or two of migrations ensued, followed in general by the slow reemergence of their culture in the historic pueblos. For a time the San Felipe people lived with the Cochitis at several locations, but the pueblos divided before the Spanish arrived.

Francisco Vasquez de Coronado may have visited the San Felipe Pueblo. In 1598, Juan de Oñate arrived in the area with settlers, founding the colony of New Mexico. Oñate carried on the process, already underway in nearby areas, of subjugating the local Indians, forcing them to pay taxes in crops, cotton, and work and opening the door for Catholic missionaries to attack their religion. The Spanish renamed the pueblos with saints' names and began a program of church construction. Oñate found two pueblos at San Felipe, on either side of the river. A church was built at the eastern village

around 1600. At the same time, the Spanish introduced new crops such as peaches, wheat, and peppers into the region. In 1620, a royal decree created civil offices at each pueblo; silver-headed canes, many of which remain in use today, symbolized the governor's authority.

The San Felipes took an active part in the 1680 Pueblo Revolt against the Spanish. For years, the Spaniards had routinely tortured Indians for practicing traditional religion. They also forced the Indians to labor for them, sold them into slavery, and let Spaniard-owned cattle overgraze Indian land, a situation that eventually led to drought, erosion, and famine. Popé of San Juan Pueblo and other Pueblo religious leaders planned the revolt, sending runners carrying cords of maguey fibers to mark the day of rebellion. On August 10, 1680, a virtually united stand on the part of the Pueblos drove the Spanish from the region. The Indians killed many Spaniards but refrained from mass slaughter, allowing them to leave Santa Fe for El Paso.

The San Felipe people abandoned their pueblo in 1681, when the Spanish attempted a reconquest. They fled to the top of Horn Mesa southwest of Cochiti, and the Spanish sacked San Felipe. The people agreed to return and accept baptism in 1692. At that time they lived on top of Santa Ana Mesa. Their friendship with the Spanish alienated them from other pueblos. After 1696, they descended from the mesa top to the site of the present pueblo.

See also Agriculture; All Indian Pueblo Council; Pueblo Revolt.

San Ildefonso Pueblo

"San Ildefonso" is the name of the Spanish mission established in 1617. The Tewa name for the Pueblo, *powhoge*, means "where the water runs through." The word "pueblo" comes from the Spanish for "village." It refers both to a certain style of Southwest Indian architecture, characterized by multistory, apartment-like buildings made of adobe (pueblo), and to the people themselves (Pueblo). Rio Grande Pueblos are known as eastern Pueblos; Zunis, Hopis, and sometimes Acomas and Lagunas are known as western Pueblos. Located roughly twenty-two miles northwest of Santa Fe, San Ildefonso shares a common boundary with Santa Clara

Pueblo. The San Ildefonso people spoke a dialect of Tewa, a Kiowa-Tanoan language.

The San Ildefonso Pueblo originally featured two- and three-story apartment-style dwellings constructed of adobe (earth-and-straw) bricks, with pine beams across the roof that were covered with poles, brush, and plaster. Floors were of wood plank or packed earth. The roof of one level served as the floor of another. The levels were interconnected by ladders. As an aid to defense, the traditional design included no doors or windows; entry was through the roof. Three pithouses, or kivas, two rectangular and one round, served as ceremonial chambers and clubhouses. The village plaza, around which the church and all dwellings were clustered, was the spiritual center of the village, a place where all the balanced forces of the world came together. The multilevel dwelling was replaced in historic times at San Ildefonso by one- and two-story adobe houses.

San Ildefonso played a leading role in the 1680 Pueblo Revolt against the Spanish. For years, the Spaniards had routinely tortured Indians for practicing traditional religion. They also forced the Indians to labor for them, sold them into slavery, and let Spaniard-owned cattle overgraze Indian land, a situation that eventually led to drought, erosion, and famine. Popé of San Juan Pueblo, as well as a San Ildefonso official named Francisco and other Pueblo leaders, planned the revolt, sending runners carrying cords of maguey fibers to mark the day of rebellion. On August 10, 1680, a virtually united stand on the part of the Pueblos drove the Spanish from the region. The Indians killed many Spaniards but refrained from mass slaughter, allowing them to leave Santa Fe for El Paso.

The San Ildefonso Pueblo was also a leader in the resistance to the Spanish reconquest under Diego de Vargas. The people of San Ildefonso and members of other pueblos moved to the top of Black Mesa and held out there until 1694, two years longer than most other pueblos. In 1696, the San Ildefonsos staged another uprising, killing two priests; this was the last of Pueblo armed resistance. Although Pueblo unity did not last and Santa Fe was officially reconquered in 1692, Spanish rule was notably less severe from then on. Harsh forced labor all but ceased, and the Indians reached an understanding with the Church that enabled them to continue practicing their traditional religion.

After the Pueblo revolt, and contrary to tradition, the San Ildefonsos relocated to the north. In

1923, when mortality rates rose and prosperity fell, the cacique led a small group of people back to the original southern village. By this time, however, a flu epidemic had reduced part of the tribe, the winter people, to two families, so the other division (the summer people) divided and absorbed what was left of the winter people. This situation gave rise to intense factionalism that greatly affected the pueblo. The traditional summer-winter division was virtually replaced by an ersatz north-south split. Each group, organized around a plaza, became autonomous but incomplete. By the late 1930s, some offices and societies had been discontinued, and some ritual had been forgotten. Secular authority remained in the hands of the north side for decades, and the situation turned violent in the 1930s when kivas were raided and burned.

At San Ildefonso, in contrast with most other pueblos, seasons were traditionally delineated not so much by the solstice as by the actual change in seasons. Formerly a summer and a winter cacique, appointed for life, oversaw the pueblo. Society was divided into two groups, summer (associated with the Squash kiva) and winter (associated with the Turquoise kiva); membership in a group was patrilineal. These groups were further divided into clans. A number of secret societies also existed. For instance, the warrior society was concerned with hunting, war, crops, fertility, and curing. Each society had its own dances and ritual paraphernalia.

See also Agriculture; All Indian Pueblo Council; Pottery; Pueblo Revolt.

San Juan Pueblo

The Tewa name for San Juan Pueblo is *Ohke,* the meaning of which is unknown. The word "pueblo" comes from the Spanish for "village." It refers both to a certain style of Southwest Indian architecture, characterized by multistory, apartment-like buildings made of adobe (pueblo), and to the people themselves (Pueblo). Rio Grande Pueblos are known as eastern Pueblos; Zunis, Hopis, and sometimes Acomas and Lagunas are known as western Pueblos. A sacred metaphorical phrase meaning "village of the dew-bedecked corn structure" also refers to the San Juan Pueblo, which is located about twenty-five miles north of Santa Fe, on the east bank of the Rio Grande. The land includes river bottomlands

and mountains. The people of the San Juan Pueblo spoke a dialect of Tewa.

When the Spanish arrived in the 1540s, the San Juan people were living at the present pueblo and at a more westerly pueblo. The appearance of Gaspar Castaño de Sosa in 1591 marked the first contact between the San Juans and non-Natives. In 1598, Juan de Oñate arrived in the area with settlers, founding the colony of New Mexico. Oñate carried on the process, already underway in nearby areas, of subjugating the local Indians, forcing them to pay taxes in crops, cotton, and work and opening the door for Catholic missionaries to attack their religion. The Spanish renamed the pueblo San Juan Bautista; it was also known as San Juan de los Caballeros. At the same time, they introduced such new crops as peaches, wheat, and peppers into the region. In 1620, a royal decree created civil offices at each pueblo; silver-headed canes, many of which remain in use today, symbolized the governor's authority.

Trade along the Santa Fe Trail began in 1821. The trader Samuel Eldodt opened a general store at San Juan in 1863. Until it burned down in 1973, it was the oldest continuously operated store in New Mexico and furthered San Juan's reputation as a trade center. By the 1880s and the arrival of railroads, the Pueblos were dependent on many American-made goods, and the Native manufacture of weaving and pottery declined and nearly died out.

At San Juan, a summer and a winter cacique, appointed for life, oversaw the pueblo. Society was divided into two groups, summer (associated with the Squash kiva) and winter (associated with the Turquoise kiva); membership in a group was patrilineal. These groups were further divided into more than thirty clans. A number of secret societies also existed. For instance, the warrior society was concerned with hunting, war, crops, fertility, and curing. Each society had its own dances and ritual paraphernalia. Numerous life cycle rites, as well as songs, crafts, and communal activities such as maintenance of irrigation canals and performing dances, also ensured that one spent one's life "becoming" a Tewa.

People of San Juan further classified themselves into three categories: ordinary earth people, youths, and made people (priests of eight separate priesthoods, half of which admit women as full members). Similarly, their physical world was divided into three corresponding categories: Village, farmlands, and other nearby lowlands, accessible to all

and particularly the woman's domain, were delineated by four shrines to ancestors. Hills, mesas, and washes, defined by four sacred mesas and in the spiritual charge of the "youths," were a mediating environment in spatial, social, sexual, spiritual, and even subsistence terms. Mountains, a male realm of hunting and religious pilgrimages, were in the charge of the made people.

San Juan Pueblo originally featured multistory apartment-style dwellings constructed of adobe (earth-and-straw) bricks, with pine beams across the roof that were covered with poles, brush, and plaster. Floors were of wood plank or packed earth. The roof of one level served as the floor of another. The levels were interconnected by ladders. As an aid to defense, the traditional design included no doors or windows; entry was through the roof. Pithouses, or kivas, served as ceremonial chambers and clubhouses. The village plaza, around which the church and all dwellings were clustered, was the spiritual center of the village, a place where all the balanced forces of the world came together.

See also Agriculture; All Indian Pueblo Council; Pueblo Revolt.

lands in response to climatic and social upheavals. A century or two of migrations ensued, followed in general by the slow reemergence of their culture in the historic pueblos. Old Santa Ana was probably established in the late sixteenth century.

Francisco Vasquez de Coronado may have visited Santa Ana Pueblo. In 1598, Juan de Oñate arrived in the area with settlers, founding the colony of New Mexico. Oñate carried on the process, already underway in nearby areas, of subjugating the local Indians, forcing them to pay taxes in crops, cotton, and work and opening the door for Catholic missionaries to attack their religion. The Spanish renamed the pueblos with saints' names and began a program of church construction. At the same time, they introduced such new crops as peaches, wheat, and peppers into the region. In 1620, a royal decree created civil offices at each pueblo; silver-headed canes, many of which remain in use today, symbolized the governor's authority.

See also Agriculture; All Indian Pueblo Council; Pueblo Revolt.

Santa Ana Pueblo

The Santa Ana people call their Old Pueblo *Tamaya*. The word "pueblo" comes from the Spanish for "village." It refers both to a certain style of Southwest Indian architecture, characterized by multistory, apartment-like buildings made of adobe (pueblo), and to the people themselves (Pueblo). Rio Grande Pueblos are known as eastern Pueblos; Zunis, Hopis, and sometimes Acomas and Lagunas are known as western Pueblos. The people spoke a dialect of Keresan.

The Old Pueblo (Tamaya) is located twenty-seven miles northwest of Albuquerque, on the north bank of the Jemez River eight miles northwest of its junction with the Rio Grande. This fairly isolated location traditionally kept residents from much contact with non-Indians. The pueblo was all but abandoned in historic times because of low-quality arable land. The people then bought land and moved to a location (Los Ranchitos) about ten miles to the southeast and just north of Bernalillo.

Keresans have been traced to an area around Chaco Canyon north to Mesa Verde. In the 1200s, the Keresans abandoned their traditional canyon home-

Santa Clara Pueblo

The Tewa name for the Santa Clara Pueblo is *Capo*, variously translated. The word "pueblo" comes from the Spanish for "village." It refers both to a certain style of Southwest Indian architecture, characterized by multistory, apartment-like buildings made of adobe (pueblo), and to the people themselves (Pueblo). Rio Grande Pueblos are known as eastern Pueblos; Zunis, Hopis, and sometimes Acomas and Lagunas are known as western Pueblos. The Santa Clara Pueblo is located on the west bank of the Rio Grande, about twenty-five miles north of Santa Fe. The people spoke a dialect of Tewa.

The Santa Clara Pueblo experienced a major political schism in the 1890s. The winter division, the more "progressive" for much of the nineteenth century, had resisted the rigid dictates of pueblo life and advocated a separation of religious from secular life. In 1894, the summer division and some winter people applied for and received recognition from the Indian agency in Santa Fe as the legitimate governing authority at the Pueblo. For the next thirty years, the summer division elected all secular officials except the lieutenant governor and tried to enforce the traditionally rigid sacred–secular con-

nection. The winter group resisted and openly defied them.

In the 1930s, each division split along progressive and conservative lines; now there were four factions, each allied with a like-minded group. Their government in shambles, the Pueblos requested arbitration by the Indian Service in Santa Fe, with the result that they incorporated under the Indian Reorganization Act (IRA) and turned to a constitution and an elected government. Thus religious and secular affairs were finally split, and participation in ceremonies was made voluntary.

See also Agriculture; All Indian Pueblo Council; Pottery; Pueblo Revolt.

Santo Domingo Pueblo

The Santo Domingo people call their pueblo *Kiuw.* The word "pueblo" comes from the Spanish for "village." It refers both to a certain style of Southwest Indian architecture, characterized by multistory, apartment-like buildings made of adobe (pueblo), and to the people themselves (Pueblo). Rio Grande Pueblos are known as eastern Pueblos; Zunis, Hopis, and sometimes Acomas and Lagunas are known as western Pueblos.

The Santo Domingo Pueblo is situated on the east bank of the Rio Grande, thirty to thirty-five miles southwest of Santa Fe, near the Camino Real and modern highways. The people spoke a Keresan dialect.

See also Agriculture; All Indian Pueblo Council; Pueblo Revolt.

Taos Pueblo

The Taos Pueblo is also known as San Geronimo de Taos, and the word "Taos" comes from a Tiwa word meaning "in the village." The word "pueblo" comes from the Spanish for "village." It refers both to a certain style of Southwest Indian architecture, characterized by multistory, apartment-like buildings made of adobe (pueblo), and to the people themselves (Pueblo). Rio Grande Pueblos are known as eastern Pueblos; Zunis, Hopis, and sometimes Acomas and Lagunas are known as western Pueblos. The Taos name for their Pueblo is *Tecuse* or *Ilaphai,* "at the mouth of Red Willow Canyon." The north-

ernmost, highest (with Picuris, at about seven thousand feet), and one of the most isolated of the eastern pueblos, Taos is seventy miles north of Santa Fe. Taos Indians spoke Northern Tiwa, a Kiowa-Tanoan language.

Francisco Vasquez de Coronado visited Taos in 1540. In 1598, Juan de Oñate arrived in the area with settlers, founding the colony of New Mexico. Oñate carried on the process, already underway in nearby areas, of subjugating the local Indians, forcing them to pay taxes in crops, cotton, and work and opening the door for Catholic missionaries to attack their religion. The Spanish renamed the pueblos with saints' names and began a program of church construction, establishing the mission of San Geronimo at Taos in the early seventeenth century. At the same time, the Spanish introduced such new crops as peaches, wheat, and peppers into the region. In 1620, a royal decree created civil offices at each pueblo; silver-headed canes, many of which remain in use today, symbolized the governor's authority.

Taos played a leading role in the Pueblo Revolt of 1680. For years, the Spaniards had routinely tortured Indians for practicing traditional religion. They also forced the Indians to labor for them, sold them into slavery, and let Spaniard-owned cattle overgraze Indian land, a situation that eventually led to drought, erosion, and famine. Popé of San Juan Pueblo and other Pueblo religious leaders planned the great revolt at Taos, sending runners carrying cords of maguey fibers to mark the day of rebellion. On August 10, 1680, a virtually united stand on the part of the Pueblos drove the Spanish from the region. The Indians killed many Spaniards but refrained from mass slaughter, allowing most of them to leave Santa Fe for El Paso.

Santa Fe was officially reconquered in 1692, after which the Taos fled to the mountains and to their Plains friends, the Kiowas. The Spanish sacked Taos Pueblo in 1693, after which the Indians returned and rebuilt it. Another short-lived rebellion occurred in 1696. Although Pueblo unity did not last, Spanish rule was notably less severe from then on. Harsh forced labor all but ceased, and the Indians reached an understanding with the Church that enabled them to continue practicing their traditional religion. By the 1700s, excluding Hopi and Zuni, only the Taos, Picuris, Isleta, and Acoma Pueblos had not changed locations since the arrival of the Spanish.

In 1906, the U.S. government included Taos's holiest site, the Blue Lake region in the Sangre de

About 150 Native Americans still live in the Taos Pueblo in practically the same buildings and under the same conditions as in the sixteenth century under Spanish rule. The mound at left is an oven. (National Archives and Records Administration)

Cristo Mountains, as part of a national forest. Under the leadership of longtime governor Severino Martinez and others, the tribe fought to get it back. In 1965 they received title to the land and were offered a cash payment, but they held out for the land. In 1970 the government returned Blue Lake, along with 48,000 surrounding acres. Since the late nineteenth century, but especially after the 1960s, the Pueblos have had to cope with onslaughts by (mostly white) anthropologists and seekers of Indian spirituality. The region is also known for its major art colonies at Taos and Santa Fe.

In traditional Pueblo culture, religion and life are inseparable. To be in harmony with all of nature is the Pueblo ideal and way of life. The sun is seen as the representative of the Creator. Sacred mountains in each direction, as well as mountain lakes and other natural places, plus the sun above and the earth below, define and balance the Taos Pueblo world. Many Pueblo religious ceremonies revolve around the weather and are devoted to ensuring adequate rainfall. To this end, Pueblo Indians evoke the power of katsinas, sacred beings who live in mountains and other holy places, in ritual and masked dance.

In addition to the natural boundaries, Pueblo Indians have created a society that defines their world by providing balanced, reciprocal relationships within which people connect and harmonize with each other, the natural world, and time itself. Unlike the situation in most Pueblos, the heads of the kiva societies, rather than the cacique, were the most important religious leaders. In fact, the cacique had both religious and secular duties.

Seven kiva or ceremonial societies were active at Taos. Each had special functions and separate religious knowledge. Feathers of birds such as eagles, hawks, and ducks, as well as wildflowers, were important ceremonially. Traditionally, all preteen boys underwent religious training, and a select few were chosen for an eighteen-month initiation, culminating in a pilgrimage to Blue Lake, into one of the kiva societies. Only initiated men could move from "boy" to "elder" status and hold secular office.

Much ceremony is also based on medicine societies, and shamans who derive powers from animal spirits use their supernatural powers for curing, weather control, and ensuring the general welfare. Corn Dances are held in the summer and animal dances in the winter. Most ceremonies at Taos are still kept secret from outsiders. Although most Taos Indians consider themselves Catholics, their form of Catholicism coexists with their traditional religion. The Native American Church was introduced at Taos in 1907. Although controversial, it remains active.

Taos was formerly walled, as a defense against the Comanche raids of the 1700s. The pueblo features two clusters of apartment-style buildings, as high as six stories, on either side of Taos Creek. The buildings are constructed of adobe (earth-and-straw) bricks, with beams across a roof covered with poles, brush, and plaster. Floors are of wood plank or packed earth. The roof of one level serves as the floor of another. The levels are interconnected by ladders. As an aid to defense, the traditional design included no doors or windows; entry was through the roof. A number of adobe houses were also scattered around the pueblo. Seven pithouses, or kivas, serve as ceremonial chambers and clubhouses. The village plaza, around which all dwellings are clustered, is the spiritual center of the village where all the balanced forces of world come together. A racetrack is part of the village, built to accommodate ceremonial footraces.

See also Agriculture; All Indian Pueblo Council; Blue Lake, New Mexico; Pueblo Revolt.

Tesuque Pueblo

"Tesuque" is a Hispanicization of the Tewa word *tecuge*, which means "structure at a narrow place" or "dry, spotted place." The word "pueblo" comes from the Spanish for "village." It refers both to a certain style of Southwest Indian architecture, characterized by multistory, apartment-like buildings made of adobe (pueblo), and to the people themselves (Pueblo). Rio Grande Pueblos are known as eastern Pueblos; Zunis, Hopis, and sometimes Acomas and Lagunas are known as western Pueblos. The Tesuque Pueblo is located nine miles north of Santa Fe, on the Tesuque River. Tesuque Indians spoke Tewa, a member of the Kiowa-Tanoan language family.

Especially after 1821, the Pueblos underwent a steady acculturation. Toward the late nineteenth century, the United States reintroduced religious repression. The government and Protestant missionaries branded Indian religious practices as obscene and immoral, and the Bureau of Indian Affairs forcibly removed Indian children to culture-killing boarding schools. As part of the effort to retain their traditions, Indians more deeply embraced customs once seen as alien, such as Catholicism. By the 1880s, railroads had ended the traditional isolation of most pueblos. Instead of treaties, the United States recognized old Spanish land grants of pueblo land. Ironically, this put them outside official treaty rights and left them particularly open to exploitation by squatters and thieves.

Tesuque ran out of water in the early twentieth century as a result of diversions by recently arrived Anglo settlers. A series of dams and basins restored much of their water by 1935. Partly because of lobbying from the All Indian Pueblo Council, Congress confirmed Pueblo title to their lands in 1924 by passing the Pueblo Lands Act. The United States also acknowledged its trust responsibilities in a series of legal decisions and other acts of Congress. In the late 1950s, the Tesuque Pueblo received no tribal income other than the interest from funds on deposit with the government. Since the late nineteenth century, but especially after the 1960s, the Pueblos have had to cope with onslaughts by (mostly white) anthropologists and seekers of Indian spirituality. The region is also known for its significant art colonies at Taos and Santa Fe.

At Tesuque, a summer and a winter cacique, appointed for life, oversaw the pueblo. Society was divided into two patrilineal groups, summer (associated with the Squash kiva) and winter (associated with the Turquoise kiva), which united in times of crisis and for the welfare of the Pueblo. These groups were further divided into relatively weak and ill defined clans. A number of secret societies also existed. For instance, the warrior society was

concerned with hunting, war, crops, fertility, and curing. Each society had its own dances and ritual paraphernalia. Numerous life cycle rites, as well as songs, crafts, communal activities such as maintenance of irrigation canals, prayer retreats, and performing dances, also ensured that one spent one's life "becoming" a Tewa.

The Tesuque Pueblo originally featured apartment-style dwellings of up to five stories constructed of adobe (earth-and-straw) bricks, with pine beams across the roof that were covered with poles, brush, and plaster. Floors were of wood plank or packed earth. The roof of one level served as the floor of another. The levels were interconnected by ladders. As an aid to defense, the traditional design included no doors or windows; entry was through the roof. Pithouses, or kivas, served as ceremonial chambers and clubhouses. The village plaza, around which the church and all dwellings were clustered, was the spiritual center of the village, a place where all the balanced forces of the world came together.

See also Agriculture; All Indian Pueblo Council; Pottery; Pueblo Revolt.

Tigua

The Tigua live on Ysleta del Sur Pueblo ("Isleta of the South"), a reference to the ancestral Isleta Pueblo in New Mexico. The Pueblo was formerly known as Tigua ('T wä) Reservation. The word "pueblo" comes from the Spanish for "village." It refers both to a certain style of Southwest Indian architecture, characterized by multistory, apartment-like buildings made of adobe (pueblo), and to the people themselves (Pueblo). Ysleta del Sur Pueblo is located within the southern boundary of El Paso, Texas. The Native language of the Tigua people is Southern Tiwa.

The Ysleta del Sur Pueblo was founded in 1682 by Pueblo refugees from the rebellion of 1680. Its original inhabitants included Indians from Isleta Pueblo as well as Piro, Manso, Apache, Suma, and Tompiro Indians, none of whom joined the revolt. These Indians retreated south with the fleeing Spaniards. They built a church at Tigua, dedicated to Saint Anthony, in 1682. Following the 1692 Spanish reconquest, in which these Indians participated, Governor Diego de Vargas planned to resettle them in their New Mexico homelands, but most preferred to remain. The Piros eventually became absorbed

into the Tigua Pueblo or into the local Spanish-American population. At some point, the Ysleta Indians received a land grant from the king of Spain.

For the next two centuries, the Tigua people practiced farming on irrigated fields. Tiguas scouted for El Paso settlements against Comanche and Apache raiders, and they also scouted for the Texas Rangers and the U.S. cavalry during the Indian campaigns. After 1848, however, Tiguas were subject to "legal" and extralegal abuses from rapacious Anglos, and much of their land was lost. When President Abraham Lincoln acknowledged the New Mexican Pueblo land grants with a second set of silver-headed canes, Tigua, standing in the Confederacy, was ignored. In any case, since Texas retained its public lands, the U.S. government was unable to create a reservation for the Tiguas.

In the late nineteenth century and into the 1920s the tribe virtually faded away, mixing with the local populace and living in extreme poverty. In 1967, the state of Texas recognized the Ysleta Indian community; federal recognition followed the next year. The receipt of federal money and recognition revitalized the tribe and provided the means by which it was able to reclaim its identity.

Tiguas practice Catholicism, with some Native elements. The pueblo's patron saint is Anthony, who was the patron of Isleta Pueblo before the 1680 revolt. A small core of people practice a more traditional religion, featuring a katsina-like entity known as the *awelo,* or "grandfather," who oversees all behavior. The tribe also possesses buffalo *awelo* masks and an ancient ceremonial drum.

The Tigua tribal government is Spanish-style civil. There is a cacique, a *cacique teniente* (lieutenant cacique, or governor), an *alguacil* (or sergeant at arms), a *capitán de guerra* (war captain), and four assistant captains. Except for the first and the last, all are elected annually. The Ysleta del Sur Pueblo also possesses the old Spanish canes, symbols of political authority, that were carried by the original settlers.

Tribal ceremonial items are stored in a *tusla,* generally the home of a tribal officer, where celebrations are often held. There is a high rate of intermarriage with outsiders, particularly with Mexicans and other Indians. The Tiguas enjoy a close relationship with the Isleta Pueblo, New Mexico, 250 miles away. They are also associated with the Tortugas community of Las Cruces, New Mexico, a Tigua community founded in the late nineteenth century and composed of Tigua, Piro, and Manso Indians. The Tiguas also have relatives in Mexico, at the former Piro

Pueblo of Senecú, near Juarez. There may have been a clan system in earlier days.

See also Agriculture; Pueblo Revolt.

Tohono O'odham

The Tohono O'odhams are also known as Papago or Desert People. The name "Papago" is derived from the Pima word *papahvio-otam,* meaning "bean people." They are also known as Two Villagers, owing to their traditional migration patterns. They, along with the Pimas (Akimel O'odhams, or River People, also known as One Villagers because of their relatively settled lives), the Sand Papagos (Hia-ced O'odhams, also known as No Villagers, because of their more or less constant migrations in search of food), and the Ak-Chin ("mouth of the arroyo") O'odhams, constitute the O'odham Indians.

The Tohono O'odhams lived originally in the Sonoran Desert near the Gulf of California. (The Sand Papagos lived in the western and most arid parts of the Sonoran Desert.) Today they live in four reservations in southern Arizona

As many as 50,000 Tohono O'odhams probably lived in the region in 1500, although their numbers had shrunk to about 3,000 by 1700. The Native language of the Tohono O'odhams is Piman, a Uto-Aztecan language.

The O'odhams are probably descended from the ancient Hohokam Indians. Unlike the Hohokams or the Pimas, the Tohono O'odhams were seminomadic. They generally spent summers in their "field villages" in the desert, usually at the mouth of an arroyo, where flash floods provided needed water. Winters were spent in "well villages," by mountain springs. The Tohono O'odhams worshiped Earth Maker (Tcuwut Makai) and Elder Brother (I'itoi, or Se'ehe), the heroes of their creation story, whose sacred home is Baboquivari Peak in southern Arizona. Ceremonies encouraged these spirits to bring the rain that made food possible. The people also made annual pilgrimages to salt flats near the Gulf of California, home of the rain spirits, to pray to them.

Their most sacred ceremony was *Nawait,* or the new year's rain ceremony, which they celebrated with saguaro wine. Other important ceremonial occasions included puberty (especially for girls), funerals, the summer cactus wine feast, the "naming" (to honor and entertain other groups), purifica-tion following childbirth, sickness, the corn harvest, the deer hunt, the early winter harvest, purification for an eagle killing, warfare, and the annual salt expeditions.

Shamans, both men and older women, derived curing power from dreams. Although many Papagos became Catholic in the eighteenth century, having clustered around Spanish presidios and missions to escape the Apaches, theirs was a Catholicism heavily mixed with traditional beliefs.

The Tohono O'odhams were organized into autonomous villages. Although each village had a chief (there was no tribal chief), decisions were made by consensus. Each village also had shamans, a headman who set the agenda for meetings and mediated conflict, and an all-male council. They also recognized a ceremonial leader, akin to the headman, called Keeper of the Smoke. Other officials included a village crier, war leader, hunt leader, game leader, and song leader.

A universal O'odham concept of the way of life (*Himdag*) centers on family, community, generosity, and modesty. The Papagos made annual visits to relatives on the Gila River or in the Sonora River Valley. In times of famine, families often moved to Pima villages along the Gila River. Every four years the Papagos and Pimas together celebrated Viikita, a holiday dedicated to ensuring their continued fortune, with dancers and clowns dressed in masks and costumes.

Each Tohono O'odham village was divided into two clans: Buzzard and Coyote. Their year began when the cactus fruit ripened. Gifts and wagering were major forms of exchange. Games and races also held cultural importance. With the exception of warriors, who were cremated, the dead were dressed in their best clothing and buried with their personal property in caves, crevices, or stone houses.

Like those of the Pimas, everyday Papago houses were circular and constructed of saguaro and ocotillo ribs and mesquite covered with mud and brush. Ceremonial houses were similar, but larger. Wall-less ramadas provided shelter for most outdoor activities in good weather. Sand Papagos used small rings of stone as temporary windbreaks.

The key to survival in the desert was diversification. The goal of the Papagos was security rather than surpluses. Men grew corn, beans, and squash. Later the Spanish introduced cowpeas, melons, and wheat. Winter wheat especially provided an edge against starvation. The people also hunted, primarily in the winter. Wild foods such as mescal,

mesquite beans, ironwood and paloverde seeds, cactus fruits, amaranth and other greens, wild chilies, acorns, and sand root provided about three-quarters of their diet. Saguaro wine was used on ceremonial occasions. During hard times the Papagos "hired out" to Pima Indians, exchanging labor for food. The Sand Papagos ate shellfish from the Gulf of California, reptiles, insects, and small mammals. A staple was the parasitic plant sand root.

The Desert People baked in pit ovens. They used long poles called *kuibits* to knock down saguaro fruit. The use of calendar sticks, with carved dots and circles to record important ceremonies, began in the early 1830s. Notches referred to secular events, such as earthquakes or Apache attacks. Other equipment included carrying nets, frame backpacks, and cradle boards. In characteristic Ak-Chin farming, men built dams to channel water runoff into a major arroyo. When the flash floods arrived, they would water the fields by erecting brush spreader dams across the arroyo. After contact with the Spanish, the Desert People adopted picks, shovels, and horse- and oxen-drawn plows and wagons.

Trade occurred mostly in the fall and winter. The Tohono O'odhams traded meat, baskets, pottery, salt, shells, mineral pigments, and macaws for corn and, later, wheat from Pimas and Quechans. The Sand Papagos also traded with Yuman peoples on the Colorado River.

The Tohono O'odhams may have first met non-Natives in the 1500s. They experienced extensive contact with the Spanish in late 1600s when Father Eusebio Francisco Kino established numerous Catholic missions and introduced cattle, horses, and wheat (1684). The Spanish also established a series of presidios against the growing Apache threat. Although too isolated to have had to endure harsh forced labor and agricultural taxes as did the Pimas, some Tohono O'odhams, such as Luis Oacpicagigua and others, participated in the Pima Revolt of 1751.

Apaches constituted the major threat from the eighteenth century through the midnineteenth century. During this time, the Sand Papagos died off or became assimilated with the Spanish or surrounding tribes. From 1840 to 1843, the Papagos fought and lost a war against Mexico in an attempt to stop the usurpation of their lands. With the Gadsden Purchase (1853), the Tohono O'odhams lost the part of their territory that remained in Mexico, although they tended to ignore the international border for many years. Despite tighter border restrictions

today, Tohono O'odham Indians living in Sonora and the United States remain in contact.

In the 1860s, the Papagos fought alongside the Pimas, the Pee-Posh, and U.S. troops against the Apaches. Still, Anglos appropriated their water holes and grazing land, resulting in conflict and some violence. San Xavier Reservation was founded in 1874, with Gila Bend Reservation following in 1882. The Papago Reservation was established in 1916 and 1917, albeit without most of the Tohono O'odhams' best lands.

The railroad came to Tucson in the 1880s, bringing an increase of cattle ranchers and miners into O'odham territory. The cattle lost by these people began important O'odham herds. By the end of the century, countless Papago (and other Indian) girls were working as domestics for whites through Bureau of Indian Affairs (BIA) programs at the Phoenix Indian School. About this time, and concurrent with the rise of many Christian schools, the O'odham culture declined markedly.

A field camp at Vecol Wash became the permanent settlement of the Ak-Chin O'odhams in the 1870s; Pimas and Maricopas lived there too. In the early wage economy, O'odham potters sold and traded watercooling ollas; men cut firewood; basketmakers sold baskets. Cotton picking became the most important economic activity through the 1950s. In the 1970s, a severe drought killed many cattle, reducing the Papagos to near starvation.

See also Reservation Economic and Social Conditions; Trade; Warfare, Intertribal.

Tortugas
See Tigua.

Walapai
See Hualapai.

Yaqui

"Yaqui" is a name established by Jesuit missionaries in the early seventeenth century. It was taken from the name of a nearby river. The traditional Yaqui name for themselves is *Yoeme*. The Yaquis originated

in the northwestern Mexican state of Sonora. They have lived in southern and southwest Arizona from the late nineteenth century.

The Yaqui population stood at perhaps 30,000 at contact (1533), the largest Native tribal population in northwest New Spain. Roughly 6,000 now live in U.S. villages out of a total U.S. tribal enrollment of almost 10,000. About 25,000 Yaquis live in Sonora, Mexico. Yaquis speak a dialect of Cahita, a member of the Uto-Aztecan language family.

The aboriginal land of the Yaquis consisted of roughly 6,000 square miles in Sonora, Mexico, approximately between the Rio Mátapa and the Arroyo de Cocoraqui. The Yaquis believe their boundaries were made sacred by singing angels (*batnaataka*) who traversed them in mythological times. Although the Sonora region is primarily a desert, Yaqui lands in the river basin were quite fertile as a result of the annual flood cycles.

The Yaqui Indians have been practicing a heavily Christian-influenced religion for nearly 400 years. They recognize a two-part universe: One is town and church, whose dwellers are mortal; the other is the Huya Aniya, spirit world and source of spiritual power, whose dwellers are immortal. The two worlds are integrated ritually. Every Christian ceremony requires the participation of ceremonialists, such as Pascola and Deer Dancers, whose power derives from the Huya Aniya.

Other important religious elements include the honoring of and concern for ancestors, the sharing of accumulated wealth for help in curing (healing), maintaining and distributing the benevolent power of Our Mother (the supernatural), honoring the patron saints of the eight towns, and affirming the sacred relationships between the Yaquis and their traditional territory.

In addition to a number of feast days, the most important and elaborate ceremony of the year is the *waehma*, or the reenactment during Holy Week of Christ's (the great curer) final days. A central theme is the accumulation of evil in the town and the destruction of the evil during a ceremonial battle on Holy Saturday, through the ritual use of flowers, followed by a great celebration.

The largest political unit was the town. Authority consisted of five groups: church, civil governors, military, "custom authorities" (*kohtumbre*), and fiesta makers (*pahkome*). Each had its own clearly defined jurisdiction, but they worked together on matters of the public good. Decision making was by consensus in town meetings, except in time of military emer-

gency, and even then the military leader's power in nonmilitary affairs was highly circumscribed. A constant process of interaction and sharing promoted continuity among the towns.

Traditional Yaqui households included any number of nuclear families related in a variety of ways. Yaqui elders were respected as the tribal spokespeople and maintained schools for young men. The godparent system, introduced by the Jesuits, has evolved into a highly complex and important institution.

Prior to 1617 the Yaquis lived in roughly eighty rancherias, most containing fewer than 250 people, consisting of clusters of dome-shaped, cane mat–covered adobe houses with flat or gently sloping roofs. Consolidation under the Jesuits of the scattered rancherias into eight towns, each with between 2,000 and 4,000 people, occurred by the mid-1600s. Each town was built around an adobe-walled church, with new civil, military, and ceremonial organizations grouped around the church and central plaza. Houses built near churches always included ramadas as well as walled rooms, surrounded by a cane fence. After 1887, the Mexicans succeeded in imposing the grid plan of settlement on Yaqui towns.

Cultivated crops such as corn, squash, beans, and amaranth were supplemented by abundant wild foods such as mesquite beans, cactus fruits, succulent roots, grass seeds, wild game (including deer and rabbits), and many kinds of shellfish and large saltwater fish from the Gulf of California. By the late seventeenth century, the Jesuits had introduced wheat, pomegranates, peaches, figs, and other crops as well as cattle (including oxen for plowing) and horses.

Rudimentary irrigation ditches were improved by the Jesuits, who also introduced the plow to the region. The Yaquis traditionally fashioned cane into a great number of articles, including mats for roof and wall materials, household compound fences, sleeping mats, cutting instruments, spoons, and shelves as well as numerous ceremonial items.

A party of Spaniards first encountered the Yaquis in 1533 but were prevented by force from trespassing on Yaqui territory. In 1609, after defeating the Spanish for the third time, the Yaquis arrived at an accommodation with them and accepted Jesuit missionaries in 1617. Over the next seven years almost all Yaquis converted to Catholicism.

The next 150 years were a period of creative cultural and economic growth for the Yaquis.

Transformations in agriculture and technology led to increasing agricultural surpluses and economic diversification (mining and sheep herding for the Spanish wool trade). In 1740, the Yaquis staged a major revolt as a result of growing tensions over land incursions, Spanish attempts to secularize and control the missions, and missionary abuses. The Indians' defeat strengthened both Spanish colonial power and the Jesuit missions, until the latter were expelled from the New World in 1767.

The 1800s were a time of semiautonomy, with the gradual loss of land and continual resistance against the Mexicans. Juan Ignacio Jusacamea, also known as Juan de la Cruz Banderas or Juan Banderas, emerged as the uncontested leader of the Yaquis and their allies in the early Mexican rebellions until his capture and execution in 1833. Further periodic revolts culminated in the so-called Cajeme era (1875–1885), a period of Yaqui cultural and economic renewal during which Yaqui society made a final defensive stand against Mexico under José María Leyva, called Cajeme.

The defeat of Cajeme in 1885 was followed by military occupation, repression, and mass deportation under the regime of Porfirio Diaz, although Yaqui bands continued guerrilla resistance in the Bacatete Mountains into the twentieth century. Most Yaquis not exiled to the Yucatan dispersed throughout rural Sonora, assisting the guerrillas and working in the mines, on the railroads, and on haciendas. Many also headed north to the United States to begin new Yaqui communities there.

The Mexican Revolution of 1910 offered the Yaquis a chance to regroup and reestablish their identity, with the formation of their own revolutionary army. Following the wars, Yaquis began a gradual return to their traditional lands and a reconstruction of their culture. For Yaquis living in Mexico, the last half of the twentieth century has been marked by the integration, albeit at the lowest levels, into that country's economy. In 1964, the U.S. Congress gave 202 acres of land to the Pascua Yaqui Association. This grant became the basis of New Pascua, which became officially recognized in 1978.

See also Agriculture; Banderas, Juan de la Cruz.

Yavapai

"Yavapai" is from the Mojave *Enyaéva Pai,* "People of the Sun." The Yavapais are sometimes confused with the Apaches, as a result of their long association together, and they are occasionally (and erroneously) referred to as Mojave Apaches or Yuma Apaches. Yavapais spoke a dialect (similar to Pai) of Upland Yuman, a Hokan-Siouan language (though culturally and historically the Yavapais were more closely related to the Tonto Apaches).

Traditionally, the Yavapais controlled roughly 10 million acres in present-day west central Arizona. This transitional area between the Colorado Plateau and the lower deserts provided them with a salubrious mixture of desert, mountain, and plateau plants and animals. Today, Yavapai Indians live on the Fort McDowell, the Camp Verde, and the Yavapai Reservations in Arizona.

The nomadic Yavapais were probably descended from the ancient Hakataya peoples. Traditionally they consisted of four major divisions: the Kewevkapayas (southeastern), the Wipukpayas (northeastern), the Tolkepayes (western), and the Yavepes (central). Each was further divided into local bands.

Contact between the Spanish and the Yavapais first occurred during 1582. After Father Francisco Garces lived with them in 1776, contact became more frequent. Nevertheless the Yavapais lived traditionally until the 1850s, largely because their country was too rough for the Spaniards, Mexicans, or Americans. Some bands, especially the Kewevkapayas, raided with the Apaches. After the Mexican cession, more non-Indian travelers and miners frequented the region, although the Yavapais tried to avoid conflict, owing primarily to their poor weaponry.

Gold was discovered in 1863. Shortly thereafter the frontier arrived and brought the permanent disruption of Yavapai traditional life. Hungry and under continuous attack, the Yavapais fought back. In 1872–1873, General George Crook's bloody Tonto Basin campaign against the Tonto Apaches and Yavapais (won with a heavy reliance on Pai scouts) ended with a massacre of Yavapais. Forced onto the Camp Verde Reservation after disease had killed an additional one-third of their number, the Yavapais and Tonto Apaches dug a five-mile irrigation ditch using discarded army tools and brought in a good harvest. For this they were forcibly relocated (again) in 1875 and settled with the Apaches on the San Carlos Reservation, 180 miles to the east. Many died or were killed on the March of Tears (within twenty-five years, their population fell from 1,500 to 200).

At San Carlos the Yavapais again tried farming. They also scouted for the Army against the Chiric-

ahua Apaches and acquired cattle. However, flooding ruined their ditches, miners and ranchers took their land, and they still wanted to go home. By 1900, most Yavapais had left San Carlos. Some returned to the Verde Valley and some to Forts McDowell and Whipple. In 1903, Fort McDowell became a reservation, inhabited mostly by the Kewevkopaya band. The Camp Verde (Weepukapa) Reservation was established in 1910, with outlying communities such as Middle Verde, Clarkdale, and Rimrock added during the following sixty years. Fort Whipple became a reservation (Yavapai–Prescott) in 1935. The western Yavapais (Tolkepayes) received no reservation and have nearly disappeared.

The Verde River ran through Fort McDowell. The Yavapais tried farming once again, but they were soon involved in a struggle for water rights. Instead of providing funds to improve irrigation and guard against floods, the government wanted to remove the Yavapais to the Salt River Pima Reservation. Largely owing to the efforts of Carlos Montezuma they were able to remain, but they secured little money or water. During this period cattle grazing and wage work, both on and off the reservation, became important sources of income. From the 1950s through the 1980s, the Yavapais also fought off a dam (Orme) that would have flooded most of the Fort McDowell Reservation, refusing $33 million in compensation. Finally, in 1990, the Yavapais won the passage of a law granting them sufficient water rights from the Verde River as well as $25 million in compensatory funds.

The Yavapais and Apaches leaving San Carlos settled at Camp Verde around the turn of the century. Camp Verde is more Apache than Yavapai in character. Unable to make a living on the inadequate reservation lands, most people worked in the nearby copper industry until the 1930s and 1940s.

In 1935 a separate reservation, primarily inhabited by the Yavepe band, was created north of Prescott. Rather than organize under the Indian Reorganization Act, this group maintained the traditional governing structure until 1988. Their land base is surrounded by the city of Prescott.

As in other Yuman groups, the veneration of the sun, dream omens, and shamanism were key aspects of Yavapai religion. Knowledge of all kinds was acquired by each person through dreaming. Shamans conducted healing rituals by singing, smoking tobacco, and sucking out bad blood. Some Yavapai rituals included the use of sandpaintings. Singing, dancing, and eagle feathers were part of

every ritual, as were certain plants and musical instruments such as rattles, drums, and flutes. "Little people" or spirits living in the mountains were thought to help people. The Yavapai place of emergence was considered to be at Montezuma Well, near Sedona.

The closest the Yavapais came to centralized authority was each local group's "civic leader." This person would orate each morning on proper ideas and behavior. Leadership was based on personal merit (wisdom, personality, and ability in war).

The Yavapais were a nomadic people who followed the ripening of wild foods. Bands camped in groups of up to ten families; winter gatherings were even larger. Elders or group leaders orated each morning from the roof of a hut, instructing people on the proper way to live. Social dances were held on occasion. Until the early 1900s the dead were customarily cremated (the house and possessions were also burned). Polygyny was rare, as was divorce. The Yavapai practiced formal puberty rites for women and men.

Yavapai people lived in caves or dome-shaped huts, framed with poles and covered with brush, thatch, or mud. Other structures included ramadas and sweat lodges.

Mescal was a staple, along with other wild plants such as cactus fruit, mesquite beans, greens, acorns, piñon nuts, walnuts, seeds, and berries. Women gathered wild foods. Game included deer, quail, fox, antelope, and rabbit; people also ate lizards, caterpillars, yellowjacket nests, and turkeys. Small amounts of corn, beans, and squash were grown or traded, mostly by the western band.

The Yavapais painted their bodies. Ornaments included necklaces, bracelets, and ear and nose rings (especially warriors). Bangs were worn to the eyebrows. Men wore hide breechclouts, leggings, and moccasins, and blankets or skin ponchos in winter (also boots and mittens). Women wore two buckskins draped over a belt and a buckskin top and moccasins (of buckskin or possibly yucca fiber). Some women tattooed their faces. Men dressed the skins for clothing.

Each local group decided for itself whether or nor to join a war. The Yavapais' traditional enemies included the Pais, Pimas, Pee-Posh, and O'odhams. Their allies included the Quechans, Mojaves, and Apaches. Unlike the Apaches, the Yavapais used few guns; instead, they mostly made do with hunting tools to fight the U.S. Army. Other weapons included clubs, hide shields, mulberry bows, and

cane arrows with obsidian points. Although they were inclined toward war, they proved to be more flexible than the Apaches regarding change, adaptation, and coexistence.

See also Agriculture; Indian Reorganization Act; Reservation Economic and Social Conditions; Relocation.

Yuma

See Quechan.

Zia Pueblo

"Zia" comes from the Spanish spelling of its Keresan name. The word "pueblo" comes from the Spanish for "village." It refers both to a certain style of Southwest Indian architecture, characterized by multistory, apartment-like buildings made of adobe (pueblo), and to the people themselves (Pueblo). Rio Grande Pueblos are known as eastern Pueblos; Zunis, Hopis, and sometimes Acomas and Lagunas are known as western Pueblos. The Zia Pueblo is located on the Jemez River, thirty miles north of Albuquerque, New Mexico. Several thousand people may have lived on the pueblo during 1540, although fewer than 300 remained in 1690 and fewer than 100 in 1890. The Zia Indians spoke a dialect of Keresan.

The Zians participated in the 1680 Pueblo Revolt against the Spanish. They suffered a bloody military defeat by Spanish forces in 1687: Six hundred were killed, and many were held captive for ten years. In 1689 the Zians received a royal land grant from Spain. In 1692 they accepted mass baptism and collaborated with the Spanish in their campaigns against other pueblos throughout the rest of the decade.

In the sixteenth century, the Zia Pueblo featured two- to three-story, apartment-style dwellings arranged around eight plazas. The buildings were constructed of adobe (earth-and-straw) bricks, with beams across the roof that were covered with poles, brush, and plaster. Floors were of wood plank or packed earth. The roof of one level served as the floor of another. The levels were interconnected by ladders. As an aid to defense, the traditional design included no doors or windows; entry was through the roof. Two pithouses, or kivas, served as ceremo-

nial chambers and clubhouses. The village plaza, around which all dwellings were clustered, was the spiritual center of the village where all the balanced forces of the world came together.

See also Agriculture; All Indian Pueblo Council; Pueblo Revolt.

Zuni

"Zuni," from the Spanish, is the name of both a people and a pueblo. The Zuni Pueblo's original name was *Ashiwi*, which might have meant "the flesh." The Zuni consisted of six pueblos along the north bank of the upper Zuni River, in western New Mexico, at least 800 years ago. It is presently in the same location. Perhaps as many as 20,000 lived there in 1500. Zuni is a language unlike that spoken at other pueblos. Scientists speculate as to a possible link to the Penutian language family.

Zunis and their ancestors, the Mogollon and the Ancestral Puebloans, and perhaps Mexican Indians as well, have lived in the Southwest for well over 2,000 years. By the eleventh century, the "village of the great kiva," near Zuni, had been built. In the fourteenth and fifteenth centuries a large number of villages existed in the Zuni Valley. By 1650 the number of Zuni villages had shrunk to six.

Zuni was probably the first Native North American village visited by Spaniards, who had heard tales of great wealth in the Kingdom of Cibola. In 1539, Estavinico, a black man in the advance guard of Fray Marcos de Niza's party, visited Zuni. He was killed as a spy, and his group quickly retreated. The following year, Francisco Vasquez de Coronado visited the pueblos, ranging all the way to present-day Kansas in search of the mythical Cibola. The Zunis resisted his demands and fled to a nearby mesa top. Other Spanish came in Coronado's wake. The first mission was established at Hawikuh in 1629. In 1632, the Zunis attacked and killed a number of missionaries, but the Spanish built a new mission, Halona, in 1643.

The Zuni participated in the Pueblo Revolt of 1680. Their main grievances were being forced to supply the Spanish with corn, women, and labor and being punished harshly for practicing their religion. At that time the Zunis lived in three of the original six pueblos. They fled to escape the Spanish, and in 1693 returned to the village at Halona on the Zuni River. A new church was built there, but shortly

abandoned, the Zunis preferring their own religion to Christianity. The ancient site of Halona is now modern Zuni.

Left on their own by the Spanish, the Zuni Pueblo was open to raids from Apaches, Navajos, and Plains tribes. As of 1850, it was still self-sufficient, although, because it was on important trade routes, it was increasingly raided by both Indians and Anglos. The U.S. government officially recognized a Zuni Reservation in 1877, although one far too small to support traditional agriculture. Three outlying summer villages established in the early nineteenth century became permanent in the 1880s, and a fourth such village was established in 1912 or 1914. In the late nineteenth and early twentieth centuries the Zuni economy shifted from agriculture to sheep and cattle herding. With the decline of warfare, their Bow society turned to warfare against supposed Zuni witches. The Bureau of Indian Affairs soon called in troops to suppress witchcraft trials, destroying the power of the Bow priests and the entire traditional government.

The opposition of tribal members as well as the failure of the government's Black Rock Reservation and Dam combined to block the implementation of the allotment process at Zuni. Erosion of arable land has been a considerable problem, especially since the debacle of counterproductive, government-mandated canal irrigation projects in the early twentieth century. By the 1930s, the government was promoting livestock as an alternative to agriculture. After World War II, the continuing shift in political power from priests to politicians led to the growth of political parties and the increased importance of the tribal council.

Religion, including membership in religious and ceremonial organizations, was at the core of Zuni existence. The sun priest was highly revered: In charge of solstice ceremonies as well as the calendar, he was held responsible for the community's welfare. The Zunis recognized six points of orientation, which corresponded to the cardinal directions as well as mythological events. Each had its own color, position, kiva group, medicine societies and priesthoods, and ceremonies. Kivas were rectangular and aboveground.

Katsinas, or benevolent guardian spirits, played a key part in Zuni religion. Katsinas represented the rain gods as well as Zuni ancestors. All boys between the ages of eleven and fourteen underwent initiation into the Katsina Society. At death, one was said to join the katsinas, especially if one was closely

A group of six Zuni men pose for a photograph in 1879. (National Archives and Records Administration)

associated with the cult. Both men and women could join the curing cult of the beast gods. Its focus was on animals of prey who lived in the east.

The Zuni new year began at the winter solstice. A twenty-day period during this time was known as *Itiwana*, or cleansing and preparing the village for the new year. Winter dances took place from February through April. Summer dances began at the solstice and lasted into September, concluding with the fertility ritual called Olowishkia. In late November or early December the Zunis celebrated Shalako, a reenactment by katsina priests of the creation and migration of the Zuni people. The people built six to eight Shalako houses and attended the Shalako katsinas—giant-sized messengers of the rain gods. This festival was accompanied by spectacular dancing and closed the Zuni year. Molawai, or the ritual dramatization of the loss and recovery of corn maidens, immediately followed Shalako.

Ruled by heads of various priesthoods and societies, the Zuni pueblo was a theocracy. Bow priests enforced the rules from at least the seventeenth

century on. A tribal council played a minor role in the nineteenth century but a more powerful one in the twentieth century. The Zunis accepted the Indian Reorganization Act (IRA) and an elected tribal council in 1934 (they ratified a constitution in 1970).

During the eighteenth century, a parallel, secular government developed at Zuni to handle mundane problems. Based on the Spanish model, it was appointed by and responsible to the religious leaders. Offices included a governor, two lieutenant governors, a sheriff, and fiscales (church assistants). These officers acted as liaisons between the pueblo and the outside world and kept order within the pueblo. Metal-topped canes with a Spanish cross served as symbols of authority. Through the years, these were augmented by more Spanish canes, Mexican canes, and then canes given by President Lincoln to reward the pueblo for its neutrality in the Civil War.

Zunis were divided into two groups: people of the north (also characterized as winter or rain) and people of the south (also characterized as summer or sun). Matrilineal clans affected ceremonial roles and certain behaviors. In general, however, ritual activity went through the father's family, and economic activity went through the mother's. There were also a number of secret cults and societies, some highly complex, each responsible for certain ceremonies. Zunis traditionally cremated their dead. In modern times the dead are buried, with their possessions burned or buried after four days, following a ceremony that includes prayer sticks and cornmeal. With the exception of certain clan and family taboos, marriage was a matter between the two people involved and was traditionally preceded by a trial period of cohabitation. Divorce was simple and easy.

Like other Pueblo Indians, Zunis lived in multistoried houses (pueblos). Men built the structures of stone and plaster, not the adobe bricks used in the pueblos to the east. Ladders led to the upper stories. Floors were of packed adobe and roofs of willow boughs, brush, and packed earth. Women kept the outsides whitewashed. Tiny windows and outside beehive ovens were introduced in the sixteenth century.

Farming was the chief Zuni mode of subsistence. Men grew at least six varieties of corn plus beans, squash, and cotton. The Spanish introduced crops such as wheat, chilies, oats, and peaches. Zunis used dams and sage windbreaks for irrigation. Corn was dried, ground into flour or meal, and served as mush or baked into breads. Food was also obtained by hunting (deer, antelope, and rabbits), fishing, and gathering wild plants (women were the gatherers, and they also kept small garden plots).

See also Agriculture; All Indian Pueblo Council; Katsinas; Pueblo Revolt.

Native Americans of California

Achumawi

"Achumawi" means "River People," who are also known, occasionally with the Atsugewis, as Pit River Indians, from their practice of hunting deer by means of pitfalls. These people were organized into eleven bands and shared several cultural characteristics of Indians of the Great Basin. With the Atsugewis, their language made up the Palaihnihan branch of the Hokan language family.

The Achumawis traditionally lived in the northeastern part of the region, from Mount Shasta and Lassen Peak to the Warner Range. This area of tremendous ecological diversity yielded a huge variety of foods, medicines, and raw materials. In the 1990s, Pit River Indians live on their own or shared reservations and rancherias, plus Pit River trust lands, in Modoc, Shasta, Mendocino, Lassen, and Lake Counties in California.

The Achumawi people were composed of about nine tribes. Though autonomous, each was connected by language, culture, and intermarriage. Chiefs were chosen on the basis of popularity, ability, and possession of supernatural powers.

At puberty, boys usually went to mountain retreats in search of a spirit vision that would bestow supernatural powers. They also had their noses pierced. On the occasion of their first menstrual period, girls sang, danced, and feasted with the community all night for ten days. This activity was repeated for nine days on the second month, eight on the third, and so on until the tenth month, when they were considered women.

Corpses were cremated and all their former possessions burned. Mourners cut their hair, darkened their faces with pitch, and refrained from speaking the name of the dead. The soul was said to head for the western mountains. When a chief died, two or three less-liked members of the tribe were sometimes killed to provide the chief with traveling companions.

When within earshot, people were generally addressed by their kin terms, not by their names. Gifts exchanged at marriage were regarded as a price for both spouses. If a married person died, the surviving spouse could still be obligated to marry another suitable person in that family. As with many North American Indians, the Achumawis played the hand game, as well as engaging in shinny (a variation of hockey), wrestling, and footraces.

Conical three-season houses were made of tule mats over a light pole framework. Wood frame winter houses were built partly underground and covered with grass, bark, or tule and a layer of earth. Both were entered by means of a ladder through the smoke hole.

The environmentally diverse Achumawi territory, which ranged from mountains to lowland swamps, contained a great variety of foods. The Achumawis regularly burned the fir and pine uplands, meadows, and grasslands to augment this richness. The fires stimulated the growth of seed and berry plants, made insects available for collecting, and drove game into accessible areas.

Food staples included fish, such as salmon, trout, bass, pike, and catfish; crawfish; and mussels. Waterfowl were caught with nets, and the people ate the eggs as well. Other important foods included

acorns, tule sprouts, various seeds, berries, roots and bulbs, and insects and their larvae. Game included deer, antelope, bear, beaver, badger, coyote, and a variety of small mammals.

Bow wood was either juniper or yew. Most points and blades were made from obsidian. Other building materials included bone and stone, including antler. Baskets were made for a number of purposes, including fish traps. The Achumawis made five kinds of tule or milkweed nets. Tule was used for many other products, including mats, twine, shoes, and rafts. Fire drills were made of juniper. Sometimes the people used a cedar rope as a slow-burning match. They also made juniper snowshoes.

Clothing included shirts, skirts, belts, caps, capes, robes, leggings, moccasins, and dresses. Clothing was made primarily of deer, badger, coyote, and antelope skin and shredded juniper bark. Colored minerals were used to decorate both objects and people.

The slave-raiding Modocs were a traditional enemy of the Achumawis. Instead of retaliating in kind, they usually hid out until the raiders went away. Weapons included elk hide armor and shields and arrows poisoned with rattlesnake venom.

Trappers entering Achumawi territory in 1828 made little impact. However, the flood of non-Natives after the gold rush provoked Achumawi resistance, which was brutally repressed by state and private militias as well as extralegal vigilantes. By the end of the century, several hundred Achumawis had been forced onto the Round Valley Reservation. Some remained in their traditional lands, however. Their acquisition of individual allotments after 1897 helped them to retain their band ties and some subsistence activities.

Most of these allotments were lost in the early twentieth century to Pacific Gas and Electric. Major health problems plagued the Achumawi Indians in the 1920s. Seven small rancherias were created between 1915 and 1938. In 1938, some Achumawi families settled on the 9,000-acre XL Ranch. As late as the 1950s, the Achumawis still retained much of their ancient knowledge and carried on a form of their aboriginal existence. It was mostly younger people who began a new activism in the 1960s, focused on the issues of sovereignty and land usurpation. The Pit River Tribe received federal recognition in 1976.

See also Demographics, Historical; Land, Identity and Ownership of, Land Rights.

Barbariño

See Chumash.

Cahto

"Cahto" is northern Pomo for "lake," referring to an important Cahto village site. The Cahtos called themselves *Djilbi*, the word in their language for that same lake and village. The Cahtos are sometimes referred to as Kaipomo Indians. The Cahtos' homeland is in northwest California, south of Rattlesnake Creek, north of the North Fork of the Ten Mile River, and between the South Fork of the Eel River and just west of the Eel River (more or less the Long and Cahto Valleys). Today, most Cahtos live in Mendocino County. Cahto was an Athapaskan language.

Like other Indian people who were overwhelmed by the sheer numbers and brutality of non-Native Californians in the 1850s, the Cahtos fought back for a brief period before being defeated. Their population declined by some 95 percent during the nineteenth century. The town of Cahto was founded in 1856, the same year reservations were created at Round Valley and Fort Bragg in Mendocino County. The town of Laytonville was established in 1880.

Cahtos prayed frequently, in part to two original beings: Nagaicho, or Great Traveler, and Tcenes, or Thunder. They also followed the Kuksu cult, which involved the acquisition of spiritual power through direct contact with supernatural beings. Tribal and intertribal ceremonies were held in winter (such as the Acorn Dance) and summer. A host who had enough food to share invited his neighbors. Then there was dancing for a week, the creation story was told, and the headman made speeches.

The Cahtos lived in approximately fifty villages. Although most were completely autonomous, six in Long Valley were united to the extent that they called themselves Grass Tribe. Each village was led by a headman or two. His authority was mainly advisory, and he was generally succeeded by his son.

Marriage was generally a matter between the couple involved, although girls were generally prepubescent when married. The Cahtos practiced polygyny as well as the taboo that prevented a man from addressing his mother-in-law directly. Divorce was easily obtained for nearly any reason. Unlike many California Indians, pregnant Cahto women

observed no food taboos. Deformed children and twins were killed at birth.

The six-day girls' puberty ceremony included dietary taboos and then a quiet life for five subsequent months. Boys, at puberty, remained in the dance house all winter to receive admonitions regarding proper behavior; "ghosts" also sang and danced for this purpose. Corpses were buried with their valuables or cremated if away from home. Both men and women mourners cut their hair, and women put pitch on their bodies.

Adult games included shinny, the grass game, stone throwing, and races. Children's games included camping, skipping rope, and playing with acorn tops. Women enjoyed singing in chorus around an evening fire. The Cahtos danced solely for pleasure as well as for ceremonial reasons. Pets included birds, coyotes, and rabbits.

The Cahtos knew three types of shamans: sucking doctors, bear doctors, and singing and dancing doctors. Bear doctors were said to be strong enough to kill enemies of the Cahtos. Various ceremonies, including magic, were practiced before all important events, such as hunting, war, birth, and funerals. Men owned hunting and war items; women owned their clothing, baskets, and cooking rocks. Men generally hunted and fished. Women gathered all foods except acorns; gathering acorns was a communal activity.

Living houses, which were privately owned by up to three families, were built over two-foot-deep pits. Slabs, bark, or earth covered wood rafters, which in turn rested on four poles. Most houses were rebuilt after two years as a vermin-control measure. Larger villages contained similarly built but larger dance houses.

Acorns, salmon, and deer served as food staples. Other important foods included other fish; bear; mink, raccoon, and other small game; birds; and some insects. Meat was generally broiled over coals or on a spit. The Cahtos also ate a variety of seeds, tubers, and berries. They also used domesticated dogs to help them hunt.

Stone, bone, and shell were the primary tool materials. Baskets were usually twined but sometimes coiled. Hunting tools included traps, snares, bows, arrows, slings, nets, and harpoons. Fish were sometimes poisoned. Musical instruments included whistles, rattles, a foot drum, a musical bow, and a six-hole elderberry flute.

The Cahtos were particularly friendly with the northern Pomos. Some Cahtos even spoke Pomo in addition to their own language. In addition to regular trade with the northern Pomos, the Cahtos gathered shellfish and seaweed in Coast Yuki territory. They also supplied these people with hazelwood bows in exchange for items such as salt, mussels, seaweed, abalone, sea fish, clamshells, and dried kelp. They traded arrows, baskets, and clothing to the Wailakis in exchange for dentalia. They also supplied clam disk beads to the Lassiks and received salt from the northern Wintuns, as well as dogs from an unknown location to the north.

Men and women dressed in a similar fashion. They both wore tanned deerhide aprons. They also wore long hair and used iris nets. Both wore bracelets, nose and ear ornaments, and occasionally tattoos.

The Cahtos seldom engaged in large-scale warfare. There were, however, frequent conflicts with the Sinkyones, Yukis, northern Pomos, Wailakis, and Huchnoms, generally over murder or trespass. When fighting occurred, close fighting was avoided whenever possible. War dances were held before each battle. Weapons included the bow and arrow, deer hide sling, and spear. All casualties were indemnified following the fighting.

See also Dams, Fishing Rights, and Hydroelectric Power; Warfare, Intertribal.

Cahuilla

"Cahuilla" is perhaps derived from the Spanish *kawiya*, or "master." The Cahuillas refer to themselves as *Iviatim*, or "speakers" of their Native language. In the eighteenth century, the Cahuillas lived generally southwest of the Bernardino Mountains, ranging over a territory including several distinct environmental zones, from mountain ranges to canyons to desert (11,000 feet to 273 feet). Today they live on ten reservations in Southern California. Cahuilla was a language from the Cupan subgroup of the Takic division of the Uto-Aztecan language family.

The Cahuilla population may have numbered as many as 10,000 in the seventeenth century, with roughly 5,000 remaining by the late eighteenth century. In 1990, the total Indian population of all reservations on which Cahuillas lived, including those they shared with other peoples, was 1,276.

Religiously, the Cahuillas recognized a supreme power, neither good nor bad, but unpredictable. According to their worldview, the entire universe and everything in it were interconnected. Cahuillas performed a large number of rituals. The most significant ones were an annual mourning ceremony, the eagle ceremony (honoring a dead chief or shaman), rite of passage rituals, and food-related rituals. Song cycles were a key part of Cahuilla ritual. They sought to reaffirm the people's place in the universe and their connections with the past and with all things. Ceremonial implements included rattles, headdresses, wands, eagle-feathered skirts, and especially the *máyswut,* a ceremonial bundle.

The Cahuillas lived in about fifty villages aboriginally. The political unit was the clan, or a group of between three and ten lineages. Each clan had a leader, usually hereditary, called the *nét.* This person had religious, economic, and diplomatic as well as political responsibilities. The *nét* also had an assistant.

Háwayniks knew and sang the ceremonial songs, including the long song cycles. Shamans (always male) had much power, including curing, through the control of supernatural power. They also controlled the weather; guarded against evil spirits; and, with the *néts,* exercised political authority. Strong as it was, however, the shaman's authority was maintained only by regular public displays of power.

The Cahuillas recognized two societal divisions, Wildcat and Coyote, each composed of a number of patrilineal clans. Female doctors complemented male shamans as curers; their methods included the use of medicinal plants and other knowledge. When a person died, the spirit was believed to travel to the land of the dead; from there, it could still be involved in the lives of the living. Old age was venerated, largely because old people taught the traditional ways and values, which were themselves venerated.

Reciprocity and sharing were two defining values. The Cahuillas frowned upon hasty behavior; conversely, it was appropriate to do things slowly, deliberately, and cautiously. They enjoyed regular interaction, including intermarriage, with other Indian groups such as the Gabrieleños and Serranos.

Although each extended family had a village site and resource area, land away from the village could be owned by anyone. Mens' games were based on endurance and the ability to withstand physical punishment. Women's games included

footraces, juggling, cat's cradle, top spinning, and balancing objects. People often bet on games.

Cahuilla songs contained tribal history and cosmology, and they accompanied all activities. Singing was common. Bathing and cleanliness in general were important. Spouses were selected by parents from the opposite division. Divorce was difficult to obtain. Everyone observed specific rules of deference and behavior toward other people.

Six varieties of acorns constituted a key food source. Other gathered food included pine nuts, mesquite and screwbeans, and a huge variety of cactus, seeds, berries, roots, and greens. Other plants were used in construction and for medicinal purposes. Rabbit, deer, antelope, rodents, mountain sheep, reptiles, and fowl were all hunted, and fish were taken. Meat was roasted, boiled, or sun-dried in strips, with the bones then cracked for marrow or ground and mixed with other foods. Blood was drunk fresh or cooked and stored. Some Cahuilla bands practiced agriculture, although this was a less important activity.

The Cocopah–Maricopa Trail, a major trade route, bisected Cahuilla territory. Two other trade routes, the Santa Fe and the Yuman, passed close by. Cahuillas traded mostly with the Mojaves, Halchidomas, Ipais, Tipais, Luiseños, Serranos, and Gabrieleños. The Cahuillas traded food products, furs, hides, obsidian, and salt for shell beads, minerals such as turquoise and tourmaline, Joshua tree blossoms, axes, and other crafts. Rituals and songs were also exchanged.

Women wore basket hats as well as skirts of mescal bark, tule, or skins. Men wore breechclouts of the same material when they wore anything at all. Both men and women wore sandals of mescal fibers soaked in mud and tied with mescal fibers or buckskin. Babies wore mesquite-bark diapers. Blankets or woven rabbit skin robes were used for warmth.

New diseases and elements of Spanish culture probably preceded the physical arrival of the Spanish, which occurred when the Juan Bautista de Anza expedition arrived in 1774. The Cahuillas were at first hostile to the Spanish. Since most routes to the Pacific at that time were by sea, the two groups had little ongoing contact, except that a few Cahuillas were baptized at nearby missions.

By the early nineteenth century, some Cahuillas worked seasonally on Spanish cattle ranches, and aspects of Spanish culture such as cattle, wage labor, clothing, and language had significantly changed the traditional Cahuilla lifestyle. The latter maintained

their autonomy until the severe smallpox epidemic of 1863. After 1877, they moved slowly onto reservations. Although initially self-supporting, they grew increasingly dependent on the Americans.

After 1891 the federal government took a much more active role in their lives. Government schools trained Cahuillas to perform menial tasks; influential Protestant missionaries suppressed Native religion and culture; allotment under the Dawes Act (1886) destroyed their agricultural capabilities; and Indian Service personnel controlled their political activities, under protest. From roughly 1891 through the 1930s, Cahuillas farmed, raised cattle, worked for wages, sold peat and asbestos, and leased their lands for income. The lack of water was a chronic obstacle to economic activities. Their tourist industry, especially that of the Agua Caliente Band, also dates from the 1920s.

Following World War II, partial termination and the severe curtailment of government services forced the Cahuillas to take a much more active role in their welfare. Renewed federal programs in the 1960s, in combination with a vitalized tribal political structure, led to a general increase in the quality of life for most Cahuillas.

> *See also* Disease, Historic and Contemporary; Gambling; Reservation Economic and Social Conditions.

Chilula

See Hupa.

Chukchansi

See Yokuts.

Chumash

"Chumash," a label chosen by an Anglo anthropologist, comes from the word used by the Coastal Chumash for either the Santa Cruz (*Mi-tcú-mac*) Indians or the Santa Rosa (*Tcú-mac*) Indians. Each Chumash regional group—Barbareños, Ynezeños, and Ventureños (eastern coastal); Obispeños and Purisimeños; Island Chumash; and Interior Chumash—has its own self-designation. The Chumash are sometimes referred to as the Santa Barbara Indians. At least six separate groups spoke related Hokan languages: Barbareños, Ventureños, Ynezeños, Purisimeños, Obispeños, and the Island language.

Traditionally, the Chumash lived along the Pacific Coast from San Luis Obispo to Malibu Canyon and inland as far as the western edge of the San Joaquin Valley. There were also Chumash Indians on the Santa Barbara Channel islands of San Miguel, Santa Rosa, Santa Cruz, and Anacapa. Today, the Santa Ynez band lives at and near Santa Ynez, California. The Chumash population was between roughly 10,000 and 18,000 in the late eighteenth century. In 1990, 213 Indians lived on the Santa Ynez Reservation.

The Chumash were organized by village rather than by tribe. Villages were led by chiefs; their limited authority was based on heredity and wealth. Coast villages maintained patrilineal descent groups. Each contained three or four captains, one of whom was head chief. Women could inherit the position of head chief. A chief's formal power was limited to leading in war, presiding at ceremonies, and granting hunting permissions.

After a mourning ceremony, the dead were buried face down (face up on the islands), head to the west, and in a flexed position. Graves were marked with rows of wood or stone. Some babies may have been killed at birth. Also, babies' noses were flattened after birth. At the onset of puberty, girls were subject to dietary restrictions, and boys were given a strong liquor to induce visions. Brides were purchased with gifts. Adultery was taboo, and only a few highly placed men could have more than one wife.

Many people smoked tobacco. Coastal people were generally gentle and slow to anger. Punishment was rare. Transvestitism was common and even esteemed. On the coast, people had more time for games, singing, and dancing

The Chumash lived in rancheria-style villages. Their houses, some of which were as large as fifty feet in diameter, were domed. They were built on poles bent inward and covered with grass. A hole in the roof let light in and smoke out. Houses in the interior were generally smaller. Reed mats covered frame beds. Reeds were also used for floor coverings, partitions, and mattresses. Other structures included storehouses, sweat houses, and ceremonial ramadas.

Live oak acorns were a staple, although fish, shellfish, and marine mammals were more

important for coastal and island Chumash. The people also hunted game such as mule deer, coyote, and fox and gathered pine nuts, cherries, and a variety of roots, bulbs, seeds, and berries.

The Chumash hunted with bow (sinew-backed) and arrow, snares, and deadfalls. They fished with seines, dip nets, and hook and line, killing larger fish and sea mammals with harpoons. They carved wood plates, bowls, and boxes; they wove water baskets and sealed them from the inside with asphaltum. Coastal residents fashioned stools of whale vertebrae.

Other cooking items and tools were made of stone, especially steatite. Musical instruments included elder wood or bone flutes, whistles, and rattles. The Chumash had no drums. For water transportation they used a *tomol*, or planked canoe. Abalone shell was used for inlay work. In general, material culture was less developed away from the coast.

Trade was active with nearby tribes. The mainland Chumash provided steatite, asphaltum, fish, wooden vessels, beads, and shells, in exchange for black pigment, antelope and elk skins, piñon nuts, obsidian, salt, beads, seeds, and herbs.

Cumash fine arts included baskets, sea animals carved in wood and soapstone, and, from roughly 1000 to 1800, ceremonial rock paintings. The latter were generally abstract but also contained highly stylized life forms. The circle was a basic theme. Rock paintings were especially well developed in mountainous regions, although the arts were generally less so away from the coast.

The Chumash are the only Native North Americans who built boats out of planks. They split cedar logs with antler or whalebone wedges and smoothed the lumber with shell and stone tools. Planks were lashed together with sinew or plant fibers and then caulked with asphaltum. The resulting boats had twelve- to thirty-foot double-bowed hulls and were moved with double-bladed paddles. They carried a crew of four and were quite oceanworthy; they traveled at least as far as San Nicholas Island, sixty-five miles offshore.

Most Chumash men wore few or no clothes. Women wore knee-length buckskin skirts ornamented with snail and abalone shell. All wore additional buckskin clothing, blankets, or robes against the cold weather. Men and women tied their long hair with strings interwoven with the hair. They pierced their noses and ears, painted their bodies, and wore shell, bone, and stone necklaces.

Reasons for war included trespass, breach of etiquette, avenging witchcraft, or defense (interior Indian peoples occasionally attacked the coastal Chumash). Rules of engagement were highly formalized. In general, however, the Chumash seldom engaged in actual warfare. The 1824 revolt against the Mexicans stands out as the major historical conflict.

The coastal Chumash were living in their traditional territory by roughly 1000. In 1542, contact was established between the Chumash and the Spanish explorers Juan Cabrillo and Bartolome Ferello. Relations were amiable, and, although the Spanish soon began using the Santa Barbara Channel as a stopover for their trans-Pacific voyages, early impact on the Chumash was minimal.

In 1772 the Franciscans built the San Luis Obispo mission. Other missions followed soon thereafter. The Chumash entered the mission period willingly, and many became completely missionized (turned into farmers, artisans, and Christians). However, for most Indians, missions were places of slave labor. Smallpox and syphilis were major killers, but even the common cold often turned into a deadly disease. Refusing either to give up their traditional ways or to be mistreated by the Spanish missionaries, some Chumash escaped into the hills either before or during the mission period. In 1824, Indians staged a major rebellion at several missions. Many sought sanctuary with the Yokut Indians or at other interior communities. Although many ultimately returned to the missions, many others did not.

Mexico seized control of the missions in 1834. Indians either fled into the interior, attempted farming for themselves and were driven off the land, or were enslaved by the new administrators. Alcoholism soon became a large problem among the Chumash. Many found highly exploitative work on large Mexican ranches. After 1849 most Chumash land was lost due to theft by Americans and a declining population, mainly as a result of the effects of violence and disease. The remaining Chumash began to lose their cohesive identity. In 1855, a small piece of land (120 acres) was set aside for just over 100 remaining Chumash Indians near Santa Ynez mission. This land ultimately became the only Chumash reservation, although Chumash individuals and families also continued to live throughout their former territory in southern California.

Chumash cemeteries along Santa Barbara Channel were looted extensively in the 1870s and 1880s.

By 1900, disease combined with intermarriage had rendered the Chumash culture virtually extinct.

See also Dams, Fishing Rights, and Hydroelectric Power; Disease, Historic and Contemporary; Pipes, Sacred; Reservation Economic and Social Conditions.

Costanoan

"Costanoan" is from the Spanish for "coast people." The term denotes a language family as opposed to a unified political entity such as a tribe. Costanoans are sometimes referred to as Ohlone, the name of one tribelet. The Costanoans traditionally lived around and south of San Francisco and Monterey Bays and to the east near the central valleys. Today many live in the same area and in Indian Canyon in San Benito County. The Costanoan population was roughly 10,000 in the mideighteenth century and about 200 in the late 1970s. There were probably thousands of Costanoan descendents in the mid-1990s. Costanoan, a group of about eight languages, belongs to the Penutian language family.

The sun was just one of many Costanoan deities that received offerings such as tobacco smoke, as well as seeds, tobacco, shell beads, and feathers. Shamans interpreted their dreams in religious terms, which were often used as a guide for future actions. Shamans also controlled weather and cured disease by sucking out offending disease objects and through the use of herbs. They could also bestow luck in economic pursuits. Much of their power depended on the performance of dances and ceremonies, including the Medicine Man's Dance, Devil's Dance, Coyote Dance, Dove Dance, and Puberty Dance.

Roughly fifty small tribes, each headed by a chief and a council of elders, spoke Costanoan languages. Each tribelet averaged about 200 people. The larger ones, of up to 500 people, had more than one permanent village.

Although men were usually chiefs, women occasionally held the office in the absence of male heirs. The position of chief was hereditary, but subject to village approval. Responsibilities included directing ceremonial, economic, and war activities; feeding visitors; providing for the poor; caring for captured grizzly bears and coyotes; and leading the council of elders. All power was advisory except in time of war. An official speaker also had ceremonial and diplomatic duties.

Costanoans maintained a clan structure as well as a division into two main groups, Deer and Bear. Small gifts given from groom to bride constituted the marriage formalities. The new couple lived in the groom's father's house. Men might have more than one wife. The dead and their possessions were either buried or cremated; their souls were said to journey across the sea. Widows cut or singed their hair, covered their heads with ashes or asphalt, and battered themselves, sometimes seriously.

Music often accompanied religious and mythological ritual. Both sexes underwent puberty rituals: Girls were confined to their houses and observed food taboos; boys used jimsonweed (datura) to seek visions. People played games such as a ball race, shinny (a variation of hockey), hoop-and-pole (in which an arrow was shot through a rolling hoop), dice, and the hand game (a traditional gambling game) and often bet on the results.

Most houses were conical in shape and built of tule, grass, or ferns around pole frames. Some Costanoan people substituted redwood slabs or bark. Sweat houses, used by men and women, were dug into the side of a stream. Large houses or brush enclosures served as dance sites.

Costanoans hunted deer using deer head disguises. They also hunted elk, antelope, bear, mountain lion, waterfowl, small mammals, and reptiles. They caught fish, especially salmon, steelhead, sturgeon, and lamprey in nets and traps. Fish were also speared by the light of a bonfire. Gathered foods included acorns, seeds, berries, nuts, insects, grapes, roots, greens, and honey. The people also ate shellfish as well as beached whales and sea lions.

Costanoans also practiced land management by controlled burning. This activity promoted the growth of seed-bearing plants, consumed dead plant material (a fire hazard), increased the grazing area for game, and facilitated acorn gathering.

Technological innovations among the Costanoans included the use of tule balsa canoes; twined baskets; musical instruments, including bird bone whistles, alder flutes, rattles, and a musical bow; earth ovens (for roasting meat, especially sea lion and whale); a variety of nets for catching rabbits, fish, and fowl; and cage-like traps to capture quail. Milkweed, hemp, or nettle fiber was used for cordage. Bedding was of tule mats and animal skins.

Men often wore no clothes; women wore tule or buckskin aprons. Rabbit skin, deerskin, duck feather,

or otter skin robes were worn in cold weather. Some men wore beards but most plucked facial hair with wooden tweezers or a pair of mussel shells or singed it with a hot coal. Both sexes painted and tattooed their bodies. Ornaments were worn in pierced ears and around the neck.

War was not uncommon among the Costanoan tribes, as well as between the Costanoans and the Esselens, Salinans, and Northern Valley Yokuts. Trespass often provoked hostilities, which began either by prearrangement or by surprise attack. Captives, except young women, were usually killed, their heads displayed on a pike in the village. Raiding parties burned enemy villages. The main weapon was the bow and arrow.

Costanoan ancestors reached the two bay areas in roughly 500. They first encountered non-Natives in the Sebastián Vizcaíno exploring expeditions of 1602. By the late eighteenth century, the Spanish had built seven missions in their territory and forced most Costanoans to join them.

In an effort to stem and reverse their cultural and physical extinction, the Costanoans in the late eighteenth century organized several incidents of armed resistance. Between 1770 and 1832, the Costanoan population fell by more than 80 percent as a result of disease, hardship, and general abuse. Their aboriginal existence disappeared during this time, as their culture and traditional practices were repressed and they mingled and mixed with other Indian peoples, including Esselens, Miwoks, and Yokuts, who were also brought by force to the missions.

After 1835, when Mexico secularized the missions, many Costanoans worked on ranches or tried to return to a hunting and gathering existence. Most, however, had become mixed with non-Natives and other Indians, establishing multiethnic Indian communities in the area. Costanoans were considered ethnologically extinct by the early twentieth century.

However, land claims cases in the 1920s and the 1960s resulted in small monetary payments and, as well, the recognition of Costanoan/Ohlone survival. Also in the 1960s, Costanoan descendents of Mission San José prevented the destruction of a burial ground that lay in the proposed path of a freeway. These people later organized as the Ohlone Indian tribe and now hold title to a cemetery in Fremont, California. A similar situation occurred in 1975, resulting in the establishment of the Pajaro Valley Ohlone Indian Council. In 1911 and again in 1988, individuals received trust allotments that became the Costanoan refuge of Indian Canyon.

See also Basketry; Land, Identity and Ownership of; Land Rights; Pipes, Sacred; Reservation Economic and Social Conditions; Warfare, Intertribal.

Cupeño

"Cupeño" is from the Spanish term for "a person who comes from Kúpa." The Cupeños traditionally lived in a mountainous area at the headwaters of the San Luis Rey River and the San Jose de Valle Valley. Today most Cupeños live on the Pala Reservation in San Diego County. Cupeño belongs to the Cupan subgroup of the Takic family of Uto-Aztecan languages.

Death ceremonies were perhaps the Cupeños' most important. Corpses were burned almost immediately, possessions were burned several weeks or months later, and images of the dead were burned every year or two as part of an eight-day festival. Also, an annual eagle-killing ritual was held in honor of the dead.

Cupeños recognized two divisions, Coyote and Wildcat, and within them a number of patrilineal clans. Each clan owned productive food-gathering sites. Each had a leader, usually hereditary in the male line, as well as an assistant leader. Kúpa and Wilákalpa were the two permanent villages prior to 1902. Each was politically independent. Decisions concerning the entire village were made by consensus of the clan leaders.

Sometimes leaders also served as shamans. Shamans were powerful, feared, and respected. They cured, witched, and divined with supernatural powers acquired in trances and dreams. Parents arranged most marriages, with the boy's parents taking the lead in mate selection, gift giving, and feasting. Girls around age ten underwent a puberty ceremony. The male initiation ceremony occurred between ten and eighteen years of age and probably involved the use of toloache, a hallucinogenic root.

Family houses were conical in shape, built partly underground, and covered with reeds, brush, or bark. Earth sweat houses were also semisubterranean. People used ramadas for ceremonies and domestic chores. Other structures included acorn granaries, mens' sweat houses, and ceremonial lodges.

Acorns, small seeds, berries, cactus fruit, deer, quail, rabbits, and other small mammals constituted the basic Cupeño diet. The Cupeños used a variety of natural materials for their technological needs, including willow or mesquite wood (bows and arrows), grasses (cooking, storage, and carrying baskets), stone (mortars, pestles, manos and metates, arrow straighteners), wood (mortars), clay (pottery for cooking, storage, eating, and pipes), pine pitch (to seal storage bins for food preservation), and mescal (fibers for rope). Other technological innovations included hunting and carrying nets, snares and traps, baking ovens or pits, and musical instruments such as elder flutes, whistles, panpipes, and rattles.

The Cupeños were part of an elaborate southern California network that dealt in economic and ritual items and activities. The Cocopah–Maricopa Trail, a major trade route, as well as the Santa Fe and the Yuman Trails, passed close by. The people traded food products, furs, hides, obsidian, and salt for shell beads, minerals such as turquoise and tourmaline, Joshua tree blossoms, axes, and other crafts. Rituals and songs were also exchanged.

Women wore basket hats as well as skirts of mescal bark, tule, or skins. Men donned breechclouts of the same material when they wore anything at all. Both wore sandals of mescal fibers soaked in mud and tied with mescal fibers or buckskin. Babies wore mesquite-bark diapers. Blankets or woven rabbit skin robes were used for warmth.

Cupeño groups generally feuded over women, trespass, and sorcery. Murder also required retribution. Tactics included ambush or simply chasing away an enemy. Weapons included the bow and arrow (possibly with a poisoned tip), poniard, thrusting sticks, and war club. Forced to resist the missions and Mexican imperialism, the people became more aggressive during the early nineteenth century.

Specific Cupeño customs and identity were derived from neighboring Cahuillas, Luiseños, Ipais, and other groups in a process that began at least 800 years ago. Non-Natives entered the area in 1795. In the early nineteenth century, the Spanish took over Cupeño lands, building a chapel, a health spa, and a meeting place and grazing their cattle. During this period, Indians worked as virtual serfs for Spanish masters.

Juan Antonio Garra, a clan leader, attempted but failed around 1850 to organize a general revolt of all southern California Indians meant to drive out or kill all non-Natives. He was captured by Cahuilla Indians and later shot by a paramilitary court. His village, Kúpa, was also burned. Between 1875 and 1877, the U.S. government created thirteen separate reservations for former "Mission Indians." Around the turn of the century, despite widespread local and even national protest, the California Supreme Court ordered all 250 or so Cupeños to move from their homes at Warner's Hot Springs to the Pala Reservation (Luiseño), awarding title to the former land to a man who was once governor of California. An influential group of non-Natives pressured the government in 1903 to purchase a 3,438-acre ranch for the Cupeños at Pala Valley, now known as New Pala. By 1973 fewer than 150 people claimed Cupeño descent.

See also Reservation Economic and Social Conditions; Trade; Warfare, Intertribal.

Diegueño
See Tipai-Ipai.

Hupa

"Hupa" comes from the Yurok name for the Hoopa Valley. Their self-designation was *Natinook-wa*, "People of the Place Where the Trails Return." The Hupas were culturally and linguistically related to three neighboring groups: the Chilulas, Whilkust, and the North Fork Hupas, who lived mainly to their east. The Hupa traditionally lived along the lower Trinity River, a main tributary of the Klamath, and especially in the Hoopa Valley. The Hoopa Valley Reservation is in this region today. Hupa is an Athapaskan language.

The Hupa celebrated annual World Renewal ceremonies during which shamans performed secret rites and dances such as the White Deerskin Dance and the Jumping Dance. This ceremony was held in specific locations for ten days in late summer or fall. It included a long narrative about Hupa history and the actions of the supernaturals. Wealthy families provided ceremonial regalia. The people also held other ceremonies for seasonal activities, such as the beginning of the salmon run. Two ceremonial divisions, northern and southern, came together in the ancient village of Takimildin, located in the heart of the Hoopa Valley.

An Athapascan Hupa female shaman from northwestern California, poses for a portrait wearing shell headbands, necklace, and holding two baskets, ca. 1923. (Library of Congress)

Curing shamans, whose methods included sucking out illness-causing objects, were almost always women. They charged high fees, which were payable in advance but refundable if the cure failed. People also used family-owned medicines for more minor ailments. Hupas also believed that male sorcerers could find many ways in which to harm a person. They recognized many spirits and supernatural beings but gave them little ritual attention. They did observe numerous daily rituals and taboos and recognized the obligation to maintain a healthy mind-set.

The Hupa recognized no formal political leadership. Instead, people were ranked according to their wealth. The family was a basic unit, but several patrilineally related households formed a larger grouping or a village. The ten to fifteen Hupa villages acted together informally and only for activities like holding religious ceremonies or building communal fish weirs.

According to Hupa tradition, all customs were formed in an earlier, mythological period of the peoples' existence. One notable custom concerned social status, which was defined by inheritable material possessions such as albino deerskins, large obsidian blades, and headdresses decorated with redheaded woodpecker scalps. Money, such as shell currency, was slightly different from material wealth and could be used to pay for items such as a dowry, a shaman's fee, or an indemnity to an injured party. Wealth could theoretically be obtained through hard work, but in practice property was difficult to accumulate and there was little movement through class lines. The legal code stated that every wrong had to be compensated for, usually with money but occasionally with blood. Family and individual wealth and power affected the terms of redress.

When a Hupa died, the body was wrapped in deerskin and buried. Clothing and utensils were placed on top of a plank-lined grave marked with a board. Close relatives cut their hair as a sign of mourning. After five days, souls departed for a dank, dark underworld (the souls of shamans and singers were fortunate to inhabit a pleasant heaven in the sky).

Hupas observed a number of life cycle prohibitions and taboos as well as magic and religious observances. Babies remained in the cradle until they walked and were not formally named at least until age five. Children knew only mild discipline. At age eight or so a boy joined his father in the sweat lodge. Pubescent girls were considered unclean and remained secluded, although girls from wealthier families might have a party to mark the occasion. Girls married at fifteen or sixteen; boys slightly later. A feast and an exchange of gifts marked the occasion. Only rich men could afford more than one wife. Sex was generally avoided for a number of reasons, except during the late summer and fall family camping trips. In case of divorce, which was fairly easy to obtain, the bride price was returned if the couple was childless.

Most men and women worked hard and steadily, although time was set aside for diversions. Men played the hand game; women bet on the mussel shell toss. Other diversions included athletic contests, storytelling, and smoking at bedtime for men. The voice was the most important musical instrument, followed by wooden clappers, bone whistles, and hoof rattles.

For most of the year, Hupas lived in cedar-planked single-family houses built around a square

hole. A stone-lined fire pit sat in the center of the house. Smoke escaped through a hole in the three-pitched roof. Earthen shelves next to the walls served as storage areas. Women and children slept in the family house; men slept in semisubterranean sweat houses, which they also used as clubhouses and workshops. People lived in roofless brush shelters during the autumn acorn-gathering expeditions.

Acorns and fish, especially salmon, were the staples. Women harvested and prepared the former, cooking it into mush or bread. Deer and elk were captured by stalking or driving them into a river and then pursuing them by canoe. Small game was also taken. Other fish included trout, sturgeon, and eel. Fish was sliced thin and smoke-dried for storage or broiled fresh. People also gathered a number of food plants, including berries, nuts, seeds, roots, and greens. They did not eat many birds, reptiles, amphibians (except turtles), insects, and larvae. Hupas rarely lacked for an adequate food supply.

The Hupas never fought together as a tribe. Even villages rarely united for war, which was generally a matter for individuals or families. Hupas kept their conflicts short, few and far between, with few casualties, except for a particularly harsh war with the Yokuts in the 1830s. Favored tactics included ambushes and surprise raids. Weapons included the bow and arrow, spears, stone knives, and rocks. Wooden or hide "armor" was sometimes worn for protection.

Little is known about Hupa pre-contact, although they are culturally related to the Yuroks and the Karuks to the north. They arrived in northern California in roughly 1000. Being fairly isolated, they had little contact with non-Natives until the midnineteenth century. There were few Spanish or Russian inroads or even American trappers. Even in 1849, the Hupas saw some miners but were spared the wholesale displacement experienced by other Natives.

After the 1849 gold rush, settlers flooded the region, but the Hupas held their ground. The construction of a fort in 1858 resulted primarily in some liaisons between soldiers and Hupa women. The government created the Hoopa Valley Reservation in 1864. Because of the relative lack of cataclysmic disruption and the location of a reservation in their traditional homeland, the Hupas were generally able to adjust slowly but steadily to their new situation. The period following World War II brought good jobs as lumberjacks and mill workers as well as the end of the traditional subsistence economy. In the 1970s and

1980s, the United States took control of tribal funds and resources for use at the government's discretion.

See also Reservation Economic and Social Conditions; Warfare, Intertribal.

Jamul Indians

See Tipai-Ipai.

Juaneño

See Luiseño.

Kamia

See Tipai-Ipai.

Karuk

"Karuk" means "upstream," as opposed to the word for their neighbors, "Yurok," which means "downstream." In the midnineteenth century, the Karuks lived on the middle course of the Klamath River in three main clusters of villages. Today, most Karuks live in Siskyou County, California, and in southern Oregon. Karuk is a Hokan language.

The acorn harvest and the salmon run provided occasions for ceremony and celebration. Specific events included the World Renewal dances: the Jumping Dance, held in the spring (associated with the salmon run), and the Deerskin Dances, held in the fall (associated with the acorn harvest and the second salmon run). Both featured priestly rituals, displays of wealth, dancing, and singing.

No political organization or formal leadership existed in the three main clusters of villages, although wealthy men enjoyed a greater degree of influence. The Karuks regulated their community through shared values.

Culturally, the Karuks were very similar to the neighboring Yuroks and Hupas. In fact, they enjoyed especially close marriage and ceremonial ties with the Yurok. Their main values were industry, thrift, and the acquisition, mostly by hunting and gambling, of property such as dentalium shells, red woodpecker scalps, and large obsidian blades. These

forms of wealth were important in and of themselves, not just for their purchasing power.

Woman doctors cured by sucking out the cause of a disease with the help of a pain, an object, recoverable at will, that she kept in her body. Other kinds of doctors of both sexes cured by using medicinal plants. Corpses were buried in a family plot, along with shell money and valuables. Clothing and tools were hung on a fence around the grave. After five days, the soul was said to ascend to a place in the sky (the relative happiness of the afterlife was said to depend on the level of a person's wealth). A dead person's name remained taboo until or unless given to a child.

Crimes were recognized against individuals only (not against society). As such they could be atoned for by making material restitution. Refusal to pay could lead to death. The Karuks considered sex to be an enemy of wealth and did not often engage in it except during the fall gathering expeditions. Sex and children outside of marriage were acceptable in this scheme: "Legitimacy," like almost everything else, had a price. Marriage was basically a financial transaction, as was divorce. A couple lived with the man's parents.

The Karuks observed many daily magical practices and taboos. They also underwent extensive ritualistic preparations for the hunt, including sweating, bathing, scarification, bleeding, smoking their weapons with herbs, fasting, and sexual continence. Games included gambling with a marked stick, shinny, cat's cradle, archery, darts, and the women's dice game.

Dwelling structures (family houses and sweat houses) were made of planks, preferably cedar. Family houses were rectangular and semisubterranean, with an outside stone-paved porch and a stone-lined firepit inside. Doors were small and low. Males from about three years of age slept, sweat, gambled, and passed the time in sweat houses, which women, except for shaman initiates, could not enter.

The Karuk diet consisted mostly of salmon, deer (caught in snares or by hunters wearing deer head masks), and acorns (as soup, mush, and bread). The people also hunted bear, elk, and small game. Meat and fish were usually roasted, although salmon and venison could be dried and stored. The only cultivated crop was tobacco. The following were never eaten: dog, coyote, wolf, fox, wildcat, gopher, mole, bat, eagle, hawk, vulture, crow, raven, owl, meadowlark, blue jay, snake, lizard, frog, caterpillar, and grasshopper.

To catch fish, Karuks stood on fishing platforms holding large dip nets (the platforms were privately owned but could be rented). They also used harpoons and gaffs. They cut planks with stone mauls and horn wedges. Wooden implements included seats, storage boxes, spoons for men (women used mussel shell spoons), and hand drills for making fire. Women wove vegetable fiber baskets, containers, cradles, and caps. Bows were made of yew wood, with sinew backings and strings. Meat and bulbs were roasted in an oven of hot stones.

Hides, usually from deer, and furs were the basic clothing materials. Women wore hides with the hair on to cover their upper bodies, and they wore a double apron of fringed buckskin. They also had three vertical lines tattooed on their chins. Men wore a buckskin breechclout or nothing at all. Both sexes wore buckskin moccasins with elkhide soles and perhaps leggings for rough traveling. Both sexes also wore basketry caps and ear and nose ornaments. They decorated their ceremonial clothing with fringe, shells, and pine nuts. Snowshoes were of hazelwood with iris cord netting and buckskin ties.

There was no war in a real sense, only retaliatory activity that might involve fellow villagers. Casualties were invariably light, and young women who may have been captured were usually returned at settlement time, when every injured party received full compensation. Weapons included yew bows, obsidian-tipped arrows, and elk hide or rod armor vests.

Contact with outsiders was largely avoided until 1850 and the great gold rush. At that time miners, vigilantes, soldiers, and assorted Anglos seized Karuk lands, burned their villages, and massacred their people. Hitherto unknown diseases also decimated their population. Many Karuk were removed to the Hoopa Valley Reservation.

Without a reservation of their own, many survivors drifted away from their traditional lands in search of work. Children were forcibly removed from their families and sent to culture-killing boarding schools. Some people did remain at home, however, and continued to live a lifestyle that included traditional subsistence and religious activities. Ceremonialism fell off after World War II but was reinvigorated beginning in the 1970s.

See also Dams, Fishing Rights, and Hydroelectric Power; Land, Identity and Ownership of, Land Rights; Reservation Economic and Social Conditions.

Konkow

See Maidu.

Konomihu

See Shasta.

Lassik

See Wailaki.

Luiseño

"Luiseño" (L i 's ny) is a name derived from the Mission San Luis Rey. Luiseño Indians who were associated with a nearby mission, San Juan Capistrano, were often referred to as Juaneño Indians. Both of these peoples are included among the groups of so-called Mission Indians. Luiseños and Juaneños belong to the Cupan group of the Takic division of the Uto-Aztecan language family.

The traditional (eighteenth-century) location of the Luiseños was a region of great environmental diversity, along the coast and inland along streams, south of present-day Los Angeles but north of the Tipai-Ipais. Today most Luiseños live on reservations in San Diego and Riverside Counties. The Luiseño population was roughly 10,000 in the late eighteenth century; in 1990, the Luiseño population on their reservations stood at 1,795.

Ritual drama and sacred oral literature controlled their environment and confirmed the Luiseños' place in the world. Ritual offices included chief, assistant chief, shamans, councilors, and members of the Chinigchinich society (most of the men in the village). A large number of ceremonies revolved around hunting, life cycle, weather control, and war and peace. Some ceremonies involved questing for visions with the help of a drink prepared from jimsonweed (datura). Religious knowledge/power was carefully guarded.

Sandpaintings were part of the secret Chinigchinich cult initiation (the cult may have been in part a response to the Spanish presence): The cosmos, sacred beings, and human spiritual phases were all represented. Sandpaintings never lasted beyond the ceremony. Ritual equipment included stone grinding bowls, clay figurines, sacred wands, head scratchers, and eagle-feather headdresses. Most participants in rituals were paid.

The Luiseños were organized into roughly fifty small, patrilineal clan-based tribes, each with an autonomous, semipermanent village led by a hereditary chief. Each village group also had its own food resource area; other resources (raw materials, sacred sites as well as food) could be owned individually or collectively. Trespass was by express permission only.

The chief supervised hunting, gathering, and war activities. He was aided by an assistant, shamans, and a council of advisers (all positions were hereditary). Band specialists managed natural resources using techniques such as controlled burning and water and erosion management. They also led various activities such as rabbit hunts and deer and antelope drives. In the eighteenth century, Spanish-style political offices (such as *generales* and *capitanes*) existed parallel to the traditional religious ones.

In addition to food and other resource areas, private property might include capital and ritual equipment, eagle nests, and songs. Social status was important and defined by many criteria. Aside from hunting (male) and gathering (female), sexual divisions of labor were ill defined. Aged women taught children crafts, whereas older men were generally more active in ceremonial affairs, including the making of hunting and ceremonial paraphernalia, and in instructing initiates. Traditional games included dice, the split stick gambling game, the ball and stick game, and cat's cradle.

The Luiseños observed various life cycle taboos, restrictions, and ritual requirements. Puberty rituals stressed correct conduct, such as dances, ordeals, learning songs and rituals (boys), and rock painting and behavior in married life (girls). Girls married an arranged partner shortly after puberty. Divorce was possible but not easy to obtain. Death ceremonies proliferated. At different times, burning an image of the deceased, purification of the relatives, feasting, and gift giving were all practiced. A person's possessions were generally destroyed when she or he died.

The Luiseños practiced controlled burning of certain areas to increase the yield of seed-bearing plants. They hunted with bow and arrow, throwing sticks, snares, and traps. Men used deer antler flakes to help flake stone points. They built canoes for ocean fishing. Other fishing equipment included seines, basketry traps, dip nets, bone or shell hooks, possibly harpoons, and poison. Utilitarian items

included pottery, coiled and twined baskets, carrying pouches of net or skin, stone grinding tools, cooking and eating utensils of wood and stone, and musical instruments, including bone and cane whistles, cane flutes, split-stick clappers, and turtle shell, gourd, or hoof rattles.

Fine arts included pottery; coiled baskets, decorated with tan, red, or black geometric designs; sandpaintings; petroglyphs, perhaps associated with hunting, from about 500 BCE to 1000; and pictographs, which featured straight and wavy lines, angles, and people. The pictographs were used in girls' puberty ceremonies after about 1400.

Trespass was a major cause for war. The Luiseños were also fairly imperialist, fighting (and marrying) to acquire territory. During war, the chief assumed commander duties along with an initiated warrior class. Weapons included the bow and arrow, small and large war clubs, lances, slings, and thrusting sticks.

The Luiseños constituted a distinct culture from at least 1400 or so. They first encountered non-Natives in 1796, with the Gaspar de Portolá expedition and the founding of Mission San Diego. Shortly thereafter, the Spanish built the missions San Luis Rey and San Juan Capistrano. Many Luiseños were missionized, and many died during this and during the succeeding Mexican and U.S. periods, which were characterized by hardship, disease, and murder.

After Mexican secularization of the missions in 1834, many Indians revolted against their continued exploitation by Mexican rancheros. In general, Luiseño villages maintained their traditional subsistence activities, with the addition of wheat and corn agriculture, irrigation, orchards, and animal husbandry. The United States created several Luiseño reservations in 1875; people either lived there or scattered. The 1891 Act for the Relief of Mission Indians led to the placement of federal administrative personnel on the reservations, including police, schools, and courts. The idea was to undermine the traditional power structure and move the people toward assimilation into mainstream U.S. culture.

Throughout the nineteenth and into the twentieth centuries, Luiseños fought to retain their land and their traditions. For instance, their resistance to government schools culminated in 1895 when a Luiseño burned the school and assassinated the teacher at Pachanga. The Luiseños rejected the Indian Reorganization Act (IRA) of 1934 because it provided for too little home rule. They were finally

forced to abandon once prosperous farms and orchards after precious water supplies were taken by non-Indians living upstream.

Still, federal control of the reservations increased, as did pressure to assimilate. The 1950s brought a partial termination of federal services, which stimulated a resurgence of local self-government and self-determination. This trend accelerated in the 1960s with the arrival of various federal economic programs. Today, the Luiseños are prominent in state and regional Indian groups.

See also Basketry; Pottery; Reservation Economic and Social Conditions; Warfare, Intertribal.

Maidu

"Maidu" describes a group of three languages (Maidu, Konkow, and Nisenan) and in modern times a tribe of Indians. "Maidu" comes from their self-designation meaning "person." "Konkow" comes from the Anglicization of their word for "meadowland." "Nisenan" comes from their self-designation meaning "among us."

Traditional Maidu territory is along the eastern tributaries of the Sacramento River, south of Lassen Peak. This country features a great variation in terrain, from river and mountain valleys to high mountain meadows. Today, most Maidus live on two small reservations in Butte County and share one in Lassen County and one in Mendocino County. Roughly 9,000 Maidus lived in the early nineteenth century. Maiduan is a Penutian language. Its three divisions—northeastern or mountain (Maidu), northwestern or foothill (Konkow), and southern or valley (Nisenan)—were probably mutually unintelligible.

The Maidu religion was closely related to their mythology. Konkows and Nisenans, but not the Maidus proper, practiced the Kuksu cult, a ceremonial and dance organization led by a powerful shaman. Only those properly initiated could join. Members followed a dance cycle in which dances represented different spirits.

Shamans trucked with the spirits, cured, interpreted dreams, and conducted ceremonies. Spirits were said to live in natural geographic sites. A shaman had at least one spirit as a guardian and source of power. Female shamans were assumed to be malevolent.

The Nisenans observed an annual fall mourning ceremony and other ritual dances as well. Doctors could be of either sex, although women were considered less likely to hurt a patient (doctors could also poison people). Religious specialists included religious shamans, poison shamans, singing shamans, and weather shamans.

Of the three main Maidu divisions, the valley people, or Nisenans, had the largest population and the most tribelets (permanent villages). Village communities (consisting of several villages, with sizes in inverse proportion to elevation) were autonomous. The central village had the largest dance or ceremonial chamber, which doubled as a home to the headman. This office, which was inheritable only among the Nisenans, was chosen by a shaman. He or she (women might become chiefs among the Nisenans) was generally wealthy and served primarily as adviser and spokesperson.

The Maidus observed many life cycle taboos and restrictions. Gender roles were fairly rigidly defined. There was no formal marriage ceremony other than mutual gift giving. Couples lived in the woman's home at first and later in a home of their own near the man's family. If a woman gave birth to twins, she and the babies were often killed. The Nisenans practiced cremation; the other two groups buried their dead with food and gifts. All three burned the dead person's house and possessions and held annual mourning ceremonies for several years thereafter.

Most fishing and hunting areas were held in common. Theft from a neighbor was severely punished, although theft from someone of another community was not punished by the home community. Murder and rape were dealt with by blood revenge (of the guilty party or of a near friend or relative) or by payment. Lying was generally avoided. The community policed its boundaries against poachers.

Games include hoop-and-pole (in which an arrow was shot through a rolling hoop), tossing games, dice games, and hand games and often contained wagering, music, and song. Tobacco was their only cultivated plant. It was smoked in elderberry pipes at bedtime and during ceremonies.

Maidus were mainly hunters and gatherers. Their staple was the acorn, from which they made mush, bread, and soup. They also ate pine nuts, manzanita, roots, and insects. Game included deer (hunted in communal drives), elk, antelope, and bear (for hides). Meat was baked, dried, or roasted. Fish included eel, salmon, and trout. Taboo foods among the Maidu proper included coyote, dog, wolf, buzzard, lizard, snake, and frog. Konkows refused to eat bear and mountain lion. The Nisenans ate neither owl, condor, nor vulture. Maidus drank wild mint tea and manzanita cider.

Prior to about 1700, when they abandoned it to the Paiutes, the Maidus also controlled the territory east of Honey Lake into present-day Nevada. Maidus first met Spanish and U.S. expeditions and trappers in the early nineteenth century. Initial contact was peaceful.

The Maidus were relatively successful in avoiding missions, but many were killed in 1833 by a severe epidemic, possibly malaria. The 1849 gold rush led directly to theft of their land, disruption of their ability to acquire food, more disease, violence, and mass murder. Most survivors were forced into ranch and farm work and onto reservations. Although some groups signed a treaty in 1851, it was never ratified; each Maidu received a land claims settlement payment of about $660 in 1971.

The Konkow Reservation was established at Nome Lackee in 1854, but its residents were forced nine years later to abandon it and march to the Round Valley Reservation. The few surviving Nisenans lived near foothill towns and worked in local low-paying industries at that time. Many Maidu children attended assimilationist boarding schools around the turn of the century. Maidu culture underwent a brief revival in the 1870s under the influence of the Ghost Dance. All rancherias were purchased between 1906 and 1937 under legislation providing for "homeless" California Indians. Following the death in 1906 of the last hereditary headman, much of the people's ceremonial regalia were sold to a local museum.

> *See also* Land, Identity and Ownership of, Land Rights; Reservation Economic and Social Conditions.

Mattole

See Wailaki; Wiyot.

Mission Indians

See Cahuilla; Luiseño; Serrano; Tipai-Ipai.

Miwok

"Miwok" is a word meaning "People" in Miwokan. The Miwoks were originally composed of three divisions: Eastern (Sierra), Lake, and Coast. The Miwoks lived in over 100 villages along the San Joaquin and Sacramento Rivers, from the area north of San Francisco Bay east into the western slope of the Sierra Nevada. The Lake Miwoks lived near Clear Lake, north of San Francisco Bay.

Today the Eastern Miwoks live in five rancherias, located roughly between Sacramento and Stockton, and in nearby cities. Lake Miwoks have one small settlement at Middletown Rancheria that they share with Pomo Indians. The Miwok population stood at about 22,000 in the eighteenth century, of whom approximately 90 percent (19,500) were Eastern Miwoks. They spoke several dialects and groups of Miwokan, a California Penutian language.

The lowland occupation of California by the Eastern Miwoks probably began as early as 2,000 years ago or more; occupation of the Sierra Nevada is only about 500 years old. The Eastern Miwoks were divided into five cultural groups: Bay Miwoks, Plains Miwoks, Northern Miwoks, Southern Miwoks, and Central Sierra Miwoks. Sir Francis Drake (1579) and Sebastian Cermeño (1595) may have met the Coast Miwoks, but no further record of contact exists until the late eighteenth century and the beginning of the mission period. Russians also colonized the region in the early nineteenth century.

With regard to religion, Eastern and probably also Coast Miwoks believed in the duality (land and water) of all things. Ceremonies, both sacred and secular, abounded, accompanied by dances held in great dance houses. The ceremonial role of each village in the tribelet was determined by geographical and political considerations. Lake Miwoks allowed only men in the dance houses.

Sacred ceremonies revolving around a rich mythology featured elaborate costumes, robes, and feather headdresses. The Miwoks recognized several different kinds of shamans, such as spirit or sucking shamans, herb shamans (who cured and helped ensure a successful hunt), and rattlesnake, weather, and bear shamans. Shamans, whose profession was inherited patrilineally, received their powers via instruction from and personal acquisition of supernatural power gained through dreams, trances, and vision quests.

The main political units were small tribes, an independent and sovereign nation of roughly 100 to 500 people (smaller in the mountains). Each group was composed of a number of lineages, or settlement areas of extended families. Larger groups, those composed of several named settlements, were led by chiefs, who were usually wealthy. Their responsibilities included hosting guests, sponsoring ceremonies, settling disputes, and overseeing the acorn harvest. In turn, chiefs were supplied with food and were expected to conduct themselves with a measure of grandness.

Among the Lake Miwoks, special ceremonial officials presided over dances. Among the Eastern and Lake Miwoks the office of chief was hereditary and male, if possible. Other officials included the announcer (elective) and messenger (hereditary). The Coast Miwoks also included two important female officials who presided over certain festivals and who supervised the construction of the dance house.

All Eastern Miwoks were members of one of two divisions (land or water). Both boys and girls went through puberty ceremonies. Marriage among Lake Miwoks was a matter arranged by the parents through gift giving. Intermarriage between neighboring groups was common. The many life cycle prohibitions and taboos included sex before the hunt or during a woman's period. Fourth and later infants may have been killed. The dead were cremated or buried. Widows cut their hair and rubbed pitch on their heads. Along the coast, property was burned along with the body. The names of the dead were never spoken again. There were no mourning ceremonies.

Men and occasionally women used pipes to smoke a gathered local tobacco. Miwoks possessed a strong feeling for property: Trespass was a serious offense, and virtually every transaction between two people involved payment. The profession of "poisoner" was widely recognized, and many people feared being poisoned more than they feared illness. People often danced, both for fun and ritual. Most songs were considered personal property. Both sexes played hockey, handball, and traditional grass games. Women also played a dice game. Children played with mud or stick dolls and used acorns and pebbles as jacks.

Miwoks built conical houses framed with wooden poles and covered with plants, fronds, bark, or grasses. Hearths were centrally located, next to an earth oven. Pine needles covered the floors; mats and skins were used for bedding. Some winter homes or dance houses, and most houses among the

Lake Miwoks, were partially below ground. Larger villages had a sweat lodge that served mostly as a male clubhouse.

The Spanish established missions in Coast Miwok and Lake Miwok territory by the early nineteenth century, to which thousands of Miwoks were forcibly removed and where most later died of disease and hardship. In the 1840s, Mexican rancheros routinely kidnapped Lake Miwok people to work on their ranches and staged massacres to intimidate the survivors. As a result of all this bloodshed, previously independent tribelets banded together and even formed military alliances with other groups such as the Yokuts, raiding and attacking from the 1820s through the 1840s.

Everything changed for the Eastern Miwoks in the late 1840s, when the United States gained political control of California and the great gold rush began. Most Miwoks were killed by disease, white violence, and disruption of their hunting and gathering environment. The Mariposa Indian War (1850), led by Chief Tenaya and others, was a final show of resistance by the Eastern Miwoks and the Yokuts against Anglo incursions and atrocities. By the 1860s, surviving Miwoks were eking out a living by mining, farm and ranch work, and low-paying work on the edges of towns. Most Miwoks remained on local rancherias, several of which were purchased for them by the U.S. government in the early twentieth century.

Coast Miwoks remained for the most part in their traditional homeland in the twentieth century, working at sawmills, as agricultural laborers, and fishing. They were officially terminated in the 1950s, but in 1992 a group called the Federated Coast Miwok created bylaws and petitioned the government for recognition.

See also Pipes, Sacred; Reservation Economic and
Social Conditions; Termination.

Monache

See Mono.

Mono

"Mono" or "Monache" is a Yokuts term of uncertain meaning. Also known as the Western Mono, they are *Nimi,* or "People," in their own language.

Before contact with Europeans, the Monos lived in central California along the Sierra Nevada, higher in elevation (by 3,000 to 7,000 feet) than the Foothill Yokuts. Today most Monos live on Big Sandy and Cold Springs Rancherias, with other Indians on the Tule River Reservation, and in several northern California communities. The Mono population stood at roughly 2,500 in the late eighteenth century. Mono is a language of the western group of the Numic family of the Uto-Aztecan language stock.

During the eighteenth century, the Monos included six independent groups (Northfork Monos, Wobonuchs, Entimbichs, Michahays, Waksachis, and Patwishas). They were in general culturally similar to the neighboring Foothill Yokuts. Since they lived in a region not highly desired by miners or non-Native settlers, they enjoyed relatively higher survival rates in the nineteenth century than did most other California Indian peoples.

The Monos believed that spirits contained supernatural powers that might be employed by people with the proper knowledge. Supernatural powers were obtained through a connection with nature or by taking jimsonweed (datura), a drug, as part of a ritual. Although shamans were especially skilled in these techniques, most people thought it a good idea to possess some powers for general success in life. Shamans used their powers for curing. However, they could also hurt or kill, and various evil activities were often ascribed to them.

Ceremonies included bear dances (by members of the Bear lineage) and the annual mourning ceremony. The Monos brought the Ghost Dance of 1870 west of the Sierra Nevada. This phenomenon ended by 1875, largely because it failed to bring back the dead as promised; the 1890 Ghost Dance revival had no impact on the Monos.

Each Mono group was composed of villages or hamlets of between one and eight huts, each led by a (usually hereditary male) chief. Patrilineal lineages, such as Eagle, Dove, Roadrunner, and Bear, were social organizations. The chief (from the Eagle lineage) arranged ceremonies, saw to the needy, and sanctioned the killing of evil shamans or others. He led by suggestion rather than by command. A messenger (Roadrunner lineage) assisted the chief and settled quarrels. They both had a symbol of office, an eight-foot-long cane with red-painted bands and string on top. Only the Northfork Monos had formal intradivision groups (Eagle and Dove), each with its own chief.

A Lake Mono basketmaker, ca. 1924. (Library of Congress)

The Monos built three types of houses: conical with an excavated floor, oval with a ridgepole, and conical with a center pole covered by thatch or cedar bark. Houses were arranged in a semicircle around the village. Most villages also contained a sweat house (male only), an acorn storehouse, and an open area used for dances and ceremonies.

Acorns were the staple food of these hunter-gatherers. They also ate roots, pine nuts, seeds, and berries (and drank cider from manzanita berries). They hunted and trapped deer, bear, rabbits, and squirrels. Good hunters shared their meat. Bears were often killed by blocking egress from their caves and then shooting them. Fish were caught with traps, weirs, nets, and spears.

As "homeless Indians," the Monos received three rancherias from the federal government in the 1910s. Some individuals also acquired parcels of land. Many people retained their traditional subsis-tence gathering patterns while working as loggers, ranch hands, miners, and domestic help. As was the case with many other Indians, a large number of Monos moved to the cities after World War II.

See also Reservation Economic and Social Conditions.

Nisenan

See Maidu.

Nomlaki

See Wintun.

Nongatl

See Wailaki.

Obispeño

See Chumash.

Okwanuchu

See Shasta.

Patwin

See Wintun.

Pit River Indians

See Achumawi.

Pomo

"Pomo," which describes a group of seven culturally similar but politically independent villages or tribelets, is taken from a Pomo word that means roughly "those who live at red earth hole," possibly a reference to a local mineral. Traditionally, the Pomos lived about fifty miles north of San Francisco Bay, on the coast and inland, especially around Clear Lake and the Russian River. Today there are roughly twenty Pomo rancherias in northern California, especially in Lake, Mendocino, and Sonoma Counties. Pomo Indians also live in regional cities and towns.

Roughly 15,000 Pomos lived during the early nineteenth century. The Pomo tongue was actually a group of seven mutually unintelligible Pomoan (Hokan) languages, including Southern Pomo, Central Pomo, Northern Pomo, Eastern Pomo, Northeastern Pomo, Southeastern Pomo, and Southwestern Pomo (Kashaya).

The Pomos' Kuksu cult was a secret religious society, in which members impersonated a god (*kuksu*) or gods in order to obtain supernatural power. Members observed ceremonies in colder months to encourage an abundance of wild plant food the following summer. Dances, related to cur-

ing, group welfare, and/or fertility, were held in special earth-covered dance houses and involved the initiation of ten- to twelve-year-old boys into shamanistic, ritual, and other professional roles. All initiates constituted an elite secret ceremonial society, which conducted most ceremonies and public affairs.

Secular in nature, and older than the Kuksu cult, the ghost-impersonating ceremony began as an atonement for offenses against the dead but evolved into the initiation of boys into the Ghost Society (adulthood). A very intense and complex ceremony, especially among the Eastern Pomos, it ultimately became subsumed into the Kuksu cult.

The Bole-Maru Religion, in turn, grew out of the Ghost Dances of the 1870s. The leader was a dreamer and a doctor, who intuited new rules of ceremonial behavior. Originally a revivalistic movement like the Ghost Dance, this highly structured, four-day dance ceremony incorporated a dualistic worldview and thus helped Indians to step more confidently into a Christian-dominated society.

Other ceremonies included a women's dance, a celebration of the ripening of various crops, and a spear dance (Southeastern, involving the ritual shooting of boys). Shamans were healing or ceremonial professionals. They warded off illness, which was thought to be caused by ghosts or poisoning, protecting individuals as well as the community. Doctors (mostly men) were a type of curing specialist, who specialized in herbalism, singing, or sucking.

The Pomos were divided into small tribes, each composed of extended family groups of between 100 and 2,000 people. Generally autonomous, each tribe had its own recognized territory. One or more hereditary, generally male, minor chiefs headed each extended family group. All such chiefs in a tribelet formed a council or ruling elite, with one serving as head chief, to advise, welcome visitors, preside over ceremonies, and make speeches on correct behavior. Groups made regular military and trade alliances between themselves and with non-Pomos. A great deal of social control was achieved through a shared set of beliefs.

The Pomos ranked individuals according to wealth, family background, achievement, and religious affiliation. Most professions, such as chief, shaman, or doctor, required a sponsor and were affiliated with a secret society. The people recognized many different types of doctors. Bear doctors, for instance, who could be male or female, could acquire extraordinary power to move objects, poison, or

Man in Pomo dance costume, ca. 1924. (Library of Congress)

cure. The position was purchased from a previous bear doctor and required much training. Names were considered private property.

Along the coast, people built conical houses of redwood bark against a center pole. Inland, the houses were larger pole-framed, tule-thatched circular or elliptical dwellings. Other structures included semisubterranean singing houses for ceremonies and councils and smaller sweat pithouses.

The Pomos participated in a vast northern California trade group. Both clamshell beads and magnesite cylinders served as money. People often traded some deliberately overproduced items for goods that were at risk of becoming scarce. One group might throw a trade feast, after which the invited group was supposed to leave a payment. These kinds of arrangements tended to mitigate food scarcities.

Exchange also occurred on special trade expeditions. Objects of interest might include finished products such as baskets as well as raw materials. The Clear Lake Pomos had salt and traded it for tools, weapons, furs, and shells. All groups used

money of baked and polished magnesite as well as strings of clamshell beads. The Pomos could count and add up to 40,000. Pomo baskets were of extraordinarily high quality. Contrary to the custom in many tribes, men assisted in making baskets. Pomos also carved highly abstract petroglyphs beginning about 1600.

Dress was minimal. Such clothing as people wore they made from tule, skins, shredded redwood, or willow bark. Men often went naked. Women wore waist-to-ankle skirts, with a mantle tied around the neck that hung to meet the skirt. Skin blankets provided extra warmth. A number of materials were used for personal decoration, including clamshell beads, magnesite cylinders, abalone shell, and feathers. Bead belts and neck and wristbands were worn as costume accessories and as signs of wealth.

Poaching (trespass), poisoning, kidnapping, or murder of women or children (usually for transgressing property lines), or theft constituted most reasons for warfare. The Pomos occasionally formed military alliances among contiguous villages. Warfare began with ritualistic preparation, took the form of both surprise attacks and formal battles, and could end after the first casualty or continue all the way to village annihilation. Women and children were sometimes captured and adopted. Chiefs of the fighting groups arranged a peace settlement, which often included reparations paid to the relatives of those killed. Hunting or gathering rights might be lost or won as a result of a battle. Pomos often fought Patwins, Wappos, Wintuns, and Yukis. They made weapons of stone, bone, and wood.

Little is known of Pomo pre-contact, except that the people became a part of a regional trading system at about 1500. By the late 1700s, the Spanish had begun raiding Southern Pomo country for converts, and Hispanic influence began to be felt in Pomo country. Russian fur traders also arrived to brutalize the Natives during this time. Their primary method of attracting Indian help was to attack a village and kidnap the women and children, who were then held as hostages (slaves) while the men were forced to hunt fur-bearing animals. In 1811 the Russians established a trading post at Fort Ross, on Bodega Bay (abandoned in 1841).

Hundreds of Pomos accepted the Catholic faith at local Spanish missions after 1817. In 1822, California became part of the Mexican Republic, and Mexicans granted land to their citizens deep within Pomo country and enforced the land grants with strict mil-

itary control. Thousands of Pomos died of disease (mainly cholera and smallpox) during the 1830s and 1840s, and Mexican soldiers killed or sold into slavery thousands more. Deaths from disease were doubly killing: Since the Pomos attributed illness to human causes, as did many Native peoples, the epidemics also brought a concurrent rise in divisive suspicions and a loss of faith in traditions.

A bad situation worsened for the Pomos after 1849, when Anglos flooded into their territory, stealing their land and murdering them en masse. Survivors were disenfranchised and forced to work for their conquerors under slavelike conditions. A number of Pomos—perhaps up to 200—were killed by the U.S. Army in 1850. In 1856, the Pomos were rounded up and forced to live on the newly established Mendocino Indian Reservation. The government discontinued the reserve eleven years later, however, leaving the Indians homeless, landless, and without legal rights.

Later in the century, the Pomos mounted a project to buy back a land base. Toward this end, they established rancherias (settlements) and worked as cheap migrant agricultural labor, returning home in winter to carry on in a semitraditional way. By 1900, however, the Pomos had lost 99 percent of these lands through foreclosure and debt. The remaining population were viewed with hatred by most whites, who practiced severe economic and social discrimination against them. This situation provided fertile ground for Ghost Dance activity and the Bole-Maru (dreamer) Religion, an adaptive structure that may have helped ease their transition to mainstream values.

Missionaries in the early twentieth century worked with Indians to promote Indian rights, antipoverty activities, education, and temperance. By that time, the Pomos had begun using the courts and the media to expand their basic rights and better their situation. A key Supreme Court decision in 1907 recognized the rancherias as Indian land in perpetuity. More Pomo children began going to school; although the whites kept them segregated, the people mounted legal challenges designed to win equal access. After World War I, Indian and white advocacy groups proliferated, and reforms were instituted in the areas of health, education, and welfare. Indians gained a body of basic legal rights in 1928.

During the 1930s, the Depression forced a return to more traditional patterns of subsistence, which led to a period of relative prosperity and revitalization. At the same time, contact with other, non-Indian migratory workers brought new ideas about industry and labor organization to the Pomos. Intermarriage also increased. Women gained more independence and began to assume a greater role in religious and political affairs about this time.

After World War II, the United States largely relinquished its role in local Indian affairs to the state of California, which was unprepared to pick up the slack. Several rancherias were terminated, and services declined drastically, leading to a period of general impoverishment. Since the 1950s, however, various Indian groups have been active among the Pomos, helping them to become more politically and economically savvy, and some state agencies have stepped in to provide services. The Clear Lake Pomos were involved in the takeovers of Alcatraz Island in 1969–1971, reflecting their involvement in the pan-Indian movement. Beginning in the 1970s, many Pomo bands successfully sued the government for recognition, on the grounds that Bureau of Indian Affairs (BIA) promises of various improvements had not been kept.

See also Bole-Maru Religion; Ghost Dance Religion; Land, Identity and Ownership of, Land Rights; Trade.

Purisimeño

See Chumash.

Salinan

The Salinans consisted of two divisions: Northern (Antoniaño) and Southern (Migueleño). A third division, extreme Coastal, may also have existed. The people traditionally lived along the south central California coast, inland to the mountains. Today's Salinan descendents live mainly in the Salinas Valley between Monterey and Paso Robles. Salinan was a Hokan language.

The Salinans offered prayer to the golden eagle, the sun, and the moon. Shamans controlled the weather. Souls went to a western land of the dead. Initiation into religious societies was important, probably in the context of the Kuksu and/or the toloache (a hallucinogenic root) cults.

Clans as well as a Deer–Bear ceremonial division may have existed in aboriginal times. Although generosity with property was considered a virtue,

loans of currency came with high rates of interest. Girls did not undergo a formal puberty ceremony. The boys' puberty ceremony involved the use of jimsonweed (datura, which was also used for pain relief). Although the Salinans observed no formal marriage ceremony, marriage was formalized by gift giving and other customs, and divorce was relatively easy to obtain. The dead were cremated. The people played a traditional bone game, shinny, ball races, games of strength, and possibly hoop-and-pole (in which an arrow was shot through a rolling hoop) games. Shamans cured. They also poisoned and specialized in black magic. Medical treatments included bleeding, scarification, herbs, and sweat baths.

Both coiled and twined baskets were used for a number of purposes. Stone tools included scrapers, choppers, points, mortars, pestles, and bowls. Bone and shell tools included awls, wedges, and fishhooks. Wooden tools included mortars, combs, and spoons. Musical instruments included cocoon rattles, elderwood rattles and flutes, musical bows, rasps, bone whistles, and drums. The Salinans also had calendars, numerical and measuring systems, and some knowledge of astronomy. They cooked basket-leached acorn meal in an earth oven.

The Salinans and Yokuts enjoyed friendly relations, including visiting, mutual use of resources, and trade. The former traded beads and unworked shells for salt-grass salt, seeds, obsidian, lake fish, and possibly tanned hides. They also traded with other groups for wooden dishes, steatite vessels, and ornaments. Trade competition for the inland market for shells led to much enmity, particularly with the Costanoans. Beads of mussel and shell formed the basis of a local currency.

In 1771 the Spanish constructed San Antonia de Padua, the first mission in Salinan territory. By 1790 this was the largest mission in California. Mission San Miguel followed in 1797 and also expanded rapidly. Under some pressure, most Salinans abandoned their aboriginal customs and became acculturated to mission life. After 1834 and the secularization of the missions, the Salinan experienced a rapid depopulation, primarily as a result of intermarriage and assimilation. Survivors either worked on the large rancheros or else remained in their original homeland as small-scale ranchers and hunters and gatherers. By the 1880s, most of the few remaining Salinans worked on the large cattle ranches that spread throughout the area, retaining a memory of their Indian heritage as well as close contact with each other. Until the 1930s there was a Salinan community not far from Mission San Antonia known as The Indians. The Northern division of Salinans became associated with the former mission; the Southern with the latter mission.

See also Basketry; Trade.

Santa Barbara

See Chumash.

Serrano

"Serrano" is a name taken from the Spanish term for "mountaineer" or "highlander." During the late eighteenth century, the Serranos lived in small, autonomous villages, near water sources in the San Bernardino Mountains and Mojave Desert. Today most live mainly on two reservations in Riverside and (especially) San Bernardino Counties in California. The Serrano population stood at roughly 2,000 in the late eighteenth century. The Serrano language belongs to the Takic division of the Uto-Aztecan language family and includes languages such as Kitanemuk, probably Vanyume, and possibly Tataviam.

The Serranos recognized a hierarchy of supernatural beings and spirits. Shamans conducted their ceremonies and acquired their powers through dreaming and datura-induced visions.

Autonomous lineages, the main political unit, claimed specific local territory. Larger social units included clans, headed by kikas who provided political, economic, and religious leadership. Kikas also had assistants. Each person belonged to one of two divisions, Wildcat and Coyote, each of which was composed of a number of patrilineal clans. In addition to conducting religious ceremonies, shamans also interpreted dreams and cured both by sucking out disease objects and by administering medicinal plants.

Both young men and women undertook puberty ceremonies. Waxan, the female ceremony, was public in the case of wealthy families and included dietary restrictions and instructions on how to be good wives. During Tamonin, the boys' ceremony, initiates ingested a jimsonweed (datura) drink and danced around a fire in the ceremonial house. After they experienced their visions, they learned special songs. The ceremony was followed

by feasting and gift giving. A new mother and child lived in a heated pit for several days, observing food taboos. The dead were cremated, and most of their possessions were burned. A month after the death, a second burning of the remaining possessions was held, accompanied by singing and dancing. There was also an annual seven-day mourning ceremony.

Parents, unmarried daughters, married sons, and sometimes extended family members lived in circular, domed tule-mat houses built around willow frames. Most household activities took place in nearby ramadas. Other structures included granaries, semisubterranean sweat houses, and a large ceremonial house where the kika lived. Men, women, and children all sweated and bathed together.

The Serranos made fine decorated coiled basketry. They also carved petroglyphs, beginning perhaps as early as 1000 BCE, that depicted big game hunting. Pictographs, consisting of geometric designs, straight and wavy lines, and people, were painted as part of the girls' puberty ceremony as early as 1400.

The Serranos may have encountered the Spanish as early as the 1770s, but the latter exerted little influence until 1819, when they constructed a settlement in the area. Most western Serranos were removed by force to the missions between then and 1834; at that point, too few remained to carry on a traditional lifestyle. The Vanyumes, a group associated with the Serranos and possibly living just to their north, became extinct well before 1900.

See also Basketry; Reservation Economic and Social Conditions.

Shasta

"Shasta" describes one of four Shastan tribes, the other three being the Konomihus, Okwanuchus, and New River Shastas. The origin and meaning of the word "Shasta" are obscure. The approximate translation for the Shastas' word for their homeland, *kahusariyeki,* is "among those who talk right." The Shastas lived on both sides of the modern California–Oregon border, roughly in Oregon's Jackson and Klamath Counties and California's Siskyou County, regions mostly of mountains and forest. Today most Shastas live on the Quartz Valley Rancheria in Siskyou County, California, in the Shasta Nation in Yreka, California, and among the general population.

Roughly 3,000 Shastas lived in their region in the eighteenth century. Shastas, Konomihus, Okwanuchus, and New River Shastas make up the Shastan division of the Hokan language family.

Shastas lived in villages of one or more families. Each of the large villages, as well as each of the four divisions, had a headman who acquired office in a loose hereditary succession and whose duties included mediating disputes among men and preaching correct behavior. The headman's wife had similar responsibilities among women.

Shamans were usually women. They cured through the use of supernatural powers, which were also the source of all disease and death (except ill will). They acquired these powers through dream trances, during which a spirit, or pain, taught the shaman its song. An extended training period followed the trance experience. Shamans acquired certain paraphernalia over the years. They diagnosed by singing, dancing, or blowing tobacco smoke and cured by sucking. If a shaman lost too many patients, she was killed. Shamans' services were also available to kill an enemy (by throwing a pain) and to find lost or stolen objects and people. Doctors, who cured by using medicinal plants, were also women.

The Shastas observed numerous life cycle food and behavior taboos. Puberty activities for boys included an optional vision-seeking quest, which ensured success in male activities such as hunting, fishing, gambling, and racing. The girls' puberty ceremony and dance were the group's most important. Marriage required the payment of a bride price. Wealthy men occasionally had more than one wife. Divorce was unusual. The dead were buried in family plots; their possessions were burned or buried. Widows cut their hair (widowers singed it), covered their head and face with a pitch and charcoal mixture until remarriage, and observed several taboos. Souls were said to travel east along the Milky Way to the home of Mockingbird, a figure in Shasta mythology.

Both bitter feuds and friendships characterized Shasta intragroup relations. Payment usually resolved interpersonal differences. Families (through the male line) owned exclusive rights to specific hunting or fishing places within the village territory at large. Money and wealth were measured in deerskins, clamshell disks, dentalia, and woodpecker scalps. Games included ring-and-pin, shinny (a variation of hockey), target games, and the men's grass (hand) and women's many-stick games.

Rectangular winter homes were set about three feet into the ground. With earth sidewalls and wooden end walls, they held between one and four families. All houses faced the water. Furnishings included tule pillows and wooden stools. Some groups used tule or raccoon skin bed coverings; others used elk skin or deerskin blankets or imported buffalo hides. The community house was similar, but larger. Boys past puberty and unmarried men slept in the sweat house if their village contained one. The menstrual hut was generally located on the west side of the village. Other structures included brush shelters in the spring and summer and bark houses during the fall acorn-gathering season.

Shastas usually ate two meals a day. Venison was a staple. Hunters also brought in bear, fowl, turtles, and various small game. Their methods included stalking and the use of drop pits and traps. Various hunting rituals and taboos included not eating one's first kill. Meat was boiled, baked (in earth ovens), broiled, or dried. Insects were parched or baked.

Men also fished for salmon, mussels, trout, and eels, using spears, nets, and traps. There were several First Fish rituals and taboos. Fresh salmon was generally roasted. Acorns were another staple. In addition to acorns, gathered foods included pine nuts, roots, seeds, greens, bulbs, and berries. Dried foodstuffs were ground into flour. Men were often served before women.

The four Shasta groups traded with each other as well as among the villages of each group. They traded acorns (Achumawis, Wintuns) and acorn paste (Rogue River Athapaskans), clamshell beads (northern peoples), and buckskin, obsidian, and dentalia (Warm Springs Indians). They obtained obsidian (Achumawis), buckskin clothing (Warm Springs Indians), otter skins (northern peoples), dentalia (Rogue River Athapaskans), and pine nut necklaces (Wintuns). Trade with their northern neighbors generally excluded the Klamaths and the Modocs. From their California neighbors, the Shastas received acorns, baskets, dentalia, obsidian blades, juniper, and Wintun beads.

Clothing was made of deerskin and shredded bark. People also wore shell necklaces, ear and nose ornaments, face and body paint, and tattoos. Heads were flattened for aesthetic reasons. Caps were of basketry (by women) and buckskin (by men). Footgear included buckskin ankle-length moccasins and snowshoes.

The four groups occasionally fought each other. They also engaged in intragroup feuds, primarily for revenge of witchcraft, murder, rape, and insult to a headman. Other occasional enemies included the Achomawis, Wintuns, and Modocs (in retaliation for the latter's raiding). Weapons included the bow and arrow, knives, and rod armor vests. Peace settlements included disarmament and payments. Young women occasionally accompanied a Shasta war party. They might be taken captive but were usually returned as part of the settlement.

Fur trappers in the 1820s were the first non-Native presence in the Shasta region. Their influence was relatively benign, in sharp contrast to that of the settlers who soon followed in their wake. Although the Shastas often fought each other and their neighbors, they all banded together in the 1850s to resist the Anglo invaders. In 1851, a treaty called for a Shasta reservation in Scott Valley, but the state of California refused to let the treaty be ratified. After the signing, Indians ate a meal at which the food had been poisoned with strychnine; thousands more Indians died during the ensuing attacks by white vigilantes.

The few surviving Shastas were forced onto the Grand Ronde and later Siletz Reservations. Among the other treaties that included the Shastas was the 1864 Klamath Treaty, in which, unbeknownst to them, their aboriginal homeland was ceded. The Shastas participated in the late-nineteenth-century religious revivals, including the Ghost Dance, Earth Lodge cult, and Big Head cult.

See also Fur Trade; Warfare, Intertribal; Women in Native Woodlands Societies.

Sinkyone
See Wailaki.

Smith River Indians
See Tolowa.

Tache
See Yokuts.

Tipai-Ipai

"Tipai-Ipai" is the common name since the 1950s of two linguistically related groups formerly known as Kamia (Kumeyaay) and Diegueño. Both terms mean "People." "Diegueño" comes from the Spanish mission San Diego de Alcala. "Kamia" may have meant "those from the cliffs." The Tipai-Ipais are sometimes referred to as Diegueño Mission Indians.

During the late eighteenth century, the Tipai-Ipai lived in southern California and Baja California, along the coast and inland almost to the Colorado River. Today, many live on thirteen reservations in San Diego County, California. The late eighteenth-century Tipai-Ipai population stood between 3,000 and 9,000. Diegueño is a member of the Yuman division of the Hokan language family.

People have been living in traditional Tipai-Ipai territory for roughly 20,000 years. A proto–Tipai-Ipai culture had been established by about 5000 BCE, and the historic Tipai-Ipais were in place about 1,000 years ago.

Shamans were the religious leaders. They performed ceremonies, interpreted dreams, were believed to control weather, and cured the sick. Evil shamans might also produce disease. Named song cycles were associated with certain ceremonial dances. Ground paintings, a feature illustrating the connection with Southwestern cultures, featured symbols of colors and their associated directions. Their most important religious ceremony was *kaurk*. This clan-based mourning ceremony lasted from four to eight days. It included gift giving, dancing with images of the dead, and feasting, and it culminated with the burning of effigies of the dead. Toloache, a hallucinogenic root, was used by adolescent boys and adult men for spiritual strengthening.

The Tipai-Ipais consisted of over thirty autonomous bands or tribelets, usually made up of a single patrilineal clan and headed by a clan chief and an assistant. Neither the tribe nor the band had a formal name. Positions of authority were sometimes inherited by the eldest sons, brothers, and, rarely, widows. Two tribal chiefs directed ceremonies, advised about proper behavior, and appointed war or gathering leaders. Band leaders and councils saw to resource management. In historic times, some chiefs ordered assistants to beat nonconformists. The Imperial Valley Tipais had a tribal chief but no clan chief.

The Tipai-Ipais' food staple was flour made from six varieties of acorn as well as from mesquite beans and seeds of sage, pigweed, peppergrass, flax, and buckwheat. Flour was cooked into mush and cakes and stewed with meat and vegetables. Other wild foods included cactus, agave, clover, cherries, plums, elderberries, watercress, manzanita berries, piñon nuts, and prickly pear. People fished where fish were available. Animal foods, which were generally roasted on coals or in ashes, included rodents and an occasional deer. The people also ate lizards, some snakes, insects, larvae, and birds. They also cultivated tobacco, which only men smoked. Imperial Valley Ipais planted maize, beans, and teparies, but they placed greater emphasis on gathering.

In 1769, the Spanish built the presidio and mission of San Diego de Alcala and began rounding up local Indians, especially those to the north and on the coast. The latter revolted regularly. In 1775, about 800 people from some seventy villages united to burn the mission. It was later rebuilt, however, and the missionization process continued. After the Mexicans secularized the missions in 1834, they treated the resident Tipai-Ipais as trespassers or rebels and continued many of the same oppressive practices that characterized mission life.

In 1852, shortly after the United States gained control of California, the U.S. Senate ratified a treaty with "the nation of Diegueño Indians," under which the latter lost their best lands. Overgrazing and water diversions soon destroyed their remaining grassland and woodland. By the late 1870s, the Tipai-Ipais were settled on about twelve small, poor reservations, although many were at least located on the site of Native villages. Coastal Ipais also lived in San Diego slums or camped in nearby hills.

At the turn of the century many Tipai-Ipais were working for low wages on ranches and in mines and towns or starving on the inadequate reservations. Traditional Tipai-Ipai government was disrupted by Indian agents who required the Indians to select a "captain." Bitter political factions had emerged by the 1930s with the formation of the rival Mission Indian Federation and the Southern Mission Indians. Frequent cross-border visits and ceremonies became difficult after 1950 and impossible after the 1970s, owing to U.S. immigration policies. In recent times, the bands have been reviving the traditional governing structure.

See also Identity; Worldviews and Values.

Tolowa

"Tolowa" is an Algonquin name given to these people by their southern neighbors, the Yuroks. Cultural and linguistic relatives in Oregon are known as Chetcos and Tututnis. Tolowas are presently associated with the Tututnis. Their name for themselves is *Xus,* or "Person." Traditionally, the Tolowas lived in approximately eight permanent villages in northwestern California, from Wilson Creek north to the Oregon border. The area included coast, rivers (especially the Smith River), and interior marshes, hills, and mountains. Today many Tolowas live in and around Humboldt and Del Norte Counties, California. The people spoke several dialects of Tolowa, an Athapaskan language.

Most important, Tolowa ceremonies were connected with diet, such as catching the season's first salmon, smelt, or sea lion. The Naydosh (Feather Dance) was performed as part of a World Renewal ceremony. Salmon, smelt, and sea lion were the staples. Other foods included seaweed, shellfish, shore bird eggs, and acorns. The people may have cultivated tobacco.

Shamans were mostly women or transvestite men. They were paid a high fee for curing disease. Their methods included dancing, trances, and sucking with the assistance of a spiritual power, or pain. Although Tolowa villages did not closely cooperate among themselves, intermarriage and ceremonial interaction between the Tolowas and their neighbors (Yuroks, Karuks, Hupas, Tututnis) was common. Male activities mostly revolved around hunting, boat building, and fishing; women generally collected and transported food, especially acorns, and prepared it for eating and storage. Corpses were removed through a loose plank in the house, wrapped in tule mats, and buried with shell beads and other objects.

The wealthiest man in the village was usually the leader. There was no formal chief or overall political organization. Prestige, in the form of gaining and displaying wealth, or treasure (such as large obsidian knives, necklaces of dentalium shell beads, and red woodpecker scalp headdresses) was of prime concern to the Tolowas. Treasure was not normally used for utilitarian purposes except for bride prices. Besides marrying off daughters, other ways to get wealth were shrewd trading, fines and indemnities (there were many occasions for this, which were watched for carefully), infant betrothal, and gambling. Wealthy men might have several wives.

The Tolowas lived in square redwood-plank houses with two-pitched roofs. The central area was slightly excavated for cooking and sleeping. An interior ground-level ledge was used for storage. Men and boys slept, gambled, and made nets and weapons in semisubterranean sweat houses. The people lived in their permanent villages about nine months a year, leaving in late summer to fish for smelt on sandy beaches and continuing on inland to catch salmon and gather acorns through the fall.

During the late eighteenth century, probably before the Tolowas had yet encountered non-Natives face to face, an epidemic contracted from non-Native explorers in the region destroyed one of their villages. The first direct contact came in June 1828 in the person of Jedediah Smith and his exploring party. However, the Tolowas continued to live relatively unaffected by outside influences until about 1850.

More than half of the Tolowa population died during that decade alone from disease and the effects of Anglo mass murders. In 1860, following the Chetco/Rogue River Indian War (begun in 1852), 600 Tolowas were forced to march onto reservations in Oregon. Some of those people were later removed to the Hoopa Valley Reservation. The 1870 Ghost Dance revival reached them in about 1872 and lasted about ten years.

Around the turn of the century, the Tolowas suffered a further dramatic population reduction as a result of disease, mostly measles and cholera. Their population at this time had been reduced by roughly 95 percent, to some 200 people. Individual Tolowas had received a few allotments in the late nineteenth century. In 1906, the government purchased tracts of land near the mouth of the Smith River that later became the Smith River and Elk Valley Rancherias. By 1913, most Tolowas were living in and around Crescent City and on the Hoopa Valley and Siletz Reservations. Beginning in 1923 and lasting for at least thirty years, owing to the government crackdown and confiscation of regalia, people held their traditional religious observances secretly.

The Indian Shaker Movement, which supported traditional healing and spiritual practices, arrived around 1930 and remained popular for a generation. About the same time, the Del Norte Indian Welfare Association was founded as a community and self-help organization. The two rancherias were terminated in 1960, with devastating cultural results. As a response to termination, Tolowa landowners in 1973 created the Nele-chun-dun Business Council and

filed for federal acknowledgment ten years later as the Tolowa Nation. The rancherias were reinstated in 1983.

See also Dams, Fishing Rights, and Hydroelectric Power; Disease, Historic and Contemporary; Women in Native Woodlands Societies.

Tubatulabal

"Tubatulabal" (T 'bät l 'ä bl) means "pine nut eaters." These people originally lived in three autonomous bands: the Pahkanapils, Palagewans, and Bankalachis, or Toloims. During the early nineteenth century, the Tubatulabals lived in the southern Sierra Nevada Mountains and their foothills and in the Kern, South Fork Kern, and Hot Springs Valleys. Today many live on reservations in Tulare County. A population of up to 1,000 Tubatulabals lived in their region in the early nineteenth century. Tubatulabal was a subgroup of the Uto-Aztecan language family.

According to traditional belief, numerous supernatural spirits often took human or animal form. They were treated with respect, in part because they could be malevolent. Shamans used jimsonweed (datura), believed to have special powers, as an aid in curing. They also used singing, dancing, herbs, blowing tobacco smoke, and sucking techniques, calling on their supernatural guardian helpers for assistance. Shamans could be either men or women, but only men could cure: Female shamans were witches, the most feared members of the community (men could also be witches). Chronically unsuccessful shamans might be accused of witchcraft and killed. Shamanism was considered an inborn quality that could not be acquired.

The three bands were composed of several family groups, mobile throughout much of the year except during winter, when they settled in hamlets of between two and six extended families. Each band was headed by a chief, generally hereditary, occasionally female. He or she arbitrated disputes, represented the band, and organized war parties. A "dance manager" or "clown" instigated public criticism of the chief preparatory to the appointment of a new chief. He also acted as the clown at ceremonies. Although the three bands were politically autonomous, people often visited and intermarried.

Each band claimed formal but unexclusive possession of a specific territory. The people played several games, most of which involved gambling on the outcome. They included a women's dice game, a men's shinny game (a variation of hockey), and a men's hoop-and-pole game (in which an arrow was shot through a rolling hoop). String figure making and storytelling provided entertainment on winter evenings. Professional male dancers performed at various ceremonies and occasions. Also, both sexes danced for enjoyment.

This group entered the region at least around 1450 and perhaps as early as 2,000 years ago. They first encountered Spanish explorers in the late eighteenth century. By the midnineteenth century, miners, ranchers, and settlers began taking their land. The Kern River gold rush began in 1857. In 1862, a few Tubatulabals joined the Owens Valley Paiutes in anti-white fighting in the Owens Valley. In the following year whites massacred Tubatulabals in the Kern River Valley.

By 1875, most male survivors were working for local ranchers. In 1893, survivors of the Pahkanapil band, the only one left of the original three, were allotted land in the Kern and South Fork Kern Valleys. The people experienced severe epidemics of measles and influenza in 1902 and 1918. During the twentieth century, many Tubatulabals moved to the Tule River Reservation and throughout California. After the last hereditary leader died in 1955, a council of elders carried on leadership through the 1960s. In the 1970s, the Tubatulabals, Kawaiisus, and Canebrake area Indians formed the Kern Valley Indian Community and Council, a goal of which is to obtain federal recognition.

See also Demographics, Historical; Worldviews and Values.

Ventureño

See Chumash.

Wailaki

"Wailaki" is a Wintun term meaning "north language." The tribe had three main subdivisions: Tsennahkennes (Eel River Wailakis), Bahnekos (North Fork Wailakis), and Pitch Wailakis (located farther up the North Fork of the Eel River). The Wailakis are culturally related to four other small tribes—the

Mattoles, Lassiks, Sinkyones, and Nongatls—who lived just to their north and west.

In aboriginal times, the Wailakis lived in northwestern California, along the Eel River and the North Fork Eel River. Today, descendents of these people live in and near Mendocino County. Roughly 2,700 Wailakis lived in their region in the midnineteenth century; the population of all five tribes may have exceeded 13,000. With the Mattoles, Lassiks, Sinkyones, and Nongatls, the Wailakis spoke a Southern Athapaskan language.

The Wailakis believed that spirits were present in all objects, inanimate as well as animate. The source of shamans' power was their ability to communicate with Katanagai (Night Traveler), the creator god. The Wailakis recognized various types of shamans, both men and women, who might attend special schools to receive visions and practice on patients. They cured the sick by sucking or with herbs, and they could find lost souls. Sucking and soul-loss doctors could also foretell the future and find lost people or objects. Singing, dancing, and smoking tobacco accompanied most shamans' rituals. Other ceremonies were connected with salmon fishing, acorn gathering, and girls' puberty.

The nuclear family was the primary social unit. Gift exchange formed the basis of the marriage formalities. Mothers-in-law and sons-in-law did not speak directly to each other out of respect. Herbal abortion was practiced and probably infanticide, especially in the case of twins, one of whom was generally killed. Divorce was relatively easy to obtain for the usual reasons: unfaithfulness, barrenness, or laziness of the wife; unfaithfulness or abuse on the husband's part. Corpses were buried with their heads facing east; the grave was later piled with stones. Wives and husbands were generally buried together. The house was destroyed, and possessions were buried or otherwise disposed of.

Retaliation or revenge for murder, witchcraft, insult, or rape could lead to war among families. Most Southern Athapaskans fought little and then usually only among themselves. Battles consisted mainly of surprise attacks. Ceremonial dances preceded and victory dances followed hostilities. All casualties and property loss were compensated for. Weapons included the sinew-backed bow and arrow, knives, clubs, sticks, slings, spears, and rocks. The Wailakis also used elk hide armor and shields.

Although human occupation of the Wailaki homeland is at least 4,000 years old, the Southern Athapaskans appear to have arrived in California around 900. They had little contact with non-Natives until the midnineteenth century, especially during the Anglo extermination raids of 1861 and 1862.

Survivors fiercely resisted being placed on reservations. Most stayed in the hills working on Anglo sheep and cattle ranches. Others worked on small parcels of land. At one point around the turn of the century, so many of their young were being kidnapped and indentured that parents tattooed their children so that they would always know their ancestry.

See also Warfare, Intertribal; Worldviews and Values.

Whilkut
See Hupa.

Wintun

"Wintun" means "person." The Wintun people consisted of three subgroups: Patwins (Southern), River and Hill Nomlakis (Central), and Wintus (Northern). Wintuns traditionally lived west of the Sacramento River, from the valley to the Coast Range. Today most Wintuns live on reservations and rancherias in Colusa, Glenn, Yolo, Mendocino, and Shasta Counties in California. The eighteenth-century population of Wintuns was roughly 15,000. The three Wintun language groups—Wintu, Nomlaki, and Patwin—are Penutian languages.

The rich Wintun mythology included recognition of a supreme being as well as numerous spirits. Wintuns prayed to the sun before washing in the morning, smoking, and eating. Spirits, present in all things, could be acquired by dreaming and going to a sacred place and engaging in ritual behavior. Among the Nomlakis, they could also be influenced by prayer, charms, magic, and ritual. Shamans provided overall religious leadership. Bear shamans could destroy enemies. They received their powers during an annual five-day initiation period of fasting, dancing, and instruction from other shamans. Their curing methods included massage, soul capture, and sucking out a disease-causing object. Some

Wintuns practiced the Kuksu cult, in which one or more secret societies, open by initiation to men and some high-status women, performed their own dances and rituals to restore the people to a perfect aboriginal state.

Wintuns did not adopt the 1870 Ghost Dance but rather the 1871 Earth Lodge cult, which preached the return of the dead, the end of the world, and the protection of the faithful. The Bole-Maru Religion came in 1872, and dream dancing was popular toward the end of the century. Among the Nomlakis, virtually every activity and life cycle phase carried with it ritual restrictions and ceremonies. Like many California peoples, Wintuns were organized into small tribes. The village was the main social, economic, and political unit. Villages were autonomous and had clearly defined territory. Each village was led by a chief, whose office was often hereditary, who arbitrated disputes, hosted ceremonies and gatherings, and engaged in diplomatic relations with the chiefs of other villages. The chief, who was materially supported by his followers, had to be a good singer and dancer and generally well liked. The Nomlakis recognized a secret society of higher-status men, who had a higher degree of authority in public matters and who controlled most of the skilled crafts and professions.

Murder, rape, or some other sexual transgression was generally capital crimes. Most intentional crimes could be atoned for by compensating the injured party. Dances were more often social than religious and were often given when food was plentiful. Gambling was also a part of social dances; activities included the grass game (for men), hand games, shinny (for women, a variation of hockey), football, hoop-and-pole (in which an arrow was shot through a rolling hoop), ring and pin, and other contests of skill. Songs could also be social or religious.

Four to seven pole-framed, bark-covered conical houses made up a village. Among the Patwins, dwellings as well as the ceremonial and domed menstrual huts were semisubterranean and earth covered. The men's clubhouse and sweat lodge was semisubterranean and circular, fifteen to twenty feet in diameter, with one center pole. In cold weather single men also slept there.

Men hunted deer and rabbits, both communally in drives and individually. They also smoked bear (except grizzly) out of their dens and captured fowl, birds, and rodents. Communal drives were held to catch salmon and trout. Women gathered grubs, grasshoppers, acorns, greens, and seeds. Men and women cooperated in gathering acorns, with men shaking acorns out of trees for women to gather. The acorns were then dried and pounded into meal, after leaching them to remove their bitter taste.

In addition to fighting neighboring villages, Wintun enemies generally included the Shastas, Klamaths, Modocs, and Yanas. The Nomlakis' main enemy was the Yuki. Wintus took no prisoners. Typical provocations for feuds or war included murder, theft of women, poaching, and trespass. Among the Nomlaki not all men fought; those who did underwent special practical and magical training. Seers determined the proper course of action, and poisoners used magic as a weapon. Wars were usually limited, and casualties were minimal. Weapons included the bow and arrow, clubs, spears, daggers, slings, and wooden rod armor. Hand-to-hand fighting was avoided if possible. When the fighting stopped, an assembly of important men decided on just compensation.

In aboriginal times, the Wintuns consisted of nine major groups within the three main subgroups. Some Nomlakis encountered the Spanish as early as 1808, although in general the Nomlakis were outside the sphere of Spanish influence.

By 1800, the Patwins were being taken by force to the missions. Wintus first met non-Natives in 1826, when the Jedediah Smith and Peter Ogden expeditions entered the region. Malaria epidemics killed roughly 75 percent of Wintuns in the early 1830s. Severe smallpox epidemics followed in 1837. By the midnineteenth century, most of their land had been stolen. Ranchers' cattle and sheep destroyed their main food sources. Miners polluted the fresh water. Then came the massacres. Captain John C. Frémont killed 175 Wintu and Yana in 1846; in 1850, whites gave a "friendship" feast with poisoned food, killing 100 Wintus. In 1851, 300 Indians died when miners burned the Wintu council house.

The so-called Cottonwood Treaty, ratified in 1852, acknowledged thirty-five square miles of Wintu land, but from 1858 to 1859, California regular and irregular troops killed at least 100 Wintus and displaced hundreds of others. Throughout the 1860s, Wintuns were hunted down and either killed or used as laborers. The 25,000-acre Nome Lackee Reservation was established in 1854 in the foothills

of western Tehama County. Indians created a stable existence there based on farming, but by 1863 the reservation had been taken over by whites, and its residents were sent to Round Valley.

Many surviving Nomlakis eventually returned to their old territory, working as farm hands and establishing a number of settlements, or rancherias. Most Patwins who survived the missions, military forays, raids, epidemics, and massacres either became assimilated into white society or were forced onto small reservations during the 1850s and 1860s, most of which have since been terminated.

A period of religious revival occurred in the 1870s, during which much traditional practice was replaced with Ghost Dance and later Big Head ceremonies. Wintus gathered en masse for the last time at the end of the nineteenth century. Copper-processing plants around the turn of the century poisoned what decent land and water remained in the region. Cortina, Colusa, Paskenta, and Grind-stone Rancherias were created between 1906 and 1909.

Wintun children were formally excluded from local schools until 1928. Termination and allotment policies during 1952 and 1953 further broke up Wintun culture; only three rancherias survived this period. In the 1930s and again in the 1970s, dam construction flooded much of their remaining land. Despite an agreement with the Wintun people, the U.S. government removed people from and destroyed their homeland, the Toyon-Wintun site, in 1984.

>   *See also* Bole-Maru Religion; Disease, Historic and Contemporary; Ghost Dance Religion; Warfare, Intertribal.

Wiyot

"Wiyot" is the name of one of three culturally and linguistically related groups on the Eel River Delta in the early nineteenth century. They were culturally similar to the Yuroks. Humboldt Bay was first occupied around 900 by Wiyots or Yuroks. The Wiyots traditionally lived near Humboldt Bay, California, from the Little River south to the Bear River and east about twenty-five miles. This environment is coastal lowland, an unusual one in California. Today, most Wiyots live in and around Humboldt

County. As many as 3,500 Wiyots may have been living in their region in the early nineteenth century. Wiyot was an Algonquian language related to Yurok.

The Wiyots' creator was known as "that old man above." The Wiyots practiced World Renewal ceremonies and dances. Although other peoples celebrated the World Renewal religion in a showy and complex manner, which involved recitations, displays of wealth, costumed dances, and various decorations, the Wiyots observed it irregularly and with less flair. Men and women also performed victory dances when an enemy was killed and conducted an elaborate girls' puberty ceremony. They did not observe a first salmon ritual (the ritualistic preparation and consumption of the season's first catch). Female berdaches played an important role in Wiyot ceremonialism.

Each Wiyot group was autonomous and self-governing. Wealth was valued as the source of social stratification and prestige, although not to the degree of the Klamath River peoples. There was no debt slavery. Most of the common menstrual taboos were absent among the Wiyots. Married couples generally lived with the father's family, except in the case of "half-marriages" (when a man worked to cover part of the bride price). Corpses were carried by stretcher to the cemetery and buried in an extended position in plank-lined graves along with money and valuables. Relatives and undertakers observed various taboos following the funeral.

Both women and men hunted. Disease was considered to be caused either by the intrusion of poisonous objects, soul loss, or breaches of taboo. Herb doctors and especially sucking doctors (shamans) cured disease. Unlike most northwest California peoples, the Wiyots did not penalize shamans for declining a curing case.

Two or more families, including men, slept in rectangular houses of split redwood planks. Each unnamed house had a two- or three-pitch roof and a smoke hole at the top. The sweat house, built like a dwelling, only smaller, was used for gambling, ceremony, and occasionally sleeping. The Wiyot built no separate birth or menstrual huts.

Women generally wore twined basket hats and either fringed and embroidered buckskin double aprons that hung to between the knee and the ankle or one-piece, inner-bark skirts or aprons. Men wore buckskin breechclouts. Robes were of deer hide and woven rabbit skin. Both sexes wore moccasins.

Murder, insult, or poaching was the typical cause of war. The Wiyots fought by surprise attack or prearranged battle and used elk hide armor, rawhide shields, and bows and arrows. Women and children were not killed in war. After the fighting, both sides paid compensation for damaged property.

In 1806, the first non-Native explorers came into the region. The first systematic murders of Wiyots began around 1852 during the Chetco/Rogue River Indian War. The regular killings of individual Indians led to wholesale massacres shortly thereafter. In 1860, a massacre at Gunther Island, perpetrated by white residents of Eureka during a Wiyot religious celebration, killed as many as 250 Indians. Survivors were forced onto reservations on the Klamath and Smith Rivers. Wiyot culture never recovered from this event; their identity became mixed with whites and other local Indian peoples.

See also Warfare, Intertribal; Women in Native
Woodlands Societies; Worldviews and Values.

Yana

"Yana" means "people." In the early nineteenth century, the Yanas lived in the upper Sacramento River Valley and the adjacent eastern foothills. The elevation of their territory ranged between 300 and 10,000 feet. The aboriginal population of Yanas probably numbered fewer than 2,000. Yana was a Hokan language. Its four divisions were Northern, Central, Southern, and Yahi.

Yana settlements consisted of a main village with several smaller satellite villages. Each village probably had a hereditary chief or headman, who lived in the main village. Chiefs were wealthy and often had two wives. They led the dances, orated from the roof of the assembly house on proper behavior, and were the only ones permitted to keep vultures as pets. The villagers provided food for chiefs and their families. Shamans, mostly male, received their power by fasting in remote places or swimming in certain pools. Trained by older shamans, they cured by singing, dancing, or sucking. Unsuccessful shamans might be accused of sorcery and killed. Various roots and teas were also used as medicines.

Land was privately owned. Men played double-ball shinny (usually a woman's game, a variation of hockey). Other games included ring and pin, cat's cradle, stick throwing at a stake, and the traditional grass or hand game.

The Northern and Central groups lived in earth-covered multifamily houses. The Southern and Yahi groups preferred smaller, conical, bark-covered houses. An assembly house was located in a tribelet's main village. All groups lived in temporary brush shelters or caves while hunting.

Acorns, fish, and venison were the Yanas' staples. Men climbed trees to shake acorns down while women gathered, shelled, and dried them. After leaching the acorn flour, it was used for mush, bread, and a soup with meat, berries, and other foods. Women also gathered roots, tubers, bulbs, berries, pine nuts, and grasshoppers. Men stalked deer using a deer head decoy and bow and arrow. Salmon was broiled on heated rocks, roasted over an open fire, or dried and stored. Rabbits were hunted in community drives. The Yanas also took other game.

Members of a Mexican expedition may have been the first non-Natives to encounter the Yanas during 1821. Hudson's Bay Company trappers almost certainly interacted with the Yanas from about 1828, and some Mexicans received land grants in Yana territory during that time. The first permanent Anglo settlement in the area came in 1845.

By the late 1840s, Anglo trails crossed Yana territory. With Anglo encroachment came increased conflict: Attacks by U.S. soldiers (John C. Frémont in 1846, for example) led to retaliations, and as food became scarcer the Yanas began raiding cabins. In the 1860s, Anglos set out to exterminate the Yanas. Through massacres, disease, and starvation, their population was reduced by 95 percent in about twenty years.

In 1911, a Yana man named Ishi walked out of the foothills of Mount Lassen to a nearby town, where two anthropologists were able to communicate with him. Ishi eventually communicated his story, which began at the time when Anglo invaders and murderers began to destroy the Yahi (a subset of Yana people). Only about a dozen or so Yahis remained alive after a massacre in 1868, six years after Ishi's birth. These people remained in the wilderness until 1908, when only four were left. Three died shortly thereafter, leaving Ishi as the only remaining Yahi in 1911. After leaving the woods, he lived and worked at the University of California Museum of Anthropology (San Francisco), demonstrating traditional crafts, providing a wealth of

information about his culture, and learning some English. Ishi died of tuberculosis in 1916.

See also Fur Trade; Worldviews and Values.

Ynezeño

See Chumash.

Yokuts

"Yokuts" is a term meaning "person" or "people." The three divisions were the Northern Valley Yokuts, the Southern Valley Yokuts, and the Foothill Yokuts. Contemporary Yokuts tribes include the Choinumnis, the Chukchansis, the Tachis (or Taches), and the Wukchumnis.

The Yokuts traditionally lived along the San Joaquin Valley and the Sierra Nevada foothills. Specifically, the Southern Yokuts inhabited a lake-slough-marsh environment in the southern San Joaquin Valley; the Northern Yokuts' territory was wetlands and grassy plains in the northern San Joaquin Valley; and the Foothill Yokuts lived approximately on the western slopes between the Fresno and Kern Rivers. Today, Yokuts live on two rancherias in Tulare and Kings Counties and in nearby communities.

The Yokuts population was between 18,000 and 50,000 in the early eighteenth century. They had one of the highest regional population densities in aboriginal North America. Yokuts people spoke various dialects of Yokuts, a California Penutian language.

The San Joaquin Valley has been inhabited for some 11,000 years. Yokuts culture is probably between 600 and 2,000 years old, with direct cultural antecedents dating back perhaps 7,000 years.

The Yokuts' most important festival was their annual six-day ritual in honor of the dead. They also celebrated the arrival of the first fruit of the season. Group ceremonies were always conducted in the open and included shamanic displays of magic powers. Many men and older women also had spiritual helpers that conferred good fortune or specific abilities. The Northern Yokuts may have practiced the Kuksu cult. Men and women of this group also drank jimsonweed (datura) annually as part of a

spring cleansing and curing ritual. Among the central Foothills group, datura was drunk once in a lifetime, by adolescents.

The Yokuts were organized into about fifty named tribelets, each with its own semipermanent villages, territory, and dialect. Each tribelet also had several hereditary chiefs (often at least one per village, usually from among the Eagle lineage). The chief, usually a wealthy man, sponsored ceremonies, hosted guests, aided the poor, mediated disputes, and authorized hunts as well as the murder of evil people such as sorcerers. Other offices included the chief's messenger. Shamans derived power from spirit animals via dreams or vision quests. They cured and presided over ceremonies. Large fees were charged for cures. Chronically unsuccessful shamans might be accused of sorcery and killed.

Among the foothill Yokuts, everyone swam at least daily, with adolescents also swimming several times at night during the winter for toughening. The divisions competed against each other in games, with men and women often gambling on the results. Both sexes played the traditional hand game. Women also threw dice or split sticks. Leisure activities also included dancing and storytelling. Men smoked tobacco, usually at bedtime. Rattles accompanied most singing, which usually occurred during rituals. Other instruments included bone and wood whistles, flutes, and a musical bow.

The Southern Yokuts built both single-family oval-shaped and ten-family dwellings, in which each family had its own door and fireplace. Both featured tule mats covering pole frames. Mats also covered the floor and raised beds. Men sweated and sometimes slept in sweat houses.

The Northern Yokuts built similar single-family and possibly ceremonial earth lodges. Conical huts thatched with grass or bark slabs characterized dwellings of the Foothills Yokuts. Beds were of pine needles. Other structures included sweat houses, gaming courts, and mat-covered granaries and ramadas. Among Foothills Yokuts, women might use the sweat houses when no men were present.

The wetland home of the Southern Valley Yokuts contained an enormous variety and quantity of wildlife. They hunted fowl, rabbits, squirrels and other rodents, turtles, and occasionally big game. They gathered tule roots, manzanita berries, pine nuts, and seeds. Seafood included lake trout, salmon, perch, and mussels. Fresh fish was broiled

on hot coals or sun-dried for storage. They also raised dogs for eating but did not eat frogs. Their salt came from salt grass.

In addition to many of these foods, Northern Valley Yokuts depended on fish, mussels, turtles, elk, antelope, and smaller mammals. Salmon and especially acorns were staples. The Foothills Yokuts ate a lot of deer, quail, acorns, and fish. They also ate pine nuts, wild oats, manzanita berries, duck, trout, wasp grubs, squirrels, and rabbits. Iris bulb and tule root were important sources of flour. Men stalked deer by using deer disguises, or they ambushed them and shot them with bow and arrow. Quail were trapped. Salmon and other fish were caught with spears, weirs, and basket traps. The Yokuts also planted tobacco and may have engaged in basic horticulture or plant management.

The Spanish came into the region of the Southern Yokuts in the 1770s and were warmly received. In the early nineteenth century, serious cultural destruction began as the northern valleys were drawn into the exploitative mission system. Yokuts' resistance and retaliation brought further Spanish repression and even military expeditions. Foothills Yokuts communities were protected by their relative isolation, and they sheltered escapees and began raiding for horses to ride and eat, activities that they continued into the Mexican period. Yokuts became excellent cattle breeders and horse breakers during this period.

In the early 1830s, malaria and cholera epidemics killed roughly three-quarters of all Indians in the region. Mexicans established land grants in the San Joaquin Valley. By then, traditional flora, fauna, and subsistence patterns had all been severely disrupted. After the United States annexed California in 1848, its citizens began a large-scale campaign of slaughter and land theft against the Yokuts. The latter, along with their Miwok allies, resisted Anglo violence and land theft by force (such as the Mariposa Indian War of 1850–1851). In 1851, the tribes signed a treaty to relinquish their land for a reservation and payment, but pressure from the state of California kept the U.S. government from ratifying the agreement.

Dispossessed, some Yokuts worked on local ranches, where they were poorly paid and kept practically in peonage. The 1870 Ghost Dance revival provided a straw of hope to a beaten people. It lasted two years; its failure probably prevented the 1890 Ghost Dance from gaining popularity. The Tule River Reservation was established 1873. The Santa Rosa Rancheria was established in 1921.

Yokuts found minimal employment as loggers, as ranch hands, and as farm laborers into the twentieth century. Their children were forcibly sent to culture-killing boarding schools in the early part of the century. By the 1950s, most Indian children were in (segregated) public schools. A cultural revival took place beginning in the 1960s.

See also Disease, Historic and Contemporary; Ghost Dance Religion; Worldviews and Values.

Yurok

"Yurok" is a Karuk word meaning "downstream" and refers to the tribe's location relative to the Karuk people. The Yuroks referred to themselves as *Olekwo'l,* or "Persons." Some Yurok villages were established as early as the fourteenth century and perhaps earlier. Traditionally, the Yurok lived in permanent villages along and near the mouth of the Klamath River, in northern California. Today, many live on several small rancherias in Humboldt County. The aboriginal Yurok population was roughly three thousand in the early nineteenth century. Yurok is an Algonquian language.

Similar to other northern California Indians, local Yurok groups practiced the World Renewal religion and the accompanying wealth-displaying white deerskin and jumping dances. Other ceremonies included the brush dance, kick dance, ghost dance, war dance, and peace dance. People who performed religious ceremonies were drawn from the ranks of the aristocracy. In general, religious training was related to acquiring not spirits, as in regions to the north, but rather real items, such as dentalia or food.

The wealthiest man was generally the village leader. About 10 percent of the men made up an aristocracy known as *peyerk,* or "real men." Selected by elder sponsors for special training, including vision quests, they lived at higher elevations than most Yuroks, spoke in a more elaborate style, and acquired treasures such as albino deerskins, large obsidian knives, and costumes heavily decorated with shells and seeds. They also wore finer clothing, imported special food, ate with a different etiquette, hosted ceremonial gatherings, and occasionally spoke foreign languages. The *peyerk* occasionally

Yurok man in canoe on the Trinity River in California, ca. 1923. (Library of Congress)

gathered as a council to arbitrate disputes. "Real women" went through a similar training experience. Since children were considered a financial drain, "real women" and their husbands practiced family limitation by sexual abstinence.

Social status was a function of individual wealth, which was itself a major Yurok preoccupation. Only individuals owned land, although other resources might be owned as well by villages and descent groups. Poor people could voluntarily submit to the status of slave to acquire some measure of wealth. Imported dentalia shells were a major measure of wealth; they were engraved, decorated, and graded into standard measures for use as money. Other forms of wealth included large obsidian blades (also imported), pileated woodpecker scalps, and albino deerskins.

Via prayer and the elicitation of wrongdoing, women doctors cured by gaining control of pains,

small inanimate, disease-causing objects within people. The misuse of curing power (sorcery) could cause individual death or group famine. Intertribal social and ceremonial relations with neighbors were frequent and friendly. Yurok villages often competed against each other in games. Unlike most offenses, certain sex crimes may have been considered crimes against the community.

The basic unit of society was a small group of patrilineally related males. Marriage was accompanied by lengthy haggling over the bride price. Most couples lived with the husband's family. Illegitimacy and adultery, being crimes against property, were considered serious. Corpses were removed from the home through the roof and buried in a family plot. If a married person died, the spouse guarded the grave until the soul's departure for the afterworld several days after death.

The Yuroks' first contact with non-Natives came with Spanish expeditions around 1775. The first known contact was among Hudson's Bay Company trappers and traders in 1827. However, the Yuroks remained fairly isolated until about 1850, when a seaport was created in Yurok territory to make travel to the gold fields more accessible. The rush of settlers after 1848 led to a wholesale slaughter and dispossession of the Yuroks. An 1851 treaty that would have established a large Yurok reservation was defeated by non-Indian interests. Shortly after the first white settlement was founded, Yuroks were working there as bottom-level wage laborers.

President Franklin Pierce established the Klamath River Reservation in the Yurok territory in 1855, and Congress authorized the Hoopa Valley Reservation in 1864. In 1891, the Klamath River Reservation was joined to the Hoopa Reservation in an extension now called the Yurok Reservation. This tract of land consisted of 58,168 acres in 1891, but allotment and the sale of "surplus" land, primarily to Anglo timber companies, reduced this total to about 6,800 acres. Three communal allotments became the rancherias of Big Lagoon, Trinidad, and Resighini.

From the midnineteenth century into the twentieth, many Yuroks worked in salmon canneries. Yuroks formed the Yurok Tribal Organization in the 1930s. Indian Shakerism was introduced in 1927, and some Yuroks joined the Assembly of God in the 1950s and 1960s. In a landmark 1988 case, the U.S. Supreme Court declined to protect the sacred sites of Yurok and other Indians from government road building. Also in 1988, the Hoopa-Yurok Settlement Act partly resolved a long-standing dispute over timber revenues and fishing rights.

See also Dams, Fishing Rights, and Hydroelectric Power; Reservation Economic and Social Conditions; Women in Native Woodlands Societies; Worldviews and Values.

Native Americans of the Northwest Coast

Bella Bella

"Bella Bella" is a term dating from 1834, not an aboriginal self-designation. The Bella Bellas (made up of at least three subgroups: the Kokaitks, Oelitks, and Oealitks), the Haihais, and the Oowekeenos are sometimes referred to as Heiltsuks. The Heiltsuks, along with the Heislas, are today identified as Bella Bellas or northern Kwakiutls. Traditionally, these groups lived in the vicinity of Queen Charlotte Sound, north of Vancouver Island and the Kwakiutl people, in the Canadian province of British Columbia. This is a wetland, marked by inlets, islands, peninsulas, mountains, and valleys, with a relatively moderate climate. Roughly 1,700 Bella Bellas lived in their territory in 1835. In 1901 the figure had shrunk to 330, but it climbed to 1,874 in 1995. The Heiltsuks spoke Heiltsuk (Haihai and Bella Bella)-Oowekyala (Oowekeeno), a Wakashan language. The two component languages were virtually mutually unintelligible.

Dancing or secret societies performed their ceremonies in winter. Initiation into the societies was by hereditary right. Dances—a first, or shamans', series, including a cannibal's dance; a "coming down again," or second, series, including war dances; and a dog-eating dance—were ranked according to the status of both the dance and the performers. Performances dramatized the encounter of an ancestor with a supernatural being. Wealthy, high-status people sponsored dances, feasts, and potlatches. A council of chiefs managed the winter dances.

As was generally the case along the Northwest Coast, the basic political unit was the autonomous local group or clan. Each such group was presided over by a chief. Parts of several clans often formed a village, where the highest-ranking chief had relative degrees of control over the others. For defensive purposes, some villages congregated to form loose confederations or tribes.

Distinctive crests and ranked titles identified each of the four crest groups, or clans—Raven, Eagle, Orca, and Wolf. These groups also had heads, or chiefs. Resource sites could be owned by families, local groups, or crest groups, and they could be rented out for some form of compensation.

In general, society was divided into status-ranked groups, such as chiefs, free commoners, and slaves. Some divisions also added another free group between commoners and slaves, as well as several levels of chief. Symbols of high rank included tattoos, ornamentation, and the possession of wealth and hereditary titles. Commoners had less prestigious names, held smaller feasts, and had no inherited rights to certain dances. The low-class free were orphans or the unambitious with no wealthy relatives.

Regular intermarriage occurred between the Bella Bellas and the Bella Coolas. Marriage between close cousins was condoned if it furthered one's status. The bride price was a key ingredient of a marriage; in cases of divorce it was generally refunded.

Semipermanent winter villages were composed of rectangular cedar plank houses. Features included vertical wall planks, a gabled roof and double ridgepole, carved interior posts, an adjustable central smoke hole, and mat-lined walls in sleeping areas. Summer camp houses were of similar but less elabo-

rate construction. When they were in small or temporary camps, people made do with bark structures.

Fish, especially salmon, was the staple. Other marine foods were also important. The Bella Bellas took stranded whales only for their blubber. They ate several varieties of berries and hunted deer, wolf, bear, mountain goat, small mammals, waterfowl, and most birds (except crow and raven) and their eggs. Other than in winter, when food stores were eaten, people migrated seasonally to various resource sites. Fishing technology included stone and wood stake weirs, traps, harpoons, dip nets, and clubs. Harpoons, clubs, and bow and arrow were used for hunting sea mammals. Land animals were hunted with the help of dogs, snares, spears, and deadfalls. Digging sticks helped people gather roots. Most woodworking tools were of stone. Women made burden and storage baskets.

The Bella Bellas traded shellfish and seaweed with more inland groups (such as the Bella Coolas) for eulachon (smelt) and eulachon products. They also obtained canoes in trade, often from the north. Bentwood boxes, chests, canoes, and horn spoons and ladles were items of fine local construction. Also important were relief carved and painted ceremonial/religious items such as totem poles and masks. The cedar dugout, a shallow-bottom canoe used with round-tipped blades, was the primary means of transportation. The Bella Bellas and Haihais also used bark canoes for lake travel.

In warm weather, women wore cedar-bark aprons; men went naked. Blankets of woven cedar bark, mountain goat wool or dog hair, or tanned, sewn skins kept people warm in cold weather. Women wore waterproof basket caps and cedar-bark ponchos in the rain. Both sexes wore their hair long. Those who could afford it wore abalone nose and ear pendants. High-status women also wore labrets, dentalia bracelets, necklaces, and anklets. They also deformed their babies' heads for aesthetic purposes. The people painted their bodies and faces against sunburn.

The Bella Bellas fought regularly, mainly against the Bella Coolas, Haidas, Tsimshians, and Kwakiutls. They were well organized militarily. The Haihais were regularly under attack, but the Oowekeenos were more geographically isolated. Revenge, trespass, violation of custom, and seasonal shortages of food were common causes of war.

Bella Bellas probably met non-Indians for the first time in 1793, when the explorers George Van-couver and Alexander Mackenzie arrived to prospect for the fur trade. Shortly thereafter, that trade brought more Anglos as well as Anglo-Indian violence. Milbanke Sound was the first local major trade center. In 1833, the Hudson's Bay Company built Fort McLoughlin on Campbell Island as a major trading post. Although it abandoned the fort ten years later, the company opened a small store on the site about 1850. During the fur trade period, the Bella Bellas emerged as intermediaries, controlling access to some interior tribes and playing the Americans and British against each other.

An 1862 smallpox epidemic set off a period of rapid change. Dramatic Indian depopulation led to village consolidation. Missionization followed, as did the growth of the commercial fishing, canning, and logging industries. In 1880, the government separated Indians from their land by unilaterally establishing reserves. The Bella Bella Reserve was run by Methodist missionaries. Village centralization and consolidation continued. Around 1900, two Oowekeeno villages were established near a sawmill and a cannery. The Haihais moved from their local villages in about 1870 to Swindle Island, a fuel depot for steamships.

In the twentieth century, northern Kwakiutls were largely displaced from the logging and fishing industries owing to a combination of factors, including competition with non-Natives, technological advances, and the loss of land rights. Increased unemployment and out-migration have been the results. However, ties remain strong between home communities and the people in regional cities and towns.

See also Disease, Historic and Contemporary; Potlatch; Salmon, Economic and Spiritual Significance of; Slavery; Trade.

Bella Coola

"Bella Coola" is an Anglicization of a Heiltsuk word for the speakers of the Bella Coola language. The Native word for the people of the Bella Coola valley was Nuxalkmx. They consisted of four or five subgroups linked linguistically, territorially, and culturally, although not politically. These people are known today as the Nuxalt Nation.

Traditionally, several permanent villages existed south and east of the Bella Bellas and the Haislas, east of the Queen Charlotte Sound coast in British Columbia. These people may also have occupied territory east of the Coastal Range. Beginning around 1800, they consolidated their villages at the mouth of the Bella Coola River. In 1936, a flood forced them to move from the north to the south shore of the river's mouth. Their traditional territory is rugged, with mountains, estuaries, and forests. The climate is cool and wet. Perhaps 1,400 Bella Coolas lived in their villages in 1780. Speaking a Salishan language, the Bella Coolas were latecomers to the region, probably arriving around 1400.

The Bella Coolas recognized four or five worlds, including a center, or human, world. A supernatural being kept this flat center world level and balanced. There were many deities and a supreme female deity, all of whom resided in the sky. All things had spirits that could intervene in the lives of people. Favorable intervention might be gained through prayer and ritual sexual intercourse.

Their extremely rich ceremonialism was dominated by two secret societies as well as the potlatch. Membership in one such society, Sisaok, was restricted to the children and relatives of certain chiefs. An extended period of seclusion accompanied initiation, as did songs and the display of carved masks with crests. The ceremony dramatized various kin-related legends. The other society, Kusiut, was based on contact with the supernaturals. Its dances, such as cannibal, scratcher, breaker, and fungus, included songs and masks representing supernatural beings. These dances dominated the ceremonial period, which lasted from November through March.

All people had the potential to become shamans; the event occurred when a supernatural being conferred power through a visit, a name, and songs. Some such power could cure sickness. Some shamans received power through ghosts and could see dead people; they cured disease caused by ghosts.

Aboriginally, the Bella Coolas inhabited between thirty and sixty autonomous villages, each consisting of from two to thirty houses arranged in a row along a river or creek bank. Each village had a chief, whose status derived from his ancestral name, prerogatives, and wealth. Chiefs had little direct ruling power. A woman who had been "rebought" several times, and who had thus helped her husband accumulate status, was also recognized as a chief.

Descent groups probably owned fish weirs in aboriginal times. Hunting, too, could only occur in an area claimed by a descent group. Hunters, some of whose ancestral prerogatives allowed them to be known as professionals, underwent ritualistic preparation.

The units of social organization included the household, village, and descent group, or all those with a common ancestral mythology. A child could inherit both parents' descent groups, but residence with the father's family tended to reinforce the patrilineal line. Social status was important and clearly delineated. The ability (and obligation) to give away gifts on ceremonial occasions (potlatches) was a key component of social status. Social mobility was possible, and even slaves might obtain dance prerogatives and thus achieve some status.

Babies were born with the assistance of midwives in a birth hut in the woods. Their heads were flattened and their bodies massaged daily. Wealthy parents gave naming potlatches. Infanticide and abortion were occasionally practiced. The Bella Coolas pierced the nasal septa of high-status children, both boys and girls; the occasion was accompanied by potlatches. Upon reaching puberty, girls were secluded, and their activity and diet were restricted for a year. There were no boys' puberty rituals, although their first hunted game was distributed and eaten ritually, as were the first berries gathered by girls.

Although the ancestral family was an important source of Bella Coola identity, they did intermarry extensively with other peoples. Parents and elderly relatives arranged marriages, around which there were many rituals and opportunities to increase status. The relatives of high-status brides were expected to "rebuy" the woman (donate goods) every time her husband gave a potlatch. Cruelty, neglect, and infidelity were considered grounds for divorce.

Music could be both sacred and secular. The former was sung by a choir, who used sticks and drums for a beat, and three main performers. Various wind instruments were also used to symbolize the supernaturals.

Permanent houses were large, planked structures. They were constructed of red cedar and often built on stilts against floods and enemies. Housefronts were decorated with the owner's crest. Houses were inhabited by extended families. Entry was through carved house posts. Some winter houses were excavated, with only the roofs showing.

The Bella Coolas enjoyed a relatively regular food supply. Fish was the staple, including five types of salmon plus steelhead trout, rainbow and cutthroat trout, eulachon (smelt), Pacific herring, and others. All fish was boiled, roasted, or smoke-dried. Eulachon was very valuable, perhaps more for its grease than as food. The first chinook salmon and eulachon of the season were eaten ritually.

Other important foods included shellfish; seals, sea lions, and beached whales; land mammals, such as mountain goat, bear, lynx, hare, beaver, marmot, and deer; and fowl. More than 135 plants were used for foods, medicines, and raw materials. Important plant foods included berries and the cambium layer of the western hemlock (steamed with skunk cabbage leaves, pounded, dried, and mixed with eulachon grease).

Wood carving was probably the preeminent Bella Coola art. Masks, entry poles, house frontal poles (with entry through a gaping mouth), and carved posts were often painted and decorated with crest figures. They had no fully developed totem pole. They also made pictographs and petroglyphs. The Bella Coolas used several types of canoes, including long, narrow canoes of a single red cedar log for rivers (the most common) and four types of seagoing canoes. Canoes were decorated with crest designs or painted black. Hunters also wore two types of snowshoes in winter.

The Bella Coolas engaged in irregular conflict with neighbors such as the Carriers, Chilcotins, and Kwakiutls. Their lack of political centralization made retaliating against raiding parties difficult. The Bella Coolas raided too, attacking at dawn, burning a village, killing all the men, and taking women and children as slaves. Weapons included moose-hide shields, wood armor, the bow and arrow, clubs, and spears.

In 1793 the Bella Coolas encountered the explorers George Vancouver and Alexander Mackenzie; the Indians traded fish and skins to them for iron, copper, knives, and other items. As the fur trade developed, Hudson's Bay Company maintained a local fort/post from 1833 to 1843. During this period, the Bella Coolas prevented furs from the Carrier Indians (an eastern group) from reaching the coast, thus maintaining a trade monopoly with the whites.

Shortly after gold was discovered in their area (1851), disease, alcohol, and hunger combined to weaken and kill many Indians. A severe smallpox epidemic in 1863 forced the abandonment of numerous villages. Hudson's Bay Company operated another local trading post from 1869 to 1882, and Protestant missionaries penetrated the Bella Coola territory in the 1870s and 1880s. In 1885, nine Bella Coolas journeyed to Germany for thirteen months, dancing and singing for European audiences and inspiring the anthropologist Franz Boas to begin his lifelong study of Northwest Coast Indians. A Norwegian colony, the first local non-Indian settlement, was established in the Bella Coola Valley in 1894.

These changes, combined with the gradual transition to a commercial (fishing and logging) economy and the replacement of traditional housing with single-family structures, weakened descent groups and led to the gradual consolidation of ceremonials and the abandonment of songs. In the 1960s and 1970s, however, the people relearned the old songs, using recordings made by anthropologists. In the 1970s, the revival of traditional culture also included new masks and dances.

See also Disease, Historic and Contemporary; Potlatch; Salmon, Economic and Spiritual Significance of; Slavery; Trade.

Chehalis
See Salish, Southwestern Coast.

Chetco
See Tolowa; Upper Umpqua.

Chinook
"Chinook" describes one of a group of Chinookan peoples whose branches included Lower Chinookan (or Chinook proper) and Upper Chinookan. The name came from a Chehalis word for the inhabitants of a particular village site on Baker Bay. In 1780, roughly 22,000 Chinookans lived in their territory, a figure that declined to less than 100 in the late nineteenth century.

Traditionally, the Chinookan peoples lived along the Pacific Coast around the Columbia River delta and upstream on both sides for about 150 miles. Lower Chinookans included the Shoalwater Chinookans (Shoalwater or Willapa Bay and the

north bank of the Columbia from Cape Disappointment to Gray's Bay) and the Clatsops (south bank of the Columbia, from Young's Bay to Point Adams). Upper Chinookans included the Cathlamets (Grays Bay to Kalama), the Multnomahs (Kalama to about Portland and up the Columbia just past Government Island), and the Clackamas (southwest of Portland and roughly along the Willamette and Clackamas Rivers). Today, most Chinookans live in southwestern Washington and locales around the Pacific Northwest.

The Chinookan family of Penutian languages was composed of Lower Chinookan (Chinook proper) and Upper Chinookan, which included the languages of Cathlamet, Multnomah, and Kiksht. In the context of historic Northwest Coast trade, Chinook, or Oregon Trade Language (consisting of elements of Chinookan, Nootkan, French, and English) was considered a trade *lingua franca* from Alaska to California.

All Chinookan males and some females sought guardian spirit powers on prepubescent quests alone at night. Special songs and dances accompanied the receipt of such powers. An elaborate ceremonialism, based on the acquisition and display of spirit powers, took place during winter, the sacred period of spiritual renewal. Shamans might rent their powers to inflict harm (bodily injury or soul loss) or to cure someone. Chinookans also observed the first salmon rite (the ritualistic preparation and consumption of the season's first catch).

Aboriginally, the Chinookans lived in more than thirty villages. Each village had a hereditary chief, but, through the deployment of the proper alliances and methods, a chief could exercise his authority over a wider area. The chief arbitrated quarrels, supervised subsistence activities, and provided for his village in time of need. His privileges included taking food, goods, or women at will. The chief was assisted by an orator who spoke directly to the lower-ranked people.

Chinookan society was clearly stratified; status rankings included slave, commoner, and chief. High status went to those who had and could display wealth (food, clothing, slaves, canoes, high-ranked spouses), such as chiefs, warriors, shamans, and traders, as well as those with hereditary privileges. Slaves were bought, sold, or captured as property. Fishing areas were usually controlled by specific descent groups, although other subsistence areas were not so clearly controlled. Ties between villages were maintained by trade and alliances through

wives. Imported dentalium shell was used for money and ornamentation. Later, beads from China were also highly prized.

All life cycle events, at least among high-status families as well as those of chiefly succession, were marked by wealth display, gift giving, feasting, singing, and dancing. The purpose of the potlatch, a word meaning "giving" in Chinookan, was to reaffirm the lineage system as well as individual and descent group rank and social status, by conferring legitimacy on an occasion. Chinookans observed numerous taboos around girls' puberty (including seclusion for five months) and menstruation. Non-slave infants' heads were flattened at birth for aesthetic reasons. Corpses were placed in cattail mats; burial with possessions took place in canoes. A slave was sometimes killed to serve as a servant in the afterlife. Mourners cut their hair and never again spoke the name of the dead. Lacrosse was a popular game.

Permanent winter dwellings were rectangular, gable-roofed, cedar plank houses, excavated and framed with cedar logs, with an average length of fifty feet. Decorations were of geometric, animal, and human designs. Floors were mat covered or planked, with an excavated central fireplace and a smoke hole above. Elevated bed platforms ran along the walls. Winter villages generally comprised around twenty houses. A light framework supported shelters of cattail mat sides and cedar-bark roofs at summer fishing, hunting, or root gathering camps.

Their strategic location at the mouth of the Columbia, as well as their business skills, enabled the Chinookans to dominate trade as far away as Puget Sound and areas to the west and south. The Dalles, a giant waterfall and rapids on the Columbia, was the site of a great aboriginal trade fair. Participants brought pelts, mountain sheep horn, baskets, woven rabbit skin robes (interior tribes); slaves (Klamaths and Modocs); salmon, bear grass, blubber, canoes, and berries (Chinookans); and dentalia (Nootkas). Connections to this trade fair stretched ultimately as far as the Great Plains. The existence of Chinook jargon, the regional trade language, was testament to the central role the Chinookans played in trade. Imported dentalium shells were a standard medium of exchange.

After contact, the Chinookans were involved in a triangular trade in which they traded elk hide cuirasses and other items to non-Natives, who traded them to other Native people for sea otter

pelts, which they in turn traded in China for items such as silk and tea. Meanwhile, the Chinookans traded guns, powder, and steel tools obtained from the non-Natives to other Indians for a fabulous profit. This trade pattern greatly increased the status of Chinook women, who played a more active trading role than men. When land-based trade in items such as beaver and other furs replaced the maritime trade, women continued their dominant roles.

Although Chinookans may have spotted Spanish ships off the Columbia River delta, early Anglo explorers first encountered and spread smallpox among them in 1792. Meriwether Lewis and William Clark lived among and wrote about the Clatsops in 1805.

The fur trade began in earnest during the next decade; Astoria was founded in 1811. During the early days of the fur trade, at least, the Indians played key roles. The acquisition of goods such as musket and powder, copper and brass kettles, cloth, tobacco, and other items increased the relative prestige of downriver groups so much that they tried to monopolize trade to the exclusion of their upriver rivals. Native culture began gradually to change, owing mainly to the acquisition of manufactured items and to enduring contact between Indians and Anglos.

Shortly after the initial contacts, Indians began to experience severe population declines due to disease. Alcohol-related disease and deaths took a further toll. The Chinookans abandoned many village sites and consolidated others, particularly around trading sites. The number of potlatches may have increased during this time, as villages had to rerank themselves in the context of the new trading society. By the 1850s, most survivors were being forced, under treaties that were never ratified, to cede their land in exchange for fishing rights. Survivors drifted to area reservations (Chehalis, Siletz, Grande Ronde, Shoalwater) or remained in their homelands.

By the twentieth century, the (Lower) Chinook had so effectively merged with the Lower Chehalis and the Shoalwater Salish that their language essentially passed out of use. Other groups also lost their identities through merger and consolidation. In 1899, the Chinookans, Clatsops, Cathlamets, and Wahkiakums (Upper Chinookans) presented a land claim to the U.S. government. They were awarded $20,000 (for almost 214,000 acres) in 1912. In 1925, the tribe established a business council to pursue its elusive treaty rights. A 1931 U.S. Supreme Court case (*Halbert v. U.S.*) held that Chinookans and other tribes had formal rights on the Quinault Reservation. Within a few years they had become that reservation's largest landholders. The Bureau of Indian Affairs (BIA), however, blocked their bid to organize a government under the Indian Reorganization Act.

In 1951, the nonreservation Chinookans combined to form the Chinook Nation and press their land claims with the newly created (1946) Indian Claims Commission. Soon, however, and without any official action, the BIA began to treat them as a terminated tribe. In 1971, this group, reconstituted in 1953 as the Chinook Indian Tribe, Inc., received an award of almost $50,000 but no land. Their petition for federal recognition, filed in 1979, is still pending.

> *See also* Disease, Historic and Contemporary;
> Fishing Rights; Salmon, Economic and Spiritual
> Significance of; Slavery; Trade.

Comox

See Salish, Northern Coast.

Coosans

"Coosans" describes the Coosans proper and Siuslaw peoples. The word is probably southwestern Oregon Athapaskan and refers to Coos Bay and the surrounding region. "Coos" may mean "on the south," "lake," or "lagoon." "Siuslaw" comes from the Siuslaw word for their region.

The Coosans lived around Coos Bay, Oregon, roughly from Twomile Creek in the south to Tenmile Lake in the north. Siuslawan speakers lived north of them, along the coast and inland, to about Tenmile Creek. Except for the immediate coast, much of the area is mountainous and densely forested. Today, most of these people live in and around Coos Bay in southwestern Oregon. The number of Coosans in the mideighteenth century may have approximated 4,000. This number had declined to roughly 465 by 1870. Coosans spoke two Coosan languages: Hanis and Miluk. The Siuslawans spoke the Siuslaw language, which consisted of the dialects Siuslaw proper and Lower Umpqua (Kuitches). Both Coosan and Siuslaw were Penutian languages.

Individuals could acquire power, mostly used to ensure luck in gaining wealth, through dreams and spirit quests. Unlike more northerly tribes, few other than shamans were actively involved with the supernatural; most people were much more interested in obtaining wealth. The most common kind of shaman was rigorously trained as a curer of disease (caused either by the intrusion of a disease-causing object, often sent by a hostile shaman, or, less often, by soul loss). The second kind of shaman was more ritualistic; in addition to curing, these shamans also found thieves and promulgated evil. They were involved in the numerous life cycle taboos and especially in the elaborate girls' puberty ceremony and various other rituals of purification.

The people regularly held large-scale ceremonies featuring dancing, feasting, games, and gambling. Their mythology included stories of a primordial trickster, of legends, and of supernatural beings of forest and water. First salmon and first elk ceremonies (the ritualistic preparation and consumption of the season's first catch or kill) were also held.

The basic political unit was the winter village group, usually a group of paternally related men with their families. Each major village had a chief and often an assistant chief. An informal council of wealthy men and women advised the chief. Succession was mainly hereditary, at least among the Coosans. Women might succeed if there were no eligible males. Chiefs arbitrated quarrels, supervised communal activities, and saw that no one went hungry. Villagers contributed food to the chief's family.

Coosan and Siuslaw society consisted of four classes: chiefly and wealthy families, a socially respectable majority, poor people, and slaves (obtained by capture or trade). The classes enjoyed similar subsistence levels; their main difference lay in nonfood wealth and status. Marriage occurred when a groom's family paid a bride price, which was later returned in a lifelong cycle of mutual gift giving and responsibilities. The dead were buried; their goods were broken and placed in and around the grave.

Permanent houses ranged between twenty and fifty or more feet long and half as wide and were excavated to a depth of about three to six feet. Two or more center posts supported a single ridgepole. Rafters sloped to the ground or to side supports. Walls and gabled roofs were of lashed cedar planks. Tule mats lined the inside walls, mat partitions divided the several families within the house, and mats or hides covered the floors. Bed platforms ran along the walls. Among the Siuslaw, two or more houses were sometimes joined.

Camp houses were of thatched grass with a gabled or one-pitch roof. Two types of sweat houses existed. One doubled as a men's clubhouse and boys' dormitory. It was square, plank-walled, excavated, and covered with dirt. The other, for use by both men and women, was in a beehive shape and heated by steam.

Most clothing was made by women from skins and various fibers. Both sexes wore leggings and moccasins but usually only for travel and in cold weather. On such occasions, they also wore headbands and waterproof fur or fiber capes. Men generally wore breechclouts or shorts and often shirts and caps. Women wore shirts and skirts or one-piece dresses and woven hats. Everyone wore rain capes of cattail or shredded bark. Wealthy people were likely to decorate their clothing. Some people wore tattoos, primarily for measuring dentalia strings. The Kuitch wore large beads in their noses and flattened the heads of their infants.

The first regional contact with non-Natives occurred in 1792, when Upper Umpquas traded with U.S. and British ships. Occasional trade-based contacts through the 1830s were generally amicable, except for a Kuitch (Lower Umpqua) massacre of the Jedediah Smith party in 1828 and their attack on a Hudson's Bay Company fort in 1838.

Tensions increased with the major influx of non-Natives in the 1850s. Although only the southernmost Coosan group, the Miluks (Lower Coquilles), participated in general in the 1855–1856 Rogue River War, all the Coosans and Siuslawans also suffered. An 1855 treaty, signed by Chief Jackson and others, though never ratified, was used to dispossess the Indians of their land and move them the following year to the Lower Umpqua River. Miluks and Kuitch were taken to the Coast (later the Siletz and the Alsea) Reservation, where about half died of starvation, exposure, and disease.

During these and subsequent years, the military continued to round up groups of Indians living in remote areas. As was the case nearly everywhere, Indian agents stole mercilessly from the Indians. Indians who practiced their traditional customs were whipped at a post. Easy access to alcohol corrupted, demoralized, and sickened the people.

In 1860, both groups were forcibly marched to the Siletz Reservation, which had been created five years earlier. In 1861, people on the southern part of

Siletz, including Coos and Kuitch, were moved to or near the Yachats River on the coast, home of the Alsea Indians. They remained there until 1875, dying of illness and starvation from trying to farm in a rain forest. In 1865, a central strip was removed from the reservation and opened for white settlement. The northern part then became the Siletz Reservation (Miluks) and the southern half became the Alsea Reservation (Coosans, Kuitches, and Alseans).

In 1875, when the Alsea Reservation was made available for non-Indian settlement, many people refused to go to Siletz. Some joined the Siuslawans while others filtered back to their original homelands and received eighty-acre homesteads from the government in 1876. As their culture and language languished, tribal members worked as loggers, laborers, clam diggers, and cranberry harvesters. Women specialized in making baskets and cattail fiber mats.

Coosans who did live at Siletz worked at subsistence activities around the turn of the century. Indian loggers cut trees that stood on their former, plundered reservation. Siletz Indians won several small land claims judgments in the 1930s and 1950s. However, the tribe and reservation were "terminated" in the mid-1950s, with devastating result. They were restored in 1977 and given a 3,630-acre reservation three years later.

The Confederated Tribes of Coos, Lower Umpqua, and Suislaw organized formally in 1916. They have spent the rest of the century petitioning the government for compensation for their aboriginal lands, in vain to date. The Coos obtained a 6.1-acre "reservation" at Coos Bay in 1940. They were involuntarily terminated in 1954 and restored thirty years later.

The Dream Dance, a local variation of the Ghost Dance, was popular in the 1870s. By the twentieth century, most Native languages were no longer spoken. In 1917, Coosans and Siuslawans created the Coos–Lower Umpqua–Siuslaw Tribal Government. A schism in the Coos tribe occurred in 1951 after a court ruled that some Miluks were eligible to share in money awarded in a land claims suit to the (upper) Coquille (Mishikhwutmetunne) Indians. These Miluks then became affiliated with the Coquille Indian tribe.

See also Fishing Rights; Ghost Dance Religion; Potlatch; Salmon, Economic and Spiritual Significance of; Slavery; Trade.

Coquille (Mishikhwutmetunne)

See Coosans; Upper Umpqua.

Cow Creek Band of Umpqua Indians

See Upper Umpqua.

Cowichan

See Salish, Central Coast.

Cowlitz

See Salish, Southwestern Coast.

Duwamish

See Salish, Southern Coast.

Grand Ronde, Confederated Tribes of

See Upper Umpqua.

Haida

"Haida" is an adaptation of their self-designation. In the late eighteenth century, Haidas lived in a number of towns, politically unorganized but distinguishable as six groups by geography, tradition, and speech. These groups included the Kaigani people, the people of the north coast of Graham island, the Skidegate Inlet people, the people of the west coast of Moresby Island, the people of the east coast of Moresby Island, and the southern (Kunghit) people. The west coast Pitch-town people stood outside this classification system.

Haida territory included the Queen Charlotte Islands and Alexander Archipelago of British Columbia. This is a region of considerable environmental variation, including coastal lowlands, plateau, and mountains. The area is fairly wet, especially

Young Haida dancer Donny Edenshaw dances while Guugaaw Edenshaw, a family member, drums out a rhythm on a beach at Masset in the Queen Charlotte Islands in 1985. (Dewitt Jones/Corbis)

in the west. The Haida population was roughly 9,000 to 10,000 in the late eighteenth century. This number dropped by almost 95 percent, to about 550, in 1915. Haidas spoke various dialects, including Skidegate and Masset, of the Haida Athapaskan language. Haida country was settled more than 9,000 years ago.

Haidas believed that animals possessed intelligence and humanlike souls, had a hierarchical ranking, lived in villages, and could change their forms at will. Haidas offered prayers, grease, tobacco, and flicker feathers to the spirits of game animals. They also conceived of three worlds: sky, sea, and land. Their ceremonies were directly related to the system of social stratification. Potlatches, feasts, and dance performances, given by high-ranking people, were the main ceremonial events. Shamans, with multiple supernatural powers, were considered to be more powerful than chiefs.

People lived in autonomous villages, some consisting of a single lineage. The basic social and political unit was the lineage, or clan; each contained up

to twelve households and was presided over by a hereditary chief. He gave permission for others to access the lineage's subsistence area and could declare war. Household chiefs (owners of plank houses) exercised control over their households, deciding when members left for fishing or hunting camps. In multilineage towns, the wealthiest, highest-ranking house chief was the town master, or town mother.

The Haidas divided most labor along sex and class lines. Women gathered, processed, and preserved all foods; prepared animal skins; and made clothing and baskets. Men fished, hunted, built houses and canoes, carved, and painted. Canoe making and carving, as well as sea otter hunting, were high-prestige occupations. Economically important slaves, captured during war, did much of the fishing.

Ambition, success in hunting and fishing, and industry were highly valued qualities. Haida society was divided into two matrilineal divisions: Raven and Eagle, each composed of lineages, or clans. Lin-

eages had mythological origins and controlled property such as subsistence areas and names, dances, songs, and crest figures. Crests were the identifying symbols of lineages and an indication of personal rank within the lineage. They were carved on totem poles and other wooden items and tattooed on the body.

At feasts and potlatches, guests were seated according to their rank. Feasts, although always part of potlatches, were also held separately to name a child, at a marriage or death, to honor a visitor, or to enhance prestige. In addition to personal rank, there was a class system. Upper-class people bore many potlatch names, because when they were children their parents had given potlatches in their honor; they owned houses and were heirs to high-ranking names and chieftainships.

The Haidas observed a number of life cycle rituals and taboos. Children were regarded as reincarnated ancestors. Uncles toughened boys by, for example, making them take winter sea swims. There was no boys' puberty ceremony, but girls were secluded for a month or longer and followed many behavioral restrictions. Marriages were arranged in childhood or infancy. Property exchange and gift giving marked the marriage. Death among high-status people was a major ceremonial occasion. After bodies were washed, costumed, and painted, they lay in state for several days. Then they were placed in bent-corner coffins constructed by men of the father's lineage and removed through a hole in the wall. Burial was either in a lineage grave or in a mortuary column, followed by a potlatch and the raising of a memorial pole. Commoners had no poles erected in their honor. Slaves were thrown into the sea.

The Haidas were a seafaring people. Fishing technology included hook and line (of gut), traps, and harpoons. Hunting equipment included snares, bows and arrows, and clubs. Women made twined basketry (for quivers and other items) of split spruce roots and cedar-bark mats and bags. Building tools included wooden wedges, stone adzes, and basalt or jade hammers. Dugout cedar canoes were up to seventy feet long and eight feet wide, carved and painted. The Haidas had a fire bow drill and began working their own iron in the late eighteenth century.

At least in the early historic period, the Haidas gained wealth from their skill as traders. They traded canoes, slaves, and shell to the Tlingits for copper, Chilkat blankets, and moose and caribou hides. Canoes, seaweed, chewing tobacco, and dried halibut went to the Tsimshians for eulachon (smelt) grease, dried eulachons, and soapberries. They acquired slaves from the Kwakiutls. There was some intravillage trade. In the mid-1830s they traded furs, dried halibut, potatoes, and dried herring spawn to the Hudson's Bay Company for blankets, rice, flour, and other staples.

The Haida were outstanding wood-carvers. Their masterpieces included canoes, totem (mortuary) poles, house fronts, walls, screens, weapons, bentwood boxes, ceremonial masks, tools, and implements. Totem pole carving burgeoned during the nineteenth century with the acquisition of metal tools; the Haidas built some of the best such poles in world history. Designs included zoomorphic crest figures as well as mythological beings and events. Black, red, and blue-green were traditional colors. Other arts included basketry, especially hats, and other excellent woven items, such as robes, capes, and blankets. They may have carved argillite in prehistoric times, but certainly for the curio trade from the nineteenth century on, at which time they also took up silver engraving.

The Natives first saw a non-Indian when the Spanish explorer Juan Pérez Hernandez arrived in 1774. Numerous trading ships followed in the late eighteenth and early nineteenth centuries. The Haidas traded sea otter pelts for European and U.S. manufactured goods. They also began cultivating potatoes at this time. By the late eighteenth century, the Haidas were rich and powerful.

Early trade was generally peaceful except for some hostilities in 1791, the probable year they first contracted smallpox. Their sea otter trade ended about 1830. It was replaced by land-based fur operations and the Hudson's Bay Company, whose 1830s post at Fort Simpson (coast Tsimshian country) became the central trading location for Tlingit, Haida, and Tsimshian traders for the next forty years. The Haidas also traded in Victoria beginning in 1858, drawn by the local gold rush. During this period, however, they fought with rival Kwakiutls and fell victim to drinking and prostitution. More disease, especially smallpox, hit hard in 1862 and led to widespread village abandonment and consolidation. By the mid-1870s, Haida culture was in full collapse.

Christian (Methodist) missionaries arrived in Haida country in 1829. The Anglican Church was active at Masset from the early 1880s; shortly thereafter the Haidas ceased erecting grave posts and

memorial totem poles. Dancing and the power of shamans also declined. In 1883, Haida villages were divided between Methodists (central and southern) and Anglican (northern) missionaries.

Under government auspices, the Presbyterian Church established Hydaburg, Alaska, around the turn of the century. It was meant to facilitate the transition among Haidas from its traditional to the dominant culture. In 1936, the Haida became the first Indian group in Alaska to adopt a constitution under the Indian Reorganization Act. They succeeded in obtaining a large reservation in 1949, but, under pressure from the salmon industry, a judge invalidated the reservation several years later.

The Haidas in Canada were granted almost 3,500 acres of land in 1882 and another 360 in 1913. By the twentieth century, Haidas were migrating seasonally to work in the commercial mining, fishing, and canning industries. Acculturation proceeded rapidly. The potlatch was outlawed in 1884, although many Indians continued clandestinely to observe this central aspect of their culture. Government land allotments, without regard to traditional lineages, undercut the latter's power, as did the growth of single-family housing.

Canada passed its first comprehensive Indian Act in 1884. Among other things, the Act established numerous small reserves for Indian subsistence and other activities. In 1912, Presbyterian Tlingits formed the Alaska Native Brotherhood (the Alaska Native Sisterhood was founded eleven years later), which worked for the abandonment of tradition, the mitigation of racial prejudice, increased educational opportunities, and land rights. These organizations reversed their stand against traditional practices in the late 1960s. Severe overt economic and social discrimination against Indians continued, however, including a virtual apartheid system during the first half of the twentieth century.

After World War II, Masset experienced a brief boom in carpentry and boatbuilding. Most villagers in the 1960s worked in the canning and processing industries for half the year and were otherwise unemployed. In general, Alaska Indians campaigned for self-government and full citizenship. Canadian Indian policy favored integration into mainstream society after World War II. In the 1960s, the government granted Indians a measure of self-determination, which sparked a period of cultural renewal. Tlingits and Haidas received a $7.5 million land claims settlement in 1970. Under the terms of the Alaska Native Claims Settlement Act (1971), the Haidas set up several corporations, although one, the Haida Corporation, declared bankruptcy in 1986.

See also Salmon, Economic and Spiritual Significance of; Slavery; Totem Poles; Trade.

Haihais

See Bella Bella.

Hoh

See Quileute.

Kikiallus

See Salish, Southern Coast.

Klallam

See Salish, Central Coast.

Kuitch (Lower Umpqua)

See Coosans.

Kwakiutl

"Kwakiutl" was originally the name of a local group and may mean "beach on the other side of the water." Once consisting of roughly thirty autonomous tribes or groups, the Kwakiutls did not think of themselves as a people until about 1900. They are sometimes referred to as *Kwakwaka'wakw* ("Kwakiutl-Speaking People") or *Kwakwala* ("Kwakiutl language"). Many Kwakiutls continue to live in or near their aboriginal territory, which is located around the Queen Charlotte Strait on the central coast of British Columbia. The Kwakiutl population in the early nineteenth century was about 8,000. Kwakiutl is a member of the northern (Kwakiutlan) branch of the Wakashan language family. The three related languages were Haisla, Heiltsuk-Oowekyala, and Kwakiutl proper.

The area around the Queen Charlotte Strait has probably been occupied for 10,000 years or longer. During the last 5,000 years, two distinct cultures arose. One was based on a simple obsidian technology and featured a broad-based subsistence economy. People of the second, or Queen Charlotte Strait culture (post-500 BCE), used bone and shell technology and ate mostly salmon, seal, and other marine foods.

Spanish, British, and U.S. explorers arrived in the Kwakiutl homeland during the late eighteenth century. By early in the next century the local sea otter trade was in full swing. The Hudson's Bay Company became active when the sea otter trade diminished, around the 1830s. At that time the Kwakiutls began serving as intermediaries in the fur trade. They and many other Indian peoples were frequent visitors to the company's post at Fort Victoria.

Changes in Kwakiutl culture during the fur trade period included the substitution of iron and steel for Native materials in tools, as well as Hudson's Bay blankets for the older style of robes. Disease epidemics leading to depopulation also took a heavy toll at that time. In the 1850s, several Kwakiutl villages consolidated around a Hudson's Bay Company coal mine at Fort Rupert; this was the genesis of the Kwakiutl tribe. In general, the 1850s and 1860s were terrible years for the Kwakiutls, marked by the destruction of several villages by the British Navy and Bella Coola raiders as well as smallpox epidemics. In the late 1880s, Canada established reserves for some Kwakiutl bands while claiming much of their aboriginal territory.

Aboriginally, trade partners were also often raiding targets. The enforced cessation of intertribal hostilities about 1865 precipitated an explosion of potlatching activity, as all Kwakiutl tribes became part of the system of social alliances and tribal ranking. The potlatch flourished despite legislation outlawing it in 1885 and 1915, as did traditional artistic expression.

Acculturation was proceeding rapidly by the 1880s. The Kwakiutl were giving up their traditional dress, subsistence activities, and many customs and were entering the local wage economy. Around 1900, Alert Bay, the site of a cannery, a school, and a sawmill, superseded Fort Rupert as the center of Kwakiutl life. The early twentieth century was a period of economic boom for Kwakiutls owing to the growth of the commercial fishing and canning industries. Another boom in the fishing industry occurred after World War II. Many people aban-

doned the potlatch and traditional culture during the Depression and converted to the Pentecostal Church. Potlatching was not significantly reestablished until the 1970s.

In traditional Kwakiutl belief, everything had a supernatural aspect that commanded respect from people in the form of individual daily prayer and thanks. Guardian spirits, which provided luck and certain skills, might be obtained through prayer or fasting. Associated with each spirit was a secret ceremonial society, such as Cannibal, Grizzly Bear, and Warrior, as well as specific dances and ceremonies.

Shamans formed an alliance with a supernatural helper and were initiated into their craft by other shamans. The Kwakiutls recognized several degrees of shamanic power, the highest being the ability to cure and cause disease; these most powerful people were usually attached to chiefs. Shamans used songs, rattles, and purification rings (hemlock or cedar) in public curing ceremonies. Witches could harm or otherwise control people without recourse to supernatural power, although knowledge similar to theirs was available to guard against such practices.

The winter ceremonials were based on complex mythological themes and involved representations of supernatural beings and stories of ancestral contact with them. The principal winter ceremonies, including the Cedar Bark Dance and the Weasel Dance, involved feasting, potlatching, entertainment, and theater. Winter was considered a sacred season because the supernaturals were said to be present at that time. People attempted to be on better behavior and even took on sacred names.

Each of the roughly thirty autonomous tribes (local groups) had its own hereditary chief, subsistence area, winter village, and seasonal sites. Tribes consisted of between one and seven (usually at least three) kin groups (numayms), each having perhaps seventy-five to 100 people aboriginally and roughly ten to fifteen in the late nineteenth and early twentieth centuries. In early historic times, some tribes formed joint winter villages without losing their individual identities.

Kin groups (tribes) owned resource areas, myths, crests, ceremonies, songs, dances, house names, named potlatching positions, and some inheritable guardian spirits. Crests, privileges, and rights were transmitted through marriage. The Kwakiutls recognized many forms of permissible marriages. Preserving the existence of crests and privileges remained all-important, and rules were

bent or broken over time to accommodate this need. There were four traditional classes or status groups: chiefs, nobles, commoners, and slaves. Society became much more equal in the midnineteenth century: As the population declined, the number of privileged positions remained constant, so that more people could rise to such positions.

Potlatches, once modest affairs, became highly complex, elaborate, and more culturally central in the late nineteenth century, helping to integrate and drive Kwakiutl society by validating social status and reciprocities. The size of a potlatch varied according to the event being marked: Life cycle events for high-status children and wiping out casual mistakes received small potlatches; the receipt of a first potlatch position, dancing the winter ceremonial, and the occasion of girls' puberty received moderately sized potlatches; and the assumption of a chiefly name and/or position within a kin group, a grease feast, the buying and selling of coppers, the erection of crest memorial poles, and marriage received the largest potlatches. All included feasting, socializing, speeches, songs, displays of wealth and crests, and dances. Such potlatches were occasionally given on credit; that is, borrowed goods (such as blankets) were usually lent at 100 percent interest.

Traditionally, the Kwakiutls practiced blood revenge, in which one or more people might be killed upon the death of a close relative. Corpses were buried in trees, caves, or canoes (chiefs), although northern groups cremated their dead.

Rows of cedar beam and plank houses with shed roofs faced the sea in traditional villages. The central house posts were carved and painted with crests. A sleeping platform extended around walls. Four families of the same kin group occupied most houses, each in a corner with its own fireplace. Private areas were partitioned off. Each village also had one or more ceremonial houses, similarly constructed. By the late nineteenth century, houses were built with milled lumber and gabled roofs.

The Kwakiutls were artists. Even in utilitarian items, visual art was joined with rhetoric, mythology, and performance art to glorify the kin groups. Wooden objects, such as massive house posts, totem and commemorative poles (nonaboriginal), masks, rattles, feast dishes, and other objects used for crest displays were carved and/or painted. The point of most Kwakiutl art was social—to display ancestral rights—rather than specifically religious, although the two are basically inseparable.

Their basic colors were black and red. The Kwakiutls experienced a golden age of art from about 1890 to 1920. They also produced some excellent twined, spruce root, and cedar-bark hats.

See also Fur Trade; Hudson's Bay Company; Slavery; Totem Poles; Trade.

Lower Umpqua

See Coosans.

Lummi

See Salish, Central Coast.

Makah

"Makah" is a Klallam word for "the People." The Makah word for themselves is *Kwe-net-che-chat*, "People of the Point." They were a whaling people, culturally similar to the Nootkans of Vancouver Island. People have lived around Cape Flattery for roughly 4,000 years. The Makahs emigrated from Vancouver Island about 500 years ago, although some Makah villages were occupied as early as 1500 BCE. The Makahs lived around Cape Flattery on the northwest tip of the Olympic Peninsula, a region of fierce, rainy winters and calm, sunny summers. The Makah Reservation is in Clallam County, Washington, within their aboriginal lands. The Makah population was roughly 2,000 in the late eighteenth century. Makah is a southern or Nootkan language of the Wakashan language family.

The acquisition of guardian spirits was central to Makah religion and ceremonialism. Adolescent boys acquired them by fasting in remote places. Shamans, both male and female, who had acquired several guardian spirits cured people and provided ceremonial leadership. Except for ritual hunting preparations, most ceremonies took place in the winter. Carved wooden masks figured prominently in a four-day Wolf ritual, during which members were initiated into the secret Klukwalle Society. A healing ceremony and complex whaling rituals follow Nootka patterns.

The Makahs lived in five permanent, semiautonomous villages, with one or more lesser satellite

villages in the same general area. Social groups included headmen, commoners, and slaves. The headmen regularly affirmed their rank through the institution of the potlatch. Commoners could advance or fall back slightly through marriage or by acquiring privileges. Alliances were formed, and privileges and subsistence areas were inherited through ranked patrilineal lineages. Whaling and fur seal hunting were particularly prestigious occupations. Only the former was an inherited privilege, but both involved substantial ritual components. Aboriginally, only men hunted and fished; women gathered shellfish and plants and cleaned, cooked, and otherwise prepared food products.

Permanent houses were built on wooden frames as large as sixty by thirty by fifteen feet high. Platforms along the wall served as sleeping and storage areas. Planks from nearly flat roofs, on which fish drying racks were located, could be easily removed for ventilation. Several families lived in one house. Privacy was provided by removable partitions. House fronts and posts were carved or painted. In summer, some people left the permanent villages for summertime residences.

The region supported abundant land and sea life, including mammals, fish and shellfish, birds, and flora. Sea mammals were the most important staple, followed by fish, particularly halibut. Oil, especially from whales and fur seals, was used to flavor dried foods. The Makahs ate some land mammals. Plant foods included several varieties of berries, roots (especially sand verbena, surf grass, and buttercup), and greens. Plants were also used as medicine, for raw materials, and in entertainment.

Makah women wove spun dog wool or bird skin and fiber cordage on a two-bar loom. Women also made baskets of cedar as well as of cattail, tule, and cherry bark. Whaling equipment included mussel shell–tipped harpoons, line made of whale sinew and pounded cedar boughs, and skin floats for floating the dead whales and towing them ashore. Fishing equipment included hooks and kelp lines, weirs, traps, and gaffs. Land mammals provided additional raw material, such as antler and bone, for manufactured items. Shell was used for cutting and eating tools and for adornment. Mats for canoe sails, blankets, and cargo wrap were made from cedar bark. Wooden implements, such as bent-corner boxes (steamed and bent), bowls, dishes, containers, clubs, harpoon and arrow shafts, and bows, were fashioned from yew, red cedar, spruce, alder, and hemlock.

The Makahs were actively involved in trade and social intercourse with all neighbors, including Klallams, Quileutes, and Nitinahts. Makahs often served as intermediaries, handling items such as dried halibut and salmon, sea otter skins, vermilion, whale and sea oil, dentalium shells, dried cedar bark, canoes, and slaves. They made an especially good profit selling whale oil. Camas, a favorite food, was obtained in trade from the north. They both imported and exported canoes.

The Makahs first encountered non-Natives around 1790, when British and Spanish ships entered the area, and the Spanish built a short-lived fort. The Makahs detained several shipwrecked Russians and Inuit around 1809, as well as three shipwrecked Japanese in 1833. They traded occasionally with Hudson's Bay Company.

The results of early contact included an intensification of trade and the use of non-Native goods as well as disease epidemics. By the 1850s, villages were being abandoned as a result of depopulation. The Makahs signed the Treaty of Neah Bay in 1855, ceding land in return for "education, health care, fishing rights" and a reservation (subsequently enlarged). The Indian Service soon moved in and tried to eradicate Makah culture. They prohibited the Native language and customs in government schools and tried, but failed, to replace maritime traditions with agriculture.

During the 1860s and 1870s, Makahs hunted fur seals for the non-Native market. In the 1880s, they were hunting on white-owned ships, at a wage so great that they temporarily abandoned whaling. By the 1890s, some Makahs had their own boats and were hiring both Indian and white crews. At this time, however, the seal population began to decline due to overhunting. As international treaties began to restrict seal hunting, Makahs turned to poaching and then abandoned the activity altogether. By this time, in any case, many of their maritime-related ceremonies had disappeared.

In 1896, when the local boarding school closed, many families moved to Neah Bay, which became the Makahs' primary village. In 1911, a treaty gave the Makahs and some other Indian groups the right to hunt seals using aboriginal methods, a practice that continued for several decades. Commercial logging began in 1926. A road connecting the reservation with the outside world opened in the 1930s, as did public schools, which replaced the hated boarding schools. Tourism and the general local cash economy increased. In the 1940s, the Army Corps of

Engineers completed a breakwater that provided a sheltered harbor for tourist boats and fishing vessels.

Major postwar economic activities were commercial fishing, logging, and tourism. Makah cultural life began to reemerge with the relaxation of the severe anti-Indian government policies. In any case, some aspects of traditional culture, such as the potlatch and the language, had never been eradicated. In 1970, archaeological excavations at the village of Ozette revealed much about the aboriginal life of the Makahs. This site has yielded over 50,000 artifacts as well as other valuable information and has encouraged many young Makahs to study anthropology.

See also Fishing Rights; Potlatch; Trade.

Muckleshoot

See Salish, Southern Coast.

Nisqually

See Salish, Southern Coast.

Nooksack

See Salish, Central Coast.

Nootkans

The Nootkans were a linguistic group of Vancouver Island Indians consisting of more than twenty-two tribes, confederacies, or sociopolitical local groups. Captain James Cook, who thought it was the Native name for what came to be called Nootka Sound, originated the term. Many Nootkans continue to live in or near their aboriginal territory, which was the western half of Vancouver Island, British Columbia, roughly 125 miles north and south of midcoast. The geography features a rocky coast and a coastal plain ("outside") as well as a series of inlets penetrating deep into the hilly interior ("inside"). The climate is wet and moderate with fierce winter storms. The Nootkan population was at least 15,000 in the mideighteenth century. Nootka and Nitinaht,

together with Makah, constitute the southern or Nootkan branch of the Wakashan language family.

Numerous categories of spirit and mythological beings were recognized as ubiquitous. They could be obtained and controlled through rituals or by spirit quests. Rituals, especially as practiced by chiefs, helped to ensure bountiful salmon runs, the beaching of dead whales, and other food resources. Long-haired shamans dived to the bottom of the sea to battle soul-stealing sea spirits. Chiefs also engaged in spirit quests (commoners' spiritual help came through minor rituals and charms). One obtained power from a spirit being by seizing it, rather than by establishing a relation with it as with a guardian spirit. Such power provided special skills, luck, or other achievements.

Nootkans prayed for power to the Four Chiefs of Above, Horizon, Land, and Undersea. They observed two primary winter ceremonies: the Dancing, or Wolf, ritual, and the Doctoring ritual (central and southern Nootkans only). Although the former was an initiation and the latter a curing ceremony, the ultimate purpose of both was to confirm the social order. The Wolf ritual, several of which might be held in a village each winter, involved masks and dramatization.

Local groups held defined territories, the legitimacy of which came from a particular legendary ancestor. The chiefly line of descent was the group's nucleus. The highest-ranking man in a local group was its chief, whose position was inheritable.

Local groups sometimes united to form tribes, with ranked chiefs and common winter villages and ceremonials. Some northern Nootkan tribes also came together to form confederacies, with each local group retaining its identity, territory, and ceremonies.

Inherited rights formed the basis of social rank and governed the ownership and use of practically everything of value. Inheritance was generally patrilineal. Nootkan social classes consisted of chief, commoners, and slaves. The chief did not work; he directed his followers, who in turn supported him and who were taken care of by them. A chief's close male relations were secondary chiefs (such as war chiefs and speakers). Chiefs received tribute for the use of resource sites. When goods accumulated, they held a feast or a potlatch. Other occasions for potlatches included life cycle and public events such as status transfer and confirmation. The participation in all life cycle rituals and ceremonies was commensurate with social rank.

Pregnancy and birth carried numerous rituals and restrictions, especially regarding twins. Infants' heads were flattened to achieve an aesthetic ideal. Children were regularly instructed on correct behavior, such as industry, peacefulness, and social responsibility, and on ritual knowledge. For high-status families, the onset of female puberty was the occasion for a great potlatch. It also entailed rituals and seclusion for the woman herself. Along with warfare, marriage was the means by which local groups sought to maximize access to subsistence areas. As such, it was mostly an alliance between families and was accompanied by great ritual, depending on rank. Although divorce was possible, adultery, unless chronic or within the chief's family, was generally smoothed over.

Multifamily cedar houses between forty and 150 feet long, between thirty and forty feet wide, and between eight and ten feet high lined the beaches. Planks were removable for use in smaller camp dwellings. Roofs were of both shed (primarily in the south) and gabled style. Individual family areas, each with its own fireplace, were set off from the others by storage chests. Sleeping platforms ringed the walls. Posts and beams were carved with hereditary designs. Local groups had house frames standing at three sites: permanent village, summertime fishing and sea hunting areas, and a main salmon stream.

Salmon, smoked and dried, was the Nootkans' staple food. Nootkans also ate herring, halibut, cod, snapper, flounder, and other fish. Other important foods included roots, berries, bulbs, ferns, crabapples, and eelgrass; shellfish, mollusks, kelp, and sea cucumbers; waterfowl; and sea mammals such as harbor seals, porpoises, sea lions, sea otters, and whales. The ritualistic preparation by whalers, who were always chiefs, included bathing, praying, and swimming, and it began months in advance of the whaling season. Land mammals included deer, elk, black bear, and small mammals. Most food was dried, smoked, steamed in pits, or broiled in wooden boxes with red-hot stones. Fish were taken with dip nets, rakes, floating fences, and weirs; waterfowl with nets, nooses, bow and arrow, and snares; marine invertebrates with yew digging and prying sticks; sea mammals with clubs, harpoons, stakes hidden in seaweed, and nets. Special whaling equipment consisted of harpoons with mussel shell blades, two forty- to sixty-fathom lines, floats, and lances. Nootkans used six types of canoes, some with cedar-bark mat sails. The uses of wood, a key raw material, included hunting and war tools, canoes, houses, utensils, buckets, and storage boxes. Mattresses and other such items were made of cedar bark.

Nootkans enjoyed a virtual monopoly on dentalia shell, an item highly prized by many peoples along and surrounding the Northwest Coast. They also supplied sea otter pelts and canoes. Their primary trading partners were the Nimpkish Kwakiutls and the Makahs. Nootkans received eulachon (smelt) oil and grease from the Tsimshians, Chilkat goat-hair blankets from the Tlingits, and furs from the Coast Salish (who obtained them from interior peoples).

Music and dance were important Nootkan arts. Vocal music, often containing complicated structures, patterns, and beats, was accompanied by drumming and rattles. Songs were sung for many different occasions, both sacred and secular.

Drama regularly included masks to represent supernatural beings. People told long, complex stories on winter evenings. House posts and fronts and many wooden objects were elaborately carved with crest designs. The decorated conical, onion-domed cedar-bark and spruce-root whaler's hat was a classic Nootkan basketry item. Painting was highly developed in the historic period.

Nootkan culture changed relatively little during the 5,000 years pre-contact with non-Natives. In the late prehistoric period they had acquired iron and other metals through trade and salvage from shipwrecks. In 1778, Captain Cook remained with the Nootkas for a month, acquiring a large collection of sea otter pelts. Cook's crew later sold the pelts to Chinese merchants at great profit, thereby laying the basis for the northwest maritime fur trade.

A few Nootkan chiefs, such as Maquinna, whose power was maintained in part by the Spanish, became very wealthy by controlling that trade. Partly by means of firearms, they established themselves as intermediaries between whites and other Indian peoples. During that time, Indians began to suffer significant population decline owing to increased warfare (competition over the fur trade) as well as epidemics, including venereal disease. By the end of the century, hunters had so depleted the sea otter stock that the local fur trade was in sharp decline. In its wake, Indians began attacking trade ships, which in turn greatly diminished their contact with non-Natives for several decades.

Population decline and general dislocation led to the formation of new tribes and confederacies in the early nineteenth century. Continued Nootkan attacks on trade ships in midcentury brought retaliation from the British navy. Gradually, without being formally conquered, the Nootkans became integrated into the new commercial economy. There was a continuing trade in the furs of animals such as deer, elk, mink, marten, and northern fur seal. Throughout the late nineteenth century, Nootkans were important suppliers of dogfish oil, which was used in the logging industry. They also became involved in the pelagic sealing industry, hunting from canoes as well as schooners. Some Nootkans became wealthy during that period and even purchased their own schooners. Commercial fishing was another important local industry, providing jobs and drawing people to canneries from their villages. Crafts for the tourist trade also became important around that time, as did seasonal hop picking in the Puget Sound area.

When British Columbia joined Canada in 1871, Nootkans became part of the federal Indian reserve system. Villages still in use received small reserves in the 1880s, though without having formally surrendered any land to the government. Missionaries arrived to carry out government health and education programs. Such programs included the establishment of Indian boarding schools, where Native culture was ruthlessly suppressed.

After World War II, further consolidation and centralization of the Nootkan population paralleled similar trends in the fishing industry. Potlatching and other forms of traditional culture continued, despite government opposition. Beginning in the 1960s and 1970s, Nootkans focused on fostering a positive self-identity and achieving control over their own destinies. In 1978, a political organization called the West Coast District Council (formerly the West Coast Allied Tribes) adopted the name Nuu-chah-nulth ("all along the mountains") for all Nootkan peoples and renamed the organization the Nuu-chah-nulth Tribal Council.

See also Potlatch; Salmon, Economic and Spiritual Significance of; Slavery; Trade.

Oowekeeno

See Bella Bella.

Puyallup

See Salish, Southern Coast.

Quileute

"Quileute" is taken from the name of a village at the site of La Push, on the present-day Washington State coast. The Hoh Indians, formerly considered a Quileute band, now have independent federal recognition. Traditionally, the Quileutes lived along the coast from south of Ozette Lake to just south of the Hoh River and west to Mt. Olympus, on the Olympic Peninsula. Most of the region is rain forest. Today, many Quileutes live on reservations on the Pacific coast of the Olympic Peninsula, in the state of Washington. In the late eighteenth century, about 500 Quileutes lived on the Olympic Peninsula. In late pre-contact times, the Quileute were members, with the Hoh and the Quinault, of a confederation that controlled most tribes from Cape Flattery to Grey's Harbor. Quileute is a Chimakuan language.

The Quileute universe was peopled with a creator-transformer and a variety of ghosts, spirits, monsters, and creatures. This interplay gave rise to a rich mythology. Entry to one of five ceremonial societies—warrior, hunter, whaler, shaman, and fisher—might be obtained by holding a potlatch or showing evidence of an appropriate guardian spirit power. Initiations, which included dances with carved wood masks, took place primarily in the winter. Potlatches also accompanied life cycle events.

Individuals could claim guardian spirits, from nature or ancestors, through special quests or by being adopted by the power. Such powers could also be lost or stolen, perhaps through the intercession of a shaman, or simply depart, in which case a shaman might bring them back (this was the lost-soul cure; shamans could also cure disease). Adolescents quested after spirit powers by fasting and visiting remote places. The Quileutes also observed first salmon rites (the ritualistic preparation and consumption of the season's first catch).

A village, made up of extended families, was the basic political unit. Each village had two hereditary chiefs. Quileute society was divided into the hereditary groups that were usual for Northwest Indians: chiefs, commoners, and slaves (acquired in raids or trade). Much social activity was devoted to maintain-

ing and pursuing status. With rank came the rights to names, dances, songs, designs, guardian spirit powers, and membership in certain secret societies.

The traits of cleanliness, moderation, and generosity were especially prized. At puberty, girls were confined to a section of the house for five days. Boys began spirit questing in their late teens. Perhaps because pre- and extramarital sex was taboo, the Quileutes recognized ten different types of marriage, including polygamy. Quileutes intermarried regularly with Makahs and Quinaults. Divorce was common.

Both parents were subject to behavioral restrictions regarding pregnancy and childbirth. The birth of twins subjected parents to eight months of additional taboos. Babies were kept in cradle boards. Noble families flattened their babies' heads. The dead were wrapped in mats or dog hair blankets and buried in canoes or hollow logs. Mourners cut their hair and painted their faces. Widows observed special taboos, such as not sleeping lying down. The names of the dead were not spoken for some time, and mourners asked those with similar names to change them. On the second anniversary of death, the remains of high-status people were reburied, and a memorial potlatch was given.

Quileutes either killed or enslaved the first non-Natives they met (Spanish in 1775, British in 1787, Russian in 1808). They had little contact with whites until 1855, when the Indians signed a treaty agreeing to move to the Quinault Reservation. They had not yet moved, however, by 1889, the year the one-square-mile La Push Reservation was created. Four years later, a reservation was established for the people of the Hoh River.

In the interim (1860s–1880s), Quileutes did the best they could to resist the invading non-Natives. Most declined to send their children to an Anglo school that opened at La Push in 1882. Symptomatic of the interracial hostility that reigned during that time was the fire set by a white person at La Push in 1889 that destroyed twenty-six houses and almost all pre-contact artifacts.

In 1895, the Quileutes embraced the Indian Shaker religion. In 1912, whites appropriated ancient fishing sites to open a canning industry on the Quillayute River. Indians were declared ineligible to obtain fishing licenses. They gave up whaling in 1904 and sealing in the 1930s. In 1936, shortly after 165 Quileutes were each allotted eighty acres of timbered land on the Quinault Reservation, the tribe adopted a constitution and bylaws.

See also Fishing Rights; Salmon, Economic and Spiritual Significance of.

Quinault

See Salish, Southwestern Coast.

Salish, Central Coast

Central Coast Salish were a group of Indians who shared a common language family and a related culture. Central Coast Salish tribes and villages included the Squamish (at least sixteen villages), the Nooksacks (at least twenty villages), the Klallams (about a dozen villages), the Halkomelems, and Northern Straits. The Halkomelems had three divisions: Island (Nanooses, Nanaimos, Chemainus, Cowichans, and Malahats), Downriver (Musqueams, Tsawwessens, Saleelwats, Kwantlens, Coquitlams, Nicomekls, and Katzies), and Upriver (Matsquis, Sumas, Nicomens, Scowlitzes, Chehalis, Chilliwaks, Pilalts, and Taits). Northern Straits had six divisions: Sookes, Songhees, Saanichs, Semiahmoos, Lummis, Samish. The discussions that follow do not apply to every group or tribe.

Traditionally, the lands inhabited by the Central Coast Salish in Canada and the United States included both sides of the southern Strait of Georgia, the San Juan Islands, the extreme northwest part of Washington east of the strait, and parts of the northern Olympic Peninsula. The region is generally wet and moderate, although it includes some drier and cooler regions. Most contemporary Central Coast Salish Indians live on reserves or reservations in or near their aboriginal lands or in cities of the Northwest. The Central Coast Salish population stood at roughly 20,000 in the mideighteenth century. Central Coast Salish, which includes the Squamish, Nooksack, Klallam, Halkomelem, and Northern Straits (Lkungen) languages, is a member of the central division of the Salishan language family.

Central Coast Salish recognized a mythological time when their legendary ancestors lived. They believed that people are composed of several components, one or more of which might occasionally get lost or lured away and had to be restored by shamans. In their everyday lives, they made a distinction between what was considered normal and anything that might connote danger or power (such

Two Salish women drying meat on a stick frame, ca. 1910. (Library of Congress)

as a deformed person, a menstruating woman, or a corpse). People sought luck or skills from an encounter with a spirit. An accompanying song provided direct access to the spirit's power.

The shamans' spirit helpers gave special powers. Men and women could be shamans. Curing, the province of shamans, entailed singing, drama, and extracting a harmful entity with the hands and mouth. Some shamans could also foretell the future. Spells or incantations were also believed to carry power. Most people used them to help perform a task, but people highly skilled in such matters could be hired for special occasions.

Intra- and intervillage spirit dances took place in the winter. The host provided food, and dancers danced their spirit songs, of which there were several categories. Dances and songs were accompanied by much ritual paraphernalia. Secret societies also held their dances in the winter. Their main ceremony was initiating new members; the right to member-

ship was hereditary. Central Coast Salish people also observed first salmon ceremonies (the ritualistic preparation and consumption of the season's first catch). Cleansing rituals were made both to erase a disgrace and to enhance a festive occasion.

Each group lived in a number of villages. Heads of the leading or established household served as local group chiefs. As such, they had little or no power to govern; they were wealthy and influential men who entertained guests, made decisions about subsistence activity, and arbitrated disputes.

Several extended families made up a household, which owned particular subsistence areas and tools, such as clam beds and fowl nets. Some particularly prestigious households, or "houses" (in the European sense), descended from a notable ancestor and shared resources, names, ceremonies, and other valuables. Some local groups may have had their own winter villages, although larger villages included several local groups. Members of different

households cooperated in some activities such as deer drives, building a salmon weir, ceremonies, and defense, but they were not necessarily culturally homogeneous. There was little intervillage cooperation. Social groups included worthy people (those with wealth, ancestry, manners, and guardian spirits), worthless people, and slaves.

The Central Coast Salish intermarried within the village and outside it. Marriages involved ritual exchanges and promoted trade. They were initiated by men; women could refuse, but they felt pressure to marry "well." A wedding usually entailed the exchange of gifts (material and/or hereditary privileges) and a cleansing ceremony. Exchanges of food and gifts between families-in-law continued throughout the marriage.

From an early age, children were "toughened" by swimming in icy water and running in storms. This process culminated in the adolescent spirit quest. Boys marked puberty by making their first kill. If possible, girls were feted with a feast and a display of hereditary privileges. They were secluded during their periods. Among the Cowichans, a girl undertook a solitary vigil; if she was joined by a boy, and their parents agreed, they could be married. Corpses were wrapped in blankets and placed in canoes or grave boxes. Among the worthy, bones were rewrapped several years later with an accompanying display of privileges.

Potlatches, as opposed to feasts, were usually held outdoors in good weather. Occasions included life crises and important life cycle or ceremonial events. Usually all or part of a village held the potlatch, with each house marking its own occasions. Goods were not expected to be returned: The point was status—that is, good relations with neighbors and good marriages for children.

Some hunters, on both land and sea, achieved a professional status and spent whole summers hunting. People generally spent the summers traveling in small groups, following seasonal food cycles and living in temporary dwellings. They enjoyed several gambling games, including the traditional hand and disk games. Sports included shinny (a variation of hockey), races, athletic competitions, and games of skill. Singing for pleasure was common.

Winter villages consisted of from one house to several rows of houses built on the beach. Houses were up to several hundred feet long. They had a permanent wooden framework with a shed roof with removable roof and wall planks. Each family had a separate fire. House posts were decorated with painted and carved images of ancestors and spirit powers. These people also built some fortified war refuges (stockades). Other structures included summer mat houses, wooden grave houses, and pole and mat sweat lodges.

Fish, especially salmon (of all species), was the staple food, although it was available to different people in different places at different times of the year. The leaner fall runs were dried for storage; otherwise fish was eaten fresh. Other important foods included sea mammals (seal and porpoise, used mostly for oil; sea lions; whales [Klallam]); shellfish; land mammals such as deer, elk, black bear, mountain goats, and beaver (smaller game as well as grizzlies, cougars, and wolves were generally avoided); waterfowl; and a large variety of plants. Camus, brake fern, wapato, and wild carrots were especially important, but other bulbs, roots, berries, sprouts, and stems were also used. Camus fields were burned and reseeded. Potato husbandry became important after 1800.

Fish were taken with reef nets, dip nets, trawl nets, harpoons, gaff hooks, spears, basket traps, weirs, tidal pounds (rows of underwater stakes), hooks, and herring rakes and in rectangular nets suspended between two canoes, a method by which several thousand fish a day might be captured. Harpoons, seal nets, and clubs served as marine mammal hunting equipment; land mammals were taken with pitfalls, snares, bow (2.5 to 3 feet, made of yew) and arrow, and spears. Waterfowl were snagged in permanent nets stretched across flyways. They were also hunted with bow and arrow, flares and nets at night, and snares.

Important raw materials included wood, hides, antler, horn, mountain goat wool, beaver teeth, wood stone, and shell. Wooden items included house materials, canoes, bent-corner boxes, dishes, tools, weapons, and ceremonial items. Shredded bark was used for towels, mattresses, and similar items. Sewn mats of cattail leaves and tule lined the interior house walls, covered the frames of summer shelters, and were made into mattresses, rain covers, and sitting or kneeling pads. Women made several types of baskets, including wrapped lattice, coiled, twined, and woven. They practiced a distinctive form of weaving, spinning wool from a special breed of dog (now extinct) plus mountain goat wool, waterfowl down, and fireweed cotton on a large spindle and weaving it on a two-bar loom.

The Central Coast Salish fought wars among themselves, with their neighbors, and with more

distant neighbors. Injury and death, intentional or not, demanded compensation. Refusal to pay might lead to fighting, and some groups, such as the Klallams, saw compensation as dishonorable. The Klallams were particularly aggressive; the impaled heads of their foes, often Snohomish, Cowichans, or Duwamish, often decorated their beaches. There was some naval warfare, in which canoes rammed and sank other canoes. At least in the early nineteenth century, the Lekwiltoks (Kwakiutls) were a common enemy.

Raids, for loot, territory, vengeance, or a show of power, were led by professional warriors with special powers. Raids featured surprise attacks. Men were killed, and women and children were captured, later to be ransomed or sold as slaves. Warriors wore elk hide armor.

> *See also* Basketry; Fishing Rights; Salmon, Economic and Spiritual Significance of; Warfare, Intertribal.

Salish, Northern Coast

The constituent groups of the Northern Coast Salish ('Sal ish) included Island Comoxes, Mainland Comoxes (Homalcos, Klahooses, and Sliammons), Pentlatches, and Sechelts. The Comoxes called themselves *Catlo'ltx*. Traditional Northern Coast Salish territory, all in Canada, included roughly the northern half of the Strait of Georgia, including east central Vancouver Island. The climate is wet and moderate. As of the 1990s, Northern Coast Salish Indians lived in villages and reserves in their traditional territory and in regional cities and towns. The Comox population in 1780 was about 1,800. In 1995, about 2,750 Northern Coast Salish from six bands (Comoxes, Homalcos, Klahooses, Sliammons, Qualicums [Pentlatches], and Sechelts) lived in the region. Northern Coast Salish, which includes the Comox, Pentlatch, and Sechelt languages, is a member of the Central division of the Salishan language family.

People sought guardian spirits (from animate or inanimate objects) to confer special powers or skills. Spirits were acquired in dreams or by fasting or other physical tests. The Northern Coast Salish Indians celebrated two forms of winter ceremonials: spirit dancing, which was inclusive and participatory, and masked dancing, which was reserved for only certain high-status families. Shamans as

well as various secret societies provided religious leadership.

Villages were headed by chiefs, who were the heads of the leading or established households. Chiefs had little or no power to govern; they were wealthy and influential men who entertained guests, made decisions about subsistence activity, and arbitrated disputes.

Among most groups, the "local group" consisted of members who traced their descent patrilineally from a mythical ancestor; it was identified with and controlled certain specific subsistence areas. The right to hold potlatches and certain ceremonies, including dances and songs, was also inheritable. Northern Coast Salish people were either chiefs, nobles, commoners, or slaves.

Both parents, but especially the mother, were subject to pregnancy and childbirth-related taboos and restrictions. Infants' heads were pressed for aesthetic effect. Pubescent girls were secluded and their behavior was restricted, but boys were physically and mentally trained to seek a guardian spirit. Those who embarked on extended training and quests became shamans.

People were considered marriageable when they reached adolescence. Men, accompanied by male relatives, first approached women in a canoe. Polygyny was common, and multiple wives resided in the same household. Corpses were washed, wrapped in a blanket, and placed in a coffin that was in turn set in a cave or a tree away from the village. Possessions were burned. The Comoxes and Pentlatches erected carved and painted mortuary poles.

Northern Coast Salish people built three types of permanent plank houses (semiexcavated and with shed and gabled roofs). Planks could be removed and transported to permanent frameworks at summer villages. Some houses were up to sixty or seventy feet long and half as wide. Most were fortified with either stockades or deep trenches. The Pentlatches and Island Comoxes had enclosed sleeping areas and separate smoke-drying sheds. Structures housed several related households, including extended families and slaves.

Fish was the staple, especially salmon. Fall salmon were smoke-dried for winter storage; the catch from summer salmon runs was eaten fresh. The people practiced the ritualistic preparation and consumption of the season's first salmon. They also ate lingcod, greenling, steelhead, flounder, sole, and herring roe. Other important foods included sea mammals (sea lion, harbor seal, porpoise); shellfish;

land mammals, such as deer, bear, and some elk and mountain goat; birds and fowl; and plant foods, including berries, shoots and leaves, roots, bulbs, and cambium.

Fish were taken with gill nets, basket traps and weirs, gaffs and harpoons, tidal basins of stakes or rocks, dip nets, and rakes (herring). Seal nets, clubs, and harpoons with an identifiable float served as marine mammal hunting equipment. Land mammals were taken with pitfalls, snares, bow (2.5 to 3 feet long, made of yew) and arrow, nets, knives, traps, and spears. Waterfowl were snagged in permanent nets stretched across flyways. They were also hunted with bow and arrow, flares and nets at night, and snares.

Important raw materials included wood, hides, antler, horn, mountain goat wool, beaver teeth, wood, bone, stone, and shell. Wooden items included house materials, canoes, bent-corner boxes, dishes, tools, weapons, and ceremonial items. Shredded bark was used for towels, mattresses, and similar items. Sewn mats of cattail leaves and tule lined interior house walls, covered frames of summer shelters, and were made into mattresses, rain covers, and sitting or kneeling pads. Women made several types of baskets of cedar limb splints or roots, including wrapped lattice, coiled, twined, and woven.

Juan de Fuca may have encountered the Northern Coast Salish in 1752. British and Spanish trade ships arrived in 1792 to a friendly reception. Owing to the lack of sea otter in the Strait of Georgia, however, most Northern Coast Salish did not participate in the local maritime fur trade.

Miners and other non-Natives founded Victoria in 1843. By this time local Indians had experienced severe epidemics with some concomitant village abandonment and consolidation. Catholic missionaries arrived in the 1860s, and many Natives converted and renounced their ceremonials, including potlatching. Some self-sufficient overtly Christian villages were established, complete with a missionary-imposed governing structure. By the end of the century, the missionaries, along with Catholic boarding schools, had largely destroyed the Native language and culture.

With their traditional economy severely damaged, many Indian men took jobs as longshoremen, loggers, and migrant farmers. They also worked in commercial fishing, including canneries. Canada officially established Indian reserves in 1876, by which time Indians had already lost much of their aboriginal land. In the early twentieth century, sev-

eral Indian organizations, such as the Allied Tribes and the Native Brotherhood of British Columbia, formed to pursue title to aboriginal lands. The Alliance of Tribal Councils continued this work in the 1970s and worked to foster a positive self-image as well as political unity. Partly as a result of its activity, in 1986 the Sechelt band became the first self-governing Indian group in Canada.

See also Fishing Rights; Salmon, Economic and Spiritual Significance of.

Salish, Southern Coast

The Southern Coast Salish included over fifty named, autonomous Indian groups or tribes inhabiting the Puget Sound region and speaking one of two languages. The component groups included (but were not limited to) Swinomish, Skagits (Lower Skagits or Whidby Island Skagits), Upper Skagits, Stillaguamish, Skykomish (perhaps once a subdivision of the Snoqualmies), and Snohomish (speakers of Northern Lushootseed); Steilacooms, Snoqualmies, Suquamish, Duwamish, Puyallups, Nisquallys, and Squaxins (speakers of southern Lushootseed); and Quilcene, Skokomish, and Duhlelips (speakers of Twana). Many of these groups themselves consisted of autonomous subdivisions. Little is known of these Indians' lives before their contact with non-Natives.

The basic Southern Coast Salish culture was in place at least 2,000 years ago. Southern Coast Salish people lived in and around the Puget Sound Basin in Washington. The climate is generally wet and moderate, with the northern areas somewhat drier. Although most of the land was timbered, some was kept open by regular burning practices. Most contemporary Southern Coast Salish Indians live on local reservations or in nearby cities and towns. The precontact population was estimated to be around 12,600. Southern Coast Salish, which includes the Lushootseed (Northern and Southern dialects) and Twana languages, is a member of the Central division of the Salishan language family.

According to the Twana, people were possessed of life souls and heart souls. Illness occurred if the former left the body. At death, life souls went to the land of the dead and were eventually reborn, whereas heart souls just disappeared. The people prayed to the sun and the earth, deities concerned

with ethics. They also regarded salmon and other animal species as "people in their own country," complete with chiefs and other such conventions.

A mythological age ended when a transformer fashioned this world. Guardian spirits, both regular (lay) and shamanistic, were believed responsible for all luck, skill, and achievement. Shamans received the same powers as lay people, plus two unique powers. Spirit helpers and their associated songs were acquired through quests (or occasionally inheritance), which might begin as early as age eight and which consisted of fasting, bathing, and physical deprivation. Following the quest, nothing happened for up to twenty years, at which time the spirit returned (temporarily causing illness), the person sang and danced, and the power was activated. Shamans cured certain illnesses (such as soul loss) and could also cause illness and death, an explanation of why they were sometimes killed.

Southern Coast Salish Indians celebrated several regular ceremonies. The Winter Dance was sponsored by someone who was ill as a result of a returning spirit. There was much ritual connected with a "cure," including dancing, singing, feasting, and gift distribution. The soul recovery ceremony was an attempt to recapture a soul from the dead. Performers sang their spirit songs and dramatized a canoe search and the rescue of soul. The potlatch was given by those who had encountered a wealthy power and were to become wealthy themselves. It was held in the summer or early fall. The leading men of nearby villages and their families were invited. Guests brought food and wealth. Potlatches lasted for several days and included games, contests, secular songs, and dances, after which the sponsor gave away gifts and sang his power song.

Among the Twanas, Suquamish, and maybe others, the *tamanawas* ceremony initiated new members (adolescents of both sexes with wealthy parents) into a secret religious society.

Each local group had one or more winter villages as well as several summer camps and resource sites. Village leaders were generally the heads of the wealthiest households; they had no formal leadership role. In Twana villages, the chief's speaker and village crier delivered brief sermons and awakened people, respectively.

Villages consisted of one or more houses, which in turn sheltered several families, each within its own special section. Village membership may have been more permanent or stable in the south than in the north. Although they were truly autonomous, neighboring groups were linked by intermarriage, by ceremonial and customary activities, and by the use of common territories. Fishing sites and equipment could be individually or communally owned. Hunting was a profession among many Coast Salish groups.

Classes, or social groups, included upper free (wealthy, high birth, sponsors of feasts and appropriate ceremonies), lower free (less wealth, common birth, fewer and less prestigious ceremonies), and slave (property). Recognition by the intervillage network was required to confirm or alter status. Possessions of woven blankets, dentalia, clamshell-disk beads, robes, pelts, bone war clubs, canoes, and slaves constituted wealth. The house posts and grave monuments of high-status people were carved and/or painted. All except slaves and the very poor had their heads flattened in infancy. Popular games included gambling (dice and the disk and traditional hand games) as well as games of skill and athletic contests. More southerly people smoked tobacco (obtained in trade) mixed with kinnikinnick (bearberry).

There were few formal birth ceremonies, although behavior was restricted for a new mother and father. At adolescence, both sexes were expected to seek visions, although a girl was subject to a greater number of behavioral restrictions, including isolation at her first period (and at all subsequent periods). Upper-class girls had "coming out parties" after their first isolation to announce their marriageability. Marriage was arranged by families, usually to people in different villages. It involved the ritual exchange of gifts. Divorce was possible but difficult, especially among the upper class. Death received the most ritualistic treatment. Professional undertakers prepared the body, which was interred in a canoe or an aboveground grave box. After the funeral there was a feast, and the deceased's property was given away.

Permanent plank houses had shed roofs (later, gambrel and gabled roofs) and were very similar to those of the Central Coast Salish. Several families (nuclear or extended, possibly including slaves) shared a house. Each family, or sometimes two, had its own fireplace. Co-wives might also share the house and have their own fireplaces. Cedar longhouses might be as large as 200 by fifty feet.

Some houses were built and used by wealthy men as potlatch houses. Temporary summertime camp houses consisted of mats covering pole frames.

Most villages had at least one sweat house. Stockades protected some villages. The famous "old man house," a Suquamish dwelling, once stood in the village of Suqua. It was about 500 feet long and sixty feet wide. The government ordered it burned in the 1870s.

Several types of cedar canoes were employed for purposes such as trolling, hunting, moving freight, and warfare. For major travel (such as travel to and from summer camps), people made a sort of catamaran by lashing some boards between two canoes. Upriver peoples used log rafts for crossing or traveling down streams. Winter hunters walked on snowshoes. Horses arrived in the area in the late eighteenth century, but only inland groups such as the Nisquallys and Puyallups used them extensively.

Most clothing was made of shredded cedar bark and buckskin. In warm weather, men wore breechclouts or nothing; women wore a cedar-bark apron and usually a skirt. In colder weather, men and some women wore hide shirts, leggings, and robes of bearskin as well as skins of smaller mammals sewn together. Both wore hide moccasins.

Some groups wore basketry or fur caps. Many wore abalone and dentalia earrings. Women also wore shell, teeth, and claw necklaces as well as leg and chin tattoos. Older men might keep hair on their faces. Intragroup violence was usually dealt with by compensation and purification. Fighting, usually resulting from revenge, the ambitions of warriors, and slave raids, was usually with nonneighboring groups. Professional warriors did exist, although warfare was largely defensive in nature. Weapons included war clubs, daggers, spears, and bow and arrow (possibly poisoned). Hide shirts were worn as armor. Rather than fight, Twanas might hire shamans to harm other groups.

At least in the early nineteenth century, the Southern Coast Salish had to deal with highly aggressive Lekwiltok Kwakiutl raiders. On at least one occasion the Salish tribes banded together to launch a retaliatory expedition against the Kwakiutls. Some groups, such as the Skagits and Snohomish, had guns before they ever saw non-Indians.

George Vancouver visited the region in 1792. By that time, evidence of metal and smallpox suggested that the Southern Coast Salish might already have encountered Europeans indirectly. Owing primarily to the lack of sea otters in their region, the Salish experienced little further contact for the next thirty years or so.

At least after 1827 and the establishment of the Hudson's Bay Company post on the Fraser River, the Southern Coast Salish were in regular contact with non-Native traders. Fort Nisqually was founded in 1833. Among the cultural changes the Indians experienced were the introduction of firearms, the move away from traditional forms of dress, and the beginning of the potato crop. They also experienced new Native ideas from remote places, such as the Plateau Prophet Dance.

Catholic missionaries arrived around 1840. The first U.S. settlers followed shortly thereafter, especially after the United States took control of the region by the Treaty of Washington (1846). In 1850, the Donation Land Act of Oregon allowed settlers to invade and claim Indian land. The Washington Territory was officially established in 1853.

In 1854 and 1855, Southern Coast Salish Indians signed a number of treaties (Medicine Creek, Point Elliot, and Point No Point) ceding land and creating seven future reservations (Squaxin, Nisqually, Puyallup, Port Madison, Tulalip, Swinomish, and Skokomish). Notable chiefs who signed included Sea'th'l (Suquamish/Duwamish, after whom the city of Seattle was named), Goliah (Skagit), and Patkanin (Snoqualmie). The Nisqually chief Leschi opposed the Medicine Creek Treaty, arguing that his people should settle near the mouth of the Nisqually River and other traditional subsistence areas. He was hanged by the Americans in 1858.

The Steilacooms were denied a reservation because of the planned development of the town of Steilacoom. Most joined other local reservations or remained in their homeland, becoming the ancestors of the modern tribe. Upper Skagits were left landless by the Point Elliot treaty; they later received and then lost several individual allotments.

In 1857, an executive order established the Muckleshoot Reservation (the Muckleshoots were an amalgam of several inland tribes and groups). During subsequent years these lands were whittled away by the Dawes Act and other legal and extralegal coercions (such as the unofficial toleration of illegal whiskey peddlers). Indians rebelled against unfair and dishonest treaty negotiations by engaging in the 1855–1856 Rogue River War and by refusing to move onto reservations.

However, by the 1850s, most Southern Coast Salish were heavily involved in the non-Native economy, and most sold their labor, furs, and other resources to non-Indians. Important and growing industries included logging, commercial fishing and

canning, and hopyards. Seattle was founded in and grew out of a Duwamish winter village (in 1962, the government paid the members of the Duwamish tribe $1.35 an acre for land that had become the city of Seattle). The Duwamishes moved around the region, refusing to settle on reservations, until some joined the Muckleshoot and Tulalip Reservations. Whites burned them out of their homes in West Seattle in 1893. In 1925, though landless, they adopted a constitution and formed a government. Furthermore, most tribes came under the control of the rigidly assimilationist Bureau of Indian Affairs.

In 1917, the government commandeered most of the 4,700-acre Nisqually Reservation for Camp (later Fort) Lewis. Displaced Nisquallys scattered to various reservations and lands. During the 1960s, clashes between Indians and non-Natives over fishing rights sometimes became violent; they were settled in the Indians' favor, however, in the 1970s. Contrary to government desires, they did not farm but maintained their hunting and fishing traditions.

The Puyallups turned to agriculture during the 1870s. For that reason, they were seen by whites as having made great progress toward civilization. The growth of the adjacent city of Tacoma fueled pressure for the sale of unallotted lands; most of the reservation had been lost by the early twentieth century. The Puyallups were at the forefront of the fishing wars of the 1960s and 1970s. Many Snohomishes left their reservation during the last years of the nineteenth century as a result of overcrowding and oppressive government policies. These Indians, plus those who never moved to the Tulalip Reservation, became the historic Snohomish tribe.

The Tulalip tribes were created in 1855, as was the Tulalip Reservation, which was intended for the Snohomishes, Snoqualmies, Stillaguamishes, Skykomishes, and others. The word "Tulalip" comes from a Snohomish word meaning "a bay shaped like a purse." Many of these Indians refused to settle on the reservation, however, and ended up landless.

By the 1860s, the Squaxins had abandoned their traditional dress but maintained other aspects of their culture. In 1874, about thirty Squaxins went to live at and became assimilated into the Twana community. Some Squaxins also owned allotments on the Quinault Reservation. In 1882, a Squaxin Indian, John Slocum, began the Indian Shaker Church, which emphasizes morality, sobriety, and honesty. This religion soon spread far and wide and continues today. The Snoqualmies were removed to the Tulalip Reservation after the Rogue River War; they slowly assimilated into that and nearby white communities.

See also Fishing Rights; Fur Trade; Potlatch; Salmon, Economic and Spiritual Significance of; Seattle.

Salish, Southwestern Coast

"Southwestern coast Salish" refers to the speakers of four closely related Salishan languages. Its component groups are Queets, Copalis, and Quinaults, who are speakers of Quinault; Humptulips, Wynoochees, Chehalis, and Shoalwater Bay, who are speakers of Lower Chehalis; Satsops and Kwaiailks, or Upper Chehalis, who are speakers of Upper Chehalis; and Cowlitzes, who are speakers of Cowlitz.

Traditionally, the Southwestern Coast Salish lived along the Pacific Coast from just south of the Hoh River delta to northern Willapa Bay, including the drainages of the Queets, Quinault, Lower Cowlitz, and Chehalis River systems, all in the state of Washington. Local environments included rain forest, mountains, open ocean, sheltered saltwater bays, forest, and prairies. Today, most of these Indians live on local reservations or in Northwest cities and towns. Around 1800, there were perhaps 2,500 Quinaults and Lower Chehalis and about 8,000 Kwaiailks and (mostly Lower) Cowlitzes. Southwest Salish, which includes the Quinault, Lower Chehalis, Upper Chehalis, and Mountain and Lower Cowlitz languages, is part of the Tsamosan (formerly Olympic) division of the Salishan language family. The Upper and Lewis River Cowlitzes spoke dialects of Sahaptian.

Southwestern Coast Salish religion centered around the relation of individuals, including slaves, to guardian spirits. Spirits lived either in the land of the dead or in animate and inanimate objects. They provided wealth, power, skill, and/or luck. Songs, dances, and paraphernalia were associated with particular spirits. Spirits not properly honored could be dangerous. Training (such as bathing, fasting in lonely places, and other physical tests) to acquire a spirit began as early as about age seven and culminated in a formal spirit quest at adolescence.

Shamans, who might be men or women, had especially powerful spirits. They diagnosed and

cured disease. They could also cause illness or death and were occasionally hired for this purpose. Feasts involved only local people; potlatches were intertribal. The latter, held in winter, were given at life cycle events or at the perceived bequest of a spirit. Social status was closely related to potlatching activity.

Spirit song ceremonials were observed in winter, accompanied among some tribes by gift giving. Some coastal groups also had secret societies. Most groups celebrated first salmon rituals (the ritualistic preparation and consumption of the season's first catch) during which they burned the salmon's heart and distributed some of the fish to all villagers.

Politically independent villages were each composed of between one and ten households, each household consisting of several families. A nonpolitical "tribe" was recognized as several villages that shared a language and a territory. Village leaders tended to come from certain families, with the eldest son often inheriting the leadership position. Leaders were wealthy and often owned several slaves so that they would not have to work as hard as others did. Their power was limited to giving advice and settling disputes. In some villages (the Quinaults, for example), speakers announced the chief's decisions and negotiated with other villages. This office was obtained by merit. Some villages also had official jokers or buffoons.

Property rights, such as the control of subsistence areas and even the use of particular parts of a whale, were inheritable and carefully controlled. One's work and social activities depended on gender, talent, status, and the possession of an appropriate spirit power. Shamans had especially powerful spirit powers.

The basic social distinction was between slave and free, although some free people were wealthier and more influential than others. Houses were owned by the man who contributed the most labor and materials to its construction. He also directed certain subsistence activities such as weir building. Upon his death, the house would be torn down; it might be rebuilt nearby, or else the former members would each build a new house.

Cedar-planked, gabled houses were arrayed along a river. A door was set at one or both ends. From two to four families, or sometimes more, lived in a house. Partitions divided sections for menstruating women. Sleeping platforms with storage space underneath ran along the interior walls. Shorter

benches in front of the houses were used for sitting and as a place for men to talk and work. Interior walls might be lined with mats. Temporary summer shelters were made of cedar-bark slabs or mat- or bough-covered pole frames. People also occasionally stayed in temporary bark or brush hunting shelters.

Fish, especially all types of salmon, was the food staple. Besides salmon, the people used sturgeon, trout, eulachon (smelt), halibut, herring, and cod. Fish were eaten fresh or smoke-dried. Eulachon was used mainly for its oil. Other important foods included shellfish; land mammals (especially in the Quinault highlands and among the Kwaiailks) such as deer, elk, and bear; waterfowl and birds; sea mammals; and plants, especially inland, such as camas, berries, crabapples, roots, and shoots. Inland people burned prairie land every two to three years.

Fishing equipment included nets (trawl, gill, drift, dip), weirs, clubs, traps, harpoons, hook and line, herring rakes, and gaffs. People hunted with bow and arrow, deadfalls, nooses, snares, and nets. Professional woodworkers made most houses and canoes as well as bent-corner and bent-bottom boxes, utensils, and tools. The basic woodworking tool was the adze. Women shredded bark and sewed and twined mats. They also made baskets, mostly of spruce root found along the coast.

Neighbors regularly traded and intermarried. Dentalium shells served as currency for durable goods, and food and raw materials were usually exchanged for them. Canoes were widely exchanged. The Copalises provided many groups with razor clams. The local trading complex stretched from Vancouver Island to south of the Columbia River and east of the Cascades.

Most disputes between villages were usually settled by some form of economic arrangement such as formal compensation or marriage. In general, the Cowlitzes were on unfriendly terms with coastal groups, and the Queets fought the Quileutes and sometimes the Quinaults. The Chehalis killed many Queets and burned their villages around 1800; they also regularly attacked the Copalises. Queets, Quinaults, Hohs, and Quileutes occasionally confederated to oppose the Klallams, Makahs, Satsops, and others.

Fighting was more regulated in the south, and there no slaves were taken. Weapons included mussel shell knives, whalebone daggers, yew spears with shell or bone points, whale rib and stone clubs, and the bow and arrow. Elk hide shirts and helmets

and cedar shields (Chehalis), as well as slatted wood breastplates, provided protection in war.

In 1775, Southwestern Coast Salish encountered and killed Spanish explorers and salvaged their ship for iron. By the late 1780s, Indians were used to trading with Europeans and had already experienced population loss from European diseases.

The Lower Chehalises were among the people who traded with Meriwether Lewis and William Clark in 1805–1806. Contact with non-Natives was commonplace after Astoria was founded on the Columbia estuary in 1811. The Hudson's Bay Company founded local posts, such as Fort Vancouver (1825), Fort Nisqually (1833), and Cowlitz Farm (1839). Some Cowlitz groups became mixed with the Klickitats, an inland group, during the early nineteenth century. As access to European goods increased, Indians also skirmished among themselves for control of the inland trade.

A malaria epidemic devastated Indian populations in the 1830s and resulted in significant village abandonment and consolidation. For instance, the Chinookan and Lower Chehalis people combined in a bilingual tribe known as Shoalwater Bay Indians; the Salishan-Chinook language (as well as the tribe's later adoption of Lower Chehalis) eventually died out altogether. The Treaty of Washington (1846) and the Donation Land Act (1850) allowed non-Natives to appropriate Indian land. Many Indians, especially inlanders, were driven away, exterminated, and/or had their food resources destroyed or taken.

The Cowlitzes refused to sign the 1855 treaty because it did not provide a reservation in their homelands. Along with many other tribes, they fought the United States in the Rogue River War of 1855–1856. After inflicting severe dislocations, the government ordered them to remove to the Chehalis Reservation, but they refused, continuing to hold out for their own reservation. Many groups refused to sign treaties or accept goods from Indian agents, fearing that such action would be seen as evidence of forfeiture of land title.

The Quinault River Treaty in 1855 did provide that tribe with a reservation in exchange for vast areas of their traditional lands. In 1864, the Chehalis Reservation was created—without treaties or the formal Indian cession of land—for Chehalis, Cowlitzes, and some southern coastal people, but most remained near their homes. These people either became assimilated into the white population or joined the Chehalis Confederated Tribes or other tribes. Most Chehalis Reservation land was later

reappropriated; the rest was homesteaded by thirty-six Indians and set aside for school purposes.

The Shoalwater Bay Tribe and Georgetown Reservation were created in 1866. The tribe was composed mainly of Chehalis and Chinook families living on Willapa (formerly Shoalwater) Bay. By 1879, these Indians all spoke the lower Chehalis dialect.

All reservation Indians experienced pressure to Christianize, take up farming, and give up their culture. Corrupt agents profited on their rations. Of necessity and desire, hunting, fishing, and gathering continued, although Indians increasingly became involved in the cash economy (logging, farming, and railroads).

The Quinaults remained relatively isolated until the late 1880s. During the early twentieth century, a legal ruling allowed members from various non-Quinault tribes to claim allotments on that reservation and to apply for (and receive) status as Quinaults. This process first resulted mostly in environmental degradation and a sharply decreased salmon run as a result of clear-cutting and then in the attendant relocation of people off the reservation.

See also Fishing Rights; Hudson's Bay Company; Potlatch; Salmon, Economic and Spiritual Significance of; Spanish Influence.

Samish
See Salish, Central Coast.

Sauk-Suiattle
See Salish, Southern Coast.

Shoalwater Bay
See Salish, Southwestern Coast.

Siltez, Confederated Tribes of
See Coosans; Upper Umpqua.

Siuslawans
See Coosans.

Skagit

See Salish, Southern Coast.

Skokomish (Twana)

See Salish, Southern Coast.

Snohomish

See Salish, Southern Coast.

Snoqualmie

See Salish, Southern Coast.

Snoqualmoo

See Salish, Southern Coast.

Squaxin

See Salish, Southern Coast.

Steilacoom

See Salish, Southern Coast.

Stillaguamish

See Salish, Southern Coast.

Suquamish

See Salish, Southern Coast.

Swinomish

See Salish, Southern Coast.

Tillamook

"Tillamook" is a Chinookan word for a Tillamook place-name, possibly meaning "land of many waters" or "People of Nehalem." These people were formerly referred to by other names, such as Calamoxes. The Tillamooks traditionally lived along a coastal strip from roughly Tillamook Head to the Siletz River, in present-day Oregon. The Tillamook population stood at about 2,200 in 1805. In 1950 it was under 250 . Tillamook is a Salishan language. Its dialects included Nehalem, Nestucca, Salmon River (Nechesnan), and Siletz (Tillamook proper).

Tillamooks attempted to gain power from spirits, whom they believed were more active and closer to humans in the winter. Shamans renewed their power in January or February by sponsoring a ceremony that included singing a power song and dispensing food and presents to guests. During the course of this five- to fifteen-day ceremony, all other "knowers" (those with spirit powers) sang their songs too. Winter was also the time for relating myth narratives. Mythological characters were particularly important because social status was dependent on one's ability to form a relationship with a mythological personage, a natural feature, or a guardian spirit. Rituals also accompanied the first seasonal consumption of various foods.

Tillamook society was divided into the many free and the few slave people as well a majority of people who had acquired guardian spirits and a minority of those who had not. The elite were wealthy and experts in doctoring, war, and hunting. Women received status from their own guardian spirits or from those of their close relatives. Older women were accorded higher status.

Depending on the particular activity, different people, including shamans, headmen, and warriors, played leadership roles in the numerous small villages. Headmen were particularly skilled orators and negotiators. Most disputes, up to and including murder, were settled by arbitration and involved payment. This was often the case even with people from other villages.

The Tillamooks recognized five types of shamans: healers (men by drawing with the hands and women, by sucking), poison doctors (men with much ritual paraphernalia to send and extract poisons), spirit doctors (men who personally retrieved lost spirits from the spirit world), love doctors (women), and baby diplomats (men who foretold events by conversing with babies).

Women wore large grass, tule rush, or shredded-bark back aprons, small front aprons, and buckskin leggings. Men wore fur or basketry caps, breechclouts, buckskin shirts, and hide pants. Beaver and painted buckskin capes and rabbit, bobcat, or sea otter fur blankets kept people warm in the winter. Footgear included both moccasins and snowshoes. Items such as menstrual pads and diapers were made of cedar bark. Both sexes painted their hair part red and wore ear pendants. Men also wore nose pendants. Women wore decorative tattoos, but men's tattoos served only to measure dentalium.

Winter villages were usually built at the mouths of rivers or streams. They typically consisted of several houses, at least one work-and-menstrual hut, sweat houses, and a graveyard. Rectangular houses, which were occupied by up to four families, were constructed of cedar planks tied together with peeled and steamed spruce roots. Roofs were gabled with overlapping planks. Each had several fires in a center pit and sleeping platforms along the sides. Some houses were built aboveground and some were semisubterranean (with a door in the roof and entry via a ladder). Mat partitions separated families and multiple wives. Floors were covered by ferns and rush mats. Pitch torches or fish head or whale oil lamps provided extra light. Roots were kept in pits beneath the floor.

Salmon and other fish were the staples. Other seafood included sea lions, seals, and shellfish. Women gathered salmonberries, huckleberries, strawberries, camas, ferns, and other plant foods. Men hunted elk, beaver, muskrat, bear, and waterfowl. Many foods were either steamed in earth ovens, stone-boiled in baskets or bowls, or dried on racks. Canoes of several sizes and shapes were used for travel and fishing. They were single-log dugouts, painted black on the outside and red on the inside, and coated with pitch. The Tillamooks were part of a flourishing regional trade. In general, they traded tanned beaver hides, canoes, and baskets to northern Columbia River peoples for abalone shell, dentalia, buffalo hides and buffalo horn dishes, and dried salmon. The Tillamooks bought wapato roots and other items from Columbia River peoples east of the Coastal Range. They traded and intermarried with the Kalapuyas, and they also raided their southern neighbors for slaves, which they sold in the north.

History records the first contact between the Tillamooks and non-Natives as occurring in 1788, although iron knives and smallpox scars told of at least indirect encounters previously. They were also visited by Meriwether Lewis and William Clark. Regular contact with traders began after 1811. Epidemics of malaria, syphilis, smallpox, and other diseases, as well as guns and liquor, diminished the Tillamook population by around 90 percent in the 1830s and greatly reduced the number of their villages.

In 1850, the Donation Land Act opened Tillamook lands for white settlement. The Indians ceded land in an unratified 1851 treaty, and the few surviving Tillamooks either remained in place, officially landless, or were removed to the Siletz or Grand Ronde Reservation. Under the leadership of the peaceful Kilchis, Tillamooks refused to participate in the wars of the 1850s. Awards from the Indian Land Claims Commission in 1958 and 1962 did little to reunite a scattered and unorganized people. Congress officially terminated its relationship with the Tillamooks in 1956.

See also Indian Claims Commission; Salmon, Economic and Spiritual Significance of; Slavery.

Tlingit

"Tlingit," meaning "human beings," is taken from the group's name for themselves. The Coastal Tlingit were a "nationality" of three main groups—Gulf Coast, Northern, and Southern—united by a common language and customs. The Interior Tlingit have never considered themselves a cohesive tribe. Total Tlingit population was at least 10,000 in 1740. Tlingit is remotely related to Athapaskan languages.

Humans have lived in Tlingit country for at least 10,000 years; the continuous occupation of the region began around 5,000 years ago. People probably came from the south, with Tlingit culture perhaps having its origins near the mouths of the Nass and Skeena Rivers about 800 years ago. The earliest Tlingit villages had disappeared by historic times, however, and a new migration into the area began in the eighteenth century, as the Haidas displaced southern Tlingit groups.

Of the three major groups of coastal Tlingits, the Gulf Coast group included the Hoonah of Lituya Bay; the Dry Bay people at the mouth of the Alsek River, who were established in the eighteenth century by a conglomeration of Tlingits and Atha-

paskans; and the Yakutats, who were composed of Eyak speakers from the Italio River to Icy Bay. In 1910 the Yakutats merged with the Dry Bay people. Northern Tlingits included the Hoonahs on the north shore of Cross Sound, the Chilkat-Chilkoots, Auks, and Takus; the Sumdums on the mainland; and the Sitkas and Huntsnuwus, or Angoons, on the outer islands and coasts. The southern Tlingits included the Kakes, Kuius, Henyas, and Klawaks on the islands and the Stikines or Wrangells, Tongasses, and Sanyas or Cape Fox along the mainland and sheltered waters.

Coastal Tlingit groups lived along the Pacific Coast from roughly Icy Bay in the north to Chatham Sound in the south, or roughly throughout the Alaskan panhandle. This country, no more than thirty miles wide, but roughly 500 miles long, is marked by a profusion of fjords, inlets, bays, and islands, most of which are mountainous. The climate is marked by fog, rain, snow, and strong winds in the fall and winter. Most Coastal Tlingits live in Alaska and in the cities of the greater Northwest.

Interior Tlingits lived along the upper Taku River, although during the nineteenth and twentieth centuries and in response to both the fur trade and the gold rush, most moved to the headwaters of the Yukon River. Many contemporary Interior Tlingits live in Teslin Village (Yukon Territory) and Atlin (British Columbia). Some also live in Whitehorse (Yukon) and Juneau (Alaska).

Animals and even natural features had souls similar to those of people. Thus they were treated with respect, either to win their help or to avoid their malice. Hunters engaged in ritual purification before the hunt, and during the hunt the hunter as well as his family back home engaged in certain formal rules of behavior. Shamans were very powerful. Most were men. Shamans could cure, control weather, bring success in hunting, tell the future, and expose witches, but only if they were consulted in time and not impeded by another shaman. Their powers came from spirits that could be summoned by a special song. A shaman underwent regular periods of physical deprivation to keep spiritually pure. Neither he nor his wife could cut their hair.

The basic political units were matrilineal clans of two divisions, Raven and Eagle. Each clan was subdivided into lineages or house groups. Thus, the tribes, or groups, listed above lacked any overall political organization and were really local communities made up of representatives of several clans.

Tlingit native woman in full potlatch dancing costume, ca. 1906. (Library of Congress)

All territory and property rights were held by the clans. Clan and lineage chiefs, or headmen, assigned their group's resources, regulated subsistence activities, ordered the death of trespassers, and hosted memorial ceremonies.

The two divisions served as opposites for marriage and ceremonial purposes. Some clans and lineages moved among neighboring groups such as the Haidas, Tsimshians, and Eyaks. A clan's crest represented its totem, or the living things, heavenly bodies, physical features, and supernatural beings associated with it. Crests were displayed on house posts, totem poles, canoes, feast dishes, and other items. All present members of an opposite division received payment to view a crest, because in so doing they legitimated both the display and the crest's associated privileges. All clan property could be bought and sold, given as gifts, or taken in war.

In general, spring brought hunting on the mainland, halibut fishing in deep waters, and shellfish and seaweed gathering. Seal hunting began in the late spring, about the time of the first salmon runs.

Summer activities generally included catching and curing salmon, berrying, and some sealing. Summer was also the time for wars and slave raids. Fall brought some sea otter hunting (land otters were never killed). In the late nineteenth century, the fall was also the time for more salmon fishing and curing, potato harvesting, and hunting in the interior. Winter villages were established by November. The winter was the season for potlatches and trading.

Individuals as well as lineages were ranked, from nobility to commoners. Slaves were entirely outside the system. (After the United States purchased Alaska, slaves were freed and brought into the social system on the lowest level.) Women had high status, probably because they controlled the food supply (not catching fish but the much harder and more laborious jobs of cutting, drying, smoking, and baling it). Any injury to someone in another clan required an indemnity. Clan disagreements were usually but not always settled peacefully. The three important feasts were the funeral feast, memorial potlatch feast, and childrens' feast.

All babies were believed to be reincarnations of maternal relatives. At about age eight, a boy went to live with his maternal uncle, who saw that he toughened and purified himself and learned the traditions and responsibilities of his clan and lineage. Girls were confined in a dark room or cellar for up to two years (according to rank and wealth) at their first period, at which time they learned the traditions of their clan, performed certain rituals, and observed behavior restrictions. At the end of this time their ears were pierced, high-status families gave a potlatch, and girls were considered marriageable.

Only people of opposite divisions but similar clans and lineages could marry. Marriage formalities included mutual gift giving. Southerners erected tall mortuary totem poles near their houses. Death initiated a mourning period and several rituals, including singing and the funeral. Cremation occurred on the fourth day, except possibly longer for a chief. Widows observed particularly restrictive mourning rituals. A person's slaves were sometimes killed. The evening after the cremation, mourners held a feast for their division opposites. Dead slaves were simply cast onto the beach. Burial was adopted in the late nineteenth century.

Tlingits usually lived in one main (winter) village and perhaps one or more satellite villages. In the early nineteenth century, the former consisted of a row of rectangular, slightly excavated, gable-roofed planked houses facing the water. Each house could hold forty to fifty people, including about six families and a few unmarried adults or slaves. Each family slept on partitioned wooden platforms that could be removed to make a larger ceremonial space.

Other features included a central smoke hole and a low, oval front doorway. The four main house posts were carved and painted in totemic or ancestral designs. Palisades often surrounded houses or whole villages. Other village structures included smokehouses, small houses for food and belongings, sweat houses, and menstrual huts.

In the nineteenth century, Inland Tlingits lived in rectangular houses similar to those of the coastal people. They also built brush lean-tos that could shelter up to ten or fifteen people.

Fish was the staple, especially all five species of salmon, as well as eulachon (smelt), halibut, and herring. Fish was boiled, baked, roasted, or dried and smoked for winter. Whole salmon might be frozen for winter use. Other important foods included shellfish, seaweed, seal, sea lion, sea otter, and porpoise.

The people also ate land mammals such as deer, bear, and mountain sheep and goat. Dogs assisted in the hunt. Inland Tlingits hunted caribou, moose, and some wood bison. Beaver were speared or netted under ice. Migrating waterfowl provided meat as well as feathers, eggs, and beaks. Some groups gathered a variety of berries, plus hemlock inner bark, roots (riceroot, fern), and shoots (salmonberries, cow parsnips). They began cultivating potatoes after the Russians introduced the food in the early nineteenth century.

People sucked on cultivated tobacco mixed with other materials; they began smoking it when the Russians introduced leaf tobacco and pipes in the late eighteenth century.

Salmon were caught in rectangular, wooden traps, trapped behind stone walls, or impaled on wooden stakes in low water. Other fishing equipment included hook and (gut) line, harpoons, and copper knives. Men hunted with spears, bow and arrow, a whip sling, and darts. Raw materials included horn (spoons, dishes, containers), wool (blankets), and wood (fire drill, watertight storage and boiling boxes). Tlingits began forging iron in the late eighteenth century, although some iron was acquired from intercontinental trade or drift wreckage in aboriginal times. Some foods were baked in earth ovens.

Imports included walrus ivory from Bering Sea Eskimos, copper from interior tribes, dentalia shell from the south, Haida canoes, Tsimshian carvings, slaves, furs, skin garments decorated with porcupine quills, and various fish products. Exports included Chilkat blankets, seaweed, leaf tobacco, and fish oil. Intragroup trade was largely ceremonial in nature. When the whites came, Tlingits tried to monopolize that trade, even going so far as to travel over 300 miles to destroy a Hudson's Bay Company post. Inland Tlingit trade partners included the Tahltans, Kaskas, Pelly River Athapaskans, and Tagish.

Tlingits excelled at wood carving, especially ceremonial partitions in house chiefs' apartments, bentwood boxes, chests, and bowls, house posts (usually shells fronting the structural posts), masks, weapons and war regalia, and utilitarian and ceremonial items used by nobles.

Chilkat Tlingit blankets were the most intricate and sought-after textiles of the Northwest Coast. They were really ceremonial robes, and the ceremonies, in which myth was dramatized through dance, were fully as artistic as the crafts themselves.

The weaving of shirts, aprons, and leggings may have come originally from the Tsimshians. Rock art probably served functions similar to those of totems. Beadwork was of very high quality. Shamans used many art objects, including carved ivory and antler and bone amulets. Baskets were also an important Tlingit art.

Tlingits preferred the great Haida canoes that were purchased by wealthy Tlingit headmen. The most common type of canoe was of spruce, except in the south, where they used red cedar. Styles included ice-hunting canoes for sealing, forked-prow canoes, shallow river canoes, and small canoes with upturned ends for fishing and otter hunting. Some Inland Tlingits also used skin canoes, but most used rafts or small dugouts when they could not walk.

Tlingits purchased Eyak and Athapaskan snowshoes. They carried burdens using skin packs with tumplines. Only a few coastal groups used Athapaskan-style sleds.

Russian explorers in 1741 were the first non-Natives to enter the region. Spanish explorers heralded the period of regular interracial contact in 1775. The Russians had established a regular presence in 1790. They built a fort at Sitka in 1799 that fell to the Indians three years later. The Russians rebuilt it in 1805, however, and made it the headquarters of the Russian-American Company from 1808 until 1867. Although the Tlingits maintained their independence during the Russian period, they acquired tools and other items. Many fell to new diseases (a particularly severe smallpox outbreak occurred from 1835 to 1839), and some were converted to the Russian Orthodox Church.

In 1839, when the Hudson's Bay Company acquired trading rights in southeastern Alaska from the Russian-American Company, the region saw an influx of European-manufactured goods. The advent of steel tools had a stimulating effect on traditional wood carving. During this time, the Tlingits successfully resisted British attempts to break their trade monopoly with the interior tribes. By the 1850s, Tlingits were trading as far south as Puget Sound and had regular access to alcohol and firearms from the Americans.

Tlingits protested the U.S. purchase of Alaska in 1867, arguing that if anyone were the rightful "owner" of Alaska, they were, not the Russians. In any case, the soldiers, miners, and adventurers who arrived after the purchase severely mistreated and abused the Indians. For much of the last half of the nineteenth century, U.S. naval authorities persecuted shamans thought to be involved with witches. Although Tlingits owned southeast Alaska under aboriginal title, they were prevented from filing legal claims during, and thus profiting from, the great Juneau gold rush of 1880. The mines ultimately yielded hundreds of millions of dollars worth of gold, of which wealth the Tlingits saw little or none.

Commercial fishing and canning, as well as tourism, became established in the 1870s and 1880s, providing jobs (albeit at wages lower than those earned by white workers) for the Indians. The Klondike gold rush of 1898–1899 brought more money and jobs to the region. Meanwhile, Christian missionaries, especially Presbyterians, waged an increasingly successful war against traditional Indian culture.

By 1900 many Tlingits had become acculturated. They had given up their subsistence economy and abandoned many small villages. Many worked in canneries in British Columbia or picked hops in Washington. Potlatches began to diminish in number and significance, and many ceremonial objects were sold to museums. Despite this level of

acculturation, however, some midnineteenth-century Tlingit villages continued to exist into the twentieth century.

In 1915, Alaska enfranchised all "civilized" Natives, but severe economic and social discrimination continued, including a virtual apartheid system during the first half of the twentieth century. Some villages incorporated in the 1930s under the Indian Reorganization Act and acquired various industries. After World War II the issue of land led to the formation of the Central Council of Tlingit and Haida, which in 1968 won a land claims settlement of $7.5 million (43 cents an acre).

Despite Tlingit efforts, Alaska schools were not integrated until 1949. The Alaska Native Brotherhood (ANB), founded in Sitka in 1912 by some Presbyterian Indians, was devoted to rapid acculturation; economic opportunity, including land rights; and the abolition of political discrimination. The Alaska Native Sisterhood (ANS) was founded soon after. Both organizations reversed their stand against traditional practices in the late 1960s.

See also Potlatch; Russians, in the Arctic/Northwest; Salmon, Economic and Spiritual Significance of; Totem Poles; Slavery and Native Americans.

Tsimshian

"Tsimshian" is a Coast and Southern Tsimshian self-designation meaning "inside the Skeena River." The Tsimshians were a group of linguistically and culturally related people. Their four major divisions were the Nishgas (Nass River), Gitksans (Upper Skeena River), Coast Tsimshians (Lower Skeena River and adjacent coast), and Southern Tsimshian (southern coast and islands). They were culturally similar to the Haidas and Tlingits. The Tsimshian population was about 8,000–10,000 in 1800. The various Tsimshian languages (Coast and Southern Tsimshian, Nishga, and Gitksan) and dialects were not all mutually intelligible.

Northwestern British Columbia, the home of the Tsimshians, is heavily forested, and the climate is wet, with coastal regions marked by numerous fjords and islands. Most villages were along the mouths of the Nass and Skeena Rivers. Some were in a subalpine zone, where drier land permitted more foot—as opposed to canoe—travel. Tsimshians live in villages and towns in northwest British Columbia and in cities throughout the Northwest.

Potlatches, feasts, and secret society dances, all highly ritualistic, were held in winter. The dances were apparently borrowed from Haisla- and Heiltsuk-speaking people in the seventeenth or eighteenth century. House chiefs also served as religious leaders, ensuring that people showed the proper respect for animals and spirits. They also served as "power," "real," and "great" dancers, in which roles they dramatized and validated the powers of their ancestors and their house and initiated young people into ritual roles.

Religious specialists, called blowing shamans, complemented the chiefs' activities. Their responsibilities included curing as well as controlling the weather. Witches worked in secret to harm people. They had no recourse to spiritual beings but used items such as bits of a corpse to make people unclean and thus unready for a supernatural encounter.

Each Tsimshian village was as autonomous from another as it was from a Haida or a Tlingit village. Local groups (twenty-six in the midnineteenth century) had permanent winter villages as well as spring and summer fishing villages and camps.

Houses (maternal extended families) were presided over by (usually male) chiefs, who, in addition to their religious responsibilities, managed the economic resources of the house. Other house members provided for their economic welfare.

Several houses made up a village. Each group of house chiefs had an established rank order, so that the village chief (a position not present in all villages) was the highest-ranking house chief in the village.

Wolf, Eagle, Raven, and Blackfish or Killer Whale constituted the four matrilineal clans, although traditionally most villages may have had a dual division. The house was the basic social unit. It controlled fishing camps and berry picking and hunting territories, and it also owned songs, crests, names, and other privileges. Tsimshian people belonged to one of the following groups: chiefs, named families of lesser rank, or free but unnamed people. Slaves were usually imported.

All important life cycle events necessitated ritual duties and wealth exchanges. Such events included birth, naming, ear (boy) and lip (girl) piercing at about age seven, second naming (and girls' seclusion) at puberty, marriage (arranged with the

purpose of advancing social rank), house building, and death. Insults or mistakes, however inadvertent, were occasions for face- and rank-saving feasts or potlatches. At puberty, boys sought guardian spirits by bathing and fasting in remote places. Men purified themselves before hunting and fishing. There were also rituals connected with the first seasonal fish catch. Corpses, along with secret society regalia, were generally burned. Ghosts were regarded as possibly dangerous to the living.

Feasts, such as potlatches, were the glue that held society together; they expressed and maintained the social order, inheritance, and succession. They generally lasted for several days and included dancing, singing, and gift giving. Slaves were often given as gifts; as a wealthy people, the Tsimshian had many of them.

Winter longhouses were typical of the area. Post-and-beam structures constructed of red cedar timbers; gabled roofs covered their roughly 2,500 square feet of living space. Inside were central fireplaces and side platforms for sleeping. Cedar-bark mats provided insulation. The door, which occasionally consisted of holes in totem poles, faced the beach. Chiefs' dwellings became dance houses in the winter.

The chief and his immediate family occupied the rear of the house. House fronts were painted with crest designs. Other structures included menstrual huts, summertime houses, and sweat lodges.

People ate halibut, salmon, herring spawn, waterbirds and their eggs, seal, sea lion, sea otter, and shellfish. Eulachon (smelt) oil ("grease") was obtained by boiling rotting eulachon and skimming the fat. Other important foods included dried seaweed, the cambium of several trees, berries, crabapples, deer, elk, mountain goat, mountain sheep, bear, caribou, and moose.

Fishing equipment included traps, bent hook and line (of cedar-bark cord), harpoons, and porpoise lures. The *yagatl*, an underwater net controlled by a ring and pole, was used to catch eulachon. Women wove clothing and other items from the inner bark of red cedar trees. They also wove plaited and twined baskets from cedar (coast) and maple and birch (inland) bark. Men carved wooden items, including totem poles, storage boxes, chests, canoes, tools, cradles, and fishing and hunting gear. Other tools and implements included bark dishes, stone chisel, and goat horn arrow points. Native copper was used for some tools and ceremonial items.

The Tsimshians enjoyed a highly profitable monopoly on the grease (eulachon oil) trade. At a huge regional trade fair held every spring at the mouth of the Nass River, Coast Tsimshian peoples traded grease with interior Tsimshians (Gitksans) for furs, dressed deer and moose skins, and porcupine quill embroidery, which the latter had obtained from interior tribes such as the Carriers. From the Haidas the Tsimshians received canoes, carved boxes, dried halibut, and chewing tobacco. Foods, carved horn spoons, and slaves were also traded.

As relatively recent arrivals to the Northwest Coast, the Tsimshians began pushing the Tlingits farther north and the Haislas farther south and fighting the Heiltsuks for coastal areas around the mideighteenth century. They had already seen European goods when a Southern Tsimshian group met a British trade ship in 1787. Interracial contact remained sporadic until the Hudson's Bay Company founded Fort Simpson in 1831. Many Coast Tsimshians subsequently relocated near the fort to strengthen and protect their key role in the local fur trade.

The basic structures of Native culture remained intact until the arrival of Christian missionaries. William Duncan, an Anglican, appeared in 1857. Five years later, he and some Indian converts founded the Christian colony of Metlakatla, which grew until it moved in 1887 to Annette Island, Alaska, and was renamed New Metlakatla. Residents there had to renounce traditional life and accept Duncan's utopian principles. Congress established the Annette Island Reserve in 1891. This community prospered until it was beset by factionalism and decline until the 1930s, when it began to recover.

Shortly after the arrival of a Methodist missionary at Fort Simpson in 1874, that community became thoroughly Christianized. As missions spread in the area, Indians replaced many Native customs, such as the erection of totem poles, with Euro-Canadian styles and customs. The gold rush of 1867 also brought increased contact with non-Natives. Although Indians still practiced some subsistence activities, they also began the switch to a wage economy. The first local salmon cannery was established in 1876, for instance.

During the late nineteenth century, Tsimshian villages became official bands with unilaterally imposed reserves under the federal Indian Act. At the end of the century, most coastal bands had been converted to Christianity and the Nass people had

abandoned their villages and became largely assimilated into Canadian society; the Gitksan, however, maintained many aspects of traditional culture.

A federal and provincial school system replaced missionary schools in the midtwentieth century. The enforced enfranchisement of women, air links to the villages (1950s), television (1960s), and satellite-enabled communications (1980s) have generally strengthened the forces of secularization, urbanization, and democratization, although more traditional cultural elements were reestablished after the 1960s.

See also Hudson's Bay Company; Potlatch; Salmon, Economic and Spiritual Significance of.

Tulalip

See Salish, Southern Coast.

Tututni

See Tolowa; Upper Umpqua.

Twana

See Salish, Southern Coast.

Upper Coquille

See Upper Umpqua.

Upper Skagit

See Salish, Southern Coast.

Upper Umpqua

The Upper Umpquas were one of several Athapaskan-speaking groups of southwest Oregon. The word "umpqua" may have meant "high and low water," "thunder," or "boat over the water." Their self-designation was *Etnemitane*. Traditionally, five Umpqua bands lived in southwest Oregon, in the valley of the south fork of the Umpqua River. Other groups lived to the west and south, including coastal areas. These included Upper Coquilles (Mishikhwutmetunnes), Chetcos, Chasta Costas, Tututnis (all four so-called Coast Rogue Indians), Galices, and Applegates. Most descendents of these people live on or near reservations in the same area. There were roughly 5,600 Oregon Athapaskans in the late eighteenth century. In 1990 there were roughly 3,000 Grande Ronde Indians as well as 850 Cow Creek Indians. Upper Umpqua, Galice-Applegate, the Tututni dialects (Mishikhwutmetunne, Tututni, Chasta Costa), and the Chetco dialect of the Tolowa language are all members of the Pacific branch of the Athapaskan language family.

The Umpquas celebrated numerous feasts and gift-giving occasions, such as birth, naming, first kills, puberty, war, death, and the make-doctor dance for new shamans. Feasts included both sacred and secular elements. Each village had a chief who had several wives and slaves. He acted as an arbiter and received a share of all financial transactions as well as a food tithe. The position of chief was generally inherited through the male line. Although they slept in sweat houses, men and boys ate in the family house, where their mothers or wives cooked for them. Women gathered firewood and plants, made baskets, prepared foods, and carried water. Men fished, hunted, tanned hides, tended tobacco, and made nets, planks, and canoes.

Although society was ranked according to wealth, the divisions were not as rigid as they were farther north. Slaves were usually acquired in raids, although a chief could enslave a villager for improper behavior.

Most shamans were women. They cured by extracting a pain, a small object filled with the patient's blood. Some groups also had common shamans, who blew smoke and waved a flicker feather over the patient. Unsuccessful cures sometimes led to the identification and murder of evil shamans (sorcerers). However, in such cases, a murder compensation had to be paid for the dead shaman. A shaman's fee was often paid to her husband. Shamans' powers derived from guardian spirits. Other powers conferred by certain spirits included the ability to cure rattlesnake bites, talk to herbs to receive remedies and love charms from them, and find lost objects.

Numerous rituals were associated with pregnancy and birth. Girls were secluded when they

reached puberty and were permitted neither to touch their hair or skin nor to eat anything except dry food for a year. They also had to swim twice a day, and their fathers also underwent certain restrictions. Women were purchased for marriage; children were illegitimate if their mothers were not paid for. Jealousy, meanness, and barrenness were acceptable reasons for divorce. Parents could also buy back their daughter, who then had considerable personal freedom.

The various death customs included the deathbed confession of wrongs, carriage of the corpse to the cemetery on a deerskin, and funeral orations. Mourners cut their hair and wore ashes and pitch on their heads and faces.

Non-Indian traders first arrived in the area in the late eighteenth century. The fur trade began around 1818, at which time a group of Umpquas was killed by traders, possibly Iroquois in the service of the North West Company. Hudson's Bay Company established Fort Umpqua in 1836. Around this time, previously unknown diseases began taking a serious toll on the Indians.

Sporadic, trade-based contact continued until the flood of settlers in the late 1840s and the Rogue River Valley gold rush of 1852. In 1851, the Tututnis traded 2.5 million acres of land for $28,500. Their bitterness when they subsequently understood the deal fueled their desire to extract revenge. They soon began killing whites and burning settlers' houses. Two years later, when a group of whites attacked some Chetco Indians after persuading them to disarm, the Chetcos attacked some soldiers, and the fighting spread.

Upper Umpquas stayed out of the war, having signed a land cession treaty in 1854, and moved two years later to the Grand Ronde Reservation. Some Upper Umpquas, along with villages of different linguistic groups, signed a treaty in 1853; in exchange for a land cession of more than 700 square miles, it recognized the existence of and called for a reservation for the Cow Creek band of the Umpqua tribe. The Rogue River War of 1855–1856 provided an opportunity for whites to destroy game trails and hunting grounds and to appropriate and clear land for farms. Cow Creeks fled the area during this period, hiding in the mountains as refugees.

After the war, local Indians, once fiercely independent, were shattered. Some Upper Umpquas, Tututnis, Chetcos, Coquilles, Chasta Costas, and others were forced to walk over the mountains in winter to the Grand Ronde Reservation. Other groups straggled in until 1857, when many Indians were moved to the Coast (or Siletz) Reservation, created two years earlier. On the way, and once there, several hundred died from exposure, starvation, and disease. Shamans who failed to cure the diseases were persecuted by their people, which gave the government an excuse to step in and disarm the Indians.

Meanwhile, the Grand Ronde Reservation was created in 1857. A school system designed to eradicate Indian culture was promptly set up. Many people left Grand Ronde for the Siletz Reservation or local communities. Those that remained worked as farmers or loggers.

Disparities between treaty and nontreaty Indians, as well as agents' promotion of alcohol and thievery, spread discord and exacerbated intertribal conflict. Many Indians escaped during this time but were rounded up by soldiers, who further abused them. Meanwhile, intermarriage further weakened tribal identities.

In 1865, a central strip was removed from the Siletz Reservation and opened for white settlement. The northern part then became the Siletz Reservation and the southern half (Coosans, Siuslawans, and Alseans) became the Alsea Reservation. The Bureau of Indian Affairs (BIA) turned all operations over to the Methodists, who worked to eradicate all vestiges of Indian culture. Indians danced the Ghost Dance in 1871; the variant Earth Lodge cult (locally known as the Warm House Dance) began in 1873. The Indian Shaker Church became popular beginning in the 1890s.

By 1894, most of the Siletz Reservation had been ceded to the public domain, and tribal languages had all but disappeared. The remaining residents worked in subsistence activities or in logging, cutting trees on their plundered reservation. By 1928, as a result of both widespread theft and the allotment processes, most of the land base was gone. Eighteen years later, the Confederated Tribes of the Siletz Reservation voted to accept termination of government recognition and services. The former reservation land base of 1.3 million acres had completely disappeared. Most of the allotments were lost shortly thereafter, due mainly to nonpayment of taxes. Tribal life for most of the former Siletz tribes virtually disappeared. At the same time, although 537 acres of land had been added to the Grand Ronde Reservation in 1936, it too was declared terminated.

Meanwhile, the Cow Creek band had intermarried extensively with other Indians as well as the French Canadian population. The group created a formal government around 1918. They pressed their case for land claims litigation, but by the time they learned of the existence of the Indian Claims Commission, they had missed the deadline for filing a claim. Officially terminated in 1956, they were formally restored in 1982. Later in that decade they accepted a land settlement of $1.5 million and, over the objections of the BIA, placed the funds in a permanent endowment.

In 1973, the Siletz reservation Indians formed a new council to work for the restoration of tribal status, which was obtained in 1977. The new 3,630-acre Siletz Reservation was created in 1980. Grand Ronde was restored in 1983, with all former rights save those pertaining to subsistence activities. A tribal council was formed the same year. Five years later, Congress gave the tribe 9,811 acres of timbered land, the income of which was used to purchase a one hundred-acre administrative land base.

See also Assimilation; Athapaskan Languages; Boarding Schools, United States and Canada; Fur Trade; Ghost Dance Religion; Indian Claims Commission.

Native Americans of the Great Basin

Paiute, Northern

"Northern Paiute" includes a number of seminomadic, culturally distinct, and politically autonomous Great Basin groups. The name is a modern construction; aboriginally, these groups were tied together only by the awareness of a common language. "Paiute" may have meant "True Ute" or "Water Ute" and was applied only to the Southern Paiute until the 1850s. Their self-designation is *Numa*, or "People." Non-Natives have sometimes called these people Digger Indians, Snakes (Northern Paiutes in Oregon), and Paviotso. The Bannock Indians were originally a Northern Paiute group from eastern Oregon.

Traditionally, the groups now known as Northern Paiute ranged throughout present-day southeast Oregon, extreme northeast California, extreme southwest Idaho, and northwest Nevada. Bannock territory included southeastern Idaho and western Wyoming (the Snake River region). The highly diverse environment included lakes, mountains, high plains, rivers, freshwater marshes, and high desert. Elements of California culture entered the region through groups living on or near the Sierra Nevada. Presently, Northern Paiutes live on a number of their own reservations, on other nearby reservations, and among the area's general population. The Paiute population in the early nineteenth century was roughly 7,500, excluding about 2,000 Bannocks. Northern Paiute is part of the Western Numic (Shoshonean) branch of the Uto-Aztecan linguistic family.

Religious power among the Northern Paiute resided in any animate or inanimate object, feature, or phenomenon. Any person could seek power for help with a skill, but only shamans acquired enough to help, or hurt, others. A power source would expect certain specific behaviors to be followed. Most power sources also had mythological roles.

Shamans, male and female, were religious leaders. Their power often came in a recurring dream. They cured by sucking, retrieving a wandering soul, or administering medicines. Disease could be caused by soul loss, mishandling power, or sorcery. Some shamans could also control weather. Special objects as well as songs, mandated by the power dream, helped them perform their tasks. Power could also be inherited or sought by visiting certain caves.

The sun was considered an especially powerful spirit, and many people prayed to it daily. Some groups celebrated rituals associated with communal food drives or other food-related events.

The nuclear family, led (usually) by senior members, was the main political and economic unit. Where various families came together, the local camp was led by a headman who advised, gave speeches on right behavior, and facilitated consensus decisions. The position of the headman was often, although not strictly, inherited in the male line. Camp composition changed regularly. Other elders were selected to take charge of various activities such as hunts and irrigation projects.

The traditional headman system was replaced at least in part by the emergence of chiefs during the mounted, raiding years of the 1860s and 1870s.

A Bannock family in Idaho during the nineteenth century. In the spring of 1878, settlers' livestock had destroyed much of the camas prairie of southeastern Idaho, an area favored by the Bannocks (originally a Northern Paiute group from eastern Oregon) for its abundance of camas roots, an important part of the tribe's diet. The conflict led to the Bannock War. (National Archives and Records Administration)

Headmen returned during the early reservation years, however, followed by elected tribal councils beginning in the 1930s.

Dwelling style and type were marked by great seasonal and regional diversity. Wickiups, used mostly in the summer, were huts of brush and reeds over willow pole frames. The winter house in the north was a cone-shaped pole framework covered with tule mats and earth. Some western groups included a mat-covered entryway. All had central fires. In the mountains, people built semi-subterranean winter houses of juniper and pine boughs covered with branches and dirt. Dispersed winter camps consisted of two or three related families (roughly fifty people). In late prehistoric times, the Bannocks used buffalo skin teepees during the winter.

Diet also varied according to specific location. Plants supplied most food needs: roots, bulbs, seeds, nuts, rice grass (ground into meal), cattails, berries, and greens. Roots were either eaten raw or sun-dried and stored. Pine nuts and acorns were especially important. Animal foods included fowl (and eggs), squirrel, duck, and other small game as well as mountain sheep, deer, buffalo, and elk. Rabbits were hunted in communal drives. Small mammals were either pit roasted, boiled, or dried for storage. Lizards, grubs, and insects were also eaten. Trout and other fish were crucial in some areas, less important in others. Fish were usually dried and stored for winter. Some groups cultivated wild seed-bearing plants. The Bannocks fished for salmon in the Snake River and hunted buffalo in the fall.

People later called the Bannocks, or Snakes, acquired horses as early as the mideighteenth century. They soon joined the Northern Shoshone in southern Idaho in developing fully mounted bands and other aspects of Plains culture, including buffalo hunting, extensive warfare, and raiding for horses.

Early Northern Paiute contacts with fur traders such as Jedediah Smith (1827) and Peter Skene Ogden (1829) were friendly, although a party led by Joseph Walker (1833) massacred about 100 peaceful Indians. When reached by whites, the Indians already had a number of non-Native items in their possession, such as Spanish blankets, horses, and Euro-American goods.

Most Northern Paiutes remained on foot until the late 1840s and 1850s. Around this time, heavy traffic on the Oregon and California Trails (in the late 1840s) and the gold rush of 1848 brought many non-Natives through their territory. These people cut down piñon trees for fuel and housing, and their animals destroyed seed-bearing plants and fouled water supplies. Mining resulted in extensive and rapid resource degradation. New diseases took a heavy toll during this period. Indians responded by moving away from the invaders or attacking wagons for food and materials. White traders encouraged thefts by trading supplies for stolen items and animals. Some Indians began to live at the fringes of and work at white ranches and settlements.

Gold and silver strikes in the late 1850s fueled the cycle of conflict and violence. Local conflicts during this period included the brief Pyramid Lake War in 1860, the Owens Valley conflicts in 1862–1863, and the Coeur d'Alene War (1858–1859), which grew out of the Yakima war over white treaty violations. In the Snake War (1866–1867), Chiefs Paulina and Weawea led the Indians to early successes, but eventually the former was killed and the latter surrendered. Survivors settled on the Malheur Reservation (Oregon) in 1871. Winnemucca, who represented

several hundred Northern Paiute in the 1860s and 1870s, participated in the Pyramid Lake War and, with his daughter Sarah, went on to serve as a negotiator and peacemaker. In 1873, he refused to take his band to the Malheur Reservation, holding out for a reservation of their own. The Bannocks, too, rebelled in a short-lived war over forced confinement on the Fort Hall Reservation and white treaty violations.

Beginning in 1859, the United States set aside land for Northern Paiute reservations. Eventually, a number of small reservations and colonies were created, but ultimately much of the designated land was lost to non-Indian settlers. Most Northern Paiutes, however, drifted between reservations, combining traditional subsistence activities with a growing dependence on local Anglo economies. Conflict on several reservations remained ongoing for decades (some issues are still pending) over issues such as water rights (Pyramid Lake, Walker River), white land usurpation, and fisheries destruction (Pyramid Lake). Refugees from the Bannock War were forced to move to the Yakima Reservation; from there many ultimately moved to the Warm Springs Reservation.

The government also established day and boarding schools from the late 1870s into the 1930s, including Sarah Winnemucca's school at Lovelock. Sarah Winnemucca, who published *Life Among the Paiutes* in 1884, also worked tirelessly, although ultimately unsuccessfully, for a permanent Paiute reservation. Northern Paiute children also attended Indian boarding schools across the United States. Most traditional subsistence activities ceased during that period, although people continued to gather certain foods. New economic activities included cattle ranching at Fort McDermitt, stock raising, haying, and various businesses.

In 1889, the Northern Paiute Wovoka, known to the whites as Jack Wilson, started a new Ghost Dance religion. It was based on the belief that the world would be reborn with all Indians, alive and dead, living in a pre-contact paradise. For this to happen, Indians had to reject all non-Native ways, especially alcohol, live together in peace, and pray and dance. The Ghost Dance followed a previous one established at Walker River in 1869.

Family organization remained more or less intact during the reservation period. By about 1900, Northern Paiutes had lost more than 95 percent of their aboriginal territory. Most groups accepted the Indian Reorganization Act (IRA) and adopted tribal

councils during the 1930s. Shamanism has gradually declined over the years. The Native American Church has had adherents among the Northern Paiutes since the 1930s, and the Sweat Lodge Movement became active during the 1960s.

> ***See also*** Dams, Fishing Rights, and Hydroelectric Power; Ghost Dance Religion; Horse, Economic Impact; Reservation Economic and Social Conditions; Sweat Lodges; Wovoka.

Paiute, Owens Valley

"Owens Valley Paiute" is the name given to a number of Paiute groups distinguished in part by their semisettled, cooperative lifestyle as well as their irrigation practices. They were largely responsible for bringing elements of California culture into the southern Great Basin. Non-Natives formerly included them with the Monache or Mono Indians. "Paiute" may have meant "True Ute" or "Water Ute" and was applied only to the Southern Paiute until the 1850s. Their self-designation is *Numa*, or "People."

Traditionally, the groups now known as Owens Valley Paiute controlled the Owens River Valley, more than eighty miles long and an average of seven miles wide. The fertile and well-watered region, east of the southern Sierra Nevada, contains a wealth of environmental diversity. Presently, Owens Valley Paiutes live on a number of their own reservations, on other nearby reservations, and among the area's general population. In the early nineteenth century there were about 7,500 total Paiutes (perhaps 1,500 to 2,000 Owens Valley Paiutes). The Owens Valley Paiutes' dialects of Mono are, with Northern Paiute, part of the Western Numic (Shoshonean) branch of the Uto-Aztecan linguistic family.

Religious observances were centered on round dances and festivities associated with the fall harvest. Professional singers in elaborate dance regalia performed in a dance corral. The girls' puberty ceremony was also important.

The cry was an annual Yuman-derived mourning ceremony for those who had died during the previous year. A ritual face washing (the first time since the death that the face was washed) marked the end of the official spousal year of mourning.

Male and female shamans were primarily doctors and religious leaders. Their power often came in a recurring dream. They cured by sucking, retrieving

a wandering soul, or administering medicines. Disease was caused by soul loss, mishandling power, or sorcery. Special objects, as well as songs mandated by the power dream, helped them perform their tasks. They might acquire a good deal of clandestine political power by making headmen dependent on them.

Owens Valley Paiutes lived in semipermanent base camps, or hamlets, named for natural features. The camps were semipermanent in that usually the same families occupied them intermittently throughout the year and from year to year. This level of social organization showed some similarities to California tribelets. Within the camps families were completely independent. Families might share or coordinate in subsistence activities, but doing so was informal and unstructured.

Hamlets in a given area cooperated in intermarriage, irrigation, rabbit and deer drives, funerals, and the use of the sweat house. The headmen or chiefs directed the communal activities. Their other duties included conducting festivals and ceremonies, overseeing construction of the assembly lodge, and determining the death penalty for a shaman accused of witchcraft. The position was hereditary, usually in the male line.

Although many people maintained the dams, an elected irrigator was responsible for watering a specific area. In the summer, most families pursued hunting and gathering activities. They generally occupied their valley dwelling places in the spring, the time of irrigation; in the fall, the time of social activities; and in the winter, unless the pine nut or Indian rice grass crops failed.

For irrigation, Owens Valley Paiutes used temporary dams and feeder streams of summer floodwaters. Their main tool was a long wooden water staff. They used nets to catch rabbits and fish. Fish were also speared or poisoned and often dried and stored for winter.

Hunting technology differed according to location, but usually featured a sinew-backed juniper bow, arrows, nets, snares, and deadfalls. Twined and coiled basketry included burden baskets with tumplines for distance (even transmountain) carrying and seed beaters. Fire was made with a drill, and smoldering, cigar-shaped fire matches were used to transport it. Roots were dug with mountain mahogany digging sticks. Nuts were ground and shelled with manos and metates or with wood or stone mortars and stone pestles. Some women made pottery, from the midseventeenth to the midnineteenth centuries.

Owens Valley Paiutes first saw non-Natives in the early nineteenth century (although they may have seen Spanish explorers earlier). These early explorers, trappers, and prospectors encountered Indians who were already irrigating wild crops.

Military and civil personnel surveyed the region in the late 1850s with an eye toward establishing a reservation for local Indians. The first non-Indian settlers arrived in 1861. These ranchers grew crops that fed nearby miners and other whites. As the white population increased, so did conflicts over water rights and irrigated lands. Whites cut down vital piñons for fuel. Hungry Indians stole cattle, and whites retaliated by killing Indians. As of early 1862, however, the Indians still controlled the Owens Valley, because they formed local military alliances.

Camp Independence was founded in July 1862 as a military outpost. Fighting continued well into 1863, until whites got the upper hand by pursuing a scorched-earth policy. Many Indians surrendered but were back in the valley in a few years. By this time, however, whites had taken over most of their best lands, and a diminished Indian population was left to settle around towns, ranches, and mining camps, working mostly as laborers. Indians on newly reserved lands, increasingly including Western Shoshone families, worked mainly as small-scale farmers.

Indian schools opened in the late nineteenth century, although formal reservations were not established until the twentieth. Too small for ranches, the early reservations supported small-scale farming as the main economic activity. However, many Indians still lived on nonreservation lands and on other, non-Paiute reservations.

From the early twentieth century through the 1930s, the city of Los Angeles bought most of Owens Valley, primarily for water rights. This development destroyed the local economy, eliminating the low-level Indian jobs. The city also proposed new ways to dispossess and consolidate the remaining Indians at that time. Ultimately, most Indian people approved of the series of land exchanges (those at Fort Independence rejected the plans). During the 1940s, the federal government built new housing and sewer and irrigation systems on the new Indian lands.

See also Dams, Fishing Rights, and Hydroelectric Power; Economic Development; Reservation Economic and Social Conditions; Water Rights.

Paiute, Southern

"Southern Paiute" is a designation for approximately sixteen seminomadic, culturally distinct, and politically autonomous Great Basin groups, such as Kaibabs, Kaiparowits, Panguitches, Shivwits, Moapas, Paranigets, and Panacas. Their self-designation is *Nuwu,* or "Person." The Chemehuevis were originally a Southern Paiute group. "Southern Paiute" is a modern construction and is more a linguistic than a cultural convention. "Paiute" may have meant "True Ute" or "Water Ute" and was applied to the Northern Paiute only after the 1850s. To the north and northeast, some Southern Paiute groups merged with the Western and Southern Utes. Numic-speaking Southern Paiutes came into their historic area around 1000, perhaps from around Death Valley. They gradually replaced Hopis in the south and may have learned agriculture from them.

Southern Paiutes lived and continue to live in southwest Utah, southern Nevada, northwest Arizona, and southeast California. The San Juan Paiutes lived east of the Colorado River. Southern Paiute territory encompasses a great environmental diversity, including canyons and high deserts of the Colorado Plateau and the Great Basin. The entire early nineteenth-century Paiute population was roughly 7,500. Southern Paiute languages belong to the Southern Numic (Shoshonean) branch of the Uto-Aztecan language family. Their languages and those of the Northern Paiutes were mutually unintelligible.

Shamans provided religious leadership; they cured and conducted ceremonies such as the girls' puberty rite. They could be men or women, although women were more often considered evil. Power dreams, perhaps dreamed in a special cave, also provided instructions and songs.

Disease was attributed to sorcerers, a ghost-inspired poisonous object (necessitating the removal of the object by sucking), or soul loss (cured by the shaman's recapturing the soul). The mourning ceremony, or cry, was undertaken by wealthy relatives of a recently deceased person (in the past three months to a year) so they could eat and sleep well. It was a feast at which many items were destroyed.

Southern Paiute posed in front of an adobe house in the early twentieth century. (Library of Congress)

Camp groups were composed of one to ten or fifteen households, many of whom were related. They were led by a headman as well as by the best hunters and gatherers. Headmen served in an advisory capacity. This position tended to remain in the family and among men but did not necessarily pass from father to son (except for the Chemehuevis and Las Vegas).

The basic social unit was the nuclear family. Each group generally gathered food, hunted, and camped together. Each was associated with a specific though nonexclusive geographic territory.

People married early; girls might be pre- or postpubescent. Most marriages were monogamous. Gender-determined rituals over infants' navel stumps underscored the priority placed on hunting for men and industry in domestic chores for women. Both new parents observed postpartum behavior and food restrictions.

Meat that a boy killed was given away to the elderly until he reached puberty. Puberty rites for both sexes included bathing, body painting, hair trimming, and physical endurance. Relatives prepared a corpse, then underwent behavior and food restrictions. Most groups cremated their dead. The dead person's possessions were burned or buried, and his or her house was torn down and moved. Some groups occasionally killed a relative as company for the deceased. There was a permanent taboo on using the name of the dead.

Springs were considered inheritable private property. People commonly gambled on traditional hand and other games such as shinny (a variation of hockey), four-stick, hoop-and-pole (in which an arrow is shot through a rolling hoop), and target. Other games included ring and pin as well as athletic contests.

Southern Paiutes migrated seasonally, following the food supply. Their diet was based on hunting, gathering, and some agriculture (mostly corn, beans, and squash, using floodplain or ditch irrigation). Tobacco patches and grasslands were burned to encourage growth.

Women gathered wild plants, including goldenrod and grass seeds, roots, pine nuts, yucca dates, cactus fruit, agave, nuts, juniper berries, mesquite, and screwbean. Grasshoppers, caterpillars, ant larvae, and insect grubs were also eaten. Seeds were parched, ground, and eaten as mush or as bread. Men hunted small game, the major source of protein, with the assistance of spirits and/or shamans. Rabbits were especially important. They were hunted individually or driven communally into 100-yard-long nets. Big game included deer, antelope, and mountain sheep. Some groups fished occasionally.

The Southern Paiutes encountered a Spanish expedition in 1776 but adopted neither horses nor much else of Spanish culture. However, diseases and some material items may have preceded actual contact. Some groups were practicing agriculture before 1800.

By 1830, the trail established by the first Spanish explorers was in heavy use. The increased traffic depleted the area's natural resources. The trail also facilitated raiding and trading parties by both Indian and non-Native peoples. Mounted Utes and Navajos, and later Spanish expeditions and American trappers were engaged in raiding for and trading in Southern Paiute slaves. Starving Southern Paiutes sometimes sold their children for food. One effect of this situation was the Paiutes' self-removal from areas that were economically productive but close to slave raiders. The loss of a significant percentage of their young also contributed to the population reduction that was well under way by this time.

Mormon settlers arrived in 1847. At first participants in the slave trade, they had it legally abolished by the mid-1850s (although they continued to "adopt" Indian children). However, their practice of establishing settlements and missions on the best land, thereby depleting Native resources and squeezing the Indians out, soon left the latter as beggars. Many Mormons alternated between seeing Indians negatively, as did most Americans, and positively, because of a perceived connection to biblical Israelites. About the same time, the Chemehuevis split off and moved down the Colorado River.

Some groups retaliated against whites by raiding their settlements. In a move to head off violence, six Mormon Southern Paiute headmen agreed in 1865 to move their people to the Uintah and Ouray Reservation, the home of their Ute enemies. The treaty remained unratified, however, and was later abandoned. By the 1870s roughly 80 percent of Southern Paiutes had died as a result of starvation and disease (Southern Paiute death rates exceeded birth rates well—in some cases, halfway—into the twentieth century). Survivors had begun the process of acculturation, gathering into larger camps and working in the new white towns.

By executive order, a reservation (Moapa) of roughly 3,900 square miles was established in Nevada for the Southern Paiutes in 1872. Although

few Indians moved there, it was expanded in 1874 with the idea that Southern Paiutes would be turned into farmers and ranchers. Soon, however, the reservation was greatly reduced in size. When promised federal support was not forthcoming, conditions began rapidly to deteriorate.

Meanwhile, Indians in southern Utah were either seeking wage work or trying desperately to hold on in their traditional locations. In the late 1880s, after a local white rancher persuaded the government to remove the Shivwits from their lands, the Shivwits Reservation was established in southern Utah. Though it was later expanded, the land was never good enough to support the population, even without the inevitable conflicts over water and range rights. Many residents eventually moved away. Several small Mormon-affiliated farming communities had also been established by 1885.

Several reservations were created for the Southern Paiutes in the twentieth century (although one, the San Juan Paiute Reservation, was returned to the public domain shortly after an oil company expressed interest in the parcel). In the mid-1950s, the Utah Paiutes (Shivwits, Indian Peaks, Koosharem, and Kanosh bands) were removed from federal control (terminated), although policy dictated that this would not happen until the people were ready and willing to take care of themselves. (The groups were restored in 1980.) The immediate effects of this action included a tremendous loss of the modest land base (through individual allotment sales and non-payment of taxes), greater impoverishment, exploitative leases to non-Indians, removal of health services, and greatly increased social problems. When people tried to hunt rabbits again for survival, they discovered that many animals had been poisoned by fallout from the Nevada nuclear test site. Perhaps not surprisingly, many people left the reservation during these years.

In 1965, Southern Paiutes were awarded $8,250,000 (27 cents an acre) as official compensation for their aboriginal land. The bands used their shares in different ways, but nearly all provided for some direct per-capita payments as well as long-term concerns. New federal programs during this time also helped lift many Indians out of dire poverty and provide them with decent housing. During the 1960s, many people were poisoned with the insecticide DDT as a result of government and farmer spraying. Women basketmakers, who pulled willow twigs through their teeth, were especially hard hit.

See also Demographics, Historical; Disease, Historic and Contemporary; Reservation Economic and Social Conditions.

Shoshone, Eastern or Wind River

Eastern, or Wind River, Shoshones make up a group grounded in Great Basin traditions who modified their culture to include elements from Plains and postcontact cultures. The Comanches broke away from the Eastern Shoshones about 1700 and moved south toward Texas. The term "Shoshone" is of dubious origin and is not a self-designation.

Beginning at least as early as 1500, the Comanche-Shoshones began expanding eastward onto the Great Plains and adopting wide-scale buffalo hunting. The Eastern Shoshones lived in present-day western Wyoming from at least the sixteenth century on, expanded into the northern Great Plains through the eighteenth century, and then retreated in the nineteenth century. They were loosely divided into two groups: Mountain Sheep Eaters to the north and west and Buffalo Eaters to the east and south. Most Eastern Shoshones now live on the Wind River Reservation, in Fremont and Hot Springs Counties, Wyoming. There were perhaps 3,000 Eastern Shoshones in 1840. The Eastern Shoshones spoke dialects of Shoshone, a Central Numic (Shoshonean) language of the Uto-Aztecan language family.

The Eastern Shoshones knew two basic kinds of religious practice. One was aimed at an individual's obtaining the assistance of supernatural powers from spirits. In exchange for power, such spirits, which could also be dangerous, demanded adherence to strict behavioral taboos. Power was gained either through dances or by sleeping in sacred places. Success in obtaining power was marked by a vision through which the power transferred skills or protections as well as songs, fetishes, and taboos. Power might also be transferred from one shaman to another by blowing. Should a person's power depart, a shaman had to recapture it lest the person die. Shamans did not so much control power as they were dependent on it.

The other kind of religious practice was designed to ensure the welfare of the community and nature as a whole by the observance of group ceremonials. The Father, the Shuffling (Ghost), and

the Sun Dances were all addressed toward beneficent beings. The first two, during which men and women sang sacred songs, often took place at night in any season except the summer. The Shuffling Dance was particularly important to Mountain Sheep Eaters.

The four-night and three-day Sun Dance was held in the summer and featured exhaustion owing to dancing and the lack of water. Introduced from the Plains around 1800, it symbolized the power and cohesion of the tribe and of the generations. It was an occasion for demonstrating virility, courage, and supernatural powers. Male dancers first participated in ritual sweats and other preparations, which began as early as the preceding winter. The ceremony itself, held around ten outer poles encircling a buffalo head mounted on a center pole, was followed by a great feast of buffalo tongues. Little boys were charged with grabbing the tongues.

Spirit places, things, and people were inherently dangerous and included ghosts, whirlwinds, old or menstruating women, death, and illness. Illness was seen as coming from either a breach of taboo or malevolent spirits. Sacred items and activities included sweating, burning certain grasses and wood, smoking wild tobacco, eagle feathers, paints, and certain songs. The peyote cult began on the reservation around 1900.

Centralization was the key to successful buffalo hunting and warfare and thus to eighteenth- and nineteenth-century Eastern Shoshone survival. During prosperous times (for instance, during periods of strong chieftainships) and when they came together seasonally as a tribe (for instance, for the spring buffalo hunt and the summertime Sun Dance), the Eastern Shoshones numbered between 1,500 and 3,000.

A chief was at least middle-aged and of military or shamanistic training. He had authority over hunting, migration, and other issues. He and his assistants controlled the two military police societies. His several distinctions included possessing a painted teepee and a special feathered headdress. He also acted as chief diplomat for external disputes.

The Eastern Shoshones separated into between three and five bands in winter, camping mainly in the Wind River Valley. Each band had a chief as well as military societies. Bands were loosely identified with particular geographic regions. Membership fluctuated, with extended family groups joining different Shoshone bands or perhaps even bands of other tribes such as the Crows.

Shoshone women were in general subordinate to men, chiefly because menstruation was believed to set them apart as sources of ritual pollution. The younger wife or wives usually suffered in instances of polygyny. Widows were dispossessed. At the same time, women gained status as individuals through their skills as gatherers, crafters, gamblers, midwives, and child care providers. Particularly during the fur trade period, alliances with white trappers and traders were made with daughters and sisters, leading to important interethnic ties.

Social status positions were earned through the use (or nonuse) of supernatural power, except that age and sex also played a role. Infants and small children were not recognized as sexually different. Boys began their search for supernatural power around adolescence. "Men" were those who were married and members of a military society.

Girls helped their mothers until marriage, which was arranged shortly after the onset of puberty. Menstrual restrictions included gathering firewood (a key female chore) and refraining from meat and daytime sleeping. A good husband was a good provider, although he might be considerably older.

Wealth and prestige accrued to curers, midwives, good gamblers, hunters and traders, and fast runners. Property was often destroyed or abandoned at death. Generosity was a central value: Giveaways for meritorious occasions were common. Men cared for war and buffalo horses, women for packhorses. High-stakes gambling games included the traditional hand and four-stick dice game, double-ball shinny (a variation of hockey, for women), and foot races.

Beginning in the eighteenth century, the state of war was more or less continuous, and warfare took a great toll on the Eastern Shoshones. There were two military societies. About 100 to 150 brave young men were Yellow Brows. The recruitment ritual included backward speech (no for yes, for example). This fearless society acted as vanguards on the march. They fought to the death in combat and had a major role keeping order on the buffalo hunt. Their Big Horse Dance was a highly ritualistic preparation for battle. Logs were older men who took up the rear on the march. Both groups were entitled to blacken their faces.

Shamans participated in war by foretelling events and curing men and horses. As many as 300 men might make up a war party. Traditional enemies included the Blackfeet and later the Arapahos, Lako-

tas, Cheyennes, and Gros Ventres. During the mid- to late nineteenth century, the principal ally of the Shoshones was the U.S. Army.

The spring and especially the fall were the times for war. At these times the Eastern Shoshones generally fought as a tribe. Men made handle-held shields from thick, young buffalo bull hide. Rituals and feasting accompanied their manufacture. Each was decorated with buckskin and fringed with feathers. Weapons included sinew-backed bows, obsidian-tipped arrows, and clubs. Successful warriors were entitled to paint black and red finger marks on their teepees.

With the acquisition of horses about 1700, the Shoshones also began widespread raiding and developed a much stronger and more centralized leadership. It was roughly at this time that the Comanches departed for places south. Armed with firearms, the Blackfeet and other tribes began driving the Eastern Shoshones off the westward Plains beginning in the late eighteenth century. Major smallpox epidemics occurred during that period, and the Eastern Shoshones adopted the Sun Dance introduced around 1800. Extensive intermarriage also occurred with the Crows, Nez Percé, and Métis.

During most of the nineteenth century, the Eastern Shoshone, under their chief, Washakie, were often allied with whites and grew prosperous. During the peak of the fur trade, from 1810 to 1840, the eastern Shoshones sold up to 2,000 buffalo skins a year. When settlers began pouring into their territory in the 1850s, the Eastern Shoshones, under Washakie, tried to accommodate them. In the Fort Bridger Treaty of 1868 they received 44 million acres; this figure was later reduced to fewer than 2 million. During the next fifteen or so years they lived in a roughly traditional way on their reservation.

Because the Shoshone fought with the U.S. Army against the Lakotas on many occasions, they felt betrayed when the government placed the Arapahos, their traditional enemies, on their reservation in 1878. The disappearance of the buffalo in the 1880s spelled the end of their traditional way of life. From the late nineteenth century and into the midtwentieth century, the Eastern Shoshones, confined to reservations, experienced extreme hardship, population loss, and cultural decline. They had no decent land, hunting was prohibited, government rations were issued at starvation levels, and they could find no off-reservation employment because of poor transportation and white prejudice.

Disease, especially tuberculosis, was rampant. Life expectancy was roughly twenty-two years at that time. The Indian Service controlled the reservation.

A slow recovery began in the late 1930s. Land claims victories brought vastly more land as well as an infusion of cash (almost $3.5 million). Concurrently, the tribal council, hitherto relatively weak, began assuming greater control of all aspects of reservation life. By the mid-1960s, the incidence of disease was markedly lower, owing in large part to the diligent efforts of women. Indicators such as housing, diet, economic resources (such as oil and gas leases), education, and real political control had all increased. Life expectancy had risen to forty to forty-five years. Traditional religious activity remained strong and meaningful. And yet severe and ongoing problems remained, including continuing white prejudice and a corresponding lack of off-reservation job opportunities, out-migration, slow economic development, and fear of the growing strength of the Arapaho.

> *See also* Buffalo; Horse, Economic Impact; Sun Dance; Warfare, Intertribal; Women in Native Woodlands Societies.

Shoshone, Northern

"Northern Shoshone" is a modern, anthropological term used to distinguish a region of Shoshone culture. The Northern Shoshones and Bannocks (originally a Northern Paiute group) shared a number of cultural traits with the Paiute and the Ute Indians as well as with so-called Eastern or Wind River Shoshones (there was no aboriginal distinction among Shoshone groups) and Northern Paiutes. Northern Shoshones incorporated elements of the Great Basin, Plateau, and Great Plains cultures. The term "Shoshone" first surfaced in 1805. Other Indians and non-Indians sometimes referred to some Shoshone and Northern Paiute groups, particularly mounted bands, as Snake Indians (sedentary Shoshones and Northern Paiutes were often referred to as Diggers), but their name for themselves is *Nomo*, or "People." Shoshone is part of the Central Numic (Shoshonean) division of the Uto-Aztecan language family. The Bannocks spoke Western Numic, also a Shoshonean language, although it was mutually unintelligible with Central Numic.

In the early nineteenth century, Northern Shoshones lived mostly in Idaho south of the

Salmon River or on the Snake River plains and the mountains to the north. This region, on the border of the Columbia Plateau, has a relatively dry climate. It contains the Sawtooth and Bitterroot Mountains, valleys, river highlands, and the Snake and other rivers and creeks. Today, most Northern Shoshones live in and around Bannock, Bingham, Caribou, and Power Counties in Idaho. The pre-contact population of up to 30,000 had been cut by 90 percent by the midnineteenth century, mainly by epidemics of European diseases.

Northern Shoshones used dreams and visions to acquire helping spirits. Such spirits instructed people on the use of medicines with which to activate their power. Certain food and other restrictions might also be imposed. Spirits might cure illness, protect an individual from arrows, or hurt other people.

Most or all men could cure, although there were also professionals. Their methods included herbs, charms, and sweats. They gained their supernatural power through dreams, visions, and visits to remote, spirit-dwelling places.

There was a concept of a creator, but creative agency was proscribed to mythological characters such as the wolf and coyote. Ceremonial occasions that featured round dances included the spring salmon return, the fall harvest, and times of adversity.

Loosely organized groups were characteristic of Great Basin culture. Traditionally, the Northern Shoshone were organized into seminomadic bands with impermanent composition and leadership. Some bands had chiefs; others, particularly in the west, had neither bands nor chiefs.

Life on the Plains called for higher forms of organization, both to hunt buffalo and to defend against enemies. In the fall, for instance, the bands in the area of the Snake and Lemhi Rivers came together for councils, feasts, and buffalo hunts. During these times, the more eastern bands were led by a principal chief and several minor chiefs. However, these offices were still nonhereditary, loosely defined, and somewhat transitory. Also, with more complex social organization, band councils arose to limit the power of the chiefs. Some "police" or soldier societies may also have existed to keep order during hunts and dances.

Equality and individual autonomy were cardinal Shoshone values. Just as social organization was fairly undeveloped, especially to the west, there was also little barrier to social interaction. Local groups were named by the foods they ate, but the same band might have several names, and the same name might apply to several bands. Many groups often intermarried, visited, and shared ceremonies and feasts. Social networks were wide and strong. Most marriages were monogamous. Both marriage and divorce were simple and common. The dead were wrapped in blankets and placed in rock crevices. Mourners cut their hair, gashed their legs, and killed one of the deceased's horses. Some private property (such as tools and weapons) was recognized, but private ownership of land or subsistence areas was not.

As a source of sustenance, roots (such as prairie turnips, yampa root, tobacco root, bitterroot, and camas) were steamed in earth ovens for several days or boiled. Berries (such as chokecherries and service berries), nuts, and seeds were also important foods, as were grasshoppers, ants and other insects, lizards, squirrels, and rabbits.

Big game included antelope, deer, elk, and mountain sheep. Buffalo were Native to parts of the region but became especially important in the seventeenth century, when people would travel for the fall hunt to the Plains (east of Bozeman) and then back to the Snake River in the winter or early spring.

Salmon was the most important fish. In fact, the salmon fishery was one of the key distinguishing features between the Northern Shoshone and the Eastern Shoshone. People also caught sturgeon, perch, trout, and other fish on Columbia and Snake River tributaries.

The Paiute-speaking Bannock were among the first local groups to acquire horses, in the late seventeenth century. At that time, they migrated from eastern Oregon to Shoshone territory near the Snake River and organized fully mounted bands and engaged in group buffalo hunts. They and the Northern Shoshones also began to raid for horses and assumed many other aspects of Plains culture, such as teepees and warrior societies, yet the Bannock continued to interact with their Northern Paiute relatives. Sacajawea, a Shoshone woman, served as a guide on the Lewis and Clark expedition of 1804. Her diplomatic and navigation skills saved the party on more than one occasion.

Continuing their move east to the western extremity of the northern Plains, the Shoshone were soon (mideighteenth century) driven back by the gun-wielding Blackfeet. Some Northern Shoshone groups did not become mounted until the nineteenth century or used the horse only as a pack animal. Such groups, particularly those away from the cen-

ters in the Snake and Lemhi River Valleys (for example, the so-called Sheepeaters), lived in scattered settlements and remained sedentary and peaceful.

The Meriwether Lewis and William Clark party (1804–1806) may have been the first non-Indians in the area. Anglos soon opened trading posts at Pend Oreille Lake (British, 1809) and the Upper Snake River (Northwest Company, 1810). Throughout the 1810s and 1820s, white trappers ranged across Shoshone territory, destroying all beaver and buffalo west of the Rockies. Other game suffered as well, as did the traditional Northern Shoshone way of life. Indians also acquired much non-Native technology during this time, including firearms, iron utensils, and alcohol, and new diseases took a heavy toll.

By the 1840s, the fur trade had collapsed. Non-Indians began arriving en masse after the California gold rush and the opening of the Oregon Trail, further stressing the delicate local ecology. In 1847, the Mormons arrived. By the 1860s, the buffalo had all but disappeared. Relatively quickly, many Northern Shoshone groups faced starvation. They began to raid white settlements and wagons in retaliation, an activity that quickly brought counterraids. This kind of conflict persisted throughout the 1860s and 1870s, although the Fort Hall Reservation (originally 1.8 million acres) was created by treaty in 1868.

The Bannocks, however, had resisted confinement to Fort Hall. Some peoples' resistance was a direct influence of the Dreamer Cult founded about 1860 by the Wanapum Smohalla. The continued destruction of their way of life—led by the wholesale slaughter of the buffalo, inadequate rations, white ranchers' crowding, and violence committed against them when they continued subsistence activities guaranteed by treaty—led to a major revolt in 1878. Its immediate cause was Anglo hog herding in a camas root area forbidden to them by treaty. The Bannocks and some Northern Paiute bands, under the Bannock chief Buffalo Born and the Paiutes Egan and Oytes, engaged the soldiers for several months that summer. Ultimately, the Paiutes were settled among the Yakima in Washington, and the Bannocks, held as prisoners of war for a while, were permitted to return to Fort Hall.

The Sheepeater War also took place in 1878, when roughly fifty central Idaho Bannocks and Shoshones, who lived primarily on mountain sheep, began raiding settlers who were encroaching on their subsistence area. At first eluding the army, they were eventually captured and placed at Fort Hall.

Other Shoshones, too, fought to retain their traditions; most ended up at Fort Hall.

The United States created the Lemhi Valley Reservation in 1875, but its people were moved to Fort Hall when the reservation was terminated in 1907. Meanwhile, the Fort Hall Reservation itself shrank by more than two-thirds as a result of encroachments by the railroads, timber, mining, highway, and other interests. Dawes Act (1887) allotments further reduced it in size. Life at Fort Hall was marked by irrigation problems; major projects in the early twentieth century benefited white farmers only. Other serious problems included the flooding of good bottomlands by the American Falls Reservoir. Major economic activities during that time included sheep and cattle ranching. A phosphate mine opened after World War II.

Fort Hall Indians acquired the Sun Dance from Plains Indians, via the Wind River Shoshone, during the 1890s. Some also adopted the Native American Church in 1915. The government awarded them a land claims settlement of more than $8.8 million in 1964; another, smaller settlement was received in 1971 by the Lemhi Valley descendents.

See also Dreamer Cult; Fur Trade; Horse, Economic Impact; Smohalla; Sun Dance.

Shoshone, Western

The Western Shoshone were a number of Shoshonean-speaking groups generally inhabiting a particular area. Many groups were known to whites as Diggers. Their self-designation is *Newe*. The Goshutes (Gosiutes) are ethnic Shoshones, despite considerable intermarriage with the Utes and the existence of a 1962 court ruling legally separating them from the Western Shoshone. Little pre-1859 scientific ethnographic data exist on the Western Shoshone. Their aboriginal population may have numbered between 5,000 and 10,000, although it had declined to roughly 2,000 by the early nineteenth century. The Western Shoshone spoke three central Numic languages—Panamint, Shoshone, and Comanche—all members of the Numic (Shoshonean) branch of the Uto-Aztecan language family.

Most Western Shoshone bands lived in harsh environments such as the Great Salt Lake area (Goshutes) and Death Valley (Panamints). Their territory stretched from Death Valley through central Nevada into northwestern Utah and southern Idaho.

celebration. In some areas the dance was associated with courtship or rainmaking. Festivals were often held in times of plenty.

Groups in small winter villages were composed of family clusters and named for an important food resource or a local geographic feature. Thus, the territory and not the composition of the group was definitive. Group membership was not fixed and groups were not bands per se. Chiefs or headmen had little authority other than directing subsistence activity.

In general, the Western Shoshone adapted very successfully to a relatively harsh environment. They used sticks to beat grasses and dig roots, as well as using seed beaters of twined willow. Coiled and twined baskets were important in grass collection, as was a twined winnowing tray. Waterproof baskets allowed people to forage far from water.

Other tools and equipment included stone metates for grinding seeds; snares, traps, and deadfalls to hunt cottontails and rodents; bows of juniper and mountain mahogany; wildcat skin quivers; stone or horn arrow straighteners; and some pottery. Western Shoshones were first visited by non-Natives—the Jedediah Smith and Peter Skene Ogden parties—in the late 1820s. Other trappers and traders passed through during the next twenty years. Despite the willingness of some groups, such as the Walker party, to massacre Indians, the latter were relatively unaffected by early contacts with non-Natives.

The Mormons, who ultimately had a huge impact on the Goshute Shoshones, began arriving to stay in 1847. The white presence increased throughout the 1840s and 1850s, but the discovery of the Comstock Lode in 1857 turned the stream into a flood. By then, degradation of the natural environment was well under way. New diseases also stalked the region, severely affecting both human and animal populations. Indians responded by either retreating farther from white activity or, less often, by raiding, stealing, and begging.

The Pony Express, established in 1860, passed through the center of Western Shoshone country. Supply depots at important springs displaced Indians, which encouraged attacks and then Army reprisals. By 1860, Mormons had invaded Goshute territory, and miners and ranchers were closing in on the rest of Western Shoshone lands. Grazing, plowing, and woodcutting (piñon and juniper pine) destroyed subsistence areas and forage land. Indians began to work for settlers as wage laborers to fend

Rabbit-Tail, Shoshone member of Captain Ray's scout company, with bracelets and ornamented vest. (National Archives and Records Administration)

Most Western Shoshones today live on a number of reservations within their aboriginal territory. They also live in nearby and regional cities and towns.

Apo, the sun, was a principal deity. Anyone could obtain supernatural powers through dreams and visions, although medicine men (*bugahant*) served as religious leaders. Most groups recognized three kinds of shamans: curers of specific ailments, general curers, and self-curers or helpers. Curing was effected by sucking and by the laying on of hands. In theory, men and women could both be shamans, although only men may have practiced curing. Shamans were also capable of capturing antelopes' souls and helping to drive them into corrals. Some groups may not have had shamans at all.

People used several hundred herbal remedies to cure nonsupernatural ailments such as cuts and bruises. The round dance was basic to ceremonial

off starvation. Euro-American clothing, technology, and shelter quickly replaced the traditional variety.

Federal negotiations with the Great Basin tribes began in the 1850s, in part to check sporadic violence against settlers. The first treaties with Western Shoshone groups were signed in 1863. They called for Indians to give up hostilities, settle down eventually, and receive goods annually worth a total of $50,000. In return, the settlers could stay. Significantly, the Indians never actually ceded any land.

The army soon began rounding up Indians. When no reservations near good land with water were established during the 1870s, some Shoshones joined Northern Paiutes and Bannocks in their wars of resistance. In 1879, the Shoshones refused an order to move to the Western Shoshone (Duck Valley) Reservation. Despite the extreme disruption of their lives, elements of traditional culture survived, such as religious beliefs (except among the Goshutes) and limited subsistence patterns. Most Shoshones still lived unconfined after 1900.

The percentage of Western Shoshones living on reservations peaked at fifty in 1927. Most carried out semitraditional subsistence activities combined with seasonal or other wage work in mines and on ranches and farms. In an effort to enlarge the reservation population, the United States encouraged Northern Paiutes to settle at Duck Valley. Finally, accepting the fact that most Western Shoshones did not and would not live at Duck Valley, the government created a series of "colonies" during the first half of the twentieth century.

In 1936, the Paiutes and most Shoshone groups organized the Paiute-Shoshone Business Council. Chief TeMoak and his descendents were considered the leaders of this effort. The U.S. government refused to recognize the traditional TeMoak council, however, and instead organized their own TeMoak Bands Council. This split culminated when the traditionalist-backed United Western Shoshone Legal Defense and Education Association (1974) argued that the TeMoak Bands Council did not represent Western Shoshone interests and further that the Western Shoshones never ceded their land. The courts rejected their claim in 1979 and ordered them paid $26 million in compensation. In 1985, the Supreme Court ruled that the 1979 payment legally extinguished their title to the disputed 24 million acres.

See also Land, Identity and Ownership of, Land Rights; Mormon Church; Reservation Economic and Social Conditions.

Shoshone, Wind River

See Shoshone, Eastern or Wind River.

Ute

The Utes consisted of roughly eleven autonomous Great Basin bands. In the eighteenth century, the eastern bands included the Uncompahgres (or Tabeguaches), Yampas and Parusanuchs (or White River Band), Mouaches, Capotes, and Weeminuches, and the western bands included the Uintahs, Timpanogots, Pahvants, Sanpits, and Moanunts. The word "Utah" is of Spanish derivation, probably borrowed originally from an Indian word. Their self-designation is *Nunt'z,* "the People." With Southern Paiute, Ute is a member of the Southern Numic (Shoshonean) division of the Uto-Aztecan language family. All dialects were mutually intelligible.

Aboriginally, Utes lived in most of present-day Utah, except the far western, northern, and southern parts; Colorado west of and including the eastern slopes of the Rockies; and the extreme north of New Mexico. Today, the three Ute reservations are in southwest Colorado, the Four Corners area, and north central Utah. From roughly 8,000 in the early nineteenth century, the Utes declined to about 1,800 in 1920. In 1990 approximately 5,000 lived on reservations, and roughly another 2,800 lived in cities and towns.

The Utes and their ancestors have been in the Great Basin for as many as 10,000 years. They lived along Arizona's Gila River from about 3000 to about 500 BCE. At that time, a group of them began migrating north toward Utah, growing a high-altitude variety of corn that had been developed in Mexico. This group, who grew corn, beans, and squash and who also hunted and gathered food, is known as the Sevier Complex. Another, related group of people, known as the Fremont Complex, lived to the northeast.

In time, the Fremont people migrated into western Colorado. When a drought struck the Great Basin in the thirteenth century, the Fremont people moved into Colorado's San Luis Valley, where they later became known as the Utes. They became one of the first mounted Indian peoples when band members escaped Spanish captivity and brought horses home in the midseventeenth century. Communal buffalo hunts began shortly thereafter. Mounted

warriors brought more protection, and larger camps meant more centralized government and more powerful leaders as well as a rising standard of living. Utes also facilitated the spread of the horse to peoples of the Great Plains.

Utes believed that supernatural power was in all living things. Curing and weather shamans, both men and women, derived additional power from dreams. A few shamans, influenced by Plains culture, undertook vision quests.

One of the oldest of Ute ceremonies, the ten-day Bear Dance, was a welcome to spring. Bear is a mythological figure who provides leadership, wisdom, and strength. Perhaps originally a hunting ritual, the dance, directed by a dance chief and his assistants, signaled a time for courtship and the renewal of social ties. It was also related to the end of the girls' puberty ceremony. An all-male orchestra played musical rasps to accompany dancers. The host band sponsored feasting, dancing, gambling, games, and horse racing. The Sun Dance, of Plains origin, was held in midsummer.

Before the midseventeenth century, small Ute hunting and gathering groups were composed of extended families, with older members in charge. There may also have been some band organization for fall activities such as trading and hunting buffalo.

With the advent of horses, band structure strengthened to facilitate buffalo hunting, raiding, and defense. Each band now had its own chief, or headman, who solicited advice from constituent group leaders. By the eighteenth century, the autonomous bands came together regularly for tribal activities. Each band retained its chief and council, and within the bands, family groups retained their own leadership.

The Western Utes lived year-round in domed willow houses. Weeminuches used them only in the summer, and all groups also used brush and conical pole-frame shelters ten–fifteen feet in diameter, covered with juniper bark or tule. Sweat houses were of similar construction and heated with hot rocks. In the east, after the seventeenth century, people lived in buffalo (or elk) skin teepees, some of which were up to seventeen feet high. Bands generally regrouped into families to hunt and gather during the spring and summer. Important plant foods included seeds, pine nuts, yampa, berries, and yucca. Some southeastern people planted corn in the late prehistoric period. Some groups burned areas to encourage the growth of wild tobacco.

Buffalo were native to the entire area and were important even before the horse. Other important animal foods included elk, antelope (stalked or driven over cliffs), rabbit (hunted with throwing sticks or communally driven into nets), deer, bear, beaver, fowl, and sage hens. Meat was eaten fresh, sun-dried, or smoked. Coyote, wolf, and bobcat were hunted for their fur only.

Other important foods included crickets, grasshoppers, and locusts (dried with berries in cake form). Some western groups ate lizards and reptiles. Some bands also fished, especially in the west, using weirs, nets, basket traps, bow and arrow, and harpoons. Important fish included cutthroat trout, whitefish, chubs, and suckers.

Before the horse, warfare was generally defensive in nature. Utes became mounted raiders in the late seventeenth century. Their usual targets were Pueblo, Southern Paiute, and Western Shoshone Indians. Weapons included a three- to four-foot bow (chokecherry, mountain mahogany, or mountain sheep horn was preferred) and arrows. Eastern Utes also used spears as well as buffalo skin shields.

Some bands were allied with the Jicarilla Apaches and the Comanches against both the Spanish and the Pueblos. Utes had generally poor relations with the Northern and Eastern Shoshones, although they were generally friendly with the Western Shoshones and Southern Paiutes, especially before they began raiding these groups for slaves in the eighteenth century. Navajos were alternately allies and enemies. The eastern Utes observed ceremonies before and after raids.

Utes also raided Western Shoshones and Southern Paiutes for slaves (mostly women and children), whom they sold to the Spanish. Moreover, they were forced to defend some hunting territory against the Comanches (formerly allies) and other Plains tribes around that time. As a result of relentless Comanche attacks, the southern Utes were prevented from developing fully on the Plains. Driven back into the mountains, they lost power and prestige, and the northern bands, enjoying a more peaceful and prosperous life, increased in importance.

A Spanish expedition in 1776 was the first of a line of non-Native explorers, trappers, traders, slavers, and miners to make contact. Non-Natives established a settlement in Colorado in 1851, and U.S. Fort Massachusetts was built the following year to protect that settlement. Utes considered non-Native livestock grazing on their (former) land fair game. In the midst of growing conflicts, treaties

(which remained unratified) were negotiated in the mid-1850s.

The flood of miners that followed the 1858 Rockies gold strikes overwhelmed the eastern Utes. At the same time, the Utes were allied with the Americans and Mexicans against the Navajos. Mormons, fighting the western Utes for land since the late 1840s, had succeeded by the mid-1870s in confining them to about 9 percent of their aboriginal territory. The United States created the Uintah Reservation in 1861 on land the Mormons did not want. They made most Utah Utes, whose population had been decimated, settle there in 1864.

In 1863, some eastern bands improperly signed a treaty ceding all bands' Colorado mountain lands. Five years later, the Eastern Utes, under Chief Ouray, agreed to move west of the continental divide, provided about 15 million acres was reserved for them. Soon, however, gold discoveries in the San Juan Mountains wrecked the deal, and the Utes were forced to cede an additional 3.4 million acres in 1873 (most of the remainder was taken in 1880). The U.S. government considered Ouray "head chief of the Utes," paid him an annual salary, and supplied him with expensive goods.

The Southern Ute Reservation was established on the Colorado–New Mexico border in 1877. At that time, the Mouache and Capote bands settled there, merged to form the Southern Ute tribe, and took up agriculture. Resisting pressure to farm, the Weeminuches, calling themselves the Ute Mountain tribe, began raising cattle in the western part of the Southern Ute Reservation (the part later called the Ute Mountain Reservation).

In the late 1870s, a new Indian agent tried to force the White River Utes to give up their traditional way of life and "become civilized" by setting up a cooperative farming community. His methods included starvation, the destruction of Ute ponies, and encouraging the government to move against them militarily. When the soldiers arrived, the Indians made a defensive stand and a fight broke out, resulting in deaths on both sides (including Agent Nathan Meeker and U.S. Army Commander Thomas Thornburgh). Chief Ouray helped prevent a general war over this affair. The engagement, subsequently called by whites the Thornburgh ambush and the Meeker massacre, led directly to the eviction of the White River people from Colorado.

By 1881, the other eastern bands had all been forced from Colorado (except for the small Southern and Mountain Ute Reservations), and the other eight bands, later known as the Northern Utes, were assigned to the Uintah and Ouray Reservation in northern Utah (the Uintah Reservation was expanded in 1882 to include the removed Weeminuche Band).

Government attempts to force the grazing-oriented Ute to farm met with little success, owing in part to a lack of access to capital and markets and in part to unfavorable soil and climate. Irrigation projects, begun early in the twentieth century, mainly benefited non-Indians who leased, purchased, or otherwise occupied Ute land. The government also withheld rations in an effort to force reservation Utes to send their children to boarding school. During the mid-1880s, almost half of the Ute children at boarding schools in Albuquerque died. In 1911, the Mountain Utes increased their acreage while ceding land that became Mesa Verde National Park.

The last traditional Weeminuche chief, Jack House, assumed his office in 1936 and died in 1971. Buckskin Charley led the Southern Utes from Ouray's death in 1880 until his own in 1936. His son, Antonio Buck, became the first Southern Ute tribal chair. During the 1920s and 1930s, Mountain Utes formed clubs to promote leadership and other skills. Disease remained a major killer as late as the 1940s.

By 1934, the Eastern Utes controlled about 0.001 percent of their aboriginal lands. In 1950, the Confederated Ute Tribes (Northern, Southern, and Mountain) received $31 million in land claims settlements. During the 1950s, the Ute Mountain people began to assume greater control over their own money, and mineral leases provided real tribal income. Funds were expended on a per-capita basis and invested in a number of enterprises, mostly tourist related. The 1960s brought federal housing programs and more land claims money, but the effectiveness of tribal leadership declined considerably. A group of mixed-bloods, called the Affiliated Ute Citizens, were legally separated from the Northern Utes in 1954.

See also Buffalo; Mormon Church; Reservation Economic and Social Conditions; Sun Dance; Warfare, Intertribal.

Washoe

Washoe is a word derived from *Washiu*, or "Person," their self-designation. Though lacking any formal institutional structures, the Washoes considered themselves a tribe, or a distinct people. Washoes

Louisa, a Washoe woman, with her baskets, ca. 1899. (Library of Congress)

lived and continue to live around Lake Tahoe, from Honey Lake in the north to about forty miles north of Mono Lake in the south, on both sides of the California–Nevada border. This mountainous and environmentally rich region was relatively compact (most groups lived within an area of 4,000 square miles, although their range exceeded 10,000 square miles). The Washoes shared many cultural traits of both California and Great Basin Indians. Washoe is a Hokan language. Ancestors of the Washoes arrived in the region roughly 6,000 years ago. Unbroken cultural continuity lasted from around 500 up to about 1800.

Spirits could be related to myths and legends as well as to death; those related to death were seen as sources of illness and bad luck. The Pine Nut Dance was the most important ceremony. It was a harvest ceremony that featured prayers, feasting, dances, and games. Other ceremonies were also related to communal subsistence activities.

Male and female shamans acquired supernatural powers through dreams and refined them through apprenticeships. The power imposed strict behavioral and dietary regulations. Shamans used their powers to cure, often by sucking after singing and praying for four days. They also used certain paraphernalia, such as rattles, feathers, and whistles. Shamans collected a fee for curing and participated in hunting and warfare by using their powers. However, they were also regarded with suspicion as potential sorcerers and were regularly killed.

In general, the Washoes maintained a strong impulse toward egalitarianism. Small, autonomous, occasionally permanent settlements were composed of family groups. These settlements were fluid in composition, since families regularly moved from one group to another. Each family group was led by temporary headmen (occasionally headwomen) who exercised wider (settlement-wide) influence only occasionally and by dint of accomplishment. Their role as diplomats was assisted by having several wives who might remain with their relatives and establish various family alliances.

Hunt leaders also played leadership roles, and shamans might acquire unofficial influence. Although some concept of a regional community did exist (in the form of local groups that occasionally cooperated), there was probably no formal division into bands, even into the twentieth century when white-imposed leadership created such a perception.

Most people moved seasonally with the food supply, but the supply was generally abundant and in predictable locations. Washoes faced little regular hunger until non-Natives destroyed their way of life. Each unit made its own decisions about when and where to procure food. The only exceptions to this rule were foods taken collectively, such as acorns, pine nuts, fish, and some animals.

Fish, including trout, suckers, whitefish, and chub, was a staple. Ice fishing was practiced in winter. Fish were caught both individually and communally and were prepared either by pit roasting, stone boiling (in baskets), or drying. Other staples usually included acorns, which were shelled, leached, and ground into flour before being used to make dumplings. Pine nuts, gathered in late fall, were made into flour for soup.

Washoe women gathered a great variety of wild plants, including roots, grasses, seeds, nuts, berries, and bulbs, for food as well as medicine. Tule and cattails were especially important. Women gathered plants with digging sticks. Family groups had traditional harvesting areas. Some rituals were associated with gathering activities.

Deer, antelope, and rabbit were hunted communally in drives. Rabbits, the most important dietary animal, were driven into corrals or over cliffs. The people also hunted mountain sheep and other large and small game, birds, and waterfowl. They collected insects, especially locusts, grasshoppers, and grubs. Men and sometimes women smoked wild tobacco or used it for poultices. Golden eagles were never killed, bears only rarely.

Although Washoes may have met Spaniards in the late eighteenth century, they were fairly removed from contact with non-Indians until the 1848 California gold rush brought people through their lands. Anglos established trading posts and settlements, complete with fenced lands and water resources, in the 1850s. Indian demands for compensation were met with refusal and/or violence.

When Anglos blamed the Washoes for Northern Paiute resistance, the Indians were forced to turn for protection to the whites who were appropriating their lands. The 1858 discovery of the Comstock silver lode brought a flood of people to nearby Virginia City. Settlers cut the pine forests, and their cattle ate all the wild grasses and scared off the game. Barely ten years after their first substantive contact with white people around 1850, the Washoes' subsistence areas, and thus the basis for their traditional lives, had been virtually destroyed.

Commercial fishing began in Lake Tahoe by the 1860s. Washoes danced the Ghost Dance in the 1870s. The government repeatedly refused to grant them a reservation on the grounds that there was no good land to give them and that, in any case, their disappearance was imminent. The Washoes were pushed farther and farther into the margins, trying to stay alive as best they could. By the late nineteenth century, whites thought of the "Washoe Tribe" as those groups around Carson City and the Carson Valley; other Washoe groups were unknown or ignored.

The Washoes eventually bought or were allotted some small plots of marginal land. Land for "colonies" was donated or purchased with government funds around 1917 and again in the 1930s. The land was always of poor quality, with little or no water. Some Washoe men worked as ranch hands, women as domestic laborers. Well into the twentieth century, desperate poverty was made even worse by white efforts to repress their culture. The Indians suffered severe discrimination and had no legal civil rights.

Some Washoes embraced the Peyote religion through the Native American Church in 1932. The strenuous opposition of whites and of some traditional shamans brought factionalism to the community. In 1935, the tribe accepted the Indian Reorganization Act and ratified a constitution and bylaws. However, tribal leadership remained ineffective through the 1960s. Throughout the period, most Washoes lived marginally in Carson Valley and around Carson City, although some small groups continued to live in their traditional territory. Public facilities, including schools, were desegregated in the 1950s. The Washoes were awarded a land claims settlement of $5 million in 1970.

See also Dams, Fishing Rights, and Hydroelectric Power; Ghost Dance Religion; Native American Church of North America; Reservation Economic and Social Conditions; Women in Native Woodlands Societies.

Native Americans of the Plateau

Cayuse

"Cayuse" (a word derived from the French *cailloux*, meaning "People of the Stones or Rocks") describes Indians who may have lived with the Molala Indians on the John Day River until the early eighteenth century. Their self-designation was *Waiilatpus*, "Superior People." At that time the Cayuses acquired horses, and by the nineteenth century they owned many horses and were disproportionately strong and dominating for the size of the tribe. They expanded northward and eastward, into the Grande Ronde and Walla Walla Valleys, subjugating the Walla Walla tribe in the process. They also regularly hunted buffalo on the Great Plains, adapting many Plains cultural attributes.

During the eighteenth century, Cayuse Indians lived along the headwaters of the Walla Walla, Umatilla, and Grande Ronde Rivers, in present-day Oregon and Washington. Today, most Cayuses live in Umatilla County, Oregon, and in regional cities and towns.

Largely because of their enormous herds of horses, the Cayuses became so wealthy during this period that they no longer bothered to fish, trading instead for fish and other necessities. They welcomed the Meriwether Lewis and William Clark expedition in 1806 and welcomed as well the fur traders who entered their territory shortly after the explorers' coming. They were not especially interested in furs but rather in the manufactured goods of non-Indians that they might trade for. Their openness to non-Natives was also due in part to their luck at having so far escaped most of the disease epidemics that ravaged other Indian peoples.

The first Presbyterian missions in the area opened in 1836. In 1843, the first emigrants traveled on the Oregon Trail. In 1847, relations between the Cayuses and whites, hitherto friendly, took a dramatic turn for the worse when a group of Indians destroyed the local mission and killed its founders, Marcus and Narcissa Whitman, and others. They blamed the missionaries for the disease epidemics that were destroying their people. They also resented the Whitmans for their intolerance to the Indians and their new wealth based on sales of former Indian land.

The Whitman "massacre" was the opening salvo in a constant struggle with non-Natives (the Cayuse War) that lasted until about 1850. Tiloukaikt, a band chief and former friend of non-Native traders, was a leader in this conflict. The tribe was ultimately defeated, and some of its members were hanged by the U.S. government. By this time, disease, warfare, and intermarriage with the Nez Percé had greatly reduced the tribe. Although the Cayuses kept up sporadic resistance into the 1850s, they were assigned by treaty to the Umatilla Reservation in 1855, and most were removed there in 1860. Some Cayuses took up farming on the reservation. Some joined the Yakimas (1855), Nez Percé (1877), and Bannocks (1878) in their various wars against the whites, but some also served with the U.S. Army during these wars.

See also Disease, Historic and Contemporary; Horse, Economic Impact; Trade.

Coeur d'Alene

"Coeur d'Alene," derived from the French for "awl heart," is reportedly a reference by an Anglo trader to the trading skills of these Indians. Their self-designation was *Skitswish*, perhaps meaning "foundling." In the eighteenth century, the Coeur d'Alenes lived along the Spokane River upstream from Spokane Falls, including Lake Coeur d'Alene. The region of over 4 million acres is fertile and well watered. In the early nineteenth century the tribe lived in central Idaho, eastern Washington, and western Montana; the mountains in this area helped to protect their horses against raiders from the Plains. Today's Coeur d'Alene Reservation is located in Benewah and Kootenai Counties in Idaho.

Like all Salish peoples, the Coeur d'Alenes probably originated in British Columbia. They migrated to the Plateau during their prehistoric period, keeping some Pacific Coast attributes even after they adopted Plateau culture. They acquired the horse around 1760, at which time they gave up their semisedentary lives to hunt buffalo, Plains-style.

Their traditional antipathy toward outsiders made it difficult for trappers to penetrate their territory. A Jesuit mission was established in 1842, however, foreshadowing the significant role the Jesuits were to play in their later history. At this time, the Jesuits successfully influenced the Indians to give up buffalo hunting and begin farming.

In the meantime, intermittent warfare with Indians and non-Indians, plus disease and crowding, had dropped their population by about 85 percent by 1850. In 1858 they fought the ill-fated Coeur d'Alene War (1858) with the help of tribes such as the Northern Paiutes, Palouses, and Spokans. Although the immediate cause of this conflict was white treaty violations, it may be seen as an extension of the Yakima War (1855–1856) and the general Plateau Indian resistance struggle during that time.

The roughly 600,000-acre Coeur d'Alene Reservation was created in 1873, at which time the Indians ceded almost 2.4 million acres. However, pressure from miners soon forced the tribe to cede almost 185,000 more acres in the late 1880s. Most of the rest of their land was lost to the allotment process in the early twentieth century. In 1894, thirty-two Spokan families joined the reservation. Most Coeur d'Alene Indians became Catholics, farmers, and stockbreeders. In 1958, the tribe was awarded over $4.3 million in land claims settlements.

See also Buffalo; Reservation Economic and Social Conditions.

Columbia
See Sinkiuse.

Columbia River Indians
See Colville; Umatilla; Yakima (Yakama).

Colville

"Colville" is a name derived from the Colville River and Fort Colville (a Hudson's Bay Company trading post), which in turn were named for Eden Colville, a governor of the company. Whites also called these Indians Basket People, after their large salmon fishing baskets, and Chaudière (kettles), after depressions in the rocks at Kettle Falls and a corruption of their self-designation, *Shuyelpee*. They were culturally similar to the Okanagon and Sanpoil Indians. They spoke a Salishan language made up of elements from the constituent tribes.

In the eighteenth century, the Colville Indians lived in northeastern Washington, around the Kettle and Columbia Rivers. Today, most live in Ferry and Okanogan Counties, Washington, and in nearby cities and towns.

As early as 1782, a smallpox epidemic destroyed large numbers of Colville Indians. Colville Indians became involved with the fur trade shortly after the arrival in the area of the first non-Indians (early traders) around 1800. By the midnineteenth century they were suffering from a sharply declining population and a deteriorating way of life due to new diseases, anti-Indian violence, land theft, and the severe disruption of their subsistence habits. Missionaries arrived in 1838. Non-Indian miners flooded into the area in the mid-1850s. Colvilles did not participate in the wars of that time.

Traditionally, autonomous villages were each led by a chief and a subchief; these lifetime offices were hereditary in theory but were generally filled by people possessing the qualities of honesty, integrity, and diplomacy. The authority of chiefs to

serve as adviser, judge, and general leader was granted mainly through consensus. As judge, the chief had authority over crimes of nonconformity such as witchcraft, sorcery, and assault.

An informal assembly of all married adults confirmed a new chief and oversaw other aspects of village life. All residents of the village were considered citizens. Other village leaders included a messenger, a speaker, and a salmon chief (often a shaman, with the salmon as a guardian spirit, who supervised salmon-related activities). By virtue of their ability to help or hurt people, shamans also acquired relative wealth and power from their close association with chiefs, who liked to keep them friendly.

Two Colville reservations were established in 1872 for local nontreaty tribes. One, created in April, was considered by local whites to have too fertile lands, so another reservation with less desirable land was established in July. The early reservation years were marked by conflict with non-Indians and among the tribes. Many Colville Indians converted to Catholicism in the later nineteenth century. In 1900, they lost 1.5 million acres, over half of their reservation. Even so, non-Natives continued to settle on the truncated reservation in large numbers until 1935.

The Confederated Tribes of the Colville Reservation was formed in 1938. The government restored some land in 1956. The tribe divided over the issue of termination through the 1950s and 1960s but ultimately decided against it. The tribe won significant land claims settlements in the later twentieth century.

See also Dams, Fishing Rights, and Hydroelectric Power; Disease, Historic and Contemporary; Reservation Economic and Social Conditions.

Flathead
See Salish.

Kalispel

"Kalispel," or Camas People, is derived from the name of an important plant food. They are also known as the Pend d'Oreilles, French for "ear drops," a term referring to the Indians' personal adornment. These people were grouped aboriginally into two divisions: lower (Kalispel proper) and upper.

In the eighteenth century, the Kalispels lived around Pend d'Oreille Lake and River. Today, most live on their reservation in Pend Oreille County, Washington. Kalispels also live on the Colville and Flathead Reservations,

Like other Salish peoples, the Kalispels probably came from British Columbia. The upper division may have moved east and south onto the plains of Montana before the Blackfeet pushed them back, in the eighteenth century, to the Pend d'Oreille Lake region. After the introduction of the horse, they joined with other Plateau groups to hunt buffalo and to organize war and raiding parties.

In the eighteenth century there were two geographical divisions: Upper Pend d'Oreilles and Lower Pend d'Oreilles, or Kalispelems. The latter were further divided into Lower Kalispel (Kalispels proper), Upper Kalispels, and Chewelahs (perhaps a separate tribe). Each division was composed of related families and was led by a chief selected on the basis of merit. Later, a tribal chief presided over a council made up of the band chiefs.

The Kalispels were masters of their white pine canoes. The lower division had distinctive low-riding canoes to meet the winds on Pend d'Oreille Lake. Although they were excellent horsemen, they had relatively few horses, even in the midnineteenth century. Most clothes were made from rabbit skins or deerskins. Men wore breechclouts and shirts, and women wore dresses. Both wore moccasins, caps, robes, leggings, and shell earrings.

The North West Trading Company opened a trading post in Kalispel country in 1809. The first Catholic mission opened in 1846 and relocated in 1854 with the upper Kalispels to the Lake Flathead area. Kalispels were forced into a major land cession in 1855, and the upper division was assigned to the Flathead Reservation in Montana, but the lower division refused to relocate, asking instead for a reservation of their own. They remained relatively isolated until 1863, when the British Columbia gold rush brought many miners through their territory.

In 1887, one of the two Lower Kalispel bands moved to the Flathead Reservation. The other, under Marcella, remained in the Pend d'Oreille Valley. Their reservation was created by executive order in 1914: It consisted of 4,629 acres, of which only 150 acres of tribal land remained after individual allotments and white encroachments. The tribe was awarded $3 million in land claims settlements in 1960, and another $114,000 in 1981.

See also Buffalo; Canoes; Reservation Economic and Social Conditions.

Klamath

"Klamath" is a word of uncertain derivation. The Klamaths' self-designation is *Maklak,* "People." The Klamaths were culturally similar to the Modocs and to other northern California Indian peoples. In the early nineteenth century, the Klamath people lived on 20 million acres in south central Oregon and northeastern California. The land included forests and mountains of the Cascade Range, highland lakes and marshes, and the headwaters of the Klamath River. Today the descendents of these people live mostly in Klamath County, Oregon, and in regional cities and towns. The Klamath language is a dialect of Lutuami, a Penutian language.

Traditionally, the Klamaths were organized into four to seven autonomous subdivisions or tribelets. Each tribelet may have consisted of about ten winter hamlets. Each had a chief (chosen either as a consequence of wealth or the ability to provide leadership in war), but shamans probably wielded more authority.

Permanent winter hamlets were generally built on lake shores and near marshes. Houses were semi-subterranean, circular multifamily structures, covered with earth on a wood frame. Entry was through the roof. Several nuclear families might have lived in one lodge. Circular, mat-covered wood-frame houses served in summer or on hunting trips. Winter and summer sweat lodges were built in a style similar to that of the dwellings.

Fish, mostly freshwater whitefish and suckers, was the food staple. The Klamaths also ate waterfowl. In the summer, women gathered roots, berries,

Klamath woman seated in front of house thatched with rush mats, ca. 1923. (Library of Congress)

and other plant foods, and men hunted deer, antelope, and small game. Wild waterlily seeds (*wokas*) were harvested in the late summer; they were eventually ground into flour.

The Klamath Indians were probably spared direct contact with non-Natives until the arrival in 1829 of Peter Skene Ogden. The white invasion of the 1850s also brought disease and scattered the game, destroying traditional subsistence patterns. In an 1864 treaty, the Klamath and Modoc people ceded over 13 million acres of land for a 1.1-million-acre reservation on former Klamath lands in southern Oregon. In addition to the Klamaths and Modocs, the reservation included Pit River Indians, Shastas, Northern Paiutes, and other groups. These Indians agreed to end the practice of slavery at that time.

Some Modocs left the reservation in 1870 because of friction between themselves and the Klamaths. The latter remained aloof from the 1872–1873 Modoc War. By the end of the nineteenth century, all Indians on the Klamath Reservation were known as the Klamath tribe. In 1901, the government agreed to pay the tribe $537,000 for misappropriated lands. Other land claims settlements, for millions of dollars, followed during the course of the century.

In 1958 the U.S. government terminated the Klamath Reservation. Although the government had long coveted the timber-rich reservation, many Klamaths were strongly against termination, but it was hastened by the then tribal leader. In 1958, 77 percent of the tribe voted to withdraw from the collective entity and take individual shares of the land proceeds. In 1974, the remaining 23 percent agreed to sell the rest of the reservation for per-capita shares. At that time, the Klamaths lost the last of their land base. Termination has had a profoundly negative effect on members of the tribe.

> *See also* Dams, Fishing Rights, and Hydroelectric Power; Reservation Economic and Social Conditions; Termination.

Klikitat

"Klikitat" is derived from a Chinook term meaning "beyond" (the Cascade Mountains). Their self-designation was *Qwulh-hwai-pum*, "Prairie People." The Klikitats were culturally similar to the Yakimas. The Klikitats lived and continue to live in the vicinity of Mount Adams in south central Washington. Klikitat was a member of the Sahaptian division of the Penutian language family.

The Klikitats may have originated south of the Columbia River, moving north in the prehistoric period to become skilled horsepeople and fighters after they acquired horses around 1700. The 1805 encounter with Meriwether Lewis and William Clark, on the Yakima and Klikitat Rivers, was friendly all around.

Nomadic bands were led by nonhereditary chiefs with advisory powers. Before the historic period, the tribe created two divisions, eastern and western, of which the latter mixed with Cowlitz Indians west of the Cascades to become Taitnapams.

Skilled with firearms, the Klikitats sometimes acted as mercenaries for other Indian tribes, taking women and horses as pay. Their effort during the 1820s to expand south of the Columbia was repulsed by the Umpquas. Later, the Klikitats had their revenge by helping whites conquer the Umpquas. They also scouted for the U.S. Army in the 1850s.

In 1855, the United States asked the Klikitats and other local Indians, including the Yakimas, to cede 10.8 million acres of land. Most tribes accepted a 1.2-million-acre reservation in exchange. Although Indians retained fishing and gathering rights at their usual off-reservation places and were given at least two years to relocate, the governor of Washington declared their land open to non-Indians twelve days after the treaty council ended.

Angered by this betrayal, a few Yakimas killed some whites. When soldiers arrived, a large group of Indians drove them away. In retaliation for the treacherous murder of a Walla Walla chief and negotiator, the Walla Walla, Klikitat, Cayuse, and Umatilla Indians joined the Yakimas in fighting non-Indians. After the war ended and twenty-four of their number were executed, the Yakimas agreed to settle on a reservation in 1859. The future Yakima Indian nation included, in addition to Yakima bands, the Klikitats, Wanapams, Wishrams, Palus (Palouse), and the Wenatchis.

Reservation Yakimas entered a brief period of prosperity but were soon pressured to sell land; most people were forced into poverty, obtaining some seasonal work at best. In 1891, about one-third of the reservation land had been allotted to individuals, but the Yakima nation, under Chief Shawaway Lotiahkan, was able to retain the "surplus" usually sold to non-Indians in such cases. Still, many of the individual allotments, including some of the best irrigated land, were soon lost. Around the turn of the

century as much as 80 percent of the reservation was in non-Indian hands.

As a result of twentieth-century dam construction (Bonneville in 1938, Grand Coulee in 1941, Dalles in 1956), the number of salmon and steelhead that returned to spawn in the Yakima River declined 98–99 percent. The issue of fishing rights remained an important and controversial one from the beginning of the reservation period through its resolution in 1974. Well into the twentieth century, Yakima nation people continued much of their traditional subsistence and ceremonial activities.

See also Dams, Fishing Rights, and Hydroelectric Power; Reservation Economic and Social Conditions.

Kootenai

The Kootenais are a nomadic people geographically divided into upper and lower divisions after their exodus from the northern Great Plains. The Upper Kootenais remained oriented toward the Plains, whereas the Lower Kootenais assumed a more Plateau-like existence. Their self-designation was *San'ka*, "People of the Waters." Kutenaian is unrelated to any language family except possibly Algonquian.

The Kootenais may once have lived east of the Rockies, perhaps as far east as Lake Michigan. In the late eighteenth century, they lived near the borders of British Columbia, Washington, and Idaho. Today, most live on the Kootenai Reservation, Boundary County in Idaho; on the Flathead Reservation, Flathead, Lake, Missoula, and Sanders Counties in Montana; and on several reserves in British Columbia.

Each of roughly eight autonomous bands was led by a chief and an assistant chief, such as a war, fish, and hunting chief. The chieftainship was hereditary into the historic period, when leadership qualities began to assume the most importance. A council of shamans chose the upper division chief. Decision making was by consensus.

Although they lived in the mountains west of the continental divide, upper division Kootenais subsisted on the Great Plains buffalo, whereas the lower division ate mostly fish (trout, salmon, and sturgeon), small game, and roots. Both divisions also hunted big and small game, and both gathered roots and berries, especially bitterroots. Most foods were dried and stored for the winter.

Men fished using weirs, basket traps, and spears. Women made a variety of baskets, including ones that could hold water. Hunting equipment included cherry and cedar wood bows, clubs tipped with antler points, stone knives, and slingshots. Buffalo were hunted with a bow and arrow or by driving them off cliffs. Leather items were prominent, especially among the upper division, whereas the lower division primarily made items of Indian hemp and tule. Kootenais also made carved wood bowls, clay pots, and stone pipes.

During the eighteenth century, the Kootenais acquired the horse and began hunting buffalo on the Plains, adopting much of Plains culture. Shortly after initial contact around 1800, Canadian traders built Kootenai House, a trading post. More traders, including Christianized Iroquois, as well as missionaries soon followed. Despite the Kootenais' avoidance of much overt conflict with whites, they suffered dramatic population declines during these years, primarily as a result of disease and alcohol abuse. The formal establishment of the international boundary in 1846 divided the tribe over time.

The Flathead Reservation was established in 1855 for the Salish and Kootenai people. Some Kootenais refused to negotiate the loss of their land, however, and did not participate in these talks. Some moved to British Columbia rather than accept reservation confinement. When the Kootenai Reservation was established in 1896, about a hundred Kootenai Indians moved to the Flathead Reservation. Of the ones who refused to move, those near Bonners Ferry were granted individual allotments in 1895. The tribe won a $425,000 land claims settlement in 1960, and the Kootenai Reservation was officially established in 1974.

See also Dams, Fishing Rights, and Hydroelectric Power; Horse, Economic Impact; Reservation Economic and Social Conditions.

Lake

See Okanagon.

Lillooet

"Lillooet," a name meaning "wild onion" or "end of the trail," was once applied only to the lower division of the tribe. The Lillooets exhibited marked

characteristics of the Northwest Coast culture. Most lived traditionally and continue to live in southwest British Columbia, Canada. Lillooet is an Interior Salish language.

Indian groups of the Plateau, including Interior Salishan speakers, have been living in their historic regions for a long time, probably upward of 9,000 years.

Lillooets were organized into upper and lower divisions, with each division composed of named bands of one or more villages. In aboriginal times, each village represented a single clan with one hereditary chief. Other leaders included war chiefs, hunting chiefs, orators, and wealthy and generous men.

Adolescents prepared for adulthood by fasting and engaging in feats of physical endurance. They also sought guardian spirits through vision quests or dreams to give them luck and skills. Girls were isolated at the time of their first menstrual periods. Like coastal groups, the Lillooets observed a caste system and kept slaves. Potlatches commemorated special life cycle events, at which the host enhanced his prestige by giving away gifts. The dead were wrapped in woven grass or fur robes and placed in painted grave boxes or in bark- or mat-lined graves. Graves were often marked with mortuary poles carved with clan totems (spiritual and mythological associates).

Men built circular winter lodges of cedar bark and earth on a wood frame. Lodges were excavated to a depth of around six feet and ranged between twenty and thirty-five feet in diameter. The floor was covered with spruce boughs. The clan totem was carved on the center pole or on an outside pole (lower division). Larger log and plank dwellings housed between four and eight families. Oblong or conical mat-covered houses served as shelter in the summer.

Salmon and other fish were the food staples. Men hunted both large and small game, including bear, beaver, rabbit, raccoon, and mountain goat. Hunters rubbed themselves with twigs to disguise their human scent. Women gathered assorted roots and berries and dried the foods for storage.

Men were known for their skill at wood carving. Stone, often soapstone, was also carved for artistic purposes, most often in the shape of a seated person holding a bowl. Women decorated clothing with porcupine quillwork. They also made excellent coiled baskets decorated with geometric motifs and colorful dyes.

Early (ca. 1809) intercourse with non-Native traders was generally friendly, although some non-native diseases had struck the people even before the beginning of the actual contact period. The people were able to live in a relatively traditional way until they were devastated by smallpox epidemics accompanying the gold rushes of the midnineteenth century. To make matters worse, famine followed the disease epidemics, striking with particular severity in the mid-1860s. Survivors gradually resettled on reserves delineated by the government of British Columbia.

See also Dams, Fishing Rights, and Hydroelectric Power; Disease, Historic and Contemporary; Worldviews and Values.

Modoc

"Modoc" comes from *Moatokni*, or "Southerners" (Klamath). Their self-designation was *Maklaks*, or "People," as was that of their neighbors and linguistic cousins, the Klamaths. Traditionally, Modocs lived around Goose, Clear, Tule, and Klamath Lakes in northern California and southern Oregon. Today, Modocs live mostly around Oregon and in Northwest cities as well as in Oklahoma. With the Klamaths, the Modocs spoke a dialect of the Lutuami division of the Penutian language family.

Each of about twenty-five Modoc villages was led by a civil and a war chief. Civil chiefs were selected on the basis of their wealth as well as their leadership and oratory skills; there were also some hereditary chiefs. An informal community assembly decided most legal matters.

Winter dwellings were permanent, semiexcavated lodges made of willow poles covered with tule mats and earth. Width averaged between twelve and twenty feet. People entered through a smoke hole in the roof. Temporary mat-covered structures were used at seasonal camping sites. Sweat houses were heated with steam; they were a place for cleansing as well as for praying.

Modocs followed the food supply in three seasons. They ate fish, especially salmon, trout, perch, and suckers. Men hunted a variety of large animals as well as rabbits and other small game. Antelope were driven into brush corrals. Fowl were taken with nets and decoys. Women gathered camas and other roots, greens, berries, and fruits. Seeds, especially those of the waterlily (*wocus*), were also

Toby Riddle, also known as "Winema," standing between an Indian agent and her husband, Frank (left), with four Modoc women in front, ca. 1873. Riddle, whose husband was white, acted as an interpreter during negotiations in the Modoc War. (National Archives and Records Administration)

important; they were gathered in the fall and ground into flour.

Fishing equipment included nets, spears, hook and line, and basket traps. Many items were made of tule or bulrushes, such as twined baskets, mats, cradles, rafts, and moccasins. The people used stone mullers and metates for grinding seeds, stone arrow straighteners, and basketry seed beaters. Modoc Indians also were actively involved in the regional trade. They especially obtained horses for slaves and plunder at the Dalles.

Modocs obtained horses early in the nineteenth century, about the time they encountered non-Natives, and by the 1830s they were aggressively raiding their neighbors for horses, slaves, and plunder. Major disease epidemics in 1833 and 1847 reduced their population considerably. Wagon trains began coming through their territory during the late 1840s, scaring the game away and disrupting their natural cycles. Hungry now, as well as anxious and resentful, they began attacking the intruders and neighboring Indians for slaves. When gold was found near their territory in 1851, miners flocked in and simply appropriated Native land, killing Indians as they liked.

The 1860s Ghost Dance brought them little comfort, and they, especially the women, drifted into debauchery during this period. In 1864, the Modocs and Klamaths ceded most of their land and moved to the Klamath Reservation. The Modocs were never comfortable there, however, and matters became worse when a food scarcity exacerbated the level of conflict with the Klamaths. They petitioned several times for their own reservation, but to no avail. In 1870, about 300 Modocs under Kintpuash (Captain Jack) reestablished a village in their former homeland on the Lost River. Increasing conflict with white settlers soon led to a military confrontation, after which the Indians escaped to the nearby lava beds.

Meanwhile, another group of Modocs under Hooker Jim also fled to the lava beds south of Tule Lake after attacking several ranches in revenge for an unprovoked army attack on their women and children. In a confrontation early in 1873, about eighty Indians held off 1,000 U.S. soldiers and irregulars. At a peace parley later that year, the Modocs killed the U.S. general and one of his negotiators. Later, another white attack was repulsed, but the Indians killed some soldiers during the negotiations. However, Modoc unity was failing, and their food was running out. Hooker Jim was captured and betrayed his people, leading troops to the hideout of Kintpuash, who was forced to surrender. At his trial, Hooker Jim provided testimony against Kintpuash and others, resulting in their being hanged. Most surviving Modocs were sent to the Quapaw Reservation in the Indian Territory (Oklahoma).

The Oklahoma Modocs became farmers and ranchers, and many adopted Christianity. Modoc tribal land ownership in Oklahoma ended in 1890 when their land was allotted to individuals. A group of forty-seven Modocs returned to the Klamath Reservation around 1905, but the reservation was terminated in 1954. Its lands were sold in 1964 and 1971. The Oklahoma Modocs lost their tribal status in 1956 as well, but they were restored in 1978.

See also Captain Jack; Ghost Dance Religion; Hooker Jim; Relocation.

Nespelem

See Sanpoil.

Nez Percé

"Nez Percé," French for "pierced nose," was a name used by non-Indian traders in the nineteenth century. Ironically, the Nez Percé did not generally pierce their noses as many other local Indians did. Their Salishan neighbors called them Sahaptin or Shahaptin. Their self-designation was *Nimipu*, "the People," or *Tsoop-Nit-Pa-Loo*, "the Walking Out People." Their early historic culture also contained Great Plains and Northwest Coast elements. Nez Percé is a member of the Sahaptian division of the Penutian language family.

Before contact with non-Indians, the Nez Percé lived on about 17 million acres between the Blue and the Bitterroot Mountains in southeast Washington, northeast Oregon, and southwest Idaho. Today, most live in the counties of Clearwater, Idaho, Lewis, and Nez Percé in Idaho; Ferry and Okanogan Counties in Washington; and in regional cities and towns.

Small, local bands each had one or more villages and fishing areas. Civil chiefs led the bands, although war chiefs exercised temporary power during periods of conflict. Chiefs were generally elected, although sons often followed fathers, and wealth (in horses) became more important in the early contact period. They had no power in purely personal matters. Women could neither be nor elect chiefs. Chiefs and old men made up the village and tribal councils; decisions were made by consensus. Ultimately, tribal cohesion grew out of the necessity to defend against fighters from the Great Plains.

Bands were called by the names of streams. Each group contained at least one permanent winter village and a number of temporary fishing camps. Some subsistence areas were considered tribal property. All handmade items were the property of the maker, except that the male was entitled to all property in unusual cases of separation or divorce.

Menstruating and late-term pregnant women were strictly segregated. Young, unmarried men slept in the sweat lodges. Young men and women, especially the latter, were married by about age fourteen. Brides were commonly purchased, and polygamy was common. Abortion was rare, as was birth out of wedlock. Adultery was a capital crime. Women did most of the domestic work, including dressing skins; men's work revolved around hunting and war.

Permanent settlements were located along rivers. Winter dwellings were semisubterranean, circular wood-frame structures covered with cedar

Four Nez Percé dressed for dance on Colville Indian Reservation, ca. 1910. (Library of Congress)

bark, sage, mats, grasses, and earth. The roof was flat or conical. Mats covered the floors. There were also teepee-like communal longhouses, up to 150 feet long, of similar construction. These houses held up to fifty families. People slept along inner walls and shared fires along the center.

Older boys and unmarried men slept and sweated in grass- and earth-covered sweat lodges; others were built for men and women to sweat in. Circular, underground menstrual huts were about twenty feet in diameter. In summer, people built temporary brush lean-tos. Some groups adopted hide teepees in the eighteenth century.

Nez Percé were seminomadic, moving with the food supply. Fish, especially salmon, was a staple, along with trout, eel, and sturgeon. Salmon was either broiled, baked, or boiled fresh or dried, smoked, and stored. Animal food included elk, deer, moose, mountain sheep, rabbits, and small game. After the Nez Percé acquired the horse, parties traveled to the Plains to hunt buffalo. Some meat was jerked for winter. Deer were run down or shot, as were other game, with a bow and arrow or killed with a spear. Some animals were hunted with the use of decoys.

Women gathered plant foods such as camas, kouse, bitterroot, wild carrot, wild onion, and

berries. Camas, dug in the midsummer, was peeled and baked in a pit oven. Most berries were dried and stored for winter. Other food included fowl, eggs, and birds. People ate horses, lichens, and tree inner bark when there was nothing else to eat. Most food was either boiled, steamed in pits, or roasted in ashes.

Fish were speared from platforms and caught using nets, spears, small traps, and weirs. Men used various nooses, snares, nets, and deadfalls for hunting as well as bows made of mountain sheep horn. Women made a range of woven and coiled baskets, some watertight, as well as woven reed bags. They also made cups, bowls, winnowing baskets, women's caps, and mats of cattails and tule. Many baskets were made of Indian hemp, bear grass, and other grasses.

Other important raw materials included bone, horn, and wood. Many tools and items, such as mortars, pestles, knives, and mauls, were made of chipping and flaking stone and also obsidian. Mattresses were cottonwood inner bark or dry grass, blankets were elk hides, and folded skins served as pillows.

Nez Percé Indians also used a fire-hardened digging stick, a fire drill, and board and buckskin cradles. Musical instruments included rattles, flageolets, whistles, and drums. They also used a twelve-month calendar and named four seasons.

In general, raiding and war, for booty, glory, and revenge, were very important to the Sahaptians. By virtue of their being the most powerful Plateau tribe, the Nez Percé played a central role in regional peace and war. At least after the late eighteenth century, they fought with the Flatheads, Coeur d'Alenes, and Spokans against the Blackfeet, Gros Ventres, Crows, and other Plains tribes. They also sometimes fought against these allies. The Cayuses, Umatillas, Yakimas, and Walla Wallas were also allies against the Shoshones, Bannocks, and other northern Great Basin tribes.

Men held intertribal dances before wars and buffalo hunts. Weapons included cedar, ash, or mountain sheep horn bows; obsidian or jasper-tipped arrows, sometimes dipped in rattlesnake venom; and spears. Elk skin shields, helmets, and armor were used for defense. The eagle feather war bonnet may or may not have come originally from the Plains. Men and horses were painted and decorated for war.

Somewhere around 1730, the Nez Percé acquired horses and began their dramatic transformation from seminomadic hunters, fishers, and gatherers to Plains-style buffalo hunters. They quickly became master horse riders and breeders. Several decades of peaceful hunting and trading ended around 1775, when the Blackfeet Indians, armed with guns they received through the fur trade, began a long period of conflict in western Montana. By 1800 or so, the Nez Percé Indians had been exposed to Euro-American technology and had heard rumors of a very powerful people to the east.

Their first encounter with non-Indians was with the Meriwether Lewis and William Clark expedition (1805). The Indians welcomed these white people as well as the hundreds of traders, missionaries, and others who poured in subsequently. The Nez Percé were involved in the fur trade during the 1820s and 1830s; they even helped to outfit settlers in the 1840s. Meanwhile, epidemics were taking a tremendous toll on their population.

In 1855, the Indians ceded several million acres of land but kept over 8 million acres for a reservation. Non-Indian miners and other intruders ignored the restrictions and moved in anyway, precipitating a crisis among the Indians over the issue of loyalty toward whites. Following gold strikes in 1860, whites wanted the Wallowa and Grande Ronde Valleys, land that equaled more than 75 percent of the reservation. In 1863, only one chief, with no authority to sell Nez Percé land, signed a treaty. The United States then used that document as an eviction notice, ending years of friendship and cooperation between the Nez Percé and whites. In the meantime, the Dreamer religion had begun influencing the Nez Percé, among others, to resist non-Native imperialism.

In 1877, the Wallowa band were unilaterally given thirty days to leave their homeland. In response to this ultimatum, some younger Indians attacked a group of whites. Young Joseph, chief with his brother, Ollikut, reluctantly sided with the resisters. When soldiers came, firing on an Indian delegation under a flag of peace, the Indians fired back. Joseph's band, about 450 Indians under the leadership of Looking Glass, knew that they could never return home or escape punishment at the hands of the United States. They decided to head for Canada.

During their two-month flight, the group traveled 1,700 miles, constantly evading and outwitting several thousand U.S. Army troops. They did fight several battles during their journey but never were defeated. They also passed through Yellowstone National Park at one point, encountering tourists but

leaving them in peace. Joseph was just one of the leaders of this flight, but he became the most important and well-known. Many Indians died along the way.

Tired, hungry, and cold, the group was forced to surrender in early October just thirty miles from Canada. Joseph and other Nez Percé were never allowed to return to their homeland. Those who survived were exiled to Kansas and the Indian Territory (Oklahoma), where many died of disease, and finally to the Colville Reservation in Washington.

The sharply rising death rate among the Nez Percé from tuberculosis after the 1870s stemmed largely from the replacement of their traditional mat houses by "modern" wooden ones. Heavy missionization had by the end of the nineteenth century resulted in factionalism and considerable loss of tribal heritage. In 1971, the Nez Percé received land claims settlements of $3.5 million.

See also Dams, Fishing Rights, and Hydroelectric Power; Fur Trade; Joseph, Yonger; Long March; Women in Native Woodlands Societies.

Okanagon

"Okanagon" means "seeing the top, or head." Another self-designation is *Isonkva'ili*, "Our People." The Okanagons were the main tribe of a culturally related group of Indians that also included the Senijextee (Lake), Colville, and Sanpoil Indians. They are occasionally known today as the northern Okanagons (Canada) and the Sinkaietks (United States). Okanagon Indians spoke a dialect of interior Salish.

Okanagons traditionally lived in the Okanagon and Similkameen River Valleys, including Lake Okanagon, in Washington and British Columbia. Today, most Okanagons live on the Colville Reservation, on reserves in British Columbia, and in regional cities and towns.

Two geographical divisions, the Similkameen and the Okanagon proper, were each composed of between five and ten autonomous bands. Each band was led by a (usually hereditary) chief with advisory powers. The true locus of authority was found in a council of older men. War, hunt, and dance chiefs were selected as needed.

Winter dwellings were of two types. One was a conical, semisubterranean, pole-frame lodge covered with earth. This type was about ten to sixteen feet in diameter, and entry was through the roof. The people also built rectangular, mat-covered, multifamily lodges. In summer they used conical, tule mats on pole frames and, later, skin teepees. Men and women used domed sweat houses for purification; the structures were also used as living quarters for youths in spirit training.

Salmon was the main staple. Large and small game, including elk, bear, bighorn sheep, and marmot, was also important. Dogs sometimes assisted in the hunt, in which animals were often surrounded and/or driven over a cliff. Meat was roasted, boiled, or dried. Buffalo was always part of the diet but became more important when groups began using horses to hunt the herds on the Great Plains. Important plant foods included camas, bitterroot, berries, and nuts.

Men caught fish with dip nets, seine nets, traps, weirs, spears, and hook and line. Stone, bone, and antler provided the raw material for most tools. Women made cedar-bark or woven spruce root baskets with geometric designs. Some baskets were woven tight enough to hold water. Women also specialized in making woven sacks. They sewed tule mats with Indian hemp.

Okanagons undertook a gradual northward expansion following their acquisition of horses in the mideighteenth century. They first encountered non-Native traders in the early nineteenth century and Catholic Indians and missionaries shortly thereafter. The tribe was artificially divided when the United States–Canada boundary was fixed in 1846. The Sinkaietks did not participate in the Yakima War (1855–1856), although some joined in fighting the United States later in that decade.

A gold strike on the Fraser River in 1858 brought an influx of miners and increased the general level of interracial conflict. Most U.S. Okanagons settled on the Colville Reservation in 1872. The Canadian Okanagons were assigned to several small reserves.

See also Dams, Fishing Rights, and Hydroelectric Power; Horse, Economic Impact; Women in Native Woodlands Societies.

Pend d'Oreille

See Kalispel.

Salish

"Salish" or Flathead, comes from the fact that they did not, like many neighboring peoples, shape their babies' foreheads (they left them "flat"). Their self-designation was *Se'lic,* or "People." Traditionally, the Salish lived in western Montana, around the Rocky Mountains and Little Belt Mountains. Today, most live in the Flathead, Lake, Missoula, and Sanders Counties in Montana. The Salish spoke a dialect of Interior Salish.

All Salish-speaking Indians probably originated in British Columbia. From their base in western Montana, the Salish may have moved farther east onto the Plains before being pushed back around 1600 by the Blackfeet. The Salish continued moving westward, into north central Idaho, throughout the following two centuries.

Various bands were formed of several related families. Each band was led by a chief, possibly hereditary in earlier times, and an assistant chief, both chosen by merit. Beginning in the late prehistoric period, as tribal cohesiveness increased, the band chiefs formed a tribal council to advise a tribal chief, and later the band chiefs themselves were relegated to the status of minor chiefs or subchiefs. In addition, individuals were selected as needed to lead various activities such as hunting and war.

Rule- or lawbreakers were punished by public whipping and/or ridicule. Premarital sexual relations were frowned on; the woman could be whipped if discovered. Although some people eloped, marriage was arranged by families and formalized by cohabitation and a formal ceremony. Polygamy was common. Women were responsible for all domestic tasks.

Winter dwellings were of two types. One was a partially excavated, conical mat (cedar bark, hemp) house on a wooden frame; the other was a long communal and ceremonial lodge. Brush shelters sufficed during camping and mountain hunting trips. Bark or skin teepees gained popularity after horse ownership turned the Salish into buffalo hunters.

Beginning in the eighteenth century, buffalo, hunted on the Great Plains, became a key food item. Before this period, however, the Salish ate a number of animals including elk, deer, antelope, and small game. Fish, including trout, salmon, and whitefish, formed an important part of their diet. Plant foods included camas, bitterroot, other bulbs, roots, and berries.

Men used hook and line, nets, traps, and weirs to catch fish. Women made birchbark and woven skin containers as well as coiled cedar baskets. They also made twined grass spoons.

Around 1700 the Salish acquired horses and assumed a great deal of the culture of Plains Indians (including buffalo hunting, stronger tribal organization, and raiding). Ongoing wars with the Blackfeet as well as several smallpox epidemics combined in the eighteenth century to reduce their population significantly. They also encountered Christian Iroquois Indians during this time.

Although disease preceded their physical arrival, non-Indians began trading in Salish country shortly after the 1805 visit of the Meriwether Lewis and William Clark expedition. The missionary period began in 1841. In 1855, a major land cession (the Hellgate Treaty) established the Flathead, or Jocko, Reservation, but most Salish Indians avoided confinement until at least 1872, in part owing to their friendliness with the Americans. During these years, other tribes were placed on the reservation, and the buffalo herds diminished rapidly. Charlot, the leader of one Salish band, held out in the Bitterroot Mountains until 1891, when his people finally joined the Flathead Reservation.

The government considered terminating the reservation in the 1950s but was successfully opposed by tribal leaders. In 1960, the tribe won roughly $4.4 million in land claims settlements.

See also Buffalo; Dams, Fishing Rights, and Hydroelectric Power; Horse, Economic Impact.

Sanpoil

"Sanpoil" or "San Poil" is derived from a Native word possibly referring to what may have been their self-designation, *Sinpauelish (Snpui'lux).* They were culturally and linguistically similar to the neighboring Nespelem Indians. Late eighteenth-century Sanpoils lived near the Columbia and the Sanpoil Rivers, in north central Washington. The environment is one of desert and semidesert. Today, most Sanpoils live in Ferry and Okanagon Counties in Washington and in regional cities and towns. With the Nespelem, the Sanpoil spoke a particular dialect of Interior Salish.

Autonomous villages were each led by a chief and a subchief; these lifetime offices were hereditary

in theory but who were generally filled by people possessing the qualities of honesty, integrity, and diplomacy. Unlike some other Plateau groups, only men could be chiefs. The authority of Sanpoil chiefs to serve as adviser, judge, and general leader was granted mainly through consensus. As judge, the chief had authority over crimes of nonconformity such as witchcraft, sorcery, and assault. His penalty usually consisted of a fine and/or lashes on the back.

An informal assembly of all married adults confirmed a new chief and oversaw other aspects of village life. All residents of the village were considered citizens. Village size averaged about thirty to forty people, or roughly three to five extended families, although some villages had as many as 100 people. Other village leaders included a messenger, a speaker, and a salmon chief (often a shaman, with the salmon as a guardian spirit, who supervised salmon-related activities). By virtue of their ability to help or hurt people, shamans also acquired relative wealth and power from their close association with chiefs, who liked to keep them allied.

Local villages had associated, nonexclusive territories or subsistence areas. Any person was free to live anywhere she or he wanted; that is, family members could associate themselves with relatives of their settlement, relatives of a different settlement, or a settlement where they had no relatives. The winter was a time for visits and ceremonies. During that season, women also made mats and baskets, made or repaired clothing, and prepared meals while men occasionally hunted or just slept, gambled, and socialized.

People rose at dawn, in the winter and summer, and began the day by bathing in the river. In spring, groups of four or five families left the village for root-digging areas; those who had spent the winter away from the main village returned. The old and the ill generally remained in camp.

Pacifism, generosity, and interpersonal equality and autonomy were highly valued. Girls fasted and were secluded for ten days at the onset of puberty, except for a nighttime running regime. The exchange of gifts between families constituted a marriage, a relationship that was generally stable and permanent. Corpses were wrapped in tule mats or deerskin and buried with their possessions. The family burned the deceased's house and then observed various taboos and purification rites. The land of the dead was envisioned as being located at the end of the Milky Way.

Sanpoil Indians used the typical Plateau-style winter houses. One was a single-family structure, circular and semisubterranean, about ten to sixteen feet in diameter, with a flat or conical roof. People covered a wood frame with planks or mats and then a layer of grass, brush, and earth. Entry was gained through the smoke hole, which could be covered by a tule mat. The interior was also covered with a layer of grass.

They also built communal houses consisting of a pole framework covered by grass, earth, and tule mats. These houses were about sixteen feet wide, between twenty-four and sixty feet long, and about fourteen feet high, with gabled roofs. Entry was through matted double doors. Each family had an individual tule-covered section, but they shared a number of fireplaces in the central passage.

Summer houses were similar in construction, but they were smaller, single-family structures. Some more closely resembled a mere windbreak. Some groups built adjoining rectangular, flat-roofed summer mat houses/windbreaks. Mat houses were always taken down after the season. Men also built sweat lodges of grass and earth over a willow frame.

Food was much more often acquired by the family than by the village. Fish was a staple. Men caught four varieties of salmon as well as trout, sturgeon, and other fish. They fished from May through October. Although women could not approach the actual fishing areas, they cleaned and dried the fish. Dried fish and sometimes other foods made up much of the winter diet. People generally ate two meals a day in summer and one in winter.

Women gathered shellfish, salmon eggs, bulbs, roots, nuts, seeds, berries, and prickly pear. Camas was eaten raw, roasted, boiled, and made into cakes. A short ceremony was performed over the first gathered crop of the season. Men hunted most large and small game in the fall. They prepared for the hunt by sweating and singing. Women came along to help dress and carry the game. Men also hunted birds and gathered mollusks. Venison and berries were pounded with fat to make pemmican.

Fish were caught using traps, nets, spears, and weirs. Spearing required the construction and use of artificial channels and platforms. Utensils were carved from wood. Women made woven cedar, juniper, or spruce root baskets, including water containers and cooking pots. Women also made the all-important mats of tule and other grasses, whose uses included houses, bedding (skins were also used), privacy screens, waterproofing, holding food, and

wrapping corpses. There was also some sun-dried pottery covered with fish skin.

Severe epidemics in the late eighteenth century and in the late 1840s and early 1850s depleted the Sanpoil population considerably. Sanpoils were among the Indians who visited Catholic missionaries at Kettle Falls in 1838. By avoiding the wars of the 1850s and by consciously eschewing contact with non-Indians, they managed to remain free until 1872, when they were moved to the Colville Reservation. Even after confinement, the Sanpoils refused government tools, preferring to hunt, fish, and gather by traditional means and to conduct small-scale farming.

> *See also* Dams, Fishing Rights, and Hydroelectric Power ; Disease, Historic and Contemporary; Women in Native Woodlands Societies; Worldviews and Values.

Shuswap

"Shuswap" means "to know, recognize" or "to unfold, spread." The word may also refer to relationships between people. They may once have called themselves *Xatsu'll*, "on the cliff where the bubbling water comes out." The people currently refer to themselves as the Great Secwepemc Nation. Shuswaps continue to live in and near their aboriginal territory in the Fraser and North and South Thompson River Valleys, British Columbia. Shuswap is a dialect of the Interior division of the Salishan language family.

The Interior Salishan people settled in their historic areas roughly 9,000 years ago. Hudson's Bay Company posts were established in the early nineteenth century. The people soon became active in the fur trade. Intertribal warfare ended in the early 1860s. About that time, the Shuswaps were decimated by epidemics, in part brought by gold miners flooding the region. Non-Natives squatted on and then claimed the land of the ailing Shuswaps. A Shuswap reserve of 176 square miles was created in 1865; it was soon reduced to one square mile. A second reserve was created in 1895. In 1945, with the Chilcotin and other groups, the Shuswaps founded the British Columbia Interior Confederation to try to persuade provincial and federal officials to be more responsive to their needs.

The Shuswaps were divided into about seven autonomous bands. All had hereditary chiefs who advised, lectured on correct behavior, and coordinated subsistence activities. There were also specialized chiefs for war, hunt, dance, and other activities.

Bands were more or less nomadic, according to their food sources. By the nineteenth century, the northern and western bands had adopted the Northwest Coast pattern of social stratification. The nobility belonged to hereditary crest groups, and commoners belonged to nonhereditary associations. Slaves were generally acquired in battle or trade. At puberty, boys undertook guardian spirit quests, whereas girls were secluded and practiced basketmaking and other skills. They also fasted and prayed, and they went out at night to run, exercise, and bathe.

Men built circular winter lodges of cedar bark and earth on a wood frame. Lodges were excavated to a depth of around six feet and ranged between twenty and thirty-five feet in diameter. The floor was covered with spruce boughs. The clan totem was carved on the center pole or on an outside pole (lower division). Larger log and plank dwellings had several rooms and housed between four and eight families. Oblong or conical mat-covered houses served as shelter in the summer.

Fish, especially salmon, was the staple in some areas. People away from rivers depended on large and small game and fowl. All groups ate roots and berries. Men caught fish with nets, basket traps, spears, weirs, and hooks. Hunting equipment included bow and arrow, traps, and spears. Utensils and some baskets were made of birchbark, coiled baskets were fashioned from cedar or spruce roots, and many tools were made of stone. People also made skin or woven grass bags. Digging sticks had wood or antler cross-handles.

> *See also* Dams, Fishing Rights, and Hydroelectric Power; Reservation Economic and Social Conditions.

Sinkaietk

See Okanagon.

Sinkiuse

"Sinkiuse" means "between people," and the Skiniuses were also known as the Columbia, Isle de Pierre, and Moses band. In late pre-contact times, the Sinkiuses lived mainly along the east bank of the

Sinkiuse-Columbia on the Colville Reservation in Washington play a game of chance in 1911. (Library of Congress)

Columbia River, although they ranged throughout the plateau south and east of the river. Today, their descendents live on the Colville Reservation, in Ferry and Okanogan Counties in Washington, and in cities and towns around central Washington. The Sinkiuses spoke a dialect of Interior Salish.

The Sinkiuses may have come either from the lower Columbia River area or from a more northerly location. They encountered non-Indians and joined the fur trade in 1811. They fought the United States in the 1850s under their chief, Moses, but adopted a peaceful stance after the war. The Columbia Reservation was established in 1879 and was abolished several years later. Four bands followed Chief Moses to the Colville Reservation; others accepted allotments and lost their geographic identity.

Autonomous villages were each led by a chief and a subchief; these lifetime offices were hereditary in theory but were generally filled by people possessing the qualities of honesty, integrity, and diplomacy. The authority of chiefs was granted mainly through consensus.

An informal assembly of all married adults confirmed a new chief and oversaw other aspects of village life. All residents of the village were considered citizens. Other village leaders included a messenger, a speaker, and a salmon chief (often a shaman, with the salmon as a guardian spirit, who supervised salmon-related activities). By virtue of their ability to help or hurt people, shamans also acquired relative wealth and power from their close association with chiefs, who liked to keep them allied.

The Sinkiuses were seminomadic for nine months a year; during the other three they lived in permanent wintertime villages. Winter was a time for visits and ceremonies. During that season, women also made mats and baskets, made or repaired clothing, and prepared meals; men occasionally hunted or just slept, gambled, and socialized.

In spring, groups of four or five families left the village for root-digging areas; those who had spent the winter away from the main village returned. People rose at dawn, in the winter and summer, and began the day by bathing in the river. The men's

realm was toolmaking, war, hunting, fishing, and, later, horses.

Pacifism, generosity, and interpersonal equality and autonomy were highly valued. Girls fasted and were secluded for ten days at the onset of puberty, except for a nighttime running regime. The exchange of gifts between families constituted a marriage, a relationship that was generally stable and permanent.

The Sinkiuses built typical Plateau-style, semi-excavated, cone-shaped wood-frame houses covered with woven matting and/or grass. Longer, lodge-style structures of similar construction were used for communal activities. Villages also contained mat-covered sweat lodges. Temporary brush shelters served as summer houses. Later, skin teepees replaced the aboriginal structures.

They also built communal tule-mat houses consisting of a pole framework covered by grass, earth, and tule mats. These houses were about sixteen feet wide, between twenty-four to sixty feet long, and about fourteen feet high, with gabled roofs. Entry was through matted doors. Each family had an individual tule-covered section, but they shared a number of fireplaces in the central passage.

Food was much more often acquired by the family than by the village. Fish was a staple. Men caught four varieties of salmon as well as trout, sturgeon, and other fish. They fished from May through October. Women cleaned, dried, and stored the fish. Dried fish and sometimes other foods made up much of the winter diet. People generally ate two meals a day in the summer and one in the winter.

Women gathered shellfish, salmon eggs, bulbs, roots, nuts, seeds, and berries. Camas was eaten raw, roasted, boiled, and made into cakes. A short ceremony was performed over the first gathered crop of the season. Men hunted most large and small game in the fall. They prepared for the hunt by sweating and singing. Women came along to help dress and carry the game. Men also hunted birds and gathered mollusks.

Men caught fish with nets, weirs, traps, and hook and line. Utensils were carved of wood. Women made coiled baskets of birchbark and/or cedar root; they also wove wallets and bags of woven strips of skin, and they sewed tule mats and other items.

See also Dams, Fishing Rights, and Hydroelectric Power; Women in Native Woodlands Societies; Worldviews and Values.

Spokan

The Spokans were a Plateau tribe having three geographic divisions: upper, lower, and middle. They have also been known as Muddy People, as well as Sun People, probably after a faulty translation of their name. Their self-designation was *Spoqe'ind*, "round head." The Spokans lived along the Spokane River in the mideighteenth century, in eastern Washington and northern Idaho. Today they live on reservations in Washington and Idaho as well as in regional cities and towns. Spokan is a dialect of the interior division of the Salishan language family.

The Spokans probably originated in British Columbia along with other Salish groups. Each division of Spokans was composed of a number of bands, which were in turn composed of groups of related families. Bands were led by a chief and an assistant chief, who were selected on the basis of leadership qualities. The office of band chief may once have been hereditary. Several bands might winter together in a village and at that time select an ad hoc village chief. Decisions were made by consensus. In the historic period, as authority became more centralized, there was also a tribal chief.

The Spokans were seminomadic for nine months a year; during the other three they lived in permanent winter villages. The men's realm consisted of toolmaking, warring, hunting, fishing, and, later, caring for horses. The dead were covered with skins and robes and buried after spending some time on a scaffold. A pole marked the grave site.

The Spokans built typical Plateau-style, semiexcavated, cone-shaped wood-frame houses covered with woven matting and/or grass. Longer, lodge-style structures of similar construction were used for communal activities. Villages also contained mat-covered sweat lodges. Temporary brush shelters served as summertime houses. Later, skin teepees replaced the aboriginal structures.

Fish, especially salmon, was the staple. Trout and whitefish were also important. These were mostly smoked, dried, and stored for the winter. Men hunted local big game and, later, buffalo on the Plains. A favorite hunting technique was for many men to surround the animal. Important plant foods included camas, bitterroot and other roots, bulbs, seeds, and berries.

Men caught fish with nets, weirs, traps, and hook and line. Women made coiled baskets of birchbark and/or cedar root; they also wove wallets and

bags of woven strips of skin, and they sewed tule mats and other items.

After they acquired horses from Kalispel Indians, around the mideighteenth century, they began hunting buffalo on the Great Plains. This was especially true of the upper division. By the time they encountered the Meriwether Lewis and William Clark expedition in 1805, their population had already declined significantly as a result of smallpox epidemics.

Following the Lewis and Clark visit, the North West, Hudson's Bay, and American Fur Companies quickly established themselves in the area. Missionaries arrived in the 1830s: They found the Spokans to be reluctant converts, and the influence of Christianity acted to create factionalism within the tribe. Interracial relations declined sharply in the late 1840s with the Whitman massacre and the closing of the Protestant mission. Severe smallpox epidemics in 1846 and again in 1852 and 1853 helped spur the rise of the Prophet Dance and the Dreamer Cult.

After miners had effectively dispossessed the Spokans from their territory, they joined with Coeur d'Alenes, Yakimas, Palouses, and Paiutes in the short-lived 1858 Coeur d'Alene, or Spokan, War. Spokan Indians then remained on their land as best they could or settled on various reservations. Despite pleas from Chief Joseph, they remained neutral in the 1877 Nez Percé War. In that year, the lower division agreed to move to the Spokan Reservation (officially declared a reservation in 1881, 154,898 acres). Ten years later, the other two divisions, as well as some remaining lower Spokans, agreed to move to either the Flathead, Colville, or Coeur d'Alene Reservation. The local fort, Fort Spokan, became an Indian boarding school from 1898 to 1906. There were also conflicts over land with non-Natives in and around the city of Spokane at this time.

In the early twentieth century, much tribal land was lost to the allotment process as well as to "surplus" land sales to non-Indians. Dams built in 1908 (Little Falls) and 1935 (Grand Coulee) ruined the local fishery. Uranium mining began in the 1950s. The Spokan tribe successfully fought off termination proceedings begun in 1955. In 1966, the tribe received a land claims settlement of $6.7 million.

See also Dams, Fishing Rights, and Hydroelectric Power; Fur Trade; Termination; Women in Native Woodlands Societies.

Thompson

The Thompson Indians are also known as Ntlakyapamuk. The Thompson Indian homeland is the Fraser, Thompson, and Nicola River Valleys in southwest British Columbia. The Thompson language is a dialect of the Interior division of the Salishan language family.

Several trading companies became established in Thompson country following the initial visit of non-Indians in about 1809. Miners flooded in after an 1858 gold strike, taking over land, disrupting subsistence patterns, and generally forcing the Indian population to the brink of ruin. Disease, too, took a heavy toll during the nineteenth century, killing as many as 70 percent of the pre-contact Indian population. The government of British Columbia confined the Thompson Indians to reserves in the late nineteenth century.

The Thompson Indians recognized two geographical divisions, located downstream and upstream of approximately the location of Cisco on the Fraser River. Within the divisions, bands were autonomous, consisted of related families, and were led by hereditary chiefs whose powers were largely advisory. A council of older men wielded real authority.

In the winter, people lived in circular, earth-covered pole-frame lodges built in pits. Each lodge was about twenty to forty feet in diameter and could hold between fifteen and thirty people. Entry was via a notched ladder inserted through the smoke hole. In the summer, people used oblong or circular lodges consisting of rush mats over a pole frame. Both men and women used domed sweat houses for purification. Sweat houses were also homes for youths during their spirit quest period.

The Thompson Indians subsisted on the typical Plateau diet of fish, especially salmon; some large and small game; and plant foods that included many roots, berries, and nuts (especially camas and bitterroot).

Men caught fish by using weirs, seine nets, traps, dip nets, and hook and line. They also carved soapstone (steatite) pipes. Bows were often made of juniper. Women made cedar-root or birchbark baskets decorated with geometric designs, as well as birch and spruce bark containers. Some were woven tight enough to hold water. Women also wove blankets of goat wool or strips of rabbit fur, and they sewed tule mats with Indian hemp cord. Digging sticks featured antler or wood cross-handles. Other

tools and utensils were also made of stone, antler, and bone.

See also Dams, Fishing Rights, and Hydroelectric Power; Women in Native Woodlands Societies; Worldviews and Values.

Umatilla

"Umatilla" is a name derived from a village name meaning "many rocks." This group is culturally similar to other Sahaptian people, such as the Klikitats, Nez Percé, Walla Wallas, and Yakimas. The Umatilla homeland was located along the lower Umatilla River and the Columbia River west of the mouth of the Walla Walla River. Today, most Umatillas live in Umatilla and Union Counties in Oregon and in regional cities and towns. The Umatilla language is a member of the Sahaptian division of the Penutian language family.

Small, local bands each had one or more villages and fishing areas. Civil chiefs led the bands, although war chiefs exercised temporary power during periods of conflict. Chiefs were generally selected by a combination of merit, heredity, and wealth. Chiefs and old men made up the village and tribal councils; decisions were made by consensus. The bands came together under a single chief in times of celebration and danger.

Each band contained at least one permanent winter village and a number of temporary fishing camps. Some subsistence areas were considered tribal property.

Permanent settlements were located along rivers. Winter dwellings were semisubterranean, circular wood-frame structures covered with cedar bark, sage, mats, grasses, and earth. The roof was flat or conical. Mats covered the floors. These houses, up to sixty feet long, held up to fifty families. People slept along inner walls and shared fires along the center. In summer, people built temporary brush lean-tos. Some groups adopted hide tipis in the eighteenth century.

Umatillas moved with the food supply. Fish, especially salmon, was the staple, along with trout, eel, and sturgeon. Salmon was broiled, baked, boiled, or dried, smoked, and stored. Animal food included elk, deer, moose, mountain sheep, rabbits, and small game. Parties also traveled to the Plains to hunt buffalo. Some meat was jerked for winter. Deer were run down or shot, as were other game, with a bow and arrow or killed with a spear. Some animals were hunted with the use of decoys.

Women gathered plant foods such as camas, kouse, bitterroot, wild carrot, wild onion, and berries. Camas, dug in the midsummer, was peeled and baked in a pit oven. Most berries were dried and stored for winter. Other food included shellfish, fowl, eggs, and birds. People ate horses, lichens, and tree inner bark when there was nothing else to eat. Most food was either boiled or steamed in pits, or roasted in ashes.

Fish were speared from platforms and caught using nets, spears, small traps, and weirs. Men used various nooses, snares, nets, and deadfalls for hunting as well as bows made of mountain sheep horn. Women made a range of woven and coiled baskets, some watertight, as well as woven reed bags. They also made cups, bowls, winnowing baskets, women's caps, and mats of cattails and tule. Many baskets were made of Indian hemp, bear grass, and other grasses.

Other important raw materials included bone, horn, and wood. Many tools and items, such as mortars, pestles, knives, and mauls, were made of chipping and flaking stone and also obsidian. Mattresses were cottonwood inner bark or dry grass, blankets were elk hides, and folded skins served as pillows. The ubiquitous digging stick was fire-hardened with a wood or antler cross-handle.

The relatively early acquisition of horses gave the Umatillas a trade advantage, although they also traded widely before they had the horse. They acquired items made as far away as British Columbia and the Mississippi Valley. Abalone was among the items they acquired from coastal Indians, along with carved wooden items, dried clams, dentalium shells, and wapato root.

As with other regional Indian groups, the Umatillas first encountered non-Natives when the Meriwether Lewis and William Clark expedition passed through their territory around 1805. Fur traders quickly moved in shortly thereafter. Severe epidemics began in the midnineteenth century, about the same time Catholic and Protestant missionaries flocked to the region.

The Umatillas enjoyed a peaceful relationship with non-Indians until the late 1840s. In 1851 a Catholic mission, previously established in 1847 and then abandoned, was rebuilt. At that time the Umatillas sent warriors to support the Cayuses in their war against whites from the Willamette Valley. In the mid-1850s they were forced, with the Walla

Wallas and the Cayuses, to cede over 4 million acres and accept the creation of a reservation. The Umatillas joined the Yakima War from 1855 to 1856. However, two decades later, they fought against the Indians in the Bannock War (1878). Umatillas were responsible for the death in that war of the Paiute Chief Egan. Despite the Indians' possible hopes for better treatment at the hands of the whites, the original reservation of over 245,000 acres was quickly pared to under 100,000 by the process of allotment and the sale of "surplus" to non-Indians.

See also Dams, Fishing Rights, and Hydroelectric Power; Fur Trade; Worldviews and Values.

Walla Walla

See Umatilla.

Warm Springs Reservation, Confederated Tribes of the

See Paiute, Northern; Umatilla; Wishram.

Wasco

See Wishram.

Wishram

The Wishrams, or Tlakluits, were a Plateau group, with many cultural attributes of Northwest Coast Indians. They were culturally similar to the neighboring Wasco people. Wishram Indians lived along the north bank of the Columbia River, several miles above and below The Dalles. Today, their descendents live on local reservations, especially the Yakima, and in regional cities and towns. Each of several villages was led by a hereditary chief. Wishram was a member of the Chinookan (Kiksht) division of the Penutian language family.

Wishram Indians observed the system of social stratification typical of Northwest Coast Indians: There were nobles, a middle class, commoners, and slaves. The slaves were acquired in war or trade, but slavery was also hereditary. Marriage was formalized by an exchange of gifts and family visits. Infants

were occasionally betrothed for purposes of creating or cementing family alliances. Corpses were wrapped in buckskin and interred in plank burial houses. Remarriage to the dead spouse's sibling was common. Fishing areas were privately owned and inheritable by groups of families.

Wishrams probably built plank houses characteristic of the coastal style. Beginning about the eighteenth century, they also built circular winter houses, holding between one and six families. These were built of a pole framework over a six-foot pit, covered with mats of grass and dirt or cedar bark. Entry was through the smoke hole. Bed platforms were located around the walls. In the summer, people built gabled-roof mat lodges with several fireplaces. Hunters and mourners purified themselves, and the sick were healed, in sweat lodges.

Fish, especially salmon, pike, eels, sturgeon, and smelts, was the most important food. Salmon eggs were also eaten. Fish were either eaten fresh or dried or smoked and ground for long-term storage. Important plant foods included roots, bulbs (especially camas), wild onions, wild potatoes, acorns, and various nuts and berries. Men hunted game to supplement the diet. In addition to nets, weirs, traps, and spears for fishing, men made a variety of carved wood tools and utensils. Women made twined baskets and bags decorated with geometric figures.

The Dalles, or Five Mile Rapids, in Wishram territory was the most important trading location in the Northwest; several thousand Northwest Coast and Plateau Indians traded there during various trade fairs. The Wishram and Wasco people acted as intermediaries in the trade of a huge amount and variety of items, including blankets, shells, slaves, canoes, fish and animal products, dried roots, bear grass, and, later, horses. Trade connections stretched from Canada to Mexico and from the Rocky Mountains west to the ocean.

Owing to their very important location at The Dalles, the Wishrams traditionally enjoyed favorable trade relations with many neighboring tribes. In the early nineteenth century, however, non-Indian traders threatened this position while the Wishram population was declining rapidly due to disease. Conflict with traders was one result. Ongoing intertribal warfare also took a population toll.

In 1855, the Wishrams and Wascos were forced to sign treaties ceding most of their land (roughly 10 million acres); the treaties established the Warm Springs Reservation in north central Oregon. Wishram Indians also became part of the Yakima

Indian nation on the Yakima Reservation. A key treaty provision allowing the Indians to fish "at all . . . usual and accustomed stations in common with the citizens of the United States . . ." served as the basis for a landmark legal ruling in 1974 that protected the Northwest Coast Indian fishery. In the 1860s members of the Warm Springs Reservation organized informally into linguistic and cultural divisions: There were Sahaptian-speaking people (Warm Springs Indians); Upper Chinookan–speaking Wascos and Wishrams; and Northern Paiutes after 1879.

See also Dams, Fishing Rights, and Hydroelectric Power; Trade; Women in Native Woodlands Societies; Worldviews and Values.

Yakima (Yakama)

"Yakima," meaning "runaway," is the common name for the people who called themselves Waptailmim, "People of the Narrow River." The Yakima people may have originated from members of neighboring tribes such as the Palouses and Nez Percé. The Yakima homeland is located along the Columbia, Wenatchee, and Yakima Rivers in southern Washington. It includes lands from the Cascade summits to the Columbia River. Yakima is a member of the Sahaptian division of the Penutian language family.

Leaders of autonomous bands were selected partly by merit and also by heredity. The bands came together under a head chief in times of celebration and danger.

Groups of families lived together in permanent winter villages, where they raced, gambled, and held festivals. During the rest of the year individual families dispersed to hunt, fish, and gather food. Corpses were buried in pits where they were sometimes cremated as well. Graves were marked by a ring of stones. More than one individual may have been buried and cremated at a time. Burials also occurred in rock slides, where they were marked with stakes.

The winter lodge consisted of a semisubterranean, rectangular, pole-frame structure covered with mats and earth. Skin-covered teepees were adopted during the eighteenth century.

Fish, especially five kinds of salmon, steelhead trout, eel, and sturgeon, was the staple. Fish was eaten fresh or dried, ground, and stored. People also ate game, roots, berries, and nuts. Men fished using platforms, weirs, dip nets, harpoons, and traps. They

Yakima woman with papoose in the early 1900s. (Library of Congress)

hunted using bow and arrow and deadfalls. Other technological items included skin bags, baskets (some watertight), and carved wooden utensils.

Yakima bands acquired horses by the early eighteenth century and began hunting buffalo on the Great Plains. Horses brought them wealth, but, even though the people acquired certain aspects of Plains culture, they did not become wholesale buffalo hunters, as some other Plateau tribes did. In 1805 the Meriwether Lewis and William Clark expedition arrived, soon followed by many trappers, missionaries, and traders. The missionaries found reluctant converts. By the early to midnineteenth century, the Yakimas had suffered dramatic population reductions owing to disease as well as to warfare with the Shoshone.

In 1855, the governor of Washington forced local Indians to cede 10.8 million acres of land. Most

tribes agreed to accept a 1.2-million-acre reservation. Shortly thereafter, gold was discovered north of the Spokane River. Although Indians retained fishing and gathering rights at their usual off-reservation places and were given two to three years to relocate after they signed the 1855 treaty, the governor declared their land open to non-Indians twelve days after the treaty council.

Friction was inevitable at this point. Miners killed some Yakimas, and the Indians retaliated in kind. When soldiers arrived, a large group of Indians drove them away. In response to the treacherous murder of a Walla Walla chief and negotiator, the Walla Walla, Palouse, Cayuse, and Umatilla Indians joined the Yakimas in fighting non-Indians. The war spread in 1856. Seattle was attacked, and southern Oregon tribes joined the fighting; that part of the conflict was called the Rogue River War (1855–1856). The Coeur d'Alene War of 1858, in which the Yakimas also participated, was essentially another part of the same conflict.

In 1859, following the end of the fighting and the execution of twenty-four Yakimas, the Indians agreed to settle on a reservation. The future Yakima Indian Nation included, in addition to the Yakima bands, the Klickitats, Wanapams, Wishrams, Palus (Palouse), and the Wenatchis. Reservation Yakimas entered a brief period of relative prosperity under a worthy Indian agent. Soon, however, facing the usual pressures to sell their land, most Indians were forced into poverty, mitigated in part by some seasonal work.

By 1891, about one-third of the reservation land had been allotted to individuals, but the Yakima Nation, under Chief Shawaway Lotiahkan, retained the "surplus" usually sold to non-Indians in such cases. Still, much land that had been allotted to Indians was soon lost, including some of the best irrigated. Around the turn of the century as much as 80 percent of the reservation was in non-Indian hands. Some Indians also established homesteads on original village sites off the reservation. Despite government attempts to eradicate it, Indians retained their Wáashat (Longhouse) religion.

Dams (Bonneville in 1938, Grand Coulee in 1941, Dalles in 1956) destroyed the Native fisheries. During the course of the twentieth century, the number of salmon and steelhead that returned to spawn in the Yakima River declined by about 99 percent. The issue of fishing rights remained an important and controversial one from the beginning of the reservation period through its resolution in the Boldt decision of 1974.

Well into the twentieth century, Yakimas continued much of their traditional subsistence and ceremonial activities. In the 1950s, their long-standing fishing place, Celilo Falls, was lost to a dam. A tribal renaissance began around that time, however. It included the development of several tribal industries such as a furniture factory, clothing manufacturers, and a ceramic center as well as an all-Indian rodeo.

See also Dams, Fishing Rights, and Hydroelectric Power; Fishing Rights; Women in Native Woodlands Societies; Worldviews and Values; Yakima.

Native Americans of the Great Plains

Alabama-Coushatta

See Alabama.

Apache, Plains

Plains Apaches have also been known to non-Natives as Kiowa Apaches, Prairie Apaches, Plains Lipans, and possibly Catakas, Palomas, Wetapahatos, and Paducas. Their self-designation is *Na-i-shan Dine*, "Our People." (*See also* Kiowa.) Plains Apaches spoke an Athapaskan language.

Ancestors of the historic Plains Apaches may have lived in northeastern Wyoming and western South Dakota as early as the twelfth century. They may also have entered the Yellowstone Valley from Canada by 1600. In the early eighteenth century, the Comanches on the west and the Pawnees on the east forced Apaches living on the central Plains to the south and southwest. Cut off from their fellow Apacheans around 1720, the people known as Plains Apaches may have joined the Kiowa for protection. Although they functioned effectively as a Kiowa band and were a Plains tribe in all senses, they maintained a separate language and never came under the jurisdiction of the Kiowa tribal council.

Sacred bundles, with their associated ceremonies, were a focus of Kiowa religious practice. Plains Apaches adopted the Sun Dance in the eighteenth century, although they did not incorporate elements of self-mutilation into the ceremony. Young men also fasted to produce guardian spirit visions.

In general, wealth remained in the family through inheritance.

Corpses were buried or left in a teepee on a hill. Former possessions were given away. Mourners cut their hair and mutilated themselves. Before the people acquired horses, they hunted nearby buffalo and ate local roots, berries, seeds, and bulbs. Buffalo became a staple after the mideighteenth century. Men also hunted other large and small game. They did not eat bear at all and fish rarely. Women gathered a variety of wild potatoes and other vegetables, fruits, nuts, and berries. Plains Apaches ate dried, pounded acorns and also made them into a drink. Cornmeal and dried fruit were acquired by trade. The buffalo and other animals provided the materials for the usual items such as parfleches and other containers. Points for bird arrows came from prickly pear thorns. The cradle board was a bead-covered skin case attached to a V-shaped frame. Women made shallow, coiled basketry gambling trays and built skin teepees.

During the eighteenth century, Plains Apaches traded extensively with the upper Missouri tribes. There was also regular trade with New Mexico, where they exchanged meat, buffalo hides, and salt for cornmeal and dried fruit. During the nineteenth century they traded Comanche horses to the Osages and other tribes. Calendric skins and beadwork were two important Native artistic traditions.

Plains Apaches are probably the Apaches del Norte named in the historical record as the group of Apaches who arrived in New Mexico by the late eighteenth century. They moved back and forth between New Mexico and the upper Missouri area

during the early nineteenth century, serving as trade intermediaries between New Mexico and the upper Missouri tribes, such as the Mandans and Arikaras. By the early 1850s, they and the Kiowas were spending more time south rather than north of the Arkansas River. They settled on the Kiowa-Comanche-Apache Reservation in 1868. In 1901, this reservation was allotted in 160-acre parcels to individual tribal members, with the "surplus" opened to non-Native settlement.

See also Na-Dene Peoples; Trade.

Arapaho

"Arapaho" is probably from the Pawnee tirapihu ("trader") or the Kiowa and Spanish word for "tattered and dirty clothing." "Kanenavish" (various spellings), a term in use around 1800, was a corruption of the French gens de vache ("Buffalo People"). The Arapahos originally called themselves Inuna-ina, "Our People." Arapaho is an Algonquin language.

At least 3,000 years ago the Arapahos, possibly united with the future Gros Ventres and other peoples, probably lived in the western Great Lakes region, where they grew corn and lived in permanent villages. They migrated by the eighteenth century to the upper Missouri River region, acquiring horses about that time.

Medicine bundles, containing various sacred objects, were said by the people to have magical powers. Medicine men (shamans or priests) used their bundles in ceremonies; other bundles belonged to secret societies or to the whole tribe. A flat pipe some two feet long, wrapped in a bundle, was the most sacred object for the tribe. Tobacco was smoked in it only as part of the most sacred ceremonies and occasions.

Each of four bands had a chief, but there was no principal chief. Bands wintered separately, along streams, and came together in the summer to hunt buffalo and celebrate ceremonies. Although menstruating women were avoided, and the subject was taboo, there was no formal girls' puberty ceremony or menstrual seclusion. Men could marry more than one woman. Marriage was generally matrilocal. Blood relative and in-law taboos were strict. Extended family members, such as uncles and aunts, had specific responsibilities concerning their nieces and nephews.

Arapahos played the hoop-and-pole game and the cup-and-ball game and held athletic contests. Curing techniques included sweating in the sweat lodge and fumigation with roots, twigs, or herbs. There was one women's society in addition to the men's societies. The dead lay in state in fine clothing before being removed by horse and buried in a nearby hill. A favorite horse was killed. Mourners cut their hair, wore old clothes, and cut their arms and legs.

Buffalo had become a staple by the nineteenth century. Women made buffalo skin teepees. Willow-framed beds covered with skins lined the interior walls. There were no permanent villages, because the tribe migrated with the buffalo herds. Men also hunted elk, antelope, deer, and small animals. Meat was boiled in a hole in the ground filled with water and hot rocks. To preserve it for the winter, women dried it and sometimes mixed it with fat and chokecherries to make pemmican. They also gathered wild mountain fruits, roots, berries, and tobacco.

Arapahos may once have made ceramics. Most raw materials came from the buffalo or other animals. They carved items such as bowls from wood, some of which had artistic and/or religious significance. They smoked black stone pipes and made shallow basketry trays. Mandan villages along the Knife River (North Dakota) were a primary regional trading center. By the early nineteenth century the Arapaho traded buffalo robes with Mexicans and Americans for items not provided by the buffalo. They also served as intermediaries in trade between northern and southern Plains Indians.

Women decorated clothing, teepees, and other items with beautiful porcupine quill embroidery and painting. Designs often included legends and spiritual beings. Designs, which often represented natural and celestial features, included diamonds with appendages such as forked trees (triangles atop a line). The Arapahos probably acquired horses in the early eighteenth century. Babies were carried on the back in a U-shaped, wood-framed buckskin cradle board. The people used oval snowshoes in the winter.

Eight military societies were graded according to age. One, the Crazy Dog Society, was noted for its extreme bravery and valor. Traditional enemies included the Shoshones, Utes, Pawnees, Crows, Lakotas, Comanches, and Kiowas. The latter three tribes had become allies, with the southern Cheyennes, by the 1840s. Counting coup, or touch-

Buffalo meat dries at an Arapaho camp near Fort Dodge, Kansas, in 1870. Once an agricultural people, the Arapaho migrated from Minnesota to the Great Plains in the late 1700s, when they began to hunt buffalo. (National Archives and Records Administration)

ing the enemy with the hand or a stick, was highly prestigious, much more so than killing an enemy. Up to four people could count coup, in descending order of prestige, on the same enemy.

In the nineteenth century, the groups separated and divided into northern and southern Arapahos. The northern branch settled around the North Platte River in Wyoming and the southern branch in the area of Bent's Fort on the Arkansas River in Colorado. The two groups remained in close contact. By this time, the Arapahos had adopted the classic Great Plains culture: They were master horse riders, buffalo hunters, and raiders.

Early Anglo traders found the Arapahos very friendly and disposed to trade. Although fur traders entered the area in the 1730s, they merely observed intertribal trade of items of European manufacture, especially knives and guns but also metal tools and other items. Furs were not an important trade commodity until around the turn of the century. Traders also brought alcohol and disease into the region,

both to devastating effect. Still, powerful chiefs like Bear Tooth, favorably disposed to non-Indians, kept the peace in the early nineteenth century.

In 1837 a major war broke out, with the southern Arapahos and southern Cheyennes fighting against the Comanches. Peace was established in 1840, largely on Arapaho–Cheyenne terms. However, the opening of the Oregon Trail brought more non-Indians to the Plains and encouraged growing conflict, based on ignorance of Indian customs, land hunger, and race hatred.

Arapahos played a major role in the nineteenth-century wars for the Plains. The northern branch fought along with the Lakotas and the southern branch with the southern Cheyennes and occasionally with the Comanches and Kiowas. Although Arapahos signed the 1851 Fort Laramie Treaty, major gold finds in 1858–1859 caused further friction between Indians and non-Natives. Despite the existence of the treaty, in 1864 a group of southern Arapahos and Cheyennes, mostly

women and children, were attacked, massacred, and mutilated by U.S. Army troops at Sand Creek, Colorado, as part of a successful campaign to drive all Indians out of Colorado. Cut off from the rich Colorado buffalo herds and under further pressure from the United States, the Cheyennes and Arapahos in 1867 signed the Medicine Lodge Treaty, under which they formally ceded their lands north of the Arkansas River and were placed on a reservation in the Indian Territory (Oklahoma). Little Raven, a skilled orator and diplomat, represented his people in these negotiations.

By the terms of the Fort Laramie Treaty (1868), the northern Arapahos were supposed to settle with the Lakotas on the Pine Ridge Reservation in South Dakota. Holding out for their own reservation, the northern Arapahos remained in Wyoming, refusing also to settle with the southern Arapahos in the Indian Territory. They finally agreed in 1878 to become part of the eastern Shoshones' Wind River Reservation.

In the eighteenth century, the annual Sun Dance became the most important single ceremony. Its purpose was the renewal of nature and tribal prosperity. Some Arapahos adopted the Peyote religion in the 1890s. Many Arapahos, especially those on the Wind River Reservation, adopted the Ghost Dance religion in the late 1880s. By this time the enormous buffalo herds had been virtually wiped out. In 1890, the Arapahos and southern Cheyennes agreed to exchange their 3.5-million-acre reservation for allotments of 160 acres each. The group formally organized in 1937 as the Cheyenne–Arapaho Tribe.

See also Buffalo; Fort Laramie Treaty (1868); Sand Creek Massacre; Sun Dance; Trade.

Arikara

"Arikara" means "horn," referring to a traditional hairstyle. Their self-designation is *Tanish*, "Original People." The Arikaras migrated from the central Plains into central South Dakota in the seventeenth and eighteenth centuries. Arikara is a Caddoan language.

The Arikaras believed in a supreme deity who shared power with four lesser gods. Most religious festivals were associated with corn, which they originally acquired from the south and southwest. Medicine men possessed particularly fine,

generations-old ears of corn, within which resided the spirit of "mother corn." Religious activity included fasting, acquiring visions, and the possession and use of personal sacred bundles. Certain religious positions, such as the priesthood and the keeper of the sacred tribal medicine bundles, were hereditary within families.

Political centralization was weak among the Arikaras. Villages combined in a loose confederation of named bands. Village chiefs made up the band council, which assisted the head chief. The Arikaras were excellent swimmers; hauling trees out of the Missouri River provided them with firewood in an area short of trees. The game of shinny (a variation of hockey) was particularly popular, as were feats of dexterity, skill, and magic.

Families owned farms and dogs as well as dwellings. There were a number of mens' societies, focused on the hunt and on keeping order, as well as women's societies. Men hunted and provided protection; women were in charge of vegetable foods (garden plots), preparing hides for clothing as well as baskets and pottery, and caring for the lodge. Descent was matrilineal, and residence was matrilocal. Social rank was hereditary to a significant degree. The dead were buried sitting, wrapped in skins, their faces painted red. A year of mourning followed a death.

Arikaras located their villages on bluffs over the Missouri River. Partially excavated earth lodges measured about forty feet in diameter and held two or more extended families. A wooden framework supported woven willow branches and grass covered with earth. A lodge might last up to twenty years. Skin teepees served as temporary field dwellings. Later villages were strongly reinforced by wooden stockades and ditches.

Women grew corn, squash, beans, and sunflowers, fertilizing their crops and rotating their fields. They also cultivated tobacco. Men hunted buffalo and other large and small game. They also fished and gathered berries and other plants. Material items included willow weirs (fish traps); farm equipment, weapons, and utensils from buffalo parts; stone mortars; pottery cooking vessels; a variety of baskets; and leather pouches and other containers.

Women traded surplus crops, pots, and baskets to the Cheyennes, Kiowas, Lakotas, and other groups for buffalo and other animal products. There was also some cultural and material exchange among the Arikaras, the Mandans, and the Hidatsas. People used boats constructed of buffalo hide stretched over

a willow frame (bull boats) to cross the Missouri. They also wore snowshoes and used dogs and later (mideighteenth century) horses to pull travois. Women made blankets, robes, and moccasins of buffalo hide. They also made clothing of white weasel or ermine skin and made winter turbans of various animal skins.

Around the beginning of the seventeenth century, the Arikaras separated from the Skidi Pawnees in Nebraska and moved north along the Missouri River, spreading knowledge of agriculture along the way. They arrived in the Dakotas in the late eighteenth century.

Contact with French traders was established in the 1730s. During the early to mideighteenth century they acquired horses and ranged even farther west, to eastern Montana, to hunt buffalo. In the 1780s the people suffered a smallpox epidemic but continued to live relatively well, despite harassment by the Teton, Dakota, and other bands.

As a result of wars with the United States, the Arikaras retreated south to join their Pawnee relatives on the Loup River in Nebraska from the early 1820s through about 1835. A devastating smallpox epidemic in 1837 brought them to the verge of extinction. About 1845, the weakened Arikaras moved farther north and occupied land formerly under Mandan control (the latter having recently moved up the Missouri River with the Hidatsa).

In 1862, the Arikaras also moved up the Missouri to the Mandan/Hidatsa village of Like-a-Fishhook and joined politically with those two tribes. Like-a-Fishhook Village was a center of trade and commerce at that time. The Fort Laramie Treaty of 1851 recognized tribal holdings of more than 12 million acres.

In 1870, the United States established the 8-million-acre Fort Berthold Reservation for the tribes. This land was reduced, mostly by allotment, to about a million acres during the 1880s. By this time, Like-a-Fishhook had been abandoned, the people scattering to form communities along the Missouri River. The Arikaras lived in Nishu and Elbowwoods, on the east side of the river.

In the 1950s, against the tribes' vehement opposition, the United States built the Garrison Dam on the Missouri. The resulting Lake Sakakawea covered much of their land, farms, and homes. This event destroyed the tribes' economic base and permanently damaged their social structure.

See also Agriculture; Trade.

Assiniboine

"Assiniboine" means "those who cook with stones" (Algonquin). Canadian Assiniboines are also known as Stoneys. Their traditional self-designation is unknown. (*See also* Nakota.) Assiniboines/Yanktonais speak the Nakota dialect of Dakota, a Siouan language. The Siouan people probably originated in the lower Mississippi Valley and moved north through Ohio and into the Lake Superior region (northern Minnesota/southwestern Ontario). In the seventeenth century, the Assiniboines lived near Lake Winnipeg. Since the eighteenth century, they have lived in present-day Montana and Saskatchewan.

Male and female specialists provided religious leadership. In the eighteenth century, the annual Sun Dance became the people's most important religious ceremony, although the custom of self-torture was not generally present. Wakonda was worshiped as a primary deity, although the Assiniboines also recognized natural phenomena such as sun and thunder. Sweat lodge purification was an important religious practice. Spirit visions could be obtained through quests or in dreams. Some ceremonies featured masked clowns.

The Assiniboines were composed of up to thirty bands, each with its own chief. The chieftainship was based on leadership skills and personal contacts rather than heredity. Each band also had a council, whose decisions were enforced by the *akitcita*, or camp police. The people valued hospitality highly. There were a number of men's and women's dance societies with various social and ceremonial importance. There may have been clans.

The dead were placed on tree scaffolds with their feet to the west. When the scaffolds fell through age, the bones were buried and the skulls placed in a circle, facing inward. Cremation was also practiced. All burial areas were treated with great respect. Dead warriors were dressed in their finest clothes. Their faces were painted red, their weapons placed beside them, and one of their horses was killed for use in the next life. Women's tools, such as those used for dressing skins, were placed beside them.

Pubescent girls were secluded for four days, during which time they observed dietary and behavioral restrictions. Brides were purchased. Marriage consisted of a simple gift-giving ceremony between parents. The people played lacrosse and games of skill and dexterity, such as shinny (a variation of hockey) and the cup-and-ball game, and held

athletic competitions. Most games were accompanied by gambling.

A village might contain up to 200 skin lodges or teepees. The average, which held two to four families, had roughly a thirty-foot circumference and was constructed of about twelve sewn buffalo hides. Assiniboine teepees had a three-pole foundation. A temporary brush field shelter was also used.

Assiniboines on the high plains lived mainly on game such as buffalo, elk, and antelope. Women often accompanied hunters to butcher the animals and cut the meat into strips to dry. Fresh meat was usually roasted on a spit, although it was sometimes boiled with hot rocks in a skin-lined hole. Other foods included wild berries, roots (turnip), fruits (grapes, plums), and nuts. The buffalo was the basis of all technology. Most items, such as clothing, tools, and utensils, were made of buffalo and other animal products. The flageolet (flute) was used in part to convey surreptitious messages between young lovers. Assiniboines also played the rasp and the drum.

The people were known as shrewd traders. Before trade began with non-Indians, they generally traded pelts and meat with farming tribes for agricultural products. Significant art included decorative beaded quillwork (nineteenth century) and designs on tree bark. Dogs (later horses) carried saddlebags and travois. The people acquired horses in about the 1730s. They also used snowshoes.

The Plains Crees were traditional allies, with whom the Assiniboines regularly fought the Dakotas, Crows, Gros Ventres, and Blackfeet. The Assiniboines were recognized as highly capable warriors. Counting coup was more important than killing an enemy; four people might count coup on the same enemy, in descending order of prestige. Weapons included war clubs (a stone in a leather pouch attached to a stick), bow and arrow, and buffalo hide shields.

Assiniboines separated from the northern Yanktonais by perhaps the late sixteenth century, moving north from the Ohio Valley through Wisconsin and Minnesota, along the edge of the Woodlands into southern and southwestern Ontario. They became involved in the French fur trade in the early seventeenth century.

By later in that century they had made peace with the Plains Crees, joining them near Lake Winnipeg, and were trading with Hudson's Bay Company posts there. Assiniboines ranged over an extremely wide territory during that period, from near the Arctic Circle to the upper Missouri River and from James Bay to the Rocky Mountains. When trade with the Hudson's Bay Company declined in the late eighteenth century, the Assiniboines became fully nomadic, continuing the westward migration and hunting around the Saskatchewan and Assiniboine Rivers and across much of the northern Plains.

Major smallpox epidemics struck the people in 1780 and 1836, and alcohol and venereal disease also took a heavy toll. During that period, the Assiniboines divided into a lower and an upper division. Decimation of the buffalo herds as well as their own sharp population decline forced them to sign the 1851 Fort Laramie Treaty, limiting Assiniboine lands to parcels in western Montana.

Some Assiniboines worked as scouts for the U.S. and Canadian Armies in their Indian wars. In 1887, upper division Assiniboines (and the Gros Ventres) were confined to the new Fort Belknap Reservation; Fort Peck, which they shared with the Yanktonais, was created in 1873. Several hundred Assiniboines died of starvation at Fort Peck in 1883–1884.

Meanwhile, in Canada, unregulated whiskey sales were taking a great toll on Indian people. In 1877, as a result of national police intervention in the whiskey trade, the Stoneys and some other tribes signed Treaty 7, exchanging their traditional territory for reserves in Alberta and Saskatchewan, although some groups attempted to maintain their autonomy. Much of the reserve land was alienated in the early twentieth century owing to allotting and permitting of non-Indian homesteads.

See also Buffalo; Counting Coup, Trade.

Atsina
See Gros Ventres.

Blackfeet

The Blackfeet are a confederacy of three closely related Plains tribes: the Pikunis (known as Peigans in Canada, where the Blackfeet are also known as "Blackfoot"), meaning "small robes" or "poorly dressed robes"; the Kainahs, "blood" or "many chiefs"; and the Siksikas, the Blackfeet proper. "Siksika," a Cree word meaning "Blackfeet People," may have referred to their moccasins, blackened by dye

or by the ashes of prairie fires. All three tribes were called the *Sakoyitapix,* "Prairie People," or the *Nitsitapix,* "Real People." The Piegans were further divided into northern and southern branches. The Blackfeet Confederacy also included the Sarcees and, until 1861, the Gros Ventres. The Blackfeet groups spoke Algonquin languages.

The Blackfeet envisioned a world inhabited by spirits, some good and some evil. Deities included sun and thunder as well as all animals. Prayers were offered regularly throughout the day. Some people had visions to benefit the tribe as a whole. Medicine bundles, including sacred pipes, were owned by individuals, societies, and bands. They were thought to ensure a long, happy, successful life and thus could be quite valuable if sold.

Ceremonies included the Sun Dance, probably acquired from the Arapahos or the Gros Ventres around the mideighteenth century. Unlike most Plains tribes, women participated in the Blackfeet Sun Dance. Religious societies were responsible for healing and curing. Individual religious activity focused on the acquisition of guardian spirits through prayerful vision quests in remote places. Sweating was considered (for men) a religious activity as well as a preparation for ceremonials.

The constituent tribes of the confederacy were completely autonomous, although all were closely related and occasionally acted in concert. The tribes were in turn organized into autonomous bands of between twenty and thirty families (200 people) before the early eighteenth century. Each band had a civil headman, or chief, chosen on the basis of acts of bravery and generosity. Each band also had a war chief, who exerted power only during military situations. All headmen together constituted a tribal council, which in turn selected a temporary tribal chief when the bands came together. All decisions were made by consensus.

Men were members of one of seven age-graded military societies. In addition, men and women could belong to numerous other religious, dance, and social societies, each with its own symbols and ceremonies. There was also a society exclusively for women. Membership in all societies was drawn from all bands and functioned mainly when the tribe came together in the summer.

Virginity in women was held in high esteem. Depending on his wealth, a man might have more than one wife. Residence after marriage was generally patrilocal. Wedding formalities centered on gift giving. Divorce was possible on the grounds of

Blackfeet man painting on skin stretched on frame as a boy watches in 1912. (Library of Congress)

laziness or infidelity (men) or cruelty or neglect (women).

Names were sometimes given by the mother but more often by a male family member based on his war experiences. Boys usually earned a new name around adolescence. Despite beliefs about the danger of contact with menstruating women, there was no particular ceremony when a girl reached puberty.

Public ridicule was generally an effective deterrent to socially unacceptable behavior. Winter nights might be filled with storytelling, gambling, or all-night smokes during which people sang their religious songs. Childrens' games included hide and seek, archery and other contests, throwing balls, playing with toys, or sledding.

The dead were placed on scaffolds in trees or in teepees if death took place there; horses were generally killed to help in the journey to the next world. Women mourners cut their hair, wailed ritualistically, and slashed their limbs. Men cut their hair and left the band for a while.

Women constructed teepees from twelve to fourteen buffalo skins over pine poles. Teepee entrances always faced east. Larger teepees, of up to

thirty buffalo skins, were a sign of wealth. Teepees were smaller when dogs pulled the travois. Food was generally abundant, although droughts or blizzards could bring hunger or even starvation. Plains Blackfeet ate mostly buffalo but also other large as well as small game. Buffalo were driven over cliffs, surrounded on foot and shot, communally hunted with bow and arrow (the most common approach after the Blackfeet acquired horses), and individually stalked. The Indians also ate waterfowl and the eggs. They did not eat fish or dog. In addition to the usual wild fruits, nuts, and berries, Blackfeet women gathered camas roots, which they steamed in an underground oven. Some tobacco was grown for ceremonial purposes.

Early, pre-Plains Blackfeet may have made pottery. The buffalo provided more than sixty material items, which the Blackfeet traded as far south as Mexico in all seasons save the winter. Skin containers were often decorated with painted designs. Musical instruments included a rattle of skin around wood as well as a flageolet (flute). The people also used stone pounding mauls and war clubs attached to wooden handles, chipped stone knives, and brushes of porcupine bristles or horsehair bound with rawhide. They also made backrests of willow sticks tied with sinew and supported by a tripod.

Men painted teepees and other leather items with stars and designs such as battle events. Women made beaded quillwork, usually on clothing. In general, the people were known for the high quality of everyday items such as clothing, tools, teepees, and headdresses. Women wore long, one-piece skin dresses, later fringed and beaded, and buffalo robes in the winter. Men dressed in skin shirts, leggings, and moccasins, as well as buffalo robes in the winter.

All men were members of age-graded military societies known as All Comrades. Blackfeet Indians were considered among the best fighters, hunters, and raiders. Although the three divisions were politically autonomous, they acted in unison to fight their enemies. Weapons included three-foot horn, sinew-backed bows, stone clubs, arrows, and buffalo hide shields. Rather than counting coup with a stick, Blackfeet warriors gathered high war honors by wresting a gun or other weapon from an enemy. Taking a horse or a scalp merited honors but of relatively low caliber.

The Blackfeet people may have originated in the Great Lakes region but had migrated to between the Bow and North Saskatchewan Rivers well before the seventeenth century. During the eighteenth century they completed their move southward into Montana, displacing the Shoshones.

Like many aboriginal peoples, the Blackfeet were transformed by the horse and the gun, both of which they acquired during the early to mideighteenth century. One result was that they had surplus buffalo products to offer for trade. Raiding, especially for horses, became an important activity. They joined in alliance with the Assiniboines, Arapahos, and Gros Ventres and were frequently at war during the historic period.

Blackfeet people first felt the influence of non-Indians in the seventeenth century. By the late eighteenth century they were engaged in the fur trade and were known as shrewd traders, playing American and British interests against each other. The people experienced severe epidemics in 1781–1782, 1837, 1864, and 1869–1870. After one of their number was killed by a member of the Meriwether Lewis and William Clark expedition in 1804, the Blackfeet fought all Americans whenever possible until they began trading with them again in 1831.

The 1868 Fort Laramie Treaty gave the Blackfeet lands south of the Missouri River, although their traditional lands had all been north of the Missouri. Still, in various treaties between 1851 and 1878 they ceded land to the United States and Canada. Epidemics, the decline of the buffalo, and, later, whiskey hurt the Blackfeet more than anything, although in 1870 they were the victims of a U.S. Army massacre in which 173 peaceful Indians, mostly women and children, were killed.

The Blackfeet Reservation was established in 1855 in northern Montana. In exchange for the northern Montana plains, the southern Piegans received fixed hunting grounds bordered by the Canadian, Missouri, and Musselshell Rivers and the Rocky Mountains; they also received promises of payments and annuities. From the 1870s into the 1890s, the United States took away much of the huge Blackfeet Reservation. In Treaty 7 (1877), the Blackfeet (and others) ceded much of southern Alberta for a number of small reserves. Roughly 600 Blackfeet, mostly southern Piegans, died of starvation in 1883 after the last great buffalo herd was destroyed.

After a farming experiment failed, the Piegans began a program of stock raising around 1890, on land individually assigned by the Bureau of Indian Affairs. A few Indians became prosperous, but the majority leased their land to non-Indians, who often did not pay. A combination of events in 1919 left the people in dire poverty and dependent on

government rations. During this period, over 200,000 acres of Indian land were lost through the nonpayment of taxes and allotments that were sold to fend off starvation. Blackfeet on both sides of the United States–Canadian border were also subject to having their children kidnapped and sent to missionary boarding schools. Log houses replaced teepees during this time. Most Canadian Blackfeet lost large portions of their reserves from 1907 to 1921.

Stock raising returned during the 1920s, accompanied by grain farming and some subsistence gardening. U.S. Blackfeet adopted an Indian Reorganization Act constitution in 1930s. Income rose as the government provided credit for ranching enterprises. After World War II, up to one-third of the population was living off-reservation. Conditions on the reservations began to improve at that time, a trend that accelerated during the 1960s. Among most people, English replaced Blackfeet as the daily language in the 1970s. At the same time, many traditions severely declined.

> *See also* Blackfeet Confederacy; Buffalo; Economic Development; Fort Laramie Treaty (1868); Horse, Economic Impact; Sun Dance; Welch, James.

Blood
See Blackfeet.

Cheyenne

"Cheyenne" is a word of Lakota origin meaning "red talkers" or "foreign talkers." Their self-designation is *Tse-tsehese-staestse*, "People." In the early nineteenth century, Cheyennes lived from the Yellowstone River to the upper Arkansas River. Cheyenne is an Algonquin language.

The Cheyennes conceived of a universe divided into seven major levels, each with resident spiritual beings that were also associated with earthly plants and animals. They also believed in a creator of all life. Through fasting and prayer, both men and women sought visions in remote places to acquire guardian spirit helpers, whose associated songs, prayers, and symbols would provide special skills or protection in times of crisis. Priests and doctors (shamans) used plants to cure disease. Annual ceremonies included the Renewal of Sacred Arrows, the Sun Dance (New Life Lodge), and the annual, five-day Sacred Buffalo Hat ceremony.

On the Plains, traditional government consisted of the Council of Forty-Four: a group of forty exceptionally wise, generous, brave, and able men, four from each of the ten bands, plus four elders/religious authorities held over from the previous council. The latter four men, plus a tribal chief chosen by them, were known as the five sacred chiefs. Council terms were ten years. Each band also had its own chief. Six military societies helped to carry out council directives and maintain strict internal discipline.

Bands lived separately in the winter so as to hunt more effectively in a wider space. In the summer, the bands came together for the communal buffalo hunt and for sacred ceremonies. At these times, the camp consisted of a large circle, within which each band had a designated position. Murder was considered among the most reprehensible of crimes as well as a sin; murderers were ostracized for life or exiled. Bravery was highly valued, as was female chastity. Games, generally accompanied by gambling, included lacrosse and the cup-and-ball game. In addition to the men's military societies, the highly prestigious buffalo society was open only to women who had embroidered at least thirty buffalo hides. Corpses were dressed in their best clothing, wrapped in robes, and placed on a scaffold, usually in a tree. While still in the northern Mississippi Valley, Cheyennes lived in bark lodges and, in North Dakota (Shyenne River area), in earth lodges. By the late eighteenth century they had begun living in buffalo hide teepees.

The Cheyennes grew corn, beans, and squash; gathered wild rice; fished; and hunted in the northern Mississippi and Shyenne valleys. From the late eighteenth century on, as the tribe became nomadic hunters, their diet depended largely on the buffalo. Cheyennes also ate other large game as well as dog. The Plains diet was supplemented by wild turnips, berries, and prickly pear cactus. The Cheyennes made pottery prior to their move to the Plains. Once there, the buffalo provided most of their clothing, dwellings, tools, containers, and utensils. They also made small, shallow basketry trays, primarily used for gambling. Cheyennes traded at both pre-contact trade centers of the northern Plains: Mandan villages on the Knife River and the Arikara villages in present-day South Dakota.

An Edward S. Curtis photo from 1910 shows Cheyenne scouts riding horses. (Library of Congress)

Traditional artists worked with leather, wood, quills, and feathers. They also carved pipes. Women dressed the skins for clothing. They made moccasins, leggings, breechclouts, shirts, and robes for men, and for themselves they made two-piece dresses and moccasins with leggings and robes in the winter. Clothing was usually decorated with beaded quillwork.

During the late eighteenth through the midnineteenth centuries, the Cheyennes were great warriors and raiders. Six interband military societies, such as the prestigious Dog Soldiers, selected a war chief. As Plains dwellers, counting coup in battle by touching an enemy counted for more prestige than killing him. Weapons included the horn bow, arrows, clubs, shields, and spears.

The Algonquin people may have come north from the lower Mississippi Valley shortly after the last ice sheet receded. Sixteenth- and seventeenth-century Cheyennes lived in the upper Mississippi Valley in permanent villages and grew corn, beans, and squash. They also fished and hunted game, including buffalo.

Some bands encountered René-Robert de La Salle in 1680, on the Illinois River. The French fur trade in the Great Lakes region was responsible for arming local Indian groups such as the Ojibwas with guns; these groups began attacking Cheyenne villages, eventually forcing them to abandon the region and undertake a slow migration westward throughout the eighteenth century. By the end of the eighteenth century, well armed Ojibwas (Anishinabes) had destroyed a main Cheyenne village. The surviving Cheyennes moved farther west, to the upper Missouri River, joining some of their number who had gone there several years earlier.

By the early nineteenth century, raids from Siouan tribes forced the Cheyennes completely out onto the Plains, where they gave up farming entirely, becoming nomadic buffalo hunters as well as fierce

fighters. Allied with the Arapahos, they settled primarily near the Black Hills and then in the upper Platte–Powder River area, where they eventually became allied with Lakota bands. About 1832, some bands moved south, attracted by trade centered around Taos, New Mexico, as well as Bent's Fort on the Arkansas River in southern Colorado. The move precipitated a tribal split into northern and southern Cheyennes. In alliance with the southern Arapahos, the southern Cheyennes controlled most of the buffalo country between western Kansas and eastern Colorado and the Platte River.

In 1837 a major war broke out, with the southern Arapahos and southern Cheyennes fighting against the Comanches; peace was established in 1840, largely on Arapaho–Cheyenne terms. The Cheyennes signed the 1851 Fort Laramie Treaty, which reaffirmed their right to land between the North Platte and Arkansas Rivers. The treaty also formalized the separation of the Cheyenne groups. Meanwhile, non-Indian leaders of territorial Colorado had decided to force all Indians from that region. Pressure against the southern Cheyennes was increased, especially after the Pike's Peak gold rush of 1859. Under Chief Black Kettle (Moketavato), the southern Cheyennes repeatedly compromised in an effort to avoid war. However, the 1864 massacre and mutilation of several hundred of their people at Sand Creek, Colorado (where they had been told to camp under the protection of the U.S. Army and met the soldiers flying a white surrender and an American flag), forced the southern Cheyennes to cede their lands in Colorado.

Black Kettle continued to seek peace but was shot down with his tribe, who offered no resistance, in the Washita Valley, Oklahoma, in 1868. At this point, the Cheyennes divided again. One group went north to the Powder River Country, and most of the rest settled on the Southern Cheyenne and Arapaho Reservation, established in 1869 in Indian Territory. This roughly 4-million-acre reservation was eliminated through allotment and non-Indian settlement by 1902. Some southern Cheyennes continued to fight with the Kiowas, Comanches, and Arapahos, until the few survivors were forced to surrender in 1875.

In the meantime, the northern Cheyennes tried to resist the onslaught of the gold seekers and land grabbers who invaded their lands, ignoring the terms of the 1851 Fort Laramie Treaty. Formerly among the tribes who held out for peace, they turned to war following the Sand Creek massacre.

The resulting Fort Laramie Treaty (1868) affirmed the exclusion of non-Indians from the Powder River region of Montana. In 1876, the northern Cheyennes joined with other Plains Indians in defeating the United States in the Battle of the Little Bighorn.

Shortly thereafter, however, the U.S. Army caught and defeated the northern Cheyennes, rounding up almost 1,000 of them and forcing them south to the Cheyenne–Arapaho Reservation in Indian Territory. Though exhausted after their forced march, sick and dying from malaria, and starving, roughly 300 desperate northern Cheyennes under Dull Knife and Little Wolf escaped and headed toward home north of the North Platte River. Fighting valiantly for their freedom, they were pursued by soldiers and had to cross lands now inhabited by white farmers and ranchers. The people were recaptured with much loss of life and relocated to the Pine Ridge area of South Dakota in 1881. Three years later, the Tongue River Reservation in eastern Montana was established for this now decimated people. Although this land was never opened to non-Indian purchase, allotments fragmented the reservation, causing long-term legal and cultural problems.

Christian missionaries, especially Mennonites, Catholics, and Southern Baptists, became active among the Cheyennes toward the end of the nineteenth century. Around the same time, the Peyote religion and the Ghost Dance became popular among the northern Cheyennes. Following confinement to reservations, most Indians lived on government rations (often inadequate at best) and marginal gardening and wage labor. In 1911, the United States organized a fifteen-member Northern Cheyenne Business Council, largely under its control. The tribe adopted an Indian Reorganization Act (IRA) constitution in 1935. In 1918, southern Cheyennes were among those who formally incorporated the Peyote religion into the Native American Church.

See also Black Kettle; Buffalo; Dull Knife; Horse, Economic Impact; Fort Laramie Treaty (1868); Native American Church of North America; Sand Creek Massacre; Sun Dance.

Comanche

"Comanche" is a name derived from either the Ute *Komantcia*, "People Who Fight Us All the Time," or the Spanish *camino ancho*, "broad trail." Their

Comanche camp ca. 1890. (Library of Congress)

self-designation was *Numinu*, "People." The Comanches lived in the Rocky Mountain regions of Wyoming and northern Colorado until the mid- to late seventeenth century, when the people moved into the central and southern Great Plains. Today, most Comanches live in Oklahoma. Comanche is part of the Uto-Aztecan language.

Comanche deities included numerous celestial objects such as the sun and moon. The Eagle Dance and Beaver ceremony were important, but Comanches did not adopt the Sun Dance until 1874. Young men undertook vision quests in remote places, hoping to attract a guardian spirit helper. When they returned, shamans helped them to interpret their visions and to prepare their personal medicine bundles.

Membership was fluid in each of the roughly thirteen bands, including four major ones. Each band had a chief or headman, who was assisted by a council of the leading men of the band. In contrast to most other Plains Indians, the fiercely independent Comanches maintained virtually no police to keep order in the camp. Leaders for buffalo hunts maintained authority for that hunt only. Men might have more than one wife. Corpses were dressed in their best clothing, face painted red and red clay on the eyes, and buried in a flexed position in a cave or shallow grave. Mourners cut their hair, arms, and legs. They gave away the dead person's possessions, burned his or her teepee, and never mentioned his or her name again.

Buffalo was the main staple on the Plains. They were driven over cliffs, stalked individually, or, most commonly after the people acquired horses, surrounded on horseback. Men also hunted other large and small game. Women gathered wild potatoes,

fruit (plums, grapes, and currants), nuts, and berries. Babies were cradled in beaded skin pockets attached to V-shaped frames. Comanches also made shallow basketry gambling trays.

Comanches frequented both northern Plains aboriginal trade centers: Mandan villages on the Knife River and the Arikara villages in present-day South Dakota. By the early eighteenth century, Comanches were trading at Taos and Santa Fe, New Mexico, although they also raided these areas mercilessly. Having acquired horses during the late sixteenth century, probably from the Utes, the Comanche became among the most highly skilled horse riders on the Plains. They were excellent breeders and trainers as well as raiders and maintained some of the largest horse herds on the Plains. Both boys and girls began riding around age five.

Women made moccasins, leggings, breechclouts, shirts, and robes for men, and for themselves they made two-piece dresses and moccasins with leggings and robes in the winter. Clothing was often decorated with beaded quillwork. Comanches used red paint for battle on their horses' heads and tails as well as themselves. Other battle gear included buffalo horn headdresses, high buffalo hide boots, and horsehair extensions to their already long hair. Weapons included feathered lances, buffalo hide shields, and bows, mainly of Osage orange wood. The people adopted military societies beginning in the eighteenth century as well as many other features of Plains warrior culture.

The Comanches were originally part of the eastern Shoshones, who had lived along Arizona's Gila River from about 3000 BCE to about 500 BCE. At that time, a group of them began migrating north toward Utah, growing a high-altitude variety of corn that had been developed in Mexico. When a drought struck the Great Basin in the thirteenth century, these people, known then as Shoshones, spread out north of the Great Salt throughout much of the Great Basin.

By about the late seventeenth century, some Shoshone bands, from the mountainous regions of Wyoming and northern Colorado, later known as Comanches, had acquired horses. The bands began migrating into New Mexico and toward the Arkansas River on the central Plains. They adopted the cycle of buffalo hunting, raiding, and fighting characteristic of Plains life. By about 1750 they had acquired vast horse herds and dominated the central high plains.

In 1780–1781 the Comanches (as well as most other Plains tribes) lost a large number of their people, perhaps as many as half, to a smallpox epidemic. In about 1790, several thousand northern Comanches and Kiowas joined in a lasting alliance. The Comanches continued southward throughout the eighteenth and into the early nineteenth century, pressured from the north by the Dakota/Lakota and other tribes and drawn by trade and raiding opportunities in the Southwest and beyond in New Spain/Mexico. During this period they continued to drive Apachean groups from the Plains. They also prevented the Spanish from colonizing Texas extensively, and they acted as a brake to French trade expansion into the Southwest.

By the midnineteenth century, Comanches were roughly separated into three divisions. The southern group lived between the Red and Colorado Rivers in Texas. The middle group wintered in Texas but followed the buffalo in the summer north toward the Arkansas River. The northern group wintered on the Red River and wandered widely during the summer. In 1840, the northern Comanches made peace with the southern Cheyennes and Arapahos, after the latter had staged several successful raids against them. As part of this agreement, the Comanches gave up land in western Kansas north of the Arkansas River.

A cholera epidemic in 1849–1850 took a heavier toll on the Comanche population than had all the battles to date. During the 1840s and 1850s, the Comanches fought bitter wars with the Texans, the latter bent on exterminating all Indian groups. The Comanches defeated Kit Carson in 1864, but they and the Kiowas signed a treaty in 1865 that reserved much of western Indian Territory (Oklahoma) for them and their allies. When the U.S. government failed to keep non-Indians out of these lands, the Indians rebelled. In the ensuing 1867 Medicine Lodge Treaty, some Comanche bands agreed to accept a reservation in southwestern Indian Territory with the Kiowa and Kiowa Apaches. Hostilities over non-Indian squatters and the difficulties of life in captivity continued for another eight years. However, by the late 1860s the Comanches were in serious trouble. The great buffalo herds had been hunted to near extinction and the U.S. Army was pursuing Indians relentlessly.

After the 1868 Battle of the Washita, in which the United States massacred a group of Cheyenne Indians, a few Comanche leaders surrendered their bands at Fort Cobb, Oklahoma; these roughly 2,500 people were later moved to Fort Sill, Oklahoma, and began farming corn. Several bands, however, remained on the Plains, holding on to the free life for

several more years. The Comanches adopted a modified version of the Sun Dance in 1874. At about the same time, a short-lived religious movement led to an unsuccessful battle against the United States at Adobe Walls.

In 1874, War Chief Quanah Parker led the last free Comanche bands, along with some Kiowa and Cheyenne refugees from Fort Sill, into Palo Duro Canyon, Texas, site of the last great buffalo range. There they lived traditionally until the Army found and destroyed their camp and horses. In 1875, Parker surrendered to mark the end of Comanche resistance.

Parker continued as an important leader on the reservation, overseeing favorable land leases and playing a major role in bringing the Peyote religion to the Comanche and many other Indian tribes after 1890. Reservation lands were allotted beginning in 1892. Nonallotted lands were sold to non-Indians, and nothing remained of the reservation by 1908.

See also Buffalo; Horse, Economic Impact; Parker, Quanah; Trade.

Cree, Plains

Plains Crees belong to a division of the Cree Indians of central Canada. The name comes from the French *Kristenaux*, a corruption of a Cree self-designation. (*See also* Cree.) Early in the seventeenth century, Crees inhabited the forests between Lake Superior and Hudson Bay. By the eighteenth and nineteenth centuries, groups of Crees had moved into western Saskatchewan and eastern Alberta and south to northern Montana. These were the northernmost of the Plains Indians. All nine Cree dialects belong to the central division of the Algonquin language family.

Cree shamans used their spirit powers to cure illness. In midsummer, bands (either individually or collectively) celebrated the Sun Dance. There were from eight to twelve bands of fluid composition among the Plains Cree, each with a headman and a loosely defined hunting territory. The leadership position required excellent hunting and speaking skills, as well as the traits of bravery and generosity, and it could be hereditary. Each band also had a warrior society.

A child's name was associated with the name givers' spirit vision. Most people also had nicknames. Girls were secluded for four nights at the onset of puberty, when they often acquired their spirit visions; a feast followed this initial period of seclusion. Married women also withdrew when menstruating. There were no male puberty ceremonies, except that boys were encouraged to fast and undertake a vision quest. For marriage gifts, the bride's family gave the couple a fully equipped teepee. The groom received a horse from his father-in-law as well as moccasins from his new wife. Plains Cree sons-in-law observed the taboo of not speaking directly to their mothers-in-law.

Corpses were dressed in their best clothing, and their faces were painted. They were taken out the side of the teepee, not the door, and buried in the ground, in log chambers, or in tree scaffolds. Some eastern bands built gabled-roof grave houses. Bundles containing ancestral locks of hair were considered extremely important and were carried by the women when the camp moved. The possessions of the dead were given away.

Plains Crees lived in buffalo hide teepees with three-pole foundations. Buffalo was the staple food. Men hunted in small groups during the winter and communally in the summer. Buffalo were driven into brush impoundments or, in the winter, into marshes or deep snow. Men also hunted other large game. Women snared a variety of small game, fished, and caught birds (and gathered their eggs). They also gathered roots, berries, fruits, and tubers. Most of these were dried and stored for the winter. At least as early as the early nineteenth century, some Plains Crees maintained gardens and even kept cattle to help ensure a constant food supply.

Crees acted as intermediaries between non-Indian traders and Indian tribes such as the Blackfeet in the late seventeenth century. Like many Plains Indians, the Crees made beaded quillwork and painted hides. Dogs carried extra goods with the help of a strap across the chest before the advent of the travois. After about 1770, horse-drawn travois were used to transport goods. The Crees also used snowshoes and canoes, which they abandoned during the seventeenth and eighteenth centuries in favor of crude, temporary buffalo hide rafts. In general, the upper body remained bare except for a robe or ceremonial garments. The people also wore one-piece moccasins as well as rawhide visors against the sun. Unlike many Plains tribes, the Cree placed a high value on scalping. One customarily gave away much of the booty captured in a raid. Weapons included sinew-backed bows and war clubs consisting of a stone in a bag on the end of a stick.

The earliest Algonquins may have come north from the lower Mississippi Valley shortly after the last ice sheet retreated from the Great Lakes and Saint Lawrence River regions. Their population grew until a large number of them lived north and west of the Great Lakes. Crees probably originated in central and northern Manitoba around 1100. By 1500 they were located at the forest's edge along and south of the Saskatchewan River. Cree bands began acquiring guns and other goods from the French in the mid-seventeenth century, trading furs, especially beaver, for them. Hudson's Bay Company opened a post in Cree territory in 1667.

During the period of the French fur trade, many Crees and French intermarried. During the later seventeenth century, the quest for furs, as well as their own growing population, pushed the Crees on toward the west until they stretched from near Labrador in the east to the Great Slave Lake and south to Alberta, northern Montana, and North Dakota in the west. During these migrations they displaced their ancient enemies to the west, the Athapaskans, and pushed Dakota bands westward as well.

Crees formed a close alliance with the Assiniboines in the late seventeenth century. They experienced severe smallpox epidemics in 1737 and 1781, particularly in the Lake Winnipeg area. By the early eighteenth century, the Crees were roughly divided into Woodland (eastern and western) and Plains divisions, having reached Lake Winnipeg and beyond. During this period they still retained much of their old Woodland culture.

Plains Crees acquired horses in the mid- to late eighteenth century and adopted much of classic nomadic Plains Indian culture. Some also intermarried with Mohawk Indians who were serving as guides for non-Indian fur trading companies, which the Crees were provisioning with buffalo meat. By the early nineteenth century, Plains Crees controlled the area north of the Missouri River and were pressuring the Blackfeet to the west and south.

A sharp decline set in during the 1850s, however, owing primarily to smallpox epidemics and warfare with the Blackfeet. Canadian officials created Cree reserves in the 1870s, on which Crees were theoretically encouraged to turn to the agricultural life. In fact, the Indians themselves were aware that the buffalo-oriented life was soon to end and wanted help in making the change to agriculture. Though they might well have adapted to this change, most were denied access to key resources, such as implements and livestock (both promised in treaties). Such items, if they were issued at all, were generally inappropriate and/or of poor quality.

Despite these obstacles, some bands made a relative success of farming, to the extent that non-Indian farmers were complaining toward the end of the 1880s about unfair competition from Native Americans. In 1890, the Canadian government turned to a policy of peasant farming, in which the reserves were subdivided. Land was allotted in severalty, "surplus" land was sold to non-Indians, and mechanized farm equipment was taken away. With this policy, Canadian officials succeeded in dramatically reducing total land under Indian cultivation, as well as the number of Indian farmers, and in keeping the reserves in poverty. Indian protests were routinely ignored or repressed.

In 1885, Poundmaker and Big Bear led the Crees in the Second Riel Rebellion (Louis Riel was a Métis nationalist leader). They and the Métis joined forces to try to stem the flow of non-Indian settlers to the vicinity of the Canadian Pacific Railway line in Saskatchewan and to create a Native state. The Crees were not defeated but surrendered shortly after their Métis allies did. One group of Crees became associated at that time with Little Shell's band of Chippewas in Montana. Big Bear, a leader of the rebellion, escaped with 200 Crees to the United States, where they wandered for three decades in Montana until joining with a band of Chippewas under the leadership of Stone Child, or Rocky Boy. In 1916, the U.S. government created the Rocky Boy Reservation in the Bearpaw Mountains of Montana for these people. Little Shell's band eventually settled in nearby towns and reservations.

See also Canada, Indian Policies of; Horse, Economic Impact; Riel, Louis.

Crow

The Crow self-designation is *Absaroke,* after a bird once native to the region. (*See also* Hidatsa.) The Crows' traditional homeland was south of Lake Winnipeg. Crow/Hidatsa is a Siouan language.

Like other Plains Indians, the Crows placed great importance on supernatural guardian helpers acquired in dreams or during vision quests. Their main ceremonies included the Sun Dance, the Medicine Lodge ceremony, and the triennial Tobacco

Eight Crow prisoners under guard at the Crow agency in Montana, 1887. Crow were relocated to the Montana reservation in 1851. (National Archives and Records Administration)

Society ceremony, performed by both men and women in honor of the tribe's sacred plant.

The existence of the Tobacco Society conferred benefits on both planters and the tribe as a whole. Planting was followed by a dance and then a feast. In a subsequent ceremony, new members were adopted into the society; this ceremony was also highly ritualized and included fees paid for various honors, painting, dancing, singing, and sweating as well as the acquisition of medicine bundles. Members observed various behavior restrictions during the year. The harvest was also accompanied by ritual.

Each of about thirteen matrilineal clans was led by a headman selected on the basis of his war record. A council of chiefs governed the tribe; one member of the council was head of the camp. Each spring, one of the men's military societies was appointed camp police force, which was charged with maintaining internal order, supervising the buffalo hunt, and regulating war parties.

Generosity was highly valued among the Crows, as with most Plains tribes. Most girls married before puberty to men outside the clan, and most men purchased their wives. Premarital or extramarital sex was not punished, but female chastity was valued. Wives were also gained by inheritance and capture. Sons-in-law did not speak directly to their mothers-in-law and fathers-in-law.

Parents spent a great deal of time nurturing, teaching, and encouraging their children to prepare for life as adults. There were no orphans, because orphans were immediately adopted by aunts or

uncles. Children rarely, if ever, received corporal punishment. Instead, "joking relatives" used pointed humor to keep people in line.

When Crows lived near Lake Winnipeg and with the Hidatsa along the Missouri River, they built earth lodges. Later, women made four-pole, twenty-five-foot-high (or higher) skin teepees of between seven and twenty buffalo skins. The larger teepees could house as many as forty people, but the average was about twelve. The teepee owner or a special guest slept at the rear (opposite the door). A draft screen around the lower inside was painted with pictures of the owner's war feats.

Pre-Plains Crows raised corn and other crops. Buffalo were hunted by driving them into impoundments or over cliffs or by means of the mounted surround. Men also hunted deer, antelope, and other large game, sometimes by wearing the skin of such an animal and stalking it. The Crows grew their ceremonial tobacco but traded for the everyday variety.

Pottery predated the move to the Plains. In addition to the usual buffalo-based items, material goods included fire drills; bows from hickory, ash, or even elk antler; and stone scrapers and other tools. With regard to trade, the Crows played the role of intermediary between the Mandans and Hidatsas to the east and Great Basin and Plateau tribes such as the Shoshones, Salish (Flatheads), Nez Percé, and Utes. The Crow–Mandan trade continued until the early nineteenth century. Weapons were extremely finely made, as were clothing, blankets, and leather items such as decorated parfleches.

Dogs carried movable goods and pulled travois. After the people acquired horses in the mideighteenth century, they became highly skilled horse riders and perhaps the best horse thieves on the Plains. Typical Plains clothing included, for men, a shirt, hiphigh leggings, moccasins, and a buffalo robe. Women wore a long dress, knee-high leggings, and moccasins. Both used rawhide visors against the sun.

The various men's societies were voluntary and not age-graded, although some were more important than others. Most or all had military, hunt, or police-related functions. The Crazy Dogs were dedicated to unusual bravery in combat. Dog Soldiers were the camp police. Some societies occasionally engaged in annual wife capturing. Traditional enemies included the Shoshones, Lakotas (after ca. 1800), and Blackfeet. Allies included the Mandans, Salish (Flatheads), and Nez Percé. Crows preferred to count coup rather than to scalp.

The Hidatsa-Crows lived originally in the Ohio country. From there, they moved to northern Illinois, through western Minnesota and into the Red River Valley, south of Lake Winnipeg. There they remained for at least several hundred years, beginning around the twelfth or thirteenth century, growing gardens and hunting buffalo.

Pressured by newly armed bands of Ojibwas and Crees, the group moved southwest to Devil's Lake in the midsixteenth century and then again toward the upper Missouri River, north of the Mandans, where they continued to hunt and grow corn. In the late seventeenth century, the Crows struck out on their own toward southwestern Montana and northern Wyoming and the vicinity of the Yellowstone, Powder, and Mussellshell Rivers. During this period, they separated into mountain (southern Montana and northern Wyoming) and river (lower Yellowstone region) divisions.

The Crow acquired horses, probably from the Shoshone, and became full-fledged nomadic Plains Indians during the mideighteenth century. Major smallpox epidemics struck the people in 1781 and 1833. Crow boundaries under the 1851 Fort Laramie Treaty included about 38.5 million acres, mostly in the Yellowstone region. The Powder River country remained in dispute between them and the Lakota. However, their lands were drastically reduced in 1868 and again in subsequent years. During that period the Crows became seminomadic, building wintertime camps that included a few log cabins. In much of the 1860s and 1870s, Crows served the United States as scouts in the Indian wars, especially against the Lakotas and the Nez Percé.

Despite their help to the United States, the U.S. government treated the Crows no differently than it did any other Indians. By the late 1880s the Crows had been forced to cede most of their remaining land. Catholic missionaries and boarding schools had made inroads into the reservation and into Crow culture. Many aspects of traditional Crow culture, such as giveaways and the Sun Dance, had been outlawed in 1884. It was also illegal to leave the reservation without permission and to sell a horse to another Indian. In the seven years from 1914 to 1921, Crow horse herds declined from roughly 35,000 to less than 1,000. Some leaders, like Chief Plenty Coups, urged accommodation, especially in the area of education.

Meanwhile, the Crows developed a tribal council that managed to keep the Bureau of Indian Affairs staff at arm's length and provide them with

a semi-independent decision-making body. In the 1950s, the government coerced the Crow into selling their rights to the Bighorn Canyon, where it built the Yellowtail Dam, ironically named for one of its chief opponents. In 1981, the legal ownership of the Bighorn River passed to the state of Montana.

See also Buffalo; Horse, Economic Impact; Plenty Coups.

Dakota

"Dakota" comes from a Siouan dialect spoken by the eastern group of the tribe commonly referred to as Sioux. The divisions of the eastern group include Sissetons ("swamp village," "lake village," or "fish-scale village"), Wahpetons ("dwellers among the leaves"), Wahpekutes ("shooters among the leaves"), and Mdewakantons ("People of the Mystic Lake"). The latter two divisions are also known as Santees (from *Isanati,* "knife") and shared a closely related culture.

The Dakotas refer to themselves as *Dakota* ("ally"), *Dakotah Oyate* ("Dakota People"), or *Ikce Wicasa* ("Natural" or "Free People"). The word "Sioux" is derived originally from an Ojibwa word *Nadowe-is-iw,* meaning "lesser adder" ("enemy" is the implication), which was corrupted by French voyageurs to *Nadoussioux* and then shortened to "Sioux." Today, many people use the term "Dakota" or, less commonly, "Lakota" to refer to all Sioux people.

All thirteen subdivisions of Dakota-Lakota-Nakota speakers (Sioux) were known as Oceti Sakowin, or Seven Council Fires, a term referring to their seven political divisions: Teton (the western group, speakers of Lakota); Sisseton, Wahpeton, Wahpekute, and Mdewakanton (the eastern group, speakers of Dakota); and Yankton and Yanktonai (the central, or Wiciyela, group, speakers of Dakota and Nakota). (*See also* Lakota and Nakota.) In the late seventeenth century, the Dakotas lived in Wisconsin and north central Minnesota, around Mille Lacs. By the nineteenth century they had migrated to the prairies and the eastern plains of Minnesota, Iowa, Nebraska, and eastern South Dakota.

Male and female shamans provided religious leadership. Depending on the tribe, their duties might include leading hunting and war parties; curing the sick; foretelling the future, including the weather; and interpreting visions and dreams. Sisse-

Dakota with calumet kneels inside a teepee in 1907. (Library of Congress)

tons and Wahpetons believed in Wakan Tanka, the Great Spirit and creator of the universe, as well as other gods and spirits. The secret Wahpeton Medicine Lodge Society performed the Medicine Dance several times a year. Other religious activities included vision quests and ritual purification in the sweat lodge. The Sissetons later adopted some Plains ceremonies, such as the Sun Dance.

All but the Wahpekutes were divided into seven bands, each usually led by a chief. For the same three bands, the *akitcita* was an elite warrior group that maintained discipline at camp and on the hunt. This police society was distinctive of Siouans and may have originated with them. The Seven Council Fires met approximately annually to socialize and discuss matters of national importance.

Mdewakantons wrapped their dead in skins or blankets and placed them on scaffolds. Remains were taken to tribal burial grounds after a few months or years and buried in mounds with tools and weapons. Sissetons treated their dead similarly but included tools, weapons, and utensils. Bodies were placed in scaffolds or trees, with their heads

facing south. Wahpetons buried their dead early on but changed to scaffolds, probably as a result of Sisseton influence. The Dakota bands may once have been clans. Favorite games, usually accompanied by gambling, included lacrosse and shinny (a variation of hockey). Descent was patrilineal.

Dakotas built small, occasionally palisaded villages near lakes and rice swamps when they lived in the Wisconsin-Minnesota area. At that time they lived in large, heavily timbered bark houses with pitched roofs. In the winter, some groups lived in small conical houses covered with skins. Both men and women helped build the houses. The Sisseton sometimes used teepees after their move to the prairies.

Siouan people in the Ohio Valley farmed corn, beans, and squash. People also ate turtles, fish, dogs, and large and small game and gathered wild rice. Buffalo, which roamed the area in small herds, was also an important food source. People burned grass around the range and forced the buffalo toward an ambush. The Sissetons, especially, turned more toward buffalo hunting with their westward migration. Bows and arrows were the main hunting weapons. The Sissetons carved pipestone (catlinite) ceremonial pipes and wove rushes into mats. The Wahpeton wove rushes into mats and also wove cedar and basswood fiber bags. All groups made pottery.

Depending on time and location, Dakota tribes traded various Woodlands, prairie, and Plains goods. Items included wild rice, pottery, and skins and other animal products. The Dakotas made fine painted rawhide trunks. They incised and painted parfleches, pipe pouches, robes, and other items. Women tended to make geometric designs, whereas men made more realistic forms. Clothing was embroidered and, later, beaded. The Sissetons made dugout canoes, and the Wahpetons made birchbark canoes. Most groups obtained horses beginning around 1760, but the eastern groups never had as many as did the western groups.

Most clothing was made from buckskin. In the Woodlands, the people wore breechclouts, dresses, leggings, and moccasins, with fur robes for extra warmth. On the Plains, they decorated their clothing with beads and quillwork in geometric and animal designs. The idea that the purpose of war was to bring glory to an individual rather than to acquire territory or destroy an enemy people was distinctive to the Siouan people and may have originated with them. Dakotas did not generally fight other Dakotas.

The *akitcita* were known particularly among the Mdewakantons.

The Siouan linguistic family may have originated along the lower Mississippi River or in eastern Texas. Siouan speakers moved to, or may in fact have originated in, the Ohio Valley, where they lived in large agricultural settlements. They may have been related to the Mound Builder culture of the ninth through twelfth centuries. They may also have originated in the upper Mississippi Valley or even the Atlantic seaboard. Siouan tribes living in the Southeast, between Florida and Virginia, around the late sixteenth and early seventeenth centuries, were destroyed either by attacks from Algonquin-speaking Indians or a combination of attacks from non-Indians and non-Indian diseases.

Dakota-Lakota-Nakota speakers ranged throughout more than 100 million acres of the upper Mississippi region, including Minnesota and parts of Wisconsin, Iowa, and the Dakotas, from the sixteenth to the early seventeenth century. Some of these people encountered French explorers around Mille Lacs, Minnesota, in the late seventeenth century, and Santees were directly involved in the great British–French political and economic struggle. Around that time, conflict with the Crees and Anishinabes, who were well armed with French rifles, plus the lure of great buffalo herds to feed their expanding population, induced bands to begin moving west into the Plains. The people acquired horses around the mideighteenth century. Dakotas were the last to leave, with most bands remaining in the prairies of western Minnesota and eastern South Dakota.

Dakotas ceded all land in Minnesota and Iowa in 1837 and 1851 (Mendota and Traverse des Sioux Treaties), except for a reservation along the Minnesota River. Santees were served by a lower agency, near Morton, and Sissetons and Wahpetons by an upper agency, near Granite Falls. At the mercy of dishonest agents and government officials, who cheated them out of food and money, and all but overrun by squatters, the Santees rebelled in 1862. Under the leadership of Ta-oya-te-duta (Little Crow), they killed hundreds of non-Indians.

Inasmuch as many Wahpetons and Sissetons remained neutral (or, as in the case of Chief Wabasha, betrayed their people), and support for the rebellion was not deep, it shortly collapsed. In reprisal, the government hanged thirty-eight Dakotas after President Abraham Lincoln pardoned over 250 others and confiscated all Dakota land and property in Minnesota. All previous treaties were

unilaterally abrogated. Little Crow himself was killed by bounty hunters in 1863. His scalp and skull were placed on exhibition in St. Paul.

Many Santees fled to Canada and to the West, to join relatives at Fort Peck and elsewhere. Many more died of starvation and illness during this period. Mdewakanton and Wahpekute survivors were rounded up and finally settled at Crow Creek, South Dakota, a place of poor soil and little game, where hundreds of removed Dakotas died in one year. Thus ended the long Santee occupation of the Eastern Woodlands/prairie region.

In 1866, Santees at Crow Creek were removed to the Santee Reservation, Nebraska, where living conditions were extremely poor. Most of the land was allotted in 1885. Missionaries, especially Congregationalists and Episcopalians, were influential well into the twentieth century. Most people lived by subsistence farming, hunting, fishing, and gathering.

Two reservations were established for Wahpetons and Sissetons around 1867: the Sisseton-Wahpeton Reservation, near Lake Traverse, South Dakota, and the Fort Totten Reservation, at Devil's Lake. By 1892, two-thirds of the Lake Traverse Reservation had been opened to non-Indians, with the remaining one-third, about 300,000 acres, allotted to individuals. In order not to starve, many sold their allotted land, so that more than half of the latter acreage was subsequently lost. For much of the early twentieth century, people eked out a living through subsistence farming combined with other subsistence activities as well as wages and trust fund payments.

Several hundred Dakotas left the Santee Reservation in 1869 to settle on the Big Sioux River near Flandreau, South Dakota, renouncing tribal membership at that time. Some federal aid was arranged by a Presbyterian minister, but by and large these people lived without even the meager benefits provided to most Indians. Some Flandreau Indians eventually drifted back to form communities in Minnesota.

See also Black Hills; Buffalo; Little Crow; Great Sioux Uprising.

Gros Ventres

"Gros Ventres" is French for "big belly," after a mistranslation of the sign language for their name. They were once known to non-Indians as Gros Ventres of the Prairie as opposed to the Gros Ventres of the Missouri (Hidatsas). The Blackfeet gave these people another of their common names, *Atsina*; their self-designation is *Haaninin*, "Lime People" or "White Clay People." Gros Ventre is an Algonquin language.

Two sacred pipes figured prominently in traditional Gros Ventre religion. Gros Ventres also observed other Plains religious customs such as vision quests, medicine bundles, and the Sun Dance. Twelve autonomous bands each had their own chief. Bands camped separately in the winter, coming together in the summer for communal buffalo hunt and celebrations, including the Sun Dance. Descent was patrilineal. People generally found marriage partners outside the parents' band. Girls were often married by age twelve, usually to men around twenty. Polygamy and divorce were common. The mother-in-law taboo was in force (out of respect, sons-in-law did not speak directly to them).

Age-graded male societies had their own costumes, dances, and paraphernalia. Men moved through the various rankings with their peers, each group purchasing the regalia of the next higher group, until the men at the top sold out and retired with a large amount of wealth. Healing, through medicines and ritual, was a job that one might attain by fasting and attaining special powers. Corpses were wrapped in robes and placed on a scaffold, in a cave, or on a high rock.

Buffalo were hunted by driving them into chutes; after about 1730, they were hunted on horseback. Women cut meat into strips and dried it or made pemmican. Fresh meat was roasted over the fire or boiled, using red-hot rocks in a water-filled hole. People also ate deer, elk, and puppies and gathered foods such as rhubarb, berries, and eggs. They did not eat fish.

On the Plains, groups of women made skin teepees with three-pole foundations. Women dressed skins with brains and liver. Men made bows of ash or cherry wood and also of horn. Horn bows were covered with rattlesnake skin. Gros Ventres participated in the regional trade complex, trading horses and animal products for agricultural items and, later, non-Indian items. Both dogs and horses pulled the travois. People made makeshift rafts of teepee covers and poles. Women made the clothing, usually of elk skin or deerskin. They wore dresses; men wore leggings, breechclouts, shirts, and moccasins. Both sexes wore buffalo skin caps and mittens in the winter.

At least 3,000 years ago the Arapahos, possibly united with the future Gros Ventres and other peoples, probably lived in the western Great Lakes region to the Red River Valley, where they grew corn and lived in permanent villages. Under pressure from the Ojibwas (Anishinabes), they migrated to the upper Missouri River region in the early eighteenth century. During the migration, perhaps around Devil's Lake, the Gros Ventres separated from the Arapahos. They acquired horses in the early to mideighteenth century. Shortly thereafter they became a Plains tribe and joined the Blackfeet Confederacy.

The people signed the 1851 Fort Laramie Treaty after spending a brief period of time with the Arapahos. Another treaty in 1855 led to further land cessions. In the early 1860s the Gros Ventres joined with their Crow enemies to fight their traditional friends, the Blackfeet, but were soundly defeated in 1867. Following a further decline caused mostly by disease, in 1888 survivors were placed on the Fort Belknap Reservation, which they shared with the Assiniboines, also former enemies.

The Gros Ventres filed a lawsuit in 1897 to gain compensation for lands seized under the 1855 treaty; in the twentieth century the tribe has received several land claims awards. Also around the turn of the century, members of the tribe sold under extreme duress a twenty-eight-square-mile strip of reservation land. Tuberculosis was a severe problem in the early twentieth century, affecting more than 90 percent of the tribal population.

See also Blackfeet Confederacy; Pipes, Sacred.

Hidatsa

"Hidatsa" is possibly taken from the name of a former village. Called Gros Ventres of the Missouri by French traders, they have also been known as the *Minitaris* (Mandan for "they crossed the water"). Most Hidatsas lived along the upper Missouri River in western North Dakota in the late eighteenth century. Hidatsa is a Siouan dialect.

The Corn Dance Feast of the Women was based on mythological concepts and offered as thanks for crops. Elderly women hung dried meat on poles and then performed a dance. Younger women fed them meat and received grains of corn to eat in return. The dried meat would be left on the poles

A portrait of Hidatsa Pehriska-Ruhpa in the costume of the Dog Band of the Hidatsa. Artwork by Karl Bodmer, 1833–1834. (National Archives and Records Administration)

until harvest time. The Hidatsas also learned the Sun Dance. There were a number of other religious societies. Hidatsas undertook vision quests from an early age.

The tribe contained several bands, including the Hidatsas proper: the Awatixas and the Awaxawis. Villages were ruled by a council, a chief, and a war chief. Descent was matrilineal, and the extended family was the primary economic unit. Land was held by groups of related families, which were in turn organized into larger groups, with formal leadership usually provided by older men. Within villages, each larger group was divided into two divisions; this organization played a key role in village leadership as well as games and other competition. The Hidatsas also recognized about seven clans.

Women controlled the gardens and were in charge of harvest distribution to their families. The White Buffalo Society, which featured dancing to

lure buffalo to the hunters, was open only to women. Age-graded men's societies had mainly military functions. Each group had its own dances, songs, and regalia, which were acquired by the youngest group and purchased en masse from the next higher group, the buyers displacing the sellers as the latter also "moved up."

Social rank was hereditary to some degree. "Joking relatives," whose fathers were in the same clan, teased or upbraided each other for deviating from normative conduct. This mechanism was very effective for maintaining social customs and proper behavior. Food, weapons, and personal items were placed on scaffolds along with corpses. Mourners cut their hair. When chiefs died, all lodge fires were extinguished.

From around 1700 on, the people lived in permanent villages on bluffs overlooking the upper Missouri River. Groups of people erected circular, dome-shaped earth lodges about forty feet in diameter. Each housed two to three families or up to about forty people. Cooking took place inside in the winter and outside in the summer. Cook kettles were suspended on poles over central fires. People also used smaller earth lodges in the winter, when they took refuge in forests. Skin teepees were used while traveling or hunting.

Women cooperated in growing corn, beans, squash, pumpkins, and sunflowers. They stored corn in earth caches, lined with logs and grass and covered with grass. Corn was boiled and eaten fresh or shelled and dried for the winter, when it was pounded and eaten as meal with other vegetables and meat. Squash was cut into strips and sun dried. Crops were harvested in the midsummer and especially in early fall. Old men grew a small tobacco crop. Tobacco was sacred and some ritual surrounded its cultivation, harvesting, and use. Only elderly men generally smoked, in pipes and for ceremonial purposes. Buffalo and other meat was acquired primarily through trade, although men did hunt buffalo and other animals. After the people acquired horses, they tracked the buffalo farther onto the plains, into present-day South Dakota and Montana.

Many material items, such as agricultural implements (bone hoes and rakes) and horn utensils and tools were made of buffalo and elk parts. Mortars, pestles, and digging sticks were made of wood. Women made twilled plaited baskets and pottery. Especially before they acquired horses, people used tumplines and chest straps for carrying burdens on their backs.

People felled and burned trees to enrich the soil for growing. Garden plots were left fallow after about three years of cultivation. Cache pits (for crop storage) were about eight feet deep, two or three feet wide at the top, and perhaps twice as wide at the bottom. Women placed ears of corn around the outside and shelled corn and squash in the center. They covered the pits with ashes, dirt, and grass. Entry was via a ladder.

Painted rawhide trunks or boxes, more typical of Woodland tribes, were about fifteen inches square and ten inches high. The people also painted parfleches and built seven-hole flageolets (flutes) from box elder wood with the pith removed. They also made music with rattles, rasps (notched wood), hand drums, or tambourines and by singing.

Village people traded agricultural products with nomads for meat and other animal products. Trade occupied an important position in Hidatsas' lives. Serviceable boats were made of buffalo hides stretched over circular willow frames. Hidatsas tended to rely more on dogs than horses to pull their travois. Women made clothing from skins and furs, particularly white weasel and ermine. Buffalo hide blankets were the main cold weather item. Traditional enemies included the Dakotas and Shoshones, whereas the Hidatsas were often allied with the Mandans.

Siouan people may have lived originally along the lower Mississippi River, slowly migrating north through Tennessee and Kentucky and into Ohio. Some then went east across the Appalachian Mountains, but most continued northwest. Originally one people, the Hidatsa-Crows were perhaps the first Siouan group to leave the Ohio country. They moved to northern Illinois, through western Minnesota, and into the Red River Valley.

For at least 400 years, beginning around the twelfth or thirteenth century, they grew gardens and hunted buffalo south of Lake Winnipeg. Finally, pressured by newly armed bands of Ojibwas and Crees, the group moved southwest to Devil's Lake in the midsixteenth century. They then moved again toward the upper Missouri River, where they continued to hunt and grow corn, encouraged by receiving seeds and acquiring new techniques from the Mandans.

In the late seventeenth century, the Crows struck out on their own, leaving the Hidatsas behind. At this time, the latter associated with other agricultural tribes such as the Mandans and Arikaras. Non-Indians also traded regularly at

Hidatsa villages, exchanging items of non-Native manufacture for furs. Early non-Indian explorers, such as Meriwether Lewis and William Clark, also lived among the Hidatsas. The people lost a significant percentage of their population in the late eighteenth century through warfare, primarily with the Dakotas, as well as from smallpox epidemics. By about 1800 they had been reduced to a few villages along the Knife River.

The smallpox epidemic of 1837 devastated the tribe; surviving Hidatsas and Mandans regrouped by 1845 into a single village called Like-a-Fishhook, located near Fort Berthold, North Dakota. They were joined there by the Arikaras in 1862. The Fort Berthold Reservation was created in 1871 for Hidatsas, Mandans, and Arikaras. Although the 1851 Fort Laramie Treaty recognized the tribes' claims to 12 million acres, the original reservation consisted of 8 million acres; by 1886 it had been reduced to about a million acres.

Like-a-Fishhook was an important regional commercial center until the 1880s, when most people left it to establish communities along the Missouri River. The Hidatsas lived on both sides of the river, in Lucky Mound, Shell Creek, and Independence. During the 1950s, against the tribes' vehement opposition, the United States built the Garrison Dam on the Missouri. The resulting Lake Sakakawea covered much of their land, farms, and homes. This event destroyed the tribes' economic base and severely damaged its social structure.

See also Agriculture; Trade.

Hunkpapa

See Lakota.

Hunkpatina

See Nakota.

Ioway

"Ioway" is from *ayuhwa*, "sleepy ones." Their self-designation is *Pahoja*, "dusty noses." Along with tribes such as Otoes, Missourias, and Winnebagos, they had elements of both Plains and Woodland cultures. In the seventeenth century, most Ioways lived in northern Iowa and southern Minnesota. Iowa-Otoe-Missouria is a member of the Chiwere division of the Siouan language.

The Ioways practiced a ceremony similar to the Grand Medicine Dance of the Woodland tribes. A candidate for admission to the secret Ojibwa medicine society, for example, was "shot" with a shell and then "revived" by members. The Ioways offered the first puff of tobacco smoke to the sky spirit. Hereditary clan and war chiefs held positions of authority. The people played lacrosse and the moccasin (guessing) game, games customarily played by Woodlands tribes. There was a dual tribal division. Patrilineal clans were divided into subclans.

Semipermanent villages consisted of earth lodges. When hunting and traveling, people used bark-covered pole-frame lodges as well as skin teepees.

The major crops were corn, beans, squash, melons, sunflowers, and pumpkins. Buffalo were taken, using the surround method, in two communal buffalo hunts a year. Men also hunted other animals such as deer, beaver, raccoon, otter, and bear. Women gathered plant foods such as nuts, berries, and roots. The Ioways also fished, using equipment including spears and possibly weirs and basketry traps. Men made a combination quiver and bow case. After the eighteenth century, women dressed skins with elk-horn scrapers. They also wove reed floor mats over a bark-cord foundation. Like Woodland tribes, Ioways made soft-twilled buffalo hair wallets and rawhide box containers or trunks.

During the early eighteenth century, Ioways sold Indian slaves, probably Pawnees, to French traders for resale to Gulf Coast plantation owners. Actively involved in the fur trade at that time, they also traded pipes to other tribes. Women made clothing of tanned animal skins. After their adoption of many Plains traits in the eighteenth century, the people gave highest war honors to those who led several successful raids. In descending order, other honors included killing an enemy, touching an enemy, and scalping. They also created rival military clubs.

According to tradition, the Ioways, Winnebagos, Missourias, and Otoes once lived together north of the Great Lakes. Migration toward their historic areas began in the sixteenth century. Moving south through Wisconsin, the Ioways crossed the Mississippi River in the late sixteenth and early seventeenth centuries and began building villages in northeastern Iowa, just south of Minnesota. Shortly thereafter, they continued west to the Des Moines

River area of northwestern Iowa and southwestern Minnesota. In the midseventeenth century, the Ioways, constantly on the move and under pressure from the Dakotas, moved west again into northern Nebraska. By the late seventeenth century they had crossed the Missouri eastward back into Iowa.

After they acquired horses in the early to mideighteenth century, they began to range farther west and take on more characteristics of Plains Indians. They were heavily engaged in the fur trade in the eighteenth and early nineteenth centuries, when some bands were living as far west as the Platte River. Around 1800 they were engaged in territorial wars with the Sauk, Fox, and Dakota tribes. They also suffered a major smallpox epidemic in 1803.

The tribe signed treaties with the United States in 1824, 1825, 1830, 1836, and 1837, eventually ceding all of their lands. In 1836, they were assigned a reservation along the Great Nemaha River (southeastern Nebraska and northeastern Kansas) that was subsequently reduced in size. In the 1870s, the tribe divided into two independent groups, the southern Ioways, in Oklahoma, and the northern Ioways, in Kansas and Nebraska. The former group preferred to live in the traditional way, on lands held in common, whereas the latter group accepted individual allotments of land. The southern Ioways were assigned a reservation in the Indian Territory in 1883, but it was opened to non-Indian settlement several years later.

See also Horse, Economic Impact; Slavery.

Itazipco (Sans Arcs)

See Lakota.

Kansa

See Kaw.

Kaw

The Kaws are also known as the Kansa (or Konza) tribe. Their self-designation is *Hutanga*, "by the edge of the shore," referring to a mythical residence on the Atlantic Ocean. The Kaws migrated from the Ohio Valley in the fifteenth century to the Kaw Valley in the sixteenth century. With the Osages, Omahsa,

Poncas, and Quapaws, the Kaws spoke a dialect of the Dhegiha branch of the Siouan language family.

Traditional religious belief held that spirits dwelt in all aspects of nature, such as celestial objects. The sun was a deity to which prayers were offered and donations made, as were the wind and a sacred salt spring in northern Kansas. Pubescent boys were taken by their fathers to a remote spot for at least three days, where they sought visions via fasting and self-deprivation.

Each village was ruled by a council-elected chief; a head chief ruled over all the villages. War chiefs led military operations. Sixteen patrilineal clans, each including several families, combined into seven larger organizational units. There were also two tribal divisions: Nata and Ictunga. Men were mostly concerned with war and hunting whereas women did most of the work around the village. Kaws placed an extremely high value on the chastity of women. Dog Soldiers served as camp police and administered public punishments as needed. After being painted and covered with bark, corpses were buried in a sitting position facing west.

Circular or oval lodges were framed in wood and covered with mats woven of reed, grass, or bark and then a layer of earth. They ranged up to sixty feet in diameter and housed five or six families. The people also used skin teepees on hunting trips. Buffalo, and other animals as well, were the most important food source. There were two large, communal buffalo hunts a year. Women grew corn, beans, squash, and sunflowers in valley bottomlands. There were generally two harvests: one in the midsummer and another in the early fall. Women also gathered prairie potatoes and other foods.

Farm implements included hoes, digging sticks, and rakes. Most items came from the buffalo, including utensils and the raw material for various woven items. The Kaws traded in buffalo skins and products. They also supplied the French with slaves in exchange for guns and other items. Dogs carried burdens before horses, which were acquired from the Apaches in 1724. Kaws dressed in typical Plains skin clothing. The men plucked or shaved all of their hair except for a single lock at the back. Weapons included bows, arrows, and buffalo hide shields. The people chose war chiefs as needed.

Perhaps at one time one people with other southern Siouans such as the Quapaws, Omahas, Poncas, and Osagse, the Kaws remained in the

Wabash Valley until driven out, possibly by the Iroquois, with the others in the early sixteenth century. They traveled down the Ohio River to the Mississippi and then north to near present-day St. Louis. Finding the lower Missouri Valley open, the Kaws moved north on that river to the Kaw Valley, where they stopped and built lodges. They lived peacefully, at least for a while, with their Pawnee and Apache neighbors.

Direct trade with the French out of New Orleans began at least as early as 1719. During the eighteenth and nineteenth centuries, the Kaws were frequently at war with both Indians and non-Indians. In 1724, at the request of French officials but also out of their own self-interest, over 1,000 Kaws traveled to Apache villages on a successful peace mission. The Kaws acquired their first horses at that time, and a brief peace was also established between the Apaches and the French, the latter hitherto actively engaged in the trade in Apache slaves. Shortly thereafter, however, French traders resumed their purchase of Apache slaves from, among others, the Kaws, the latter preferring good trade relations with the French to peace with the declining Apaches.

By the late eighteenth century, the well armed Kaw, along with other tribes such as the Osages, Pawnees, and Wichitas, represented the eastern boundary of the huge Comanche country. The Kaws ceded all of their Missouri land in 1825 in exchange for a 2-million-acre reservation in Kansas. That land in turn was ceded in 1846, and they were removed to a 265,000-acre reservation farther west, at Council Grove, on the Neosho River. The United States took those lands in 1873, and the remaining Kaws were removed to the Indian Territory. Their remaining lands were allotted in 1902, and the tribe was legally dissolved. A significant number of the full-bloods, such as Chief Al-le-go-wa-ho, had opposed allotment, a situation that exacerbated factionalism and the legal struggles that followed tribal dissolution. An example of the "progressive" faction was Congressman and later Vice President Charles Curtis, who was largely responsible for the Kaw Allotment Act of 1902 that stripped the Kaw people of their tribal lands.

The tribe reconstituted itself in 1959 under the auspices of the Department of the Interior. Tribal holdings at that time included 260 acres near the mouth of Beaver Creek. In the mid-1960s, the U.S. Army built the Kaw Reservoir, flooding most of these lands. The cemetery and council house were moved, the latter to a fifteen-acre tract that was subsequently enlarged by Congress to 135.5 acres.

See also Curtis, Charles; Horse, Economic Impact; Trade.

Kiowa

"Kiowa," "Principal People," is a derivation of *Ka'i gwu*, their self-designation. The Kiowas migrated in the seventeenth century from the Gallatin-Madison Valleys in southwestern Montana to the Black Hills. By the early nineteenth century, their territory included southeast Colorado, extreme northeast New Mexico, southwest Kansas, northwest Oklahoma, and extreme north Texas. Kiowa is considered a linguistic isolate that might be related to Tanoan, a Pueblo language, as well as Shoshonean.

Kiowas gained religious status through shield society membership and/or guardianship of sacred tribal items, such as the Ten Grandmother Bundles.

Portrait of Satank, also known as Sitting Bear, a Kiowa leader, ca. 1868–1874. (National Archives and Records Administration)

According to legend, the bundles originated with Sun Boy, the culture hero. With their associated ceremonies, they were a focus of Kiowa religious practice. Kiowas adopted the Sun Dance in the eighteenth century, although they did not incorporate elements of self-mutilation into the ceremony. Young men also fasted to produce guardian spirit visions.

There were traditionally between ten and twenty-seven autonomous bands, including the Kiowa Apaches, each with its own peace and war chiefs. Occasionally, especially later in their history, a tribal chief presided over all the bands. Beginning in the nineteenth century the Kiowas adopted a social system wherein rank was based especially on military exploits and also on wealth and religious power. Generosity was valued, and wealthy men regularly helped the less fortunate, but general wealth remained in the family through inheritance. Sons from wealthy families could begin their military training earlier and thus, through military success, gain even more wealth. There were numerous specialized men's and women's societies.

Bands lived apart in the winter but came together in the summer to celebrate the Sun Dance. Corpses were buried or left in a teepee on a hill. Former possessions were given away. Mourners cut their hair and gashed themselves, even occasionally cutting off fingers. A mourning family lived apart during the appropriate period of time.

Buffalo supplied most of the food, shelter, and clothing for Kiowas on the Plains. Buffalo hunts were highly organized and ritualized affairs. After the hunt, women cut the meat into strips to dry. Later, they mixed it with dried chokecherries and fat to make pemmican, which remained edible in skin bags for up to a year or more. Men also hunted other large and small game. They did not eat bear or, usually, fish. Women gathered a variety of wild potatoes and other vegetables, fruits, nuts, and berries.

Kiowas made pictographs on buffalo skins to record events of tribal history. They used the buffalo and other animals to provide the usual material items such as parfleches and other containers. Women made shallow coiled basketry gambling trays. They also built and owned skin teepees, and they dressed buffalo, elk, and deer hides to make robes, moccasins, leggings, shirts, breechclouts, skirts, and blouses.

During the eighteenth century, Kiowas traded extensively with the upper Missouri tribes (Mandans, Hidatsas, and Arikaras). They exchanged meat, buffalo hides, and salt with Pueblo Indians for cornmeal and dried fruit. During the nineteenth century they traded Comanche horses to the Osages and other tribes. Calendric skins and beadwork were two Kiowa artistic traditions.

The highest status for men was achieved through warfare. Counting coup and leading a successful raid or fight were the most prestigious military activities. The numerous military societies included the Principal Dogs (or Ten Bravest), a group of ten extremely brave and tested fighters. Satank (Sitting Bear) was the leader of the Principal Dogs during the last phase of Kiowa resistance. Kiowas beginning a raid sometimes appealed to a group of women for their prayers, feasting them upon their return. The tribe was allied with the Crows in the late seventeenth century and with the Comanches beginning around 1790.

The Kiowas may have originated in Arizona or in the mountains of western Montana. They began drifting southeast from western Montana in the late seventeenth century, settling near the Crows. In the early eighteenth century, the Kiowa Apaches became cut off from their fellow Apacheans, at which time (if not a generation before) they joined the Kiowas for protection. Although they maintained a separate language and identity, they functioned effectively as a Kiowa band.

Meanwhile, the Kiowas had acquired horses, probably through trade with upper Missouri tribes, and were living in the Black Hills as highly successful buffalo hunters, warriors, and horse riders. Individual Kiowas and Kiowa Apaches also lived in northern New Mexico, probably brought there originally by Comanches and others as prisoners or slaves. Later in the century, the Kiowas, still in the Black Hills, acted as trade intermediaries between Spanish (New Mexican) traders and the upper Missouri tribes.

The people suffered a smallpox epidemic in 1781, from which they gradually recovered. A large group of Kiowas and Kiowa Apaches migrated south during that period, to be followed by the rest around the turn of the century. At that time, the Kiowas were pushed south to the Arkansas River area by the Dakotas, Arapahos, and Cheyennes (southeastern Colorado), where they ran into the Comanche barrier. They were also drawn south by raiding opportunities provided by Spanish and Pueblo settlements in New Mexico and Mexico. In the early nineteenth century they ranged between New Mexico and the upper Missouri River area.

In 1814 they concluded a treaty with the Dakotas defining the boundary between the two groups. Making peace also with the Comanches, these two groups raided for horses, guns, and food as far south as Durango, Mexico. By the midnineteenth century, the Kiowas spent more time south of the Arkansas than north of it. In the 1830s they made peace with their longtime enemies, the Cheyennes, Osages, and Arapahos.

In the early 1860s, the Kiowas strongly resisted non-Native intruders, land thieves, and immigrants. In 1865 they agreed to a reservation south of the Arkansas River. In the 1867 Medicine Lodge Treaty, they ceded tribal lands and, in exchange for a shared reservation in the Indian Territory, agreed to hunt buffalo only south of the Arkansas and withdrew opposition to a railroad. After the U.S. massacre of Cheyennes called the Battle of the Washita (December 1868), Kiowas and others were ordered to Fort Cobb, Oklahoma. Kiowas, citing provisions in the Medicine Lodge Treaty that allowed then to continue to live and hunt south of the Arkansas, refused. During a peace meeting in 1869, the Kiowa negotiators, Satanta (White Bear) and Lone Wolf, were taken prisoner and placed under a death sentence unless the Kiowas surrendered, which they did.

Two thousand Kiowas and 2,500 Comanches were placed on a reservation at Fort Sill, Indian Territory (Oklahoma). The United States encouraged them to farm, but the Kiowas were not farmers. With starvation looming, the United States permitted them to hunt buffalo. In 1870 and 1871, the Kiowas went on a buffalo hunt and continued their old raiding practices to the south. Some argued for remaining free while others spoke for cooperating with the United States. In 1871, soldiers arrested Kiowa leaders Satanta, Satank, and Big Tree for murders committed during the raids. Satank was killed on the way to his trial in Texas. The other two were convicted and sentenced to life imprisonment. During a meeting in Washington the following year, Lone Wolf won their release as a condition for keeping the Kiowas peaceful.

In 1873, a party of Kiowas and Comanches raided in Mexico for horses. The following year, a group of Indians including Kiowas fought a losing battle against whites at Adobe Walls. By this time, most of the great buffalo herds, almost 4 million buffalo, had been killed by non-Indians. That summer, a large group of Kiowas and Comanches left Fort Sill for the last great buffalo range at Palo Duro Canyon, Texas, to live as traditional Indians once again. In the fall, U.S. soldiers hunted them down and killed 1,000 of their horses. Fleeing, scattered groups of Indians were hunted down in turn.

The last of these people surrendered in February 1875. They were kept in corrals. Satanta was returned to prison in Texas, and twenty-six others were exiled to Florida. Kicking Bird died mysteriously two days after the exiles he selected had departed, possibly poisoned by those who resented his friendship with the whites. Within a few years, the great leaders were all gone, and the power of the Kiowas was broken.

The late 1870s saw a major measles epidemic and the end of the Plains buffalo; more epidemics followed in 1895 and 1902. Many Kiowas took up the Ghost Dance in the late 1880s and early 1890s. In 1894, Kiowas offered to share their reservation with their old Apache enemies who were exiles in Florida; Geronimo and other Chiricahua Apaches lived out their lives there.

Almost 450,000 acres of the reservation were allotted to individuals in 1901, with the remaining more than 2 million acres then sold and opened for settlement to non-Natives. Kiowas were among the group of Indians who organized the Native American Church in 1918, having adopted ritual peyote use around 1885. Thanks to the legacy of Kicking Bird and others, Kiowas in the twentieth century have concentrated on education, sending their children to boarding schools (including Riverside, still active in the 1990s) and several nearby mission schools.

See also Buffalo; Horse, Economic Impact; Kicking Bird; *Lone Wolf v. Hitchcock;* Momaday, N. Scott; Native American Church of North America; Warfare, Intertribal.

Kiowa Apache

See Apache, Plains.

Lakota

"Lakota" is a name in a Siouan dialect spoken by the western or Teton (Titunwan, "prairie dwellers") group of the tribe commonly referred to as Sioux. The subdivisions of the western group include Oglalas ("they scatter their own"), Sicangus ("burned thighs," also known by the French name Brûlé),

Lakota camp at Pine Ridge, South Dakota, on November 28, 1890. Conflicts over the Ghost Dance, coupled with a government bent on repression and a military seeking to avenge General Custer, led to the infamous Wounded Knee Massacre. (National Archives and Records Administration)

Hunkpapas ("end village"), Minneconjous ("plant beside the stream"), Itazipcos ("no bows," also known by the French name Sans Arcs), Sihasapas ("black feet"), and O'ohenonpas ("two kettles").

The Lakotas refer to themselves as *Lakota* ("ally"), as *Lakotah Oyate* ("Lakota People"), or as *Ikce Wicasa* ("Natural" or "Free People"). The word "Sioux" is derived originally from an Ojibwa word *Nadowe-is-iw*, meaning "lesser adder" ("enemy" is the implication) that was corrupted by French voyageurs to *Nadousssioux* and then shortened to "Sioux." Today, many people use the term "Dakota" or, less commonly, "Lakota" to refer to all Sioux people.

All thirteen subdivisions of Dakota-Lakota-Nakota speakers (Sioux) were known as Oceti Sakowin, or Seven Council Fires, a term referring to their seven political divisions: Tetons (the western group, speakers of Lakota); Sissetons, Wahpetons, Wahpukutes, and Mdewakantons (the eastern group, speakers of Dakota); and Yanktons and Yanktonais (the central, or Wiciyela, group, speakers of Dakota and Nakota). (*See also* Dakota; Nakota.)

According to legend, White Buffalo Calf Pipe Woman brought the people seven ceremonies: the Sweat Lodge (*Inipi*), Making of Relatives (*Hunka*),

Vision Quest (*Hanbleceya*), Girls' Puberty Ritual (*Isnati alowanpi*), Throwing of the Ball (*Tapa wankayeyapi*), Keeping of the Soul (*Wakicagapi*), and the Sun Dance (*Wiwanyang wacipi*).

Given originally by a legendary personage, the Sacred Pipe is a symbol of the vitality of the nation and its relationship with the creative forces of the universe. Pipes, carried by members of a special society, were used in peace ceremonies and to "sanctify" decisions and agreements.

Shamans, or medicine people (men or women), were healers and curers as well as interpreters of visions. They also found lost objects, divined the future, and provided important leadership during war or hunts. They received their powers from especially powerful guardian spirits and had a particularly close relationship with all of the deities. They were especially familiar with all legends, symbols, rituals, ceremonies, and cosmology.

A guardian spirit, usually in the guise of an animal, appeared to people on a vision quest, which was a period of self-deprivation in a remote place, or perhaps in a dream. Spirits were associated with particular songs, prayers, and symbols that, properly used, could bring the individual luck, skills, and/or

protection from evil or danger. Women as well as men sought visions. Personal medicine bundles were made up of objects dictated by the guardian spirit during the vision quest.

Shamans also led the Sun Dance, the most important of Plains ceremonies after about the mideighteenth century, when the horse transformed Plains dwellers into full-time nomadic buffalo hunters. Among the Lakotas the Sun Dance brought together their most important beliefs about themselves and the universe. Wakan Tanka, or the Great Spirit, as the supreme creator of the universe, or the sacred hoop, was first among sixteen gods representing the forces of nature. The number four was particularly sacred to the Lakota, representing the four cardinal directions, the pantheon of gods (four groups of four), and the four stages of life. The highly symbolic, twelve-day-long Sun Dance brought benefits both to the participants and to the nation as a whole. Individually sponsored as the result of a vow taken the previous winter, the dance itself contained elements of dancing, feasting, praying, fasting, and self-torture.

Elected chiefs in the Woodlands gave way to leadership by warriors. The subdivisions became more autonomous and divided into bands and their basic units. These were known as *tiyospaye,* a group of fluid composition composed of relatives and led by a warrior chief. Each had its own recognized hunting area. Chiefs were older men who had distinguished themselves in hunting and battle and were noted for their wisdom, well-spokenness, and generosity. Each band also had a council of such men, who governed without any force to back them up except the respect engendered by their position and a consensus-style decision making.

In the later historical period, the Oglalas had a society composed of older men, who elected seven lifelong chiefs. In practice, authority was delegated to four highly respected "shirt wearers," who also served for life. There were also four *wakikun,* or camp police, who were temporary officials assisted by the members of the *akitcita.*

The seven Teton divisions met regularly, ideally annually in the summer, from at least the late eighteenth century to about 1850. At these times there was a Sun Dance, and people socialized and generally renewed acquaintances. A supreme council of four chiefs met to discuss national policies. Still, the nation was very decentralized, with no overall political or military coordination, and the supreme council's power was largely symbolic.

On the Plains, patrilineal clans gave way to bilaterally descended extended families. Generosity was highly valued, as were bravery, fortitude, wisdom, and fidelity. In the giveaway custom, people shared generously, especially with the less able or fortunate and during important times in their lives. Thus did people achieve prestige while actually reducing individual suffering and want. Social control was effected mostly by peer pressure and ridicule, although serious crimes were punished by revenge and/or adjudication by the council. Various voluntary societies included those for men (mostly war related); feast and dance societies (which included social groups of both sexes and groups for women only); dream cult societies (such as the Heyoka, or clown, society); and craft societies. Games included various guessing games, cup-and-ball, and competitions. Adult games were usually accompanied by gambling. Toys included conical tops and sleds. In general, storytelling was a favorite pastime.

Marriage was mainly a matter of parental agreement, often based on the couple's choice, and divorce was common and easy to obtain. Fidelity in marriage was an ideal, and a disloyal woman might have the end of her nose cut off. Children, especially boys, were always welcomed. Infants were allowed to nurse on demand. Children were treated with love and affection and were rarely struck. Boys and girls (except for brothers and sisters) generally played together until puberty. Games revolved around future adult activities.

During menstruation, girls and women were secluded for a few days, as men considered them dangerous. Girls having their first period were seen only by women and instructed on proper womanly behavior. Several weeks later, fathers who were able gave a ceremony, presided over by a shaman, for their daughters. The relative lavishness of the ceremony reflected on the whole family. Girls who had reached puberty were considered marriageable.

Boys did not have a specific puberty ceremony. Their vision quests, first successful buffalo hunt, first war party, and so forth might be marked by feasts and gifts and were considered rites of passage. Men generally married slightly older than did women, having first to prove their manhood and perhaps acquire enough goods to distribute.

As a matter of respect there was no verbal communication between a man and his mother-in-law. Aged people were generally accorded a great deal of respect. When people reached what they considered

to be the end of their functional lives, they might elect to remain behind the migrating band, although sometimes this action was taken involuntarily.

In the Woodlands, Lakotas lived in pole-frame lodges covered with woven mats or bark. Once on the Plains, they shifted to conical buffalo skin teepees in both the summer and the winter. The average teepee was made of about twelve buffalo skins, dressed and sewn together by women and placed over a pole framework. A teepee held one family. The interior fire was slightly off center. Two skin flaps at the top, attached to long poles, regulated the smoke hole. A small, elevated doorway was covered by a rawhide door.

Large and small game, wild rice, maple sugar, and fish constituted the bulk of the Woodland diet. On the Plains, people mostly ate buffalo. No part of the animal went to waste. The communal hunt, which was often but not always very successful, was accomplished by fire surrounds, shooting with bow and arrow, clubbing, or driving the animals off cliffs. Men also hunted individually or in family groups.

Lakotas also ate antelope, deer, and other large and small game as well as birds, eggs, turtles, tortoises, and fish. Young dog, considered a delicacy, was often eaten at feast times. Women gathered foods such as wild potatoes and turnips, berries, chokecherries, cactus, acorns, and wild onions. Some Teton women occasionally planted a little maize. There were also many medicinal herbs and plants.

Women tanned skins using elk antler scrapers with an attached stone (or iron) blade; the hair was either left on or soaked and scraped off. Rawhide was often used to attach items to each other, such as clubs and mauls. People made willow back rests for use in teepees. Lakotas traded at Arikara villages, north of the mouth of the Grand River, in present-day South Dakota, until about 1800, when they completely subjugated the Arikaras. They acted as intermediaries for the catlinite (red pipestone) trade between the Yanktons and most northern Plains tribes. Part of an extensive trade complex stretching throughout the West, the Tetons traded buffalo products to the eastern Dakotas for non-Indian goods the latter had obtained through the fur trade.

Art was integral to all Lakota materialism. Winter counts were pictographs on hides that recorded annual events. Clothing and bags were decorated with painting and porcupine quillwork, later beadwork. Bags, robes, and teepees were also painted. Designs were either realistic (generally painting, often made by men) or geometrical (generally quill-work and beadwork, often made by women). Musical instruments included flageolets, rattles, rasps, and drums.

Lakotas used birchbark and dugout canoes and snowshoes in the Woodlands. On the Plains, dogs served as the first beast of burden; the original migrations of the seventeenth and early eighteenth centuries were accomplished with the aid of dogs pulling travois. They still played a role in transportation even after the Lakotas acquired horses during the mideighteenth century, probably from the Arikaras. Tetons became extremely skilled riders, and horse travois carried teepees and other goods.

Men wore deerskin or elk skin breechclouts, leggings, and soft sole moccasins. They braided their hair, and they often wore face and body paint. Some wore their hair in a roach. In the winter, women wore long elk skin dresses, knee-length leggings, and moccasins. They braided and parted their hair in the middle. They also wore face paint and earrings. Both sexes wore buffalo hide robes. Some of this clothing was discarded in the summer.

Plains clothing often was fringed and decorated with colorful beadwork, especially in the later historical period and for ceremonial purposes. People made ornaments of bone, dentalium shell, elk and grizzly bear teeth, beads, copper and obsidian, and perhaps turquoise.

From about the midnineteenth century on, certain war leaders wore long eagle-feathered war bonnets for ceremonial purposes, although even before that period young men wore eagle feathers in their hair to signify achievements in battle. Chiefs and other people of authority also often wore special clothing and other paraphernalia at official occasions.

Tetons were feared fighters but did not fight each other. The *akitcita* was an elite warrior society that kept order in camp and especially on the hunt. Severe penalties were meted out to those who disrupted the summer hunt.

Warfare and raiding were the primary means to gain prestige. Military societies had their own songs, paraphernalia (such as feathered headgear), and ceremonies. War leaders, generally young men, had absolute authority but only over the war party while on a sortie. War and raiding parties were completely voluntary, motivated mainly by the desire to attain prestige. Men generally engaged in ritual purification in the sweat lodge before battle. Large battles involving hundreds of warriors occurred only in the late historical period.

As practiced in the early nineteenth century, counting coup meant achieving bravery in a hand-to-hand encounter with the enemy or some other feat of daring such as stealing a horse within a village. Killing and scalping generally merited less honor than did counting coup, although, in the nineteenth century, scalping was important to the Lakotas for ritualistic purposes.

Dakota-Lakota-Nakota speakers inhabited over 100 million acres, mostly prairie, in the upper Mississippi region, including Minnesota and parts of Wisconsin, Iowa, and the Dakotas, in the sixteenth to early seventeenth centuries. They largely kept clear of the British–French struggles. Conflict with the Crees and Anishinabes, who were well armed with French rifles, plus the lure of great buffalo herds to feed their expanding population, induced bands to begin moving west onto the Plains in the midseventeenth century. The Teton migration may have begun in the late seventeenth century, in the form of extended hunting parties into the James River basin.

Lakotas acquired horses around 1740; shortly after that time the first Teton bands crossed the Missouri River. They entered the Black Hills region around 1775, ultimately displacing the Cheyennes and Kiowas, and made it their spiritual center. As more and more Teton bands became Plains dwellers (almost all by 1830), they helped establish the classic Plains culture, which featured highly organized bands, almost complete dependence on the buffalo, and the central role of raiding and fighting. The Tetons became subdivided into their seven bands during that time.

In 1792, by defeating the Arikara Confederacy, the Lakotas were able to expand into the Missouri Valley and western South Dakota. In 1814 they concluded a treaty with the Kiowas, marking boundaries between the two peoples, including recognition that the Lakotas controlled the Black Hills (known to them as *Paha Sapa*). By that time, at the latest, the Lakotas were well armed with rifles.

Around 1822, the Lakotas joined with the Cheyennes to drive the Crows out of eastern Wyoming north of the Platte. During that period, the Tetons were engaged in supplying furs for non-Indians, although contacts were usually limited to trading posts, particularly Fort Laramie after 1834. In the 1840s, wagon trains passing through Teton territory began disrupting the buffalo herds, and the Indians began attacking the wagons. In the 1851 Fort Laramie Treaty, the Indians agreed to give the wagons free access in exchange for official recognition of Indian territory.

Conflict continued throughout the 1850s. In one series of incidents, in which a group of Sicangus ate and offered to pay for a stray Mormon cow, the U.S. Army attacked Sicangu villages and killed over a hundred people. In the early to mid-1860s, the Oglala Chief Red Cloud (Makhpiya-luta) led and ultimately won a brutal and protracted fight to force the United States to close the Bozeman Road through the Powder River country, the last great hunting ground of the Lakotas. The 1868 Fort Laramie Treaty was an admission by the United States of the Indian victory in the so-called Red Cloud's War. The government agreed to close the Bozeman Road and stay out of Teton territory. In exchange, the Indians agreed to stop their raids and remain on a Great Sioux Reservation. Both Red Cloud and the Sicangu leader Spotted Tail remained committed to peace, although they often spoke against easy accommodation to U.S. terms.

In 1874, gold was discovered in the Black Hills during an illegal military expedition. This event brought swarms of miners and other non-Indians in direct violation of the treaty. With Red Cloud and Spotted Tail settled on reservations, it fell to new leaders, young and free, such as the medicine man Sitting Bull (Tatanka Yotanka) and Crazy Horse (Tashunka Witco), to protect the sacred and legally recognized Teton lands against invasion. The United States rebuffed all Indian protests, and the Indians rejected U.S. efforts to purchase the Black Hills.

In 1876, Army units ceased protecting the Black Hills against non-Indian interlopers and went after Teton bands who refused to settle (which they were under no obligation to do under the terms of the Fort Laramie Treaty). In March, Tetons under Crazy Horse repelled an attack led by Colonel Joseph Reynolds. At Rosebud Creek the following June, Crazy Horse and his people routed a large force of soldiers as well as Crow and Shoshone scouts under the command of General George Crook. Later that month, Teton and Cheyenne Indians, led by Oglalas under Crazy Horse and Hunkpapas under Sitting Bull and Gall, wiped out the U.S. Seventh Cavalry under General George Custer at the Little Bighorn River.

Here the Indian victories came to an end. The Army defeated a large force of Cheyennes in July, and in September General Crook's soldiers captured a combined force of Oglalas and Minneconjous under American Horse. Two months later, Dull

Knife and his northern Cheyennes lost an important battle, and Crazy Horse himself was defeated in January 1877 by General Nelson Miles. Finally, Miles defeated Lame Deer's Minneconjou band in May 1877. Meanwhile, Sitting Bull, tired of the military harassment, had taken his people north to Canada. With his people tired and starving, Crazy Horse surrendered in April 1877. In August he was placed under arrest and was assassinated on September 5. He is still regarded as a symbol of the Lakotas' heroic resistance and as their greatest leader.

Defeated militarily and under threat of mass removal to the Indian Territory, Red Cloud, Spotted Tail, and the other Lakota and Santee chiefs signed the treaty ceding the Black Hills and the Powder River country. Shortly thereafter, the Army confiscated all Lakota weapons and horses and then drove the people into exile to reservations along the Missouri River.

After unilateral "cessions" in 1877, the Great Sioux Reservation consisted of 35,000 square miles of land, but a coalition of non-Indians, including railroad promoters and land speculators, maneuvered to break up this parcel. Meanwhile, Canada proved completely inhospitable to the exiled Lakotas, and gradually they began drifting back to the United States. Sitting Bull returned to surrender formally in 1881.

The giant landgrab came in 1888, when the United States proposed to carve the great reservation up into six smaller ones, leaving about 9 million acres open for non-Indian settlement. The government unsuccessfully offered the Lakotas 50 cents an acre for the land. They then offered $1.50 an acre and prepared to move unilaterally if the offer was rejected. The government needed three-quarters of the adult male votes for approval. Despite the opposition of Red Cloud, about half of the Oglalas signed the treaty. With Spotted Tail dead (assassinated in 1881), most of the Sicangus signed. Sitting Bull was the loudest voice opposed, but he was physically restrained from attending a meeting presided over by accommodationist chiefs, and the signatures were collected. The Great Sioux Reservation was no more.

Deprived of their livelihood, Lakotas quickly became dependent on inadequate and irregular U.S. rations. The United States also undermined traditional leadership and created their own subservient power structure. A crisis ensued in 1889 when the government cut off all rations. The general confusion provided fertile ground for the Ghost Dance.

Fearing that the Ghost Dance would encourage a new Indian militancy and solidarity, white officials banned the practice. In defiance, Oglala leaders in 1890 planned a large gathering on the Pine Ridge Reservation. To keep Sitting Bull, the last strong Lakota leader, from attending, the Indian police arrested him in December. During the arrest he was shot and killed.

The Minneconjou leader Big Foot once supported the dance, and for this reason General Miles ordered his arrest. Big Foot led his band of about 350 people to Pine Ridge to join Red Cloud and others who advocated peace with the United States. The Army intercepted him along the way and ordered him to stop at Wounded Knee Creek. The next morning (December 29) the soldiers moved in to disarm the Indians. When a rifle accidentally fired into the air, the soldiers opened fire with the four Hotchkiss cannons on the bluffs overlooking the camp, killing between 260 and 300 Indians, mostly women and children. The Wounded Knee Massacre marked the symbolic end of large-scale Native American armed resistance in the United States.

From the 1880s into the 1950s, most Lakota children were forced to attend mission or Bureau of Indian Affairs (BIA) schools. There the children were taught menial skills, and their culture was violently repressed. During the twentieth century, teepees slowly gave way to government-issued tents and then log cabins. Many Lakotas became Catholics or Episcopalians, although traditional customs and religious practices also continued, including the officially banned Sun Dance.

Bands were broken up, in part by the allotment process. As the United States worked to replace traditional leadership, education, religion, and other cultural and political structures, Lakota society underwent a profound demoralization. Most Lakotas were fed government-issued beef, which they had trouble eating after a steady diet of buffalo. In general, government rations were of low quality and quantity.

Lakotas were ordered to begin raising cattle. Despite some success in the early twentieth century, U.S. agents encouraged them in 1917 to sell their herds and lease their lands to non-Indians. When the lessees defaulted in 1921, the government urged Indians to sell their allotments for cash. By the 1930s, devoid of cattle and land, general destitution had set in.

Lakotas adopted the Indian Reorganization Act in 1934, after which reservations were governed by an elected tribal council, although the traditional system of chief-led *tiyospayes* (subbands) was still in place. A tribal court system handled minor problems; more serious offenses fell under the control of the U.S. court system.

> *See also* Black Elk; Black Hills; Buffalo; Counting Coup; Crazy Horse; Fort Laramie Treaty (1868); Horse; Battle of the Little Bighorn; Red Cloud; Sitting Bull; Spotted Tail; Standing Bear, Luther; Sun Dance; Warfare; Intertribal; Wounded Knee Massacre: Testimony of the Sioux; Occupation of Wounded Knee.

Mandan

Mandan is a Dakota word. Their self-designation was *Numakiki,* "People." For centuries before the coming of non-Indians, Mandans lived along the upper Missouri River and near the mouth of the Heart River, in central North Dakota. Mandan, related to but unintelligible with Hidatsa, is a Siouan language.

Medicine bundles (called Mother) symbolized fertility and crop productivity. They were owned by individual men who passed them down to their descendents or sold them. All bundles had a mythological component and were considered so sacred that the welfare of the entire village depended on their safety and proper care. They were associated with specific ceremonies, songs, and activities.

The four-day Okipa ceremony, similar to and a likely precursor of the Sun Dance, was a ritual enactment of their worldview. Its dual purpose was tribal renewal and bringing the buffalo. Prompted by their vision, individuals pledged to offer the summer ceremony, which included periods of fasting and ritual self-torture. The preparation period lasted several months at least. The ceremony contained masked performers representing animals, and required a special lodge fronting the village plaza. Creation legends were told during this time but in an unintelligible language; the uninformed could pay for a translation. Participants hoped to receive a vision afterward.

Other agricultural and hunting festivals included the women's Corn Dance and the men's Buffalo Dance. Clan chiefs were in charge of ceremonial activities, aspects of which were overseen by dual (summer and winter) divisions. The Mandans also had secret religious societies.

There were nine villages in the early nineteenth century. Villages had two hereditary chiefs, one from each division, roughly the same as a war and a peace chief. The people were also governed by a council of older males who made decisions by consensus. In the eighteenth century there were about five bands, each speaking slightly different dialects. There was also a police group called the Black Mouth Society.

Women grew the crops and processed animal skins into clothing. Households controlled the garden plots, but the land was actually held by lineages composed of several extended families. About thirteen matrilineal clans, composed of extended family lineages, were loosely ranked by status, depending on their ritual importance. The tribe was also divided into two groups, each producing a village leader, which competed against each other in games and contests.

Social class determined status to a far greater degree than did war deeds. High individual rank was affirmed through lavish giveaways and brave personal acts, but a high inherited status did not always need this sort of affirmation. Similarly, a commoner could not rise to be a chief despite the most extensive gift giving and remarkable personal exploits. Age-graded societies and ranked social clubs united nonrelatives. Organized around hunting, dancing, or curing, membership was purchased from existing members, who then purchased their way up to the next level. Only a few reached the highest level, which in any case was open by invitation only.

Grandparents largely brought up the children. Marriage, which consisted of an exchange of gifts between the two families, took place outside the division and clan. Corpses were buried in the earth, although the people adopted scaffold burial in later times. After a four-day mourning period, and when the bones had dried, people placed the skulls in circles around the village.

People lived where there was arable land and a supply of wood. Permanent villages, composed of between a dozen to as many as 150 earth lodges, were on high bluffs overlooking the river, often where tributary streams joining the Missouri were protected on two sides by the steep riverbanks. Heavily fortified with wooden stockades and barrier ditches, they were fairly impervious to attack.

Buffalo dance of the Mandan tribe of the American Plains. Artwork by Karl Bodmer, ca. 1833–1834. (National Archives and Records Administration)

The main lodges were semiexcavated. A heavy wooden frame was overlaid with willow branches and overlapping strips of sod and covered with an outer layer of earth. These lodges sheltered as many as fifty people but usually about twenty to forty extended family members. The lodges were about forty feet or more in diameter. A set of planks in front of the rawhide door further protected against cold winds. Animals occasionally stayed in the lodges as well.

Men hunted elk, deer, and smaller mammals. Buffalo were hunted in the summer communally as well as individually. Women grew maize, sunflowers, beans, squash, and tobacco. Burned trees provided additional soil fertilizer to the already rich bottomlands. Mandan maize was a variety adapted by the people to their short growing season. Women parched sunflower seeds and then ground them into meal used for thickening boiled dishes. Men also ate balls of this meal as travel food. Dogs were eaten in times of want, although puppy stew was considered a delicacy. Tobacco was considered sacred and grown only by the older men.

Material items included willow fish weirs, buffalo horn and bone utensils, pointed digging sticks, antler or willow rakes, hoes made from the shoulder blade of a buffalo or elk, and clay and stone pipes. Women made baskets (twilled plaited carrying and coiled gambling) and pottery. Mandan villages on the Knife River were a major center of aboriginal trade. Mandans were famous for their painted buffalo robes and their fine baskets.

Horses began pulling sleds or travois toboggans around 1745. Bull boats were made of hide stretched over a wooden framework. Women made the clothing, such as blankets, robes, and moccasins. In addition to buffalo, deer, and elk, they also used white weasel or ermine skin. The Mandans wore animal skin head wraps in the winter. Traditional allies were the Hidatsas and the Crows. Enemies included

Dakota tribes from the eighteenth century on. Weapons included bows and arrows, clubs, and buffalo hide shields.

The Mandans arrived in the Missouri River region from the southeast (Ohio Valley) between about the year 1000 and the thirteenth century, perhaps as early as the seventh century. They gradually moved upriver and away from other Siouan-speaking people.

The first smallpox epidemics arrived in the early sixteenth century. The acquisition of horses in the early to mideighteenth century allowed the Mandans to expand their buffalo hunting, but they did not give up their sedentary lifestyle. During the mideighteenth century, the Mandans became intermediaries between French and Indian traders, dealing in furs, horses, guns, crops, and buffalo products.

The Mandans suffered a gradual decline beginning in the late eighteenth century, owing primarily to smallpox and warfare with the Dakotas and other tribes. In the early nineteenth century, Mandans were friendly to non-Indians, even allowing visitors to study their religious ceremonies. In 1837, a major smallpox epidemic dropped the Mandan population by over 90 percent, to just about 125 people. In 1845, the surviving Mandans joined the Hidatsa people to establish Like-a-Fishhook village on the Missouri. They were joined by the Arikaras in 1862. Like-a-Fishhook was a significant commercial center at this time.

Although the 1851 Fort Laramie Treaty recognized Native holdings of more than 12 million acres, the 1870 Fort Berthold Reservation, created for the Three Affiliated Tribes (Mandans, Hidatsas, and Arikaras) consisted of only 8 million acres, which was reduced, mostly by allotment, to about 1 million during the 1880s. By that time, the people had abandoned Like-a-Fishhook to form communities along the Missouri River.

In 1910, the United States unilaterally removed a large section of land from the reservation. During the 1950s, the United States built the Garrison Dam on the Missouri, against the tribes' vehement opposition. The resulting Lake Sakakawea covered much of their land, farms, and homes. This event destroyed the tribe's economic base and severely damaged its social structure as well as its infrastructure.

See also Agriculture; Trade.

Mdewkanton

See Dakota.

Métis

See Ojibwa, Plains.

Minneconjou

See Lakota.

Missouria

"Missouria" or "Missouri" is an Algonquin term, probably meaning "People with Dugout Canoes." Their self-designation was *Niutachi,* or "People of the River Mouth." They were closely related to Poncas, Ioways, Otoes, and Winnebagos. All southern Siouans had elements of both Plains and Woodland cultures. Iowa-Otoe-Missouria was a member of the Chiwere division of the Siouan language family.

The people recognized Wakonda as a universal spirit, to which they could draw closer through fasting and vision seeking. There were secret curing and dance societies and a hereditary priesthood. As part of a Woodland ceremony related to the Ojibwa Midewiwin, or Medicine Lodge Society, members of a particular religious society "shot" a prospective member with a magic shell. The candidate was later restored by older shamans.

Political authority was vested in hereditary clan and war chiefs. Each of about ten patrilineal clans had specific social and religious responsibilities. Missourias lived in small farming villages of between forty and seventy semiexcavated earth lodges. From the eighteenth century on, the people used skin teepees on hunting trips.

Women grew corn, beans, and squash in river bottomlands. Men assisted with the crops but mainly hunted buffalo (twice a year from the eighteenth century on), deer, and small game. The people also gathered plant foods such as nuts, berries, and roots, and they ate fish. Crops were stored in underground bell-shaped caches. People speared fish or caught them in weirs and basketry traps.

Women dressed skins with elk antler scrapers. Other material items included buffalo wool bags;

reed floor mats woven over a bark-cord foundation; twined rectangular storage bags; rawhide trunks or containers, bent and sewn into place; and buffalo-hair wallets. During the late seventeenth and early eighteenth centuries, Missourias traded heavily with the French, supplying Indian slaves and wood-worked goods, among other items. On the Plains, Missourias dressed similarly to other local Indians. Men wore skin leggings and a breechclout; women wore a one-piece dress. Both wore moccasins. Cold weather gear included shirts, robes, and fur caps.

According to tradition, the Winnebagos, Ioways, Missourias, and Otoes once lived together north of the Great Lakes. In the sixteenth century, the groups began migrating south toward their historic areas. The Otoes and Missourias continued past the Ioways and especially the Winnebagos until they reached the junction of the Missouri and Grand Rivers around 1600. There the tribes had a falling-out ascribed to a love affair between the two chiefs' children.

After the split, the Missourias were under constant attack from such tribes as the Sauks and Foxes. They were also regularly struck by smallpox and other diseases. Jacques Marquette encountered the Missouria in 1673 by the Missouri and Grand Rivers. Trade with the French soon developed and continued for about a century.

In 1730, after the Sauks killed several hundred of their people, the Missourias moved across the Missouri River and settled near the Osages. After they acquired horses in the early to mideighteenth century, their lives became much more focused on hunting buffalo. The Missourias were nearly all killed in a 1798 Fox ambush on the Missouri River. Many rejoined the Otoes at that time. Some also went to live with the Osages and the Kaws. Several years later, the rest of the tribe, including the fewer than 100 survivors of the devastating 1829 smallpox epidemic, joined the Otoes.

Several difficult decades followed, during which the people continued to battle disease as well as Indians and non-Indians. By treaties in the 1830s and 1854, the Otoes and Missourias ceded all land and moved to a 162,000-acre reservation on the Kansas–Nebraska border, along the Big Blue River. Additional land cessions in occurred in 1876 and 1881.

Two factions developed in 1880 over the issue of acculturation. The Coyote, or traditional faction, moved to the Indian Territory (Oklahoma). The Quakers ceded their land for a 129,000-acre reserva-

tion near Red Rock in north central Oklahoma. Most Coyotes joined them by 1890, having lived for a time in a separate village on the Iowa Reservation. The reservation was allotted by 1907.

Many people lived by growing grains and potatoes. After oil was discovered on their land in 1912, the United States forced many Otoe-Missourias to give up their allotments. During the early to midtwentieth century, intermarriage truly created one tribe. Many Indians left the region during the 1930s. The tribe received a $1.5 million land claim settlement in 1955 and another payment in 1964. Both were divided on a per capita basis.

See also Horse, Economic Impact; Trade.

Nakota

"Nakota" is from a Siouan dialect spoken by the central group—whose divisions include Yankton ("end village") and Yanktonai ("little end village")—of the tribe commonly referred to as Sioux. The Yanktonais were divided into upper Yanktonais and lower Yanktonais (Hunkpatina), from which Assiniboine/ Stoney was derived. Nakota is a dialect of Dakota, a Siouan language. (*See also* Dakota; Lakota.)

Wakan Tanka was known as the great spirit and creator of the universe. There were other deities as well; Nakotas were a very prayerful people. Access to the supernatural world was provided in part by guardian spirits obtained through quests and in dreams. From the eighteenth century on, Nakotas performed the Sun Dance.

The Yanktons were organized into eight bands. The upper division Yanktonais consisted of six bands, and the Hunkpatinas had seven bands. The governing band council was composed of band chiefs and clan leaders. The Seven Council Fires met approximately annually to socialize and discuss matters of national importance. Nakota bands were composed of patrilineal clans.

Small villages were located near lakes and rice swamps when the people lived in the Wisconsin–Minnesota area. In the summer they lived in large houses of timbered frames with pitched roofs and bark-covered sides, whereas in the winter they lived in small mat-covered houses. From the mid- to late eighteenth centuries, the Yanktonais lived in earth lodges like the Arikaras, as well as in teepees

While still in the Great Lakes region, women grew corn, beans, and squash. People also gathered wild rice and ate turtles, fish, and dogs. Large and small game, especially buffalo, which roamed the area in small herds, was also an important food source. With the westward migration, buffalo became increasingly important, although men still hunted deer, elk, and antelope. Women also grew some corn, beans, and squash along river bottomlands and gathered fruits and berries.

As the Missouri River trade developed, the Yanktons controlled the catlinite, or red pipestone, quarry in southwest Minnesota, supplying its clay to most of the northern Plains groups. During the early nineteenth century, the Yanktonais traded along the Jones River, acting as intermediaries for British goods between the Sisseton and Wahpeton Dakotas and the Tetons farther west.

Nakotas plied the northern Woodlands in birchbark and dugout canoes. On the Plains, horses replaced dogs as travois carriers around 1760. They also used round bull boats when crossing water. Most clothing was made from buckskin. In the Woodlands, the people wore breechclouts, dresses, leggings, and moccasins, with fur robes for extra warmth. On the Plains, they decorated their clothing with beads and quillwork in geometric and animal designs.

Dakota-Lakota-Nakota speakers ranged throughout more than 100 million acres in the upper Mississippi region, including Minnesota and parts of Wisconsin, Iowa, and the Dakotas, in the sixteenth to early seventeenth centuries. At this time the Yanktons and Yanktonais were one tribe, the Assiniboines having separated from the Yankton/Yanktonais, probably by the midsixteenth century.

French explorers encountered Eastern group tribes around Mille Lacs, Minnesota, in the late seventeenth century. Shortly afterward, the latter probably became directly involved in the fur trade. But conflict with the Crees and Ojibwas, who were well armed with French rifles, in addition to the lure of great buffalo herds to feed their expanding population, induced bands to begin moving west onto the Plains.

The Yanktons and Yanktonais separated near Leech Lake in the late seventeenth century. The Yanktons had moved out of the northern Woodlands and onto the southern prairies (near the pipestone quarries of southwest Minnesota and then west of the Missouri in northwest Iowa) by the early eighteenth century. A hundred years later, the Yanktons ranged north and northwest into Minnesota and South Dakota.

Meanwhile, the Yanktonais left their homes in Mille Lacs by the early eighteenth century to follow Teton tribes west, making winter villages on the James River (South Dakota) at least as early as 1725. They acquired horses in the mid- to late eighteenth century. By the early nineteenth century they were hunting buffalo between the Red and the Missouri Rivers and north to Devil's Lake.

A general Yankton decline set in during the 1830s. Its causes were smallpox, the growing scarcity of game, and war, particularly with the Pawnees, Otoes, and Omahas. Yanktons ceded their Iowa lands (2.2 million acres) to the United States in 1830 and 1837 treaties and ceded over 11 million acres in 1858. They did retain a 430,000-acre reservation near Fort Randall, South Dakota. They also claimed the 650-acre Pipestone Reservation in Minnesota.

By 1860, the Yanktons had ceded all of their remaining lands. Most moved to the Yankton Reservation in South Dakota; others went to the Crow Creek and Lower Brûlé Reservations in South Dakota and to the Fort Totten (now Devil's Lake) Reservation in North Dakota. The Yanktonais ceded their remaining lands in 1865. They were removed to a number of reservations, including Standing Rock (South Dakota), Devil's Lake (North Dakota), Crow Creek (South Dakota), and Fort Peck (Montana). In 1866 they replaced the Santees at Crow Creek when the latter were moved to Nebraska. The Yanktons sold the Pipestone Reservation in 1929 for almost $330,000 plus guarantees of Indian access.

See also Pipes, Sacred; Trade.

Oglala
See Lakota.

Ojibwa, Plains

"Ojibwa," a term that means "puckered up," refers to a distinctive style of moccasin seam. The Plains Ojibwas were also known as "Bungi." Their self-designation is *Anishinabe*, "First People." People of Ojibwa/Cree/French ancestry are known as Métis, or Mitchif. The Plains Ojibwas are the westernmost branch of the widespread Ojibwa people, also

Native Americans of the Ojibwa tribe paddle a handmade canoe, ca. 1913. The lightweight construction and shallow draft of the canoe made it an ideal craft for navigating the lakes and small rivers of North America. (Library of Congress)

known variously as Ojibwe, Ojibway, Chippewa, and Anishinabe. (*See also* Anishinabe.) Ojibwa is an Algonquin language.

Gitchi Manito, the Great Spirit, and other spirits pervaded all nature. Children were encouraged to attract guardian spirit helpers by fasting in remote places. The people adopted the Sun Dance in the nineteenth century.

The Midewiwin, or Medicine Lodge Society, included both men and women. Candidates, who usually had to have experienced dream spirit visions, were initiated in a dance ceremony lasting several days. The main event included being "shot" by a member with a white shell that, taken from the medicine bag, carried supernatural power into the initiate. Upon being "revived" by older members, the initiate would spit out the shell. Members "shot" at one another as well to demonstrate their magical power. The meeting events were recorded on birch-bark scrolls with bone awls dipped in red paint. Members wore special medicine bags, usually of otter skin.

While still living around Lake Superior, the Ojibwas lived in small hunting bands of about ten people, each with its own hunting area. On the Plains, government conformed largely to the Plains model, including the presence of soldier societies. Patrilineal clans gave way to bilaterally descended extended families. Wealth and kin connections also played a part, however, and status ultimately rested on a combination of individual and family qualities.

The winter was generally a time for repairing tools and weapons and making crafts and clothing. Social control was effected mostly by peer pressure and ridicule, although serious crimes were punished by revenge and/or council action. Among the various social and religious groups were men's dance societies. Games included various guessing games, cup-and-ball, and competitions. Adult games were usually accompanied by gambling. Toys included conical tops and sleds. In general, storytelling was a favorite pastime.

Polygamy was practiced, although it was expensive. Each wife might or might not have a sep-

arate teepee. Marriage was mainly a matter of parental agreement, often based on the couple's choice, and divorce was common and easy to obtain. Children were treated permissively. Boys and girls (except for brothers and sisters) generally played together until puberty. Games revolved around future adult activities.

During menstruation, girls and women were secluded for a few days. Several weeks later, fathers who were able gave a ceremony, presided over by a shaman, for their daughters. Girls who had reached puberty were considered marriageable. Boys did not have a specific puberty ceremony. Their vision quests, first successful buffalo hunt, first war party, and other such events were considered rites of passage. As a matter of respect there was no direct verbal communication between a man and his mother-in-law. Aged people were generally accorded a great deal of respect.

On the Plains, the people lived in conical buffalo skin teepees in both the summer and the winter. The skins were dressed and sewn together by women and placed over a pole framework. A teepee held one family. Tanned buffalo robes served as beds and blankets and buffalo robes as carpeting. Women erected and took down the teepees, which could be moved quickly and easily. Tipis were often painted with special symbols and war exploits and also decorated with feathers, quills, or other items.

While in the vicinity of Lake Superior, rabbits and wild rice were staples. On the Plains, buffalo became the main food. Men also hunted other large and small game. Women gathered local roots, berries, and nuts. Sugar syrup came from box elder or maple trees.

Bone fishhooks were fastened onto sinew lines attached to willow poles. Many tools were also made of stone, until iron became available from non-Indian traders. On the Plains, most manufactured items came from the buffalo. Women tanned the skins using elk antler scrapers with an attached stone (or iron) blade; the hair was either left on or soaked and scraped off. Rawhide was often used to attach items to each other, such as two-piece clubs and mauls. Plains Ojibwas exchanged sugar syrup with tribes that had no such traditions. Among the products they imported were pipes.

Some people used a pointed tool (or occasionally pieces of wood) to cut into the inner layer of birchbark to produce line drawings; most such drawings related to the Midewiwin, or Medicine Lodge Society. Such pictograms also combined to illustrate song texts. People occasionally used incised drawings to decorate prayer sticks and weapons. Some groups also used a different style of decoration, consisting of zigzags and bands of triangles combined with symbolic shapes. On the Plains, the people decorated clothing and hides with paint, beads, and quillwork.

The Plains Ojibwas originated in the eastern Great Lakes region. The so-called Salteaux Anishinabe bands had their origin in the vicinity of Sault Sainte Marie. During the late sixteenth century, the people came into friendly, trade-based contact with Dakota bands west and south of Lake Superior. The first French traders and missionaries arrived in the early seventeenth century. Later in that century, the Anishinabes became heavily involved in the fur trade.

The Anishinabes also began to expand their territory during the seventeenth century, an event caused in part by pressure from the Iroquois as well as the overtrapping of food and pelts. One migration route was westward into the upper Mississippi basin, displacing Dakotas, Sauks, Foxes, and Kickapoos along the way—where these people became influenced by the Crees. Wild rice became an important part of their diet during this time. This group emerged from the forest about 1690.

Anishinabe groups that continued into the Red River area during the eighteenth century, such as the Pembina band of Chippewas, were armed with French guns and thus able to displace Hidatsa, Arikara, and Cheyenne bands. From this base there were four separate migrations to Montana.

During the eighteenth century, Red River Valley Ojibwas, Crees, and Métis traveled west in response to the continued overtrapping of small game. They acquired horses in the late eighteenth century and became buffalo hunters, fully adapting to life on the Plains by the early nineteenth century. After a failed effort to establish a Native state in Manitoba, Canada, in 1868, about 4,000 Chippewa-Crees from the Pembina band moved into present-day Montana. During the 1880s, the United States forced many Crees out of the United States into Canada. Many Chippewas and Métis were also forced out; their homes were burned behind them.

In 1885, the Chippewas, Crees, and Métis, now back in Canada, again attempted to create a Native state in Manitoba under the leadership of the Métis Louis Riel. When this effort failed, the Chippewa Chief Stone Child, or Rocky Boy, led a group of people back into Montana. In the late 1870s another

group of Chippewa-Crees followed the buffalo into Montana from the Turtle Mountain area in North Dakota. They generally moved between Montana and North Dakota Chippewa-Cree communities.

In 1882, the United States recognized the Turtle Mountain band's claim to twenty townships in north central North Dakota. Two years later, however, it decided that the reservation was too large. The Little Shell band, away hunting buffalo in Montana, was excluded from a government census, as were all Métis, who were declared to be Canadian. Despite the existence of these roughly 5,000 people, the North Dakota Reservation was reduced by about 10 million acres, or about 90 percent.

In the early twentieth century, following the negotiations over the Turtle Mountain Reservation, many of those people were forced to accept allotments on the public domain in North and South Dakota and eastern Montana. In 1904 the United States paid the Turtle Mountain band $1 million for their land cession, or about 10 cents an acre, but they refused to reenroll the Métis. By 1920, many of the exiled Turtle Mountain and Pembina Chippewas, having lost their allotments through tax foreclosure, returned to the North Dakota community. During the next several decades the situation became, if anything, worse, with the poverty-stricken people squeezed onto an inadequate land base. Many left the reservation during those years in search of work, never to return. The Turtle Mountain people were saved from termination in the 1950s only by the deplorable example of the Menominee termination fiasco.

See also Anishinabe Algonquin National Council; Canada, Indian Policies of; Erdrich, Louise; Horse, Economic Impact; Fur Trade; Riel, Louis.

Omaha

"Omaha" comes from *Umon'hon,* "those going against the current," a reference to the people's migration down the Ohio River and then north on the Mississippi. They were closely related to the Poncas. The Omahas inhabited the Ohio and Wabash Valleys in the fifteenth century. In the late eighteenth century they had migrated to northeast Nebraska. Omaha is a member of the Dhegiha division of the Siouan language family.

The people considered Wakonda to be the supreme life force, through which all things were related. People sought connection to the supernatural world through visions, which were usually requisite for membership in a secret society. Two pipes featuring mallard heads attached to the stems were the tribe's sacred objects. There were two religious organizations: the Shell and Pebble societies, which enacted a classic Woodlands ceremony of "shooting" a candidate with a shell and having him revived by the older members.

Each of the two tribal divisions, sky people and earth people, were represented by a head chief and a sacred pipe, symbolized by a sacred pole. A tribal council of seven chiefs acted as arbitrators of disputes, with the ability to pronounce sentences that included banishment and the death penalty, and as representatives to other tribes. They also chose the buffalo hunt leader and a group of camp and hunt police.

The two divisions were each composed of five patrilineal clans. There were numerous social and secret societies. Marriage took place outside the division. A man might have as many as three wives. Homicide was considered a crime against the wronged family; murderers were generally banished but allowed to return when the aggrieved family relented. The people played shinny (a variation of hockey) and other games, including guessing and gambling games. People gained status both in war and through their generosity.

In villages located along streams, men and women built earth lodges similar to those of (and probably adopted from) the Arikaras. In the nineteenth century, the Omahas built embankments around four feet high around their villages when they learned of an impending attack. Women also built skin teepees, which were mostly used during hunting trips—including the tribal spring and the late summer buffalo hunt—or in sheltered winter camps.

Women grew corn, beans, and squash. Dried produce was stored in underground caches. After planting their crops, people abandoned the villages to hunt buffalo. The spring and summer buffalo hunts provided meat as well as hides for robes, teepees, and many other material items. Men also hunted deer and small game.

Especially after the mideighteenth century, most material items were derived from buffalo parts. Women dressed the skins for and made all the clothing. They wore fringed tunics that left the arms free. Men wore leggings and breechclouts. Both sexes wore smoked skin moccasins as well as cold weather

gear such as robes, hats, and mittens. The Omahas made pottery until metal containers became available from non-Indian traders. They speared fish or shot them with tipless arrows. Nettle fibers were made into ropes. Bowls, mortars and pestles, and utensils were fashioned occasionally from horn but usually from wood.

The group of Siouan people known as the Omahas left the Wabash and Ohio River regions in the early sixteenth century. Shortly thereafter, they reached the Mississippi River and split into five separate tribes. The initial exodus was prompted in part by pressure from the Iroquois. Those who continued north along the Mississippi became known as Osages, Kaws, Poncas, and Omahas; the people who headed south were known as Quapaws.

The Omahas and Poncas, accompanied by the Skidi Pawnees, followed the Des Moines River to its headwaters and then traveled overland toward the Minnesota catlinite (pipestone) quarries, where they lived until the early to midseventeenth century. Then, driven west by the Dakotas, they moved to near Lake Andes, South Dakota. The two tribes traveled south along the Missouri to Nebraska, where they separated, probably along the Niobrara River, in the late seventeenth century. The Omahas settled on Bow Creek, in northeast Nebraska. After acquiring horses about 1730, the people began to assume many characteristics of typical Plains Indians.

During the eighteenth century, the Omahas visited French posts as far north as Lake Winnipeg. Well supplied with horses (from the Pawnees) and guns (from French traders), the Omahas were able to resist Dakota attacks, even acting as trade intermediaries with their enemies. In 1791–1792, the two warring groups signed a peace treaty. By the early nineteenth century, heavy involvement in the non-Native trade had altered Omaha material culture. A severe smallpox epidemic in 1802 reduced the population to around 300. In 1854 they were forced to cede their land and the following year to take up residence on a reservation. In 1865 the government created the Winnebago Reservation from the northern Omaha Reservation. In 1882 the reservation was allotted.

By 1900 most Omahas knew English, and many spoke it well. All lived in houses, and nearly all wore nontraditional clothing. Most children attended school, and a significant number of adults were succeeding as farmers or in other occupations in the nontraditional economy. Still, throughout the twentieth century, the Omahas fought further encroachments on the reservation and advocated tribal sovereignty.

See also Horse, Economic Impact; LaFlesche, Susan Picotte; LaFlesche, Susette Tibbles; Trade.

O'ohenonpa (Two Kettles)

See Lakota.

Osage

"Osage" is the French version of "Wazhazhe," the name for one of the Osages' three historical bands (Great Osage, Little Osage, and Arkansas Osage). Their self-designation was *Ni-U-Ko'n-Ska*, "Children of the Middle Waters." In the late seventeenth century, Osage Indians lived along the Osage River in western Missouri. Osage is a member of the Dhegiha division of the Siouan language family.

Wakonda was considered to be the supreme life force, with which people might connect through the acquisition of supernatural visions. Shamans provided religious leadership. There was a secret religious society to which both men and women belonged. Ceremonies revolved around planting, peace, and war. The oral history of the tribe was recounted in the Rite of Chiefs.

Two divisions, Sky/Peace (*Tzi-sho*) and Land/War (*Hunkah*) people, encompassed a total of twenty-one patrilineal clans, each of which held distinctive ceremonial and political functions. Each of the two divisions had a peace and a war chief. In certain cases, clan leadership was hereditary. There was also a council of older men to make laws and arbitrate disputes. From the nineteenth century on, the tribe was divided into three political divisions (bands): Great Osage, Little Osage, and Arkansas Osage.

The Osage located their villages along wooded river valleys. They built oval or rectangular pole-frame houses, thirty-six to 100 feet long, fifteen to twenty feet wide, and ten feet high, covered with woven rush mats or bark. People lived in teepees while on buffalo hunts. Women grew corn, squash, pumpkins, and beans, and they gathered foods such as persimmons, wild fruits and berries, and acorns and other nuts. In addition to buffalo, men hunted deer, wild fowl, beaver, and wildcat.

Osage orange was considered the best wood for bows. The people also built carved wooden cradleboards, cattail and rush mats, and buffalo hair bags. By around 1700, the Osages were supplying the French with Indian slaves (mainly Pawnees and then Apaches), in exchange for guns, among other items. In the later eighteenth and into the nineteenth centuries, Osages had a surplus of horses to trade, in part because they did not require as many as did the truly nomadic Plains buffalo hunters. Being short on winter pastureland, they generally traded most of their horses in the fall, restocking again in the spring.

Most clothing was made of deerskin. Women wore a shirt and a cape; men wore leggings and a breechclout. Men wore their hair in a roach. Men also wore body paint, jewelry, and scalp locks. Through acts of bravery, a warrior gained the privilege to tattoo himself and his wife and daughter(s).

A group of Siouan people, known as Omahas, split into five separate tribes after they reached the Mississippi in the late sixteenth century from the Wabash and Ohio River regions. The initial exodus was prompted in part by pressure from the Iroquois. Those who continued north along the Mississippi and Missouri Rivers became known as the Osages, Kaws, Poncas, and Omahas; the people who headed south were known as Quapaws.

The French explorers Jacques Marquette and Louis Joliet encountered the Osages in 1673, when the Indians were living in two villages along and nearby the south fork of the Osage River. Around 1700, the Osages acquired horses and began hunting buffalo. In the early eighteenth century, the Osages formed a strong alliance with the French, who gave them special trade treatment in exchange for pelts and slaves. Osage warriors helped the French fight Fox Indians, the English, and various other enemies. During the mideighteenth century, the Osages were well armed and powerful, able both to defend their farming villages and to hunt buffalo on the western Plains. The Spanish, a presence in the later eighteenth century, also tried to stay on good terms with the Osages, despite Osage raids on their outlying settlements.

In 1802, half of the Great Osage band, under Chief Big Track, moved to the Arkansas River in Oklahoma to be near a trading post opened by the friendly Chouteau family. Thereafter they were known to non-Indians as the Arkansas Osages. In 1808, however, following the large-scale arrival of non-Indians in the region, the Osages ceded most of Missouri and northern Arkansas to the United States. The Little and Great bands then moved to the Neosho River in Kansas.

By treaties in 1818 and 1825, the Osages ceded all of their lands except for a reservation in extreme southern Kansas, to which all bands had relocated by 1836. In the 1850s, in alliance with Plains tribes such as the Cheyennes, Kiowas, and Comanches, they fought and lost a battle to stem the tide of eastern bands, such as the Cherokees, Choctaws, and Chickasaws, who had been moved to their lands by the United States. During the Civil War, the Osages fought for both the United States and the Confederacy. Following that war, Osage men scouted for the United States in its wars against the Cheyennes in 1868–1869.

By 1870, the Osages had sold their Kansas lands and bought roughly 1 million acres of land from the Cherokees in northeastern Indian Territory (Oklahoma). There, they settled in five villages and retained a structure of twenty-four clans and two divisions. Many Osages embraced the Native American Church in the 1890s.

Large oil deposits were discovered on the reservation in 1897, and the Osages became very wealthy during the 1920s. In 1906, influenced by the prospect of oil wealth, the Osages created and implemented a voluntary allotment plan, dividing the tribal land individually, with the tribe retaining mineral rights. By the 1960s, however, half of the allotted parcels were lost. Although the oil wealth conferred many benefits, it also brought a large measure of corruption, through which people were cheated out of land and money, as well as greatly increased substance abuse. There was a general decline in revenues during the Depression and a resurgence during the Arab oil embargo of the early 1970s.

See also Horse, Economic Impact; Native American Church of North America; Osage, and Oil Rights.

Otoe

"Otoe" or "Oto" is from *Wahtohtata*, "lovers" or "lechers," referring to an alleged incident between the children of an Otoe and a Missouria chief. An earlier self-designation may have been *Che-wae-rae*. Otoes are closely related to Poncas, Ioways, Missourias, and Winnebagos. Otoe-Iowa-Missouria is a member of the Chiwere division of the Siouan language family.

Otoe delegation of five wearing claw necklaces and fur turbans. Photographed by John K. Hillers, January 1881. (National Archives and Records Administration)

Wakonda was the universal spirit to which people could draw closer by fasting and acquiring visions. There were a number of secret curing and dance (religious) societies as well as a hereditary priesthood. In a ceremony related to the Ojibwa (Woodland) Midewiwin, members of the Medicine Lodge Society "shot" an initiate with a magic shell. He was later "restored" by older shamans.

Political and military leadership was provided by hereditary clan and war chiefs. There were about ten patrilineal clans, each with particular responsibilities. The people played lacrosse, among other games. Corpses were placed in a tree or buried in the ground. A four-day mourning period followed funerals, during which a horse was occasionally killed to provide transportation to the spirit world.

Otoe villages were composed of from forty to seventy semiexcavated earth lodges. Each lodge was about forty feet in diameter. People caked clay or earth over a wooden framework interwoven with brush and grass. Skin teepees were used on hunting trips.

Women grew corn, beans, and squash in river bottomlands. Crops were stored in underground, bell-shaped caches. Women also gathered plant foods such as nuts, berries, and roots. Men assisted in farming but mainly hunted buffalo (twice a year), deer, and small game. Hunting, in fact, was a major occupation, and once on the Plains the people gradually shifted to rely more on buffalo than on crops. The people also ate fish.

On the Plains, the Otoes dressed similarly to other local Indians. Skins tanned by women formed the basis of most clothing. Men wore leggings and breechclouts, and women wore a one-piece dress. Both wore moccasins. Cold weather gear included shirts, robes, and fur caps. During the late seventeenth and early eighteenth centuries, the Otoes traded heavily with the French, supplying Indian slaves, among other commodities.

According to tradition, the Winnebagos, Ioways, Missourias, and Otoes once lived together north of the Great Lakes. In the sixteenth century, groups began migrating toward their historic areas. The Otoes and Missourias continued past the Ioways, especially the Winnebagos, until they reached the junction of the Missouri and Grand Rivers in the late sixteenth to early seventeenth century.

There the two tribes had a falling-out, traditionally ascribed to a love affair between the two chiefs' children. After the split, the Otoes moved west along the Missouri. Trade with the French began soon after Jacques Marquette and Louis Joliet encountered the Otoes in 1673 and continued for about a century. Between 1680 and 1717, the Otoes lived along the upper Iowa River and then the Blue Earth River. From 1717 to 1854 they lived along the Platte in various locations, including its mouth at the Missouri River. The people acquired horses early in that period and became much more involved in hunting buffalo.

The Otoe people absorbed the smallpox-decimated Missourias, with whom they had been fighting the Sauks and Foxes for years, in 1829. Several difficult decades followed, during which the people battled disease as well as Indians and non-Indians. By treaties in the 1830s and 1854, the Otoe-Missourias ceded all land and moved to 162,000-acre reservation on the Kansas-Nebraska border, along the Big Blue River. Two more land cessions occurred in 1876 and 1881.

Two factions developed in 1880 over the issue of acculturation. The Coyote, or traditional faction, moved to the Indian Territory (Oklahoma). The Quakers ceded their land for 129,000-acre reservation near Red Rock in north central Oklahoma. Most Coyotes joined them by 1890, having lived for a time in a separate village on the Iowa Reservation. The reservation was allotted by 1907.

Many individuals grew crops of grains and potatoes at that time. After oil was discovered on their land in 1912, the United States forced many Otoe-Missourias to give up their allotments. During the early to midtwentieth century, intermarriage truly created one tribe. Many Indians left the region during the 1930s. The tribe received a $1.5 million land claim settlement in 1955 and another payment in 1964. Both were divided on a per-capita basis.

See also Agriculture; Horse, Economic Impact.

Pawnee

"Pawnee" comes from the Caddoan *pariki* ("horn"), referring to the distinctive male hairstyle, or from *parisu* ("hunter"). Their self-designation was *Chahik-sichahiks*, "Men of Men." By about 1700, if not sooner, the Pawnees had divided into four independent subtribes: the Panimahas (Skidis), the Kitkehakis (Republicans), the Chauis (Grands), and the Pita-hauerats (Tappages). All but the Skidis spoke a similar dialect and were sometimes known as the southern Pawnees. The Skidis were also known as Loups (French), Lobos (Spanish), and Wolves (English). The Pawnees were closely related to the Wichitas and the Arikaras, and they maintained attributes characteristic of southwestern and Mesoamerican cultures. Panian (Skidi Pawnee, southern Pawnee, and Arikara) is a Caddoan language.

Tirawa, the sun, was the great spirit or creator and ruler of lesser deities. Among the Skidis, the morning and evening stars represented the masculine and feminine elements respectively. Much of the rich ceremonial life revolved around the heavenly bodies as well as planting, cultivating, and harvesting corn and hunting buffalo.

Hereditary priests were a large and powerful class of people. They conducted the rituals, knew sacred songs and rituals, and were associated with the sacred bundles. Shamans obtained powers from supernatural beings. They performed a large ceremony in the late summer or early fall at which they impressed people with feats such as handling live coals and plunging their hands in boiling water. Sacred bundles, connected with various rituals and associated with specific villages, dominated Pawnee life. There were also many secret societies, each with its own paraphernalia and rituals. Sacred animal lodges were associated with the southern people.

The chieftaincy was inherited through the female line. Villages were political units, each of which had chiefs, priests, bundles, and a council. Councils made all final civil and military decisions. They were established at the different levels of societal organization (village, tribe, confederacy). Each successive level of council was composed of members of the preceding level. All but two of the Skidi villages were joined in a political and religious confederation before they were forced to consolidate into one village following the smallpox epidemic of 1780–1781.

A dual division, winter and summer people, came into play during games and ceremonies. Most

Pawnee lodges at Loup, Nebraska, ca. 1873. The Pawnee were members of the Caddoan family and the oldest of the Great Plains tribes. The Pawnee tended to ally with European powers during conflicts with Native Americans and became some of the first western Indians to serve as U.S. Army scouts. (National Archives and Records Administration)

people married within the village. Corpses were wrapped in matting and buried in a sitting position, usually on high ground away from the village. People owned the right to perform dances and ceremonies. A society of single and elderly women affected shabby dress and tortured prisoners of war. There were various men's societies as well, generally revolving around military and religious themes.

By 1500, some Pawnees were living in permanent villages of between five and fifteen earth lodges. The lodges were round, semiexcavated, and about forty to sixty feet in diameter. They featured a pole framework interwoven with brush and grass, covered with a thick layer of soil and clay. By the early nineteenth century, most Pawnees used temporary semicircular summertime tents that differed from standard teepees. After driving small, arched poles into the ground along the circumference, people placed four larger posts vertically across the front. They also used standard skin teepees on buffalo hunting trips.

Unlike their neighbors who lived at similar longitudes, Pawnee women grew corn, beans, pumpkins, and sunflowers in small gardens. The people also hunted buffalo in the early summer and winter. They preferred two or three small drives to one massive slaughter. Meat was quickly butchered and dried. Men also hunted antelope, elk, deer, and small game, including fowl and birds. Women gathered roots, berries, plums, grapes, chokecherries, and nuts.

Before the seventeenth century, the Skidis traded with the Omahas and other related Siouan tribes. In the early to mideighteenth century, they exchanged Apache slaves, buffalo robes, and animal pelts with the New Orleans French for guns, tools, and other items. By later in the century they were trading guns for Comanche horses, which they traded in turn to the Omahas, Poncas, and other tribes.

Pawnee art included basketry and incised pottery. They occasionally smoked their fine tanned

hides. Teepees, robes, and shields were painted with heraldic designs. Women made most clothing of antelope or elk rather than buffalo hide. Men wore breechclouts and moccasins, plus leggings and a robe in the cold or on special occasions. Women wore moccasins, a skirt and cape, and leggings and a robe in the winter. Both sexes painted their faces.

Pawnee tradition has the people originating in the Southwest, but they may have their origin in the Southeast, perhaps in the Gulf region of southern Texas, and may have been associated very early on with Iroquoian people. Caddoan people occupied the Plains, from Texas to the Arkansas River region of Oklahoma and Kansas, inconsistently for perhaps several thousand years. Caddoans had major ceremonial centers by 500, including large temple mounds.

Upon leaving east Texas (thirteenth century), the Skidi Pawnees separated from the other bands and traveled east across the Mississippi, following the trail of the Iroquois to the northeast and settling in the Ohio Valley. In the sixteenth century, pressured by the initial stages of Iroquois expansion, the Skidis headed down the Ohio River. They were joined along the way by the Omahas. Together, the two people traveled to the Des Moines River, where the Skidis left the Omahas, continuing west to join their cousins and settling on the Loup fork of the Platte River.

Despite a separation of several hundred years, the Skidis reintegrated smoothly among the other Pawnee groups and soon became the largest and most powerful Pawnee tribe. They encountered the Spanish during the sixteenth century. Residents of western Pawnee villages were victims of Apache raiders from the midseventeenth century into the eighteenth century. The men were killed, and the women and children were sold as slaves. Thus occurred a gradual abandonment of Pawnee villages in western Nebraska and northeastern Colorado. The Illinois and other tribes also raided them for slaves in the eighteenth century.

Pawnees acquired a few horses around 1700, and within a generation they became great raiders and buffalo hunters, slowly relying less on crops and more on the buffalo for their food. Direct contact with French traders began in the early eighteenth century and expanded rapidly. By the 1750s, the French switched from buying Pawnees to buying Apaches, which the Pawnee, among other tribes,

gladly provided. The guns they received in trade helped protect them against Apache attacks against them, which soon ended.

From about 1770 to 1800, the Skidi Pawnees, reduced from eight villages to only one, lived with the Taovayas band of Wichita Indians on the Red River in northeastern Texas. Pawnees first met Anglo-Americans, including Meriwether Lewis, William Clark, and Zebulon Pike, in the early nineteenth century. After the Louisiana Purchase, more and more Americans entered Pawnee land. Most generally received a friendly and peaceful welcome.

By the terms of the 1805 Treaty of Table Rock, all Pawnees were relocated to a reservation in Genoa, Nebraska. During the 1830s and 1840s, they often fought and raided in the vicinity of the Arkansas River in southeastern Colorado and southwestern Kansas. Many also served as scouts for the U.S. Army during that period and later. Presbyterian missionaries arrived in 1834. Three years later, the Pawnees suffered a major smallpox epidemic.

By 1850, cholera and warfare with the Dakota tribes had greatly reduced the Pawnee population. They held their last tribal hunt in 1873. Pressured in 1876 to cede their reservation, the tribe moved to a new one, of over 200,000 acres, in north central Indian Territory (Oklahoma). Part of this reservation was allotted in 1892, with more than half then opened for non-Indian settlement. In 1906, the tribal population had declined 94 percent, to about 600 from about 10,000 just a century before. In 1966, the tribe won a land claims award of over $7 million, and in the 1970s they forced the return of tribal lands given by the United States to the city of Pawnee.

See also Agriculture; Horse, Economic Impact; Slavery.

Peigan

See Blackfeet.

Ponca

"Ponca" is a word possibly meaning "sacred head." With Kaw, Omaha, Osage, and Quapaw, Ponca is part of the Dhegiha division of the Siouan language family.

Wakonda was the Great Spirit or universal creator. All things had supernatural power, which could be accessed through guardian spirits obtained in vision quests. The original tribal Sacred Pipe was carved of catlinite when the Poncas lived in Minnesota. It was used in the Pipe Dance and on other occasions, as were its later replacements. Other important events included the Medicine Lodge ceremony, Sun Dance, and War Dance. The Ponca Sun Dance included self-torture.

Hereditary chiefs governed the clans. On the Plains, buffalo police kept order during the hunt. Two divisions, Chighu and Wazhazha, were each subdivided into four patrilineal clans. The Poncas built permanent villages on bluffs over rivers and fortified them with log and earth stockades. They lived in east-facing earth or hide-covered lodges.

There was also a ceremonial earth lodge. Skin teepees were used on buffalo hunts. Women grew corn, beans, squash, pumpkins, and tobacco in gardens located on river bottomlands. There were two annual communal buffalo hunts. Before the people acquired horses, buffalo were often stampeded over cliffs. Men also hunted other large and small game. The people ate fish as well as a variety of wild foods.

Notable art items included carved wooden goods, blue clay pottery, woven mats and baskets, and work in quills and beads in floral and geometric designs.

Women tanned the skins and made the clothing. They wore a one-piece dress and moccasins. Men wore leggings and breechclouts, as well as moccasins. Cold weather gear included shirts, mittens,

Ponca skinning a buffalo in the early 1900s. (Library of Congress)

robes, and caps. On the Plains men wore their hair long, a custom they probably adopted from the Dakotas. Weapons included the bow and arrow, buffalo hide shield, and wooden war club. On the Plains, the Poncas acquired the institution of rival military clubs, probably from the Tetons.

Dhegiha speakers probably originated in the Southeast and entered the Plains from the Ohio Valley. After arriving at the Mississippi in the midsixteenth century, the Poncas traveled upriver with the Kaws, Omahas, and Osages. Continuing north with the Omahas into Iowa and Minnesota, the groups settled on the Big Sioux River near the pipestone quarries. Pressure from the Dakotas forced them to the Lake Andres area of South Dakota, where they separated from the Omahas in the early to midseventeenth century. From there they traveled west to the Black Hills and then east again, rejoining the Omahas and moving south along the Missouri River to Nebraska. They settled on the mouth of the Niobrara River around 1763. The Omahas left them soon after to settle on Bow Creek.

Epidemics had reduced the Ponca population by over 90 percent by the time they encountered the Meriwether Lewis and William Clark expedition in 1804. Treaties with the United States, beginning in 1817, cost them over 2 million acres of land. In 1858, the people accepted a reservation of about 100,000 acres and promises of protection against Lakota tribes. However, ten years later the Lakotas successfully claimed most of this land in the 1868 Fort Laramie Treaty. Lakota attacks were worse then ever, since they now controlled the disputed land by treaty. In contravention of the treaties and in the face of active resistance of the chiefs, the United States forced the Poncas to remove to the Indian Territory (Oklahoma). There the Indians received a reservation of just over 100,000 acres near the Arkansas and Salt Fork Rivers. Within a year, about a quarter of the tribe died in those new lands from hunger and disease.

In 1877, Chief Standing Bear and others led their people on a 500-mile walk back to the Niobrara River to bury their dead. They were arrested and detained, but a precedent-setting trial established their rights both to legal standing and to their Nebraska land, to which they soon returned. Fearing for the very survival of the reservation system, however, not to mention the corrupt system of supplying reservation Indians with substandard food and materials, the United States refused permission for the rest of the Poncas to return to Nebraska.

From then on, the Poncas living in Nebraska were known as northern Poncas, and the southern Poncas remained in Oklahoma.

The Oklahoma land was allotted in 1908. Most people later sold their allotments or leased them to non-Indians. Among the southern Poncas, strong antiallotment sentiment led to factionalism within the tribe. Two Poncas were among those who established the Native American Church in the 1910s; the church's first president was a Ponca. The northern Poncas were formally "terminated" in the 1950s. By the mid-1960s, over 400 Poncas had lost all of their remaining 834 acres of land. The Ponca Clyde Warrior and the Paiut, Mel Thom formed the National Indian Youth Council, a group dedicated to advancing Indian rights, in 1961.

See also Native American Church of North America; Pipes, Sacred; *Standing Bear v. Crook;* Sun Dance; Warrior, Clyde.

Quapaw

"Quapaw" comes from *Ugakhpa,* "Downstream People," referring to their migration south along the Mississippi. The Quapaws were also known as Arkansas Indians. Quapaw is a member of the Dhegiha division of the Siouan language family.

Wakonda was the great universal spirit who encompassed any number of other spirits or deities. Pipes featured prominently in their ceremonies, and the Green Corn Dance celebrated the beginning of the harvest. There were also numerous other agriculture-related ceremonies. A hereditary chief and a council of elders governed each village. Beginning in the eighteenth century, the people created an overall tribal chief. Two divisions were subdivided into twenty-two patriarchal clans. People were buried with tools, weapons, and other items, both in and above the ground. Some villages were protected with palisades. Women built rectangular houses with domed roofs covered with cypress bark, grass, woven mats, and hides. Several families lived in each house.

Women grew three crops of corn a year, plus beans, squash, and tobacco. They also gathered foods, including persimmons, walnuts, berries, and plums. Men hunted buffalo, fowl, and other large and small game. The people also ate fish, which they captured in weirs. The people carved stone pipes, made pottery, wove mats, and stored corn in gourds

or cane baskets. Quapaws traded pottery and other items primarily to the Chickasaws, the Tunicas, and, later, the French. Painted and incised pottery was a Quapaw specialty. Before the onset of Plains culture, Quapaws made walnut and cypress dugout canoes. Prior to the eighteenth century, men generally went naked, pierced their nose and ears, and wore their hair short. On the Plains, men and women adopted the typical dress, including breechclouts, leggings, shirts, dresses, and robes.

Quapaw ancestors may have been the Indian Knoll people of Kentucky and the vicinity, of about the year 500, who lived along rivers and ate mainly shellfish. In the sixteenth century, with the Omahas and other Siouan groups, the Quapaws migrated through the Ohio Valley to the Mississippi River. When the others continued north along the Mississippi, the Quapaws struck out toward the south.

Shortly after the people met Jacques Marquette and Louis Joliet in 1673, they were decimated by smallpox and ongoing warfare. They acquired horses in the early eighteenth century and adopted much of the Plains buffalo culture. Although in general the Quapaws avoided taking sides in the regional European colonial struggles, they fought the Chickasaws in the eighteenth century as French allies as well as to avenge raids made against them.

In 1818 the Quapaws ceded their claims to southern Arkansas, southern Oklahoma, and northern Louisiana. They did reserve about 1 million acres of land in Arkansas but were forced to give that up by 1824. Landless now, they went to live with the Caddos south of the Red River, but, following several crop failures as a result of floods, they drifted back to Arkansas. The Quapaws were forced to relocate to a reservation in the Indian Territory (Oklahoma and Kansas) in 1833. In 1867 they lost their Kansas lands when that territory became a state. The tribe voted in 1893 to liquidate the reservation by allotting 240 acres each to 230 tribal members. About this time, a variant of the Peyote religion was introduced to the people.

Rich mineral deposits (zinc and lead) were found on Quapaw land in 1905. For a few years non-Indians defrauded the Quapaws out of land and money. After the government finally stepped in and exercised its trust responsibility, considerable monetary benefits began to accrue, despite the fact that royalties were paid to the federal government, not to the tribe. Many individuals who managed to share in the wealth spent most or all of their money in the

1920s. The tribe received a land claims payment in the early 1960s of roughly $1 million.

See also Agriculture; Horse, Economic Impact.

Santee
See Dakota.

Saulteaux
See Ojibwa, Plains.

Sicangu (Brulé)
See Lakota.

Sihasapa (Blackfeet Teton)
See Lakota.

Sioux
See Dakota; Lakota; Nakota.

Sisseton
See Dakota.

Stoney
See Assiniboine.

Teton
See Lakota.

Tonkawa
"Tonkawa" is a Waco word possibly meaning "they all stay together." Their self-designation was *Titska Watitch,* possibly meaning "Most Human People." Tonkawan is considered a language isolate but

may relate to the Hokan-Coahuiltecan group of languages.

The Tonkawas recognized numerous deities. They may have engaged in cannibalism, possibly for religious reasons. Psychotropic plants also played a part in their religious practice. There were at least twenty autonomous bands with loose, decentralized governing structures. The Tonkawas were excellent runners. For most of their existence they were nomadic hunters. On the Plains, the people lived in skin teepees.

Men hunted large and small game, especially buffalo and deer. Women gathered roots, seeds, nuts, prickly pear, and other wild foods. The people also ate fish, shellfish, and rattlesnake meat but neither wolf nor coyote. Like all Plains tribes, most of their material goods came from the buffalo and other animals. Tonkawas traded buffalo-derived materials for feathers and other items. They were also well-known horse traders. Pueblo groups were among their trade partners. They imported copper from the north. Painting—of shields, teepees, and their own bodies—was a major part of Tonkawa art.

Women made all clothing from animal skins. They wore short wraparound skirts and either let their hair hang long or made one braid. Men wore long breechclouts and long, braided hair. Men also plucked their beards and eyebrows. Moccasins or fiber sandals were rarely worn. Both sexes wore buffalo robes, and both tattooed and painted their bodies and wore many personal ornaments.

Tonkawa men had a reputation as fierce raiders, with many enemies, especially the Apaches and Comanches. Their weapons included the bow and arrow, hide vests, feathered helmets, and hide shields. They were considered excellent shots. They painted for war in red, yellow, green, and black. Warriors may have cut their hair on the left side, leaving the long hair on the right to be tied with a thong.

The Tonkawa may be descended from Indians who lived in southern Texas and northern Mexico. They had contact with the Spanish in the 1530s. Beginning in the late seventeenth century, the people were caught up in the colonial struggle between Spain and France for control of Texas. The Tonkawas lived around Mission San Gabriel in east Texas for a time before it was abandoned in 1758. They acquired horses in the late seventeenth or early eighteenth century.

El Mocho was a captured Apache who became a Tonkawa chief in the late eighteenth century. His dream was to unite the Apaches and the Tonkawas against the Spanish. At a council attended by over 4,000 Indians, the two peoples failed to resolve their differences. El Mocho was captured and killed by the Spanish.

After Mexican independence in 1821, the Tonkawas became allied with Anglo-Texans against the Comanche and Waco Indians. Along with other Texas tribes, the Tonkawas were assigned two small reservations on the Brazos River in 1855. Despite their past alliance with non-Native Texans, in 1859 the Tonkawas were deported from Texas and relocated to Fort Cobb on the Washita River, Indian Territory (Oklahoma). From there some fought for the Confederacy during the Civil War, and in 1862 more than half of the tribe were killed in a raid by Unionist Caddo, Shawnee, and Delaware people.

Survivors returned to Texas, where they remained until 1884, when they were assigned to the former Nez Percé Reservation in the Indian Territory. This reservation was allotted in 1896. Some Tonkawas participated in the Pawnee Ghost Dance in the early twentieth century.

See also Horse, Economic Impact; Trade.

Wahpekute

See Dakota.

Wahpeton

See Dakota.

Wichita

"Wichita" is the name of one band of a loose confederacy of several tribes living in separate villages. The Spanish called them *Jumanos*. They have also been called Black Pawnees as well as by the names of related tribes such as Wacos, Tawakonis, Tawehashes, and Akwits. Their self-designation was *Kitikiti'sh*, meaning "Men." Wichita is a Caddoan language.

Kinnikasus was the great creator. Other deities were recognized, too, particularly those related to the celestial bodies. The people held a deer dance three times a year. They also performed a calumet (pipe) ceremony. There were many secret societies, for both men and women, each with its own ceremonies and dances.

The Wichita were traditionally a loose confederation of several bands or tribes occupying independent villages. A chief and a subchief, chosen by a council of warriors, presided over each village. The smallest economic unit was the family. Descent was matriarchal. Corpses were buried in a nearby hill with various goods associated with their earthly activities. Mourners cut their hair and gave away some of their possessions.

The various Wichita bands lived in separate villages near rivers. In the sixteenth century, settlements consisted of up to 1,000 round houses, each fifteen to thirty feet in diameter and built of a pole framework tied with branches or reeds and thatched with grass. The houses had two doors, a smoke hole in the center of the roof, and sleeping platforms along the walls. The people also used ramadas in the summer and for some occasions, as well as skin teepees during the fall buffalo hunts.

Women grew corn, beans, squash, and tobacco. Crops were stored in underground caches. Pumpkins were cut, dried, and woven into mats for storage. Women also gathered foods such as plums, grapes, and nuts. Men hunted buffalo, usually twice a year—in June and following the harvest—after they obtained horses. They also hunted deer, elk, rabbit, antelope, and bear. Women made all clothing of animal skins. Both sexes practiced extensive body and facial tattooing.

The Wichita traded agricultural goods to nomadic tribes in exchange for animal goods. There was little trade with the New Mexico pueblos, although the two societies communicated. After 1720, the Wichitas acted as intermediaries between the French (tools, guns) and the western nomadic tribes (hides, furs). Following a 1746 friendship treaty, they traded guns to the Comanches for horses, which went eventually to the plantations on the lower Mississippi or Southeastern states.

The people who were to become the historic Wichitas split from the proto-Pawnees about 1,500 years ago. These people may have lived near the Washita River of western Oklahoma about 1,000 years ago. They probably moved north from eastern Texas in the fourteenth century to the Great Bend of the Arkansas River. There they were visited by Francisco Vasquez de Coronado in 1541, when he referred to their villages as Quivira. The people acquired horses by 1700.

During the eighteenth century, under pressure from the well-armed Osage, the Wichitas began moving south toward Oklahoma and Texas. Trade with the French began after 1720; with the southern Pawnees, the Wichitas dominated the gun trade out of New Orleans. However, in the mid- to late eighteenth century the French trade was suspended while the Wichitas were engaged in periodic wars with the Spanish. A severe smallpox epidemic crippled the people in 1801. Osage and non-Indian raids depleted their population even further in subsequent years. An 1835 treaty between the United States and the Wichitas, Comanches, and several eastern tribes marked the first time that the Wichitas were officially referred to by that name.

In 1854, several Wichita bands settled with the Shawnees and Delawares on a reservation on the Brazos River, although the non-Native Texans soon forced them out. The United States established a Wichita reservation in Indian Territory (Oklahoma), south of the Canadian River, in 1859. Wichitas left the Indian Territory for Kansas (near present-day Wichita) during the Civil War but returned in 1867. They formally ceded all their non-reservation land in 1872 in exchange for a 743,000-acre reservation along the Washita River. However, the agreement was never ratified by Congress. Tribal lands were allotted in 1901. The government paid them $1.25 an acre for the "excess" and then opened that land to non-Indian settlement.

See also Pipes, Sacred; Trade.

Yankton

See Nakota.

Yanktonai

See Nakota.

Native Americans of the Southeast

Alabama

"Alabama" is derived from *Alibamu*, "plantgatherers," "medicine gatherers," or "thicket clearers." Alabamas were culturally related to the neighboring Creeks and Choctaws. Alabamas spoke a Muskogean language.

The people worshipped the sun (fire), as well as a host of lesser deities and beings. Alabamas conducted the Green Corn ceremony as well as other ceremonies throughout the spring, summer, and fall. Most councils and ceremonies began with an emetic tea (black drink). Priests, doctors, and conjurers underwent a rigorous training period that included healing techniques, songs, and formulas.

Alabamas were part of the Creek Confederacy, although each village was politically sovereign. In most towns of the confederacy, a chief (*miko*) was chosen largely by merit. He was head of a democratic council that had ceremonial and diplomatic responsibilities.

Chunkey (a variety of hoop-and-pole in which an arrow was shot through a loop) was one of many popular games, most of which involved gambling. The dead were buried with their heads to the east and sometimes a knife in the hand for fighting eagles on the way to the afterworld. Alabamas had over fifty clans in the eighteenth century, although probably fewer before contact. Infidelity in marriage was an offense punishable by public whipping and exile.

Towns were laid out in a square and enclosed by walls up to several hundred feet long. By design, entry and egress were difficult: On one side the

gate was too low for a horse to enter, and another side might open onto a steep embankment. Many towns were surrounded by mud-covered wooden stockades.

Dwellings were pole-frame structures with plastered walls and bark-covered or shingled, gabled roofs. The outer covering was of mud and grass or mats. Many families had a winter house and a summer house. These buildings, plus a granary and possibly a storehouse, were placed to form a square, in the manner of the ceremonial square ground.

Alabamas ate fish, squirrels and other small game, deer and other large game, and their crops. The winter hunt, during which men traveled up to 250 miles or more, lasted from after the harvest until the spring planting. Fish were taken with spears, bows and arrows, and poison. Women wove cane or palmetto baskets. Many points and knives were made of flint, although mortars and pestles were generally wooden. Bows were also made of wood (cedar was considered the best), with strings of hide (perhaps of bark in earlier times). Men also hunted with blowguns and possibly spears.

Alabamas exported flint and animal products and imported pipes and shells. Women made pottery and wove geometric designs into their baskets. Artisans worked silver ornaments from the sixteenth century on. Most pre-contact transportation was via dugout pirogues. Personal adornment included ornaments in pierced ears and noses, body paint, and various armbands, bracelets, and necklaces. In the late eighteenth century, women wore cloth skirts, as well as shawls, or capes. Men wore

breechclouts, cloaks or shirts, and bear or buffalo robes in the winter. In battle, the war chief carried along the sacred war ark or medicine bundle. Life (of one's own people) was considered precious, and warriors were extremely careful not to risk inopportune or imprudent fighting or capture.

Alabamas probably descended from Mound Builder cultures and may have originated north and west of the Mississippi. They encountered a hostile Spanish party under Hernando de Soto in 1540. By the early eighteenth century they had become allies of the French, who built Fort Toulouse in Alabama country in 1713.

Many Alabamas left their homeland following the French defeat in 1763. Some joined the Seminoles in Florida. Some resettled north of New Orleans, and later some of that group moved on to western Louisiana and Texas. Land given them in recognition of their contribution in the 1836 fight against Mexico was promptly stolen by non-Natives. In 1842, the Alabamas and the Coushatta Indians were given a 1,280-acre reservation along the Trinity River. The United States added 3,081 acres to that reservation in 1928. In 1954 the tribe voluntarily terminated its relationship with the federal government, at which time the state took over control of the reservation. The tribe reverted to federal status in 1986.

Those who remained in Alabama fought unsuccessfully with the Creeks against non-Natives in the 1813–1814 Creek War. Survivors of that conflict settled in the Alabama town of Tawasa. Most were resettled in Indian Territory (Oklahoma) with the Creeks in the 1830s. Part of the Creek Nation until 1938, the Alabama-Quassartes at that time received a federal charter, several hundred acres of land, and political, but not administrative, independence.

Louisiana Alabamas maintained a subsistence economy during the early twentieth century, gradually entering the labor market. Tourism and tourist-related sales of cane baskets and woodcrafted items began to grow in midcentury.

See also Creek War; Mound Cultures of North America; Muskogean Language; Seminole Wars.

Biloxi
See Tunica.

Caddo

"Caddo" means "true chiefs," from *Kadohadacho*, "principal tribe." The Caddo Indians included people of the Natchitoches Confederacy (Louisiana), the Hasinai (Tejas or Texas) Confederacy (Texas), the Kadohadacho Confederacy (Texas and Arkansas), and the Adai and Eyish people. There were about twenty-five Caddo tribes in the eighteenth century. Caddos spoke a Caddoan language.

The people's supreme deity was known as Ayanat Caddi. There were also other deities and spirits, including the sun. Most annual ceremonies revolved around the agricultural cycle. Each Caddo tribe was headed by a powerful chief, who was assisted by other people of authority. Among the Hasinais (at least), a high priest had supreme authority. Clans were more hierarchical and social classes more pronounced among the western Caddos than in the east. Shell beads were used as a medium of exchange. Premarital sexual liaisons were condoned. In some tribes, men were allowed to have more than one wife, although in others a woman might not allow it. Divorce was easily obtained and occurred regularly.

At least one seventeenth-century town had over 100 houses. Some villages may have been reinforced with towered stockades. Houses in the east were round, about fifteen feet high and between twenty and sixty feet in diameter. They were constructed of a pole frame covered with grass thatch, through which smoke from the cooking fires exited; roofs came all the way to the ground. Western Caddos built earth lodges, with wooden frames and brush, grass, and mud walls reaching to the top. There were also outside arbors. Sacred fires always burned in circular temples.

Women grew two corn crops a year, as well as beans, pumpkins, sunflowers, and tobacco. They also gathered wild foods such as nuts, acorns, mulberries, strawberries, blackberries, plums, pomegranates, persimmons, and grapes. Agricultural products were most important in the diet, although buffalo grew in importance as the group moved westward. Men hunted deer, bear, raccoon, turkey, fowl, and snakes. They stalked deer using deer disguises. Dogs may have assisted them in the hunt. Fish were caught where possible.

Caddos exported Osage orange wood and salt, which they obtained from local mines (licks) and boiled in earthen (later iron) kettles. They imported Quapaw wooden platters, among other items. Their

fine arts included basketry, pottery, and carved shells, and they used single-log dugout canoes and cane rafts to navigate bodies of water.

Most clothing was made of deerskin. Men wore breechclouts, untailored shirts, and cloaks. Women wore skirts and a poncho-style upper garment and painted their bodies. They parted their hair in front and fastened it behind. Both wore blankets or buffalo robes and tattooed their faces and bodies, especially in floral and animal patterns.

Caddoans are thought to have originated in the Southwest. They reached the Great Plains in the midtwelfth century and the fringes of the Southeast cultural area shortly thereafter. They gave the Spanish under Hernando de Soto a mixed reception in 1541. Few of the Spanish missions in their country had any success.

Trade with the French began in the early seventeenth century. The Indians traded their crops for animal pelts, which they then traded to the French for guns and other items of non-Native origin. During the eighteenth century, Caddo villages suffered from Spanish-French colonial battles. Many tribes were wiped out by disease during that period.

In 1835, the Caddos ceded their Louisiana land and moved to Texas. In the 1850s, however, non-Native Texans drove all Indians out of Texas, and the Caddos fled from their brutality to the Indian Territory (Oklahoma). In 1859, the United States confined them to a reservation along the Washita River, which the Wichitas and Delawares later joined.

Rather than support the Confederacy, most Caddos fled to Kansas during the Civil War, returning in 1868. Some scouted for the U.S. Army during the Plains wars, in part as a strategy of supporting farmers against nomads. The boundaries of their reservation were secured in 1872, but, despite Caddo objections, most of the reservation was allotted around 1900. After extensive litigation and appeals, the tribe won over $1.5 million in land claim settlements in the 1980s.

See also Agriculture; Confederacies; Fur Trade.

Catawba

The Catawba people were also known as *Issa* or *Esaw,* "People of the River." Catawbas traditionally lived along the North Carolina–South Carolina border, especially along the Catawba River. Catawba is probably a Siouan language.

The people made use of wooden images in their ceremonies, which were relatively unconnected to the harvest. Enemies were killed to accompany the dead to an afterworld. There were two Catawba bands in the early eighteenth century. Some of their chiefs—men and women—were quite powerful.

Catawbas may have practiced frontal head deformation. The chunkey game was a variety of hoop-and-pole (in which an arrow was shot through a loop), played with a stone roller. They also played stickball (lacrosse). At puberty, young women learned the proper way to wear decorative feathers. Doctors and conjurers cured and detected thieves by consorting with spirits. Men alone were punished in cases of adultery. Divorce was easy to obtain, and widows could remarry at once.

Six early villages were located in river valleys. People lived in bark-covered pole-frame houses. The town houses were circular, as were the temples. Open arbors were used in the summer. Women grew corn, beans, squash, and gourds. Men hunted widely for large and small game, including buffalo, deer, and bear. The people also ate fish, pigeons, acorns, and various other wild plant foods. Blowguns with an average length of five to six feet and with an effective range of no more than thirty feet were used to bring down birds.

The main regional aboriginal trade routes ran right through Catawba territory. The Catawbas became heavily involved with British traders, especially in the mideighteenth century but beginning at least in 1673. Pottery was an ancient and highly developed Catawba art. It was often stamped with a carved piece of wood before firing. Rivers were navigated on dugout and possibly birchbark canoes. Chiefs wore headdresses of wild turkey feathers. Women may have worn leggings as well, when mourning, as special clothing made from tree moss.

Catawbas may have come to the Carolinas from the northwest. They first encountered non-Natives—Spanish explorers—in the midsixteenth century. Extensive contact with British traders in the late seventeenth and early eighteenth centuries transformed their lives. A dependence on non-Native goods caused them to hunt ever farther afield for pelts with which to purchase such goods. Encroachment on other peoples' hunting grounds combined with the heavy volume of goods carried along the trade routes encouraged increased attacks by enemy Indians. Catawbas also underwent severe depopulation from disease.

Catawba potter Sarah Jane Ayers Harris and seven grandchildren, seated on her porch with her pottery, ca. 1910. (Library of Congress)

To maintain trade relations with the colonists, the Catawbas took their side in a 1711–1713 war with the Tuscarora Indians. By 1715, however, some Catawbas had taken the Indian side in the Yamasee War, rebelling against unfair trade practices, forced labor, and slave raids. The non-Native victory in this conflict broke the power of the local Indians.

In the mideighteenth century smallpox epidemics almost wiped the tribe out: Their pre-contact population of about 6,000 had declined by over 90 percent to 500 or fewer. Alcohol sold and aggressively promoted by Anglo traders took many more lives. Catawbas tended to absorb local tribes who suffered the same fate, such as the Cheraws, Sugarees, Waxhaws, Congarees, Santees, Pedees, and Waterees.

In 1760–1761 the Catawbas were forced by their dependence on the state of South Carolina to fight against the powerful Cherokees in the French and Indian War. By 1763 they were confined to a fifteen-square-mile (144,000-acre) reservation, as non-Natives continued to take their former lands. Part of the agreement creating the reservation stipulated that non-Indians would be evicted from it (which never happened) and that the Catawbas continued to enjoy hunting rights outside the area. Their last great chief, Haigler, or Arataswa, died at that time.

The declining tribe took the patriot side in the American Revolution. In 1840, the few remaining Catawbas signed a treaty with the state of South Carolina, agreeing to cede lands in that state and move to North Carolina. Unable to buy land there, however, most dispersed among the Cherokees and Pamunkeys, although a very few remained in South Carolina. In the 1850s, however, most Catawbas who had gone to live with the Cherokees returned to South Carolina. A few families moved to Arkansas, the Indian Territory, Colorado, Utah, or elsewhere. Those in South Carolina acquired a reservation of 630 (of the original 144,000) poor-quality

acres. They also obtained the promise of annual payments from the state.

Many South Carolina Catawbas began share-cropping at that time but returned occasionally to live on the reservation. They also continued to speak their language and to make their traditional crafts. The Catawba Indian School opened in 1896 and ran until 1962. Mormons also played a large role in educating Catawba children beginning in the 1880s.

Many Catawbas worked in textile mills beginning after World War I. The Indians added to their reservation by purchasing land in the midtwentieth century. By that time, however, traditional Catawba culture had all but expired. Although the federal trust relationship was formally begun only in 1943 as a result of Catawba legal pressure, in 1962 the tribe voluntarily ended its relationship with the federal government, at which time individuals took over possession of the recently purchased tribal lands.

See also Pottery; Mormon Church; Trade.

Cherokee

"Cherokee" is probably from the Creek *tciloki*, "people who speak differently." Their self-designation was *Ani-yun-wiya*, "Real People." With the Creeks, Choctaws, Chickasaws, and Seminoles, the Cherokees were one of the so-called Five Civilized Tribes; this non-Native appellation arose because by the early nineteenth century these Indians dressed, farmed, and governed themselves nearly like white Americans. At the time of contact the Cherokees were the largest tribe in the southeast. Cherokees were formerly known as Kituhwas.

Cherokee is an Iroquoian language. The lower towns spoke the Elati dialect; the middle towns spoke the Kituhwa dialect; the upper (overhill and valley) towns spoke the Atali dialect. The dialects were mutually intelligible with difficulty.

The tribe's chief deity was the sun, which may have had a feminine identity. The people conceived of the cosmos as being divided into three parts: an upper world, this world, and a lower world. Each contained numerous spiritual beings that resided in specific places. The four cardinal directions were replete with social significance. Tribal mythology, symbols, and beliefs were complex, and there were also various associated taboos, customs, and social and personal rules.

Many ceremonies revolved around subsistence activities as well as healing. The primary one was the annual Green Corn ceremony (Busk), observed when the last corn crop ripened. Medicine people (men and women) could, by magical means, influence events and the lives and fortunes of people. Witches, when discovered, were summarily killed. Learning sorcery took a lifetime. Medicine powers could be used for good or evil, and the associated beads, crystals, and formulas were a regular part of many people's lives.

The various Cherokee villages formed a loose confederacy. There were two chiefs per village: a red, or war, chief, and a white chief (Most Beloved Man or Woman), who was associated with civil, economic, religious, and juridical functions. Chiefs could be male or female, and there was little or no hereditary component. There was also a village council, in which women sat, although usually only as observers. The Cherokees were not a cohesive political entity until the late eighteenth century at the earliest.

There were seven matrilineal clans in the early historic period. Cherokees regularly engaged in ceremonial purification, and they paid careful attention to their dreams. Both men and women, married and single, enjoyed a high degree of sexual freedom. Divorce was possible; men who were thrown out returned to their mothers. Children were treated gently, and they behaved with decorum. In general, Cherokees, valuing harmony as well as generosity, tried to avoid conflict.

Intraclan, but not interclan, murder was a capital offense. Names were changed or added to frequently. As with chiefs, towns may also have been considered red and white. Women owned the houses and their contents; this custom, along with matrilineal descent and the clan system, weakened with increasing exposure to non-Native society. People did not address each other directly. In place of public sanctions, Cherokees used ostracism and public scorn to enforce social norms.

Towns were located along rivers and streams. They contained a central ceremonial place and in the early historic period were often surrounded by palisades. People built rectangular summer houses of pole frames and wattle, walls of cane matting and clay plaster, and gabled bark or thatch roofs. The houses, about sixty or seventy feet by fifteen feet, were often divided into three parts: a kitchen, a dining area, and bedrooms. Some were two stories high, with the upper walls open for ventilation.

In a recreated Cherokee village, Cherokee tour guides show visitors the daily life and crafts of the Cherokees approximately 300 years ago. (Raymond Gehman/Corbis)

There was probably one door. Beds were made of rush mats over wood splints, and animal skins served as bedding.

Cherokees were primarily farmers. Women grew corn (three kinds), beans, squash, sunflowers, and tobacco, the latter used ceremonially. Wild foods included roots, crab apples, persimmons, plums, cherries, grapes, hickory nuts, walnuts, chestnuts, and berries. Men hunted various animals, including deer, bear, raccoon, rabbit, squirrel, turkey, and rattlesnake. They fished occasionally, and they collected maple sap in earthen pots and boiled it into syrup. Hunting gear included the bow and arrow, stone hatchet, and flint knife. Smaller animals and birds were shot with darts blown out of hollow nine- to ten-foot-long cane stems; these blowguns were accurate up to sixty feet.

Cherokee pipes were widely admired and easily exported. The people also traded maple sugar and syrup. They imported shell wampum that was used as money. Their plaited cane baskets, pottery, and masks carved of wood and gourds were especially fine.

Men built thirty- to forty-foot-long canoes of fire-hollowed pine or poplar logs. Each canoe could hold between fifteen and twenty people. Women made most clothing of buckskin and other skins and furs as well as of mulberry-bark fibers. Men wore breechclouts; women wore skirts. In the winter, both wore bear or buffalo robes. Men also wore shirts and leggings, and women wore capes. Both sexes wore moccasins as well as nose ornaments, bracelets, and body paint.

Each village had a red (war) chief as well as a War Woman, who accompanied war parties. She fed the men, gave advice, and determined the fate of prisoners. Women also distinguished themselves in combat and often tortured prisoners of war. The people often painted themselves, as well as their canoes and paddles, for war. The party carried an ark or medicine chest to war, and it left a war club engraved with its exploits in enemy territory.

The Cherokees probably originated in the upper Ohio Valley, the Great Lakes region, or someplace else in the north. They may also have been related to the Mound Builders. The town of Echota,

on the Little Tennessee River, may have been the ancient capital of the Cherokee Nation.

They encountered Hernando de Soto about 1540, probably not long after they arrived in their historic homeland. Spanish attacks against the Indians commenced shortly thereafter, although new diseases probably weakened the people even before Spanish soldiers began killing them. There were also contacts with the French and especially the British in the early seventeenth century. Traders brought guns around 1700, along with debilitating alcohol.

The Cherokees fought a series of wars with Tuscarora, Shawnee, Catawba, Creek, and Chickasaw Indians early in the eighteenth century. In 1760 the Cherokees, led by Chief Oconostota, fought the British as a protest against unfair trade practices and violence practiced against them as a group. Cherokees raided settlements and captured a British fort but were defeated after two years of fighting by the British scorched-earth policy. The peace treaty cost the Indians much of their eastern land, and, in fact, they never fully recovered their prominence after that time.

Significant depopulation resulted from several mideighteenth century epidemics. Cherokee support for Britain during the American Revolution encouraged attacks by North Carolina militia. Finally, some Cherokees who lived near Chattanooga relocated in 1794 to Arkansas and Texas and in 1831 to Indian Territory (Oklahoma). These people eventually became known as the western Cherokees.

After the American Revolution, Cherokees adopted British-style farming, cattle ranching, business, and government, becoming relatively cohesive and prosperous. They also owned slaves. They sided with the United States in the 1813 Creek War, during which a Cherokee saved Andrew Jackson's life. The tribe enjoyed a cultural renaissance between about 1800 and 1830, although they were under constant pressure for land cession and riven by internal political factionalism.

The Cherokee Nation was founded in 1827 with "Western" democratic institutions and a written constitution (which specifically disenfranchised African Americans and women). By then, Cherokees were intermarrying regularly with non-Natives and were receiving increased missionary activity, especially in education. Sequoyah (also known as George Gist) is credited with devising a Cherokee syllabary in 1821 and thus providing his people with a written language. During the late 1820s, the people began publishing a newspaper, the *Cherokee Phoenix*.

The discovery of gold in their territory led in part to the 1830 Indian Removal Act, requiring the Cherokees (among other tribes) to relocate west of the Mississippi River. When a small minority of Cherokees signed the Treaty of New Echota, ceding the tribe's last remaining eastern lands, local non-Natives immediately began appropriating the Indians' land and plundering their homes and possessions. Indians were forced into internment camps, where many died, although over 1,000 escaped to the mountains of North Carolina, where they became the progenitors of what came to be called the eastern band of Cherokees.

The removal, known as the Trail of Tears, began in 1838. The Indians were forced to walk 1,000 miles through severe weather without adequate food and clothing. About 4,000 Cherokees, almost a quarter of the total, died during the removal, and more died once the people reached the Indian Territory, where they joined—and largely absorbed—the group already there. Following their arrival in Indian Territory, the Cherokees quickly adopted another constitution and reestablished their institutions and facilities, including newspapers and schools. Under Chief John Ross, most Cherokees supported slavery and also supported the Confederate cause in the Civil War.

The huge "permanent" Indian Territory was often reduced in size. When the northern region was removed to create the states of Kansas and Nebraska, Indians living there were again forcibly resettled. One result of the Dawes Act (late 1880s) was the "sale" (the virtual appropriation) of roughly 2 million acres of Indian land in Oklahoma. Oklahoma became a territory in 1890 and a state in 1907. Although the Cherokees and other tribes resisted allotment, Congress forced them to acquiesce in 1898. Their land was individually allotted in 1902, at about the same time their Native governments were officially "terminated."

Ten years after the Cherokee removal, the U.S. Congress ceased efforts to round up the eastern Cherokees. The Indians received North Carolina state citizenship in 1866 and incorporated as the eastern band of Cherokee Indians in 1889. In the early twentieth century, many eastern Cherokees were engaged in subsistence farming and in the local timber industry. Having resisted allotment, the tribe took steps to ensure that it would always own

its land. Although the Cherokees suffered greatly during the Depression, the Great Smoky Mountain National Park (1930s) served as the center of a growing tourist industry.

In the 1930s, the United Keetoowah Band (UKB), a group of full-bloods opposed to assimilation, formally separated from the Oklahoma Cherokees. (The name "Keetoowah" derives from an ancient town in western North Carolina.) The group originated in the antiallotment battles at the end of the nineteenth century. In the early twentieth century the UKB reconstructed several traditional political structures, such as the seven clans and white towns, as well as some ancient cultural practices that did not survive the move west. They received federal recognition in 1946.

See also Cherokee Nation v. Georgia; Cherokee Phoenix and Indian Advocate; Creek War; Indian Removal Act; Mankiller, Wilma; Ross, John; Sequoyah; Trail of Tears.

Chickasaw

"Chickasaw" is a Muskogean name referring to the act of sitting down. The Chickasaws were culturally similar to the Choctaws. Along with the Cherokees, Choctaws, Creeks, and Seminoles, the Chickasaws were one of the so-called Five Civilized Tribes. Chickasaw is a Muskogean language.

The supreme deity was Ababinili, an aggregation of four celestial beings: Sun, Clouds, Clear Sky, and He That Lives in the Clear Sky. Fire, especially the sacred fire, was a manifestation of the supreme being. Two head priests (*hopaye*) presided over ceremonies and interpreted spiritual matters. Healers (*aliktce*), who combated evil spirits by using various natural substances, and witches were two types of spiritual people.

Political leadership was chosen in part according to hereditary claim but also according to merit. The head chief, chosen from the Minko clan, was known as the High Minko. Each clan also had a chief. There was also a council of advisers, which included clan leaders and tribal elders. The fundamental units were local groups.

Key Chickasaw values included hospitality and generosity, especially to those in need. Two divisions were in turn divided into many ranked matrilineal clans. The people played lacrosse, chunkey (in which an arrow was shot through a hoop), and other games, most of which included gambling and had important ritual components. Tobacco was used ritually and medicinally. Murder was subject to retaliation.

Boys were toughened by winter plunges into water and special herbs. Women were secluded in special huts during their menstrual periods. Marriage involved various gift exchanges, mainly food or clothing. A man might have more than one wife. Men avoided their mothers-in-law out of respect. In cases of adultery only the woman was punished, often by a beating or by an ear or nose cropping. Chickasaws practiced frontal head deformation.

The dead were buried in graves under houses, along with their possessions, after an elaborate funeral rite. They were placed in a sitting position facing west, with their faces painted red. After death they were only vaguely alluded to and never directly by name. All social activities ceased for three days following a death in the village. Chickasaws maintained the concept of a heaven generally in the west, the direction of witchcraft and uneasy spirits.

Chickasaws built their villages on high ground near stands of hardwood trees. They were often palisaded and more compact during periods of warfare. Rectangular summer houses were of poleframe construction, notched and lashed, with clapboard sides and gabled roofs covered with cypress or pine-bark shingles.

Winter houses were semiexcavated and circular, about twenty-five feet in diameter, with a narrow, four-foot-high door. They were plastered with at least six inches of clay and dried grass. Bark shingles or thatch covered conical roofs with no smoke holes. Furniture included couches and raised wood-frame beds, under which food was stored. Town houses or temples were of similar construction.

Crops—corn, beans, squash, and sunflowers—were the staple foods. Men also hunted buffalo, deer, bear, and numerous kinds of small game, including rabbits but probably not beaver or opossum. Birds and their eggs were included in the diet. Women gathered nuts, acorns, honey, onions, persimmons, strawberries, grapes, and plums. Tea was made from sassafras root. Chickasaws ate a variety of fish, including the huge Mississippi catfish (up to 200 pounds).

Earthen pots of various sizes and shapes served a number of purposes. Men stunned fish with buckeye or green walnut poison. Women wove mulberry bark in a frame and used the resulting textile in

floor and table coverings. Most clothing was made of deerskin, although other hides, including beaver, were also used. Men wore breechclouts, with deerskin shirts and bearskin robes in cold weather. Most kept their hair in a roach soaked in bear grease. There were also high boots for hunting. Women wore long dresses and added buffalo robes or capes in the winter. People generally went barefoot, although they did make moccasins of bear hide and occasionally elk skin.

Chickasaws traded as far away as Texas and perhaps even Mexico. Among other items, they traded deerskins for conch shell to use as wampum. Cloth items (from woven mulberry inner bark) were decorated with colorful animal and human figures and other designs. The people also made exceptional dyed and decorated cane baskets. Men hollowed dugout canoes out of hardwood trees.

Chickasaws were known as fierce, enthusiastic, and successful warriors. Raiding parties usually consisted of between twenty and forty men, their faces painted for war. They engaged in ritual preparation before they departed, and, upon their return, ritual celebration, which might include the bestowal of new war names.

The Chickasaws may once have been united with the Choctaws. The people encountered Hernando de Soto in 1541. At first welcoming, as their customs dictated, they ultimately attacked the Spanish when the latter tortured some of them and tried to enslave others.

In the late seventeenth and early eighteenth centuries, warfare increased with neighboring tribes as the Chickasaws expanded their already large hunting grounds to obtain more pelts and skins for the British trade. Increasingly dependent on this trade, they did not shrink from capturing other Indians, such as the Choctaws, and selling them to the British as slaves. In general, the Chickasaws' alliance with the British during the colonial period acted as a hindrance to French trade on the Mississippi.

Constant warfare with the French and their Choctaw allies during the eighteenth century sapped the people's vitality. In part to compensate, they began absorbing other peoples, such as several hundred Natchez as well as British traders. A pattern began to emerge in which descendents of British men and Chickasaw women (such as the Colbert family) became powerful tribal leaders. Missionaries began making significant numbers of converts during that time.

Tribal allegiance was divided during the American Revolution, with some members supporting one side, some the other, and some neither. The overall goal was to preserve traditional lands. With game growing scarce, many Chickasaws became exclusively farmers during the early to midnineteenth century. Some also began cotton plantations, and the tribe owned up to 1,000 African-American slaves during that period. By 1830 they had a written code of laws (which banned whiskey) and a police force.

As non-Native settlement of their lands increased during the 1820s, many Chickasaws migrated west, ceding land in several treaties (1805, 1816, 1818) during the period. Finally they ceded all lands east of the Mississippi in 1832. Roughly 3,000 Chickasaws were forcibly removed to Indian Territory (Oklahoma) after 1837, where many died of disease, hunger, and attacks by Plains Indians who resented the intrusion. The Chickasaws fared somewhat better than the Cherokees, being able to purchase many supply items, including riverboat transportation, with tribal funds. Most settled in the western part of Choctaw lands.

Survivors of the ordeal resumed farming and soon, with the help of their slaves, grew a surplus of crops. However, as a tribe the people had lost most of their aboriginal culture. Their own reservation and government were formally established in 1855 and lasted until Oklahoma statehood in 1907. In the years before the Civil War, the people operated schools, mills, and blacksmith shops, and they had started a newspaper. Chickasaws fought for the Confederacy in the Civil War. Unlike some other Oklahoma tribes of southeast origin, the Chickasaws never adopted their freed slaves.

Their lands were allotted around 1900. All tribal governments in Oklahoma were dissolved by Congress in 1906. By 1920, of the roughly 4.7 million acres of preallotment Chickasaw land, only about 300 remained in tribal control, a situation that severely hampered tribal political and economic development well into the century. Many prominent twentieth-century Oklahoma politicians were mixed-blood Chickasaws. From the 1940s on, individuals received payments from the sale of land containing coal and asphalt deposits.

See also Agriculture; Indian Removal Act; Muskogean Language; Slavery; Trade.

Chitimacha

"Chitimacha" may have meant "those living on Grand River," "those who have pots," or "men altogether red." They may have comprised three or four separate tribes in the early sixteenth century. The Chitimachas traditionally lived along the lower Louisiana coast, especially around Grand Lake, Grand River, and Bayou Teche. Chitimacha may be a language isolate, or it may be related to Tunican.

Chitimachas recognized a sky god, possibly feminine in nature. Boys and girls sought and obtained guardian spirits through solitary quests. Priests oversaw religious life. A twelve-foot-square temple on Grand Lake served as a center of religious activity, especially for the annual six-day midsummer festival. The main event here was the male adult initiation ceremony, during which the young men fasted and danced until exhausted.

There was a chief in each town and a subchief in each village; leadership was largely hereditary. Head chiefs possessed a large measure of authority and power and were fed, at least in part, by others. Among the different social classes, priests, headmen, and curers constituted a nobility. There may also have been clans. Women might obtain any religious or political position. The dead may have been laid on scaffolds, where special people (Buzzard Men) disposed of flesh and returned cleaned bones to the families, where they were eventually buried under mounds of earth.

Village populations reached up to 500 in the early historic period. Pole-frame houses were covered with palmetto thatch. The people ate bear, alligators, turtles (and their eggs), and deer, among other animals. They were highly dependent on fish and shellfish. Women grew sweet potatoes as well as beans, squash, sunflowers, and possibly four varieties of corn. They also gathered water lily seeds, palmetto seeds, nuts, and various wild fruits and berries.

Exports included fish and salt; imports, mainly from inland tribes, included flint, stone beads, and arrow points. They traded often with the Atakapa and the Avoyel Indians. Patterned black-and-yellow cane baskets, made with a unique double weaving technique, were especially fine arts. Extensive canoe transportation was made easier by the natural harbor provided by Grand Lake. Nose ornaments, bracelets, and earrings were common personal adornments. Both sexes kept their fingernails long.

Men wore their hair in roaches, or perhaps long, and decorated with feathers and lead weights.

Resident in their historic area for at least 2,500 years, the Chitimachas may have migrated south from the region of Natchez at some early time and east from Texas still earlier. Their decline began with the French arrival in the late seventeenth century. French slaving among the Indians created a generally hostile climate between the two peoples, especially in the early eighteenth century. Peace was established in 1718, but by then the Chitimacha population had suffered great losses through warfare and disease. Survivors were forcibly relocated north or taken away as slaves.

The influx of French Acadians in the late eighteenth century led to intermarriage (with Acadians as well as with other surviving local Indian groups), further land thefts, and the increased influence of Catholicism. In 1917, the Indians' remaining land base was privately purchased and sold to the United States. Throughout the twentieth century, chiefs have continued to govern the people and struggle to retain tribal land and sovereignty.

See also Basketry; New France and Natives; Slavery.

Choctaw

"Choctaw" was originally *Chahta*. An early name for the tribe might have been *Pafallaya*, or "long hair." They were culturally related to the Chickasaws and Creeks. With the Cherokees, Chickasaws, Creeks, and Seminoles, they were regarded by whites as one of the Five Civilized Tribes. Choctaw is a Muskogean language.

Choctaws worshipped the sun and fire as well as a host of lesser deities and beings. They celebrated the Green Corn ceremony and other festivals, mainly in the late summer and fall. The tribe was organized into two divisions. Three or four districts were each headed by a chief and a council. Also, each town had a lesser chief and a war chief. The power of these chiefs was relatively limited, and the Choctaws were among the most democratic of all southeastern Indians. Although there was no overall head chief, a national council did meet on occasion.

The people placed a high priority on peace and harmony. Lacrosse, played with deerskin balls and raccoon-skin-thong stick nets, was a huge spectator

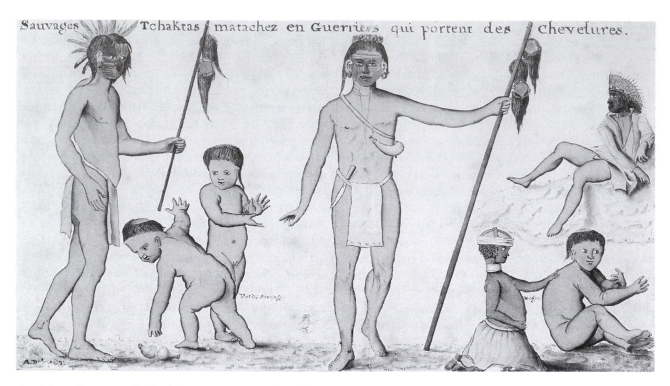

An eighteenth-century sketch of Choctaw warriors and children. One of the Five Civilized Tribes of the Old South, the Choctaws were an ethnically mixed people who occupied three river valleys in modern Mississippi. Although the Choctaws' assistance was vital to the victories of Major General Andrew Jackson's army in the south, their land was stolen and they were removed to the Indian Territory in the 1830s. (Corbis)

sport as well as a means for settling disputes. Rituals and ceremonies began days before a game. There was always gambling; sometimes the stakes included a person's net worth.

Women adulterers were severely punished; some contributed to a class of prostitutes. Both men and women observed food taboos when a child was born. Infants' heads were generally shaped at birth. Maternal uncles taught and disciplined boys. At puberty, boys were tattooed, and some wore bear claws through their noses. Homosexuality was accepted.

Perhaps 100 or more Choctaw villages (summer and winter) existed in the seventeenth century. Border towns, especially in the northeast, were generally fortified, whereas interior towns were more spread out. Towns, which were groups of villages and houses surrounded by farms, usually contained a public game/ceremonial area.

Men built pole-frame houses roofed with grass or cane reed thatch and walled with a number of materials, including crushed shell, hide, bark (often pine or cypress), and matting. Summer houses were oblong or oval with two smoke holes. The winter houses were circular and insulated with clay.

Choctaws farmed bottomland fields along the lower Mississippi. They often realized food surpluses. Women, with the assistance of men, grew corn, beans, squash, sunflowers, tobacco, and later potatoes and melon. Also, in the eighteenth century they grew leeks, garlic, cabbage, and other garden produce, the latter strictly for trade. Corn was also made into bread, as was sweet potato seed.

Large game, such as buffalo, deer, and bear (killed mainly for their fat), were particularly important when the harvest was poor. Small game included squirrel, turkey, beaver, otter, raccoon, opossum, and rabbit. Other foods included birds' eggs, fish, and wild fruits, nuts, seeds, and roots.

Fields were cleared using slash-and-burn technology. People fished using spears, nets, stunning poison, and buffalo hide traps. They carved bows, mortars, and stools of wood; made skin-covered gourd and horn pouches; and wove bags from twisted tree bark. Women wove and dyed baskets. Spun buffalo wool was also used as a fabric. Cane, another important raw material, was used for such items as knives, blowguns, darts, and baskets. Musical instruments included drums of skins stretched over hollowed logs, rattles, and rasps. Traders devel-

oped a regional trade language mixed with sign language for wide communication.

Choctaws followed the general Southeastern dress of deerskin breechclouts, skirts, and tunics and buffalo or bear robes and turkey feather blankets for warmth. Some women made their skirts of spun buffalo wool plus a plant fiber. Both men and women wore long hair except for men in time of mourning. Both also tattooed their bodies. The Choctaws partook less of war than did many of their neighbors, although they did not shirk from defensive fighting. Adult captives were regularly burned; others were enslaved.

Choctaws probably descended from the Mississippian Temple Mound Builders and may once have been united with the Chickasaws. Early encounters with the Spanish, starting with Hernando de Soto about 1540, were not peaceful, as de Soto generally burned Choctaw villages as he passed through the region.

The French established a presence in Choctaw territory in the late seventeenth century, and the two groups soon became important allies, although there was always a faction of Choctaws friendly to the British. Fighting along with the French and other Indian tribes, the Choctaws helped defeat the Natchez revolt of 1729. Bitter internal fighting around 1750 between French and British supporters was resolved generally in favor of the former.

Intertribal war continued with the Chickasaws and the Creeks until the French cession in 1763 (at the conclusion of the French and Indian War). Choctaws fought the Creeks even after that, until the United States took "possession" of greater "Louisiana" in the early nineteenth century. Small bands of Choctaws began settling in Louisiana in the late eighteenth century. At the same time, alcohol, supplied mainly by British traders, was taking a great toll on the people.

Largely under the influence of their leader, Pushmataha, the Choctaws refused to join the pan-Indian Tecumseh confederacy. However, non-Natives continued pushing into the Choctaws' territory. One strategy that non-Natives used to gain Indian land was to encourage trade debt by offering unlimited credit. Under relentless pressure and threats, the Choctaws began ceding land in 1801. Although treaties usually called for an exchange of land, in practice the Indians seldom received the western land they were promised, in part because the United States traded land that was not the government's to give or that it had no intention of allowing the Indians to have.

By the 1820s, the Choctaws had adopted so many lifeways of the whites that the latter regarded them as a "civilized tribe." Nevertheless, and although the Choctaws had never fought the United States, President Andrew Jackson signed the Indian Removal Act of 1830, requiring the Choctaws and other Southeast tribes to leave their homelands and relocate west of the Mississippi. A small minority of unrepresentative Choctaws signed the Treaty of Dancing Rabbit Creek, ceding all of their land in Mississippi, over 10 million acres. Articles in the treaty providing for Choctaws to remain in Mississippi were so full of loopholes that most of those who did so were ultimately dispossessed. At the same time, the state of Mississippi formally made the Indians subject to state laws, thus criminalizing tribal governments.

Removal of roughly 12,000 Choctaws took place between 1831 and 1834. Terrible conditions on this forced march of several hundred miles caused about a quarter of the Choctaws to die of fatigue, heartbreak, exposure, disease, and starvation. Many more died once they reached the Indian Territory (Oklahoma). Roughly 3,000 to 5,000 Choctaws escaped to the back country rather than join the removal. Many of these people were removed in the 1840s, but some remained. Although they continued living as squatters in a semitraditional manner, their condition declined. Officially illegal, they were plied with alcohol and relentlessly cheated, and they became disheartened.

The bulk of the people reestablished themselves out west and prospered in the years before the Civil War, with successful farms, missionary schools, and a constitutional government. Most Choctaws fought for the Confederacy; the war was a disaster for them and the other tribes. A relatively high percentage of Indians died in the war, and further relocations and dispossessions followed the fighting. After the war, the Choctaws paid for the removal of African Americans living on their territory, although most were eventually adopted into the tribe.

In the last two decades of the nineteenth century, the General Allotment Act and the Curtis Act were passed over the opposition of the tribes. These laws deprived Oklahoma Indians, including the Choctaws, of most of their land. The "permanent" Indian Territory became the state of Oklahoma in 1907 (the name "Oklahoma," a Muskogean word for "Red People," was introduced by a Choctaw

Indian), at which time the independent Choctaw nation became subject to U.S. control. The tribe spent decades attempting to reassert control over its institutions.

After the Reconstruction period, the Mississippi and Louisiana Choctaws lived by sharecropping, subsistence hunting, some wage labor, and selling or bartering herbs and handicrafts. Their community and traditions were kept alive in part by the retention of their language and their rural isolation, both from Euro-Americans, who branded them nonwhite, and African Americans, with whom the Choctaw refused to identify.

The government finally recognized the Mississippi Choctaws in the early twentieth century, and the Bureau of Indian Affairs began providing services, such as schools and a hospital, during the 1920s and 1930s. It began purchasing land for them as well. Reservations were created in 1944, and the tribe adopted a constitution and bylaws in 1945. Educational and employment opportunities remained severely limited until the 1960s owing to Mississippi's Jim Crow policies.

See also Agriculture; Forced Marches; Indian
    Removal Act; Mississippian Culture;
    Muskogean Language.

Coushatta
See Alabama.

Creek

"Creek," taken from Ochesee Creek, is the British name for the Ocmulgee River. The so-called Creeks were actually composed of many tribes, each with a different name, the most powerful of which was called the Muskogee (or Mvskoke), itself a collection of tribes who probably migrated from the Northwest. With the Cherokees, Choctaws, Chickasaws, and Seminoles, the Creeks became known by non-Natives in the early nineteenth century as the Five Civilized Tribes.

The Creek confederacy was a loose organization that united many Creek and non-Creek villages. Muskogee-speaking towns and tribes formed the core of the confederacy, although other groups joined as well. It was founded some time before 1540 but strengthened significantly in the seventeenth

and eighteenth centuries. Traditionally, Upper Creeks lived along the Coosa and Tallapoosa Rivers, in Alabama. Creeks spoke two principal Muskogean languages.

The Green Corn ceremony, also called the Busk, marked the new year. It was both a thanksgiving ceremony and one of renewal. Some participants drank a black drink that was mainly caffeine and that induced vomiting when consumed in quantity; it was designed to purify the body. The ceremony also included dancing, fasting, feasting, games, and contests. It ended with a communal bath and an address from the head chief. Other ceremonies in the spring and early summer included "stomp dances." Another group of feasts culminated in the late fall Dance of the Ancient People.

The supreme being, "master of breath," presided over the Land of the Blessed Dead. It received an offering of the first buck killed each season and also a morsel of flesh at each meal. Its representative on earth was the Busk fire. There were also many spiritual beings, particularly dwarfs, fairies, and giants.

Tribal towns (*talwas*) were the main political unit. Each contained about 100 to over 1,000 people, and each was politically sovereign, the alliance among them determining the nature of the confederacy. Towns chiefs (*mikos*) were largely chosen by merit. The power of the chiefs was to influence (and to carry out certain duties), not to command. They were head of the democratic council, which had ceremonial and diplomatic responsibilities. Decisions were made by consensus. There was also a subchief and a war chief. A town crier announced governmental decisions to the people.

The council met daily in the square ground or the town house. The people drank "black drink" and smoked tobacco before each important council meeting. Part of the council was a group of elders known as the Beloved Men. There were also Beloved Women, although women generally did not have formal power. Another council, composed of white clan members, oversaw internal public works affairs.

A dual division within most tribes manifested itself in the existence of red towns and white towns. Red was associated with war, white with peace. There were also about forty matrilineal clans, unequal in prestige, with animal names. Clans were the fundamental social unit.

Lacrosse games were played between towns of different divisions, in part to relieve tensions. Games also had significant political and ritualistic signifi-

cance. Unmarried women had considerable sexual freedom. Men could marry more than one wife. Marriage was formalized by gift giving, repeatedly in the case of multiple wives. Divorce was unusual, especially if there were children. Both parties were killed or punished in cases of adultery, unless they could escape punishment until the next Busk. Rape, incest, and witchcraft were capital offenses, as was nonseclusion during a woman's periods. Infanticide was permitted within the first month of life.

Women made pottery, baskets, mats, and other such items; prepared food and skins; made clothing; helped with the communal fields; and grew all the garden crops. Men also helped with the communal fields, and they hunted, fished, fought, played ball games, led ceremonies, built houses and other structures, and made tools. Men also carried skin pouches containing medicines, tobacco, and knives that hung by their sides.

Fifty towns, each with between thirty and 100 houses and located on river or creek banks, formed the original core of the confederacy. Each town was organized around a central square or plaza, which contained several features: a circular town (or hot) house; a game field; and a summer ceremonial house, or square ground. The square ground was actually four sheds around a square of one-half acre or so, in the center of which was the sacred fire. Private homes were clustered in groups of up to four. Each reasonably prosperous family had a winter house and a summer house, both generally rectangular.

A third structure was a two-story granary, one end of which was used for storing grain and roots (lower) and for meetings (upper). The other end, with open sides, was a general storage area (lower) and a reception area (upper). A fourth building, if one could afford it, was a storehouse for skins. The four buildings were placed to form a square, after the ceremonial square ground design.

Crops—corn, beans, and squash—were the staples. Hunting was important for meat and skins. Most men left the villages during the winter to hunt. Women often accompanied the hunting parties, mostly to attend to the meat and skins along the way. The people also ate fish.

Creeks utilized the Choctaw trade language. Some groups exported flint and salt. A pictographic system represented historical events. Women made pottery, glazed with smoky pitch, and cane and hickory splint baskets. Men made large cypress dugout canoes. Except on the Georgia coast, where they used tree moss, women made their clothes largely from skins and textiles. Skirts that reached below the knee were tied around the waist. Men wore breechclouts and often leggings. Some young men wore nose ornaments and enlarged their ears with copper wire. Both sexes wore buffalo hide and deerskin moccasins as well as extensive tattoos. Boys often went naked until puberty. Rank was reflected in clothing and adornment.

There were three levels of warriors: war chiefs, big warriors, and little warriors, depending on their level of accomplishment. Most fighting took place in spring. The purpose was generally honor and revenge. Men painted their bodies black and red for war. A successful war party left signs to indicate who had done the deeds. Parties that resulted in the loss of many men, no matter how successful otherwise (captured horses, war honors, and so on) were considered failures. Enemies were often scalped and dismembered; those remaining alive might be enslaved or whipped and otherwise tortured by the women, unless they could escape.

The Creek people probably descended from Mississippian Temple Mound Builders, entering their historic area from the west. Hernando de Soto passed through the region in 1540. In the colonial wars, Creeks were traditional allies of the British, although they were often successful in playing the European nations against one another. Early on, the Creeks were grouped very informally into a lower section, located in eastern Georgia and more accommodating to Anglo society, and an upper section, more traditional and resistant to assimilation.

As British allies in the late seventeenth and early eighteenth centuries, the Creeks fought the Spanish as well as other Indian tribes, such as the Apalachees, the Timucuas, the Choctaws, and the Cherokees. They also absorbed some of the tribes they defeated in battle, such as part of the Apalachicolas and the Apalachees about 1704. Creeks took part in the 1715 Yamasee War, because years of British abuse, including slaving, rape, and cheating, had temporarily disrupted the Creek–British alliance. Following the Yamasee defeat, the bulk of the Creeks moved inland to the Chattahoochee River.

The Creeks were more cautious about choosing sides in the French and Indian War and the American Revolution. Few favored the colonists, however, which was reason enough for the victors to demand land cessions after the fighting. In the late eighteenth century, the Creek leader Alexander McGillivray

dominated the confederacy's diplomatic maneuvering and attempted to reorganize its political structure to his advantage. In 1790 he signed a treaty, later repudiated by the leaders of the confederacy, accepting U.S. protection and involvement in the people's internal affairs.

Many Creeks resisted joining Tecumseh's plan for a united Indian attack against the Americans, but in 1813 and 1814 they mounted their own military challenge. This was actually a civil war resulting from continuing diplomatic pressures and relentless encroachments from the Georgians as well as their own political and economic decline. The White Stick faction (mainly Lower Creeks) supported the United States and the Red Sticks the British. Despite early successes, the war was put down. As punishment, the Creeks, both Red and White, were made to sign the Treaty of Horseshoe Bend, ceding 23 million acres of land. Many Creeks migrated to Florida around that time to become part of the newly formed Seminole people.

In 1825, thirteen chiefs ceded all remaining Creek lands to the state of Georgia. These chiefs were later condemned by their people for high treason, and two were shot. Although the treaty was illegal, the state of Georgia proceeded to act as if it owned the land, and the United States soon backed the state, calling for complete Indian removal. President Andrew Jackson signed the Indian Removal Act in 1830. Non-Natives obtained the remaining Indian lands in the usual way: fraud, intimidation, and outright theft.

In 1832, Creeks signed the Treaty of Washington, ceding 5 million acres of land. Farcically, the treaty offered the Creeks a choice to remain or move and stated that white usurpers would be removed if the Indians chose to stay. In the mid-1830s, more Creeks joined the Seminoles in Florida while others made a last-ditch military stand. Forced relocation began in 1836. The Indians were taken to a place between the Canadian and the Arkansas Rivers. Of the roughly 14,000 who were relocated, almost 4,000 died of starvation, disease, exposure, and heartbreak during the march and shortly after their arrival in Indian Territory.

Once there, the people began to rebuild, accepting missionary schools and reestablishing towns, fields, and government. Christianization proceeded rapidly after removal. In 1856 the Creek lost over 2 million acres along the Canadian River to the Seminoles. Although the Creeks split in their allegiance during the Civil War, they suffered with the other members of the Five Civilized Tribes, which had largely supported the South, and lost land, goods, crops, and political power.

The 1867 constitution of the Muskogee Nation reaffirmed the sovereignty of tribal towns and provided for a democratic governmental structure. Following the war, a full-blood, pro-Northern, traditional faction emerged that took a hard line on land cessions, as did a moderate Muskogee party and a number of other parties. Creeks also pressed for intertribal cooperation among Oklahoma tribes. Their land base was gradually whittled away until they lost all of it in 1907, as well as their political independence, when Oklahoma became a state.

From 1907 until 1970, the federal government recognized only the Creek nation, an entity of the accommodationist Lower Creeks. Its principal chiefs were appointed by the U.S. government. Around 1900, an upper Creek named Chitto Harjo (Crazy Snake) led a rebellion against allotment, the process that gave tribal holdings to individuals and made the "surplus" available for non-Native purchase. In 1917, the Upper Creeks again took up arms as part of the Green Corn Rebellion, a movement of African-Americans, Indians, and whites dedicated to obtaining federal help for the rural poor.

In the 1930s, three tribal towns, including the Alabama-Quassartes, opted out of the Creek confederacy to accept charters under the Indian Reorganization Act. Many people left the Creek communities for cities during and after World War II. By 1970, 95 percent of preallotment tribal land was owned by non-Natives, and non-Natives held petroleum leases worth $50 billion. In 1970, a new law allowing for the democratic election of the principal chief gave rise to the Creek Nation of Oklahoma.

See also Agriculture; Confederacies; Creek War; Forced Marches; Harjo, Chitto; Indian Removal Act; Mississippian Cultures; Muskogean Language; Seminole Wars; Warfare, Intertribal.

Houma

"Houma," or *Ouma*, means "red" in Choctaw and Chickasaw, but it may have been a shortened form of Chakchiuma, a tribe from whom they probably

descended. It may also be an abbreviation of their tribal symbol, *sakti homma,* or "red crawfish." Many Houmas prefer simply the word "Indian" as a self-designation. In the late seventeenth century, Houmas lived on the east side of the Mississippi River, opposite the mouth of the Red River. Houma is a Muskogean language.

Temples were fronted with carved wooden figures. There may also have been earthen images of deities inside. The people probably worshiped a number of gods, in particular the sun, thunder, and fire. Young people may have sought guardian spirits through quests. Houma head chiefs, if they existed at all, were less powerful than the Natchez Suns. Women were known to have served as war chiefs.

Each town may have had over 100 cabins, possibly arrayed in a circle. Houses were square, pole-frame structures, from fifteen to more than thirty feet on a side, and with walls of adobe and Spanish moss. Traditionally horticulturists, the Houmas grew corn and other crops. They also collected shrimp and other marine food as well as a variety of wild plant food, and they ate muskrat and other small game.

Palmetto was used in the manufacture of baskets, mats, and other items. Hunters used a two-piece blowgun. Musical instruments included clay pot drums with skins stretched over the top. The Caddos were significant trade partners. Marine food was an important export. The people probably imported flint and bow wood. They may also have traded in salt and bird feathers.

Houmas carved wooden satyrs and animals, some in relief, and painted in black, white, red, and yellow on their temple vestibules. Men wore deerskin cloaks or went naked. Some men and women wore turkey feather or woven muskrat skin mantles. They may also have worn skin leggings and moccasins and possibly bearskin blankets in the winter. Girls, from about eight to ten years of age until marriage or the loss of their virginity, may have worn a waist-to-ankle–length mulberry thread net garment, fringed and ornamented.

Shortly after they made their initial alliance with the French, in 1686, more than half the tribe was killed by disease. Catholic missionaries began operating among the Indians after 1700. The Tunica Indians, to whom the Houmas had given permission to settle in the area in 1706, soon killed more than half of their hosts. The survivors moved south after the massacre.

In 1718, shortly after the conclusion of the Chitimacha War, the Houma joined some Chitimachas and members of other tribes and migrated south again, to the vicinity of New Orleans, and then north again to present-day Ascension parish. After the Natchez defeat at the hands of the French, Houmas, who aided the Indian refugees, were in their turn attacked by French forces; hundreds were captured and sold as slaves in New Orleans.

By the early eighteenth century the Houmas had begun a process of absorbing some smaller, neighboring tribes, such as the Acolapissas, Bayogoulas, Biloxis, and Chitimachas. Beginning some time in the early nineteenth century, the people still in Ascension parish moved south and settled on the Gulf Coast (in the present-day Lafourche and Terrebonne parishes). Other portions of the tribe intermarried with the Atakapas and moved to their territory or migrated to Oklahoma or to the north, toward their original homeland, and became lost to history.

The Houmas remained generally isolated well into the twentieth century. In the 1930s, oil speculators began taking advantage of the Indians' illiteracy and lack of understanding to obtain their land. In response, local Indian leaders pushed their people to learn English. Still, most Houmas did not attend school until after World War II. Schools in the area were desegregated in the 1960s. Centuries of intermarriage thoroughly integrated Catholicism and the French language into Houma identity.

See also Basketry; Warfare, Intertribal.

Lumbee

The Lumbees were a historical Indian people whose ancestors were Indians of indeterminate tribal affiliations, Anglos, and African Americans. Their name is taken from the Lumber (formerly Lumbee) River. From colonial times to the present, Lumbee Indians have lived in and near Robeson County, in southeastern North Carolina, and also in several counties in northeastern South Carolina. The Lumbee have always spoken English.

Lumbee Indians are probably descended from Cheraw Indians and other local Siouan speakers. Their ancestors may also include British settlers from

the "lost" colony of Roanoke, Virginia (1587), who may have joined Hatteras Indians living on Croatoan Sound. There are at least twenty surnames of Roanoke colonists among contemporary Lumbees. Their ancestors may also include Cherokee, Tuscarora, and Croatoan Indians.

The marshy character of the Lumber and Pee Dee River area made it a likely haven for refugees of all sorts. Lumbee Indians, free frontier farmers, were first encountered by British and Scots settlers in the early eighteenth century. At that time they had no Indian traditions or customs, although their skin color was suggestive of an Indian origin. They maintained little contact with Anglo settlers, most of whom were more interested in the better and more accessible land farther west.

In the 1760s, the Lumbees experienced increasing competition with Highland Scots settlers. Land incursions were resisted where possible, but Lumbees soon lost much land to the Scots and to the tidewater planters, often by fraudulent means. The state of North Carolina formally disenfranchised them, along with other "persons of color," in 1835.

During the Civil War, Lumbees were conscripted into service as forced labor; when they resisted, they were attacked by soldiers. Lumbee resistance to this oppression was led by Henry Berry Lowry (or Lowerie), who led raids on plantations to feed the poor of all races. Lowry kept up his campaign for justice even after the war, taking on as well the Republican (Reconstruction) party, which sided with the Democrats and branded Lowry's organization as bandits. He eluded capture at least until his disappearance in 1872.

The Lumbees pressed their claim for state and federal recognition after war's end, but with the defeat of the multicultural Lowry movement, their identity turned more inward. They accepted a status as a third racial caste, with more rights than African Americans but not as many as whites. In 1885 the North Carolina General Assembly recognized them as Croatoan Indians and allowed them to operate their own schools, segregated from whites but apart from African Americans. A normal (teacher training) school was also opened, which later became a college and, around 1970, Pembroke State University. In 1911 the North Carolina legislature dubbed them Robeson County Indians. This name was changed to Cherokee Indians of Robeson County until protests by the Cherokees forced its withdrawal. The people filed an unsuccessful request for federal recognition as the Siouan Tribes of the Lumber River.

Most Lumbees continued farming until after World War II. They were recognized by the state of North Carolina as Lumbee Indians in 1953. Partial federal recognition came in 1956, although the tribe was prohibited from receiving federal benefits. In 1958, thousands of Lumbees stood up to the Ku Klux Klan and drove them from Robeson County. They lost control of their school system in the 1960s. The tribe formed the Lumbee River Regional Development Association, a nonprofit corporation, in 1968.

See also Identity; Economic Development.

Miccosukee
See Seminole.

Muskogee
See Creek.

Natchez

The Natchez are an extinct tribe that had a marked similarity to Mississippian Mound Builder culture in the early historic period. They were the largest, most powerful tribe on the Mississippi in the mid-sixteenth century. The early historic location of the Natchez was along St. Catherine's Creek, near present-day Natchez, Mississippi. Natchezean languages may have been related to the Muskogean language family, with possible Tunican influences.

The sun was the supreme deity. Its son was said to be responsible for Natchez culture, and its authority was continued in the sun caste. The people also recognized many minor servant spirits. Natchez society was ruled by an absolute, hereditary monarch called the Great Sun. A ceremonial center in the main village included a partitioned, rectangular sun temple and the house of the Great Sun, each

Depiction of Natchez hunting deer from the eighteenth century. (Library of Congress)

built on mounds of adobe and covered with woven mats.

The Natchez also offered human sacrifices, especially upon the death of a chief. They observed the Great Corn ceremony, which corresponded to the Creek Busk, in mid- to late summer. Most ceremonies were led by the Great Sun and/or other suns. There was also a priesthood, whose members shaved their heads.

The Natchez recognized two social classes: nobles and commoners. The former included the Great Sun (king); the king's brothers and uncles (little suns), from whom were chosen the war chief and head priest; hereditary nobles; and honored men and women, a status obtainable by merit. Commoners (or Stinkards) farmed, built the mounds, and did most of the manual labor. They gave food and other presents to the suns, and the Great Sun redistributed some of it.

There were elaborate deferential codes of behavior and speech between the classes. Members of the higher classes, even the Great Sun, were required to marry commoners. The offspring of a male of high rank and a commoner were a step below the man's rank, but the offspring of a highly ranked woman and a male commoner kept the mother's rank.

When a person of high rank died, his or her commoner spouse, if there was one, and several servants were killed for companions in the afterlife. Much ritual attended the deaths of nobility. The afterlife destination was based on earthly conduct: There was a paradise of equality and freedom from want and a hell full of mosquitoes.

Women enjoyed a high degree of sexual license before marriage, although fidelity after marriage was the norm, and divorce was rare. The Natchez practiced infant head flattening. Babies nursed until they stopped voluntarily or the mother became pregnant.

Men engaged in generally cooperative work, such as hunting, fishing, cultivating the sacred fields, fighting, playing games, dressing skins, building houses, and making canoes and weapons. They were fed before women and generally enjoyed a higher status. Women prepared food; kept the fires going; made pottery, baskets, mats, clothing, and beadwork; and tended crops. Much of their work was performed alone. Berdaches assumed women's economic as well as sexual roles.

Nine villages were scattered among woods and fields. Low, windowless square adobe houses with domed, thatched roofs over cane matting were built in rows around a central plaza. Diet was agriculture based. Men and women grew corn as well as pumpkins and beans and also melons and peaches in the historic period. Sowing and harvesting were highly ritualistic activities. Women gathered wild rice, nuts, berries, grapes, mushrooms, and persimmons; the latter were made into bread. Men hunted deer, turkey, and buffalo as well as a host of other game. The people also ate duck, other fowl, fish, and shellfish.

Women made incised pottery, dyed cane baskets and mats, and white fabric from the inner bark of

mulberry trees. They also wove baskets and nets. Men carved and painted religious figures, such as birds and rattlesnakes. They also made pipes from a black stone, especially in the later eighteenth century, and they burned logs to fashion dugout canoes, some up to forty feet long.

Clothing and personal adornment indicated differences in rank. Most clothing was made of mulberry tree inner bark fabric and/or deerskin. Women wore a knee-length skirt. Men wore a deerskin breechclout. Both wore high, laced moccasins, a long deerskin shirt, and leggings in colder weather. Other winter wear included buffalo robes and feather mantles.

Warriors were tattooed from head to foot; they slit the lower part of their ears and decorated them with wire. The Natchez recognized three classes of warriors, and war was seen as a means of social advancement. Most war parties were led by the head war chief. There were various prewar rituals, including drinking an emetic, feasting on dog meat, dancing and relating war stories, and planting the war post. Warriors carried fetishes of war spirits with them. Male captives were generally scalped and burned alive, whereas women were kept as slaves.

With other Muskogean people, the Natchez may have come to their historical territory from the northwest. The Natchez had clear cultural ties to the Mississippian Mound Builder civilization, which may in turn have been influenced by Mesoamerican Indian cultures.

Contact with the Hernando de Soto party in 1542 was likely casual and not particularly friendly. French explorers entered the region in the later seventeenth century, and Catholic missionaries soon followed. The little nation soon divided its loyalties between France and Britain. By 1715 it was raiding nearby Indians such as the Chawashas in the service of British slave traders.

The Natchez population was greatly reduced by wars with the French, beginning in 1716. The final conflict began when a governor of Louisiana moved to take over the site of the Natchez Great Village. In late 1729, partly at British instigation, Natchez warriors sacked Fort Rosalie and other French settlements, killing and capturing hundreds of people. The Yazoo Indians soon joined in, but the Choctaws sided with the French. In 1731 the French achieved a decisive victory. They killed many people and sold even more (including the last Great Sun) into slavery. Some people managed to escape to local tribes,

especially to the Chickasaws and also to the Creeks and Cherokees.

Three to five Natchez towns continued among the Creek into the nineteenth century. After removal to Oklahoma, Natchez descendents formed communities in the eastern part of the reservation. By about 1900, intermarriage had ended a distinct Natchez identity. The Natchez held their last formal ceremony in 1976; the last Native speaker died in 1965.

See also Berdaches; Confederacies; Mississippian Culture; Natchez Culture.

Pamunkey
See Powhatan.

Powhatan
"Powhatan" means "falls in a current of water." The Powhatans are part of a group of Algonquin speakers from North Carolina to New Jersey known as Renápe ("human beings") or Lenápe in the L dialect. The Powhatan tribes (Renápe of Virginia) were culturally intermediate between the Southeast and Northeast regions. Powhatan was also the main tribe and village of the roughly thirty-tribe Powhatan Confederacy. Powhatan Indians spoke an Algonquin language.

The chief deity was known as Okee. There were carved images of various kings and deities in the temples, as well as carved idols, dressed in various clothing and ornaments. There was at least one priest and temple in every village. Priests made sacrifices of meat and tobacco at outdoor stone altars. Two or three children may have been sacrificed annually to propitiate the gods. There were regular communal ceremonies, including singing and dance, especially in times of triumph or crisis and at the harvest. Common people were thought to have no afterlife, but chiefs and priests were said to inhabit a western paradise until they were born again.

Each town, or kingdom, was led by a chief, or king. Sometimes, when kings controlled more than one town, a regent did the king's bidding in his absence and paid him tribute. Chiefly descent was mainly matrilineal. Children were bathed daily in

cold water for strengthening. Furthermore, male children may have been beaten as part of a general toughening ceremony.

Men had many wives. Men announced their intentions by bringing the women a quantity of fresh food. After the woman's family received presents and promises of more to come, she was brought to the man for a small wedding ceremony, followed by a feast. Once she had a baby, the king's wife was given a quantity of goods and dismissed, after which she was free to marry someone else; the child was taken from her and raised in the king's household.

Villages, often palisaded in the early seventeenth century, were usually located along a river. There were between two and about 100 houses and between fifty and 500 families per village/kingdom. Houses were constructed by bending and tying off saplings and then covering them with bark or woven mats. Houses were generally built under trees. Some elongated houses may have reached more than 100 feet in length, but most were much smaller. Several families lived in each house. There may also have been a combination raised storage/drying area under which men congregated.

Fish and shellfish constituted a major part of the diet. Agriculture was somewhat less intensive than in other parts of the Southeast. Women grew corn (three varieties), beans, and squash in fields of up to 200 acres. Some nuts and fruits were dried and stored for the winter. A milky drink was made from walnuts. Men hunted deer, beaver, opossums, otters, squirrels, and turkeys, among other animals.

Powhatans' main arts were basketry, beadwork, and pottery as well as ceremonial clothing woven from turkey feathers. Their dugout canoes were up to fifty feet long. Women made the clothing, mostly from skins. Married women wore hairstyles that were different—longer in front—than those of unmarried women. Both sexes painted their bodies, particularly black, yellow, and red. The chief priests wore turkey feather cloaks and snake and weasel skin headdresses. Priests, but not common men, may have worn beards. Weapons included tomahawks, bows and arrows, clubs, and shields. Priests had the final say about making war.

Aside from a short-lived Spanish mission in 1570, the British were the first European power in the region. By 1607, Chief Wahunsonacock (known to early British colonists as Powhatan) had expanded

the confederacy by conquest from six or eight tribes to more than thirty. Shortly after the establishment of the Jamestown colony in 1607, the settlers began wide-scale cultivation of tobacco to sell in Europe. Because tobacco rapidly depletes the soil, the British constantly needed more land and did not shrink from obtaining it by fraud and trickery from the Indians.

In 1622, the Powhatans determined to break the cycle of land thefts. Now led by Opechancanough, Wahunsonacock's brother, they organized a revolt that killed almost 350 colonists and destroyed all settlements except Jamestown. In response, the colonial militia began a push to sweep the Indians farther inland. At one point, the British attacked a group of Indians who had come to attend a peace council. After years of bitter fighting, during which the Powhatans lost many people, peace was restored in 1636, but Opechancanough organized another revolt in 1644, at which time he may have been over 100 years old. Over 500 colonists died during this campaign. After Opechancanough was captured and shot in 1644, his people were forced out of Virginia or placed on reservations, and the confederacy came to an end.

The Powhatan people were attacked by whites in 1675 after being falsely accused of depredations; the following year the whites massacred a large number of Powhatan men, women, and children living at a fort near Richmond. By this time, most Powhatan people and towns had disappeared. The people lost several of their reservations in the early eighteenth century. In 1722, Iroquois Indians agreed to stop attacking the Powhatans. Beginning in the 1770s, surviving Powhatans began migrating north to New Jersey, a movement that accelerated during and after the Civil War.

Pamunkey and Mattaponi Reservations of about 800 and 1,000 acres, respectively, remained in 1800. The reservations existed as a result of treaties signed with colonial governments. In 1831, most surviving Powhatans, many of whom had intermarried with African Americans, were chased away by whites in the aftermath of the Nat Turner slave rebellion. Few Powhatan Indians fought in the Civil War; those who did mainly did so on the Union side.

Following the Civil War, Virginia's Indians fought successfully for a social—and legal—status higher than that of African Americans; the result was a three-way segregation system. This negotiation

affected their legal identity as Indians. For instance, during World War I, Pamunkey and Mattaponi Indians protested the fact that they were drafted, since they were not citizens. The courts ruled in their favor. Having made their legal point, many proceeded to enlist.

Prior to World War II, many Pamunkeys continued to live by fishing, hunting, and trapping. Also during that time, the attention paid to Virginia Indians by anthropologists stimulated a renewal of their ethnic identity and political organization, although this soon provoked a fierce white backlash. Powhatans began a community in the Philadelphia-Camden area, maintaining their Native identity in part through a close network of families. They frequently intermarried with the Nanticokes of Delaware and members of other tribes. Formal organization began in the 1930s, culminating in the emergence of the Powhatan Indians of the Delaware Valley in the 1960s and the Powhatan-Renápe Nation in the 1970s.

See also Confederacies; Pocahontas; Powhatan.

Renápe

See Powhatan.

Seminole

"Seminole" means "pioneer" or "runaway," possibly from the Spanish *cimarrón* ("wild"). The Seminoles, known as such by 1775, formed in the eighteenth century from members of other Indian peoples, mainly Creeks, but also Oconees, Yamasees, and others. The Creeks, Choctaws, Chickasaws, Cherokees, and Seminoles were known by non-Natives in the nineteenth century as the Five Civilized Tribes.

Until 1962, the Miccosukee Indians were part of the Seminoles. According to their traditions, they were descended from Chiaha Indians. The name "Miccosukee" means "Red Person." Located in north Florida in the early eighteenth century, the Seminoles and Miccosukees were forced southward into the swamps and westward to Oklahoma from the midnineteenth century on. Seminoles spoke two

Portrait of Billy Bowlegs, a Seminole, ca. 1895. (Library of Congress)

mutually unintelligible Muskogean languages: Hitchiti, spoken by Oconee Indians and today mostly by Miccosukees, and Muskogee.

The Seminoles considered themselves children of the sun. They observed the Green Corn ceremony as early as May or June. This ritual helped to unify the tribe after the wars. Seminoles believed that a person's soul exited the body when he or she slept. Illness occurred when the soul failed to return, in which case a priest was called to coax the soul back.

Before the wars, Seminole towns had chiefs and councils of elders. Afterward, there were three bands, based on language (two Miccosukee and one Creek). Each had its own chief and council of elders. Matrilineal clans helped provide cultural continuity among widely scattered bands after the wars. There was also a dual division among the people. Particularly after 1817, the Seminoles lived in small extended families.

Owing to a fairly mobile and decentralized existence, the early towns were much less organized than were those of the Creeks. For example, there

were no yards for chunkey (a variety of hoop-and-pole in which an arrow was shot through a loop) and only a vague public square. People living in these towns generally owned a longhouse, divided by mats into a kitchen, dining area, and sleeping area, and another, smaller house of two stories, similar to the Creek granary.

People in south Florida built their villages on hammocks and near rivers. Houses, or *chickees*, had pole foundations of palmetto trunks and palmetto-thatched roofs, platforms raised about three feet off the ground, and open walls. The thatch was watertight and could resist very strong winds.

Women grew corn, beans, squash, and tobacco. They made hominy and flour from corn and "coontie" from certain roots. They also grew such non-Native crops as sweet potatoes, bananas, peanuts, lemons, melons, and oranges. They also gathered wild rice; cabbage palmetto; various roots and wild foods, such as persimmon, plum, honey, and sugarcane; and nuts, such as hickory and acorns. Men hunted alligator, bear, opossum, rabbit, squirrel, wild fowl, manatee, and turkeys (using calls for the turkeys). The people ate fish, turtles, and shellfish.

Traditional trade items included alligator hides, otter pelts, bird plumes, and foods. Bird plumes and alligator hides in particular were very much in demand in the late nineteenth century. Seminoles were known for their patchwork clothing and baskets. Their geometric designs were often in the pattern of a snake. Ribbon appliqué, previously consisting mainly of bands of triangles along borders, became much more elaborate during the late nineteenth century.

Men built fire-hollowed cypress dugout canoes, often poled from a stern platform. Canoes were relatively flat to accommodate the shallow, still water of the swamps. Some had sails, for journeys on Lake Okeechobee and even to the Bahamas. The Seminoles eventually developed their own breed of horses. There was no intertribal warfare: Seminoles fought only with the U.S. Army and local non-Native settlers.

Women made colorful patchwork clothing beginning around 1900. Some clothing was made of tanned deerskin as well. Women wore short shirts and long skirts, both generally of cloth. They also wore as many as 200 bead necklaces around the neck. Men, especially among the Miccosukee, wore turbans made of wrapped shawls. Other clothing

included shirts, neckerchiefs, breechclouts, and, occasionally, buckskin moccasins. Both sexes wore ornaments of silver and other metals and painted their faces and upper bodies.

The Apalachee and Timucua Indians were the original inhabitants of north Florida. By about 1700, most had been killed by disease and raids by more northerly tribes. Non-Muskogee Oconee Indians from south Georgia, who moved south during the early eighteenth century, formed the kernel of the Seminole people. They were joined by Yamasee refugees from the Carolina Yamasee War (1715–1716), as well as by some Apalachicola, Calusa, Hitchiti, and Chiaha Indians and escaped slaves. The Chiahas were known as Miccosukees by the late eighteenth century. Several small Muskogean groups joined the nascent Seminoles in the late eighteenth century.

Seminoles considered themselves Creek; they supported the Creeks in war and often attended their councils. They experienced considerable population growth after the 1814 Creek War, mainly from Muskogeans from Upper Creek towns. From this time on, the dominant language among the Seminoles was Muskogee, or Creek. However, Seminole settlements, mainly between the Apalachicola and the Suwannee Rivers, were too scattered to permit the reestablishment of Creek towns and clan structures.

Prior to the Civil War some Seminoles owned slaves, but the slaves' obligations were minimal, and Seminoles welcomed escaped slaves into their communities. Until 1821, U.S. slaves might flee across an international boundary to Florida. Even after that year, the region remained a haven for escaped slaves because of the presence of free African American and mixed African American and Seminole communities.

Seminoles first organized to fight the United States in 1817–1818. The conflict was begun by state militias chasing runaway slaves, and it resulted in the Spanish cession of Florida. In the Treaty of Moultrie Creek (1823), the Seminoles traded their north Florida land for a reservation in central Florida. The 1832 Treaty of Payne's Landing, which was signed by unrepresentative chiefs and was not supported by most Seminoles, called for the tribe to relocate west to Indian Territory. By 1838, up to 1,500 Seminoles had been rounded up and penned in concentration camps. These people were forcibly marched west, during which time as many as 1,000

died from disease, starvation, fatigue, heartbreak, and attacks from whites. Although under pressure to do so, the Seminoles consistently refused to give up the considerable number of African Americans among them. In 1856, the western Seminoles were given a strip of land of about 2 million acres west of the Creeks.

Resistance to relocation and to white slave-capturing raids led to the second Seminole War of 1835–1842. Under Osceola, Jumper, and other leaders, the Seminoles waged a guerrilla war against the United States, retreating deep into the southern swamps. Although Osceola was captured (at a peace conference) and soon died in captivity, and although at war's end most Seminoles, about 4,500 people, were forced into Indian Territory, the Seminoles were not militarily defeated. The war ended because the United States decided not to spend more than the $30 million it had already spent or to lose more than the 1,500 soldiers that had already been killed.

A third Seminole war took place from 1855 to 1858. From their redoubt in the Everglades, the Indians attacked non-Native surveyors and settlers. The Army, through its own attacks and by bringing in some Oklahoma Seminoles, succeeded in persuading another 100 or so Seminoles to relocate, but about 300 remained, undefeated, in Florida. There was never a formal peace treaty.

In the 1870s, as the first non-Natives began moving south of Lake Okeechobee, there was another call for Seminole removal, but the government decided against an attempt. In the late nineteenth century, a great demand for Seminole trade items led to close relationships being formed between Florida Indians and non-Native traders.

Western Seminoles settled in present-day Seminole County, Oklahoma, in 1866. By the 1890s the people had formed fourteen bands, including two composed of freedmen, or black Seminoles. Each band was self-governing and had representation on the tribal council. Most of the western Seminole reservation, almost 350,000 acres, was allotted in the early twentieth century. Through fraud and other questionable and illegal means, non-Natives by 1920 had acquired about 80 percent of the land originally deeded to Indians. Tribal governments were unilaterally dissolved when Oklahoma became a state in 1907. An oil field opened on Seminole land in 1923, but few Indians benefited. Many Oklahoma Seminoles moved away from the community during and after World War II in search of jobs.

Indian Baptists from Oklahoma achieved the first large-scale successes in Christianizing Florida Seminoles in the early twentieth century. Most Florida Seminoles lived by subsistence hunting, trapping, and fishing, as well as by trading, until non-Natives overhunted and trapped out the region. Around the time of World War I, the subsistence economy disintegrated even further as Florida began to drain the swamps and promote agriculture. By the 1920s, the new land boom, in conjunction with the drainage projects, led to significant Indian impoverishment and displacement.

Most Seminoles relocated to reservations during the 1930s and 1940s. There they quickly acculturated, adopting cattle herding, wage labor, schools, and Christianity. With the help of Florida's congressional delegation, the tribe avoided termination in the 1950s. At that time they adopted an Indian Reorganization Act–style corporate charter. Formal federal recognition came in 1957. By the 1950s, a group of more traditional Mikasuki-speaking Indians, mostly living deep in the Everglades, moved to separate themselves from the Seminoles, whom they regarded as having largely renounced their Indian traditions. After a great deal of struggle, the Miccosukees were given official permission by the federal government to form their own government, the Miccosukee Tribe, which they did in 1962.

See also African Americans; Black Seminoles; Canoes; Creek War; Economic Development; Indian Removal Act; Muskogean Language; Osceola; Seminole Wars; Slavery.

Tunica

"Tunica" means "Those Who Are the People." The Tunicas were culturally similar to the Yazoos. The people lived anciently in northwestern Mississippi and Arkansas as far as the Washita River. Tunica was one of several Tunican languages.

Tunicas worshipped the sun, among other deities. They celebrated the Green Corn feast. Clay figures stood inside thatched temples built atop mounds. They may have engaged in sacrificial killing. Chiefs were relatively authoritarian, although not at the level of the Natchez. Men planted, harvested, and dressed skins. Women made

pottery, clothing, and mulberry tree bark fabric. The custom of infant head deformation was probably acquired in the late pre-contact period. If personally witnessed, adultery was severely punished.

Villages were located on the Mississippi floodplain in the midsixteenth century but on the bluffs overlooking the floodplain in the late seventeenth century. At least in the early eighteenth century, towns were laid out in a circle. Thatched houses were partly square and partly round and contained no smoke holes. Granaries, possibly square, were built on posts.

The Tunica economy was based on agriculture. Men and women grew corn as well as pumpkins and beans. They integrated crops such as melons and peaches after contact with non-Natives. Corn was made into at least forty-two different dishes, including gruel (hominy) and bread. The people also grew a particular grain-bearing grass. Women gathered wild rice, berries, fruits, grapes, mushrooms, and nuts. In season, persimmon bread was a staple food item for at least a month. Deer, turkey, and buffalo were the most important animal foods. Other foods included ducks and other fowl, fish, and possibly dogs.

Cloth fabric woven from mulberry bark was used in a number of items. Women also made pottery and pine straw baskets. Men hollowed logs for mortars and cut saplings for pestles. Tunicas mined and boiled down salt from licks to trade with other tribes, particularly the Quapaws and Taensas. The people made very fine pottery as well as dressed skins. Carved dugout canoes enabled them to move around the many rivers and lakes.

Most clothing was made from deerskin. Men wore breechclouts, and women wore a wrapped waist-to-knee skirt made from deerskin or mulberry cloth. Mantles or cloaks were made from turkey feathers or muskrat skins. Girls wore a two-piece tasseled mulberry net apron, like those of the Natchez. Most men wore their hair long. Women blackened their teeth. Both sexes tattooed their bodies.

Tunicas had ancient links to southern Hopewell culture. Hernando de Soto came through their territory in 1541. Around 1700, the French claimed the lower Mississippi area, at which time Jesuit missionaries established a presence. The Tunicas became loyal French allies, in part to counter pro-British Chickasaw slave traders.

Out of fear of the Chickasaws and other tribes, the Tunicas moved south to a Houma town, opposite the mouth of the Red River, around 1705. Despite being given a friendly reception, after several years they killed most of their Houma hosts and forced the others to move away. The Tunicas were important French allies in the 1729 Natchez War and fought the Yazoos and several other tribes in 1731.

The Tunicas fought the British as part of the Pontiac uprising when the French lost political control of the region in 1763. For years after that event, the Tunicas attempted to maintain a delicate diplomatic balance between the European powers. They sided with France and the colonies in the American Revolution. Their existence and their rights ignored, at best, by the U.S. government, the Tunicas dispersed in the later eighteenth century, moving up the Red River to the Avoyelles prairie. Others joined the Atakapa, and still others joined the Choctaws in Indian Territory.

The tribe hired a lawyer to protect its interests in the early nineteenth century. Still, ignoring federal law, the United States denied the Tunicas long established title to their land. The Indians lived in relative harmony with their neighbors, however, until their chief was murdered in 1841 for resisting the theft of tribal land. In a state trial, centering on the land dispute, the Indians were formally awarded some of their own land, which became the basis of their reservation.

The Tunicas continued to hunt, farm, fish, and practice traditional healing and religion into the twentieth century. They merged with the Biloxis, a small Siouan tribe, in the 1920s. Participation in several court cases in the early twentieth century underscored the need for literacy and formal recognition. Faced with a severely diminished population, one chief proposed in the 1940s to sell all tribal lands and move the people to Texas, for which he was removed from office. The last chief died in 1976.

See also Agriculture; Canoes; Hopewell Culture; Trade.

Tuscarora

"Tuscarora" comes from *Skaroo'ren*, "hemp gatherers," their self-designation and possibly the name of one of the constituent tribes or villages. (*See also* Oneida.) In the sixteenth century, the Tuscaroras were living near Cape Hatteras on the Roanoake,

Neuse, Tar, and Pamlico Rivers, in North Carolina. Tuscaroras spoke an Iroquoian language that changed markedly following the northward migration.

Tuscaroras believed that after death the immortal soul traveled to a western paradise. There were a number of planting and harvest festivals. The "tribe" was a collection of autonomous villages, each with its own chief, or headman, and council. The office of chief may or may not have been hereditary. Women served in some political capacity. Ultimate political authority was vested in the people and the council. The Tuscaroras were at first represented by the Oneidas in the Iroquois League's annual council.

There were eight matrilineal clans in New York. Women nominated the clan chiefs. For five or six weeks, once in their lives, older children were secluded in a cabin and tortured with hunger and emetic plants. The people may have played a mathematical reed game, in which high-stakes gambling figured prominently. A great deal of ceremony was associated with the burial of men, the degree of ritual and expense being related to a person's social standing.

Curing methods included shaking gourd rattles, sucking blood and fluids, and using snakes. Curers also used many herbal and plant medicines. The cures were often quite effective, and early non-Native observers noted that these Indians were generally much healthier than were the colonists and other Europeans.

Some villages were palisaded, at least in the early historical period. A village might have hundreds of houses; the average early eighteenth-century village population was around 400. A village consisted of several hamlets, or cabins near an open ceremonial area surrounded by fields. People who lived in "the country" had more distant neighbors.

Corn was the staple food, north and south. People also grew beans and squash. Women gathered wild fruits, nuts, berries, and roots. Men hunted game, including deer, bear, beaver, otter, rabbit, cougar, opossum, raccoon, partridge, pheasant, geese, and ducks. Seafood also played an important dietary role. Bows were carved from black locust wood whenever possible. Animal bones were used as hoes. Men made bowls, dishes, spoons, and utensils from tulip, gum, and other wood. Women made pottery and wove baskets of bark and hemp as well as mats of rush and cane.

Men wore hand-tanned breechclouts; women wore a wraparound skirt and a tunic. Both were made from Spanish moss or softened tree bark. Outerwear consisted of turkey feather, fur, or deerskin mantles. Men, especially among the wealthy, wore copper bracelets and other ornaments. Both men and women painted their bodies extensively. Tuscaroras were very active traders, at least in the early to midseventeenth century. Their arts included carved wooden items, woven mats and baskets, and pottery. The people navigated rivers and marshes in cypress log canoes.

The Tuscarora people came originally from the north, perhaps around the Saint Lawrence Valley–Great Lakes region. They may have moved southward as late as around 1400. In the sixteenth century, and for some time thereafter, they were the dominant tribe in eastern North Carolina, despite losing upward of 80 percent of their population to European diseases during the seventeenth and early eighteenth centuries. Their somewhat inland location kept them from extensive contact with non-Native settlers until the midseventeenth century.

Tuscaroras were traditionally friendly to the British settlers, even to the point of helping them fight other Indians. Active involvement in the deerskin, rum, and slave trade led to a growing factionalism within the tribe, which was the most intense in villages closest to trade centers. Involvement with rum also contributed significantly to a general decline of the people. Throughout the seventeenth and into the eighteenth centuries, non-Natives regularly took advantage of Indian generosity, taking their best lands, cheating them in trade, and stealing their children for slaves.

War between the two groups broke out in 1711. It was largely a reaction to years of British abuse and to continuing population loss due to disease. Led by Chief Hancock, the Indians raided settlements and killed perhaps 200 British, who took their revenge as they could. Some Tuscarora villages remained neutral because of especially pro-British contact and sympathies; the "neutral" and "hostile" camps each had their Indian allies from other tribes. Freed African Americans played a significant role in the construction of European-style forts among the Indians.

The conflict soon became a general war, with some tribes, such as the Coree and Pamlico, fighting with the Tuscaroras and others, mainly Algonquins, fighting with the Carolina militias. In 1713, as a

result of a betrayal by Tuscarora leader Tom Blount, Carolina soldiers killed or captured almost 1,000 Tuscaroras. Many of the captives were sold into slavery. Most survivors migrated to New York to live among their Iroquoian-speaking relatives. Those who did not join the initial exodus lived for some additional years on the Susquehannah and Juniata Rivers, and some neutrals continued to live for a time in North Carolina. Virtually all Tuscaroras had left by 1802.

In 1722 or 1723, under the sponsorship of the Oneidas, the Tuscaroras were formally admitted into the Iroquois League, although their chiefs were not made official sachem chiefs. The former southerners soon adopted much of northern Iroquois culture. With the Oneidas, most Tuscaroras remained neutral or sided with the colonists in the American Revolution, although the rest of the league supported the British. The Senecas and a non-Native land company donated land to the Tuscaroras consisting of three square miles near Niagara Falls. The tribe purchased over 4,000 acres in 1804. It also received over $3,000 from the North Carolina legislature from the sale of Tuscarora land in that state.

Most Tuscaroras had become farmers and Christians by the end of the nineteenth century. Meanwhile, those loyal to Britain in the war settled in Oshweken, Ontario, on the Six Nations Reserve. The Tuscarora rejected the Indian Reorganization Act in the 1930s. In the 1950s, the government proposed that a massive reservoir be built on their land. The Indians' refusal to sell led to many protests and a court battle. Although they ultimately lost, and the reservoir was constructed, the process contributed significantly to their own, as well as other tribes', sense of empowerment and national identity.

See also Agriculture; Haudenosaunee Confederacy; Trade.

Yuchi

"Yuchi" possibly either means "from far away" or is derived from *Hitchiti* for "People of Another Language." The tribe consisted of several distinct, named bands, one of which may have been called Chisca. They were culturally similar to the Catawba Indians. Yuchis lived in the eastern Tennessee hills in the midsixteenth century. Yuchean was a linguistic isolate, possibly related to the Siouan language family.

The sun was recognized as the chief deity and power. The three-day corn harvest festival included dancing, a new fire ceremony, and deep male scarring. The Green Corn festival included a stickball game as well as the formal initiation of boys into manhood. Disease was said to be caused by offended animal spirits; shamans cured with herbs, chants, and dancing. One of the four souls possessed by each person could pass to another life.

Each band had its own chief and leadership structure. Yuchis belonged to one of two societies: chief and warrior. Membership was determined by patrilineal descent. Babies were named on the fourth day of life. Matrilineal clans may or may not antedate their associations with the Creeks.

Yuchis built their villages—stockaded in the midseventeenth century—near streams. They grouped their houses around a central square used for ceremonial and social purposes. Houses were wood-frame structures covered with clay or woven mats and roofed with cypress bark or shingles.

Corn, beans, and squash were planted in river valleys. Corn was the staple food. It was served in many ways and often mixed with other foods, including powdered hickory nuts and meat. Wood ash was added for flavor. Men hunted buffalo, bear, elk, deer, turkey, and birds. Men hunted using bows and arrows and blowguns (for birds and small game). Most men owned two large leather pouches decorated with beads and slung over the shoulder on straps. Turkey feather fans were used mostly by men to keep insects away and as a sign of leadership. Especially fine pottery included pipes and decorated bowls. Women also made fine cane and split hickory baskets. Turtles and snakes were a common design.

The Yuchis may have been a link in moving copper south from the Great Lakes. Some groups, using the Choctaw trade language, traded in flint or salt. Their pipes came from the Cherokees and Natchez, and they also traded for catlinite pipes from the early eighteenth century on.

Men wore deerskin leggings, sashes, and moccasins, although they frequently went barefoot. In the later eighteenth century they wore brightly colored cloth shirts and jackets, modified breechclouts, leggings tied to a belt, cloth turbans, and various ornaments. Women wore cloth dresses, short leggings, belts, moccasins, and personal ornaments.

Yuchis may have descended from Siouan peoples. They may have encountered Hernando de Soto around 1540 but were certainly attacked by the Spanish in 1566. In the 1630s, Yuchi bands began leaving the Appalachian highlands to raid Spanish settlements in Florida. Some of the bands remained in the south, settling in west Florida among the Upper Creeks. The people encountered British settlers in Tennessee and North Carolina in the 1670s.

In the mid- to late seventeenth century, under pressure by the Shawnees, many Yuchi bands left the high country and followed the Savannah River toward coastal Georgia. They joined Yuchis who had migrated there earlier. With the Creek, both groups became British allies, conducting slave raids for them on Spanish settlements and among other tribes, such as the Apalachees, Timucuas, Calusas, Guales, and Cusabos. This wave was soon driven away from the Savannah, however, and moved west toward the Chattahoochee River in central Alabama.

A final wave of Yuchis migrated south in the early eighteenth century. By the late 1700s, most Yuchis were living near the Coosa and Tallapoosa Rivers, although some remained in southeast Georgia.

By the nineteenth century, Yuchis in Tennessee and North Carolina had merged with the Cherokee. The Georgia Yuchis joined the Creeks, and the Florida Yuchis joined the Seminoles. As many as 900 Yuchis were removed with the Creeks to Indian Territory in 1836. They formed eleven communities in present-day Creek County, Oklahoma.

In the early twentieth century, the Yuchis remained legally united with the Creeks but maintained their own stomp grounds and churches. They refused their own charter in 1938, fearing the motives of the federal government. They maintained their own language and customs, as well as ties to religious sites in Georgia, through the 1950s.

See also Creek War; Forced Marches; Trade.

Native Americans of the Northeast Woodlands

Abenaki

"Abenaki" or more properly "Wabenaki," means "Dawn Land People" or "Easterners." The Abenakis were a group of Algonquin tribes, sometimes discussed as Eastern Abenaki (including Kennebecs, Penobscots, Arosagunticooks, and Pigwackets) and Western Abenakis (including Penacooks, Winnipesaukees, and Sokokis). There was also a seventeenth- and eighteenth-century Abenaki Confederacy consisting of these and other tribes, such as the Maliseets, Micmacs, and Passamaquoddy.

Abenakis lived near major rivers of northern New England and southern Quebec in the early seventeenth century. There were perhaps 10,000 eastern and 5,000 western Abenakis at that time. They spoke dialects of eastern Algonquin languages.

Western groups tended to believe in a supreme creator, and both eastern and Western Abenakis enjoyed a rich mythology. Many ceremonies were based on crops or the hunt as well as on greeting visitors, weddings, and funerals. At least among the western group, boys might seek the help of supernatural beings by obtaining a guardian spirit through a vision quest around the time of puberty. Dances were often associated with the spirit power. Shamans, often employing drums, foretold the future, located game, and cured illness.

Authority was gained as a result of leadership qualities, although there was also an element of patrilineal descent. Eastern chiefs of extended families were also sometimes shamans and after the seventeenth century were known as sagamores. Western groups recognized lifelong civil and war chiefs as well as a council of elders. The chiefs' powers were relatively limited.

Several related nuclear families living together made up a household, which was the basic social and economic unit. Descent was patrilineal. Social status was somewhat hierarchical, especially in the east, where chiefs might have more than one wife. In general, men provided animal foods, fought, and made tools and houses; women grew crops, gathered foods, prepared and cooked food, made clothing, and took care of children. Men engaged in frequent races and archery contests.

The use of stories and gentle group pressure was sufficient to discipline children. Marriage, considered official after gifts were given to the bride's family, was celebrated by feasting and dancing (as were many occasions). The dead were buried as soon as possible with weapons and/or tools for use in the afterlife.

Villages were located along streams and, among the western group, near meadows. Easterners lived in dome-shaped and square houses with pyramid roofs shingled with bark. There were smoke holes at the top, and deerskins covered the two doors. Westerners tended to live in birchbark longhouses with arched roofs. Several families lived in each house. They also built dome-shaped sweat lodges.

A shorter growing season and poorer soil meant that Abenakis depended less on crops than did southern Algonquins. In small family groups they

hunted caribou, deer, and bear and trapped beaver and other small game as well as birds. Western groups called and ran down moose.

Women gathered berries, nuts, potatoes, and wild cherries and other fruits. They also boiled maple and birch sap for syrup and sugar. In spring, the eastern group fished along the coast for salmon, shad, eel, sturgeon, smelt, and other fish. They also gathered shellfish and other marine foods and hunted sea mammals. Fish were also important to the western group, who grew more corn, beans, squash, and tobacco.

Men made birchbark and dugout canoes, snowshoes, and toboggans. Many items, including pottery and bark containers, were carefully decorated. From the early seventeenth century on, wampum beads were used to record treaties and major council decisions. Abenakis generally traded with neighboring groups until the beginning of the fur trade period, when they traded furs for corn from southern New England. At that time, wampum became a medium of exchange and political status.

Women tanned skins to make most clothing. Men wore beaver pelt breechclouts and belts. Western women wore skirts and blouses in addition to cold weather gear. Both wore moccasins, leggings, moose hide coats, and fur robes and caps. Tunics were also common. Both sexes painted their faces and bodies and wore their hair long.

Abenakis originally came from the Southwest, according to their legends. They may have met early explorers such as Giovanni da Verrazano in the sixteenth century. They were definitely visited by Samuel de Champlain and others, including missionaries, early in the seventeenth century, shortly after which time the Abenakis became heavily involved in the fur trade. Western groups traded with the Dutch and entered the fur trade later than the eastern groups.

Almost immediately, many eastern villages disappeared as a result of war (mostly Micmac attacks) and disease. Among the survivors, material culture and subsistence economy changed rapidly with the availability of non-Native items. Indians and the French regularly intermarried. Western groups came into conflict with the Iroquois from the mid- to late seventeenth century. Abenakis first arrived in Quebec from Maine in the late seventeenth century. They lived on the banks of the Chaudière River before moving to their present territory in the early eighteenth century.

Abenakis were staunch allies of the French in the colonial wars, although eastern groups needed to cover their bases with the British in the interest of preserving trade. Fierce Abenaki fighters sacked many British settlements throughout New England in the late seventeenth and early eighteenth centuries. The Western Abenakis, in particular, played a significant role in much of the history of New France, including fur trading, exploring, and fighting the Senecas and Mohawks.

The Indians steadily lost land during the late seventeenth and eighteenth centuries. The Penobscots slowly emerged as the strongest eastern tribe. When the town of Norridgewalk fell to the British in 1724, many Eastern Abenakis withdrew to Quebec. Although the Penobscots urged Abenaki neutrality in the French and Indian War, other Eastern Abenakis, now living in Quebec, fought with the French. The Penobscots were eventually drawn in: The treaty of 1763 marked the British victory and the Penobscot defeat. Meanwhile, after the fighting ended in 1763, Western Abenakis returned to their territory to find British squatters. They abandoned most of these lands after 1783, settling near a reserve on the Ste. Francois River in Quebec.

In the nineteenth and early twentieth centuries, most Western Abenakis sought to avoid anti-Indian sentiment by speaking French, selling ash splint baskets to tourists, and keeping to themselves. Some hunted in a large territory north of the Saint Lawrence River, and some returned to northern New England for seasonal cash work and subsistence activities. Many Western Abenakis attended Dartmouth College in the nineteenth century.

In 1941, the establishment of a wildlife refuge by the state of Vermont ended the people's ancient hunting and fishing rights. A postwar resurgence of the western group was based on controversies over fishing and hunting rights and a lack of official recognition. These groups held fish-ins to dramatize their situation. State recognition in 1976 was withdrawn the following year.

See also Canoes; Maine Indian Claims Settlement Act.

Algonquin

"Algonquin" or "Algonkin" probably comes from a Micmac word meaning "at the place of spearing fish and eels from the bow of a canoe." It is the name of a

A 1645 portrait of a 23-year-old Algonquin man wearing necklace and head ornaments, and with facial markings. (Library of Congress)

northeastern group of bands that also gave its name to an important language family. The original self-designation was *Anishinabeg,* or "true men." Principal Algonquin bands included the Weskarinis (the Algonquins proper), Abitibis, and Temiskamings. In the early seventeenth century, Algonquins lived in the Ottawa Valley of Quebec and Ontario, particularly along the northern tributary rivers. Algonquins spoke an Algonquin language.

The people believed in a great creator spirit and a host of lesser spirits, both good and evil. Both shamans and hunters sought guardian spirits to help them with their work, which included interpreting dreams and healing the sick. Small bands were composed of one or more clans with local chiefs. People smoked tobacco silently before council meetings. Algonquins entertained visitors with the annual Feast of the Dead, a dance with a war theme. When entertaining guests, the host did not eat. Clan descent as well as the inheritance of hunting territo-

ries may have been patrilineal. Bands tended to come together in the summer and disperse in the winter. People lived in cone-shaped, teepee-like dwellings. They also built rectangular birchbark hunting shelters.

Men fished in both the summer and winter (through holes cut in the ice). They hunted game such as moose, deer, caribou, and beaver. Agricultural crops played a small role in their diet. Important material items included birchbark containers sewn with spruce roots, basswood bags and mats, wooden cradle boards, bows and arrows, and double-headed drums. Algonquins imported fish nets and cornmeal from the Hurons and traded extensively with Iroquoian tribes. They traded animal pelts and porcupine quills to nearby groups in exchange for corn, tobacco, fishing gear, and wampum.

Men made birchbark canoes, snowshoes, and toboggans. Dress varied according to location. Most clothing was made of buckskin or moose skin. Clothing included breechclouts, skirts, ponchos, leggings, robes, and moccasins; moccasins were often dyed black. Fur garments were added in cold weather.

Algonquins lived on the north shore of the Saint Lawrence River from about 1550 to 1650. They began trading with the French in the early sixteenth century and later provoked a war with the Mohawks. The Algonquins won that skirmish with the assistance provided by the French in order to maintain an important trade partner.

However, the French had made a powerful enemy in the Mohawks, and within a few decades the local military situation had been reversed, with the Iroquois now firmly in control. Meanwhile, the Hurons had replaced the Algonquins as the key French trade partner. The Mohawks, needing to expand their trapping area, soon attacked again. The Algonquins were forced to abandon the upper Saint Lawrence and, after about 1650, the Ottawa Valley. They returned in the 1660s when peace was reestablished. An epidemic in the 1670s left them further weakened.

During the late seventeenth century, some Algonquin bands merged with the Ottawa Indians. French trading posts were established, and missionaries became a permanent presence in their territory by the early eighteenth century. Some Algonquins traveled to the far west to trap for Canadian companies. After the final French defeat in 1763, the Algonquins became staunch British allies. Reserves

for the group were created in the nineteenth century, when their lands were overrun by British settlers. The decline of the fur trade and of their hunting grounds (mainly owing to local logging operations), as well as a growing dependence on non-Natives, led many Algonquins to adopt a sedentary lifestyle.

> *See also* Canoes; French and Indian War;
> Haudenosaunee Confederacy, Political System;
> Wampum.

Anishinabe

"Anishinabe" means "People." The Anishinabes are also variously known by the band names Ojibwe/Ojibwa/Ojibway/Chippewa, Mississauga, and Salteaux. The name "Ojibwa" means "puckered up," probably a reference to a style of sewn moccasin. Northern groups had a Subarctic as well as a Woodlands cultural orientation. In the early seventeenth century, at least 35,000, and maybe double that number, of Anishinabes lived north of Lake Huron and northeast of Lake Superior (present-day Ontario, Canada). The various Anishinabe groups spoke dialects of Algonquin languages.

Some groups may have believed in the existence of an overarching supreme creative power. All animate and inanimate objects had spirits that could be good or evil (the latter, like the cannibalistic Windigo, were greatly feared). People attempted to keep the spirits happy through prayer, by the ritual use of tobacco, and with the intervention of shamans. Tobacco played a significant role in many rituals.

By fasting and dreaming in a remote place, young men sought a guardian spirit that would assist them throughout their lives. In general, dreams were considered of extreme importance. There was probably little religious ceremonialism before people began dying in unprecedented numbers as a result of hitherto unknown diseases of Old World origin. The Midewiwin, or Medicine Dance, was a curing society that probably arose, except among the northern Ojibwas, in response to this development.

Men led autonomous bands of perhaps 300 to 400 people on the basis of both family and ability. Band headman were often war captains but had little direct authority before the fur trade period; for their own advantage, traders worked to increase the power of the headman. These efforts ultimately led to the creation of a patrilineal line of chiefs.

About fifteen to twenty-five patrilineal clans were linked into the larger divisions. Bands came together in villages during the summer and dispersed for the winter hunting season. Within the context of a social organization that was relatively egalitarian, there were people with higher status than others, such as chiefs, accomplished warriors, and shamans.

Although a special feast was held to celebrate a boy's first kill, the major male puberty rite was the vision quest, which entailed a four-day fast deep in the forest to await a propitious dream. Girls might also have visions, but they were not generally required to undergo a quest.

Corpses were washed and well presented. Wrapped in birchbark, they were removed from the wigwam, after a period of lying in state, through an opening in the west side. A priest gave a funeral ceremony, after which the body was buried with tools and equipment. The soul was said to travel for four days to a happy location in the west. The mourning period lasted one year.

The Anishinabes enjoyed regular visiting as well as social dancing (although on such occasions men often danced apart from women). They also enjoyed various sports, such as lacrosse and a game in which they threw a pole along frozen snow, and contests; gambling invariably played a part in these activities. Lacrosse was rough and carried religious overtones.

The traditional Anishinabe dwelling was a domed wigwam of cattail mats or birchbark over a pole frame. There were also larger, elliptical wigwams that housed several families. Hunters also used temporary bark-covered A-frame lodges, and people built smaller sweat lodges, used for purification or curing, as well as menstrual huts and Midewiwin, or Medicine Lodge Society, lodges.

Women grew small gardens of corn, beans, and squash in the south. Men hunted and trapped a variety of large and small game, mostly in the winter, as well as birds and fowl. Meat was roasted, stone boiled, or dried and stored. Some was dried and mixed with fat and chokecherries to make pemmican, an extremely nourishing, long-lasting food. Men fished year round, especially for sturgeon, sometimes at night by the light of flaming birchbark torches. People also ate shellfish where available.

In the fall, women in canoes gathered wild rice, which became a staple in the Anishinabe southwest and important as well around Lake Winnipeg. They also gathered a variety of berries, fruits, and nuts, and some groups collected maple sap for sugar, which they used as a seasoning and in water. Northern Ojibwas had access neither to wild rice nor to maple sap.

Trade items included elm-bark bags and assorted birchbark goods, carved wooden bowls, food, and maple sugar. As they expanded west, the people began to trade Woodland items for buffalo-derived products. Clothing and medicine bags were decorated with quillwork. Men carved wooden utilitarian as well as religious items (figurines). They also made birchbark canoes and snowshoes. Northern Ojibwas used toboggans and canoe sleds, sometimes hauled by large dogs, from the nineteenth century on. The Anishinabe were also known for their soft elm-bark bags. Lake Winnipeg women made fine moose hide mittens, richly decorated in beads. As with many Native peoples, storytelling evolved to a fine art.

Dress varied according to location. Most clothing was made of buckskin. Ojibwas tended to color their clothing with red, yellow, blue, and green dyes. In the southwestern areas, women wore woven fiber shirts under a sleeveless dress. Other clothing included breechclouts, leggings, robes, and moccasins, the last often dyed and featuring a distinctive puckered seam. Fur garments were added in cold weather.

The Anishinabes probably came to their historical location from the northeast and had arrived by about 1200. They encountered Frenchmen in the early seventeenth century and soon became reliable French allies. From the later seventeenth century on, the people experienced great changes in their material and economic culture as they became dependent on guns, beads, cloth, metal items, and alcohol.

Pressures related to the fur trade, including Iroquois attacks, drove the Anishinabes to expand their territory by the late seventeenth century. With French firearms, they pressured the Dakotas to move west toward the Great Plains. They also drove tribes such as the Sauks, Foxes, and Kickapoos from Michigan and replaced the Hurons in lower Michigan and extreme southeast Ontario. With the westward march of British and especially French trading posts, Ojibwa bands also moved into Minnesota and north central Canada, displacing Siouan and other Algonquin groups. Many people also intermarried

with Cree Indians and French trappers and became known as Métis, or Mitchif. By the eighteenth century, Anishinabe bands stretched from Lake Huron to the Missouri River.

The people were most deeply involved in the fur (especially beaver) trade during the eighteenth century. They fought the British in the French and Indian War and in Pontiac's Rebellion. In 1769, in alliance with neighboring tribes, they utterly defeated the Illinois Indians. They fought on the British side in the Revolutionary War. Following this loss, they kept up anti-American military pressure, engaging the non-Natives in Little Turtle's War, Tecumseh's Rebellion, and the War of 1812.

By the early nineteenth century, scattered, small hunter-fisher-gatherer bands of northern Ojibwas and Salteaux were located north and west of the Great Lakes. These people experienced significant changes from the early nineteenth century, such as a greater reliance on fish and hare products and on non-Native material goods.

The Plains Ojibwas (Bungis) had moved west as far as southern Saskatchewan and Manitoba and North Dakota and Montana. They adopted much of the Great Plains culture. The southeastern Ojibwas (Mississaugas), living in northern and southern Michigan and nearby Ontario, were hunters, fishers, gatherers, and gardeners. They also made maple sugar and, on occasion, used wild rice. Their summer villages were relatively large. Finally, the southwestern Ojibwas had moved into northern Wisconsin and Minnesota following the departing Dakotas. They depended on wild rice as well as hunting, fishing, gathering, gardening, and maple sugaring.

The Anishinabes living in the United States ceded much of their eastern land to that government in 1815 upon the final British defeat. Land cessions and the establishment of reservations in Wisconsin and Minnesota followed during the early to midnineteenth century. Two small bands went to Kansas in 1839. In the 1860s, some groups settled with the Ottawas, Munsees, and Potawatomis in Indian Territory.

Michigan and Minnesota Anishinabe groups (with the exception of the Red Lake people) lost most of their land (90 percent or more in many cases) to allotment, fraud, and other irregularities in the mid- to late nineteenth century. They also suffered significant culture loss as a result of government policies encouraging forced assimilation. In the late nineteenth century, many southwestern Ojibwas worked as lumberjacks. Many in the southeast

concentrated more on farming, although they continued other traditional subsistence activities when possible. Transition to non-Native styles of housing, clothing, and political organization was confirmed during this period.

Plains Ojibwas took part in the Métis rebellion of Louis Riel in 1869–1870. These groups were finally settled on the Turtle Mountain Reservation in the late nineteenth century and on the Rocky Boy Reservation in the early twentieth century. Around the turn of the century, the Turtle Mountain Chippewas, led by Chief Little Shell, worked to regain land lost in 1884 and to reenroll thousands of Métis whom the United States had unilaterally excluded from the tribal rolls. In 1904, the tribe received $1 million for a 10-million-acre land claim. Soon thereafter, most of the Turtle Mountain land was allotted. One result of that action was that many people, denied adequate land, were forced to scatter across the Dakotas and Montana. Most of the allotments were later lost to tax foreclosure, after which the tribal members, now landless, drifted back to Turtle Mountain.

The growing poverty of Michigan bands was partially reversed after most accepted the Indian Reorganization Act (IRA) in the 1930s and the United States reassumed its trust relationship with them. Many of these people moved to the industrial cities of the Midwest, especially in Michigan and Wisconsin, after World War II, although most retained close ties with the reservation communities.

See also Fur Trade; Indian Reorganization Act; Lacrosse; Riel, Louis; Tecumseh; Trade.

Brothertown
See Pequot.

Cayuga

The Cayugas, from their word for "People of Oiogouen," were one of the five original tribes of the Iroquois League. The name Iroquois ("real adders") comes from the French adaptation of the Algonquin name for these people. Their self-designation was *Kanonsionni*, "League of the United (Extended) Households." Iroquois today refer to themselves as Haudenosaunee, "People of the Longhouse." There

were about 1,500 Cayugas in 1660 and possibly as many as several thousand or more a century earlier, among perhaps 20,000 members of the Iroquois League. Cayugas spoke a northern Iroquois dialect.

The Cayugas recognized Orenda, a supreme creator. Other animate and inanimate objects and natural forces were also considered of a spiritual nature. They held important festivals to celebrate maple sap and strawberries as well as corn planting, ripening (Green Corn ceremony), and harvest. These festivals often included singing, male dancing, game playing, gambling, feasting, and food distribution.

The eight-day new year's festival may have been most important of all. Held in midwinter, it was a time to give thanks, to forget past wrongs, and to kindle new fires, with much attention paid to new and old dreams. A condolence ceremony had quasi religious components. Curing societies also conducted ceremonies, since illness was thought to be of supernatural origin. In the early nineteenth century, many Iroquois embraced the teachings of Handsome Lake.

The Iroquois League comprised fifty hereditary chiefs, or sachems, from the constituent tribes. Each position was named for the original holder and had specific responsibilities. Sachems were men, except when a woman acted as regent, but they were appointed by women. The Cayugas sent ten sachems to meetings of the Iroquois Great Council, which met in the fall and for emergencies. Their symbol at this gathering was the Great Pipe.

Tribes were divided into two divisions within the league, the Cayugas belonging to the "younger brothers." Debates within the great council were a matter of strict clan, division, and tribal protocols, in a complex system of checks and balances. Politically, individual league members often pursued their own best interests while maintaining an essential solidarity with the other members. The creators of the U.S. government used the Iroquois League as a model of democracy.

Locally, the village structure was governed by a headman and a council of elders (clan chiefs, elders, wise men). Matters before the local councils were handled according to a definite protocol based on the clan and division memberships of the chiefs. Village chiefs were chosen from groups as small as a single household. Women nominated and recalled clan chiefs. Tribal chiefs represented the village and the nation at the general council of the league. The entire system was hierarchical and intertwined, from the family up to the great council. Decisions at

all levels were reached by consensus. There were also a number of nonhereditary chiefs ("pine tree" or "merit" chiefs), some of whom had no voting power. Their existence may have been a postcontact phenomenon.

The Cayugas recognized a dual division, each composed of two matrilineal, animal-named clans. The Cayugas probably had nine clans. Each owned a set number of personal names, some of which were linked with particular activities and responsibilities. Women enjoyed a high degree of prestige, being largely equated with the "three sisters" (corn, beans, and squash), and they were in charge of most village activities, including marriage. Great intravillage lacrosse games included heavy gambling. Other games included snowsnake, or sliding a spear along a trench in the snow for distance. Food was shared so that everyone had roughly the same to eat.

Personal health and luck were maintained by performing various individual rituals, including singing and dancing, learned in dreams. Members of the False Face medicine society wore wooden masks carved from trees and used rattles and tobacco. Shamans also used up to 200 or more plant medicines to cure illness. The condolence ceremony mourned dead league chiefs and installed successors. A modified version also applied to common people.

Boys began developing war skills at a young age. Prestige and leadership were often gained through war, which was in many ways the most important activity. All aspects of warfare, from the initiation to the conclusion, were highly ritualized. Women had a large, sometimes decisive, say in the question of whether or not to fight. Male prisoners were often forced to run the gauntlet: Those who made it through were adopted, but those who did not might be tortured by widows. Some captives were eaten.

In the early eighteenth century, Cayugas lived in at least three villages of thirty or more longhouses, each village with 500 or more people. The people built their villages near water and often on a hill after about 1300. Some villages were palisaded. Other Iroquois villages had up to 150 longhouses and 1,000 or more people. Villages were moved about twice in a generation, when firewood and soil were exhausted.

Iroquois Indians built elm-bark longhouses, fifty to 100 feet long, depending on how many people lived there, from about the twelfth century on. The longhouses held two or three or as many as twenty families, as well as their dogs. The people also built some single-family houses.

Women grew corn, beans, squash, and gourds. Corn was the staple and was used in soups, stews, breads, and puddings. It was stored in bark-lined cellars. Women also gathered a variety of greens, nuts, seeds, roots, berries, fruits, and mushrooms. Tobacco was grown for ceremonial and social smoking. After the harvest, men and some women took to the woods for several months to hunt and dry meat. Men hunted large game and trapped smaller game, mostly for the fur. They also caught waterfowl and other birds, and they fished.

Iroquois used porcupine quills and wampum belts as a record of events. Wampum was also used as a gift connoting sincerity and, later, as trade money. Other important material items included elm-bark containers, cordage from inner tree bark and fibers, and levers to move timbers. Men steamed wood or bent green wood to make many items, including lacrosse sticks. Elm-bark canoes were roughly twenty-five feet long. The people were also great runners and preferred to travel on land. They used snowshoes in the winter.

Women made most clothing from deerskins. Men wore breechclouts and shirts; women wore skirts. Both wore leggings, moccasins, and cornhusk slippers in the summer. Clothing was decorated with feathers and porcupine quills. Both men and women tattooed their bodies extensively.

The Iroquois began cultivating crops shortly after the first phase of their culture in New York was established around 800. Deganawida, a Huron prophet, and Hiawatha, a Mohawk shaman living among the Onondagas, founded the Iroquois League or Confederacy some time between 1000 and 1150. It originally consisted of five tribes: Cayugas, Mohawks, Oneidas, Onondagas, and Senecas; the Tuscaroras joined in the early eighteenth century.

Iroquois first met non-Natives in the sixteenth century. There were sporadic Jesuit missions in Cayuga country throughout the midseventeenth century. During those years, the Cayuga were more friendly toward the French than were some other Iroquois tribes. The people became heavily involved in the fur trade during the seventeenth and eighteenth centuries. Trading, fighting, and political intrigue characterized those years. Although they were good at playing the European powers against each other, the Iroquois increasingly became British allies in trade and in the colonial wars and were

instrumental in the ultimate British victory over the French.

Diplomatic success allowed the Iroquois to concentrate on expanding their trapping territory and increasing their trade advantages, mainly by fighting many tribes to their west and south. The Cayuga warpath led as far south as Virginia. Iroquois power blocked European westward expansion. Two Siouan tribes, the Tutelos and the Saponis, joined the Cayugas in 1753.

The British victory in 1763 meant that the Iroquois no longer controlled the regional balance of power. Despite their long-standing allegiance, some Indians joined anti-British rebellions in an effort to protect their land. One such rebellion took place in 1774 and was led by Logan, a Cayuga chief of the Iroquoian Mingos of Pennsylvania.

The confederacy split its allegiance in the Revolutionary War, with most Cayugas siding with the British. This split resulted in the council fire's being extinguished for the first time in some 200 years. The Iroquois suffered a major defeat in 1779. After the final U.S. victory, many Cayugas migrated to Ontario, Canada, where they established two villages on the Six Nations Reserve. Others settled with the Senecas in western New York. Still others remained for several more years in their homelands. However, by 1807 the Cayugas had sold all their land to the United States. After the Buffalo Creek and Tonawanda Reservations were sold in 1842, Indians who had been living there, including many Cayugas, relocated to the Cattaraugus and Allegany Reservations. Most Cayugas went to Cattaraugus.

The Iroquois council officially split into two parts during that time. One branch was located at the Six Nations Reserve and the other at Buffalo Creek. Gradually, internal reservation affairs, as well as relations with the United States and Canada, assumed more significance than intraconfederacy matters. In the 1840s, when the Buffalo Creek Reservation was sold, the fire there was rekindled at Onondaga.

In Canada, the Cayugas, known with the Onondagas and Senecas as the lower tribes, tended to retain more of their traditional beliefs than did the upper Iroquois tribes. Many subsequently adopted the Handsome Lake religion. Traditional structures were further weakened by the allotment of reservation lands in the 1840s; the requirement under Canadian law, from 1869 on, of patrilineal descent; and the transition of league councils and other political structures to a municipal government. In 1924, the Canadian government terminated confederacy rule entirely, mandating an all-male elected system of government on the reserve.

The Native economy gradually shifted from primarily hunting to farming, dependence on annuities received for the sale of land, and some wage labor. The people faced increasing pressure from non-Natives to adopt Christianity and sell more land. The old religion declined during that time, although on some reservations the Handsome Lake religion grew in importance.

In 1817, some of the New York Cayugas, along with other Iroquois and Delaware Indians, moved west to near the Sandusky River in Ohio. They were removed to Indian Territory (Oklahoma) in 1831. Some other Cayugas moved to Wisconsin in 1832 with a group of Oneidas. The Cayugas in Oklahoma maintained a separate tribal government until 1937. Mainly because of fraud and outright theft, their 65,000-acre reservation had been reduced to 140 acres of tribal land by 1936. In 1937, the Seneca-Cayuga incorporated under Oklahoma law, adopting a constitution and bylaws and electing a business committee. Although their land base quickly grew, almost 300 acres were later taken away as a result of reservoir construction. The tribe successfully resisted termination in the 1950s. With other members of the confederacy, the Cayugas resisted the 1924 citizenship act, selective service, and all federal and state intrusions on their sovereignty.

See also Deganawidah; Deskaheh; French and Indian War; Handsome Lake; Haudenosaunee Confederacy, Political System; Hiawatha.

Chippewa
See Anishinabe.

Delaware
See Lenápe.

Fox
"Fox" is possibly from one of the tribe's clans. Their self-designation was *Mesquaki*, "Red Earth People."

The Foxes were culturally related to the Kickapoos. (*See also* Sauk.) In the seventeenth century, roughly 2,500 Foxes were located in a wide area on the border between the Woodlands and the prairie, centered in eastern Wisconsin near Lake Winnebago. The Fox people speak an Algonquin language.

The Fox recognized an upper and a lower cosmic region. The former was ruled by the great or gentle manitou. There were also any number of other nature-related spirits, or manitous, the most important of which were connected with the four directions. People might gain the attention and assistance of the manitous by offering tobacco, blackening their faces with charcoal, fasting, and wailing.

The vision quest, undertaken at puberty, was another way to attract spiritual power. Those who were especially successful assembled a medicine pack or bundle; certain packs represented power that affected and were the property of entire lineages. Two annual ceremonies were related to the medicine packs. The Midewiwin, or Medicine Dance, was a key ceremony. Others included the Green Corn and Adoption ceremonies. The calumet, or sacred pipe, played a vital role in all sacred activities, including peace negotiations.

Fox society was divided into bands or villages, of fluid composition, that formed in the summer but broke up in the winter. There were dual political divisions of peace and war. Officers were the main chief, subchiefs, and criers. A hereditary peace chief held authority over gatherings, treaties, peace councils, intertribal negotiations, and rituals. War chiefs were chosen by other warriors on the basis of merit, although there may have been a hereditary component.

The Foxes recognized about fourteen patrilineal clans. Membership in one of the two tribal divisions was determined by birth order. Each summer house was an economic unit as well as a social one.

Parents rarely inflicted corporal punishment on their children. At the onset of puberty, girls were secluded for ten days and were subject to various restrictions. Both sexes marked puberty by undertaking a vision quest. Marriages were generally arranged by the couple in question and were formalized when the families exchanged gifts. Some men had more than one wife. Adultery was generally cause for divorce. Burial took place after various rituals had been performed. All people were buried in their finest clothing, wrapped in bark or mats, with their feet toward the west.

Summer villages were located near crop fields in river bottoms. Extended families of some ten people lived in houses about fifty feet long by twenty feet wide and covered with elm bark. These houses were oriented in an east-west direction and were built in parallel rows, with an open game and ceremonial area in between. People moved the villages when firewood became scarce or when attacks forced them to move. When in their winter camps, people lived in small, dome-shaped wigwams covered with reed mats and located in sheltered river valleys. The camps ranged in size from just one or two families to an entire band.

Fox women grew corn, beans, squash, and tobacco. They also gathered a number of wild plant foods, including nuts, honey, berries, fruits, and tubers. Men hunted a variety of large and small game, especially deer, as well as buffalo from at least the eighteenth century until about 1820. Clothing was generally light and consisted mainly of buckskin breechclouts, dresses or aprons, leggings, and moccasins. Hide or fur robes were added for extra warmth. The people also tattooed and painted their bodies.

Reasons for war included conflict over territory, retaliation, and the achievement of status. War parties had to be authorized by the war council. Leaders of war parties began by fasting to obtain a vision and undertook several more ritualistic activities before the party departed. The leader carried his sacred ark, which was said to provide the party with spiritual power. Warriors were subject to a number of rituals on their return as well. Prisoners were often adopted.

The Foxes may once have lived just west and/or south of Lake Erie and, before that, along the southern shore of Lake Superior. They were driven by Iroquois raids into the upper Fox River–Chicago River area, perhaps in the early seventeenth century.

After non-Natives first appeared among them in the midseventeenth century, the Foxes quickly joined the fur trade. Unlike most Algonquins, however, they refused to settle near trading posts or missions. They also made enemies by requiring a toll from French traders plying the Fox River and were even able to block French access to the Mississippi if and when they chose.

The Foxes fought the French and their Indian allies in the early to mideighteenth century. They were almost destroyed during that period by warfare and disease, which was in fact the goal of French forces. Survivors took refuge with the Sauks in 1733,

beginning an alliance that lasted until the 1850s. In 1769, the Sauks, Foxes, and other tribes dealt a permanent defeat to the Illinois tribes and moved south and west into some of their former territory and ultimately back into Iowa. By that time they had become highly capable buffalo hunters.

The Foxes took an active part in Little Turtle's war (1790–1794) and in Tecumseh's Rebellion (1809–1811), two defensive actions in which the tribes of the old west made a last-ditch effort to hold onto their lands. Lead mines near Dubuque, Iowa, at which the Foxes had been mining up to two tons of lead a year, were illegally seized by non-Native interests in the early nineteenth century. In 1842, the Sauks and Foxes ceded their remaining lands and were relocated to a reservation in Kansas.

Some Foxes remained with the Sauks in Kansas and went with them in 1869 to the Indian Territory (Oklahoma). However, after a series of disputes with the Sauks, most Foxes returned to Iowa in the late 1850s, settling near Tama and acquiring land there. Ownership of their own land prevented future allotment and enabled the people to maintain their physical boundaries and thus much of their traditional culture. The people generally refused to enroll their children when the Bureau of Indian Affairs opened a boarding school in the late nineteenth century, but they did accept a day school after 1912. They adopted an Indian Reorganization Act–based government in 1937. Traditional and progressive factions have struggled for control of the tribe for much of the twentieth century.

See also Algonquin; Indian Reorganization Act; Thorpe, Jim.

Huron

See Wyandotte.

Illinois

The Illinois were a group of bands, probably all Algonquins, that included but were not limited to the Cahokias, Kaskaskias, Michigameas, Moingwenas, Peorias, and Tamaroas. The word "Illinois" is a French adaptation of their self-designation, *Inoca*. The Illinois were a borderline Eastern Woodlands group, with much of their territory consisting of prairie. They were culturally similar to the Miamis. Roughly 10,000 Illinois lived south of Lake Michigan in the early seventeenth century. Illinois was an Algonquin language.

Manitou, a supreme being or creator, dwelled to the east and may have been identified with the sun. Men probably undertook a vision quest at adolescence, during which they hoped to attract a personal guardian spirit. At the onset of puberty, girls fasted in a special lodge until they received a personal guardian spirit. Shamans, or medicine people (they could be men or women and were usually older), conducted religious ceremonies. They acquired their powers from powerful animal spirits. Most ceremonies included dancing and smoking tobacco from a sacred pipe (calumet).

Each tribe was an independent entity and lived either in a separate village or in a separate section of a multitribe village. There may have been peace and war chiefs as well as criers to make announcements. Camp police during the summer buffalo hunt enforced strict discipline.

Illinois tribes recognized patrilineal clans. Hospitality was a primary value. A ritual feast followed a boy's first game kill. Boys who showed such an inclination might become berdaches (men who dressed like women and assumed all of their roles). Berdaches were regarded as having a particularly sacred element. Men usually refrained from marriage until they had proven themselves as warriors and hunters. Women could destroy the property of men who attempted to marry without the proper lineage controls. Female adultery was punished by death, mutilation, or mass rape.

Each gender was responsible for burying its own dead. After the face and hair were painted, corpses were dressed in fine clothing, wrapped in skins, and buried in the ground or on scaffolds. Tools, pipes, and other goods were set by the grave, which was marked by two forked sticks with a crossstick or, in the case of a chief, by a painted log. Various ceremonies were then performed that honored the dead by reenacting a favorite activity.

Capturing prisoners rated higher war honors than killing them. Male prisoners were usually burned and eaten, whereas women and children were distributed among the population. Some were ultimately adopted, but some maintained a slavelike identity.

The Illinois built semipermanent summer villages strung out for miles along river banks. The villages consisted of up to 300 or more lodges, each

with one to four fireplaces and housing up to twelve families. There were also small menstrual/birth huts and possibly an additional structure used for political or ceremonial purposes.

Large, rectangular summer houses were built of woven mats over a pole frame. Mats were also placed on the ground as flooring. The people also built temporary summer and winter hunting camps. Summer huts were bark-covered buildings, whereas winter lodges were covered with rush mats.

Meat formed the most important part of the Illinois diet. Men hunted elk, bear, buffalo, deer, mountain lion, turkey, beaver, and other animals. Women grew corn, beans, and squash. They also gathered a variety of wild fruits, nuts, berries, and roots.

Men fashioned dugout canoes of up to fifty feet in length from butternut trees. They wore breechclouts, while women wore long dresses. Both sexes wore buffalo robes and blankets. They also tattooed and painted their bodies and wore various personal adornments of animal teeth, colored stones, feathers, and other items.

The Illinois may have come to their historic territory from the Northeast. They may have mixed with the Cahokian (Mississippian) people when they moved into Illinois in the midseventeenth century. The people fought two major wars with the Winnebagos from about 1630 to 1645: They lost the first and won the second.

Iroquois attacks drove the people west of the Mississippi about 1660. After this time they began slaving raids on Siouan and Pawnee tribes west of the Mississippi. The Illinois tribes first met French explorers in the 1670s and became French allies shortly thereafter. The abandonment of the Illinois River region and a southward movement began around 1700, marking a general defeat at the hands of tribes such as the Kickapoos, Foxes, and Sauks, who also sought French favor. With the exception of the Peorias, who held out in the north until the later eighteenth century, most Illinois tribes became associated with specific French agricultural settlements. By 1800, the Michigameas, Cahokias, and Tamaroas merged with the Kaskaskias and Peorias.

The Wisconsin tribes maintained more or less continuous pressure on the Illinois tribes during the eighteenth century. The final battle may have come after an Illinois Indian, said to be in the pay of Britain, killed Chief Pontiac in 1769. In any case, those Illinois still free of French protection were all but wiped out, suffering upward of 90 percent casualties. Meanwhile, the southern Illinois, through their contact with the French, had become missionized, poor, and alcoholic.

Survivors of the wars with the Great Lakes Algonquins, mainly members of the Kaskaskia and Peoria bands, signed treaties in the early nineteenth century ceding their lands to the United States. Their culture practically gone, these people moved to eastern Kansas in 1833, where they lived with the Wea and Piankashaw (Miami) bands until 1867, when they all bought land in northeastern Oklahoma. In 1873 they took the name United Peoria and Miami. Their lands were allotted in 1893, and any remaining tribal land was lost when Oklahoma became a state in 1907. The group reincorporated as the Peoria Tribe of Oklahoma in 1940. They were terminated in 1950 but restored in 1978.

See also Algonquin; Cahokia; Termination.

Iroquois

See Cayuga; Mohawk; Oneida; Onondaga; Seneca, Tuscarora.

Kickapoo

"Kickapoo" is possibly from *kiwegapaw*, "he moves about, standing now here, now there." The Kickapoos were culturally similar to the Sauks and Foxes and may once have been united with the Shawnees. Several thousand Kickapoos lived around the Fox and Wisconsin Rivers (present-day southern Wisconsin) in the midseventeenth century, although they inhabited present-day Michigan and Ohio earlier and Illinois and Kansas somewhat later. Kickapoos spoke an Algonquin language similar to Sauk and Fox.

All things, animate and inanimate, contained spirits, or manitou. Kicitiata, the supreme manitou, or creator, dwelled in the sky. Tobacco facilitated communication with the manitous. Young people may have undertaken vision quests. Dreams, which may have been encouraged by fasts, also had spiritual significance.

The main ceremony was a weeklong renewal and thanksgiving in early spring, at which time sacred bundles were opened and repaired. The people also celebrated the Green Corn and Buffalo Dances. Priests were in charge of religious

A Kickapoo wichiup, Sac and Fox Agency, Oklahoma, ca. 1880. (National Archives and Records Administration)

observances. There may have been a ritual office, held by a woman, which gave approval to hold certain ceremonies.

The Kickapoos were divided into constituent bands, which were probably led by chiefs. A council of clan heads made decisions by consensus. Kickapoo society was organized in patrilineal clans. Furthermore, a dual division formed the basis for various cultural features such as "joking" (informal enforcement of social norms), games, races, and ritual seating. Personal names were tied to dreams or visions. Menstrual seclusion was particularly long and rigorous the first time, at which time the woman was advised by older women on how to behave as an adult. After killing their first game, boys were given a feast, which included songs and prayers.

Courting may have involved the use of a flute. Marriage was finalized by gift giving between the families. Funeral or death ceremonies included feasting, song, and prayer as well as quiet moments. People left the village for four days following a death,

after which time ceremonial adoptions were often performed.

Rectangular summer and round or oval winter houses were framed with green saplings. Summer houses were covered with elm bark and often attached to an arbor. Sleeping platforms lay along the sides. Doors faced east, and there was a smoke hole in the roof. Temporary winter houses were covered with woven cattail or tule mats.

Kickapoos were heavily dependent on crops. Women grew corn, beans, and squash, and they gathered various wild foods. Men hunted deer, bear, and other game, including some buffalo, and they fished. Carved wooden prayer sticks recorded prayers and myths as well as events. Pottery containers could hold water. Kickapoos served as intermediaries in the midnineteenth century Comanche horse trade. Kickapoo dress depended largely on their location. The basic items were breechclout, dress or apron, leggings, and moccasins, although they tended to borrow local customs, especially with

regard to personal ornamentation. Kickapoo warriors were known as extremely fierce, able, and enthusiastic fighters.

The Kickapoos may have originated in southeast Michigan. In the seventeenth century, pressure from the Iroquois drove them west to southern Wisconsin, where they encountered French missionaries. They may have shared villages with the Miamis at that time. Kickapoos entered the fur trade, but throughout the later seventeenth and early eighteenth centuries they resisted pressure to assimilate and cede their lands. They were often at war with the French during that period, although the two groups established an alliance in 1729. They also fought various Indian tribes.

In the early eighteenth century, the Kickapoos joined tribes such as the Ojibwas, Ottowas, Sauks, and Foxes to defeat the Illinois Confederacy and occupy their territory. The Kickapoos moved south to the Illinois River, where the tribe soon divided. One group headed farther south to the Sangamon River. Known as the Prairie band, they increased their buffalo hunting. The other group moved east toward the Vermillion Branch of the Wabash River. This band retained their forest hunting practices. The band also absorbed the Mascouten, or Prairie Potawatomi, tribe of Indians.

Part of the Prairie band moved into southwest Missouri in the mid-1760s. Following the French defeat in 1763, the Kickapoos transferred their allegiance to the Spanish. They participated in Pontiac's Rebellion and later accepted British aid against the United States, with whom they never had good relations.

The early nineteenth century saw greatly increased non-Native settlement in the region. Most Kickapoos participated in Little Turtle's war. The Vermillion band also supported Tecumseh's Rebellion, which the Prairie band opposed. Both groups, however, were drawn into the War of 1812. Some chiefs of each band ceded the people's Illinois land in 1819, a move that forced most Kickapoos to join the group already living in Missouri.

Some Kickapoos, however, under Chief Mecina and the prophet Kenakuk, continued to resist relocation by passive means as well as guerrilla tactics. They were finally forced to move to Kansas in the early 1830s following their defeat in Black Hawk's war. Most Missouri Kickapoos had accepted a reservation in Kansas in 1832. Some later fought with the United States against the Seminole in 1837.

From their base in Kansas, the tribe broke into several smaller groups, some remaining in Kansas and some migrating to Oklahoma, Texas, and Mexico. Horse-stealing raids, particularly in Texas, were an important activity throughout much of the nineteenth century. In 1862, some Kickapoo land was allotted and some was sold to a railroad company.

In the early to mid-1860s, fighting erupted between Mexican Kickapoos and Texas Rangers attempting to prevent some Kansas Kickapoos from crossing Texas to join their relatives. In the 1870s, the U.S. Army illegally crossed the Mexican border and destroyed the main Kickapoo village in Mexico. They also brought a group of women and children back to the Indian Territory as hostages; many men then agreed to leave Mexico and join them there.

In 1883, these people were granted a 100,000-acre reservation in Oklahoma. However, when that reservation was allotted ten years later and pressure to assimilate increased, many people returned to Mexico, first to Nacimiento and then to northern Sonora. In 1908, the Kansas reservation was allotted to individuals. In 1937, the Kansas Kickapoos reorganized under the Indian Reorganization Act. They successfully resisted termination in the 1950s.

See also Agriculture; Algonquin; Horse, Economic Impact; Termination.

Lenápe

"Lenápe," or Leni Lenápe, means "Human Beings" or "Real People" in the Unami dialect. The Lenápes were part of a group of Algonquin speakers from North Carolina to New York. This group numbered around 10,000 in 1600. The Lenápe tribes who lived around the Delaware River are more commonly known as Delaware Indians. This central group of northeastern Algonquin Indians was referred to as "grandfather" by other Algonquin tribes, in recognition of its position as the group from which many local Algonquin tribes diverged.

Like many Algonquins, the Lenápes believed in a great spirit (manitou) as well as the presence of other spirits in all living things. Personal guardian spirits were acquired in adolescence and were said to be connected with future success. The bear sacrifice, held in the midwinter, was the most important of at least five annual religious festivals. Others revolved around foods, such as maple sugar (early

spring), corn (late spring and late summer), and strawberries (early summer), as well as curing.

After death, spirits were said to travel to an afterlife. Names were given with the benefit of a personal vision by the name giver, which enhanced his or her status. Chiefs often served as religious as well as political leaders of the village. Shamans of both sexes were responsible for holding the curing ceremonies.

Each of the three autonomous divisions maintained its own territory; there was never any political unity. Each village group of several hundred people had its own hereditary chief (sachem or sagamore). The chief had no coercive powers, instead acting as mediator, adviser, and hunt leader. With the chief, other lineage leaders and elders formed a council. Village groups were autonomous, but they often acted in concert for purposes of hunting drives and defense.

There were traditionally three matrilineal clans. Women grew and prepared foods, took care of children, gathered firewood, and prepared skins. Men hunted, fished, traded, fought, cured, made houses and most tools, and served as chiefs. People from the coast tended to visit the interior in the spring, when they moved to fishing and hunting camps, whereas people from the interior visited the coast in the summer. Murder was generally expiated by a payment.

Premarital girls were secluded and observed strict behavioral taboos during their periods. Premarital sexual relations were condoned, but adultery was not, except when consent was given, such as in wife lending on the part of a polygynous chief. Divorce was easily and frequently obtained. Corpses were buried in a sitting position with some possessions. Mourners blackened their faces and visited the grave annually.

Each of thirty to forty villages, located on river and tributary meadows, was surrounded by fields and hunting grounds. Houses were circular, domed wigwams or thirty- to sixty-foot (but up to 100-foot) multifamily, grass or bark-covered, single-doorway longhouses with both pitched and arched roofs. Both dwellings contained smoke holes. Interior longhouses may have been palisaded in times of war.

From at least about 1300, inland groups depended mostly on corn; beans and squash were also important. Game hunted in seasonal trips included deer, elk, bear, raccoons, rabbit, wolves, squirrel, and fowl. Fire surrounds were used as part of a general practice of burning the undergrowth of certain lands. Men also trapped various small mammals, turkeys, and other birds. Coastal people depended mainly on fish and shellfish (generally dried and preserved), seaweed, birds, berries, and meat and oil from stranded whales. Women gathered various roots, greens, wild fruits, and nuts as well as maple sap. Tobacco was also grown.

The Walum Olum ("red score") was a pictographic history, painted or engraved on wood or bark, of the people's legends and early migrations. A later manuscript, the only one that survives in any form, interpreted the pictographs in the Lenápe language. Men made dugout and bark canoes. The Lenápes traded in, among other items, rounded-bottom pots; grass mats, bags, and baskets; wampum (polished shell); and bark and skin containers. Woven items, such as baskets, were decorated with painted spruce roots or porcupine quills.

Women made clothing of deerskins and furs. People generally wore few clothes, such as breechclouts for men and skin kilts for women, in warm weather. Both added leggings, deerskin moccasins, and robes of bear or other skins in the winter. Other items of clothing included turkey feather cloaks, leather belts, and temporary cornhusk footwear. People dressed their hair and bodies with bear or raccoon grease mixed with onion, in part as a protection against the sun and insects. Various personal adornments included earrings and necklaces, tattoos, and body paint.

According to the Walum Olum, the Lenápes may have originated to the northeast, possibly in Labrador, where they were united with the Shawnees and the Nanticokes. They may have passed through the eastern Great Lakes region and the Ohio Valley, where they met and possibly defeated Hopewell Mound Builder people. They likely encountered non-Natives in the early to mid-sixteenth century.

Contact with Henry Hudson in 1609 was followed by the people's rapid involvement in the fur trade. In short order, their dependence on items of non-Native manufacture, such as metal items, guns, and cloth, fundamentally altered their economy as well as their relations with neighboring peoples. Other changes in material culture included the introduction of new foods such as pigs, chickens, and melons. In 1626, the Manhattan band of Lenápes traded the use of Manhattan Island to a Dutchman for about $24 worth of goods. This arrangement was quickly interpreted as a sale by the Dutch, who, unlike the Lenápes, valued property ownership.

Growing numbers of non-Natives, Indian land cessions and pressure for more, and intertribal rivalries brought on by competition over furs led to conflict with the Dutch from the 1640s until the British took possession of the colony in 1663. In 1683, the Lenápe people, represented by Chief Tamanend (from whose name the designation of Tammany Hall was taken), signed a treaty of friendship with the Quaker William Penn (who gave his name to the state of Pennsylvania).

By the late seventeenth century, the Lenápe population had been decimated by disease and warfare. In the early eighteenth century, the Iroquois Confederacy dominated the Lenápe people, even going so far as to sell some of their land to the British. By the middle of that century, more and more Lenápes had moved into western Pennsylvania and the Ohio River Valley. A group of Lenápes established farms in eastern Ohio, but hostilities with non-Natives increased as the frontier moved west. About 100 Lenápes were slaughtered by Kentucky frontiersmen at a Moravian mission in 1782.

Unami speakers living in the lower Allegheny and upper Ohio Valleys in the mideighteenth century formed the nucleus of the emerging Lenápe or Delaware tribe. These people were organized into three groups, or clans—Turkey, Turtle, and Wolf—each with a chief living in a main village. One of the chiefs acted as tribal spokesman. The Lenápes fought the British in the French and Indian War and were generally divided in the Revolutionary War. In 1762, a Lenápe medicine man called Delaware Prophet helped to unite the local Indians to fight in Pontiac's Rebellion. Some Lenápe also participated in Little Turtle's war (1790–1794) and in Tecumseh's Rebellion (1809–1811).

As the non-Natives kept coming, groups of Lenápes continued west into Missouri and even Texas, where they remained until forced into western Oklahoma in 1859. These "absentee Delawares" began hunting buffalo and assumed some aspects of Plains life.

After the Lenápes remaining in Ohio were defeated, with their Indian allies, in the 1794 Battle of Fallen Timbers, they moved to Indiana, Missouri, and Kansas. From their base in Kansas they fought with the Pawnees, who claimed their land, as well as with other Plains tribes. Many also served as scouts in the U.S. Army. After living in Kansas for a couple of generations as farmers, trappers, and guides, they were forced to relocate to Oklahoma in the 1860s.

Following a court battle, these Lenápes became citizens of the Cherokee Nation.

Meanwhile, groups of Munsee speakers had joined the Stockbridge Indians in Massachusetts and New York and moved with them to a reservation in Wisconsin. Others joined the Cayugas in New York and migrated with them to the Six Nations Reserve in Ontario in the late eighteenth century. Still others moved to Canada as well, one group founding a Moravian village in 1792 along the Thames River and another group living at Munceytown. Yet another group joined the Swan Lake and Black River Chippewas near Ottawa, Kansas.

> *See also* Algonquin; French and Indian War; Little Turtle; Tecumseh; Women in Native Woodlands Societies.

Mahican

"Mahican" comes from *Muh-he-con-ne-ok*, "People of the Waters That Are Never Still." This tribe is often confused with the Mohegans, a Connecticut tribe, in part because of the James Fenimore Cooper book *Last of the Mohicans*, a fictional story about a fictional tribe of Indians. There were originally several members of the Mahican confederacy, including, in the late seventeenth century, the Housatonics, Wyachtonocs, and Wappingers.

The Mahican proper (roughly 4,000 to 5,000 in 1600) lived on both sides of the northern Hudson (Mahicanituck) River, in present-day eastern New York and western Vermont. The confederacy was centered around Schodac, near present-day Albany, and included tribes living along the lower Hudson River as well as in western Massachusetts and Connecticut. Mahican was an Algonquin language.

Manitou, the Great Spirit, was present in all things. Some families owned sacred dolls whose spirits were said to protect the owners. The Mahicans celebrated the Green Corn Dance at the beginning of harvest season as well as various first fruits and first game rituals.

Each autonomous village had its own chief and councilors. The positions of lineage leaders and clan chiefs (who may also have been village chiefs) were inherited matrilineally. The head chief, or sachem, kept the tribal bag of peace, which contained wampum, at least in the historical period. As Mahican local and regional power grew, the sachem

acquired three assistants: owl, or orator and town crier; runner, or messenger; and hero, or war chief.

The three matrilineal clans may have inhabited separate villages. Men helped women with the harvest after celebrating the Green Corn festival. Families scattered into the woods in the late fall and remained through the midwinter, when they returned to the villages. Old people remained in the villages all winter long, generally doing craft work. There may have been a recognized system of social status. People were buried in a sitting position. Graves were stocked with provisions for use in the afterlife.

Villages were often located on a hill near a river. At least from the seventeenth century on they were often palisaded. Roughly 200 people lived in a village. Each village contained from three to sixteen long, rectangular bark lodges, as well as domed wigwams, framed with hickory saplings and covered with birch, elm, or basswood bark pressed flat. Longhouses averaged three fireplaces and as many nuclear families. Animal skins were hung on the interior walls for insulation. Villages were moved every ten years or so owing to exhaustion of the land and firewood.

The Mahicans practiced slash-and-burn field clearing and regular rotation of fields. They used fish and ash as fertilizer. Women grew beans, squash, probably sunflowers, and several varieties of corn. Women also gathered waterlily roots, greens, mushrooms, nuts, and berries and made sassafras and wintergreen tea. Maple sap may have been boiled into sugar.

Men hunted game such as bear, deer, moose, beaver, rabbit, otter, squirrel, raccoon, turkey, passenger pigeons, and many other birds. Deer were hunted in fall, moose in spring. In the summer, men gathered mussels and caught herring, shad, and other fish.

Corn was stored in bark containers or bark-lined pits. Most Mahican technology was wood based: Wooden or bark items included bowls, utensils, and containers. Mortars were fire-hollowed stumps. Men made dugout and birchbark canoes as well as snowshoes. Women made pottery and wove baskets, bags, and mats. Containers and clothing were decorated with porcupine quills and paints. Mahicans acted as intermediaries in the shell bead trade from the coast to the Saint Lawrence Valley.

Women made most clothing from finely tanned skins. Men wore breechclouts, and women wore skirts. Both wore shirts, blankets, high leggings, and

moccasins. Both also wore long braids dressed with bear grease and tattooed their faces.

The Mahicans were drawn into the fur trade shortly after they encountered Henry Hudson in 1609. They soon began collecting tribute from the Mohawks for access to a Dutch trade post established in Mahican country in 1614. Shell beads, or wampum, came into use at that time as currency. For a time the Mahicans, trading with the Algonquins to the north, monopolized the regional fur trade.

As nearby fur areas became trapped out, the European powers had some success encouraging their Indian partners to expand through intertribal conflict. With the help of French firearms, for instance, Mohawks drove the Mahicans east of the Hudson River Valley in 1628. The latter reestablished their council fire to the north, around Schaghticoke. Some defeated New England tribes joined this group in the 1670s.

Throughout the late seventeenth century, the Mahicans fought the Munsees, Iroquois, and others in the Piedmont and the Ohio Valley in their quest for pelts. They even ranged as far west as Miami territory, where some of them remained. By 1700 or so, Mahican culture was in retreat, and the people began to sell or otherwise abandon traditional lands to non-Natives. Traditional social and political structures began to break down owing to the demands of the fur trade, as did traditional manufacture and economies. The people also underwent a general moral breakdown, due in part to the influence of alcohol and the general cultural disruption.

In the 1670s, some groups withdrew to live among the Housatonic band of Mahicans, in Westenhunk, although Mahicans also remained in the Hudson River Valley. Some Mahicans also merged with the Saint Francis Abenakis in the Saint Lawrence Valley and joined other Indian communities as well. In the mid-1730s, a group migrated to Wyoming, Pennsylvania, and some resettled in the mission town of Stockbridge, Massachusetts. The so-called Stockbridge Indians fought with the British in the French and Indian War and with the Patriots in the American Revolution. In the mid-1740s, Moravian missionaries persuaded local Indians to remove to the area of Bethlehem, Pennsylvania. This group ultimately settled in Ottawa, Canada.

By the mid- to late eighteenth century, the Mahicans had completely lost their subsistence economy. Most survived by selling splint baskets, other crafts, and their labor. Despite assisting the colonies in their various wars of this period, the Stockbridge Mahi-

cans were soon dispossessed, and many joined their relatives in the Susquehanna River area in Pennsylvania, there to merge with other tribes, especially the Algonquin Delawares.

By the end of the American Revolution, most of the dispirited remnant of the Mahican nation had left Stockbridge and nearby areas and settled near the Oneida Indians in New York, where they established a thriving non-Native–style farm and craft community. Between 1818 and 1829, these Indians left the Oneida country and migrated west to Wisconsin, where missionaries had purchased land for them. They moved again several years later, after the Wisconsin Indians repudiated their land sales.

Some of this group dispersed to Kansas or died along the way after an abortive move to the Missouri River in 1839. In 1856, they were granted a reservation in Wisconsin, with the Munsee band of Delaware Indians and, later, a group of Brothertown Indians. (*See also* Pequot.) The community was marked by factionalism and various removals for years.

The tribe lost a significant amount of land in the post-1887 allotment process. It was officially terminated in 1910. In the 1930s, the Stockbridge-Munsee, landless and destitute, reorganized under the Indian Reorganization Act and acquired 2,250 acres of land.

Longtime president of the tribe Arvid Miller helped establish the Great Lakes Intertribal Council in the 1960s. Today, the people observe a traditional twelve-day new year celebration. Most Stockbridge-Munsees are Christians, although some participate in sweat lodge ceremonies. Some people study the Munsee-Mahican language and would like to teach it. Most traditional culture has been lost. The tribe hosts a large powwow in early August.

> *See also* American Revolution, Native American Participation; Cooper, James Fenimore; Fur Trade.

Maliseet

"Maliseet," or "Malicite," is probably a Micmac word for "lazy speakers" or "broken talkers." The tribe may be of Passamaquoddy (maritime) and Natick (inland) extraction. Together with the Passamaquoddys, they have also been known as the Etchemin tribe. (*See also* Abenaki; Micmac; Passamaquoddy.) The Maliseets (roughly 1,000 in 1600) traditionally lived along the Saint John River

drainage in present-day New Brunswick, Canada, as well as in northeastern Maine. Maliseets and Passamaquoddys spoke dialects of the same Algonquin language.

Guardian spirits gave people the ability to protect subsistence areas from trespass. They also gave shamans the power to cure, which they did by chanting, blowing, and possibly sucking. Sweat lodges and dances were associated with spiritual power.

Skilled hunters generally provided local leadership. In the seventeenth century there was a supreme hereditary chief who lived at the main village. In general, leadership was more formalized under the confederacy, with graduated civil offices and a war chief. The Maliseets were part of the Abenaki Confederacy from the mideighteenth century to the mid- to late nineteenth century, when the confederacy ceased to exist.

The people came together in large villages in the summer and dispersed into small hunting camps in the winter. They preferred football, a kicking game, to lacrosse. They also played any number of dice gambling games. Herb doctors could be men or women.

Men served their prospective in-laws for at least a year before marriage. During this period, the woman made the man's clothing and footgear. Weddings were marked by feasting, oratory, and the formal recognition of the groom's ancestry. At least in the historical period, sexual mores were strict, and divorce was rare. Children were generally treated gently and with a high degree of freedom, at least when compared with the early French in the area.

Some summer villages were palisaded. They included multi- and single-family dwellings. The former were conical, pole-frame wigwams covered with birchbark; the latter, as well as council houses, were rectangular log-frame structures with birchbark roofs. Council houses could hold up to 100 people.

Farming, especially of corn, was the key economic activity. Harvested corn was either stored or taken on the winter hunts. Men hunted inland animals such as moose, bear, otter, and muskrat. They also fished for salmon, bass, and sturgeon. This, with wild grapes and roots gathered by the women, made up most of the summer diet. Women also gathered fiddlehead ferns in early spring.

Corn was stored in bark-lined pits. Various birchbark items included canoes, containers, baskets, dishes, and boxes, some of which were decorated

with porcupine quills. Cordage came from spruce roots or cedar bark. The crooked knife was an important woodworking tool. Men made lightweight canoes of birchbark, moose hide, or spruce bark. They also made snowshoes. They summoned moose with a birchbark calling instrument. Musical instruments included boards (for beating time), drums, rattles, flageolets, and flutes. Although part of a wide-ranging network, the Maliseets traded mainly among local groups.

The basic dress was breechclouts for men, dresses for women, and moccasins. Furs and heavy skins were used in cold weather. Beaverskin caps protected people's heads from the cold. There were also temporary raincoats made of birchbark.

The Maliseet people may have come to their historical territory from the southwest, where they probably had contact with the Ohio Mound Builders in ancient times. They may also have been united with the Passamaquoddys in the distant past. Their first contact with non-Natives probably occurred in the early seventeenth century when they met Samuel de Champlain, although they may have encountered fishers from northern and western Europe as much as a century earlier.

A growing involvement in the French fur trade led to a parallel dependence on items of non-Native manufacture. The people also accepted Catholic missionaries in the seventeenth century. Throughout the eighteenth century, the Maliseet population declined sharply as a result of disease, abuse of alcohol, and loss of land. They joined the pro-French Abenaki Confederacy in the mideighteenth century. They also sided with the French in the colonial wars and intermarried with them.

By the late eighteenth century, British settlers had pushed the Maliseets out of many of their best subsistence areas, and the traditional annual round of subsistence activities had been seriously disrupted. Reserves were established from 1876 on, although the Maliseets resisted a sedentary lifestyle for a long time. In the mid- to late nineteenth century, many Maliseets worked as loggers, stevedores, craftspeople, guides, and farm laborers. Logging and potato farming transformed the region in the 1870s. Local Maliseets, such as the several families who roamed around Houlton, Maine, also worked as house cleaners and in the mills, made baskets, and hunted, fished, and gathered foods where possible.

In the twentieth century, some old communities were abandoned, as many people congregated in a few reservations or moved off the reservations alto-gether. Along with other landless Indians, Maliseets formed the Association of Aroostook Indians in 1970.

Services by the state of Maine date from 1973. Although the Houlton band receives numerous benefits as a party to the 1980 Maine Indian Land Claims Settlement Act, such as cash, land, and access to federal services, many unaffiliated Maliseet families remain without services or recognition. Maliseets and Passamaquoddys have long enjoyed close relations and continue to intermarry. Canadian Maliseets have largely assimilated into French society. Few people outside of New Brunswick speak the Native language fluently. The Tobique Reservation operates its own school as well as shops selling locally made arts and crafts. The Wabanaki Aboriginal Music Festival is held there over Labor Day weekend. Saint-Anne Day is celebrated in July.

See also Agriculture; Maine Indian Claims Settlement Act; Ohio Valley Mound Culture.

Menominee

"Menominee" comes from *Manomini,* Anishinabe for "Wild Rice People." The Menominees were culturally related to the Winnebagos and Anishinabes. Prior to contact with non-natives, roughly 3,000 Menominees controlled nearly 10 million acres along the northwestern shore of Lake Michigan and west into central Wisconsin. Menominees speak an Algonquin language.

Mecawetok, who may have been identified with the sun, was the Great Spirit and supreme creative force. There were many levels of deities and spirits, some friendly and some evil; the latter were assumed to reside below the earth. Most people sought to obtain spiritual power with the help of a guardian spirit, which one acquired in a vision through fasting and dreaming. Dreams were in some ways the entire basis of living: They determined an individual's sacred songs, dances, and ceremonies. One's power was said to increase with age.

Medicine bundles contained various personal sacred charms. There may have been several old religious cults made up of medicine men or people with outstanding power. People with particularly strong powers included witches and "jugglers." The latter were curers and diviners.

The Midewiwin, or Medicine Lodge Society, was a secret society of shamans. Membership was by invitation or inheritance; initiation was highly ritual-

ized. Each member possessed a medicine bag as well as strong and benevolent medicines. The Dream Dance or Drum Dance contained some pre-contact elements.

Clan chiefs were probably hereditary. Chiefs of the Bear Clan served as tribal chiefs, and the various lineage chiefs made up the village council. Non-hereditary chiefs achieved status through their dreams or war exploits. These people might be war leaders, lead public celebrations, or enjoy other duties and responsibilities.

A band system replaced clans and villages during the late seventeenth century and early eighteenth century. Bands tended to follow clan lines but were mostly based on friendships. The hereditary system of leadership became less important, replaced by skills such as excellence in trapping and an ability to negotiate with non-Natives. There was also a tribal council from this time on.

The Menominees were divided into two divisions: Bear and Thunderbird. Each was in turn divided into patrilineal clans. Smoking tobacco accompanied nearly every important activity. Certain relatives were allowed or encouraged to joke with each other as a means of maintaining social mores and order.

The male sphere included ceremonies, tool and weapon manufacture, and war. Women saw to the home and children; grew, collected, and prepared all food; were responsible for firewood, water, and carrying goods; and made clothing and items associated with food and the home. Women could also participate in many male activities, such as fishing, hunting, dancing, and some power ceremonies.

Boys and girls undertook ten-day dream fasts at puberty; these were the culmination of short childhood fasts. There was also a feast following a boy's first game kill. Children were toughened by icy plunges into water and other ordeals. Women were isolated during their menstrual periods and after childbirth because they were thought to threaten the balance of spiritual power.

Marriages were generally arranged by elders, who took their lead from a couple to a greater or lesser degree. Men might have more than one wife. Corpses were placed on scaffolds, but in the later historical period they were painted red and placed in birchbark coffins, along with personal items. Mourners blackened their faces with charcoal, but funerals were accompanied by feasting and sport.

Winter houses were domed wigwams, with cattail and reed mats placed over bent saplings. These structures were especially used after contact with non-Natives in winter hunting camps. Rectangular summer houses were made of bark over a pole framework. Other hut-type buildings were used for sweat lodges, for women's seclusion, and for ceremonial purposes. Permanent villages usually contained a lacrosse field.

Wild rice—which is not rice but a grass seed—gave this tribe its name and was a staple, along with fish. It was collected in the summer by people, usually women, in canoes. The method entailed bending the plants over and knocking them with paddles; the seeds fell into the bottom of the canoes. They were then dried, pounded, and winnowed, with the grain boiled and served in a stew or with maple syrup.

Men hunted large game, such as deer and buffalo. They also hunted small game from canoes. Men also fished for sturgeon and other fish in Green Bay and in nearby streams. They fished through the ice in the winter. Women grew small gardens of corn, beans, squash, and tobacco. They also gathered berries and maple sap.

Fish were caught using traps, hooks, spears, and woven bark fiber gill nets. Women wove pouches of plant fibers and buffalo hair. They also wove and dyed cattail, rush, or cedar-bark mats and winnowing trays, and they made pottery. Menominee women made especially fine pottery, pouches, and clothing decorated with porcupine quills and animal hair. Men made bark and dugout canoes as well as snowshoes. Wild rice was a major export, as were items made of stone and wood. The people imported buffalo hides and other Prairie items, catlinite (pipestone), and copper.

Men wore deerskin breechclouts, shirts, leggings, and moccasins. Women wore woven nettle shirts as well as deerskin robes, leggings, and moccasins. Both decorated their clothing with paint and porcupine quills. Both also wore copper jewelry and rubbed oil and grease on their hair and bodies.

Shortly after the first non-Natives made contact with the Menominee people in the midseventeenth century, Iroquois warriors drove the Menominees into the Green Bay area, possibly from Michilimackinac. Jesuit missionaries arrived among them in 1671. The people maintained generally friendly relations with non-Natives, especially the French, with whom they occasionally intermarried.

Participation in the fur trade from the late seventeenth century through the early nineteenth century broke the tribe into small, mobile bands of hunters-trappers. They avoided many of the colonial

and other wars of the eighteenth and nineteenth centuries, although some sided with the British in the American Revolution and the War of 1812. With the fur-bearing animals depleted, and under pressure from non-Natives, the Menominees in 1854 ceded all of their remaining lands except for a reservation on the Wolf River in north central Wisconsin.

On the reservation, a split soon developed between traditionalists and progressives. Some people tried farming in the later nineteenth century, but because this was generally unsuccessful, many soon turned to lumbering. In the early twentieth century, with the help of the U.S. Forest Service, the Menominees began harvesting their prime timber resources for sustained yield. Their sawmill became the center of economic activity and the tribe's most important employer. Despite the government's mismanagement of the tribe's timber resources (for which the tribe won a legal judgment and collected an award of over $7.5 million in 1951), the Menominees were among the country's most economically stable and prosperous tribes by the early 1950s.

However, in 1961, the tribe was officially terminated (removed from its special relationship with the federal government). The reservation became a county and the tribe a corporation. The Menominees are perhaps the classic termination disaster. Termination-related expenses soon depleted their cash reserves. When the hospital was forced to close, the people experienced a sharp rise in tuberculosis and other health problems. The low tax base could not finance needed government services, and the tribe sank into poverty. Faced with total financial collapse, it was forced in the late 1960s to sell off prime waterfront real estate to non-Natives—perhaps the point of the termination in the first place.

In reaction to these developments and to the related possibility that non-Natives would make up a majority of the county's voters, a new organization, the Determination of Rights and Unity for Menominee Shareholders (DRUMS), called for a new federal trust relationship for the tribe as well as tribal self-determination. Although termination was reversed in 1973, and most of the former reservation was restored, the tribe has yet to recover from the devastating effects of the termination.

Today, most tribal members are Christians, although the Big Drum religion is also popular, as are the Ojibwa-based Warrior's Dance, the Native American Church, and Medicine Lodge ceremonies. A renewed clan structure exists among the people. The language is in use and taught in school. The College of the Menominee Nation is located in Keshena. The people host an annual powwow. Substance abuse remains a daunting challenge. The tribe is committed to maintaining its sovereignty and its Indian identity.

See also Fur Trade; Language and Language Renewal; Termination.

Miami

"Miami" is possibly from the Ojibwa word *Omaumeg* ("People of the Peninsula") or from their own word for pigeon. Their original name may have been Twaatwaa, in imitation of a crane. The traditional bands were the Atchatchakangouens, Kilatikas, Mengakonkias, Pepicokias, Weas, and Piankashaws. Miamis were culturally and linguistically related to the Illinois. From a position possibly south of Lake Michigan, roughly 4,500 Miamis moved into northern Illinois and southern Wisconsin in the midseventeenth century. Miami is an Algonquin language.

In addition to the supreme Miami deity, the sun, there were also lesser manitous, or spirits. Both sexes undertook a vision quest at puberty, for which they began training by fasting at a young age. Some men were directed by their guardian spirit to act and dress like women; this role was generally accepted, although if they engaged in warfare they did so as men. Priests who cured with magic powers made up the Midewiwin, or Grand Medicine Society. There were also shamans who cured with herbs and plant medicines. The most important ceremonies focused on the harvest and the return from the winter hunt.

The six traditional bands had consolidated by the eighteenth century into four: the Miamis proper, the Pepicokias, the Weas, and the Piankashaws. Of these, the second soon merged into the last two, which by the nineteenth century acted as separate tribes. Even in the nineteenth century, each of the three Miami tribes was divided into bands.

Each village had a council made up of clan chiefs; the council in turn confirmed a village chief, generally a patrilineally inherited position, who was responsible for civil functions and was in turn supported by the people. There was also a war chief who oversaw war rituals. This person generally inherited his position but might obtain it by merit (as was the case with Little Turtle). There were also parallel female peace and war chiefs: The former

supervised feasts, and the latter provisioned war parties and could demand an end to various types of hostilities.

The village council also sent delegates to the band council, which in turn sent delegates to the tribal council. All leaders enjoyed respect and a great deal of authority. In fact, early tribal chiefs may have had a semidivine status, reflecting the influence of Mound Builder culture.

The Miamis recognized roughly five patrilineal clans and possibly a dual division. Names were clan specific, although adults might change names to alter their luck or to avert bad luck. Children were rarely punished; parental instruction and discipline consisted mostly of lectures and behavior modeling. Marriages were either arranged or initiated by couples. Killing an adulterous wife (or clipping off the end of her nose) or an abusive husband was condoned; however, other murders were avenged either by blood or by money or property.

Burial, either extended or seated, took place on scaffolds, in hollowed-out logs, and in small, sealed huts. Only food and water and perhaps some personal adornments went with the corpse. Postfuneral activities included a performance of the dead's favorite dance or activity and, if a parent, a ceremonial adoption of a new parent a year later.

The people built small summer villages along river valleys. Private houses were made of an oval pole framework covered with woven cattail or rush mats. There were also village council houses. Structures in winter hunting camps tended to be covered with elm bark or hides. Miamis developed and grew a particularly fine variety of corn, in addition to beans, squash, and, later, melons. Men hunted buffalo on the open prairies, using fire surrounds and bow and arrow before they acquired horses. Women also gathered wild roots and other plant food.

Miamis exported agricultural products, pipes, and buffalo products. They imported shell beads, among other items. Except for soft-soled moccasins, men often went naked in the summer; women wore a wraparound skirt, leggings, and a poncho. In the winter, men wore deerskin shirts and breechclouts. Men wore their hair in a roach and were extensively painted and tattooed. Some items of clothing were decorated by quillwork with bands in a twining or geometric pattern. Buffalo skin robes were also painted with representational and geometric designs.

With the help of the council, war chiefs decided whether to wage war. War rituals, such as the all-night war dance and the homecoming of a successful war party, were clan based, and leaders of war parties were not considered responsible for deaths or members of their own clan. Warriors carried large buffalo hide shields.

Miami culture evolved at least in part from the prehistoric Ohio Mound Builders. In the midseventeenth century, the people effected a temporary retreat west of the Mississippi in the face of Iroquois war parties; Dakota pressure, including a huge military defeat, sent them back east (with French assistance). Peace was established between the Miamis and the Iroquois in 1701.

Miamis traded with the French from the midseventeenth century on but tended to side with the British in the colonial wars. Some Miamis guided Jacques Marquette and Louis Joliet down the Mississippi in the 1670s. The tribe experienced early factionalism over the issue of Christianity. The Miamis participated in Pontiac's Rebellion (1763), after which they ceded most of their Ohio lands and concentrated in Indiana. They fought with the British against the Americans in the Revolutionary War.

The Miami War, also known as Little Turtle's War, was led by the great strategist Michikinikwa, or Little Turtle. The Indian coalition included Objibwas, Ottawas, Lenápes, Shawnees, Potawatomis, and Illinois as well as Miamis. The war was a defensive one, fought to contain non-Native settlement of the Ohio Valley. The coalition enjoyed significant victories in the early years, thanks mainly to Michikinikwa's strategy of guerrilla warfare. In the end, however, sheer numbers of non-Native soldiers wore the Indians down. Although Michikinikwa foresaw the inevitable defeat and advised a cessation of hostilities, the coalition replaced him with another leader and was decisively defeated at the Battle of Fallen Timbers in 1794. The ensuing Treaty of Greenville forced local Indians to cede all of Ohio and most of Indiana to the United States.

The Miamis underwent a dramatic population decline beginning in the late eighteenth century. Groups of Weas and Piankashaws began moving to Missouri as early as 1814. The United States forcibly removed a group of about six hundred Miamis to Kansas in 1846. In 1854, these groups came together to join the remnants of the Illinois tribe, forming the Confederated Peoria Tribe. They were later relocated to Oklahoma. There, in 1873, the Miamis joined that confederacy, which changed its name to the United Peoria and Miami. The group that remained in Indiana consisted of about 1,500 people whose chiefs had been granted private land.

By the early twentieth century, Miami land in both Oklahoma and Indiana had largely been lost through allotment and tax foreclosure. With the loss of their lands, both communities, but especially the one in Indiana, suffered significant population loss, as people moved away to try to survive. Forty years after the Indiana Miamis lost federal recognition in 1897, they organized a nonprofit corporation in an effort to maintain their identity.

The Indiana Miamis meet twice annually and hold an annual picnic in August. Their agenda for years has focused on reinstating federal recognition, reacquiring land, and economic development. Both Miami tribes, in Indiana and Oklahoma, helped found the Minnetrista Council for Great Lakes Native American Studies, in Muncie, Indiana, an organization dedicated to preserving and promoting Woodlands culture.

See also Algonquin; Little Turtle; Ohio Valley Mound Culture; Pontiac.

Micmac

"Micmac," or "Mi'kmaq," means "allies." The Micmacs called their land *Megumaage* and may have called themselves *Souriquois*. They were members of the Abenaki Confederacy in the eighteenth and nineteenth centuries. Culturally similar to the Maliseets, Penobscots, and Passamaquoddys, they were known to the seventeenth-century British as Tarantines, possibly meaning "traders." The people were traditionally located in southeast Quebec, the Maritime Provinces, and the Gaspé Peninsula of eastern Canada. The Micmac population was between 3,000 and 5,000 in the sixteenth century. Micmac was an Algonquin language.

Manitou, the ubiquitous creative spirit, was identified with the sun. Other deities in human form could be prevailed upon to assist mortals. All animals, but especially bears, were treated with respect, in part because it was believed that they could transform themselves into other species. The Micmacs' rich mythology included Gluscap, the culture hero, as well as several types and levels of magical beings, including cannibalistic giants. Shamans were generally men and could be quite powerful. They cured, predicted the future, and advised hunters.

Small winter hunting groups, composed of households, came together in the summer as bands, in seven defined districts. They also joined forces for war. Bands were identified in part through the use of distinctive symbols. There were three levels of chiefs, all with relatively little authority. Local hunting groups of at least thirty to forty people were led by a hereditary headman (sagamore), usually an eldest son of an important family. These groups were loosely defined and of flexible membership. Chiefs of local groups provided dogs for the hunt, canoes, and food reserves. Sagamores also kept all game killed by unmarried men, and some of the game killed by married men.

The general Micmac worldview valued moderation, equality, generosity, bravery, and respect for all living things. When the people gathered together from the spring through the fall, each group camped at a traditional place along the coast. There was a recognized social ranking in which commoners came below three levels of chiefs but above slaves, who were taken in war.

Children as well as the elderly were treated with respect and affection, although little or no effort was made to help ill or old people remain alive. There were many occasions for feasting and dancing, especially as part of life cycle events. The Micmacs probably observed a woman's puberty ceremony; boys were considered men when they had killed their first large game. There were elaborate menstrual taboos, including seclusion. Older brothers and sisters generally avoided each other. Men used the sweat lodge for purification.

Marriages were generally arranged. A prospective husband, usually no less than twenty years of age, spent at least two years working for his future father-in-law as a hunter and general provider. After the probationary period, he provided game for a big wedding feast, including dancing (first marriages only). The birth of children formalized a marriage. Adultery was rare, although polygyny was practiced. Longevity (life spans over 100 years) was not unusual before contact with Europeans.

Micmacs built their inland winter camps near streams. Single extended families lived in conical wigwams of birchbark, skins, or woven mats. Each had a central indoor fireplace. The inside was divided into several compartments for cooking, eating, sleeping, and other activities. Floors were covered with boughs, and fur-covered boughs served as beds. The people may have had rectangular, open, multifamily summer houses.

In the winter, small bands hunted game such as moose, bear, caribou, and porcupine. They also

trapped smaller game and ate land and water birds (and their eggs). Meat and fish were eaten fresh, roasted, broiled, boiled, or smoked. Pounded moose bones yielded a nutritious "butter." People fished in the spring and summer for eel, salmon, cod, herring, sturgeon, and smelt. They also collected shellfish and hunted seals and other marine animals. They also gathered a number of wild berries, roots, and nuts. They occasionally ate dog, especially at funeral feasts, but they generally avoided snakes, amphibians, and skunks.

Men made birchbark moose calls and boxes. They also made double-edged moose-bone-blade spears and bows and stone-pointed arrows for hunting as well as snares and deadfalls for trapping. Women made reed and coiled spruce-root baskets, woven mats, and possibly pottery. Micmacs generally served as trade intermediaries between northern hunters and southern farmers. Men built eight- to ten-foot-long, seaworthy birchbark and caribou skin canoes. They made two types of square-toed snowshoes, one for powder and one for frozen surfaces.

People dressed in skin robes fastened with one (men) or two (women) belts, moose skin or deerskin leggings, and moccasins. Men also wore loincloths. Both sexes wore their hair long. People tattooed band symbols on their bodies.

Small population groups came together as bands for war. The people were allied with southern Algonquins as members of the Abenaki Confederacy. The Micmacs adopted some Iroquois war customs, such as the torture of prisoners by women. There was some interband fighting (intraband disputes were generally resolved by individual fighting or wrestling). Captives were taken as slaves, tortured and killed, or, especially in the case of young women, adopted.

The Micmacs were originally from the Great Lakes area, where they probably had contact with the Ohio Mound Builders and were exposed to agriculture. They may have encountered Vikings around 1000. The Cabots, early explorers, captured three Micmacs at their first encounter. Friendly meetings with Jacques Cartier (1523) and Samuel de Champlain (1603) led to a long-term French alliance.

The Micmacs were involved with the fur trade by the seventeenth century, becoming intermediaries between the French and Indian tribes to the south. A growing reliance on non-Native manufactured metal goods and foods changed their cultural and economic patterns, and war, alcohol, and disease vastly diminished their population. In 1610, the Grand

Chief Membertou converted to Catholicism after being cured by priests.

In the eighteenth century, the French armed Micmacs with flintlocks and encouraged them, with scalp bounties, to kill people from the neighboring Beothuk tribe. This they did to great effect, nearly annihilating those Indians, after which they occupied their former territory in Newfoundland. British attempts at genocide against the Indians included feeding them poisoned food, trading them disease-contaminated cloth, and indiscriminate individual and mass murder.

By the mideighteenth century, most Micmacs had become Catholics. They continued fighting the British until 1763. Much of this fighting took place at sea, where the people showed their excellent nautical skills. Following the American Revolution and the end of the fur trade, Micmacs remained in their much diminished traditional area, which was increasingly invaded by non-Natives.

In the nineteenth century, Micmacs were forced to accept non-Indian approval of their leadership as well as a general trimming of lands guaranteed by treaty. The people continued some traditional subsistence activities during the nineteenth century but also moved toward working in the lumber, construction, and shipping industries and as migrant farm labor. They were generally excluded from higher-paying skilled or permanent jobs. Starvation and disease also stalked the people during those years.

Micmacs had lost most of their Canadian reserves by the early 1900s. Schools were located on many of those that remained. Hockey and baseball became very popular before the Depression. Significant economic activities in the early to midtwentieth century included logging, selling splint baskets, and local seasonal labor, such as blueberry raking and potato picking. An administrative centralization of reserves in the 1950s led to increased factionalism and population flight.

In the 1960s, many Micmac men began working in high-steel construction, on projects mainly in Boston. Women used vocational training to find work as nurses, teachers, and social workers. They also became increasingly active in band politics. Canadian Micmacs formed the Union of New Brunswick Indians and the Union of Nova Scotia Indians in 1969 to coordinate service programs and document land claims. They and other landless tribes formed the Association of Aroostook Indians in 1970 to try to raise their standard of living and

fight discrimination. The tribe formed the Aroostook Micmac Council in 1982.

Many Micmacs still speak the Native language, and they tend to be active in various pan-Indian organizations. Most are Catholics. There have been some gains in Canadian Micmacs' quest to regain their hunting and fishing rights. Canadian Micmacs still face severe problems such as substance abuse, discrimination, and a high suicide rate.

See also Algonquin; French and Indian War; Maine Indian Claims Settlement Act.

Mohawk

"Mohawk" is Algonquin for "eaters of men." The Mohawk self-designation was *Kaniengehawa,* "People of the Place of Flint." The Mohawks are one of the five original tribes of the Iroquois League and the Keepers of the Eastern Door of the League. The name "Iroquois" ("real adders") comes from the French adaptation of the Algonquin name for these people. Their self-designation was *Kanonsionni,* "League of the United (Extended) Households." Iroquois today refer to themselves as Haudenosaunee, "People of the Longhouse."

The Mohawks were located mainly along the middle Mohawk River Valley but also north into the Adirondack Mountains and south nearly to Oneonta. At the height of their power, the Iroquois controlled land from the Hudson to the Illinois Rivers and from the Ottawa to the Tennessee Rivers. Today, Mohawks live in southern Quebec and Ontario, Canada, and in the extreme north of New York. There were perhaps 15,000 to 20,000 members of the Iroquois League around 1500 and roughly four thousand Mohawks in the midseventeenth century. Mohawks spoke a northern Iroquois dialect.

The Mohawks recognized Orenda as the supreme creator. Other animate and inanimate objects and natural forces were also considered to be of a spiritual nature. The Mohawks held important festivals to celebrate maple sap and strawberries, as well as corn planting, ripening (Green Corn ceremony), and harvest.

The eight-day new year's festival may have been most important of all. Held in the midwinter, it was a time to give thanks, to forget past wrongs, and to kindle new fires, with much attention paid to new and old dreams. A condolence ceremony had quasi religious components. Medicine groups such as the False Face Society, whose members wore carved wooden masks, and the Medicine, Dark Dance, and Death Feast Societies (the last two controlled by women) also conducted ceremonies, since most illness was thought to be of supernatural origin. In the early nineteenth century, many Iroquois embraced the teachings of Handsome Lake.

The Iroquois League comprised fifty hereditary chiefs, or sachems, from the constituent tribes. Each position was named for the original holder and had specific responsibilities. Sachems were men, except where a woman acted as regent, but they were appointed by women. The Mohawk sent nine sachems (three from each clan) to meetings of the Iroquois Great Council, which met in the fall and for emergencies. Their symbol at this gathering was the shield.

Debates within the great council were a matter of strict clan, division, and tribal protocols, in a complex system of checks and balances. Politically, individual league members often pursued their own best interests while maintaining an essential solidarity with the other members. The creators of the U.S. government used the Iroquois League as a model of democracy.

Locally, the village structure was governed by a headman and a council of elders (clan chiefs, elders, wise men). Matters before the local councils were handled according to a definite protocol based on the clan and division memberships of the chiefs. Village chiefs were chosen from groups as small as a single household. Women nominated and recalled clan chiefs. Tribal chiefs represented the village and the nation at the general council of the league. The entire system was hierarchical and intertwined, from the family up to the great council. Decisions at all levels were reached by consensus.

Mohawk society was composed of three matrilineal, animal-named clans (Wolf, Bear, and Turtle). The clans in turn were composed of matrilineal lineages. Each owned a set number of personal names, some of which were linked with particular activities and responsibilities.

Women enjoyed a high degree of prestige, being largely equated with the "three sisters" (corn, beans, and squash), and they were in charge of most village activities, including marriage. Great intravillage lacrosse games included heavy gambling. Personal health and luck were maintained by performing various individual rituals, including singing and danc-

ing, learned in dreams. Shamans also used up to 200 or more plant medicines to cure illness.

Young men's mothers arranged marriages with a prospective bride's mother. Divorce was possible but not readily obtained because it was considered a discredit. The dead were buried in a sitting position, with food and tools for use on the way to the land of the dead. A ceremony was held after ten days. The condolence ceremony mourned dead league chiefs and installed successors. A modified version also applied to common people.

In the seventeenth century, Mohawks lived in three main villages (Caughnawagas, Kanagaros, and Tionnontoguens) of thirty or more longhouses, each village with 500 or more people, and other smaller villages as well. The people built their villages near water and often on a hill after about 1300. Some villages were palisaded. Other Iroquois villages had up to 150 longhouses and 1,000 or more people. Villages were moved about twice in a generation, when the firewood and soil were exhausted.

Iroquois Indians built elm-bark longhouses, fifty to 100 feet long, depending on how many people lived there, from about the twelfth century on. The houses held generally two or three but as many as twenty families. There were smoke holes over each two-family fire. Beds were raised platforms; people slept on mats, their feet to the fire, covered by pelts. Upper platforms were used for food and gear storage. Roofs were shingled with elm bark. The people also built some single-family houses.

Women grew corn, beans, squash, and gourds. Corn was the staple and was used in soups, stews, breads, and puddings. It was stored in bark-lined cellars. Women also gathered a variety of greens, nuts, seeds, roots, berries, fruits, and mushrooms. Tobacco was grown for ceremonial and social smoking.

After the harvest, men and some women took to the woods for several months to hunt and dry meat. Men hunted large game and trapped smaller game, mostly for the fur. They also caught waterfowl and other birds, and they fished. The people grew peaches, pears, and apples in orchards from the eighteenth century on.

Iroquois used porcupine quills and wampum belts as a record of events. Wampum was also used as a gift connoting sincerity and, later, as trade money. These shell disks, strung or woven into belts, were probably a postcontact technological innovation. Mohawks obtained birchbark products from the Huron. Elm-bark canoes were roughly twenty-

five feet long. The people were also great runners and preferred to travel on land. Women used woven and decorated tumplines to support their burdens. They used snowshoes in the winter.

Women made most clothing from deerskins. Men wore shirts and short breechclouts and tunics in cooler weather; women wore skirts. Both wore leggings, moccasins, and corn husk slippers in the summer. Robes were made of lighter or heavier skins or pelts, depending on the season. These were often painted. Clothing was decorated with feathers and porcupine quills. Both men and women tattooed their bodies extensively. Men often wore their hair in a roach, whereas women wore theirs in a single braid doubled up and fastened with a thong.

Boys began developing war skills at a young age. Prestige and leadership were often gained through war, which was in many ways the most important activity. Mohawks were known as particularly fierce fighters. In traditional warfare, at least among the Mohawk, large groups met face to face and fired a few arrows after a period of jeering, then engaged in another period of hand-to-hand combat using clubs and spears.

All aspects of warfare, from the initiation to the conclusion, were highly ritualized. War could be decided as a matter of policy or undertaken as a vendetta. Women had a large, sometimes decisive, say in the question of whether or not to fight. During war season, generally the fall, Iroquois war parties ranged up to 1,000 or more. Male prisoners were often forced to run the gauntlet: Those who made it through were adopted, but those who did not might be tortured by widows. Women and children prisoners were regularly adopted. Some captives were eaten.

The Iroquois began cultivating crops shortly after the first phase of their culture in New York was established around 800. Deganawida, a Huron prophet, and Hiawatha, a Mohawk shaman living among the Onondaga, founded the Iroquois League or Confederacy some time between 1000 and 1150.

The Iroquois first met non-Natives in the sixteenth century. There were sporadic Jesuit missions in Mohawk country throughout the midseventeenth century. During these and subsequent years, the people became heavily involved in the fur trade. Trading, fighting, and political intrigue characterized the period. Although they were good at playing the European powers against each other, the Iroquois increasingly became British allies in trade and in the

colonial wars and were instrumental in the ultimate British victory over the French.

Shortly after 1667, a year in which peace was concluded with the French, a group of Mohawk and Oneida Indians migrated north to La Prairie, a Jesuit mission on the south side of the Saint Lawrence River. This group eventually settled south of Montreal at Sault Saint Louis, or Kahnnawake (Caughnawaga). Although they were heavily influenced by the French, most even adopting Catholicism, and tended to split their military allegiance between France and Britain, they remained part of the Iroquois League. Some of this group and other Iroquois eventually moved to Ohio, where they became known as the Seneca of Sandusky. They ultimately settled in Indian Territory (Oklahoma).

At about the same time, a group of Iroquois settled on the island of Montreal and became known as Iroquois of the Mountain. Like the people at Caughnawaga, they drew increasingly close to the French. The community moved in 1721 to the Lake of Two Mountains and was joined by other Indians at that time. This community later became the Oka reserve. Other Mohawks traveled to the far west as trappers and guides and merged with Indian tribes there.

Early in the eighteenth century, the first big push of non-Native settlers drove into Mohawk country. Mohawks at that time had two principal settlements and were relatively prosperous from their fur trade activities. The establishment of St. Regis in the mideighteenth century by some Iroquois from Caughnawaga all but completed the migration to the Saint Lawrence area. Most of these people joined the French in the French and Indian War, and their allegiance was split during the American Revolution.

The British victory in 1763 meant that the Iroquois no longer controlled the balance of power in the region. Despite the long-standing British alliance, some Indians joined anti-British rebellions as a defensive gesture. The confederacy split its allegiance in the Revolutionary War, with most Mohawks, at the urging of Theyendanegea (Joseph Brant), siding with the British. This split resulted in the council fire's being extinguished for the first time in roughly 200 years.

The British-educated Mohawk Joseph Brant proved an able military leader in the American Revolutionary War. Despite his leadership and that of others, however, the Mohawks suffered depredations throughout the war, and by war's end their villages had been permanently destroyed. When the 1783 Treaty of Paris divided Indian land between Britain and the United States, British Canadian officials established the Six Nations Reserve for their loyal allies, to which most Mohawks repaired. Others went to a reserve at the Bay of Quinté, which later became the Tyendinaga (Deseronto) Reserve.

The Iroquois council officially split into two parts during that time. One branch was located at the Six Nations Reserve and the other at Buffalo Creek. Gradually, the reservations, as well as relations with the United States and Canada, assumed more significance than intraconfederacy matters. In the 1840s, when the Buffalo Creek Reservation was sold, the fire there was rekindled at Onondaga.

In Canada, traditional structures were further weakened by the allotment of reservation lands in the 1840s; the requirement under Canadian law, from 1869 on, of patrilineal descent; and the transition of league councils and other political structures to a municipal government. In 1924, the Canadian government terminated confederacy rule entirely, mandating an all-male elected system of government on the reserve.

The Native economy gradually shifted from primarily hunting to farming, dependence on annuities received for the sale of land, and some wage labor. The people faced increasing pressure from non-Natives to adopt Christianity and sell more land. The old religion declined during that time, although on some reservations the Handsome Lake religion grew in importance. During the nineteenth century, Mohawks worked as rowers with shipping companies, at one point leading an expedition up the Nile in Egypt. They also began working in construction during that period, particularly on high steel scaffolding.

At Akwesasne (*see* Reservation Economic and Social Conditions), most people farmed, fished, and trapped during the nineteenth century. Almost all resident Indians were Catholic. Government was provided by three United States–appointed trustees and, in Canada, by a mandated elected council. With other members of the confederacy, Mohawks resisted the 1924 citizenship act, selective service, and all federal and state intrusions on their sovereignty.

Mohawks, particularly those from Kahnawake, have earned a first-rate reputation as high-steel workers throughout the United States since the late nineteenth century. People from Kahnawake have pursued self-determination particularly strongly. In 1990 there was a major incident, sparked by the

expansion of a golf course, that resulted in an armed standoff involving local non-Natives and the communities of Oka, Kahnawake, and Kanesatake. Akwesasne Mohawks have continued to battle the U.S. and Canadian governments over a number of issues. In 1968, by blocking the Cornwall International Bridge, they won concessions making it easier for them to cross the international border. The same year, a Mohawk school boycott brought attention to the failure of Indian education. In 1974, they and others established a territory called Ganienkeh on a parcel of disputed land. In 1977, New York established the Ganienkeh Reservation in Altoona. The Akwesasne community has also been beset by fighting from within. Community leaders have had difficulty uniting around divisive issues such as gambling, state sales and cigarette taxes, pollution, sovereignty, and land claims.

As a result of generations having worked in high steel, Mohawk communities exist in some Northeastern cities. Most of these people remain spiritually tied to their traditions, however, and frequently return to the reservations to participate in ceremonies, including Longhouse ceremonies, which have been active at least since the 1930s.

In general, traditional political and social (clan) structures remain intact. One major exception is caused by Canada's requirement that band membership be reckoned patrilineally. The political structure of the Iroquois League continues to be a source of controversy for many Iroquois (Haudenosaunee). Some recognize two seats—at Onondaga and Six Nations—whereas others consider the government at Six Nations a reflection of, or corollary to, the traditional seat at Onondaga. Important issues concerning the confederacy in the later twentieth century include Indian burial sites, sovereignty, gambling casinos, and land claims.

The Six Nations Reserve is still marked by the existence of progressive and traditional factions, with the former generally supporting the elected band council and following the Christian faith and the latter supporting the confederacy and the Longhouse religion. Traditional Iroquois Indians celebrate at least ten traditional or quasi traditional events, including the Midwinter, Green Corn, and Strawberry ceremonies. Iroquois still observe condolence ceremonies as one way to hold the League together after roughly 500 years of existence. The code of Handsome Lake, as well as the Longhouse religion, based on traditional thanksgiving ceremonies, is alive on the Six Nations Reserve and in other Iroquois communities.

See also Agriculture; Brant, Joseph; French and Indian War; Haudenosaunee Confederacy, Political System; Hiawatha; Wampum.

Mohegan
See Mahican; Pequot.

Nanticoke

"Nanticoke" comes from *Nentego,* "Tidewater People." The Nanticokes were one of a group of similar Algonquin Indian tribes that also included the Choptanks, Assateagues, Pocomokes, Patuxents, Conoys, and Piscataways. (*See also* Lenápe.) In 1600, roughly 12,000 Nanticokes lived on the peninsula between Delaware and Chesapeake Bays. Nanticokes and their neighbors spoke Algonquin languages.

The people recognized good and evil deities, and there may have been a formal priesthood. First fruits ceremonies were directed at a benevolent deity. A great chief or sachem was the overall leader. Each village may also have been ruled by a lesser chief, who might be a woman. The office of chief was probably inherited. The people also recognized war captains.

Descent was matrilineal. There may have been a social hierarchy, with the chiefs and their councilors having more material worth and respect. The people poisoned their enemies and even other tribal members. Shell bead money could be used as compensation for crimes and to purchase trade goods. The people may have observed a male puberty ceremony as well as polygyny.

Corpses were buried or placed on scaffolds. In the historical period, their bones were stored temporarily in log houses, whose shelves also held pipes and other personal belongings. Bones of up to several hundred people were later buried to the accompaniment of a spirit dance, which was meant to send them off to the afterlife. Chiefs' bones were preserved in temples.

There were at least five Nanticoke towns in the early seventeenth century. These were built along stream banks, and some were palisaded, especially those closest to the Iroquois. The Nanticokes were notable traders. Their art included pottery, woven baskets, and carved wood bowls. Baskets were decorated with spruce or porcupine quills.

Women planted corn, beans, and pumpkins. They pounded corn in mortars to make meat, fish, or vegetable hominy. They also gathered nuts and other wild foods. Fishing and shellfishing took place in the summer. The whole village removed to the woods for the fall hunt for deer, bear, turkey, squirrel, and other small game and fowl.

Skin clothing consisted of breechclouts and knee-length aprons fastened with a belt. Children generally remained naked. People wore fur cloaks in the winter and cloaks without fur in the summer. They painted their faces and bodies and covered themselves with bear grease.

The Nanticokes may have originated toward the northeast, possibly in Labrador, with the Shawnees and the Lenápes. They may also have passed through the eastern Great Lakes region and the Ohio Valley, where they met and possibly defeated Hopewell Mound Builder people.

Contact in 1608 with British Captain John Smith probably came a generation or two later than their neighbors' encounters with earlier British and Spanish explorers. In any case, the people soon became involved in the local beaver trade. Some groups allied themselves with the British as protection against Iroquois raids. In eastern Maryland, some groups, including the Nanticokes, continued to have problems with the British, based on the presence of alcohol and disease, throughout most of the seventeenth century.

British settlers granted the Nanticokes a reservation in 1684 between Chicacoan Creek and the Nanticoke River. The British also reserved the right to confirm Nanticoke leaders and to collect a formal tribute. Nanticokes and other neighboring tribes also became subordinate to the Iroquois Confederacy during that time. After non-Natives usurped their original reservation, in 1707 the people obtained a 3,000-acre tract on Delaware's Broad Creek, which was sold in 1768. In 1742, they were forced to eliminate the position of grand chief. In 1744, with Iroquois permission, they settled near Wyoming, Pennsylvania, and along the Juniata River, although ten years later they were living farther up the Susquehanna in a former Onondaga town. At about that time they merged with the Piscataways and became administratively linked with the Iroquois Confederacy.

Nanticokes (and many Conoys who had joined them in the 1740s) remained neutral in the French and Indian War, but they sided with the British during the American Revolution. In 1778, about 200 Nanticokes moved to Fort Niagara and subsequently to the Six Nations Reserve in Canada. Some Nanticokes also remained at Buffalo Creek, New York, while another group of Nanticokes and Conoys went west with the Lenápes, ending up in Kansas and, after 1867, in Oklahoma.

Throughout the later nineteenth century and into the twentieth century, the Nanticokes remaining in Delaware gradually lost their official tribal status and were in danger of losing their Indian identity completely. In 1922, the Delaware Nanticokes incorporated as the Nanticoke Indian Association. They elected a chief and assistant chief and began to recapture interest in some of their former traditions. The annual powwow dates from that time.

The Nanticoke Indian Heritage Project, dating from 1977, established a tribal museum and encourages the continued exploration of Indian traditions. The Nanticoke Leni-Lenápe Indians maintain a museum and library, and they host an annual powwow.

See also Agriculture, Algonquin; French and Indian War; Smith, John.

Narragansett

"Narragansett" means "People of the Small Point." It was the name both of a specific tribe and a group of tribes—such as Shawomets, Pawtuxets, Cowesets (Nipmucs), and eastern Niantics—dominated by Narragansett sachems. (*See also* Pequot.) In the sixteenth century, at least 3,000 Narragansetts were located in south central Rhode Island, although the greater Narragansett territory extended throughout all but northwest and the extreme southwest of Rhode Island. Narragansetts spoke an eastern Algonquin language.

Cautantowwit, the supreme deity, lived to the southwest. There were also numerous other spirits or deities, who could and did communicate with people through dreams and visions. Priests or medi-

cine men (powwows) were in charge of religious matters. They were usually men who realized their profession in a dream or a vision experience. Their main responsibilities included curing, bringing rain, and ensuring success in war. A harvest ritual was held in a longhouse near the sachem's house. At one important ceremony, possibly held in the winter, participants burned their material possessions.

Narragansetts recognized a dual (junior and senior) chief or sagamore. Power was shared with a council of elders, sachems, and other leaders. Sachems were responsible for seeing to the public welfare and defense and for administering punishment. The office of sagamore may have been inheritable and was occasionally held by a woman. Within the larger administrative body there were smaller groups presided over by lesser sachems.

People changed their names at various life cycle ceremonies. They were generally monogamous. The dead were wrapped in skins or woven mats and then buried with tools and weapons to accompany them to an afterworld located to the southwest. Narragansetts lived in dome-shaped, circular wigwams about ten to twenty feet in diameter, covered with birch and chestnut bark in the summer and with mats in the winter. Smoke passed through an opening at the top. Winter hunting lodges were small and built of bark and rushes. People erected temporary field houses where they stayed when guarding the crops. Villages were often stockaded.

Women grew corn, beans, squash, and sunflowers; men grew tobacco. The men also hunted moose, bear, deer, wolves, and other game, and they trapped beaver, squirrels, and other small animals and fowl. Deer were stalked and may have been hunted communally. People fished in freshwater and saltwater. They gathered much marine life, including the occasional stranded whale, as well as strawberries and a number of other wild foods.

The Narragansetts were notable traders. They dealt in wampum, skins, clay pots, carved bowls, and chestnuts. They imported carved stone and wooden pipes from the Mohawks. People generally wore deerskin breechclouts, skirts, and leggings. They might also wear turkey feather mantles and moccasins. In the winter they donned bear and rabbit skin robes, caps, and mittens.

This group may have originated well to the southwest of their historical territory. They were the most powerful New England tribe until 1675, dominating neighbors such as the Niantics and Nipmucs.

They may have encountered non-Natives in 1524, although there was no significant contact for another century or so afterward.

Trade with the British and Dutch was under way by 1623. Although the Narragansetts largely avoided the epidemics of 1617–1619, smallpox and other diseases dramatically weakened the people in 1633 and thereafter. As British allies, some Narragansetts fought against the Indians in the Pequot War of 1636–1637. In 1636, the grand sachem Canonicus sold land to Roger Williams, on which he established the future state of Rhode Island.

In an effort to protect themselves from non-Native depredations, the tribe voluntarily submitted to Britain in 1644. Despite Williams's entreaties to treat the Indians fairly, many British remained extremely hostile. Eventually, they forced the Narragansett people to join the Nipmucs and Wampanoags in King Philip's War (1675–1676). A huge defeat in December 1675, in which more than 600 Narragansetts were killed and hundreds more captured and sold into slavery, signaled the beginning of the end of the war as well as the virtual destruction of the tribe itself.

After the war, survivors dispersed among the Mahicans, Abenakis, and Niantics, the last group thenceforth assuming the name Narragansett. Some of the Mahicans joined the Brotherton Indians in 1788 (see Pequot) and later moved with them to Wisconsin. Those who remained in Rhode Island (probably fewer than 100) worked as servants or slaves of the non-Native settlers, who moved quickly to occupy the vacated Narragansett lands.

The people underwent a general conversion to Christianity in the mideighteenth century, at which time a Christian reservation community was established in Charlestown. After the last hereditary sachem died during that period, government changed to an elected president and council. The last Native speaker died in the early nineteenth century. A constitution was adopted in 1849. All of the Narragansett Reservation, except for two acres, was sold in 1880, and the tribe was terminated by the state at that time. The Rhode Island Narragansetts incorporated in 1934 under the terms of the Indian Reorganization Act.

In 1985, the state of Rhode Island returned two pieces of land of about 900 acres each. The August annual meeting and powwow have been held for the last 250 or more years on the old meeting ground in Charlestown. Other ceremonies are both religious

(such as the Fall Harvest Festival held in the long-house) and secular (such as the commemoration of the 1675 battle) in nature. There are tribal programs for the elderly and for children. Tribal representatives are involved in local non-Native cultural and educational programs.

See also Metacom and King Philip's War; Trade; Williams, Roger.

Ojibwa

See Anishinabe.

Oneida

"Oneida" means "People of the Standing Stone," in reference to a large boulder near their main village. The Oneidas are one of the five original tribes of the Iroquois League. The name Iroquois ("real adders") comes from the French adaptation of the Algonquin name for these people. Their self-designation was *Kanonsionni,* "League of the United (Extended) Households." Iroquois today refer to themselves as Haudenosaunee, "People of the Longhouse."

The Oneidas were located between the Mohawks and the Onondagas, between Lake Ontario and the upper Susquehanna River, especially around Oneida Creek. There were perhaps 15,000–20,000 members of the Iroquois League around 1500, and roughly 1,000 Oneidas in the midseventeenth century. The Oneidas spoke a northern Iroquois dialect.

The Oneidas recognized Orenda as the supreme creator. Other animate and inanimate objects and natural forces were also considered of a spiritual nature. They held important festivals to celebrate maple sap and strawberries as well as corn planting, ripening (Green Corn ceremony), and harvest. The eight-day new year's festival may have been the most important of all. Held in the midwinter, it was a time to give thanks, to forget past wrongs, and to kindle new fires, with much attention paid to new and old dreams. Medicine groups such as the False Face Society, which wore carved wooden masks, and the Medicine, Dark Dance, and Death Feast Societies (the last two controlled by women) also conducted ceremonies, since most ill-ness was thought to be of supernatural origin. In the early nineteenth century, many Iroquois embraced the teachings of Handsome Lake.

The Iroquois League comprised fifty hereditary chiefs, or sachems, from the constituent tribes. Each position was named for the original holder and had specific responsibilities. Sachems were men, except when a woman acted as regent, but they were appointed by women. The Oneidas sent nine sachems to meetings of the Iroquois Great Council, which met in the fall and for emergencies. Their symbol at this gathering was the great tree.

Locally, the village structure was governed by a headman and a council of elders. Matters before the local councils were handled according to a definite protocol based on the clan and division memberships of the chiefs. Village chiefs were chosen from groups as small as a single household. Women nominated and recalled clan chiefs. Tribal chiefs represented the village and the nation at the general council of the league. The entire system was hierarchical and intertwined, from the family up to the great council. Decisions at all levels were reached by consensus.

The Oneidas recognized a dual division, each composed of probably three matrilineal, animal-named clans. The clans in turn were composed of matrilineal lineages. Each owned a set number of personal names, some of which were linked with particular activities and responsibilities.

Women enjoyed a high degree of prestige, being largely equated with the "three sisters" (corn, beans, and squash), and they were in charge of most village activities, including marriage. Personal health and luck were maintained by performing various individual rituals, including singing and dancing, learned in dreams. Shamans also used up to 200 or more plant medicines to cure illness.

Young men's mothers arranged marriages with a prospective bride's mother. Divorce was possible but not readily obtained because it was considered a discredit. The dead were buried in a sitting position, with food and tools for use on the way to the land of the dead. A ceremony was held after ten days. The condolence ceremony mourned dead league chiefs and installed successors. A modified version also applied to common people.

The main aboriginal village, Oneniote, had over sixty longhouses and was palisaded. The people built their villages near water and often on a hill after about 1300. Some Iroquois villages had up to 150 longhouses and 1,000 or more people. Villages

were moved about twice in a generation, when firewood and soil were exhausted.

Iroquois Indians built elm-bark longhouses, fifty to 100 feet long, depending on how many people lived there, from about the twelfth century on. They held around two or three but as many as twenty families, related maternally (lineage segments), as well as their dogs. The people also built some single-family houses.

Women grew corn, beans, squash, and gourds. Corn was the staple and used in soups, stews, breads, and puddings. It was stored in bark-lined cellars. Women also gathered a variety of greens, nuts, seeds, roots, berries, fruits, and mushrooms. Tobacco was grown for ceremonial and social smoking.

After the harvest, men and some women took to the woods for several months to hunt and dry meat. Men hunted large game and trapped smaller game, mostly for the fur. They also caught waterfowl and other birds, and they fished. The people grew peaches, pears, and apples in orchards from the eighteenth century on.

The Iroquois used porcupine quills and wampum belts as a record of events. Wampum was also used as a gift connoting sincerity and, later, as trade money. These shell disks, strung or woven into belts, were probably a postcontact technological innovation.

Oneidas obtained birchbark products from the Huron. They imported copper and shells and exported carved wooden and stone pipes as well as dried salmon. They also raised and traded ginseng with other tribes. Elm-bark canoes were roughly twenty-five feet long. The people were also great runners and preferred to travel on land. They used snowshoes in the winter.

Women made most clothing from deerskins. Men wore shirts and short breechclouts and tunics in cooler weather; women wore skirts. Both wore leggings, moccasins, and corn husk slippers in the summer. Robes were made of light or heavy skins or pelts, depending on the season. These were often painted. Clothing was decorated with feathers and porcupine quills. Both men and women tattooed their bodies extensively. Men often wore their hair in a roach; women wore theirs in a single braid doubled up and fastened with a thong.

Boys began developing war skills at a young age. Prestige and leadership were often gained through war, which was in many ways the most important activity. The title of Pine Tree Chief was a historical invention to honor especially brave warriors. Oneidas were known as particularly fierce fighters. In traditional warfare, large groups met face to face and fired a few arrows after a period of jeering, then engaged in another period of hand-to-hand combat using clubs and spears. Population losses were partially offset by the adoption of captives. Former enemies became Oneidas because they were brought in to fill specific roles in specific lineages; the clan mothers could order the death of anyone who did not do what was expected of him.

All aspects of warfare, from the initiation to the conclusion, were highly ritualized. War could be decided as a matter of policy or undertaken as a vendetta. Women had a large, sometimes decisive, say in the question of whether to fight. During war season, generally the fall, Iroquois war parties ranged up to 1,000 miles or more. Male prisoners were often forced to run the gauntlet: Those who made it through were adopted, but those who did not might be tortured by widows. Some captives were eaten.

The Iroquois began cultivating crops shortly after the first phase of their culture in New York was established around 800. Deganawida, a Huron prophet, and Hiawatha, a Mohawk shaman living among the Onondaga, founded the Iroquois League or Confederacy some time between 1000 and 1150. Iroquois first met non-Natives in the sixteenth century. During these and subsequent years, the people became heavily involved in the fur trade. Trading, fighting, and political intrigue characterized the period. Although they were good at playing the European powers against each other, the Iroquois increasingly became British allies in trade and in the colonial wars and were instrumental in the ultimate British victory over the French.

In the late seventeenth century, battles with the French and allied Indian tribes as well as disease epidemics severely reduced the Oneidas' already small population. As much as two-thirds of the tribe members in those years were enemies, such as Hurons and Algonquins. Following the Tuscarora Wars in 1711–1713, people of that tribe began resettling on Oneida land. The Oneidas sponsored the Tuscarora tribe as the sixth member of the Iroquois Confederacy in the early 1720s. Some Oneidas began to drift into the Ohio Valley as early as the mideighteenth century. By that time, longhouse living had seriously declined, with houses of nuclear families taking their places.

The British victory in 1763 meant that the Iroquois no longer controlled the balance of power in

the region. Despite the long-standing British alliance, some Indians joined anti-British rebellions as a defensive gesture. From 1767 on, evangelical missionaries provided a theoretical/religious basis for the new Pine Tree Chiefs/warriors, such as the Susquehannock Shenendoah, to oppose the traditional chiefs. The missionaries attacked traditional religion and politics, and in this were aided by the warriors, who saw a way to topple control by the clan mothers and traditional chiefs. The 1760s were also a time of famine, increased pressure from non-Natives for land, and growing alcohol abuse, all of which provided fertile ground for the missionaries and their new converts.

The confederacy split its allegiance in the Revolutionary War, with most Oneidas (and Tuscaroras), after a period of neutrality, siding with the patriots at the warriors' urging. This split resulted in the council fire's being extinguished for the first time in roughly 200 years. The Oneidas participated in American attacks on the Onondaga, Cayuga, and Seneca villages. The Iroquois suffered a defeat in 1779 that broke the power of the confederacy. The Oneidas ended the war a scattered people, alienated from their fellow Iroquois, with little food and their traditional social, political, and economic systems in ruins.

The Oneidas welcomed two more groups of Indians in the late eighteenth century. Stockbridge Indians arrived to build the community of New Stockbridge, New York, in 1785. Three years later, a group of Mohegans, Mahicans, Narragansetts, Pequots, Montauks, and other Algonquin Indians, as well as some Oneidas, formed the Brothertown Community near New Stockbridge.

Following the Revolutionary War, New York State and the new U.S. government guaranteed the territorial integrity of nearly 6 million acres of Oneida land. However, the Oneidas bowed to pressure and sold most of their lands in New York, gradually relocating westward. Under the influence of an Episcopal missionary and despite the objections of most Oneidas, about half of the tribe settled around Green Bay, Wisconsin, in the 1820s and 1830s, on land they purchased from the Menominee tribe. Following the Treaty of Buffalo Creek (1838), which called for the removal of all Iroquois from New York to Kansas, other Oneidas moved to the Six Nations Reserve in Ontario, Canada, to the Thames River near London, Ontario, to the Onondaga Reservation near Syracuse, and to their original territory near Utica.

The Iroquois council officially split into two parts during that time. One branch was located at the new Six Nations Reserve and the other at Buffalo Creek. Gradually, the reservations as well as relations with the United States and Canada assumed more significance than intraconfederacy matters. In the 1840s, when the Buffalo Creek Reservation was sold, the fire there was rekindled at Onondaga.

In Wisconsin, most people practiced Christianity, with few elements of their traditional religion. Political leadership was based mainly on personal qualities and affiliations, although a hereditary council maintained considerable power. Most land had been allotted by 1908; as usual, the allotments were lost through tax default and foreclosure. At the same time, municipal governments began to replace the tribal structures. Although many people left the community permanently or seasonally to find work, Indian life remained centered on family, medicine societies, church, and several associations.

The Oneida community in Ontario reestablished the traditional tribal council shortly after they arrived in 1839 (although most power was exercised by a general assembly). Clan leaders also represented the tribe at the Council held at the Six Nations Reserve. Kinship ties and traditional medicine societies remained strong. Most people farmed throughout the nineteenth century, with perhaps seasonal lumbering in the winter. In the twentieth century, the economic focus shifted to wage labor in white communities. This development led to increased factionalism and the eventual creation of a parallel tribal council supported by adherents of the Longhouse religion. After a third faction arose in the 1930s, the Canadian government unilaterally mandated an elective system. With other members of the confederacy, the Oneidas have tried to resist governmental intrusions on their sovereignty.

In Wisconsin, most Oneidas are either Episcopalians or Methodists, although some follow the Longhouse religion. Few people speak Oneida, although the tribal school teaches classes in the Native language. Although most people are Christian, there are also many adherents of the Handsome Lake religion among the Ontario Oneida community. Descent is patrilineal by Canadian law, and clan identification has lost much of its significance.

In New York, leadership has been in dispute since at least the 1950s, when a newly organized elective system was more or less successfully challenged by traditionalists. Sachems and clan mothers now hold the leadership positions. Most members

are Christians, although many are also members of the Longhouse religion. The nation operates a health center, youth and elderly programs, and a housing development. Some New York Oneidas still speak the language.

The political structure of the Iroquois League continues to be a source of controversy for many Iroquois (Haudenosaunee). Some recognize two seats—at Onondaga and Six Nations—whereas others consider the government at Six Nations a reflection of or corollary to the traditional seat at Onondaga. Important issues concerning the confederacy in the later twentieth century include Indian burial sites, sovereignty, gambling casinos, and land claims. The Six Nations Reserve is still marked by the existence of progressive and traditional factions, with the former generally supporting the elected band council and following the Christian faith and the latter supporting the confederacy and the Longhouse religion.

Traditional Iroquois Indians also celebrate at least ten traditional or quasi traditional ceremonies, including the Midwinter, Green Corn, and Strawberry. Iroquois still observe condolence ceremonies as one way to hold the League together after roughly 500 years of existence. Many Iroquois continue to see their relationship with the Canadian and U.S. governments as one between independent nations and allies, as opposed to one marked by paternalism and dependence.

> *See also* American Revolution, Native American Participation; Deganawidah; Gambling; French and Indian War; Haudenosaunee Confederacy, Political System.

Onondaga

"Onondaga" means "People of the Hill." The Onondagas were one of the five original tribes of the Iroquois League. As Keepers of the Council Fire, they hosted the annual great council. The name Iroquois ("real adders") comes from the French adaptation of the Algonquin name for these people. Their self-designation was *Kanonsionni*, "League of the United (Extended) Households." Iroquois today refer to themselves as Haudenosaunee, "People of the Longhouse."

The Onondagas were the geographically central tribe of the Iroquois confederacy, located near Onondaga Lake and the Oswego River, near present-day Syracuse. There were perhaps 15,000 to 20,000 members of the Iroquois League around 1500, and approximately 1,000 Onondagas in the midseventeenth century. Onondagas spoke a northern Iroquois dialect.

The Onondagas recognized Ha-wah-ne-u as the supreme creator. Other animate and inanimate objects and natural forces were also considered of a spiritual nature. They held important festivals to celebrate maple sap and strawberries as well as corn planting, ripening (Green Corn ceremony), and harvest.

The eight-day new year's festival may have been the most important of all. Held in the midwinter, it was a time to give thanks, to forget past wrongs, and to kindle new fires, with much attention paid to new and old dreams. Medicine groups such as the False Face Society and the Medicine, Dark Dance, and Death Feast Societies (the last two controlled by women) also conducted ceremonies, since most illness was thought to be of supernatural origin. In the early nineteenth century, many Iroquois embraced the teachings of Handsome Lake.

The Iroquois League comprised fifty hereditary chiefs, or sachems, from the constituent tribes. Each position was named for the original holder and had specific responsibilities. Sachems were men, except when a woman acted as regent, but they were appointed by women. The head of the council was always an Onondaga. This person was assisted by a council of two other Onondagas, and a third Onondaga kept the council wampum. The Onondagas sent fourteen sachems to the meetings of the Iroquois Great Council, which met in the fall and for emergencies.

Locally, the village structure was governed by a headman and a council of elders. Matters before the local councils were handled according to a definite protocol based on the clan and division memberships of the chiefs. Village chiefs were chosen from groups as small as a single household. Women nominated and recalled clan chiefs. Tribal chiefs represented the village and the nation at the general council of the league. The entire system was hierarchical and intertwined, from the family up to the great council. Decisions at all levels were reached by consensus.

The Onondagas probably recognized a dual division, each composed of eight matrilineal, animal-named clans. The clans in turn were composed of matrilineal lineages. Each owned a set number of personal names, some of which were linked with particular activities and responsibilities.

Women enjoyed a high degree of prestige, being largely equated with the "three sisters" (corn, beans, and squash), and they were in charge of most village activities, including marriage. Personal health and luck were maintained by performing various individual rituals, including singing and dancing, learned in dreams. Members of the False Face medicine society wore wooden masks carved from trees and used rattles and tobacco. Shamans also used up to 200 or more plant medicines to cure illness.

Dancing was popular; the Onondagas had up to thirty or more different types of dances. Young men's mothers arranged marriages with a prospective bride's mother. Divorce was possible but not readily obtained because it was considered a discredit. The dead were buried in a sitting position, with food and tools for use on the way to the land of the dead. A ceremony was held after ten days. The condolence ceremony mourned dead league chiefs and installed successors. A modified version also applied to common people.

In the seventeenth century, Onondagas probably lived in two villages, a large one (roughly 140 longhouses) and a small one (roughly twenty-four longhouses). The people built their villages near water and often on a hill after about 1300. Some villages were palisaded. Other Iroquois villages had up to 150 longhouses and 1,000 or more people. Villages were moved about twice in a generation, when firewood and soil were exhausted.

Women grew corn, beans, squash, and gourds. Corn was the staple and used in soups, stews, breads, and puddings. It was stored in bark-lined cellars. Women also gathered a variety of greens, nuts, seeds, roots, berries, fruits, and mushrooms. Tobacco was grown for ceremonial and social smoking.

After the harvest, men and some women took to the woods for several months to hunt and dry meat. Men hunted large game and trapped smaller game, mostly for the fur. Hunting was a source of potential prestige. They also caught waterfowl and other birds, and they fished. The people grew peaches, pears, and apples in orchards from the eighteenth century on.

Onondagas obtained birchbark products from the Huron. They imported copper and shells and exported carved wooden and stone pipes. Women made most clothing from deerskins. Men wore shirts and short breechclouts and tunics in cool weather; women wore skirts. Both wore leggings, moccasins, and corn-husk slippers in the summer. Robes were made of light or heavy skins or pelts, depending on the season. Clothing was decorated with feathers and porcupine quills. Both men and women tattooed their bodies extensively. Men often wore their hair in a roach; women wore theirs in a single braid doubled up and fastened with a thong.

Boys began developing war skills at a young age. Prestige and leadership were often gained through war, which was in many ways the most important activity. The title of Pine Tree Chief was a historical invention to honor especially brave warriors. All aspects of warfare, from the initiation to the conclusion, were highly ritualized. War could be decided as a matter of policy or undertaken as a vendetta. Women had a large, sometimes decisive, say in the question of whether to fight. Male prisoners were often forced to run the gauntlet: Those who made it through were adopted, but those who did not might be tortured by widows. Women and children prisoners were regularly adopted. Some captives were eaten.

There were Indians in upper New York at least 10,000 years ago. The Iroquois began cultivating crops shortly after the first phase of their culture in New York was established around 800. Deganawida, a Huron prophet, and Hiawatha, a Mohawk shaman living among the Onondagas, founded the Iroquois League or Confederacy some time between 1000 and 11500.

Iroquois first met non-Natives in the sixteenth century. During those and subsequent years, the people became heavily involved in the fur trade. Trading, fighting, and political intrigue characterized the period. Although they were good at playing the European powers against each other, the Iroquois increasingly became British allies in trade and in the colonial wars and were instrumental in the ultimate British victory over the French.

Still, as a result of trade-motivated efforts to make peace with the French, a pro-French faction existed among the Onondagas from the midseventeenth century on. The French also established a Catholic mission in their territory about that time. By the midseventeenth century, war with the Susquehannocks was taking a heavy toll on the Onondagas and other Iroquois tribes. In fact, captive foreigners outnumbered Onondagas in the tribe by the time the war ended in 1675.

Fighting with the French at the end of the seventeenth century led to the torching and temporary abandonment of the main Onondaga village. In the mideighteenth century, a number of Onondagas and

other Iroquois went to live at Oswegatchie, a mission on the upper Saint Lawrence River. These people became French allies in the French and Indian War, although they sided with the British in the American Revolutionary War.

The British victory in 1763 meant that the Iroquois no longer controlled the balance of power in the region. Despite the long-standing British alliance, some Indians joined anti-British rebellions as a defensive gesture. The Onondagas and the confederacy as a whole split their allegiance in the Revolutionary War. This split resulted in the council fire's being extinguished for the first time in roughly 200 years.

The Iroquois suffered a defeat in 1779 that broke the power of the confederacy. By war's end most of their villages had been destroyed. When the 1783 Treaty of Paris divided Indian land between Britain and the United States, British Canadian officials established the Six Nations Reserve for their loyal allies, to which over 200 Onondagas repaired. Several hundred others moved to Buffalo Creek, New York, where groups of Senecas and Cayugas were living. A 100-square-mile Onondaga Reservation was established in 1788, although most of it had been lost by the early nineteenth century. In 1806, the Oswegatchies were removed. They scattered to St. Regis, Onondaga, and elsewhere in New York.

The Iroquois council officially split into two parts during that time. One branch was located at the Six Nations Reserve and the other at Buffalo Creek. Gradually, the reservations as well as relations with the United States and Canada assumed more significance than intraconfederacy matters. In the 1840s, when the Buffalo Creek Reservation was sold, the fire there was rekindled at Onondaga.

In Canada, the Onondagas, referred to along with the Cayugas and Senecas as the lower tribes, tended to retain more of their traditional beliefs than did the upper Iroquois tribes. Many subsequently adopted the Handsome Lake religion. Slowly, the general influence of non-Natives increased, as tribal councils, consensus decision making, and other aspects of traditional culture fell by the wayside. Traditional structures were further weakened by the allotment of reservation lands in the 1840s. The council eventually came to resemble a municipal government. In 1924, the Canadian government terminated confederacy rule entirely, mandating an all-male elected system of government on the reserve.

In the midnineteenth century there were significant Onondaga communities at Onondaga (Onondaga Reservation), on the Six Nations Reserve, and on Seneca and Tuscarora land, especially the Allegany Reservation. The Native economy gradually shifted from primarily hunting to farming, dependence on annuities received for the sale of land, and some wage labor. There was also increasing pressure for Indians to sell more land and adopt Christianity, although the Onondagas remained fairly resistant to both. The old religion declined in importance during that time, though among some Iroquois, including many Onondaga, the Handsome Lake religion grew in importance.

In 1898, the wampum belts remaining among the Onondaga were placed in the keeping of the New York State Museum. With other members of the Confederacy, the Onondagas resisted the 1924 citizenship act, selective service, the Indian Reorganization Act, and all federal and state intrusions on their sovereignty.

Onondagas today are considered to be the most conservative of the Six Nations. The Onondaga Reservation is again the capital of the Iroquois Confederacy. The leader of the Iroquois League, who alone can summon meetings of the Great Council, is always an Onondaga. Recent political activism has resulted in the return of wampum belts, education reforms, and the prevention of the acquisition of reservation land for road widening by New York State. In 1994 the tribe ceased seeking or accepting federal grants.

Although most Onondagas are Christian, all chiefs must adhere to the Longhouse religion. This requirement ties them to other Iroquois Longhouse communities throughout the United States and Canada. A hereditary council heads both political and religious life. Many people speak Onondaga, although English is the official tribal language. The community is known for its artists and athletes, especially its lacrosse players. Mutual aid remains strong.

In general, traditional political and social (clan) structures remain intact. One major exception is caused by Canada's requirement that band membership be reckoned patrilineally. The political structure of the Iroquois League continues to be a source of controversy for many Iroquois (Haudenosaunees). Some recognize two seats—at Onondaga and Six Nations—whereas others consider the government at Six Nations a reflection of or corollary to the traditional seat at Onondaga.

Important issues concerning the confederacy in the later twentieth century include Indian burial sites, sovereignty, gambling casinos, and land claims.

The Six Nations Reserve is still marked by the existence of progressive and traditional factions, with the former generally supporting the elected band council and following the Christian faith and the latter supporting the confederacy and the Longhouse religion. Traditional Iroquois Indians celebrate at least ten traditional or quasi traditional events, including the Midwinter, Green Corn, and Strawberry ceremonies. Iroquois still observe condolence ceremonies as one way to hold the league together after roughly 500 years of existence.

Many Iroquois continue to see their relationship with the Canadian and U.S. governments as one between independent nations and allies, as opposed to one marked by paternalism and dependence. Occasionally, the frustrations inherent in this type of situation boil over into serious confrontations.

See also American Revolution, Native American Participation; Deganawidah; French and Indian War; Haudenosaunee Confederacy, Political System; Treaty Diplomacy, with Summary of Selected Treaties; Wampum.

Ottawa

"Ottawa," or "Odawa," is from *adawe*, "to trade." Before about 1600, the name was loosely applied to several groups of upper Algonquins. Their self-designation was *Anishinabe* ("People"). (*See also* Anishinabe.) Roughly 8,000 Ottawas lived in the northern Lake Huron region, specifically Manitoulin Island, Georgian Bay, and the Bruce Peninsula, in the early seventeenth century. Ottawas spoke a dialect of Anishinabe, an Algonquin language.

The Ottawas recognized Manitou, the great spirit, along with many lesser spirits, both good and evil. Around puberty, boys and girls sought visions through dreams or in isolated areas. There were three religious cults, as well as the Midewiwin, or Medicine Lodge Society; the latter, open to both men and women initiates, was designed to channel spiritual power toward the well-being of members. Shamans cured through their intercession with the spirits.

At least four, or possibly up to seven bands, had their own relatively weak chief or chiefs. These bands were composed of local villages, each with their own leadership. Small hunting groups left the villages during the winter, returning to plant crops in spring. Men might have more than one wife. The dead were cremated, buried, or placed on scaffolds. A feast honoring the dead was held every year or so.

Permanent villages were sometimes palisaded. The Ottawas built longhouses of fir or cedar bark on pole frames with barrel roofs. They also used temporary mat-covered conical lodges while on trips. People navigated lakes and rivers in birchbark canoes. They wore two kinds of snowshoes—round for women and children and tailed for men—when traveling in snow. Men carved various wooden objects. The Ottawas were also known for their woven mats. The people decorated many birchbark items with the use of templates. Decorative styles included zigzag bands and floral motifs. Most designs were symmetrical. Southern bands decorated items with porcupine quillwork.

Men hunted and trapped large and small game and birds. Game was often taken in fire drives. Fishing was of key importance, especially around the lake shores. Women gathered various berries and other plant food. They also grew corn, beans, and squash and collected maple sap. They baked cornmeal bread in ashes and hot sand.

In the summer, men went naked or wore a light robe; they added fitted, decorated breechclouts for special occasions. They added leggings and heavier robes made of skin or pelts in the winter. They wore their hair short and brushed up in front. Women wore wraparound skirts, with added ponchos and robes in the winter. They generally wore their hair in one braid wrapped with fur or snakeskin. Moccasins were of deer or moose skin, with attached retractable cuffs.

According to legend, the Ottawas migrated from the Northwest as one people with the Anishinabes and the Potawatomis. They probably arrived on the east side of Lake Huron in about 1400. They first encountered non-Natives in 1615, in the person of Samuel de Champlain. The people traded furs to Huron intermediaries, in exchange for European goods, until the 1649 Iroquois defeat of the Huron. At that point, the Ottawas took over direct trade with the French, taking their canoes up the Saint Lawrence River to Montreal.

In 1660, the Ottawas suffered their own military defeat at the hands of the Dutch-armed Iroquois, at which time they moved west to the Green Bay area. Some groups continued even farther west, to around

Lake Superior and the Mississippi River (these were soon driven back by Dakota warriors). With a guarantee of French protection, many returned to their old homes in 1670. By 1680, most had joined the Hurons at Mackinaw. There were many Ottawa settlements around Lakes Michigan and Huron in the eighteenth century.

Like most Algonquins, the Ottawas took the French side in the colonial wars. The Ottawa chief Pontiac led a coalition of regional Indians in an anti-British rebellion in 1763, after the latter's decisive victory over French forces. The coalition at first enjoyed much success, although the end result was failure. The people tried to remain neutral during the American Revolution, although some actively sided with the Americans; they were similarly divided in the War of 1812. Most Ottawas had converted to Catholicism by the early nineteenth century. By the terms of an 1833 treaty, Ottawas south and west of Lake Michigan, about 500 people, were relocated to Iowa and Kansas with some Chippewas and Potawatomis, with whom they had united in an alliance called the Three Fires.

Other groups, forced to move by the scarcity of game and pressure from non-Natives, relocated to the Lake Huron islands or to Michigan reservations or allotments. In 1867, most Kansas Ottawas bought land on the Quapaw Reservation in Indian Territory (Oklahoma). This land was allotted in severalty in the 1890s. The tribe was officially terminated in 1956 but was reinstated in 1978. In 1965, the people received just over $400,000 in land claims settlements pertaining to their time in Kansas.

During the mid- and later nineteenth century, when many Ottawa groups merged or otherwise became associated with the Ojibwa and Potawatomi Indians, the United States created an ersatz tribal entity called the Ottawa and Chippewa Bands. This bogus "tribe" was the basis on which the Michigan Ottawas were wrongly but effectively assumed to have been officially terminated. These people have been seeking redress for the loss of various benefits and payments for over 100 years. The government has consistently refused to recognize them, even under the Indian Reorganization Act.

Northern Ottawas farmed or worked in lumbering throughout most of the twentieth century. After World War II, however, many moved from local communities to regional cities in search of employment. In 1948 the people created the Northern Michigan Ottawa Association (NMOA) to represent them in all litigation.

Michigan Ottawas have regularly suffered arrest and other actions for asserting their treaty rights to hunt and fish. The language survives in Michigan mainly among elders, although the people have instituted various language and cultural preservation programs (many Ontario Ottawas speak their Native Algonquin language). Most Michigan Ottawas are Christian, although some celebrate quasi traditional feasts, naming ceremonies, and other festivals. The Oklahoma Ottawas are highly acculturated. Few people speak the Native language.

See also Algonquin; Dams, Fishing Rights, and Hydroelectric Power; Trade.

Passamaquoddy

"Passamaquoddy" means "those who pursue the pollack" or "pollack-spearing place." Together with the Maliseets, the Passamaquoddys have also been known as the Etchemin tribe. (*See also* Abenaki; Maliseet; Penobscot.) The traditional location of the Passamaquoddys is in the vicinity of Passamaquoddy Bay and the St. Croix River. With the Maliseets, their population reached about 1,000 in the early seventeenth century. Maliseets and Passamaquoddys spoke dialects of the same Algonquin language.

Guardian spirits, acquired through vision quests, gave shamans the power to cure and regular people the ability to protect subsistence areas from trespass. Any number of supernatural beings included Kuloscap, the culture hero. Dances were mainly associated with spiritual power.

Skilled hunters provided local leadership. The people recognized a supreme hereditary chief in the seventeenth century who lived at the main village. The last such chief died in the 1870s. Leadership became more formalized under the confederacy, with graduated civil offices and a war chief. The people remained part of the Abenaki Confederacy from the mideighteenth century to the mid- to late nineteenth century, when the confederacy ceased to exist. War chiefs existed at least from the eighteenth century on. This position was never inherited or elected.

The people came together in large villages in the summer and dispersed into small hunting camps in the winter. They preferred football, a kicking game, to lacrosse. They also enjoyed any number of dice gambling games. Men served their prospective

in-laws for at least a year before marriage. Weddings were marked by feasting and oratory recognizing the groom's ancestry. At least after contact, sexual mores were strict, and divorce was rare. Children were generally treated gently and with a high degree of freedom, at least when compared with the region's early French. When death was expected, it was sometimes hastened by pouring cold water on the victim, who may also have been buried alive.

Summer villages were sometimes palisaded. They included multi- and single-family dwellings. The former were conical pole-frame wigwams covered with birchbark; the latter, as well as council houses, were rectangular log-frame structures with birchbark roofs. Council houses could hold up to a hundred people.

Farming, especially of corn, was the key economic activity. Harvested corn was stored and taken on the winter hunts. There was some hunting of inland animals such as moose, bear, otter, and muskrat. More important was the capture of marine animals such as seal and porpoise. The people also ate stranded whales as well as other marine foods, including lobster, shellfish, and sea birds and their eggs. Marine mammals were hunted in canoe teams. They also fished for salmon, bass, and sturgeon and gathered wild grapes, roots, and fiddlehead ferns. Maple sugaring may have predated contact with non-Natives.

Lightweight canoes were made of birchbark, moose hide, or spruce bark. Clothing was made from skins. Beaverskin caps shielded people's heads from the cold. They also wore temporary birchbark raincoats. Snowshoes were worn in the winter.

The Passamaquoddys may once have been united with the Maliseets. First contact with non-Natives probably occurred with Samuel de Champlain in the early seventeenth century, although the people may have met fishers from northern and western Europe as much as a century earlier.

With their growing involvement in the French fur trade, the people soon became dependent on items of non-Native manufacture. They also accepted Catholic missionaries. Their population declined severely throughout the eighteenth century, owing to disease, the abuse of alcohol, and the loss of land.

They joined the pro-French Abenaki Confederacy in the mideighteenth century. Many Passamaquoddys married French men and women. By the late eighteenth century, British settlers had pushed them out of many of their best subsistence areas, and the traditional annual round of subsistence activites had been seriously disrupted. The state of Massachusetts set aside 23,000 acres of land for them in 1794 as part of a treaty never ratified by the federal government. The two reservations were founded around 1850 by competing political factions, the progressive one based at Sipayik and the conservatives at Motahkokmikuk.

In the mid- to late nineteenth century, many Passamaquoddys worked in sea-related industries and as farmers, loggers, and guides. They also worked as migrant laborers (picking potatoes and blueberries) and made baskets, paddles, moccasins, and other items for sale to the tourist trade. Both reservations became enclaves of poverty in a poor region, and by the 1960s many Indians had left to pursue economic opportunities elsewhere. During World War II, the government used part of Indian Township as a German prisoner of war camp; this land was later sold to non-Natives. This and other such actions ignited the Native rights struggle in Maine and led ultimately to the Maine Indian Claims Settlement Act.

Today, while the people enjoy free health care, the Native language is falling into disuse, with most speakers among the older population. It is taught in school, as are traditional crafts and tribal history. Alcoholism, high unemployment, and anti-Indian prejudice are obstacles that need be fully conquered. Most Passamaquoddys are Catholic. The tribe holds an annual festival.

See also Agriculture; Maine Indian Claims Settlement Act; Trade and Intercourse Acts.

Penobscot

"Penobscot" means "where the rocks widen," referring to the falls on the Penobscot River. The Penobscots were members of the Abenaki Confederacy and sometimes referred to as being among the Eastern Abenaki people (others include the Kennebecs, Arosagunticooks, and Pigwackets). They are culturally similar to the Micmacs and Passamaquoddys. (*See also* Abenaki.)

Penobscots traditionally lived along the Penobscot River, from the headwaters to the mouth, including tributaries. There were perhaps 10,000 Eastern Abenakis around 1600 and about 1,000 Penobscots in the early eighteenth century. Penobscots spoke an eastern Algonquin language.

The summer was the time for religious ceremonies, led by shamans, who also cured illness of spiritual origin by blowing and dancing. Common ailments (those without a spiritual component) were cured with herbs and plant medicines. Tribal organization traditionally consisted of a loose grouping of villages, each with its own sagamore. These leaders, who might or might not be shamans, consolidated their power through multiple marriages and by supporting and making alliances with nonrelatives. Leaders were chosen by merit, although there was a weak hereditary component. Sagamores had various social obligations that included feasting the band.

The Eastern Abenakis were politically united prior to and through the time of the first European contact under one chief sagamore named Bashabes. Penobscots had a chief sagamore, sometimes in name only, from at least the early seventeenth century to 1870.

Penobscots were divided into patrilineal lineages, each with its own winter hunting territory that became more strictly defined in the fur trade era. They may have recognized a dual division. The tribe broke into small hunting groups in the winter but came together in summer villages along rivers.

Most socializing, such as playing the hoop-and-pole game (in which an arrow is shot through a hoop), took place in the summer gatherings. Women were secluded during their menstrual periods. The first kill of the season was given away, as was the first kill of any boy. Gifts to the bride's family formalized a marriage; the quantity and quality of the gifts reflected the desirability of the bride and the status of her family. Leading men might have more than one wife.

Common illness was treated by means of sweating, herbs, and plant medicines. An anticipated death might be hastened by starvation. Those material goods not given away before death were buried with the body.

There were no permanent villages until at least the eighteenth century. Some villages were palisaded, at least in the historical period. People lived in both square houses with pyramid roofs and cone-shaped wigwams. Both were covered with birchbark sheets and were about twelve feet in diameter.

Men hunted and trapped deer, moose, bears, beaver, otter, and other animals, especially in the winter. Most meat and fish were dried and stored for the winter. The people boiled maple sap for syrup. They gathered wild tubers, fruits, and berries, and they fished. On the spring and summer trips to the ocean, they gathered shellfish and hunted porpoise, seals, and fowl. There may have been a small amount of corn cultivation.

Birchbark was a key material; in addition to houses and canoes, the people made it into folded containers, baskets, and other important items. They also made smaller containers of bark, sweetgrass, and hide. Pipes might have been made of clay or stone, but most vessels were of clay. Utensils were carved of wood.

Penobscots were part of a trade network that reached past the Mississippi to the west, almost to the Gulf Coast to the south, and north into Labrador. Still, most trade was local and included items such as canoes, pipes, pottery, and birchbark goods.

Most clothing, such as tunics, breechclouts, long skirts, and moccasins, came from tanned skins. In the winter people wore removable sleeves and leggings and moose hide coats. Beaver pelts were sometimes used for breechclouts and robes. Sagamores might wear special headgear. Men and women also engaged in extensive face and body painting.

Tribal tradition has these people originating in the Southwest. Shortly after their first encounter with non-Natives, in the sixteenth century, a story began to circulate in parts of Europe about Norumbega, a fantastic (and mythical) Penobscot town. This tale greatly encouraged British interest in the region.

Because early British visitors mistreated the Indians, the Penobscots showed a preference for contacts with French traders. Intertribal war with the Micmacs ended in 1615, about the same time that devastating epidemics drastically reduced the local Indian population. Involvement in the fur trade from the seventeenth century on signaled the virtual end of many aspects of traditional material culture, as the Indians became dependent on cloth, glass beads, corn, metal items, guns, and items of non-Native manufacture. Wampum became a currency as well as an important status symbol.

The winter dispersal into the forests and summer trips to the shore became less necessary, as village Indians could eat corn and other foods obtained in trade for furs. Some groups started growing their own corn at that time. Penobscots were often at war with the British, some of whom were pushing into Penobscot territory, during the later seventeenth and the eighteenth centuries. However, since they needed the British as trade partners, they refrained from establishing a full-blown alliance with the French until the mideighteenth century, when they joined the Abenaki Confederacy. By that time, many

Penobscots had exchanged their traditional dwellings for log cabins. Much of western Maine was in British hands, and other Eastern Abenakis had left the area for residence in Quebec.

Although the Penobscots tried to remain neutral in the French and Indian War, British bounties on their scalps pushed them into the French camp. The British victory ended their access to the ocean, among other calamities. Around that time, the Penobscots joined a confederacy of former French allies whose center was at Caughnawaga, Quebec. They remained members until 1862, when regional intertribal affairs could no longer hold their interest sufficiently.

Although Penobscots fought with the Patriots in the American Revolution, Massachusetts took possession of most of their land in the late eighteenth century in exchange for in-kind payments (food, blankets, ammunition, and so on). An Indian agent appointed by the state of Maine was responsible for conducting the tribe's business after 1820.

In 1833, the tribe sold all but about 5,000 acres to Maine. Their traditional economy in ruins, Penobscots became farmers, seasonal wage laborers (loggers, hunting guides), artisans (snowshoes, canoes, moccasins), and basketmakers for the tourist trade. Traditional government was superseded by state-mandated elections in 1866, and the last sagamore (chief) died in 1870.

In the 1920s, the tribe actively sought to bring tourists to the reservation by means of pamphlets and pageants. They also benefited from increasing work in local industries (canoes, shoes, textiles). With other Maine Indians, the Penobscots in the 1960s pushed for and won improved services through a new state Indian Affairs department.

Recognition in 1980 brought a host of new projects and improvements in infrastructure and standards of living. Substance abuse remains a significant problem. There is some interest in traditional crafts and religious ideas, although most traditional culture was lost over 100 years ago. Although only a few elders still know the Native language, the people are attempting to preserve it. Most Penobscots are Catholic. The people regularly intermarry with Maliseets and Passamaquoddys as well as with people from other tribes and non-Natives.

See also Agriculture; French and Indian War; Maine Indian Claims Settlement Act; Trade and Intercourse Acts.

Peoria

See Illinois.

Pequot

Pequot, "destroyers." The tribe known as Mohegan ("wolf") sprang from a Pequot faction in the early seventeenth century. (*See also* Narragansett.) Roughly 4,000 Pequots lived in eastern Connecticut and extreme northeastern Rhode Island in the early seventeenth century. Their main villages were situated on the Thames and Mystic Rivers. Pequots spoke an Eastern Algonquin language.

The people recognized a supreme deity as well as lesser deities. Medicine men called powwows used herbs, sweats, plants, and songs to cure illness and banish evil spirits. The people also celebrated a variety of the Green Corn festival.

Village bands were led by sagamores, or chiefs, who maintained their influence through generosity and good judgment. A council of important men together took all major decisions. There may have been a hereditary component to the position of village sagamore. There may or may not have been a grand sachem who led the bands in precontact times. Certainly, that was the case in the early seventeenth century, when Sassacus dominated the Pequots as well as some Long Island bands.

Unlike many northeastern tribes, the Pequots dispersed in the summer to designated resource sites such as fishing weirs, shellfish gathering places, gardens, and marshlands and came together in winter villages. They also dispersed in the early winter to hunting camps. Leading men might have more than one wife, in part so that they could entertain more frequently and more lavishly and in part to build alliances with other families. Corpses were wrapped in skins and woven mats and buried in the ground with weapons, tools, and food. The ultimate destination was the land of the dead. Houses were abandoned after a death.

Villages were usually located on a hill and were often palisaded. Consisting of at least several houses, they were moved when the supply of firewood was exhausted. People lived in bark or woven mat houses, framed with saplings or poles bent and lashed together. Smaller houses (roughly fifteen feet in diameter) held two families. Larger bark-covered longhouses (up to 100 feet long and thirty feet wide) with multiple fires held up to fifty people. Tempo-

rary villages were located along the coast in the summer and in the woods in the winter.

Women grew corn, beans, and squash; men grew tobacco. Corn was used in stew; cornmeal was also made into cakes and baked in hot ashes. The people gathered shellfish along the coast in the summer. They also ate an occasional beached whale. Although deer was the animal staple, men hunted an enormous variety of large and small game as well as fowl, the latter including turkey, quail, pigeon, and geese.

Deer, especially the white-tailed deer, furnished most of the people's clothing. Men generally wore breechclouts, leggings (in the winter), and moccasins; women wore skirts or dresses and moccasins. Both donned fur robes in cold weather. Clothing was often decorated with quillwork as well as feathers, paints, and shells. Pottery was generally basic although often decorated by incision. Canoes were of the birchbark and more commonly the dugout variety.

The Pequots may have arrived in their historical territory from the Hudson River Valley–Lake Champlain area, wresting land from the Narragansetts and the Niantics in the late sixteenth century. In the early seventeenth century, the grand sachem Sassacus dominated twenty-six subordinate sagamores. However, the people were driven out of Rhode Island by the Narragansetts in 1635. About that time Uncas, son-in-law of Sassacus, led a group of Pequots to establish another village on the Thames River; that group became known as Mohegans.

Soon after the Dutch arrived in the region, they began trade with the Pequots, who sold them land at the future site of Hartford. However, control of that land had been disputed, and the British favored more local Indians. As tensions worsened, the Mohegans saw a chance to end their subordinate status. In 1637, they and the Narragansetts aided British forces in attacking a Pequot village, killing between 300 and 600 people. Sassacus and a large group of followers were killed by Mohawks while trying to escape. Many were captured, however, and sold into slavery or given to allied tribes as slaves. The rest of the tribe fled to the southwest. Some escaped to Long Island and Massachusetts, where they settled with other Algonquins. The surviving Pequots were forced to pay tribute to the Massachusetts Bay Colony and were prohibited from using the name "Pequot." Uncas then became chief of the Pequots and Mohegans, now all known as Mohegans. He remained firm in his friendship with the colonists,

fighting the Narragansetts in 1657 and Britain's enemies in King Philip's War.

Although the Pequot/Mohegans survived that conflict, they and other local Indians were severely diminished, and they ceased to have a significant independent role other than as servants or indigents. Some joined other Indian tribes, such as those who passed through Schaghticoke in upstate New York to join the Western Abenakis. In 1655, freed Pequot slaves in New England resettled on the Mystic River. The people suffered a continuing decline until well into the twentieth century.

The tribe divided in the late seventeenth century, into an eastern group (Paucatucks) and a western group (Mashantuckets). The former received a reservation in 1683, and the latter were granted land in 1666. Most of their land was later leased to non-Natives and lost to Indian control.

In the 1770s, some Mohegans joined a group of Narragansetts, Mahicans, Wappingers, and Montauks in creating the Brotherton (or Brothertown) tribe in Oneida territory (New York). The community was led by Samson Occom, an Indian minister. In the early nineteenth century, this community, joined by groups of Oneidas and Stockbridge (Mahican) Indians, was forced to migrate to Wisconsin, where they received a reservation on Lake Winnebago that they shared with the Munsee band of Delaware Indians. The reservation was later divided and sold.

By the early twentieth century, most Brotherton Indians had been dispossessed, but the community remained intact, mainly because members kept in close contact and returned regularly for gatherings and reunions. Mohegan Indians began a political revival in the early twentieth century, forming the Mohegan Indian Council and becoming involved with the Algonquin Indian Council of New England.

Paucatuck Pequots continue to fight for full federal recognition as well as full recognition by the state of Connecticut of their rights and land claims. They are also attempting to ease the factionalism that has troubled them for some time. The Mashantucket Pequots were recognized and their land claims settled by Congress in 1983. A museum and cultural center are planned. They publish the *Pequot Times* and own and operate Foxwoods, the largest resort casino in the world.

Elements of the Pequot language exist on paper and are known by some of the people, especially tribal elders. Various gatherings and family reunions continue among the Brotherton people of Wisconsin.

The spiritual center of the tribe is in Gresham, Wisconsin. Traditional culture has disappeared, but these people remain proud of their heritage.

The Mohegans have a land claim pending against the state of Connecticut for roughly 600 acres of land alienated in the seventeenth century. The Tantaquidgeon museum is a central point of reference for the tribe, as is the Mohegan church (1831) and the Fort Shantok burial ground. The people celebrate the wigwam festival or powwow, which has its origins in the Green Corn festival of ancient times.

See also Gambling; Land, Identity and Ownership of, Land Rights; Metacom and King Philip's War; Pequot War.

Pokanoket

See Wampanoag

Potawatomi

Potawatomi, a word of uncertain meaning. The commonly ascribed translation, "People of the Place of Fire" or "Keeper of the Fire" is probably apocryphal and refers to their traditional obligation to maintain a council fire uniting them with the Ottawas and Anishinabes. Their own self-designation was *Weshnabek*, "the People." (*See also* Anishinabe; Ottawa.) In the early seventeenth century, roughly 8,000 Potawatomis lived in southwest Michigan. Potawatomi is an Algonquin language.

The people may have recognized a chief deity that corresponded with the sun. Religion was based mainly on obtaining guardian spirits through fasting. Sacred bundles were probably part of religious practice from prehistoric times on; at some point they became associated with the supernatural power of clans. There were three types of shamans: doctors, diviners, and advisor-magicians. The people observed the calumet (peace pipe) ceremony. Other festivals included the Midewiwin Dance, the War Dance, and the Sacred Bundle ceremony.

There were clan chiefs, but the decision makers were generally the clan's warriors, elders, and shamans. Chiefs of semiautonomous villages, who were chosen from among several candidates of the appropriate clans, lacked authority, since the democratic impulse was strong among the Potawatomis. There was no overall tribal chief, although a village chief, through his personal prestige, might lead a large number of villages. The chief was aided by a council of men. Women occasionally served as village chiefs. There was also an intratribal warrior society that exercised police functions in the villages.

At least thirty patrilineal clans owned certain supernatural powers, names, and ritual items. Over time, the clans died out, and new ones were created. They were a source of a child's name as well as part of his or her personal spirit power. A dual division by birth order had significance in games and some rituals. Lacrosse was a popular game, as were the woman's double ball game and dice games.

After the harvest, people generally broke into small hunting camps for the winter. Polygyny was common. Marriages were formalized by gift exchange between clans and by the approval of senior clan members. Babies were named after a year and weaned after several years. Both sexes were recognized as adults at puberty when they went through a time of isolation, women during their periods and men to fast and seek a vision. Young women might also have visions at this time. Corpses were dressed in their best clothes and buried in an east-west alignment (one clan practiced cremation) with considerable grave goods that included food, tools, and weapons.

Summer villages, numbering up to 1,500 people of several clans, were built along lakes and rivers and often contained members of the Anishinabe and Ottawa groups. Small winter camps lay in sheltered valleys. Some villages may have been palisaded. Summer houses were bark-covered rectangular structures with peaked roofs. The people built smaller, dome-shaped wigwams with mats covering a pole framework for their winter dwellings. They also built ramadas with roofs of bark or limbs for use as cooking shelters. Rush-mat menstrual huts were built away from the main part of the village.

Women grew corn, beans, squash, and tobacco, and they gathered wild rice, maple sap for sugar, beechnuts (which were pounded into flour), berries, roots, and other wild plant foods. Men fished and hunted buffalo (especially from the eighteenth century on), deer, bear, elk, beaver, and many other animals, including fowl. People made bark food storage containers, pottery, and stone or fired-clay pipes with wooden or reed stems. Pictographs on birch-bark scrolls served as mnemonic devices.

Group portrait of Potawatomi men, women, and children dressed in western clothes, ca. 1906. (Library of Congress)

Potawatomis used both dugout and bark-frame canoes. The latter were up to twenty-five feet long; construction and ownership of these vessels were limited. A litter slung between two horses could carry materials or ill people; woven rush mat saddlebags also held goods. Clothing was made of skins and furs. Men were tattooed, and both sexes painted their bodies. The Potawatomis wore personal adornments made of Native copper and shell.

Tradition has the people, once united with the Anishinabes and the Ottawas, coming to their historical territory from the northeast. Driven from southwest Michigan around 1640 by the Iroquois, Hurons, and others, the Potawatomis took refuge in upper Michigan and then the Green Bay area, where they met other refugee groups and built advantageous alliances and partnerships, notably with the French but also with other tribes. At this time they occupied a single village and became known to history as a single tribe with their present name.

By the late seventeenth century, however, having consolidated their position as French trade and political allies, the single village had collapsed, mainly under trade pressures. Forced by Dakota raiding parties, Potawatomi groups began moving southward to occupy former lands of the Illinois Confederacy and the Miamis. By the early eighteenth century there were multiclan Potawatomi villages in northern Illinois and southern Michigan. By the mideighteenth century, southern groups had acquired enough horses to make buffalo hunting a significant activity.

The French alliance remained in effect until 1763. The Potawatomis fought the British in Pontiac's Rebellion. They also joined the coalition of tribes to administer the final defeat to the Illinois about that time, evicting them from northern Illinois and moving into the region themselves. The Potawatomis fought on the side of the British, however, in the Revolutionary War and continued to

fight the American invasion of their territory in a series of wars in the late eighteenth and early nineteenth centuries that included Little Turtle's War (1790–1794), Tecumseh's Rebellion (1809–1811), and the Black Hawk War of 1832. By that time, many southern Potawatomis had intermarried with non-Natives.

After all these Indian losses, the victorious non-Natives demanded and won significant land cessions (the people ultimately signed at least fifty-three treaties with the United States). The Potawatomis were forced to remove west of the Mississippi. Bands from the Illinois-Wisconsin area went to southwest Iowa while Michigan and Indiana Potawatomis went to eastern Kansas. In 1846 both groups were placed on a reservation near Topeka, Kansas. Some remained in Michigan and Wisconsin, however, and some managed to return there from the west. Others joined the Kickapoos in Mexico, and still others went to Canada.

Some of the Potawatomis in Kansas became relatively successful merchants and farmers. In 1861, a group of these people formed the Citizen Band as a separate entity from the Prairie Band. They were moved to Indian Territory in the 1870s, and their land there was allotted by 1890. Since much of the land was of marginal quality, however, people tended to leave the community in the early to midtwentieth century. Many Citizen Band Potawatomis were educated in Catholic boarding schools in the early twentieth century.

The Prairie Potawatomis remained in Kansas. Despite their strong resistance, lands along the Kaw River in Kansas were allotted by 1895. The tribal council disbanded by 1900, and all government annuities ended in 1909. By 1962, less than one-quarter of their former lands remained in their possession, and much of this was leased to non-Natives. The tribe rejected the 1934 Indian Reorganization Act (IRA) and was able to avoid termination in the 1950s.

Among those who refused to leave their homelands, a large group of Potawatomi refugees was still in Wisconsin in the midnineteenth century. These people had been joined by several Ottawa and Anishinabe families. With the help of an Anishinabe man, they obtained land and money to build a community, called Hannaville, in the 1880s. The U.S. Congress purchased additional land for them in 1913. The community adopted an IRA constitution and bylaws in 1936. Most people were farmers, and many also worked seasonally in the lumber industry.

By the early twentieth century, the land was exhausted, the lumber industry had declined, and the state refused them all services, contributing to the onset of widespread poverty and exacerbating anti-Indian prejudice.

In 1839, the Huron Potawatomis who had escaped removal purchased land for a community. The state of Michigan added another forty acres in 1848. The Methodist Episcopal church served as the focus of community life. Near Waterviliet, Michigan, members of the future Pokagon band bought land near Catholic churches. They continued a subsistence economy based on small game hunting; gathering berries, maple sap, and other resources; and small-scale farming. They also worked on nearby farms when necessary. They created a formal government as early as 1866, which later pursued land claims against the United States. They and the Huron Potawatomis were denied federal recognition in the 1940s based on an arbitrary administrative ruling.

See also Black Hawk's War; Little Turtle; Tecumseh; Thorpe, Jim.

Sauk

Sauk, or Sac, from *Osakiwugi,* "People of the Outlet" or "Yellow Earth People." The Sauks were culturally related to the Kickapoos and Potawatomis. (*See also* Fox.) For much of their history, the Sauks straddled the area between the Northeast Woodlands and the Prairie. In the sixteenth century they lived around Saginaw Bay in eastern Michigan. There were approximately 3,500 Sauks in the midseventeenth century. Sauk is an Algonquin language.

The Sauks recognized any number of nature-related spirits, or manitous, the most important of which were Wisaka, founder of the Medicine Dance, and those connected with the four directions. People might gain the attention and assistance of the manitous by offering tobacco, blackening their faces with charcoal, fasting, and wailing. A vision quest at puberty was meant to attract manitous. Those who obtained especially powerful spirits assembled a medicine pack or bundle; certain packs represented spiritual power that affected and were the property of entire lineages.

The Midewiwin, or Medicine Dance, was a key ceremony. Others included Green Corn, Naming, and Adoption. In the last, there was a formal adop-

tion to replace a family member who had died. The calumet, or sacred pipe, played a key role in all solemn activities, including peace negotiations. A head shaman instructed others in curing, in hunting, and in agricultural and other ceremonies.

The Sauks were divided into bands or villages, of fluid composition, that came together as one unit in the summer. There was also a dual peace and war political division. A hereditary, clan-based village peace chief held authority over gatherings, treaties, peace councils, intertribal negotiations, and rituals. In return for access to his property, the people regularly gave him gifts. Two war chiefs were chosen by other warriors on the basis of merit, although there may have been a hereditary component. The war chief commanded the camp police and presided over war councils.

Sauks recognized about twelve patrilineal clans. Membership in the dual division—peace/white and war/black—was determined by birth order. Birth took place in special lodges in the company of only women; the mother remained subject to special postpartum restrictions for up to a year or more. An elderly relative named a baby from the stock of clan names. As adults, people might acquire additional, nonclan names as a result of dreams or warfare.

Parents rarely engaged in corporal punishment of their children. At the onset of puberty, girls were secluded for ten days and were subject to various other restrictions. Boys marked puberty by undertaking a vision quest. Girls also sought visions, although not in seclusion. Vermilion face paint indicated adult status.

Marriages were generally arranged by the couple and were formalized when the families exchanged gifts. The couple lived with the wife's family for a year before establishing their own household. Some men had more than one wife.

Burial took place after various rituals had been performed. Warriors might be buried in a sitting position. All people were buried in their finest clothing and wrapped in bark or mats with their feet toward the west. The mourning period lasted for at least six months, during which time mourners were subject to a variety of behavioral restrictions.

Summer villages were located near fields in river bottoms. At least in the early nineteenth century, almost the entire tribe assembled at the summer villages. Each summer house was an economic unit as well. Extended families of some ten people lived in houses about fifty feet long and twenty feet wide and covered with elm bark. Houses were ori-

ented in an east-west direction and were built in parallel rows, with an open game and ceremonial area between the rows. Villages were moved when firewood became scarce or when attacks forced the people to move. In their winter camps, people lived in small, dome-shaped wigwams covered with reed mats and skins and located in sheltered river valleys. The camps ranged in size from one or two families to an entire band.

Women grew corn, beans, squash, and tobacco. They also gathered a number of wild plant foods, including nuts, honey, berries, fruits, and tubers. Men hunted a variety of large and small game, especially deer, as well as buffalo until about 1820. The Sauks mined and traded lead. They also exported corn. They imported deer tallow, feathers, and beeswax. Water transportation was by bark and dugout canoe. Clothing was made of skin and furs and consisted mainly of breechcouts, dresses, leggings, and moccasins. The people decorated their clothing with quillwork and paint. Body tattooing and painting were common.

The Sauks may once have been united with the Foxes and the Kickapoos. The Anishinabes and/or the Iroquois pushed the Sauks out of eastern Michigan and toward the lower Fox River sometime in the late sixteenth or early seventeenth century. French explorers arrived around 1667.

The Sauks got along well with the British. They also maintained good relations with the French until they began sheltering the Foxes and other French enemies. Fox Indians fleeing the French took refuge with the Sauks in 1733, beginning an alliance that lasted until the 1850s. At that time, the Sauks and Foxes moved away from the Green Bay area into eastern Iowa. They moved back to northern Illinois and southern Michigan after peace with the French was established in 1737.

In 1769 the Sauks, Foxes, and other tribes, under pressure from the French as well as the Menominees and Anishinabes, dealt a permanent defeat to the Illinois tribes. At that point the Sauks and Foxes moved south and west into some of the Illinois tribes' former territory. Later they headed back into Iowa, where they adapted rapidly to a prairie/plains existence, becoming highly capable buffalo hunters. Their parties traveled far to the west of the Mississippi in search of the herds. They also continued to grow corn.

In 1804, one Sauk band (the Missouri band) ceded all tribal lands, although they claimed they were ceding only a small parcel of land. The action

was not binding, however, because the tribal council, in whom authority for land cessions was vested, refused to ratify the treaty. Anger over this treaty on the part of the rest of the Sauk people forced the Missouri band to remain separate from the main group, ultimately settling on the eastern border of Kansas and Nebraska.

The Sauks took an active part in Little Turtle's War (1790–1794), but most remained neutral in Tecumseh's Rebellion (1809–1811). They sided with the British in the War of 1812. After the war, the Sauks divided into two factions. Black Hawk headed the anti-United States band, which refused to accept the treaty of 1804, and Keokuk headed the accommodationist party. In the 1820s, the United States exercised an increasingly important role in Sauk internal politics, ultimately vesting Keokuk as tribal chief, a man with no hereditary claim to the position.

Black Hawk's War (1832) resulted directly from the controversy over the 1804 treaty. Black Hawk (Makataimeshekiakiak), a Saukenuk (Rock Island) Sauk leader, attempted to form a pan-Indian alliance to defend his homeland against illegal non-Native usurpation. Despite the fact that Keokuk had agreed to relocate west of the Mississippi, Black Hawk and his people were determined to occupy their own lands. Some fighting ensued, after which the Sauks decided to retreat beyond the Mississippi. However, a U.S. steamer caught up with and shelled the Indians, many of whom were women and children, as they attempted to cross the river in rafts, slaughtering hundreds. Black Hawk himself surrendered several months later. Following his release from prison in 1833, he toured several cities and dictated his autobiography.

The Sauks and Foxes soon defeated Dakota warriors in Iowa (who had themselves killed many of the survivors of the Mississippi shelling) and occupied their land. Over the next few years, the factions hardened, and relations became strained with the Foxes, who resented the United States–backed Keokuk's control over the tribe. In 1842, the people were forced to cede their lands in Iowa and were relocated to a reservation in Kansas. They were joined by some members of the Missouri band at that time. Most Foxes returned to Iowa in the late 1850s. In 1867, the Sauks were forced into Indian Territory (Oklahoma). In 1890, most of the reservation was allotted in severalty, with the rest, almost 400,000 acres, opened to non-Native settlement.

Eleven clans remain in existence. Education will increase the number of people who speak the Native language, now estimated at about 200. Many traditions continue, including seasonal ceremonies, adoptions, and naming. Most people are Christians, but many adhere to the Native American Church. The tribe maintains its own police and court system. It publishes the *Sac and Fox News*. Local groundwater has been contaminated by oil. There is an annual all-Indian stampede and rodeo. Most of the Kansas Sauks are acculturated and assimilated into the local economy.

See also Black Hawk's War; Little Turtle; Thorpe, Jim.

Schaghticoke

See Pequot.

Seneca

The Senecas were the largest, most powerful, and westernmost of the five original tribes of the Iroquois League. Their self-designation was *Onotowaka*, "Great Hill People." The name Iroquois ("real adders") comes from the French adaptation of the Algonquin name for these people. Their self-designation was *Kanonsionni*, "League of the United (Extended) Households." Iroquois today refer to themselves as Haudenosaunee, "People of the Longhouse." (*See also* Cayuga.)

The Seneca homeland stretched north to south from Lake Ontario to the upper Allegheny and Susquehanna Rivers and west to east from Lake Erie to Seneca Lake, but especially from Lake Canandaigua to the Genesee River. There were perhaps 15,000 to 20,000 members of the Iroquois League around 1500 and about 5,000 Senecas in the midseventeenth century. The Senecas spoke a Northern Iroquois dialect.

The Senecas recognized an "earth holder" as well as other animate and inanimate objects and natural forces of a spiritual nature. They held important festivals to celebrate maple sap and strawberries as well as corn planting, ripening (Green Corn ceremony), and harvest. These festivals often included

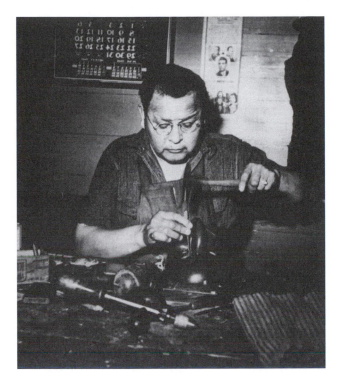

Jesse Cornplanter, descendent of Cornplanter, the famous Seneca chief, making a ceremonial mask in 1940, Tonawanda Community House, Tonawanda, New York. (National Archives and Records Administration)

singing, male dancing, game playing, gambling, feasting, and food distribution.

The eight-day new year's festival may have been most important of all. Held in the midwinter, it was a time to give thanks, to forget past wrongs, and to kindle new fires, with much attention paid to new and old dreams. Medicine groups such as the False Face Society, and the Medicine, Dark Dance, and Death Feast Societies (the last two controlled by women) also conducted ceremonies, since most illness was thought to be of supernatural origin. In the early nineteenth century, many Iroquois embraced the teachings of Handsome Lake.

The Iroquois League comprised fifty hereditary chiefs, or sachems, from the constituent tribes. Each position was named for the original holder and had specific responsibilities. Sachems were men, except where a woman acted as regent, but they were appointed by women. The Seneca sent eight sachems to meetings of the Iroquois Great Council, which met in the fall and for emergencies.

Debates within the great council were a matter of strict clan, division, and tribal protocols, in a complex system of checks and balances. Politically, individual league members often pursued their own best interests while maintaining an essential solidarity with the other members. The creators of the U.S. government used the Iroquois League as a model of democracy.

Locally, the village structure was governed by a headman and a council of elders (clan chiefs, elders, wise men). Matters before the local councils were handled according to a definite protocol based on the clan and division memberships of the chiefs. Village chiefs were chosen from groups as small as a single household. Women nominated and recalled clan chiefs. Tribal chiefs represented the village and the nation at the general council of the league. The entire system was hierarchical and intertwined, from the family up to the great council. Decisions at all levels were reached by consensus.

The Senecas recognized a dual division, each composed of eight matrilineal, animal-named clans. The clans in turn were composed of matrilineal lineages. Each owned a set number of personal names, some of which were linked with particular activities and responsibilities.

Women enjoyed a high degree of prestige, being largely equated with the "three sisters" (corn, beans, and squash), and they were in charge of most village activities, including marriage. Great intravillage lacrosse games included heavy gambling. Personal health and luck were maintained by performing various individual rituals, including singing and dancing, learned in dreams. Members of the False Face medicine society wore wooden masks carved from trees and used rattles and tobacco. Shamans also used up to 200 or more plant medicines to cure illness. People committed suicide on occasion for specific reasons (men who lost prestige, women who were abandoned, children who were treated harshly). Murder could be revenged or paid for with sufficient gifts.

Young men's mothers arranged marriages with a prospective bride's mother. Divorce was possible but not readily obtained because it was considered a discredit. The dead were buried in a sitting position, with food and tools for use on the way to the land of the dead. A ceremony was held after ten days. The condolence ceremony mourned dead league chiefs and installed successors. A modified version also applied to common people.

From the early sixteenth century on, scattered Seneca villages were consolidated into two large (100 or more houses) villages (one eastern and one western) and one or two smaller (about twenty-five houses) ones. Gandagaro, the large eastern village,

was also the main tribal village. The people built their villages near water and often on a hill after about 1300. Some villages were palisaded.

Iroquois Indians built elm-bark longhouses, fifty to 100 feet long, depending on how many people lived there, from about the twelfth century on. They held around two or three but as many as twenty families, related maternally (lineage segments), as well as their dogs. There were smoke holes over each two-family fire. Beds were raised platforms; people slept on mats, their feet to the fire, covered by pelts. Upper platforms were used for food and gear storage. Roofs were shingled with elm bark. The people also built some single-family houses.

Women grew corn, beans, squash, and gourds. Corn was the staple and was used in soups, stews, breads, and puddings. It was stored in bark-lined cellars. Women also gathered a variety of greens, nuts, seeds, roots, berries, fruits, and mushrooms. Tobacco was grown for ceremonial and social smoking.

After the harvest, men and some women took to the woods for several months to hunt and dry meat. Men hunted large game and trapped smaller game, mostly for the fur. Hunting was a source of potential prestige. They also caught waterfowl and other birds, and they fished. The people grew peaches, pears, and apples in orchards from the eighteenth century on.

The Iroquois used porcupine quills and wampum belts as a record of events. Wampum was also used as a gift connoting sincerity and, later, as trade money. These shell disks, strung or woven into belts, were probably a postcontact technological innovation. Other important material items included elm-bark containers, cordage from inner tree bark and fibers, and levers to move timbers. Men steamed wood or bent green wood to make many items, including lacrosse sticks. Unstable elm-bark canoes were roughly twenty-five feet long. The people were also great runners and preferred to travel on land. They used snowshoes in the winter and wood-frame backpacks to carry heavy loads such as fresh meat.

Women made most clothing from deerskins. Men wore shirts and short breechclouts and tunics in cool weather; women wore skirts. Both wore leggings, moccasins, and corn-husk slippers in the summer. Robes were made of light or heavy skins or pelts, depending on the season. These were often painted. Clothing was decorated with feathers and porcupine quills. Both men and women tattooed their bodies extensively. Men often wore their hair in a roach; women wore theirs in a single braid doubled up and fastened with a thong. Some men wore feather caps or, in the winter, fur hoods.

Boys began developing war skills at a young age. Prestige and leadership were often gained through war, which was in many ways the most important activity. The title of Pine Tree Chief was a historical invention to honor especially brave warriors. All aspects of warfare, from the initiation to the conclusion, were highly ritualized. War could be decided as a matter of policy or undertaken as a vendetta. Women had a large, sometimes decisive, say in the question of whether to fight. During war season, generally the fall, Iroquois war parties ranged up to 1,000 miles or more. Male prisoners were often forced to run the gauntlet: Those who made it through were adopted, but those who did not might be tortured by widows. Women and children prisoners were regularly adopted. Some captives were eaten.

The Iroquois began cultivating crops shortly after the first phase of their culture in New York was established around 800. According to legend, Deganawida, a Huron prophet, and Hiawatha, a Mohawk shaman living among the Onondagas, founded the Iroquois League or Confederacy some time between 1000 and 1150. It originally consisted of five tribes: Cayugas, Mohawks, Oneidas, Onondagas, and Senecas; the Tuscaroras joined in the early eighteenth century. The league's purpose was to end centuries of debilitating intertribal war and work for the common good.

There were two Seneca groups in the sixteenth century and perhaps as early as the founding of the league, each of which had its own large village. The people first encountered Jesuit missionaries shortly before the latter established a mission in Seneca country in 1668. During the seventeenth and eighteenth centuries, the people became heavily involved in the fur trade. Trading, fighting, and political intrigue characterized this period.

In the course of their expansion to get more furs, especially beaver, the Iroquois, often led by the Senecas, wiped out tribes, such as the Hurons and Eries, and fought many generally pro-French tribes, such as the Algonquins, Ottawas, Miamis, and Potawatomis. The Iroquois also fought and defeated the Iroquoian Susquehanna (or Conestoga) Indians during the early to midseventeenth century. Their power effectively blocked European westward expansion.

Although they were good at playing the European powers against each other, the Iroquois increasingly became British allies in trade and in the colonial wars, and they were instrumental in the ultimate British victory over the French. The western Senecas (Chenussios) remained pro-French, however, even in the French and Indian War and Pontiac's Rebellion of 1763.

The British victory in 1763 meant that the Iroquois no longer controlled the balance of power in the region. Despite the long-standing British alliance, some Indians joined anti-British rebellions as a defensive gesture. The confederacy split its allegiance in the Revolutionary War, with most Senecas siding with the British. This split resulted in the council fire's being extinguished for the first time in roughly 200 years.

Despite the leadership of Cornplanter and others, however, the Senecas suffered depredations throughout the war, and by war's end their villages had been permanently destroyed. When the 1783 Treaty of Paris divided Indian land between Britain and the United States, British Canadian officials established the Six Nations Reserve for their loyal allies, to which many Seneca repaired.

Seneca lands were formally defined in the 1794 Canandaigua (Pickering) Treaty. Most Seneca lands (except for 310 square miles) were sold in 1797. This action was the genesis of the Buffalo Creek, Tonawanda, Allegheny, Cattaraugus, and several other small reservations, most of which were soon sold. Chief Cornplanter also received a land grant from the Commonwealth of Pennsylvania around that time, in consideration of services rendered during the war. After the war, both Cornplanter and the Pine Tree Chief Red Jacket recognized the sovereignty of the United States. Cornplanter favored alliance with the new government, whereas Red Jacket urged his people to continue to live as traditionally as possible.

The Iroquois council officially split into two parts during that time. One branch was located at the Six Nations Reserve and the other at Buffalo Creek. Gradually, the reservations as well as relations with the United States and Canada assumed more significance than intraconfederacy matters. In the 1840s, when the Buffalo Creek Reservation was sold, the fire there was rekindled at Onondaga. Some Senecas who had settled with the Cayuga at Buffalo Creek traveled to Ohio and were removed from there to the Indian Territory (Oklahoma) in the early 1830s.

The Seneca Handsome Lake (half brother of Cornplanter) founded the Longhouse religion in 1799. In 1838, the U.S. Senecas lost most of their remaining land in a fraudulent procedure. Four years later, a new treaty replaced the fraudulent one. However, it still included the sale of the Buffalo Creek and Tonawanda Reservations.

In 1848, an internal dispute over the payment of annuities led to the formal creation of the Seneca Nation of Indians (Allegany and Cattaraugus) and the adoption of a U.S.-style constitution and government. With this action the people effectively withdrew from the Iroquois Confederacy and separated from the Tonawanda Reservation as well. In 1857, the Tonawanda Senecas won a long-standing fight to retain their reservation. In the midnineteenth century, illegal land leases led to the formation of several non-Native towns on the Allegany reservation, the largest being Salamanca.

In Canada, the Senecas, referred to along with the Onondagas and Cayugas as the lower tribes, tended to retain more of their traditional beliefs than did the upper Iroquois tribes. Many subsequently adopted the Handsome Lake religion. Slowly, the general influence of non-Natives increased, as tribal councils, consensus decision making, and other aspects of traditional culture fell by the wayside. Traditional structures were further weakened by the allotment of reservation lands in the 1840s; the requirement under Canadian law, from 1869 on, of patrilineal descent; and the transition of league councils and other political structures to a municipal government. In 1924, the Canadian government terminated confederacy rule entirely, mandating an all-male elected system of government on the reserve.

In 1869, the Seneca Donehogawa (Ely Parker), a general in the U.S. Army, became the first Native American Commissioner of Indian Affairs. He stood for peace with the western tribes and fairness in general, shaking up the corrupt Indian Ring. However, trumped-up charges, of which he was fully exonerated, led to a congressional investigation and ultimately to his resignation in 1871.

The Native economy gradually shifted from primarily hunting to farming, dependence on annuities received for the sale of land, and some wage labor. By 1900 there were a number of missionary and state-supported schools on the reservations. Although there were also several churches, relatively few Senecas attended services. Instead, longhouses served as the place where the old ceremonies were maintained and continue to fill that role today. Most

Senecas spoke English by that time. With other members of the confederacy, the Senecas resisted the 1924 citizenship act, selective service, and all federal and state intrusions on their sovereignty.

The Senecas in Oklahoma elected a tribal council from the 1870s to 1937. By that time their land base had shrunk, mostly through allotment and outright theft, from about 65,000 acres to 140 acres. At that time they incorporated under state law as the Seneca–Cayuga tribe, adopted a constitution and bylaws, and elected a business committee. The tribe resisted termination in the 1950s.

In the 1960s, despite massive protests, the Army flooded over 9,000 acres of the Cornplanter tract and the Allegany Reservation to build the Kinzua Dam. Many important cultural and religious sites were lost. The tribe eventually received over $15 million in damages.

Today in the Seneca Nation, the language remains intact, as do traditional political and social (clan) structures, with the exception of Canada's requirement that band membership be reckoned patrilineally. The people participate in Longhouse and many other celebrations, such as the midwinter, maple, Green Corn, and harvest ceremonies. Not all ceremonies are observed at all reservations, and, of those that are, there are occasionally local differences. A number of medicine ceremonies also continue to be performed.

There are a museum and library on the Allegany Reservation. The Cattaraugus Reservation features a museum, a library, and a sports arena. The community hosts a fall festival, an Indian fair, and two bazaars. Cayugas and Senecas have yet to resolve issues of Cayuga land ownership on the Cattaraugus Reservation. Few people there speak the Native language, but the community retains various traditional ceremonies.

Many Iroquois continue to see their relationship with the Canadian and U.S. governments as one between independent nations and allies, as opposed to one marked by paternalism and dependence. Occasionally, the frustrations inherent in this type of situation boil over into serious confrontations.

See also American Revolution, Native American Participation; Canandaigua (Pickering) Treaty; Cornplanter; French and Indian War; Handsome Lake; Haudenosaunee Confederacy, Political System; Treaty Diplomacy, with Summary of Selected Treaties; Wampum.

Shawnee

"Shawnee" is derived from *Shawanwa,* "southerner," their self-designation. These people acted in many ways as agents of cultural change and adaptation between the Northeast Woodlands and the Southeastern and Plains tribes. They were variously known to non-Natives as Ouchaouanags, Chaouanons, Satanas, and Shawanos. They were culturally related to the Sauks, Foxes, and Kickapoos.

The Shawnees migrated often, but their territory in the late seventeenth century, when they may have numbered 50,000 or more, may have ranged from the Illinois River east to the Delaware, Susquehannah, and Savannah Rivers. Some scholars place them on the Cumberland River at or before that time. Shawnee villages have been located throughout an enormous area, ranging from the present states of New York and Illinois south to South Carolina, Georgia, and Alabama. Their aboriginal home may have been around the south shore of Lake Erie, and they lived in southern Ohio during the second half of the eighteenth century. Shawnees spoke an Algonquin language.

A supreme deity, possibly female, controlled a large number of other deities, who in turn all had their places in Shawnee mythology. The people recognized twelve fundamental laws with religious/ mythological origins. The Piqua division of the tribe was in charge of religious ceremonies. Each division was conceived of as ritually discrete, and each held a sacred pack.

Important communal ceremonies included the Bread Dance, held at planting and harvest times and organized by women. The ceremony featured dancing and a feast of meat hunted by twelve men and cooked by twelve women. The people also celebrated the Green Corn Dance (a harvest/thanksgiving/renewal ceremony) and various other sacred ceremonies.

The five Shawnee divisions were the Chillikothes, Kispokothas, Piquas, Hathawekelas, and Spitothas. They were linked through specific responsibilities, such as politics, ceremonialism, and war, and they were associated with specific territories and towns. Division membership was inherited patrilineally.

Political functions fell under either the peace or war organization. Tribal, clan, and division chiefs were hereditary (clan chiefs may have been associated more with ritual than politics) prior to the nine-

teenth century, although the office of war chief also had a merit component. There was also a tribal council made up of the chiefs as well as elderly men. Town councils probably existed as well.

Women related to male leaders could be chiefs on the town level. Women were also associated with peace and war organizations. Among their prerogatives were the right to ask for the cancellation of a war party, the right to spare prisoners, and direction over feasts and planting crops.

Another type of tribal division was geographical in nature. These groups were fluid in number, size, and composition as the tribe shifted its territory. This system was eventually responsible for the three formal Shawnee divisions of the late nineteenth century.

Up to twelve patrilineal clans controlled names; certain qualities associated with certain names also belonged to particular clans. Ritual and political appointments might follow from these qualities and were thus associated with clans. Birth occurred in a special, secluded hut, where mother and child remained for ten days, after which a naming ceremony was held. Marriage was probably arranged, at least in part, and was associated with gift giving. Only men buried Shawnee men, but both men and women buried women. Corpses were buried in their best clothing and usually prone, with the head facing west. Tobacco was sprinkled over the body. The mourning period of twelve days was bracketed with two feasts (spouses mourned for up to a year). Diverse death customs might include a condolence ceremony and, if a husband died, a replacement ceremony, when the widow chose a new husband about a year after the death.

The Shawnee created various house styles, depending on the period and location. Typical summer dwellings were bark-covered extended lodges. Town organization by division included ceremonial aspects as well, on the Southeast "town" model. Each Shawnee town had a large, wooden council house used for a number of purposes, including sacred and secular group functions and the ritual seclusion of warriors after fighting. Towns varied in size according to time and location, but the largest consisted of hundreds of houses and over one thousand people.

Women grew several varieties of corn. They also gathered a number of foods, including berries, cherries, and persimmon, and they tapped maple trees for their sap. Men hunted deer, bear, buffalo, and turkey. They also trapped a number of smaller mammals. The people left their summer towns in the fall to establish winter camps. From there, able-bodied men and women left on months-long hunting trips. There was also a summer deer hunt. The Shawnee diet also included fish.

The people generally adopted the clothing of their neighbors, incorporating some styles of their former environs as well. In general, they wore little clothing. Items included buckskin breechclouts, aprons, and moccasins. Body painting and tattooing were extensively practiced. Personal ornamentation varied according to location.

According to tradition, the Shawnee people were once united with the Lenápes and the Nanticokes, perhaps in Labrador. They may have originated north of or in the Ohio Valley. They were probably associated with the Fort Ancient cultural complex (1000–1700), which was characterized by a mixed subsistence economy, including agriculture, with fortified villages having central courtyards. Town populations may have ranged up to 1,000 people.

The Iroquois may have begun pushing scattered Shawnee bands south into Ohio as early as the sixteenth century. Iroquois attacks on Shawnees in Ohio lasted until the mid- to late eighteenth century, when the Iroquois forced the last Shawnees out of that area. Shawnees pushed into Pennsylvania in the late seventeenth century, and a population center was established on the Savannah River by that time as well. In the early eighteenth century, bands began a general westward movement again, settling on the north bank of the Ohio River. By about 1750 most Shawnees had come to that location, with Iroquois permission. Some groups also joined the Creek Nation in Alabama about that time.

Heavy involvement in the fur trade from the early eighteenth century on soon left many Shawnee in the clutches of alcohol and debt. Most Shawnee bands were pro-French in the colonial wars, but some were steadfast British trade partners and military allies, especially the bands that came under the control of the Iroquois. Most Shawnees participated in Pontiac's Rebellion of 1763–1764. Under Chief Cornstalk, they also fought the British later in 1764 over the issue of land. Pressured by the colonies to cede land, the Shawnees joined the British cause in the American Revolution, hoping that the country that promulgated the Proclamation Line of 1763 would defend their interests against the rapacious colonials. The loss in that war and in Little Turtle's War (1794) led to further land cessions in Ohio and Indiana. In the 1790s, a group of Shawnees and

Lenápes moved to Missouri to occupy a Spanish land grant.

In the early nineteenth century, two Shawnees—twins by birth—achieved renown as among the last great military defenders of Indian land in the entire region. The shaman Tenskwatawa, or Shawnee Prophet, encouraged his people to return to their traditions and eschew all non-Native elements, particularly Christianity and alcohol. He also claimed to have special medicine that would help repulse the whites. His brother was Tecumseh, a brilliant orator and military strategist. Envisioning an Indian country from Canada to the Gulf of Mexico, he encouraged pan-Indian solidarity and resistance to the domination of the United States. In particular, he believed that no single Native American had the moral right to sell or cede any Indian land.

In 1812, Tenskwatawa foolishly moved against a non-Native military expedition before the alliance was complete. The Indian forces were defeated, and Tenskwatawa's power proved to be ineffective. This action fatally disrupted the alliance before it had a chance to coalesce. Tecumseh quickly joined the British cause in the War of 1812, hoping that what remained of his alliance, in conjunction with British forces, could defeat the Americans. Although as a general in the British Army he led many successful campaigns, many Indians refused to join the war. Tecumseh was fatally shot in October 1813.

Their power broken, many Ohio tribes, including the Shawnees, became refugees, drifting in scattered bands throughout the present-day states Kansas, Missouri, Arkansas, Oklahoma, and Texas. Meanwhile, the Missouri Shawnees living on Spanish land were slowly joined by other Shawnee groups. Resulting tensions forced the groups apart once again. About 1845, groups of Shawnees gathered near Oklahoma's Canadian River and later became known as the Absentee Shawnees (this tribe was composed mostly of the former divisions of Hathawekelas, Kispokothas, and Piquas). Most members accepted allotments soon after the reservation was officially established in 1872, and by 1900 most had assimilated into the dominant society. Factionalism between progressives and traditionals kept the two sides apart throughout the early twentieth century.

In 1825 the United States established a reservation in Kansas for the Indians still living on the Spanish land grant. Shawnees still in Ohio moved there in the early to mid-1830s, although they were eventually forced into Oklahoma, where the groups split up. One part joined the Cherokees (known thereafter as the Cherokee Shawnees or Loyal Shawnees, from their Unionist stance during the Civil War), and the other joined the Absentee Shawnees.

In 1831, a group of Shawnees and Senecas who had been living in Ohio settled in Ottawa County, Oklahoma. When the groups separated in 1867, the Shawnees became known as the Eastern Shawnees. They organized formally as the Eastern Shawnee Tribe of Oklahoma in 1937, when they officially broke apart from the Senecas. Despite their loyalty to the Union in the Civil War, most Shawnees were forced out of Kansas and into Oklahoma, where they merged with the Cherokees in 1869. During the nineteenth and twentieth centuries, scattered Shawnee communities in Ohio and Indiana retained their Indian identity and some of their traditions. These communities came together politically in 1971 as the United Remnant Band (URB).

The URB's main land holdings now serve as a ceremonial and cultural center, where the tribe conducts powwows, youth programs, and ceremonies. Most are well integrated into the surrounding non-Native population. The Absentee Shawnees maintain a police force, a tribal court system, and a clinic. Most of the people are Christians, especially Baptists and Quakers. The Native language is still spoken. The more traditional Big Jim band holds quasi traditional dances every year.

The facilities of the Eastern Shawnees include a tribal headquarters, a recreational park, and an eye clinic. The tribe also runs a nutrition clinic for the elderly, provides most of its own health care, and publishes a newsletter. Few speak their Native language. The Loyal Shawnees maintain a cultural center and several traditions, such as the Bread, Green Corn, and Buffalo Dances. The Native language among these people is practically defunct.

See also Agriculture; Algonquin; Tecumseh; Tenskwatawa

Stockbridge-Munsee
See Mahican.

Tuscarora
See Iroquois.

Wampanoag

"Wampanoag" means "Eastern People." They were formerly known as Pokanokets, which originally was the name of Massasoit's village but came to be the designation of all the territory and people under that great sachem. The Wampanoags or Pokanokets also included the Nausets of Cape Cod, the Sakonnets of Rhode Island, and various tribes of the offshore islands. (*See also* Narragansett.)

Traditionally, Wampanoags lived in southern New England from just north of Cape Cod, but including Nantucket and Martha's Vineyard, to Narragansett Bay. There were approximately 6,500 Wampanoags in 1600, including tributary island tribes. Wampanoags spoke the Massachusett dialect of an Algonquin language.

The people recognized a supreme deity and many lesser deities. Priests, or medicine men, provided religious leadership. Their duties included mediating with the spirit world to cure, to forecast the weather, and to conduct ceremonies.

A chief sachem led the tribe. In theory his power was absolute, but in practice he was advised by a council of village and clan chiefs (sagamores). The village was the main political unit. Village leadership had a hereditary element, which may be responsible for the existence of women chiefs. Villages may have made their own temporary alliances. Overall political structure consolidated and became more hierarchical after the epidemics of 1616–1619.

Wampanoags were organized into a number of clans. Their annual round of activities took them from winter villages to gathering sites at summer fields. Women had clearly defined and significant political rights. Social stratification was reflected in leadership and marriage arrangements. Leading men might have more than one wife. The dead were wrapped in mats and buried with various possessions, mourners blackened their faces, and the souls of the dead were said to travel west.

There were at least thirty villages in the early seventeenth century, most of which were located by water. People lived in wigwams, both circular and rectangular. The largest measured up to 100 feet long; smaller ones were about fifteen feet in diameter. The houses consisted of pole frames covered with birchbark, hickory bark, or woven mats.

Wigwams tended to have central fires, but longhouses featured rows of several fires. Some houses may have been palisaded. Their larger structures were probably built in winter villages. Mat beds stood on platforms against the walls or directly on the ground. Skins served as bedding. All towns featured a central open space used for ceremonies and meetings. The people also built sweat houses.

Men hunted fowl, as well as small and large game, with the white-tailed deer being the most important. They stalked, trapped, and snared deer and may have hunted them in communal drives. They also grew tobacco. The people ate seals and beached whales, and they gathered shellfish, often steaming them over hot rocks. They fished for freshwater and saltwater species in the winter (through the ice) and in the summer. Women gathered roots, wild fruits, berries, and nuts as well as maple sap for sugar. Women began growing corn, beans, and squash in the late prehistoric period. Fish may have been used as fertilizer.

Dugout canoes could hold up to forty passengers, with the average being ten to fifteen. There may also have been some number of birchbark canoes. Women wore skirts and poncho-style blouses as well as soft-soled moccasins. They donned rabbit and beaver robes in cold weather. Men wore skin leggings and breechclouts and soft-soled moccasins. They also wore turkey feather cloaks and bone and shell necklaces. They tended to pull out all their hair except for a scalp lock.

Wampanoag/Pokanoket culture developed steadily in their approximate historical location for about 8,000 years. They had already been weakened from disease and war with the Penobscots when they encountered non-Natives in the early seventeenth century. They had also been forced by the Narragansetts to accept tributary status.

The people greeted the Pilgrims in 1620, although there had been contact with the British some years earlier. The Grand Sachem Massasoit made a treaty of friendship with the British. His people helped the Europeans survive by showing them how to grow crops and otherwise survive in a land alien to them. Men named Squanto and Samoset are especially known in this regard. Largely as a result of Massasoit's influence, the Wampanoags remained neutral in the Pequot War of 1636. Many Indian residents of Cape Cod and the islands of Nantucket and Martha's Vineyard were Christianized during the midseventeenth century.

Massasoit died in 1662. At that time his second son, Metacomet, also known as Philip, renewed the peace. However, relations were strained by British abuses such as the illegal occupation of

land; trickery, often involving the use of alcohol; and the destruction of resources, including forests and game. Diseases also continued to take a toll on the population.

Finally, local tribes reached the breaking point. The Pokanoket, now mainly relocated to the Bristol, Rhode Island, area and led by Metacomet, took the lead in uniting Indians from southern and central New England in King Philip's War (1675–1676). This was an attempt by the Wampanoag, Narragansett, and other tribes to drive the British out of their territory. However, the fighting began before all the preparations had been completed. In the end, hundreds of non-Native settlers died, but the two main Indian tribes were nearly exterminated. The tribal name of Pokanoket was also officially banned.

Most Wampanoags were either enslaved or killed. Survivors fled into the interior or onto the Cape and the islands, whose tribes had not participated in the war. Some also fled to the Great Lakes region and Canada. For centuries following this event, local Indians were cheated, discriminated against, used as servants, or, at best, ignored.

The Indian population on Nantucket Island declined from possibly 1,500 in 1600 to 358 in 1763 to twenty in 1792, mainly owing to disease. The last of the indigenous population died in 1855. Indians at Mashpee, on Cape Cod, were assigned fifty square miles of land in 1660. Self-government continued until 1788, when the state of Massachusetts placed the Indians under its control. Most of their lands were allotted in 1842. Trespass by non-Natives was a large problem during the entire period. Near Mashpee, the 2,500-acre Herring Pond Reservation was allotted in 1850.

Indian land in Fall River was divided into lots in 1707, and a 160-acre reservation was created in 1709. The people's right of self-government was abrogated in the early nineteenth century. The reservation was eliminated entirely in 1907. Of the three reservations on Martha's Vineyard in the nineteenth century—Chappaquiddick, Christiantown, and Gay Head—only the latter remained by 1900. This group was never governed by non-Native overseers, and its isolation allowed the people to retain their identity and cohesion to a far greater extent than other Wampanoag communities.

Other groups of Wampanoag descendents maintained a separate existence until the nineteenth century, when most became fully assimilated. The Wampanoag Nation was founded in 1928 in response to the pan-Indian movement of the times.

Contemporary Wampanoag events, many of which have both sacred and secular/public components, include a powwow on the Fourth of July (Mashpee), Indian Day and Cranberry Day (Gay Head), and a new year's ceremony and the Strawberry Festival (Assonet). Many Gay Head people have left the island, but many also plan to return. The Mashpee people continue to seek a land base and hope that federal recognition will advance their prospects. The community is in the process of working out a fair relationship with the increasingly non-Native population of the town. The Pokanoket tribe, led by descendents of Massasoit, seeks federal recognition, as well as stewardship of 267 acres of land in Bristol, Rhode Island.

See also Canoes; Massasoit; Pequot War; Squanto.

Winnebago

"Winnebago" is Algonquin for "People of the Filthy Water," referring to the lower Fox River and Lake Winnebago, which became clogged with dead fish every summer. This name was translated by the French into *Puants* and back into English as "Stinkards." The people's self-designation was *Hochungra,* "People of the Big (Real, or Parent) Speech (Voices)" or "Great Fish (Trout) Nation." Today they are known as the Ho-Chunk Nation.

The Winnebagos shared cultural characteristics with Plains Siouans such as the Otoes, Iowas, and Missourias as well as with Woodland/Plains Algonquins such as the Sauks, Foxes, and Menominees. Little is known of Winnebago culture prior to their brush with annihilation in the early seventeenth century. In the early seventeenth century, perhaps 3,000 Winnebagos were located in Wisconsin on the Door Peninsula, Green Bay, just south of the Menominees. The Winnebagos may also once have lived in west central Wisconsin. Winnebago belongs or is related to the Chiwere division of the Siouan language family.

The primary deity was the sun, or earth maker. The people also recognized other deities, some sex identified, and many lesser spirits. Winnebago cosmology was intricate and complex, and, although most people were unfamiliar with the details, most also observed the various rituals associated with aspects of traditional religious belief having to do with personal visions, clan membership, and life cycle events.

Young people undertook vision quests to acquire guardian spirits. These were said to provide luck and success in hunting, war, or curing. The Midewiwin (Medicine Dance) ceremony differed from the Algonquin version in that it dealt mainly with life and death as well as life after death. Clan feasts focused on making offerings to the clan animal. There was also a winter feast.

War bundle ceremonies, held under clan auspices, resulted from particular visions. They included ritual offerings and were meant to enhance the spiritual power of the military enterprise. There were several kinds of shamans: Those associated with war and curing were considered good, but those associated with hunting might be good or bad (witches). Certain older people used both medicinal plants and spiritual power to cure disease.

There was a hereditary head chief in former times. As the population dispersed during the eighteenth century, population centers became more autonomous. Dual chieftainships (peace and war chiefs) existed in villages and among head chiefs. Both civil and war chiefs were selected from hereditary candidates according to merit. One clan, the Bear, served as a tribal police force.

Generosity may have been the people's highest value. The tribe was organized into two divisions, earth and air. There were also twelve patrilineal clans, four among the air division and eight among the earth division. Clans were related to animals and were represented by mounds in the shape of animals. They governed marriage, leadership, and games such as lacrosse. Each clan also owned certain names, ceremonies, responsibilities, and restrictions. Descent may have been matrilineal in the distant past.

Berdaches (transvestites), thought to be divinely inspired, were accorded respect. The mother's brother(s) played an important role in raising a boy. Although menstruating women were isolated, some degree of courtship may have taken place at those times. Marriages were often arranged by close male relatives of a woman. In-laws were generally avoided out of respect.

People enjoyed various sports, such as lacrosse, as well as gambling games such as the moccasin game. The Winnebagos were cannibals. At four-night wakes held for the dead, people told stories and gambled for the souls of enemies, which would later assist the dead on their way to the afterlife. Corpses were buried on scaffolds.

The few large late seventeenth-century villages became forty or so scattered settlements by the early nineteenth century. People lived in rectangular bark- or mat-covered lodges. There was also a rectangular council house for meetings and ceremonies and similarly built sweat houses. From the eighteenth century on, as populations became less concentrated, people began to build domed wigwams.

Women grew gardens of corn, beans, and squash as well as tobacco. Men hunted buffalo communally on the nearby prairie and trapped small game. Other large game included deer and bear. Hunting parties probably included women. Runners traveled between winter hunting parties and the villages, exchanging fresh meat for dried vegetables. Fish was often caught at night by the light of pine pitch torches. Women gathered fruit, berries, and tubers as well as wild rice from canoes.

Most clothing was made from tanned buckskin. Men wore deer hair headdresses dyed red. They also wore breechclouts, leggings, and soft-soled moccasins, possibly fringed and/or decorated with quillwork. Women wore sleeveless dresses (consisting of two skins sewed together at the shoulder and belted) over a nettle fiber undershirt, leggings, and moccasins with a distinctive flap over the toe.

Winnebagos were known as enthusiastic fighters. Captured enemies were regularly eaten. Clans owned sacred war bundles, which contained items dictated in a vision by a particular war-related spirit. One clan, the Hawk, had the power of life and death over prisoners of war. War honors included counting coup.

According to tradition, the Winnebagos were united with the Chiwere Siouans in the distant past. Their ancestors were in Wisconsin as early as around 700. As the groups moved north and west, and then south and west, the Winnebagos may have remained in the forest while the other Chiwere speakers moved onto the prairie and Plains in the early to midseventeenth century. They probably participated in the fifteenth-century Mound Builder culture. They were also probably allied with the sixteenth-century Temple Mound people, based at Cahokia, near present-day St. Louis, and borrowed some of their cultural elements (perhaps including cannibalism).

The Winnebagos may have defeated the Illinois in the early seventeenth century. Shortly after the French arrival, around 1634, Michigan-area Algonquins fleeing from Iroquois attacks swarmed into Winnebago territory. Winnebago warfare against these people led to the defeat of most of the refugee

groups. Despite their strength and military capability, by the midseventeenth century the Winnebagos had been reduced to near extinction by disease and war with the Illinois, Ottawa, and other Algonquin tribes. At that point, the Winnebagos were forced to sue for peace with their enemies, adopting and marrying many of them to make up for their losses and in the process incorporating many aspects of Algonquin culture.

They became involved in the fur trade from the mid- to late seventeenth century. That development tended to disperse the tribe west and south of Lake Winnebago. Material changes and technological dependence soon followed. They were French allies during the colonial wars, but pro-British in the American Revolution. They participated in Tecumseh's Rebellion (1809–1811) and tentatively in Black Hawk's War (1832).

Unstable relations between the European and Euro-American powers had aided the Indian cause. The end of fighting between the United States and Britain in 1815 ushered in the era of land cessions and removals for the Winnebagos. They were powerless to prevent the United States from pressuring the Menominees to cede land traditionally belonging to the Winnebagos so that Indians from New York might have a home in the west.

Crowding by non-Natives and pressure from the U.S. government led the Winnebagos to cede their Wisconsin lands between 1825 and 1837 (at least the final treaty was blatantly fraudulent). By then two factions had developed within the tribe: those agreeing to removal and those determined not to leave. The former group, determined to acculturate, soon moved onto several successive reservations in Iowa, Minnesota, South Dakota, and finally Nebraska. Up to one-third of the people died during the removals, particularly on the move to South Dakota. There was an especially severe smallpox epidemic in 1836.

In Nebraska, people continued to grow gardens and hunt. Most of the land was allotted by 1900. Allotments were generally leased to non-Natives, who profited by the towns that grew up in the area, most notably the town of Winnebago. In the early twentieth century, most Winnebago land was sold to non-Natives. At the same time, forced attendance at boarding schools had a particularly destructive effect on the Winnebago. Demoralization set in, and factionalism, based on religious differences (such as Christian sects and the Native American Church), rent the tribe. As was the case

so often, educational and employment opportunities were closed to Indians.

The tribe reorganized in 1936 under the Indian Reorganization Act but was unable to stem the tide of despair, poverty, and growing social problems. Many aspects of traditional culture had vanished by that time. The government soon began a program of purchasing homes in scattered counties for tribal members. In the 1960s, the tribe benefited from both federal antipoverty programs and its own community development work.

Meanwhile, by the 1870s over half of the tribe had returned to Wisconsin, which some members had never left. In the 1880s, many members received scattered forty-acre parcels of land under the Homestead Act, most of which were later sold. The people lived in a semitraditional manner until well into the twentieth century, despite the growing presence of missionaries and missionary schools. In 1906, the people lost much of their land to tax foreclosure.

In 1908, many Wisconsin Winnebagos became involved with the Native American Church. As in Nebraska, the tribe soon developed bitter factions based at least in part on religious differences. The people continued to gather berries and harvest fruit and vegetables where they could. Tourism—mainly craft sales (especially ash splint baskets)—became increasingly important after World War I.

The Wisconsin Winnebagos have retained their clan structure in the context of the two divisions, earth and air (or sky). Many people still observe traditional religious ceremonies such as the vision quest and various festivals. They celebrate a powwow around Labor Day. Gaming remains controversial, but even traditionalists defend it on grounds of sovereignty. Wisconsin Winnebagos are known in part for their dedicated service in the U.S. armed forces. The Native American Church remains popular in both locations.

See also Berdaches; Disease, Historic and Contemporary; Fur Trade; Native American Church of North America.

Wyandotte

"Wyandotte" or "Wyandot" is from *Wendat*, "islanders" or "People of the Peninsula," the self-designation of the Huron people. "Huron" is an archaic French reference to the hair on the head of a wild

boar, meaning "boarlike" or "boorish" and referring to the roached hairstyle, which is a slur to many Wyandottes. The Wyandottes are a successor tribe to the Huron Confederacy, which was destroyed in 1650 and which consisted of four or five tribes: Attignaouantans ("People of the Bear"), Attigneenongnahacs ("Barking Dogs or People of the Cord"), Arendahronons ("People of the Rock"), Tohontaenrats ("People of the Deer"), and possibly Ataronchronons ("People of the Marshes"). Contemporary Canadian Hurons are known as Hurons-Wendats.

In the sixteenth century, Hurons lived in the Saint Lawrence River Valley. By 1600 at the latest, they inhabited an area known as Huronia, which included land between Georgian Bay (Lake Huron) and Lake Ontario. From a level between 16,000 and 30,000 people in the early seventeenth century, the Huron population dropped to about 10,000 in the midseventeenth century and to fewer than 200 in Canada in the early nineteenth century. Huron/Wyandottes spoke mutually intelligible dialects of a Northern Iroquoian language.

The Hurons recognized an almost unlimited number of spirits and deities, the most powerful of which were the sun and sky. Dreams were considered important as foreshadowing good or evil. There were four types of annual religious feasts: prewar singing, the departure of a dying man, thanksgiving, and healing. Of these, the last were related to medicine societies.

The Dance of the Fire, which involved physical contact with boiling water and hot stones or coals, was meant to attract the assistance of a curing spirit. The most important celebration was the Feast of the Dead, held every ten years or so. Relatives cleaned, rewrapped, and buried bones in a common tribal grave. Then they feasted and honored their ancestors' lives in story. This ceremony was accompanied by games, contests, and gift giving.

The tribes of the Huron Confederacy were led by a council of chiefs from each tribe. This council had no jurisdiction in purely local matters. The position of chief was inherited matrilineally, but within that context it was subject to merit criteria and a confirmation process. Large villages were governed by clan civil and war chiefs. The chiefs' male relatives acted as their councilors. Decisions were made by consensus and were not, strictly speaking, binding on individuals or, if a tribal-level decision, on villages.

Generosity was valued to the point where stinginess could leave one open to charges of witchcraft, a capital offense. Each of the constituent clan families was led by the senior mother. Collectively, these women also selected the chiefs from within the appropriate families. Certain lineages in clans were more important than others; holding feasts was a means to achieve status. Crimes against the body politic, such as witchcraft or treason, were punishable by death, but serious crimes like murder were subject to settlement, including compensation.

Premarital sexual relations, beginning shortly after puberty, were common and accepted, within certain clan restrictions. A couple need not marry in the eyes of society, but, if they chose to, marriages were apparently monogamous. Divorce was unusual after children had been born.

Corpses, wrapped in furs, lay in state for several days, during which time people gave speeches and feasted. A mourning period lasted a year, during which time a surviving spouse could not remarry. Every ten years or so the tribe held a feast of the dead.

There were at least eighteen villages in the early seventeenth century. Villages were located on high ground near waterways and woods. The larger ones were often palisaded with up to five rows of sharpened stakes. Public spaces were located between the longhouses. Larger villages had up to 100 longhouses and 2,000 people or more; the average size was perhaps 800 people. Villages were moved every ten to twenty years, after the local soil and firewood were exhausted.

The people built pole-frame, bark houses, twenty-five to thirty feet wide and high and about 100 to 150 (even up to 240) feet long. Each longhouse was home to eight to twenty-four families, with an average of about six people per family. The longhouses tended to be smoky, and fleas and mice were particular pests. The larger house of chiefs also served as council/ceremonial houses.

Villages were economically self-sufficient. Women grew corn, beans, squash, and sunflowers. Men may have grown some tobacco. Corn, the staple food, was eaten mainly as soup with some added foods. Women also gathered blueberries, nuts, and fruits as well as acorns in times of famine.

Men hunted deer, bear, numerous other large and small game, and fowl. Bears were occasionally trapped and then fattened for a year or two before being eaten for special feasts. Dogs were also eaten, as were fish, clams, crabs, and turtles.

The digging stick and an antler or bone hoe were the primary agricultural tools. Women wove mats, baskets, and nets of Indian hemp, reeds, bark, and

corn husks. They also made leather bags; these and the baskets were painted or decorated with porcupine quills. Men made wooden items such as utensils, bowls, and shields as well as stone or clay pipes and heavy stone tools such as axes. Pottery and wooden mortars were related to food preparation.

Most people traded to acquire goods to give away and thus acquire status. The Hurons were important traders even before the French arrived. They had a monopoly on corn and tobacco. They also dealt in furs and chert, wampum beads, dried berries, mats, fish, and hemp. Extensive trade routes took the Hurons all over much of the eastern Great Lakes and the Saint Lawrence River region and kept their society rich and stable. Trade routes were owned or controlled by the people who had made them as well as by other members of their lineage. Intratribal use of the trails entailed payment of a fee. Intertribal use was prohibited. Rivers were navigated via birchbark canoe.

Women made clothing from buckskin. It consisted generally of shirts, breechclouts, leggings, skirts, and moccasins. Fur capes were added in the winter. Clothing was decorated with fringe and brightly painted designs. Face painting and tattooing were popular, especially among men.

Hurons never achieved the kind of unity of purpose and command essential for defeating or even realistically engaging an enemy as powerful as the Iroquois. People fought mainly for blood revenge as well as to gain personal status. Most fighting was practiced by surprise attacks on small groups. Captives were often ritually tortured and sometimes eaten. Some, especially women and children, might be adopted.

The Hurons probably originated with other Iroquoians in the Mississippi Valley. They encountered Jacques Cartier in 1534 and Samuel de Champlain in 1609. The Iroquois wars probably began sometime in the sixteenth century, if not earlier, when those people drove the Huron tribes out of the Saint Lawrence Valley, lands that they may originally have taken by warfare from the Iroquois. Thereafter the Hurons sided with the Algonquins against the Iroquois.

The people entered the fur trade in the early seventeenth century, mainly as intermediaries between the French and other tribes. Catholic missionaries soon followed the traders, as did venereal disease and alcohol. Until the late 1640s, the Hurons dominated the French beaver pelt trade. The French, however, were reluctant to sell arms to unconverted Hurons, a policy that was to have disastrous conse-

quences. Severe epidemics in the late 1630s were followed by more Christian conversions and increased factionalism.

The Iroquois, armed with Dutch firearms, launched their final invasion in 1648. These tribes were allied with the British and sought to expand their trapping area and their control over neighboring tribes. Within two years they had destroyed the Hurons. Some Hurons escaped to Lorette, near Quebec City, where they were granted land. They continued to grow crops, hunt, and trap until the end of the nineteenth century, when craft sales and factory work became the most important economic activities. They also intermarried regularly with the French.

Other Hurons settled among tribes such as the Eries, who were themselves later destroyed by the Iroquois. Many were adopted by the victorious Iroquois nations. Some Hurons escaped to the west, where they joined with the Tionotati (Petun, or Tobacco nation), a related tribe. Under continuing pressure from the Iroquois, they began wandering around the Michilimackinac–Green Bay region, where they hunted and remained active in the fur trade. Although never a large tribe, membership in various alliances allowed them to play an important role in regional affairs.

Jesuits continued to minister to these people, who migrated to Detroit around 1700. They split into pro-British (at Sandusky) and pro-French groups in the mideighteenth century. The latter group became known as the Wyandottes and claimed territory north of the Ohio River, where they allowed Shawnee and Lenápe bands to settle. Wyandottes fought the British in Pontiac's Rebellion (1763).

Land cessions to non-Natives began in 1745 and continued into the nineteenth century. Wyandottes sold their lands on the Canadian side of the Detroit River in 1790 in exchange for reserves, most of which were ceded in the early nineteenth century; the rest were allotted in severalty later in the century. These people sided with the British in the Revolutionary War and split their allegiance in the War of 1812.

Their land in Ohio and Michigan was recognized by the United States after the War of 1812, but the tribe ceded most of it by 1819. With the decline of the fur trade, many Wyandottes began farming and acculturating to non-Native society. More land was ceded in 1832, and in 1842 the people had ceded all Ohio and Michigan lands and moved to the Indian Territory (Kansas), on land purchased from the Lenápes and on individual sections. During this

period, the question of slavery increased factionalism among tribal members; some were slaveholders, whereas others were adamant abolitionists.

An 1855 treaty provided for land allotment (most allotments were soon alienated) and divided the tribe into citizens and noncitizens. Three years later, roughly 200 Wyandottes settled on the Seneca Reservation. The more traditional (noncitizen) group relocated to the new Indian Territory (Oklahoma) in 1867, after the Seneca-Cayugas agreed to donate part of their reservation there. This reservation was allotted in 1893. The Wyandotte Tribe of Oklahoma was created in 1937. It was terminated in the 1950s but was rerecognized in 1978. The citizen group remained in Kansas, incorporating as the Wyandot Nation of Kansas in 1959.

The tribe in Oklahoma provides several important services, including student scholarships and meals for the elderly. The people are working on identifying and preserving aspects of their cultural traditions. The Hurons of Lorette (Quebec) are all Catholic and part French. The Canadian National Railway bisects the reserve. Most Indians own property. Children attend school on the reserve through grade four. The reserve is similar to neighboring towns in Quebec. There is some effort to revive the Native language.

See also Fur Trade; Disease, Historic and Contemporary; Deganawidah; Haudenosaunee Confederacy, Political System.

Native Americans of the Subarctic

Beaver

"Beaver" comes from *Tsattine*, "dwellers among the beaver." Today the people refer to themselves as *Deneza* or *Dunne-za*, "Real People." They were culturally similar to the Chipewyans and Sekanis. Traditional Beaver territory (in the mideighteenth century) is the prairies south of the Peace River and east of the Rocky Mountains and on the upper Peace River (present-day Alberta and British Columbia). They may once also have lived in the Lake Claire area and the upper parts of the Athapaska River. The Beaver population may have been between 1,000 and 1,500 in the seventeenth century. The Beaver people speak a Northern Athapaskan language.

A well-defined cosmology and mythology were intimately connected with vision quests. Young people fasted to acquire guardian spirits, mainly in dreams. Various food and behavioral taboos, as well as songs and medicine bundles, were associated with a particular animal spirit. The most important festival took place twice a year and involved the fire sacrifice of food to ensure continued bounty. Dreamers, or prophets—people in touch through dreams with the past and future—had special powers. Shamans were those who had acquired especially powerful guardian spirits. They cured by singing, blowing, and sucking illness-linked objects from the body.

Three or four independent bands had their own hunting areas and leaders. Leadership was based on skill and knowledge, which was in turn gained partly through experience and partly through dreaming. Bands were composed of hunting groups of roughly thirty people; the size and composition of the bands varied. Groups grew in size during the summer and broke into constituent parts in the winter and early spring.

Men might have more than one wife. Newlyweds lived with the woman's family and served her parents for a period of time, but descent was patriarchal. Corpses were placed on birchbark strips and buried in tree scaffolds or on platforms. Mourners gave away their possessions.

The typical dwelling was a three-pole conical moose or caribou skin teepee. Winter lodges of logs were covered with moss and earth. In the summer, people mainly lived in conical brush shelters or simple lean-tos.

The Beaver people were basically nomadic hunters of moose, caribou, beaver, and other animals. Men drove buffalo into enclosures as late as the early nineteenth century. Fish were not an important part of the diet except in emergencies. People also snared smaller animals, such as rabbits, and women gathered berries and other plant food.

Food was often hot-rock boiled in containers of spruce or birch bark or woven spruce roots. Bags were generally made of moose and caribou skins. Bark containers were important as well. Arrowheads were mostly flint, as were knife blades, although people also used moose horn or beaver teeth for this purpose. To encourage certain plants and animals, people regularly burned parts of the prairie.

Favorite trade locations included Vermilion and the mouth of the Smoky River. The relation of oral tradition was taken very seriously and considered a fine art. Women made most clothing from moose skin. Clothing consisted of shirts, leggings, fur-lined

moccasins, and a knee-length coat. Men added breechclouts after being influenced by the Crees. Women sometimes wore a short apron. Clothing was decorated with porcupine quill embroidery. Women drew toboggans before the advent of dog power in the twentieth century. People traveled in spruce-bark and birchbark canoes as well as on snowshoes.

Ancestors of the Beavers were in their historical territory 10,000 years ago. The Beaver and Sekani people may once have been united. By the mideighteenth century, Crees, armed with guns, had confined the Beaver Indians to the Peace River basin. At that time, eastern Beaver groups joined the Crees, adopting many of their customs and habits, while western groups moved farther up the Peace River, toward the eastern slopes of the Rocky Mountains. The Sarcees probably branched off from the Beaver Indians about that time as well.

In 1799, the leader Makenunatane (Swan Chief) sought to attract both missionaries and a trading post. The people became more and more involved in the fur trade during the nineteenth century. Most people had accepted Catholicism by about 1900, although many retained a core of their former religious ideas.

Although they had been obtaining arms and other items of non-Native manufacture for years, direct contact between the people and non-Native traders occurred only in 1876. New foods were introduced, and for the first time the people's subsistence activities were fundamentally altered. The Beavers signed Treaty 8 with Canada in 1899, under which the Indians accepted reserves but retained extensive subsistence rights. Canadian officials began appointing nominal chiefs after that.

In the early twentieth century, some Beaver people were raising horses and trapping for a living. By 1930, non-Native farmers had settled much of their territory. Construction of the Alaska Highway in the early 1940s disrupted the nomadic life of the last traditional Beaver bands, and in the 1950s and 1960s, oil and gas became major regional industries.

The ancient prophet tradition has waned in recent years, although dreamers' songs remain the basis for much ceremonialism as well as an important part of the summer gatherings known as Treaty 8 Days. The Alaska and Mackenzie Highway has separated the Beavers of Alberta and British Columbia from one another. Younger people are literate in English, although Beaver remains the first language for most.

Effective rule by Indian agents came to an end in the 1980s, when the people began to administer their own affairs through such organizations as the Treaty Eight Tribal Association. Children attend band and/or provincial and/or private schools. Most people have high school educations. In general, housing and social services are considered adequate.

See also Athapaskan Languages; Athapaskan Peoples; Canada, Indian Policies of; Fur Trade.

Carrier

"Carrier" comes from the French *Porteur* and is originally from a Sekani word referring to the custom among certain bands for widows to carry their dead husbands' bones on their backs in a birchbark container. They called themselves *Takulli* ("People Who Go upon the Water") in the nineteenth century, apparently a word given to them from without. The people usually refer to themselves by the subtribe or band name.

The Carriers were strongly influenced by Northwest Coast tribes and were culturally similar to the Sekanis and the Chilcotins. Carrier territory is the region of Eutsuk, Francis, Babine, and Stuart Lakes and the upper Skeena and Fraser Rivers in north central British Columbia. Their population numbered approximately 8,500 in the late eighteenth century. Carriers spoke dialects (Lower, Central, and Upper) of a Northern Athapaskan language.

Traditional religious belief may have included recognition of a supreme deity in the sky. Of key importance were a host of supernatural beings, mostly animal based, with whom the people tried to communicate through fasting and dreams. Through their rituals, the people sought to gain the favor and power of these spiritual beings. The people also believed in life after death, perhaps in a land to the west. Some especially Tsimshian-influenced groups adopted a secret cannibal society.

Young men fasted and dreamed in remote places in an effort to attract a guardian spirit protector (optional in the southern regions). Those with special power became shamans, who could cure illness, although they themselves might be killed if a patient died. Shamans could also retrieve lost souls and forecast the future.

Each of roughly fifteen independent subtribes/ regional bands was composed of one or more villages/local bands. The subtribes were associated with specific subsistence areas. In the south, leaders were heads of extended families who acted as spokesmen and subsistence coordinators. Shamans were also politically important in the south.

The most important political unit in central and northern areas was the hereditary matrilineal clan, of which there were roughly twenty. They were divided into houses, which had hereditary chiefs who supervised subsistence areas, provided for the poor, and represented clan interests in councils.

Society was divided into ranked, hereditary social classes of nobles, commoners, and a few slaves. Depending on the specific location, descent could be through the mother's or father's line. Except on the Tsimshian border, commoners had the possibility of obtaining sufficient goods to give potlatches and attain the noble rank. Crests were displayed on totem poles, houses, and regalia. Crests, titles, and honors were considered clan property and could usually be bought and sold.

Trespass was considered a serious offense, but chiefs could often work out an arrangement or decide on appropriate compensation. The extended family was the main social and economic unit. Potlatching occurred in the north. Feasts were given and presents distributed at important life cycle events. The installation of a new chief was considered the most important occasion of all, requiring numerous potlatches. The entire potlatch complex became especially important from the late eighteenth through the late nineteenth centuries.

Women were responsible for most domestic tasks, such as carrying water and firewood, cooking, tanning skins, and sewing clothing. Men made houses, tools, and weapons; fought; and acquired animal foods. Women gave birth in a specially constructed hut assisted by their husbands and/or other women. Names were taken from a hereditary stock, if available, or from dreams if not.

At adolescence, boys were encouraged to increase their level of physical activity, whereas girls were secluded and their activity restricted for up to two years. Young women selected a mate with their parents' assistance. The couple was engaged after the man gave valuable items to his prospective mother-in-law, and married after the couple spent the night together at a later date. They lived with the woman's parents for up to a year while the new husband helped provide for his new in-laws.

Corpses were cremated. Widows were expected to hold their husband's burning body for as long as they could. In the east, women carried the charred bones of their husbands on their backs for several years.

Semipermanent villages served as bases for hunting and fishing expeditions. Rectangular winter houses were built of pole frames covered with spruce bark, whose gabled roofs extended to the ground. These houses held several families. Some southern groups built underground winter lodges similar to those of the Chilcotins and Shuswaps. Summer houses had low, plank walls and plank or bark gabled roofs. There were also specialty menstrual, fishing, sweat, and smoking structures.

Fish, especially salmon, was perhaps the most important item in the diet, although this was less true in the south. People fished through the ice for carp and other species. Before the snow fell, men hunted caribou, mountain goats, and bear as well as smaller game such as beaver, marmot, and hare. Women gathered a number of roots, bulbs, greens, and berries.

The Carriers imported woven baskets from the Bella Coolas, Chilcotins, and Shuswaps; Chilkat blankets, cedar boxes, and stone labrets from the Tsimshians; and wooden cooking boxes, eulachon (smelt) oil, shell ornaments, and copper bracelets from other coast tribes. There was also some intratribal trade. The people mainly exported prepared hides and furs.

Men made spruce- and birchbark canoes as well as cottonwood dugouts. Goods were carried overland with the help of a tumpline and backpack. Snowshoes and toboggans arrived with the non-Natives. Skin clothing consisted of robes, leggings, and moccasins, with fur caps and mittens added in cold weather. In warm weather, men sometimes went naked; women wore a knee-length apron. High-status men wore Chilkat blankets for special occasions, and similarly ranked northern women wore wooden labrets in their mouths. Other ornaments were made of dentalium, bone, and haliotis shell.

The Carriers may have originated east of the Rocky Mountains and were probably in their historic location for at least several centuries before contact with non-Natives. Major epidemics began in the late eighteenth century, about the time they met the Scotch trader and explorer Alexander Mackenzie (1793).

Beginning in the late eighteenth century, the Carriers began to acquire iron and other items of non-Native manufacture. With the growing value of the pelts of interior animals (beaver, marten, and lynx), Carrier wealth increased with their ability to export these products. Carrier control of some local trade networks in the early nineteenth century allowed some chiefs to amass wealth and power. Some high-ranking people began to intermarry with Bella Coola and Gitksan families around this time, as Northwest Coast cultural influences became much more pronounced.

The first local trade fort (James) was built in 1806 at Stuart Lake. A quasi Christian prophet movement arose among the Carriers beginning in the 1830s. An entire band was exterminated by smallpox in 1837. Catholic missionaries arrived in the 1840s. Penetration by miners, farmers, and ranchers from the midnineteenth century on led to increased disease and general problems for the Indians.

Another ramification of increased contact was the decline of the potlatching complex. Retention of material goods became more important than status gained by giving them away. Also, there was a growing need to accumulate items of non-Native manufacture just to survive, so giving them away became difficult. The Catholic Church also worked to eliminate potlatching.

Wage work, such as on ranches, as guides, in canneries, in sawmills, and at construction sites, began to take the place of traditional subsistence activities. The Carriers were prevented by law from preempting land after 1866. The Canadian Pacific Railway, completed in 1885, bisected Carrier territory. Most reserves were created in the later nineteenth century, although additional ones were established in the early twentieth century. Subsistence activities were increasingly government regulated by then.

Another railway line, completed in 1914, led to an influx of settlers and speculators. Commercial mining and lumbering began in the early twentieth century. Lumbering, including clear-cutting, expanded sharply after World War II. In the 1970s, the Carriers began organizing politically over the chronically unresolved issues of Native land title and rights.

Most Carriers today live in individual houses. Many still speak Carrier. Clans exist today, especially among the northern and central groups, although they are vastly less important than they used to be. Potlatch privileges and responsibilities are rarely observed except among the groups nearest the Tsimshian people. Most people are Christian, at least nominally, although ancient beliefs linger as well, including the power of dreams and the efficacy of shamans. Children attend band and/or provincial and/or private schools.

Local anti-Indian sentiment remains deeply entrenched. Carrier bands along the Nechako River have strongly opposed the completion of a hydroelectric project, the initial stages of which created forced relocations and other hardships for the people beginning in the 1950s. Struggles also continue over issues such as land title and rights. One example is the development of the so-called Mackenzie Grease Trail, which continues against Indian wishes and portrays them (when they are not ignored entirely) as little more than tourist attractions.

See also Athapaskan Languages; Athapaskan Peoples; Fur Trade; Canada, Indian Policies of; Potlatch.

Chilcotin

"Chilcotin" means "Inhabitants of Young Man's River." The Chilcotins were culturally related to the Carriers, the Interior Salish tribes, the Bella Coolas, and the Kwakiutls. The territory of the Chilcotins is along the headwaters of the Chilcotin River and the Anahim Lake district and from the Coast Range to near the Fraser River, British Columbia.

The Chilcotin population stood at approximately 1,500 in the seventeenth century. It increased to possibly 3,500 in the late eighteenth century. Chilcotin is a Northern Athapaskan language.

Boys, and girls to some extent, went into seclusion at adolescence to acquire a guardian spirit. Spirits, which could be any natural phenomenon, gave the person songs and dances as well as protective power. A person who acquired many spirits might become a shaman and engage in curing and seeing what most people could not. Shamans could use their power for evil as well as good, although evil against an individual was generally considered to be practiced only for the general good. Illnesses that were not soul related were treated by medical specialists.

Three or four autonomous bands were each composed of camp groups. Bands were defined as

people sharing a wintering territory. There was no overall leadership, and the people never joined or acted together in any way.

Bands were divided into social classes of nobles, commoners, and slaves. Nobles and commoners were arranged into clans, the most powerful of which was Raven. Descent was bilateral. Although sharing was highly valued, some people accumulated more material goods than did others. In those cases, the surplus was generally given away—effectively exchanged for prestige—in feasts. High rank was obtained by giving potlatches.

Early adolescence was a time for adult training. Boys focused on endurance and survival skills. Girls were isolated during their first menstrual period, at which time they observed several behavioral restrictions and performed domestic tasks. Marriage occurred shortly after this adult training. Most marriages were arranged by parents with input from the children.

Women generally did all the camp work; men were responsible for getting animal foods, fighting, and making tools. The dead were buried in the ground, cremated, or simply left under a pile of rocks or branches. Social control was largely internalized. Extreme violators were ostracized or, rarely, killed.

People generally lived in rectangular, pole-framed, earth-covered lodges with bark or brush walls and gable roofs. An open space at the top served as a smoke hole. There were also small, subterranean winter houses and dome-shaped sweat houses.

Men hunted a variety of animals including caribou, elk, mountain goat, sheep, and sometimes bear. Small animals like marmots, beaver, and rabbits were trapped, as were fowl. Men and women caught fish such as trout, whitefish, and salmon. Women gathered camas and other roots as well as a variety of berries.

Chilcotins acquired salmon from the Shuswaps and Bella Coolas. They also imported shell ornaments, cedar-bark headbands, wooden containers, and stone pestles from the Bella Coolas. They sent dried berries, paints, and furs to the Bella Coolas and furs, dentalium shells, and goat hair blankets woven by the Bella Coolas to other tribes. The people made fine coiled basketry with designs of humans and animals as well as geometric shapes. Although most travel was overland, men carved spruce-bark and dugout canoes, some with pointed

prows like those of the interior Salish. Snowshoes were used for winter travel.

Dress generally consisted of moccasins, buckskin aprons, belts, and leggings. Cold weather gear included caps; robes of marmot, hare, or beaver; and woven wool and fur blankets. Men's hair was generally no longer than shoulder length, although women grew their hair long and often wore it in two braids. The people used a number of personal ornaments of bone, shell, teeth, and claws.

Trespass was a reason to fight, as were murder and feuding. Fighters wore red and black face paint. Ritual purification, including vomiting, took place after a raid. Those who had killed lived apart from others for a time.

Chilcotins first encountered non-Natives in either 1793 or 1815. Fort Alexandria, a trading post, was established in 1821. A gold strike around the Fraser River about 1860 led to the large-scale invasion of Indian lands and the widespread destruction of resources, with no compensation. Indian villages and even graves were looted by the newcomers.

There was a serious smallpox epidemic about 1862. Chilcotins sent out war parties to attack road builders. Several warriors, including Chiefs Tellot, Elexis, and Klatsassin, were captured and hanged. After the epidemics and the fighting, many survivors worked on non-Native–owned ranches, since Indians were explicitly excluded from preempting land, and much of their land was confiscated.

Missionaries helped establish villages that became reserves. They also significantly influenced the selection of chiefs, or headmen. Some groups merged with the Shuswaps and Carriers on the Fraser River at that time. Most were located on three reserves by 1900 and were largely acculturated. Stonies, or Stone Chilcotin bands, remained semitraditional in the western mountains. In the early twentieth century, most people hayed and/or sold a few head of cattle or some furs for a living. There was little contact with the outside world until the 1960s.

The westernmost people still cross the mountains to visit the Bella Coolas. Public lands containing natural resources from which Chilcotins traditionally derived subsistence have steadily decreased since the 1960s. Children attend various band and/or provincial and/or private schools.

See also Athapaskan Languages; Athapaskan Peoples; Basketry; Canada, Indian Policies of; Potlatch.

Chipewyan

"Chipewyan" meaning "pointed skins," comes from the Cree word *chipwayanewok*, referring to a style of drying beaver skins that left shirts pointed at the bottom. Their self-designation was *Dene*, "the People." Geographical divisions included the Athabaskans (Chipewyan proper), Desnedekenades, Ethaneldis (Caribou Eaters), and Thilanottines. The Yellowknifes (Tatsanottines) are sometimes considered to be a Chipewyan division. The people were known to the French as Montagnais, not to be confused with the people of eastern Canada.

There were probably between 4,000 and 5,000 Chipewyans in the seventeenth century. In the early eighteenth century, Chipewyans occupied a huge expanse north of the Churchill River between the Great Slave Lake and Hudson Bay, in the present-day Northwest Territories and northern Manitoba, Alberta, and Saskatchewan. Chipewyan land straddled the northernmost taiga and the southern tundra. The people spoke an Athapaskan language. The word "Athapascan" is taken from one of their divisions.

Communication with the spirit world through dreams and visions provided success in hunting and other activities. Owing to the harsh environment there were no herbal curers: All illness was considered a function of witchcraft, and shamans, by virtue of their spirit powers, acted as curers. After death, only good souls were said to inhabit an island full of game.

There were many autonomous bands of various sizes in each division. Regional bands (at least 200 to 400 people) came together during caribou migration periods and broke into smaller local bands (perhaps fifty or so people) at other times. Bands were associated with particular subsistence areas. Leaders had little or no authority beyond an immediate activity such as hunting or war.

Men were named after seasons, animals, or places, but women's names always included the word for "marten." In general, weaker men were at the mercy of the stronger, and women fared worst of all. Girls were separated from boys around late childhood, and women did most of the hardest work and were the first to go without food in lean times. Women were segregated during their first menstrual periods and, on subsequent occasions, were subjected to behavioral taboos. Women were married at the onset of adolescence, often to considerably older men.

Good hunters had more than one wife. Old and/or sick people were often abandoned to starve to death. The dead were generally left on the ground. When someone died, their property was destroyed. Widows cut off their hair and observed a year-long mourning period.

People lived in temporary encampments in open country in the summer and in the woods in the winter. Dwellings were conical caribou skin tents with a smoke hole at the top. Spruce boughs and caribou skins served as floors. The teepees were semi-insulated with snow around the base in winter.

The annual round of subsistence activities revolved around following the caribou, which was the main food for all Chipewyan groups. Caribou were driven into pounds, snared with ropes, and shot from canoes or by men on foot. Men also hunted buffalo, deer, bear, musk oxen, and moose. Some groups mixed dried meat with fat to make pemmican, which they stored in caribou intestines.

The people also snared and trapped small game and fowl. They fished for trout, whitefish, and pike. Most fish were smoked or sun dried. There were also some plant foods, such as moss and lichen (the latter generally eaten fermented in an animal's stomach).

Most tools were of stone and bone. The use of copper for tools such as hatchets, awls, knives, and arrow and spearheads probably came from the Yellowknife people. Water could be stone boiled in birchbark and caribou skin pots. Moss was used for baby diapers. The people also made drums.

Birchbark items were acquired from the Crees. The people also imported shell, including dentalium, mainly for decorative purposes. There was some trade in copper in the late prehistoric period. Trade chiefs (captains) emerged in the mideighteenth century. Birchbark and spruce-bark canoes served as river transport. Snowshoes made from summer tent poles featured right and left sides. Women dragged heavy toboggans in the winter and served as pack animals in the summer, carrying goods, food, and skins on their backs. Dogs were not widely used as pack animals until the twentieth century.

Well-tanned caribou skin clothing consisted of shirts, leggings (sometimes joined to moccasins), breechclouts (for men), dresses (for women), caps, and mittens. Caribou robes were hooded and trimmed with fur. The hair on the hides was shaved off in the summer but left on and worn on the inside in the winter. Children wore body suits of rabbit skin.

The Chipewyans may have originated in the Rocky Mountains. The Hudson's Bay Company forced an uneasy truce between Chipewyans and Crees to their south in 1715, although fighting remained intermittent for another forty-five years. In 1717, the Hudson's Bay Company established a post at Churchill in Chipewyan territory.

The Chipewyans acquired firearms soon after contact with non-Natives, and they then expanded northward at the expense of the coast Inuits. They also harassed the Dogribs and the Yellowknifes by excluding them from the fort, cheating them of goods, and kidnapping their women. Chipewyans generally served as intermediaries in the fur trade between the British and the Yellowknifes and Dogribs until their monopoly was ended in the late eighteenth century. Chipewyans, such as the guides Thanadelther and Matonabbee, helped non-Natives explore the northland.

The people suffered a mortality rate of up to 90 percent in a 1781 smallpox epidemic. Survivors continued to trade at Fort Chipewyan, a closer North West Company fort, after 1788. Some groups moved into the boreal forest, where there were more fur-bearing animals, but in so doing they gave up their traditional dependence on the caribou.

Their subsequent lives were characterized by dependence on non-Native goods and poor health caused by malnutrition and disease. Missionaries worked among them from the midnineteenth century. They accepted reserves and $5 per-capita annuities in treaties signed from 1876 through 1906. Log cabin settlements were established in the 1920s. The post–World War II era saw increased school attendance, better health care, and the spread of social services among the people. In the 1960s, forcible relocation brought severe disruption to the most traditional group, the Caribou Eaters.

Hunting, fishing, and trapping remain important activities, although the bands live in permanent villages of log or frame houses. Most people are at least nominal Christians. Most people still speak Chipewyan as their first language. Some groups have moved from the more settled communities they were forced to inhabit back to more traditional areas, mainly to be closer to caribou.

See also Athapaskan Languages; Athapaskan Peoples; Basketry; Canada, Indian Policies of; Canoes; Hudson's Bay Company; North West Company.

Cree

"Cree" comes from from *Kristeneaux,* a French word for the name (possibly Kenistenoag) of a small Cree band. The self-designation is either *Ininiw* ("person"), *Nehiyawak* (among the Woodland Crees, "those who speak the same language"), *Atheneuwuck* ("People"), or *Sackaweé-thinyoowuk* ("Bush People"). Crees are commonly divided into Woodland (or Western Woods) Crees (west) and Muskegon (from Omaskekow), Swampy, or West Main Crees (east). Another division, the Plains Cree, is described elsewhere. The Eastern Crees, who live just east of James Bay, are generally regarded as being a division of the Naskapi/Montagnais (Innu). Cree speakers whose territory included land northwest of Quebec and Trois Rivières are known as Tête-de-Boules, or Attikameks. It should be noted, however, that all such labels are spurious and that originally such groups consisted of autonomous groups or "nations."

Three divisions make up the Woodland Crees: Rocky Crees, Western Swampy Crees, and Strongwoods Crees. Information about the traditional lives of these people should be considered sketchy and incomplete. There may also have been a fourth group, the Athabaska-Crees. Traditional Swampy Cree bands include the Abitibi, Albany, Attawapiskat, Monsoni, Moose River (Mousousipiou), Nipigon, Piscotagami, Severn, Winisk, and Winnipeg Indians.

Around 1700, the Crees lived from south of James Bay westward into eastern Alberta, north to around Fort Churchill and Lake Athabaska, and south to a line running roughly from just north of Lake of the Woods to the Lesser Slave Lake. Swampy Cree land was roughly the easternmost 330 kilometers of this territory, including a considerable portion of coastline along James and Hudson Bays. There were at least 20,000 Crees in the sixteenth century. Crees spoke dialects of a Central Algonquin language.

Woodland Crees believed in the ubiquitous presence of Manitou, the great spirit power. Some coastal people also believed in a number of powerful creatures such as dwarfs and cannibalistic giants (Windigo). Some groups may have had the Midewiwin (Medicine Dance), which they probably borrowed from the Anishinabe.

Adolescents fasted and secluded themselves to obtain dream visions; the guardian spirits that they

Interior of a Cree tent, ca. 1822. (Historical Picture Archive/Corbis)

obtained in these visions were said to provide luck. Secret religious societies were dedicated to propitiating animal spirits. Shamans, or conjurers, wielded much authority, in part because of the general fear that they would use their powers for evil purposes (sorcery). Their legitimate functions were to divine the future and cure illness. The latter activity was often associated with a "shaking tent" ritual. Both men and women could become shamans. (Herbalists also cured illness.)

Small local bands, consisting of several extended families, were the basic political units. Bands remained separated except during the summer season, at which time they united on lake shores for ceremonies and councils. Band membership was fluid, and the bands probably had no clearly defined hunting territories. During the summer gatherings, temporary regional bands were led by chiefs, whose authority was based on merit as well as the possession of spiritual power.

In the west, local band chiefs might have as many as seven wives. Parents had a great deal of influence regarding their childrens' mates. Girls were often married before they reached puberty. Newly married men worked for their wives' parents for a period of time. Among the eastern people, divorce was easily obtained. Men might temporarily exchange their wives with others and/or "lend" them to strangers as an act of hospitality, although adultery by the wife was severely punished.

Both twins were not permitted to live. If twins of both sexes were born, the girl was killed (infant girls may have been killed under other circumstances as well). Children were generally raised with great affection and without physical punishment. Girls were subjected to isolation and a number of behavioral restrictions during and immediately following their first menstrual periods; a feast was held when a young man killed his first big game.

Widows and orphans were protected by the group. Death was not generally feared, and the very old or sick were often abandoned or killed. Corpses were wrapped in bark and buried in the ground or

on a scaffold. The people held an annual feast of the dead.

Murder was avenged by relatives. Crees were forced into cannibalism during periods of starvation. They learned tobacco smoking from the people of the Saint Lawrence Valley, and this custom became important among some groups. All groups held numerous athletic contests and games of skill. Singing and dancing occurred both socially and for luck (as in hunting).

Toward the south, the people lived in conical or dome-shaped birchbark wigwams with a three-pole foundation. Farther north and west, the lodges were covered with pine bark or caribou, elk, or moose skin. These structures sheltered extended families of ten or more people. There were also sweat lodges (used in curing and for cleanliness), menstrual lodges, and various caches and ceremonial pavilions.

Cree men were considered superb hunters. They targeted caribou, elk, moose, and beaver. They killed bear when they could get them, and hare when they could not. Some southern groups also hunted buffalo. There were many behavioral taboos and customs designed to mollify spirits related to the hunt. Every hunter carried his personal medicine pouch, and hides were often painted with red stripes and dots.

Fowl were plentiful, especially in certain areas. Woodland people fished only out of necessity, but Swampy Crees relied on fish such as lake trout, pike, whitefish, and pickerel. People on the coast occasionally ate seals and beluga whales, spearing them with harpoons. Seal fat was often added to meat and fish in the east.

The people made birchbark cooking vessels, except in the east, where woven spruce-root pots or soapstone pots (around James Bay) were used. Some vessels were also made of clay. Some groups used an Inuit-style curved knife for scraping hides, although farther west the women used a Plains-style tool shaped more like a chisel. A balancing stick was used while walking on snowshoes or pulling toboggans. Fire was generally kept alive as coals in a birchbark container.

People made birchbark canoes, toboggans (of juniper in the west), and elongated birch-frame snowshoes.

Artistic expression took the forms of fine moose hair, bird feather, and porcupine quill embroidery, of carved wood items, and of face and body tattooing and painting. Clothing generally contained painted geometric patterns and, later, beaded floral designs. There was some rock painting of both realistic and stylized animals, people, and mythological personages.

Moose, caribou, or elk skin clothing was often fringed. Clothing generally consisted of breechclouts (belted in the east), shirts, dresses, belts, moccasins (extended in the winter), and long leggings. Winter gear included beaver and caribou robes, socks, mittens, and hats as well as woven hare skin coats and blankets and caribou coats. Women generally tattooed the corners of their mouths and men their entire bodies. Eastern men and women plucked facial hair, and head hair was often braided.

The Crees and Anishinabes probably share a common origin. Crees have been in their known aboriginal territory for at least 4,000 years. They first encountered non-Natives when the Henry Hudson exploration arrived in 1610.

The first trade forts were founded among the Swampy Crees beginning around 1670 and in the west from the mideighteenth century on. Crees serving as guides and trappers increased their importance to local fur trade companies. French and Scottish trappers and traders regularly intermarried with Cree Indians. The mixed-race offspring, known as Métis, eventually developed their own culture. Some fought two wars with Canada in the mid- to late nineteenth century over the issues of land rights and sovereignty.

In the early trade days (seventeenth century in the east and mideighteenth to early nineteenth centuries in the west), the Indians prospered in part by playing the French and British against each other. Their acquisition of firearms from the Hudson's Bay Company, as well as the completion of an alliance with the Assiniboines, precipitated a tremendous expansion almost to the Arctic Sea, the Rocky Mountains, and the Red River region. Groups of Crees arriving on the Great Plains, near the end of the seventeenth century, adopted many elements of classic Plains culture, especially including dependence on the buffalo.

Jesuit missionaries began working among the Swampy Crees for a short time in the late seventeenth century. The region was devoid of missionaries, however, from then until 1823, when the Church of England established a presence. By 1717, the Swampy Crees had become dependent on non-Native traders for necessities such as cloth, blankets,

and even food, in addition to trade goods. New foods included sugar and flour; alcohol and tobacco were also valued. Many traditional customs changed or disappeared during the trade period.

The people were devastated by smallpox in the early 1780s. Survivors succumbed to alcohol and were often attacked by enemies, including the Blackfeet Confederacy. Furthermore, the Crees' strong trade position led to overtrapping as well as the depletion of the moose and caribou herds by the early nineteenth century. Although the effects were partially offset by the Indians' growing dependence on items of non-Native manufacture, these trends combined to shrink the Indians' land base. Also about that time, western Crees, now using an iron chisel and moving on dogsleds, began taking more of an interest in fishing.

When the Hudson's Bay Company and the North West Company merged in 1821, many Crees began to abandon their traditional nomadic lives in favor of settlement at or near trade posts. Eventually, all-Indian communities arose in these areas. There was a second devastating smallpox epidemic in 1838. The people never fully recovered from this event. Severe tuberculosis and influenza epidemics struck in the early twentieth century as well.

Heavy missionary activity began in the mid-nineteenth century. Most Indians were at least nominally Christian by the midtwentieth century, although many western groups retained a core of traditional beliefs and practices. In the midnineteenth century, northern and eastern groups adopted a missionary-devised syllabary that soon gained wide acceptance. Parallel to this development was the elimination of practically all traditional religion in favor of the Churches of Rome and England.

The treaty and reserve period began in the 1870s. People began slowly to settle into all-Native log cabin communities, and the election of chiefs was made mandatory in the 1920s. Although their land and resources were being gradually but steadily whittled away, Crees were able to use their land in at least a semitraditional way well into the twentieth century.

After World War II, however, many Swampy Crees, their land essentially trapped out, began working in local cities and towns such as Moosonee and Churchill. Many Woodland Crees altered their lives fundamentally for the first time, attending school, using non-Native medicine, accepting government financial assistance, and becoming connected to the outside world via road and air links. The advent of relatively extensive roads and rail lines in the 1950s and 1960s, as well as the expansion of the forestry industry, greatly increased pollution. At the same time there was a dramatic reduction in game animals. In 1975, the Eastern Crees and Inuits ceded over 640,000 square kilometers of land to the James Bay Hydroelectric Project, in exchange for promises of hundreds of millions of dollars and various other provisions.

In recent years, Crees have attained greater control over local services and resources and the ability to maintain legal pressure on non-Native governments. The Cree school system in Quebec is under Native control. Perhaps half of all Crees speak their Native language. Yet the people face several crises, including the destruction of natural resources, the need for appropriate economic development, and the need to forge a viable relationship with provincial and national governments. Crees still face severe morale problems stemming from over a century of chronic disease, ill treatment at the hands of non-Natives, and a diminished capability to pursue their traditional way of life. Clear- and overcutting of forests have also negatively affected Cree hunting and trapping lands.

The Lubicon band of Treaty 8 area never received the reserve promised them in 1939. The region around Lubicon Lake, in northern Alberta, is rich in oil. In the 1970s, the band unsuccessfully fought to prevent road construction into the drilling site. By the early 1980s there were hundreds of oil wells in and near the community, creating dangerous levels of pollution.

The band is pressing for compensation for "irreparable damage to their way of life." Once a self-sustaining hunting community, its people now depend on welfare to survive. However, two subgroups have settled with the government. The newly created Woodland Cree band (unrecognized by treaty chiefs) received a reserve of 142 square kilometers and a financial settlement of almost $50 million. The Loon Lake people are negotiating for a $30 million settlement.

See also Buffalo; Canada, Indian Policies of; Canoes; Coon Come, Matthew; Cree-Naskapi Act; James Bay and Northern Quebec Agreement; Métis Nation Accord; Husdon's Bay Company; Trade.

Dogrib

"Dogrib," from their self-designation *Thlingchadinne* ("Dog Flank People"), signifies their legendary descent from a dog. The people also call themselves *Done*, "Men" or "People." They are culturally related to the Slaveys. In the nineteenth and twentieth centuries, Dogribs lived between Great Slave and Great Bear Lakes, Northwest Territories, an area that included both forest and tundra. There were perhaps 1,250 Dogribs in the late seventeenth century. Dogrib is a Northeastern Athapaskan language.

People acquired guardian spirits in dreams. They also made offerings to spirits that inhabited bodies of water. Shamans caused and cured disease and foretold the future.

There were traditionally four autonomous bands, or divisions (Lintchanres, Takfwelottines, Tsantieottines, and Tseottines). Band leadership was informal; a chief hunter had helpful spiritual power but little authority. Bands were composed of local hunting groups. Membership in all groups was fluid. When a young man killed his first game, his peers would strip him and wish him continued good luck. Only indirect address was considered polite. The people enjoyed games and dancing, the latter often accompanied by group male singing.

People's names often changed at the birth of their children. Brothers and sisters remained reserved with each other, as did a man with his brother-in-law and father-in-law. Men might have more than one wife, but they were required to serve their new in-laws for a period of time after the marriage. There may have been a practice of wrestling for wives as well as some female infanticide.

The elderly or ill were often abandoned. Streamers attached to burial scaffolds were meant to placate the spirits of the dead. Mourners destroyed most of their own property, and the women slashed their bodies. A memorial feast was held a year following the death.

Dogribs lived in conical teepees covered with as many as forty caribou skins sewn together with sinew or *babiche*. The sides were covered with snow in the winter. There were also some rectangular pole-and-brush winter huts. In the coldest weather, people often slept outside in skin bags to avoid the interior drafts.

Men hunted mainly caribou, which they snared in pounds and speared in lakes, in the forests, and on short trips onto the tundra. They also hunted musk ox, moose, hare and other small game, fowl,

A Dogrib man carries home meat after a successful caribou hunt in the late 1990s. (Lowell Georgia/Corbis)

and birds. There was some fishing; later, with decreasing game in the nineteenth century, fish gradually assumed a greater importance in the diet. Women gathered some berries and other plant foods as well as poplar sap. Food taboos included the weasel, wolf, skunk, and dog.

The people exported Native copper to the Slaveys and Yellowknifes, among other groups. They also traded in caribou skins, flint, chert, and pyrites as well as Inuit bone and ivory knives. They exported moose and fish products. Women decorated a number of items, such as moccasins, shirts, and bags, with woven quillwork or moose hair. Musical instruments included drums and caribou hoof rattles. Most transportation was overland using sleds and snowshoes. Birchbark canoes were caulked with spruce gum. Typical clothing included a tailored skin shirt, breechclout, leggings, and moc-

casins. Winter items included moose hide blankets, fur robes, hats, and mittens.

The people may have come to their historic location from the south and east. They first encountered non-Natives in either 1744 or 1771. The first trade posts were built in the 1790s.

The fur trade and provisioning were the dominant economic activities throughout the nineteenth century, during which time the people gradually began settling around trade posts. Fort Rae (1852) marked the first permanent local post and the beginning of extensive contact for most Dogribs with non-Natives. Fur trading became much more important at that time, especially after 1900 and the end of the Hudson's Bay Company monopoly. In addition to the usual fur-bearing animals, musk ox robes were also in demand.

The people suffered severe epidemics from 1859 onward. Most Dogribs had been baptized Catholic by 1870. The first treaty with Canada was signed in 1900. In 1920, the Dogribs stopped accepting government payments as a protest against hunting and fishing restrictions. This issue was resolved when they accepted a special designation, but the signed agreement was later lost.

As part of a 1921 treaty, the leader Monphwi became a "government chief," and band leaders formed an official council. There was a brief local gold rush, at Great Bear Lake, in 1930. The people were largely monolingual and semitraditional through the 1940s.

Band membership is still recognized and considered important. Although the language is still in use, there is a high degree of acculturation among the people. Modern housing, non-Native education, welfare eligibility, and medical services date from the 1960s. Their lands are being rapidly developed, mainly by mineral extraction industries, without Dogrib input. This had led to a decision to negotiate a land claim settlement with the Canadian government in an effort to gain some control over development.

See also Athapaskan Languages; Athapaskan People; Canada, Indian Policies of; Fur Trade; Hudson's Bay Company.

Gwich'in

"Gwich'in" means "People." The Gwich'ins were a group of tribes or bands who called themselves by various names, each having the suffix "-*kutchin*."

The name of one band—*Tukkuth,* or "People of the Slanting Eyes"—was translated by the French to *Loucheux,* a name now commonly used to designate the Gwich'in people. Their self-designation is *Dindjie,* "Person." They were culturally related to the Hans, Tutchones, and Tananas and were culturally influenced by the Inuits as well as the Tlingits.

Gwich'in territory is the Peel River Basin to its junction with the Mackenzie River as well as the Yukon River drainage (Alaska and Yukon). The Gwich'in population was between 3,000 and 5,000 in the eighteenth century. Gwich'ins spoke dialects of Kutchin, a Northern Athapaskan language.

Shamans acquired spiritual power through fasting and dreaming. They could foretell the future, cure illness, and control the weather. They were quite powerful in the west but less so in the east. In general, most people seldom came in "official" contact with the shamans.

Spirits inhabiting nature were mollified with offerings of beads. Hunters prayed to moon-related deities, offering pieces of caribou fat thrown into the fire. Ceremonial feasts, including singing and dancing, were held on various occasions. The main ceremonies revolved around life cycle events, lunar eclipses, and memorial potlatches. Bear and caribou were considered to be especially deserving of respect, in part owing to a supposed physical connection (shared hearts) between people and caribou.

Tribal chiefs were chosen for their leadership qualities or wealth. In some cases the positions were hereditary, but leaders had no real power. Local groups (two or so extended families) lived in a defined area and used its resources.

Animal-associated matrilineal clans declined in importance from west to east. The clans had marriage and ceremonial functions, playing significant roles in feasts and games. There were three social classes that may have been ranked: the "dark people" (Crow), "fair people" (Wolf), and "halfway people" (no crest). There were also some slaves, although they probably were not purchased.

Women carried babies in their coats or in birch-bark containers. They also performed most of the hard work (except for cooking, which men did) and ate only after the men had finished. Women generally selected husbands for their daughters. Female infants, as well as the elderly, were sometimes killed. From shortly before puberty until marriage, young men moved away from their parents to live in a lodge with other such young men. This was a period of self-denial and skill sharpening.

Young women were segregated during their menstrual periods. At that time they observed many taboos, such as not looking at others, designed to prevent others from being "contaminated" by their "condition." The dead were cremated. Their ashes were hung in bags from poles, or, if the person were particularly influential, the body was placed in a coffin in a tree until it decayed and then it was burned. Relatives destroyed their own property and cut their bodies.

Hospitality was a key value. The nuclear family was the basic unit, but grandparents might sleep in a nearby lodge and spend a great deal of time with the family. Rich men of certain tribes gave potlatches but usually only at funerals. Everyone enjoyed singing, dancing, games, and contests. Games included stick and hand games, ball games, and athletic contests. Witches were greatly feared.

Dome-shaped, caribou skin tents were stretched over curved spruce poles painted red. These portable lodges were about twelve to fourteen feet long and six to eight feet high. There was a smoke hole at the top, fir boughs for flooring, and bough and snow insulation. Some groups covered the lodges with birchbark instead of caribou skin. Some groups built semisubterranean dwellings of moss blocks covering a wood frame, with gabled roofs. When traveling, men sometimes built dugout snow houses glazed with fire.

Fishing took place mainly in the summer. Men hunted mainly caribou but also moose, hare, beaver, muskrat, and other game. Dogs often assisted in the hunt. People also ate waterfowl and plant foods, such as berries, rhubarb, and roots.

In addition to the many nonfood items derived from the caribou, important material items included wooden and birchbark trays, woven spruce and tamarack root baskets and cooking vessels, and other containers made of bentwood and birchbark. There were any number of tools with which to work hides, bone, and wood. Blades were mostly of stone and bone. Musical instruments included wooden gongs, drums, and willow whistles.

Sleds were made with high-framed runners, which might be covered with bone or frozen sod coated with water or blood. Inuit-style birchbark canoes had flat bottoms and nearly straight sides. The people also used moose skin canoes, toboggans, and particularly well-made long, narrow snowshoes with *babiche* netting.

Most clothing came from white caribou skin as well as furs. Shirts were pointed both front and rear.

Wide (Inuit-style) leggings attached to moccasins were beaded or embroidered with porcupine quill designs along the sides. Winter gear included long mittens, headbands, fur hats, and winter hoods. Most clothing was fringed and/or decorated with seeds or dentalium shell beads and/or painted and embroidered with porcupine quills.

Both sexes, but especially men, wore quill and dentalium shell personal ornamentation. Men also skewered their noses; women simply wore nose decorations. People took particular care of their hair. Men applied a large amount of grease to their hair and wore it in a ball at the neck, covered with bird down and feathers. They also painted their faces red and black. Women tattooed lines on their chins.

Gwich'in people encountered the Mackenzie expedition in 1789. The North West Company founded Fort Good Hope in 1806; other trading posts followed in 1839 (Fort MacPherson) and 1847 (Fort Yukon). Fur trapping gained in importance among the people during the nineteenth century. Catholic and Protestant (Church of England) missions worked in Gwich'in territory from the mid-nineteenth century on. Missionaries introduced a system of reading and writing (called Tukudh) in the 1870s.

Major epidemics stalked the people during the 1860s and 1870s, and again in 1897 and into the twentieth century. Many Gwich'ins left their immediate region to take advantage of the local whaling boom at the end of the nineteenth century. The Klondike gold rush (1896) brought an influx of non-Natives into the region, many of whom abused the Indians and stole their land. Religious residential schools existed from 1905.

Some groups live in small wood-frame houses. Although some have access to modern inventions such as snowmobiles, televisions, and satellite dishes, more than most other Indians the Gwich'ins have been able to retain a semiaboriginal lifestyle and culture, including religious beliefs, to a considerable degree (although less so in Fort Yukon). Most are fluent in English, although there are efforts to retain the Native language. The people are fighting to maintain the health and existence of the Porcupine caribou herd, which is threatened by development-related resource destruction.

See also Athapaskan Languages; Athapaskan People; Canada, Indian Policies of; North West Company.

Han

See Ingalik; Gwich'in.

Hare

"Hare" comes from the people's reliance on the Arctic or snowshoe hare. Their self-designation was *Kawchottine*, "People of the Great Hares," or *Kasogotine*, "Big Willow People." They were culturally similar to the Kutchins and Dogribs. This description of "aboriginal" culture includes some postcontact influences.

Hare Indians lived and continue to live west (to just past the Mackenzie River) and northwest of Great Bear Lake, in the present-day Northwest Territories. They ranged in parts of Alberta, the Yukon, and Alaska. This territory includes tundra, taiga, mountains, and intermediary areas. There were probably no more than 800 Hares in the early eighteenth century. Hare is a Northern Athapaskan language.

Guardian spirits formed the basis of Hare religious belief. Spirit helpers were not formally sought out but appeared in dreams. Shamans were able to attract particularly powerful guardians through dreams and visions. Cures were effected by using medicinal plants, singing, and sucking. Shamans sometimes hung by ropes from trees or tent poles when communicating with the spirits. Religious feasts included a memorial to the dead a year after death and on the occasion of a new moon.

There were perhaps five to seven small, autonomous, nomadic bands of fluid size and composition. The bands had defined hunting territories but only informal leaders, with little authority other than their people's respect for their hunting and/or curing abilities.

Sharing and generosity were highly valued. The bands gathered together several times a year for ceremonies, socializing, and hunting and fishing during migration and spawning seasons. Girls entering puberty were isolated in special huts and required to observe food and behavior taboos. Certain of these taboos, such as those regarding fish and animals, were continued during every monthly period. A feast would be held for young men who killed their first big game.

Intermarriage was common with several peoples, such as the Bearlake Mountain (Kaska and other tribes) and Kutchin Indians. Marriage occurred in the early teens and was generally arranged, although divorce was readily available. There was some period of bride service after marriage.

The elderly as well as some female babies were killed or left to die. Corpses were wrapped in blankets or moose skin and placed in aboveground enclosures. Relatives cut their hair and disposed of their own property. Ghosts were feared and provided with offerings to keep them at bay. Souls were said to be reborn at a later date.

In the winter, people lived in rectangular or A-frame pole-frame houses with gabled roofs, covered with spruce boughs, brush, and snow. Caribou hide teepees date from the nineteenth century. Summer lean-tos were common as well.

Caribou and musk ox were staples, although small animals (especially hare) and fish (such as trout and whitefish) contributed the bulk of the diet. Surpluses might be frozen or smoke dried. There was a severe lack of food every seven years or so when hares became scarce. Women gathered a few plant foods, such as berries and material predigested by caribou and other animals. Mosses and lichens were used to make beverages and medicines. Wolves and dogs were not eaten.

Trade partners probably included fellow Athapaskans such as the Yellowknife, Dogrib, Beaver, and Slavey Indians. Items exchanged included animal skins, copper, and various minerals. There may have been some trade in Inuit knives. Women decorated a number of items, such as moccasins, shirts, belts, and bags, with fringe and woven quillwork or moose hair. Musical instruments included drums and caribou hoof rattles. Most travel was overland. Snowshoes were used in the winter. Women pulled wooden toboggans before dogs took over in the twentieth century. Men also made spruce, birchbark, and occasionally moose hide canoes.

Most clothing came from hare pelts, supplemented by caribou and moose hides. The standard summer wardrobe was shirt, leggings, moccasins, and possibly a breechclout. In the winter, the people wore robes, mittens, and hats and added hoods to their shirts. The people wore caribou or hare hairbands. There was very little personal ornamentation except for facial tattooing and painting.

Shortly after the people encountered Alexander Mackenzie in 1789, the North West Company built Fort Good Hope (1806) in the area. Rapid involvement in the fur trade brought dependence on items of non-Native manufacture. Non-Native traders created trade chiefs among the people, so that their political organization eventually became more hierarchical.

The people were decimated by epidemics throughout the nineteenth century. A local Catholic church was built around 1866. Gradually, nomadic band life was mitigated in favor of a growing concentration around the trade posts. As the government created "bands" for administrative purposes and assigned subsistence areas for such groups, ethnic and group identity became stronger. The people were largely acculturated, as Hare Indians, by 1900.

Treaties signed with the Canadian government in the early twentieth century provided for payments and services in exchange for land title, although the Indians retained the right to use land for subsistence activities. Children began attending Catholic boarding school in 1926. Tuberculosis was rampant between the 1930s and the 1960s, and the people suffered periodic outbreaks of other diseases as well.

During the 1920s, many people built log homes and left traditional manufacture further and further behind. The fur trade continued to flourish until World War II. People increasingly worked at seasonal wage labor after the war, mainly in the oil and construction industries. The more traditional Colville Lake community dates from around 1960.

See also Athapaskan Languages; Athapaskan People; Canada, Indian Policies of; Fur Trade; North West Company.

Ingalik

"Ingalik" comes from the Russian for an Inuit word for "Indian." The name has been loosely used to include such culturally related—but separate—tribes as Koyukons, Tananas, and Hans. Their self-designation is *Deg Hit'an,* "People from Here." They were heavily influenced by their Yup'ik neighbors.

The Ingalik shared the eastern parts of their traditional territory—the banks of the Anvik, Innoko, Kuskokwim, Holitna, and lower Yukon Rivers—with the Kuskowagamiut Inuits. The land consists of river valleys as well as forest and tundra. The Holikachuks, a related though distinct people, lived to their north. There were between 1,000 and 1,500 Ingaliks in the nineteenth century. Ingaliks speak a Northern Athapaskan language. However, by the later twentieth century most Kuskokwim Ingaliks spoke the language of their Kuskowagamiut Inuit relatives.

Everything, animate or inanimate, was thought to have spirits. The Ingalik universe consisted of four levels, one higher and two lower than earth. Spirits of the dead might travel to any of the levels, depending on the method of death. A creator, spirits associated with nature, and various spiritual and superhuman beings, as well as people, inhabited the four worlds.

Most ceremonies were designed to maintain equilibrium with the spirit world. They included the two- to three-week Animals ceremony, the Bladder ceremony, the Doll ceremony, and four potlatch-type events with other villages. The single-village Bladder and Doll ceremonies involved paying respects to animal spirits and learning the future. Of the potlatch ceremonies, the Midwinter Death potlatch was the most solemn. Accompanying this ceremony was the so-called Hot Dance, a night of revelry.

The feast of the animals, involving songs, dances, costumes, and masks, was most important. Major roles were inherited. It involved a ritual enactment of hunting and fishing, with a clown providing comic relief. Other, more minor, ceremonies involved sharing food and occurred at life cycle events and on occasions such as eclipses.

Songs, or spells—which could be purchased from older people—helped keep the human, animal, and spiritual worlds in harmony. Songs were also associated with amulets, which could be bought, inherited, or made. Male and female shamans were said to have more powerful souls than other people. They acquired their powers through animal dream visions. Shamans' powerful songs, or spells, could be used for good or evil.

Each of four geographical groups contained at least one village that included a defined territory, and a chief society was divided into ranked status groups or social classes known as wealthy, common people, and idlers. People in the first group were expected to be generous with their surpluses and held potlatches as a redistributive method. The idlers were considered virtually unmarriageable; however, the classes tended to be fluid and were noninherited. Wealth consisted mostly of fish but also of items such as furs, meat, and any particularly well wrought item, such as a carved bowl, a canoe, or a drum.

Ingaliks often intermarried with, and borrowed culturally from, the nearby Inuits. Marriage depended in part on the ability of the man to per-

form bride service. With a first wife's permission, a wealthy man might have two wives. Both parents observed food and behavioral restrictions for at least three weeks following a birth. Young women endured segregation for a year at the onset of adolescence, during which time they mastered all the traditionally female tasks. The Ingaliks were a relatively peaceful people.

Punishments for inappropriate social behavior, such as theft, included banishment or death. This was a group decision, on the part of the men and older women, whereas murder required individual blood revenge. Corpses were placed in wooden coffins and buried in the ground or in vaults. Cremation was practiced on rare occasions. The dead's personal property was disposed of. Following funerals, the people observed a twenty-day mourning period and often held memorial potlatches.

Ingaliks maintained summer and winter villages, as well as canoe or spring camps. The winter dwelling was dome shaped and covered with earth and grass. Partially underground, it housed from one to three nuclear families. Ten to twelve such houses made up a winter village. Men used a larger, rectangular, semisubterranean communal house for sleeping, eating, working, sweating, and conducting ceremonies. This *kashim* was adapted from their Yup'ik neighbors.

Canoe camps, containing cone-shaped spruce pole and bough shelters, were built while people went in search of fresh fish. Summer houses were built of spruce plank, spruce bark, or cottonwood logs. There were also gabled-roof smoke houses and fish-drying racks. Temporary brush houses were located away from the village.

Among most groups, fish were the most important part of the diet. The people also ate a variety of large and small animals. Caribou, hunted by communal surround, were the most important. Others included moose, bear, sheep, and numerous fur-bearing animals, especially hare. Ingaliks also ate birds, mainly waterfowl, and their eggs, as well as berries and other plant foods. "Ice cream," a mixture of cottonwood pods, oil, snow, and berries, was eaten ceremonially and with some restrictions on who could receive it from whom.

Ingaliks moved around in birchbark canoes and on sleds and snowshoes. They did not trade extensively because they possessed rich natural resources. When they exchanged goods, it was mostly with Inuit groups, exporting wooden bowls, wolverine skins, and furs for seal products and caribou hides.

They might also trade furs, wolverine skins, spruce gum, and birchbark canoes for fish products and dentalia.

Most clothing was made from squirrel and other skins. Shirts and pants were common, as were parkas. Women's moccasins were attached to their pants; the men's were separate. Personal adornment included dentalium earrings and nose and neck decorations.

The people probably originated in Canada. They were driven west by the Crees to settle in present-day Alaska around 1200. They encountered Russian explorers in 1833. A trade post was constructed either around then or in 1867. There were Russian Orthodox missionaries in the region during that period. The major epidemics began in 1838–1839.

Steamboats began operating on the Yukon, expanding the fur trade, beginning in about 1867, the year the United States took possession of Alaska. Catholic and Anglican missionaries arrived in the 1880s and soon opened boarding schools. The caribou disappeared in the 1870s, leading to even more fishing and closer ties with the Kuskowagamiut Inuits. Non-Natives flooded into the region during the Yukon gold rush of the late 1890s. Most Ingaliks had accepted Christianity by the midtwentieth century.

For most people, life still revolves around the seasons. Frame or log houses have replaced traditional structures. Although many people struggle with a number of social problems related to high unemployment and cultural upheaval, and the people retain little aboriginal culture, traditional values remain palpable among the Ingaliks.

See also Alaska Native Claims Settlement Act; Athapaskan Languages; Athapaskan People; Fur Trade; Potlatch; Russians, in the Arctic/Northwest.

Innu

See Naskapi/Montagnais.

Kaska

"Kaska" is taken from the local name for McDame Creek. The Kaskas were culturally related to the Sekanis. They are also known, or included, with the

Tahltans and others, among the people called Nahani (Nahane) or Mackenzie Mountain People. Kaskas lived and continue to live in northern British Columbia and the southern Yukon Territory, in a rough triangle from the Pelly River south to Dease Lake and east to the Fort Nelson River. The Kaskas probably numbered around 500 before contact with non-Natives. Kaska, along with Tahltan and Tagish, is a Northern Athapaskan language.

Young men and women fasted to acquire animal guardian spirits in dreams and visions. Illness was said to be caused by breaking taboos. Shamans cured and foretold the future with recourse to their powerful spirit guides. Curing methods included blowing water onto the body or transferring the illness to another object.

There were at least four divisions. Each was composed of independent regional bands that had no fixed membership but generally consisted of local bands of extended families. Local band leadership was provided by the best hunters. Women occasionally served in important leadership positions.

Two matrilineal clans, Wolf and Raven, were borrowed from coastal tribes, as was the institution of the memorial potlatch. Also from coastal cultures, women acquired the custom of attacking symbolic enemies while their husbands were away at war.

Birth took place apart from the community out of fear of spiritual contamination. From late childhood on, boys began training for the vision quest, as well as building strength, with icy water plunges and other physically demanding activities. Women were secluded and observed various taboos during their menstrual periods. Girls married in their mid-teens, boys slightly later or as soon as they could provide for a family. Men served their prospective in-laws for a year before the wedding; thereafter, they avoided speaking to one another. Though frowned upon, divorce was common. The dead were wrapped in skins and left under a pile of brush; later the tribe adopted cremation and underground burial.

The people enjoyed many games and contests. Most life cycle events were marked by feasts. Names were inherited, as were some material items. Peer pressure usually sufficed as a means of social control; more serious offenses might be dealt with by exile, payments, or revenge.

Two or more families lived in conical or A-frame lodges covered with sod, brush, or skin. Most people used simple brush lean-tos in the summer. From coastal groups, Kaskas learned to weave blankets and ropes of sheep wool and goat hair. Babies were carried in skin bags padded with moss and rabbit fur. Men hunted with the bow and arrow as well as with spears, clubs, and especially *babiche* snares. Some groups may have used the atlatl. Men built dugouts and spruce-bark canoes; sewn caribou skin toboggans; two different types of snowshoes, depending on the quality of the snow; and moose skin boats.

Men hunted mainly caribou, but also buffalo, mountain goat, bighorn sheep, and numerous smaller types of game. They drove large game into pounds, snared them, or caught them in deadfalls or pitfalls. Beavers were clubbed to death. Salmon and other fish were caught in the summer. Women gathered berries and a few other wild plant foods, such as mushrooms, onions, lily bulbs, and rhubarb.

Most clothing was made of sewn caribou skins. Both sexes wore belted breechclouts, skin shirts (hooded in the winter), and leggings, belted and fastened to moccasins in the winter. Other winter gear included mittens and hide robes. Clothing was often decorated with porcupine quill embroidery, sewn fringe, and hard material obtained from moose stomach. People tattooed their bodies and wore ear and nose rings for personal ornamentation.

Wars were fought either to steal women or to avenge violent acts performed by strangers. War party leadership was selected on an ad hoc basis. Younger men carried the supplies while seasoned warriors did the fighting. There was some limited ceremonial cannibalism.

The people traded with non-Natives through Tlingit intermediaries until Fort Simpson, on the Laird and Mackenzie Rivers, was established in the early nineteenth century as the local trade center. Forts Laird and Nelson opened soon afterward. Fort Halkett, the first trade fort located directly in Kaska territory, was established soon after 1821. The people gradually came to rely on metal pots, nails, wire, and tools as well as items such as flour, soap, candles, guns and ammunition, and kerosene.

Kaska territory was invaded by gold seekers in the 1870s and again during the Klondike gold rush of 1897, seriously disrupting their traditional way of life. A Catholic mission was established in 1926. In the early 1940s the Alaskan Highway was built through their territory. Trapping remained important well into the contemporary period.

See also Athapaskan Languages; Athapaskan People; Canada, Indian Policies of.

Koyukon

See Ingalik.

Mackenzie Mountain People

See Kaska.

Nahani

See Kaska; Tahltan.

Naskapi/Montagnais

"Naskapi/Montagnais" is a compound name. "Naskapi" is a Montagnais word that may mean "rude or uncivilized people." "Montagnais" is French for "mountaineers." Their self-designation was *Nenenot*, "the People." Contemporary Naskapis and Montagnais refer to themselves as Innus.

The territory of these groups, including the Eastern Crees, ran from the Gulf of Saint Lawrence to James Bay, along the northeastern coast of Hudson Bay to Ungava Bay, and east to the Labrador Sea. The division was more or less that the Eastern Crees occupied the west of this region, the Naskapis the north, and the Montagnais the south and east. Much of this territory is extremely rugged and remote. Moose lived in the wooded Montagnais country, whereas Naskapi country, more open and grassy, was favored by caribou. There were perhaps 4,000 Montagnais and 1,500 Naskapis in the fifteenth century. Montagnais and Naskapi are dialects of Cree, an Algonquin language.

People may have believed in a great sky spirit to whom pipe smoke was occasionally offered. The people certainly believed in any number of spirits or supernatural beings. The key to Naskapi/Montagnais religion was to maintain a healthy and respectful relationship with the spirit world. This could be done both by observing the various taboos and by mastering certain techniques.

They especially attempted not to offend the spirits or souls of the animals on which they depended for food, mainly by being as respectful as possible toward them. Ceremonies included the Mokosjan, in which people ate caribou bone marrow.

Feasting was considered a religious practice, as was drumming.

Prayer was always offered before beginning any important activity. Boys fasted to obtain spirit helpers. Male and female shamans cured and kept away evil spirits. Shamans sometimes demonstrated their magic powers. In the shaking tent rite, shamans communicated with their spirits in specially built lodges to learn of good hunting areas. People feared cannibalistic monsters called Windigo (Montagnais) or Atsan (Naskapi).

Society consisted of perhaps twenty-five to thirty small, independent winter hunting bands related by marriage. There were several lodge groups (families of fifteen to twenty people) to a band. A named band, or division, probably consisted of two or three of these winter bands (up to three hundred people or so) who shared a general area. Several named bands came together in the summer on lake shores or river mouths for fishing, group hunting, and socializing. In all cases, band affiliation was fluid. Traditional chiefs or headmen had little or no formal authority, and all decisions were made by consensus.

Within the context of group cooperation for survival, individuals answered to no one about their personal behavior. Most people were generous, patient, and good-natured. Joking, or kidding, was effective in maintaining social mores, because real criticism was taken very seriously and avoided if possible. Montagnais had defined and patrilineally inherited family hunting grounds. Although groups were associated with specific subsistence areas, in lean times they readily gave permission to share.

Within the lodge groups there was no real dependence of one individual on another, since sexual relations were not limited to marriage, divorce was easy to obtain, and children were in many ways considered a group responsibility. These structures and relations encouraged a general egalitarianism.

Although gender roles were not especially rigid, men generally worked with wood and stone and women with leather. Men hunted big game while women set snares and gathered berries. Women were secluded during their menstrual periods. Parents generally arranged marriages. Men tended to marry in their early twenties, and women in their late teens. Some men had two wives, but a few had more. Men were obligated to perform bride service for a year or so. Joking, or familiar, relationships with cousins sometimes led to marriages.

Children were raised with tolerance and gentleness by both men and women, regardless of whether or not they were "legitimate." The old and sick were sometimes killed out of a sense of compassion. Dead Montagnais were wrapped in birchbark and buried in the ground. A memorial feast followed the funeral. Naskapis placed their dead on platforms or in trees.

The people tended to live in conical dwellings covered mainly in birchbark (Montagnais) and caribou skin (Naskapis). These held between fifteen and twenty people and featured central fires with top smoke holes. The ground was covered with branches and then mats or skins. The people also used temporary lean-tos, some made of snow. The Naskapis also built large A-frame or rectangular lodges to house several families and for winter dancing. This structure was covered with caribou skins and floored with boughs.

Men hunted primarily moose (Montagnais), caribou (Naskapis), and fowl as well as bear and other animals. The people used birchbark canoes to pursue big game after driving the animals into the water, and they wore snowshoes to run the game down. Small game, snared by women and sometimes men, included hares, porcupines, and beaver. The people also fished for salmon, eels, and trout. The Montagnais and Naskapi of Labrador also harpooned seals and fished through the ice, both activities probably borrowed from the Inuits. Some Montagnais had gardens and may have made maple syrup. Wild foods, such as berries, grapes, apples, and bulbs, played a small role in people's diet. Food was unsparingly shared when necessary.

The Montagnais traded meat and skins at Tadoussac and other places with Great Lakes people for tobacco, corn, and even some wild rice. Northern bands acquired cedar to use for canoe ribbing. Some groups also traded for birchbark.

The Naskapis wore clothing of caribou skin that had been dressed, smoked, and sewn. Some southern groups wore breechclouts; leggings (sometimes attached with a belt); bear, moose, or beaver robes; and moccasins as well as attachable sleeves for winter wear. Clothing also included fur pants, sewn hare blankets, fur or hide headbands, and hide caps.

In the north, hooded winter coats had fur inside. Moccasins in the north were sometimes made of sealskin. The Naskapis tattooed themselves by simply rubbing charcoal or soot into a cut on the skin, unlike many neighboring groups, who ran a charcoal-coated thread through the skin. Red ochre and greasepaint were applied to clothing in geometrical patterns with bone or antler pens or stamps. Skin objects, including clothing and bags, were painted with groups of parallel lines, triangles, and leaf shapes.

Humans—likely the direct ancestors of the Naskapi/Montagnais—have lived on the Labrador Peninsula for at least 5,000 years. Indians may have lived peacefully alongside the Inuits in ancient times. The Naskapi/Montagnais were among the first North American groups to come into contact with non-Natives, probably Basque and other European fishermen, in the early sixteenth century.

The Montagnais welcomed Champlain in 1603, whose French muskets proved to be of some help against the crippling Iroquois war parties. The people soon became heavily involved in the fur trade. They found it very competitive and profitable and soon began acquiring a large number of non-Native goods. Europeans created Indian trade chiefs, or captains. Missionaries arrived among the Montagnais in 1615. Tadoussac remained a key trade town from the midsixteenth century until Quebec was founded in 1608.

However, both moose and caribou were soon overhunted. As food supplies became less certain, some starvation ensued. Problems with alcohol abuse exacerbated the situation. The people were able to trade furs for supplies until non-Natives took over the best trapping grounds. Devastating disease epidemics reduced and weakened the Indian population, and further mass deaths resulted from relocating to the coast at the urging of missionaries.

The fur trade remained important during the eighteenth and early nineteenth centuries. The Naskapis became involved in the fur trade during that period. As they quickly increased their dependence on the trading posts and forsook the caribou hunt, they began to lose important elements of their traditional lives. By the midnineteenth century, traditional small local bands had generally become associated with a particular Hudson's Bay Company trading post. As forestry operations began replacing the fur trade, and non-Natives continued to move into the Saint Lawrence Valley, the people's hunting grounds became severely diminished. At that time the government created the first official Indian villages.

By the midtwentieth century, the trading post communities were being replaced by larger, permanent settlements. Also, well-defined trapping areas of at least several hundred square miles had

evolved. People generally remained around a settlement in the summer, retiring to their territory in small groups (ten to twenty people) to hunt and trap during the other seasons.

Since 1940, Canada has built over twenty hydroelectric dams and plants in Labrador. The government created several new reserves in the 1950s. In 1975, the Eastern Crees and Inuits ceded over 640,000 square kilometers of land to the James Bay Hydroelectric Project, in exchange for promises of hundreds of millions of dollars and various other provisions.

Among the Eastern Crees, many people retain elements of traditional religious belief either along with or instead of Christianity. Parts of these people's territory, such as north central Labrador, have only recently been explored by non-Natives. Most Innus, however, are Christian. In a marked departure from the pre-contact period, they have discarded former ideas about personal independence and duty to the group in favor of duty to individuals (women must obey men, children their parents, people their leaders). Few people remain self-sufficient.

Southeastern bands live in permanent framehouse villages. Hunting and trapping trips into the interior are far less important than they used to be, yet the cooperative ethic remains strong. Most people wear non-Native dress, and most children go to non-Native schools and are largely acculturated.

The Cree-Naskapi Act of Quebec (1984) replaced the Indian Act and provides for local self-government. The Labrador Innus (North West River) won an injunction in 1989, later overturned, preventing the military from continuing low-flying exercises over their region. The Naskapi-Montagnais Innu Association work for, among other issues, the sovereignty of the Davis Inlet Innus and the Sheshatshiu Montagnais. The Conseil Attikamek/Montagnais (twelve bands in Quebec) is also negotiating with the Canadian government for specific rights.

In 1974, the people formed the Grand Council of the Crees (of Quebec) to deal with the ramifications of the James Bay Hydroelectric Project, which had been allowed to proceed over Indian opposition. The people of Davis Inlet, led by the Mushuau Innu Band Council and the Mushuau Innu Renewal Committee (1993), have worked to address serious health and safety issues. They have constructed and renovated houses, instituted job training, and increased social services. Furthermore, in 1995 a multilateral agreement was signed calling for the return of the provincial court to Davis Inlet. This is part of the community's plan to assume greater responsibility in policing its own affairs.

> *See also* Canada, Indian Policies of; Cree-Naskapi Act; Department of Indian Affairs and Northern Development; Fur Trade; Hudson's Bay Company; James Bay and Northern Quebec Agreement; Trade.

Ojibwa, Northern
See Anishinabe.

Salteaux
See Anishinabe.

Sekani

"Sekani" means "People of the Rocks" (Rocky Mountains), and it comes from the people's self-designation. The Sekanis were culturally related to the Beavers and the Kaskas. Traditional Sekani territory is the Parsnip and Finlay River Basins, British Columbia. An eighteenth-century expansion to the south was largely checked by the Shuswaps. There were probably around 3,000 Sekanis in the eighteenth century and around 200 in the early nineteenth century, not counting 300 or so people in groups living west of the Arctic-Pacific divide. Sekanis spoke an Athapaskan language.

Young men fasted and dreamed alone in the wilderness to acquire supernatural guides, which were associated with animals or birds. These guides were of help only in emergencies. However, men might obtain other guides later in life, associated with either animals or natural forces, that might provide more regular assistance. These men became shamans, who were able to cause and cure disease, the latter for pay. Women could not become curers but they could, through dreaming, acquire the power to foretell the future. Disease was considered to be caused by soul loss, taboo breaking, or malice.

Several autonomous bands were led by a headman of little real authority. "Sekani" was the name of one such band. Regional bands in the nineteenth century were, from north to south, Tselonis, Sasuchans, Yutuwichans, and Tsekanis.

Other groups may have been Meadow Indians and Baucannes (*Says-Thau-Dennehs*). Bands owned hunting territories.

Names were derived ultimately from guardian spirits. Most children were nursed for about three years. At puberty, girls were secluded and forced to observe special food and behavioral taboos, all designed to keep them apart from men and animals. Boys fasted and dreamed for spirit guides.

Men might have more than one wife, especially if the wives were sisters. Newly married men served their in-laws for a year or so but lived apart from them during that time. The dead may anciently have been buried in the ground or covered in brush huts; they were later cremated. Chiefs or other people of authority were placed in hollow-log coffins deposited in trees or on platforms. Daily mourning (wailing) could last for years after a death. The Sekanis adopted matrilineal divisions and even quasi potlatches for a short time in the nineteenth century, in imitation of the Carriers and Gitksans.

Temporary conical lodges were covered with spruce bark or, later, moose hide. The people also built lean-tos covered with brush, bark, or skins as well as brush menstrual huts. Large game, such as moose, caribou, mountain sheep, and bear, constituted the bulk of the Sekani diet. Many other animals were also hunted, including porcupine, beaver, and marmot. There was some buffalo hunting, at least around 1800, in the eastern foothills and prairies. Some groups hunted in both the summer and the winter.

Trout and whitefish were the most important fish species. Fish were occasionally taken at night, from canoes, in the light of pine torches. Other foods included fowl and berries. Surplus food was cached in trees.

The Sekanis traded with Carrier groups. They exported mainly products of the hunt. Most people traveled overland, carrying their possessions on their backs. They used snowshoes in the winter and, occasionally, some spruce-bark canoes.

Men wore a sleeveless skin shirt, which they sometimes laced together between their legs, high skin leggings, and moccasins lined with fur. They added a breechclout after sustained contact with the Crees. Women wore similar clothing, although their leggings were shorter and their shirts were longer. Sometimes they wore a short apron as well. Sekanis decorated their clothing with porcupine quill and moose hair embroidery. Items of personal adornment included horn and bone bracelets. Hunters wore grizzly bear claws around their necks. Both sexes painted their bodies and wore marmot or hare robes, caps, and mittens in the winter.

The Sekanis may have originated east of the mountains and may have been driven west by the Crees. They may once have been united with the Beaver. They probably first encountered non-Natives in 1793. Around the same time, Shuswaps stopped the southward expansion of the people.

The North West Company established two posts in 1805, including Trout Lake (Fort McLeod). Trade forts continued to be established for the next several decades. The people began a decline shortly after the trade posts opened that was mainly linked with alcohol abuse and disease.

The Omineca gold rush occurred in 1861. By 1870, over 1,000 non-Native trappers and miners had occupied the territory of the Senakis. Environmental degradation and the decline of natural resources, including game animals, were the result. In consequence of these trends, mal- and undernourishment were added to the people's woes, and their population declined even more sharply. Still armed mainly with traditional weapons, the people at that time were forced to give up their winter grounds east of the Rocky Mountains to the Beavers and Crees, who had access to firearms. Catholic missionaries were active in the area from about 1870.

Two new bands or groups created around the turn of the century were the T'lotona (Sasuchans intermarried with Gitksans) and Davie's band (Otzanes), people organized around the son of a French Canadian man and a Sasuchan woman. A large dam created in the 1960s displaced many bands and separated several traditionally linked Sekani groups.

See also Athapaskan Languages; Athapaskan People; Canada, Indian Policies of; North West Company.

Slavey

"Slavey," or "Slave," is a translation of a name (*Awakanak*) given by the Cree enemies of these people. Their self-designation was *Dine'é*, "People." They were also known as *Etchareottine*, "People Dwelling in the Shelter." They are culturally related to the Dogribs and, like them, were not considered a "tribe" until relatively recently.

In the early eighteenth century, Slaveys lived between Lake Athabaska and Great Slave Lake. Their midnineteenth-century territory included the Mackenzie and Laird River Basins, from western Great Slave Lake south to around Hay Lake and north to Fort Norman, boreal forestland in present-day northeast British Columbia, northwest Alberta, and southwest Northwest Territories. The Slavey population was possibly 1,250 in the late seventeenth century. Slaveys spoke dialects of a Northeastern Athapaskan language.

People sought to acquire a guardian animal spirit in a dream, which would provide them with luck and assistance. Special songs usually accompanied powers provided by the guardian spirits. There were also malevolent spirits or supernatural beings, such as giants, who abducted young children. Quasi medicine bundles, or collections of items inspired by the dream vision, were kept in a pouch or a box. With few herbal remedies, medicine men were primary curers through removing physical manifestations of illness from a patient. Souls were said to live again after death.

People with little real authority led several autonomous bands, each with perhaps 200 people, that came together only in the summer, and even then only when conditions permitted. The bands were composed of local hunting groups of ten to fifteen people, within which food and other items were shared. Membership in all groups was fluid. An informal council of hunters settled disputes.

Within the local group, all people fared roughly equally well or poorly in terms of subsistence. Most personal disputes were settled by compensation or, in extreme cases, banishment. Local groups often resolved differences by playing a game, such as the traditional hand game, or through ritual competition by medicine men. The meeting of two local groups might be an occasion to feast and dance.

Individuals chose their own marriage partners, although parents also played a key role. A yearlong bride service for men followed a wedding. Men sometimes engaged in the custom of wrestling each other for their wives. Divorce was rare.

Women generally gave birth in a kneeling position attended only by women. There was some female infanticide. At her first menstrual period, a young woman left the camp and lived in a separate shelter for about ten days; she returned to the shelter every month. During this time she was subject to several food and behavioral taboos, such as avoiding eye contact with others and not traveling on an existing trail. Boys marked the passage into adulthood by making their first big game kill.

Unlike many regional groups, men did much of the hard work, such as obtaining firewood and preparing the lodge, in addition to hunting and fighting. Grandparents were important in the lives of children, often "joking" with them to teach proper behavior. The elderly and ill were rarely abandoned. Many people confessed wrongs on their deathbeds. The entire camp remained awake to witness a person's death. Death was greatly feared and was considered, with illness, to be the result of sorcery. Corpses were placed on scaffolds or covered with leaves and snow and placed with their property under a hut.

The winter dwelling was a low pole-frame structure covered with moss, with a pitched spruce bough roof and two doorways. There was an open smoke hole at the top. These structures might be twenty feet long and ten feet wide and were inhabited by extended families. In the summer, people built conical spruce, moose hide, bark, or brush lodges.

Men hunted mainly moose, but they also hunted woodland caribou, running them down and shooting them with bow and arrow in spring and snaring them with the help of dogs in the summer and winter. Beavers were caught in wooden traps in the fall and speared or clubbed in the winter. Men also hunted numerous small animals as well as birds. Fish were also very important. Women gathered berries, roots, and some other plant foods. Food to be stored was cached in the ground (during the winter) or hung in a bag from a pole.

Most animals were caught with *babiche* or sinew snares. Other hunting gear consisted of the bow and arrow, clubs, and spears. People fished with twisted willow bark or *babiche* nets and weirs as well as with hook and line. Other important items included stone adzes, beaver tooth knives, bone or antler projectile points, woven spruce root or bark cooking vessels, and moose hide, calfskin, or hare pelt diapers. Babies were carried in moose hide bags lined with moss.

Slaveys imported some Native copper from the Yellowknife and Dogrib people. They also imported some caribou skins, flint, chert, and pyrites as well as Inuit bone and ivory knives. They exported moose and fish products. The people used two types of snowshoes, beaver hide or birch toboggans, birch- or spruce-bark canoes, and some moose hide rafts. Much travel took place overland, with goods carried

on a person's back by means of a tumpline around the forehead.

Clothing was mainly of moose skins and consisted of pointed shirts and coats, leggings joined to moccasins, tassels (men), dresses (women), robes, caps, and mittens. In some areas, women's clothing was made mostly of woven hare skins. Clothing was heavily fringed, with moose hair and porcupine quill decoration. People also wore moose hide and rabbit skin blankets.

Faces were tattooed with parallel lines on the cheek. Women wore woven spruce root caps. Men plucked their facial hair and skewered their noses with wood or goose quills. Both sexes wore embroidered leather waist, wrist, and arm ornaments.

Despite their peaceful reputation, the Slaveys were known to massacre Kaskas and other mountain Indian enemies. Neighboring tribes were reluctant to attack them for fear of witchcraft reprisals. The people also fought the Crees. War garments included bear claw headdresses or feather caps. Weapons included willow twig shields. War leaders were chosen on an ad hoc basis.

The Crees, carrying firearms, drove the people north from the Lake Athabaska area in the late eighteenth century. They encountered Alexander Mackenzie in 1789. The first trade post in the area was built in 1796, with additional posts following in the next fifteen years. Anglican and Catholic missionaries arrived in 1858; Christianization was virtually complete by 1902.

Treaties signed with Canada in 1900, 1911, 1921, and 1922 generally called for land cessions in return for payments, services, and reserves. The high cost of trade items, as well as the relatively limited non-Native presence in the area, kept the people from dramatically changing many aspects of their culture until well into the twentieth century. Slaveys adopted non-Native material goods (such as metal items, firearms, flour, and tobacco) on a large scale after World War I, when many began trapping for income for the first time. At about the same time, groups began gathering for the summer at trade posts rather than at traditional lakeshore places, and gatherings were added for Christmas and Easter.

Permanent, significant governmental intrusion began only after World War II for some more remote groups, when the fur market collapsed. Oil and gas exploitation replaced furs as the region's most important commercial resource at about the same time. Traditional nomadic patterns have been replaced by a sedentary existence, especially since the 1960s. Since about the same time, the Slavey have become politically active to maintain control of their own affairs. The nature of local development, such as a controversial oil and gas pipeline, may be the biggest issue of all.

Contemporary life is marked in part by a number of problems, including substance abuse and general ill health, substandard housing, limited educational and economic opportunities, crime, and racism. Most of these problems can be attributed to the tension between the loss of traditional culture and replacement by spiritually and materially inadequate non-Native institutions, programs, and attitudes.

See also Athapaskan Languages; Athapaskan People; Canada, Indian Policies of.

Tahltan

"Tahltan" comes from the Tlingit for "basin-shaped hollow," referring to a place at the mouth of the Tahltan River. There are also other possible origins and meanings of the name. Their self-designation was *Titcakhanotene*, "People of Titcakhan." They are sometimes classified, with the Kaskas, as Nahani Indians and were culturally related to the Carriers.

The Tahltans lived, and continue to live, in northwest British Columbia, specifically the upper Stikine River drainage. They also shared the Stikine River Valley below Telegraph Creek with the Tlingits. The Tahltans hunted in the region in the winter, whereas the Tlingits fished and gathered there in the summer. There were perhaps 2,000 Tahltans in the late eighteenth century. Tahltan is a dialect of Tahltan-Kaska, an Athapaskan language.

The people recognized a sky god and a sun god. Adolescent boys fasted in wilderness vision quests to obtain guardian animal or bird spirits and songs. Shamans dreamed powerful guardian animal spirits.

Six autonomous bands were each associated with a particular hunting territory. Leadership was relatively weak, and band membership was fluid. Eventually, under Tlingit influence, the bands became clans, which were led by a chief who inherited his office through his mother's line. (In the mideighteenth century a seventh clan was created, but it remained more of a Tlingit than a Tahltan entity.) Family and possibly clan leaders might be

women. Clan leaders constituted an informal council. In about 1875, a single "tribal" leader emerged.

Two matrilineal divisions, Raven and Wolf, each contained three of the clans. Eventually, the three clans in each division came to share hunting territories. People were socially ranked as either nobles, commoners, or slaves. The latter category was permanent, and the children of slaves were born slaves.

Commoners, however, could enter the nobility by accumulating wealth and giving potlatches and/or through marriage. Titles, which confirmed social status, could be inherited but also had to be earned, mainly by potlatching. Three kinds of potlatches existed among the Tahltans: those given by parents to acknowledge their childrens' rank, those given by rivals to increase their status, and memorial potlatches.

Men toughened themselves with icy water plunges and by self-flagellation with willow switches. Girls reaching adolescence remained secluded for up to two years, receiving intensive training in the female tasks during that time and enduring a number of food and behavior taboos, such as keeping their faces covered. Young men served a prospective wife's family for a period of time before the wedding.

Widowers often married a sister of their late wife. Women were supported—and often married—by their nephews when their husbands died. The dead were cremated, after which the bones were placed on a post or in a small box raised off the ground. Death chants were sung for the dying and the dead. When a prominent person died, one of his slaves might be killed or, alternatively, freed.

Tahltans lived in pole-frame lean-tos with bark roofs and earth-and-bough packing. Those who could covered the poles with moose hide. At semipermanent fishing villages, the people built barkroofed huts with straight sapling walls and gabled roofs. In the main village, clans built structures up to 100 or more feet long that housed the clan's main families and served as a ceremonial hall. There were also special living and clubhouses for young, unmarried men.

Tahltans ate mainly game, including caribou, moose, bear, buffalo, and a range of smaller animals, such as marmot and beaver. Dogs assisted in hunting. Fish, especially salmon, were an important part of the diet. Women gathered roots, berries, and other plant foods.

Tahltans had long-standing trade and other personal contacts with the Tlingit, Kaska, and Sekani groups. They imported eulachon (smelt) and salmon oil, dentalium and abalone shells and ornaments, stone axes, woven blankets, and slaves (who originated among the Haidas). Exports included moose and caribou products (such as cured hides and *babiche*) and furs.

The people made a few relatively poor-quality spruce-bark canoes and temporary rafts. During overland travel, which they preferred to water travel, they might use snowshoes and carry baskets with tumplines. Women pulled a rough toboggan.

Tanned skin and fur clothing included shirts and leggings, often with attached moccasins, for men and dresses (long shirts), leggings, and moccasins for women. Both sexes wore goatskin and woven rabbit fur robes as well as various personal adornments. Clothing and other objects were often decorated with quillwork in geometric designs.

Tahltans periodically fought the Inland Tlingits, Taku River Tlingits, and the Tsimshians (Ness River branch), mostly over trade and the use of subsistence areas. They took scalps and held women prisoners for ransom. There was also some ceremonial cannibalism. Allies included other Tlingit groups, the Dease River Kaskas, and the Bear Lake Sekanis.

Tahltan history is in part a process of continuous adaptation of their Native Athapaskan traditions to those of Pacific Coast cultures. Tahltans probably moved into their known territory in the seventeenth century. The rich natural resources of the region encouraged population growth, larger and more permanent habitations, the acquisition of more material goods, increased social stratification, and a more complex culture in general.

Tlingit-Tahltan contact intensified after non-Natives established a presence along the coast in the early nineteenth century. At that time, trade and the production of furs became increasingly important. As wealth grew, stratification became more pronounced. At the same time, with so many people dying, opportunities were rife for social mobility.

Major epidemics began in the early nineteenth century when coastal people brought germs into the interior. Up to 75 percent or more of Tahltans died from epidemics during the nineteenth century. Sustained contact with non-Natives came when gold was discovered below Glenora in 1861 and especially after the 1874 gold strike at Cassiar. At that point, the Tahltans no longer controlled the Stikine River territory. In the late nineteenth century, survivors of various bands coalesced into one unit,

or tribe, with a head chief. They built the Tahltan village, a log house community.

The trend toward the loss of land and control over their own destinies became even stronger following the Klondike gold rush of 1898, as thousands of non-Native prospectors, missionaries, tourists, and entrepreneurs rushed into the region. Although many people were drawn into the wage economy as guides, wranglers, and government employees, most Indians remained engaged in traditional subsistence activities through the midtwentieth century. Major employment opportunities during and after World War II included highway construction and asbestos mining.

See also Athapaskan Languages; Athapaskan People; Canada, Indian Policies of; Warfare, Intertribal.

Tanaina

"Tanaina," or "Dena'ina," means "the People." The Tanainas were also known as Knaiakhotana. Their designation as a single tribe is a non-Native convention, the people having consisted traditionally of various related tribes, or divisions, such as Kachemaks, Kenai-tyoneks, Upper Inlets, and Iliamna-susitnas. They were culturally related to local Northwest Coast tribes such as the Tlingits.

Before contact with non-Natives, the Tanainas lived around the drainage of Cook Inlet, Alaska. From perhaps 4,500 in the mideighteenth century, the Tanaina population dropped to around 3,000 in 1800. Tanaina, an Athapaskan language, includes two major divisions—Upper Inlet and Lower Inlet—as well as many subdialects.

Everything in nature was said to have a spirit. The people recognized three groups of beings in particular: mythological beings; supernatural beings, such as giants and tree people; and beings that interacted closely with people, such as loon, bear, and wolf spirits. There was also a fourth group of creatures, including Hairy Man and Big Fish. Ceremonies included memorial potlatches and first salmon rites.

Male and female shamans mediated between the human and spiritual worlds, using spiritual powers acquired in dreams to cure illness and to divine the future. To cure illness, shamans wore carved wooden masks and used dolls to locate and exorcise evil spirits. Shamanic power could be used for good or for evil. In addition to their spiritual power, many shamans enjoyed a great deal of political power, occasionally serving as the village leader ("rich man"), usually the wealthiest members of their clan lineage groups.

Tanainas traditionally organized into three distinct societies: Kenai, Susitna, and Interior. The three developed separately because of the difficulty of communicating across the hazardous Cook Inlet. The village was the main political unit. It was headed by one or more leaders ("rich men"). Leadership functioned mainly as a redistributive mechanism, wherein goods flowed to the rich man and were redistributed by him according to need. The leader was also responsible for the moral upkeep of his people.

The power of these leaders was noncoercive, and their "followers" were bound to them only out of respect. Leadership qualities, in addition to wealth, included generosity, bravery, and hunting ability. A man who aspired to this position needed help and material support from his relatives.

Relatively stable winter villages gave rise to social hierarchy and other complex organizations. A dual societal division was further broken into matrilineal clans, approximately five in one division and ten in the other. Clans owned most property and controlled marriage as well as most hunting and fishing areas. Social control was maintained primarily by peer pressure, although revenge, physical retribution, and payments played a role also.

"Rich men" gave potlatches as an important means of economic redistribution and of increasing or maintaining their prestige. They were provided crucial support by their relatives. Potlatch occasions included life cycle events as well as other opportunities to express generosity. Dentalium shells, certain furs, and, later, glass beads were the primary symbols of prestige. "Rich men" had several wives as well as slaves. The latter were generally well treated and not kept for more then several years. In general, women had a relatively high degree of prestige and honor and could become wealthy in their own right.

Men served their future in-laws for at least a year. Children were born in a separate house, and adoption was common. Puberty recognition was accorded to both sexes. Boys fasted, either in a room (Interior) or in the woods (Susitna), and ran in the morning. Girls were confined for the better part of a year, during which time they learned appropriate skills and proper behavior. They also endured vari-

ous behavioral taboos during this time, including the prohibition against looking directly at anyone else.

People made loud noises around the sick and dying to keep malevolent spirits at bay. Corpses were cremated, their ashes placed either in boxes on posts or buried and their possessions destroyed or given away. Members of another clan were responsible for making all the funeral arrangements. A mourning period of several weeks followed funerals. Memorial potlatches were held about a year after death.

A winter village consisted of from one to ten or more partially excavated houses with tunnel entries, and the population averaged between fifty and 200 people. These rectangular houses had log walls covered with grass and dirt. Spruce-bark or planked gabled roofs were also covered with dirt. There was a large main room with several side sleeping chambers. The total length ranged from ten to 100 feet.

The houses featured rooms for several families, including a main room with a fire and sleeping platforms for adolescent boys. Compartments for married couples and their young children as well as adolescent girls were located underneath the platforms. Other chambers were for sweating, menstrual isolation, and sleeping for the elderly. Villages were often concealed or camouflaged against enemy attack.

Summer houses were similarly designed, but lighter. The people also built temporary houses, such as birchbark or skin tents or log and sod structures, at fish and hunting camps. These houses held only nuclear or small extended families. House styles began to change in the nineteenth century with Russian influence.

There was a wide dietary divergence among groups. Some, such as those in the extreme south, depended mainly on marine life, whereas the northern interior people were mainly hunters and fishers. Most groups depended on fish, especially all five kinds of salmon. Other important species included eulachon (smelt), halibut, and catfish.

Important sea animals included seals, otter, and beluga whale. Land animals included caribou, bear, moose, beaver, and rabbit. Caribou herds were driven into lakes and speared or shot, or they were channeled with fences into snares and surrounds. The people also ate birds and fowl as well as various roots and berries. Coastal people gathered shellfish.

The Tanainas acquired kayaks and umiaks from the Alutiiqs, serving also as intermediaries between those people and interior groups. The Tanainas participated in regional trade networks stretching across Alaska. Informally and at trade fairs, they traded with other Tanaina groups as well as with groups farther away. Wealthy men with established trade partners were especially successful. Traditional exports included wolverine skins, porcupine quills, and moose products. Imports included copper, dentalium shell, and cedar arrow shafts.

Water transportation included birchbark canoes and moose skin boats as well as Inuit-style sealskin kayaks and umiaks. People traveled overland in the winter on foot (snowshoe) and on dogsleds, which date from the midnineteenth century.

Tailored clothing was made of tanned caribou or sheepskins. Both sexes wore a knee-length undergarment, a shirt, and boots. Fur coats and shirts were added in the winter. Rain gear included a whale membrane parka and waterproof salmon skin boots. In the winter, the long undergarment had knee-high bear or beluga whale–soled boots attached. Blankets were made of sewn rabbit skins. Skin shirts were worn in the summer.

Clothing was often dyed brown or red, embroidered with porcupine quills, and decorated with fur trim and shells. Decoration often reflected social rank. Tattooing and face painting were common, especially among the wealthy. Women wore bone labrets in their lower lips. Both sexes pierced their ears and septa for shell decorations.

Captain James Cook entered the area in 1778, followed by more British traders. Local Indian groups already possessed iron and other items of non-Native manufacture when Cook arrived. Although Indians welcomed the Europeans as traders, they strongly and, for some time, successfully opposed non-Native settlement.

Russians built the first trading posts in the late eighteenth century. Relations between the Russians and Native Americans were difficult, even though the two groups regularly intermarried. Russians often attacked the Native people and took them as hostages, ultimately turning many Indian and Inuit groups into forced labor. Russian control was generally brutal. As the violence subsided and more posts were built in the early to midnineteenth century, many Native people became active in the fur trade.

A severe smallpox epidemic in 1838 took thousands of Indian lives. Other non-Native diseases such as syphilis and tuberculosis also killed many Indians. The people had guns by the 1840s. Russian Orthodox missionaries arrived in force about 1845; the people were nominally converted within two generations, especially along the coast.

Although population decline and game shortages caused interior groups to consolidate their villages, the late nineteenth century was generally a time of increasing prosperity, owing mainly to the extension of credit and growing involvement in the fur trade. The peak years were between 1867 (when the United States purchased Alaska) and the fur market crash of 1897. As a consequence, traditional "rich men," or Indian trade leaders, became even wealthier and more powerful. One consequence of the U.S. purchase of Alaska was that the Tanainas lost legal rights as Russian citizens. U.S. citizenship was not granted until 1924.

The discovery of gold in the area around 1900 brought a flood of miners and other non-Natives. Other factors, such as the growth of commercial fishing and canning industries (with their attendant pollution and resource monopolization), improved transportation, and continuing population declines and game shortages, weakened social distinctions and contributed to the people's general decline.

These developments also hastened the transition from a subsistence to a wage economy. Canneries and commercial salmon fishing boomed by the midtwentieth century. Schools, at least through the eighth grade, have been available to most Tanainas since the 1960s.

Tanainas are generally acculturated, although many retain a strong pride in their heritage and traditions. The three traditional societies are no longer distinct. The clan system is still important in most areas. Most people are Russian Orthodox Chris-

tians, although some elements of traditional religion survive. The Kenai-tynecks used revenue from oil leases in part to modernize village facilities. Local concerns include bridge construction and road improvement. A Tanaina Athapaskan Indian cultural facility has been proposed, perhaps to be built in Iliamna.

See also Alaska Native Claims Settlement Act; Athapaskan Languages; Athapaskan People; Canada, Indian Policies of; Potlatch; Russians, in the Arctic/Northwest; Slavery; Trade.

Tanana
See Ingalik.

Tlingit, Inland
See Tlingit.

Tutchone
See Gwich'in.

Yellowknife
See Chipewyan.

Native Americans of the Arctic

Aleut

See Alutiiq; Unangan.

Alutiiq

"Alutiiq" means "a Pacific Eskimo person"; the plural form is "Alutiit." The Alutiit were a maritime people, also known as Pacific Eskimos, Pacific Yup'ik, South Alaska Inuit, Yuit (with the Yup'ik), or Aleut. However, "Aleut" (of Russian origin) is easily confused with the culturally and linguistically separate Native people of the Aleutian Islands.

The self-designation of the Alutiiq people is *Sugpiaq* ("real person"). The three traditional subgroups are the Chugachmiuts (Prince William Sound), Unegkurmiuts (lower Kenai Peninsula), and Qikertarmiuts or Koniagmiuts (Kodiak Island). There are many similarities to Unangan culture. The Alutiit lived and continue to live along coastal southern Alaska, between Prince William Sound and Bristol Bay. Kodiak Island was one of the most densely populated places north of Mexico. The aboriginal (mid- to late eighteenth-century) population was between 10,000 and 20,000 people. Alutiit spoke the Sugcestun, or Suk, dialect of the Pacific Gulf Yup'ik branch of Eskimo, an Eskaleut language.

The people recognized one or several chief deities, as well as numerous supernatural beings. Success in hunting required a positive relationship with the spirits of game animals. Human spirits were reincarnated through birth and naming.

Trances, as well as certain masks and dolls, allowed contact with the supernatural.

A large variety of dances, ceremonies, and rituals, including masked performances, songs, and feasts, began in the early winter. Specific ceremonies included a memorial feast, a ritual to increase the animal population, the Messenger's Feast (a potlatch-like affair that took place between two closely related villages), life cycle events, the selection of chiefs, and preparation for the whale hunt. Wise men (Kodiak Island) were in charge of most religious ceremonies, although a dance leader might direct ceremonies and instruct children in dances.

Male and female shamans forecast weather and other events, and they cured disease. Berdaches were often shamans as well. Women also acted as healers through bloodletting and herbal cures.

Despite the existence of fifty or more villages or local groups, there was no strong central government. Most important decisions were made by consensus agreement of a council. Village leaders were chosen on the basis of merit, although there was a hereditary component. They were expected to earn respect and retained their offices by giving gifts and advice. Some controlled more than one village. Their primary responsibilities were to lead in war and guide subsistence activities. From the nineteenth century on, chiefs (*toyuq*) and secondary chiefs (*sukashiq*) were appointed by a consensus of elders.

Descent was weakly matrilineal. Women generally had relatively high status, although they did not participate in formal governing structures such as councils. Society was divided into ranked classes:

noble, commoner, and slave. Slaves might be acquired through trade or war, especially among the Chugaches and the Koniags. High-stakes gambling was a favorite pastime.

Women were secluded in special huts during their menstrual periods and at the birth or death of a child. Seclusion during the initial menstrual period could extend for several months or more. Women's chins were tattooed when they reached puberty. Male transvestites were esteemed and performed the woman's role for life. Some girls were also raised as boys and performed male roles.

Marriage was formalized when gifts were accepted and the man went to live, temporarily, with his wife's family. A woman might have two husbands, although the second would have very low status. Men might also have multiple wives. Divorce and remarriage were possible. Babies' heads were flattened in the cradle, perhaps intentionally for aesthetic purposes. Children were generally raised gently, with no corporal punishment, but toughened with icy water plunges.

Corpses were wrapped in seal or sea lion skin and kept in a special death house. High-status people were mummified. Slaves were sometimes killed and buried with a person of high rank. Mourners blackened their faces, cut their hair, and removed themselves from society. Graveside ceremonies went on for a month or more. Pieces of the corpse of a great whale hunter were sometimes cut up and rubbed on arrow points or used as talismans on hunting boats.

Houses were semisubterranean, with planked walls and sod- and straw-covered roofs. A common main room also served as a kitchen and workshop. Side sleeping rooms, heated with hot rocks, were also used by both sexes for ritual and recreational sweats. Up to twenty people (several families) lived in each house. Winter villages were composed of up to ten or so houses. Some villages had large ceremonial halls (*kashim*). In fishing and other temporary camps, people lived in bark shelters or even under skin boats.

Salmon was a staple, although other fish, such as herring, halibut, cod, and eulachon (smelt), were also important. Sea mammals, such as whales, porpoises, sea lions, sea otters, and seals, were also key. Dead whales were not pulled ashore but were allowed to drift in the hope that they would come back to camp. The people also ate sea birds. There was some gathering of shellfish and seaweed, as well as greens, roots, and berries. Land mammals,

such as caribou, moose, squirrel, mountain goat, and hare, also played a part in the diet.

Woven spruce root baskets were decorated with grass and fern embroidery. Men carved and painted wooden dance masks. Two-hatch skin kayaks were the main vehicle for transportation, whaling, and sealing. They were made of sealskin stretched over branches. The people also used some dugout canoes, umiaks, and plank toboggans pulled by dogs. The Alutiit acquired dentalia and slaves from the Northwest Coast. They exported caribou, mountain goats, and marmot parts. Messenger Feasts/potlatches also involved trade.

In cold weather, the Alutiiq people wore long parkas made of squirrel or sea lion fur and bird skin, rain parkas made of sewn eagle skin or eagle intestine, and boots made of sea lion, salmon, or bearskin. Men's conical bentwood or woven spruce root hats, worn at sea, may reflect a Tlingit influence. Men also wore Unangan-style wooden visors.

Women wore labrets and nose pins. Men also wore ornaments, such as sea lion whiskers, in their ears and noses. Other types of ornaments included coral, shell, and bone. Men braided their long hair, whereas women wore it tied up on their heads.

The Alutiiq people had been living in their historic territory for at least 2,000 and perhaps as many as 7,000 years when the Dane Vitus Bering, working for Russia, arrived in 1741. Although he may not have actually encountered any people, contact became regular in the 1760s and 1770s—and generally resisted by the Alutiit. The first permanent Russian settlement was established in 1784, on Kodiak Island. By that time British and Spanish seamen had also visited the area.

In part by keeping their children as hostages, Russians soon forced the Natives to hunt sea otter pelts and do other work for them. Disease and general oppression soon cut the Alutiiq population dramatically. Many people were acculturated to the Russian religion and customs when the United States gained political control of Alaska in 1867.

At that time there began a renewed push for acculturation in another direction. Children were soon sent to mission and Bureau of Indian Affairs boarding schools, where they were forced on pain of punishment to accommodate the U.S. model. Economically, canneries and commercial fishing dominated the region from the late nineteenth century on.

Several Alutiiq villages suffered a devastating earthquake and tsunami in 1964. The Alaska Native Claims Settlement Act (ANCSA, 1971) had a pro-

found influence on the people. The act established twelve formal culture areas, of which three fell in Alutiiq territory. In 1989 the *Exxon Valdez* ran aground and spilled nearly 11 million gallons of crude oil in Alutiiq territory, resulting in a tremendous loss of sea life, among other things.

Many villages remain accessible only by air or water. Most people are Russian Orthodox, many older people speak Russian (along with English and Alutiiq), and there are considerable other Russian influences. Most village social activities are church related.

Some Alutiit are more identified with the ANCSA corporate entities than with the original Alutiiq culture. Village concerns include protecting the local fisheries, road construction, and the construction of a boat harbor. Efforts to preserve the Native culture include the formation of the Kodiak Alutiiq Dancers, language classes, oral histories, and craft (woodworking and kayak-making) projects.

> *See also* Alaska Native Claims Settlement Act; Demographics, Historical; Russians, in the Arctic/Northwest; Salmon, Economic and Spiritual Significance of; Women in Native Woodlands Societies.

Eskimo, Bering Strait

See Inupiat.

Eskimo, Kotzebue Sound

See Inupiat.

Eskimo, Nunivak

See Yup'ik.

Eskimo, Pacific

See Alutiiq.

Eskimo, South Alaska

See Yup'ik.

Eskimo, Southwest Alaska

See Yup'ik.

Eskimo, Saint Lawrence Island

See Yup'ik.

Eskimo, West Alaska

See Yup'ik.

Iglulik

"Iglulik" is a name derived (with their main settlement, Igloolik) from the custom of living in snow houses, or igloos. (*See also* Inuit, Baffinland.) Traditional Iglulik territory is north of Hudson Bay, including northern Baffin Island, the Melville Peninsula, Southhampton Island, and part of Roes Welcome Sound. It lies within the central Arctic, or Kitikmeot. The Iglulik population in the early nineteenth century was roughly 500. Igluliks speak a dialect of Inuit-Inupiaq (Inuktitut), a member of the Eskaleut language family.

Religious belief and practice were based on the need to appease spirit entities found in nature. Hunting and specifically the land-sea dichotomy were the focus of most rituals and taboos, such as that prohibiting sewing caribou skin clothing in certain seasons. The people also recognized generative spirits, conceived of as female and identified with natural forces and cycles. A rich body of legends was related during the long, dark nights.

Male and female shamans (*angakok*) provided religious leadership by virtue of their connection with guardian spirits. They could also control the weather, improve conditions for hunting, cure disease, and divine the future. Illness was due to soul loss, the violation of taboos, and/or the anger of the dead. Curing methods included interrogation about taboo adherence, trancelike communication with spiritual helpers, and dramatic performance.

There was little real political organization; nuclear families came together in the fall to form local groups, or settlements, that in turn were grouped into three divisions—Iglulingmiuts, Aivilingmiuts, and Tununermiuts—associated with

geographical areas (-*miuts*). Local group leaders were usually older men, with little formal authority and no power. Leaders generally embodied Inuit values, such as generosity, and were also good hunters.

Descent was bilateral. People came together in larger group gatherings in late autumn; that was a time to sew and mend clothing and renew kinship ties. Spring was also a time for visiting and travel. People married simply by announcing their intentions, although infants were regularly betrothed. Prospective husbands often served their future in-laws for a period of time. Men might have more than one wife, but most had only one. Divorce was easy to obtain. The people also recognized many other types of formal and informal partnerships and relationships. Some of these included wife exchanges.

A woman gave birth in a special shelter and lived in another special shelter, in which she observed various taboos for some time after the birth. Because infant mortality was high, infanticide was rare, and usually practiced against females. Babies were generally named after a deceased relative. Children were highly valued and loved, especially males. They were generally given a high degree of freedom. After puberty, siblings of the opposite sex acted with reserve toward each other. This reached an extreme in the case of brothers- and sisters-in-law.

The sick or aged were sometimes abandoned, especially in times of scarcity, or the aged might commit suicide. Corpses lay in state for three days, after which they were wrapped in skins, taken out through the rear of the house, and buried in the snow. The tools of the deceased were left with him or her. No activities, including hunting, were permitted for six days following a death.

Feuds, with blood vendettas, were a regular feature of traditional life. Tensions were relieved in various ways: through games; through duels of drums and songs, in which the competing people tried to outdo each other in parody and song; "joking" relationships; and athletic contests. Outdoor games included ball, hide-and-seek, and contests. There were many indoor games as well. These activities also took place on regular social occasions, such as visits. Ostracism and even death were reserved for the most serious cases of socially inappropriate behavior.

The people lived in domed snow houses for part of the winter. They entered through an above-ground tunnel that trapped the warm air inside. Snow houses featured porches for storage and some-

times had more than one room. Ice or gut skin served as windows. Some groups lined the snow house with sealskins. Snow houses were often joined together at porches to form multifamily dwellings. People slept on raised packed snow platforms on caribou hide bedding. Some larger snow houses were built for social and ceremonial purposes. People generally lived in sealskin tents in the summer. In the spring and fall, some groups used stone houses reinforced with whalebone and sod and roofed with skins.

The Igluliks were nomadic hunters. The most important game animals were seals, whales, walrus, and narwhal. Men hunted seals at their breathing holes in the winter and from boats in the summer, as they did whales and walrus. In the summer, the people traveled inland to hunt caribou, musk ox, and birds and to fish, especially for salmon and trout. Other foods included some berries and birds and their eggs. Meat, which might not be very fresh, was cooked in soapstone pots over soapstone blubber lamps or eaten raw or frozen. In the summer, people burned oil-soaked bones for cooking fuel.

Men used bone knives to cut blocks for snow houses, and they caught fox and wolf in stone or ice traps. Many tools were made from caribou antlers as well as stone, bone, and driftwood. Blades were made of bone or copper. Fires were started with flint and pyrite or a wooden drill. The people carved soapstone cooking pots and seal oil lamps as well as wooden utensils, trays, dishes, spoons, and other objects.

Men hunted in one- or two-person sealskin kayaks. Occasionally, several might be lashed together to form a raft. Umiaks were larger, skin-covered open boats. Dogs pulled wooden sleds, the whalebone or wood runners of which were covered with ice. Dogs also carried small packs during seasonal travel.

Women sewed most clothing from caribou skins, although sealskins were commonly used on boots. Apparel included men's long, gut sealing coats and light swallowtail ceremonial coats. The people wore a double skin suit in the winter and only the inner layer in the summer. Most men's parkas had a long flap in the back; the woman's had two long, narrow flaps. Women's clothing featured large shoulders and hoods for accommodating infants as well as one-piece, attached leggings and boots. They wore high caribou skin and sealskin boots containing square pouches. Men wore small loon beak dancing caps with weasel skin tassels.

They sometimes shaved their foreheads. Both sexes wore tattoos and ivory or bone snow goggles.

The people encountered Scottish whalers early in the nineteenth century. Eventually, Scottish celebrations partly supplanted traditional ones. By the time American whalers arrived in the 1860s, the Igluliks had acquired whaleboats, guns, iron items, tea, and tobacco. Later in the century, the people became involved with fox trapping and musk ox hunting. They also intermarried with non-Natives and acquired high rates of alcoholism and venereal disease.

Regular contact with other Inuits, such as the Netsiliks, was established at local trading posts and missions. These arrived in the early twentieth century, as did a permanent presence of the Royal Canadian Mounted Police (RCMP). Improved medical care followed these inroads of non-Native influence.

The far north took on strategic importance during the Cold War, about the same time that vast mineral reserves became known and technologically possible to exploit. These developments encouraged population movements. Also, as non-Natives increased their influence, such aspects of traditional culture as shamanism and wife exchange began to disappear. In 1954, the federal Department of Northern Affairs and Natural Resources officially encouraged the Inuits to abandon nomadic life. It built housing developments, schools, and clinics. Local political decisions were made by a community council subject to non-Native approval and review.

The snowmobile, introduced in the early 1960s, increased the potential trapping and hunting area and diminished the need for meat (fewer dogs to feed). Such employment as the Inuits could obtain was generally unskilled and menial. With radical diet changes (including flour and sugar), the adoption of a sedentary life, and the appearance of drugs and alcohol, the people's health declined markedly.

The Baffin Regional Association was formed to press for political rights. In 1993, the Tungavik Federation of Nunavut (TFN), an outgrowth of the Inuit Tapirisat of Canada (ITC), signed an agreement with Canada providing for the establishment in 1999 of a new, mostly Inuit, territory on roughly 36,000 square kilometers of land, including Baffin Island.

The people never abandoned their land, which is still central to their identity. Traditional and modern coexist, sometimes uneasily, for many Inuits. Although people use television (there is even radio and television programming in Inuktitut), snowmobiles, and manufactured items, women also carry babies in the traditional hooded parkas, chew caribou skin to make it soft, and use the semilunar knives to cut seal meat. Full-time doctors are rare in the communities. Housing is often of poor quality. Most people are Christians. Culturally, although many stabilizing patterns of traditional culture have been destroyed, many remain. Many people live as members of extended families. Adoption is widely practiced. Decisions are often made by consensus. However, with access to the world at large, social problems, including substance abuse and suicide among the young, have increased. Fewer than half of the people finish high school.

Politically, community councils have gained considerably more autonomy over the past decade or two. There is also a significant Inuit presence in the Northwest Territories legislative assembly and some presence at the federal level. The disastrous effects of government-run schools have been mitigated to some degree by local control of education, including more culturally relevant curricula in schools. Many people still speak Inuktitut, which is also taught in most schools, especially in the earlier grades. Children attend school in their community through grade nine; the high school is in Frobisher Bay. Adult education is also available.

See also Assimilation; Canada, Indian Policies of; Nunavut Land Claims Agreement; Women in Native Woodlands Societies.

Inuit, Baffinland

"Baffinland Inuit" means "Baffinland People." The people call themselves *Nunatsiaqmiut*, "People of the Beautiful Land." The Baffin region today, including Baffin Island, and the eastern High Arctic Islands, is known as Qikiqtaaluk. The Baffinland Inuits live on mainly the coastal parts of southern and central Baffin Island and the eastern Northwest Territories. The land is rugged and includes mountains, plains, rolling hills, fjords, lakes, and rivers. The weather is also rugged and extreme, and the tides, especially in the east, are very high. There were approximately 27,000 Baffinland Inuits in the mideighteenth century, most of whom lived on Cumberland Sound. The Native language is Inuit-Inupiaq (Inuktitut), a member of the Eskaleut language family.

Inuit woman in 1903 wearing native garb. (Library of Congress)

Religious belief and practice were based on spirit entities found in nature and needing to be treated with respect. Rituals showing respect to an animal just killed focused on these beliefs, which were also the basis of most taboos and the use of amulets. People could acquire the spirits of objects as protectors. There were also more overarching, generative spirits identified with natural forces and cycles. These were largely female identified. Souls were said to be reincarnated.

Male and female shamans (*angakok*) provided religious leadership by virtue of their direct connection with guardian spirits. They led group religious activities. They could also cure disease and see into the future. Illness was perceived as having to do with soul loss and/or the violation of taboos. Curing methods included interrogation about taboo adherence, trancelike communication with spiritual helpers, and dramatic performance.

There was no formal political organization; instead, nuclear families combined to form villages in distinct geographical areas (*-miuts*). Villages occasionally came together as small, fluid, kinship-related bands. The bands were also geographically identi-fied—the *-miut* suffix—although other groups were not specifically excluded. Larger but ill defined population regions included the Sikosuilarmiuts, Akuliarmiuts, Qaumauangmiuts, Nugumiuts, Oqomiuts, Padlimiuts, and Akudnirmiuts.

Band leaders (*isumataq*) were usually older men with little formal authority and no power. Leaders embodied Inuit values, such as generosity, and were also good hunters.

Sharing was paramount in Inuit society. All aspects of a person's life were controlled by kinship relationships. People married by announcing their intentions, although infants were regularly betrothed. Some men might have more than one wife, and divorce was easy to obtain. Wife exchange was practiced as part of formal male partnerships. Infanticide was rare and usually practiced against females. Names were taken from deceased people and given by elders. A person might have several names, each denoting a kinship relationship and particular behaviors. Names were not sex specific. Children were generally raised gently.

The sick or aged were sometimes abandoned, especially in times of scarcity. Corpses were wrapped in skins and covered with rocks. People brought weapons and food to the grave after four days. No work, including hunting, was performed during the days of mourning. Tensions were relieved through games, such as feats of strength, and duels of drums and songs, in which one person tried to outdo another in parody and song. Joking relationships also helped keep people's emotions in check. Ostracism and even death were reserved for the most serious cases of socially inappropriate behavior.

Domed snow houses were used in the winter, although people might also build stone houses covered with skin and plant material. Entry through a tunnel kept the warm air inside. These houses sometimes had more than one room and had storage porches as well. Beds were raised snow platforms covered with branches and skins. The people also built some larger snow or sod and bone houses for ceremonial purposes. Skin tents were generally used in the summer.

The Baffinland Inuits were nomadic hunters. The most important marine animals were seals and beluga whales, but they also hunted walrus, narwhal, and polar bear. Seals were hunted at their breathing holes and also on floe ice. In the summer, the people traveled inland to hunt caribou and birds (and eggs) as well as some small game. They fished year-round and gathered some berries, roots, and shellfish.

Men used bone knives to cut snow blocks for houses. Hunting equipment included harpoons, lances, spears, and the bow (driftwood or antler) and arrow. Wood and leather floats and drags were also used in whale hunting. Birds (their bones made excellent needles) were caught with wood and leather nets as well as whalebone snares; fish were caught with hooks and stone weirs. Most tools were made of caribou antlers as well as stone, bone, and driftwood. Sinew served nicely as thread. Other important items included carved soapstone cooking pots and lamps that burned seal oil/blubber and carved wooden trays, dishes, spoons, and other objects.

The Baffinland Inuits engaged in some trade and other intercourse with nearby neighbors; for instance, the people of Cumberland Sound were in contact with the Iglulik Inuits and those of southern Baffin Island with the Inuits of Labrador (Ungavas), where they obtained wood for their kayaks and umiaks. Other trade items included copper and ivory. Some groups carved wooden and ivory figurines. Storytelling was also considered a high art. Drum dancing, a performance art, combined music, story, dance, and song. Some Inuit women also practiced a form of singing known as throat singing.

Men hunted using one- or two-person kayaks of driftwood frames and sealskin. Umiaks were larger, skin-covered open boats. Wooden sleds carried people and belongings to and from the interior. Dog traction dates generally from the early twentieth century to the 1960s.

Most clothing consisted of caribou skin and sealskin clothing and boots. Women's sealskin parkas had a larger hood for accommodating an infant. Some people were able to acquire pants made of polar bear skin. Waterproof seal intestine suits, partially lined with dog fur, were used for whale hunting. Women coiled or braided their hair.

Parts of Baffin Island were settled over 4,000 years ago. The Thule, or pre-Inuit culture, entered the region about 1200. Norsemen may have visited Baffin Island around the year 1000, but definite contact with non-Natives was not established until the people met early explorers in the late sixteenth century.

Non-Native whaling began in the east (Davis Strait) in the eighteenth century. The Inuit people shortly began to experience high rates of tuberculosis and other diseases, such as measles. Whaling centers established in the nineteenth century employed Inuits and slowly changed their economy, marking the shift to dependency.

Anglican missionaries arrived in the early twentieth century and conducted the first baptisms. A missionary-derived syllabary was created and persisted well into the twentieth century. The Hudson's Bay Company built trading posts from 1911 on, signaling the end of whaling and the beginning of fur trapping as the most important economic activity. This period also saw the beginning of the outside control of the people's lives by traders, missionaries, and police.

The far north took on strategic importance during the Cold War, about the same time that vast mineral reserves became known and technologically possible to exploit. The federal Department of Northern Affairs and Natural Resources (1954) encouraged the Inuits to abandon their nomadic life. It saw to the construction of housing developments, schools, and a general infrastructure. Local political decisions were made by a community council subject to non-Native approval and review. Inuits found generally menial and poorly paying employment. With radical diet changes, the adoption of a sedentary life, and the appearance of drugs and alcohol, health declined markedly.

The Baffin Regional Association was formed to press for political rights. In 1993, the Tungavik Federation of Nunavut (TFN), an outgrowth of the Inuit Tapirisat of Canada (ITC), signed an agreement with Canada providing for the establishment in 1999 of a new, mostly Inuit, territory on roughly 36,000 square kilometers of land, including Baffin Island.

The people never abandoned their land, which is still central to their identity. The traditional and modern lifeways coexist, sometimes uneasily, for many Inuits. Although people use television (there is even radio and television programming in Inuktitut), snowmobiles, and manufactured items, women also carry babies in the traditional hooded parkas, chew caribou skin to make it soft, and use the semilunar knives to cut seal meat. Full-time doctors are rare in the communities. Housing is often of poor quality. Most people are Christians. Culturally, although many stabilizing patterns of traditional culture have been destroyed, many remain. Many people live as members of extended families, and adoption is widely practiced. Decisions are often made by consensus.

Politically, community councils gained considerably more autonomy around the turn of the century. There is also a significant Inuit presence in the Northwest Territories legislative assembly and some presence at the federal level. The disastrous effects of

government-run schools have been mitigated to some degree by the local control of education, including more culturally relevant curricula in schools. Many people still speak Inuktitut, which is also taught in most schools, especially in the earlier grades. Children attend school in their community through grade nine; the high school is in Frobisher Bay. Adult education is also available.

See also Canada, Indian Policies of; Norse Exploration of North America; Nunavut Land Claims Agreement; Trade.

Inuit, Caribou

"Caribou Inuit" is a non-Native name reflecting the people's reliance on caribou. The Inuit self-designation was *Nunamiut*, "inlanders." The Caribou Inuit homeland is located on the southern Barren Grounds west of Hudson Bay (Keewatin District, Northwest Territories). The early population was centered along the coast near Whale Cove. As the population grew during the nineteenth century, the trend was to expand to the north, south, and west (interior), especially as the Chipewyan Indians abandoned the latter region. This windy land consists mainly of gently rolling plains. It is very well watered, although little plant life exists there. There were between 300 and 500 Caribou Inuits in the late eighteenth century. The Caribou Inuits speak a dialect of Inuit-Inupiaq (Inuktitut), part of the Eskaleut language family.

The Caribou Inuits recognized a supreme creative force that took an interest in the affairs of people. This deity may have been associated with the female caribou. The souls of people who had lived well (observed all the taboos, of which there were many) were thought to rejoin this force when they died, thence to be reincarnated on earth. The souls of those who had not lived well were said to be eternally damned.

Religion was essentially hunting based. Respect was owed to all things in nature but especially game animals. People left offerings for the spirits of slain animals. A number of ceremonial dances reinforced these ideas. Shamans specialized in such matters, acting as spiritual intermediaries. They could find out, by communicating with the spirits, who had broken which taboo and how a problem could be rectified (curing).

Political leadership, such as it was, took place in the context of the family. The leader was generally

an older man who sat atop the family kinship network. He was also likely to be strong, wise, highly skilled in hunting, and familiar with the spirit world. Other than this, informal, ad hoc leaders advised small groups on hunting matters and when to move camp. There were five bands or societies in the midnineteenth century: Paatlirmiuts, Qairnitmiuts, Ahiarmiuts, Hauniqturmiuts, and Harvaqturmiuts. The societies were separate but related by marriage and descent.

Betrothal took place as early as infancy. Cross cousins (children of a mother's brothers or a father's sisters) were regarded as highly desirable marriage partners. There was some regular intermarriage with other Inuit groups such as the Netsiliks and Igluliks. There was little or no marriage ceremony. Newly married couples might live with either set of parents. Men might have more than one wife; widows tended to marry their brothers-in-law.

Although children were highly valued and generally treated very well, and although childless couples often adopted children, there was some female infanticide. Corpses were wrapped in skins and placed within a circle of stones, along with various possessions. The mourning period was highly ritualized.

The extended family was the basic unit. The people displayed a distinct fondness for singing, feasting, and social drum dancing, sometimes in a large snow house or tent. They played several games, many of which included gambling, and took part in athletic contests.

For most of their prehistory, coastal people used stone winter houses, chinked with moss and dirt and covered with snow. Around 1880 they learned, from the Igluliks, to build domed snow houses. These houses generally held ten people at most. Storage was available on the sides of a long entryway, which itself was placed below ground level to keep the cold drafts out. Furniture consisted of snow platforms covered with skins and willow mats. Some people built a small connected kitchen with a smoke hole, although many cooked, when they cooked at all, outside on fires of moss and willow. Houses of family members might be linked by tunnels.

In other seasons, the people used conical skin tents (hair side out for waterproofing), as well as temporary brush windbreaks. Most settlements were occupied by only one extended family, although groups might grow in size in the spring and summer.

Men engaged in extensive summer seal, walrus, and whale hunting before the early to midnineteenth

Inuit spearing salmon in Canada in the early 1900s. (Library of Congress)

century. A few coastal people continued these activities even after that time. Meat was sun-dried and stored in sealskin bags and retained for winter use.

Especially from the midnineteenth century on, the people depended almost totally on the migrating herds of caribou, which reached their peak numbers in autumn. People intercepted the animals at water crossings, drove them into lakes, and directed them down courseways where hunters waited. The men continued to hunt while women processed the meat and skins. Excess meat was covered with skins and hidden under rocks. When necessary, especially when the caribou meat began to run out, men also hunted musk ox, which were hunted to extinction by about 1900.

Most winter food was eaten frozen and raw. Fishing took place mostly in the winter and spring. Other foods included birds and their eggs, some summer berries, and the plant foods taken from caribou stomachs.

Most material items, such as tools, scrapers, needles, hooks, and arrowheads, were derived from the caribou. Other raw materials included wood and soapstone. Small, weak lamps burned caribou fat or fish oil. Cooking fires burned dwarf shrubbery. Musical instruments included drums and tambourine.

All trade took place in the summer. The people traded caribou skins and soapstone with the

Chipewyans and Crees for snowshoes, moccasins, and pyrite. They also traded with the Aivilik Iglulik Inuits from about 1800 on. Exports included driftwood and seal dog traces and boot soles, among other items. Long, narrow, skin-covered kayaks were sometimes tied together to form rafts for crossing larger bodies of water. After around 1800, the people used dogsleds whose runners were coated with ice-covered peat. Most transportation was overland with the help of tumplines, the Caribou Inuits being particularly strong walkers.

Six to eight caribou skins provided an adult suit of well-tailored clothing, including pants, boots, mittens, and outer and inner parkas. Furs and fur trim came from polar bears, wolves, wolverines, and foxes. Women wore bone or copper headbands. Women's parka hoods were extra large to accommodate babies carried high on the back.

The historic Caribou Inuits descended directly from the ancient Thule people, in local residence since about the twelfth century. The first non-Native explorers arrived in the early seventeenth century, although there may not have been direct contact between the two peoples.

Regular trade with non-Natives began shortly after the people were first visited by Hudson's Bay Company representatives in 1717. Ships brought foreign goods from Churchill, and the Inuits traded for

items such as metal knives and axes, beads, tobacco, and, later, guns and powder. At that time they often acted as intermediaries between non-Natives and the Igluliks, Netsiliks, and Copper Inuits. Regular trade began at Churchill in 1790.

By the early nineteenth century, Caribou Inuit society had begun to reorient itself, with southerners focusing on the Churchill area and the non-Native trade, and northerners making stronger ties with the Aivilik Iglulik Inuits. The two groups divided about 1810. Shortly thereafter, the two societies became five.

The Hudson's Bay Company conducted commercial whaling from about 1860 to 1915. The Inuit people killed seals and whales each summer, trading most oil and other products, while shifting to almost total dependence on caribou, as well as musk ox and fish to a lesser extent.

Canada established a formal presence in 1903. Trading posts and Catholic missionaries arrived in 1912, followed by various non-Native settlements in the region. A severe famine from 1915 to around 1924 killed perhaps two-thirds of the people. After that event, the people turned to trapping (mainly fox fur) and the wage/trade economy as a means of survival. This marked the end of their independence.

Gradually, continuing hunger and epidemics began to fragment the societies, and the population continued to decline. The situation attracted governmental intervention in the 1950s. Administrative centers were established. Most people relocated by choice to one of five settlements, most of which contained a minority of Caribou Inuits (although a majority of Inuits).

The shift to towns was completed in the 1960s. The people lived in prefabricated housing, generally wore nontraditional clothing, and ate nontraditional foods. With the breakdown of the traditional economy and nothing to take its place, many experienced for the first time problems of substance abuse. Children began learning English in school but little about their traditional culture. Acculturation quickly took hold among the young. The arrival of television in the 1970s and then other electronic media accelerated these trends.

The people never abandoned their land, which is still central to their identity. Traditional and modern coexist, sometimes uneasily, for many Inuits. Although people use television (there is even radio and television programming in Inuktitut), snowmobiles, and manufactured items, women also carry babies in the traditional hooded parkas, chew cari-

bou skin to make it soft, and use the semilunar knives to cut seal meat.

Full-time doctors are rare in the communities. Housing is often of poor quality. Most people are Christians. Culturally, although many stabilizing patterns of traditional culture have been destroyed, many remain. Many people live as members of extended families. Adoption is widely practiced. Decisions are often made by consensus. Intermarriage among the Inuit groups in the five population centers has blurred ethnic identity; people now tend to identify with their settlement.

Politically, community councils have gained considerably more autonomy over the past decade or two. There is also a significant Inuit presence in the Northwest Territories legislative assembly and some presence at the federal level. The disastrous effects of government-run schools have been mitigated to some degree by local control of education, including more culturally relevant curricula in schools. Many people still speak Inuktitut, which is also taught in most schools, especially in the earlier grades. Caribou overhunting has prompted increased government regulations, which are resisted by the Caribou Inuits, who still identify to a significant extent with the caribou.

See also Boarding Schools, United States and Canada; Canada, Indian Policies of; Hudson's Bay Company; Nunavut Land Claims Agreement; Trade.

Inuit, Copper

"Copper Inuit," meaning "People," is a name bestowed by non-Native explorers who found them using Native copper in tools and weapons. (*See also* Netsilik.) In the eighteenth century the Copper Inuits were living between Cape Parry and Queen Maude Gulf, especially on southern Victoria Island and along Coronation Gulf. The region is almost entirely tundra, except for some forest to the south and along the Coppermine River. Many Copper Inuits still live in this area of the central Arctic, known as Kitikmeot. The Native population was probably between 800 and 1,300 in the late eighteenth century. Copper Inuits speak a dialect of Inuit-Inupiaq (Inuktitut), a member of the Eskaleut language family.

Religious belief and practice were based on the need to appease spiritual entities found in nature. Hunting and specifically the land-sea dichotomy

were the focus of most rituals and taboos, such as that prohibiting sewing caribou skin clothing in certain seasons. The people also recognized generative spirits, conceived of as female and identified with natural forces and cycles.

Male and female shamans (*angakok*) provided religious leadership by virtue of their connection with guardian spirits. They could also control the weather, improve conditions for hunting, cure disease, and divine the future. Illness was due to soul loss, the violation of taboos, and/or the anger of the dead. Curing methods included interrogation about taboo adherence, trancelike communication with spiritual helpers, and dramatic performance.

Nuclear families were the basic economic and political unit. Families were led by the oldest man. They were loosely organized into small local groups associated with geographical areas (*-miuts*). Local groups occasionally came together as perhaps six or seven small, fluid bands. The bands were also geographically identified, their names carrying the *-miut* suffix as well.

Sharing was paramount in Inuit society. All aspects of a person's life were controlled by kinship relationships. The people recognized many types of formal and informal partnerships and relationships. Some of these included wife exchanges. People came together in larger group gatherings in late autumn; this was a time to sew and mend clothing and to renew kinship ties. Men hunted, made and repaired weapons and tools, and built kayaks, sleds, and shelter. Women prepared skins and made clothing, sewed hides for coverings, caught and prepared fish, raised children, and gathered moss, berries, and other items.

Descent was bilateral. People married simply by announcing their intentions, although infants were regularly betrothed. Prospective husbands often served their future in-laws for a period of time. Men might have more than one wife, but most had only one. Divorce was easy to obtain. Names were taken from deceased people and given by elders.

People often adopted orphans. Children were highly valued and loved, especially males. When a boy killed his first seal, the seal's body was ritually dragged over his. The sick or aged were sometimes abandoned, especially in times of scarcity. Corpses were wrapped in skins and buried in stone or snow vaults or, later, left outside within a ring of stones. No work, including hunting, was performed during the days of mourning.

Tensions were relieved through games, such as feats of strength and duels of drums and songs, in which one person tried to outdo another in parody and song. "Joking" relationships also helped keep people's emotions in check. Ostracism and even death were reserved for the most serious cases of socially inappropriate behavior.

Men built domed snow houses in the winter. Entry through a straight-sided, flat-topped tunnel kept the warm air inside. Some houses had more than one room. Snow platforms covered with the skins of caribou, musk ox, or bear served as beds. The people used larger snow or sod-and-bone houses for ceremonial purposes. They also used caribou skin and sealskin tents built over raised sod rings in the summer and over pits in the autumn.

Copper Inuits were nomadic hunters. The most important game animals were seals and whales. Some polar bears were caught in the winter as well. The people also hunted caribou, musk ox, small game, and fowl, mainly in small groups in the summer and autumn. One- or two-person kayaks, propelled with a double-bladed paddle, were generally used for hunting. Several men could hunt whales in umiaks, which were larger, skin-covered open boats. Fishing was a year-round activity. Some berries were available in the summer.

The summer was trade season. The people exchanged goods, particularly copper and driftwood, with the Inuvialuits, the Caribou Inuits, and the Netsiliks. There were occasional contacts with Athapaskan Indians to their south. Dogs carried burdens in the summer and pulled wooden sleds in the winter. The sleds had wooden runners covered with whalebone, mud, or peat and then ice. Toboggans were occasionally made of skin. The most important artistic traditions were carved wooden and ivory figurines.

Women sewed most clothing from caribou skins, although sealskins were commonly used on boots. Apparel included men's long, gut sealing coats and light swallowtail ceremonial coats. The people wore a double skin suit in the winter and only the inner layer in the summer. Women's clothing featured large shoulders and hoods for accomodating infants as well as one-piece, attached leggings and boots. Men wore small loon beak dancing caps with weasel skin tassels. Both sexes wore tattoos and ivory or bone snow goggles. Clothing decoration consisted mainly of bands of white fur or skin. There was some skin fringing.

Historical Copper Inuit people are descended from ancient pre-Dorset, Dorset, and Thule cultures. They first encountered non-Natives in the late eighteenth and early nineteenth centuries. Although they obtained some non-Native trade goods, such as iron, and caught new diseases, traditional life remained relatively unchanged for some time thereafter.

Local trading posts were established in the 1920s, bringing items such as rifles, fish nets, and steel traps as well as cloth, tea, and flour. These material changes had the result of extending the caribou season and generally reorienting the people away from the sea. This development, plus the regular presence of trade ships, began to undermine traditional self-sufficiency and social structures. The region's first missionaries arrived at about the same time, as did a permanent presence of the Royal Canadian Mounted Police (RCMP).

It was not until the 1950s, however, that the root aspects of traditional culture began to disappear. Some mixing with western Inuit newcomers occurred during that time. The far north took on strategic importance during the Cold War, about the same time that vast mineral reserves became known and technologically possible to exploit. These two industries offered some wage labor and contributed to the decline of the nomadic life. Other factors contributed as well, such as the decline of the caribou herds.

The federal Department of Northern Affairs and Natural Resources (1954) began constructing wood-frame housing developments, clinics, and schools and encouraged resettlement in these permanent communities. Local political decisions were made by a community council subject to non-Native approval and review. Population centralization was largely completed by the 1970s. Most job opportunities for Inuits were unskilled and menial, although hunting and trapping remained important. With radical diet changes, the adoption of a sedentary life, and the appearance of drugs and alcohol, health declined markedly.

The people never abandoned their land, which is still central to their identity. Traditional and modern coexist, sometimes uneasily, for many Inuit. Full-time doctors are rare in the communities. Housing is often of poor quality. Most people are Christians. Culturally, although many stabilizing patterns of traditional culture have been destroyed, many remain. Many people live as members of extended families. Adoption is widely practiced. Decisions are often made by consensus.

Politically, community councils have gained considerably more autonomy over the past decade or two. There is also a significant Inuit presence in the Northwest Territories legislative assembly and some presence at the federal level. In 1993, the Tungavik Federation of Nunavut (TFN), an outgrowth of the Inuit Tapirisat of Canada (ITC), signed an agreement with Canada providing for the establishment, in 1999, of the new, mostly Inuit, territory of Nunuvut on roughly 36,000 square kilometers of land, including Kitikmeot.

See also Canada, Indian Policies of; Department of Indian Affairs and Northern Development; Nunavut, Land Claims Agreement; Trade.

Inuit, Labrador or Ungava

Labrador or Ungava Inuits are actually two groups of northeastern Inuits once differentiated by dialect and custom. Reflecting recent political developments, many people of the latter group now refer to themselves as Inuit Kapaimiuts, "People of Quebec."

From the late sixteenth century on, these people have lived on the northern half of the Labrador peninsula, especially along the coasts and the offshore islands. There is some controversy as to whether Inuit groups ever occupied land bordering the Gulf of Saint Lawrence. The Labrador Inuit population in the mideighteenth century was between 3,000 and 4,200, about two-thirds of whom lived in the south. The people speak dialects of Inuit-Inupiaq (Inuktitut), a member of the Eskaleut language family.

Religious belief and practice were based on the need to appease spiritual entities found in nature. Hunting and specifically the land-sea dichotomy were the focus of most rituals and taboos, such as that prohibiting sewing caribou skin clothing in certain seasons. The people also recognized generative spirits, conceived of as female and identified with natural forces and cycles. Their rich cosmogony and mythology were filled with spirits and beings of various sizes, some superhuman and some subhuman.

Male and female shamans (*angakok*) provided religious leadership by virtue of their connection with guardian spirits. They could also control the weather, improve conditions for hunting, cure disease, and divine the future. Illness was perceived as stemming from soul loss, the violation of taboos,

and/or the anger of the dead. Curing methods included interrogation about taboo adherence, trancelike communication with spiritual helpers, and dramatic performance.

Nuclear families were loosely organized into local groups of twenty to thirty people associated with geographical areas (-miuts). These groups occasionally came together as roughly twenty-five (perhaps ten among the Ungavas) small, fluid bands that were also geographically identified. The Ungava Inuits also recognized three regional bands (Siqinirmiuts, Tarramiuts, Itivimiuts) that were identified by intermarriage and linguistic and cultural similarities.

The harpooner or boat owner provided leadership for whaling expeditions. The best hunters were often the de facto group leaders. The abuse of their authority was likely to get them killed. Still, competition for leadership positions was active, with people dueling through song and woman exchange. Women also competed with each other through singing. Local (settlement) councils helped resolve conflicts that arose in situations without a strong leader, especially in the south.

Women were in charge of child rearing as well as skin and food preparation. They made the clothes, fished, hunted small animals, gathered plant material, and tended the oil lamps. Men hunted and had overall responsibility for all forms of transportation. They made and repaired utensils, weapons, and tools. They also built the houses.

Children were named for dead relatives regardless of gender; they were generally expected to take on the gender roles of their namesake, as opposed to those of their own sex. Children were occasionally brought up in the roles of the opposite gender for economic reasons. People married simply by announcing their intentions, although infants were regularly betrothed. Good hunters might have more than one wife (especially in the south), but most had only one. Divorce was easy to effect. Some wife exchanges were permitted within defined family partnerships; these relationships were considered a kind of marriage.

Infanticide was rare and usually practiced against females; cannibalism, too, occasionally occurred during periods of starvation. Children were highly valued and loved, especially males. Adoption was common. The sick or aged were sometimes abandoned, especially in times of scarcity. Corpses were buried in stone graves covered by broken personal items.

The typical winter house was semiexcavated and made of stone, whalebone, and wood frames filled with sod and stone with a skin roof. Floors were also stone; windows were made of gut. Each house held up to twenty people; spaces were separated by skin partitions. The people also built mainly temporary domed snow houses. Conical and/or domed sealskin or caribou skin tents served as summer housing. There were also large ceremonial and social structures (kashim) as well.

Labrador Inuits were nomadic hunters, taking game both individually and collectively. Depending on location, they engaged in a number of subsistence activities, such as the late summer and fall caribou hunting, whaling, and breathing hole sealing in the winter. They hunted seals from kayaks in the spring and summer. Men and women fished year-round. People also ate birds and their eggs as well as walrus and bear (polar and black). Women gathered numerous berries and some roots as well, as some shellfish and sea vegetables. Coastal hunters traveled into the interior in the spring to hunt caribou, reemerging on the coast in the fall. The results of a hunt were divided roughly equally, with those who played more important roles getting somewhat better (but not generally larger) shares. Drinks included blood and water.

Special harpoons, floats, and drags were used in whaling. Caribou were generally shot with bow and arrow or speared from kayaks. Birds were shot, snared, or brought down with bolas. Fish were caught with hooks, weirs, and spears.

Soapstone lamps burned beluga oil (in the north) or caribou fat (in the south and interior). The latter provided light but not much heat. In the interior and more southern areas, people also molded caribou tallow candles in goose leg skins. They started fires with pyrite, flint, and moss. Coiled baskets and woven willow mats were made around Hudson Bay.

Southeastern groups imported wood for bows and arrows from the Beothuk Indians of Newfoundland. Inlanders and coastal residents exchanged dogs, ivory, caribou, and sealskins. Art objects included woven grass baskets and carved ivory figures. There were also some petroglyphs in steatite quarries.

Travel was fairly well developed, allowing people to move with relative ease to exploit the various regions of their territory. Several types of kayaks were used, generally for hunting sea mammals, birds, and caribou. Umiaks (larger, skin-covered

open boats that might hold up to thirty people) were generally rowed by women on visits to offshore islands or during seasonal migrations. They were also used in the south for autumn whale hunting. Wooden sleds were pulled by dogs, who also carried some gear. Temporary boats might be made of caribou skin stuffed with branches. Long-distance walking, on snowshoes in the winter, was common (snowshoes may not be native).

Dress throughout Labrador was originally similar to that of the Baffinland Inuits. It consisted mainly of caribou skin and sealskin clothing and boots. Skins of other animals were used as needed. Some island people made clothing of bird skins, especially those of ducks.

Better hunters had newer and better clothing. Decoration was also age and sex appropriate. Ivory, wood, and other materials were used in clothing decoration. Some items were used as amulets or charms, whereas others were basically decorative. Women generally tattooed their faces, arms, and breasts after reaching puberty. Men occasionally tattooed noses or shoulders when they had killed a whale. Both men and women wore hair long, but women braided, rolled, and knotted theirs.

This region has been occupied since about 2500 BCE, probably at first by people emigrating in waves from the northwest. Norse explorers arrived about 1000. The ancient Dorset culture lasted until around the fourteenth century, when it was displaced by Thule immigrants from Baffin Island. Around 1500, some Thule groups began a slow migration to the southern Labrador coast.

The people encountered Basque and other European whalers in the late fifteenth century, when Inuit whaling technology was more advanced than it is now. Contacts with non-Native explorers, particularly those looking for the fabled northwest passage to Asia, continued throughout the sixteenth century. Early contacts between the Inuits and non-Natives were generally hostile.

Whale and caribou overhunting, combined with the introduction of non-Native diseases, led to population declines in the north by the late seventeenth century. The first trade centers were established in the north during the eighteenth century, although trade did not become regular there until close to the midnineteenth century.

In the eighteenth century, especially after the 1740s, sporadic trade began with the French fishery in the south. Moravian missions, schools, and trading posts, especially to the south, gradually became

Inuit population centers after the mid- to late eighteenth century. Missionization began in Arctic Quebec in the 1860s. A mixed British-Inuit population (known as "settlers") also became established in the south from the mideighteenth century on. This influential group slowly grew in size and spread northward as well. Increased trade activity in the south in the midnineteenth century led to Inuit population declines as a result of alcohol use and disease epidemics.

In the north, by later in the century, some families intermarried with non-Native traders and otherwise established close relations with them. Fur trade posts became widespread in the north in the early twentieth century. Native technology began to change fundamentally and permanently during that period. Shamanism, too, had all but disappeared; most people had by then accepted Christianity, although not without much social convulsion.

In the south, the Moravians turned the Inuit trade over to the Hudson's Bay Company in 1926. There was an increasing government presence in the 1930s and 1940s. Few or no inland groups remained in Arctic Quebec after 1930, the people having moved to the coast. About the same time, the bottom dropped out of the fox fur market. Trade posts disappeared, and many people went back to a semitraditional mode of subsistence and technology.

The far north took on strategic importance during the Cold War, about the same time that vast mineral reserves became known and technologically possible to exploit. The federal Department of Northern Affairs and Natural Resources (1954) encouraged the Inuits to abandon their nomadic life. Extensive Canadian government services and payments date from that time. Local Moravian missions ceded authority to the government when Labrador and Newfoundland entered the Canadian confederation in 1949.

Some of Labrador's Native communities were officially closed in the 1950s and their residents relocated. Most wage employment was of the unskilled and menial variety. By the 1960s, most people had abandoned the old ways. With radical diet changes, the adoption of a sedentary life, and the appearance of drugs and alcohol, their health declined markedly.

The entire region has experienced growing ethnopolitical awareness and activism since the 1970s. During that period, the Labrador Inuit Association (LIA) reached an accommodation with local biracial residents ("settlers") regarding representation and rights. The LIA is associated with the Inuit

Tapirisat of Canada (ITC). This advocacy group works to settle land claims and to facilitate interracial cooperation. It also supports and funds local programs and services, including those relating to Inuit culture.

The Northern Quebec Inuit Association (1971) approved the James Bay and Northern Quebec Agreement (JBNQA) in 1975. It provided for local and regional administrative power as well as some special rights in the areas of land use, education, and justice. There was also monetary compensation. This controversial agreement divided the Inuits on the issue of aboriginal land rights. The opposition, centered in the locally based cooperative movement, formed the Inuit Tungavingat Nunami (ITN). This group rejects the JBNQA, including the financial compensations, funding its opposition activities through local levies on carvings.

A cultural revival beginning in the 1980s led to the creation of museums, cultural centers, and various studies and programs. Newspapers, air travel, television, and telephone reach even remote villages. Education is locally controlled in grades one through twelve, although the curriculum differs little from those in non-Native communities. Issues there include mineral and other development versus protecting renewable resources.

Traditional and modern coexist, sometimes uneasily, for many Inuits. Full-time doctors are rare in the communities. Housing is often of poor quality. Most people are Christians. Culturally, although many stabilizing patterns of traditional culture have been destroyed, many remain. Many people live as members of extended families. Adoption is widely practiced. Decisions are often made by consensus.

> *See also* Canada, Indian Policies of; Department of Indian Affairs and Northern Development; Hudson's Bay Company; L'Anse aux Meadows Viking Settlement; Norse Exploration of North America; Trade.

Inuit, Mackenzie Delta

See Inuvialuit.

Inuit, North Alaska

See Inupiat.

Inupiat

"Inupiat," meaning "the People," is an Inuit name covering the Eskimo or Inuit groups formerly known to anthropologists as Bering Strait, Kotzebue Sound, sometimes West Alaska, and North Alaska Eskimos. The last group has also been divided into two groups: coastal people, or Tareumiuts, and the land-oriented Nuunamiuts.

The Inupiats lived in northwest and northern Alaska, from about Norton Sound and the Seward Peninsula (with offshore islands) north and east to about the Canadian border, including the North Slope–Barrow region. This is considered to have been one of the world's most productive sea mammal regions. Many Inupiats still live in this area. There were perhaps 9,500 Inupiats in the midnineteenth century. Inupiat people speak dialects of Inupiaq (Inuktitut), an Eskaleut language. Some Bering Strait Inuit speak Yup'ik dialects.

Religious belief was based on the existence of spiritual entities found in nature. In particular, the spirits of game animals allowed themselves to be caught only if they were treated properly. Respect was expressed in behaviors such as maintaining a separation between land and sea hunting, opening the head of an animal just killed to allow its spirit to escape, speaking well of game animals, and offering sea mammals a drink of cold water and land animals knives or needles; respect was also expressed by observing many taboos, rituals, and ceremonies including certain songs and charms.

Among whale hunters, personal spirit songs that were purchased or inherited were used to make the hunt more successful. Whale and caribou hunters and their wives were required to observe many rituals and taboos. Whaling ceremonies along the north coast and caribou ceremonies inland were the most important rituals, representing a sort of world renewal. Male and older female shamans (*angakok*) provided religious leadership by virtue of their connection with the spirit world. They also participated in regular economic activities.

Nuclear or small extended families were loosely organized into fluid local groups (*-miuts*) associated with geographical areas. These local groups occasionally came together as small, fluid, autonomous bands (family groups; tribes) of between twenty and 200 bilaterally related people. The bands were also geographically identified but not political entities; their names carried the *-miut* suffix. People within them depended on each other for subsistence

support and spoke the same subdialect. Several distinct societies of bands had formed in the interior north by the midnineteenth century.

Family heads (*umialik*, literally umiak captain, or whaling leader) were usually older men, with little formal authority and no power. Leaders generally embodied Inuit values, such as generosity, and were also good hunters. Within the context of a basically egalitarian society, they were relatively wealthier (owing to their following) and had more status than other men. Their main responsibilities included directing hunting, trading, and diplomatic activities. The *umialik* and his wife were also responsible for food redistribution.

Among the northern Inupiats, leaders might also impose their will on women as well. Potential leaders often competed with each other to hold their crews or hunters by such means as wife exchange and gift giving. Additional wives generally meant additional followers, wealth, and power. Leaders there might oversee not only the hunt but also religious ceremonies, festivals, and trade.

The northern Inupiats came together briefly for large hunting (sea and land) forays, but mainly they remained in family groups. The Bering Strait and Kotzebue Sound tribes had principal winter villages. Each had one or more chiefs for each local group residing in the village. The chief(s) and a council oversaw local and intertribal affairs.

Kinship networks were the most important social structure as well as the key to survival in terms of mutual aid and cooperative activity. This arrangement also led to ongoing blood feuds: An injury to one was perceived as an injury to the whole kin group and called for revenge.

Nonkin men teamed up for hunting or trade purposes. Such defined partnerships might include temporary wife exchanges, which were considered a kind of marriage (interestingly, at least among the Bering Strait people, relations considered adulterous were harshly dealt with). "Joking" relationships between unrelated men also furthered mutual aid and support and served to reduce tension and conflict. Nonkin relationships also included adopted people and people who had the same name.

In some Bering Strait Inuit villages, family groups lived on patrilineally inherited plots of land. In larger groups, food was generally turned over to the *umialik* and his wife, who redistributed it according to various priorities. Generosity was highly valued. When hunters brought in a whale or caribou, no one went hungry. Hard work and individual freedom were other key values, the latter in the context of kinship associations.

Southerners especially celebrated the fall and winter Messenger Feasts, in which a neighboring group was invited to feast and dance. Social status was related to largesse on these occasions, which were similar to potlatches. They brought some north Alaska Inuits together with some Athapaskan Indians.

Marriage was considered to be mainly a kinship-building exercise. Successful hunters might have more than one wife, but most had only one. Divorce, or the end of cohabitation, was easy to obtain, especially before many children had been born. It was also the case that men might try to dominate women, including raping them, in their or another's household. In this endeavor the "bully" was usually backed by members of his kinship group (as, in fact, older women might occasionally, by virtue of their supposed magical powers, capture a young man for a husband).

Infanticide was rare and usually practiced against females. Children were highly valued and loved, especially males. They were raised by the women with a great deal of liberty. Names, usually of dead relatives, were associated with specific food taboos. The sick or aged were sometimes abandoned, especially in times of scarcity. Death was attended by a minimum of ritual. Corpses were removed through skylights and left on the tundra. A mourning period of four or five days ensued, during which all activity ceased, and a feast was often held a year after a relative's death.

The regular winter dwelling was a semiexcavated, domed, driftwood-and-sod house, roughly twelve to fifteen feet long. Moss was placed between the interior walls and the sod for insulation. There was a separate kitchen with a smoke hole and storage niches off the entrance tunnel, which descended into a meat cellar and ended at a well that led up to the main room. The houses held from eight to twelve people (two families). Inside were raised sleeping platforms and suspended drying racks. Stretched gut or ice served as windows.

Some groups also used a dome-shaped wooden structure covered with skins or bark and also temporary snow or ice houses. Interior groups also used willow-frame dome tents covered with caribou skin, bark, or grass. Some Bering Strait people built woodframe summer houses.

Larger men's houses (*kashim*) were present in communities with more than a few families.

Reserved for men and boys by day, they became a family social center at night. They were also used for ceremonies and other activities and, along the coast, were associated with whaling crews.

The Tareumiuts and some Bering Strait and Kotzebue Sound people depended mainly on marine life such as seals, bowhead and beluga whales, and walrus, whereas the Nuunamiuts hunted mainly caribou. Whale meat was stored in the permafrost and generally provided a reliable food source from season to season. Northern groups hunted whales from umiaks in the spring and seal and walrus through the ice in the winter.

The Kotzebue Sound and some Bering Strait people had a mixed land and marine hunting economy. Game animals included fowl, mountain sheep, bear, wolves, wolverines, hares, squirrels, and foxes. Men and women fished year-round. The Bering Strait and Kotzebue Sound people also gathered a variety of greens, berries, and roots in the summer.

Stone-tipped, toggle-headed harpoons were attached to wooden floats and inflated sealskins to create drag on a submerging whale. Floats were also used to keep a slain whale from sinking before it could be towed to shore.

Hunting equipment included spears, bow and arrow, bolas (strings attached to stone balls to bring down birds), deadfalls, traps, and snares. The atlatl was used to throw sealing darts or harpoons. Fishing equipment included hooks, weirs, nets, traps, and spears. People used a variety of mainly stone and ivory butchering tools; some were fashioned of antler and driftwood as well. The key women's tool was a crescent-shaped knife. The Bering Strait people made some grass baskets and mats.

Boiling pots might be made of driftwood or pottery. Other important items included baleen seal nets; bone needles and sinew thread; carved wooden trays, dishes, spoons, and other objects; a bow drill to start fires and drill holes; sun goggles; and carved soapstone (in the north) or pottery (in the Bering Strait and Kotzebue Sound) cooking pots and lamps (the latter burned seal oil using moss wicks). Local stone around Kotzebue Sound included chert, slate, and jade. There was also some birchbark around Kotzebue Sound that the people made into containers.

The two groups of northern Inupiats were mutually dependent, trading whale products, such as skin, oil, and blubber, for caribou skins on a regular basis. Summer trade fairs were widely attended. The one at Sheshalik, on Kotzebue Sound, may have attracted 2,000 or more people. The other large northern Alaska trade fair was held in Nigalik (Colville River Delta) and was attended by Yup'ik people as well as Athapaskan Indians. In addition to trade, fairs included private contact between various partners, dancing, feasts, and competitions.

Kotzebue trade fairs were also attended by Siberians, who exchanged jade, pottery, reindeer skins, and beads for local products. Native Siberians (Chukchis) also provided Russian goods from the late seventeenth century on.

The basic hunting vehicle was the one- or two-person closed skin kayak. Several men could hunt whales in umiaks (skin-covered open boats with a driftwood frame between fifteen and fifty feet long). Umiaks might also hold 2,000 pounds of cargo. The people also used wooden sleds with iced runners. Dogs pulled (or helped pull) the sleds after about 1500. Some interior people used snowshoes.

Women tanned skins and made sealskin and caribou skin clothing, some with fur trim. In the winter, people wore two suits of parkas and pants: The inner suit was worn with the fur turned in, whereas the outer had the fur turned out. Other winter clothing included mittens and hoods (women's were extra large for carrying babies). Clothing in the Kotzebue Sound area was sewn from untanned skins.

Other items of clothing included skin socks, boots of caribou skin and chewed seal hide soles, and waterproof outer jackets of sewn sea mammal intestine. Men wore labrets, the lip being pierced around puberty. Many women had three lined tattoos down the chin.

Fighting was generally a matter of kin group involvement and remained limited in scope if not in time. Strangers outside the kinship or alliance system were considered potential enemies and could be killed on sight, their goods and women taken. Blood feuds were the result of the lack of overall conflict-resolution structures. Fighting also took place among rival trade groups. Also, territory was defended against neighboring groups.

The historic Nuunamiuts (interior North Alaska people) moved into their region from the south and west from about 1400 through about 1800. Russian explorers and traders arrived in the early to mideighteenth century and remained for the next 100 years or so. Whalers and traders from other countries plied the local waters from about the 1840s (1880s in the far north). Among other things, they introduced alcohol, tobacco, and non-Native

diseases. Traditional patterns began to break down as well after that time.

The Nuunamiuts began a sharp decline from the midnineteenth century on, largely owing to disease and starvation (smaller caribou herds). Most families had left the interior by 1820, drawn to the coast, although a few families began moving back around 1840. There were severe epidemics throughout the region in the 1870s and 1880s. A severe famine struck the Kotzebue Sound region in 1880–1881.

Mining began in the Bering Strait area in the 1880s. Meanwhile, imported reindeer herding, fur trapping, missionaries, and schools began to attract people to local settlements from the mid- to late nineteenth century on. Reindeer herding proved ultimately to be unsuccessful in the area. The Nome gold rush of 1898 saw the migration of many Inuits to the Nome area to sell crafts and eventually to work and to attend school. Anti-Inuit sentiment remained strong in Nome for some time thereafter.

Fur traders arrived around 1900, about the time of a severe measles epidemic and the near depletion of the caribou herds. Another severe influenza epidemic struck in 1918. In the early twentieth century, the federal government assumed responsibility for Inuit education. To a greater extent than even the churches, the government increased the pressure to acculturate. For instance, government schools punished people severely for speaking their Native language. The only high schools were located away from Inupiat-speaking centers.

The people experienced a general population growth after World War II, attributable to the return of the caribou, the introduction of moose into the region, and government efforts against disease. The far north took on strategic importance during the Cold War, about the same time that vast mineral reserves became known and technologically possible to exploit. Oil was discovered on the North Slope in 1968. Most of the jobs that Inuits were able to obtain were unskilled and menial. Furthermore, with radical diet changes, the adoption of a sedentary life, and the appearance of drugs and alcohol, their health declined markedly.

In the late 1950s, the Inupiat people began organizing politically in reaction to the U.S. government's threat to use nuclear weapons in the preparation of a deep-water port as well as its bird hunting restrictions. The Seward Peninsula Native Association, Alaska Federation of Natives, Inupiat Paitot, Northwest Alaska Native Association, and North Slope Native Association formed as a result of this activism. Land issues also gave rise to the Alaska Native Claims Settlement Act (ANCSA) in 1971. The settlement gave the people legal rights to millions of acres of land and shares in corporations worth millions of dollars in exchange for their cession of aboriginal title. Major land conservation laws were enacted in 1980.

In response to severe problems with substance abuse, several communities have restricted or eliminated the sale of alcohol. Other efforts to remedy the problems are ongoing. Severe radioactive pollution exists around the Cape Thompson area, caused by the Atomic Energy Commission's (predecessor to the Nuclear Regulatory Commission) use of the area as a nuclear dump and its conduct of nuclear experiments using local plant and animal life, as well as by Soviet nuclear waste dumping. Negotiations over cleanup are ongoing.

Curricula and in fact the control of education shifted to local authorities beginning in the 1970s. The preservation and instruction of Native culture are part of this effort. Most Inupiat people have access to all modern air and electronic transportation and communication. Most speak English as a first language, although most adults are bilingual.

See also Alaska Native Claims Settlement Act; Alcoholism and Substance Abuse, Fur Trade.

Inuvialuit

"Inuvialuit" is the Inuit name for the people formerly known as Mackenzie Delta Eskimos or western (Canadian) Arctic Eskimos. The homeland of this group is the Mackenzie Delta region, specifically from Herschel Island to the Baillie Islands, northwest Northwest Territories. From between 2,000 and 2,500 people in the mideighteenth century, the Inuvialuit population was reduced to about 150 in 1910 and perhaps ten in 1930. Inuvialuits speak a dialect of Inuit-Inupiaq (Inuktitut), a member of the Eskaleut language family.

Religious belief and practice were based on the need to appease spiritual entities found in nature. Hunting and specifically the land-sea dichotomy were the focus of most rituals and taboos. The people also recognized generative spirits, conceived of as female and identified with natural forces and cycles.

Male and female shamans (*angakok*) provided religious leadership by virtue of their connection with guardian spirits. They could also control the weather, improve conditions for hunting, cure disease, and divine the future. Illness was perceived as stemming from soul loss, the violation of taboos, and/or the anger of the dead. Curing methods included interrogation about taboo adherence, trancelike communication with spirit helpers, and dramatic performance.

Nuclear families were loosely organized into local groups associated with geographical areas (-*miuts*). These groups occasionally came together as perhaps five small, fluid bands or subgroups: Kittegaryumiuts, Kupugmiuts, Kigirktarugmiuts, Nuvouigmiuts, and Avvagmiuts. The bands were also geographically identified. Informal or ad hoc village leaders (*isumataq*) were usually older men, with little formal authority and no power. They embodied Inuit values, such as generosity, and were also good hunters, perhaps especially good whalers.

Contact with neighboring Inuit groups may have influenced the development of a somewhat stronger village leadership structure, including inheritance in the male line, around the time of contact. The Inuvialuit population was generally less dispersed than that of other Inuit groups. Their largest summer village, for instance, contained up to 1,000 people.

Descent was bilateral. Intermarriage was common among members of the five bands. People married simply by announcing their intentions, although infants were regularly betrothed. Men might have more than one wife, but most had only one. Divorce was easy to obtain. Some wife exchanges took place within defined partnerships between men; the relationship between a man and his partner's wife was considered a kind of marriage.

Infanticide was rare and, when practiced, usually directed against females. Children were highly valued and loved, especially males. Their names generally came from deceased relatives and were bestowed by shamans. Male adolescents had some teeth filed down and their cheeks and earlobes pierced. The sick or aged were sometimes abandoned, especially in times of scarcity. Corpses were not removed from houses through the door but rather through a specially made hole in the wall. They were then placed on the ground and covered with driftwood.

Tensions were relieved through games, through duels of drums and songs, in which the competing people tried to outdo each other in parody, and through "joking" relationships. Ostracism and even death were reserved for the most serious cases of socially inappropriate behavior, such as murder, wife stealing, and theft. Relations between the Inuvialuits and their Indian neighbors were both cordial, including intermarriage, and hostile.

The typical winter dwelling was a semiexcavated, rectangular, turf-covered, log-frame house. Each one held about three families. Sleeping chambers were appended, giving the structure a cross shape. Each family had a separate cooking area as well. Entry was via an underground tunnel. Houses were named. Windows or skylights were made of gut. Storage was located along the tunnel or in niches inside.

The people occasionally used temporary domed snow houses in the winter, mainly when traveling. Entry was gained through a door. There were some larger open-roofed sod-and-wood houses as well for ceremonial purposes, although these may reflect a later Inupiat influence. Conical caribou skin tents used in the summer were strengthened by a hoop lashed to the frame about six feet from the ground. Also, each village had a men's house (*kashim*) up to sixty feet long.

The Inuvialuits were nomadic hunters. The most important game animals were seals and baleen whales, especially beluga. Whales were hunted communally by driving up to 200 of them into shallow water with kayaks. Seals were netted on the edges of ice floes and hunted at their breathing holes in the winter.

The people also hunted caribou, moose, mountain sheep, hares, bears, musk ox, muskrat, beaver, and birds. Fishing took place especially in the spring and summer, mainly for whitefish and herring. Other foods included berries and some roots. People generally drank water or stock.

Goods were exchanged with the Kutchin and Hare Indians as well as with the Inupiats to the west. Individual formal trade partnerships were a part of this process. The people exported wood, which they procured in the southern part of their territory. Sewn clothing and carved wooden and ivory figurines were developed to artistic levels. One- or two-person kayaks were used mostly for sea mammal hunting. Several men hunted whales in umiaks, or large open boats covered with beluga skin. Overland travel was facilitated by the use of wooden dogsleds with iced-over runners of bone or antler.

Clothing consisted mainly of sewn caribou skins. Men and women wore two layers, the under layer with the hair turned in and the outer layer with the hair turned out. Coats and pants were trimmed with fur, as were parka hoods. Men's hoods were made from caribou or wolf-head skin, the latter with the ears left on. Women's parkas were knee length and double flapped, as opposed to mens', which ended at the hip. Women's parka hoods were also made bigger to cover their double bun–shaped hairstyles. Other clothing included caribou leg boots with beluga skin soles and caribou mittens.

In the summer, most people wore old inner garments with the hair turned out. Men who had killed a bear wore pieces of stone or ivory through their cheeks. Most men also wore polished stone or ivory labrets in their lips. Both sexes wore ornaments in pierced ears and nasal septa. Both men and women applied small tattoos on their faces and bodies. Children who had reached puberty had their teeth filed down; boys' cheeks and ears were pierced as well.

The people offered a generally friendly reception when they first met non-Native traders in the late eighteenth and early nineteenth centuries. However, relations soon soured. Missionaries were active in the region by the midnineteenth century, although few Inuvialuits accepted Christianity before 1900.

The heyday of the whaling period began in 1888, when some 1,000 non-Native whalers wintered near the Mackenzie River; the region soon became a trade center as well as a haven for "frontier living" that included alcohol abuse, sexual promiscuity, and death from firearms. Traditional life declined sharply, as did the population, which was further beset by a host of hitherto unknown diseases such as scarlet fever, syphilis, smallpox, and influenza. By 1920 the Inuvialuits had all but disappeared from the Yukon. Most modern Inuvialuits are descended from Inupiat groups who moved east from Alaska about that time. Indians and non-Natives moved in as well.

The far north took on strategic importance during the Cold War. In 1954, the federal Department of Northern Affairs and Natural Resources encouraged the Inuits to abandon their nomadic life. The department oversaw the construction of housing developments, schools, and clinics. Local political decisions were made by a community council subject to non-Native approval and review. In 1959, the "government" town of Inuvik was founded as an administrative center.

Inuits generally found only unskilled and menial work. They also survived through dependence on government payments. With radical diet changes, the adoption of a sedentary life, and the appearance of drugs and alcohol, health declined markedly. The Committee for Original People's Entitlement (COPE), founded in 1969, soon became the political voice of the Inuvialuits. Oil and gas deposits were found in the Beaufort Sea in the 1970s.

The people never abandoned their land, which is still central to their identity. Traditional and modern coexist, sometimes uneasily, for many Inuits. Although people use television (there is even radio and television programming in Inuktitut), snowmobiles, and manufactured items, women also carry babies in the traditional hooded parkas, chew caribou skin to make it soft, and use the semilunar knives to cut seal meat. Full-time doctors are rare in the communities. Housing is often of poor quality. Most people are Christians. Culturally, although many stabilizing patterns of traditional culture have been destroyed, many remain. Many people live as members of extended families.

Politically, community councils have gained considerably more autonomy over the past generation. There is also a significant Inuit presence in the Northwest Territories legislative assembly and some presence at the federal level. The disastrous effects of government-run schools have been mitigated to some degree by local control of education, including more culturally relevant curricula in schools. Many people still speak Inuktitut, which is also taught in most schools, especially in the earlier grades.

See also Boarding Schools, United States and Canada; Canada, Indian Policies of; Department of Indian Affairs and Northern Development; Hudson's Bay Company; Language and Language Renewal; Trade.

Netsilik

"Netsilik" means "People of the Seal" or "there are seals." (*See also* Inuit, Copper.) Netsilik territory, entirely within the Arctic Circle, is north of Hudson Bay, especially from Committee Bay in the east to Victoria Strait in the west, north to Bellot Strait, and south to Garry Lake. The sea begins to freeze as early as September, and the thaw is generally not completed until the end of July. The summer tundra

remains wet, because permafrost not far below the surface prevents drainage. Many Netsilik Inuits still live in this area of the central Arctic, known as Kitik-meot. The Netsilik population numbered roughly 500 in the late nineteenth century. The Native language is a dialect of Inuit-Inupiaq (Inuktitut), a member of the Eskaleut language family.

Overarching, generative, female-identified deities or spirits were associated with natural forces and cycles. Another level of spirit entities consisted of human and animal souls or spirits. Most religious activities were designed to propitiate the spirits of game animals specifically and potentially dangerous supernatural forces in general. Yet another group of supernatural beings was made up of numerous monsters and ghosts. Hunting and life cycle events, particularly childbirth and death, were the basis of most taboos.

Magic spells, generally applicable to a single subject, were personal and secret, and they could be purchased or transmitted between generations. Souls were considered to be immortal. Those of people who died violently, including by their own hand, as well as those of good hunters and beautifully tattooed women were able to inhabit a paradise. The souls of lazy hunters and women without tattoos went to a sad and hungry place.

Male and female shamans (*angakok*) provided religious leadership by virtue of their connection with personal guardian spirits. They led group religious activities. They could also cure disease, see into the future (including such things as the location of game), and harm people.

Nuclear families, loosely combined into extended families or local groups, were associated with geographical areas (*-miuts*). Local group leaders (*isumataq*) were usually older men with little formal authority and no power. Leaders embodied Inuit values, such as generosity, and were also good hunters. Older women played a leadership role in food distribution.

Local groups occasionally traveled together as fluid hunting regional bands. The bands were also geographically identified, and they included Arvertormiuts, Arviligjuarmiuts, Ilivilermiuts, Kitdlinermiuts, Kungmiuts, Netsilingmiuts, and Qegertarmiuts.

Although the nuclear family was the basic social unit, survival required the regular association of extended families and, in fact, the existence of numerous complex relationships. For instance, although the people were generally monogamous, wives were exchanged within various defined male partnerships, such as song partnerships; these relationships were considered a kind of marriage. The precise workings of wife (and husband) exchange were varied and ranged from short to long (or even permanent) and from willing to acrimonious.

Young women married around age fourteen or fifteen, boys around age twenty. People married simply by announcing their intentions, although infants and even fetuses were regularly betrothed. Women usually moved in with the husband's household. Men might have more than one wife, but most had only one. Divorce was easy to obtain. In general, the Netsiliks enjoyed a high degree of sexual freedom. There was some in-law avoidance.

Infanticide was usually practiced against females, but the high rate of adult male mortality somewhat evened the gender balance. Children were highly valued and loved, especially males, and adoption was common. The sick or aged were sometimes abandoned, especially in times of scarcity. Suicide for those and other reasons, such as a general sense of insecurity or perceived weakness, was a regular occurrence. Corpses were abandoned, because the camp generally moved after a death. No work, including hunting, could be done within several days following a death.

Food was generally shared within the extended family or local group. In cases of collaborative hunting, such as winter sealing, food was shared according to precise rules. Strangers or people without direct relatives were feared and might be summarily killed.

Villages of domed snow houses contained about fifty people but could hold up to 100. Entry to the houses was gained through a tunnel that kept the warm air inside. Windows were made of freshwater ice. Two related nuclear families generally occupied a snow house, which had more than one room and even a porch. The average house size was between nine and fifteen feet in diameter, although sizes varied widely. People slept on raised packed snow platforms covered with skins and furs.

Other structures included large ceremonial or dance snow houses, a platform for storing dog feed, and a toilet room or outhouse. Some groups built ice houses in the fall. In the spring, people used a combination snow house and skin tent, which were snow houses with a skin roof. Summer dwellings were conical sealskin tents held down by stones.

The Netsiliks were nomadic hunters. The most important game animals were seals, which were hunted communally at their breathing holes in the

winter and stalked in the spring. A hunter might have to stand motionless next to a breathing hole for hours in the dark and bitter cold. The people also hunted caribou, polar bear, and musk ox (in the east). Smaller animals included fox and squirrel. Meat was eaten raw, frozen, or, preferably, cooked. Large animals' stomach contents were eaten as well.

Fishing, particularly for salmon trout (Arctic char) and lake trout, occurred mainly in the summer and autumn, individually or communally at inland weirs. Fish was mainly eaten raw, although it might be boiled or dried and cached for the winter. Other food resources included fowl, gulls, and some berries. In the winter, people drank melted old sea ice, which loses its salinity after a year or so. Blood was another common drink.

Womens' semilunar knives were used mainly for skin preparation and fish cleaning. Men used antler knives to cut snow blocks for houses and to butcher caribou. Hunting equipment included various harpoons, spears, the bow and arrow, breathing hole finders and protectors, down or horn seal motion indicators (also used for breathing hole sealing), and other hunting equipment. Fish were caught with hooks, spears, prongs, weirs, and traps.

Netsiliks engaged in some trade with Iglulik bands. Western groups traded with their neighbors for items such as pots and lamps. Some groups imported copper and driftwood from the Copper Inuits and wood from the Caribou Inuits. Some people carved fine wooden and ivory figurines. Men hunted seals and caribou from long, slender, one-person kayaks covered with sealskin. Umiaks were larger, skin-covered open boats. There were some wooden dogsleds, whose runners were covered with ice-coated peat or made of fish wrapped in sealskin. Polar bearskins were also used for sleds, especially in the east and in spring when the snow deteriorated.

Men skinned the caribou, and women did most of the hide preparation and sewed the clothing. They also prepared sealskins for summer clothing as well as boots and mittens. About twenty caribou skins were needed to outfit a family of four.

Mens' coats had short, fringed flaps, and womens' coats had long wide flaps. All were two-layered and had pointed hoods. The hair of the inner layer was turned in, and that of the outer layer was turned out. The outer coat had a sewn-in hood, although for women both layers had extra large shoulders and sewn-in hoods to fit over babies, who were carried in a pouch at the back of a coat.

Four layers of caribou fur socks protected people's feet in the winter. Men wore knee-length, two-layered pants; women made do with one layer. All outer coats (parkas) and womens' pants might be decorated with white fur. Women often braided their hair around two sticks. They also tattooed their faces and limbs. Childrens' clothing was often a one-piece suit.

Netsiliks are descended from the ancient Thule culture. In about 1830 they encountered non-Natives looking for the northwest passage. Still, contact with non-Natives remained only sporadic until the early twentieth century. About that time, the people obtained firearms from the neighboring Igluliks. More productive hunting enabled them to keep more dogs, changing their migration and subsistence patterns.

The establishment of trading posts in their territory around 1920 heralded the economic switch to white fox fur trapping and trade for additional items of non-Native manufacture, such as woolen clothing, tobacco, steel traps, fishing nets, canoes (which replaced kayaks), tea, and canvas tents. Game killed with rifles came to belong to the hunter, a practice that eroded and ultimately destroyed traditional exchange.

Missions established in the 1930s soon became permanent settlements. The Netsiliks quickly accepted Christianity (Anglicanism and Catholicism), ending the taboo system and shamanic practices, not to mention infanticide and other social practices. The authority of traders, missionaries, and eventually the Royal Canadian Mounted Police (RCMP) undermined traditional leadership, such as it was.

The far north took on strategic importance during the Cold War, about the same time that vast mineral reserves became known and technologically possible to exploit. In 1954, the federal Department of Northern Affairs and Natural Resources began a program of population consolidation and acculturation. Coastal settlements were abandoned, and all people moved to one of three towns. The department oversaw the construction of housing developments, schools, and a general infrastructure. Local political decisions were made by a community council subject to non-Native approval and review. The Natives were offered generally unskilled employment. With radical diet changes, the adoption of a sedentary life, and the appearance of drugs and alcohol, their health declined markedly.

In 1993, the Tungavik Federation of Nunavut (TFN), an outgrowth of the Inuit Tapirisat of Canada (ITC), signed an agreement with Canada providing for the establishment in 1999 of the new, mostly Inuit, territory of Nunuvut on roughly 36,000 square kilometers of land, including Kitikmeot.

The people never abandoned their land, which is still central to their identity. Traditional and modern coexist, sometimes uneasily, for many Inuits. Although people use television (there is even radio and television programming in Inuktitut), snowmobiles, and manufactured items, women also carry babies in the traditional hooded parkas, chew caribou skin to make it soft, and use the semilunar knives to cut seal meat. Full-time doctors are rare in the communities. Housing is often of poor quality. Most people are Christians. Culturally, although many stabilizing patterns of traditional culture have been destroyed, many remain. Many people live as members of extended families.

Politically, community councils have gained considerably more autonomy over the past decade or two. There is also a significant Inuit presence in the Northwest Territories legislative assembly and some presence at the federal level. The disastrous effects of government-run schools have been mitigated to some degree by local control of education, including more culturally relevant curricula in schools. Many people still speak Inuktitut, which is also taught in most schools, especially in the earlier grades.

See also Boarding Schools, United States and Canada; Canada, Indian Policies of; Department of Indian Affairs and Northern Development; Trade.

Unangan

"Unangan" means "People." The Unangans were formerly and are occasionally known as Aleuts, possibly meaning "island" in a Siberian language. The Unangans consisted of perhaps nine named subdivisions, each of which spoke an eastern, a central, or a western dialect. Unangan territory included the Pribilof, Shumagin, and Aleutian (west toward the International Date Line) Islands and the extreme west of the Alaska Peninsula. Fog and wind, perhaps more than anything else, characterized the climate. In contrast to most of the Arctic region, the ocean remains ice free year-round. In the early eighteenth

century, the Unangan population was between 16,000 and 20,000 people, although there may have been fewer. Unangans spoke three dialects of Aleut, a member of the Eskaleut language family.

The people may have recognized a generative deity associated with the sun that had overall responsibility for souls as well as hunting success. They also recognized good and evil spirits, including animal spirits. These were the supernatural beings that influenced people's lives on a day-to-day basis. Adult men made offerings to the spirits at special sacred places and used a number of charms, talismans, and amulets for protection. They also undertook spirit dances, although mainly to intimidate women and children into proper behavior.

Souls were said to migrate among three worlds: earth, an upper sphere, and a lower sphere. Shamans mediated between the material and spiritual worlds. Their vocations were considered to be predetermined; that is, they did not seek a shamanic career. They had the usual responsibilities concerning hunting, weather, and curing.

Various winter masked dances and ceremonies were designed to propitiate the spirits. Perhaps the major ceremony was a memorial feast held forty days following a death. Death was an important rite of passage. Some groups mummified dead bodies to preserve the person's spiritual power. A whaler might even remove a piece of the mummy for assistance, but this custom was also considered potentially dangerous.

The eldest man usually led an independent house group, although collectively all household leaders functioned as a council. One house group in a village was generally considered first among equals, the head of that group functioning as village chief if he merited the position. These leaders had little or no coercive power but mainly coordinated decision making over issues of war and peace and camp moves. They might become wealthy in part from receiving a share of their subordinates' catch (wealth consisted not only of furs and skins but also of dentalium shells, amber, and slaves). Their position could be inherited in the male line. In addition, there were also special leaders known as strong men, who received special training.

Among the Unangans, descent was probably matrilineal. Their class structure was probably derived from Northwest Coast cultures. The three hereditary classes were wealthy people (chiefs and nobles), commoners, and a small number of slaves, mainly women. The first two groups were usually

related. Harmony, patience, and hard work were key values. Speech was judicious in nature, and silence was generally respected.

Villages claimed certain subsistence areas and evicted or attacked trespassers. Numerous formal partnerships between men and women served to bind the community together. Berdaches were men who lived and worked as women. Women sewed and processed and prepared food. Truly incorrigible people might be put to death upon agreement by the village elders.

Boys moved from their mother's to their maternal uncle's home in midchildhood. The uncle took over primary responsibility for raising the boy, with the father playing more of a supporting role. Boys were strengthened, toughened, and rigorously trained from a very early age for the life of a kayak hunter. When a girl began menstruating, she was confined for forty days, during which time her joints were bound, in theory so that they would not ache in her old age. She was also subject to a number of food and behavioral restrictions and admonishments and was allowed to cure minor illness, the people believing that she possessed special curative powers during these times.

Girls could marry even before they reached puberty, but boys were expected to wait until they were at least eighteen, that is, when they were capable providers. Most marriages were monogamous, except that particularly wealthy men might have more than one wife. Men performed a one- or two-year bride service. Cross cousins (children of a mother's brothers or a father's sisters) were considered potential, even preferred, spouses. Divorce was rare.

Some men paddled out to sea at the end of their lives, never to return. In fact, suicide tended to be seen in a positive light for a number of reasons. The insides of most corpses were removed and replaced with grass. Following this procedure, bodies would remain in the house, either in a corner or in a cradle over the bed, for up to several months. They were eventually buried in a flexed position in the house, either under the floor or within the walls. Central and eastern people also mummified some corpses, caching the mummies in warm, dry, volcanic caves. Widows and widowers were subject to a period of special behavioral restrictions, including some joint binding.

Typical villages contained roughly 200 people, although up to 2,000 people may have populated some eastern communities. Rectangular, semiexcavated houses (barabara) were framed with driftwood and whalebone, covered with matting and turf. Sizes varied widely. The average may have been about thirty-five to sixty feet long by about fifteen to thirty feet wide. These houses held perhaps forty people or several nuclear families related through the male line. The largest houses may have been up to 240 feet long by forty feet wide, holding up to 150 people.

Sleeping compartments separated by grass mats ringed a large central room. Mats also served as flooring. Entry was gained via a ladder placed through an opening in the roof. Cooking was generally outside the house. Large houses also served as dance halls.

Depending on location, the people ate mainly sea lions, but also seals, sea otter, octopus, and some walrus. Most sea mammals were hunted by men in kayaks. There was also some highly ritualized whaling, especially in the west. Other types of food included large and small game on the eastern islands and mainland. Important fish species included cod, flounder, halibut, herring, trout, and salmon. People ate birds, fowl, and their eggs, the latter collected mainly by climbing up or down steep cliffs. They also gathered seaweed, shellfish, roots, and berries, depending on location. Unangans tended to eat much of their food raw, although there was some pit cooking.

Sea mammals were harpooned or clubbed. Atlatls helped give velocity to a harpoon throw. Eastern people hunted large game with the bow and arrow. Whale lances may have had poisonous tips. Most tools were made from stone and bone. Other important material items included sewn skin bags and pouches, some wooden buckets and bowls, sea lion stomach containers, tambourine drums, and spruce root and grass baskets. Stone lamps burned sea lion blubber for light and heat. Cordage came from braided kelp or sea lion sinew. The people started fires with a wooden drill and flint sparks on sulphur and bird down. A highly developed counting system allowed them to reckon in five figures.

Unangnan people traded both goods and ideas with Northwest Coast groups, such as the Tlingits and Haidas, as well as with the Yup'ik and Alutiiq peoples. Exports included baskets, sea products, and walrus ivory. The people imported shells, slaves, blankets, and hides.

Art objects included carved wooden dancing masks and decorative bags. Women wove fine spruce root and grass baskets and decorated mats with geometric designs. Ivory carvings of the great creative

spirit were hung from ceiling beams in houses, and other objects were decorated with ivory carvings as well. The Unangans were also known for their painted wooden hats. Men hunted in one- or possibly two-person kayaks. Larger skin-covered open boats were used for travel and trade but not for whaling.

Women and men wore long parkas of sea otter or bird skin (men wore only the latter material). The women's version had no hood, only a collar. Men also wore waterproof slickers made of sewn sea lion gut, esophagus, or other such material. Particularly in the east, sealskin boots had soles of sea lion flippers. Boots were less common in the west. Men also wore wooden visors, painted and decorated with sea lion whiskers. They wore painted conical wooden hats on ceremonial occasions. Other ceremonial clothing was made of colorful puffin skins. Both sexes wore labrets of various materials. They tattooed their faces and hands and wore bone or ivory nose pins.

The Unangans fought their Inuit neighbors, especially the Alutiiqs, as well as among themselves (especially those who spoke different dialects). Small parties often launched raids for women and children slaves or to avenge past wrongs. Slain enemies were often dismembered, in the belief that an intact body, though dead, could still be dangerous. Prisoners might be tortured. On the other hand, high-status captives might be held for ransom or used as slaves.

Ancestors of the Unangans probably moved east and then south across the Bering Land Bridge and then west from western Alaska to arrive in their historical location, where people have lived for at least 7,000 years. Direct cultural relationships have been established to people living in the region as long ago as 4,000 years.

The Russians, arriving in the 1740s, quickly recognized the value of sea otter and other pelts. For about a generation, they tried to compel the Unangans to hunt for them, mainly by taking hostages and threatening death. The Natives resisted, and there was much bloodshed during that time. However, after losing between a third and half of their total population, they gave up the struggle and did the Russians' bidding. Unangan men were forced to hunt sea mammals from Alaska to southern California for the Russian-American company. Large-scale population movements date from that period and lasted well into the twentieth century.

The strong influence of Russian culture dates from that period and includes conversion to the Russian Orthodox Church by the early nineteenth century, when the worst of the Russian excesses ended. Other significant Russian influences include metal tools, steam baths, and larger kayaks, with sails. A Unangan orthography was created about that time, allowing the people to read and write in their own language.

Unangan hunters had come into increasing conflict with their Inuit and Indian neighbors as they were forced to go farther and farther afield for pelts. By the early nineteenth century, disease as well as warfare had diminished their population by about 80 percent. Survivors were consolidated onto sixteen islands in 1831, but, by that time, Unangan culture had suffered a near fatal blow.

The Russians left and the Americans took over around 1867, increasing fur hunting and driving the sea otter practically to extinction. The town of Unalaska had become an important commercial center by 1890. Fox trapping and canneries had become important to the local economy by the early twentieth century. Much of the Aleutian chain was designated as a national park in 1913. Some religious and government schools were opened in the early to midtwentieth century. Still, the people endured high tuberculosis rates in the 1920s through the 1940s, and there were few, if any, village doctors.

The Japanese attacked the Aleutian Islands during World War II, capturing residents of Attu. The United States removed almost all Unangans west of Unimak Island, interning them in camps in southeast Alaska. Many people, especially elders who normally transmitted cultural beliefs and practices to the young, died during that period owing to the poor conditions in the camps. When the people returned home after the war, they found that many of their homes and possessions had been destroyed. As a result, many villages were abandoned.

The commercial fishing and cash economy grew sharply after the war. Most Unangans worked at the lowest levels of the economy. By then, Unangan children were attending the Bureau of Indian Affairs high school in Sitka and Anchorage. Alaska received statehood in 1958. Nine years later, the Native people founded the Alaska Federation of Natives (AFN) and the Aleut League. Unangans were included in the 1971 Alaska Native Claims Settlement Act (ANCSA), after initial rejection because of their high percentage of Russian blood.

Most Unangans are of the Russian Orthodox faith. Most also live in wood-frame houses. There is

a considerable degree of intermarriage with non-Unangans. The position of the corporations vis-à-vis the tribes has made for bitter interfamily and inter-village divisions. Political sovereignty remains a major goal for most people. Some public schools feature courses in the Unangan language.

> *See also* Alaska Native Claims Settlement Act; Basketry; Russians, in the Arctic/Northwest; Trade.

Yup'ik

"Yup'ik" means "Real People." The Yup'ik people were formerly known as Nunivak Inuits (or Eskimos), Saint Lawrence Island Eskimos, West Alaska Eskimos, South Alaska Eskimos, and Southwest Alaska Eskimos. They are also known as Bering Sea Yuits and, with the Alutiit (Pacific Eskimos), simply as Yuits. The Saint Lawrence Islanders were culturally similar to Siberian Eskimos. (*See also* Alutiiq.)

Yup'ik territory was located in southwestern Alaska, between Bristol Bay and Norton Sound, including Nunivak and Saint Lawrence Islands. The early nineteenth-century Yup'ik population was between about 15,000 and 18,000. The people spoke the Yuk or Central Alaskan Yup'ik (including Saint Lawrence Island or Central Siberian Yup'ik) branch of Yup'ik. With Inuit-Inupiaq (Inuktitut), Yup'ik (or Western Eskimo) constitutes the Eskimo division of the Eskaleut language family.

Religious belief and practice were based on the conception of spiritual entities found in nature and needing to be treated with respect. Most rituals focused on this belief, such as those that showed respect to an animal just killed. It was also the basis of most taboos as well as related objects and songs.

Souls were said to be reincarnated through naming. Spirits not yet reincarnated also needed to be treated with respect lest they cause harm. In some areas, secret, spirit-based knowledge, objects, and songs, all thought to bring success in hunting, were passed on from father to son. The people also believed in various nonhuman, nonanimal supernatural beings.

Male and female shamans (*angakok*) provided religious leadership by virtue of their connection with guardian spirits. They led group religious activities. They could also cure disease and see into the future.

Illness was thought to be due to soul loss and/or the violation of taboos. Professional curing methods included interrogation about taboo adherence, trance-like communication with spiritual helpers, extraction (such as sucking), and dramatic performance, including masked dances. Shamans were relatively powerful people, in part owing to their ability to use their spiritual power to harm people.

The Messenger Feast, a major ceremony, included dancing and gift exchange between two villages. The Saint Lawrence Islanders held a spring whaling ceremony. When the successful crew returned, the umiak owner's wife offered the whale a drink of water as a token of respect. Then followed another feast and a thanksgiving ceremony. Some groups held memorial feasts about a year following a death.

In general, Yup'iks living along the Bering Sea had their main ceremonial season in the winter and early spring. The festivities featured spirit masks and dances. The Bladder Feast was another important ceremony dedicated to respect for animals, in this case, seals. This festival also underscored the ritual sexual division in society.

Nuclear families were loosely organized into extended families or local groups associated with geographical areas (-*miuts*). Local groups on the mainland occasionally came together as perhaps seven small, fluid subgroups or bands. From north to south, they were Kuigpagmiuts, Maarmiuts, Kayaligmiuts, Kukquqvagmiuts, Kiatagmiuts, Tuyuryarmiuts, and Aglurmiuts. Older men, with little formal authority and no power, led *kashim* (men's houses) and kin groups (generally the same as villages on Saint Lawrence Island). These leaders generally embodied Inuit values, such as generosity, and were also good hunters.

The family was the most important economic and political unit. Descent was bilateral, except patrilineal on Saint Lawrence Island. There, secret songs, ceremonies, house ownership, and hunting group membership were passed through patrilineal clans and lineages. Status was formally ranked within the *kashim* and depended on hunting and leadership skills.

People married simply by announcing their intentions, although infants were regularly betrothed. Men might have more than one wife, but most had only one. Divorce was easy to obtain. Both men and women remained respectful and distant toward their in-laws. Wife exchange was a part of

certain defined male partnerships, such as mutual aid, "joking," and trade. Some of these relationships were inheritable. The alliance between the wife and the exchanged husband was considered a kind of marriage. Formal female partnerships existed as well.

Infanticide was rare and usually practiced against females. Children were highly valued and loved, especially males, and adoption was common. Life cycle events, such as berry picking and grass gathering by girls and seal killing by boys, were recognized by the community. Childbirth, girls' puberty, and death were the occasions for special taboos.

The sick or aged were sometimes abandoned, especially in times of scarcity. Corpses were generally removed through an alternate exit (not the door) and left on the ground with certain grave goods. Along the Bering Sea, some groups placed their dead in painted wooden coffins and erected carved wooden memorial poles to keep their spirits at bay. The mourning period generally lasted four or five days, during which time activities, including hunting, were severely restricted.

Work was fairly gender specific. Women made food and clothing and cared for children; men fished and hunted land animals. Use of a person's real name was generally avoided, perhaps for religious reasons. Tensions were relieved through games, through duels of drums and songs, in which the competing people tried to outdo each other in parody, and through "joking" relationships. Ostracism and even death were reserved for the most serious cases of socially inappropriate behavior.

The people created larger settlements in the winter to take advantage of group subsistence activities. Villages ranged in size from just two to more than a dozen houses, plus one or more *kashim* and storehouses.

There were several kinds of dwellings throughout the area, depending on location. Houses were generally semiexcavated, roughly twelve to fifteen feet by fifteen feet and made of sod, grass, and/or bark over wooden posts and beams. They were mainly inhabited by related women and children. Some might have plank walls with benches placed along them. Entry was via an anteroom connected to the main room by an underground tunnel. A hearth and cooking area stood at one end of the room, and raised sleeping platforms were at the other end. Windows were often made of sewn fish skins.

Except on Saint Lawrence Island, men worked, bathed, slept, and ate in *kashim*, which were also used as ceremonial houses, to which women delivered the food. Political decisions were made there as well. Some groups built cut-sod spring camp houses, about 100 square feet in size. Skin tents were generally the norm in the summer.

Yup'ik people were nomadic hunters with either a land or a sea orientation, although most people also exploited the region opposite their own. The most important game animals were seals, walrus (especially on Saint Lawrence and Nunivak Islands), and whales. Men hunted seals at their breathing holes in the winter. On Nunivak, men hunted them from kayaks in spring and with nets under shore ice in the fall. Some groups also hunted caribou (especially away from the coast and major rivers and on Nunivak Island until about 1900) and moose, especially in the fall.

Fish, especially salmon, trout, smelt, and whitefish, was the most important dietary item in many locations and was generally taken in all seasons but the winter. Fish were especially important inland, with marine mammals more important on the coasts and islands. Shellfish were gathered where possible. Birds and fowl, such as ptarmigan, were speared or netted and their eggs gathered. Some groups were able to obtain berries, roots, and greens.

Most tools were fashioned from caribou antlers as well as stone, bone, and driftwood (on Saint Lawrence and Nunivak Islands, many items were made from walrus parts). Men and women had their own specialty stone knives. People cooked in pottery pots and burned seal or walrus oil in saucer-shaped pottery lamps. They carved wooden trays, boxes, dishes, spoons, and other objects.

Various kinds of containers were made out of gut, wood, and clay. Saint Lawrence Islanders often used baleen as a raw material. Some groups made twined and coiled baskets of grasses and birchbark. In fact, grass was used extensively for items such as mats, baskets, socks, and rope, although some cordage also came from beluga sinew. The ceremonial tambourine drum was made of seal gut stretched over a wooden frame.

The people made finely carved wooden and ivory figurines. The Yup'iks engaged in a general coastal–interior interregional trade, including trade with the Unangan and Northwest Coast peoples. Saint Lawrence Island people traditionally traded and otherwise interacted with those from Siberia.

Men hunted from one- or two-person sealskin-covered kayaks. Umiaks were larger, skin-covered open boats; several men could hunt whales or walrus in these. They were also used for trade voyages. Wooden sleds were used for overland winter travel. Some interior groups also used canoes.

Women made most clothing of caribou and sealskin. Yup'ik clothing tended to fit relatively loosely. Some groups used the skins of other animals, such as marmot and muskrat, as well as bird and even fish skins. Most people wore long hooded parkas and inner shirts and pants. Women's parkas were often shorter and featured front and rear flaps. Other items included sealskin (some groups used salmon skin) boots and mittens, skin or grass socks, fish skin parkas and pants in the summer, waterproof gut raincoats, and wooden snow goggles.

Men on Saint Lawrence Island wore distinctive hairdos in which they shaved the tops of their heads but retained a circle of hair around the forehead. Women generally tattooed three lines on their chins. Personal ornaments included labrets and other items of walrus and bird parts.

People have lived on Nunivak Island since at least 150 BCE, making pottery and using mainly stone tools. The mainland has been inhabited for at least 4,000 years, with cultural continuity since about 300 BCE.

Most groups avoided direct contact with non-Natives until Russian traders established trading posts in Yup'ik territory, generally in the early nineteenth century. The Russians exchanged clothing, metal tools, and beads for beaver pelts. The Inuits began spending more time trapping beaver and less time on subsistence activities, eventually becoming dependent on the posts even for food. In general, Russian Orthodox missionaries followed the early traders. Most Inuits had accepted Christianity by the 1860s.

This process was uneven throughout the region. Saint Lawrence Island people first met non-Natives in the 1850s, whereas people on the Yukon Delta did not do so until the late nineteenth century. About one thousand people (roughly two-thirds of the total population) of Saint Lawrence Island died in 1878 from a combination of natural causes combined with a high incidence of alcohol abuse. Nunivak Island was similarly insulated (contact occurred in 1821 but perhaps not again until 1874), in part owing to the shallowness of the surrounding sea. The first trading post, which included a reindeer herd, was established there in 1920; missionaries and schools dated from about the 1930s. The people experienced various epidemics throughout the early to midtwentieth century.

Little changed with the sale of Alaska to the United States until the advent of commercial fishing in Bristol Bay in the 1880s. Moravian missionaries appeared on the Kuskokwim River in 1885; those of other sects soon followed. Like most missionary schools, theirs forbade children to speak their Native language. In an effort to undermine the traditional lifestyle, the U.S. government introduced reindeer to the region around 1900.

In addition to commercial fishing, fox hunting for the fur trade plus the manufacture of baleen and carved ivory objects formed the basis of a local cash economy from the late nineteenth century through the early twentieth century. Nunivak Islanders experienced the full cash economy only after World War II. By then the people had incorporated under the Indian Reorganization Act (IRA). The Bureau of Indian Affairs managed their reindeer herd.

The far north took on strategic importance during the Cold War, about the same time that mineral reserves became known and technologically possible to exploit. Saint Lawrence Island became exposed to mainland life and tied to Alaska only after military installations were built there in the 1950s. Inuits generally found only unskilled menial labor. With radical diet changes, the adoption of a sedentary life, and the appearance of drugs and alcohol, health declined markedly. The Yukon Kuskokwim Health Corporation serves the people's health needs with culturally appropriate programs and care.

The Alaska Native Claims Settlement Act (ANCSA) was passed in 1971. Bilingual education has been in force since the 1970s, and most Yup'ik people still speak the Native language. Some communities have been more severely disrupted and are consequently less cohesive than others. Most Saint Lawrence Islanders had been converted to Christianity by the midtwentieth century, although many of the old ideas still resonate for the people.

The issue of subsistence hunting rights remains very important to the Yup'iks. Chignik area villages share certain concerns, such as the decline of the local caribou herd, possibly owing to excess sport hunting, and the threat to subsistence activities from industrial development. Togiak area villages seek to

conduct a permanent annual walrus hunt on Round Island, and they seek funds to maintain their reindeer herd. They are also trying to prevent the desecration of ancient burial sites.

Local concerns in the Iliamna area include road improvement, bridge construction, and air links. Concerns in the Kvichak Bay area include the maintenance of subsistence fishing rights, the use and contamination cleanup of the former air force base site, the construction and management of a visitor center at Katmai National Park, and the decline of the local caribou herd. Issues in the Nushagak Bay area include the possible formation of a Nuchagak and Togiak area borough, land allotments within Wood-Tikchik State Park, and the proper management of the local caribou herd.

See also Alaska Native Claims Settlement Act; Alcoholism and Substance Abuse; Russians, in the Arctic/Northwest.

Discontinued Indian Mascots, 1969–2002

Date	School	Change in Mascot or Team Name
1969	Dartmouth College (New Hampshire)	Drops nickname "Indians" in favor of "Big Green."
1969	Oklahoma State University	Retires "Little Red" mascot.
1971	Marquette University (Wisconsin)	Abolishes mascot "Willie Wampum" and changes its Indian-related nicknames.
1971	Mankato State College (Minnesota)	Drops Indian caricature mascot.
1972	Stanford University (California)	Drops "Indians" team name and "Chief Lightfoot" mascot.
1979	Syracuse University (New York)	Drops "Saltine Warrior" mascot.
1988	Siena College (New York)	Changes team name from "Indians" to "Saints."
1988	St. John's University (New York)	Retires Indian mascot.
1988	St. Mary's College (Minnesota)	Drops nickname "Redmen" in favor of "Cardinals."
1988	Bradley University (Illinois)	Abandons costumed Indian mascot.
1989	Montclair State College (New Jersey)	Drops Indian nickname and mascot.
1991	Eastern Michigan University	Changes nickname from "Hurons" to "Eagles."
1993	Arvada High School (Colorado)	Drops "Redskins" nickname for "Reds."
1995	St. John's University (New York)	Changes nickname from "Redmen" to "Redstorm."
1996	University of Tennessee at Chattanooga	Abandons Chief Moccanooga mascot.
1996	Miami University (Ohio)	Drops "Redskins" nickname for "RedHawks."
1996	Adams State University (Colorado)	Changes Indian mascot to a grizzly bear.
1996	Syracuse AAA baseball team (New York)	Changes nickname from "Chiefs" to "Skychiefs."
1996	Hull Western Christian School (Iowa)	Retires Indian mascot and logo.
1997	Los Angeles Board of Education (California)	Eliminates Indian-related mascots from four schools.
1997	Akron AA baseball team (Ohio)	Replaces "Indians" nickname with "Aeros."
1998	Yakima College (Washington)	Retires race-related mascot.
1998	Southern Nazarene University (Oklahoma)	Abandons "Redskins" nickname in favor of "Crimson Storm."
1999	Oklahoma City University	Replaces "Chiefs" nickname with "Stars."
2000	Seattle University (Washington)	Changes "Chieftains" nickname to "Redhawks."
2001	Illinois Valley Community College	Changes "Apache" nickname to "Eagles."
2001	Southwestern College (California)	Changes "Apache" nickname to "Jaguars."
2002	Hendrix University (Arkansas)	Eliminates references to American Indians though retains "Warriors" nickname.

Source: Anti-defamation and Mascots. Available at:
http://www.ncai.org/ncai/resource/documents/governance/mastimeline.htm. Accessed June 21, 2006.

Indian Mascots

Professional Sports Teams with Indian Mascots

City	League	Team Name
Atlanta, Georgia	Major League Baseball	Braves
Chicago, Illinois	National Hockey League	Blackhawks
Cleveland, Ohio	Major League Baseball	Indians
Kansas City, Missouri	National Football League	Chiefs
Washington, D.C.	National Football League	Redskins

Colleges and Universities with Indian Mascots

School	State	Team Name
Alcorn State University	Mississippi	Braves
Arkansas State University	Arkansas	Indians
Bacone College	Oklahoma	Warriors
Bradley University	Illinois	Braves
California State University, Stanislaus	California	Warriors
Catawba College	North Carolina	Indians
Chowan College	North Carolina	Braves
Central Michigan University	Michigan	Chippewas
College of William & Mary	Virginia	Tribe
East Stroudsberg University	Pennsylvania	Warriors
Florida State University	Florida	Seminoles
Goldey-Beacom College	Delaware	Braves
Hendrix College	Arkansas	Warriors
Indiana Institute of Technology	Indiana	Warriors
Indiana University of Pennsylvania	Pennsylvania	Indians
Keuka College	New York	Warriors
Life Bible College	California	Warriors
McMurry University	Texas	Indians
Miami Christian University	Florida	Warriors
Morningside College	Iowa	Maroon Chiefs
Northeastern State University	Oklahoma	Redmen
Oklahoma City University	Oklahoma	Chiefs
Ottawa University	Kansas	Braves
Pembroke State University	North Carolina	Braves
San Bernardino Valley College	California	Indians
San Diego State University	California	Aztecs
Southeastern Oklahoma State University	Oklahoma	Savages
Southwestern College	Kansas	Moundbuilders
State University of West Georgia	Georgia	Braves
Sterling College	Kansas	Warriors
Trinity International University	Florida	Warriors
Union College	Nebraska	Warriors
University of Alaska, Fairbanks	Alaska	Nanooks
University of Illinois	Illinois	Fighting Illini
University of North Dakota	North Dakota	Fighting Sioux
University of Rio Grande	Ohio	Redmen
University of Utah	Utah	Utes
Westmont College	California	Warriors

Source: American Indian Sports Team Mascots, http://www.aistm.org/. Accesssed June 21, 2006.

Tribal Governments in the United States, 2006

Absentee-Shawnee Tribe of Indians of Oklahoma
    [Southern Plains)
2025 S. Gordon Cooper Drive
Shawnee, OK 74801

Agdaagux Tribe of King Cove (Alaska)
P.O. Box 249
King Cove, AK 99612

Agua Caliente Band of Cahuilla Indians (Pacific)
600 East Tahquitz Canyon Way
Palm Springs, CA 92262
Website: www.aguacaliente.org

Ak Chin Indian Community (Western)
42507 W. Peters & Nall Road
Maricopa, AZ 85239

Akiachak Native Community (Alaska)
P.O. Box 70
Akiachak, AK 99551-0070

Akiak Native Community (Alaska)
P.O. Box 52127
Akiak, AK 99552

Alabama-Coushatta Tribes of Texas (Southern
    Plains)
571 State Park Road 56
Livingston, TX 77351

Alabama-Quassarte Tribal Town (Eastern
    Oklahoma)
P.O. Box 187, 117 North Main
Wetumka, OK 74883

Aleut Community of St. Paul Island (Alaska)
P.O. Box 86
St. Paul Island, AK 99660

Algaaciq Native Village (Alaska)
P.O. Box 48
St. Mary's, AK 99658

Allakaket Village (Alaska)
P.O. Box 30
Allakaket, AK 99720

Alturas Rancheria (Pacific)
P.O. Box 340
Alturas, CA 96101

Angoon Community Association (Alaska)
P.O. Box 188
Angoon, AK 99820

Anvik Village (Alaska)
P.O. Box 10
Anvik, AK 99558

Apache Tribe of Oklahoma (Southern Plains)
P.O. Box 1220
Anadarko, OK 73005

Arctic Village Council (Gwich'in Artic Village)
    (Alaska)
P.O. Box 22069
Arctic Village, AK 99722

Aroostook Band of Micmacs (Northeast)
7 Northern Road
Presque Isle, ME 04769

Asa'carsarmiut Tribe (Alaska)
P.O. Box 32249
Mountain Village, AK 99632

Augustine Band of Mission Indians (Pacific)
P.O. Box 846
Coachella, CA 92236

Bad River Band of Lake Superior Tribe of Chippewa
    Indians (Midwest)
P.O. Box 39
Odanah, WI 54861

Barona Band of Mission Indians (Pacific)
1095 Barona Road
Lakeside, CA 92040
Website: www.baronatribe.org

Battle Mountain Band (Western)
37 Mountain View Drive, #C
Battle Mountain, NV 89820

Bay Mills Indian Community of Michigan
(Midwest)
12140 W. Lakeshore Drive
Brimley, MI 49715
Website: www.4baymills.com

Bear River Band of Rohnerville Rancheria (Pacific)
32 Bear River Road
Loleta, CA 95551

Beaver Village Council (Alaska)
P.O. Box 24029
Beaver, AK 99724

Benton Paiute Reservation (Pacific)
Star Route 4, Box 56-A
Benton, CA 93512

Berry Creek Rancheria (Pacific)
5 Tyme Way
Oroville, CA 95966

Big Lagoon Rancheria (Pacific)
P.O. Box 3060
Trinidad, CA 95570

Big Pine Reservation (Pacific)
P.O. Box 700, 825 S. Main Street
Big Pine, CA 93513

Big Sandy Rancheria (Pacific)
P.O. Box 337
Auberry, CA 93602

Big Valley Rancheria (Pacific)
2726 Mission Rancheria Road
Lakeport, CA 95453

Birch Creek Village (Alaska)
P.O. Box KBC
Fort Yukon, AK 99740

Bishop Tribe (Pacific)
50 Tu Su Lane
Bishop, CA 93515
Website: www.paiutepalace.com

Blackfeet Nation (Rocky Mountain)
P.O. Box 850
Browning, MT 59417
Website: www.blackfeetnation.com

Blue Lake Rancheria (Pacific)
P.O. Box 428
Blue Lake, CA 95525

Bois Forte Reservation Business Committee
(Midwest)
P.O. Box 16 5344 Lakeshore Drive
Nett Lake, MN 55772
Website: www.boisforte.com

Bridgeport Indian Colony (Pacific)
P.O. Box 37
Bridgeport, CA 93517

Buena Vista Rancheria of Me-Wuk Indians (Pacific)
P.O. Box 162283
Sacramento , CA 95816

Burns Paiute Tribe (Northwest)
100 Pasigo Street
Burns, OR 97720

Cabazon Band of Mission Indians (Pacific)
84-245 Indio Springs Drive
Indio, CA 92203

Caddo Indian Tribe of Oklahoma (Southern Plains)
P.O. Box 487
Binger, OK 73009

Cahuilla Band of Mission Indians (Pacific)
P.O. Box 391760
Anza, CA 92539-1760
Website: www.cahuilla.com

California Valley Miwok Tribe (Pacific)
10601 Escondido Place
Stockton, CA 95212
Website: www.californiavalleymiwoktribe-nsn.gov

Campo Band of Kumeyaay Indians (Pacific)
36190 Church Road, Suite 1
Campo, CA 91906
Website: www.kumeyaay.com/links.html

Carson Community (Western)
2900 South Curry Street
Carson City, NV 89703

Catawba Indian Tribe (Southeast)
996 Avenue of the Nations
Rock Hill, SC 29730

Cayuga Nation (Northeast)
P.O. Box 11
Versailles, NY 14168-0011

Cedarville Rancheria (Pacific)
200 South Howard Street
Alturas, CA 96101

Central Council Tlingit & Haida Indian Tribes of
    Alaska (Alaska)
320 W. Willoughby Avenue, Suite 300
Juneau, AK 99801
Website: www.ccthita.org

Chalkyitsik Village Council (Alaska)
P.O. Box 57
Chalkyitsik, AK 99788

Chemehuevi Indian Tribe (Western)
P.O. Box 1976
Havasu Lake, CA 92362
Website: www.havasulanding.com

Cherokee Nation of Oklahoma (Eastern Oklahoma)
P.O. Box 948
Tahlequah, OK 74465
Website: www.cherokee.org

Cherokees of Southeast Alabama (Southeast)
P.O. Box 36302
Dothan, AL 36302-0717

Chevak Native Village (Alaska)
P.O. Box 140, Aurora Street
Chevak, AK 99563

Cheyenne and Arapaho Tribes of Oklahoma
    (Southern Plains)
P.O. Box 38
Concho, OK 73022

Cheyenne River Sioux Tribe (Great Plains)
P.O. Box 590
Eagle Butte, SD 57625
Website: www.sioux.org

Chickahominy Indian Tribe, Inc. (Northeast)
8200 Lott Cary Road
Providence Forge, VA 23140

Chickaloon Native Village (Alaska)
P.O. Box 1105
Chickaloon, AK 99674-1105

Chickasaw Nation (Eastern Oklahoma)
P.O. Box 1548
Ada, OK 74821

Chicken Ranch Rancheria (Pacific)
P.O. Box 1159
Jamestown, CA 95327

Chignik Lake Village (Alaska)
P.O. Box 33
Chignik Lake, AK 99548

Chilkat Indian Village (Klukwan) (Alaska)
P.O. Box 210
Haines, AK 99827-0210

Chilkoot Indian Association (Alaska)
P.O. Box 490, 207 Main Street, Suite 2
Haines, AK 99827-0490
Website: http://thorpe.ou.edu/IRA/chilkchrtr.html

Chinik Eskimo Community (aka Golovin) (Alaska)
P.O. Box 62020
Golovin, AK 99762

Chinook Indian Tribe (Northwest)
P.O. Box 228
Chinook, WA 98614

Chippewa Cree Tribe of the Rocky Boy's
    Reservation (Rocky Mountain)
Rural Route 1, P.O. Box 544
Box Elder, MT 59521

Chitimacha Tribe of Louisiana (Southeast)
P.O. Box 661
Charenton, LA 70523

Chitina Traditional Village Council (Alaska)
P.O. Box 31
Chitina, AK 99566

Choctaw Nation of Oklahoma (Eastern Oklahoma)
Drawer 1210
Durant, OK 74702

Chuloonawick Native Village (Alaska)
General Delivery
Chuloonawick, AK 99581

Circle Native Community (Alaska)
P.O. Box 89
Circle, AK 99733

Citizen Potawatomi Nation (Southern Plains)
1601 S. Gordon Cooper Drive
Shawnee, OK 74801
Website: www.potawatomi.org

Cloverdale Rancheria of Pomo Indians of California
    (Pacific)
555 S. Cloverdale Boulevard, Suite A
Cloverdale, CA 95425

Cocopah Tribe (Western)
County 15 & Avenue G
Somerton, AZ 85350

Coeur d'Alene Indian Tribe (Northwest)
850 A Street, P.O. Box 408
Plummer, ID 83851

Cold Springs Rancheria (Pacific)
32535 Sycamore Road
Tollhouse, CA 93667

Colorado River Indian Reservation (Western)
Route 1 Box 23-B
Parker, AZ 85344

Colusa Rancheria (Pacific)
50 Wintun Road, Dept. D
Colusa, CA 95932

Colville Tribe (Northwest)
P.O. Box 150
Nespelem, WA 99155-0150

Comanche Indian Tribe (Southern Plains)
P.O. Box 908
Lawton, OK 73502

Confederated Tribes of Coos, Lower Umpqua and
    Siuslaw Indians (Northwest)
1245 Fulton Avenue
Coos Bay, OR 97420

Confederated Tribes of the Chehalis Reservation
    (Northwest)
P.O. Box 536
Oakville, WA 98568

Confederated Tribes of the Grand Ronde
    Community of Oregon (Northwest)
9615 Grand Ronde Road
Grand Ronde, OR 97347-0038
Website: www.grandronde.org

Confederated Tribes of the Salish & Kootenai
    (Northwest)
Box 278
Pablo, MT 59855

Confederated Tribes of the Umatilla Indian
    Reservation (Northwest)
P.O. Box 638
Pendleton, OR 97801-0638

Confederated Tribes of the Warm Springs
    Reservation (Northwest)
P.O. Box C
Warm Springs, OR 97761-3001
Website: www.warmsprings.org

Coquille Indian Tribe (Northwest)
P.O. Box 783
North Bend, OR 97459
Website: www.coquilletribe.org

Cortina Rancheria (Pacific)
P.O. Box 1630
Williams, CA 95987

Coushatta Indian Tribe of Louisiana (Southeast)
P.O. Box 818
Elton, LA 70532

Cow Creek Band of Umpqua (Northwest)
2371 NE Stephens Street, Suite 100
Roseburg, OR 97470-1338
Website: www.cowcreek.com

Cowlitz Indian Tribe (Northwest)
1417 15th Avenue #5, P.O. Box 2547
Longview, WA 98632-8594

Coyote Valley Band of Pomo Indians (Pacific)
P.O. Box 39
Redwood Valley, CA 95470
Website: www.coyotevalleycasino.com

Craig Community Association (Alaska)
P.O. Box 828
Craig, AK 99921

Crooked Creek Traditional Council (Alaska)
P.O. Box 69
Crooked Creek, AK 99575

Crow Creek Sioux Tribe (Great Plains)
P.O. Box 50
Fort Thompson, SD 57339

Crow Nation (Rocky Mountain)
P.O. Box 159
Crow Agency, MT 59022

Curyung Tribal Council (Alaska)
P.O. Box 216
Dillingham, AK 99576

Delaware Nation (Southern Plains)
P.O. Box 825
Anadarko, OK 73005
Website: www.delawaretribeofindians.nsn.us/

Delaware Tribe of Indians (Eastern Oklahoma)
220 NW Virginia Avenue
Bartlesville, OK 74003
Website: www.delawaretribeofindians.nsn.us

Dot Lake Village Council (Alaska)
P.O. Box 2279
Dot Lake, AK 99737-2279

Douglas Indian Association (Alaska)
P.O. Box 240541
Douglas, AK 99824

Dresslerville Community (Western)
585 Watasheamu Road
Gardnerville, NV 89410

Dry Creek Rancheria Band of Pomo Indians
    (Pacific)
P.O. Box 607
Geyserville, CA 95441
Website: www.drycreekrancheria.com

Duckwater Shoshone Tribe (Western)
P.O. Box 140068
Duckwater, NV 89314

Eastern Band of Cherokee Indians (Southeast)
P.O. Box 455
Cherokee, NC 28719
Website: www.cherokee-nc.com

Eastern Pequot Tribal Nation (Northeast)
391 Norwich Westerly Road, P.O. Box 208
North Stonington, CT 06359

Eastern Shawnee Tribe of Oklahoma (Eastern
    Oklahoma)
P.O. Box 350
Seneca, MO 64865

Eastern Shoshone Tribe of Wind River Indian
    Reservation (Rocky Mountain)
P.O. Box 538
Fort Washakie, WY 82514

Egegik Village (Alaska)
P.O. Box 29
Egegik, AK 99579

Ekwok Village Council (Alaska)
P.O. Box 70
Ekwok, AK 99580

Elem Indian Colony (Pacific)
P.O. Box 1997
Clearlake Oaks, CA 95423
Website: www.elemnation.com

Elk Valley Rancheria (Pacific)
2332 Howland Hill Road
Crescent City, CA 95531
Website: www.elkvalleycasino.com

Elko Band (Western)
1745 Silver Eagle Drive
Elko, NV 89801

Ely Shoshone Tribe (Western)
16 Shoshone Circle
Ely, NV 89301

Emmonak Village (Alaska)
P.O. Box 126
Emmonak, AK 99581

Enterprise Rancheria (Pacific)
1940 Feather River Boulevard, Suite B
Oroville, CA 95965-5723

Evansville Tribal Council (Alaska)
P.O. Box 26087
Bettles Field, AK 99726

Ewiiapaayp Community of Kumeyaay Indians
    (Cuyapaipe Band of Mission Indians) (Pacific)
P.O. Box 2250
Alpine, CA 91903-2250

Fallon Paiute Shoshone Tribe (Western)
565 Rio Vista Road
Fallon, NV 89406-9159

Federated Indians of Graton Rancheria (Pacific)
P.O. Box 14428
Santa Rosa, CA 95402
Website: www.gratonrancheria.com

Flandreau Santee Sioux Tribe (Great Plains)
P.O. Box 283
Flandreau, SD 57028

Fond du Lac Reservation Business Committee
    (Midwest)
105 University Road
Cloquet, MN 55720

Forest County Potawatomi Community of
    Wisconsin (Midwest)
P.O. Box 340
Crandon, WI 54520

Fort Belknap Tribe (Rocky Mountain)
Rural Route 1 Box 66
Harlem, MT 59526
Website: www.fortbelknapnations-nsn.gov

Fort Bidwell Reservation (Pacific)
P.O. Box 129
Fort Bidwell, CA 96112

Fort Independence Indian Reservation (Pacific)
P.O. Box 67
Independence, CA 93526

Fort McDermitt Tribe (Western)
P.O. Box 457
McDermitt, NV 89421

Fort McDowell Yavapai Tribe (Western)
P.O. Box 17779
Fountain Hills, AZ 85269

Fort Mojave Tribe (Western)
500 Merriman Avenue
Needles, CA 92363

Fort Peck Tribes of Assiniboine and Sioux (Rocky
    Mountain)
P.O. Box 1027
Poplar, MT 59255
Website: www.fortpecktribes.org

Fort Sill Apache Tribe of Oklahoma (Southern
    Plains)
Rt. 2, Box 121
Apache, OK 73006

Four Winds Tribe, Louisiana Cherokee Confederacy
    (Southeast)
P.O. Box 395
New Llano, LA 71461

Gila River Indian Community (Western)
P.O. Box 97
Sacaton, AZ 85247
Website: www.gric.nsn.us

Goshute Tribe (Western)
P.O. Box 6104
Ibapah, UT 84034

Grand Portage Reservation Business Committee
    (Midwest)
P.O. Box 428
Grand Portage, MN 55605

Grand Traverse Band of Ottawa and Chippewa
    Indians of Michigan (Midwest)
2605 North W Bay Shore Drive
Peshawbestown, MI 49682

Greenville Rancheria (Pacific)
P.O. Box 279
Greenville, CA 95947

Grindstone Indian Rancheria (Pacific)
P.O. Box 63, County Road 305 #13A
Elk Creek, CA 95939

Guidiville Band of Pomo Indians (Pacific)
P.O. Box 339
Ukiah, CA 95481

Gulkana Village (Alaska)
P.O. Box 254
Gulkana, AK 99586

Gwichyaa Zhee Gwichi'in Tribal Gov't (Fort Yukon)
    (Alaska)
P.O. Box 126
Fort Yukon, AK 99740

Haliwa-Saponi Indian Tribe, Inc. (Southeast)
P.O. Box 99
Hollister, CA 27844

Hannahville Indian Community of Michigan
    (Midwest)
N14911 Hannahville B1 Road
Wilson, MI 49896-9728
Website: www.hannahville.com

Havasupai Tribe (Western)
P.O. Box 10
Supai, AZ 86435

Healy Lake Traditional Council (Alaska)
P.O. Box 60300
Fairbanks, AK 99706-0300

Ho-Chunk Nation (Midwest)
W9814 Airport Road, P.O. Box 667
Black River Falls, WI 54615

Hoh Tribe (Northwest)
2464 Lower Hoh Road
Forks, WA 98331

Holy Cross Village (Alaska)
P.O. Box 89
Holy Cross, AK 99602

Hoonah Indian Association (Alaska)
P.O. Box 602
Hoonah, AK 99829

Hoopa Valley Tribe (Pacific)
P.O. Box 1348
Hoopa, CA 95546
Website: www.hoopa-nsn.gov

Hopi Tribe (Western)
P.O. Box 123
Kykotsmovi, AZ 86039
Website: www.hopi.nsn.us

Hopland Band of Pomo Indians (Pacific)
P.O. Box 610, 3000 Shanel Road
Hopland, CA 95449
Website: www.shokawah.com

Houlton Band of Maliseet Indians (Northeast)
88 Bell Road
Littleton, ME 04730

Hualapai Tribe (Western)
P.O. Box 179
Peach Springs, AZ 86434

Hughes Village (Alaska)
P.O. Box 45029
Hughes, AK 99745

Huron Potawatomi, Inc. (Midwest)
2221 1-1/2 Mile Road
Fulton, MI 49052

Huslia Village (Alaska)
P.O. Box 70
Huslia, AK 99746

Hydaburg Cooperative Assn. (Alaska)
P.O. Box 349
Hydaburg, AK 99922-0349

Igiugig Village (Alaska)
P.O. Box 4008
Igiugig, AK 99613

Inaja-Cosmit Band of Mission Indians (Pacific)
309 S. Maple Street
Escondido, CA 92065

Inupiat Community of Arctic Slope (Alaska)
P.O. Box 934
Barrow, AK 99723

Ione Band of Miwok Indians (Pacific)
P.O. Box 1190
Ione, CA 95640

Iowa Tribe of Kansas & Nebraska (Southern Plains)
3345-B Thrasher Road
White Cloud, KS 66094

Iowa Tribe of Oklahoma (Southern Plains)
Rt. 1, Box 721
Perkins, OK 74059
Website: www.iowanation.org

Iqurmiut Traditonal Council (Alaska)
P.O. Box 9
Russian Mission, AK 99657

Ivanoff Bay Village Council (Alaska)
P.O. Box 500
Perryville, AK 99648

Jackson Rancheria (Pacific)
P.O. Box 1090
Jackson, CA 95642

Jamestown S'Klallam Tribe (Northwest)
1033 Old Blyn Highway
Sequim, WA 98382
Website: www.jamestowntribe.org

Jamul Indian Village (Pacific)
P.O. Box 612
Jamul, CA 91935
Website: www.jamulindianvillage.com

Jena Band of Choctaw Indians (Southeast)
P.O. Box 14
Jena, LA 71342

Jicarilla Apache Nation (Southwest)
P.O. Box 507
Dulce, NM 87528-0507
Website: www.jicarillaonline.com

Kaguyak Village (Alaska)
P.O. Box 5078
Akhiok, AK 99615

Kaibab Paiute Tribe (Western)
HC65, Box 2
Fredonia, AZ 86022

Kaktovik Village (Alaska)
P.O. Box 130, 834 8th Street
Kaktovik, AK 99747

Kalispel Business Committee (Northwest)
P.O. Box 39
Usk, WA 99180-0039

Karuk Tribe of California (Pacific)
P.O. Box 1016
Happy Camp, CA 96039

Kaw Nation (Southern Plains)
P.O. Box 50
Kaw City, OK 74641
Website: www.kawnation.com

Kenaitze Indian Tribe (Alaska)
P.O. Box 988, 225 N. Ames Road
Kenai, AK 99611-0988

Ketchikan Indian Corporation (Alaska)
2960 Tongass Avenue
Ketchikan, AK 99901

Keweenaw Bay Indian Community of Michigan
    (Midwest)
107 Beartown Road
Baraga, MI 49908
Website: www.kbic-nsn.gov

Kialegee Tribal Town (Eastern Oklahoma)
P.O. Box 332
Wetumka, OK 74883

Kickapoo Traditional Tribe of Texas (Southern
    Plains)
8C1 Box 9700
Eagle Pass, TX 78853

Kickapoo Tribe in Kansas (Southern Plains)
1117 Goldfinch Road
Horton, KS 66439
Website: www.kickapoonation.com

Kickapoo Tribe of Oklahoma (Southern Plains)
P.O. Box 70
McCloud, OK 74851

King Island Native Community (Alaska)
P.O. Box 992
Nome, AK 99762

King Salmon Tribe (Alaska)
P.O. Box 68, 1/2 Mile King Salmon Creek Road
King Salmon, AK 99613-0068

Kiowa Indian Tribe of Oklahoma (Southern Plains)
P.O. Box 369
Carnegie, OK 73015

Klamath General Council (Northwest)
P.O. Box 436
Chiloquin, OR 97624-0436

Klawock Cooperative Assn. (Alaska)
P.O. Box 430
Klawock, AK 99925-0430

Knik Tribal Council (Alaska)
P.O. Box 871565
Wasilla, AK 99687

Kobuk Traditional Council (Alaska)
P.O. Box 51039
Kobuk, AK 99751

Kokhanok Village (Alaska)
P.O. Box 1007
Kokhanok, AK 99606

Kongiganak Traditional Council (Alaska)
P.O. Box 5069
Kongiganak, AK 99559-5069

Kootenai Tribal Council (Northwest)
P.O. Box 1269
Bonners Ferry, ID 83805-1269

Koyukuk Tribal Council (Alaska)
P.O. Box 109
Koyukuk, AK 99754

La Jolla Band of Luiseno Indians (Pacific)
22000 Highway 76
Pauma Valley, CA 92061
Website: www.lajollaindians.com

La Posta Band of Mission Indians (Pacific)
P.O. Box 1120
Boulevard, CA 91905

Lac Courte Oreilles Band of Lake Superior
    Chippewa Indians of Wisconsin (Midwest)
13394 West Trepania Road, Building #1
Hayward, WI 54843

Lac du Flambeau Band of Lake Superior Chippewa
    Indians of Wisconsin (Midwest)
P.O. Box 67
Lac du Flambeau, WI 54538

Lac Vieux Desert Band of Lake Superior Chippewa
    Indians of Michigan (Midwest)
P.O. Box 249
Watersmeet, MI 49969
Website: www.lacvieuxdesert.com

Larsen Bay Tribal Council (Alaska)
P.O. Box 50
Larsen Bay, AK 99624

Las Vegas Paiute Tribe (Western)
One Paiute Drive
Las Vegas, NV 89106-3261

Laytonville Rancheria (Cahto Tribe) (Pacific)
P.O. Box 1239
Laytonville, CA 95454

Leech Lake Reservation Business Committee
    (Midwest)
6530 US Highway 2 NW
Cass Lake, MN 56633
Website: www.llojibwe.com/llojibwe/History.html

Lesnoi Village (Alaska)
P.O. Box 9009, 3248 Mill Bay Road
Kodiak, AK 99615
Website: www.woodyisland.com

Levelock Village (Alaska)
P.O. Box 70
Levelock, AK 99625

Lime Village Traditional Council (Alaska)
P.O. Box LVD
Lime Village, AK 99627

Little River Band of Ottawa Indians (Midwest)
375 River Street
Manistee, MI 49660-2729

Little Traverse Bay Bands of Odawa Indians
    (Midwest)
7500 Odawa Circle
Harbor Springs, MI 49740

Lone Pine Paiute Shoshone Reservation (Pacific)
P.O. Box 747
Lone Pine, CA 93545

Los Coyotes Band of Indians (Pacific)
P.O. Box 189, 3000 Isil Road
Warner Springs, CA 92086

Louden Tribal Council (Alaska)
P.O. Box 244
Galena, AK 99741

Lovelock Tribe (Western)
P.O. Box 878
Lovelock, NV 89419

Lower Brule Sioux Tribe (Great Plains)
187 Oyate Circle, P.O. Box 187
Lower Brule, SD 57548

Lower Elwha Klallam Tribe (Northwest)
2851 Lower Elwha Road
Port Angeles, WA 98363
Website: www.elwha.org

Lower Lake Rancheria (Pacific)
P.O. Box 3162, 131 Lincoln Street
Healdsburg, CA 95448

Lower Sioux Indian Community of Minnesota
    (Midwest)
39527 Res. Hwy 1, P.O. Box 308
Morton, MN 56270

Lumbee Tribe of North Carolina (Southeast)
P.O. Box 2709
Pembroke, NC 28372
Website: www.lumbeetribe.com

Lummi Indian Business Council (Northwest)
2616 Kwina Road
Bellingham, WA 98226

Lytton Band of Pomo Indians (Pacific)
1250 Coddingtown Center, Suite 1
Santa Rosa, CA 95401

Ma-Chris Lower Creek Indian Tribe of Alabama
    (Southeast)
Rt 1, 708 South John Street
New Brockton, AL 36351

Makah Indian Tribal Council (Northwest)
P.O. Box 115
Neah Bay, WA 98357-0115

Manchester–Point Arena Rancheria (Pacific)
P.O. Box 623
Point Arena, CA 95468

Manley Hot Springs Village (Alaska)
Box 105
Manley Hot Springs, AK 99756

Manokotak Village (Alaska)
P.O. Box 169
Manokotak, AK 99628

Manzanita Band of Mission Indians (Pacific)
P.O. Box 1302
Boulevard, CA 91905

Mary's Igloo Traditional Council (Alaska)
P.O. Box 629
Teller, AK 99778

Mashantucket Pequot Tribe (Northeast)
P.O. Box 3060
Mashantucket, CT 06338
Website: www.foxwoods.com/TheMashantucket
    Pequots/Home/

Match-E-Be-Nash-She-Wish Band of
    Pottawatomi Indians of Michigan
    (Midwest)
P.O. Box 218
Dorr, MI 49323
Website: www.mbpi.org

McGrath Native Village Council (Alaska)
P.O. Box 134
McGrath, AK 99627

Mechoopda Indian Tribe of the Chico Rancheria
    (Pacific)
125 Mission Ranch Boulevard
Chico, CA 95926

Menominee Indian Tribe of Wisconsin
    (Midwest)
P.O. Box 910
Keshena, WI 54135-0910
Website: www.menominee-nsn.gov/

Mentasta Traditional Tribal Council (Alaska)
P.O. Box 6019
Mentasta Lake, AK 99780-6019

Mesa Grande Band of Mission Indians (Pacific)
P.O. Box 270
Santa Ysabelle, CA 92070

Mescalero Apache Tribe (Southwest)
P.O. Box 227
Mescalero, NM 88340

Metlakatla Indian Community (Alaska)
P.O. Box 8
Metlakatla, AK 99926-0008

Miami Tribe of Oklahoma (Eastern Oklahoma)
P.O. Box 1326
Miami, OK 74355

Miccosukee Indian Tribe of Florida (Southeast)
P.O. Box 440021, Tamiami Station
Miami, FL 33144

Middletown Rancheria (Pacific)
P.O. Box 1035
Middletown, CA 95461

Mille Lacs Band (Midwest)
43408 Oodena Drive
Onamia, MN 56539
Website: www.millelacsojibwe.org

Minnesota Chippewa Tribe (Midwest)
P.O. Box 217
Cass Lake, MN 56633

Mississippi Band of Choctaw Indians (Southeast)
P.O. Box 6010
Choctaw, MS 39350
Website: www.choctaw.org

Moapa Tribe (Western)
P.O. Box 340
Moapa, NV 89025-0340

Modoc Tribe of Oklahoma (Eastern Oklahoma)
515 G St. Southeast
Miami, OK 74354

Mohegan Indian Tribe (Northeast)
5 Crow Hill Road
Uncasville, CT 06382
Website: www.mohegan.nsn.us

Monacan Indian Nation, Inc. (Southeast)
P.O. Box 1136
Mission Heights, VA 24572

Mooretown Rancheria (Pacific)
1 Alverda Drive
Oroville, CA 95966

Morongo Band of Mission Indians (Pacific)
11581 Potrero Road
Banning, CA 92220-2965

Mowa Band of Choctaw Indians (Southeast)
1080 W. Red Fox Road
Mt. Vernon, AL 36560

Muckleshoot Tribal Council (Northwest)
39015 172nd Avenue, S.E.
Auburn, WA 98092

Muscogee (Creek) Nation (Eastern Oklahoma)
P.O. Box 580
Okmulgee, OK 74447

Naknek Native Village Council (Alaska)
P.O. Box 106
Naknek, AK 99633

Nanticoke-Lenni Lenape Tribal Nation (Northeast)
18 East Commerce Street, P.O. Box 544
Bridgetown, NJ 08032
Website: http://www.nanticoke-lenape.org

Narragansett Indian Tribe (Northeast)
P.O. Box 268
Charlestown, RI 02813

Native Village of Afognak (Alaska)
P.O. Box 968
Kodiak, AK 99615

Native Village of Akhiok (Alaska)
P.O. Box 5050
Akhiok, AK 99615

Native Village of Akutan (Alaska)
P.O. Box 89
Akutan, AK 99553-0089

Native Village of Alakanuk (Alaska)
P.O. Box 149
Alakanuk, AK 99554-0149

Native Village of Alatna (Alaska)
P.O. Box 70
Alatna, AK 99720

Native Village of Aleknagik (Alaska)
P.O. Box 115
Aleknagik, AK 99555

Native Village of Ambler (Alaska)
P.O. Box 47
Ambler, AK 99786

Native Village of Atka (Alaska)
P.O. Box 47030, 116 Laavkix Road
Atka, AK 99547

Native Village of Atqasuk (Alaska)
P.O. Box 91109
Atqasuk, AK 99791

Native Village of Barrow (Alaska)
P.O. Box 1139
Barrow, AK 99723

Native Village of Belkofski (Alaska)
P.O. Box 57
King Cove, AK 99612

Native Village of Brevig Mission (Alaska)
P.O. Box 85063
Brevig Mission, AK 99785

Native Village of Buckland (Alaska)
P.O. Box 67
Buckland, AK 99727

Native Village of Cantwell (Alaska)
P.O. Box 940
Cantwell, AK 99729

Native Village of Chenega (Alaska)
P.O. Box 8079, 623 Cato Street
Chenega Bay, AK 99574-8079

Native Village of Chignik (Alaska)
P.O. Box 48
Chignik, AK 99564

Native Village of Chignik Lagoon (Alaska)
P.O. Box 57
Chignik Lagoon, AK 99565

Native Village of Chistochina (Cheesh-na Tribal
    Council) (Alaska)
P.O. Box 241
Chistochina, AK 99586

Native Village of Chuathbaluk (Alaska)
P.O. Box CHU
Chuathbaluk, AK 99557

Native Village of Council (Alaska)
P.O. Box 2050
Nome, AK 99762

Native Village of Deering (Alaska)
P.O. Box 89
Deering, AK 99736

Native Village of Diomede (aka Inalik) (Alaska)
P.O. Box 7079
Little Diomede, AK 99672

Native Village of Eagle (Alaska)
P.O. Box 19
Eagle, AK 99738

Native Village of Eek (Alaska)
P.O. Box 89
Eek, AK 99581

Native Village of Eklutna (Alaska)
26339 Eklutna Village Road
Chugiak, AK 99567

Native Village of Ekuk (Alaska)
P.O. Box 530
Dillingham, AK 99576

Native Village of Elim (Alaska)
P.O. Box 70
Elim, AK 99739

Native Village of Eyak (Alaska)
P.O. Box 1388
Cordova, AK 99574-1388

Native Village of False Pass (Alaska)
P.O. Box 35
False Pass, AK 99583

Native Village of Gakona (Alaska)
P.O. Box 303
Copper Center, AK 99573

Native Village of Gambell (Alaska)
P.O. Box 90
Gambell, AK 99742

Native Village of Georgetown (Alaska)
1400 Virginia Court
Anchorage, AK 99501

Native Village of Goodnews Bay (Alaska)
P.O. Box 3
Goodnews Bay, AK 99589

Native Village of Hamilton (Alaska)
P.O. Box 20248
Kotlik, AK 99620

Native Village of Hooper Bay (Alaska)
P.O. Box 36
Hooper Bay, AK 99604

Native Village of Kalskag (Alaska)
P.O. Box 50
Kalskag, AK 99607

Native Village of Kanatak (Alaska)
P.O. Box 875910, MSC 230
Wasilla, AK 99687
Website: www.kanatak.org

Native Village of Karluk (Alaska)
P.O. Box 22
Karluk, AK 99608

Native Village of Kasaan (Alaska)
P.O. Box 26–Kasaan
Ketchikan, AK 99950

Native Village of Kasigluk (Alaska)
P.O. Box 19
Kasigluk, AK 99609

Native Village of Kiana (Alaska)
P.O. Box 69
Kiana, AK 99749

Native Village of Kipnuk (Alaska)
P.O. Box 57
Kipnuk, AK 99614

Native Village of Kivalina (Alaska)
P.O. Box 50051
Kivalina, AK 99750

Native Village of Kluti-Kaah (aka Copper Center)
    (Alaska)
P.O. Box 68
Copper Center, AK 99573

Native Village of Kotzebue (Alaska)
P.O. Box 296
Kotzebue, AK 99752

Native Village of Koyuk (Alaska)
P.O. Box 53030
Koyuk, AK 99753

Native Village of Kwigillingok (IRA) (Alaska)
P.O. Box 49
Quinhagak, AK 99622

Native Village of Kwinhagak (Alaska)
P.O. Box 149
Quinhagak, AK 99655

Native Village of Marshall (aka Fortuna Ledge)
    (Alaska)
P.O. Box 110
Marshall, AK 99585

Native Village of Mekoryuk (Alaska)
P.O. Box 66
Mekoryuk, AK 99630

Native Village of Minto (Alaska)
P.O. Box 26
Minto, AK 99758-0026

Native Village of Nanwalek (aka English Bay)
    (Alaska)
P.O. Box 8026
Nanwalek, AK 99603

Native Village of Napaimute (Alaska)
P.O. Box 96
Aniak, AK 99557

Native Village of Napakiak (Alaska)
P.O. Box 34069
Napakiak, AK 99634

Native Village of Napaskiak (Alaska)
P.O. Box 6009
Napaskiak, AK 99559

Native Village of Nikolski (Alaska)
P.O. Box 105
Nikolski, AK 99638

Native Village of Noatak (Alaska)
P.O. Box 89
Noatak, AK 99761

Native Village of Nuiqsut (Alaska)
P.O. Box 187
Nuiqsut, AK 99723

Native Village of Nunapitchuk (Alaska)
P.O. Box 130
Nunapitchuk, AK 99641

Native Village of Ouzinkie (Alaska)
P.O. Box 130
Ouzinkie, AK 99644

Native Village of Paimiut (Alaska)
P.O. Box 100193
Anchorage, AK 99510

Native Village of Pauloff Harbor (Alaska)
P.O. Box 97
Sand Point, AK 99661

Native Village of Perryville (Alaska)
P.O. Box 101
Perryville, AK 99648-0101

Native Village of Pitka's Point (Alaska)
P.O. Box 127
St. Mary's, AK 99658

Native Village of Point Hope (Alaska)
P.O. Box 109
Point Hope, AK 99766

Native Village of Point Lay (Alaska)
P.O. Box 101
Point Lay, AK 99759

Native Village of Port Heiden (Alaska)
P.O. Box 49007
Port Heiden, AK 99549

Native Village of Port Lions (Alaska)
P.O. Box 69
Port Lions, AK 99550

Native Village of Red Devil (Alaska)
P.O. Box 61
Red Devil, AK 99656

Native Village of Savoonga (Alaska)
P.O. Box 120
Savoonga, AK 99769

Native Village of Scammon Bay (Alaska)
P.O. Box 126
Scammon Bay, AK 99662

Native Village of Shaktoolik (Alaska)
P.O. Box 100
Shaktoolik, AK 99771-0100

Native Village of Sheldon Point (Alaska)
P.O. Box 09
Sheldon's Point, AK 99666

Native Village of Shishmaref (Alaska)
P.O. Box 72110
Shishmaref, AK 99772

Native Village of Shungnak (Alaska)
P.O. Box 64
Shungnak, AK 99773

Native Village of South Naknek (Alaska)
P.O. Box 70029
South Naknek, AK 99670

Native Village of Stevens (Alaska)
P.O. Box 74016
Stevens Village, AK 99774

Native Village of St. Michael (Alaska)
P.O. Box 59050
St. Michael, AK 99659

Native Village of Tanacross (Alaska)
P.O. Box 76009
Tanacross, AK 99776
Website www.nativevillageoftanacross.com

Native Village of Tanana (Alaska)
P.O. Box 130
Tanana, AK 99777

Native Village of Tatitlek (Alaska)
P.O. Box 171
Tatitlek, AK 99677

Native Village of Tetlin (Alaska)
P.O. Box TTL
Tetlin, AK 99779

Native Village of Tuntutuliak (Alaska)
P.O. Box 8086
Tuntutuliak, AK 99680

Native Village of Tununak (Alaska)
P.O. Box 77
Tununak, AK 99681

Native Village of Tyonek (Alaska)
P.O. Box 82009
Tyonek, AK 99682-0009

Native Village of Unalakleet (Alaska)
P.O. Box 270
Unalakleet, AK 99684-0270

Native Village of Venetie Tribal Government
   (Alaska)
P.O. Box 81080
Venetie, AK 99781-0080

Native Village of Wales (Alaska)
P.O. Box 549
Wales, AK 99783

Native Village of White Mountain (Alaska)
P.O. Box 84082
White Mountain, AK 99784

Navajo Nation (Navajo Region)
P.O. Box 9000
Window Rock, AZ 86515
Website: www.navajo.org

Nelson Lagoon Tribal Council (Alaska)
P.O. Box 13
Nelson Lagoon, AK 99571

Nenana Native Association (Alaska)
P.O. Box 356
Nenana, AK 99760

New Koliganek Village Council (Alaska)
P.O. Box 5057
Koliganek, AK 99576

New Stuyahok Village (Alaska)
P.O. Box 49
New Stuyahok, AK 99636

Newhalen Tribal Council (Alaska)
P.O. Box 207
Newhalen, AK 99606

Newtok Traditional Council (Alaska)
P.O. Box 5565
Newtok, AK 99559

Nez Percé Tribe (Northwest)
P.O. Box 305
Lapwai, ID 83540-0305
Website: www.nezperce.org

Nightmute Traditional Council (Alaska)
P.O. Box 90021
Nightmute, AK 99690

Nikolai Edzeno' Village Council (Alaska)
P.O. Box55
McGrath, AK 99627

Ninilchik Traditional Council (Alaska)
P.O. Box 39070
Ninilchik, AK 99639

Nisqually Indian Community Council (Northwest)
4820 She-Nah-Num Drive, S.E.
Olympia, WA 98513-9199

Nome Eskimo Community (Alaska)
P.O. Box 1090
Nome, AK 99762

Nondalton Village (Alaska)
P.O. Box 490
Nondalton, AK 99640

Nooksack Indian Tribal Council (Northwest)
P.O. Box 157
Deming, WA 98244-0157

Noorvik Native Community (Alaska)
P.O. Box 209
Noorvik, AK 99763

North Fork Rancheria (Pacific)
P.O. Box 929
North Fork, CA 93643-0929

Northern Arapaho Tribe (Rocky Mountain)
P.O. Box 396
Fort Washakie, WY 82514

Northern Cheyenne Tribe (Rocky Mountain)
P.O. Box 128
Lame Deer, MT 59043

Northway Village (Alaska)
P.O. Box 516
Northway, AK 99764

Northwestern Band of Shoshone Nation
    (Northwest)
427 North Main, Suite 101
Pocatello, ID 83204-3016

Nulato Tribal Council (Alaska)
P.O. Box 65049
Nulato, AK 99765-0049

Nunakauyak Traditional Council (Alaska)
P.O. Box 37048
Toksook Bay, AK 99637-7048

Oglala Sioux Tribe (Great Plains)
P.O. Box 2070
Pine Ridge, SD 57770

Ohkay Owingeh (formerly Pueblo of San Juan)
    (Southwest)
P.O. Box 1099
San Juan Pueblo, NM 87566

Omaha Tribe of Nebraska (Great Plains)
P.O. Box 368
Macy, NE 68039

Oneida Indian Nation (Northeast)
5218 Patrick Road
Vernona, NY 13478
Website: www.oneida-nation.net

Oneida Tribe of Indians of Wisconsin (Midwest)
P.O. Box 365
Oneida, WI 54155-0365
Website: www.oneidanation.org

Onondaga Indian Nation (Northeast)
RR#1 Box 319-B
Nedrow, NY 13120

Organized Village of Grayling (Alaska)
General Delivery
Grayling, AK 99590

Organized Village of Kake (Alaska)
P.O. Box 316
Kake, AK 99830-0316

Organized Village of Kwethluk (Alaska)
P.O. Box 129
Kwethluk, AK 99621-0129

Organized Village of Saxman (Alaska)
Route 2, Box 2–Saxman
Ketchikan, AK 99901

Orutsararmuit Native Council (Alaska)
P.O. Box 927
Bethel, AK 99559

Osage Tribal Council (Eastern Oklahoma)
627 Grandview
Pawhuska, OK 74056

Oscarville Tribal Council (Alaska)
P.O. Box 6129
Napaskiak, AK 99559

Otoe-Missouria Tribe of Indians (Southern Plains)
8151 Highway 177
Red Rock, OK 74651

Ottawa Tribe of Oklahoma (Eastern Oklahoma)
P.O. Box 110
Miami, OK 74355

Paiute Indian Tribe of Utah (Western)
440 N. Paiute Drive
Cedar City, UT 84720-2613

Pala Band of Mission Indians (Pacific)
P.O. Box 50
Pala, CA 92059
Website: www.palaindians.com

Pascua Yaqui Tribe (Western)
7474 South Camino De Oeste
Tucson, AZ 85746

Paskenta Band of Nomlaki Indians (Pacific)
P.O. Box 398
Orland, CA 95963

Passamaquoddy Tribe–Indian Township
    Reservation (Northeast)
P.O. Box 301
Princeton, ME 04668
Website: www.passamaquoddy.com/

Passamaquoddy Tribe–Pleasant Point Reservation
    (Northeast)
P.O. Box 343
Perry, ME 04667-0343
Website: www.wabanaki.com

Pauma/Yuima Band of Mission Indians (Pacific)
P.O. Box 369
Pauma Valley, CA 92061

Pawnee Nation of Oklahoma (Southern Plains)
P.O. Box 470
Pawnee, OK 74058

Pechanga Band of Luiseno Indians (Pacific)
P.O. Box 1477
Temecula, CA 92593

Pedro Bay Village (Alaska)
P.O. Box 47020
Pedro Bay, AK 99647

Penobscot Indian Nation (Northeast)
12 Wabanaki Way
Indian Island, ME 04468

Peoria Tribe of Oklahoma (Eastern Oklahoma)
P.O. Box 1527
Miami, OK 74355
Website: www.peoriatribe.com

Petersburg Indian Association (Alaska)
P.O. Box 1418
Petersburg, AK 99833

Picayune Rancheria of Chukchansi Indians (Pacific)
46575 Road 417
Coarsegold, CA 93614

Pilot Point Traditional Council (Alaska)
P.O. Box 449
Pilot Point, AK 99649

Pilot Station Traditional Village (Alaska)
P.O. Box 5119
Pilot Station, AK 99650

Pinoleville Reservation (Pacific)
367 No. State Street, Suite 204
Ukiah, CA 95482

Pit River Tribe (Pacific)
37014 Main Street
Burney, CA 96013

Platinum Traditional Village Council (Alaska)
P.O. Box 8
Platinum, AK 99647

Poarch Band of Creek Indians (Southeast)
5811 Jack Springs Road
Atmore, AL 36502

Pokagon Band of Potawatomi Indians of Michigan
    (Midwest)
58620 Sink Road
Dowagiac, MI 49047
Website: www.pokagon.com

Ponca Tribe of Indians of Oklahoma (Southern
    Plains)
20 White Eagle Drive
Ponca City, OK 74601

Ponca Tribe of Nebraska (Great Plains)
P.O. Box 288
Niobrara, NE 68760

Portage Creek Village (Alaska)
General Delivery
Portage Creek, AK 99576

Port Gamble S'Klallam Tribe (Northwest)
31912 Little Boston Road NE
Kingston, WA 98346

Port Graham Village Council (Alaska)
P.O. Box 5510
Port Graham, AK 99603-5510

Potter Valley Rancheria (Pacific)
2251 South State Street
Redwood Valley, CA 95482-4809

Prairie Band of Potawatomi Indians (Southern
    Plains)
16281 Q Road
Mayette, KS 66509

Prairie Island Indian Community (Midwest)
5636 Sturgeon Lake Road
Welch, MN 55089

Pueblo of Acoma (Southwest)
P.O. Box 309
Acoma, NM 87034

Pueblo of Cochiti (Southwest)
P.O. Box 70
Cochiti, NM 87072

Pueblo of Isleta (Southwest)
P.O. Box 1270
Isleta, NM 87022

Pueblo of Jemez (Southwest)
P.O. Box 100
Jemez Pueblo, NM 87024

Pueblo of Laguna (Southwest)
P.O. Box 194
Laguna Pueblo, NM 87026

Pueblo of Nambe (Southwest)
Route 1, Box 117-BB
Nambe Pueblo, NM 87506

Pueblo of Picuris (Southwest)
P.O. Box 127
Penasco, NM 87553

Pueblo of Pojoaque (Southwest)
17746 US 84/285
Santa Fe, NM 87506

Pueblo of Sandia (Southwest)
Box 6008
Bernalillo, NM 87004
Website: www.sandiapueblo.nsn.us

Pueblo of San Felipe (Southwest)
P.O. Box 4339
San Felipe Pueblo, NM 87001

Pueblo of San Ildefonso (Southwest)
Route 5, Box 315-A
Santa Fe, NM 87501

Pueblo of Santa Ana (Southwest)
2 Dove Road
Santa Ana Pueblo, NM 87004
Website: www.santaana.org

Pueblo of Santa Clara (Southwest)
P.O. Box 580
Espanola, NM 87532

Pueblo of Santo Domingo (Southwest)
P.O. Box 99
Santo Domingo Pueblo, NM 87052

Pueblo of Taos (Southwest)
P.O. Box 1846
Taos, NM 87571

Pueblo of Tesuque (Southwest)
Route 42, Box 360-T
Santa Fe, NM 87506

Pueblo of Zia (Southwest)
135 Capitol Square Drive
Zia Pueblo, NM 87053-6013

Pueblo of Zuni (Southwest)
P.O. Box 339
Zuni, NM 87327
Website: www.ashiwi.org

Puyallup Tribal Council (Northwest)
1850 Alexander Avenue
Tacoma, WA 98421

Pyramid Lake Paiute Tribe (Western)
P.O. Box 256
Nixon, NV 89424
Website: www.plpt.nsn.us

Qagan Tayagungin Tribe (Alaska)
P.O. Box 447
Sand Point, AK 99661

Qawalangin Tribe of Unalaska (Alaska)
P.O. Box 334
Unalaska, AK 99685

Quapaw Tribal Business Committee (Eastern
    Oklahoma)
P.O. Box 765
Quapaw, OK 74355

Quartz Valley Reservation (Pacific)
P.O. Box 24
Fort Jones, CA 96032

Quechan Tribe (Western)
P.O. Box 1899
Yuma, AZ 85366-1899

Quileute Tribe (Northwest)
P.O. Box 279
LaPush, WA 98350-2079

Quinault Indian Nation (Northwest)
P.O. Box 189
Taholah, WA 98587-0189

Ramona Band of Cahuilla Indians (Pacific)
P.O. Box 391372
Anza, CA 92539

Rampart Village (Alaska)
P.O. Box 67029
Rampart, AK 99767

Red Cliff Band of Lake Superior Chippewa Indians
    of Wisconsin (Midwest)
88385 Pike Road, Highway 13
Bayfield, WI 54814

Redding Rancheria Tribe (Pacific)
2000 Redding Rancheria Road
Redding, CA 96001

Red Lake Band of Chippewa Indians of Minnesota
    (Midwest)
P.O. Box 550
Red Lake, MN 56671

Redwood Valley Little River Band of Pomo Indians
    (Pacific)
3250 Road I
Redwood Valley, CA 95470-9526

Reno-Sparks Tribe (Western)
98 Colony Road
Reno, NV 89502

Resighini Rancheria (Pacific)
P.O. Box 529
Klamath, CA 95548

Rincon Band of Mission Indians (Pacific)
P.O. Box 68
Valley Center, CA 92082

Robinson Rancheria of Pomo Indians (Pacific)
P.O. Box 4015
Nice, CA 95464

Rosebud Sioux Tribe (Great Plains)
P.O. Box 430
Rosebud, SD 57570
Website: www.rosebudsiouxtribe-nsn.gov

Round Valley Reservation (Pacific)
P.O. Box 448
Covelo, CA 95428

Ruby Tribal Council (Alaska)
P.O. Box 210
Ruby, AK 99768

Rumsey Indian Rancheria (Pacific)
P.O. Box 18
Brooks, CA 95606
Website: www.rumseyrancheria.org

Sac & Fox Tribe of the Mississippi in Iowa
    (Midwest)
349 Meskwaki Road
Tama, IA 52339-9629

Sac and Fox Nation of Missouri (Southern Plains)
305 N. Main Street
Reserve, KS 66434

Sac and Fox Nation of Oklahoma (Southern Plains)
Rt. 2, Box 246
Stroud, OK 74079

Saginaw Chippewa Indian Tribe of Michigan
    (Midwest)
7070 East Broadway Road
Mt. Pleasant, MI 48858
Website: www.sagchip.org

Salt River Pima-Maricopa Indian Community
    (Western)
10005 E. Osborn Road
Scottsdale, AZ 85256
Website: www.saltriver.pima-maricopa.nsn.us

Samish Indian Nation (Northwest)
P.O. Box 217
Anacortes, WA 98221

San Carlos Apache Tribe (Western)
P.O. Box 0
San Carlos, AZ 85550

San Juan Southern Paiute Tribe (Western)
P.O. Box 1989
Tuba City, AZ 86045

San Manuel Band of Mission Indians (Pacific)
P.O. Box 266, 26569 Community Center Drive
Highland , CA 92346

San Pasqual Band of Diegueno Mission Indians
    (Pacific)
P.O. Box 365
Valley Center, CA 92082

Santa Rosa Band of Mission Indians (Pacific)
325 N. Western Avenue
Hemet, CA 92543

Santa Rosa Rancheria (Pacific)
P.O. Box 8
Lemoore, CA 93245

Santa Ynez Band of Mission Indians (Pacific)
P.O. Box 517
Santa Ynez, CA 93460

Santa Ysabel Band of Mission Indians (Pacific)
P.O. Box 130
Santa Ysabel, CA 92070

Santee Sioux Tribe (Great Plains)
108 Spirit Lake Avenue West
Niobrara, NE 68760-7219

Sauk-Suiattle Tribe (Northwest)
5318 Chief Brown Lane
Darrington, WA 98241-9421

Sault Ste. Marie Tribe of Chippewa Indians of
    Michigan (Midwest)
523 Ashmun Street
Sault Ste. Marie, MI 49783
Website: www.sootribe.org

Schaghticoke Tribal Nation (Northeast)
P.O. Box 335
Derby, CT 06418-0335

Scotts Valley Band of Pomo Indians (Pacific)
301 Industrial Avenue
Lakeport, CA 95453

Selawik IRA Council (Alaska)
P.O. Box 59
Selawik, AK 99770

Seldovia Village Tribe (Alaska)
P.O. Drawer L
Seldovia, AK 99663

Seminole Indian Tribe of Florida (Southeast)
6300 Stirling Road
Hollywood, FL 33024
Website: www.seminoletribe.com

Seminole Nation of Oklahoma (Eastern Oklahoma)
P.O. Box 1498
Wewoka, OK 74884

Seneca-Cayuga Tribe of Oklahoma (Eastern
    Oklahoma)
P.O. Box 1283
Miami, OK 74355

Seneca Nation of Indians (Northeast)
12837 Route 438
Irving, NY 14081
Website: www.sni.org

Shageluk Native Village (Alaska)
P.O. Box 35
Shageluk, AK 99665

Shakopee Mdewakanton Sioux Community of
    Minnesota (Midwest)
2330 Sioux Trail NW
Prior Lake, MN 55372
Website: www.ccsmdc.org

Shawnee Tribe (Eastern Oklahoma)
P.O. Box 189
Miami, OK 74355

Sherwood Valley Rancheria (Pacific)
190 Sherwood Hill Drive
Willits, CA 95490

Shingle Springs Rancheria (Pacific)
P.O. Box 1340
Shingle Springs, CA 95682-1340

Shoalwater Bay Tribe (Northwest)
P.O. Box 130
Tokeland, WA 98590-0130

Shoonaq' Tribe of Kodiak (Alaska)
713 East Rezanof Drive #B
Kodiak, AK 99615

Shoshone-Bannock Tribes/Fort Hall Business
    Council (Northwest)
P.O. Box 306
Fort Hall, ID 83203-0306
Website: www.shoshonebannocktribes.com

Shoshone-Paiute Tribe (Western)
P.O. Box 219
Owyhee, NV 89832

Siletz Tribal Council (Northwest)
P.O. Box 549
Siletz, OR 97380-0549

Sisseton-Wahpeton Oyate Tribe (Great Plains)
P.O. Box 509
Agency Village, SD 57262-0509

Sitka Tribe of Alaska (Alaska)
456 Katlian Street
Sitka, AK 99835-7505

Skagway Village (Alaska)
P.O. Box 1157
Skagway, AK 99840

Skokomish Tribe (Northwest)
N. 80 Tribal Center Road
Skokomish Nation, WA 98584

Skull Valley Band of Goshute Indians (Western)
3359 South Main Street, #808
Salt Lake City, UT 84029

Sleetmute Traditional Council (Alaska)
P.O. Box 34
Sleetmute, AK 99668

Smith River Rancheria (Pacific)
P.O. Box 239
Smith River, CA 95567-9525

Snoqualmie Tribe (Northwest)
P.O. Box 280
Carnation, WA 98014-0280

Soboba Band of Luiseno Indians (Pacific)
P.O. Box 487
San Jacinto, CA 92581

Sokaogon Chippewa Mole Lake Band of Lake
    Superior Chippewa Indians (Midwest)
3051 Sand Lake Road
Crandon, WI 54520

Solomon Traditional Council (Alaska)
P.O. Box 243
Nome, AK 99762

South Fork Band (Western)
HC 30, Box B-13–Lee
Spring Creek, NV 89815

Southern Ute Indian Tribe (Southwest)
P.O. Box 737, 116 Capote Drive
Ignacio, CO 81137
Website: www.southern-ute.nsn.us

Spirit Lake Sioux Tribe (Great Plains)
P.O. Box 359
Fort Totten, ND 58335

Spokane Tribe of Indians (Northwest)
P.O. Box 100
Wellpinit, WA 99040-0100

Squaxin Island (Northwest)
10 SE Squaxin Lane
Shelton, WA 98584-9200

St. Croix Chippewa Indians of Wisconsin (Midwest)
24663 Angeline Avenue
Hertel, WI 54893

St. George Traditional Council (Alaska)
P.O. Box 940
St. George, AK 99591

St. Regis Band of Mohawk Indians (Northeast)
412 State Route 37
Akwesasne, NY 13655

Standing Rock Sioux Tribe (Great Plains)
P.O. Box D
Fort Yates, ND 58538
Website: www.standingrock.org

Stebbins Community Association (Alaska)
P.O. Box 71002
Stebbins, AK 99671

Stewart Community Council (Western)
5300 Snyder Avenue
Carson City, NV 89701

Stewarts Point Rancheria (Pacific)
1420-D Guerneville Rd, Suite 3
Santa Rosa, CA 95403

Stillaguamish Tribe (Northwest)
P.O. Box 277
Arlington, WA 98223-0277

Stockbridge Munsee Community of Wisconsin
    (Midwest)
N8476 Mo He Con Nuck Road
Bowler, WI 54416
Website: www.mohican.com

Summit Lake Paiute Tribe (Western)
653 Anderson Street
Winnemucca, NV 89445

Suquamish Tribe (Northwest)
P.O. Box 498
Suquamish, WA 98392-0498
Website: www.suquamish.nsn.us

Susanville Indian Rancheria (Pacific)
745 Joaquin Street
Susanville, CA 96130

Swinomish Indian Tribal Community (Northwest)
P.O. Box 817
LaConner, WA 98257-0817

Sycuan Band of Mission Indians (Pacific)
5459 Dehesa Road
El Cajon, CA 92021

Table Bluff Reservation–Wiyot Tribe (Pacific)
1000 Wiyot Drive
Loleta, CA 95551
Website: www.wiyot.com

Table Mountain Rancheria (Pacific)
P.O. Box 410
Friant, CA 93626

Takotna Tribal Council (Alaska)
General Delivery
Takotna, AK 99675

Tazlina Village Council (Alaska)
P.O. Box 87
Glennallen, AK 99588-0087

Telida Native Village Council (Alaska)
P.O. Box 32
McGrath, AK 99627

Teller Traditional Council (Alaska)
P.O. Box 567
Teller, AK 99778

Te-Moak Tribe of Western Shoshone (Western)
525 Sunset Street
Elko, NV 89801

Thlopthlocco Tribal Town (Eastern Oklahoma)
P.O. Box 188
Okemah, OK 74859

Three Affiliated Tribes of Mandan, Hidatsa &
    Arikara Nation (Great Plains)
404 Frontage Road
New Town, ND 58763
Website: www.mhanation.com

Timbisha Shoshone Tribe (Pacific)
P.O. Box 206
Death Valley, CA 92328

Tohono O'odham Nation (Western)
P.O. Box 837
Sells, AZ 85634

Tonawanda Band of Seneca (Northeast)
7027 Meadville Road
Basom, NY 14013

Tonkawa Tribe of Indians of Oklahoma (Southern
    Plains)
P.O. Box 70
Tonkawa, OK 74653

Tonto Apache Tribe (Western)
Tonto Apache Reservation #30
Payson, AZ 85541

Torres-Martinez Desert Cahuilla Indians (Pacific)
P.O. Box 1160, 66725 Martinez Rd.
Thermal, CA 92274

Traditional Village of Togiak (Alaska)
P.O. Box 310
Togiak, AK 99678

Trinidad Rancheria (Pacific)
P.O. Box 630
Trinidad, CA 95570

Tulalip Board of Directors (Northwest)
6700 Totem Beach Road
Marysville, WA 98271-9715
Website: www.tulalip.nsn.us

Tule River Reservation (Pacific)
P.O. Box 589
Porterville, CA 93258

Tuluksak Native Community (Alaska)
P.O. Box 95
Tuluksak, AK 99679-0095

Tunica-Biloxi Tribe of Louisiana (Southeast)
P.O. Box 1589
Marksville, LA 71351
Website: www.tunica.org

Tuolumne Me-Wuk Tribe (Pacific)
P.O. Box 699
Tuolumne, CA 95379

Turtle Mountain Band of Chippewa Indians (Great
    Plains)
P.O. Box 900
Belcourt, ND 58316

Tuscarora Nation (Northeast)
2006 Mt. Hope Road
Lewistown, NY 14092

Twenty-Nine Palms Band of Mission Indians
    (Pacific)
46-200 Harrison Street
Coachella, CA 92236

Twin Hills Village Council (Alaska)
P.O. Box TWA
Twin Hills, AK 99576

Ugashik Traditional Village Council (Alaska)
206 East Fireweed Lane, Suite 204
Anchorage, AK 99503

Uintah & Ouray Ute Indian Tribe (Western)
P.O. Box 190
Ft. Duchesne, UT 84026

Umkumiut Native Village (Alaska)
General Delivery
Nightmute, AK 99690

Unga Tribal Council (Alaska)
P.O. Box 508
Sand Point, AK 99661

United Auburn Indian Community (Pacific)
575 Menlo Drive, Suite 2
Rocklin, CA 95765

United Keetoowah Band of Cherokee Indians
    (Eastern Oklahoma)
P.O. Box 746
Tahlequah, OK 74465
Website: www.ukb-nsn.gov

Upper Lake Rancheria (Pacific)
P.O. Box 516
Upper Lake, CA 95485

Upper Mattaponi Tribe (Southeast)
13383 King William Road
King William, VA 23086

Upper Sioux Community of Minnesota (Midwest)
P.O. Box 147
Granite Falls, MN 56241-0147

Upper Skagit Tribe (Northwest)
25944 Community Plaza Way
Sedro Woolley, WA 98284-9739

Ute Mountain Ute Tribe (Southwest)
P.O. Box 6
Towaoc, CO 81334
Website: www.utemountainute.com

Viejas Band of Kumeyaay Indians (Pacific)
P.O. Box 908
Alpine, CA 91903
Website: www.viejasbandofkumeyaay.org

Village of Anaktuvuk Pass (Alaska)
P.O. Box 21065
Anaktuvuk Pass, AK 99721

Village of Aniak (Alaska)
P.O. Box 176
Aniak, AK 99557

Village of Atmautluak (Alaska)
P.O. Box 6568
Atmautluak, AK 99559

Village of Bill Moore's Slough (Alaska)
P.O. Box 20037
Kotlik, AK 99620

Village of Chefornak (Alaska)
P.O. Box 110
Chefornak, AK 99561-0110

Village of Clarks Point (Alaska)
P.O. Box 90
Clarks Point, AK 99569-0090

Village of Iliamna (Alaska)
P.O. Box 286
Iliamna, AK 99606

Village of Kaltag (Alaska)
P.O. Box 129
Kaltag, AK 99748

Village of Kotlik (Alaska)
P.O. Box 20210
Kotlik, AK 99620

Village of Lower Kalskag (Alaska)
P.O. Box 27
Lower Kalskag, AK 99626

Village of Ohogamiut (Alaska)
P.O. Box 26
Marshall, AK 99585

Village of Old Harbor (Alaska)
P.O. Box 62
Old Harbor, AK 99643

Village of Salamatoff (Alaska)
P.O. Box 2682
Kenai, AK 99611

Village of Stony River (Alaska)
P.O. Box SRV
Stony River, AK 99557

Village of Wainwright (Alaska)
P.O. Box 143
Wainwright, AK 99782

Waccamaw Siouan Development Assn., Inc.
    (Southeast)
P.O. Box 221
Bolton, NC 28423

Walker River Paiute Tribe (Western)
P.O. Box 220
Schurz, NV 89427

Wampanoag Tribe of Gay Head (Aquinnah)
    (Northeast)
20 Black Brook Road
Aquinnah, MA 02535-1546
Website: www.wampanoagtribe.net

Washoe Tribe (Western)
919 Highway 395 South
Gardnerville, NV 89410

Wells Band (Western)
P.O. Box 809
Wells, NV 89835

White Earth Reservation Business Committee
    (Midwest)
P.O. Box 418
White Earth, MN 56591

White Mountain Apache Tribe (Western)
P.O. Box 700
Whiteriver, AZ 85941
Website: www.wmat.nsn.us

Wichita and Affiliated Tribes (Southern Plains)
P.O. Box 729
Anadarko, OK 73005
Website: www.wichita.nsn.us

Winnebago Tribe of Nebraska (Great Plains)
100 Bluff Street, P.O. Box 687
Winnebago, NE 68071
Website: www.winnebagotribe.com

Winnemucca Tribe (Western)
P.O. Box 1370
Winnemucca, NV 89446

Woodfords Community Council (Western)
96 Washoe Boulevard
Markleeville, CA 96120

Wrangell Cooperative Association (Alaska)
P.O. Box 1198
Wrangell, AK 99929

Wyandotte Tribe of Oklahoma (Eastern Oklahoma)
P.O. Box 250
Wyandotte, OK 74370

Yakama Nation (Northwest)
P.O. Box 151
Toppenish, WA 98948-0151

Yakutat Tlingit Tribe (Alaska)
P.O. Box 418
Yakutat, AK 99689

Yankton Sioux Tribe (Great Plains)
P.O. Box 248
Wagner, SD 57380
Website: www.yanktonsiouxtribe.org

Yavapai-Apache Tribe (Western)
2400 W. Datsi Road
Camp Verde, AZ 86322
Website: www.yavapai-apache-nation.com

Yavapai-Prescott Indian Tribe (Western)
530 E. Meritt Street
Prescott, AZ 86301-2038

Yerington Paiute Tribe (Western)
171 Campbell Lane
Yerington, NV 89447

Yomba Shoshone Tribe (Western)
HC61, Box 6275
Austin, NV 89310

Ysleta del Sur Pueblo (Southwest)
119 S. Old Pueblo Rd.
El Paso, TX 79907

Yupiit of Andreafski (Alaska)
P.O. Box 88, Westdahl Street
St. Mary's, AK 99658-0088

Yurok Tribe (Pacific)
P.O. Box 1027
Klamath, CA 99548

Source: National Congress of American Indians. Available at: http://www.ncai.org/Tribal_Governments.119.0.html. Accessed June 21, 2006.

Largest Tribes in the United States, 1980–2000

Tribe	1980	1990	2000
Cherokee	232,080	369,035	281,069
Navajo (Dine')	158,633	225,298	269,202
Canadian and Latin American	7,804	27,179	108,802
Sioux (Lakota, Dakota)	78,608	107,321	108,272
Chippewa (Ojibwa)	73,602	105,988	105,907
Choctaw	50,220	86,231	87,349
Pueblo (Hopi, Jemez, Keres, Pecos, Piro, Tewa, Tiwa, Zuni)	42,552	55,330	59,533
Apache	35,861	53,330	57,060
Lumbee	28,631	50,888	51,913
Iroquois (Cayuga, Mohawk, Oneida, Onondaga, Seneca, Tuscarora)	38,218	52,557	45,212
Creek (Muskogee)	28,278	45,872	40,223
Blackfeet (Blackfoot)	21,964	37,992	27,104
Chickasaw	10,317	21,522	20,887
Tohono O'odham (Papago)	13,297	16,876	17,466
Potawatomi	9,715	16,719	15,817
Yaqui	5,197	9,838	15,224
Tlingit	9,509	14,417	14,825
Alaskan Athapascans	10,136	14,198	14,520
Seminole	10,363	15,564	12,431
Cheyenne	9,918	11,809	11,191
Puget Sound Salish	6,591	10,384	11,034
Comanche	9,037	11,437	10,120
Paiute	9,523	11,369	9,705
Pima	11,722	15,074	8,619
Osage	6,884	10,430	7,868

Source: U.S. Census Bureau. Available at: http://www.census.gov. Accessed June 21, 2006.

National Indian Organizations

American Indian Business Association
Tel: 505-277-8889
Website: http://www.unm.edu/~aiba

American Indian College Fund
Tel: 303-426-8900
Website: www.collegefund.org

American Indian Disability Technical Assistance
    Center
Tel: 406-243-5764
Website: aidtac.ruralinstitute.umt.edu

American Indian Higher Education Consortium
Tel: 703-838-0400
Website: www.aihec.org

American Indian Resources Institute
Tel: 209-460-0924

American Indian Science and Engineering Society
Tel: 505-765-1052
Website: www.aises.org

American Indian Society
Tel: 804-448-3707
Website: www.aisdc.org

Americans for Indian Opportunity
Tel: 505-842-8677
Website: www.aio.org

Catching The Dream Inc.
Tel: 505-262-2351
Website: www.catchingthedream.org

Center for World Indigenous Studies
Tel: 360-407-1095
Website: www.cwis.org

Council of Energy Resource Tribes
Tel: 303-282-7576
Website: www.certredearth.com

First Nations Development Institute
Tel: 540-371-5615
Website: www.firstnations.org

Indian Land Tenure Foundation
Tel: 651-766-8999
Website: www.indianlandtenure.org

Indian Law Resource Center
Tel: 406-449-2006
Website: www.indianlaw.org

Indigenous Language Institute, The
Tel: 505-820-0311
Website: www.indigenous-language.org

Institute for Indian Estate Planning and Probate
Tel: 206-398-4284
Website: www.indianwills.org

Institute for Tribal Government—The Hatfield
    School of Government, The
Tel: 503-725-9000
Website: www.tribalgov.pdx.edu

Intertribal Agriculture Council
Tel: 406-259-3525
Website: www.indianaglink.com

InterTribal Bison Cooperative
Tel: 605-394-9730
Website: www.intertribalbison.org

Intertribal Tax Alliance
Tel: 918-287-5392

Intertribal Timber Council
Tel: 503-282-4296
Website: www.itcnet.org

Intertribal Trust Fund Monitoring Association
Tel: 505-247-1447
Website: www.itmatrustfunds.org

National American Indian Court Judges Association
Tel: 605-342-4804
Website: www.naicja.org

National American Indian Housing Council
Tel: 202-789-1754
Website: www.naihc.net

National Association of Tribal Historic Preservation
    Officers
Tel: 202-628-8476
Website: www.nathpo.org

National Center for American Indian Enterprise
    Development
Tel: 480-545-1298
Website: www.ncaied.org

National Congress of American Indians
Tel: 202-466-7767
Website: www.ncai.org

National Indian Business Association
Tel: 202-233-3766
Website: www.nibanetwork.org

National Indian Child Welfare Association
Tel: 503-222-4044
Website: www.nicwa.org

National Indian Council on Aging
Tel: 505-292-2001
Website: www.nicoa.org

National Indian Education Association
Tel: 202-544-7290
Website: www.niea.org

National Indian Gaming Association
Tel: 202-547-7711
Website: www.indiangaming.org

National Indian Health Board
Tel: 202-742-4262
Website: www.nihb.org

National Indian Justice Center
Tel: 707-579-5507
Website: www.nijc.indian.com

National Native American AIDS Prevention Center
Tel: 510-444-2051
Website: www.nnaapc.org

National Native American Law Enforcement
    Association
Tel: 800-948-3863
Website: www.nnalea.org

National Tribal Environmental Council
Tel: 505-242-2175
Website: www.ntec.org

National Tribal Justice Resource Center
Tel: 303-245-0786
Website: www.tribalresourcecenter.org

Native American Boys and Girls Club of America
Tel: 301-261-6925
Website: www.naclubs.org

Native American Contractors
Tel: 202-349-9845
Website: www.nativeamericancontractors.org

Native American Finance Officers Association
Tel: 602-532-6295
Website: www.nafoa.org

Native American Fish & Wildlife Society
Tel: 303-466-1725
Website: www.nafws.org

Native American Journalists Association
Tel: 605-677-5282
Website: www.naja.com

Native American Rights Fund
Tel: 303-447-8760
Website: www.narf.org

Seventh Generation Fund for Indian Development,
    Inc.
Tel: 707-825-7640
Website: www.7genfund.org

Tribal Child Care Technical Assistance Center
Tel: 580-762-8850
Website: www.nccic.org/tribal

United National Indian Tribal Youth (Unity)
Tel: 405-236-2800
Website: www.unityinc.org

Source: National Congress of American Indians. Available
at: http://www.ncai.org/National_Indian_Organizations
.190.0.html. Accessed June 21, 2006.

American Indian Population 1860–1990

Year	Total U.S. Population	American Indian, Eskimo, and Aleut	Percentage
2000	281,421,906	2,475,956	0.9
1990	248,709,873	2,015,143	0.8
1980	226,545,805	1,534,336	0.7
1970	203,210,158	760,572	0.4
1960	179,325,671	546,228	0.3
1950	150,216,110	342,226	0.2
1940	131,669,275	333,969	0.3
1930	122,775,046	332,397	0.3
1920	105,710,620	244,437	0.2
1910	91,972,266	265,683	0.3
1900	75,994,575	237,196	0.3
1890	62,947,714	248,253	0.4
1880	50,155,783	66,407	0.1
1870	38,558,371	25,731	0.1
1860	31,443,321	44,021	0.1

Note: For 1950 to 1970, Eskimo and Aleut population figures are not included.
Source: U.S. Census Bureau, Population Division.

Poverty on American Indian Reservations and Trust Lands

Name	1990 Population	Land Area (Square Miles)	Persons For Whom Poverty Status Determined	Percent Below Poverty Level
Acoma Pueblo and Trust Lands, NM	2590	416.7	2578	49.65
Acoma Pueblo, NM	2590	411.3	2578	49.65
Acoma Trust Lands, NM	0	5.4	0	0.00
Agua Caliente Reservation, CA	20206	49.6	19575	10.46
Alabama and Coushatta Reservation, TX	478	7.0	548	23.36
Alamo Navajo Reservation, NM	1271	99.0	1259	58.86
Allegany Reservation, NY	7315	41.0	7128	18.73
Alturas Rancheria, CA	5	0.0	3	0.00
Annette Islands Reserve, AK	1469	128.9	1458	9.81
Augustine Reservation, CA	0	1.0	0	0.00
Bad River Reservation, WI	1070	192.0	1031	45.30
Barona Rancheria, CA	537	9.2	573	14.14
Bay Mills Reservation, MI	461	3.5	438	35.16
Benton Paiute Reservation, CA	63	0.2	75	64.00
Berry Creek Rancheria, CA	2	0.1	0	0.00
Big Bend Rancheria, CA	3	0.1	5	0.00
Big Cypress Reservation, FL	484	81.9	449	19.38
Big Lagoon Rancheria, CA	22	0.0	12	0.00
Big Pine Rancheria, CA	452	0.4	455	23.30
Big Sandy Rancheria, CA	51	0.4	59	32.20
Big Valley Rancheria, CA	108	0.2	81	29.63
Bishop Rancheria, CA	1408	1.4	1428	25.21
Blackfeet Reservation, MT	8549	2371.4	8278	46.96

(continues)

Poverty on American Indian Reservations and Trust Lands (cont.)

Name	1990 Population	Land Area (Square Miles)	Persons For Whom Poverty Status Determined	Percent Below Poverty Level
Blue Lake Rancheria, CA	58	0.0	53	11.32
Bois Forte (Nett Lake) Reservation, MN	358	163.0	333	39.64
Bridgeport Colony, CA	49	0.1	28	64.29
Brighton Reservation, FL	524	57.0	524	19.08
Burns Paiute Reservation and Trust Lands, OR	163	18.9	198	34.34
Burns Paiute Reservation, OR	163	1.3	198	34.34
Burns Paiute Trust Lands, OR	0	17.6	0	0.00
Cabazon Reservation, CA	819	3.4	850	27.76
Cahuilla Reservation, CA	104	28.6	107	57.94
Campo Reservation, CA	281	25.8	261	24.90
Camp Verde Reservation, AZ	618	1.0	609	62.56
Canoncito Reservation, NM	1189	121.6	1189	59.80
Capitan Grande Reservation, CA	0	20.5	0	0.00
Carson Colony, NV	248	0.2	262	33.59
Catawba Reservation, SC (state)	174	1.1	170	27.06
Cattaraugus Reservation, NY	2178	33.7	2180	28.17
Cedarville Rancheria, CA	8	0.0	10	100.00
Chehalis Reservation, WA	491	7.0	486	40.95
Chemehuevi Reservation, CA	358	49.5	325	24.92
Cheyenne River Reservation, SD	7743	4265.3	7705	46.32
Chicken Ranch Rancheria, CA	73	0.1	66	0.00
Chitimacha Reservation, LA	286	0.4	311	37.30
Cochiti Pueblo, NM	1342	80.4	1404	19.80
Cocopah Reservation, AZ	515	10.0	578	55.19
Coeur d'Alene Reservation and Trust Lands, ID	5802	598.1	5760	16.25
Coeur d'Alene Reservation, ID	5800	598.1	5757	16.26
Coeur d'Alene Trust Lands, ID	2	0	3	0.00
Cold Springs Rancheria, CA	192	0.2	163	48.47
Colorado River Reservation, AZ, CA	7865	432.7	7870	27.38
Colusa (Cachil Dehe) Rancheria, CA	22	0.3	20	0.00
Colville Reservation, WA	6957	2116.6	6935	27.53
Coos, Lower Umpqua, and Siuslaw Reservation, OR	4	0.0	0	0.00
Cortina Rancheria, CA	30	1.2	29	17.24
Coushatta Reservation, LA	36	0.4	42	50.00
Cow Creek Reservation, OR	58	0.1	89	48.31
Coyote Valley Reservation, CA	135	0.1	139	66.19
Crow Reservation and Trust Lands, MT	6370	3574.1	6305	41.67
Crow Reservation, MT	6366	3543.5	6294	41.74
Crow Trust Lands, MT	4	30.6	11	0.00
Crow Creek Reservation, SD	1756	421.7	1745	48.83
Crow/Northern Cheyenne Area, MT	7	18.6	0	0.00
Cuyapaipe Reservation, CA	0	7.9	0	0.00
Deer Creek Reservation, MN	186	35.1	166	25.90
Devils Lake Sioux Reservation, ND	3588	392.0	3516	43.37

(continues)

Poverty on American Indian Reservations and Trust Lands (cont.)

Name	1990 Population	Land Area (Square Miles)	Persons For Whom Poverty Status Determined	Percent Below Poverty Level
Dresslerville Colony, NV	152	0.1	153	25.49
Dry Creek Rancheria, CA	75	0.1	75	0.00
Duck Valley Reservation, NV	1101	505.8	1076	35.13
Duckwater Reservation, NV	135	6.2	151	24.50
Eastern Cherokee Reservation, NC	6527	81.1	6216	33.74
Elk Valley Rancheria, CA	77	0.1	124	0.00
Ely Colony, NV	59	0.2	85	30.59
Enterprise Rancheria, CA	5	0.1	0	0.00
Fallon Colony, NV	165	0.1	158	48.73
Fallon Reservation, NV	381	12.8	367	32.15
Flandreau Reservation, SD	279	3.5	280	22.50
Flathead Reservation, MT	21259	1938.2	20604	22.86
Fond du Lac Reservation, MN	3229	165.0	3177	25.24
Fort Apache Reservation, AZ	10394	2627.7	10385	50.78
Fort Belknap Reservation and Trust Lands, MT	2508	1013.8	2474	45.27
Fort Belknap Reservation, MT	2508	969.0	2474	45.27
Fort Belknap Trust Lands, MT	0	44.8	0	0.00
Fort Berthold Reservation, ND	5395	1318.9	5216	35.08
Fort Bidwell Reservation, CA	118	5.1	136	47.06
Fort Hall Reservation and Trust Lands, ID	5114	814.9	5045	33.34
Fort Hall Reservation, ID	5060	814.5	4994	33.68
Fort Hall Trust Lands, ID	54	0.4	51	0.00
Fort Independence Reservation, CA	69	0.6	58	22.41
Fort McDermitt Reservation, NV, OR	396	54.6	397	69.52
Fort McDowell Reservation, AZ	640	38.6	628	28.18
Fort Mojave Reservation and Trust Lands, AZ, CA, NV	758	51.3	685	42.19
Fort Mojave Reservation, AZ, CA, NV	496	51.2	470	45.32
Fort Mojave Trust Lands, CA	262	0.1	215	35.35
Fort Peck Reservation, MT	10595	3289.1	10504	31.58
Fort Yuma (Quechan) Reservation, AZ, CA	2084	68.4	2086	43.67
Gila Bend Reservation and Trust Lands, AZ	0	0.7	0	0.00
Gila Bend Reservation, AZ	0	0.7	0	0.00
Gila Bend Trust Lands, AZ	0	0.1	0	0.00
Gila River Reservation, AZ	9540	583.9	9482	63.01
Golden Hill Reservation, CT (state)	10	0.2	9	0.00
Goshute Reservation, NV, UT	99	177.4	79	89.87
Grand Portage Reservation, MN	306	73.2	299	25.08
Grand Ronde Reservation, OR	57	15.4	49	6.12
Grand Traverse Reservation and Trust Lands, MI	228	0.5	263	69.58
Grand Traverse Reservation, MI	12	0.0	0	0.00
Grand Traverse Trust Lands, MI	216	0.4	263	69.58
Greenville Rancheria, CA	24	0.1	25	0.00
Grindstone Creek Rancheria, CA	103	0.1	101	48.51

(continues)

Poverty on American Indian Reservations and Trust Lands (cont.)

Name	1990 Population	Land Area (Square Miles)	Persons For Whom Poverty Status Determined	Percent Below Poverty Level
Hannahville Community and Trust Lands, MI	181	6.8	196	28.57
Hannahville Community, MI	152	5.6	171	29.82
Hannahville Trust Lands, MI	29	1.3	25	20.00
Hassanamisco Reservation, MA (state)	1	0.0	0	0.00
Havasupai Reservation, AZ	423	273.9	433	30.02
Hoh Reservation, WA	96	0.7	116	50.00
Hollywood Reservation, FL	1394	0.7	1407	31.91
Hoopa Valley Reservation, CA	2143	136.9	2182	37.35
Hopi Reservation and Trust Lands, AZ	7360	2436.1	7164	48.24
Hopi Reservation, AZ	7360	2435.7	7164	48.24
Hopi Trust Lands, AZ	0	0.4	0	0.00
Hopland Rancheria, CA	189	0.1	208	72.60
Hualapai Reservation and Trust Lands, AZ	822	1601.0	816	54.66
Hualapai Reservation, AZ	822	1590.8	816	54.66
Hualapai Trust Lands, AZ	0	10.2	0	0.00
Inaja-Cosmit Reservation, CA	0	1.3	0	0.00
Indian Township Reservation, ME	617	37.5	619	34.41
Iowa Reservation, KS, NE	172	19.5	227	15.42
Isabella Reservation and Trust Lands, MI	22944	217.5	22439	17.91
Isabella Reservation, MI	22870	216.8	22325	17.97
Isabella Trust Lands, MI	74	0.7	114	6.14
Isleta Pueblo, NM	2915	328.0	2934	26.79
Jackson Rancheria, CA	21	0.5	27	0.00
Jamestown Klallam Reservation and Trust Lands, WA	22	0.0	34	5.88
Jamestown Klallam Reservation, WA	8	0.0	13	0.00
Jamestown Klallam Trust Lands, WA	14	0	21	9.52
Jamul Village, CA	0	0.0	0	0.00
Jemez Pueblo, NM	1750	139.7	1734	36.79
Jicarilla Apache Reservation, NM	2617	1286.4	2584	28.06
Kaibab Reservation, AZ	165	188.8	120	27.50
Kalispel Reservation, WA	100	7.3	90	40.00
Karok Reservation and Trust Lands, CA	421	0.7	394	7.61
Karok Reservation, CA	0	0.0	0	0.00
Karok Trust Lands, CA	421	0.6	394	7.61
Kickapoo Reservation, KS	478	29.8	476	32.77
Kootenai Reservation, ID	65	0.0	101	39.60
Lac Courte Oreilles Reservation and Trust Lands, WI	2408	107.0	2412	42.66
Lac Courte Oreilles Reservation, WI	2408	106.9	2412	42.66
Lac Courte Oreilles Trust Lands, WI	0	0.1	0	0.00
Lac du Flambeau Reservation, WI	2434	107.8	2390	39.00
Lac Vieux Desert Reservation, MI	124	0.0	145	21.38
Laguna Pueblo and Trust Lands, NM	3731	760.9	3693	31.11
Laguna Pueblo, NM	3731	758.1	3693	31.11
Laguna Trust Lands, NM	0	2.8	0	0.00

(continues)

Poverty on American Indian Reservations and Trust Lands (cont.)

Name	1990 Population	Land Area (Square Miles)	Persons For Whom Poverty Status Determined	Percent Below Poverty Level
La Jolla Reservation, CA	152	13.5	135	31.85
Lake Traverse (Sisseton) Reservation, ND, SD	10733	1449.7	10568	28.43
L'Anse Reservation and Trust Lands, MI	3293	92.0	3239	19.39
L'Anse Reservation, MI	3273	92.0	3217	19.52
L'Anse Trust Lands, MI	20	0.1	22	0.00
La Posta Reservation, CA	10	6.4	0	0.00
Las Vegas Colony, NV	80	6.2	86	37.21
Laytonville Rancheria, CA	142	0.3	137	58.39
Leech Lake Reservation, MN	8669	972.4	8754	30.98
Likely Rancheria, CA	0	0.0	0	0.00
Lone Pine Rancheria, CA	244	0.4	234	27.35
Lookout Rancheria, CA	17	0.1	62	0.00
Los Coyotes Reservation, CA	58	39.2	181	18.23
Lovelock Colony, NV	94	0.0	92	26.09
Lower Brule Reservation, SD	1123	338.7	1081	49.58
Lower Elwha Reservation and Trust Lands, WA	137	0.7	112	33.93
Lower Elwha Reservation, WA	137	0.7	112	33.93
Lower Elwha Trust Lands, WA	0	0	0	0.00
Lower Sioux Community, MN	259	2.7	239	36.82
Lummi Reservation, WA	3147	21.0	3150	19.75
Makah Reservation, WA	1214	42.7	1204	31.23
Manchester (Point Arena) Rancheria, CA	200	0.6	212	56.13
Manzanita Reservation, CA	84	5.6	44	45.45
Maricopa (Ak-Chin) Reservation, AZ	446	32.9	444	44.59
Mashantucket Pequot Reservation, CT	83	1.9	71	0.00
Mattaponi Reservation, VA (state)	70	0.1	74	24.32
Menominee Reservation, WI	3397	355.9	3349	52.13
Mesa Grande Reservation, CA	96	11.9	63	39.68
Mescalero Apache Reservation, NM	2695	719.1	2649	48.43
Miccosukee Reservation, FL	94	127.9	72	29.17
Middletown Rancheria, CA	79	0.2	76	17.11
Mille Lacs Reservation, MN	470	5.3	380	76.58
Minnesota Chippewa Trust Lands, MN	43	0.7	31	16.13
Mississippi Choctaw Reservation and Trust Lands, MS	4073	33.0	4126	42.34
Mississippi Choctaw Reservation, MS	3782	29.1	3879	42.15
Mississippi Choctaw Trust Lands, MS	291	4	247	45.34
Moapa River Reservation, NV	375	112.0	377	50.66
Montgomery Creek Rancheria, CA	11	0.1	8	0.00
Morongo Reservation, CA	1072	49.2	1100	28.91
Muckleshoot Reservation and Trust Lands, WA	3841	6.1	3814	18.25
Muckleshoot Reservation, WA	3841	6.1	3814	18.25
Muckleshoot Trust Lands, WA	0	0	0	0.00

(continues)

Poverty on American Indian Reservations and Trust Lands (cont.)

Name	1990 Population	Land Area (Square Miles)	Persons For Whom Poverty Status Determined	Percent Below Poverty Level
Nambe Pueblo and Trust Lands, NM	1402	32.3	1356	14.75
Nambe Pueblo, NM	1402	32.0	1356	14.75
Nambe Trust Lands, NM	0	0.3	0	0.00
Narragansett Reservation, RI	31	3.4	30	0.00
Navajo Reservation and Trust Lands, AZ, NM, UT	148451	24426.0	147535	56.22
Navajo Reservation, AZ, NM, UT	128356	21877.8	127337	54.84
Navajo Trust Lands, AZ, NM	20095	2548.3	20198	64.96
Nez Percé Reservation, ID	16160	1195.1	15616	15.72
Nisqually Reservation, WA	578	7.9	639	25.67
Nooksack Reservation and Trust Lands, WA	556	4.2	686	41.55
Nooksack Reservation, WA	19	0.7	16	0.00
Nooksack Trust Lands, WA	537	3.5	670	42.54
Northern Cheyenne Reservation and Trust Lands, MT, SD	3923	700.3	3859	48.17
Northern Cheyenne Reservation, MT	3923	697.1	3859	48.17
Northern Cheyenne Trust Lands, MT, SD	0	3.2	0	0.00
North Fork Rancheria, CA	4	0.1	0	0.00
Northwestern Shoshoni Reservation, UT	0	0.3	0	0.00
Oil Springs Reservation, NY	5	1.0	4	75.00
Omaha Reservation, IA, NE	5227	312.0	5117	30.25
Oneida (East) Reservation, NY	37	0.1	41	0.00
Oneida (West) Reservation, WI	18033	102.3	17722	7.61
Onondaga Reservation, NY	771	9.2	771	2.85
Ontonagon Reservation, MI	0	3.7	0	0.00
Osage Reservation, OK	41299	2242.7	40136	15.83
Ozette Reservation, WA	12	1.2	0	0.00
Paiute of Utah Reservation, UT	645	51.0	624	27.08
Pala Reservation, CA	1071	25.4	1115	25.11
Pamunkey Reservation, VA (state)	49	1.7	47	25.53
Papago Reservation, AZ	8730	4342.0	8471	65.13
Pascua Yaqui Reservation, AZ	2412	1.4	2344	62.88
Passamaquoddy Trust Lands, ME	3	146.7	7	0.00
Paucatuck Eastern Pequot Reservation, CT (state)	18	0.3	16	0.00
Pauma Reservation, CA	148	9.4	148	38.51
Payson (Yavapai-Apache) Community, AZ	102	0.1	103	12.62
Pechanga Reservation, CA	398	7.0	391	26.34
Penobscot Reservation and Trust Lands, ME	485	100.7	467	37.04
Penobscot Reservation, ME	476	7.8	462	37.45
Penobscot Trust Lands, ME	9	92.9	5	0.00
Picayune Rancheria, CA	32	0.1	0	0.00
Picuris Pueblo, NM	1882	27.4	1895	39.47
Pine Creek Reservation, MI (state)	24	0.2	22	18.18

(continues)

Poverty on American Indian Reservations and Trust Lands (cont.)

Name	1990 Population	Land Area (Square Miles)	Persons For Whom Poverty Status Determined	Percent Below Poverty Level
Pine Ridge Reservation and Trust Lands, NE, SD	12215	3468.4	11885	62.64
Pine Ridge Reservation, SD	11385	3159.1	11136	62.72
Pine Ridge Trust Lands, NE, SD	830	309.3	749	61.42
Pinoleville Rancheria, CA	130	0.2	70	30.00
Pit River Trust Lands, CA	7	0.4	4	0.00
Pleasant Point Reservation, ME	572	0.8	542	17.16
Poarch Creek Reservation and Trust Lands, AL	212	0.4	255	62.35
Poarch Creek Reservation, AL	212	0.4	255	62.35
Poarch Creek Trust Lands, AL	0	0	0	0.00
Pojoaque Pueblo, NM	2556	21.1	2472	12.78
Poospatuck Reservation, NY (state)	136	0.1	196	30.61
Port Gamble Reservation, WA	552	1.9	541	20.89
Port Madison Reservation, WA	4834	11.7	4812	8.27
Potawatomi (Kansas) Reservation	1082	120.1	1072	26.87
Potawatomi (Wisconsin) Reservation and Trust Lands, WI	279	18.8	266	62.41
Potawatomi (Wisconsin) Reservation, WI	279	18.6	266	62.41
Potawatomi (Wisconsin) Trust Lands, WI	0	0.2	0	0.00
Prairie Island Community, MN	60	0.8	30	63.33
Puyallup Reservation and Trust Lands, WA	32406	28.5	32259	16.91
Puyallup Reservation, WA	32392	28.5	32243	16.92
Puyallup Trust Lands, WA	14	0	16	0.00
Pyramid Lake Reservation, NV	1388	553.9	1349	38.18
Quartz Valley Rancheria, CA	124	1.0	57	5.26
Quileute Reservation, WA	381	1.6	352	55.40
Quinault Reservation, WA	1216	325.2	1263	32.38
Ramah Navajo Community, NM	194	27.7	175	64.00
Ramona Reservation, CA	0	0.9	0	0.00
Rankokus Reservation, NJ (state)	0	0.4	0	0.00
Red Cliff Reservation and Trust Lands, WI	857	22.7	874	48.40
Red Cliff Reservation, WI	857	21.9	874	48.40
Red Cliff Trust Lands, WI	0	0.9	0	0.00
Redding Rancheria, CA	101	0.0	72	0.00
Red Lake Reservation, MN	3699	880.1	3633	49.46
Redwood Valley Rancheria, CA	142	0.1	111	38.74
Reno-Sparks Colony, NV	264	3.2	242	39.26
Resighini Rancheria, CA	28	0.4	51	52.94
Rincon Reservation, CA	1352	6.1	1468	40.74
Roaring Creek Rancheria, CA	18	0.1	20	100.00
Robinson Rancheria, CA	139	0.4	163	41.72

(continues)

Poverty on American Indian Reservations and Trust Lands (cont.)

Name	1990 Population	Land Area (Square Miles)	Persons For Whom Poverty Status Determined	Percent Below Poverty Level
Rocky Boy's Reservation and Trust Lands, MT	1954	168.3	1927	47.48
Rocky Boy's Reservation, MT	1547	88.5	1527	48.46
Rocky Boy's Trust Lands, MT	407	79.8	400	43.75
Rohnerville Rancheria, CA	14	0.0	0	0.00
Rosebud Reservation and Trust Lands, SD	9696	1974.6	9532	53.58
Rosebud Reservation, SD	8352	1388.2	8254	50.19
Rosebud Trust Lands, SD	1344	586.4	1278	75.43
Round Valley Reservation and Trust Lands, CA	1183	94.9	1178	26.32
Round Valley Reservation, CA	1183	78.2	1178	26.32
Round Valley Trust Lands, CA	0	16.6	0	0.00
Rumsey Rancheria, CA	8	0.1	19	0.00
Sac and Fox (Iowa) Reservation	577	5.9	585	28.55
Sac and Fox (KS-NE) Reservation and Trust Lands, KS, NE	210	24.0	162	9.26
Sac and Fox (KS-NE) Reservation, KS, NE	209	23.1	159	9.43
Sac and Fox (KS-NE) Trust Lands, KS, NE	1	0.9	3	0.00
St. Croix Reservation, WI	505	2.9	483	49.48
St. Regis Mohawk Reservation, NY	1978	19.0	1974	26.44
Salt River Reservation, AZ	4852	80.0	4722	40.15
San Carlos Reservation, AZ	7294	2910.6	7174	61.99
Sandia Pueblo, NM	3971	39.0	3918	26.70
Sandy Lake Reservation, MN	37	0.4	28	25.00
San Felipe Pueblo, NM	2434	78.6	2517	35.28
San Felipe/Santa Ana joint area, NM	0	1.1	0	0.00
San Felipe/Santo Domingo joint area, NM	0	1.2	0	0.00
San Ildefonso Pueblo, NM	1499	43.7	1585	11.42
San Juan Pueblo, NM	5209	26.7	5231	30.70
San Manuel Reservation, CA	80	1.0	59	54.24
San Pasqual Reservation, CA	512	2.2	514	31.71
Santa Ana Pueblo, NM	593	101.2	624	13.14
Santa Clara Pueblo, NM	10193	76.8	10081	24.08
Santa Rosa Rancheria, CA	323	0.3	319	48.59
Santa Rosa Reservation, CA	50	17.1	58	70.69
Santa Ynez Reservation, CA	279	0.2	317	16.09
Santa Ysabel Reservation, CA	169	14.4	165	10.30
Santee Reservation, NE	758	172.9	740	41.08
Santo Domingo Pueblo, NM	2992	107.2	2773	33.32
San Xavier Reservation, AZ	1172	111.4	1123	64.92
Sauk-Suiattle Reservation, WA	124	0.1	112	26.79

(continues)

Poverty on American Indian Reservations and Trust Lands (cont.)

Name	1990 Population	Land Area (Square Miles)	Persons For Whom Poverty Status Determined	Percent Below Poverty Level
Sault Ste. Marie Reservation and Trust Lands, MI	768	1.3	720	38.06
Sault Ste. Marie Reservation, MI	385	0.9	357	42.30
Sault Ste. Marie Trust Lands, MI	383	0.4	363	33.88
Schaghticoke Reservation, CT (state)	10	0.4	10	20.00
Seminole Trust Lands, FL	114	0.1	105	45.71
Shakopee Community, MN	203	0.5	225	4.44
Sheep Ranch Rancheria, CA	0	0.0	0	0.00
Sherwood Valley Rancheria, CA	15	0.5	6	0.00
Shingle Springs Rancheria, CA	18	0.3	12	0.00
Shinnecock Reservation, NY (state)	375	1.3	397	15.11
Shoalwater Reservation, WA	131	1.2	124	80.65
Siletz Reservation, OR	5	5.8	0	0.00
Skokomish Reservation, WA	614	8.2	607	46.13
Skull Valley Reservation, UT	32	28.2	17	0.00
Smith River Rancheria, CA	104	0.2	179	2.79
Soboba Reservation, CA	369	9.1	435	25.98
Sokaogon Chippewa Community and Trust Lands, WI	357	2.9	333	64.26
Sokaogon Chippewa Community, WI	266	2.4	298	67.11
Sokaogon Chippewa Trust Lands, WI	91	0.4	35	40.00
Southern Ute Reservation, CO	7804	1058.6	7855	17.91
Spokane Reservation, WA	1502	237.5	1435	37.14
Squaxin Island Reservation and Trust Lands, WA	157	2.5	194	29.90
Squaxin Island Reservation, WA	0	2.2	0	0.00
Squaxin Island Trust Lands, WA	157	0.3	194	29.90
Standing Rock Reservation, ND, SD	7956	3567.3	7917	44.81
Stewarts Point Rancheria, CA	91	0.1	89	62.92
Stillaguamish Reservation, WA	113	0.0	112	76.79
Stockbridge Reservation, WI	581	34.8	563	25.04
Sulphur Bank (El-Em) Rancheria, CA	93	0.1	96	50.00
Summit Lake Reservation, NV	7	17.4	8	0.00
Susanville Reservation, CA	454	0.2	490	20.61
Swinomish Reservation, WA	2282	11.4	2277	15.42
Sycuan Reservation, CA	4	1.0	0	0.00
Table Bluff Rancheria, CA	48	0.0	45	64.44
Table Mountain Rancheria, CA	51	0.2	44	22.73
Tama Reservation, GA (state)	22	0.1	20	70.00
Taos Pueblo and Trust Lands, NM	4745	156.1	4682	32.14
Taos Pueblo, NM	4681	154.9	4610	31.91
Taos Trust Lands, NM	64	1.2	72	47.22
Te-Moak Reservation and Trust Lands, NV	949	27.8	950	35.68
Te-Moak Reservation, NV	918	16.6	923	36.08
Te-Moak Trust Lands, NV	21	11.2	27	22.22
Tesuque Pueblo and Trust Lands, NM	697	27.0	700	15.43
Tesuque Pueblo, NM	697	26.5	700	15.43

(continues)

Poverty on American Indian Reservations and Trust Lands (cont.)

Name	1990 Population	Land Area (Square Miles)	Persons For Whom Poverty Status Determined	Percent Below Poverty Level
Tesuque Trust Lands, NM	0	0.5	0	0.00
Tonawanda Reservation, NY	501	11.8	483	15.53
Torres-Martinez Reservation, CA	1462	34.5	1628	51.29
Trinidad Rancheria, CA	78	0.1	71	4.23
Tulalip Reservation, WA	7103	35.2	7060	10.44
Tule River Reservation, CA	798	84.4	798	43.86
Tunica-Biloxi Reservation, LA	29	0.2	32	6.25
Tuolumne Rancheria, CA	135	0.5	85	25.88
Turtle Mountain Reservation and Trust Lands, ND, SD	7106	138.8	7022	54.00
Turtle Mountain Reservation, ND	4987	69.9	4952	52.40
Turtle Mountain Trust Lands, ND, SD	2119	68.8	2070	57.83
Tuscarora Reservation, NY	772	9.3	709	5.22
Twenty-Nine Palms Reservation, CA	0	0.2	0	0.00
Uintah and Ouray Reservation, UT	17224	6768.2	17105	22.95
Umatilla Reservation, OR	2502	271.1	2474	22.03
Upper Lake Rancheria, CA	76	0.7	68	47.06
Upper Sioux Community, MN	49	1.2	26	34.62
Upper Skagit Reservation, WA	180	0.2	173	50.87
Ute Mountain Reservation and Trust Lands, CO, NM, UT	1320	900.6	1352	48.30
Ute Mountain Reservation, CO, NM, UT	1314	888.9	1344	48.59
Ute Mountain Trust Lands, UT	6	11.6	8	0.00
Vermillion Lake Reservation, MN	91	1.6	35	0.00
Viejas Rancheria, CA	411	2.5	422	26.30
Walker River Reservation, NV	802	534.4	703	27.88
Warm Springs Reservation and Trust Lands, OR	3076	1019.3	3033	28.59
Warm Springs Reservation, OR	3076	1010.5	3033	28.59
Warm Springs Trust Lands, OR	0	8.8	0	0.00
Washoe Reservation, NV	157	4.5	112	16.07
White Earth Reservation, MN	8727	1088.4	8677	30.78
Wind River Reservation, WY	21851	3471.4	21568	22.44
Winnebago Reservation, NE	2341	173.4	2339	27.45
Winnemucca Colony, NV	67	0.6	54	11.11
Wisconsin Winnebago Reservation and Trust Lands, WI	700	5.0	603	42.95
Wisconsin Winnebago Reservation, WI	506	1.3	449	51.00
Wisconsin Winnebago Trust Lands, WI	194	3.7	154	19.48
Woodfords Community, CA	14	0.6	20	0.00
XL Ranch Reservation, CA	35	14.4	23	34.78
Yakima Reservation and Trust Lands, WA	27668	2137.6	26691	32.81
Yakima Reservation, WA	27522	2104.3	26654	32.84
Yakima Trust Lands, WA	146	33.3	37	10.81
Yankton Reservation, SD	6269	665.8	6072	37.30

(continues)

Poverty on American Indian Reservations and Trust Lands (cont.)

Name	1990 Population	Land Area (Square Miles)	Persons For Whom Poverty Status Determined	Percent Below Poverty Level
Yavapai Reservation, AZ	176	2.2	190	17.89
Yerington Reservation and Trust Lands, NV	428	2.6	401	30.17
Yerington Reservation, NV	275	2.5	244	24.59
Yerington Trust Lands, NV	153	0	157	38.85
Yomba Reservation, NV	95	7.3	94	39.36
Ysleta Del Sur Pueblo, TX	292	0.2	370	26.22
Yurok Reservation, CA	1357	84.7	1218	38.92
Zia Pueblo and Trust Lands, NM	637	189.9	638	33.39
Zia Pueblo, NM	637	186.6	638	33.39
Zia Trust Lands, NM	0	3.3	0	0.00
Zuni Pueblo, AZ, NM	7412	654.3	7422	50.59

Source: United States Census, www.census.gov/geo/www/ezstate/airpov.pdf, accessed April 27, 2007.

Native American Terminated Tribes, 1955–1969

Tribe	Date of Termination	Tribal Membership	Tribal Land (acres)
Alabama-Couchatta Tribes, Texas	1955	450	3,200
California Rancherias and Reservations	1969	1,107	4,316
Catawba of South Carolina	1962	631	3,388
Klamath Tribe of Oregon	1961	2,133	862,662
Menominee Tribe of Wisconsin	1961	3,270	233,881
Ottawa Tribe of Oklahoma	1959	630	0
Paiute Indians of Utah	1957	232	42,839
Peoria Tribe of Oklahoma	1959	640	0
Ponca Tribe of Nebraska	1966	442	834
Uintah and Ouray Utes of Utah	1961	490	211,430
Western Oregon Indians (60 bands)	1956	2,081	3,158
Wyandot Tribe of Oklahoma	1959	1,157	94
Totals		13,263	1,365,802

Source: Hirschfelder, Arlene, and Martha Kreipe de Montaño, *The Native American Almanac* (1993). Macmillan General Reference, New York.

Canadian First Nations

British Columbia
Yavs9
Akisq'nuk First Nation
P.O. BOX 130
WINDERMERE, BC, V0B 2L0

Adams Lake
P.O. BOX 588
BC, CHASE, BC, V0E 1M0

Ahousaht
GENERAL DELIVERY
AHOUSAHT, BC, V0R 1A0

Aitchelitz
8150 AITKEN ROAD
CHILLIWACK, BC, V2R 4H5

Alexandria
7 - 423 Elliot Street
Quesnel, BC, V2J 1Y6

Alexis Creek
P.O. BOX 69
CHILANKO FORKS, BC, V0L 1H0

Ashcroft
P.O. BOX 440
ASHCROFT, BC, V0K 1A0

Beecher Bay
4901B EAST SOOKE ROAD
RR 6, SOOKE, BC, V0S 1N0

Blueberry River First Nations
P.O. BOX 3009
BUICK, BC, V0C 2R0

Bonaparte
P.O. BOX 669
CACHE CREEK, BC, V0K 1H0

Boothroyd
P.O. BOX 295
BOSTON BAR, BC, V0K 1C0

Boston Bar First Nation
P.O. BOX 369
BOSTON BAR, BC, V0K 1C0

Bridge River
P.O. BOX 190
LILLOOET, BC, V0K 1V0

Burns Lake
BAG 9000
BURNS LAKE, BC, V0J 1E0

Burrard
3075 TAKAYA DRIVE
NORTH VANCOUVER, BC, V7H 2V6

Campbell River
1400 WEIWAIKUM ROAD
CAMPBELL RIVER, BC, V9W 5W8

Canim Lake
P.O. BOX 1030
100 MILE HOUSE, BC, V0K 2E0

Canoe Creek
GENERAL DELIVERY
DOG CREEK, BC, V0L 1J0

Cape Mudge
P.O. BOX 220
QUATHIASKI COVE, BC, V0P 1N0

Cayoose Creek
P.O. BOX 484
LILLOOET, BC, V0K 1V0

Chawathil
4-60814 LOUGHEED HIGHWAY
HOPE, BC, V0X 1L3

Cheam
52130 OLD YALE ROAD
ROSEDALE, BC, V0X 1X0

Chehalis
4690 Salish Way
CHEHALIS ROAD, AGASSIZ, BC, V0M 1A0

Chemainus First Nation
12611-A TRANS CANADA HIGHWAY
LADYSMITH, BC, V9G 1M5

Cheslatta Carrier Nation
P.O. BOX 909
BURNS LAKE, BC, V0J 1E0

Coldwater
P.O. BOX 4600
MERRITT, BC, V1K 1B8

Comox
3320 COMOX ROAD
COURTENAY, BC, V9N 3P8

Cook's Ferry
P.O. BOX 130
SPENCES BRIDGE, BC, V0K 2L0

Cowichan
5760 ALLENBY ROAD
DUNCAN, BC, V9L 5J1

Da'naxda'xw First Nation
P.O. BOX 330
ALERT BAY, BC, V0N 1A0

Ditidaht
P.O. BOX 340
PORT ALBERNI, BC, V9Y 7M8

Doig River
P.O. BOX 56
ROSE PRAIRIE, BC, V0C 2H0

Douglas
P.O. BOX 606
MOUNT CURRIE, BC, V0N 2K0

Ehattesaht
P.O. BOX 59
ZEBALLOS, BC, V0P 2A0

Esketemc
P.O. BOX 4479
WILLIAMS LAKE, BC, V2G 2V5

Esquimalt
1189 Kosapsum Crescent
VICTORIA, BC, V9A 7K7

Fort Nelson First Nation
MILE 293 ALASKA HWY
RR 1, FORT NELSON, BC, V0C 1R0

Gitanmaax
P.O. BOX 440
HAZELTON, BC, V0J 1Y0

Gitanyow
P.O. BOX 340
KITWANGA, BC, V0J 2A0

Gitsegukla
36 CASCADE AVENUE
RR 1, SOUTH HAZELTON, BC, V0J 2R0

Gitwangak
P.O. BOX 400
KITWANGA, BC, V0J 2A0

Gitxaala Nation
P.O. BOX 149
KITKATLA, BC, V0V 1C0

Glen Vowell
RR 1 SITE J COMP 43
HAZELTON, BC, V0J 1Y0

Gwa'Sala-Nakwaxda'xw
P.O. BOX 998
PORT HARDY, BC, V0N 2P0

Gwawaenuk Tribe
P.O. BOX 344
PORT MCNEIL, BC, V0N 2R0

Hagwilget Village
P.O. BOX 460
NEW HAZELTON, BC, V0J 2J0

Halalt
8017 CHEMAINUS ROAD
CHEMAINUS, BC, V0R 1K5

Halfway River First Nation
P.O. BOX 59
WONOWON, BC, V0C 2N0

Hartley Bay
GENERAL DELIVERY
445 HAYIMIISAXAA WAY, HARTLEY BAY, BC,
   V0V 1A0

Heiltsuk
P.O. BOX 880
WAGLISLA, BC, V0T 1Z0

Hesquiaht
P.O. BOX 2000
TOFINO, BC, V0R 2Z0

High Bar
P.O. BOX 458
CLINTON, BC, V0K 1K0

Homalco
1218 BUTE CRESCENT
CAMPBELL RIVER, BC, V9H 1G5

Hupacasath First Nation
P.O. BOX 211
PORT ALBERNI, BC, V9Y 7M7

Huu-ay-aht First Nations
P.O. BOX 70
BAMFIELD, BC, V0R 1B0

Iskut
P.O. BOX 30
ISKUT, BC, V0J 1K0

Ka:'yu:'k't'h'/Che:k:tles7et'h' First Nations
GENERAL DELIVERY
KYUQUOT, BC, V0P 1J0

Kamloops
202 - 355 YELLOWHEAD HWY
KAMLOOPS, BC, V2H 1H1

Kanaka Bar
P.O. BOX 210
LYTTON, BC, V0K 1Z0

Katzie
10946 KATZIE ROAD
PITT MEADOWS, BC, V3Y 2G6

Kispiox
COMP 25, SITE K, RR 1
HAZELTON, BC, V0J 1Y0

Kitamaat
P.O. BOX 1101
HAISLA, BC, V0T 2B0

Kitasoo
GENERAL DELIVERY
KLEMTU, BC, V0T 1L0

Kitselas
5500 GITAUS ROAD, RR 2
TERRACE, BC, V8G 3Z9

Kitsumkalum
P.O. BOX 544
TERRACE, BC, V8G 4B5

Klahoose First Nation
P.O. BOX 9, SQUIRREL COVE
MANSONS LANDING, BC, V0P 1K0

Kluskus
P.O. BOX 4639
QUESNEL, BC, V2J 3J8

Kwadacha
207 - 513 AHBAU STREET
PRINCE GEORGE, BC, V2M 3R8

Kwakiutl
P.O. BOX 1440
PORT HARDY, BC, V0N 2P0

Kwantlen First Nation
23690 GABRIEL LANE, P.O. BOX 108
FORT LANGLEY, BC, V1M 2R4

Kwaw-kwaw-Apilt
P.O. BOX 2065 STN MAIN, 8775 ASHWELL ROAD
CHILLIWACK, BC, V2R 1A5

Kwiakah
1440 OLD ISLAND HWY
CAMPBELL RIVER, BC, V9W 2E3

Kwicksutaineuk-ah-kwaw-ah-mish
P.O. BOX 10, 1 Front Street
ALERT BAY, BC, V0N 1A0

Kwikwetlem First Nation
65 COLONY FARM ROAD
COQUITLAM, BC, V3C 3V4

Lake Babine Nation
P.O. BOX 879
BURNS LAKE, BC, V0J 1E0

Lake Cowichan First Nation
1609 DOUGLAS ST
VICTORIA, BC, V8W 2G5

Lax-kw'alaams
206 SHASHAAK STREET
PORT SIMPSON, BC, V0V 1H0

Leq' a: mel First Nation
43101 Leq'a:mel Way
DEROCHE, BC, V0M 1G0

Lheidli T'enneh
1041 WHENUN ROAD
PRINCE GEORGE, BC, V2K 5X8

Little Shuswap Lake
P.O. BOX 1100
CHASE, BC, V0E 1M0

Lower Kootenay
830 SIMON ROAD
CRESTON, BC, V0B 1G2

Lower Nicola
181 NAWISHASKIN LANE
MERRITT, BC, V1K 1N2

Lower Similkameen
P.O. BOX 100
KEREMEOS, BC, V0X 1N0

Lyackson
9137 CHEMAINUS ROAD
CHEMAINUS, BC, V0R 1K5

Lytton
P.O. BOX 20
LYTTON, BC, V0K 1Z0

Malahat First Nation
110 Thunder Rd. RR4
MILL BAY, BC, V0R 2P4

Mamalilikulla-Qwe'Qwa'Sot'Em
1441A OLD ISLAND HWY
CAMPBELL RIVER, BC, V9W 2E4

Matsqui
P.O. BOX 10
MATSQUI, BC, V4X 3R2

McLeod Lake
GENERAL DELIVERY
MCLEOD LAKE, BC, V0J 2G0

Metlakatla
P.O. BOX 459
PRINCE RUPERT, BC, V8J 3R2

Moricetown
205 BEAVER ROAD
SMITHERS, BC, V0J 2N1

Mount Currie
P.O. BOX 602
MOUNT CURRIE, BC, V0N 2K0

Mowachaht/Muchalaht
P.O. BOX 459
GOLD RIVER, BC, V0P 1G0

Musqueam
6735 SALISH DRIVE
VANCOUVER, BC, V6N 4C4

N'Quatqua
P.O. BOX 88
D'ARCY, BC, V0N 1L0

Nadleh Whuten
P.O. BOX 36
FORT FRASER, BC, V0J 1N0

Nak'azdli
P.O. BOX 1329
FORT ST. JAMES, BC, V0J 1P0

Namgis First Nation
P.O. BOX 210
ALERT BAY, BC, V0N 1A0

Nanoose First Nation
209 MALLARD WAY
LANTZVILLE, BC, V0R 2H0

Nazko
P.O. Box 4129
QUESNEL, BC, V2J 3J2

Nee-Tahi-Buhn
RR 2 SITE 7 COMP 28
BURNS LAKE, BC, V0J 1E0

Neskonlith
P.O. BOX 608
CHASE, BC, V0E 1M0

New Westminster
105 - 3680 RAE AVENUE
VANCOUVER, BC, V5R 2P5

Nicomen
P.O. BOX 670
LYTTON, BC, V0K 1Z0

Nisga'a Village of Gingolx
1304 BROAD STREET
KINCOLITH, BC, V0V 1B0

Nisga'a Village of Gitwinksihlkw
P.O. BOX 1
GITWINKSIHLKW, BC, V0J 3T0

Nisga'a Village of Laxgalt'sap
P.O. BOX 200
GREENVILLE, BC, V0J 1X0

Nisga'a Village of New Aiyansh
P.O. BOX 233
NEW AIYANSH, BC, V0J 1A0

Nooaitch
18 SHACKELLY ROAD
MERRITT, BC, V1K 1N9

Nuchatlaht
P.O. BOX 40
ZEBALLOS, BC, V0P 2A0

Nuxalk Nation
P.O. BOX 65
BELLA COOLA, BC, V0T 1C0

Okanagan
12420 WESTSIDE ROAD
VERNON, BC, V1H 2A4

Old Massett Village Council
P.O. BOX 189
OLD MASSET, BC, V0T 1M0

Oregon Jack Creek
P.O. BOX 940
ASHCROFT, BC, V0K 1A0

Osoyoos
RR 3 SITE 25 COMP 1
OLIVER, BC, V0H 1T0

Oweekeno/Wuikinuxv Nation
P.O. BOX 3500
OWEEKENO VILLAGE RIVERS INLET, PORT
          HARDY, BC, V0N 2P0

Pacheedaht First Nation
GENERAL DELIVERY
PORT RENFREW, BC, V0S 1K0

Pauquachin
9010 WEST SAANICH ROAD
SIDNEY, BC, V8L 5W4

Penelakut
P.O. BOX 360
CHEMAINUS, BC, V0K 1K0

Penticton
RR 2 SITE 80 COMP 19
PENTICTON, BC, V2A 6J7

Peters
16870 PETERS ROAD
RR 2, HOPE, BC, V0X 1L2

Popkum
C/O STO:LO NATION, 1-7201 VEDDER ROAD
CHILLIWACK, BC, V2R 4G5

Prophet River First Nation
P.O. BOX 3250
FORT NELSON, BC, V0C 1R0

Qualicum First Nation
5850 RIVER ROAD
QUALICUM BEACH, BC, V9K 1Z5

Quatsino
P.O. BOX 100
COAL HARBOUR, BC, V0N 1K0

Red Bluff
1515 ARBUTUS ROAD, P.O. BOX 4693
QUESNEL, BC, V2J 3J9

Saik'uz First Nation
RR 1 SITE 12 COMP 26
VANDERHOOF, BC, V0J 3A0

Samahquam
P.O. BOX 610
MOUNT CURRIE, BC, V0N 2K0

Saulteau First Nations
P.O. BOX 330
MOBERLY LAKE, BC, V0C 1X0

Scowlitz
P.O. BOX 76
LAKE ERROCK, BC, V0M 1N0

Seabird Island
P.O. BOX 650
AGASSIZ, BC, V0M 1A0

Sechelt
P.O. BOX 740
SECHELT, BC, V0N 3A0

Semiahmoo
16049 BEACH ROAD
SURREY, BC, V4P 3C5

Seton Lake
SITE 3 BOX 76
SHALALTH, BC, V0N 3C0

Shackan
2160 SETTLER'S ROAD
LOWER NICOLA, BC, V1K 1M9

Shuswap
P.O. BOX 790
INVERMERE, BC, V0A 1K0

Shxw'ow'hamel First Nation
58700A ST ELMO ROAD
HOPE, BC, V0X 1L2

Shxwhá:y Village
44680 SCHWEYEY ROAD
CHILLIWACK, BC, V2R 5M5

Simpcw First Nation
P.O. BOX 220
BARRIERE, BC, V0E 1E0

Siska
P.O. BOX 519
LYTTON, BC, V0K 1Z0

Skatin Nations
P.O. BOX 190
PEMBERTON, BC, V0N 2L0

Skawahlook First Nation
58611A LOUGHEED HWY
AGASSIZ, BC, V0M 1A2

Skeetchestn
P.O. BOX 178
SAVONA, BC, V0K 2J0

Skidegate
P.O. BOX 1301
SKIDEGATE, BC, V0T 1S1

Skin Tyee
P.O. BOX 131
SOUTHBANK, BC, V0J 2P0

Skowkale
P.O. BOX 2159
SARDIS, BC, V2R 1A7

Skuppah
P.O. BOX 400
LYTTON, BC, V0K 1Z0

Skwah
P.O. BOX 178
CHILLIWACK, BC, V2P 6H7

Sliammon
RR 2, SLIAMMON RD
POWELL RIVER, BC, V8A 4Z3

Snuneymuxw First Nation
668 CENTRE STREET
NANAIMO, BC, V9R 4Z4

Soda Creek
3405 MOUNTAIN HOUSE ROAD
WILLIAMS LAKE, BC, V2G 5L5

Songhees First Nation
1500D ADMIRALS ROAD
VICTORIA, BC, V9A 2R1

Soowahlie
4172 SOOWAHLIE ROAD
CULTUS LAKE, BC, V2R 4Y2

Spallumcheen
P.O. BOX 460
ENDERBY, BC, V0E 1V0

Spuzzum
SITE 3, C-11, RR 1
YALE, BC, V0K 2S0

Squamish
P.O. BOX 86131
NORTH VANCOUVER, BC, V7L 4J5

Squiala First Nation
8528 ASHWELL ROAD
CHILLIWACK, BC, V2P 7Z9

St. Mary's
7470 MISSION ROAD
CRANBROOK, BC, V1C 7E5

Stellat'en First Nation
P.O. BOX 760
FRASER LAKE, BC, V0J 1S0

Stone
GENERAL DELIVERY
HANCEVILLE, BC, V0L 1K0

Sumas First Nation
3092 SUMAS MOUNTAIN ROAD, RR 4
ABBOTSFORD, BC, V3G 2J2

T'Sou-ke First Nation
P.O. BOX 307, 2154 LAZZAR ROAD
SOOKE, BC, V0S 1N0

T'it'q'et
P.O. BOX 615
LILLOOET, BC, V0K 1V0

Tahltan
P.O. BOX 46
TELEGRAPH CREEK, BC, V0J 2W0

Takla Lake First Nation
P.O. BOX 2310
PRINCE GEORGE, BC, V2L 3N2

Tl'azt'en Nation
P.O. BOX 670
FORT ST. JAMES, BC, V0J 1P0

Tl'etinqox-t'in Government Office
P.O. BOX 168
ALEXIS CREEK, BC, V0L 1A0

Tla-o-qui-aht First Nations
P.O. BOX 18
TOFINO, BC, V0R 2Z0

Tlatlasikwala
P.O. BOX 578
PORT HARDY, BC, V0N 2P0

Tlowitsis Tribe
106-1434 ISLAND HIGHWAY
CAMPBELL RIVER, BC, V9W 8C9

Tobacco Plains
P.O. BOX 76
GRASMERE, BC, V0B 1R0

Toosey
P.O. BOX 80
RISKE CREEK, BC, V0L 1T0

Toquaht
P.O. BOX 759, 1316 PINE STREET
UCLUELET, BC, V0R 3A0

Ts'kw'aylaxw First Nation
P.O. BOX 2200
LILLOOET, BC, V0K 1V0

Tsartlip
P.O. BOX 70, 800 STELLYS CROSS ROAD
BRENTWOOD BAY, BC, V8M 1R3

Tsawataineuk
GENERAL DELIVERY
KINGCOME INLET, BC, V0N 2B0

Tsawout First Nation
P.O. BOX 121
SAANICHTON, BC, V8M 2C3

Tsawwassen First Nation
131 TSAWWASSEN DRIVE NORTH
DELTA, BC, V4M 4G2

Tsay Keh Dene
11 - 1839 1ST AVENUE
PRINCE GEORGE, BC, V2L 2Y8

Tseshaht
P.O. BOX 1218
PORT ALBERNI, BC, V9Y 7M1

Tseycum
1210 TOTEM LANE
SIDNEY, BC, V8L 5S4

Tzeachten
45855 PROMONTORY ROAD
CHILLIWACK, BC, V2R 4E2

Uchucklesaht
P.O. BOX 1118
PORT ALBERNI, BC, V9Y 7L9

Ucluelet First Nation
P.O. BOX 699
UCLUELET, BC, V0R 3A0

Ulkatcho
P.O. BOX 3430
ANAHIM LAKE, BC, V0L 1C0

Union Bar
P.O. BOX 788
HOPE, BC, V0X 1L0

Upper Nicola
P.O. BOX 3700
MERRITT, BC, V1K 1B8

Upper Similkameen
P.O. BOX 310
KEREMEOS, BC, V0X 1N0

West Moberly First Nations
P.O. BOX 90
MOBERLY LAKE, BC, V0C 1X0

Westbank First Nation
301-515 HWY 97 SOUTH
KELOWNA, BC, V1Z 3J2

Wet'suwet'en First Nation
P.O. BOX 760
BURNS LAKE, BC, V0J 1E0

Whispering Pines/Clinton
615 WHISPERING PINES DRIVE
KAMLOOPS, BC, V2B 8S4

Williams Lake
2672 INDIAN DRIVE
WILLIAMS LAKE, BC, V2G 5K9

Xaxli'p
P.O. BOX 1330
LILLOOET, BC, V0K 1V0

Xeni Gwet'in First Nations Government
GENERAL DELIVERY
NEMIAH VALLEY, BC, V0L 1X0

Yakweakwioose
RR 2, 7176 CHILLIWACK RIVER ROAD
SARDIS, BC, V2R 1B1

Yale First Nation
P.O. BOX 1869
HOPE, BC, V0X 1L0

Yekooche
1890 - 3RD AVENUE
PRINCE GEORGE, BC, V2M 1G4

Alberta
Alexander
P.O. BOX 3419
MORINVILLE, AB, T8R 1S3

Alexis Nakota Sioux Nation
P.O. BOX 7
GLENEVIS, AB, T0E 0X0

Athabasca Chipewyan First Nation
P.O. BOX 366
FORT CHIPEWYAN, AB, T0P 1B0

Bearspaw

Beaver First Nation
P.O. BOX 2700
HIGH LEVEL, AB, T0H 1Z0

Beaver Lake Cree Nation
P.O. BOX 960
LAC LA BICHE, AB, T0A 2C0

Bigstone Cree Nation
P.O. BOX 960
DESMARAIS, AB, T0G 2K0

Blood
P.O. BOX 60
STANDOFF, AB, T0L 1Y0

Chiniki
P.O. BOX 40
MORLEY, AB, T0L 1N0

Chipewyan Prairie First Nation
GENERAL DELIVERY
CHARD, AB, T0P 1G0

Cold Lake First Nations
P.O. BOX 1769
COLD LAKE, AB, T9M 1P4

Dene Tha'
P.O. BOX 120
CHATEH, AB, T0H 0S0

Driftpile First Nation
GENERAL DELIVERY
DRIFTPILE, AB, T0G 0V0

Duncan's First Nation
P.O. BOX 148
BROWNVALE, AB, T0H 0L0

Enoch Cree Nation #440
P.O. BOX 29
ENOCH, AB, T7X 3Y3

Ermineskin Tribe
P.O. BOX 219
HOBBEMA, AB, T0C 1N0

Fort McKay First Nation
P.O. BOX 5360
FORT MCMURRAY, AB, T9H 3G4

Fort McMurray #468 First Nation
P.O. BOX 6130
CLEARWATER STATION, FORT MCMURRAY, AB,
    T9H 4W1

Frog Lake
GENERAL DELIVERY
FROG LAKE, AB, T0A 1M0

Heart Lake
P.O. BOX 447
LAC LA BICHE, AB, T0A 2C0

Horse Lake First Nation
P.O. BOX 303
HYTHE, AB, T0H 2C0

Kapawe'no First Nation
P.O. BOX 10
GROUARD, AB, T0G 1C0

Kehewin Cree Nation
P.O. BOX 220
KEHEWIN, AB, T0A 1C0

Little Red River Cree Nation
P.O. BOX 30
JOHN D'OR PRAIRIE, AB, T0H 3X0

Loon River Cree
P.O. BOX 189
RED EARTH CREEK, AB, T0G 1X0

Louis Bull
P.O. BOX 130
HOBBEMA, AB, T0C 1N0

Lubicon Lake
P.O. BOX 6731
PEACE RIVER, AB, T8S 1S5

Mikisew Cree First Nation
P.O. BOX 90
FORT CHIPEWYAN, AB, T0P 1B0

Montana
P.O. BOX 70
HOBBEMA, AB, T0C 1N0

O'Chiese
P.O. BOX 1570
ROCKY MOUNTAIN HOUSE, AB, T4T 1B2

Paul
P.O. BOX 89
DUFFIELD, AB, T0E 0N0

Piikani Nation
P.O. BOX 70
BROCKET, AB, T0K 0H0

Saddle Lake
P.O. BOX 100
SADDLE LAKE, AB, T0A 3T0

Samson
P.O. BOX 159
HOBBEMA, AB, T0C 1N0

Sawridge
P.O. BOX 326
SLAVE LAKE, AB, T0G 2A0

Siksika Nation
P.O. BOX 1100
SIKSIKA, AB, T0J 3W0

Smith's Landing First Nation
P.O. BOX 1470
FORT SMITH, NT, X0E 0P0

Sturgeon Lake Cree Nation
P.O. BOX 757
VALLEYVIEW, AB, T0H 3N0

Sucker Creek
P.O. BOX 65
ENILDA, AB, T0G 0W0

Sunchild First Nation
P.O. BOX 747
ROCKY MOUNTAIN HOUSE, AB, T4T 1A5

Swan River First Nation
P.O. BOX 270
KINUSO, AB, T0G 1K0

Tallcree
P.O. BOX 100
FORT VERMILION, AB, T0H 1N0

Tsuu T'Ina Nation
9911 CHULA BLVD SW, SUITE 200
TSUU T'INA, AB, T2W 6H6

Wesley
Whitefish Lake
GENERAL DELIVERY
ATIKAMEG, AB, T0G 0C0

Woodland Cree First Nation
GENERAL DELIVERY
CADOTTE LAKE, AB, T0H 0N0

Saskatchewan
Ahtahkakoop
P.O. BOX 220
SHELL LAKE, SK, S0J 2G0

Beardy's and Okemasis
P.O. BOX 340
DUCK LAKE, SK, S0K 1J0

Big Island Lake Cree Nation
P.O. BOX 309
PIERCELAND, SK, S0M 2K0

Big River
P.O. BOX 519
DEBDEN, SK, S0J 0S0

Birch Narrows First Nation
GENERAL DELIVERY
TURNOR LAKE, SK, S0M 3E0

Black Lake
P.O. BOX 27
BLACK LAKE, SK, S0J 0H0

Buffalo River Dene Nation
GENERAL DELIVERY
DILLON, SK, S0M 0S0

Canoe Lake Cree First Nation
GENERAL DELIVERY
CANOE NARROWS, SK, S0M 0K0

Carry The Kettle
P.O. BOX 57
SINTALUTA, SK, S0G 4N0

Clearwater River Dene
P.O. BOX 5050
CLEARWATER RIVER, SK, S0M 3H0

Cote First Nation 366
P.O. BOX 1659
KAMSACK, SK, S0A 1S0

Cowessess
P.O. BOX 100
COWESSESS, SK, S0G 5L0

Cumberland House Cree Nation
P.O. BOX 220
CUMBERLAND HOUSE, SK, S0E 0S0

Day Star
P.O. BOX 277
PUNNICHY, SK, S0A 3C0

English River First Nation
GENERAL DELIVERY
PATUANAK, SK, S0M 2H0

Fishing Lake First Nation
P.O. BOX 508
WADENA, SK, S0A 4J0

Flying Dust First Nation
8001 FLYING DUST RESERVE
MEADOW LAKE, SK, S9X 1T8

Fond du Lac
P.O. BOX 211
FOND DU LAC, SK, S0J 0W0

Gordon
P.O. BOX 248
PUNNICHY, SK, S0A 3C0

Hatchet Lake
GENERAL DELIVERY
WOLLASTON LAKE, SK, S0J 3C0

Island Lake First Nation
P.O. BOX 240
ISLAND LAKE, SK, S0M 3G0

James Smith
P.O. BOX 1059
MELFORT, SK, S0E 1A0

Kahkewistahaw
P.O. BOX 609
BROADVIEW, SK, S0G 0K0

Kawacatoose
P.O. BOX 640
RAYMORE, SK, S0A 3J0

Keeseekoose
P.O. BOX 1120
KAMSACK, SK, S0A 1S0

Kinistin Saulteaux Nation
P.O. BOX 2590
TISDALE, SK, S0E 1T0

Lac La Ronge
P.O. BOX 480
LA RONGE, SK, S0J 1L0

Little Black Bear
P.O. BOX 40
GOODEVE, SK, S0A 1C0

Little Pine
P.O. BOX 70
PAYNTON, SK, S0M 2J0

Lucky Man
103B PACKHAM AVENUE
SASKATOON, SK, S7N 4K4

Makwa Sahgaiehcan First Nation
P.O. BOX 340
LOON LAKE, SK, S0M 1L0

Mistawasis
P.O. BOX 250
LEASK, SK, S0J 1M0

Montreal Lake
BOX 106
MONTREAL LAKE, SK, S0J 1Y0

Moosomin
P.O. BOX 98
COCHIN, SK, S0M 0L0

Mosquito, Grizzly Bear's Head, Lean Man
     Fst.Natns.
P.O. BOX 177
CANDO, SK, S0K 0V0

Muscowpetung
P.O. BOX 1310
FORT QU'APPELLE, SK, S0G 1S0

Muskeg Lake
P.O. BOX 248
MARCELIN, SK, S0J 1R0

Muskoday First Nation
P.O. BOX 99
MUSKODAY, SK, S0J 3H0

Muskowekwan
P.O. BOX 249
LESTOCK, SK, S0A 2G0

Nekaneet
P.O. BOX 548
MAPLE CREEK, SK, S0N 1N0

Ocean Man
P.O. BOX 157
STOUGHTON, SK, S0G 4T0

Ochapowace
P.O. BOX 550
WHITEWOOD, SK, S0G 5C0

Okanese
P.O. BOX 759
BALCARRES, SK, S0G 0C0

One Arrow
P.O. BOX 147
BELLEVUE, SK, S0K 3Y0

Onion Lake
P.O. BOX 100
ONION LAKE, SK, S0M 2E0

Pasqua First Nation #79
P.O. BOX 79
PASQUA, SK, S0G 5M0

Peepeekisis
P.O. BOX 518
BALCARRES, SK, S0G 0C0

Pelican Lake
P.O. BOX 399
LEOVILLE, SK, S0J 1N0

Peter Ballantyne Cree Nation
GENERAL DELIVERY
PELICAN NARROWS, SK, S0P 0E0

Pheasant Rump Nakota
P.O. BOX 238
KISBEY, SK, S0C 1L0

Piapot
GENERAL DELIVERY
ZEHNER, SK, S0G 5K0

Poundmaker
P.O. BOX 610
CUTKNIFE, SK, S0M 0N0

Red Earth
P.O. BOX 109
RED EARTH, SK, S0E 1K0

Red Pheasant
P.O. BOX 70
CANDO, SK, S0K 0V0

Sakimay First Nations
P.O. BOX 339
GRENFELL, SK, S0G 2B0

Saulteaux
P.O. BOX 159
COCHIN, SK, S0M 0L0

Shoal Lake Cree Nation
BOX 51
PAKWAW, SK, S0E 1G0

Standing Buffalo
P.O. BOX 128
FORT QU'APPELLE, SK, S0G 1S0

Star Blanket
P.O. BOX 456
BALCARRES, SK, S0G 0C0

Sturgeon Lake First Nation
RR 1 SITE 12, P.O. BOX 5
SHELLBROOK, SK, S0J 2E0

Sweetgrass
P.O. BOX 147
GALLIVAN, SK, S0M 0X0

The Key First Nation
P.O. BOX 70
NORQUAY, SK, S0A 2V0

Thunderchild First Nation
P.O. BOX 600
TURTLEFORD, SK, S0M 2Y0

Wahpeton Dakota Nation
P.O. BOX 128
PRINCE ALBERT, SK, S6V 5R4

Waterhen Lake
P.O. BOX 9
WATERHEN LAKE, SK, S0M 3B0

White Bear
P.O. BOX 700
CARLYLE, SK, S0C 0R0

Whitecap Dakota First Nation
RR 5 SITE 507, P.O. BOX 28
SASKATOON, SK, S7K 3J8

Witchekan Lake
P.O. BOX 879
SPIRITWOOD, SK, S0J 2M0

Wood Mountain
P.O. BOX 1792
ASSINIBOIA, SK, S0H 0B0

Yellow Quill
P.O. BOX 40
YELLOW QUILL, SK, S0A 3A0

Manitoba
Barren Lands
GENERAL DELIVERY
BROCHET, MB, R0B 0B0

Berens River
GENERAL DELIVERY
BERENS RIVER, MB, R0B 0A0

Birdtail Sioux
P.O. BOX 22
BEULAH, MB, R0M 0B0

Bloodvein
GENERAL DELIVERY
BLOODVEIN, MB, R0C 0J0

Brokenhead Ojibway Nation
GENERAL DELIVERY
SCANTERBURY, MB, R0E 1W0

Buffalo Point First Nation
P.O. BOX 1037
BUFFALO POINT, MB, R0A 2W0

Bunibonibee Cree Nation
GENERAL DELIVERY
OXFORD HOUSE, MB, R0B 1C0

Canupawakpa Dakota First Nation
P.O. BOX 146
PIPESTONE, MB, R0M 1T0

Chemawawin Cree Nation
P.O. BOX 9
EASTERVILLE, MB, R0C 0V0

Cross Lake First Nation
P.O. BOX 10
CROSS LAKE, MB, R0B 0J0

Dakota Plains
P.O. BOX 1246
PORTAGE LA PRAIRIE, MB, R1N 3J9

Dakota Tipi
2020 DAKOTA DRIVE
DAKOTA TIPI, MB, R1N 3X6

Dauphin River
P.O. BOX 58
GYPSUMVILLE, MB, R0C 1J0

Ebb and Flow
GENERAL DELIVERY
EBB AND FLOW, MB, R0L 0R0

Fisher River
P.O. BOX 367
KOOSTATAK, MB, R0C 1S0

Fort Alexander
P.O. BOX 3
FORT ALEXANDER, MB, R0E 0P0

Fox Lake
P.O. BOX 369
GILLAM, MB, R0B 0L0

Gamblers
P.O. BOX 250
BINSCARTH, MB, R0J 0G0

Garden Hill First Nations
GENERAL DELIVERY
ISLAND LAKE, MB, R0B 0T0

God's Lake First Nation
GENERAL DELIVERY
GOD'S LAKE NARROWS, MB, R0B 0M0

Grand Rapids First Nation
P.O. BOX 500
GRAND RAPIDS, MB, R0C 1E0

Hollow Water
GENERAL DELIVERY
WANIPIGOW, MB, R0E 2E0

Keeseekoowenin
P.O. BOX 100
ELPHINSTONE, MB, R0J 0N0

Kinonjeoshtegon First Nation
BOX 359
HODGSON, MB, R0C 1N0

Lake Manitoba
GENERAL DELIVERY
VOGAR, MB, R0C 3C0

Lake St. Martin
P.O. BOX 69
GYPSUMVILLE, MB, R0C 1J0

Little Black River
GENERAL DELIVERY
O'HANLEY, MB, R0E 1K0

Little Grand Rapids
GENERAL DELIVERY
LITTLE GRAND RAPIDS, MB, R0B 0V0

Little Saskatchewan
GENERAL DELIVERY
GYPSUMVILLE, MB, R0C 1J0

Long Plain
P.O. BOX 430
PORTAGE LA PRAIRIE, MB, R1N 3B7

Manto Sipi Cree Nation
GENERAL DELIVERY
GOD'S RIVER, MB, R0B 0N0

Marcel Colomb First Nation
P.O. BOX 1150
LYNN LAKE, MB, R0B 0W0

Mathias Colomb
GENERAL DELIVERY
PUKATAWAGAN, MB, R0B 1G0

Mosakahiken Cree Nation
GENERAL DELIVERY
MOOSE LAKE, MB, R0B 0Y0

Nisichawayasihk Cree Nation
GENERAL DELIVERY
NELSON HOUSE, MB, R0B 1A0

Northlands
GENERAL DELIVERY
LAC BROCHET, MB, R0B 2E0

Norway House Cree Nation
P.O. BOX 250
NORWAY HOUSE, MB, R0B 1B0

O-Chi-Chak-Ko-Sipi First Nation
GENERAL DELIVERY
CRANE RIVER, MB, R0L 0M0

O-Pipon-Na-Piwin Cree Nation
Box 13
South Indian Lake, MB, R0B 1N0

Opaskwayak Cree Nation
P.O. BOX 1000
OTINEKA MALL, THE PAS, MB, R9A 1L1

Pauingassi First Nation
P.O. BOX 60
PAUINGASSI, MB, R0B 2G0

Peguis
P.O. BOX 10
PEGUIS RESERVE, MB, R0C 3J0

Pinaymootang First Nation
P.O. BOX 279
FAIRFORD, MB, R0C 0X0

Pine Creek
P.O. BOX 70
CAMPERVILLE, MB, R0L 0J0

Poplar River First Nation
GENERAL DELIVERY
VIA NEGGINAN, NEGGINAN, MB, R0B 0Z0

Red Sucker Lake
GENERAL DELIVERY
RED SUCKER LAKE, MB, R0B 1H0

Rolling River
P.O. BOX 145
ERICKSON, MB, R0J 0P0

Roseau River Anishinabe First Nation Government
P.O. BOX 30
GINEW, MB, R0A 2R0

Sandy Bay
P.O. BOX 109
MARIUS, MB, R0H 0T0

Sapotaweyak Cree Nation
GENERAL DELIVERY
VIA PELICAN RAPIDS, PELICAN RAPIDS, MB,
    R0L 1L0

Sayisi Dene First Nation
GENERAL DELIVERY
TADOULE LAKE, MB, R0B 2C0

Shamattawa First Nation
P.O. BOX 210
SHAMATTAWA, MB, R0B 1K0

Sioux Valley Dakota Nation
P.O. BOX 38
GRISWOLD, MB, R0M 0S0

Skownan First Nation
GENERAL DELIVERY
SKOWNAN, MB, R0L 1Y0

St. Theresa Point
GENERAL DELIVERY
ST THERESA POINT, MB, R0B 1J0

Swan Lake
P.O. BOX 368
SWAN LAKE, MB, R0G 2S0

Tataskweyak Cree Nation
GENERAL DELIVERY
SPLIT LAKE, MB, R0B 1P0

Tootinaowaziibeeng Treaty Reserve
GENERAL DELIVERY
SHORTDALE, MB, R0L 1W0

War Lake First Nation
GENERAL DELIVERY
ILFORD, MB, R0B 0S0

Wasagamack First Nation
GENERAL DELIVERY
WASAGAMACK, MB, R0B 1Z0

Waywayseecappo First Nation Treaty Four – 1874
P.O. BOX 9
WAYWAYSEECAPPO, MB, R0J 1S0

Wuskwi Sipihk First Nation
P.O. BOX 220
BIRCH RIVER, MB, R0L 0E0

York Factory First Nation
GENERAL DELIVERY
YORK LANDING, MB, R0B 2B0

Ontario
Aamjiwnaang
978 TASHMOO AVENUE
SARNIA, ON, N7T 7H5

Albany
P.O. BOX 1
FORT ALBANY, ON, P0L 1H0

Alderville First Nation
P.O. BOX 46
ROSENEATH, ON, K0K 2X0

Algonquins of Pikwakanagan
P.O. BOX 100
GOLDEN LAKE, ON, K0J 1X0

Animbiigoo Zaagi'igan Anishinaabek
P.O. BOX 120
BEARDMORE, ON, P0T 2G0

Anishinabe of Wauzhushk Onigum
P.O. BOX 1850
KENORA, ON, P9N 3X8

Anishnaabeg of Naongashiing
GENERAL DELIVERY
MORSON, ON, P0W 1J0

Aroland
P.O. BOX 10
AROLAND, ON, P0T 1B0

Attawapiskat
P.O. BOX 248
ATTAWAPISKAT, ON, P0L 1A0

Aundeck-Omni-Kaning
P.O. BOX 21, RR 1
LITTLE CURRENT, ON, P0P 1K0

Batchewana First Nation
236 FRONTENAC STREET
SAULT STE MARIE, ON, P6A 5K9

Bay of Quinte Mohawk

Bearfoot Onondaga

Bearskin Lake
GENERAL DELIVERY
BEARSKIN LAKE, ON, P0V 1E0

Beausoleil
GENERAL DELIVERY
CEDAR POINT, ON, L0K 1C0

Big Grassy
P.O. BOX 414
MORSON, ON, P0W 1J0

Biinjitiwaabik Zaaging Anishinaabek
GENERAL DELIVERY
MACDIARMID, ON, P0T 2B0

Brunswick House
P.O. BOX 1178
CHAPLEAU, ON, P0M 1K0

Caldwell
10297 TALBOT ROAD
BLENHEIM, ON, N0P 1A0

Cat Lake
P.O. BOX 81
CAT LAKE, ON, P0V 1J0

Chapleau Cree First Nation
P.O. BOX 400
CHAPLEAU, ON, P0M 1K0

Chapleau Ojibway
P.O. BOX 279
CHAPLEAU, ON, P0M 1K0

Chippewas of Georgina Island
RR 2, P.O. BOX 13
SUTTON WEST, ON, L0E 1R0

Chippewas of Kettle and Stony Point
RR 2
FOREST, ON, N0N 1J0

Chippewas of Mnjikaning First Nation
5884 RAMA ROAD, SUITE 200
RAMA, ON, L0K 1T0

Chippewas of Nawash First Nation
RR 5
WIARTON, ON, N0H 2T0

Chippewas of the Thames First Nation
RR 1
MUNCEY, ON, N0L 1Y0

Constance Lake
GENERAL DELIVERY
CALSTOCK, ON, P0L 1B0

Couchiching First Nation
RR 2 RMB 2027
FORT FRANCES, ON, P9A 3M3

Curve Lake
GENERAL DELIVERY
CURVE LAKE, ON, K0L 1R0

Deer Lake
GENERAL DELIVERY
DEER LAKE, ON, P0V 1N0

Delaware

Dokis
RR 1
MONETVILLE, ON, P0M 2K0

Eabametoong First Nation
P.O. BOX 298
FORT HOPE, ON, P0T 1L0

Eagle Lake
P.O. BOX 1001
MIGISI SAHGAIGAN, ON, P0V 3H0

Flying Post
P.O. BOX 1027
NIPIGON, ON, P0T 2J0

Fort Severn
GENERAL DELIVERY
FORT SEVERN, ON, P0V 1W0

Fort William
90 ANEMKI DRIVE, SUITE 200
THUNDER BAY, ON, P7J 1L3

Garden River First Nation
7 SHINGWAUK STREET, RR 4
GARDEN RIVER, ON, P6A 6Z8

Ginoogaming First Nation
P.O. BOX 89
LONGLAC, ON, P0T 2A0

Grassy Narrows First Nation
GENERAL DELIVERY
GRASSY NARROWS, ON, P0X 1B0

Gull Bay
GENERAL DELIVERY
GULL BAY, ON, P0T 1P0

Henvey Inlet First Nation
GENERAL DELIVERY
PICKEREL, ON, P0G 1J0

Hiawatha First Nation
RR 2
KEENE, ON, K0L 2G0

Iskatewizaagegan #39 Independent First Nation
GENERAL DELIVERY
KEJICK, ON, P0X 1E0

Kasabonika Lake
GENERAL DELIVERY
KASABONIKA LAKE, ON, P0V 1Y0

Kee-Way-Win
GENERAL DELIVERY
KEEWAYWIN, ON, P0V 3G0

Kingfisher
GENERAL DELIVERY
KINGFISHER LAKE, ON, P0V 1Z0

Kitchenuhmaykoosib Inninuwug
GENERAL DELIVERY
BIG TROUT LAKE, ON, P0V 1G0

Konadaha Seneca

Lac Des Mille Lacs
1100 MEMORIAL AVENUE, SUITE 328
THUNDER BAY, ON, P7B 4A3

Lac La Croix
P.O. BOX 640
FORT FRANCES, ON, P9A 3M9

Lac Seul
P.O. BOX 100
HUDSON, ON, P0V 1X0

Long Lake No.58 First Nation
P.O. BOX 609
LONGLAC, ON, P0T 2A0

Lower Cayuga

Lower Mohawk

M'Chigeeng First Nation
P.O. BOX 2
M'CHIGEENG, ON, P0P 1G0

Magnetawan
P.O. BOX 15, RR 1
BRITT, ON, P0G 1A0

Martin Falls
GENERAL DELIVERY
OGOKI, ON, P0T 2L0

Matachewan
P.O. BOX 208
MATACHEWAN, ON, P0K 1M0

Mattagami
P.O. BOX 99
GOGAMA, ON, P0M 1W0

McDowell Lake
P.O. BOX 321
RED LAKE, ON, P0V 2M0

Michipicoten
P.O. BOX 1
WAWA, ON, P0S 1K0

Mishkeegogamang
GENERAL DELIVERY
OSNABURGH, ON, P0V 2H0

Missanabie Cree
7 SHINGWAUK STREET
GARDEN RIVER, ON, P6A 6Z8

Mississauga
P.O. BOX 1299
BLIND RIVER, ON, P0R 1B0

Mississauga's of Scugog Island First Nation
22521 ISLAND ROAD
PORT PERRY, ON, L9L 1B6

Mississaugas of the Credit
RR 6
HAGERSVILLE, ON, N0A 1H0

Mohawks of Akwesasne
P.O. BOX 579
CORNWALL, ON, K6H 5T3

Mohawks of the Bay of Quinte
RR 1
DESERONTO, ON, K0K 1X0

Moose Cree First Nation
P.O. BOX 190
MOOSE FACTORY, ON, P0L 1W0

Moose Deer Point
P.O. BOX 119
MACTIER, ON, P0C 1H0

Moravian of the Thames
RR 3
THAMESVILLE, ON, N0P 2K0

Munsee-Delaware Nation
RR 1
MUNCEY, ON, N0L 1Y0

Muskrat Dam Lake
GENERAL DELIVERY
MUSKRAT DAM, ON, P0V 3B0

Naicatchewenin
P.O. BOX 15
DEVLIN, ON, P0W 1C0

Naotkamegwanning
GENERAL DELIVERY
PAWITIK, ON, P0X 1L0

Neskantaga First Nation
GENERAL DELIVERY
VIA PICKLE LAKE, LANSDOWNE HOUSE, ON,
    P0T 1Z0

Nibinamik First Nation
GENERAL DELIVERY
VIA PICKLE LAKE, SUMMER BEAVER, ON,
    P0T 3B0

Nicickousemenecaning
P.O. BOX 68
FORT FRANCES, ON, P9A 3M5

Niharondasa Seneca

Nipissing First Nation
36 SEMO ROAD
GARDEN VILLAGE, ON, P2B 3K2

North Caribou Lake
GENERAL DELIVERY
WEAGAMOW LAKE, ON, P0V 2Y0

North Spirit Lake
GENERAL DELIVERY
NORTH SPIRIT LAKE, ON, P0V 2G0

Northwest Angle No.33
P.O. BOX 1490
KENORA, ON, P9N 3X7

Northwest Angle No.37
P.O. BOX 267
SIOUX NARROWS, ON, P0X 1N0

Obashkaandagaang
P.O. BOX 625
KEEWATIN, ON, P0X 1C0

Ochiichagwe'babigo'ining First Nation
RR 1, DALLES ROAD
KENORA, ON, P9N 3W7

Ojibway Nation of Saugeen
GENERAL DELIVERY
SAVANT LAKE, ON, P0V 2S0

Ojibways of Onigaming First Nation
P.O. BOX 160
NESTOR FALLS, ON, P0X 1K0

Ojibways of the Pic River First Nation
GENERAL DELIVERY
HERON BAY, ON, P0T 1R0

Oneida

Oneida Nation of the Thames
RR 2
SOUTHWOLD, ON, N0L 2G0

Onondaga Clear Sky

Pays Plat
10 CENTRAL PLACE
PAYS PLAT, ON, P0T 3C0

Pic Mobert
GENERAL DELIVERY
MOBERT, ON, P0M 2J0

Pikangikum
GENERAL DELIVERY
PIKANGIKUM, ON, P0V 2L0

Poplar Hill
GENERAL DELIVERY
POPLAR HILL, ON, P0V 3E0

Rainy River First Nations
P.O. BOX 450
EMO, ON, P0W 1E0

Red Rock
P.O. BOX 1030
NIPIGON, ON, P0T 2J0

Sachigo Lake
GENERAL DELIVERY
SACHIGO LAKE, ON, P0V 2P0

Sagamok Anishnawbek
P.O. BOX 610
MASSEY, ON, P0P 1P0

Sandpoint
682 CITY ROAD
THUNDER BAY, ON, P7J 1K3

Sandy Lake
GENERAL DELIVERY
SANDY LAKE, ON, P0V 1V0

Saugeen
RR 1
SOUTHAMPTON, ON, N0H 2L0

Seine River First Nation
P.O. BOX 124
MINE CENTRE, ON, P0W 1H0

Serpent River
48 VILLAGE ROAD
CUTLER, ON, P0P 1B0

Shawanaga First Nation
RR 1
NOBEL, ON, P0G 1G0

Sheguiandah
P.O. BOX 101
SHEGUIANDAH, ON, P0P 1W0

Sheshegwaning
GENERAL DELIVERY
SHESHEGWANING, ON, P0P 1X0

Shoal Lake No.40
GENERAL DELIVERY
KEJICK, ON, P0X 1E0

Six Nations of the Grand River
P.O. BOX 5000
OHSWEKEN, ON, N0A 1M0

Slate Falls Nation
48 LAKEVIEW DR
SLATE FALLS, ON, P0V 3C0

Stanjikoming First Nation
P.O. BOX 609
FORT FRANCES, ON, P9A 3M9

Taykwa Tagamou Nation
P.O. BOX 3310, RR 3
COCHRANE, ON, P0L 1C0

Temagami First Nation
GENERAL DELIVERY
VIA BEAR ISLAND, TEMAGAMI, ON, P0H 2H0

Thessalon
P.O. BOX 9
THESSALON, ON, P0R 1L0

Tuscarora

Upper Cayuga

Upper Mohawk

Wabaseemoong Independent Nations
GENERAL DELIVERY
WHITEDOG, ON, P0X 1P0

Wabauskang First Nation
P.O. BOX 418
EAR FALLS, ON, P0V 1T0

Wabigoon Lake Ojibway Nation
RR 1, SITE 115, P.O. BOX 300
DRYDEN, ON, P8N 2Y4

Wahgoshig
P.O. BOX 629
MATHESON, ON, P0K 1N0

Wahnapitae
P.O. BOX 1119
CAPREOL, ON, P0M 1H0

Wahta Mohawk
P.O. BOX 260
BALA, ON, P0C 1A0

Walker Mohawk

Walpole Island
RR 3
WALLACEBURG, ON, N8A 4K9

Wapekeka
GENERAL DELIVERY
ANGLING LAKE, ON, P0V 1B0

Wasauksing First Nation
P.O. BOX 250
PARRY SOUND, ON, P2A 2X4

Wawakapewin
C/O SHIBOGAMA FIRST NATION COUNCIL,
    P.O. BOX 449
SIOUX LOOKOUT, ON, P8T 1A5

Webequie
P.O. BOX 176
WEBEQUIE, ON, P0T 3A0

Weenusk
P.O. BOX 1
PEAWANUCK, ON, P0L 2H0

Whitefish Lake
P.O. BOX 39
NAUGHTON, ON, P0M 2M0

Whitefish River
GENERAL DELIVERY
BIRCH ISLAND, ON, P0P 1A0

Whitesand
P.O. BOX 68
ARMSTRONG, ON, P0T 1A0

Wikwemikong
P.O. BOX 112
WIKWEMIKONG, ON, P0P 2J0

Wunnumin
P.O. BOX 105
WUNNUMIN LAKE, ON, P0V 2Z0

Zhiibaahaasing First Nation
GENERAL DELIVERY
SIVLER WATER, ON, P0P 1Y0

Quebec
Abénakis de Wôlinak
10120 RUE KOLIPAIO
BÉCANCOUR, QC, G0X 1B0

Algonquins of Barriere Lake
GENERAL DELIVERY
RAPID LAKE, QC, J0W 2C0

Atikamekw d'Opitciwan
CP 135
OBEDJIWAN, QC, G0W 3B0

Betsiamites
2 RUE ASHINI, CP 40
BETSIAMITES, QC, G0H 1B0

Communauté anicinape de Kitcisakik
CP 5206
VAL D'OR, QC, J9P 7C6

Conseil de la Première Nation Abitibiwinni
45 RUE MIGWAN
PIKOGAN, QC, J9T 3A3

Conseil des Atikamekw de Wemotaci
CP 221
WEMOTACI, QC, G0X 3R0

Cree Nation of Chisasibi
P.O. BOX 150
CHISASIBI, QC, J0M 1E0

Cree Nation of Mistissini
ISAAC SHECAPIO SR ADMIN BLDG,
      187 MAIN STREET
MISTISSINI, QC, G0W 1C0

Cree Nation of Nemaska
1 LAKESHORE ROAD
NÉMISCAU, QC, J0Y 3B0

Cree Nation of Wemindji
16 BEAVER ROAD, P.O. BOX 60
WEMINDJI, QC, J0M 1L0

Eagle Village First Nation – Kipawa
P.O. BOX 756, EAGLE VILLAGE FIRST NATION
TÉMISCAMING, QC, J0Z 3R0

Eastmain
P.O. BOX 90
EASTMAIN, QC, J0M 1W0

Innu Takuaikan Uashat Mak Mani-Utenam
1089 DEQUEN, CP 8000
SEPT-ÎLES, QC, G4R 4L9

Innue Essipit
32 RUE DE LA RESERVE, CP 820
LES ESCOUMINS, QC, G0T 1K0

Kahnawake
P.O. BOX 720
KAHNAWAKE, QC, J0L 1B0

Kitigan Zibi Anishinabeg
P.O. BOX 309
MANIWAKI, QC, J9E 3C9

La Nation Innu Matimekush-Lac John
CP 1390
SCHEFFERVILLE, QC, G0G 2T0

La Nation Micmac de Gespeg
783 BOUL POINTE NAVARRE, CP 69
FONTENELLE, QC, G4X 1J0

Les Atikamekw de Manawan
135 RUE KICIK
MANOUANE, QC, J0K 1M0

Les Innus de Ekuanitshit
35 RUE MANITOU
LONGUE-POINTE-DE-MINGAN, QC, G0G 1V0

Listuguj Mi'gmaq Government
17 RIVERSIDE DRIVE WEST, P.O. BOX 298
LISTUGUJ, QC, G0C 2R0

Long Point First Nation
P.O. BOX 1
WINNEWAY RIVER, QC, J0Z 2J0

Micmacs of Gesgapegiag
P.O. BOX 1280
MARIA, QC, G0C 1Y0

Mohawks of Kanesatake
681 RANG SAINTE-PHILOMÈNE, RR 1
OKA, QC, J0N 1E0

Montagnais de Natashquan
159A RUE DES MONTAGNAIS
NATASHQUAN, QC, G0G 2E0

Montagnais de Pakua Shipi
CP 178
ST-AUGUSTIN-SAGUENAY, QC, G0G 2R0

Montagnais de Unamen Shipu
GENERAL DELIVERY
GETHSÉMANI, QC, G0G 1M0

Montagnais du Lac St.-Jean
1671 RUE OUIATCHOUAN
MASHTEUIATSH, QC, G0W 2H0

Naskapi of Quebec
P.O. BOX 5111
KAWAWACHIKAMACH, QC, G0G 2Z0

Nation Anishnabe du Lac Simon
1026 BOUL CICIP, CP 139
LAC SIMON, QC, J0Y 3M0

Nation Huronne Wendat
255 PLACE CHEF MICHEL LAVEAU
WENDAKE, QC, G0A 4V0

Odanak
102 RUE SIBOSIS
ODANAK, QC, J0G 1H0

Première Nation Malecite de Viger
112 RUE DE LA GRÈVE, P.O. BOX 10
CACOUNA, QC, G0L 1G0

Première nation de Whapmagoostui
P.O. BOX 390
KUUJJUARAPIK, QC, J0M 1G0

The Crees of the Waskaganish First Nation
P.O. BOX 60
WASKAGANISH, QC, J0M 1R0

Timiskaming First Nation
P.O. BOX 336
NOTRE-DAME-DU-NORD, QC, J0Z 3B0

Waswanipi
DIOM BLACKSMITH BUILDING, P.O. BOX 8
WASWANIPI, QC, J0Y 3C0

Wolf Lake
P.O. BOX 998
HUNTER'S POINT, TÉMISCAMING, QC, J0Z 3R0

New Brunswick
Buctouche
9 RESERVE ROAD
BUCTOUCHE RESERVE, NB, E4S 4G2

Burnt Church
620 BAYVIEW DRIVE
BURNT CHURCH, NB, E9G 2A8

Eel Ground
47 CHURCH RD
EEL GROUND, NB, E1V 4E6

Eel River Bar First Nation
11 MAIN STREET, Unit 201
EEL RIVER BAR, NB, E8C 1A1

Elsipogtog First Nation
RR 1, 373 BIG COVE ROAD
ELSIPOGTOG FIRST NATION, NB, E4W 2S3

Fort Folly
P.O. BOX 1007
DORCHESTER, NB, E4K 3V5

Indian Island
61 INDIAN ISLAND DRIVE
INDIAN ISLAND, NB, E4W 1S9

Kingsclear
77 FRENCH VILLAGE RD
KINGSCLEAR FIRST NATION, NB, E3E 1K3

Madawaska Maliseet First Nation
1771 MAIN STREET
MADAWASKA MALISEET FIRST NAT, NB, E7C
    1W9

Metepenagiag Mi'kmaq Nation
P.O. BOX 293
Metepenagiag Mi'kmaq Nation, NB, E9E 2P2

Oromocto
P.O. BOX 417
OROMOCTO, NB, E2V 2J2

Pabineau
1290 PABINEAU FALLS ROAD
PABINEAU FIRST NATION, NB, E2A 7M3

Saint Mary's
150 CLIFFE STREET
FREDERICTON, NB, E3A 0A1

Tobique
13156 ROUTE 105
TOBIQUE FIRST NATION, NB, E7H 5M7

Woodstock
3 WULASTOOK COURT
WOODSTOCK FIRST NATION, NB, E7M 4K6

Nova Scotia
Acadia
10526 Highway 3
YARMOUTH, NS, B5A 4A8

Annapolis Valley
P.O. BOX 89
CAMBRIDGE STATION, NS, B0P 1G0

Bear River
P.O. BOX 210
BEAR RIVER, NS, B0S 1B0

Chapel Island First Nation
P.O. BOX 538
CHAPEL ISLAND, NS, B0E 3B0

Eskasoni
P.O. BOX 7040, 63 MINI MALL DRIVE
ESKASONI, NS, B1W 1A1

Glooscap First Nation
P.O. BOX 449
HANTSPORT, NS, B0P 1P0

Membertou
111 MEMBERTOU STREET
SYDNEY, NS, B1S 2M9

Millbrook
P.O. BOX 634
TRURO, NS, B2N 5E5

Paq'tnkek First Nation
RR 1
AFTON, NS, B0H 1A0

Pictou Landing
SITE 6, BOX 55, RR 2
TRENTON, NS, B0K 1X0

Shubenacadie
GENERAL DELIVERY
MICMAC POST OFFICE, HANTS CO., NS,
    B0N 1W0

Wagmatcook
P.O. BOX 30001
WAGMATCOOK, NS, B0E 3N0

Waycobah First Nation
P.O. BOX 149
WHYCOCOMAGH, NS, B0E 3M0

Prince Edward Island
Abegweit
P.O. BOX 36
MOUNT STEWART, PE, C0A 1T0

Lennox Island
P.O. BOX 134
LENNOX ISLAND, PE, C0B 1P0

Newfoundland
Miawpukek
P.O. BOX 10
BAY D'ESPOIR, CONNE RIVER, NF, A0H 1J0

Mushuau Innu First Nation
P.O. BOX 190
NATUASHISH, NF, A0P 1A0

Sheshatshiu Innu First Nation
P.O. BOX 160
Sheshatshiu First Nation, NF, A0P 1M0

Northwest Territories and Nunavut
Acho Dene Koe
GENERAL DELIVERY
FORT LIARD, NT, X0E 0A0

Aklavik
P.O. BOX 118
AKLAVIK, NT, X0E 0A0

Behdzi Ahda" First Nation
P.O. BOX 53
COLVILLE LAKE, NT, X0E 0L0

Dechi Laot'i First Nations
P.O. BOX 69
WEKWETI, NT, X0E 1W0

Deh Gah Gotie Dene Council
GENERAL DELIVERY
FORT PROVIDENCE, NT, X0E 0L0

Deline First Nation
P.O. BOX 158
DELINE, NT, X0E 0G0

Deninu K'ue First Nation
BOX 1899
FORT RESOLUTION, NT, X0E 0M0

Dog Rib Rae
P.O. BOX 8
FORT RAE, NT, X0E 0Y0

Fort Good Hope
P.O. BOX 80
FORT GOOD HOPE, NT, X0E 0H0

Gameti First Nation
P.O. BOX 1
RAE LAKES, NT, X0E 1R0

Gwichya Gwich'in
P.O. BOX 4
TSIIGEHTCHIC, NT, X0E 0B0

Inuvik Native
P.O. BOX 2570
INUVIK, NT, X0E 0T0

Jean Marie River First Nation
GENERAL DELIVERY
JEAN MARIE RIVER, NT, X0E 0N0

K'atlodeeche First Nation
P.O. BOX 3060
HAY RIVER RESERVE, NT, X0E 1G4

Ka'a'gee Tu First Nation
P.O. BOX 4428
HAY RIVER, NT, X0E 1G3

Liidlii Kue First Nation
P.O. BOX 469
FORT SIMPSON, NT, X0E 0N0

Lutsel K'e Dene First Nation
P.O. BOX 28
LUTSEL K'E, NT, X0E 1A0

Nahanni Butte
GENERAL DELIVERY
NAHANNI BUTTE, NT, X0E 0N0

Pehdzeh Ki First Nation
GENERAL DELIVERY
WRIGLEY, NT, X0E 1E0

Salt River First Nation #195
P.O. BOX 960
FORT SMITH, NT, X0E 0P0

Sambaa K'e (Trout Lake) Dene
P.O. BOX 10, VIA FORT SIMPSON
TROUT LAKE, NT, X0E 0N0

Tetlit Gwich'in
P.O. BOX 30
FORT MCPHERSON, NT, X0E 0J0

Tulita Dene
P.O. BOX 118
TULITA, NT, X0E 0K0

West Point First Nation
1 - 47031 MACKENZIE HWY
HAY RIVER, NT, X0E 0R9

Wha Ti First Nation
P.O. BOX 92
WHA TI, NT, X0E 1P0

Yellowknives Dene First Nation
P.O. BOX 2514
YELLOWKNIFE, NT, X1A 2P8

Aishihik, Yukon
Carcross/Tagish First Nations
P.O. BOX 130
CARCROSS, YT, Y0B 1B0

Champagne

Champagne and Aishihik First Nations
P.O. BOX 5309
HAINES JUNCTION, YT, Y0B 1L0

Dease River
GENERAL DELIVERY
GOOD HOPE LAKE, BC, V0C 2Z0

First Nation of Nacho Nyak Dun
P.O. BOX 220
MAYO, YT, Y0B 1M0

Kluane First Nation
BOX 20
BURWASH LANDING, YT, Y0B 1H0

Kwanlin Dun First Nation
35 McIntyre Street
WHITEHORSE, YT, Y1A 5S5

Liard First Nation
P.O. BOX 328
WATSON LAKE, YT, Y0A 1C0

Little Salmon/Carmacks First Nation
P.O. BOX 135
CARMACKS, YT, Y0B 1C0

Ross River
GENERAL DELIVERY
ROSS RIVER, YT, Y0B 1S0

Selkirk First Nation
BOX 40
PELLY CROSSING, YT, Y0B 1P0

Ta'an Kwach'an
117 Industrial Road
WHITEHORSE, YT, Y1A 2T8

Taku River Tlingit
P.O. BOX 132
ATLIN, YT, V0W 1A0

Teslin Tlingit Council
BOX 133
TESLIN, YT, Y0A 1B0

Tr'ondëk Hwëch'in
P.O. BOX 599
DAWSON CITY, YT, Y0B 1G0

Vuntut Gwitchin First Nation
GENERAL DELIVERY
OLD CROW, YT, Y0B 1N0

White River First Nation
GENERAL DELIVERY
BEAVER CREEK, YT, Y0B 1A0

Source: Indian and Northern Affairs Canada, http://
pse2-esd2.ainc-inac.gc.ca/FNProfiles/ FNProfiles
_home.htm, accessed April 27, 2007.

Heads of Indian Affairs, 1824–2007

Name	Title	Term
Thomas L. McKenney	Head of Office of Indian Affairs[1]	1824–1829
Samuel S. Hamilton	Head of Office of Indian Affairs	1830–1831
Elbert Herring	Head of Office of Indian Affairs	1831–1832
Elbert Herring	Commissioner of Indian Affairs[2]	1832–1836
Carey A. Harris	Commissioner of Indian Affairs	1836–1838
Thomas H. Crawford	Commissioner of Indian Affairs	1838–1845
William Medill	Commissioner of Indian Affairs	1845–1849
Orlando Brown	Commissioner of Indian Affairs[3]	1849–1850
Luke Lea	Commissioner of Indian Affairs	1850–1853
George W. Manypenny	Commissioner of Indian Affairs	1853–1857
James W. Denver	Commissioner of Indian Affairs	1857–1859
Charles E. Mix	Commissioner of Indian Affairs (interim)	1858
Alfred B. Greenwood	Commissioner of Indian Affairs	1859–1861
William P. Dole	Commissioner of Indian Affairs	1861–1865
Dennis N. Cooley	Commissioner of Indian Affairs	1865–1866
Lewis Vital Bogy	Commissioner of Indian Affairs	1866–1867
Nathaniel G. Taylor	Commissioner of Indian Affairs	1867–1869
Ely S. Parker (Seneca)	Commissioner of Indian Affairs	1869–1871
Francis A. Walker	Commissioner of Indian Affairs	1871–1872
Edward P. Smith	Commissioner of Indian Affairs	1873–1875
John Q. Smith	Commissioner of Indian Affairs	1875–1877
Ezra A. Hayt	Commissioner of Indian Affairs	1877–1880
Rowland E. Trowbridge	Commissioner of Indian Affairs	1880–1881
Hiram Price	Commissioner of Indian Affairs	1881–1885

(continues)

Heads of Indian Affairs, 1824–2007 (cont.)

Name	Title	Term
John D. C. Atkins	Commissioner of Indian Affairs	1885–1888
John H. Oberly	Commissioner of Indian Affairs	1888–1889
Thomas J. Morgan	Commissioner of Indian Affairs	1889–1893
Daniel M. Browning	Commissioner of Indian Affairs	1893–1897
William A. Jones	Commissioner of Indian Affairs	1897–1905
Francis E. Leupp	Commissioner of Indian Affairs	1905–1909
Robert G. Valentine	Commissioner of Indian Affairs	1909–1912
Cato Sells	Commissioner of Indian Affairs	1912–1920
Charles H. Burke	Commissioner of Indian Affairs	1921–1929
Charles J. Rhoads	Commissioner of Indian Affairs	1929–1932
John Collier	Commissioner of Indian Affairs	1933–1945
William A. Brophy	Commissioner of Indian Affairs	1945–1948
John R. Nichols	Commissioner of Indian Affairs	1949–1950
Dillon S. Myer	Commissioner of Indian Affairs	1950–1953
Glenn L. Emmons	Commissioner of Indian Affairs	1953–1961
Philleo Nash	Commissioner of Indian Affairs	1961–1966
Robert LaFollette Bennett (Oneida)	Commissioner of Indian Affairs	1966–1969
Louis R. Bruce Jr. (Mohawk/Oglala Sioux)	Commissioner of Indian Affairs	1969–1972
Morris Thompson (Athabascan)	Commissioner of Indian Affairs	1973–1976
Benjamin Reifel (Brulé Sioux)	Commissioner of Indian Affairs	1976–1977
Forrest J. Gerard (Blackfeet)	Assistant Secretary for Indian Affairs[4]	1977–1981
Raymond Butler (Blackfeet)	Acting Commissioner of Indian Affairs	1977
Martin Seneca Jr. (Seneca)	Acting Commissioner of Indian Affairs	1978
William E. Hallett (Chippewa)	Commissioner of Indian Affairs[5]	1979–1981
Tom Fredericks (Mandan-Hidatsa)	Temporary Assistant Secretary for Indian Affairs	1981
Kenneth L. Smith (Wasco)	Assistant Secretary for Indian Affairs	1981–1985
Ross Swimmer (Cherokee)	Assistant Secretary for Indian Affairs	1985–1989
Eddie Brown (Pascua Yaqui)	Assistant Secretary for Indian Affairs	1989–1993
Ada Deer (Menominee)	Assistant Secretary for Indian Affairs	1993–1997
Kevin Gover (Pawnee)	Assistant Secretary for Indian Affairs	1997–2001
Neil McCaleb (Chickasaw)	Assistant Secretary for Indian Affairs	2001–2003
David Anderson (Lake Superior Chippewa)	Assistant Secretary for Indian Affairs	2003–2005
Carl J. Artman (Oneida)	Assistant Secretary for Indian Affairs[6]	2007–Present

[1]From 1789 to 1832, the secretary of war was officially in charge of Indian affairs, but in 1824, an Office of Indian Affairs was created within the War Department, and a head of Indian affairs was appointed to oversee it.

[2]In 1832, the secretary of war created the position of commissioner of Indian affairs within the War Department to manage Indian affairs.

[3]In 1849, the Bureau of Indian Affairs and its head, the commissioner of Indian affairs, moved from the War Department to the Department of the Interior.

[4]In 1977, Congress created the position of assistant secretary of the interior for Indian affairs to aid the interior secretary with Indian policy. The commissioner of Indian affairs continued to oversee the operations of the Bureau of Indian Affairs.

[5]William E. Hallett served as the last commissioner of Indian affairs. Since 1981, the position has remained vacant, and the assistant secretary for Indian affairs has assumed responsibility for Indian affairs.

[6]The position of Assistant Secretary for Indian Affairs was vacant from 2005–2007.

Sources: Bureau of Indian Affairs (http://www.doi.gov/bureau-indian-affairs.html); Grossman, Mark, ABC-CLIO, *Companion to the Native American Rights Movement,* 1996; Hirschfelder, Arlene, and Martha Kreipe de Montaño, The Native American Almanac, 1993. Accessed April 24, 2007

Native American Treaties with the United States, 1778–1883

Treaty	Year	Treaty	Year
Treaty with the Delawares	1778	Treaty with the Wea	1809
Treaty with the Six Nations	1784	Treaty with the Kickapoo	1809
Treaty with the Wyandot, etc.	1785	Treaty with the Wyandot, etc.	1814
Treaty with the Cherokee	1785	Treaty with the Creeks	1814
Treaty with the Choctaw	1786	Treaty with the Potawatomi	1815
Treaty with the Chickasaw	1786	Treaty with the Piankashaw	1815
Treaty with the Shawnee	1786	Treaty with the Teton	1815
Treaty with the Wyandot, etc.	1789	Treaty with the Sioux of the Lakes	1815
Treaty with the Six Nations	1789	Treaty with the Sioux of St. Peter's River	1815
Treaty with the Creeks	1790	Treaty with the Yankton Sioux	1815
Treaty with the Cherokee	1791	Treaty with the Makah	1815
Agreement with the Five Nations of Indians	1792	Treaty with the Kickapoo	1815
Treaty with the Cherokee	1794	Treaty with the Wyandot, etc.	1815
Treaty with the Six Nations	1794	Treaty with the Osage	1815
Treaty with the Oneida, etc.	1794	Treaty with the Sauk	1815
Treaty with the Wyandot, etc.	1795	Treaty with the Foxes	1815
Treaty with the Seven Nations of Canada	1796	Treaty with the Iowa	1815
Treaty with the Creeks	1796	Treaty with the Kansa	1815
Treaty with the Mohawk	1797	Treaty with the Cherokee	1816
Agreement with the Seneca	1797	Treaty with the Cherokee	1816
Treaty with the Cherokee	1798	Treaty with the Sauk	1816
Treaty with the Chickasaw	1801	Treaty with the Sioux	1816
Treaty with the Choctaw	1801	Treaty with the Winnebago	1816
Treaty with the Creeks	1802	Treaty with the Wea and Kickapoo	1816
Treaty with the Seneca	1802	Treaty with the Ottawa, etc.	1816
Treaty with the Seneca	1802	Treaty with the Cherokee	1816
Treaty with the Choctaw	1802	Treaty with the Chickasaw	1816
Treaty with the Delawares, etc.	1803	Treaty with the Choctaw	1816
Treaty with the Eel River, etc.	1803	Treaty with the Menominee	1817
Treaty with the Kaskaskia	1803	Treaty with the Oto	1817
Treaty with the Choctaw	1803	Treaty with the Ponca	1817
Treaty with the Delawares	1804	Treaty with the Cherokee	1817
Treaty with the Piankeshaw	1804	Treaty with the Wyandot, etc.	1817
Treaty with the Cherokee	1804	Treaty with the Creeks	1818
Treaty with the Sauk and Foxes	1804	Treaty with the Grand Pawnee	1818
Treaty with the Wyandot, etc.	1805	Treaty with the Noisy Pawnee	1818
Treaty with the Chickasaw	1805	Treaty with the Pawnee Republic	1818
Treaty with the Delawares, etc.	1805	Treaty with the Pawnee Marhar	1818
Treaty with the Cherokee	1805	Treaty with the Quapaw	1818
Treaty with the Cherokee	1805	Treaty with the Wyandot, etc.	1818
Treaty with the Creeks	1805	Treaty with the Wyandot.	1818
Treaty with the Choctaw	1805	Treaty with the Peoria, etc.	1818
Treaty with the Piankashaw	1805	Treaty with the Osage	1818
Treaty with the Sioux	1805	Treaty with the Potawatomi	1818
Treaty with the Cherokee	1806	Treaty with the Wea	1818
Treaty with the Ottawa, etc.	1807	Treaty with the Delawares	1818
Treaty with the Osage	1808	Treaty with the Miami	1818
Treaty with the Chippewa, etc.	1808	Treaty with the Chickasaw	1818
Treaty with the Delawares, etc.	1809	Agreement with the Piankeshaw	1818
Supplementary Treaty with the Miami, etc.	1809	Treaty with the Cherokee	1819

(continues)

Native American Treaties with the United States, 1778–1883 (cont.)

Treaty	Year	Treaty	Year
Treaty with the Kickapoo	1819	Treaty with the Miami	1828
Treaty with the Kickapoo	1819	Treaty with the Western Cherokee	1828
Treaty with the Chippewa	1819	Treaty with the Winnebago, etc.	1828
Treaty with the Chippewa	1820	Treaty with the Potawatomi	1828
Treaty with the Ottawa and Chippewa	1820	Treaty with the Chippewa, etc.	1829
Treaty with the Kickapoo	1820	Treaty with the Winnebago	1829
Treaty with the Wea	1820	Treaty with the Delawares	1829
Treaty with the Kickapoo of the Vermilion	1820	Treaty with the Delawares	1829
Treaty with the Choctaw	1820	Treaty with the Sauk and Foxes, etc.	1830
Treaty with the Creeks	1821	Treaty with the Choctaw	1830
Treaty with the Creeks	1821	Treaty with the Chickasaw	1830
Treaty with the Ottawa, etc.	1821	Treaty with the Menominee	1831
Treaty with the Osage	1822	Treaty with the Menominee	1831
Treaty with the Sauk and Foxes	1822	Treaty with the Seneca	1831
Treaty with the Florida Tribes of Indians	1823	Treaty with the Seneca, etc.	1831
Agreement with the Seneca	1823	Treaty with the Shawnee	1831
Treaty with the Sauk and Foxes	1824	Treaty with the Ottawa	1831
Treaty with the Iowa	1824	Treaty with the Wyandot	1832
Treaty with the Quapaw	1824	Treaty with the Creeks	1832
Treaty with the Choctaw	1825	Treaty with the Seminole	1832
Treaty with the Creeks	1825	Treaty with the Winnebago	1832
Treaty with the Osage	1825	Treaty with the Sauk and Foxes	1832
Treaty with the Kansa	1825	Treaty with the Appalachicola Band	1832
Treaty with the Ponca	1825	Treaty with the Potawatomi	1832
Treaty with the Teton, etc. Sioux	1825	Treaty with the Chickasaw	1832
Treaty with the Sioune and Oglala Tribes	1825	Treaty with the Chickasaw	1832
Treaty with the Cheyenne Tribe	1825	Treaty with the Kickapoo	1832
Treaty with the Hunkpapa Band of the Sioux Tribe	1825	Treaty with the Potawatomi	1832
Treaty with the Arikara Tribe	1825	Treaty with the Shawnee, etc.	1832
Treaty with the Belantse-Etoa or Minitaree Tribe	1825	Treaty with the Potawatomi	1832
		Treaty with the Kaskaskia, etc.	1832
Treaty with the Mandan Tribe	1825	Treaty with the Menominee	1832
Treaty with the Crow Tribe	1825	Treaty with the Piankashaw and Wea	1832
Treaty with the Great and Little Osage	1825	Treaty with the Seneca and Shawnee	1832
Treaty with the Kansa	1825	Treaty with the Western Cherokee	1833
Treaty with the Sioux, etc.	1825	Treaty with the Creeks	1833
Treaty with the Oto and Missouri Tribe	1825	Treaty with the Ottawa	1833
Treaty with the Pawnee Tribe	1825	Treaty with the Seminole	1833
Treaty with the Makah Tribe	1825	Treaty with the Quapaw	1833
Treaty with the Shawnee	1825	Treaty with the Appalachicola Band	1833
Agreement with the Creeks	1825	Treaty with the Oto and Missouri	1833
Treaty with the Creeks	1826	Treaty with the Chippewa, etc.	1833
Treaty with the Chippewa	1826	Treaty with the Pawnee	1833
Treaty with the Potawatomi	1826	Treaty with the Chickasaw	1834
Treaty with the Miami	1826	Treaty with the Miami	1834
Treaty with the Chippewa, etc.	1827	Treaty with the Potawatomi	1834
Treaty with the Potawatomi	1827	Treaty with the Potawatomi	1834
Treaty with the Creeks	1827	Treaty with the Potawatomi	1834
		Treaty with the Potawatomi	1834

(continues)

Native American Treaties with the United States, 1778–1883 (cont.)

Treaty	Year	Treaty	Year
Treaty with the Caddo	1835	Treaty with the Chippewa	1842
Treaty with the Comanche, etc.	1835	Treaty with the Sauk and Foxes	1842
Treaty with the Cherokee (Treaty of New Echota)	1835	Agreement with the Delawares and Wyandot	1843
Agreement with the Cherokee	1835	Treaty with the Creeks and Seminole	1845
Treaty with the Potawatomi	1836	Treaty with the Kansa Tribe	1846
Treaty with the Ottawa, etc.	1836	Treaty with the Comanche, Aionai, Anadarko, Caddo, etc.	1846
Treaty with the Potawatomi	1836	Treaty with the Potawatomi Nation	1846
Treaty with the Potawatomi	1836	Treaty with the Cherokee	1846
Treaty with the Potawatomi	1836	Treaty with the Winnebago	1846
Treaty with the Wyandot	1836	Treaty with the Chippewa of the Mississippi and Lake Superior	1847
Treaty with the Chippewa	1836	Treaty with the Pillager Band of Chippewa Indians	1847
Treaty with the Potawatomi	1836	Treaty with the Pawnee-Grand Loups Republicans, etc.	1848
Treaty with the Menominee	1836	Treaty with the Menominee	1848
Treaty with the Sioux	1836	Treaty with the Stockbridge Tribe	1848
Treaty with the Iowa, etc.	1836	Treaty with the Navaho	1849
Treaty with the Potawatomi	1836	Treaty with the Utah	1849
Treaty with the Potawatomi	1836	Treaty with the Wyandot	1850
Treaty with the Potawatomi	1836	Treaty with the Sioux–Sisseton and Wahpeton Bands	1851
Treaty with the Sauk and Fox Tribe	1836	Treaty with the Sioux–Mdewakanton and Wahpakoota Bands	1851
Treaty with the Sauk and Foxes	1836	Treaty of Fort Laramie with Sioux, etc.	1851
Treaty with the Sauk and Foxes	1836	Treaty with the Chickasaw	1852
Treaty with the Oto, etc.	1836	Treaty with the Apache	1852
Treaty with the Sioux	1836	Treaty with the Comanche Kiowa and Apache	1853
Treaty with the Chippewa	1837	Agreement with the Rogue River	1853
Treaty with the Choctaw and Chickasaw	1837	Treaty with the Rogue River	1853
Treaty with the Potawatomi	1837	Treaty with the Umpqua-Cow Creek Band	1853
Treaty with the Kiowa, etc.	1837	Treaty with the Oto and Missouri	1854
Treaty with the Chippewa	1837	Treaty with the Omaha	1854
Treaty with the Sioux	1837	Treaty with the Delawares	1854
Treaty with the Sauk and Foxes	1837	Treaty with the Shawnee	1854
Treaty with the Yankton Sioux	1837	Treaty with the Menominee	1854
Treaty with the Sauk and Foxes	1837	Treaty with the Iowa	1854
Treaty with the Winnebago	1837	Treaty with the Sauk and Foxes of Missouri	1854
Treaty with the Iowa	1837	Treaty with the Kickapoo	1854
Treaty with the Chippewa	1837	Treaty with the Kaskaskia Peoria, etc.	1854
Treaty with the New York Indians	1838	Treaty with the Miami	1854
Treaty with the Chippewa	1838	Treaty with the Creeks	1854
Treaty with the Oneida	1838	Treaty with the Chippewa	1854
Treaty with the Iowa	1838	Treaty with the Choctaw and Chickasaw	1854
Treaty with the Miami	1838	Treaty with the Rogue River	1854
Treaty with the Creeks	1838	Treaty with the Chasta, etc.	1854
Treaty with the Osage	1839		
Treaty with the Chippewa	1839		
Treaty with the Stockbridge and Munsee	1839		
Treaty with the Miami	1840		
Treaty with the Wyandot	1842		
Treaty with the Seneca	1842		

(continues)

Native American Treaties with the United States, 1778–1883 (cont.)

Treaty	Year	Treaty	Year
Treaty with the Umpqua and Kalapuya	1854	Treaty with the Eastern Shoshoni	1863
Treaty with the Confederated Oto and Missouri	1854	Treaty with the Shoshoni–Northwestern Bands	1863
Treaty with the Nisqualli Puyallup, etc.	1854	Treaty with the Western Shoshoni	1863
Treaty with the Kalapuya, etc.	1855	Treaty with the Chippewa–Red Lake and Pembina Bands	1863
Treaty with the Dwamish Suquamish, etc.	1855	Treaty with the Utah–Tabeguache Band	1863
Treaty with the S'klallam	1855	Treaty with the Shoshoni-Goship	1863
Treaty with the Wyandot	1855	Treaty with the Chippewa–Red Lake and Pembina Bands	1864
Treaty with the Makah	1855		
Treaty with the Chippewa	1855	Treaty with the Chippewa, Mississippi, and Pillager and Lake Winnibigoshish Bands	1864
Treaty with the Winnebago	1855	Treaty with the Klamath, etc.	1864
Treaty with the Wallawalla Cayuse, etc.	1855	Treaty with the Chippewa of Saginaw Swan Creek and Black River	1864
Treaty with the Yakima	1855		
Treaty with the Nez Percés	1855	Treaty with the Omaha	1865
Treaty with the Choctaw and Chickasaw	1855	Treaty with the Winnebago	1865
Treaty with the Tribes of Middle Oregon	1855	Treaty with the Ponca	1865
Treaty with the Quinaielt, etc.	1855	Treaty with the Snake	1865
Treaty with the Flatheads, etc.	1855	Treaty with the Osage	1865
Treaty with the Ottawa and Chippewa	1855	Treaty with the Sioux–Miniconjou Band	1865
Treaty with the Chippewa of Sault Ste. Marie	1855	Treaty with the Sioux–Lower Brulé Band	1865
Treaty with the Chippewa of Saginaw, etc.	1855	Agreement with the Cherokee and Other Tribes in the Indian Territory	1865
Treaty with the Blackfeet	1855	Treaty with the Cheyenne and Arapaho	1865
Treaty with the Molala	1855	Treaty with the Apache Cheyenne and Arapaho	1865
Treaty with the Stockbridge and Munsee	1856		
Treaty with the Menominee	1856	Treaty with the Comanche and Kiowa	1865
Treaty with the Creeks, etc.	1856	Treaty with the Sioux–Two-Kettle Band	1865
Treaty with the Pawnee	1857	Treaty with the Blackfeet Sioux	1865
Treaty with the Seneca Tonawanda Band	1857	Treaty with the Sioux–Sans Arc Band	1865
Treaty with the Ponca	1858	Treaty with the Sioux–Hunkpapa Band	1865
Treaty with the Yankton Sioux	1858	Treaty with the Sioux–Yanktonai Band	1865
Treaty with the Sioux	1858	Treaty with the Sioux–Upper Yanktonai Band	1865
Treaty with the Sioux	1858		
Treaty with the Winnebago	1859	Treaty with the Sioux—Oglala Band	1865
Treaty with the Chippewa, etc.	1859	Treaty with the Middle Oregon Tribes	1865
Treaty with the Sauk and Foxes	1859	Treaty with the Seminole	1866
Treaty with the Kansa Tribe	1859	Treaty with the Potawatomi	1866
Treaty with the Delawares	1860	Treaty with the Chippewa–Bois Fort Band	1866
Treaty with the Arapaho and Cheyenne	1861	Treaty with the Choctaw and Chickasaw	1866
Treaty with the Sauk and Foxes, etc.	1861	Treaty with the Creeks	1866
Treaty with the Delawares	1861	Treaty with the Delawares	1866
Treaty with the Potawatomi	1861	Agreement at Fort Berthold	1866
Treaty with the Kansa Indians	1862	Treaty with the Cherokee	1866
Treaty with the Ottawa of Blanchard's Fork and Roche de Boeuf	1862	Treaty with the Sauk and Foxes	1867
Treaty with the Kickapoo	1862	Treaty with the Sioux–Sisseton and Wahpeton Bands	1867
Treaty with the Chippewa of the Mississippi and the Pillager and Lake Winnibigoshish Bands	1863		
Treaty with the Nez Percés	1863	Treaty with the Seneca, Mixed Seneca, and Shawnee Quapaw, etc.	1867

(continues)

Native American Treaties with the United States, 1778–1883 (cont.)

Treaty	Year	Treaty	Year
Treaty with the Potawatomi	1867	Treaty with the Navaho	1868
Treaty with the Chippewa of the Mississippi	1867	Treaty with the Eastern Band Shoshoni and Bannock	1868
Treaty with the Kiowa and Comanche	1867	Treaty with the Nez Percés	1868
Treaty with the Kiowa, Comanche, and Apache	1867	Agreement with the Sisseton and Wahpet on Bands of Sioux Indians	1872
Treaty with the Cheyenne and Arapaho	1867	Amended Agreement with Certain Sioux Indians	1873
Treaty with the Ute	1868	Agreement with the Crows	1880
Treaty with the Cherokee	1868	Agreement with the Sioux of Various Tribes	1882–1883
Treaty with the Sioux–Brûlé, Oglala, Miniconjou, Yanktonai, Hunkpapa, Blackfeet, Cuthead, Two Kettle, Sans Arcs, and Santee–and Arapaho (Treaty of Fort Laramie)	1868	Agreement with the Columbia and Colville	1883
Treaty with the Crows	1868		
Treaty with the Northern Cheyenne and Northern Arapaho	1868		

Source: Kappler's Indian Affairs: Laws and Treaties (1906). Compiled and edited by Charles J. Kappler. Washington, D.C.: Government Printing Office, 1904.

Index

Note: Page locators in **boldface** type indicate the location of a main encyclopedia entry.

Abenaki Confederacy, 1235, 1251, 1252, 1256, 1257, 1271, 1272, 1273
Abenaki Indians, 355, 370, **1235–1236**
    Eastern, 113, 1272–1274
    Western, 112, 113
Aboriginal Healing Foundation, 724–725
Aboriginal Peoples Television Network, **631–632**
Aboriginal rights. *See* Indigenous rights
Abourezk, James, 305, 363, 364, 495
Abraham (Black Seminole), 314, 314 (photo)
Abramoff, Jack, 140
Absentee Shawnees, 1286
Abuse/atrocities
    and boarding schools, 79, 97, 98–102, 331–332
    and California Indians, 227, 229
    and Clark, George Rogers, 681–682
    and the Spanish, 677–678
    against women, 384–385
    See also Genocide
"Academic Squaw," 834–835
Acculturation. *See* Assimilation
Achumawi Indians, **1047–1048**
Acoma Pueblos, 19–20, 220, 414, **998–1001,** 999 (photo)
Acomita, 998
Act for the Gradual Enfranchisement of Indians and the Better Management of Indian Affairs (1869), 537
Act for the Relief of Mission Indians (1891), 1060
Activism, political, 66, 67–68, 75, 293 (photo)
    and the Achumawis, 1048
    and the Arctic Indians, 1325, 1327, 1332, 1334–1335, 1338
    and education policy, 127
    fishing rights and anti-Indian, 389

    and the Fort Laramie Treaty, 530–531
    and Indian/indigenous rights, 71–74 (*see also* Indian rights)
    and Indian religious freedom, 497–498 (*see also* Religious freedom)
    and international bodies, 618–619
    and James Bay hydroelectric project, 565, 568
    and lacrosse, 418
    and the Mohawks, 1261
    and Native Hawai'ians, 533
    occupation of Alcatraz Island, 288–292
    and the Onondagas, 1269
    and radiation exposure, 602
    Red Power movement, 292–297
    Trail of Broken Treaties, 297–300
    Ward Valley protest, 307–309, 308 (photo)
    See also Activists; Pan-Indianism; Political organizations; *specific protests*
Activists
    Collier, John, 689, 690–691
    Erasmus, George, 724
    Mad Bear, 647
    Mankiller, Wilma, 779–780
    McNickle, D'Arcy, 785
    Means, Russell, 785–787
    Montezuma, 793–794
    Oakes, Richard, 806–807
    Peltier, Leonard, 817–819
    Warrior, Clyde, 871–872
Actors
    Rogers, Will, 833–834
    Standing Bear, Luther, 855
    Thorpe, Jim, 866
Adai people, 1209
Adair, John, 772
Adak Island, 144–145, 144 (photo)
Adams, Hank, 298–299, 798
Adams, John Quincy, 252, 526
Adams-Onís Treaty (1819), 249
Adena culture, 8, 9–10, 166, **311–313,** 312 (photo). *See also*

    Moon-Eyed People
Adobe Walls, Battle of, 815–816, 1170, 1183
Adonwentishon, Catharine, 668
Adoption, 124, 409, 870
    and captives, 192, 359, 483, 484
    and the Iroquois, 219, 370, 745
Africa, 178
African Americans, **314–315**
    Black Seminoles, 344–346, 1229, 1230
    See also Slaves
Agnew, Spiro, 347
Agriculture, **315–319,** 316 (photo)
    and the Great Basin Indians, 1124
    and the Great Plains Indians, 660–661, 1160, 1165, 1171, 1178, 1180, 1190, 1191, 1207
    and the Northeast Woodland Indians, 192–193, 386, 1241, 1250, 1259, 1282
    and the Northwest Coast Indians, 1106
    policies encouraging, 540
    pollution from, 131
    and pre-contact Indians, 4, 7–11, 313, 328, 330, 350, 400–401, 402, 432, 434, 435–436
    and the Southeast Indians, 1209, 1213, 1216, 1218, 1229, 1231
    and the Southwest Indians, 1003, 1009, 1011, 1012–1013, 1016, 1017, 1018, 1019, 1024–1025, 1026, 1028, 1039, 1041, 1042, 1043, 1046
    See also Environment management; Irrigation
Ak-Chin Him-Dak EcoMuseum, 804
Akins, J. D. C., 421
Akwesasne, 161–162, 174, 1260, 1261
    Freedom School, **632–633**
    pollution and, 129–131, 513
Akwesasne Notes, **633–634,** 791
Al-le-go-wa-ho, 1181

Alabama-Coushatta. *See* Alabama
    Indians
Alabama Indians, **1208–1209,** 1222
    language of, 438
Alarcón, Hernando de, 1029
Alaska
    alcohol abuse in, 158
    Athapaskans in, 336
    and the Haidas, 1092
    hazardous waste in, 132–133,
        144–145
    identity issues and Natives of,
        409
    land claims and treaty rights in,
        72, 491–493, 606–607 (*see
        also* Alaska Native
        Claims Settlement Act
        [ANCSA] [1971])
    Reorganization Act (1936), 557
    Statehood Act (1958), 491
    and the Tlingits, 1111, 1113–1114
    trade in, 19, 395
    U.S. purchase of, **263–265,** 264
        (photo)
    *See also specific Alaskan Indian
        groups*
Alaska Federation of Natives (AFN),
    492, 493, 636, 1338, 1345
Alaska National Interest Land
    Conservation Act, 492
Alaska Native Brotherhood (ANB),
    634–636, 1092, 1114
Alaska Native Claims Settlement
    Act (ANCSA) (1971), 72,
    491–493, 607, 636, **965**
    and the Alutiiqs, 1322–1323
    and the Haidas, 1092
    and the Inupiats, 1338
    and the Unangans, 1345
    and the Yup'iks, 1348
Alaska Native Sisterhood (ANS),
    1092, 1114
Alaskan Highway, 1295, 1310
Albany Congress, **493–495,** 569, 616
    and Franklin, Benjamin, 730
    and Hendrick, 747, 748
Alberni Indian Residential School,
    100
Albuquerque, 145–146
Alcatraz Island occupation, 71, 154,
    287–292, 288 (photo), 639
Alcatraz Proclamation, **964**
    and the Fort Laramie Treaty, 531
    and Mad Bear, 647
    and Mankiller, Wilma, 779
    and Means, Russell, 785
    as model for Indian activism,
        293, 294, 295

and Oakes, Richard, 806, 807
and the Pomos, 1067
Alcohol/alcohol abuse, 48, **77–81,**
    158
    and Alaskan Natives, 133
    and the Arctic Indians, 1325,
        1334, 1338, 1348
    and the Assiniboines, 1162
    and boarding schools, 97
    campaigns/arguments against,
        766, 806
    and the Carlisle Treaty Council,
        513–514
    and the Chumash, 1052
    and crime, 156
    death rate from, 112
    and epidemic disease, 111
    and the Great Basin Indians,
        1129
    and the Northeast Woodland
        Indians, 1250, 1252, 1257,
        1266, 1272, 1285, 1292
    and the Northwest Coast
        Indians, 1084, 1086, 1088
    and the Southeast Indians, 1211,
        1219, 1232
    and the Subarctic Indians, 1303,
        1312, 1314
    as a trade item, 394, 535–536, 832
    and treaty negotiations, 173
Aleut League, 1345
Aleut Native Corporation, 145
Aleutian-Fox dictionary, 223
Aleutian Islands, 144–145, 1345
Aleutian/Pribilof Island
    Association, 144–145
Aleuts, 222, 222 (photo). *See also*
    Alutiiq Indians;
    Unangan Indians
Alexander, John, 830
Alexander (Wampanoag), 787
Alexander I, Czar (Russia), 264
Alexander VI, Pope, 17, 208, 215,
    232
Alexie, Sherman, 407
Alfonso V, King (Portugal), 208
Algonquin Indian Council of New
    England, 1275
Algonquin Indians, 5, 9, 11,
    1236–1238, 1237 (photo)
Anishinabe Algonquin National
    Council, 648–649
    and the Council of the Three
        Fires, 368
    and the French, 212, 356
    and Massachusetts praying
        villages, 719–720
    migration westward, 219

See also Algonquin language
    family
Algonquin language family, 419,
    1237
    and California Indians, 1076,
        1079
    Cree dialects, 1170, 1300, 1311
    Eastern dialects, 1235, 1262,
        1272, 1274
    Fox, Sauk, and Kickapoo
        dialects, 1243, 1245, 1278
    and the Illinois, 1244
    and the Lenápes, 1247
    Mahican, 1249
    and the Maliseets and
        Passamaquoddys, 1251,
        1271
    and the Menominees, 1252
    and the Miamis, 1254
    and the Micmacs, 1256
    and the Nanticokes, 1261
    Ottawa and Anishinabe dialects,
        1238, 1270
    and Plains Indians, 1158, 1163,
        1165, 1176, 1194
    Potawatomi, 1276
    Powhatan, 1226
    and the Shawnees, 1284
    Wampanoag and Massachusetts
        dialect, 1287
All Indian Pueblo Council (AIPC),
    637, 998, 1001, 1028, 1037
Allegany Reservation, 1242, 1269,
    1283, 1284
Allen, John, 153
Alliance of Tribal Councils, 1103
Alliances, 367–371
    activist and environmental
        groups, 338, 639, 693
    and the American Revolution,
        237–239, 240 (*see also*
        Revolutionary War)
    French and Indian, 356–357
    and the French and Indian War,
        225, 226 (*see also* French
        and Indian War)
    international, 73
    and King Philip's War, 789
    and Little Turtle's War, 771–772
    and Massasoit, 784
    and the Northwest Territory
        Indians, 853
    Ohio Union pan-Indian, 682
    and the Pequot War, 217–218
    and Pontiac, 825–826
    spiritual underpinnings of, 396
    and Tecumseh, 31–32, 661,
        860–862, 864

trade and political, 167
and War of 1812, 357–358 (*see also* War of 1812)
See also Pan-Indianism; *specific Indian groups and confederacies*
Allied Tribes and the Native Brotherhood of British Columbia, 1103
Allotment, 147, 175, 278–282, 690–691
abolishment of, 554–555, 556
and assimilation efforts, 89, 117
and the Blackfeet, 661
and the Comanches, 816
and the Crazy Snake Movement, 739
and the Five Civilized Tribes of Oklahoma, 707
and fragmenting reservation land, 47–48, 123
and Jackson, Helen Hunt, 756
and the Kaws, 1181
and Leupp, Francis Ellington, 769
and *Lone Wolf v. Hitchcock*, 570–571
and the Osage, 448
Aloha Hawai'i, 533
Alsea Reservation, 1089, 1117
Alutiiq Indians, **1321–1323**
Alvarado, Hernando de, 1000
Alvarado, Pedro de, 676
Amalgamation, cultural, 320–321, 410. *See also* Assimilation
Ambrister, Robert, 249
American Anthropological Association, 552, 710
American Board of Commissioners for Foreign Missions (ABCFM), 877
American Civil Liberties Union, 555
American Diabetes Association, 378
American Fur Company, 264, 394, 526, 1152
American Horse, 103 (photo), 1187
American Indian Baskets, 339
American Indian Chicago Conference (AICC), 124, 293, 734–735, 798
and Warrior, Clyde, 871, 872
American Indian Contemporary Arts, 407
American Indian Council, Inc., 288
American Indian Defense Association (AIDA), 553–554, 555, 576, 690, 691

American Indian Development Corporation, 785
American Indian Federation, 558
American Indian Higher Education Consortium (AIHEC), 72, 126, **638,** 868
American Indian Historical Society, 700
American Indian Magazine, 666
American Indian Movement (AIM), 154, 293 (photo), 497–498, **638–646,** 639 (photo)
and Aquash, Anna Mae Pictou, 651–653
and Banks, Dennis, 656–657
formation of, 291–292, 295–296
and the ITC, 618
leadership of, 289
and Means, Russell, 785–786
and Peltier, Leonard, 817–818
and Pine Ridge conflicts, 71, 300–303
protests by, 296
Three-Point Program, **968**
and Trail of Broken Treaties, 297–300
and the Ward Valley protest, 309
and Wilson, Richard, 879–880
and Wounded Knee II, 303–305
American Indian Movement Youth Organization, 165
American Indian Progressive Association, 855
American Indian Quarterly, 835
American Indian Religious Freedom Act (AIRFA) (1978), 62, 91, 460, **495–499,** 582, 867
1994 amendment to, **975**
American Indian Science and Engineering Society, 155
American Indian Stories, 666
American Indian studies, 155, 294, 710
The American Indian's Sacred Ground, 425
American Museum of Natural History, 679
American Political Science Association's Indigenous Studies Network, 155
American Professional Football Association, 866
America's Second Tongue, 666
Amherst, Jeffrey, 806
Amiott, Roger, 302

Amnesty International, 817
Anasazi, 326–330
Anawak, Jack, 593
Anaya, James, 799
Ancestral Puebloan culture, **326–330,** 998
and the Hopi, 1013
Mogollon culture, 433 (*see also* Mogollon culture)
and the Pueblos, 1018
and the Zunis, 1044
Andean weavers, 486
Andersen, Magnus, 207
Anderson, Clinton P., 347
Anderson, Michael, 818
Andrus, Cecil B., 496
Angeline, 840
Anglican Church, 99, 102, **331–332**
and the Northwest Coast Indians, 1091, 1115
and the Subarctic Indians, 1302
Anglican Old Sun's School, 100
Anishinabe Algonquin National Council, **648–649**
Anishinabe/Anishnabe Indians, **1238–1240**
French alliance, 356–357
and the Seven Nations of Canada, 370
and War of 1812, 357–358
See also Chippewa/Chipewya Indians; Ojibwa/Ojibway, Northern, Indians
Annette Island Reserve, 1115
Anthony, Aaron, 314
Anthony, Scott, 262–263
Anthony, Susan B., 383 (photo), 384, 387
Anthropology
and Boas, Franz, 664–665
and the Bureau of American Ethnology, 500
and Deloria, Vine, Jr., 710–711
and the Indian Reorganization Act, 552, 691
and Kennewick Man, 416
and McNickle, D'Arcy, 785
and Parker, Ely, 814
and Rose, Wendy, 834–835
Antiquities Act (1909), 459, 581
Antone, Wally, 308–309
Anza, Juan Bautista de, 1050
Aoghyatonghere, Neggen, 668
Apache Indians, 8, 40, 272 (photo)
as Athapaskan cultural group, 335
and Baptists, 265

Apache Indians *(cont.)*
    Chiricahua, 271–273, 705,
        778–779, **1001–1003**, 1006
    Cibecue (*see* Apache Indians,
        Western)
    Cochise, 683–685
    enslavement of, 168, 1181
    Eskiminzin, 728–729
    Fort Sill (*see* Apache Indians,
        Chiricahua)
    Geronimo, 730–732
    and horses, 39, 404, 406
    and humor, 407
    Jicarilla, 266, **1003–1004**, 1005,
        1006
    and the Kiowas, 1183
    Lipan, **1004–1005**, 1006
    Mescalero, 260, 265, 675,
        1005–1006
    Mimbreño (*see* Apache Indians,
        Chiricahua)
    and missionaries, 234
    and Mount Graham, 398–399
    Northern Tonto (*see* Apache
        Indians, Western)
    Plains, 8, **1157–1158**
    raids on Pueblos, 233
    San Carlos (*see* Apache Indians,
        Western)
    Southern Tonto (*see* Apache
        Indians, Western)
    and the Spanish, 109, 215
    and the Tiguas, 1038
    and the Tonkawans, 1206
    and the U.S. Army, 705
    Western, 270–271, **1006–1007**,
        1006 (photo)
    White Mountain (*see* Apache
        Indians, Western)
    and the Yavapais, 1042
Apache Pass, Battle of, 273, 685, 871
Apache Wars, **271–273**, 1002–1003
Apachean language family, 333, 419,
    1003, 1005, 1006
Apalachee Indians, 18–19, 438, 1229
Apalachicola Indians, 1229
Apess, William, **650–651**
Aquash, Anna Mae Pictou, 300, 302,
    645, **651–653**
Aquash, Nogeeshik, 652
Aquila, Richard, 173, 238
Aranda, Conde de, 22
Arapaho/Arapahoe Indians,
    1158–1160, 1159 (photo)
    and Baptists, 265
    and the Battle of Little Bighorn,
        274–276
    and the Ghost Dance, 361
        (photo)

    and Gros Ventres Indians, 1177
    sacred pipe of the, 454
    and the Sand Creek Massacre,
        261–263
    and the Shoshonis, 874, 1127
    spirituality and language, 420
    and the Sun Dance, 471
    and treaties, 23, 176
    and the Washita Massacre, 268
    See also Wind River Reservation
Arbuthnot, Alexander, 249
Archaeological Resources Protection
    Act (ARPA) (1979), 459,
    581
Archaeology, **82–87**
    and agriculture, 317
    and the Ancient Pueblo, 326–330
    and Athapaskan migrations, 335
    and Cahokia, 350–352
    and Dalles trading area, 201
    and the Hohokam culture, 400
    and the Hopewell culture, 402
    and Kennewick Man, 416
    and the Makahs, 1096
    migration theory and, 93–94,
        200, 201, 441
    and Mississippian culture,
        432–433
    and Mogollon culture, 433–435
    and mound builders, 436–437,
        446
    and museums, 803
    and the Norse, 205–206, 206–207
    North American sites, 2, 83,
        84–85, 85 (figure)
    and Paleo-Indians, 2–3, 451–452
    and Parker, Arthur C., 813
    and pipes, 453
    and pottery, 457
    and weaving, 485
Architecture, 319, 324, 327–329. *See
    also* Houses/housing
Arctic Athabaskan Council (AAC),
    336
Arctic Brotherhood, 635
Arctic region, 11–12
    Indian groups in the, 1321–1349
    and pollution, 132–133
Arendaronon Indians, 369
Arens, William, 352, 353–354
Arikara Indians, **1160–1161**
Arizona, 138–139, 148–151, 165
Arkansas, 138
Arkansas Indians. *See* Quapaw
    Indians
Armistead, Walker K., 250
Armstrong, Samuel C., 766
Army, U.S.
    and the Apaches, 271–273, 871

    and Black Hawk, 251–252
    and buffalo extermination,
        349–350
    and the Camp Grant massacre,
        270–271
    and the Cheyenne, 715
    and Cochise, 683–685
    and Cody, William, 686
    and the Crows, 822–823
    expansionism and the, 39, 45, 46,
        47
    and the factory system, 525
    and the genocide of California
        Indians, 229, 1067
    and the Ghost Dance massacre,
        362
    Indian scouts for the, 1038,
        1042–1043, 1140, 1202,
        1210, 1249
    and the Modoc wars, 674, 752
    and the Navajos, 261, 780–781
    and the Nez Percé, 276–277,
        762–763
    and the Plains Indians, 255, 266,
        273–275, 320, 828
    and removal, 551
    and the Seminoles, 248–249, 315
    and the Shoshonis, 873, 874, 1127
    and Smohalla, 846
    treaty enforcement and the, 41,
        44
    and Wounded Knee, 283–285,
        398, 497
Army Corps of Engineers, U.S., 415,
    1095–1096
    and dam projects, 374, 375, 700
Arn, W. F. M., 714
Aroostook Micmac Council, 1257
Arrow Worship, 472
Art, 24
Adena, 313
    and the Ancient Pueblo, 328, 329
    beadwork, 339–340
    and the Hohokam culture, 400,
        402
    and the Hopewell culture,
        403–404
    and Indian humor, 407–408
    Katsina, 414
    and the Kwakiutls, 1094
    and Mississippian culture, 432
    and Mogollon culture, 434–435
    and pottery, 457–458
    and pre-contact Indians, 4–6,
        8–10, 12
    totem poles, 477–479
    weaving, 485–487
    See also Artists; Basketry; *specific
        Indian groups*

Arthur Andersen & Co., 614
Arthur Bremer Foundation, 561
Articles of Confederation, 239
The Artifact Piece, 774
Artists
    Catlin, George, 678–679
    Gorman, R. C., 732–734
    Luna, James Alexander, 773–774
    Lyons, Oren, 774
    Means, Russell, 787
    Momaday, N. Scott, 792
    Scholder, Fritz, 838–839
Arvide, Martin de, 1017
Asatru Folk Assembly, 415, 416
Ashley, William, 394
Askew, Patricia Gladys, 866
Askin, John, Sr., 357
*The Assault on Assimilation: John
        Collier and the Origins of
        Indian Policy Reform*, 552
Assembly of First Nations (AFN),
        101, **653–654**, 724
Assimilation, 48, 65, 71, 78, **87–92**
    and the Alaska Native
        Brotherhood, 635
    and allotment, 278–282
    and Athapaskans, 336
    and the BIA, 501
    and Canadian policies, 505, 506,
        537–538
    and the Cherokees, 252–253, 835
    and citizenship, 103–104
    and the Creeks, 246
    and early Indian activists, 292
    and education policy, 96–98,
        127–128, 143
    and ending sovereignty, 180
    and Episcopal missionaries, 723
    as federal policy, 43, 47, 50, 117,
        146, 689–690
    and the Fort Laramie Treaty, 530
    and Grant's peace policy,
        268–270
    and the Indian Civilization Fund
        Act, 540–541
    and the IRA, 558
    and language loss, 418, 422
    and Massachusetts praying
        villages, 599–600
    Meriam Report on, 576
    and pan-Indian organizations,
        154
    and the Society of American
        Indians, 847
    and termination policy, 66–68,
        79, 137, 607–610
Assiniboine Indians, 151–153, 404,
        1161–1162, 1193
Association of American Indian

Physicians (AAIP), 155,
        378, 379
Association of Aroostook Indians,
        1252, 1257
Astor, John Jacob, 264, 394–395, 526
Astoria, 1086, 1108
Astronomy, 321, 436, 444–445
Ataronchronon Indians, 369
Athapaskan/Athabaskan Indians,
        335–336, 335 (photo)
    and the Apaches, 1001
    in California, 5
    Dene, 332, 335, 592, 617, 724–725
    in the Northwest Coast area, 6,
        332
    in the Subarctic region, 11
Athapaskan/Athabaskan language
        family, **332–334,** 336, 419
    and California Indians, 1048,
        1055, 1072, 1074
    Chipewyan, 1299
    and Na-Dene, 440–441
    Navajo, 1021
    Northeastern dialects, 1304, 1315
    Northern dialects, 1294, 1295,
        1297, 1305, 1307, 1308,
        1310
    and Northwest Coast Indians,
        1090, 1110, 1116
    and Plains Apaches, 1157
    and the Sekanis, 1313
    Tahltan-Kaska, 1316
    Tanaina, 1318
Athletes
    Mills, William M., 790–791
    Thorpe, Jim, 865–867
Atkins, J. D. C., 282
Atkinson, Henry, 251, 662–663
Atkinson, Theodore, 494
Atomic Energy Commission (AEC),
        132, 134, 184, 1338
Atsina. *See* Gros Ventres Indians
Attigeenongnahac Indians, 369
Attignawantan Indians, 369
Attucks, Crispus, 314
August Snake Dance, 1012
Augustine, 353
Australia, 380
Awatovi, 1014
Axelrod, Beverly, 642
Aztalan, 8
Aztec Indians, 425, 427, 678
Aztec-Tanoan language phyla, 419
Azul family, 1026

Babbitt, Bruce, 139, 562
Bad Axe, Battle of, 251 (photo), 252
Bad Heart Bull, Sarah, 641
Bad Heart Bull, Wesley, 303, 641

Badlands National Monument
        occupation, 295
Baffin Island, 1325, 1327
Baffin Regional Association, 1325,
        1327
Bagley, Clarence B., 840
Bailey, F. Lee, 776
Bailey, Harriet, 314
Baja California, 108, 234–235
Baker, E. M., 660
Baker, Leonard, 36
Baker Massacre, 561, 660
Balance of power, 22, 23, 173, 358,
        505, 760
Bald Eagle Protection Act, 363
Baldwin, Henry, 515
Ball, Milner, 597
Ballanger, Pat, 638
Baller, Pearl Capoeman, 705, 706
Balme, Augustin de la, 771
Baltimore, Lord, 821
Banderas, Juan de la Cruz (Juan
        Ignacio Jusacamea), **655,**
        1042
Banks, Dennis, 289, **656–657,** 657
        (photo)
    and AIM, 303, 498, 638, 639,
        785–786
    and Aquash, Anna Mae Pictou,
        652
    and the FBI, 817
    and the Longest Walk, 645
    and Onondaga sanctuary, 513
    and Pine Ridge conflict, 300,
        301–302, 304
    and Trail of Broken Treaties, 297,
        298 (photo), 299
    and the Wounded Knee siege,
        296, 640–641, 642
Banks, Kamook, 642
Banks, Native-owned, 156, 560, 561
Banning, Evelyn I., 755
Bannock Indians, 873, 1119, 1120,
        1120 (photo), 1121, 1127,
        1128, 1129
    and the Ghost Dance, 396, 398
    See also Paiute, Northern;
        Shoshone Indians,
        Northern
Bannock War, 41, 1154
Baptist Church, **265–266,** 526
Baranov, Alexander, 221
Barbariño. *See* Chumash Indians
Barbé-Marbois, François, 16
Barboncito, 260
Barona Band (Mission Indians), 137
Barreiro, José, 475, 634
Barry, G., 99–100
Barry, Tom, 184–185

Barsh, Russel, 170
Bartlett, John R., 778
Bartram, John, 381–382
Bascom, George, 272, 684–685
Bashabes, 1273
Basket Maker people, 4
Basket Tales of the Grandmothers, 339
Basketry, 4–7, 9, **336–339,** 337
　　　(photo), 454
Basques, 1334
Battey, Thomas C., 763
Battice, Walter, 793
Battle, R. F., 521
Battlefield and Classroom: Four Decades
　　　with the American Indian,
　　　1867–1904, 96
Bausch, Edward, 813
Bay Area Indian Association, 290
Bdewakantunwan Dakota, 257, 258
Beadwork, **339–340**
Beans, 316, 318
　　　and pre-contact Indians, 4, 7, 8,
　　　　　10, 328
　　　See also "Three sisters" complex
Bear Dance, 1132
Bear Flag Revolt, 229
Bear Lodge, 458–459, 459 (photo),
　　　460
Bear Tooth, 1159
Bearskin, Leaford, **657–658**
Beauchamp, William, 382
Beaufort Sea, 1340
Beaver ceremony, 1168
Beaver Indians, **1294–1295**
Beaver Wars, **218–220,** 483
Bedford, David, 782, 783
Begaye, Kelsey, 91
Behind the Trail of Broken Treaties: An
　　　Indian Declaration of
　　　Independence, 618
Belcourt, Tony, 579 (photo)
Belgarde, Daniel B., 595
Bella Bella Indians, **1082–1083**
Bella Bella Reserve, 1083
Bella Coola Indians, **1083–1085**
Bellecourt, Clyde, 297, 303, 656, 785
Bellecourt, Vernon, 297, 299, 656
Belloni, Robert C., 849
Ben Mannasseh, Israel, 93
Ben Wright Massacre, 673
Benedict, Ernie (Kaientaronkwen),
　　　634
Benedict, Jeff, 135–136
Bennett, Robert, 503
Benson, Paul, 645, 818
Benson, Robby, 791
Bent, George, 39, 663
Benteen, Frederick, 275
Beothuk Indians, 212, 728, 1257

Berdaches, **340–342,** 341 (photo)
　　　and Arctic Indians, 1322, 1344
　　　and California Indians, 1051,
　　　　　1072, 1076
　　　and the Natchez, 1225
　　　and the Northeast Woodland
　　　　　Indians, 1244, 1289
Berglud, Bob, 496
Bering, Vitus, 19, 1322
Bering Sea, 133
Bering Strait migration theory, 83,
　　　92–95, 199–201, 335
Beringia, 2, 3, 86
Beringian Mid-Continental
　　　migration route, 83
Bernal, Paul J., 346
Beyond Traplines, 332
Big Bear, 1171
Big Blue River Reservation, 1192
Big Drum religion, 1254
Big Eagle, 258
Big Foot/Bigfoot, 283, 284, 284
　　　(photo), 362, 398, 687, 1188
Big Head cult, 1070, 1076
Big Hole Valley, 276–277
Big Lagoon Rancheria, 1081
Big Mouth, 850
Big Sandy Rancheria, 1063
Big Snake, 605, 854
Big Track, 1198
Big Tree, 1183
Big Warrior, 247
Bilateral descent
　　　and Arctic Indians, 1324, 1331,
　　　　　1339, 1346
　　　and the Plains Indians, 1185,
　　　　　1194
　　　and the Subarctic Indians, 1298
Bilingual Education Act, 91, 422
Bill of Rights, U.S., 363
Billings, Richard "Mohawk,"
　　　642–643
Biloxi Indians, 1231. *See also* Tunica
　　　Indians
Birchbark, 355
Bird, Gloria, 740
Birth control, 193
Birth rates, 107
Bissonette, Pedro, 640, 643
Bkejwanong Indians, 354, 509
Black Canyon of the Gunnison
　　　National Park, 670
Black Elk, 148, **658–659**
Black Elk: Holy Man of the Oglala, 659
Black Elk Speaks, 443, 658
Black Hawk, 251–252, **661–663,** 662
　　　(photo), 1280
　　　and Harrison, William Henry,
　　　　　742

surrender speech, **915**
Black Hawk's War, **251–252,** 251
　　　(photo), 794
　　　and the Kickapoos, 1247
　　　and the Potawatomis, 1278
　　　and the Sauks, 1280
　　　and the Winnebagos, 1290
Black Hills (Paha Sapa), **342–344,**
　　　343 (photo)
　　　and Black Elk, 658–659
　　　and Congress, 843
　　　and Crazy Horse, 703
　　　and the Fort Laramie Treaty,
　　　　　530, 828
　　　Indian land claims and the,
　　　　　176–177, 274, 275–276,
　　　　　531–532, 646
　　　and the Lakotas, 1187
　　　and Sitting Bull, 842
　　　and uranium, 183
Black Hills Treaty (1876), 851
Black Jim, 674
Black Kettle, **663–664,** 1167
　　　and the Sand Creek Massacre,
　　　　　261–263
　　　and the Washita Massacre, 266,
　　　　　267–268
Black Mesa, 148–151
　　　and the Hopi, 1012, 1014
　　　and the San Ildefonso Pueblos,
　　　　　1032
Black Mesa Pipeline, Inc., 150–151
Black Mouth Society, 1189
Black Rock Reservation, 1045
Blackbear, Eugene, Sr., 454, 471,
　　　472, 474
Blackface, Jackie, 98
Blackfeet/Blackfoot Confederacy,
　　　367–368, **659–661,** 1177
Blackfeet/Blackfoot Indians, 115
　　　(photo), 349 (photo),
　　　484 (photo), **1162–1165,**
　　　1163 (photo)
　　　and Baker's Massacre, 561
　　　and the Battle of the Little
　　　　　Bighorn, 275
　　　economic development and,
　　　　　156
　　　and horses, 404
　　　and land losses, 53
　　　starvation and, 564
　　　and the Sun Dance, 471
　　　and sweat lodges, 474
　　　Welch, James, 875–876
　　　and written language, 425
Blackfeet Reservation, 1164–1165
Blackgoat, Roberta, 151
Blacks. *See* African Americans
Blackwater, Willy, 102

Blatchford, Herbert, 797, 798
Blount, Tom, 1233
Blue Corn, 458
Blue Jacket (Weyapiersenwah), 244, 772
Blue Lake, New Mexico, **346–347,** 1035–1036
Blue Licks, Battle of, 682
Blue Water People, 1010
Board of Indian Commissioners, 270, 497, 554
Boarding schools, **96–102**
    and addiction patterns, 78–79
    allotment/assimilation policy and, 78–79, 89, 96–102, 127–128, 143, 278, 281, 282, 501
    and the Anglican Church, 331–332
    and Arctic Indians, 1322
    and Banks, Dennis, 656
    and Bonnin, Gertrude Simmons, 666
    Canadian, 507, 725
    and destruction of family structure, 123–124
    and the Great Basin Indians, 1121, 1133
    and Katsina art, 414
    and the Lakotas, 1188
    and MacDonald, Peter, 776
    and McNickle, D'Arcy, 784
    and the Northwest Coast Indians, 1098
    and pan-Indianism, 154, 497
    and the Plateau Indians, 1152
    and self-determination, 559
    and Southwest Indians, 1001, 1014, 1020, 1023
    and the Subarctic Indians, 1308, 1309
    and termination policies, 608
Boas, Franz, 90, 420, 500, **664–665,** 665 (photo), 1084
Boats, plank, 1052. *See also* Canoes
Boldt, George, 72, 171, 176, 375, 391–392, 560, 849
Boldt decision, 171, 176, 389, 391–392, 517, **969**
Bole-Maru Religion, **347–348,** 1065, 1067, 1075
Bolivia, 109
Bolon, A. J., 255
Bombs, unexploded, 144–145, 144 (photo)
Bone Game, 812
Bonneville Power Administration, 517

Bonnin, Gertrude Simmons (Zitkala-sa), **665–666,** 666 (photo), 847
Book of Mormon, 445
Bosque Redondo (Fort Sumner), 260, 261, 1004, 1005, 1023
Boston Charley, 674
Boston Indian Council, 651–652
Boston Tea Party, **236–237,** 237 (photo), 239, 430
Boudinot, Elias, 253, 680, 777, 874
Boundaries
    and Nunavut, 591–594, 617
    Russian America/Oregon Territory, 264
    U.S.-Canadian, 239, 505–506, 659
Bow society, 1045
Bowerman, Dr., 133
Bowlegs, Billy, 250–251, 1228 (photo)
Boxberger, Daniel, 462, 463
Boyer, LaNada, 290
Boyle, David, 382
Bozeman Trail, 530, 1187
    War (1866–1867), 45
Braddock, Edward, 224–225, 825
Bradford, William, 218, 476, 783, 784
Bradley, Hannah, 359
Bradley University, 431
Brando, Marlon, 289, 872
Brandon, William, 377
Brant, Joseph, 238, 238 (photo), **667–669,** 667 (photo), 699, 760, 857, 1260
    and Red Jacket, 829, 830, 831
Brant, Molly (Mary), 16, 238, 667, 760
Brébeuf, Jean de, 214
Brenner, William, 101
Brewer, Duane, 643, 644
Breyer, Stephen, 182
Bridger, Jim, 394
Brigham Young University (BYU), 795
Brightman, Lehman, 884
British
    and the Arctic Indians, 1322
    conquest and sovereignty issues, 17, 179
    and the French and Indian War, 21, 224–226
    and Indian trade relations, 78, 116, 394, 395
    and the Iroquois, 667–669, 713, 857
    and the Northwest Coast, 263, 840, 1098
    and the Pontiac alliance, 356–357, 806, 816
    and the Southeast Indians, 247,

249, 1210, 1214, 1216, 1221, 1226, 1227, 1232, 1234
    violence and warfare and the, 14–15, 142
    See also Canada; *specific Northeast Woodland Indian groups*
British Columbia Interior Confederation, 1149
British Indian Department, 520, 537
British North America Act (1867), 507
Brodhead, Daniel, 682, 856–857
Brookings Institute, 124
Brooks, William, 780–781
Brophy, William, 607
Brothertown/Brotherton Indians, 1251, 1266, 1275–1276. *See also* Pequot Indians
Brown, Adella Katherine, 733
Brown, Dee, 659
Brown, George E., Jr., 287, 289
Brown, Jerry, 301, 642, 656
Brown, Joseph Epes, 659
Brown, Michele, 145
Brown, W. O., 302
Brown, Zonnie Maria, 733
Browning, Montana, 561
Bruce, Louis, 503
Brule, Etienne, 356
Brûlé Lakota, 275, 850–851
Brunot, Felix, 811
Bubonic plague, 14, 107
Buck, Antonio, 1133
Buckskin Charley, 1133
Buffalo Bill's Wild West Show, 687, 843, 855
Buffalo/bison, **348–350,** 349 (photo)
    and the Blackfeet, 368, 660
    Cody, William, and hunting, 686
    expansionism and destruction of the, 41, 45, 46, 143, 395
    and Métis in Canadian northern Plains, 832
    and Paleo-Indians, 452
    and pre-contact Indians, 8–9, 11
    and the Sun Dance, 471
    See also specific Indian groups
Buffalo Born, 1129
Buffalo Creek Reservation, 1242, 1260, 1266, 1269, 1283
Buffalo Dance, 1189, 1190 (photo), 1245
Buffalo Soldiers, 871
Bull, John, 242–243
Bull Head, 283
Bunting, Doris, 185
Bureau of American Ethnology, **499–500**

Bureau of Indian Affairs (BIA),
        501–503
    and Black Seminoles, 345–346
    and the Choctaws, 1220
    cultural repression by the, 98,
        554
    and dams, 374
    doctrines of trust and wardship
        and the, 36, 67, 68, 515,
        614, 616–617, 623–624
    and education, 124, 128 (see also
        Boarding schools)
    Establishing the Existence of an
        Indian Tribe, **987**
    and gaming operations, 138
    and Grant's peace policy,
        268–269
    harassment of AIM by, 641–646
    and the IIM scandal, 560–561,
        562
    Indian occupation of
        headquarters, 71, 294,
        295, 297, 299–300, 640,
        656, 786, 817
    and the Indian Reorganization
        Act, 147, 556
    and the Marshall Trilogy, 36, 514
    Meriam Report criticisms of the,
        577
    occupation of Alcatraz Island
        and the, 291
    recent policy and the, 68–69, 74,
        559
    and the Southwest Indians, 1001,
        1011, 1024–1025, 1026,
        1028–1029, 1037, 1045
    and termination, 610
    and testing Indian intelligence,
        97
    and urban relocation programs,
        66, 285–287
    and the Wounded Knee
        occupation, 817
Bureau of Land Management
        (BLM), 152, 308–309,
        621–622
Bureau of Reclamation (BOR), 189,
        600, 626
Burger, Warren E., 595
Burgoyne, John, 852
Burial/funerary practices, 361
    Adena burial mounds, 311–312
    and the Hohokam culture, 401
    and the Hopewell culture, 403
    and lacrosse, 417
    and Mogollon culture, 433
    and mound builders, 435,
        444–445
    and pre-contact Indians, 5, 8, 9

See also specific Indian groups
Burial sites, 364, 374
Burke, Charles, 53, 54–56, 58
Burke, Charles H., 553, 690
Burnette, Robert, 297, 298, 299
Burnham, Carrie, 385
Bursum, Holm, 637
Bursum Bill, 576, 637
Bury My Heart at Wounded Knee, 659
Busby School, 125
Bush, George H. W., 498
Bush, George W., 638, 799
    administration of, 134, 416, 562,
        563
Businesses, Native, 70, 775, 1023
Butler, Dino, 644–645, 652, 818
Butler, Elizur, 627
Butler, John, 857

Cabazon Band (Mission Indians), 74,
        137, 580
Cabeza de Vaca, Alvar Nuñez, 232
Cabrillo, Juan, 1052
Cactus Hill archaeology site, 83, 84
Caddo Indians, 8, 265, 1202,
        1209–1210
Caddoan language family, 419, 1160,
        1200, 1206, 1209
Cage, Nicolas, 367
Cahokia, 8, 10, **350–352**, 351 (photo),
        432, 435, 1289
Cahokia Mounds State Historic Site,
        352
Cahto Indians, **1048–1049**
Cahuilla Indians, **1049–1051**
Cajeme (José María Leyva), 1042
Calder v. Attorney General of British
        Columbia, 508, 589
Caldwell, Joseph R., 404
California
    effect of the 1763 Treaty of Paris
        on, 21–22
    and gambling operations, 137,
        139–140, 543–544
    genocide of Indians in, 226–231
    indenture law in, 168–169
    and Indian affairs, 1067
    Indian groups in, 5, 340,
        1047–1081
    mining in, 44
    reservation encroachment in, 41
    and termination, 67, 288
    tribal federal recognition in, 72
California Indian Basketweavers
        Association (CIBA), 338
California Trail, 1120
California v. Cabazon Band of Mission
        Indians, 74, 543–544, **979**
Calloway, Colin, 111, 168

Calnimptewa, Cecil, 414
Calumet. See Pipes
Calusa Indians, 21, 1229
Cameahwait, 837
Camp, Carter, 299, 642
Camp Grant Massacre, **270–271**, 728
Camp Independence, 1122
Camp Verde Reservation, 1007, 1042,
        1043
Campbell, Albert, 669
Campbell, Ben Nighthorse, 564,
        669–671, 670 (photo)
Campbell, Linda Price, 670
Campbell, Maria, 408
Campbell, Thomas, 668
Canada
    Aboriginal Diabetes Initiative,
        379
    aboriginal television in, 631–632
    alcoholism in, 158
    Anglican Church in, 331–332
    and the Assembly of First
        Nations, 653–654
    Athapaskans in, 335–336
    and the Blackfeet, 660–661
    and boarding schools, 98–102
    and the Constitution Act,
        518–519
    and Erasmus, George, 724
    and the Haidas, 1092
    and the Hurons, 1293
    and the Indian Act, 537–539
    Indian confederacies in,
        368–371
    Indian policies, 89, 90, **503–511**,
        537–539
    and the Iroquois, 712–713, 1242,
        1266, 1269, 1283
    Jay Treaty and, 174
    and the JBNQA, 565–568
    land claims in, 648–649
    and the Métis, 578–579, 716–717,
        831–833
    and the Mohawks, 161–162, 1260
    Native museums in, 804
    and the Northwest Coast
        Indians, 1098, 1102–1103
    and Nunavut, 617–618
    Pikangikum, 157–158
    and the Plains Cree, 1171
    and religious repression, 362,
        471
    role of canoe in history of,
        355–357
    and the Royal Commission on
        Aboriginal Peoples,
        602–604
    Thanksgiving in, 474
    treaties, **928**

See also specific Subarctic and Arctic Indian groups
Canada Firsters, 832
Canadian Indian Act, 471
Canadian Pacific Railroad (CPR), 832
Canalla, 812
Canandaigua (Pickering) Treaty (1794), 482, **511–513,** 1283
Canary Islands, 178
Canassatego, 173, 239, 493, 494, 568–569, **671–672,** 729
Canby, Edward R. S., 674, 752
Canby, William S., Jr., 172
Cannibal dance, 456
Cannibalism, **352–354**
    and the Carriers, 1295
    and the Crees, 1302
    and the Inuit, 1333
    and Jamestown, 823
    and the Kaskas, 1310
    and the Spanish, 678
    and the Tonkawans, 1206
Cannon, T. C., 839
Canoes, **354–358,** 536, 1113, 1138, 1194 (photo)
Canonicus, 217, 218, **672–673,** 1263
Canyon de Chelly, 1022, 1023
Cape Cod, 206
Cape Thompson, Alaska, 133, 1338
Capilano, Joseph, 759
Capital Conference on Indian Poverty, 798
Capitalism, 324
Captain Jack (Kintpuash), 229–230, **673–674,** 673 (photo), 751, 752, 1143
Captain Pollard, 830
Captivity narrative, **358–360,** 359 (photo)
Cardinal, Harold, 290
Caribou, 1299, 1306, 1329, 1330, 1338, 1348
Carleton, James H., 259, 260, 275, 675, 685, 781, 1005
Carlisle Indian Industrial School, 79, 88 (photo), 89, 96, 96 (photo), 97–98, 497
    and Standing Bear, Luther, 854
    and Thorpe, Jim, 865
Carlisle Treaty Council, **513–514,** 730
Carmichael, Stokely, 639
Carpenter, David O., 132
Carpenter, Mary, 100
Carr, Eugene A., 267, 686
Carrier Indians, **1295–1297**
Carrillo, Leopoldo, 271
Carroll, Henry, 871

Carson, Christopher "Kit," **674–676,** 675 (photo)
    and the Comanches, 1169
    and the Navajos, 259, 260, 529, 781, 1023
    and Ouray, 811
Carson National Forest, 346–347
Carter, Jimmy, 363, 495, 496, 573, 574 (photo)
Cartier, Jacques, 113, 212–213, 213 (photo), 393, 528, 1257, 1292
Casas, Bartolome de las, **676–678,** 677 (photo)
Casas, Pedro de las, 676
Cass, Lewis, 526, 695
Caste system, 5–6, 109, 455
Castro, Fidel, 647
Cataract Canyon, 1010, 1011
Catawba Indian School, 1212
Catawba Indians, **1210–1212,** 1211 (photo)
Catch the Bear, 283
Catherine II (Russia), 221
Catholicism
    and Black Elk, 659
    and boarding schools in Canada, 99, 102
    and Grant's peace policy, 270
    and legitimizing rule, 17, 178
    and the Spanish, 215
    and Tekakwitha, Kateri, 862–863
    and the Tiguas, 1038
Catlin, George, **678–679,** 810, 865
Catlin, Putnam, 678
Catlinite. *See* Pipes
Cattaraugus Reservation, 1242, 1284
Caughnawaga, 1274
Cavelier, René-Robert, 443
Cayanguileguoa, 730
Cayuga Indians, **1240–1242**
    and the American Revolution, 238, 239
    and Cattaraugus Reservation, 1284
    Deskaheh, 712–713
    and the Iroquois Confederacy, 11, 14, 369, 412, 428, 743–747
    and the Lenápes, 1249
    See also Iroquois Confederacy (Haudenosaunee)
Cayuse Indians, 202, 876–877, **1136**
Cayuse War, 1136, 1153
Celilo Falls, 202, 203, 517, 848, 1156
Celilo Fish Committee (CFC), 517
Cell, J. W., 503
Center for Addiction and Substance Abuse (CASAA),

University of New Mexico, 77
Central Council of Tlingit and Haida, 1114
Ceremonies/festivals
    agricultural, 317
    and Blue Lake, 346
    criminalization of, **360–364,** 497, 553–554, 689–690
    ending repression of, 555
    and the False Face Society, 382
    Ghost Dance, 154
    and horse economies, 406
    and Katsina religion, 414
    Northwest region and fishing, 462
    peyote use in, 801–802
    pipes and, 454
    potlatches, 454–456
    and sacred sites, 458–461
    and Seven Drums Religion, 465–466
    Sun Dance, 90, 471–472
    sweat lodges, 473–474
    thanksgiving, 474–476
    and weaving, 486
    See also Religion; *specific ceremonies and Indian groups*
Cermeño, Sebastian, 1062
Cetanwakanmani, 769
Chaco Canyon, 4, 317, 318, 329, 1031, 1034
    and petroglyphs, 425
Champagne, Duane, 456
Champlain, Samuel de, 212, 213, 317
    and the Abenakis, 1236
    False Face Society and, 381
    and Indian alliances, 356
    and the Maliseets, 1251, 1252
    and the Micmacs, 1257
    and the Naskapi/Montagnais, 1312
    and the Ottawas, 1270
    and the Passamaquoddys, 1272
    and the Wyandottes, 1292
Chapell, James, 159
Chapman, Oscar, 542 (photo)
Charbonneau, Jean Baptiste, 837
Charbonneau, Toussaint, 836, 837
Charles, Norman, 818
Charles I, King (Spain), 676
Charles II, King (England), 534
Charlot, 1147
Charlottetown Accord (1992), 510, 511, 578, 654
Chartrand, Paul, 603
Chase, Hiram, 847
Chatters, James C., 415

Checks and balances, 745–746
Chehalis Indians. *See* Salish Indians,
        Southwestern Coast
Chehalis Reservation, 1108
Chemehuevi Indians, 308,
        1007–1008, 1020
Cherokee Advocate, 836
Cherokee Indians, **1212–1215,** 1213
        (photo)
    artwork by, 337, 340
    and assimilation, 33, 35, 89, 549
    and Baptists, 265
    and the Creek War, 248
    diplomacy efforts, 23
    and European trade goods, 168
    and Jackson, Andrew, 753
    language of the, 419
    Major, Ridge, 777
    Mankiller, Wilma, 779–780
    and the Marshall Trilogy,
            514–517, 626–627
    as mound builders, 444
    oral history, 95, 446
    Owens, Louis, 812–813
    and protecting burial sites, 364
    removal from homelands, 32,
            34, 36–37, 117, 142,
            252–254, 528, 549–552
    Rogers, Will, 833–834
    role of women, 16
    Ross, John, 835–836
    and slaves, 20, 466
    and sovereignty issues, 146,
            179–180
    and thanksgiving festivals, 474
    and treaties, 174, 175
    Watie, Stand, 874–875
    writing system of the, 420,
            840–841
    and the Yuchis, 1234
Cherokee Nation, 1214, 1249
Cherokee Nation Memorial, **914**
Cherokee Nation v. Georgia, 36, 117,
        136–137, 146, 179–180,
        253, **514–517,** 522–523,
        526, 548, 550, 614, **905**
*Cherokee Phoenix and Indian
        Advocate,* 420, 551,
        679–680, 680 (photo),
        841, 1214
Cherum, 1015
Chester, Peter, 78
Chetco Indians, 1117. *See also*
        Tolowa Indians; Upper
        Umpqua Indians
Cheyenne-Arapaho Tribe, 1160
Cheyenne-Arapaho War (1864–
        1865), 45
Cheyenne Autumn, 715, 716

Cheyenne Indians, **1165–1167,** 1166
        (photo)
    and Baptists, 265
    and the Battle of the Little
            Bighorn, 274–276
    and the Black Hills, 659
    Black Kettle, 663–664
    buffalo economy of, 348
    Campbell, Ben Nighthorse,
            669–671
    and Cody, William, 686
    and the Colorado gold rush, 45
    and Crazy Horse, 703
    Dull Knife, 715–716
    and the Ghost Dance, 361
            (photo)
    and the Great Sioux War, 842
    horses and, 39, 405–406
    language, 420
    migration onto the Plains, 219
    and minimizing contagion,
            111–112
    and the Plains Wars, 1187–1188
    and the Sun Dance, 471, 471
            (photo), 472
    and trade, 167
    and treaties, 176
    and the U.S. Army, 705
    See also Dog Soldiers; Southern
            Cheyenne Indians
Cheyenne River Reservation, 53
Chiaha Indians, 1228, 1229
Chickasaw Indians, **1215–1216**
    and assimilation, 33
    and the Civil War, 47
    and common Creek language,
            369
    and the Creek War, 248
    enslavement of, 466
    language of, 438, 439
    and removal, 142, 252, 753
Chilcotin Indians, **1297–1298**
Child, Brenda, 123–124
Children
    and assimilation efforts, 50
    and boarding schools, 78–79,
            278, 281, 282
    and diabetes, 378, 379
    disease and, 107, 108
    effect of death rates on, 123–124
    of intermarriages, 394, 408
    treatment of captured, 19–20
    See also Education
Chillicothe, Ohio, 31, 436, 445
Chiloco School, 125
Chilula Indians. *See* Hupa Indians
Chimakuan language group, 6, 1098
Chimney Rock area, 572
Chinigchinich cult, 1059

Chinook Indians, 168, 201–203,
        1085–1087
Chinook jargon, 202, 1086
Chippewa, Battle of, 358
Chippewa/Chipewya Indians,
        1299–1300
    and the American Revolution,
            240
    and the Battle of Fallen Timbers,
            245
    Erdrich, Louise, 725–726
    and fishing rights, 392
    and Little Turtle's War, 853
    migration westward, 219
    and the Old Northwest
            Confederacy, 369
    and the Plains Cree, 1171
    and treaties, 174, 175
    See also Anishinabe/Anishnabe
            Indians
Chiricahua Apaches, 271–273, 705,
        778–779, **1001–1003**
Chitimacha Indians, 337, **1217,** 1223
Chivington, John M., 142, 259,
        262–263, 262 (photo), 664
Chiwere Siouans, 1289
Choctaw Academy, 541
Choctaw Indians, **1217–1220,** 1218
        (photo)
    and assimilation, 33
    and Baptists, 265
    and basketry, 337
    and the Civil War, 47
    and common Creek language,
            369
    and the Creek War, 248
    economic development and, 70
    and gaming operations, 138
    and lacrosse, 417 (photo)
    language of, 419, 438, 439
    Owens, Louis, 812–813
    and removal, 142, 753
    and treaties, 174, 175, 252
Choteau, Luzena, 793
Chrétien, Jean, 91, 603
Christianity
    and captivity narratives, 358
    conflict with Native cosmology,
            190
    conversion imperative in,
            360–361
    Deloria, Vine, Jr. on, 712
    and the Ghost Dance, 885
    and Handsome Lake, 736–737
    and migration theories, 93
    and the Native American
            Church of North
            America, 803
    and pipes, 454

role in reconciling worldviews,
15
and traditional views, 232
and utopianism, 791
and the Washani religion,
380–381, 845
See also Catholicism; Conversion,
religious; Missionaries;
specific Christian groups
Chukchansi Indians. *See* Yokuts
Indians
Chukchi Sea, 133
Chumash Indians, 339, **1051–1053**
Church Missionary Society (CMS),
331
Churchill, Manitoba, 1300, 1330
Churchill, Ward, 354
Churchill, Winston, 534–535, 713
Cibola regional system, 330
Citizens Against Nuclear Threats,
185
Citizenship, **102–104,** 854
and Alaskan Natives, 265, 635
in Canada, 538
congressional extension of, 576
and Curtis, Charles, 707
and *Elk v. Wilkins,* 524
and General Allotment Act, 281,
282
and the Indian Citizenship Act,
58
Indians and dual, 73, 74
and land allotment, 53
and the Seminoles, 345
and the Society of American
Indians (SAI), 154
and sovereignty issues, 146, 147
and *Standing Bear v. Crook,* 605
and the Treaty of Guadalupe
Hidalgo, 175
*City of Sherrill, New York v. Oneida
Indian Nation of New York
et al.,* 17
Civil disobedience, 154
Civil Rights Division, Justice
Department, 643, 644
Civil rights movement, 68, 91, 118,
154, 294, 423, 867
Civil Service Reform League, 768
Civil War, American, 44, 47
and the Caddoes, 1210
and Carson, Christopher "Kit,"
675
and the Cherokees, 836, 874–875,
1214
and the Chickasaws, 1216
and the Choctaws, 1219
and Cody, William, 686
and the Creeks, 1222, 1224

and the Osage, 1198
and Parker, Ely, 814
and the Powhatans, 1227
and the Shawnees, 1286
and the Tonkawans, 1206
Civilization and Enfranchisement
Act (1859), 537
Civilization program, 116. *See also*
Assimilation;
Conversion, religious
Claims, Indian
and Alaska, 336, 491–493,
635–636
and the Arctic Indians, 1335,
1338
and the battle for Blue Lake,
346–347
and the Black Hills, 646
and California Indians, 1054,
1061
in Canada, 508–511, 649
and the Great Basin Indians,
1127, 1129, 1131, 1133,
1135
and the IRA, 556, 558
and the James Bay hydroelectric
project, 565, 566
and *Lone Wolf v. Hitchcock,*
569–571
and the Northeast Woodland
Indians, 564, 573–575,
658, 1240, 1271, 1272,
1276, 1278
and the Northwest Coast
Indians, 1086, 1089, 1092,
1114, 1118
Nunavut, 588–594, 617–618
and the Plains Indians, 1200,
1202, 1205
and the Plateau Indians, 1137,
1138, 1140, 1141, 1146,
1147, 1152
and the Southeast Indians, 1210,
1233
and the Southwest Indians, 637,
1004, 1008, 1011
and the Subarctic Indians, 1297,
1303, 1305
Tee-Hit-Ton v. United States,
606–607
and *United States v. Dann,*
619–622
and the White Earth Land
Recovery Program,
764–765
Clan Mothers, Iroquois, 16, 191–194,
387, 412–413, 737,
757–758
Clapp Act, 54n

Clark, George Rogers, **681–683,** 682
(photo)
Clark, John and Ann Rogers, 681
Clark, Joshua, 751
Clark, Malcolm, 660
Clark, Ramsey, 290
Clark, William, 30, 681, 1086, 1108,
1110, 1202
and Catlin, 678
and Sacagawea, 837
See also Lewis and Clark
expedition
Class action suit, 560–564
Clatsops, 1086
Claus, William, 669
Clay, Henry, 549
Clayton, Augustin, 627
Clean Water Act, 152
Clearwater, Frank, 304, 641
Cleveland, Grover, 279, 769, 843
Cleveland Indians, 430
Clinch, Duncan L., 810
Clines, Charlie, 100
Clink, D. L., 100
Clinton, James, 856–857
Clinton, William Jefferson, 156, 157
(photo)
and Indian religious freedom,
498, 499
and Kennewick Man, 416
and LaDuke, Winona, 766
pardon of MacDonald, Peter, 776
and Peltier, Leonard, 645
and protecting sacred sites, 460
and tribal colleges, 638
Clothing, 6, 7, 9, 11. *See also specific
Indian groups*
Cloud, Reverend Henry Roe, 577,
847
Cloud, Millie Horn, 157 (photo)
Clovis complex, 3, 8, 82 (photo), 86,
86 (figure), 451–452
discovery of the, 2, 93
Clum, John P., 728, 729, 731
Coal, 129, 148–151, 701
Coalition for Navajo Liberation
(CNL), 184
Coast Guard, U.S., 291
Coast Reservation. *See* Siletz
Reservation
Cobell, Alvin, 561
Cobell, Elouise, 156, 560–564
Cobell v. Norton, 560–564
Cochabamba region, 109
Cochimí-Yuman language phyla,
419
Cochise, 272, 273, **683–685,** 684
(photo), 778, 1002–1003
Cochiti Pueblo, **1008–1009**

Cocke, John, 248
Cocoacoochee, 250
Cocopah Indians, **1009–1010**
Cocopah-Maricopa Trail, 1050, 1055
Cocopah Quechan Indians, 308
Cocopah Reservation, 1029
Code talkers, Navajo, **364–367,** 365
    (photo)
Code Talkers Association, 367
The Codex Nuttal, A Picture
    Manuscript from Ancient
    Mexico, 427
Cody, William Frederick "Buffalo
    Bill," 267, **686–687,** 687
    (photo)
Coeur d'Alene Indians, 134, 256,
    1137
Coeur d'Alene Reservation, 1137,
    1152
Coeur d'Alene (Spokan) War, 1120,
    1137, 1152, 1156
Cohen, Abe, 339
Cohen, Felix, 51–52, 320, 409, 515,
    609–610, 615, 616, 623,
    688
Cohen, Morris Raphael, 688
Cohoninas culture, 1010
Coiling, 338
Coke, Richard, 280
Colbert family, 1216
Colborne, John, 506
Cold Springs Rancheria, 1063
Cold War, 1325, 1327, 1332, 1334,
    1338, 1340, 1342, 1348
Coler, Jack, 301, 644, 817, 818
College of the Menominee Nation,
    1254
Collier, John, 115 (photo), **689–692,**
    690 (photo)
    and the AIPC, 637
    and the BIA, 501–502
    and Blue Lake, 346
    and changing U.S. Indian policy,
       58–59
    and Cohen, Felix, 688
    and definitions of Indianness, 61
    and education, 90–91, 124
    and halting fee patents, 55
    and humane treatment of
       Indians, 18
    and Indian religious freedom, 497
    and the Indian Reorganization
       Act, 118, 147, 180,
       552–558
    and the Navajo Nation, 714
    opposition to the Bursum Bill,
       576
    and restoring Indian traditions,
       577

Collins, Anita, 298, 299
Colonial records, 212, 214
Colorado Historical Society (CHS),
    427
Colorado Plateau, 327
Colorado River, 1010
Colorado River Indian Tribes (CRIT),
    308, 580, 1008, 1020
Colorado River Reservation, 1008,
    1015, 1018, 1020
Colorado Ute Settlement Act
    Amendments (2000), 670
Colton, Harold S., 414
Columbia Gorge Discovery Center,
    203
Columbia Indians. *See* Sinkiuse
    Indians
Columbia Reservation, 1150
Columbia River, 133–134, 201–202,
    203, 375, 388 (photo), 389
Columbia River Indians. *See* Colville
    Indians; Umatilla
    Indians; Yakima/
    Yakama Indians
Columbia River Inter-Tribal Fish
    Commission (CRITFC),
    375, 392, **517–518**
Columbus, Christopher, 178, 178
    (photo), 208, 232
    and depiction of Native
       cannibalism, 353
    and Indian enslavement, 466
    journal of, **890**
    and the myth of the noble
       savage, 439–440
Columbus Day, campaign to abolish,
    646, 787
Colville, Eden, 1137
Colville Indians, 134, **1137–1138**
Colville Lake community, 1308
Colville Reservation, 277, 1138, 1146,
    1149, 1150, 1152
Colyer, James, 271
Comanche Indians, 171 (photo),
    1167–1170, 1168 (photo)
    and Baptists, 265
    and Carson, Christopher "Kit,"
       675
    and the Eastern Shoshones, 1125,
       1127
    and horses, 404
    and the Indian slave trade, 20
    Parker, Quanah, 815–816
    raids against Navajos, 260
    and the Spanish, 215
    treaties, 175
Committee for Original People's
    Entitlement (COPE),
    1340

Committee of One Hundred, 58
Communication
    Canadian aboriginal television,
       631–632
    and humor, 407
    Indian publications, 633–634 (*see*
       also Writers/publishing)
    and the National Museum of the
       American Indian, 801
    and totem poles, 478
    and Western expansionism, 39,
       40
    See also Language; Media
Community, 81, 123
    action program (CAP) grants, 68
    colleges, 71–72
Comox Indians. *See* Salish Indians,
    Northern Coast
Compact negotiations (gaming), 138,
    139
Compensation
    and Alaskan Natives, 492, 607,
       636
    and the Black Hills, 344
    and Blue Lake, 347
    and the Cree-Naskapi Act, 519
    and dam projects, 375, 513, 566,
       568
    and the Indian Claims
       Commission, 541–543,
       796
    and land cessions during
       Jackson term, 754
    and Maine Indian claim
       settlement, 573
    and Nunavut land claims, 588,
       592, 593, 594
    and radiation exposure, 601–602
    to Seminoles, 345
    and termination, 607
    and treaties, 42, 43
    for Western Shoshone land
       claims, 621
    and Wyandotte Nation land
       claims, 658
    See also Claims, Indian; *specific*
       Indian groups
Competency commissions, 53–54
Comstock, Anthony, 385
Condolence Ceremony, 172, 480,
    708–709, 749, 750
Confederacies, **367–371.** *See also*
    Alliances
Confederated Peoria Tribe, 1255
Confederated Tribes of Coos, Lower
    Umpqua, and Suislaw,
    1089
Confederated Ute Tribes, 1133
Conflict. *See* Warfare/violence

Congress, U.S.
 and assimilation, 88
 and authority to abrogate
       treaties, 571
 and the Covenant Chain, 482
 and dam projects, 374, 375
 and education policy, 124–125
 and the Individual Indian
       Monies (IIM scandal),
       561, 563
 and Indian economic
       development, 116–119
 and Indian religious freedom,
       363–364
 and the Indian Reorganization
       Act, 60, 691
 and Indian treaties, 41–42, 43
 Northwest Ordinance and,
       586–587
 and plenary power, 596–598
 and protecting sacred sites,
       459–460
 and sovereignty issues, 180–181,
       182
 and termination policy, 66
Connecticut, 72, 138, 160, 1275, 1276
Connor, Howard, 366
Conoy Indians, 1262
Conquering Bear, 170–171
Constitution, U.S., 412
Constitution Act (1980), **518–519**
Constitutional Alliance of the
       Northwest Territories
       (CA), 591
Contract schools, 125
Contributions, American Indian,
       319–325
 and Franklin, Benjamin, 729–730
 and the Iroquois Confederacy,
       743–747
 and political philosophy,
       721–722
 and unity concept, 568–569
Convention for the Protection of Fur
       Seals in Alaska (1892),
       395
Convention on the Prevention and
       Punishment of the Crime
       of Genocide, 141,
       226–227
Converse, Harriet M., 382, 384, 385
Conversion, religious, 71, 87
 and the Anglican Church in
       Canada, 331–332
 and the Arctic Indians, 1334,
       1342, 1348
 and assimilation efforts, 540
 and the Baptist Church, 265–266
 Christianity on, 360–361

and education policy/boarding
       schools, 79, 96, 127
 and Episcopal missionaries, 723
 and the factory system, 525–526
 and government policy, 269, 279,
       496–497
 and Jesuit missionaries, 211
 and Massachusetts praying
       villages, 599–600, 719–720
 and New France, 213–214
 and Northeast Woodland
       Indians, 784, 1257, 1260,
       1263, 1266–1267, 1269,
       1271, 1287, 1292
 and the Plateau Indians,
       876–877, 1138
 Red Jacket opposition to,
       830–831
 and Russian Orthodox Church,
       221–224, 222 (photo)
 and Seattle, 840
 and Seven Drums Religion, 465
 and the Southeast Indians, 1222,
       1230
 and the Spanish mission system,
       227–228, 232–235
 and the Subarctic Indians, 1295,
       1303, 1305, 1309, 1313,
       1316
 and Tekakwitha, Kateri, 862–863
 and the Tlingits, 1113
 and the Yaquis, 1041
 See also Missionaries; Religion;
       Repression, religious;
       specific Christian groups
Cook, James, 395, 1096, 1097, 1319
Cook, Katsi, 130–131
Cook, Sherburne, 226, 230, 231
Coolican Task Force Report, 592
Coolidge, Calvin, 449 (photo), 707
       (photo), 834
Coolidge, Reverend Sherman, 847
Coon Come, Matthew, **692–693**
Cooper, James Fenimore, 225,
       693–696, 694 (photo),
       698, 1249
Cooper, Susan Augusta De Lancey,
       694–695
Cooper, William, 693–694
Coosans Indians, **1087–1089**
Copinger, Polly, 809
Copper industry, 1043, 1076
Copper Pass, Battle at, 780
Copway, George, **697–698,** 697
       (photo)
Coquille (Mishikhwutmetunne)
       Indians. *See* Coosans
       Indians; Upper Umpqua
       Indians

Cora Indians, 801–802
Corbin, Bob, 139
Cordero, Helen, 458
Cornelius, Laura, 793
Cornell, Stephen, 289
Corn/maize, 4, 7–10, 315, 318–319,
       432, 476. *See also* "Three
       sisters" complex
Cornplanter, Jesse, 1281 (photo)
Cornplanter (Gaiant'waka), 512,
       698–700, 699 (photo),
       829, 1283
 and the American Revolution,
       238, 239
 and Handsome Lake, 428, 429,
       735, 737
Cornstalk, 860, 1285
Cornwallis, Charles, 239
Coronado, Francisco Vasquez de,
       232
 and the Pueblos, 1030, 1031,
       1034, 1035
 and the Wichitas, 1207
 and the Zunis, 1044
Corporations, tribal, 58–59, 60, 121,
       492–493, 556, 1092. *See
       also* Businesses, Native
Corruption/fraud
 and the BIA, 501, 640
 in Canada, 505
 and the Doolittle report, 814
 Euro-American tolerance of, in
       Indian affairs, 41, 43
 and Grant's peace policy, 270
 and the IIM scandal, 560–564
 Indian Rings, 829
 and Kiowa reservation
       allotment, 570–571
 and mineral deposits on
       Quapaw land, 1205
 and Navajo politics, 1023
 and oil wealth of the Osage, 1198
 and Pine Ridge politics, 643, 880
 and Seneca land sales, 831
 and treaty negotiations, 170
Cortéz, Hernán, 108, 466, 676, 678
Cosmology
 Black Hills in Sioux, 342
 and Blue Lake, 346
 and Cahokia, 351, 352
 and Mississippian culture, 432
 and mound builder cultures,
       436, 444–445
 Northeast Woodland, 190–191,
       745
 Pueblo creation stories, 232
 See also Religion; Worldviews
Costanoan Indians, **1053–1054**
Costo, Jeannette Henry, 700

Costo, Rupert, **700–701**
Cote, E. A., 521
Cottier, Allen, 288
Cottier, Belva, 807
Cotton, 4, 32, 516
Cotton Petroleum Corporation, 547–548
Cotton Petroleum v. New Mexico, 547–548
Cottonwood Treaty, 1075
Coulter, Robert C., 614–615, 616, 623
Council of Energy Resource Tribes (CERT), 183, **701–702,** 776
Council of the Three Fires, 368, 371
Counting coup, **372–373.** *See also specific Indian groups*
Courthouse Rebellion, 831
Courts of Indian Offenses (CFR courts), 471, 612
Coushatta Indians, 337. *See also* Alabama Indians
Covenant Chain, 172, 356, 357, 482, 821
    and the Albany Congress, 494
    and Canadian policies, 503–504
Cow Creek Band of Umpqua Indians. *See* Upper Umpqua Indians
Cow Creek Indians, 1117, 1118
Cowichan Indians. *See* Salish Indians, Central Coast
Cowlitz Farm, 1108
Cowlitz Indians, 1108. *See also* Salish Indians, Southwestern Coast
Cowpox vaccine, 106
Cram, Reverend Jacob, 830
Crandell, Barbara, 445
Crawford, William, 243
Crazy Dogs, 1173
Crazy Horse, 343, **702–704,** 828, 851, 1187, 1188
    and the Battle of the Little Bighorn, 277, 822
    and the Battle of the Rosebud, 842, 873
Crazy Snake Movement, 52, 739
Cree Indians, 157–158, **1300–1303,** 1301 (photo)
    and the Blackfeet, 660
    Coon Come, Matthew, 692–693
    and the Council of the Three Fires, 368
    and the Cree-Naskapi Act, 519–520, 1313
    and horses, 404
    and the James Bay hydroelectric project, 375, 565–568

and the Northwest Rebellion, 832
Plains, **1170–1171**
and the Plains Ojibwa, 1195–1196
Cree-Naskapi Act (1984), **519–520,** 1313
Creek Confederacy, 1208, 1220
Creek (Muscogee) Indians, 265, 369–370, **1220–1222**
    assimilation and, 33
    and beadwork, 340
    and the Creek War, 246–248
    diplomacy and the, 15, 16, 23
    Emathla, Charley, 720–721
    Harjo, Chitto, 739–740
    Harjo, Joy, 740–741
    and the horse trade, 18–19
    language of, 438–439
    Osceola, 808–810
    and pre-contact cultural collapses, 14
    and removal, 142, 552, 753
    and the Seminoles, 344, 1229
    and slavery, 20, 466
    and treaties, 174–175, 176, 252, 549
    warfare with Tuscarora Indians, 484
    and the Yuchis, 1234
Creek Nation, 1209, 1222
Creek War (Red Stick War), 34, **246–248,** 1209, 1214, 1222
Crevecoeur, Hector Saint Jean de, 748
Crime
    addiction problems and, 79, 158
    murders on Pine Ridge, 639, 643–645
    and rape in woodland traditions, 192
    rate at reservations, 156
    smuggling and money laundering, 161–162
Criminal justice
    and the Canandaigua Treaty, 512–513
    and the Indian Civil Rights Act, 540
    state administration of, 66–67, 137, 147, 181
    trade and intercourse acts and jurisdiction of, 616
    and *United States v. Kagama,* 622
    See also Judiciary; Law enforcement
Crockett, Davy, 325
Croghan, George, 513, 668
Cronon, William, 317
Crook, George, **704–706,** 704 (photo)

and the Battle of the Rosebud, 703, 873, 1187
and Geronimo, 273, 731
and the Great Sioux War, 822, 842
and Montezuma, 793
and Spotted Tail, 850
and Standing Bear (Ponca), 605, 854
and the Tonto Basin campaign, 1042
Crooks, Lynn, 645
Crow Creek Reservation, 1193
Crow Dog, 851
Crow Dog, Leonard, 297, 640, 642, 656
Crow Foot, 283
Crow Indians, 473 (photo), **1171–1174,** 1172 (photo)
    and the Hidatsas, 1178
    and horses, 406
    and the IRA, 558
    land losses, 53
    and the Nez Percé Long March, 277
    and the Plains Wars, 873
    Plenty Coups, 822–823
    and Sioux conflict with Euro-Americans, 45
    and the Sun Dance, 471
    and trade, 167, 202
Crowstand School, 100
Crowther, Bosley, 716
Cruz, Joseph de la, **705–706**
Cultural collapse, 14, 115, 216
    and California Indians, 226, 229–231
Cultural pluralism, 690, 691, 723
Cultural relativism, 90, 377
Cultural Resources Center, 800–801
Cultural traditions
    boarding school attacks on, 97–98, 99
    effect of European trade goods on, 167–168
    Indian retention of, 70–71
    youth and loss of Native, 156
    See also Religion; Sociocultural relations; Sociopolitical structure; *specific Indian groups*
Cummins, Jim, 869
Cuneo, Michele de, 677–678
Cupeño Indians, **1054–1055**
Curry, Reginald, 542 (photo)
Curtis, Charles, 104, **706–708,** 707 (photo), 1181
Curtis, Oren A., 706
Curtis, Samuel R., 262

Curtis Act (1898), 52, 707, 739
Cushing, Frank Hamilton, 500
Cushing, Howard B., 731
Custer, George Armstrong, 176
    and the Battle of the Little
        Bighorn, 273, 275, 703,
        843, 1187
    and the Black Hills, 343, 658–659
    and Cody, William, 686
    and Crow scouts, 822
    and the Washita Massacre, 266,
        267–268, 664
Custer Died for Your Sins, 290, 406,
        709, 710, 803

Dade, Francis, 250, 721, 810
Daganett, Charles E., 847
Dakota Indians, 219, 529, **1174–1176**,
        1175 (photo), 1184
    Bonnin, Gertrude Simmons,
        665–666
    Great Sioux Uprising, 256–259,
        529
    and horses, 405, 406
    language of, 419
    Little Crow, 769–771
    and the Sacred Hoop, 279–280
    See also Santee Sioux Indians;
        Sisseton/Sisitunwan
        Dakota; Wahpekute
        Dakota; Wahpetunwan
        Dakota
Dakota Reservation, 67
Dakota War, 1175–1176
Dalles trading area, 7, 168, **201–203,**
        1086, 1154
Dams, **373–375,** 793, 795
    and James Bay hydroelectric
        project, 565–568
    and the Northeast Woodland
        Indians, 292, 700, 1233,
        1284
    and the Northwest Coast, 203,
        517, 848
    and Plains Indians, 1161, 1174,
        1179, 1181, 1191
    and the Plateau Indians, 1141,
        1152, 1156
    and Pyramid Lake controversies,
        600
    and Southwest Indians, 1007,
        1008, 1010, 1020, 1030
    and the Subarctic Indians, 1297,
        1313, 1314
    and the Wintuns, 1076
Daniels, Harry, 102
Dann family, 620 (photo)
Dark River, 812–813
Darling, Sir Charles Henry, 506

Dartmouth College, 421, 429, 431,
        1236
Dat so la lee, 339
Davin Report, 331
Davis, California, 295
Davis, Gray, 140
Davis, Jefferson, 663, 850
Davis, Sylvia, 345–346
Davis Inlet, 1313
Davy, Sir Humphrey, 321
Dawes, Henry L., 51, 278–279, 280,
        345
Dawes Act. *See* General Allotment
        Act (Dawes Act) (1887)
Dawes Commission, 707
Dawson, Beadie Kanahele, 533
de Acosta, Fray, 82
de las Casas, Bartolome, 142
de Soto, Hernando, 168, 432
    and the Alabamas, 1209
    and the Caddos, 1210
    and the Cherokees, 1214
    and the Chickasaws, 1216
    and the Choctaws, 1219
    and the Creeks, 16, 1221
    and the Natchez, 443, 1226
    and the Tunicas, 1231
de Tocqueville, Alexis, 34–35, 754
de Vaca, Cabeza, 341
de Victoria/Vitoria, Franciscus, 170,
        178–179
Debassige, Blake, 355
Debt
    fur trade and Indian, 525
    and gaining Choctaw land, 1219
    IRA and cancellation of, 555
    Jefferson and Indian, 741–742
    and the Shawnees, 1285
Decker, George, 713
Declaration of Indian Purpose, 124
Deere, Philip, 656
Deganawidah (Peacemaker), 11, 14,
        319, **708–709,** 1241, 1259,
        1264, 1268, 1282
    and Hiawatha, 749
    and Jigonsaseh, 757–758
    oral history and, 411–412,
        480–481
Deganawidah-Quetzalcoatl
        University (D-Q U),
        125–126, 302, 656
Del Norte Indian Welfare
        Association, 1072
DeLancey, James, 493, 494, 748
Delaware Confederacy. *See* Old
        Northwest Confederacy
Delaware Indians (Len-pe/Leni-
        Lenápe), 1247
    and Baptists, 265

    and the Battle of Fallen Timbers,
        245–246
    and the Carlisle Treaty Council,
        513–514
    and the French and Indian War,
        225, 226
    and the Goschochking Massacre,
        240–243
    and the Iroquois League, 191, 192
    and Little Turtle's War, 853
    and the Mahicans, 1251
    and medicine, 322
    as mound builders, 444, 445
    Neolin, 805–806
    and the Old Northwest
        Confederacy, 369
    oral history, 446
    and Penn, William, 819, 821,
        859–860
    and Pontiac, 816
    and the Tecumseh alliance, 860
    and treaties, 173, 174
    and the Wabash Confederacy,
        371
Delaware Prophet, 1249
Delgamuukw v. British Columbia, 510,
        991
DeLong, Sidney R., 271
Deloria, Vine, Jr., 290, **709–712,** 711
        (photo)
    on citizenship and plenary
        power, 104, 524, 597, 598
    on humor, 406
    and international appeals, 618
    on the IRA, 60, 553, 555
    and migration theory, 94
    and Native spirituality, 499, 783,
        803
    and the NCAI, 798
    on treaties, 170
    on tribal land losses, 57
DeMain, Paul, 302
Democracy, **376–378,** 411–413, 436
Demographics, historical, **104–110**
    agriculture and population
        densities, 317
    and California, 226, 229, 230, 231
    depopulation, 16, 141–142 (*see
        also* Genocide)
    growth during Holocene era, 3
    growth in Great Plains and
        Prairie region, 8
    nineteenth-century Indian *versus*
        Euro-American, 39, 40
    pre-contact population
        estimates, 2, 5, 12,
        112–113, 330
    Spanish America and Native
        population collapse, 216

Denaina Indians, 336
Denali complex, 86, 451
Dene Nation, 291. *See also*
        Athapaskan/Athabaskan
        Indians, Dene
Denetsosie, Louis, 151
Densmore, Christopher, 829, 831
Department of Indian Affairs and
        Northern Development,
        520–522
Department of Interior, U.S., 189,
        449, 460, 562–564. *See also*
        Bureau of Indian Affairs
        (BIA)
Department of Northern Affairs and
        Natural Resources, 1325,
        1327, 1332, 1334, 1340,
        1342
Department of Treasury, U.S.,
        562–564, 614
Dermer, Thomas, 783, 851
DeSersa, Byron, 643
Deskaheh/Deskaheah (Levi
        General), 618, **712–713**
Determination of Rights and Unity
        for Menominee
        Shareholders (DRUMS),
        1254
Detroit, 356, 358, 816
*The Devastation of the Indies: A Brief
        Account*, 676–677
Devil's Tower, 458–459, 459 (photo),
        460
Devlin, Arnold, 157
Diabetes, **378–380**
Diaz, Porfirio, 1042
Dickason, Olive, 213
Dickinson, Emily, 755, 757
Dickinson, John, 859
Dickson, Brian, 602
Diegueño. *See* Tipai-Ipai Indians
Diet, and diabetes, 379
Dinetah, 1021
Dion-Buffalo, Yvonne, 792
Dioxins, 145
Diplomacy
    and Canassatego, 671
    and Creek meeting with English
        king, 15
    and Franklin, Benjamin, 729–730
    and Mohawk, John C., 791
    and Ouray, 811–812
    and trade items, 806
    and treaty negotiations, 23,
        172–173
    wampum, 354–355, 481–482
    See also Politicians; Politics
Discrimination
    and addiction problems, 79

and the Alaska Native
        Brotherhood, 636
    and the Carriers, 1297
    and education, 128
    and the National Indian Youth
        Council (NIYC), 799
    and the Pomos, 1067
    and the Tlingits, 1114
    and the Washoes, 1135
    See also Racism
Disease, 21–22, 105–110, **111–113,**
        166, 394, 535
    and Athapaskan depopulation,
        336
    and boarding schools, 97
    and the Creek Confederacy, 369
    and depopulation of California
        Indians, 227, 228, 230,
        231
    diabetes, 378–380
    and Jamestown colonists, 827,
        844
    and the Long Walk, 260
    and Natives of New France, 213
    and New England Indians, 851
    in the 1970s, 796
    and the Plains Indians, 822, 853,
        855
    and the Plateau region, 876, 877
    socioeconomic effects of,
        114–115
    and Spanish America, 216, 234,
        235
    as thwarting Indian
        enslavement, 466
    and the Trail of Tears, 528
    See also specific Indian groups
Ditidaht language, 479, 480
Divorce, 193, 385–386. *See also specific
        Indian groups*
Dixon, Roland, 420
Dobyns, Henry F., 105, 112, 113
Doctrine of Discovery, 17–18, 22–23,
        178, **208–210,** 527
    and the occupation of Alcatraz
        Island, 290
    and the Supreme Court, 36, 117,
        179, 606
    and the trade and intercourse
        acts, 615
Dodge, Ben, 714
Dodge, Henry, 662
Dodge, Henry Chee, **713–714,** 1023
Dodge, Mabel, 689, 690
Dodge, Richard I., 343
Dodge, Thomas, 714
Doer, Gary, 701
Dog Soldiers, 686, 1166, 1173, 1180
    ledger book of, 427

Dogrib Indians, **1304–1305,** 1304
        (photo)
Dogs, 660
Domestic dependent nation,
        522–523, 548, 551. *See also*
        Trust, doctrine of;
        Wardship, doctrine of
Dominican missionaries, 108, 215,
        235
Donation Land Act (1850), 202–203,
        1105, 1108, 1110
Donnacona, 213
Doolittle, James B., 814
Dorris, Michael, 725, 726
Dorset culture, 12, 1332, 1334
    and the Norse, 205, 206, 728
Douglass, Frederick, 314
Downey, Hal, 54
Drake, Sir Francis, 20–21, 1062
Dream Dance, 1089
Dreamer cult. *See* Washani religion
        (Dreamer cult)
Dreams, 1018, 1029
Drew, Neil, 161
Dryden, John, 440
DuBray, Dan, 564
Duceppe, Gilles, 649
Dueñas, Roque, 818
Dull Knife, **715–716,** 715 (photo),
        1167, 1187–1188
Dull Knife, Guy, 643
Dumont, Gabriel, **716–717**
Duncan, William, 1115
Dundy, Elmer S., 177, 605, 755,
        854
Durant, Paul "Skyhorse," 642–643
Durham, Jimmie, 618, 639, 641–642,
        645
Duro v. Reina, 182, 596
Dussault, René, 603, 724
Dustan, Hannah, 359
Dutch, 166 (photo), 172–173
    and the Abenakis, 1236
    and the Lenápes, 1248
    and the Narragansetts, 1263
    and the Pequots, 216, 218, 1275
Dutch Reformed Church of
        America, 1004
Duwamish Indians, 169, 1106
    Seattle (Sea'th'l), 839–840
    See also Salish Indians, Southern
        Coast

Eagle, Jimmy, 644, 818
Eagle Dance, 1168
Eagle feathers, 363, 496, 498
Eagle Lodge, 81
Eagle Village First Nation–Kipawa,
        648–649

Earth Lodge cult, 1070, 1075, 1117
Earthquakes, 1322
Earthworks/mounds
    Adena culture and, 311–313, 312
        (photo)
    at Cahokia, 350–352, 351 (photo)
    Hohokam, 401
    Hopewell, 403
    Mayan, 317
    and the Mississippian culture,
        432
Eastern Abenakis, 113, 1272–1274
Eastern Shawnee Tribe of
        Oklahoma, 1286
Eastern Shoshone. *See* Wind River
        Reservation
Eastman, Charles A., 52, 766, 847,
        847 (photo)
Eastman, George, 666
Easton, Bill, 790
Eaton, John, 627
EchoHawk, John, 718
EchoHawk, Larry, **717–718**
Echota, 1213–1214
Economic development, **114–122**
    at Akwesasne, 162
    and the Aleutian Islands, 145
    and the Blackfeet, 661
    and gambling operations, 135,
        137, 140, 158–161,
        545–546
    and the IRA, 553, 556, 558
    on reservations, 156
    tribal government involvement
        in, 70
    and tribal sovereignty, 182
    and Wyandotte Nation, 658
    See also Businesses, Native;
        Corporations, tribal;
        Reservations, economic
        and social conditions on
Economy, traditional, 114–119
    assimilation and Creek, 246
    Athapaskan, 336
    Blackfeet, 660–661
    buffalo, 348–350
    fishing, 388, 461–463
    horse, 406
    and Natives of New France,
        212
    specialized production in, 167
    See also Material culture; *specific*
        Indian groups
Edenshaw, Donny, 1090 (photo)
Edenshaw, Guugaaw, 1090 (photo)
Edson, Caspar, 397, 885
Education, **122–127**, 123 (photo)
    American Indian studies, 155,
        294, 710

and assimilation, 88–90, 501
and CERT, 702
and the Cherokee in Oklahoma,
    254
and Dodge, Henry Chee, 714
and Episcopal missionaries, 723
factory system and encouraging,
    525–526
and the Indian Civilization Fund
    Act, 540–541
and the IRA, 556
and the James Bay and Northern
    Quebec Agreement
    (JBNQA), 567
and the Kiowa, 763
and Leupp, Francis Ellington,
    769
and the Mormons, 794–795
and museums and cultural
    learning centers, 801,
    804
and Native languages, 420–424
and the NCAI, 797
and religious repression, 497
Russians and Native, 223
and social control, **127–128**
and Standing Bear, Luther, 855
and termination policies,
    608–609
tribal colleges, 71–72, 638,
    867–869
tribal schools and self-
    determination, 69, 91,
    559–560, 632–633, 635,
    637
urban relocation program and,
    285–286
See also Boarding schools
Educational institutions, Indian
    imagery in, 429, 431
Edwards, Harold, Sr., 718–719
Edwards, J. R., **718–719**
Edwards, Silas John, 1007
Egan, 1129, 1154
Egmont, Earl of, 15
Egushawa, 562
Eichstaedt, Peter, 186
Eisenhower, Dwight, 91, 137, 609
Eisler, Kim Isaac, 136
El Mocho, 1206
Eldodt, Samuel, 1033
Electricity generation, 148–151. *See*
    also Dams
Elementary and Secondary
    Education Act (1965),
    125, 128
Eleventh Amendment, 138
Elexis, 1298
Elías, Jesus Maria, 271

Eliot, John, 87, 419–420, 599,
    719–720, 719 (photo)
Elizabeth, Queen (England), 504
    (photo)
Elk, John, 104, 524
Elk v. Wilkins, 104, 175, **524**
Elk Valley Rancheria, 1072–1073
Elliott, Joel H., 268
Ellis Island occupation, 295
Ellsworth, William, 550
Emathla, Charley, 34, 250, **720–721,**
    721 (photo), 810
Embroidery, 1020, 1158
Emergency Conservation Work
    (ECW), 554
Emerson, Ralph Waldo, 37, 755
Emissary of Peace, 192
Emmons, Glenn, 608, 647
Employment
    and gambling operations, 135,
        140, 159, 160
    and the IRA, 554, 556
    and mining/electricity
        generation, 151, 546
    urban relocation and, 66,
        285–287
    See also Unemployment
Employment Division, Department of
    Human Resources of
    Oregon v. Smith, 362–363,
    498
Encyclopedia of American Indian
    Contributions to the World,
    320
Engels, Friedrich, 378, **721–722,** 722
    (photo), 782
English for the Children
    propositions, 91
Enlightenment, the, 376–378, 722
Enron Corporation, 149
Enslavement, 15, 324, **466–468,** 467
    (photo)
    and California/Northwest Coast
        Indians, 5, 6, 1067
    and captured Indians, 19–20
    and the Christian conversion
        imperative, 360
    and the Pawnees, 1202
    and the Pequots, 789, 870, 1275
    role in demographic collapse of,
        105, 107
    and Southeast Indians, 369, 443,
        1217, 1223, 1226
    of Southern Paiutes, 1124
    and Southwest Indians, 259, 271,
        780, 1002, 1022
    and the Tuscaroras, 1232, 1233
    and the Wampanoags, 1288
    See also Slaves

Environment
    and bald eagle feathers, 363
    degradation of Hawai'ian, 533
    fishing and concerns regarding
        the, 203, 392, 848
    hunting/trapping and species
        depopulation, 395
    industrial materialism and effect
        on the, 792
    and the James Bay
        hydroelectric project,
        375, 567, 692–693
    Mount Graham and concerns
        regarding, 398–399
    and pollution, **129–134**
    protecting basketry, 338
    and water diversion, 600–601
    See also Pollution
Environment management, 5, 7, 11
Environmental Achievement Award,
    203
Environmental Protection Agency
    (EPA), 130, 144, 152, 185
Environmentalists
    LaDuke, Winona, 764–766
    Lyons, Oren, 775
Episcopal Church, 331, **723–724**
Equality, Indian contribution to idea
    of, 324
Erasmus, George Henry, 603,
    724–725
Erdrich, Louise, 407, **725–726**
Erdrich, Ralph, 725, 726
Erickson, Leif, 207, **727–728**
Erickson, Thorvald, 207
Erie Indians, 444, 446, 1292
Erik the Red, 727
Erik's Saga, 727
Ervin, Sam, 540
Eschief, Bernadine, 798
Eskaleut language family, 419
    Aleut, 1343
    Inuit-Inupiaq, 1323, 1325, 1328,
        1330, 1332, 1335, 1338,
        1341
    Yup'ik branch, 1321, 1335, 1346
Eskiminzin (Haské Bahnzin),
    728–729
Eskimo, Bering Strait. *See* Inupiat
    Indians
Eskimo, Kotzebue Sound. *See*
    Inupiat Indians
Eskimo, Nunivak. *See* Yup'ik
    Indians
Eskimo, Pacific. *See* Alutiiq Indians
Eskimo, St. Lawrence Island. *See*
    Yup'ik Indians
Eskimo, South Alaska. *See* Yup'ik
    Indians

Eskimo, Southwest Alaska. *See*
    Yup'ik Indians
Eskimo, West Alaska. *See* Yup'ik
    Indians
Estavinico, 1044
Estes, James, 419
Estevan, 1000
Etchemin tribe, 1271
Ethnocentrism, 89–90, 526–527,
    782–783, 877
*An Ethnologic Dictionary of the Navajo
    Language*, 420
Etowah, 10
Eugenics, 51, 54
Eurocentrism, 352–354, 353 (photo)
Europe, 14–15, 15–16, 105, 107
Evans, Andrew W., 267
Evans, James, 697
Evans, John, 262
Everglades, 250, 251, 315, 345, 439
Ex Parte Crow Dog, 612, **938**
Exiled in the Land of the Free, 775,
    791
Expansionism, 30–31, 39–48
    and Apache territory, 272–273
    and captivity narratives, 359
    and forced removal, 528–529
    and Harrison, William Henry,
        741–743
    and Jackson, Andrew, 752–754
    and land allotment policy, 278
    myth of the noble savage as
        justifying, 439–440
    and the Oregon Trail, 254–255
    and sovereignty issues, 527
    See also Land encroachment/
        speculation
*The Experiences of Five Christian
    Indians of the Pequot Tribe*,
    651
Exxon Valdez, 1323
Eyak language, 333, 419, 441
Eyish culture, 1209
Eyre, Chris, 773

Factionalism
    and Cherokee leadership, 253
    and the Northeast Woodland
        Indians, 1251, 1254, 1255,
        1257, 1261, 1266, 1267,
        1270, 1275, 1286, 1290,
        1292, 1293
    and the Ogala Sioux, 296, 300,
        303–304
    and Plateau Indians, 1146, 1152
    and the Southeast Indians, 1214,
        1219, 1232
    and the Southwest Indians, 1033,
        1034–1035

    and the Tipai-Ipais, 1071
    and the Washoes, 1135
    See also Red Sticks
Factory system, **524–526**, 540–541
Fadden, John Kahionhes, 688
Fadden, Ray, 688
Fall, Albert, 553, 690
Fallen Timbers, Battle of, 174,
    244–245, 244 (photo), 853
    and the Lenápes, 1249
    and Little Turtle, 772
    and the Miamis, 1255
    and the Shawnee, 24
    and the Wabash Confederacy,
        371
False Face Society, **381–382**
Famine/starvation, 107
    American Revolution and, 240,
        245
    and the Arctic Indians, 223, 1330,
        1338
    and California Indians, 230, 1077
    and genocide by the Spanish,
        678
    and genocide of the Iroquois,
        858
    and the Great Basin Indians,
        1124, 1129
    and Jamestown, 823
    and the Long Walk, 259, 260
    and the Northeast Woodland
        Indians, 219, 1266
    and the Northwest Coast
        Indians, 1084, 1088, 1117
    and the Plains Indians, 257–258,
        564, 770, 853, 1162, 1164,
        1167, 1176, 1183, 1188
    and the Plateau Indians, 1142,
        1143
    and the Southeast Indians, 1219
    and the Southwest Indians, 220,
        1015, 1023, 1024, 1040
    and the Subarctic Indians, 1302,
        1312
Farmer, Gary, 773
Federal Bureau of Investigation
    (FBI)
    and AIM, 640–646, 652, 817–818
    and the Pine Ridge conflict, 155,
        300–301, 302
    and Wilson, Richard, 879
    and the Wounded Knee
        occupation, 303–305, 656
Federal Employment Assistance
    Program, 286
*Federal Indian Law: Cases and
    Materials*, 409
Federal Lands Policy Management
    Act, 459

Federal Power Commission v. Tuscarora Indian Nation, 647
Federal recognition, 72–73
  and the Achumawis, 1048
  and Alaskan Native corporations, 493
  and the Chinooks, 1086
  and gaming operations, 138
  and identity issues, 409
  and the Lumbees, 1224
  and Maine Indian claim settlement, 573, 575
  and Native Hawai'ians, 533
  and the Penobscots, 1274
  and the Pequots, 1275
  and the Seminoles, 1230
  and the Tiguas, 1038
  and the United Keetoowah Band, 1215
Federal Trade Commission (FTC), 129, 183
Federally Impacted Areas Aid Act (1951), 608–609
Federated Coast Miwok, 1063
Fells Cave, 94
Feminism, **383–387,** 721
Fenton, William N., 382, 750
Ferdinand, King (Spain), 232
Ferello, Bartolome, 1052
Fernando, Andy, 462
Fetterman, William J., 828
Fewkes, Jesse Walter, 414
Fields, Anita, 458
Fields, Jerry, 319
Fifteenth Amendment, 104
Fight Back: For the Sake of the People, for the Sake of the Land, 808
Fillmore, Millard, 230
Fish and Wildlife Service, U.S., 144, 460
Fishing
  Athapaskans and, 336
  and Northwest traditions, 201–202, 455
  pollution and, 130, 145
  and pre-contact Indians, 5–11
  and Pyramid Lake controversy, 600
  and salmon economies, 461–463, 462 (photo)
Fishing rights, **388–392,** 388 (photo)
  in Alaska, 492
  Boldt decision, 72, 126
  and Columbia River dams, 375
  and de la Cruz, Joseph, 706
  and fish-ins, 293
  and the Great Basin Indians, 1121

and the Northeast Woodland Indians, 1236, 1271
  and the Plateau Indians, 1141, 1155, 1156
  and the Salish, 1106
  and Schuylkill Fishing Company, 860
  and Sohappy, David, Sr., 848–849
  and Treaty of Medicine Creek, 176
  and Warrior, Clyde, 872
Five Civilized Tribes, 1212, 1215, 1217, 1220, 1228
  and assimilation, 33, 89
  and the Civil War, 47
  and contesting treaty violations in court, 42
  and Euro-American technologies, 40
  and land allotment, 48
  and removal, 252, 549
Five Civilized Tribes of Oklahoma, 707
Five Nations Confederacy. *See* Iroquois Confederacy (Haudenosaunee)
Fixco, Donald, 541–542
Flathead Indians, 53, 202, 660
  1832 delegation to St. Louis, 877
  McNickle, D'Arcy, 784–785
  See also Salish Indians
Flathead Reservation, 1138, 1141, 1147, 1152
Fletcher, Alice, 51, 385, 386, 387
Fletcher v. Peck, 35, **526–527**
Flint Ridge, Ohio, 445
Florida, 137, 248–251, 344
Floyd, John, 248
Flynt, Larry, 786
Folsom complex, 2, 86, 86 (figure), 93, 452
Fonda, Jane, 289
Fontaine, Phil, 101, 654 (photo)
Food
  American native, 476
  expansionism and, 40
  and Jamestown colonists, 844
  and Lewis and Clark expedition, 837
  Mino-Miijim project and, 765
  and Northwest Coast Indians, 454–455, 462–463
  and Paleo-Indians, 3
  and the Pilgrims, 852
  and Plateau Indians, 465
  and pre-contact Indians, 4–10, 12
  as a trade item, 167
  See also Agriculture;

Famine/starvation; *specific Indian groups*
Fools Crow, Frank, 643, 656
Forbes, Jack, 125
Forbes, John, 226
Forced marches, **528–529.** *See also* Removal
Ford, John, 716
Foreman, Stephen, 680
"Forgotten Americans," 181
Forsyth, James W., 283–284, 285
Fort Alexandria, 1298
Fort Ancient cultural complex, 444, 1285
Fort Apache Reservation, 1006, 1007
Fort Belknap Reservation, 151, 624–625, 1162, 1177
Fort Berthold Reservation, 374, 1161, 1179, 1191
Fort Bowie, 273
Fort Bragg Reservation, 1048
Fort Bridger Treaty (1868), 1127
Fort Bridger Treaty (1869), 873
Fort Chipewyan, 1300
Fort Dalles, 202
Fort Defiance, 780–781
Fort Duquesne (Pittsburgh), 224, 226. *See also* Fort Pitt
Fort Frontenanc, 226
Fort Garrison Dam, 374
Fort Good Hope, 1306, 1307
Fort Halkett, 1310
Fort Hall Reservation, 1129
Fort Harmar Treaty, 853
Fort Laramie Treaty (1851), 45, 170–171, 175, 261, 624, 828, **916**
  and the Arapahos, 1159
  and the Arikaras, 1161
  and the Assiniboines, 1162
  and the Cheyennes, 1167
  and the Crows, 1173
  and the Gros Ventres, 1177
  and the Hidatsas, 1179
  and the Lakotas, 1187
  and the Mandans, 1191
Fort Laramie Treaty (1868), 23, 45, 46, 171, 176–177, 274, **529–532,** 531 (photo), 828, **927**
  and the Arapahos, 1160
  and the Black Hills, 342–343
  and Blackfeet Indians, 1163
  and the Cheyennes, 1167
  and the Lakotas, 1187
  and occupation of Alcatraz Island, 289–290
  and the Poncas, 1204
  and Spotted Tail, 850

Fort Lawton, 295, 639
Fort Lee, 202
Fort Lewis, 295, 1106
Fort Louisbourg, 226
Fort Massachusetts, 1132
Fort McDowell Reservation, 139,
        1042, 1043
Fort Miamis (Toledo), 244
Fort Michilimackinac, 356, 358
Fort Mojave Reservation, 308, 1018
Fort Niagara, 226
Fort Nisqually, 1105, 1108
Fort Oswego, 225
Fort Peck Reservation, 53, 1162, 1193
Fort Pitt, 240–243
Fort Rae, 1305
Fort Ross, 1066
Fort Rupert, 1093
Fort Sackville, 681
Fort Sill, Oklahoma, 1001, 1003,
        1169, 1183
Fort Simpson, 1091, 1115, 1310
Fort Snelling, 257, 258
Fort Stanwix Treaty (1784), 512, 699,
        898
Fort Sumner. *See* Bosque Redondo
        (Fort Sumner)
Fort Ticonderoga (Fort Carillon),
        226, 852
Fort Totten (Devil's Lake)
        Reservation, 1176, 1193
Fort Toulouse, 1209
Fort Umpqua, 1117
Fort Vancouver, 1108
Fort Victoria, 1093
Fort Whipple Reservation, 1043
Fort William Henry, 225
Fort Yuma Reservation, 1029, 1030
Fountain, John "Chick," 161
Four Corners, 148
Fourteenth Amendment, 104
Fowke, Gerald, 437
Fowler, Emily, 755
Fox, George, 819
Fox Indians, 46, 175, 368, **1242–1244**
        and Black Hawk's War, 251–252,
                661
        and gambling operations, 580
        and the Sauks, 1279, 1280
Foxwoods Resort Casino, 135–136,
                136 (photo), 160, 314,
                1275
Francis, Josiah, 246–247
Franciscans, 87
        in California, 228
        and the Chumash, 1052
        and epidemic diseases, 108
        and Indian enslavement,
                466–467

and the Navajo language, 420
and New France, 213–214
in Spanish America, 215, 216,
        232, 233, 234–235
François I, King (France), 213
Frankfurter, Felix, 688
Franklin, Benjamin, 30, 377, 378,
        729–730, 729 (photo)
        and the Albany Congress, 493,
                494–495, 616
        and Canassatego, 239, 671
        and the Carlisle Treaty Council,
                513–514
        and Hendrick, 747, 748
        Indian influences on, 412, 721,
                722, 743
        and Indian rights, 18
        and Indian treaties, 569
        and Philadelphia, 821
        and the Tammany Society, 859
Fred Harvey Company, 458
Frederici, Louisa Maude, 686
Freedom, concept of, 324
Freeman, Milton, 590
Freemasonry, 813
Frémont, John C., 675, 1075, 1077
Fremont culture complex, 8, 327,
        1131
French
        and Arctic Indians, 1334
        and the French and Indian War,
                21, 224–226
        and the fur trade, 394
        and New France, 212–214
        and the Northeast Woodland
                Indians, 219 (*see specific
                Northeast Woodland
                groups*)
        and the Plains Indians, 1171,
                1181, 1191, 1198, 1199,
                1200, 1201, 1202, 1205,
                1207
        and Pontiac, 825
        and the right of discovery, 17
        and the Southeast Indians, 443,
                1209, 1210, 1214, 1217,
                1219, 1223, 1226, 1231
        and Subarctic Indians, 1302
        warfare and Indian alliances,
                356–357
French, Mary, 359
French and Indian War, 116, 214,
        224–226
        and the Carlisle Treaty Council,
                514
        and Cornplanter, 699
        and Hendrick, 747
        and the Northeast Woodland
                Indians, 1236, 1239, 1249,

        1250, 1260, 1262, 1269,
        1274, 1283
        and Pontiac, 825
        role of canoes in, 356–357
        and the Southeast Indians, 1211,
                1219, 1221
Freudenthal, Dave, 701
Friends of the Indian, 51
Frobisher, Benjamin and Joseph, 585
Frobisher, Martin, 528
From Every Zenith, 552
from Sand Creek, 808
Fuca, Juan de, 1103
Funds, government
        and education, 128, 331, 638
        and fiscal conservatism, 74
        Indian Reorganization Act and
                shortfalls in, 60, 118
        and negotiated settlements over
                water rights, 189
        Reagan administration and, 148
        and termination policy, 67
        and tribal governments, 68–69
Fur trade, 166, 167, **393–395,** 393
        (photo)
        and Alaska, 264–265
        and the Arctic Indians, 1334,
                1338, 1342, 1345, 1348
        and Athapaskans, 336
        and the Beaver Wars, 218–220
        in Canada, 357
        as clashing with Indian
                worldview, 15
        and the Dalles area, 202
        factory system, 524–526
        and the Great Basin Indians,
                1120, 1126, 1127
        and the Hudson's Bay Company,
                534–536
        and the North West Company,
                584–585
        and the Northeast Woodland
                Indians, 1236, 1239,
                1241–1242, 1243, 1247,
                1248, 1250, 1252, 1253,
                1257, 1259, 1262, 1264,
                1268, 1270, 1272, 1273,
                1282, 1285, 1290, 1292
        and the Northwest Coast
                Indians, 1083, 1084, 1086,
                1093, 1095, 1097–1098,
                1115, 1117
        and the Pequot War, 216
        and the Plains Indians, 1159,
                1166, 1171, 1179, 1180,
                1193
        and the Plateau Indians, 845,
                1137, 1145, 1149, 1150
        and Russian colonization, 222

and the Shastas, 1070
and Sitting Bull, 842
and the Southeast Indians, 1210
and the Subarctic Indians, 1295,
    1300, 1302, 1305, 1306,
    1307–1308, 1309, 1312,
    1317, 1319, 1320

Gage, Matilda Joslyn, 383, 384, 385,
    386, 387
Gage, Thomas, 20
Gahahno (Caroline Mountpleasant),
    758
Gaines, Edmund P., 248–249
Gaiwí:yo. *See* Longhouse religion
    (Gaiwí:yo)
Galbraith, Thomas, 258
Gall, 275, 1187
Gambill, Jerry, 634
Gambling/gaming operations,
    135–140, 158–162
    and Akwesasne violence,
        718–719
    and EchoHawk, Larry, 718
    economic development and,
        74–75, 156
    Lyons, Oren, on, 775
    and the Maine Indian claim
        settlement, 575
    and the Osage, 450
    regulating, 543–546, 580–581
Games, 401, 417–418. *See also*
    Lacrosse
Gandagaro, 1281–1282
Gandhi, Mahatma, 487
Ganienkeh Reservation, 1261
Garces, Francisco, 1011, 1018, 1042
Garcia, Bobby, 818
Gardiner, W. H., 695
Garra, Juan Antonio, 1055
Garrison Dam, 1161, 1179, 1191
Garry, Charles, 643
Gathering Strength: Canada's
    Aboriginal Action Plan,
    603–604
Gay Head, 1288
Gelelemund, 242
Gender, and berdaches, 340–342
Gendering, 191
General, Alexander, 713
General Allotment Act (Dawes Act)
    (1887), 47, 50–54, 89, 117,
    146, 180, **278–282, 941**
    and the BIA, 501
    and the doctrine of trust, 614
    effect on education of, 123
    and Indian Territory, 552
    and Jackson, Helen Hunt, 756
    and *Lone Wolf v. Hitchcock,* 570

See also Allotment
General Federation of Women's
    Clubs, 555, 690
General Mineral Lands Leasing Act
    (1920), 55–56, 553
General Mining Law (1872), 152
General Motors foundry, 130
Genocide, **141–143**
    and the British, 1257
    and California Indians, 226–227,
        231
    and Canadian policies, 507
    and intertribal warfare, 484
    of Iroquois during American
        Revolution, 856–858
    and Mexicans, 778
    myth of the noble savage as
        justifying, 439–440
    Ortiz, Simon J., on, 808
    and the Spanish, 676–678
    U.S. policy as facilitating, 89,
        142
Genocide, cultural, 142–143, 720,
    756, 795. *See also*
    Repression, cultural
Gentile, Carlos, 793
Gentlemen, P. H., 100
Gentles, William, 703
George, Ros, 414
George II, King (England), 15, 747
George III, King (England), 356
George VI, King (England), 504
    (photo)
George Gustav Heye Center, 800
George-Kanentiio, Doug, 159, 634,
    719
Georgetown Reservation, 1108
Georgia, 515 (photo), 516
    and the Cherokees, 253, 514–515,
        523, 836
    and the Creeks, 1222
    and *Worcester v. Georgia,* 626–628
Germans, 678
Geronimo, 273, 293, **730–732,** 731
    (photo), 1003
Geronimo: His Own Story, **947**
    and the Kiowas, 1183
    and Naiche, 683
Gerusky, Tom, 133
Getches, David H., 409
Ghost Dance, 154, 361 (photo),
    396–398, 397 (photo)
    and California Indians, 1061,
        1063, 1070, 1072, 1076,
        1079
    and the Great Basin Indians,
        1121, 1135
    and the Massacre at Wounded
        Knee, 283, 362, 497

and the Northwest Coast
    Indians, 1117
and the Plains Indians, 1160,
    1167, 1183, 1188, 1206
and the Plateau Indians, 1143
and Sitting Bull, 843
and Wovoka, 884–885
Ghost Ridge, 564
Gibbon, John, 842
Gibbons v. Ogden, 596
Gibson, John, 243
Giddings, Joshua, 344
Gila River Reservation, 156, 1040
Gill, Aurilien, 566 (photo)
Gilmer, George, 627
Gingold, Dennis, 560, 561, 563–564
Ginsburg, Ruth Bader, 17, 182
Glacier National Park, 660
Global Energy Decisions, 702
Globalization, 91, 792
Gnadenhutten, 240–243
Gold, 39, 41, 44–45, 148, 151–153
    in Alaska, 606, 1113, 1115
    and the Arctic Indians, 1338
    in the Black Hills, 176, 274, 342,
        343, 530, 659, 1187
    and California, 226, 227 (photo),
        229, 673, 1048, 1057,
        1058, 1061, 1063, 1073,
        1081
    and the Cherokees, 1214
    and Colorado, 261, 663, 1159,
        1167
    and the Great Basin area, 620,
        1120, 1129, 1130, 1133,
        1135
    in Mimbres Apache territory, 271
    and the Mojaves, 1020
    on the Nez Percé Reservation,
        762
    and the Northwest Coast
        Indians, 1084
    and the Plateau Indians, 1138,
        1143, 1145, 1146, 1152,
        1156
    in Rogue River Valley, 1117
    and the Subarctic Indians, 1298,
        1305, 1306, 1309, 1310,
        1314, 1317, 1318, 1320
    Tonto Apache and the Prescott
        strike, 1007
Goldenweiser, A. A., 382
Goldtooth, Tom, 309
Goldwater, Barry, 776
Goliah, 1105
Gonzales, Barbara, 458
Gonzales, Rodolfo "Corky," 639
Goodloe, Robert, 526
Goodnight, Charles, 816

Goodyear, Charles, 321
Gordon, Frank, 139
Gorman, Carl Nelson, 733
Gorman, Rudolph Carl, **732–734,** 733
    (photo)
Goschochking Massacre, **240–243,**
    241 (photo)
Goshute Indians. *See* Shoshone
    Indians, Western
Gould, Canon S., 100
Gourneau, Rita, 725
Gover, Kevin, 503
Government misconduct. *See*
    Corruption/fraud
Gracia Real de Santa Teresa de
    Mose, 314
Gradual Civilization Act (1857), 537
Graham, John, 645
*Grammar and Dictionary of the Dakota
    Language,* 420
Grand Canyon, 1010
Grand Council of Nations (1764), 505
Grand Council of the Cree, 565–566,
    1313
Grand Ronde Reservation, 1070,
    1110, 1117, 1118
    Confederated Tribes of (*see* Upper
        Umpqua Indians)
Grande, Sandy, 209, 783
Grant, Peter, 101
Grant, Ulysses S., 89
    and the Camp Grant Massacre,
        271
    and the Fort Laramie Treaty, 530
    Indian policy of, 268–270, 1007
    Indian Rings and, 829
    and Manuelito, 781
    and the Nez Percé, 762
    and Parker, Ely, 814
Grant's Peace Policy, **268–270,** 1007
Grattan, John Lawrence, 850
Grattan Fight, 255
Great Basin Native Basketweavers
    Association, 338
Great Basin region, 7–8, 327
    Indian groups in the, 1119–1135
    and Paleo-Indians, 452
Great Hopewell Road, 436, 445
Great Lakes Indian Basket & Box
    Makers Association
    (GLIBBA), 338
Great Lakes Indian Fish and Wildlife
    Commission, 392
Great Lakes Intertribal Council
    (GLITC), **734–735,** 1251
Great Lakes region
    and the American Revolution,
        357

and fishing rights, 389, 392
and the French and Indian War,
    356
and the fur trade, 394
Great Nemaha River reservation,
    1180
Great Plains region, 8–9
    Indian groups in the, 1157–1207
    and Paleo-Indians, 452
    See also Plains Indians
Great Serpent Mound, 312–313, 312
    (photo), 403, 436, 445
Great Sioux Reservation, 282–283,
    342–343, 530, 1188
Great Sioux Uprising (Minnesota),
    256–259, 257 (photo),
    529
Great Sioux War (1875-1877), 45,
    842–843, 850–851. *See also*
    Little Bighorn, Battle of
    the (Battle of Greasy
    Grass)
Great Smoky Mountain National
    Park, 1215
Great Southwest Revolt, 153
Great Sun, 442
Great Swamp Massacre, 879
Great Treaty (1682), 821
Green, Rayna, 163
Green Corn ceremony
    and the Northeast Woodland
        Indians, 1240, 1245, 1249
    and the Quapaws, 1204
    and the Southeast Indians, 1208,
        1212, 1217, 1220, 1228,
        1230, 1233
Green Corn Rebellion, 1222
The Green Light, 866
Green Party, 765
Greenberg, Joseph, 441
Greene, Graham, 773
Greenland, 205, 727
The Greenlanders' Saga, 727
Gregory, Clara, 678
Grimm, Lloyd, 304
Grinnell, George Bird, 51, 663
Groghan, George, 662
Gros Ventres Indians, 151–153, 368,
    404, **1176–1177**
    Welch, James, 875–876
    See also Blackfeet/Blackfoot
        Indians
Guarani Indians, 108–109
Guardians of the Oglala Nation
    (GOONs), 155, 300, 304,
    817, 879, 880
    and reign of terror on Pine
        Ridge, 643, 644

and Wounded Knee occupation,
    640, 641
Guillette, Elizabeth, 131, 132
Gulf Branch language family, 419
Gunther Island massacre, 1076
Gutiérrez, Dolores, 655
Gwich'in Indians, 336, 535 (photo),
    1305–1306

Haida Indians, 635–636, **1089–1092,**
    1090 (photo)
Haida language family, 6, 333
    and Na-Dene, 440–441
Haig, Alexander, 641
Haigler (Arataswa), 1211
Haihais Indians. *See* Bella Bella
    Indians
Haisla language, 479
Hakataya culture, 1010, 1014, 1042
Halbritter, Raymond, 159–160
Haldiman Treaty (1784), 713
Haldimand, Frederick, 668
Hale, Kenneth, 420
Hale, Matthew, 385
Halfbreed, 408
Hall, G. Stanley, 90
Hall, Tex, 701–702
Haller, Granville O., 255
Halona, 1044–1045
Hamilton, Henry, 464, 681–682
Hampton Normal and Agricultural
    Institute, 766
Han Indians. *See* Gwich'in Indians;
    Ingalik Indians
Hancock, 1232
Hancock, John, 482, 569
Handbook of Federal Indian Law, 320,
    409, 609–610, 688
Handley, Joseph L., 701
Handsome Lake, 158, 382, 428–429,
    735–738, 1283
Hanford Environmental Dose
    Reconstruction (HEDR),
    134
Hanford Nuclear Reservation, 129,
    129 (photo), 133–134
Hannaville, 1278
Hannon, T. E., 289, 290
Hare, Melvin and Leslie, 639
Hare, William Hobart, 723
Hare Indians, **1307–1308**
Harjo, Chitto (Crazy Snake), 34, 52,
    739–740, 740 (photo),
    1222
Harjo, Coa, 810
Harjo, Joy, **740–741**
Harmar, Josiah, 244, 771–772, 853
Harmon, Moses, 385

Harney, William S., 250, 530, 850
Harrington, J. P., 420
Harrington, M. R., 382
Harris, Fred, 347
Harris, LaDonna, 347
Harris, Sarah Jane Ayers, 1211 (photo)
Harrison, Benjamin, 682
Harrison, William Henry, 661,
    741–743, 742 (photo), 772
    and Tecumseh, 31–32, 861–862,
    864–865
Hasinai Confederacy, 1209
Hastings, Doc, 416
Hauptman, Lawrence, 552–553
Haury, Emil W., 433
Havasupai Indians, **1010–1011,** 1014,
    1015
Hawai'ians, Native, 379, 409
    land claims, **532–533**
    and language, 422, 423
Hawkins, Benjamin, 246, 247, 540
Hayes, Alan, 332
Hayes, Rutherford B., 280, 705, 882,
    883
Hayworth, J. D., 563
Hazardous waste, 129–134, **144–146,**
    150, 184–186, 307–309.
    See also Nuclear waste
Hazen, William Babcock, 268
Head, Sir Francis Bond, 506
Healing v. Jones, 306–307
Health issues
    addiction treatment and
        recovery, 80–81, 158
    and the Arctic Indians, 1325,
        1327, 1332, 1334, 1338,
        1340, 1342, 1348
    care improvements after 1900,
        109–110
    and diabetes, 378–380
    and effect of James Bay
        hydroelectric project,
        692–693
    at end of twentieth century, 57
    European treatments, 105–106
    and the Menominees, 1254
    and pollution, 130–134, 144,
        145–146, 150, 153,
        184–186, 601–602, 1125
    See also Alcohol/alcohol abuse;
        Medicine
Heard Museum Show, 414
Heckewelder, John, 695
Heirship, 56–57, 556
Helgeson, Gus, 151
Henderson, James, 170
Hendrick (Tiyanoga), 482, 493, 494,
    616, **747–748,** 748 (photo)

and Johnson, Sir William, 238,
    760
Hendry Report, 332
Henige, David, 113
Hennepin, Louis, 341
Henry, Patrick, 681
Herjulfsson, Bjarni, 207
Herman (Russian monk), 221–222,
    223
Hernandez, Juan Pérez, 1091
Hernando, Francisco, 321
Herring, Elbert, 501
Herring Pond Reservation, 1288
Hertzberg, Hazel W., 408
Hewitt, J. N. B., 382
Heye, George Gustav, 799–800
Hiawatha (Hiawanthe/
    Aionwantha), 11, 319,
    411, 480, 708, **749–751,**
    750 (photo), 1241, 1259,
    1264, 1268, 1282
    and Jigonsaseh, 758
Hiawatha Belt, 481, 750–751
Hickok, James "Wild Bill," 686
Hickory Ground, 739
Hicks, Charles, 680
Hidatsa Indians, 167, 341, 837,
    1177–1179, 1177 (photo)
Hieltsuk language, 479
Hill, Aaron (Kanonraron), 22–23
Hill, Charlie, 407 (photo), 408
Hill Patwin Indians, 347
Hinton, Leanne, 420
Historic Sites, Buildings, and
    Antiquities Act (1935),
    459
History
    Colonial and American
        Revolution eras, **14–24**
    early nineteenth-century
        removals and conquests,
        30–37
    early twentieth-century
        assimilation efforts,
        50–62
    late twentieth-century, **65–75**
    pre-contact, **2–12**
    Western expansionism and late
        nineteenth century,
        39–48
Hitchiti Indians, 438, 1229
Ho-Chunk Nation. *See* Winnebago
    Indians
Hobbes, Thomas, 440
Hodge, W. Frederick, 500
Hoeven, John, 701
Hoh Indians, 1098. *See also* Quileute
    Indians

Hohokam culture, 4, 327, **400–402,**
    401 (photo), 1026, 1039
    and the Mogollon culture, 433
Hokan-Siouan language family
    in California, 5
    and the Chumash, 1051
    in the Great Basin, 7
    Karuk, 1057
    Palaihnihan branch, 1047
    Pomoan, 1065
    Salinan, 1067
    Shastan division, 1069
    Washoe, 1134
    Yana, 1077
    Yuman division, 1071
        Pee-Posh and River Yuman,
            1009, 1018, 1024
        Quechan and River Yuman,
            1029
        Yavapai and Upland Yuman,
            1010, 1014, 1042
Holder, Stan, 642
Holocene era, 3, 4–12
Homan, Paul, 561–562
Homicide, 133, 156, 300–303, 817
Homily, 846
Homli, 381
Honey Lake Valley agreement,
    881–882
Honyuti, Ronald and Brian, 414
Hooker Jim, 674, **751–752,** 1143
Hoopa Valley Reservation, 572, 1055,
    1057, 1058, 1072, 1081
Hoopa-Yurok Settlement Act (1988),
    1081
Hoover, Herbert, 707, 796
Hoover Dam, 1008
Hopewell culture, 8, 10, 166,
    402–404, 402 (photo), 444
    and the Adenas, 313
    and the Tunicas, 1231
Hopi Indians, 59, **1012–1014,** 1013
    (photo)
    and coal mining, 148–151
    and the Colorado River Indian
        Tribes, 1008, 1020
    crafts and, 337, 338, 458, 485–486
    and the IRA, 557, 558
    land dispute with the Navajos,
        306–307, 776
    oral history and religion, 95,
        413–414
    Rose, Wendy, 834–835
    and urban relocation, 285
Hopi Reservation, 148–151, 1014
Hopi Roadrunner Dancing, 834
Hopi-Tewa Indians, **1014**
Hopkins, L. H., 883

Horses, 39, 214, 349, **404–406**
    and Blackfeet Indians, 660
    and the Cayuses, 1136
    and Dalles trade area, 202
    as a trade item, 18–19, 166–167, 168
    and the Utes, 1131–1132
    See also specific Indian groups
Horseshoe Bend, Battle of, 248, 753, 777
Hosmer, Brian C., 764
Houma Indians, **1222–1223,** 1231
House, Jack, 1133
House Concurrent Resolution 108, 608, 609, **960**
House Made of Dawn, 290, 792–793
Houser, Allan, 785
Houses/housing
    Adena, 313
    and the Hohokam culture, 400, 401–402
    and horse economies, 406
    Indian substandard, 156, 157, 796
    at L'Anse aux Meadows, 205
    and Mississippian culture, 432
    and Mogollon culture, 433, 434
    and pre-contact Indians, 4, 6–8, 10, 11
    See also specific Indian groups
Howard, Oliver O., 685, 762–763, 873, 882
Howato, Walter, 414
Howe, Oscar, 838
Howell, Elizabeth, 697
Howells, Emily Susannah, 759
Hoxie, Frederick E., 768
Hrdlicka, Ales, 54, 93
Hu-DeHart, Evelyn, 655
Hualapai Indians, 1010, **1014–1015**
Hualapai War, 1011, 1015
Hubbard, Niles, 831
Hudson, Henry, 528, 1248, 1250, 1302
Hudson's Bay Company, 357, 394, 395, **534–536,** 535 (photo)
    and the Arctic Indians, 1327, 1329–1330, 1334
    and California Indians, 1077, 1081
    and the Northwest Coast Indians, 1083, 1084, 1088, 1091, 1093, 1105, 1108, 1113, 1115, 1117
    and the Plains Indians, 1162, 1171
    and the Plateau Indians, 1137, 1149, 1152
    and Puget Sound, 840

    rivalry with the North West Company, 585
    and the Subarctic Indians, 1300, 1302, 1312
Hughes, Langston, 314
Hughes, Samuel, 271
Hull, William, 358
Human remains, 581 (photo)
    and museums, 803
    and the NAGPRA, 581–584
    repatriation of, 437, 446, 496, 498, 692, 716
Human rights
    de las Casas on, 676–678
    and *Standing Bear v. Crook,* 854
    U.S. *versus* Iroquois views on, 412
    See also Indian rights
Humor, **406–408**
Humphrey, Hubert H., 688
Hunkpapa Lakota Indians
    and the Battle of Little Bighorn, 275
    Deloria, Vine, Jr., 709–712
    Sitting Bull, 842–844
    See also Lakota Indians
Hunkpatina Indians. *See* Nakota Indians
Hunt, Edward B., 755
Hunt, Thomas, 851
Hunting, 336, 406
    and Paleo-Indians, 85–86, 451–452
    and pre-contact Indians, 3, 5, 7–12
Hupa Indians, 462 (photo), **1055–1057,** 1056 (photo)
Hurd, R. D., 300–301
Huron Wyandot Indians, 1291–1293
    and the Council of the Three Fires, 368
    False Face Society and, 381–382
    French alliance, 356
    and the fur trade, 394
    and lacrosse, 417
    matrilineal social structure of, 370
    and the Ottawas, 1271
    and Pontiac, 816
    and the Seven Nations of Canada, 370
    and the Wabash Confederacy, 371
    See also Wyandotte/Wyandot (Huron) Indians
Huron-Wendat Confederacy, 369, 1291
Huronia, 1291
Hurons of Lorette, 1293

Husis-Kute, 276
Husk, Gary, 139
Hyde, George E., 829
Hydroelectric power, **373–374,** 519
    and James Bay, 375, 565–568, 567 (photo)

Iberian *reconquista,* 214–215, 232
Ickes, Harold, 554, 691
Idaho, 717, 718
Identity, **408–410**
    addiction problems and loss of, 78, 79, 81
    boarding school attacks on, 96, 97–98, 99
    and Bole-Maru religion, 348
    Canadian repression and Indian, 538
    and Christian conversion imperative, 360
    Indian retention of, 70–71
    and Indian youth, 92, 156
    Indians and U.S., 236
    and lacrosse, 418
    oppositional, 90
    and pan-Indian movements, 155, 292, 293–294
    and scalping, 464
    Tammany Society and national, 859, 860
    urban relocation and pan-Indian, 287
    and works by Momaday, N. Scott, 792–793
If You Poison Us: Uranium and American Indians, 186
Iglulik Indians, **1323–1325**
Ignatius of Loyola, Saint, 210
Illini Indians, 367, 484
Illinois, 681–682
Illinois Indians, 341, **1244–1245**
Inca Empire, 105
The Increase of the Kingdom of Christ: A Sermon, 651
Indenture, 231, 466
Indian Act of 1876, 507, 518, 521, **537–539**
Indian Affairs Branch (IAB), 521
Indian and Eskimo Association (IEA), 589
Indian Association of Alberta (IAA), 661
Indian Baskets, 339
Indian Bible, 420
Indian Brotherhood of the North West Territories, 724
Indian Canyon, 1054
Indian Child Welfare Act (1978), 62, 91, 867

Indian Citizenship Act (1924), 58, 102, 104, 281, 707, **952**

Indian Civil Rights Act (1968), 363, **539–540, 962**

amendment to, 182

Indian Civilization Fund Act (1819), 88, **540–541**

Indian Claims Commission (ICC), 177, 347, **541–543,** 688, 796

Act (1946), 607

and Northwest Coast Indians, 1086, 1110

and Western Shoshone land claims, 620–621

Indian Commerce Clause, 179

Indian Country Crime Report, 156

Indian Education Acts (1972, 1974), 91, 125, 128, 867

Indian Empowerment Assistance Program, 867

Indian Financing Act (1974), 867

Indian Full Gospel Church, 411

Indian Gallery, Catlin's, 678, 679

Indian Gaming Regulatory Act (IGRA) (1988), 74, 135, 137–138, **543–546**

Indian Givers, 324

Indian Health Service (IHS), 143, 559

sterilization program, 640, 884

Indian Humor, 407

Indian Island massacre, 230

Indian Knoll people, 1205

Indian Linguistic Families of America North of Mexico, 420

Indian Man: The Story of Oliver La Farge, 785

Indian Mineral Development Act, 546

Indian Mineral Leasing Act (1938), **546–548**

Indian Nationalist Movement of North America, 647

Indian New Deal. *See* Indian Reorganization Act (IRA) (1934)

Indian Oil and Gas Leasing Act (1924), 56

Indian Peace Commission Act (1867), 171 (photo)

Indian Progressive Organization, 793

Indian Pueblo Cultural Center, 637

Indian relations

and Canada's Royal Commision on Aboriginal Peoples (RCAP), 603–604

and doctrine of trust, 614–617

and farmers, 39–40

and Jamestown, 844–845

Northwest Ordinance and, 586–587

and the Oregon Trail, 254–255

and Penn, William, 821

ranchers and, 39, 46

and Seattle, 840

and Trade and Intercourse Acts, 610–612

and Williams, Roger, 878–879

Indian Religious Crimes Code, 497

Indian Removal Act (1830), 252, 345, 528, **548–552, 914**

and the Cherokees, 1214

and the Choctaws, 1219

and the Creeks, 1222

Indian Reorganization Act (IRA) (1934), 36, 48, 57–62, 118, 180, **552–558, 958**

and the Alaska Native Brotherhood, 636

and the Blackfeet, 661

as change in U.S. Indian policy, 147

and Collier, 502, 689, 691

Costo, Rupert on, 700

and definitions of Indianness, 409

and the NCAI, 795

and religious freedom, 346, 497

and tribal courts, 612

Indian rights, 18, 44, 50, 72–74

in Canada, 518–519

and Costo, Rupert, 700

and dam projects, 374–375

and Erasmus, George, 724–725

and the Indian Civil Rights Act, 539–540

Indian Reorganization Act and, 57–58

and LaFlesche, Susette Tibbles, 767–768

and the United Nations, 618–619

See also Activism, political; Indigenous rights

Indian Rights Association, 278, 555, 689, 690, 796, 847

and the Bursum Bill, 576

and Episcopal missionaries, 723

and the IRA, 553

and Leupp, Francis Ellington, 768

Indian Rings, 829

Indian Self-Determination and Education Assistance Act (ISDEAA) (1975), 57, 91, 125, 126, 128, 502–503, **559–560,** 867, **974**

Indian Shaker religion, **410–411,** 465

and California Indians, 1072, 1081

and the Northwest Coast Indians, 1098, 1117

and Slocum, John, 1106

Indian Territory

allotment and encroachment on, 44, 552, 570, 707

citizenship and, 104

dissolution of, 52

Northeast Woodlands Indian removal to, 1239, 1242, 1244, 1271, 1278, 1280, 1283, 1293

Plains Indian removal to, 277, 1160, 1169–1170, 1180, 1181, 1183, 1192, 1198, 1200, 1202, 1204, 1205, 1206, 1207

Southeast Indian removal to, 37, 439, 1209, 1211, 1214, 1216, 1219, 1222, 1229–1230, 1234

Indian Territory Naturalization Act, 104, 524

Indian Trade and Intercourse Acts, 116

Indian Voices, 872

Indianness, 50–54, 54n, 61–62, 408–410

Canada and defining, 507–508, 518–519, 522, 538–539

Deloria and defining, 711

IRA and definition of, 557

self-identification and, 110

Spanish definitions of, 109

Indians, 290

Indians of All Tribes (IAT), 287, 288 (photo), 289, 290, 639, 807

Indians of the Americas, 552, 691

Indigenous rights, 66, 73, 641–642, 653

and the *Calder* decision, 589–590

Draft Declaration on the Rights of Indigenous Peoples, 619

and Means, Russell, 786–787

and the Métis, 578–579

See also Indian rights

Individual Indian Monies (IIM) scandal, **560–564,** 614

Ingalik Indians, **1308–1309**

Ingalls, Reverend G. W., 793

Ingstad, Benedicte, 205

Ingstad, Helge, 204–205, 207, 727

Innocent, Bishop, 264

Innu Indians. *See* Naskapi/Montagnais Indians

Inoculation by variolation, 106
Inouye, Daniel, 580, 849
Institute for Government Research, 576
Institute for Pueblo Indian Studies, 637
Institute for Social and Religious Research, 576
Institute for the Development of Indian Law, 710
Institute of Ethnic Affairs, 691
Institute of the American West, 552
Instructions of 1786, 234
Inter Caetera, 208
Intermarriage
    and the French, 213
    and fur traders, 394, 585
    and Indian identity, 408, 409
    and Northeast Indians, 20
    and removal, 549
    role in demographics of, 105, 109
    Seminoles and escaped slaves, 34
    and U.S. policy, 282
    See also Métis Indians; *specific Indian groups*
International Council of Women, 385, 386, 387
International Covenant on Civil and Political Rights, 58
International Covenant on Economic, Social and Cultural Rights (1966), 57–58
International Indian Treaty Council (IITC), 131, 618–619, 641–642, 645
International Indian Youth Conference, 798
An Introduction to the Study of Indian Languages, 420
Inuit, Baffinland, **1325–1328**, 1326 (photo)
Inuit, Caribou, **1328–1330**, 1329 (photo)
Inuit, Copper, **1330–1332**
Inuit, Labrador or Ungava, **1332–1335**
Inuit, Mackenzie Delta. *See* Inuvialuit Indians
Inuit, North Alaska. *See* Inupiat Indians
Inuit Committee on National Issues, 519
Inuit Tapirisat of Canada (ITC), 589–590, 591, 1325, 1327, 1332, 1334–1335, 1343
Inuit Tungavingat Nunami (ITN), 1335

Inuit, 11, 101
    and Canadian recognition, 518
    and the Cree-Naskapi Act, 519–520
    and the James Bay hydroelectric project, 375, 565–568
    and Nunavut, 588–594, 617–618
    and Point Hope nuclear dump, 129, 132–133
    See also specific Inuit groups
Inuktitut language, 1325, 1328, 1330, 1340, 1343
Inupiat Indians, 19, **1335–1338**
Inupiat Paitot, 1338
Inuvialuit Indians, 590, 592, 617, **1338–1340**
Ioasaph, Archimandrite, 221
Ioway Indians, 175, **1179–1180**
Iqaluit Agreement, 592, 617
Iroquoian language family, 419
    and the Cayugas, 1240
    Cherokee, 1212
    Huron/Wyandottes and, 1291
    and the Mohawks, 1258
    Oneidas and, 1264
    Onondagas and, 1267
    Senecas and, 1280
    and the Tuscaroras, 1232
Iroquois Confederacy
        (Haudenosaunee), 11, 14, 219 (photo), 369–370, 744 (photo)
    and adoption, 110, 219
    and agriculture, 10–11, 319
    and the Albany Congress, 493–495
    and the American Revolution, 107, 237–239, 240, 699
    and the Beaver Wars, 218–220
    and the Cayugas, 1240–1242
    and the Council of the Three Fires, 368
    diplomacy, wampum, and the, 23, 172–173, 174, 355–356, 480–482
    and Franklin, Benjamin, 729–730
    and the French, 212
    and the French and Indian War, 225, 226
    Great Law of Peace, **411–412**, 481, 743–747, 757, **887**
    and the holocaust of 1779, **856–858**
    international appeals by the, 618, 712–713
    Jigonsaseh and, 757–758
    Johnson, Sir William, and the, 760–761
    and lacrosse, 417

    and the Lancaster Treaty Councils, 568–569, 671
    and the Lenápes, 1249
    Longhouse religion, 428–429
    and Lyons, Oren, 774–775
    and the Mohawks, 1258, 1259
    and the Nanticokes, 1262
    of New France, 212
    and the Oneidas, 1264
    and the Onondagas, 1267
    Parker, Ely, on U.S. debt to the, 815
    and the Peacemaker, 708–709 (*see also* Deganawidah [Peacemaker])
    political philosophy and the, 721–722
    political protests by, 292
    publications and, 634
    and Quakers, 819, 821
    role of women in, 16, 383–387
    and the Senecas, 1280, 1281
    and the *Sherrill* court case, 17
    sociopolitical system of the, 321, **743–747**
    traditional culture and, 191, 192 (*see also* Northeastern Woodland Indians)
    and treaties, 511–513
    and the Tuscaroras, 1232, 1233, 1264
    two seats of the, 1261, 1266, 1267, 1269
    and the War of 1812, 357–358
    See also Iroquois Indians
Iroquois Great Council
    and the Cayugas, 1240
    and the Mohawks, 1258
    and the Oneidas, 1264
    and the Onondagas, 1267
    and the Senecas, 1281
Iroquois Indians
    agriculture and, 316–317
    and the Carlisle Treaty Council, 513–514
    craftwork, 337, 339, 340
    False Face Society and, 381–382
    and the fur trade, 394
    and the IRA, 558
    and the Mourning War, 483
    oral history, 446
    and the Powhatans, 1227
    and scalping, 464
    and the Seven Nations of Canada, 370
    and thanksgiving festivals, 475
    and the Wyandottes, 1292
    See also Cayuga Indians; Mohawk Indians;

Oneida Indians;
Onondaga Indians;
Seneca Indians;
Tuscarora Indians
Iroquois Nationals, 418
Iroquois of the Mountain, 1260
Iroquois White Corn Project, 791
Irrateba, 1020
Irrigation
    and the Ancient Pueblo, 330
    and the Great Basin Indians,
        1122
    and the Hohokam culture,
        400–401
    Mayan, 317
    Navajo-Hopi Rehabilitation Act
        (1950) and, 187 (photo)
    and the Pimas, 1028
    and pre-contact Indians, 4, 5, 7
    and the Pueblos, 317–318, 1000
    and the Quechans, 1029
    and water rights, 600–601,
        624–626 (see also Water
        rights)
    and the Yaquis, 1041
Irvine, William, 243
Irving, Danielle, 783
Irving, Washington, 698
Isabella, Queen (Spain), 215, 232
Isbister, Alexander Kennedy, 536
Ishi, 230, 1077–1078
Ishi in Two Worlds, 230
Island Mountain Protectors, 151,
    152
Isleta Pueblo Indians, 144, 145–146,
    1015–1016, 1038
Itazipco (Sans Arcs) Indians. See
    Lakota Indians
Iverson, Peter, 124–125

Jackson (Chief), 1088
Jackson, Andrew, 31, 116, **752–754,**
    753 (photo)
    and the Cherokees, 836
    contempt of Supreme Court by,
        564
    and the Creek War, 248, 1214
    and ethnic cleansing, 89
    Indian Removal Message to
        Congress, **911**
    and Indian removals, 32–36, 146,
        252, 253, 528, 548–550
    and the Marshall Trilogy, 514,
        516
    and Ridge, Major, 777
    and the Seminoles, 249, 314, 315,
        344
Jackson, Bruce, 791
Jackson, Helen Hunt, 18, **755–757,**

756 (photo), 767
A Century of Dishonor, **936**
Jackson, Jack, 165
Jackson, Jesse, 314
Jackson, William S., 755
Jacobs, Leo David, 161
Jacobson, Richard Karen, 798
James, George Wharton, 338
James Bay and Northern Quebec
    Agreement (JBNQA)
    (1975), 519, **565–568,** 1335
James Bay hydroelectric project, 375,
    519, 565–568, 567 (photo)
    and Coon Come, Matthew,
        692–693
    and the Crees, 1303
    and the Naskapi/Montagnais,
        1313
James River, Virginia, 206
Jamestown, 823–824, 827, 844–845,
    1227
Jamul Indians. See Tipai-Ipai Indians
Janklow, William, 642, 644
Japanese Americans, 168, 608, 1020
Jarvis, Annie, 348
Jay, John, 22
Jay Treaty (1794), 161, 174, 525
Jefferson, Thomas, 93, 116, 377, 378
    and expansionism, 278
    and Handsome Lake, 428, 737
    on Indian debt, 525, 741–742
    Indian influences on, 721, 722
    and Native word lists, 419
    and the Northwest Ordinance,
        482
    and removal policy, 252, 528
    and the Tammany Society, 859
    and the trade and intercourse
        acts, 611
Jeffords, Tom, 685
Jelderks, John, 415, 416
Jemez Pueblos, 337, **1016–1017**
Jemison, Mary, 381–382, 858
Jenks, Albert E., 54
Jenner, Edward, 106
Jerome Commission, 570
Jesuit Relations, 211, 212, 214
Jesuits, 87, 108, **210–211,** 210 (photo)
    and Indian enslavement,
        466–467
    and the myth of the noble
        savage, 440
    in New France, 214
    and the Northeast Woodland
        Indians, 1241, 1253, 1259,
        1282, 1292
    and the Plateau Indians, 1137
    and the Southeast Indians, 1231
    in Spanish America, 215,

233–234
    and the Subarctic Indians, 1302
    and Tekakwitha, Kateri, 863
    and the Yaquis, 1041–1042
Jesup, Thomas S., 250, 315, 345, 810
Jicarilla Apaches, 266, **1003–1004,**
    1005, 1006
Jigonsaseh, **757–758**
Jim, Ella, 466
Jim Thorpe, All-American, 866
John Collier's Crusade for Indian
    Reform, 1920–1954, 552
John D. MacArthur Foundation, 561
Johnson, Andrew, 260
Johnson, Charles, 669
Johnson, Emily Pauline, **759–760**
Johnson, Floyd, 415
Johnson, George Henry Martin, 759
Johnson, Guy, 668, 761
Johnson, Jed, 60
Johnson, Lyndon B., 68, 118, 181,
    422, 502, 540
Johnson, Napoleon, 795
Johnson, Nicholas, 596–597
Johnson, Sir William, 504, 505, 520,
    760–761, 761 (photo), 806
    and the American Revolution,
        238
    and the Anishinabe nations, 356
    and Brant, Joseph, 667, 668
    and the Council of the Three
        Fires, 368
    and the French and Indian War,
        225, 226
    and Hendrick, 747, 748
    on Indian trade goods, 19
    report regarding the Iroquois
        Confederacy, **895**
Johnson, William (Justice), 515–516,
    527
Johnson and Graham's Lessee v.
    William M'Intosh, 17
Johnson-O'Malley (JOM) Act (1934),
    559, 608–609
Johnson v. M'Intosh, 36, 116–117,
    136–137, 179, 514, 526,
    903
    and the Doctrine of Discovery,
        208–210
Johnston, Philip, 364–365, 366
Johnstown, Battle of, 239
Joliet, Louis, 443, 1198, 1200, 1205,
    1255
Jones, Harold, 723
Jones, James E. (Lieutenant Colonel),
    365
Jones, James Earl, 314
Jones, John B., 420
Joseph, Old (Tu-ya-kas-kas), 761–762

Joseph, Younger (Hinmaton Yalatik), 256, 276, 277, **761–763,** 762 (photo), 1145, 1146
    I Will Fight No More Forever Speech, **936**
Josephy, Alvin, Jr., 291, 702
Juaneño Indians. *See* Luiseño Indians
Judiciary
    in Eastern Woodland cultures, 191, 192
    and trials of AIM leaders, 642–643
    tribal courts, 182, 612–613
    See also Criminal justice
Juh, 731
Jumper, 1230
Jumping Bull, Cecelia and Harry, 644, 818
Jusacamea, Juan María, 655
Justice Department, U.S., 189

Kabotie, Fred, 90, 414
Kadohadacho Confederacy, 1209
Kahnawake Mohawks, 510, 1260–1261
Kainai/Kainah (Blood) Indians, 368, 659–661, 1162. *See also* Blackfeet/Blackfoot Indians
Kaleak, Jeslie, 133
Kalispel Indians, **1138–1139**
Kalm, Peter, 322
Kamia Indians. *See* Tipai-Ipai Indians
Kamiakin, 255
Kanaka Maoli, 532–533
Kanesatake Mohawks, 510, 1261
Kaniatse, 811
Kansa Indians. *See* Kaw Indians
Kap-kap-on-mi, 762
Karlsefni, Thorfinn, 207
Karuk Indians, **1057–1058**
Kaska Indians, **1309–1310**
Kaskaskia Indians, 246, 371
Kastenmeier, Robert W., 289
Katanski, Amelia V., 666
Katmai National Park, 1349
Katsinas/katchinas, 216, **413–414,** 413 (photo)
    and the Hopi, 1012
    and Toas Pueblos, 1036
    and the Zunis, 1045
Kaurk, 1071
Kaw Indians, **1180–1181,** 1197
Kaw Reservoir, 1181
Kearny, Stephen, 778
Keefe, Tom, Jr., 849

Keeping Slug Woman Alive, 347
Keeswood, Esther, 184
Keetoowah NightHawks, 52
Kelly, Fred, 654 (photo)
Kelly, Lawrence, 552
Kelsay, Isabel, 669
Kemnitzer, Louis, 807
Kenakuk, 1247
Keneschoo, 672
Kennedy, Anthony M., 182, 596
Kennedy, John F., 68, 126, 735, 796
Kennedy, Mary Jean, 348
Kennedy, Ted, 347
Kennedy, William, 536
Kennedy Report, 124, 125
Kennewick Man, 200, **414–416**
Kentucky, 681, 682
Keoke, Emery Dean, 320, 321, 324–325
Keokuk, 662, 663, 1280
Keresan culture, 1017, 1031, 1034
Keresan language family, 998, 1008, 1018, 1031, 1034, 1035, 1044
Kern Valley Indian Community and Council, 1073
Kerr-McGee Company, 184–185
Kescoli, Maxine, 149
Kettle Falls, 848, 1149
A Key into the Language of America, 879
Kickapoo Indians, 246, 265, 371, 860, **1245–1247,** 1246 (photo)
Kicking Bear, 398
Kicking Bird, **763–764,** 1183
Kickingbird, Kirke, 622
Kidder, Alfred V., 327
Kikiallus Indians. *See* Salish Indians, Southern Coast
Kilchis, 1110
Kill Eagle, 659
Killbuck's Island, 240, 242
Killdeer Mountain, Battle of, 842
Killsright, Joe Stuntz, 644
Kilroe, Patricia, 425–426
King, Matthew, 643
King Philip. *See* Metacom/Metacomet (King Philip)
King Philip's War, 20, 142, 153, 599–600
    and Massachusetts praying towns, 720
    and the Mohegans, 869, 870
    and the Narragansetts, 1263
    and the Pequots, 1275
    and the Wampanoags, 1288
    and Williams, Roger, 879

Kino, Eusebio Francisco, 228 (photo), 234, 1026, 1029, 1040
Kinzua Dam, 374, 513, 700, 1284
Kiowa Apache Indians, 175, 1182. *See also* Apache Indians, Plains
Kiowa-Comanche-Apache Reservation, 1158
Kiowa Indians, 9, 171 (photo), 265, 675, **1181–1183,** 1181 (photo)
    and the Comanches, 1169
    and gambling operations, 580
    and the Ghost Dance, 398
Kicking Bird, 763–764
    and *Lone Wolf v. Hitchcock,* 570–571
    and Plains Apaches, 1157
    and the Sun Dance, 471
    and treaties, 175
Kiowa-Tanoan language family, 419
Kiowa, 1181
    Tewa, 1014, 1020, 1028, 1032, 1033, 1034, 1037
    Tiwa, 1015, 1025, 1030, 1035, 1038
    Towa, 1016
Kirkland, Samuel, 667, 668
Kirkpatrick, Freeda, 866
Kitcisakik First Nation, 648–649
Kitigan Zibi Anishinabeg, 648–649
Kitikmeot, 1330, 1332, 1341, 1343
Klallam Indians. *See* Salish Indians, Central Coast
Klamath Indians, **1139–1140,** 1139 (photo)
    and basketry, 338
    and the IRA, 558
    and the Modocs, 1143
    oral history, 95
    removal and, 751–752
    and the slave trade, 168, 202
    and termination, 67, 147, 288, 609
Klamath Reservation, 1081, 1140, 1143
Klamath Termination Act, 609
Klamath Treaty (1864), 1070
Klatsassin, 1298
Klein, Ralph, 701
Klikitat Indians, **1140–1141**
Klukwali (Wolf) society, 169
Kneale, Albert, 89–90
Knox, Henry, 280, 587, 615
Knutson, Paul, 207–208
Koasati Indians, 438
Kodiak Alutiiq Dancers, 1323

Kodiak Island, 221, 264, 1321, 1322
Konkow Indians. *See* Maidu Indians
Konkow Reservation, 1061
Konomihu Indians. *See* Shasta
        Indians
Kootenai House, 1141
Kootenai Indians, 134, 176, 660, **1141**
Kootenai Reservation, 1141
Koots, Jimmy, 414
Kopit, Arthur, 290
Koppedrayer, K. I., 863
Kosciuszko, Tadeusz, 772
Koster site, 94
Kotiakan, 381
Koyukon Indians. *See* Ingalik
        Indians
Krasheninnikov, Stephan Petrovich,
        19
Krauss, Michael, 441
Kroeber, Alfred, 93, 420
Kroeber, Theodora, 230
Kropotkin, Peter, 689
Kuitch (Lower Umpqua) Indians.
        See Coosans Indians
Kuksu cult, 5, 347–348, 1048, 1060,
        1065, 1075, 1078
Kunstler, William, 643
Kuskowagamiut Inuits, 1308, 1309
Kutenaian language, 1141
Kwakiutl/Kwakwaka'wakw
        Indians, 407, 456,
        1092–1094, 1105
Kwakiutlan language group, 479

La Barre, Weston, 802
La Farge, Oliver, 1012
La Flesche, Susan, 91
La Nation Anishnabe de Lac Simon,
        649
La Previère Nation Abitibiwinni,
        648–649
La Purisima, 227
La Push Reservation, 1098
La Salle, René-Robert (Cavelier),
        443, 1166
Labor, forced, 227, 228, 231. *See also*
        Enslavement
Labrador Inuit Association (LIA),
        1334–1335
Lac Courte Oreilles v. Voight, 389
Lacrosse, **417–418,** 417 (photo)
        and Lyons, Oren, 774
LaDuke, Winona, 112, **764–766,** 765
        (photo), 883
LaFarge, Oliver, 346, 688
LaFlesche, Joseph, 766, 767
LaFlesche, Mary Gale, 767
LaFlesche, Susan Picotte, **766–767**

LaFlesche, Susette Tibbles, 756, 757,
        767–768
Laguna Pueblo Indians, 1000,
        1017–1018
Laing, Arthur, 521
Laird, David, 100
Lake Baikal, 94
Lake Indians. *See* Okanagon Indians
Lake Mohonk Conference of the
        Friends of the Indian, 847
Lake Traverse Reservation, 1176
Lakota Indians, 219, 348, 1174,
        1183–1189, 1184 (photo)
        and Black Elk, 658–659
        and Crazy Horse, 702–704
        effect of IRA on, 691
        and the Ghost Dance, 362,
                397–398
        and the Grattan Fight, 255
        and the Great Sioux War, 842 (*see
                also* Great Sioux War
                [1875-1877])
        and horses, 405, 406
        Means, Russell, 785–787
        Mills, William M., 790–791
        oral history, 95
        Red Cloud, 827–829
        Sacred Calf Pipe of the, 454
        Standing Bear, Luther, 854–855
        and the Sun Dance, 472
        and sweat lodges, 473, 474
        and termination, 67
        and thanksgiving festivals, 474
        treaties and the, 23, 530–532
        See also Brûlé Lakota; Hunkpapa
                Lakota Indians; Oglala
                Lakota Indians
Lamberth, Royce C., 560, 562, 563
Lame Deer, 1188
Lamont, Buddy, 641
Lamont, Lawrence, 304
Lamson, Chauncey, 259, 771
Lamson, Nathan, 259, 771
Lanápe Indians, **1247–1249**
Lancaster, Burt, 866
Lancaster (Pennsylvania) treaty
        councils, 173, **568–569,**
        729
Land encroachment/speculation, 39,
        41–48, 45–46, 89, 219
        in Canada, 505
        and Clark, George Rogers, 681
        and Jackson, Andrew, 752,
                753–754
        and King Philip's War, 787–788
        and Mormons, 794
        and the Plains Indians, 658–659,
                770, 828

        and removal, 32–33, 34, 516, 550
        and St. Clair, Arthur, 852, 853
        and sovereignty issues, 526–527
        and Washington, George, 856
        See also Expansionism; Land
                losses/cessions;
                Removal
Land losses/cessions
        allotment and, 50, 53–57,
                278–282, 553, 554 (*see also*
                Allotment)
        and the Bursum Bill, 576
        and California Indians, 230–231
        and Canadian Indians, 505,
                506–508
        and the Creeks, 369, 809
        and dam projects, 374
        and the Iroquois, 239, 240,
                668–669, 830–831
        and Massasoit, 784
        and the Narragansetts, 673
        and Ohio, 772
        and the Plains Indians, 151–152,
                256–257, 368, 450, 660,
                663, 770, 816
        and the Plateau Indians, 762,
                845, 877
        and Sheep Mountain Gunnery
                Range, 644
        and the trade and intercourse
                acts, 615–616
        and treaties, 116, 244, 245–246,
                248, 261, 512, 549 (*see also
                specific treaties*)
        and the Utes, 811
        and the Yakima War, 255
Land of the Spotted Eagle, 855
Land Ordinance of 1785, 116
Land ownership, **146–148**
        and allotment, 117
        citizenship and, 103
        Indian activism and, 72
        inheritance and, 281–282
        and sovereignty issues, 179–181,
                291
        Supreme Court on Indian, 117
        and termination policy, 67
        and water rights, 187–189
        and women in woodland
                cultures, 192
        See also Land losses/cessions
Land use/management
        controlled burning, 1053, 1059
        and the ISDEAA, 560
        and the JBNQA, 566–567
        protection of sacred sites,
                459–461
Landusky, Pike, 151

Language
    assimilation and prohibiting
        Native, 89, 90, 98, 282
    and Bonnin, Gertrude Simmons,
        666
    and Canada, 604
    ending repression of, 555
    gendering and, 191
    Holocene regional groups, 4–12
    and the Hopewell culture, 404
    migration theory and, 199, 200,
        201
    and Navajo code talkers,
        364–367
    Nunavut official, 594
    Penn, William, and Native, 821
    pre-contact written, **425–427**
    programs and Native museums,
        804
    renewal/revitalization of, 71, 91,
        418–424, 632–633, 1269,
        1271, 1274, 1275, 1280,
        1284, 1286
    Russians and Native, 223, 224
    and self-determination, 125
    squaw as a derogatory term,
        163–165
    state names derived from
        Native, 468–469
    Williams, Roger and the
        Narragansett, 879
    word borrowing, 320, 325, 419
    youth and loss of Native, 156
    See also Sign language/signaling
        systems; *specific languages
        and language families*
Lannan, J. Patrick, 561
Lanphear, Kim M., 113
L'Anse aux Meadows, **203–206**, 204
        (photo), 207, 727–728
Largo-Gallina peoples, 327
Las Casas, Bartolomé de, 18
Lassik Indians. *See* Wailaki Indians
Last of the Mohicans, 225, 787, 1249
Laughing, Tony, 161
Laurel culture, 11
Law enforcement
    and the IRA, 556–557
    and peyote use, 362–363
    and sovereignty issues, 182,
        594–596
    and substance abuse, 80
    See also Criminal justice;
        Judiciary
Law of Innocents, 192
Law of Nations, 208
Laws of the Indies, 232
Lawson, John, 322
Le Jeune, Paul, 212, 214

Leadership
    Cherokee and factionalism in,
        253
    and the Creek War, 246–247
    and Deloria, Vine, Jr., 709, 712
    and intertribal warfare, 484
    and the Iroquois Confederacy,
        412–413
    legitimacy issues and, 140
    and Mississippian culture,
        432–433
    negotiating treaties and Indian,
        42
    and the Nez Percé, 276
    and political activism, 288–289,
        292, 638–646, 798, 807
    and tribal colleges, 868
    and tribal governments, 69
    urban relocation and
        reservation, 287
    See also Activism, political; Tribal
        government
League of Nations, 618, 712–713
League of the Ho-De-No-Sau-Nee, 384
Leakey, Louis, 93
Lean Elk, 276, 277
Learning to Write "Indian," 666
Leasing, 55–56, 60, 61
    BIA fraud and, 640
    and Blackfeet land in Canada,
        661
    and the Comanches, 816
    and General Allotment Act, 281
    and government
        mismanagement of
        Indian funds, 560–564
    and the Great Basin Indians,
        1133
    and mineral extraction, 129, 183,
        185, 546–548
    and pollution, 131
Leatherstocking Tales, 695
Leavitt, Scott, 554
LeBlanc, Romeo, 588 (photo)
LeClaire, Antonine, 663
Lee, George P., 795
Left Hand, 261, 262, 263
Legends/stories
    Athapaskan, 335
    corn in, 318
    and the False Face Society, 382
    Iroquois Great Peacemaker,
        480–481 (*see also*
        Deganawidah
        [Peacemaker])
    role of canoes in, 354–355
    and totem poles, 478–479
Leighton, Elliott, 289–290
Lejac School, 100

Lemhi Valley Reservation, 1129
Lemkin, Raphael, 141
Len-pe/Leni-Lenápe Indians. *See*
        Delaware Indians
        (Len-pe/Leni-Lenápe)
Leschi, 1105
Lester, A. David, 701, 702
Leupp, Francis Ellington, 50, 54, 55,
        501, 541, **768–769**, 768
        (photo)
Lewis, Lucy Martin, 458
Lewis, Meriwether, 30, 1086, 1108,
        1110, 1202. *See also* Lewis
        and Clark expedition
Lewis and Clark expedition
    and the Blackfeet, 660, 1163
    and Dalles trading area, 202
    and the Hidatsas, 1179
    journals, **901**
    and the Northern Shoshone,
        1128, 1129
    and the Plateau Indians, 1136,
        1140, 1145, 1152, 1153,
        1155
    and the Poncas, 1204
    and Sacagawea, 836–837
    on trade relations, 167
Libertarian party, 787
Lickers, Henry, 130
Licking Reservoir, 437, 445
Liette, Pierre, 341–342
Life Among the Paiutes, 883, 1121
Like-a-Fishhook Village, 1161, 1179,
        1191
Lili'uokalani, Queen (Hawai'i), 532
Lillooet Indians, **1141–1142**
Lincoln, Abraham, 1038, 1175
Lindquist, G. E. E., 576
Lipan Apaches, **1004–1005**, 1006
Lipe, William, 436
Little, Jim, 643
Little Big Man, 290
Little Bighorn, Battle of the (Battle of
        Greasy Grass), **273–276**,
        274 (photo), 530, 659, 850
    account by Two Moon, **934**
    and the Cheyennes, 715, 1167
    and Crazy Horse, 703
    and the Lakotas, 1187
    and the Shoshonis, 873
    and Sitting Bull, 843
    as a symbol of resistance, 293
Little Crow (Taoyateduta), 258, 259,
        769–771, 770 (photo),
        1175, 1176
Little Mountain, 763
Little Prince, 247
Little Raven, 261, 262, 1160
Little Rocky Mountains, 151–153

Little Salt Springs archaeology site, 84
Little Shell, 1171, 1196, 1240
Little Six Casino, 159
Little Thunder, 850
Little Turtle (Michikinikwa), **771–772,** 771 (photo), 853, 1254, 1255
Little Turtle's War, 853
    and the Anishinabe, 1239
    and the Foxes, 1244
    and the Lenápes, 1249
    and the Miamis, 1255
    and the Potawatomis, 1278
    and the Sauks, 1280
    and the Shawnees, 1285
Little Wolf, 715, 1167
Littlebear, Richard, 91–92, 424
Litzau, Dawn, 165
Locke, John, 376, 377, 440
Locker, Corinne, 346
Loco, 731
Lode Star Casino, 156
Loe, Thomas, 819
Logan, 1242
Logan, William R., 624
Lomawaima, K. Tsianina, 122, 209, 597, 598
Lone Wolf, 570–571, 570 (photo), 764, 1183
Lone Wolf v. Hitchcock, 50, 66, 146, 523, **569–571,** 614, **945**
Long March, **276–277,** 763, 1145–1146
Long Point First Nation, 649
Long Walk (1864), **259–261,** 439, 529, 674–675, 676, 781, 1023
Longest Walk (1977), 71, 293 (photo), 296–297, 645, 657
Longfellow, Henry Wadsworth, 698, 751, 755, 767
Longhouse religion (Gaiwí:yo), **428–429,** 736–738, 1240
    and the Cayugas, 1242
    and the Mohawks, 1258, 1260, 1261
    and the Oneidas, 1264, 1266, 1267
    and the Onondagas, 1267, 1269
    and the Plateau Indians, 1156
    Quaker influence in, 819
    and the Senecas, 1281, 1283, 1284
    See also Handsome Lake; Seven Drums Religion
Looking Cloud, Arlo, 302, 645
Looking Glass, 276, 277, 1145
Looks Twice, Lucy, 659
Lopez, Barry, 142
Lopez, Steve, 308

Lord Dunmore's War, 24, 681
Loreto, 108–109, 234
Los Angeles, 1122
Losh, Angela, 165
Lotiahkan, Shawaway, 1140, 1156
Loud Hawk, Kenny, 642
Louis, Adrian, **772–773**
Louis, Max, 566 (photo)
Louisiana Purchase, 30, 116
Loupe Fork, Battle at, 686
Lower Brûlé Reservation, 156, 1193
Lower Umpqua Indians. *See* Coosans Indians
Lowry, Henry Berry, 1224
Loyal Shawnees (Cherokee Shawnees), 1286
Lubicon band, Crees, 1303
Luiseño Indians, **1059–1060**
Lumbee Indians, **1223–1224**
Lumbee River Regional Development Association, 1224
Lummi Aquatic Training Program, 126–127
Lummi Indian School of Aquaculture (LISA), 126–127
Lummi Indians, 126–127, 462, 463, 476. *See* Salish Indians, Central Coast
Luna, James Alexander, **773–774**
Luoma, Jon R., 131–132
Lydia, or, Filial Piety, 671–672
Lydick, Lawrence, 818
Lyng v. Northwest Indian Cemetery Protective Association, 364, 499, **572–573,** 646
Lyons, Oren, **774–775,** 791
Lytle, Clifford, 553, 555, 597, 598

MacDonald, Peter (Hoshkaisith Begay), **776,** 1023
MacDonald, Robert, 332
Mackenzie, Alexander, 585
    and the Bella Bellas, 1083
    and Bella Coolas, 1084
    and the Carriers, 1296
    and the Gwich'ins, 1306
    and the Hares, 1307
    and the Slaveys, 1316
Mackenzie Grease Trail, 1297
Mackenzie Mountain People. *See* Kaska Indians
Maclean, Allan, 22–23
Macleod, Roderick C., 717
Macomb, Alexander, 250
Macro-Algonkian language phyla, 419
Macro-Siouan language phyla, 419

Mad Bear, **647,** 648 (photo)
Mader, Andy, 309
Madison, James, 859
Magnus, King (Norway and Sweden), 207–208
Mahican Indians, 240–243, **1249–1251,** 1263
Maidu Indians, **1060–1061**
Maine, 72, 144, 145, 1274
    ban on "squaw" in place names, 164 (photo), 165
    Indian Land Claims Settlement Act (1980), 573–575, 574 (photo), 1252, 1272
Maine Indian Basketmakers Alliance (MIBA), 338
Major, Ridge (Nunna Hidihi), **777,** 777 (photo)
Major Crimes Act (1885), 50, 180, 612, 622
Makah Cultural and Research Center, 804
Makah Indians, 169, **1094–1096** language, 479–480
Makah Reservation, 1094
Makenunatane (Swan Chief), 1295
Malatare, Lewis, 465
Malecite Indians, 356
Malheur Reservation, 1120
Maliseet Indians, 370, **1251–1252,** 1271, 1272
    and Maine Indian claim settlement, 573, 574
Maloney, Jake, 651
Mamanti, 764
Mammoths, 86
The Man-Eating Myth, 352
Management of Indian Lands and Property Act (1867), 537
Mandan Indians, 318, **1189–1191,** 1190 (photo)
Mandeville, John, 353
Mangas Coloradas, 271–272, 273, **778–779,** 870, 1002
    and Cochise, 683, 685
    and Geronimo, 730
Manhattan Island, 1248
Manifest Destiny. *See* Expansionism
Manis Mastodon archaeology site, 84
Manitoba, 832
Manitoba Treaty, 536
Mankiller, Wilma, **779–780,** 779 (photo)
Mann, Barbara, 319
Mann, James, 284
Mann, Mary Tyler Peabody, 883
Manso Indians, 1038
A Manual for History Museums, 813

Manuel, George, 99, 566 (photo)
Manuelito (Hastiin Ch'iil Hajiin),
        260, **780–781,** 781
        (photo), 1023
Manypenny, George, 175, 570
Maori, 423, 477
Maquinna, 1097
March, Othniel C., 828–829
March of Tears, 1042
Maricopa Indians, 266. *See also* Pee-
        Posh Indians
Maricopa Wells, Battle at, 1024
Mariposa War (1850–1851), 44, 1063
Markham, William, 820
Marquette, Jacques, 443, 1192, 1198,
        1200, 1205, 1255
Marquette, Pierre, 341
Marquette University, 431
Marriage, 167, 193. *See also specific
        Indian groups*
Marshall, John, 117, 146, 179–180,
        623 (photo)
    and the Doctrine of Discovery,
        208–209
    and the doctrine of trust, 614
    and the doctrine of wardship,
        616, 623
    and domestic dependent nation,
        522–523
    and *Fletcher v. Peck,* 527
    and the Marshall Trilogy, 32,
        35–36, 514–517, 626, 627
    and removal, 548
    and sovereignty issues, 550–551
Marshall, Thurgood, 595
Marshall Trilogy, 36, 116–117,
        136–137, 146, 179–180,
        514–517
    and domestic dependent nation,
        522–523
Marshel, James, 243
Martha's Vineyard, 1288
Martinez, Julian, 458
Martinez, Maria, 458
Martinez, Martin, 288
Martinez, Paddy, 185
Martinez, Seferino, 346, 1036
Martyr, Peter, 378
Marx, Karl, 721, **782–783,** 782 (photo)
Marxism, 782–783, 791–792
Mascots, **429–431,** 430 (photo)
Masham, Sir William, 878
Mashantucket Pequots, 1275
Mashpee, Cape Cod, 1288
Mashpee revolt, 651
Mason, C. H., 255
Mason, John, and the Pequot War,
        892
Mason, Otis, 338, 500

Massachusetts, 1272, 1274, 1288
    depopulation of, 112, 113
Massachusetts Bay Colony, 599–600,
        720, 878–879
Massachusetts Indians, 217
    and praying villages, 599, 719–720
Massacres
    at Acoma, 1000
    of Apaches by Mexicans, 684
    attack on Sicangu Lakota, 1187
    of Blackfeet Indians by U.S.
        Army, 1164
    and California gold rush period,
        229–230
    and California Indians, 1072,
        1073, 1075, 1076, 1077
    and the Karuks, 1058
    of the Lenápes, 1249
    and the Miwoks, 1063
    Ortiz, Simon J., on, 808
    and the Powhatans, 1227
    at Pyramid Lake, 882
    of San Carlos Apache, 1007
    and the Sauks, 1280
    and the Shastas, 1070
    and the Walker party, 1120
    and the Whitmans, 876–877
    of Yavapais, 1042
    See also Genocide; *specific
        massacres*
Massasoit (Ousa Mequin), **783–784,**
        784 (photo), 787, 852,
        1287
    peace treaty, **891**
Masset, 1091–1092
Matachina Dance, 216
Material culture
    expansionism and, 39, 40
    and fishing economies, 462–463
    Indian inventions, 321
    and Mississippian culture, 432
    and Paleo-Indians, 3, 85–86, 86
        (figure), 451–452
    and travel, 355–356
    See also Agriculture; Economy,
        traditional; *specific Indian
        groups*
Mather, Cotton, 93, 359
Matonabbee, 1300
Matoush, Maryann, 692
Matrilineal descent/matrilocal
        residence, 385–386, 409,
        412
    and Arctic Indians, 1321, 1343
    and the Northeast Woodland
        Indians, 191, 193, 370,
        745, 1241, 1248, 1250,
        1258, 1261, 1264, 1267,
        1281, 1291

    and the Northwest Coast
        Indians, 1090, 1111, 1114
    and the Plains Indians, 1158,
        1160, 1172, 1177, 1189,
        1207
    and Southeast Indians, 442, 1212,
        1226, 1228, 1232, 1233
    and Southwest Indians, 998,
        1001, 1002, 1010, 1012,
        1016, 1022
    and the Subarctic Indians, 1296,
        1305, 1310, 1314, 1317
Mattaponi Reservation, 1227–1228
Mattole Indians. *See* Wailaki Indians;
        Wiyot Indians
Mawedopenais, 507
Maximilian, 406
Mayan Indians, 317, 321, 425–427,
        486
Mayflower II, seizure of, 296, 639, 786
Mayo Indians, 655
McAvoy, Thomas, 161, 162
McCain, John, 416
McCartys, 998
McCool, Daniel, 189
McEntire, Carl, 298 (photo)
McGillivray, Alexander, 1221–1222
McGillycuddy, V. T., 828
McIntosh, William, 174–175, 247,
        248, 549
McKenna, Joseph, 624–625
McKenney, Thomas, 88, 540, 831
McKenzie, Richard Delaware Dior,
        288, 290
McKinley, Howard, Jr., 798
McKosato, Harlan, 562
McLaughlin, James, 283, 843
McLean, John, 515
McNamee, Steve, 138–139
McNickle, D'Arcy, **784–785,** 795
McNickle, William, 784
McPhee Village, 328
McQueen, Peter, 246–247, 809
McTavish, Simon, 585
Mdewakanton Indians. *See* Dakota
        Indians
Meachum, Albert, 674
Meachum, Alfred B., 752
Mead, Jonn V., 271
Meadowcroft Rockshelter, 83, 84, 451
Means, Russell, 289, **785–787,** 786
        (photo)
    and AIM, 639, 646, 656
    and the FBI, 817
    and the International Treaty
        Council, 618
    and *Means v. Chinle District
        Court,* 596
    and Pine Ridge conflict, 300, 643

and Trail of Broken Treaties, 297,
    298–299
and tribal politics, 880
and Wounded Knee siege, 296,
    304, 305, 640–641, 642
Means, Theodora Louise Feather,
    785
Means, Walter, 288–289, 785
Means v. Chinle District Court, 596
Mecina, 1247
Media
    Aboriginal Peoples Television
        Network, 631–632
    and inciting genocide, 142
    and Indian activism, 295–296
    and Indian gambling, 136
    and occupation of Alcatraz
        Island, 287, 289
    and the Osage, 450–451
    Rogers, Will, and radio, 834
    Television Northern Canada
        (TVNC), 631
    See also Writers/publishing
Medicine
    and California Indians, 1056,
        1058
    False Face Society and, 381–382
    Indian contributions to, 321–323
    and LaFlesche, Susan Picotte,
        766–767
    and Lewis and Clark expedition,
        837
    and Montezuma, 793
    and Northeast Woodland
        tradition, 191
    and sweat lodges, 473
    Western, 105–106, 109–110
    See also Health issues;
        Shamanism
Medicine, Bea, 163
Medicine Dance, 1174, 1238, 1243,
    1278
Medicine Lodge ceremonies, 1171,
    1203, 1254
Medicine Lodge Society, 1191, 1194,
    1199
Meech Lake Accord, 510, 511, 653
Meeds, Lloyd, 596
Meek, Joe, 877
Meeker, Nathan, 812, 1133
Meekison, Peter, 603
Membertou, 1257
Menawa, 246–247
Mendocino Indian Reservation, 1067
Menominee Indians, 72, 175, 368,
    1252–1254
    and termination, 67, 147, 288,
        609
Meredith, Thomas, 247

Meriam, Lewis, 58, 285, 576
Meriam Report, 124, 128, 147,
    285–286, 501, 541, 553,
    554, **576–577, 952**
    and Bonnin, Gertrude Simmons,
        666
    and Collier, John, 690–691
    and the Society of American
        Indians, 847
Merivale, Herman, 506
*Merrion v. Jicarilla Apache Indian
    Tribe*, 547
Mesa Verde, 4, 328, 329–330
    National Park, 1031 (photo), 1133
Mescalero Apache Indians, 260, 265,
    675, **1005–1006**
Mescalero Apache Reservation, 553
    and the Chiricahua Apache,
        1001, 1003
    and the Jicarilla Apache, 1004
    and the Lipan Apache, 1004,
        1005
Meskwaki Casino, 580
Messiah Letter, 397
Metacom/Metacomet (King Philip),
    20, 600, **787–789,** 788
    (photo), 879, 1287, 1288
Methamphetamine (meth), 79–80
Methodist Church, 697, 1091, 1115,
    1117
Methodist Episcopal church, 1278
Métis Indians, 101, 357, 535
    and the Anishinabes, 1239, 1240
    and Canadian recognition, 518,
        519
    and the Crees, 1302
    Dumont, Gabriel, 716–717
    McNickle, D'Arcy, 784–785
    and Nunavut, 617
    Riel rebellions, 831–833, 1171,
        1240
    See also Ojibwa, Plains, Indians
Métis Nation Accord (1992), **578–579**
Métis National Council (MNC), 578
Metlakatla, 1115
Mexican-American War, 675
Mexico/Mexicans
    and the Apaches, 778
    and California Indians,
        1066–1067, 1071, 1077
    and the Chumash, 1052
    and Cochise, 684
    demographic collapse in, 105
    Indian policy and, 228–229
    and the Navajos, 780
    and the Pueblos, 1000
    and the Treaty of Guadalupe
        Hidalgo, 175
    and the Yaquis, 655, 1042

Meyer, Dillon S., 502
Miami Confederacy, 174
Miami Indians, 265, 342, **1254–1256**
    and the American Revolution,
        240
    and the Battle of Fallen Timbers,
        245–246
    and Brant, Joseph, 668
    Little Turtle, 771–772, 853
    and the Old Northwest
        Confederacy, 369
    and the Wabash Confederacy,
        371
Miantonomo, 672–673
Miccosukee Indians, 251, 344,
    1228–1229, 1230. *See also*
        Seminole Indians
Michigan, 72, 1278
Michilimackinack, 368
Micmac/Mi'kmaq Indians, 212, 355,
    370, 482, **1256–1258**
    and Maine Indian claim
        settlement, 573, 575
Middleton, Frederick, 717
Midgette, Sally, 421, 424
Migration
    and the Ancient Pueblo, 329,
        330
    and the Athapaskans, 333, 335
    role in demographic collapse,
        107
    theory on arrival in the
        Americas, 2–3, 82–85, 84
        (figure), 451
        Bering Strait, 92–95, 199–201
        and Kennewick Man, 416
        and linguistics, 441
    See also specific Indian groups
Mikasuki Indians, 438
Miles, John, 715
Miles, Nelson, 273, 277, 687, 705,
    731, 1003, 1188
Miller, Arvid, 1251
Miller, Christopher, 462
Miller, Iva, 866
Miller, Larry, 162
Miller, Samuel, 622
Mills, Sid, 298–299
Mills, William M., **790–791,** 790
    (photo)
Miluk Indians, 1089. *See also*
        Coosans Indians
Mimbres Apache Indians, 271–273,
    870–871
Mimbres Valley, 434–435
Mims, Samuel, 248
Miners, 39, 44–45
Mingos, 245
Miniconjous, 275

Mining, 55–56, 61, **148–153**
   and Alaska, 491
   Foxes and lead, 1244
   and gold in California, 229
   and the Great Basin Indians,
      1120, 1129
   and the Hopi, 1014
   and the Inupiat, 1338
   and the Navajos, 1023
   Nunavut and mineral rights,
      593, 617
   and the Osage, 448–451
   pollution and, 144
   and reservations, 129
   uranium, 183–186, 184 (photo),
      1152
   and Ute land, 811–812
Minneconjou Lakota Sioux. *See*
      Lakota Indians
Minnesota, 67, 81, 165
   and the Great Sioux Uprising,
      256–259
Minnesota v. Mille Lacs Band, 389
Minnetrista Council for Great Lakes
      Native American
      Studies, 1256
Miscegenation. *See* Intermarriage
Miskito Indians, 786–787
Mission Dolores, 228
Mission Indians, 337 (photo). *See also*
      Cahuilla Indians;
      Luiseño Indians; Serrano
      Indians; Tipai-Ipai
      Indians
Mission of San Francisco Sandia, 1030
Mission San Miguel, 1068
Missionaries
   and the Arctic Indians, 1327,
      1330, 1332, 1334, 1340,
      1348
   and assimilation efforts, 540, 541
   and Athapaskans, 336
   and California Indians, 21–22,
      227–228, 1052, 1067, 1079
   and Christian conversion
      imperative, 360–361
   and conversion as U.S. policy,
      496–497
   and epidemic diseases, 108
   and Indian enslavement,
      466–467, 468
   and Indian languages, 419–420,
      421
   and the Indian Reorganization
      Act, 691
   and lacrosse, 418
   misinterpretation of Native
      cosmology by, 190
   and New France, 213–214

   and the Northeast Woodland
      Indians, 1236, 1237, 1252,
      1266, 1268, 1272, 1292
   and the Northwest Coast
      Indians, 1084, 1091, 1098,
      1103, 1105, 1113, 1115
   and Plains Indians, 257, 1167,
      1173, 1176, 1202
   and the Plateau Indians, 1137,
      1138, 1149, 1152, 1153,
      1155
   Russian, in Alaskan interior, 224
      (*see also* Russian
      Orthodox Church)
   and the Southeast Indians, 1214,
      1216, 1223, 1226
   and Southwest Indians, 1000,
      1001, 1005, 1013, 1014,
      1017, 1022, 1024, 1026,
      1031–1032, 1037, 1041,
      1044
   Spanish, 215, 228 (photo),
      231–235
   and Subarctic Indians,
      1296–1297, 1298, 1300,
      1303, 1306, 1310, 1312,
      1314, 1316
   and the Washani religion, 845
   and the Whitman Massacre,
      876–877
   See also specific Protestant groups
      and Catholic brotherhoods
Missionary Society of the Church of
      England in Canada, 331
Mississauga Indians. *See*
      Anishinabe/Anishnabe
      Indians
Mississippi, 1219–1220
Mississippian culture, 10, 350–352,
      432–433
Missouri River Basin Development
      Program, 374
Missouria Indians, **1191–1192,** 1200
Mistissini First Nation, 692
Mitchell, George, 289, 297, 299, 498,
      638
Mitchell v. United States, 209–210
Miwok Indians, **1062–1063**
Mixanno, 217
Mixtec pictography, 426, 427
Moche Indians, 321
Modoc Indians, 229–230, 1140,
      1142–1143, 1143 (photo)
   Captain Jack, 673–674
   Hooker Jim, 751–752
Modoc Wars, 673–674, 752, 1143
Mofford, Rose, 139
Mogollon culture, 4, 327, **433–435,**
      998, 1018, 1044

Mohawk, John C., 634, 775, **791–792**
Mohawk Indians, **1258–1261**
   at Akwesasne, 129–131, 161–162,
      632–633 (*see also*
      Akwesasne)
   and the Algonquins, 1237
   and the American Revolution,
      238–239
   and the Beaver Wars, 218, 219
   Brant, Joseph, 667–669
   disease and, 112, 113
   and European trade goods, 18,
      168
   Hendrick, 747–748
   and the Iroquois Confederacy,
      11, 14, 369, 412, 428,
      743–747
   Johnson, Emily Pauline, 759–760
   and Johnson, Sir William, 760
   and King Philip's War, 789
   and the Mahicans, 1250
   Oakes, Richard, 806–807
   and the Plains Cree, 1171
   Tekakwitha, Kateri, 862–863
   and trade with the Dutch,
      172–173
   U.S. imagery and, 236
   and the Wabanaki Confederacy,
      370, 371
   See also Iroquois Confederacy
      (Haudenosaunee)
Mohegan Indians, 1275–1276
   gambling operations, 160–161
   and King Philip's War, 789
   and the Narragansetts, 672–673
   and the Pequot War, 217
   Uncas, 869–870
   See also Mahican Indians; Pequot
      Indians
Mohegan Sun Casino, 161
Mohican Indians, 72
Mojave Generating Station, 148, 149,
      151
Mojave/Mohave Indians, 1008,
      1018–1020, 1019 (photo)
   as River Yumans, 1010, 1014
Mojave Valley, 1018
Molawai, 1045
Momaday, Alfred and Natachee
      Scott, 792
Momaday, N. Scott, 290, **792–793**
Monache Indians. *See* Mono Indians
Monk's Mounds, 432
Mono Indians, **1063–1064,** 1064
      (photo)
Monphwi, 1305
Monroe, James, 33, 252, 501, 541, 626
   and the Monroe Doctrine, 264,
      265

Montaigne, 377, 378
Montana, 151–153, 165, 547, 548
Montana v. Blackfeet Tribe of Indians,
    547, 548
Montana v. United States, 181
Montcalm, Louis-Joseph de, 226
Monte Verde, 83, 94, 451
Montesquieu, 376
Montezuma, Carlos, 766, **793–794,**
    847, 1043
Montezuma Valley, 329–330
Montileaux, Martin, 786
Montreal, 212
Moogk, Peter, 213
Moon-Eyed People, 444, 446
Mooney, James, 36–37, 51, 112–113,
    500, 551, 802, 885
Moore, James, 168
Moorehead, Warren King, 402
Mootzka, Waldo, 414
Moravians, 525
    as missionaries, 240–243, 1250,
        1334, 1348
More, Sir Thomas, 17, 377
Morgan, Colonel, 713
Morgan, George, 482
Morgan, Jacob, 714
Morgan, Lewis Henry, 51, 384, 698,
    721, 738, 814
Morgan, Michael Oliver, 807
Morgan, Ron, 148–149
Morgan, Thomas J., 282, 497, 502
    (photo)
Mormons, **794–795**
    and Bole-Maru religion, 348
    and the Catawbas, 1212
    and EchoHawk, Larry, 717–718
    and the Great Basin Indians,
        1124, 1129, 1130, 1133
    and Washakie, 873, 874
Morongo Band, Mission Indians, 702
Morongo Indian Reservation, 544
    (photo)
Morris, Alexander, 507
Morris, Glenn, 646
Morris, Thomas, 831
Morrison, Pitcairn, 684
Mortality rates, 123–124, 796
    and allotment policies, 554
    and removal, 528–529, 548, 551
    See also Alcohol/alcohol abuse;
        Disease;
        Famine/starvation;
        Suicide
Morton, Thomas, 476
Moses, Chief, 846, 1150
Mott, James, 383
Mott, Lucretia, 383, 387
Mound Builder cultures, 14, **435–437**

Adena culture, 9, 10, 311–313
    and the Alabamas, 1209
    and Cahokia, 10, 350–352
    and the Cherokees, 1213
    and the Creek Confederacy,
        369–370
    Hopewell culture, 402–404, 1262
    Mississippian culture, 432–433,
        1219, 1221
        the Natchez and the,
            442–443, 1224, 1226
        Ohio Valley, **444–447**
        Maliseets and the, 1252
        Miamis and the, 1255
        Micmacs and the, 1257
    and Plains Indians, 8
    and the Winnebagos, 1289
Moundbuilders State Memorial
    Park, 445
Moundville, 10
Mount Graham, **398–399,** 399
    (photo)
Mount Rushmore protest, 295, 303,
    639, 786
Mountain Horse, Mike, 661
Mountain Meadows Massacre, 794
Mourning War, 483
Muckleshoot Indians. *See* Salish
    Indians, Southern Coast
Muckleshoot Reservation, 1105
Mud Bay Louis (Luis Yowaluck),
    410
Mud Bay Sam, 410
Mulatto King, 345
Mulroney, Brian, 602
Muni, 655
Munro, John, 591
Murah, Guera, 811
Murkowski, Frank, 133, 701
Murray, Julius, 542 (photo)
Muscogee Baptist Association, 265
Muscogee Indians. *See* Creek
    (Muscogee) Indians
Museum of the American Indian
    Act, 498
Museums, Native American, 414,
    774, **803–805,** 813. *See also*
        National Museum of the
        American Indian
        (NMAI)
Mushuau Innu Band Council, 1313
Mushuau Innu Renewal Committee,
    1313
Music/musical instruments
    and the Arctic Indians, 1329
    and California Indians, 1049,
        1052, 1053, 1055, 1056,
        1068, 1078
    and Harjo, Joy, 741

and the Northeast Woodland
        Indians, 1252
    and the Northwest Coast
        Indians, 1084, 1097
    and Plains Indians, 1162, 1163,
        1178, 1186
    and the Plateau Indians, 1145
    and the Southeast Indians, 1223
    and Southwest Indians,
        1009–1010, 1043
    and the Subarctic Indians, 1307
Muskogean language family, 9,
    438–439
    and the Alabamas, 1208
    Chickasaw, 1215
    Choctaw, 1217
    Creeks, 1220
    Houma, 1223
    and the Seminoles, 1228
Muskogee Indians. *See* Creek
    (Muscogee) Indians
My Indian Boyhood, 96
My Lai, 808
Myer, Dillon S., 285, 607–608
Myrick, Andrew, 258
Mythology. *See* Legends/stories;
        Oral history

Na-Dené/Dené Indians, 4, 333, 1001
Na-Dené language phyla, 419,
    440–441
Naha, Raymond, 414
Nahani Indians. *See* Kaska Indians;
        Tahltan Indians
Naiche, 273, 683, 731
Nakota Indians, 219, **1192–1193**
    divisions of Sioux, 1174, 1184
    and horses, 405, 406
    See also Yankton Sioux;
        Yanktonnai Sioux
Nambé Pueblo, **1020**
Names, stereotypical, 797. *See also*
        Place names
Nampeyo, 458
Nana, 1003
Nananawtunu, 788
Nanticoke Indian Association, 1262
Nanticoke Indian Heritage Project,
    1262
Nanticoke Indians, **1261–1262**
Nantucket Island, 1288
Napolitano, Janet, 701
Narbona, 780
Narragansett Indians, 72, 672–673,
    852, 870, **1262–1264**
    and King Philip's War, 788–789
    and the Pequot War, 216–218
    and Williams, Roger, 879
Narragansett Reservation, 1263

Narvaz, Panfilo de, 676
Naskapi/Montagnais Indians, 212,
          356, 375, 519–520,
          1311–1313
Naskapi-Montagnais Innu
          Association, 1313
Nat Turner slave rebellion, 1227
Natchez Indians, **442–443,** 442
          (photo), **1224–1226,** 1225
          (photo)
     revolt by the, 1219, 1231
Natchezean language family, 1224
Natchitoches Confederacy, 1209
National American Indian
          Movement, 646
National American Journalists
          Association, 155
National American Language Act
          (1990), 128
National Association of the
          Advancement of
          Colored People
          (NAACP), 847
National Association on Indian
          Affairs, 555
National Coalition on Racism in
          Sports and Media, 429
National Collegiate Athletic
          Association, 431
National Congress of American
          Indians (NCAI), 67, 124,
          154, 292, 293, 701–702,
          734, **795–797**
     and the American Indian
          Chicago Conference, 798
     and de la Cruz, Joseph, 705
     and Deloria, Vine, Jr., 709, 710
     and McNickle, D'Arcy, 785
     and termination, 91, 147
National Council of American
          Indians, 555, 576
National Forest Management Act
          (1976), 459
National Historic Preservation Act
          (1966), 459–460, 582
National Indian Brotherhood (NIB),
          519, 521, 653
National Indian Brotherhood from
          Canada, 297
National Indian Committee of
          Alcohol and Drug
          Abuse, 297
National Indian Council (NIC), 653
National Indian Gaming
          Association, 159
National Indian Gaming
          Commission (NIGC),
          137, **580–581**
National Indian Institute, 691

National Indian Leadership
          Training, 297
National Indian Lutheran Board, 297
National Indian Republican
          Association, 793
National Indian Youth Council
          (NIYC), 154, 185, 297,
          497, **797–799,** 1204
     and Warrior, Clyde, 871, 872
National League for Justice to the
          American Indian, 855
National Museum of the American
          Indian (NMAI), 160, 500,
          799–801, 800 (photo)
     and basketry, 336, 339
     and Deloria, Vine, Jr., 710
National Park Service (NPS), U.S.,
          460, 583, 1011
National Survey on Drug Use and
          Health (2005), 79
National Tribal Chairmen's
          Association, 640, 705
National Woman Suffrage
          Association (NWSA),
          384, 385
The Nations Within: The Past and
          Future of American Indian
          Sovereignty, 553, 555
Native American Business
          Development, Trade
          Promotion, and Tourism
          Act (2000), 182
Native American Church, 460, 553,
          801–803, 802 (photo), 846
     and the Great Basin Indians,
          1121, 1129, 1135
     and the Northeast Woodland
          Indians, 1254, 1280, 1290
     and peyote use, 80, 154, 362
     and the Plains Indians, 1167,
          1183, 1198, 1204
     and the Southwest Indians, 1022,
          1037
Native American Graves Protection
          and Repatriation Act
          (NAGPRA) (1990), 414,
          415, 460, 498, **581–584,**
          980
     and mound builder remains, 446
     and museums, 803
     and wampum belts, 480
Native American Journalists
          Association (NAJA), 772
Native American Languages Act
          (1990), 91, 422, **982**
Native American Law Students
          Association, 155
Native American Rights Fund
          (NARF), 72, 297

Native American Support
          Committees (NASCs),
          639
Native Americas, 475
Native Council of Canada, 519
Native Roots, 324
Native Women's Association of the
          Northwest Territories,
          101
Natural resources
     and CERT, 701–702, 776
     and the Navajos, 1023
     See also Resource management
Nault, Robert, 539
Navajo Community College
          (NCC)/Diné College, 71,
          125
Navajo Community College Act
          (1971), 125
Navajo-Hopi Land Dispute
          Settlement Act (1996),
          990
Navajo-Hopi Rehabilitation Act
          (1950), 187 (photo)
Navajo (Diné/Dine'é) Indians, 69,
          91, 125, 335, **1021–1024,**
          1021 (photo)
     and agriculture, 316, 318
     and alcoholism/substance
          abuse, 78, 80
     and Baptists, 265–266
     code talkers, 364–367, 365
          (photo)
     and the Colorado River Indian
          Tribes, 1008, 1020
     and Episcopal missionaries, 723
     Gorman, R. C., 732–734
     Grand Council of the, 58
     and Hopi land dispute,
          306–307
     and the IRA, 558
     and the Long Walk, 259–261,
          529, 674–675, 676
     MacDonald, Peter, 776
     Manuelito, 780–781
     and mining issues, 61, 148–151,
          183–185, 547, 601
     and peyote use, 80
     and the Pueblos, 233, 1017
     and removal/relocation issues,
          285, 548
     and sacred sites, 361–362, 364
     and thanksgiving festivals, 474
     and tribal courts, 613
     and weaving, 485, 486–487, 486
          (photo)
Navajo language, 419, 421
     renewing the, 422, 423–424
     and World War II code, 332

Navajo Nation
    and Collier, John, 691
    Dodge, Henry Chee, 713–714
Navajo Times, 184
Navajo Way, 1021–1022
Neah Bay, 1095
Nebraska, 67
Negro Fort, 248–249
Neihardt, John, 443, 658
Nele-chun-dun Business Council,
        1072–1073
Nenana complex, 451
Neolin, 153–154, 380, 396, 802,
    805–806
Nesmith, J. W., 256
Nespelem Indians. *See* Sanpoil
        Indians
The Netherlands, 713
Netsilik Indians, **1340–1343**
Neutral Confederacy, 367
Nevada, 67
Nevada v. Hicks, 181–182
New Agers, **443–444**
New France, **212–214**
The New Indians, 798
New Laws (Spain), 676–677
New Mexico, 144, 145–146, 147,
        183–185
New Pala, 1055
New Pascua, 1042
New Tidings, 398
New Ulm, 257 (photo)
New York Evening Post, 280
New York State, 693
New York Times, 136, 289
New York Times v. Sullivan, 744
Newark, Ohio, mounds, 435, 437, 445
Newfoundland, 203–206, 204
        (photo), 206–207, 727
Newlands, Francis, 600
Newtown, Battle of, 239, 857
Nez, James, 799
Nez Percé Indians, 177, 202, 338, 406,
        1144–1146, 1144 (photo)
    1832 delegation to St. Louis, 877
    and the inter-tribal fish
            commission, 517–518
    Joseph, Younger, 761–763
    Long March, 41, 276–277
    and the Yakima War, 255
Nez Percé Reservation, 1206
Nicaragua, 786–787
Nichol, Fred J., 300–301, 642
Nicholas I, Csar (Russia), 223
Nicholas V, Pope, 466
Nichols, Joanna, 441
Nichols, John, 607
Nightland, 812
Nijoras, 109

Niman, 1012
Nipmuck Indians, 599
Nippissing Indians, 368
Nisenan Indians. *See* Maidu Indians
Nishga Treaty (2003), 508
Nisqually Indians, 95. *See also* Salish
        Indians, Southern Coast
Nisqually Reservation, 1106
Nixluidix (village), 202
Nixon, Richard M., 69, 118
    and Blue Lake, 347
    and Menominee Restoration Act,
        609
    and occupation of Alcatraz
            Island, 287–288, 289, 291
    and occupation of BIA
            headquarters, 640, 656
    and self-determination, 181, 502
Nixon administration
    and the ANCSA, 491
    and Indian activism, 300, 305
    and the Indian Empowerment
            Assistance Program, 867
    Indian policy, 126
Niza, Fray Marcos de, 232, 1026,
        1044
No Child Left Behind Act (NCLB),
        128
No Cross, No Crown, 820
Noble, Joan, 798
Noble savage, myth of the, **439–440**
Nocona, Pete, 815
Nome, 1338
Nome Lackee Reservation,
        1075–1076
Nomlaki Indians. *See* Wintun
        Indians
Nongatl Indians. *See* Wailaki Indians
Nooksack Indians. *See* Salish
        Indians, Central Coast
Nootka Sound Convention, 263
Nootkan Indians, **1096–1098**
Nootkan language, 479
Nordwall, Adam, 807
Norse
    and the Arctic Indians, 1327,
        1334
    at L'Anse aux Meadows,
        203–206, 204 (photo)
    and Leif Erickson, 727–728
North American explorations,
        206–208
North, Frank, 686
North American Energy Summit
        (2004), 701
North American Indian Unity
        Caravan, 647
North Atlantic migration route, 83
North Carolina, 1224

North Dakota Reservation, 1196
North Reservation, 1010
North Slope, 1338
North Slope Native Association,
        1338
North West Company, 394, 536,
        584–585
    and the Plateau Indians, 1138,
        1152
    and the Subarctic Indians, 1300,
        1306, 1307, 1314
North West Territories (NWT), 336,
        590–594, 724
    Inuit Land Claims Commission
            (ILCC), 590
    and Nunavut, 617
Northeast Woodland Indians, 10–11
    craftwork, 337, 339
    and the fur trade, 393–394
    Native groups in the, 1235–1293
    women in, 190–194
    See also Mound Builder cultures
Northeastern Quebec Agreement
        (NQA), 519
Northern Arapaho Indians, 1159,
        1160
Northern Cherokee Indians, 138
Northern Cheyenne Indians, 1167
Northern Michigan Ottawa
        Association (NMOA),
        1271
Northern Quebec Inuit Association,
        1335
Northern Ute Indians, 422
Northwest Alaska Native
        Association, 1338
Northwest Coast migration route, 83
Northwest Coast region, 5–6, 169,
        201–203, 479–480
    crafts, 337, 338, 340, 477–479
    and fishing, 389–392, 461–463
    and the fur trade, 395
    Indian groups in the, 1082–1118
    and potlatches, 454–456
Northwest Indian College (NWIC),
        126–127
Northwest Indian Fisheries
        Commission, 392, 517
Northwest Native American
        Basketweavers
        Association (NNABA),
        338
Northwest Ordinance (1787), 116,
        586–587, 899
Northwest Rebellion, 832–833
Northwest Territory, 244–246,
        852–853
Norton, Gale, 562
Norton, John, 667, 669

Norton culture, 12
Norumbega, 1273
Novo-Arkhangel'sk (Sitka), 221
Nuclear waste, 185–186, 307–309,
    620, 1338
   and Hanford Nuclear
      Reservation, 129,
      133–134
   and Point Hope, Alaska, 129,
      132–133
Numic (Shoshonean) language
    group, 7
Nunavut, 508, 588–594, 588 (photo),
    589 (photo), 617–618,
    1332, 1343. *See also*
    Tunngavik Federation of
    Nunavut (TFN)
Nunavut Land Claims Agreement
    Act (1993), **588–594, 985**
Nunavut Land Claims Project
    (NLCP), 590
Nunavut Tunngavik Inc. (NTI),
    617–618
Nunivak Island, 1347, 1348
Nuttal, Zelia, 427
Nuu-chah-nulth Tribal Council, 1098
Nuuchalnulth language, 479
Nuunamiuts, 1337, 1338
Nuxalt Nation, 1083

Oacpicagigua, Luis, 1026, 1040
Oahe Dam, 374
Oakes, Richard, 287, 289, 290–291,
    806–807
O'Bail, John, 698
Obispeño Indians. *See* Chumash
    Indians
O'Brien, Robert, 646
Occom, Samson, 1275
O'Clock, George, 643–644
Oconee Indians, 1229
O'Connor, Sandra Day, 182, 499
Oconostota, 1214
Odawa Indians, 219
"Of Cannibals," 377
Office for Economic Opportunity
    (OEO), 68, 735
Office of Federal Acknowledgment,
    72–73
Office of Navajo Economic
    Opportunity (ONEO),
    1023
Ogbu, John, 90
Ogden, Peter Skene, 395, 1075
   and the Great Basin Indians,
      1120, 1130
   and the Plateau Indians, 1140
Ogden Land Company, 830, 831
Oglala Lakota College, 125

Oglala Lakota Indians
   and the Battle of the Little
      Bighorn, 275
   tribal conflict at Pine Ridge, 296,
      300–303, 303–304
   Wilson, Richard, 879–881
   See also Lakota Indians
Oglala Sioux Civil Rights
    Organization (OSCRO),
    640, 641
Ohio, 240–243, 436–437, 445, 682
Ohio Canal, 437, 445
Ohio Company, 856
Ohio Historical Society (OHS), 445
Ohio Railroad, 437, 445
Ohio River Valley, 224, 356, 394,
    444–447
Ohio Union of Iroquois League, 240
Oil, 553, 714
   and Alaska, 491
   and the Arctic Indians, 1338,
      1340
   and CERT, 701
   and the Creeks, 1222
   and MacKenzie River Valley
      pipeline, 724
   and the Osage, 448–451, 1198
Ojibwa, Plains, Indians, 1166,
    1193–1196, 1194 (photo)
Ojibwa/Ojibway, Northern, Indians,
    157–158
   and Baptists, 265
   and Canadian treaties, 507
   Copway, George, 697–698
   and the Council of the Three
      Fires, 368
   language, 419
   and Little Turtle's War, 771–772
   mythology and canoes, 355
   and the Tecumseh alliance, 860
   and the Treaty of Greenville, 246
   and the Two Row Wampum belt,
      356
   and War of 1812, 358
   See also Anishinabe/Anishnabe
    Indians
Oka occupation, 508, 510, 511, 602,
    724, 774–775
Oka Reserve, 1260, 1261
Okanagon Indians, **1146**
Okipa ceremony, 1189
Oklahoma
   and the Cherokees, 1214
   and the Choctaws, 1219–1220
   and the Creeks, 1222
   land rush, 45, 279 (photo)
   pan-Indian movement and, 154
   and the Seminoles, 1230
   and the Senecas, 1284

   See also Indian Territory
Oklahoma Indian Welfare Act
    (1936), 557
Oklahoma Indians, 379
Oklahoma Native American
    Basketweavers (ONAB),
    338
Okwanuchu Indians. *See* Shasta
    Indians
Old Crow/Bluefish Cave complex,
    94
Old Indian Legends, 666
Old Northwest Confederacy, 369
Oliphant, Mark David, 594–595
Oliphant v. Suquamish Indian Tribe
    (1978), 181, **594–596, 977**
Oliver, Frank, 98
Ollokot/Ollikut, 276, 277, 762, 1145
Olmec Indians, 339
Olowishkia, 1045
Olympic Games, 865–867
Omaha Indians, 265, 342, 405,
    1196–1197, 1202, 1204
   and agriculture, 318
   LaFlesche family, 766–768
Omaha Reservation, 1197
Omaha World Herald, 284–285
O'Mahoney, Joseph C., 542 (photo)
Omnibus Tribal Lands Leasing Act,
    61
Oñate, Juan de, 19–20, 232
   and the Acoma Pueblos, 1000
   and the San Felipe Pueblos, 1031
   and the San Juan Pueblos, 1033
   and the Sandia Pueblos, 1030
   and the Santa Ana Pueblos, 1034
   and the Taos Pueblos, 1035
Oneida, town of, 159
Oneida Indians, 20, 168, 265, 384,
    564, **1264–1267**
   and the American Revolution,
      237–239
   and gambling operations,
      159–160
   and the Iroquois Confederacy,
      11, 14, 369, 412, 428,
      743–747
   See also Iroquois Confederacy
    (Haudenosaunee)
O'Neill, Dan, 133
Oneniote, 1264
Oneota Indians, 8
The Only Method of Attracting
    Everyone to the True
    Religion, 676
Onondaga Indians, 384, 581,
    1267–1270
   and the American Revolution,
      238, 239

and the Great Council Fire of the
	Confederacy, 708–709,
	749
and the Iroquois Confederacy,
	11, 14, 369, 412, 428,
	743–747
Lyons, Oren, 774–775
See also Iroquois Confederacy
	(Haudenosaunee)
Onondaga Reservation, 1266, 1269
O'odham (Papago) Indians, 1026,
	1039
O'ohenonpa (Two Kettles). *See*
	Lakota Indians
Oowekeeno Indians. *See* Bella Bella
	Indians
Oowekyala language, 479
Opechancanough, 827, 844, 1227
Oral history
	and Athapaskans, 333, 335
	and Canadian land claims,
		510–511
	corn in Iroquois, 319
	and the Goschochking Massacre,
		242
	Hopi, 329
	and the Iroquois Peacemaker,
		411–412
	and the Long Walk, 260
	and migration theory, 3, 82, 201,
		451
	and mound builder cultures,
		436, 444, 446
	and Native writers, 808
	Norse, 204–205, 206–207
	Pueblo, 330
	role of canoes in, 354–355
	and the Sand Creek Massacre, 263
	and the Sun Dance, 471
	See also Legends/stories
Oregon, 67, 849
Oregon Trail, 202, **254–255,** 845, 1120,
	1129
Organization of American States,
	622
*The Origin of the Family, Private
	Property and the State,* 721
Oriskany, Battle of, 239, 857
Ortega, José, 801–802
Ortiz, Simon J., **807–808**
Osage Act of 1906, 448–449, 450
Osage Indians, 265, 449 (photo), 548,
	1197–1198
	and oil rights, **448–451,** 614
Osage Membership Act (2004), 450
Osceola, 34, 250, 345, **808–810,** 809
	(photo), 1230
	and Emathla, Charley, 720–721
Oshara subtradition, 328

Ossernenon, 863
Oswegatchie, 1269
Oto/Otoe Indians, 19, 265, 1192,
	1198–1200, 1199 (photo)
Ottawa and Chippewa Bands, 1271
Ottawa/Odawa Indians, 103, 265,
	356, 392, **1270–1271**
	and the Algonquins, 1237
	and the American Revolution,
		240
	and the Battle of Fallen Timbers,
		245–246
	and the Council of the Three
		Fires, 368
	and Little Turtle's War, 853
	and the Old Northwest
		Confederacy, 369
	Pontiac, 825–826
	and the Tecumseh alliance, 860
	and termination, 288
	and treaties, 174, 175
	and the Wabanaki Confederacy,
		370, 371
	and War of 1812, 358
Ouray, 43, **811–812,** 811 (photo), 1133
Oury, William, 271
Ovando, Nicholas de, 676
Owen, John, 820
Oweneco, 870
Owens, Bill, 701
Owens, Louis, **812–813**
Owens Valley, 1120
	Paiutes, 1073, 1121–1122
	Shoshone, 7
Owhi, 381
Oytes, 1129

Pacific Coast region. *See* Northwest
	Coast region
Pacific Fur Company, 202, 395
Pacific Gas and Electric, 1048
Pacific Salmon Fisheries Treaty, 706
Pagan party, 830
Paine, Thomas, 377, 378, 721
Pais Indians, 1010, 1014
Paiute, Northern, 44, **1119–1121,** 1120
	(photo)
	Winnemucca, 881–882
	Winnemucca, Sarah, 882–883
	Wovoka, 884–885
Paiute, Owens Valley, **1121–1122**
Paiute, Southern, 7, **1123–1125,** 1123
	(photo)
Paiute Indians, 202, 306, 558
	and the Ghost Dance, 396–397,
		398
	Louis, Adrian, 772–773
	and Warm Springs Indian
		Reservation, 203

See also Paiute, Northern; Paiute,
	Owens Valley; Paiute,
	Southern
Paiute-Shoshone Business Council,
	1131
Pajaro Valley Ohlone Indian
	Council, 1054
Pala Reservation, 1054, 1055
Paleo-Indians, 3, 85–86, 328, **451–452**
Palmer, Joel, 255
Palouse Indians, 256
Pamunkey Indians. *See* Powhatan
	Indians
Pamunkey Reservation, 1227–1228
Pan-Indianism, **135–155**
	activism and, 291–292, 293–294
	boarding schools and, 124
	and Brant, Joseph, 668
	and distorting Native
		cosmology, 190
	and the Native American Church
		of North America, 803
	Shawnee and, 23–24
	and the Society of American
		Indians, 846–847
	and urban relocation, 287
	See also Alliances; Political
		organizations
Pancoast, Henry, 723
Papago. *See* Tohono O'odham
	(Papago) Indians
Papago Reservation, 1040
Pappan, Helen, 706
Paraguay, 108–109
Parenteau, Philomena, 784
Parker, Arthur C. (Gawasowaneh),
	382, 738, **813–814,** 829,
	831, 847
Parker, Cynthia Ann, 815
Parker, Ely S. (Donehogä'wa), 176,
	737, 738, **814–815,** 814
	(photo), 1283
Parker, John, 592
Parker, Quanah, 803, **815–816,** 816
	(photo), 1170
Parker Dam, 1008
Parkman, Francis, 698
Parrish, Essie, 348
Parrish, Jasper, 831
Parrón, Fernando, 234–235
Pascua Yaqui, 139
Pascua Yaqui Association, 1042
Pasego, 872
Passamaquoddy/Passamaquoddie
	Indians, 337, 370,
	1271–1272
	land-claim settlement, 72,
		573–575
	and the Maliseets, 1251, 1252

Passports, Haudenosaunee, 173
Pastrana, Julia, 835
Patayan culture, 4, 1014
Patkanim/Patkanin, 839–840, 1105
Patrilineal descent/patrilocal
     residence
     and the Arctic Indians, 1336,
          1346
     and California Indians, 1056,
          1059, 1063, 1071, 1080
     and Canadian law, 1242, 1260,
          1261, 1266, 1269, 1283
     and the Northeast Woodland
          Indians, 1235, 1238, 1243,
          1244, 1255, 1273, 1276,
          1279, 1284, 1289
     and the Northwest Coast Indians,
          1084, 1095, 1096, 1102
     and the Plains Indians, 1163,
          1175, 1176, 1179, 1180,
          1191, 1192, 1196, 1197,
          1199, 1203, 1204
     and Southwest Indians, 1025,
          1027, 1029, 1033, 1037
     and the Subarctic Indians, 1311
Pattea, Clinton, 139
Patuxet Indians, 851
Patwin Indians. See Wintun Indians
Paucatuck Pequots, 1275
Pauketat, Timothy, 350
Paul, Ron, 787
Paul, William, 635
Paul III, Pope, 676
Paulina, 1120
Pawnee Indians, 8, 265, 454, 1197,
          1200–1202, 1201 (photo)
     EchoHawk, Larry, 717–718
     enslaved by French, 168
     and the Ghost Dance, 398
     and horses, 19, 166, 167, 404
     and warfare with Sioux, 373
Pawtucket Indians, 599
Paxton Boys, 240
Payne, John Howard, 36, 551
Payson Reservation, 1007
Peabody, Elizabeth, 883
Peabody Coal Company, 148–151,
          547, 1014
Peabody Museum, Harvard
          University, 336, 339
Peacemaker. See Deganawidah
          (Peacemaker)
Pearson, John, 152
Pecos Classification, 327, 328
Pecos Pueblos. See Jemez Pueblos
Pee-Posh Indians, **1024–1025,** 1026
Pegasus Gold Corporation, 152
Peigan/Piegan Indians, 368, 373
          (photo), 659–661

North, 368, 659–661, 1162–1163,
     1164 (see also
          Blackfeet/Blackfoot
          Indians)
Peltier, Leonard, 155, 300, 301,
          644–645, 657, **817–819,**
          818 (photo)
Pembroke State University, 1224
Pend d'Oreille Indians. See Kalispel
          Indians
Pend Oreille Lake, 1129
Penn, Margaret, 819
Penn, William, 93, 322, 527, **819–821,**
          820 (photo), 1249
     and Indian relations, 859–860
Penn, William, Sr., 819
Pennacook Confederacy, 599
Pennsylvania, 820–821
Penobscot Indians, 337, 370,
          573–575, 1236,
          1272–1274
     and dioxin pollution, 144, 145
Pensoneau, William, 798
Pentecostal Church, 1093
Penutian language family, 5, 6, 1044
     Chinookan division, 1086, 1154
     Coosan and Siuslaw, 1087
     Costanoan, 1053
     Lutuami division, 1139, 1142
     Maiduan, 1060
     Miwokan, 1062
     Sahaptian division, 1140, 1144,
          1153, 1155
     Wintun, 1074
     Yotus, 1078
People's Institute, 689
Peoria Indians. See Illinois Indians
Peoria Tribe of Oklahoma, 1245
Pepys, Samuel, 819
Pequot Indians, 72, 314, 869–870,
          1274–1276
     Apess, William, 650
     gambling operations, 135–136,
          160
     and the Pequot War, 216–218
     and Williams, Roger, 879
Pequot Times, 1275
Pequot War, 142, 168, **216–218,** 217
          (photo), **892**
     and the Mohegans, 869, 870
     and the Narragansetts, 672, 1263
     and the Wampanoags, 1287
Performance art, 1094
Perrin v. United States, 598
Pesticides, 131–132
Peters, Isaac, 513
Peters, Richard, 513, 568, 671
Peterson, Gary, 302
Peterwegeschick, 354

Petroglyphs/pictographs, 425–427,
          426 (photo)
Peyote, 80, 154
     access to, 496, 498–499
     criminalization versus religious
          freedom and, 362–363
     and the Great Basin Indians,
          1126
     and the Native American
          Church of North
          America, 801–803
     and the Plains Indians, 1160,
          1167, 1170
Phillips, Loren, 414
Philosophy, 376–378, 440, 487. See
          also Political philosophy;
          Worldviews
Philp, Kenneth, 552, 557, 689
Phipps, Bill, 101–102
Phoenix Indian School, 125
Piankeshaws, 246
Pick, Lewis A., 374
Pickering, Timothy, 511–512, 512
          (photo)
Picotte, Henri, 766
Picuris Pueblo, **1025–1026**
Pierce, Franklin, 1081
Piikani/Pikuni. See Peigan/Piegan
          Indians
Pikangikum, 157–158
Pike, Zebulon, 1202
Pilgrims, 475 (photo), 476, 783–784,
          851–852, 1287
Pima Indians, 4, 266, 1024,
          1026–1028, 1027 (photo),
          1039
     and diabetes, 378, 379
Pima Revolt of 1751, 1040
Pine Nut Dance, 1134
Pine Ridge Reservation, 53, 80, 156,
          157 (photo)
     murders on, **300–303,** 639,
          643–645, 651, 652
     Oglala Lakota College, 125
     reign of terror at, 154–155, 296,
          817–818
     and Wilson, Richard, 879–881
     and Wounded Knee occupation,
          71, 640–642
     See also Wounded Knee,
          occupation of
Pine Tree Chiefs/warriors, 1266
The Pioneers, 694
Pipes, 167, **453–454,** 453 (photo)
     Adena, 313
     and pipestone, 679, 1186, 1193
Pipestone Creek, 454
Pipestone Reservation, 1193
Piro Indians, 1038

Piro Pueblo of Senecú, 1039
Piscataway Indians, 1262
Pit River Indians, 807. *See also*
        Achumawi Indians
Pitt, William, the Elder, 225–226
Pizzaro, Francisco, 105
Place names, 163–165, 325, 419,
        468–469. *See also* Names,
        stereotypical
Plains Apaches, 8, **1157–1158**
Plains Indians
    and alcoholism, 158
    and beadwork, 340
    buffalo economy of, 348–350
    Catlin's depictions of, 678
    and counting coup, 372–373
    groups of, 1157–1207
    and horses, 405, 406
    and the IRA, 558
    and ledger books, 427
    and poverty, 156
    resistance and, 255, 266–267
    settlement patterns and disease,
        110
    and the Sun Dance, 471–472
    treaties with, 175, 529–532
    See also Sign language/signaling
        systems
Plains Wars, 770, 873. *See also* Great
        Sioux War (1875-1877)
Plaiting, 337
Plateau region, 6–7
    crafts, 338, 340
    Indian groups in the, 1136–1156
    and missionaries, 876–877
    and Seven Drums Religion,
        465–466
    and trade, 202
    and the Washani religion,
        380–381, 845–846
    and the Yakima War, 255–256
Plenary power, **596–598**, 614, 623
Plenty Coups, **822–823,** 822 (photo),
        873, 1173
Plint, Arthur, 101
Pliny, 353
*Ploughed Under: The Story of an Indian
        Chief,* 767
Pocahontas, 192, 322, **823–824,** 824
        (photo), 844
Pohl, Frederick, 207
Point Hope, Alaska, 129, 132–133
Pojoaque Pueblo, **1028–1029**
Pokanoket Indians, 783–784,
        851–852. *See also*
        Wampanoag Indians
Policy, U.S.
    allotment and, 278–282, 570
    assimilation and, 43, 47, 48, 50,

65, 88–90, 540–541
    and the BIA, 501–503
    and education, 124–127, 127–128
    eugenics, 884
    as facilitating genocide, 89, 142
    and fiscal conservatism, 74
    Grant's Peace, **268–270,** 269
        (photo)
    and Indian economic
        development, 116–122
    and Indian religious freedom,
        496–498
    and the Indian Reorganization
        Act, 552–558, 691
    and language preservation, 422
    Meriam Report on, 576–577
    and the NCAI, 795–797
    and Parker, Ely, as Indian
        Commissioner, 814–815
    on sovereignty and land
        ownership issues, 69,
        146–148, 179–182,
        287–289, 291
    termination, 66–68, 91, 137,
        541–542, 607–610
    and trade and intercourse acts,
        610–612
    and water rights, 187–189
Political mobilization. *See* Activism,
        political
Political organizations
    AIM, 638–646
    the Alaska Native Brotherhood,
        635–636
    the All Indian Pueblo Council
        (AIPC), 637
    in Canada, 653–654
    and James Bay hydroelectric
        project, 692–693
    the National Indian Youth
        Council, 797–799
    the NCAI, 795–797
    and termination and urban
        relocation policies, 734
    and Women of All Red Nations
        (WARN), 883–884
    See also specific organizations
Political philosophy, 155, 721–722,
        782–783, 791–792
Politicians
    Campbell, Ben Nighthorse,
        669–670
    Curtis, Charles, 706–708
    EchoHawk, Larry, 718
    LaDuke, Winona, 765–766
    St. Clair, Arthur, 852
Politics
    and the Alaska Native
        Brotherhood, 635–636

captivity narratives as
        metaphors in, 359
    Cherokee, 835–836, 874–875
    economic development and
        tribal, 120, 121
    Mankiller, Wilma, and Cherokee,
        780
    Navajo, 1023
    on Pine Ridge reservation,
        786–787, 879–881
    See also Factionalism; Tribal
        government
Polk, James K., 395
Pollution, 129–134, 144, 145–146
    at Akwesasne, 633
    and Cape Thompson area, 1338
    and coal, 148–151
    and Cree lands, 1303
    effect on basketry of, 338
    and fishing, 849
    on Iroquois lands, 513
    mining on Navajo lands and,
        1023
    and uranium mining, 184–186
    and Ward Valley hazardous
        waste dump, 307–309
Polo, Marco, 353
Pombo, Richard, 563
Pommersheim, Frank, 614
Pomo Indians, 347, 807, 1049,
        1065–1067, 1066 (photo)
Ponca Indians, 548, 604–605, 1197,
        1202–1204, 1202 (photo)
    fund raising by the, 755–756, 767
    Standing Bear, 853–854
    and Treaty of Fort Laramie
        (1868), 171, 177
    Warrior, Clyde, 871–872
Pond, Peter, 357
Pontiac, 153–154, 225 (photo), 356,
        825–826, 825 (photo),
        1271
    killing of, 1245
    and Neolin, 805, 806
    Reasons for Making War on the
        English Speech, **896**
    Seneca alliance with, 173
    spiritualism underpinnings of
        alliance, 396
Pontiac's Rebellion, 736, 826
    and the Anishinabes, 1239
    and the Kickapoos, 1247
    and the Lenápes, 1249
    and the Miamis, 1255
    and the Potawatomis, 1277
    and the Senecas, 1283
    and the Shawnees, 1285
    and the Wyandottes, 1292
Pony Express, 686, 1130

Pooley, Orin, 414
Poor Bear, Myrtle, 301, 818
Poor Peoples' Campaign, 798
Popé, 220, 1000, 1017, 1028, 1030, 1032, 1035
Poppleton, A. J., 605, 854
Population. *See* Demographics, historical
Port Alberni Residential School, 101
Porter, Pleasant, 739
Porter, Tom, 412, 475
Porterfield, Kay Marie, 320, 321, 324–325
Portolá, Gaspar de, 1060
Portugal, 178, 208
Post, Wiley, 834
Post-traumatic stress disorder (PTSD), 378–379
Potatoes, 315, 316
Potawatomi Indians, 103, 174, 219, 265, **1276–1278,** 1277 (photo)
    and the American Revolution, 240
    and the Battle of Fallen Timbers, 245–246
    and the Council of the Three Fires, 368
    and lacrosse, 417
    and Little Turtle's War, 771–772, 853
    and the Old Northwest Confederacy, 369
    and the Two Row Wampum belt, 356
    and Van Horne captivity narrative, 360
Potlatch, 6, **454–456,** 455 (photo), 478
    criminalization of, 362, 538, 1092
    and the Northwest Coast Indians, 1086, 1091, 1093, 1094, 1095, 1096, 1098, 1101, 1104, 1107, 1115
    and the Plateau Indians, 1142
    and the Subarctic Indians, 1296, 1297, 1298, 1308, 1310, 1314, 1317, 1318
Pottery, **456–458**
    and the Ancient Pueblo, 328, 329
    and the Arapahos, 1158
    and Blackfeet Indians, 1163
    and the Hohokam culture, 401, 402
    and Mississippian culture, 432
    and Mogollon culture, 433, 434–435
    and pre-contact Indians, 4, 5, 8, 10–12

and Pueblos, 999 (photo), 1000
    and the Quapaws, 1205
    San Ildefonso, 1020
Potts, Gary G., 356
Poundmaker, 1171
Poverty, 57, 67, 120, 124, 796
    and addiction problems, 77, 79
    and the Great Basin Indians, 1135
    and land sales, 554, 668
    and Native Hawai'ians, 532–533
    and the Northeast Woodland Indians, 1254, 1272, 1278
    at Pikangikum, 157
    and Plains Indians, 156
    and the Plateau Indians, 1156
Poverty Point, 9
Poverty Point Earthworks, 435
Powder River country, 274, 275–276, 530, 828
Powder River War, 176
Powell, John Wesley, 51, 90, 420, 500
Powell, Peter, 280
Powell, William, 809
Powhatan (Wahunsonacock), 823, **826–827,** 827 (photo), 1227
    Remarks to Captain John Smith, **891**
Powhatan Confederacy, 823, 826–827, 844–845, 1226
Powhatan Indians, **1226–1228**
Powley, Roddy, 519, 579
Powley, Steve, 519, 579, 579 (photo)
Pownall, Thomas, 747
Pratt, Richard Henry, 89, 96, 97, 127, 143, 497
    and Bonnin, Gertrude Simmons, 666
    and the Hampton Normal and Agricultural Institute, 766
Praying Villages of Massachusetts, **599–600**
Presbyterian Church, 526
    and boarding schools in Canada, 99, 101–102
    and the Northwest Coast Indians, 1092, 1113
    and the Plateau Indians, 1136
    and the Southwest Indians, 1024, 1026
Price, David, 301
Price, Hiram, 497
Principal Dogs, 1182
Prior appropriation (water rights), 187–189, 625–626

Prisoners, 499
The Problem of Indian Administration, 58
Property rights, 582–584, 775, 803
Prophet movement, 396, 1105, 1152, 1296
Prophetstown, 864, 865
Protestant missionaries, 47, 87, 541
Proto-Athapaskan language, 333
Prucha, Francis Paul, 610, 611–612
Prudden, T. M., 329
Public Law 280 (1953), 66–67, 137, 147, 180–181, 609, 613, **961**
Public schools, 123 (photo), 124–125, 128
Puckeshinwa, 860, 864
Pueblo Grande Museum and Park, 401 (photo)
Pueblo Indians, 4, 40, 216, 266
    and agriculture, 317–318
    and Collier, John, 690
    and crafts, 458, 485–486
    and horses, 19, 404
    land losses and, 553, 576
    and the Navajos, 259, 1022
    Ortiz, Simon J., 807–808
    and political activism, 637
    and sovereignty/land rights, 146–147
    and Spanish missions, 232, 233
    and water rights, 187
    See also Ancestral Puebloan culture; Pueblo Revolt (1680); *specific Pueblo groups*
Pueblo Lands Act (1924), 1001, 1028, 1037
Pueblo Revolt (1680), 153, **220,** 233, 1009
    and the Hopi, 1014
    and the Jemez Pueblos, 1017
    Ortiz, Simon J., on, 808
    and the Pojoaque Pueblos, 1028
    and the San Felipe Pueblo, 1032
    and the San Ildefonso Pueblos, 1032
    and the Sandia Pueblos, 1030
    and the Taos Pueblos, 1035
    Tigua Indians and refugees from the, 1038
    and the Zia Pueblos, 1044
    and the Zunis, 1044
Pulling, John, 236
Purisimeño Indians. *See* Chumash Indians
Puritans, 216–218, 319, 719–720, 787–789

Pushmataha, 1219
Puyallup Indians, 390, 1106. *See also* Salish Indians, Southern Coast
Pyke, Mathew, 718
Pyramid Lake Paiute Tribe v. Morton, **600–601**
Pyramid Lake War, 882, 1120, 1121

Quakers, 46, 269–270, 525, **819–821**, 860
Qual-chin, 255
Qualla Cooperative, 338
Quapaw Indians, 1197, **1204–1205**
Quapaw Reservation, 1143, 1271
Quartz Valley Rancheria, 1069
Quebec, 375, 519–520, 565–568
    Battle of, 226
Quebec Association of Indians, 565
Quechan Indians, 1010, 1014, **1029–1030**
Quechua language, 419
Queen Charlotte Strait, 1093
Queenston Heights, 357
Quileute Indians, **1098–1099**
Quinault Indians, 705–706. *See also* Salish Indians, Southwestern Coast
Quinault Reservation, 1086, 1098, 1106
Quinault River Treaty (1855), 1108
Qukiqtaaluk, 1325

Rabbit-Tail, 1130 (photo)
Racial identification, 416
    and Indianness, 50–54, 52n, 54n, 61–62 (*see also* Indianness)
    and the Seminoles, 345–346
    See also Racism
Racism, 44, 142, 723
    and California gold rush, 229
    and Canadian policy, 505, 507, 511
    and Clark, George Rogers, 682
    and competency proceedings, 53–54
    and interpreting mound building cultures, 437, 445
    and the Law of Nations, 208
    and mascots, 431
    Meriam Report on, 577
    and squaw as a derogatory term, 163
    and theory of racial hierarchy, 665

Radiation Exposure Compensation Act (1990), **601–602**
Radioactivity, 184–186, 601–602. *See also* Hazardous waste
Rafinesque, Constantine Samuel, 93
Raids. *See* Warfare/violence
Railroads
    in Canada, 832
    and Cody, William, 686
    expansionism and, 39, 40, 41, 43–44, 45
    and the Hopi, 1014
    and the Hualapais, 1015
    and the Pueblos, 1001, 1025, 1037
    and the Subarctic Indians, 1297, 1303
    and the Tohono O'odham, 1040
Rainbow Bridge, 364
Rains, Gabriel, 255, 256
Ramah Navajo High School, 125
Ramirez, Juan, 1000
Ramona, 756
Ramsey, Alexander, 258, 259, 529, 770
Ranápe Indians. *See* Powhatan Indians
Rancherias
    and the Achumawis, 1048
    and the Miwoks, 1062, 1063
    and the Monos, 1064
    and the Pomos, 1067
    recognition by the Supreme Court, 1067
    and the Wintuns, 1076
Ration, Norman, 799
Readings in Jurisprudence and Legal Philosophy, 688
Reagan, Ronald, 148, 979
Real Bird, Edison, 798
Red Cloud (Makhpyia-luta), 703, 815, **827–829**, 828 (photo), 1187, 1188
    and the Fort Laramie Treaty, 176, 530, 531 (photo)
Red Deer School, 100
Red Dog, 815
Red Jacket (Sagoyewatha), **829–831**, 830 (photo), 1283
    and the American Revolution, 238, 699
    and the Canandaigua Treaty, 512
    and Handsome Lake, 735, 737
Red Lake Reservation, 92
Red Man in the United States, 576
Red Power movement, 71, **292–297**, 779–780
Red Rock Reservation, 1200

Red Sticks, 246–248, 247 (photo), 809, 1222. *See also* Creek War (Red Stick War)
Red Thunder, 152
Red Tomahawk, 283
The Redeemed Captive, 359
Redford, Robert, 289
Redman's Appeal for Justice, 713
Redner, Russell, 642
Rehnquist, William, 182, 594, 595
Reid, Bill, 355
Reid, Harry, 138
Reindeer herding, 1338, 1348
Religion
    and Black Elk, 659
    boarding schools and, 79
    Bole-Maru, 347–348
    and Cahokia, 352
    and Christianity in legitimizing conquest, 179
    and clashing Indian/European worldviews, 15–16
    Deloria, Jr., Vine, on, 712
    and the Hopewell culture, 403
    Indian retention of, 71
    and interfaith services, 775
    and the Iroquois Confederacy, 428–429
    and Marxism, 783
    Native American, 361–364
    Native prophets, 806
    New Agers, 443–444
    Northeast Woodland cosmology, 190–191
    and Parker, Quanah, 816
    and pre-contact Indians, 4–12
    Quakers, 819–820
    role in addiction treatment, 81
    role of corn in, 318
    and salmon, 462
    Seven Drums, 381, 465–466, 846
    spiritual significance of lacrosse, 417
    and syncretism in Spanish America, 216
    See also Ceremonies/festivals; Ghost Dance; Indian Shaker religion; Katsinas/katchinas; Longhouse Religion (Gaiwí:yo); Native American Church; Repression, religious; Sacred sites; *specific Indian groups*; Sun Dance; Washani religion (Dreamer cult)
Religious Crimes Act (1883), 346

Religious freedom
   congressional action and, 495–499
   and legacy of John Collier, 691–692
   and *Lyng v. Northwest Indian Cemetery Protective Association,* 572–573
   and Quakers, 819–821
   and Williams, Roger, 878
   See also Repression, religious
Religious Freedom Restoration Act (1993), 498
Religious groups, Euro-American, 269–270, 541. *See also specific religions*
Religious Land Use and Institutionalized Persons Act (2000), 499
Relocation, urban, 66, 71, 79, **285–287**
   activism against, 294, 734
   and the BIA, 502
   and Mankiller, Wilma, 779
   and the NCAI, 796
   termination and, 91, 609
"Remarks Concerning the Savages of North America," 377
Removal
   and Canadian policies, 506
   and dam projects, 374
   forced marches, 528–529
   as a form of genocide, 142–143
   and Jackson, Andrew, 752–754
   and mining activities, 149, 150, 151–152
   and pan-Indianism, 497
   and Southeast Indians, 32–37, 1219, 1222, 1229–1230, 1234
   and Western expansionism, 46
   and *Worcester v. Georgia,* 626–628
   See also Indian Territory; *specific Indian groups;* Trail of Tears
Removal Act (1830), 32, 752
Renewal of Sacred Arrows, 1165
Reno, Marcus, 275
Repression, cultural
   boarding school attacks on identity, 96, 97–98, 99
   Canada and, 538
   and Indian confederacies, 371
   myth of the noble savage as justifying, 439–440
   and Native languages, 421–422
Repression, religious, 360–364, 496–497, 553–554

   ban on ceremonies, 89, 90, 98, 689–690
   and peyote use, 803
   Religious Crimes Act, 346
   reversal of, 91
   and Seven Drums Religion, 465
   and Spanish America, 220, 227
   and the Sun Dance, 471
   and the Washani religion, 381
Reservations
   allotment and, 56–57, 278–282 (*see also* Allotment)
   boarding schools on, 98
   economic and social conditions on, **156–162**
   expansionism and, 41–48
   gaming operations and revenue for, 140
   and Grant's peace policy, 269
   and *Lone Wolf v. Hitchcock,* 569–571
   mineral and metal extractions from, 129 (*see also* Mining)
   and the Spanish, 215
   termination of, 67 (*see also* Termination)
   and water rights, 187–189
   See also Land ownership; Removal; *specific reservations and Indian groups*
Reserves, Canadian
   and the Northeast Woodland Indians, 1236, 1237–1238, 1252, 1293
   and the Plateau Indians, 1141, 1142, 1149, 1152
   and the Subarctic Indians, 1297, 1298, 1300, 1303, 1313
Resighini Rancheria, 1081
Resistance, Native
   to allotment, 570–571
   Anishinabe nations and, 356–357
   and the Cherokee syllabary, 841
   and the Crazy Snake Movement, 739
   non-violent, 228
   and pan-Indianism, 153–154
   to removal, 548
   and Spanish missions, 227–228, 234
   and the Washani religion, 845–846, 848
   See also Warfare/violence
Resource management
   and CERT, 701–702
   and the Columbia River Inter-

   Tribal Fish Commission, 517–518
   dams and conflict over, 373–375
   fishing rights and environmental concerns, 392
   and the ISDEAA, 560
   timber, 1254
   See also Fishing rights; Water rights
The Return of the Native: American Indian Political Resurgence, 289
Revenge of the Pequots, 136
Revenue
   coal mining/electricity generation, 149, 151
   gambling operations and, 140, 158–159, 160, 545–546
   and mining, 546, 547
   the Osage and oil, 448–451
   See also Economic development; Funds, government
Revere, Paul, 236–237
Revitalization movements
   and Bole-Maru, 347
   and the Ghost Dance, 398
   and renewing language, 418, 422–424 (*see also* Language)
   and the Washani religion, 380–381
Revolutionary War
   and the Battle of Fallen Timbers, 244–246
   Boston Tea Party, 236–237, 237 (photo)
   and Brant, Joseph, 667, 668
   and the Cherokees, 174
   and Clark, George Rogers, 681–682
   and the Goschochking Massacre, 240–243
   and the Great Lakes region, 357
   and Handsome Lake, 736
   and the Iroquois, 699, 856–858
   Native American participation in, **237–239**
   and the Northeast Woodland Indians, 1239, 1242, 1249, 1250, 1254, 1255, 1260, 1266, 1269, 1271, 1274, 1277–1278, 1283, 1285, 1290, 1292
   and Red Jacket, 829
   and St. Clair, Arthur, 852
   and the Southeast Indians, 1211, 1214, 1216, 1221, 1231, 1233

Reynolds, John, 662
Reynolds, Joseph, 1187
Rhoads, Charles, 55, 501
Rhode Island, 72
Ribault, Jean, 341
Rich, E. E., 534
Richardson, Bill, 701
Richardson, John, 830
Riddle, Frank, 674, 1143 (photo)
Riddle, Toby (Winema), 674, 1143
        (photo)
Ridge, John, 253, 680, 777, 874
Ridge, Major, 253, 874
Riel, Louis, 101, 717, **831–833,** 832
        (photo), 1171, 1195, 1240
Riggs, Stephen, 420, 421
Riley, Del, 653
Rio Grande Pueblo Indians, 558, 998
Rio Grande River Valley, 145, 232,
        233, 327
Rio Puerco, 185–186
River Yumans, 1010, 1014
Roanoke Colony, 20–21, 827
Roberts, Lawrence, 799
Robideau, Bob, 644–645, 818
Robinson, Fred, 398
Robinson, Viola, 603
Rochester Museum, 813
Rock paintings, 1052
Rock Point Community School, 423
Rocky Boy Reservation, 80, 1171,
        1240
Rocky Mountain region, trapping
        system in, 394, 395
Roe, Frank Gilbert, 406
Rogers, Richard, 441
Rogers, Robert, 225 (photo), 825
        (photo), 826
Rogers, Rox, 100–101
Rogers, Will, **833–834,** 833 (photo)
Rogin, Michael Paul, 516
Rogue River War (1855-1856), 44,
        1072, 1077, 1088, 1117,
        1156
    and the Salishes, 1105, 1108
Rolfe, John, 824
Rolfe, Thomas, Jr., 824
Rolling Thunder, 647
Roman Nose, 266, 267
Romanus Pontifex, 208
Romer, Querino, 346–347
Romero, Francisco, 271
Romero, Juan de Jesus, 347
Rominger, Mac, 156
Roosevelt, Franklin D., 497, 691, 834
Roosevelt, Theodore, 50, 346, 739,
        768, 769
Rose, Wendy, **834–835**

Rosebud, Battle of the, 705, 842, 873,
        1187
Rosebud Reservation, 53, 80, 125
Ross, Alexander, 202
Ross, John, 32, 33, 36–37, 254, 549,
        551, 626, **835–836**
    and *The Cherokee Phoenix,* 680
    and the Civil War, 1214
    and the Treaty of New Echota,
        253, 777
    and Watie, Stand, 874–875
Rough Rock Demonstration School,
        125
Round Valley Reservation, 1048,
        1061
Rounds, Mike, 701
Rousseau, Jean-Jacques, 376, 377,
        440
Rowland, Bill, 715
Rowlandson, Mary, 359
Royal Canadian Mounted Police
        (RCMP), 1325, 1332, 1342
Royal Commission on Aboriginal
        Peoples (RCAP), 99–100,
        102, 510, **602–604,** 724
Royal Commission on the Economic
        Union and Development
        Prospects for Canada,
        592
Royal Proclamation of 1763, 116,
        356–357, 505, 520, **897**
Rumsey v. Wilson, 139
*Runner in the Sun: A Story of Indian
        Maize,* 785
Running Brave, 791
Running Strong for American Indian
        Youth, 790–791
Rupert's Land, 534–536, 565
Rush, Benjamin, 859
Russell, Charles M., 405 (photo)
Russell, Peter, 669
Russian American Company,
        221–224, 264, 395, 1113
Russian Orthodox Church
    in Alaska, 221–224, 222 (photo),
        264
    and the Arctic Indians, 1323,
        1345, 1348
    and the Subarctic Indians, 1309,
        1319–1320
    and the Tlingits, 1113
Russians, 19, 168, **221–224**
    and the Arctic Indians, 1322,
        1323, 1337, 1345, 1348
    and California Indians, 1062,
        1066
    and Northwest Coast Indians,
        1095, 1113

    and the Subarctic Indians, 1309,
        1319
    and U.S. purchase of Alaska,
        263–265

Sac and Fox News, 1280
Sac Indians. *See* Sauk/Sac Indians
Sacagawea/Sakakawea, 30, **836–838,**
        837 (photo), 1128
Sacred Buffalo Hat ceremony, 1165
Sacred Hoop, 279–280
The Sacred Pipe, 659
Sacred sites, 458–461, 459 (photo),
        692
    access to, 496, 498, 499
    and the Black Hills, 646
    Blue Lake, 1035–1036
    and *Lying v. Northwest Indian
        Cemetery Protective
        Association,* 572–573
    and the Yurok, 1081
Sacred Sites Executive Order, 582
Sacred Soul, 657
Sahaptin language group, 6
Saint Lawrence Island, 1346–1348
Saint Lawrence River, 130
Saint Paul residential school, 98
Salem, 240–243
Salinan Indians, **1067–1068**
Salish Indians, 410, **1147**
    Central Coast, **1099–1102,** 1100
        (photo)
    Northern Coast, **1102–1103**
    Southern Coast, **1103–1106**
    Southwestern Coast, **1106–1108**
Salish language family, 176, 419
    Bella Coola, 1084
    central division, 1099, 1102, 1103
    and the Colvilles, 1137
    interior division, 1147, 1149,
        1150, 1151, 1152
        Lillooet, 1142
    and the Okanagons, 1146
    and the Plateau region, 6
    in the Northwest Coast area, 6
    and the Southwestern Coast
        Salish, 1106
    Tillamook, 1109
Salmon, **461–463**
    and fishing rights controversies,
        389
    and Northwest tribes, 201–202
    and pre-contact Indians, 5, 6, 7
    and the Wanapam, 848–849
    See also Fishing rights
Salt Lake (New Mexico), 458–459
Salt River Pima-Maricopa Indian
        community, 139, 156

Salt River Reservation, 1024, 1026
Salteaux Indians, 1195. *See also*
      Anishinabe/Anishnabe
      Indians; Ojibwa, Plains,
      Indians
Salvatierra, Juan Maria de, 234
Samek, Hana, 368
Samish Indians. *See* Salish Indians,
      Central Coast
Samoset, 851–852, 1287
San Antonia de Padua, 1068
San Carlos Project, 1026–1027
San Carlos Reservation, 1003,
      1006–1007
San Diego de Alcalá, 22, 1071
San Felipe Pueblo, **1031–1032,** 1031
      (photo)
San Fernando mission, 108
San Francisco, social services in,
      294
San Francisco Chronicle, 290
San Geronimo at Taos, 1035
San Ildefonso Pueblo, **1032–1033**
San Joaquin Valley, 1078
San Juan Capistrano Mission, 1060
San Juan Pueblo, **1033–1034**
San Lorenzo Martir mission, 108
San Luis Rey Mission, 1060
San Pedro Valley, 270
San Xavier Del Bac Mission, 228
      (photo)
San Xavier Reservation, 1040
Sand Creek Massacre, 142, **261–263,**
      262 (photo), 664
    apology/compensation for, 176
    and the Arapahos, 1160
    and the Cheyennes, 1167
    Ortiz, Simon J., on, 808
    Report of the Joint Committee
      on the Conduct of the
      War, **920**
Sand Creek Massacre National
      Historic Site, 670
Sand Creek Reservation, 663
Sand Papago/Hia-ced O'odham. *See*
      Tohono O'odham
      (Papago) Indians
Sanday, Peggy Reeves, 353
Sandia Pueblo, **1030–1031**
Sandoz, Mari, 715
Sandpaintings, 1059
Sangre de Cristo Mountains, 1025
Sanpoil Indians, **1147–1149**
Sans Arcs, 275
Santa Ana Pueblo, **1034**
Santa Barbara, 227
Santa Barbara Indians. *See* Chumash
      Indians

Santa Clara Pueblo, **1034–1035**
Santa Fe Indian Market, 339
Santa Fe Trail, 1000, 1009, 1022,
      1033
Santa Gertrudis mission, 108
Santa Rosa Rancheria, 108, 1079
Santa Ynez Reservation, 1051, 1052
Santa Ysabel Indians, 557
Santee Reservation, 1176
Santee Sioux Indians, 80, 275. *See
      also* Dakota Indians
Santo Domingo Pueblo, 339, **1035**
Sapir, Edward, 420, 441
Saponi Indians, 1242
Sarcee Indians, 333, 1163, 1295
Sargent, Bill, 299
Sarracino, Marvin, 184 (photo)
Sarris, Greg, 347
Saskatchewan, 832
Sassacus, 1274, 1275
Sassafras root, 322
Satanta (White Bear), 764, 1183
Sauk/Sac Indians, 46, 175, 742,
      1278–1280
    and Black Hawk, 251–252, 661
    and the Council of the Three
      Fires, 368
    and the Fox Indians, 1243–1244
Sauk-Suiattle Indians. *See* Salish
      Indians, Southern Coast
Sayres, Ken, 302
Scalia, Antonin Gregory, 182
Scalping, 324–325, **463–464,** 464
      (photo), 483, 484
Scarfaced Charley, 674
Scarrooyady, 158, 513–514, 730
Schaaf, Angie Yan, 339
Schaaf, Gregory, 339
Schaefer and Hebior archaeology
      sites, 84
Schaghticoke Indians. *See* Pequot
      Indians
Schmidt, Harold, 303
Schneider, Andrew, 151, 152
Schneider, Iyawata Britten, 150
Schneider, Keith, 134
Scholder, Fritz, **838–839**
Schonchin John, 673, 674
Schoolcraft, Henry Rowe, 387, 695,
      698, 751
Schurz, Carl, 280–281, 882, 883
Schuylkill Fishing Company, 860
Schwarzenegger, Arnold, 140
Schweig, Eric, 773
Science
    Deloria, Jr., Vine, on, 711, 712
    Indian contributions to, 321
    and Kennewick Man, 415–416

    and Mount Graham observatory,
      398–399
    See also Human remains
Scorched-earth strategy, 142, 239,
      858, 1122, 1214
    against Navajos, 259, 260, 529,
      675, 1023
Scots, 584–585, 1224, 1302, 1325
Scott, Duncan Campbell, 712–713
Scott, Jennifer, 706
Scott, Randy, 706
Scott, Thomas, 832
Scott, Winfield, 253
Scout, Warner, 98
Sea mammals, 222, 336, 395, 455,
      1345
    and pre-contact Indians, 10, 11,
      12
    whaling, 1327, 1328–1329, 1330,
      1334, 1340
*The Search for an American Indian
      Identity,* 408
Sea'th'l/Seattle, 169, **839–840,** 839
      (photo), 1105
    Farewell Speech, **918**
Seattle, 1106
Secakuku, Ferrell, 150–151
Sekani Indians, **1313–1314**
Self-determination. *See*
      Sovereignty
Self-Determination and Education
      Act (1975), 69
Selkirk, Lord, 585
Sells, Cato, 53, 54, 55
Seminole Indians, 34, 265,
      1228–1230, 1228 (photo)
    and beadwork, 340
    Black, 314–315, 314 (photo),
      344–346
    and the Creeks, 1222
    Emathla, Charley, 720–721
    and gambling operations, 137,
      138, 158
    language of, 438–439
    Osceola, 808–810
    and removal, 33, 142, 548, 753
    and the Seminole Wars, 248–251,
      249 (photo) (*see also*
      Seminole Wars)
    and slaves, 466
    and treaties, 176, 252
    and the Yuchis, 1234
Seminole Nation of Oklahoma
      (SNO), 345–346
Seminole Negro Indian Scouts, 315
Seminole Tribe of Florida v. Florida,
      138, 139, 545
Seminole v. Butterfield, 137

Seminole Wars, **248–251**, 315, 344, 345, 1229–1230
   first, 777, 809
   second, 808, 810
Senate Special Subcommittee on Indian Education, 124
Seneca Indians, 193, 383, 548, **1280–1284**, 1281 (photo)
   alliance with Pontiac, 173, 816
   and the American Revolution, 238–239, 240
   and the Beaver Wars, 219
   and the Canandaigua Treaty, 511–513
   Cornplanter, 698–700
   and dam project, 374
   Handsome Lake, 735–738
   and the Iroquois Confederacy, 11, 14, 369, 412, 428, 743–747
   Mohawk, John C., 791–792
   as mound builders, 444, 446
   Parker, Arthur C., 813–814
   Parker, Ely, 814–815
   Red Jacket, 829–831
   See also Iroquois Confederacy (Haudenosaunee)
Seneca Nation of Indians, 1283
Seneca of Sandusky, 1260
Seneca Reservation, 1293
Sequasson, 672
Sequoyah, 35, 420, 679–680, **840–841**, 841 (photo), 1214
Sequoyah v. T.V.A., 364
Serra, Junípero, 108, 234–235
Serrano Indians, **1068–1069**
Settlement patterns
   Adena, 313
   agriculture and village relocation, 212
   Ancient Puebloan, 328–329, 330
   and Athapaskans, 336
   and epidemics, 106, 110, 111
   and the Hopewell culture, 403
   and Mogollon culture, 434
Seven Council Fires, 1184, 1192
Seven Drums Religion, 381, **465–466**, 846, 848
Seven Nations of Canada, 370
Seven Oaks, Battle of, 585
Seven Years' War. *See* French and Indian War
Sevier Complex, 1131
Seward, William H., 264 (photo), 265
Seward Peninsula, 144
Seward Peninsula Native Association, 1338
Shakespeare, William, 378

Shakopee Mdewakanton Sioux tribe, 159
Shakpe, 258
Shalako, 1045
Shamanism, 5, 98, 322, 363, 403. *See also specific Indian groups*
The Sharpest Sight, 812
Shasta Indians, **1069–1070**
Shaw, Benjamin F., 840
Shawnee Indians, 23–24, 265, **1284–1286**
   and the American Revolution, 240
   and the Battle of Fallen Timbers, 245–246
   and Brant, Joseph, 668
   and the Carlisle Treaty Council, 513–514
   and Clark, George Rogers, 681, 682
   and Fort Ancient culture, 444, 446, 447
   and Little Turtle's War, 771–772, 853
   and the Old Northwest Confederacy, 369
   and Penn, William, 821
   and Pontiac, 816
   Tecumseh, 860–862
   and treaties, 174
   and the Wabash Confederacy, 371
   See also Tecumseh
Shebbeare, John, 671–672
Sheep herding, 1004, 1023
Sheepeater War (1879), 41, 1129
Shelikov, Grigorii I., 221, 222–223
Shenandoah, Joanne, 159
Sheridan, Philip, 256, 266–267, 349, 664, 843
Sheridan, William, 142
Sherman, William Tecumseh, 260, 267, 342, 530, 531 (photo)
Report on the End of the Indian Problem, **940**
Shipley, David, 714
Shirley, Joe, 92, 734
Shivwits Reservations, 1125
Shoalwater Bay Indians, 1108. *See also* Salish Indians, Southwestern Coast
Shoalwater Bay Tribe Reservation, 1108
Shoshone Indians
   and the Blackfeet, 660
   and the Comanches, 1169
   Eastern, or Wind River, **1125–1127**

   and the Ghost Dance, 396, 398
   and the IRA, 558
   Northern, **1127–1129**
   Sacagawea, 836–838
   Washakie, 872–874
   Western, 619–622, **1129–1131**, 1130 (photo)
   and written language, 425
Shot Both Sides, 661
Shoup, George L., 263
Shuffling Dance, 1126
Shuswap Indians, **1149**
Siberians, 1337
Sibley, Henry, 258, 770
Sicangus (Brûlé) Lakota. *See* Brûlé Lakota
Sierra Blanca Mountains, 1005
Sign language/signaling systems, 320, 329
   Plains Sign Language (PSL), 425–427
Sihasapa Lakota. *See* Lakota Indians
Siksika First Nation Reserve, 98
Siksika Indians, 368, 659–661, 1162. *See also* Blackfeet/Blackfoot Indians
Sikytaki pattern, 458
Siletz, Confederated Tribes of. *See* Coosans Indians; Upper Umpqua Indians
Siletz Reservation, 138, 1070, 1072, 1088–1089, 1110, 1117, 1118
Sillett, Mary, 603
Simcoe, John Graves, 505
Simmons, M. T., 840
Simpson, George, 224, 536
Sinkaietk Indians. *See* Okanagon Indians
Sinkiuse Indians, **1149–1151**, 1150 (photo)
Sinkyone Indians. *See* Wailaki Indians
Sinte Gleska College, 125
Siouan language family, 419
   Catawba, 1210
   Chiwere division, 1179, 1191, 1198, 1288
   Crow/Hidatsa, 1171, 1177
   Dakotan division, 1161, 1174, 1183, 1192
   Dhegiha division, 1180, 1196, 1197, 1202, 1204
   Mandan, 1189
   in the Southeast, 9
Sioui, Georges, 353

Sioux Indians, 45, 46, 484 (photo), 705, 723
  and the Battle of the Little Bighorn, 274–276
  and the Black Hills, 342–344
  and Cody, William, 687
  and the Council of the Three Fires, 368
  and horses, 404, 406
  and intertribal warfare, 373, 484, 822
  and the Massacre at Wounded Knee, 283–285
  and the Missouri River Basin Development Program, 374
  and occupying Alcatraz Island, 289–290
  and the Sun Dance, 471
  and treaties, 175, 176–177
  See also Dakota Indians; Lakota Indians; Nakota Indians
Sisseton/Sisitunwan Dakota, 257. *See also* Dakota Indians
Sisseton-Wahpeton Reservation, 1176
Sitka, 1113
Sitting Bear (Satank), 1181 (photo), 1182, 1183
Sitting Bull, 154, 283, 343, **842–844,** 843 (photo), 851, 1187, 1188
  death of, 687
  speech on keeping treaties, **943**
Siuslawans Indians. *See* Coosans Indians
Six Nations Confederacy. *See* Iroquois Confederacy (Haudenosaunee)
Six Nations of the Grand River, 371
Six Nations Reserve
  and the Iroquois, 1233, 1242, 1260, 1261, 1266, 1267, 1269, 1270, 1283
  and the Lenápes, 1249
  and the Nanticokes, 1262
  revolt, 647
Six Rivers National Forest, 572
638 contracts, 69, 559, 560
Skagit Indians, 462. *See also* Salish Indians, Southern Coast
Skenandoah, 238–239, 384
Skenandore, Rod, 299
Skins, 773
Skokomish (Twana) Indians. *See* Salish Indians, Southern Coast
Sky City (Old Acoma), 998
Slany, John, 851

Slaughter, W. A., 255
Slaves, 20–21, 168–169, 466
  and the cotton economy, 516
  and Jackson, Andrew, 33, 752
  and the Northwest Coast Indians, 202, 456, 1086, 1091, 1112, 1115, 1116
  and Penn, William, 821
  Plains Indians and trade in, 1132, 1179, 1180, 1181, 1198, 1199
  and the Plateau Indians, 1143
  and the Seminoles, 34, 248–249, 314–315, 753, 1229
  and the Southeast Indians, 1214, 1216, 1234
  and the Spanish, 676–678
  and the Wyandottes, 1293
  See also Enslavement
Slavey Indians, **1314–1316**
Sloan, Thomas L., 793, 847
Sloan, William G., 374
Slocum, John, 410, 1106
Slocum, Mary, 410
Smallpox. *See* Disease
Smith, Gerrit, 384
Smith, Henry A., 840
Smith, Jean Edward, 550
Smith, Jedediah, 394, 1072, 1075, 1088, 1120, 1130
Smith, John, 192, 823–824, 827, **844–845,** 845 (photo)
  and Indian medicine, 322
  and the Nanticokes, 1262
  on warfare, 14–15
Smith, Joseph, 93, 445
Smith, Margaret, 765
Smith, Paul Chaat, 645
Smith, Peter Skenandoah, 384
Smith, RedBird, 52
Smith, Rex Alan, 283, 284
Smith River Indians. *See* Tolowa Indians
Smith River Rancheria, 1072–1073
Smithsonian Institute, 336, 500, 679
Smohalla, 381, 396, 465, **845–846,** 848
Smohalla, Wanapum, 1129
Smoke Signals, 407
Smyth, John, 265
Snake, Reuben, 297, 299
Snake Creek, Battle of, 277
Snake War, 1120
Snohomish Indians, 1106. *See also* Salish Indians, Southern Coast
Snoqualmie Indians, 1106. *See also* Salish Indians, Southern Coast

Snoqualmoo Indians. *See* Salish Indians, Southern Coast
Snow, Dean, 113, 404–405
Social evolutionary theory, 51, 89
Social services
  and California Indians, 1067
  and Canada, 332, 522
  and the Choctaws, 1220
  counseling and urban relocation programs, 287
  Great Lakes Intertribal Council (GLITC) and delivery of, 735
  and the Great Basin Indians, 1125
  and the Indian Self-Determination Education Assistance Act (ISDEAA), 559
  and the James Bay and Northern Quebec Agreement (JBNQA), 567
  and the Navajos, 776, 1023
  and Parker, Arthur C., 813
Society for the Propagation of the Gospel (SPG), 331
Society of American Indians (SAI), 154, 292, 576, 794, **846–847**
  and Bonnin, Gertrude Simmons, 666
  and Parker, Arthur C., 813
  and Standing Bear (Ponca), Luther, 855
Sociocultural relations, 406–408, 417–418, 455–456
Socioeconomic conditions, 156–162, 577, 609, 796–797
  effect of removal on, 110, 117
Sociology, 689
Sociopolitical structure
  Adena and Hopewell cultures, 312, 403
  Albany Congress and intercolony unity, 494–495
  and the Ancient Pueblo, 329
  and Athapaskans, 336
  and buffalo economies, 349
  and Cahokia, 351
  and the Cherokee in Oklahoma, 254
  and confederacies, 367–371
  Creeks and transformation in, 246
  and early Pennsylvania, 820–821
  effects of the fur trade on, 393–394
  and epidemic recovery, 107

IRA and differences in Indian, 558

Iroquois, 319, 386–387, 411–412, 743–747

Iroquois contributions to U.S., 239, 321

and irrigation, 318

and Mississippian culture, 432

and the Natchez, 442–443

and Natives of New France, 212

and Northeast Woodland cultures, 190–194, 191–192, 193

and Northwest Coast Indians, 455

and Nunavut, 593–594

and Paleo-Indians, 452

and salmon economies, 461–463

See also Matrilineal descent/matrilocal residence; Patrilineal descent/patrilocal residence; *specific Indian groups*

Sockbeson, Rebecca, 145

Soctomah, Donald, 165

Sohappy, David, Sr., **848–849**

Sohappy, Richard, 849

Sohappy v. Smith (Belloni decision), 389, 849

Sokolov, Aleksei, 221

Solutreans, 3, 83

A Son of the Forest, 650–651

Sonora, Mexico, 131–132, 1041

Sons of Liberty, 236

Sosa, Gaspar Castaño de, 1033

Sos'heowa, 737, 738

Sou-i-hat, 477 (photo)

Souter, David, 182

Southard, Henry, 540

Southeast region, 9–10, 14, 337
    Indian groups in the, 1208–1234

Southern Arapaho Indians, 1159–1160

Southern California Indian Basketweavers Organization (SCIBO), 338

Southern Cheyenne and Arapaho Reservation, 1167

Southern Cheyenne Indians, 176, 1167
    and the Sand Creek Massacre, 261–263
    and the Washita Massacre, 266–268

Southern Ute Reservation, 1133

Southwest region, 4–5, 14, 340
    the Ancestral Pueblo, 326–330

Indian groups in the, 998–1046

Southwestern Regional Indian Youth Council, 797, 872

Sovereignty, **177–182**
    and the battle for Blue Lake, 347
    and the BIA, 501–503
    in Canada, 503–505, 510, 522, 578–579, 603–604, 653–654
    and the Canandaigua Treaty, 512–513
    citizenship as violating, 103–104
    and Costo, Rupert, 700
    and the Crees, 520, 692
    and de la Cruz, Joseph, 706
    and definitions of Indianness, 409
    and Deloria, Vine, Jr., 709
    and doctrine of trust, 614–617
    versus domestic dependent nation, 522–523
    and economic issues, 115–121
    and education issues, 122, 124, 127, 423, 559–560
    and Erasmus, George, 724–725
    and *Fletcher v. Peck*, 526–527
    and Haudenosaunee passports, 173
    and Indian activism, 292, 735
    and the Indian Civil Rights Act, 539–540
    and Indian gambling, 136, 138, 545
    and the Indian Mineral Leasing Act, 546
    and the Indian Reorganization Act, 57–60, 553, 555–556, 691
    Iroquois appeal to League of Nations for, 712–713
    and the James Bay and Northern Quebec Agreement (JBNQA), 567
    Mad Bear on, 647
    and the Maine Indian claim settlement, 573, 575
    and the Marshall court, 514–517, 550–551, 626–628
    and migration theory, 416
    and Native Hawai'ians, 533
    and Nunavut, 588–594
    Oliphant case and, 594–596
    and plenary power, 597–598
    and Red Jacket, 829, 831
    and treaties, 170
    and tribal colleges, 867
    and the Two Row Wampum belt, 356
    and *United States v. Kagama*, 622

U.S. policy and, 69, 118–119, 146–148, 181, 291
    and water rights, 188–189

The Sovereignty and Goodness of God . . ., 359

Soviet Union, pollution from the, 133

Soyal, 1012

Spack, Ruth, 666

Spanish, 14, 142
    and the Arctic Indians, 1322
    and California Indians, 1050, 1052, 1054, 1055, 1063, 1066, 1068, 1071, 1073, 1075, 1079, 1081
    and the Christian conversion imperative, 360
    de las Casas on genocide by the, 676–678
    and the Doctrine of Discovery, 17, 18, 178–179, 208
    and Florida, 214, 344
    and the Great Basin Indians, 1124
    and Indian demographics, 108–109, 227–228
    and Indian enslavement, 466–468, 467 (photo)
    and Indian trade relations, 116
    influence, **214–216**
    mapping of Northwest coast, 263
    mission on York River, 823
    mission system, **231–235**
    and the Northwest Coast Indians, 1095, 1108, 1113
    and the Plains Indians, 1198, 1202, 1206, 1207
    and the Seminole Wars, 248, 249
    and the 1763 Treaty of Paris, 21–22
    and slaves, 21, 168
    and the Southeast Indians, 1209, 1210, 1214, 1216, 1219, 1221, 1234
    and the Southwest Indians, 220, 1000, 1002, 1009, 1011, 1013–1014, 1015, 1017, 1018, 1022, 1026, 1028, 1029, 1030, 1031–1032, 1033, 1035, 1040, 1041–1042, 1044

Spanish-American War, 48

Spanish language, 422

Spear points, 82 (photo)

Special Olympics, 160

Speck, Frank G., 382

Spicer, Edward Holland, 655

Spirit Mountain, 151–153

"The Spirit of Haida Gwaii," 355
Spirit of the Laws, 376
Spiro, 10
Spokan Reservation, 1152
Spokan/Spokane Indians, 134, 256,
    1151–1152
Spokane Prophet, 876
Sports
    Indian imagery in, 429, 430–431
    lacrosse, 417–418, 417 (photo)
    See also specific Indian groups
Spotted Elk, Garfield, 288
Spotted Tail, 703, **850–851,** 850
    (photo), 1187, 1188
Squanto (Tisquantum), 476, 783,
    851–852, 1287
Squash, 4, 7–10. *See also* "Three
    sisters" complex
Squaw, **163–165,** 164 (photo)
Squaxin Indians, 1106. *See also* Salish
    Indians, Southern Coast
St. Clair, Anthony, 174
St. Clair, Arthur, 24, 244, 772,
    852–853
St. George's School, 99
St. John's University, 431
St. Mary's Creek, Battle at, 853
St. Regis, 1260
Stadacona, 113
Standing Bear, 171, 177, 604–605, 605
    (photo), 755–756, 767,
    853–854, 1204
Standing Bear, Henry, 794
Standing Bear, Luther, 96, 97, 666,
    854–855, 855 (photo)
Standing Bear v. Crook, 548, **604–605,**
    755, **853–854**
Standing Rock Reservation, 53, 1193
Stanford University, 431
Stanton, Elizabeth Cady, 383, 383
    (photo), 384, 385–386,
    387
Starvation. *See* Famine/starvation
State names, **468–469**
States
    and gambling operations,
        543–546
    Indian relations and, 32, 34, 36
    and jurisdictional issues, 587,
        609, 796 (*see also* Public
        Law 280 [1953])
    and sovereignty issues, 516,
        550–551 (*see also* Marshall
        Trilogy)
    and taxation issues, 547–548
Steilacoom Indians, 1105. *See also*
    Salish Indians, Southern
    Coast
Steimetz, Father Paul, 454

Steiner, Stan, 798
Steltenkamp, Michael, 659
Stereotypes
    and alcoholism, 77, 78
    and educational failure, 869
    and mascots, 429–431
    and the myth of the noble
        savage, 376–378, 439–440
    and squaw as a derogatory term,
        163
Sterilization, 640, 884
Stevens, Isaac, 168, 176, 255,
    761–762, 839–840
Stevens, John Paul, 182
Steward, Julian, 500
Stewart, James M., 366
Stewart, Jane, 101
Sticks, Duncan, 100
Sticks, Johnny, 100
Stillaguamish Indians. *See* Salish
    Indians, Southern Coast
Stillman's Run, Battle of, 251,
    662–663
Stine Ingstad, Anne, 204, 205–206
Stockbridge Indians, 265, 1249,
    1250–1251, 1266
Stockbridge-Munsee Indians. *See*
    Mahican Indians
Stoeckl, Edouard de, 265
Stone, Chester, 643
Stone, Ward, 130
Stone, William Leete, 669, 830, 831
Stone Child (Rocky Boy), 1171, 1195
Stoney Indians. *See* Assiniboine
    Indians
Story, Joseph, 515
Straits Salish Indians, 462–463
Strauss, Alexis, 150
Strauss, Lewis L., 134
Strom, Stephen, 740
Strong, Ted, 518
Stuart, John, 520
Student Non-Violent Coordinating
    Committee (SNCC), 294
Students for a Democratic Society
    (SDS), 294
Stuntz, Joe, 818
Stuyvesant, Peter, 166 (photo)
Subarctic region, 11
    Indian groups in the, 1294–1320
Substance abuse, **77–81,** 157–158,
    378, 1274, 1330. *See also*
    Alcohol/alcohol abuse
Substance Abuse and Mental Health
    Services Administration,
    77
Suhtai Indians, 471
Suicide, 79, 97, 156, 158
    and Alaskan Natives, 133

    and the Arctic Indians, 1344
    and Black Mesa mining, 150
    and genocide by the Spanish,
        678
    and post-traumatic stress
        disorder, 379
    rates at Pikangikum, 157–158
Sullivan, John, 238, 239, **856–858,** 857
    (photo)
Suma Indians, 1038
Sumner, Edwin V., 778
Sun Dance, **471–472,** 471 (photo),
    842, 874
    and the Great Basin Indians,
        1126, 1127, 1129, 1132
    and the Plains Indians, 661, 1157,
        1161, 1163, 1165, 1170,
        1171, 1173, 1174, 1176,
        1177, 1182, 1185, 1192,
        1194, 1203
    repression of the, 90, 362, 538,
        553
    and the Southwest Indians, 1160
Supreme Court, U.S.
    on citizenship and voting rights,
        104
    and the Doctrine of Discovery,
        17, 208–210
    and fishing rights, 389–390, 392
    and gambling operations, 137,
        138, 139
    and jurisdiction issues, 50, 622
    and land claims, 344, 569–571,
        606–607, 619, 621, 1086,
        1131
    and mining issues, 547–548
    and plenary power, 596–598
    and pollution cases, 146
    on rancherias, 1067
    and religious freedom issues,
        362–363, 364, 498, 499,
        1081
    and sovereignty issues, 118, 119,
        146, 179–180, 181–182,
        526–527, 594–596
    and treaties, 170, 171–172
    and water rights, 187, 188,
        624–625
    See also Marshall Trilogy; *specific*
        court cases
Suquamish Indians. *See* Salish
    Indians, Southern Coast
Suquamish Port Madison
    Reservation, 594–595
Suquamish Tribal Museum, 804
The Surrounded, 785
Survival of American Indians
    Association (SAIA), 293,
    298

Susquehannock (Conestoga) Indians, 821, 1282
Sutter's Creek, 227 (photo)
Sutton, Polly, 678
Swamp, Jake, 411, 412
Swan Point archaeology site, 84
Swanton, John, 500
Swarton, Hannah, 359
Sweat Lodge Movement, 1121
Sweat lodges, **473–474,** 473 (photo)
Swift Hawk Lying Down, 663
Swimmer, Ross O., 780
Swinomish Indians. *See* Salish Indians, Southern Coast
Sword Bearer, 822–823
Symbols, 236, 239
    Adena mounds as, 312–313
    canoe, 355
    of Indian resistance, 293
    mascots, 429–431
    and scalping, 464
    Tammany Society and Indian, 859, 860
    and totem poles, 477–479
    and wampum, 481–482
Symington, Fife, 139
Syncretism
    and Bole-Maru religion, 347
    and New Agers, 443–444
    and Seven Drums Religion, 465
Syphilis, 325
Szasz, Margaret Connell, 124

Table Mountain Rancheria, 801
Tabotem, 218
Tache Indians. *See* Yokuts Indians
Tacoma, 1106
Tadodaho (Adodaroh), 708–709, 749, 758
Tadoussac, 1312
Tafoya, Margaret, 458
Tahltan Indians, **1316–1318**
Tahontaenrat Indians, 369
Tall Bull, 686
Tallapoosa River, 247 (photo)
Talton v. Mayes, 180
Tamanend, 1249
Tammany, 859–860
Tammany Society, 698, 699, **859–860**
Tanaina Indians, **1318–1320**
Tanana Indians. *See* Ingalik Indians
Tanoan language. *See* Kiowa-Tanoan language family
Taos Pueblo Indians, 291, 453 (photo), 554, **1035–1037,** 1036 (photo)
    and Blue Lake, 346–347
Taos trade fair, 1000, 1009
Tapia, Antonio José, 1028

Tappan, S. F., 260
Tarahumara (Ramamuri), 433
Tashtasick, 672
Tax, Sol, 293, 734
Taylor, Graham, 552–553, 558
Taylor, Richard, 347
Taylor, Wayne, Jr., 151
Taylor, Zachary, 250, 662
Taza, 683
Te-Moak tribe, 620–621
Technology. *See* Material culture
Tecumseh, 24, 31–32, 154, **860–862,** 1286
    and Black Hawk, 661
    and the Creeks, 246
    and Harrison, William Henry, 742
    and Little Turtle's War, 772
    Northeast Woodland Indians and alliances with, 1239, 1244, 1247, 1249, 1278, 1290
    Speech to Governor William Henry Harrison, **902**
    spiritual underpinnings of alliance, 396
    and the Treaty of Greenville, 371
    and War of 1812, 357, 358
Tee-Hit-Ton v. United States, **606–607**
Tehanna, Frank, 1010
Teillet, Jean, 579 (photo)
Tekakwitha, Kateri, **862–863**
Tekarihoga, Henry, 668
Telegraph, 39, 40
Television, 136, 631
Television Northern Canada (TVNC), 631
Teller, Henry Moore, 281, 497
Tellot, 1298
TeMoak, 1131
TeMoak Bands Council, 1131
Tenaya, 1063
Teninos, 201
Tenskwatawa/Tenskwataya (The Prophet), 32, 380, 396, 802, 862, **864–865,** 864 (photo), 1286
    System of Religion Speech, **902**
Termination, 66–68, 126, 180–181, 540, **607–610**
    activism against, 124, 288, 734, 796
    and assimilation, 91, 137
    and the BIA, 502
    and the Indian Claims Commission, 541–542
    and the Menominees, 1254
    and the Narragansetts, 1263
    and the Plateau Indians, 1140

    and the Southeast Indians, 1209, 1214
    and the Southern Paiutes, 1125
    and urban relocation, 285
    as U.S. policy, 118, 147
Termination and Relocation, 541–542
Terry, Alfred, 275, 530, 842, 843
Tesuque Pueblo, **1037–1038**
Teton Lakota. *See* Lakota Indians
Tewa, Dennis, 414
Tewa language. *See* Kiowa-Tanoan language family, Tewa
Texas, 41
Texas Rangers, 1247
Thames, Battle of the, 32, 862, 865
Thanadelther, 1300
Thanksgiving holiday, **474–476,** 475 (photo)
Thatcher, John Boyd, 750
Theodoratus Report, 572
Thiebaud, Wayne, 838
Third World Liberation Strikes, 807
Thom, Melvin, 797, 798, 1204
Thomas, Clarence, 182
Thomas, Cyrus, 437, 445
Thomas, Eleazar, 674
Thomas, Jacob, 738
Thompson, David, 585
Thompson, Loran, 161
Thompson, Smith, 515
Thompson, Wiley, 250, 720, 721, 809–810
Thompson Indians, **1152–1153**
Thornburgh, Thomas, 1133
Thornburgh ambush (Meeker massacre), 1133
Thornton, Russell, 62
Thorpe, Charles, 865
Thorpe, Hiram, 865
Thorpe, Jim, 97, **865–867,** 866 (photo)
Three Fires Confederacy, 240, 358, 1271
"Three sisters" complex, 212, 317, 319
    and the Iroquois, 1241, 1258, 1264, 1268, 1281
Thule culture, 12, 1327, 1329, 1332, 1334, 1342
Thundershield, Dallas, 818
Tiama-Tiama, 83
Tibbles, Thomas Henry, 605, 756, 767, 854
Tigua Indians, **1038–1039**
Tillamook Indians, **1109–1110**
Tiloukaikt, 877, 1136
Tilson, Ken, 642
Time, 136
Timucua Indians, 1229
Tinker, George, 720

Tionantates (Petun), 212
Tipai-Ipai Indians, **1071**
Tippecanoe, 32
Tlingit, Inland, Indians. *See* Tlingit
        Indians
Tlingit and Haida Technology
        Industries, 564
Tlingit-Haida Central Council
        (THCC), 636
Tlingit Indians, 169, 224, 456,
        1110–1114, 1111 (photo)
    and the Alaska Native Brotherhood,
        635–636
    and *Tee-Hit-Ton v. United States,*
        606–607
Tlingit language family, 333
        and Na-Dene, 440–441
Tobacco, 5, 8–10, 322, 454, 1227
Tobacco Indians, 212
Tobique Reservation, 1252
Toboggans, 356
Tohono O'odham Basketweavers
        Organization (TOBO),
        338
Tohono O'odham Desert Diamond
        Casino, 139
Tohono O'odham (Papago) Indians,
        4, 95, 139, 266, **1039–1040**
    and the Camp Grant Massacre,
        271
    and pottery, 457
Tolowa Indians, **1072–1073**
Tomahas, 877
Tomochichi, 15
Tompiro Indians, 1038
Tomsho, Rupert, 130
Tonawanda Indians, 265
Tonawanda Reservation, 513, 1242,
        1283
Tongass National Forest, 606
Tongue River Reservation, 1167
Tonkawa Indians, **1205–1206**
Tonto Apaches, 1042
Tonto Basin campaign, 1042
Toohoolhoolzote, 276, 277
Topper site, 2
Topsannah, 815
Torpy, Sally, 884
Tortugas, 1038. *See also* Tigua
        Indians
Totem poles, **477–479,** 477 (photo),
        1091
Toughkamiwon Indians, 368
Tourism, 457–458
Towns/villages
        and the Ancient Pueblo, 328–329
        Cahokia, 350–352
        and pre-contact Indians, 4, 8, 9,
        11

Trade, **166–169,** 166 (photo)
    in Adena culture, 313
    and alcohol, 698, 832
    and the Ancient Pueblo, 329, 330
    and beads, 339–340
    and the Blackfoot Confederacy,
        368
    at Cahokia, 350
    and canoe transportation, 354,
        357
    confederacies and, 367
    and the Crows, 822
    Dalles trading area, 201–203
    and diplomacy, 806
    and the Hohokam culture, 401
    Hopewell Interaction Sphere,
        402, 404
    in horses, 404–405, 406
    and Mississippian culture, 432
    and Mogollon culture, 434
    and Penn, William, 821
    and pre-contact Indians, 4–11
    relations and European balance
        of power, 115–116
    relationships, 39, 44, 172–173
    role in spreading disease, 106
    and the trade and intercourse
        acts, 610–612, 615–616
    and tribes along the Oregon
        Trail, 254
    turquoise, 318
    See also Fur trade; *specific Indian
        groups;* Trade items
Trade and intercourse acts, 146–147,
        573, **610–612,** 615–616
Trade items
    alcohol, 78
    European, 167
    and the factory system, 525
    impact of European, 18–19,
        167–168
    Northwest Coast, 202
    and the Spanish, 216
    traditional, 166, 167
Trafzer, Clifford, 277
Trail of Broken Treaties, 294, 295,
        297–300, 298 (photo),
        303, 640
    and Banks, Dennis, 656
    and Means, Russell, 786
    and Peltier, Leonard, 817
Trail of Tears, 32, 36–37, 107, 117,
        252–254, 517, 528, 551,
        836, 1214
    as a form of genocide, 142
    and Sequoyah, 841
    and Watie, Stand, 874
Transportation
    and canoes, 354–358

    Euro-American systems of, 39
    and expansionism, 40, 45
    and horses, 404–406
    and pre-contact Indians, 5, 6, 7,
        11
    roads and the Ancient Pueblo,
        329
    See also specific Indian groups
Traveling Hail, 258
Treaties, **170–177**
    balance of power inequities and,
        23
    breaking, 24, 41–44, 66, 374, 571
    and the California Indians, 230,
        1105
    and Canada, 503–505, 507–508,
        509, **928**
    and citizenship, 103
    and Cornplanter, 699
    as expansionism tools, 527
    and fishing rights, 375, 390–391
        (table)
    government use of alcohol as
        incentive, 78
    and the Great Basin Indians,
        1131, 1132–1133
    and Harrison, William Henry,
        31–32, 861–862
    and identity issues, 409–410
    IRA and return to, 553
    Iroquois negotiation procedure,
        355–356
    and Jackson, Andrew, 33, 34,
        548–549, 754
    and the James Bay and Northern
        Quebec Agreement
        (JBNQA), 565–568
    Lancaster treaty councils,
        568–569
    land losses/cessions through,
        116, 244, 245–246, 248,
        261, 512, 541, 549
    and the Northeast Woodland
        Indians, 20, 1278, 1280,
        1290, 1293
    and the Northwest Coast
        Indians, 839–840, 1110
    and Northwest Territory land
        encroachment, 741–742
    as "pen and ink witchcraft," 562
    and Penn, William, 821
    and the Plains Indians, 368, 1180
    and the Plateau Indians,
        761–762, 845, 1154–1155,
        1156
    and plenary power, 597–598
    and the Southeast Indians, 369,
        1216, 1222
    and Southwest Indians, 261

and the Subarctic Indians, 1308, 1316
U.S. cessation to negotiating, 117, 180, 269
and water rights, 624–625
and water transportation rights, 357
See also Land losses/cessions; *specific treaties*
Treaty 7 (Canada), 660, 1162, 1164
Treaty 8 (Canada), 1295
Treaty at Fort Wayne (1803), 742
Treaty at Prairie du Chien (1825), 175
Treaty between the Cherokee Nation and the United States (1817), 174
Treaty Eight Tribal Association, 1295
Treaty of 1804, 251
Treaty of 1805, 256–257
Treaty of 1867, 606
Treaty of Big Tree (1797), 830
Treaty of Buffalo Creek (1838), 1266
Treaty of Canandaigua (1794), 23, 830
Treaty of Conejos (1863), 811
Treaty of Dancing Rabbit Creek (1830), 1219
Treaty of Easton, 226
Treaty of Fort Atkinson (1853), 175
Treaty of Fort Gibson (1833), 720, 809
Treaty of Fort Jackson (1814), 248, 809
Treaty of Fort Wayne (1809), 742
Treaty of Fort Wise (1861), 261, 663
Treaty of Greenville (1795), 174, 244, 245–246, 371, 587, 772, 1255
Treaty of Guadalupe Hidalgo (1848), 146–147, 175, 187, 229, **916**
Treaty of Hell Gate (1855), 176, 1147
Treaty of Holston (1791), 174
Treaty of Hopewell (1785), 174
Treaty of Horseshoe Bend (1814), 1222
Treaty of Indian Springs (1825), 174–175, 344, 549
Treaty of Little Arkansas (1865), 176, 763
Treaty of Medicine Creek (1854), 176, 1105
Treaty of Medicine Lodge (1867), 176, 570, 664, 1160, 1169, 1183
Treaty of Moultrie Creek (1823), 250, 315, 345, 809, 1229
Treaty of Mount Dexter (1805), 174
Treaty of Neah Bay (1855), 1095

Treaty of New Echota (1835), 36, 175, 253, 528, 836, 1214
and Ridge, Major, 777
and Ross, John, 551
and Watie, Stand, 874
Treaty of New York, 344
Treaty of Paris (1763), 21–22, 226
Treaty of Paris (1783), 21, 22, 239, 244
Treaty of Payne's Landing (1832), 250, 315, 720, 809, 1229
Treaty of Point Elliot (1855), 126, 595, 840
Treaty of Ruby Valley (1863), 619–620
Treaty of Table Rock (1805), 1202
Treaty of Tordesillas (1494), 215
Treaty of Washington (1832), 1222
Treaty of Washington (1846), 1105, 1108
Treaty Party, 253, 777
Treaty with the Choctaws, 175
Treaty with the Creeks (1866), 176
Treaty with the Creeks and Seminoles (1856), 176
Treaty with the Delaware Tribe (1778), 173
Treaty with the Kiowa, Comanche, and Apache (1867), **923**
Treaty with the Makah, 389
Treaty with the Navajo (1868), **925**
Treaty with the Nez Percé (1871), 177
Treaty with the Oto and Missouri Indians (1854), 175
Treaty with the Wyandots, et al. (1785), 174
Trevino, Juan Francisco de, 220
Tribal College Journal (TCJ), 638
Tribal colleges, **867–869,** 881
controlled community colleges (TCCC), 124, 125–127
Tribal courts, 182, **612–613,** 1023
Tribal government, 48, 65–66, 68–69
AIM and legitimacy of, 154–155
and Alaska, 493
economic development and, 70, 114, 119–122 (*see also* Economic development)
Indian Reorganization Act and creation of, 502
regulatory authority of, 594–596
and religion, 363
and tribal membership issues, 450
See also Factionalism; Sovereignty; Tribal courts
Tribally Controlled Community College Assistance Act (1978), 71–72, 126, 128, 867
Tribute, 468

Trickster characters, 3
Trigger, Bruce G., 166
Trimble, Al, 300
Trinidad Rancheria, 1081
Trout Lake, 1314
Truckee, 881, 882
Trudeau, Pierre, 518, 538
Trudell, John, 639, 645
Truganinny, 835
Truman, Harry S., 542, 542 (photo)
Trust, doctrine of, **614–617**
Tsalages people, 446
Tsegi Canyon, 330
Tsimshian Indians, **1114–1116**
Tsimshian language family, 6, 1114
Tsis-tsis-tas, 471, 472
Tubatulabal Indians, **1073**
Tuberculosis, 8, 112, 1004, 1146, 1177
Tulalip Indians. *See* Salish Indians, Southern Coast
Tulalip Reservation, 1106
Tule River Reservation, 1063, 1073, 1079
Tulee v. State of Washington, 390
Tullberg, Steven B., 614–615
Tully, James, 355
Tunica Indians, 1223, **1230–1231**
Tunican languages, 1230
Tunngavik Federation of Nunavut (TFN), 591, 592, **617–618,** 1325, 1327, 1332, 1343
Turkey, as food native to the Americas, 476
Turnbaugh, Sarah Peabody, 339
Turnbaugh, William A., 339
Turner, Tina, 314
Turning Stone, 159
Turquoise trade, 318, 329
Turtle Mountain Reservation, 67, 1196, 1240
Tuscarora Indians, 265, 484, 647, **1231–1233**
and the American Revolution, 238, 239
and the Iroquois Confederacy, 192, 369–370, 412, 428, 1264
See also Iroquois Confederacy (Haudenosaunee)
Tutchone Indians. *See* Gwich'in Indians
Tutelo Indians, 1242
Tututni Indians. *See* Tolowa Indians; Upper Umpqua Indians
Twana Indians. *See* Salish Indians, Southern Coast
Twenty Points, 299, 300
Twightwee Indians, 513–514
Twin Cities Naval Air Station, 295

Twining, 337–338
Two Kettles, 275
Two Moon, **934**
Two Row Wampum, 481–482, 503
Tyendinaga (Deseronto) Reserve, 1260
Tyler, Oren, 384

Udall, James, 495, 496
Udall, Morris, 137, 580
Udall, Stewart, 491
Uintah Reservation, 1133
Umatilla Indians, 134, 877, **1153–1154**
Umatilla Reservation, 375, 517–518, 1136
Umpqua language family, 419
Unalaska, 1345
Unangan Indians, **1343–1346**
Unangan language, 1346
Unca Indians, 672–673, **869–870,** 1275
Underhill, Ruth, 90
Unemployment, 57, 119, 796
    and Blackfeet, 561
    and the Navajos, 1023
    rates at Pikangikum, 157
    and substance abuse, 79, 158
Uneven Ground: American Indian Sovereignty and Federal Law, 209
Unification Church, 787
Union of New Brunswick Indians, 1257
Union of Nova Scotia Indians, 1257
United Church of Canada, 101–102
United Keetoowah Band (UKB), 1215
United Nations, 73, 149, **618–619,** 641–642
    and the Dann case, 622
    Declaration on the Granting of Independence to Colonial Countries and Peoples (1960), 57–58
    Declaration on the Rights of Indigenous Peoples, 73, 460, 619, 642
    on genocide, 141
    on the Hiawatha Belt, 481
    and Lyons, Oren, 775
    Working Group on Indigenous Populations, 533
United Native Americans, 154
United Nuclear mill, 186
United Remnant Band (URB), 1286

United States Civil Rights Commission, and mascots, 431
United States of America v. Robert Lawrence Boyll, **983**
United States Pharmacopoeia, 321
United States v. Dann, **619–622**
United States v. Kagama, 598, **622**
United States v. Lara, 118, 182
United States v. Michigan (Fox decision), 389, 392
United States v. Navajo Nation, 547
United States v. Nichols-Chisolm Lumber, 54
United States v. Oregon, 517
United States v. State of Washington. See Boldt decision
United States v. Wheeler, 181
United States v. Winans, 389–390
United Western Shoshone Legal Defense and Education Association, 1131
Unity concepts, 671, 729–730, 746, 748
University of Alaska, Reindeer Research Program, 144
University of Arizona, 398–399
University of California, 700
University of Chicago, 97
University of Illinois, 429
University of Miami, 431
University of Oklahoma, 431
University of Utah, 429, 431
The Unjust Society, 290
Unz, Ron, 91
Upland Yumans, 1010, 1014
Upper Coquille Indians. See Upper Umpqua Indians
Upper Skagit Indians, 1105. See also Salish Indians, Southern Coast
Upper Snake River, 1129
Upper Umpqua Indians, **1116–1118**
Uranium, 129, 148, **183–186,** 184 (photo), 601, 644
    and CERT, 701
Urban areas, social services in, 155, 294
Urban relocation. See Relocation, urban
Urbom, Warren, 642
U.S. Forest Service, 572
U.S. Geological Survey, 500
Ute Indians, 147, 259, 675, 811–812, **1131–1133**
    and the Ghost Dance, 396, 398
    horses and, 39, 404
Ute language, 422

Ute War (1878-1879), 41, 811–812
Utley, Robert M., 283
Uto-Aztecan language family, 419
    Cahita, 1041
    in California, 5
    Central Numic branch, 1125, 1127, 1129, 1168
    Cupan group, Takic division of, 1049, 1054, 1059
    Hopi, 1012
    Piman, 1026, 1039
    Serrano, 1068
    Southern Numic branch, 1008, 1123, 1131
    Tubatulabal, 1073
    Western Numic branch, 1063, 1119, 1121, 1127
Uto-Aztecan O'odham, 4
Utopia, 17
Utopian Legacies, 791–792
Utopianism, 791–792

Vacuum domicilium, 17
Valaam monastery, 221
Valencia, Angel, 131
Values, **487–488**
    boarding school attacks on, 97–98, 99
    counting coup and warrior honor, 372–373
    cultural clashes in, 149
    education and conflicting, 122, 128
    humor as a, 406–408
    retaining and reclaiming Indian, 70–71, 633
    role in addiction treatment, 81
    and the Tammany Society, 859
    and tribal colleges, 868
    See also specific Indian groups
Van Buren, Martin, 253, 836
Van den Bogaert, Harmen Meyndertsz, 18
Van Horne, James, 359–360
Van Schaich, Goose, 856–857
Vancouver, George, 111, 1083, 1084, 1105
Vancouver Island, 479, 480, 1096
Vandegrift, Alexander, 366
Vandevelder, Paul, 145–146
Vanyumes, 1069
Vargas, Diego de, 1032, 1038
Velasquez, Diego de, 676
Veniaminov, Ivan, 223–224
Ventureño Indians. See Chumash Indians
Verelst, John, 747
Vermont, 1236

Verona, town of, 159
Victoria, 1103
Victorio, **870–871,** 1003, 1005, 1007
Victorio War, 871
Vierra, Mary, 669
Vigil, Martin, 637
Viikita, 1027, 1039
Vikings. *See* Norse
Village of the Great Kivas, 329
Villages. *See* Towns/villages
Vincent, Thomas, 332
Vinland, 204–205
Vision quests, 6, 7, 9, 472
Vizcaíno, Sebastián, 1054
Voltaire, 377, 819
Voting rights
    in Canada, 538
    Cohen, Felix, and Indian, 688
    and General Allotment Act, 281
    and Navajo code talkers,
        366–367
    and the NCAI, 795
    and public school boards, 125
    Supreme Court on, 104, 524
    for women, 387

Wa-win-te-piksat, 762
Wabanaki Confederacy, 370–371
Wabanaki Indians, 573–575
Wabash Confederacy, 371
Wabash River, 861–862
Wabasha, 258
Waddle, Delena, 165
Wahgoshig First Nation, 649
Wahpekute Dakota, 257. *See also*
        Dakota Indians
Wahpeton Indians. *See* Dakota
        Indians
Wahpetunwan Dakota, 257. *See also*
        Dakota Indians
Wailaki Indians, **1073–1074**
Wakan Tanka, 9
Wakashan language family, **479–480**
    Heiltsuk-Oowekyala, 1082
    Kwakiutl, 1092
    Nootkan branch, 1094, 1096
    in the Northwest Coast area, 6
Wakinyantanka, 769
Walam Odum, 93
Walapai Indians. *See* Hualapai
        Indians
Waldie, Jerome R., 287, 289
Walker, Joseph, party, 1120
Walker River Reservation, 396–397
Walla Walla Indians, 203, 877. *See
        also* Umatilla Indians
Walla Walla Treaty (1855), 762
Walum Olum, 1248

Wampanoag Confederation, 783–784
Wampanoag Indians, 475 (photo),
        787–789, 879, **1287–1288**
Wampum, 339, **480–482,** 481 (photo)
    and the Condolence Ceremony,
        708–709
    and Hiawatha, 749, 750–751
    and the Iroquois Confederacy,
        743, 775, 1269
    and treaty negotiations, 172
    Two Row, 355–356
    and written language, 425
Wanapam Indians, 845–846, 848–849
War of 1812, 116, 357–358
    and Black Hawk, 661
    and Canadian policies, 505
    and Cornplanter, 699
    and the Creek War, 247
    and Harrison, William Henry,
        742–743
    and the Northeast Woodland
        Indians, 1239, 1247, 1254,
        1271, 1280, 1286, 1292
    and Red Jacket, 829–830
    and Tecumseh, 862
    and Tenskwatawa, 865
Ward, Felix, 684
Ward, John, 684
Ward, Nancy, 16
Ward Valley, **307–309**
Wardship, doctrine of, 515, 523, 537,
        614, 616–617, **623–624**
Warfare/violence
    and the Apaches, 233, 683, 685,
        778, 871, 1002, 1007
    the Beaver Wars, 218–220
    Black Hawk's War, 251–252,
        662–663
    and the Black Hills, 342, 343, 659
    canoes in, 356–358
    and the Cayuse Indians, 877
    confederacies and, 367
    and conflicts over the fur trade,
        394, 464
    counting coup and, 372–373
    as a European tradition, 14–15
    over fishing rights, 391–392
    gambling-related, 161, 634,
        718–719
    gold rushes, settlement, and,
        44–45, 229–230, 674
    and horse economies, 406
    and Indian enslavement, 466,
        468
    intentional biological, 21
    intertribal, **483–485**
    and King Philip's War, 788–789
    lacrosse as surrogate for, 418

    and Mayan cultural collapse, 317
    in Mississippian culture, 432
    and mound builders, 436, 446
    Native-Norse, 206, 207
    and the Navajos, 233, 675, 1022
    in Northeast Woodland
        traditions, 192, 193
    and Ohio country Indians, 116,
        853
    and the Oregon Trail, 255
    and Pine Ridge Reservation,
        300–303, 643–645, 652,
        817–818
    and Plains Indians, 261, 530, 687,
        842–843, 882
    and Pontiac, 826
    and post-traumatic stress
        disorder, 379
    and the Powhatan Confederacy,
        826–827
    and pre-contact Indians, 5, 7, 11
    role in demographic collapse,
        105, 107
    and Shoshone land
        encroachment, 619
    and trade in firearms, 168
    and treaty violations, 41, 42–43
    against women, 163, 384–385
    and Yaqui resistance, 655
    See also Resistance, Native;
        *specific Indian groups and
        wars*
Warm Springs Indians, 134, 291
Warm Springs Reservation, 67, 203,
        375, 517–518, 1121,
        1154–1155
Warm Springs Reservation,
        Confederated Tribes of
        the. *See* Paiute, Northern;
        Umatilla Indians;
        Wishram Indians
Warner, "Pop," 865
Warrior, Clyde, 797, 798, **871–872,**
        1204
Warrior's Dance, 1254
Wasco County Historical Museum,
        203
Wasco Indians, 201–203, 338. *See also*
        Wishram Indians
Washakie, **872–874,** 873 (photo), 1127
Washani religion (Dreamer cult),
        380–381, 396, 845–846
    and the Great Basin Indians,
        1129
    and the Plateau Indians, 762,
        1145, 1152
    and Seven Drums Religion, 465
Washat. *See* Seven Drums Religion

Washington, George, 142
    and the Canandaigua Treaty, 513
    and Clark, George Rogers, 682
    and Cornplanter, 698, 699–700
    and the French and Indian War, 224
    and genocide of the Iroquois, 856
    and the Goschochking Massacre, 243
    and the Iroquois Confederacy, 238–239
    and Little Turtle, 772
    and the Northwest Ordinance, 587
    and Red Jacket, 830
    and seizing Northwest Territory lands, 240, 244
    and St. Clair, Arthur, 852
    and the trade and intercourse acts, 611, 615
Washington (state), 72, 126–127, 293, 389–392, 849
Washington Redskins, 431
Washington v. Washington State Commercial Passenger Fishing Vessel Association, 170
Washita Massacre, **266–268,** 267 (photo), 664
    and the Cheyennes, 1167
    and the Comanches, 1169
Washoe Indians, 7, **1133–1136,** 1134 (photo)
Wasik, John, 151
Wassaja, 794
Water
    and Ancient Puebloan variability, 327
    aquifer depletion, 148–149, 150–151, 185
    in creation stories, 355
    pollution, 130, 133–134, 145–146, 148, 152–153, 185–186, 309
Water rights, **186–189**
    and the Colorado River Indian Tribes, 1020
    and the Great Basin Indians, 1121
    and *Pyramid Lake* court case, 600–601
    and the Southwest Indians, 1001, 1020, 1024–1025, 1026–1027, 1030, 1037, 1043
Waters, Frank, 825
Watie, Stand, 680, 777, 836, **874–875,** 875 (photo)

Watkins, Arthur, 147, 608
Wauneka, Annie, 714
Wax, Murray L., 710–711
Wayne, "Mad" Anthony, 174, 244–245, 772, 853
We-Wa, 341 (photo)
Wea Indians, 246
Weapons, 40–41, 168
    and the Beaver Wars, 218
    and intertribal warfare, 485
    and mound builders, 446
    and reign of terror on Pine Ridge, 643
    and the Spanish, 216
Weatherford, Jack, 324
Weatherford, William, 246–247
Weaving, **485–487,** 486 (photo), 1000, 1023, 1101, 1113
Weawea, 1120
Webster, J. L., 605, 854
Webster, William, 645
Weiser, Conrad, 172, 513
Welch, James, **875–876**
Welhik Tuppeek (Schonbrunn), 240–243
Weller, LaVonna, 298, 799
Wells, William, 742, 772
Welsh, Herbert, 723, 768
Wendat Indians, 212, 214, 354
Wessonsuoum, 672
West Coast District Council, 1098
Western Abenakis, 112, 113
Western Apaches, 270–271, **1006–1007,** 1006 (photo)
Western Iroquois groups, 218
Western Lakes Confederacy, 368
Western Shoshone (Duck Valley) Reservation, 1131
Wewa, Wilson, 465
Wheeler, Burton, 557
Wheeler-Howard Act. *See* Indian Reorganization Act (IRA) (1934)
Wheelock, Eleazar, 667
Whilkut Indians. *See* Hupa Indians
Whipple, H. Benjamin, 723
White, Barry, 791
White Antelope, 261, 263
White Bison, 81
White Buffalo Calf Pipe Woman, 1184
White Buffalo Society, 1177–1178
White Cloud, 662
White Earth Land Recovery Program, 764–765
White Earth Reservation, 54
White Mountain Apache, 139
White River Apaches, 266
White Roots of Peace, 807

White Stick faction, 1222
Whitebear, Bernie, 706
Whitebird, 276, 277
Whitebird Canyon, Battle of, 276
Whitman, Marcus and Narcissa, **876–877,** 877 (photo), 1136
Whitman, Royal F., 270–271
Whitman, Walt, 320
Whitman Massacre, 876–877, 1136, 1152
Whitside, Samuel, 283
Wichita Indians, 265, **1206–1207**
Wickersham, James, 410
Wilkie, Bruce, 798
Wilkie, Madeline, 716
Wilkins, David, 209, 596, 597–598
Wilkinson, Charles, 36, 170, 514, 712
Wilkinson, Gerald, 798–799
Wilkinson, James, 683
Williams, John, 359
Williams, Roger, 18, 378, 672, **878–879,** 878 (photo)
    and Metacom, 787, 788–789
    and the Narragansetts, 1263
    and the Pequot War, 217–218
    and religious freedom, 819
Williams, Ronald, 301, 644, 817, 818
Williams, Stephen, 206
Williams Lake Industrial School, 100
Williamson, David, 240, 241, 243
Williamson, H. E., 822
Wilson, Bertha, 603
Wilson, David and Abigail, 884–885
Wilson, Mary Jane, 303, 638
Wilson, Mona, 880
Wilson, Pete, 139
Wilson, Richard "Dick," 296, 300, 303–304, 305, 817, **879–881,** 880 (photo)
    and Pine Ridge land transfer, 644
    and Wounded Knee occupation, 640, 641, 643, 656
Wilson, Woodrow, 834, 847
Wilson, Yvonne, 880
Winchester, James, 662
Winchester, John R., 798
Wind Cave National Park, 342
Wind River Reservation, 80, 1125, 1160
Wind Talkers, 367
Windmiller culture, 5
Window Rock School District's Diné immersion program, 423–424
Winnebago Indians, 53, 175, 368, 474, **1288–1290**
Winnebago Reservation, 1197

Winnemucca, **881–882,** 881 (photo), 1120–1121
Winnemucca, Sarah, **882–883,** 883 (photo), 1121
Winslow, Edward, 784
Wintergreen, 323
Winters, Yvor, 792
Winters doctrine, 188–189, 374, 600
Winters v. United States, 188, **624–626, 950**
Winthrop, John, 317, 319
Winthrop, John, Jr., 719
Winthrop, Margaret, 719
Wintun Indians, 347, **1074–1076**
Wisaka, 1278
Wisconsin, 72
Wishram Indians, 95, 201, 202, **1154–1155**
Witch hazel, 323
Witchcraft, 1045, 1073
Without Reservation, 135
Witt, Shirley Hill, 798, 799
Wiyot Indians, 230, **1076–1077**
Wodziwob (Gray Hair), 347, 396, 885
Wolf Necklace, 340 (photo)
Wolfe, James, 226
Wolfsong, 812
Wollock, Jeffrey, 156
Woman of Cofitachique, 16
Women, **190–194**
    and the Iroquois Confederacy, 412–413, 744–745, 757–758
    in Mississippian culture, 432
    Native influences and rights for, 383–387
    and Navajo culture, 734
    and Penn, William, 821
    and pottery, 458
    societal role as balance to men, 15–16
    squaw as a derogatory term, 163–165
    status in Canada, 538
    and Tlingit slavery, 169
    and tribal colleges, 867
    and WARN, 883–884
Women of All Red Nations (WARN), **883–884**
Wood, Bill, 301
Wood carving, 1084, 1091, 1113
Wood-Tikchik State Park, 1349
Woodland Cree band, 1303
Worcester, Reverend Samuel, 420, 627, 627 (photo), 680
Worcester v. Georgia, 36, 117, 137, 146, 180, 209–210, 253, 514, 516, 526, 548, 550–551, 616, 623, **626–628, 908**

Work, Hubert, 58, 285, 553–554, 576
Workshop on American Indian Affairs, 872
World Council of Indigenous Peoples, 724
World Renewal, 1055, 1057, 1072, 1076, 1079
World War I, 55, 1228
World War II, 90–91, 795
    and the Aleutian Islands, 1345
    and Navajo code talkers, 332, 364–367, 1023
    and the Passamaquoddys, 1272
Worldviews, 15–16, **487–488**
    Athapaskan, 335
    Boas, Franz, effect on, 665
    and the French, 213
    land and Indian, 279–280, 508
    life essence in Indian, 317
    Native influences on American, 688
    role of language in, 420–421
    and tribal colleges, 867–868
    See also Cosmology; Religion
Worster, Donald, 626
Worthington, Thomas, 311
Wounded Knee, occupation of, 294, 296, 301 (photo), **303–305,** 639 (photo), 640–642, 656
    and Aquash, Anna Mae, 652
    and the Fort Laramie Treaty, 531
    and Means, Russell, 786
    and Peltier, Leonard, 817
    and Wilson, Richard, 879
Wounded Knee Massacre, 142, 154, **282–285,** 284 (photo), 398, 497, 530, 687, 835
    and the Lakotas, 1188
    and Sitting Bull, 843
    as a symbol of resistance, 293
    Testimony of the Sioux, **943**
Wovoka (Jack Wilson), 97, 283, 362, 396–397, 802, **884–885,** 1121
Wratten, George, 732
Writers/publishing, 666, 697–698
    Akwesasne Notes, 633–634
    Apess, William, 650–651
    Cooper, James Fenimore, 694–696
    Costo, Rupert, 700
    Deloria, Vine, Jr., 709–712
    Erdrich, Louise, 725–726
    Gorman, R. C., 734
    Harjo, Joy, 740–741
    Jackson, Helen Hunt, 755–757
    Johnson, Emily Pauline, 759–760
    Louis, Adrian, 772–773

Lyons, Oren, 774–775
McNickle, D'Arcy, 784–785
Mohawk, John C., 791
Momaday, N. Scott, 792–793
Montezuma, 794
and the NIYC, 798
Ortiz, Simon J., 807–808
Owens, Louis, 812–813
Parker, Arthur C., 813–814
Rogers, Will, 834
Rose, Wendy, 834–835
Standing Bear, Luther, 855
Thorpe, Jim, 866
Welch, James, 875–876
Winnemucca, Sarah, 882–883
Writing-on-Stone Provincial Park, 425
Writing systems, 419–420, 425-427
    Cherokee, 35, 420, 679–680, 840–841, 1214
    Inuit syllabaries, 1327
    Tukudh, 1306
    Unangan orthography, 1345
Wyandot Nation of Kansas, 1293
Wyandots of Anderdon, 506
Wyandotte Tribe of Oklahoma, 1293
Wyandotte/Wyandot (Huron) Indians, 103, 174, 369, 513–514, **1290–1293**
    and the American Revolution, 240, 243
    and the Battle of Fallen Timbers, 245
    Bearskin, Leaford, 657–658
    and the Beaver Wars, 218–220
    and Little Turtle's War, 853
    and the Tecumseh alliance, 860
    See also Huron Indians
Wynkoop, Edward W., 262, 266
Wyoming Valley, Battle at, 239

Yahi Indians, 230
Yakima Reservation, 1121, 1154, 1155
Yakima War (1855), 41, 176, **255–256,** 762, 1137, 1140, 1154, 1156
Yakima/Yakama Indians, 291, 338, **1155–1156,** 1155 (photo)
    and fishing, 375, 389–390, 517–518
    and the Klikitats, 1140–1141
    and pollution, 129, 133–134
    and the Washani religion, 381
    and the Yakima War, 255–256
Yamamoto, Akira, 420
Yamasee Indians, 1229
Yamasee War, 1211, 1221
Yana Indians, **1077–1078**
Yankton Reservation, 80, 1193

Yankton Sioux, 60. *See also* Nakota Indians
Yanktonnai Sioux, 275. *See also* Nakota Indians
Yanomami Indians, 112
Yaqui Indians, 129, 131–132, 655, **1040–1042**
Yavapai Indians, 705, 793–794, 1010, 1014, **1042–1044**
Yavapai-Prescott Indian tribe, 139
Yavapai Reservation, 1042
Yazoo Indians, 1230
Yazzie, Emma, 149
Yazzie, Evangeline Parsons, 424
Yazzie, Robert, 596
Yazzie, Terry, 186
Yeigh, Frank, 759
Yellow Bird, 284
Yellow Bird Steele, John, 787
Yellow Hair (Yellow Hand), 686
Yellow Thunder, Raymond, 303, 639, 880

Yellowknife Indians. *See* Chippewa/Chipewya Indians
Yellowstone National Park, 1145–1146
Yellowtail Dam, 1174
Ynezeño Indians. *See* Chumash Indians
Yokuts Indians, 1063, 1068, **1078–1079**
Young, Brigham, 873
Young, John, 564
Young, Robert, 420
Young Bear, Severt, 643
Young King, 830
Young Man Afraid of His Horses (Tasunka Kokipapi), 530
Ysleta del Sur Pueblo, 1038
Yuchean language, 1233
Yuchi Indians, **1233–1234**
Yukian language group, 5

Yukon Kuskokwim Health Corporation, 1348
Yuma Indians, 4, 457. *See also* Quechan Indians
Yup'ik Indians, **1346–1349**
Yurok Indians, 1057, **1079–1081**, 1080 (photo)
Yurok Reservation, 1081

Zah, Peterson, 422, 1023
Zapotec Indians, 486
Zapotec pictographs, 427
Zia Pueblo, **1044**
Zortman, Pete, 151
Zuni Indians, 318, 414, 485–486, 998, **1044–1046**, 1045 (photo)
Zuni language, 419, 1044
Zuni Pueblos, 69, 338
Zuni Reservation, 1045

About the Editors

Bruce E. Johansen is Frederick W. Kayser Research Professor of Communication and Native American Studies at the University of Nebraska at Omaha. He is the author of dozens of books; his publishing efforts are concentrated in Native American studies and in environmental issues. His most recent publication is *The Praeger Handbook on Contemporary Issues in Native America* (Praeger, 2007).

Barry Pritzker is Director of Foundation and Corporate Relations at Skidmore College, where he occasionally teaches courses on contemporary Native America. He has authored books on Ansel Adams, Mathew Brady, and Edward Curtis, as well as *Native Americans: An Encyclopedia of History, Culture and Peoples* (ABC-CLIO, 1998). His most recent publication is *Native America Today* (ABC-CLIO, 1999).